SUBLIME CONCLUSIONS
LAST MAN NARRATIVES FROM APOCALYPSE TO DEATH OF GOD

LEGENDA

LEGENDA is the Modern Humanities Research Association's book imprint for new research in the Humanities. Founded in 1995 by Malcolm Bowie and others within the University of Oxford, Legenda has always been a collaborative publishing enterprise, directly governed by scholars. The Modern Humanities Research Association (MHRA) joined this collaboration in 1998, became half-owner in 2004, in partnership with Maney Publishing and then Routledge, and has since 2016 been sole owner. Titles range from medieval texts to contemporary cinema and form a widely comparative view of the modern humanities, including works on Arabic, Catalan, English, French, German, Greek, Italian, Portuguese, Russian, Spanish, and Yiddish literature. Editorial boards and committees of more than 60 leading academic specialists work in collaboration with bodies such as the Society for French Studies, the British Comparative Literature Association and the Association of Hispanists of Great Britain & Ireland.

The MHRA encourages and promotes advanced study and research in the field of the modern humanities, especially modern European languages and literature, including English, and also cinema. It aims to break down the barriers between scholars working in different disciplines and to maintain the unity of humanistic scholarship. The Association fulfils this purpose through the publication of journals, bibliographies, monographs, critical editions, and the MHRA Style Guide, and by making grants in support of research. Membership is open to all who work in the Humanities, whether independent or in a University post, and the participation of younger colleagues entering the field is especially welcomed.

ALSO PUBLISHED BY THE ASSOCIATION

Critical Texts
Tudor and Stuart Translations • *New Translations* • *European Translations*
MHRA Library of Medieval Welsh Literature

MHRA Bibliographies
Publications of the Modern Humanities Research Association

The Annual Bibliography of English Language & Literature
Austrian Studies
Modern Language Review
Portuguese Studies
The Slavonic and East European Review
Working Papers in the Humanities
The Yearbook of English Studies

www.mhra.org.uk
www.legendabooks.com

STUDIES IN COMPARATIVE LITERATURE

Editorial Committee
Dr Duncan Large, British Centre for Literary Translation,
University of East Anglia (Chair)
Dr Emily Finer, University of St Andrews
Dr Dorota Goluch, Cardiff University
Dr Priyamvada Gopal, Churchill College Cambridge
Professor Timothy Mathews, University College London
Professor Wen-chin Ouyang, SOAS, London
Professor Elinor Shaffer, School of Advanced Study, London

Studies in Comparative Literature are produced in close collaboration with the British Comparative Literature Association, and range widely across comparative and theoretical topics in literary and translation studies, accommodating research at the interface between different artistic media and between the humanities and the sciences.

ALSO PUBLISHED IN THIS SERIES

11. *Singing Poets: Literature and Popular Music in France and Greece*, by Dimitris Papanikolaou
12. *Wanderers Across Language: Exile in Irish and Polish Literature*, by Kinga Olszewska
13. *Moving Scenes: The Aesthetics of German Travel Writing on England*, by Alison E. Martin
14. *Henry James and the Second Empire*, by Angus Wrenn
15. *Platonic Coleridge*, by James Vigus
16. *Imagining Jewish Art*, by Aaron Rosen
17. *Alienation and Theatricality: Diderot after Brecht*, by Phoebe von Held
18. *Turning into Sterne: Viktor Shklovskii and Literary Reception*, by Emily Finer
19. *Yeats and Pessoa: Parallel Poetic Styles*, by Patricia Silva McNeill
20. *Aestheticism and the Philosophy of Death: Walter Pater and Post-Hegelianism*, by Giles Whiteley
21. *Blake, Lavater and Physiognomy*, by Sibylle Erle
22. *Rethinking the Concept of the Grotesque: Crashaw, Baudelaire, Magritte*, by Shun-Liang Chao
23. *The Art of Comparison: How Novels and Critics Compare*, by Catherine Brown
24. *Borges and Joyce: An Infinite Conversation*, by Patricia Novillo-Corvalán
25. *Prometheus in the Nineteenth Century: From Myth to Symbol*, by Caroline Corbeau-Parsons
26. *Architecture, Travellers and Writers: Constructing Histories of Perception*, by Anne Hultzsch
27. *Comparative Literature in Britain: National Identities, Transnational Dynamics 1800-2000*, by Joep Leerssen with Elinor Shaffer
28. *The Realist Author and Sympathetic Imagination*, by Sotirios Paraschas
29. *Iris Murdoch and Elias Canetti: Intellectual Allies*, by Elaine Morley
30. *Likenesses: Translation, Illustration, Interpretation*, by Matthew Reynolds
31. *Exile and Nomadism in French and Hispanic Women's Writing*, by Kate Averis
32. *Samuel Butler against the Professionals: Rethinking Lamarckism 1860–1900*, by David Gillott
33. *Byron, Shelley, and Goethe's Faust: An Epic Connection*, by Ben Hewitt
34. *Leopardi and Shelley: Discovery, Translation and Reception*, by Daniela Cerimonia
35. *Oscar Wilde and the Simulacrum: The Truth of Masks*, by Giles Whiteley
36. *The Modern Culture of Reginald Farrer: Landscape, Literature and Buddhism*, by Michael Charlesworth
37. *Translating Myth*, edited by Ben Pestell, Pietra Palazzolo and Leon Burnett
38. *Encounters with Albion: Britain and the British in Texts by Jewish Refugees from Nazism*, by Anthony Grenville
39. *The Rhetoric of Exile: Duress and the Imagining of Force*, by Vladimir Zorić

Sublime Conclusions

Last Man Narratives from Apocalypse to Death of God

❖

Robert K. Weninger

LEGENDA

Studies in Comparative Literature 43
Modern Humanities Research Association
2017

*Published by Legenda
an imprint of the Modern Humanities Research Association
Salisbury House, Station Road, Cambridge CB1 2LA*

ISBN 978-1-91088-721-9 (HB)
ISBN 978-1-78188-423-2 (PB)

First published 2017

All rights reserved. No part of this publication may be reproduced or disseminated or transmitted in any form or by any means, electronic, mechanical, photocopying, recording or otherwise, or stored in any retrieval system, or otherwise used in any manner whatsoever without written permission of the copyright owner, except in accordance with the provisions of the Copyright, Designs and Patents Act 1988, or under the terms of a licence permitting restricted copying issued in the UK by the Copyright Licensing Agency Ltd, Saffron House, 6–10 Kirby Street, London EC1N 8TS, England, or in the USA by the Copyright Clearance Center, 222 Rosewood Drive, Danvers MA 01923. Application for the written permission of the copyright owner to reproduce any part of this publication must be made by email to legenda@mhra.org.uk.

Disclaimer: Statements of fact and opinion contained in this book are those of the author and not of the editors or the Modern Humanities Research Association. The publisher makes no representation, express or implied, in respect of the accuracy of the material in this book and cannot accept any legal responsibility or liability for any errors or omissions that may be made.

Trademark notice: Product or corporate names may be trademarks or registered trademarks, and are used only for identification and explanation without intent to infringe.

© Modern Humanities Research Association 2017

Copy-Editor: Dr Birgit Mikus

CONTENTS

	List of Illustrations	ix
	Preface and Acknowledgements	xi
	Introduction	1
1	Theism 1805: Franz von Sonnenberg and the Presence of God	42
2	From Theism to Deism 1805: Jean-Baptiste Cousin de Grainville and the Absence of God	103
3	From Theism to Atheism and Nihilism 1805: The German Romantics and the Death of God	187
4	Atheism, Science and Religion 1811/1826: The Shelleys and the Death of Man	252
5	'The Earth Void of Man': Variations on a Theme 1945 and Beyond	358
	Sublime (?) Conclusions	470
	Bibliography	537
	Index	563

LIST OF ILLUSTRATIONS

❖

FIG. I.1   The opening page of the 1756 edition of Voltaire's *Poème sur le désastre de Lisbonne*

FIG. I.2.   Title page of the 1755 first edition of Immanuel Kant's *Allgemeine Naturgeschichte und Theorie des Himmels, oder Versuch von der Verfassung und dem mechanischen Ursprung des ganzen Weltgebäudes nach Newtonischen Grundsätzen abgehandelt*

FIG. I.3.   John Martin, *The Great Day of His Wrath* (1852)

FIG. 1.1.   Title page of the 1713 first edition of Edward Young's *A Poem on the Last Day*

FIG. 1.2.   The frontispiece of Vol. 2 of the 1813 edition of *The Works of Edward Young*

FIG. 1.3.   First page of Archbishop James Ussher's 1650 *Annals of the Old Testament deduced from the first origin of the world*

FIG. 1.4.   Title page of Franz von Sonnenberg's 1801 *Das Welt-Ende*

FIG. 1.5.   Title page of the 1806 first volume of Franz von Sonnenberg's *Donatoa. Epopöie*

FIG. 1.6.   William Blake's watercolour design *The Day of Judgment* for the 1808 painting *A Vision of the Last Judgment*

FIG. 2.1.   Title page of the 1805 first French edition of Jean-Baptiste Cousin de Grainville's *Le Dernier Homme*

FIG. 2.2.   '"Behold, where we shall be tomorrow!"' — illustration in Nicolas Camille Flammarion's 1894 *Omega: The Last Days of the World*

FIG. 2.3.   Title page of the 1804 French translation of Edward Young's 1713 *A Poem on the Last Day*

FIG. 2.4.   Title page of the 1670 Latin first edition of Spinoza's *Tractatus theologico-politicus*

FIG. 2.5.   Frontispiece to the 1791 first edition of Comte de Volney's *Les Ruines, ou Méditation sur les Révolutions des Empires*

FIG. 3.1.   Caspar David Friedrich, *Der Mönch am Meer* (1808–1810)

FIG. 3.2.   Caspar David Friedrich, *Meeresstrand mit Fischer* (1807)

FIG. 3.3.   Caspar David Friedrich, *Wanderer über dem Nebelmeer* (around 1818)

FIG. 3.4.   The first page of the 'First Flower-Piece' in the 1796 first edition of Jean Paul's novel *Siebenkäs*

FIG. 3.5.   Second title page of the 1804/1805 first edition of August Klingemann's *Nachtwachen*, published under the pseudonym Bonaventura

FIG. 3.6.   Percy Bysshe Shelley's poem 'Ozymandias' as published pseudonymously in the 12 January 1818 issue of *The Examiner*

FIG. 3.7.   Gustave Doré, 'The New Zealander', detail of the last plate of Gustave Doré and Blanchard Jerrold's 1872 volume *London: A Pilgrimage*

FIG. 4.1.   Title page of the 1821 pirated 'London' edition of Percy Bysshe Shelley's *Queen Mab*

FIG. 4.2.   Title page of Mary and Percy Shelley's 1817 *History of a Six Weeks' Tour through a part of France, Switzerland, Germany, and Holland, with Letters*

FIG. 4.3.   Title page of the 1826 anonymously published first British edition of Mary Shelley's *The Last Man*

FIG. 4.4.   Frontispiece to James Parkinson's 1804 *Organic Remains of a Former World. An examination of the Mineralized Remains of the Vegetables and Animals of the Antidiluvian World*

FIG. 4.5. Film Poster of the 2009 Hollywood blockbuster *2012*, directed by Roland Emmerich
FIG. 5.1. Ferdinand Barth's 1882 illustration to Goethe's poem 'Der Zauberlehrling'
FIG. 5.2. Illustrations from the 1950 U.S. Government Science Service pamphlet *Atomic Bombing. How To Protect Yourself*
FIG. 5.3. Karl Staudinger's cover graphics for the 1949 first edition of Arno Schmidt's *Leviathan*
FIG. C.1. John Martin, *The Opening of the Seventh Seal* (1837)
FIG. C.2. John Martin, *The Last Man* (1850)

PREFACE AND ACKNOWLEDGEMENTS

Researched and written over more than two decades, a book of this kind will inevitably be autobiographical in nature; having preoccupied me for a good third of my lifetime it reflects not just my development and growth as a person and academic but — spanning literature, philosophy, theology, art history, and film history as well as the history of science and science fiction — also my interests, tastes and opinions. My fascination with what I call Last Man narratives dates back to a period shortly after I entered university when I encountered Arno Schmidt's virtuoso Last-Man-meets-Last-Woman yarn *Dark Mirrors* (*Schwarze Spiegel*, 1951). My early penchant for Arno Schmidt's tales of post-World-War-III survival and subsistence — besides *Dark Mirrors* Schmidt wrote three further novels of nuclear apocalypse, one more original and imaginative than the other — led me into other aspects of his work and, eventually, to my 1982 Frankfurt doctoral dissertation on Arno Schmidt and James Joyce. My subsequent major project, taking the next ten years of my life, comprised a theoretical and historical examination of literary conventions; the resulting monograph *Literarische Konventionen. Theoretische Modelle / Historische Anwendung* was published in 1994. I have since published three further monographs, but for my part I consider the work that I now lay before my reader the capstone of my academic journey, in scale as well as in scope. Only late in that journey — in the late 1990s — did I begin to consider turning my fascination with the Last Man theme into a manifest 'research outcome', as British university lingo economically designates it. By then I had advanced sufficiently in my research on the material to offer a (post)graduate seminar; entitled 'The End(s) of Humanity' and taught at Washington University in Saint Louis in the Spring semester of 1999, the course — offered as an 'Introduction to Comparative Literary Thematology' — took us through Mary Shelley's *The Last Man*, George Stewart's *Earth Abides*, Nevil Shute's *On the Beach*, Arno Schmidt's *Dark Mirrors*, Samuel Beckett's *Happy Days* and *Endgame*, Marlen Haushofer's *The Wall*, David Markson's *Wittgenstein's Mistress* and Kobo Abe's *The Ark Sakura*, some of which will have principal roles to play also in *Sublime Conclusions*, as we shall see. Written late that same year, a 24-page article in German on the subject was published in 2000 in the comparative literature journal *Arcadia*, an article that would — of course unbeknownst to me at the time — later come to serve as the pilot study for today's nearly 600-page book.

But my project has changed significantly since the days of its inception. Arguing that Mary Shelley's 1826 novel *The Last Man* was premised on the notion of the Death of God, the maiden article was, on the whole, literary and philosophical in scope. It was only after I decided to revisit the topic some ten years ago in order to expand it into a monograph-length study for an English-language audience that I came to realize that my initial research had failed to appreciate the significance of the role played by theology and Enlightenment science in what I consider to be the Last Man narrative's gestation period, 1775 to 1825, that crucial half century in which, for Michel Foucault, 'the great hiatus occurred in the modern *episteme*' ('la grande rupture qui s'était produite dans l'*épistémè* moderne').[1] This realization led me to broaden my perspective and include, on the one hand, seventeenth- and eighteenth-century theology (and within it specifically its partitioning into theism and deism, both of which were coming under pressure from an ever more strident atheism) and, on the other, late eighteenth- and early nineteenth-century natural philosophy and natural science (and within the latter specifically the stirrings of early geology); this expansion into the terrain of theology and science constitutes the most conspicuous difference — aside from the obvious amplification of detail that space now allows — between the current study and its predecessor of 2000. The trajectory of theology from theism through deism to atheism, as I now unfold it in its relevance for early nineteenth-century literary and intellectual history, may originally have been implied, but it was neither the explicit subject of my original article nor did I accord it the attention that I subsequently came to realize it merited. So while the actual thesis and result — the differentiation of three successive paradigms of Last Man narratives — may not have changed in substance, the arc, focus and detail of my exposition have shifted considerably. What has by consequence also changed is the title: accentuating my initial literary and philosophical line of reasoning the original article was entitled 'Last Men and the Death of God. A Philosophical and Literary Genealogy' ('Letzte Menschen und der Tod Gottes. Eine philosophische und literarische Genealogie'); giving emphasis to the current book's more theological focus, by contrast, the monograph is entitled *Sublime Conclusions. Last Man Narratives from Apocalypse to Death of God*. Cutting a long story short — a story whose many twists and turns I hope to disentangle in my study's five chapters as well as its Introduction and Conclusion — the keyword Apocalypse and the catchphrase Death of God together spell out the alpha and omega of my approach, the beginning and end point of the narrative I am about to relate.

Having said that, I should add that when I first embarked on this project I never expected it later to take me in its current direction. For the early decades of my career religion was at best peripheral to my interests. However, it is perhaps precisely because religion has not played a decisive role in my life, personal or academic, that I have been able dispassionately and equably to generate and explore the thesis underpinning this book, namely that the worldview of atheism and the attendant notion of the 'death of God' laid the groundwork for Mary Shelley in the early nineteenth century to conjure up those two foundational narratives of modern science fiction, *Frankenstein* and *The Last Man*. A lesson I have learnt from

---

[1] Michel Foucault, *The Order of Things. An Archaeology of the Human Sciences* (New York: Random House/Vintage, 1973), p. 325; *Les Mots et les choses. Une archéologie des sciences humaines* (Paris: Gallimard, 1966), p. 366.

researching and writing this book is that each subject matter has its own unique dynamic and requirements; in this book's case it is thus an instance not of someone bringing their particular philosophical penchant or religious predisposition to bear on a given literary historical topic, but rather of the project's literary historical materials asking for an interpretive methodology underpinned also by theology and the philosophy of religion. I will reveal no more for now and will let my chapters speak for themselves; but prior to that I shall use my book's Introduction to contour some of the prime constituents, literary, philosophical and theological, and launch us into the fuller story as I have come to see it, as well as what I see as this story's larger significance and ramifications for us today.

Before I proceed to amplify on my original essay and thesis two brief notes on methodology and purpose may be in order: first, I prefer to call the approach I take in *Sublime Conclusions* 'transdisciplinary' rather than interdisciplinary. The use of the uncustomary term 'transdisciplinary' relates to my hope to reach out to readers beyond the fields of literary studies. My ambition was to produce research that would prove illuminating and relevant not just for students and scholars of literature, but also for students and scholars in the fields of philosophy and theology (as well as the history of philosophy and theology), art history, European intellectual history, the history of science and science's relationship with literature, and of course — last but not least — science fiction studies. Second, when I study history I enjoy listening to the voices behind that history; as important as it is to attend to the (literary) historian's retrospective summary and critical analysis, it is no less important in my view to grant readers access to the original utterances through which the subjects of history expressed their opinions, concerns and beliefs, and on which the (literary) historian bases her or his judgments. For this reason I have opted to include what some may consider as rather generous quantities of citations from historical source materials; I hope my readers will agree that they enrich the argument rather than dilute it. This puts me in a quandary nonetheless. Because the target audience for this book is an English-language readership, and because I make abundant use of foreign-language materials which require translation, I must beg the forbearance of my reader for the frequent intrusion of both original and translation into the body of my text; in this I am following the specifications of the MHRA style guide on which Legenda volumes are based. Yet the benefit of readability should outweigh the inconvenience of reduplication even for the multilingual reader who is here spared the annoyance of having perpetually to consult the footnotes, or an appendix, in order to retrieve the originals' foreign-language wording. When not indicated otherwise, translations are my own.

★ ★ ★ ★ ★

One collection of essays I will be drawing on later in my study is the American psychiatrist Robert Jay Lifton's 1987 *The Future of Immortality and Other Essays for a Nuclear Age*. In the opening sentence of his 'Introduction' he relates something that very much struck a chord with me when I first came across it; he observes: 'After collecting these essays, my feeling was: "So *this* is what I have been doing for the past fifteen years!" There are surely more pleasant ways to spend one's time than worrying about war, mass murder, and nuclear threat, but I seemed to have made a choice to spend much of mine doing just that'.[2] In Chapters Four and Five I too will be mulling over murderous monsters and nuclear threats, in earlier chapters I add to those vexations the menaces of the Deluge, the Apocalypse and the Last Judgment. No light fare indeed, and I sometimes wonder how I ever managed to maintain my sanity and equilibrium in light of the gloomy and depressing subject matter behind my study. Aside perhaps from my own generally sanguine disposition — albeit tinged with recurrent lapses into caustic misanthropy whenever I tune into the daily news, which I do too often — it was largely due to other people that I escaped becoming depressed; it was people too who helped me to navigate the plethora of materials and avoid the ever-looming danger of my drowning in excess. I have hence many persons to thank who have, in one way or another, supported me over the long haul and have given me advice and encouragement, or provided information that had succeeded in eluding me, or even — more pecuniarily but no less importantly — helped me to secure the necessary research leave and attendant peace of mind without which a project of this magnitude cannot come to fruition. Beyond the countless literary historians, philosophers, intellectual historians and literary theorists whose works have inspired me over the years and taught me what can be achieved — as many of whom are cited in this volume as are not — there are many individuals and institutions I would like to acknowledge here by name for their backing and assistance (even if some of them may be unaware of it, or have long forgotten it).

The persons I would like to single out for thanks are, in alphabetical order: Jeremy Adler (King's College London); Matthew Bell (King's College London); Erica Carter (King's College London); Ingo Cornils (University of Leeds); Ghoncheh Dolatshahi (Royal Holloway College, London); Patrick ffrench (King's College London); Michael C. Finke (University of Illinois, Urbana-Champaign); Susanne Fischer (Arno Schmidt Stiftung, Bargfeld); Monika Fludernick (Albert-Ludwigs-Universität Freiburg); Gerald Gillespie (Stanford University); Anne Green (King's College London); Christopher Hamilton (King's College London); Nick Harrison (King's College London); Emma Kafalenos (Washington University, Saint Louis); Betsy Kim (Yale Center for British Art); Monsieur M. L. Larnaudie (Archives Diocesaines, Cahors); Graham Nelson (University of Oxford and Legenda); Michael Perraudin (University of Sheffield); Terence James Reed (University of Oxford); Zoe Roth (Durham University); Susanne Schmid (Johannes Gutenberg-Universität Mainz); and Elinor Shaffer (School of Advanced Study, University of London, and Clare Hall, University of Cambridge). Special thanks also go to my three graduate research assistants, Meghan Barnes, Michaela Gelsenkirchen and Miriam Steuer, whose support I enjoyed during the early stages of this project. I am grateful, too, to the following institutions and organisations for their generous

---

2 Robert Jay Lifton, *The Future of Immortality and Other Essays for a Nuclear Age* (New York: Basic Books, 1987), p. 3.

financial support: the Department of Germanic Languages and Literatures at Washington University in Saint Louis for granting the crucial research sabbatical in the developmental stages of this project; the German Department of King's College London for granting the crucial research sabbatical in the final stages of this project; King's College's Faculty of Arts and Humanities for providing publication and copyright subsidies; and the British Comparative Literature Association (BCLA) for their support. But I owe the most profound debt to three colleagues and academic friends among those mentioned above, not alone for their careful reading of my chapter manuscripts as the project gradually matured and for providing ever astute and helpful feedback, but also for giving so altruistically and bounteously of their time and wisdom when, so I am sure, they had more pressing obligations than to read my interminable ruminations. These three are Jeremy Adler, Ingo Cornils, and Elinor Shaffer; Elinor in particular has been a most sympathetic tutelary patron of my project.

I must, finally, make one admission: fifteen years ago I counted myself among the sceptics as regards Google's project of digitalizing our libraries' holdings; at the time I did not fully understand the need. I must say that doing the research for this book has radically changed my mind. I have liberally and gratefully used such online digital collections as those provided by Gallica of the Bibliothéque Nationale in Paris, the MDZ (Münchener DigitalisierungsZentrum) of the Bayerische Staatsbibliothek Munich, ECCO (Gale's Eighteenth-Century Collections Online), JSTOR, and the innumerable Google digitalizations found on the Internet Archive, to name just some. Without them I would never have had such easy and convenient access — on my personal computer at home — to the first or early editions of such works as Thomas Burnet's *The Sacred Theory of the Earth*, Franz von Sonnenberg's *Donatoa*, Jean-Baptiste François Xavier Cousin de Grainville's *The Last Man (Le Dernier Homme)*, Karl Heinrich Heydenreich's *Letters on Atheism (Briefe über den Atheismus)*, Joseph Priestley's *Letters to a Philosophical Unbeliever*, Mary Shelley's *The Last Man*, Percy Bysshe Shelley's *The Necessity of Atheism* and *Queen Mab*, Constantin de Volney's *The Ruins: Or a Survey of the Revolutions of Empires (Les Ruines, ou, revolutions des empires)*, John Wesley's *Serious Thoughts Occasioned by the Earthquake at Lisbon*, Edward Young's *A Poem on the Last Day*, or that anonymous late eighteenth-century German author's historical curio *The approaching End of the World, described through its Remarkable Events, since the Time of Creation (Das nahe Ende der Welt aus den merkwürdigen Begebenheiten derselben von ihrer Erschaffung an)*, to mention just a small sampling of the texts that will be discussed later in this volume and that came to me via the World Wide Web completely without charge and without the need for costly and time-consuming travel to far-flung archives. I thank all those involved in making it possible for these texts to be conveyed to me so freely through digital means.

★ ★ ★ ★ ★

I dedicate this book to my closest family members: my parents, my brothers and my wife. It is they who started me off and accompanied me longest on that extraordinarily enriching yet wondrously unpredictable journey of intellectual discovery that my life continues to be; may this book stand as a record of where that journey has taken me thus far, a journey yet to be continued.

INTRODUCTION

> These are the two proper subjects of Science Fiction: the
> Present Future and the End of Man.
> LESLIE FIEDLER (1968)[1]

> As long as modernity lasts, *all* days will feel to someone like
> the last days of humanity.
> JONATHAN FRANZEN (2013)[2]

To Be or Not To Be?

The much-cited nucleus of Hamlet's famous soliloquy 'To Be or Not To Be' acquired new significance in August 1945. On the sixth day of that month the first nuclear bomb was set off in warfare, exploding above a Japanese city far away from the Pacific front lines of the Second World War and killing thousands of innocent civilians. From this day on Hamlet's question was no longer one of a riven lone individual mulling pathologically over his existential quandary; it had become instead the existential question of the whole human race. With this day a new uncertainty arose, one that would be predestined to remain suspended above each and every one of us as long as humankind exists: it is the question whether the human species will survive on planet Earth or annihilate itself through technologies of its own contriving. Were it to be mankind's fate not to survive, 'not to be', it must find itself at some point in the near or distant future facing terminal death; such is the scenario of the terminal narratives that form one of the two key subject matters of this study, narratives in which mankind is shown being wiped out completely and irrevocably, either through man-made technologies or through some cataclysmic natural event such as a lethal pandemic or a devastating comet strike. There is of course an alternative scenario, one in which mankind faces such a catastrophic event but does not perish and lives on, emerging from the cataclysm bruised and battered but not annihilated, reduced instead, as countless

---

1 'Cross the Border — Close the Gap' (1970), in *A Fiedler Reader* (New York: Stein and Day, 1977), pp. 270–94 (p. 283). This essay first appeared in German as 'Das Zeitalter der neuen Literatur' in *Christ und Welt*, 13 September and 20 September 1968. The full context reads: '[Science Fiction] is a very young genre, indeed, having found itself (after tentative beginnings in Jules Verne, H. G. Wells etc.), its real meaning and scope, only after World War II. At that point, two things become clear: first, that the Future was upon us, that the pace of technological advance had become so swift that a distinction between Present and Future would get harder and harder to maintain; and second, that the End of Man, by annihilation or mutation, was a real, even an immediate possibility. But these are the two proper subjects of Science Fiction: the Present Future and the End of Man' (pp. 282–83).

2 'Rage against the machine', *Guardian*, 14 September 2013, *Review* section pp. 2–4 (p. 4).

fictions revel in picturing, to motley bands of survivors struggling to eke out an existence in the debris of civilization; this I call the semi-terminal narrative, which comprises the second key subject matter of this study, a celebrated recent literary example of which is the American writer Cormac McCarthy's 2006 novel *The Road*. Opposed to these scenarios is a third possibility, namely that humankind might get a grip on itself — as well as on its technologies of destruction — and avoid the self-made brand of catastrophe, as a result of which it would continue 'to be', holding on to its civilizational achievements. But with the bombs of 1945 even such a continuing to be takes on a new significance; because Hiroshima and Nagasaki have made us conscious of our vulnerability, we find ourselves, since 1945, existing in a state of perpetual anxiety and apprehension, awaiting our possible terminal extinction without knowing when or even whether it will occur. As the most vocal and scathing of all so-called nuclear critics, the German philosopher and essayist Günther Anders emphasized as early as 1962 that we are sentenced to exist forthwith in a perpetual state of 'respite', as he calls it, a suspended 'mode of being' that is defined by our 'not yet being non-existent'.[3] This is the world we live in today, this is our current *conditio humana*, one we can reverse only at the cost of complete relinquishment of all technologies of mass destruction — and how likely is that?

McCarthy's *The Road* is, incidentally, not a typical representative of our subject matter, the Last Man genre, because the author consciously avoids naming the precise cause of the disaster that has obliterated the United States. Most of the narratives that I will be discussing over the course of this study are less equivocal; they are premised by and large on one of three kinds of causes of disaster, establishing three discrete paradigms of annihilation, as I shall call them.[4] Man's self-annihilation through either the technologies of his own invention, most commonly scientific experimentation (including, among other things, nuclear fusion and fission, robots and super-computers, artificial viruses and chemical agents, or bioengineering), or — less precipitously — man-made ecological disaster represents only the third and historically most recent of these paradigms. The first and earliest is — from the perspective of European intellectual history that forms the backdrop to my study

---

3 Günther Anders, 'Theses for the Atomic Age', *The Massachusetts Review*, 3 (Spring 1962), pp. 493–505 (p. 493).

4 For the sake of evenhandedness I should perhaps add here that W. Warren Wagar in the most comprehensive study of terminal fictions to date (*Terminal Visions. The Literature of Last Things*. Bloomington: Indiana University Press, 1982) also uses the term 'paradigm', of which he distinguishes four; but the worldviews or '*Weltanschauungen*' that he works with are of a completely different order to mine, underscoring the differential in our approaches. His four paradigms are Enlightenment rationalism which 'inspired the production of few terminal visions — perhaps none' (p. 134); 'the romantic *Weltanschauung*' (p. 134); 'positivism' (p. 135); and 'irrationalism' (p. 136). My focus by contrast is theophilosophical, using philosophical and theological patterns of thinking as stimuli for the literary progression of the Last Man theme. Thus my particular interest lies in investigating precisely the transition from Wagar's first to his second paradigm — the shift from Enlightenment rationalism to romanticism — in order to provide an answer to the question why Enlightenment rationalism remained unable to produce terminal visions, and why it was precisely romanticism that originated the idea and literary theme.

— the Christian paradigm; in it the Christian God or a designated proxy of the Almighty such as Jesus Christ or the archangel Gabriel embodies the agency that wields the power to eradicate our species through Apocalypse and Last Judgment. Thus Franz von Sonnenberg in his apocalyptic verse epic *Donatoa* of 1806/1807 (which forms the literary centrepiece of Chapter One) accords this role to the all-powerful 'Angel of Death' Donatoa whom God has tasked with extinguishing the human race. The Christian paradigm forms this study's first subject; it appears most characteristically in the form of the eighteenth- and nineteenth-century sub-genre of eschatological poetry and verse epics that sought to give literary shape to the unfolding of the Last Judgment, Christianity's rendering of the obliteration of mankind once the Apocalypse is unleashed. Where the first paradigm entails God's active intervention in the world's affairs, the second involves nature as a less vengeful and more disinterested agent of destruction. The prime example of nature's paradigm and its earliest manifestation, to be discussed at length in Chapter Four, is Mary Shelley's 1826 novel *The Last Man* in which a plague wipes out mankind, save one, the 'Last Man' Lionel Verney. If with *The Last Man* Mary Shelley creates the blueprint for nature's paradigm, it is — remarkably — another novel by Mary Shelley that prefigures the third of the three paradigms. In *Frankenstein, or The Modern Prometheus* (1818) the scientist Victor Frankenstein creates a monster that later takes revenge on his maker by hunting down and murdering Frankenstein's loved ones; and as intimated at the end of the novel, it is in pursuit of this monster that Frankenstein will also find his own death. Mankind's Frankenstein-like self-eradication through the technological machinery he himself has concocted is, as I indicated above, the most recent of the three paradigms that underpin my argument and determine this study's overall structure and progression. By the time we reach the twenty-first century we find these three paradigms coexisting in our time as competing modes and matrices of how to envision humankind's ultimate or near-ultimate, terminal or semi-terminal end in literary (and filmic) fiction. It is a key objective of *Sublime Conclusions* — one of its key 'research questions', in research grant parlance — to show not just that these three paradigms arose consecutively in time, but also why they came about when they came about and what their significance is for us today. In short, the core purpose of this book is to examine the origins and trajectories of these three paradigms across three centuries of European intellectual history.

Standard dictionaries of the English language tell us that the noun 'subject' possesses a range of meanings chief among which are 'the central substance or core of a thing as opposed to its attributes'; 'a person or thing that is being discussed, described, or dealt with'; 'a thinking or feeling entity, the conscious mind, the ego'; and 'a branch of knowledge studied or taught'.[5] If the 'central substance or core' of my study comprises the historical analysis and survey of those three paradigms of Last Man narratives I just briefly outlined, an obvious extension of this — being in many ways reflective of my book's signature theme — is the scrutiny accorded

---

5 I have adapted these short definitions from *Oxford Dictionary of English*'s entry 'Subject' (2nd edn, ed. by Catherine Soanes and Angus Stevenson (Oxford: Oxford University Press, 2006)).

to the fictional protagonists who populate these narratives, the 'persons being discussed, described, or dealt with'. We can distinguish two distinct types of such Last Men (or, more rarely, Last Women): the first is the 'terminal' survivor in the strict sense; here *Homo sapiens* is wiped out either completely or completely bar one, the 'Last Man' (or 'Last Woman') protagonist from whom the genre takes its name and who makes his first appearance in Mary Shelley's appropriately titled novel *The Last Man*. In this futuristic tale set between the years 2073 and 2100 the lone survivor of a world-encompassing plague is a man named Lionel Verney; he is the last remaining witness of the epidemic that arose 'on the shore of the Nile' in 2092, tore through Asia, the Americas and of course Europe, finally crossing the Channel to reach Verney's native Britain. In 2096, Verney and a small group of survivors decide to escape to more favourable climes and make their way to Italy; but with the plague still virulent their numbers dwindle as they proceed south via France and Switzerland, and by the end of the novel only Lionel and his close friend Adrian remain alive together with two girls, Clara and Evelyn, who seem to be the only humans immune to the plague. But then Evelyn dies of typhus, and Adrian and Clara drown in a storm while attempting to cross to Greece in a boat; Verney now finds himself the sole survivor, the solitary heir to a once thriving humankind: 'For a moment', he reflects,

> I compared myself to that monarch of the waste — Robinson Crusoe. We had been both thrown companionless — he on the shore of a desolate island: I on that of a desolate world. I was rich in the so called goods of life. If I turned my steps from the near barren scene, and entered any of the earth's million cities, I should find their wealth stored up for my accommodation — clothes, food, books, and a choice of dwelling beyond the command of princes of former times — every climate was subject to my selection. [...] Yet he was far happier than I: for he could hope, nor hope in vain — the destined vessel at last arrived, to bear him to countrymen and kindred, where the events of his solitude became a fire-side tale. To none could I ever relate the story of my adversity; no hope had I.[6]

No hope had he, nor had mankind: for due to the absence of a female companion for the Last Man, the archetypal Eve, it has lost all chance to regenerate. In 'terminal' narratives of this drastic kind — rare as they are — mankind is wiped out totally and in perpetuity, or at least will be once the protagonist, the last specimen of his (or her) species, expires.

The semi-terminal type of Last Man or Last Woman, by contrast, may like Verney initially find him- or herself alone in the world following the catastrophe — whatever shape it may take — only soon to discover that there are other survivors, scattered lone men and women who like him- or herself roam the 'desolate world' scavenging in civilization's flotsam and jetsam. Prime avatars of this figure are

---

6 Mary Shelley, *The Last Man*, ed. by Hugh J. Luke, with an introduction by Anne K. Mellor (Lincoln and London: University of Nebraska Press, 1965), p. 326; all further page references are to this edition. Ahead of my discussion of Susan Sontag's essay 'The Imagination of Disaster', published in *Commentary* (October 1965, pp. 42–48), I might add here that Sontag discusses one grouping of end-time movies 'as devoted to the fantasy of occupying the deserted city and starting all over again — Robinson Crusoe on a world-wide scale' (p. 45).

the miserable remnants of humankind we encounter in the nuclear wasteland California of Aldous Huxley's 1948 novel *Ape and Essence*, the male and female Natty Bumppo-like nomads of Arno Schmidt's 1951 vision of post-World War III devastation entitled *Dark Mirrors* (*Schwarze Spiegel*), the lone female homestead builder in Marlen Haushofer's 1968 novel *The Wall* (*Die Wand*), or the wretched father and son in Cormac McCarthy's above-cited *The Road*, all of whom may one day, assuming they can sustain themselves for long enough, begin to rebuild society. Some of these individuals will opt not to engage in procreation; others will band together seeking to rebuild community and society, and by the third or fourth generation after 'The Great Disaster' their offspring will, if all goes well, have reverted to hunting, dressing and living like native Americans, reintegrating, as the occasionally moralizing narrators like to depict it, more harmoniously into their natural habitats than their civilizational forebears — so the storyline of two of this tradition's most classic texts, Jack London's 1912 *The Scarlet Plague* and George R. Stewart's 1949 *Earth Abides*.

Moving from the protagonists of those tales to the protagonists of my tale brings us to yet another subject of my book, the real-life authors of the terminal and semi-terminal narratives without whom the literary genre would not exist. Among these historical individuals we will encounter two lesser known Catholic poets, Franz von Sonnenberg and Jean-Baptiste François Xavier Cousin de Grainville, whose early nineteenth-century verse epics, published in 1806/1807 and 1805 respectively (and covered in Chapters One and Two), presage the downfall and demise of the Christian eschatological verse epic; George Gordon Lord Byron (covered also in Chapter Two) who, in his 1816 futuristic poem 'Darkness', was among the earliest English-language writers to feature man's distant-future demise through natural means, the natural means in this instance being the extinction of our sun; the German writer August Klingemann (covered in Chapter Three), the author of the surprisingly irreverent 1805 *The Nightwatches of Bonaventura*, a Black Romantic nihilistic satire in which the narrator-cum-night-watchman in jest first calls down the Last Judgment on his town's inhabitants only to then pronounce the death of God and the reign of Nothingness; and Mary Shelley (covered in Chapter Four) who with her novel *The Last Man* created the original template for the secular Last Man genre. Auxiliary roles will be played (in approximate chronological order) by such literary notables as Edward Young, William Wordsworth, Percy Bysshe Shelley, Georg Büchner, Nicolas Camille Flammarion, H. G. Wells, Aldous Huxley, Nevil Shute, Mordecai Roshwald, Arno Schmidt, Günter Grass and — as the latest representatives of the family tree — Cormac McCarthy and Emily St. John Mandel.

Inasmuch as the word 'subject' means 'a thinking or feeling entity, the conscious mind, the ego', I must key into my reflections the psychological and moral question why humans take so much 'morbid pleasure'[7] from imagining the death, or even

---

7 The formulation is by Ingo Cornils who, in an article on German end-time science fiction, speaks of the 'morbid pleasure of watching the world go to ruins'; see his 'Alles kaputt? Visions of the End in West German and Austrian Science Fiction', originally published in 2001 in the international review of science fiction *Foundation*, but cited here from its 2009 reprint in *Twentieth-Century Literary*

only partial death, of their species. What is it that attracts the readers of Last Man fictions or viewers of apocalyptic films to these narratives, and what is it that makes authors want to concoct ever new twists and turns to the by now well-established plots of annihilation? One of the earliest and most incisive answers given to this question is contained in an essay the literary critic Susan Sontag published in 1965; fittingly entitled 'The Imagination of Disaster', Sontag's essay scrutinizes specifically the emotional functions underlying the end-time plots of science fiction films; she thus observes:

> Science fiction films are one of the most accomplished of the popular art forms, and can give a great deal of pleasure to sophisticated film addicts. Part of the pleasure, indeed, comes from the sense in which these movies are in complicity with the abhorrent. It is no more, perhaps, than the way all art draws its audience into a circle of complicity with the thing represented. But in science fiction films we have to do with things which are (quite literally) unthinkable. Here, 'thinking about the unthinkable' [...] becomes, however inadvertently, itself a somewhat questionable act from a moral point of view.[8]

That 'science fiction films reflect powerful anxieties about the condition of the individual psyche' is, for Sontag, self-understood; indeed (and as my discussion of Stanley Kubrick's 1964 film *Dr. Strangelove or: How I Learned to Stop Worrying and Love the Bomb* and Mordecai Roshwald's 1959 novel *Level 7* in later chapters will corroborate), some fictions serve as vehicles for the 'metaphoric expression of sexual desire', others as a 'model of technocratic man, purged of emotions, volitionless, tranquil, obedient to all orders'. In sum Sontag designates end-time science fiction movies 'as a popular mythology for the contemporary *negative* imagination about the impersonal', adding:

> science fiction films can be looked at as thematically central allegory, replete with standard modern attitudes. [...] [But] it is not enough to note that science fiction allegories are one of the new myths about — that is, ways of accommodating to and negating — the perennial human anxiety about death. (Myths of heaven and hell, and of ghosts, had the same function.) Again, there is a historically specifiable twist which intensifies the anxiety, or better, the trauma suffered by everyone in the middle of the twentieth century when it became clear that from now on to the end of human history, every person would spend his individual life not only under the threat of individual death, which is certain, but of something almost unsupportable psychologically — collective incineration and extinction which could come any time, virtually without warning.

'What I am suggesting', Sontag concludes in her article written during the heyday of the Cold War and nuclear proliferation, 'is that the imagery of disaster in science fiction films is above all the emblem of an *inadequate* response', a point upon which I will enlarge in Chapter Five as well as in my Conclusion.

Criticism, vol. 218, ed. by Thomas L. Schoenberg and Lawrence J. Trudeau (Detroit: Gale, 2009), pp. 67–77 (p. 68).
 8 Sontag, 'The Imagination of Disaster', this passage p. 42, the subsequent passages pp. 47 and 48.

The fourth and final meaning of the word 'subject' was 'a branch of knowledge studied or taught'. The 'branches of knowledge' touched upon in *Sublime Conclusions* are both manifold and diverse, so diverse in fact that researching and writing this study forced me to branch out from my usual disciplines — German, English and comparative literature combined with philosophy and art history — into fields well beyond the compass of those customary safe havens. Lacunae in knowledge and coverage are an inescapable result; I am convinced every reader will find things that he or she feels should have been included or that received less attention than they deserved. Such are the intrinsic gains and hazards of comparativism, which is as much about interdisciplinary enrichment as about inadvertent omission and improvisation. Historical and modern theology are surely the most obvious cases in point in my study; here especially I must beg forbearance for any gaps in knowledge and coverage. A comparable challenge was keeping the near limitless literary subject matter in check. Under the heading 'List of apocalyptic and post-apocalyptic fiction' Wikipedia itemizes more than 960 titles within thirteen genre categories, under the heading 'List of nuclear holocaust fiction' no fewer than 370 titles within 9 rubrics. In the list of 'Selected Sources' appended to the most wide-ranging study to date of post-apocalyptic fiction, *Terminal Visions. The Literature of Last Things*, its author W. Warren Wagar catalogues 'more than three hundred novels, stories, plays, and poems that comprise the primary source material' for his book.[9] There would be little gain in trying to aspire to more exhaustive coverage; indeed, Wagar himself conceded already in 1982 that a 'complete list of terminal visions of modern speculative literature' (which is more or less coextensive with what I call terminal and semi-terminal literature) would easily 'run into the thousands' — and this was thirty-five years ago.

For that reason alone an alternative approach was called for, one that would concentrate on exemplary cases rather than seeking to provide a comprehensive survey; not everyone will therefore find their particular hobby horse, their favourite specimen of end-time science fiction, mentioned or discussed. (In fact, many of my own favourites did not make their way into my discussion.) This is because my priority also lies elsewhere. The analysis of terminal and semi-terminal fictions is only one half of my interest; the other is the intersection of literary, philosophical and theological discourses from the Enlightenment to the present as it manifests itself in the genesis and trajectory of the Last Man theme. If one of my aims is thus to interpret the genre of Last Man narratives as a 'metaphor for our own cultural crises', as George Levine once aptly formulated it in the volume *The Endurance of Frankenstein*, another is to chart the seismic shifts in European thought between the mid-eighteenth century and the early twenty-first century which enabled the thinking of a godless world. For the core proposition at the heart of *Sublime Conclusions* is the claim that the 'Death of God' is the precondition of our modern ability to conjure up narratives of the extinction of humankind. For so long as the European public persisted in the belief either that an all-powerful Christian God governed the progress of history and determined beginning and end (this being

---

9 *Terminal Visions*, p. 221; the following passages also p. 221.

the essence of Christian theism), or that some powerful 'Supreme Being' — often collapsed with 'Nature' herself — instigated the beginning but then withdrew from all involvement in our planet's daily affairs (this being the essence of the various brands of seventeenth- and eighteenth-century deism and pantheism), people remained incapable of imagining themselves as extinguishable as a species. This core proposition is embedded in the subtitle of this volume, 'Last Man Narratives from Apocalypse to Death of God'; and I can provide no better introduction to this guiding proposition than the prehistory itself of that notion of the 'Death of God'.

'Shaken to its Foundations': A Theophilosophical Overture

To locate the wellspring of Last Man narratives we need to go back in time to a point half a century before the first literary text entitled 'The Last Man' — the French priest Jean-Baptiste François Xavier Cousin de Grainville's *Le Dernier Homme* — was published in 1805, and nearly three quarters of a century before Mary Shelley's *The Last Man*, the founding novel of the secular Last Man genre, was published in 1826. The story of how we became able to imagine the extinction of mankind begins with a mid-eighteenth-century real-life disaster, obviously not one in which all of mankind was eradicated — else we would not be here today — but a more localized one, one that wiped out, depending on the estimate, between ten and one hundred thousand denizens of Portugal, Spain and Morocco. It was an event that was to embed itself deep within European consciousness, putting Enlightenment philosophy on a new trajectory. This event was the so-called 'Earthquake of Lisbon', although it actually affected large swathes of southwest Europe and northern Africa. Striking on 1 November 1755 with a magnitude today estimated at between 8.5 and 9.0 its most destructive damage centered on Lisbon, a city that was regarded at the time as one of the wealthiest and most majestic capitals of Europe. To make matters worse, it struck on All Saints Day; the earthquake's tremors hence hit the city just as a large part of its population was celebrating this Christian holy day in the town's churches, chapels and cloisters. (An allegorical depiction of the aftermath of the earthquake is given by the painter João Glama Stroberle in his 1755/56 *Allegory to the 1755 Earthquake* held by Lisbon's Museu Nacional de Arte Antiga and easily retrievable on the World Wide Web.) The earthquake began with three strong tremors which were soon followed by devastating fires and a tsunami that together caused more damage and killed more people than did the tremors themselves — indeed, the tsunami waves were registered in places as far away as Iceland, Finland and even across the Atlantic in the West Indies. News of the earthquake began to filter through to central Europe and Britain three weeks later, the first reports of it being published in Paris and London newspapers on 22 November.[10] Reflecting back on his childhood, Johann Wolfgang Goethe, born 1749, recalls

---

10 A fascinating account of the (delayed) impact of the earthquake in British media is given by Matthias Georgi in 'Das Erdbeben von Lissabon in der englischen Publizistik', in *Das Erdbeben von Lissabon und der Katastrophendiskurs im 18. Jahrhundert*, ed. by Gerhard Lauer and Thorsten Unger (Göttingen: Wallstein, 2008), pp. 96–109.

in his autobiographical *Poetry and Truth* how strongly he was affected as a six-year old by the reports of this tragedy, much perhaps as a child today might remember witnessing the horrifying images of the collapse of the World Trade Center on 11 September 2001 or the images of the tsunami that hit the Indian Ocean and South-East Asia on Boxing Day 2004:

> However, the boy's tranquillity of mind was deeply shaken for the first time by an extraordinary event. On the first of November, 1755, occurred the great earthquake of Lisbon, spreading enormous terror over a world grown accustomed to peace and quiet. A large, splendid city, both a port and trade center, is hit without warning by the most fearful calamity. The earth quivers and rocks, the sea rages, ships collide, houses collapse, churches and towers fall on top of them, the royal palace is partly swallowed up by the sea, and the severed earth seems to spit flames, for everywhere the ruins begin to smoke and burn. Sixty thousand human beings, who were calm and content just a moment before, perish together, and the happiest man among them is he who had no time to feel or consider his misfortune. The flames rage on, and with them rages a mob of criminals, now coming out into the open, or perhaps set free by the disaster. The unfortunate survivors are exposed to robbery, murder, and every possible mistreatment; and so nature on every hand asserts her arbitrary will. [...] Hereupon, God-fearing persons were moved to wise observations, philosophers offered consoling arguments, and clergymen preached fiery sermons. [...] Indeed, the demon of terror has perhaps at no other time spread its chill over the world as quickly and powerfully. Having to hear all of this repeatedly, I was more than a little disconcerted by it in my boyish mind. God, the Creator and Preserver of heaven and earth, who had been presented to me as so very wise and merciful in the explanation of the first article of the Creed, had shown Himself by no means fatherly when He abandoned both the just and the unjust in the same destruction. My young mind tried in vain to resist these impressions, and it was not made any easier for me by the philosophers and scholars when they themselves could not agree on the way to view such a phenomenon.
>
> [Durch ein außerordentliches Weltereignis wurde jedoch die Gemütsruhe des Knaben zum erstenmal im tiefsten erschüttert. Am ersten November 1755 ereignete sich das Erdbeben von Lissabon und verbreitete über die in Frieden und Ruhe schon eingewohnte Welt einen ungeheuren Schrecken. Eine große, prächtige Residenz, zugleich Handels- und Hafenstadt, wird ungewarnt von dem furchtbarsten Unglück betroffen. Die Erde bebt und schwankt, das Meer braust auf, die Schiffe schlagen zusammen, die Häuser stürzen ein, Kirchen und Türme darüber her, der königliche Palast zum Teil wird vom Meer verschlungen, die geborstene Erde scheint Flammen zu speien. Sechzigtausend Menschen, einen Augenblick zuvor noch ruhig und behaglich, gehen miteinander zugrunde, und der Glücklichste darunter ist der zu nennen, dem keine Empfindung, keine Besinnung über das Unglück mehr gestattet ist. Die Flammen wüten fort, und mit ihnen wütet eine Schar sonst verborgener, oder durch dieses Ereignis in Freiheit gesetzter Verbrecher. Die unglücklichen Übriggebliebenen sind dem Raube, dem Morde, allen Mißhandlungen bloßgestellt; und so behauptet von allen Seiten die Natur ihre schrankenlose Willkür. [...] Hierauf ließen es die Gottesfürchtigen nicht an Betrachtungen, die Philosophen nicht an Trostgründen, an Strafpredigten die Geistlichen

nicht fehlen. [...] Ja vielleicht hat der Dämon des Schreckens zu keiner Zeit so schnell und so mächtig seine Schauer über die Erde verbreitet. Der Knabe, der alles dieses wiederholt vernehmen mußte, war nicht wenig betroffen. Gott, der Schöpfer und Erhalter Himmels und der Erden, den ihm die Erklärung des ersten Glaubensartikels so weise und gnädig vorstellte, hatte sich, indem er die Gerechten mit den Ungerechten gleichem Verderben preisgab, keineswegs väterlich bewiesen. Vergebens suchte das junge Gemüth sich gegen diese Eindrücke herzustellen, welches überhaupt um so weniger möglich war, als die Weisen und Schriftgelehrten selbst sich über die Art, wie man ein solches Phänomen anzusehen habe, nicht vereinigen konnten.][11]

Goethe does not name the philosophers, but the disagreement he is alluding to refers most likely to the mid-century debate incited by Voltaire that revolved around the philosophy of Gottfried Wilhelm Leibniz and Alexander Pope, respectively their followers (Leibniz had died in 1716, Pope in 1744, both witnessing neither the Lisbon earthquake nor the controversy that they sparked with their works). In his 1755/1756 *Poem on the Disaster of Lisbon, or Inquiry into the Maxim: 'Whatever Is, Is Right'* (*Poème sur le désastre de Lisbonne ou examen de cet axiome: «Tout est bien»*) and his later satire *Candide, or Optimism* (*Candide ou l'optimisme*, 1759) Voltaire attacked the foundations of the theophilosophical optimism that had come to dominate rationalist thought over the preceding decades. Eighteenth-century optimism is epitomized by two classic formulations, Leibniz's maxim that ours is 'the best of all possible worlds' and Pope's supplementary adage 'Whatever Is, Is Right'. In an abridgement of his standpoint, Leibniz declares: 'Out of all the possible ways in which the universe or series of things is able to exist, one way is the most perfect, and that way is without doubt the one that really exists', a declaration he elsewhere enlarges upon thus: 'Given the most perfect being, namely God (as I now suppose), that the most perfect operation is that of the most perfect being, and that the world is the work of God, then the world is the most perfect, and hence no other series of things can be imagined which is more perfect than this one'.[12]

This has stark implications for Leibniz's concept of theodicy, the explanation and justification of why evil exists in our world. The following passage from a 1712 letter to Louis Bourguet provides a useful abbreviation of Leibniz's thinking in this regard: 'I do not believe that a world without evil, preferable in order to ours, is possible', he writes, 'otherwise it would have been preferred. We must believe that the mixture of evil has produced the greatest possible good: otherwise the evil

---

11 *From My Life. Poetry and Truth*, trans. by Robert R. Heitner, in *Goethe's Collected Works*, ed. by Thomas P. Saine and Jeffrey L. Sammons (New York: Suhrkamp, 1987), vol. 4, pp. 34–35. *Dichtung und Wahrheit*, Teil 1, Buch 1, *Hamburger Ausgabe*, ed. by Erich Trunz (Hamburg: Wegner, 1955), vol. 9, pp. 29–30. It is worth mentioning here the insightful article by Bernd Hamacher ('Strategien narrativen Katastrophenmanagements. Goethe und die "Erfindung" des Erdbebens von Lissabon', in *Das Erdbeben von Lissabon*, pp. 162–72), in which Hamacher argues that Goethe, from his 1811 retrospective when he wrote *Poetry and Truth*, is able to stage the Lisbon earthquake as a point of cultural shock and rupture as well as a loss of innocence.

12 Gottfried Wilhelm Leibniz, 'The elements of true piety, or, on the love of God over everything' (written around 1677/1678), in *The Shorter Leibniz Texts. A Collection of New Translations*, ed. by Lloyd Strickland (London: Continuum, 2006), pp. 189–95 (p. 194).

would not have been permitted'.[13] Because God, 'this supreme wisdom, united to a goodness that is no less infinite, cannot but have chosen the best' from all possible alternative options, as Leibniz states in §8 of his key work on this issue, *Theodicy: Essays on the Goodness of God, the Freedom of Man and the Origin of Evil* (*Essais de theodicée sur le bonté de Dieu, la liberté de l'homme et l'origine du mal*, written in 1705, first published edition Amsterdam 1710), and because 'There is nothing without a reason', the logical conclusion for him is that 'God would not permit evil unless he could procure a greater good from evil'. 'I am effectively of the opinion', Leibniz amplifies in a letter to André Morell, 'that God could not do better than he does, and that all the imperfections we think we find in the world only originate from our ignorance'.

In 1733, some two decades after the publication of Leibniz's *Theodicy*, the British critic and poet Alexander Pope effectively codifies Leibniz's philosophical views in poetic form in his — at the time much celebrated and widely translated — 'Essay on Man'. The crucial passage that Voltaire will pick up on and scoff at over and again in his philippic against eighteenth-century optimism is perhaps the most famous segment of 'An Essay on Man'; it is the concluding section of 'Epistle I' which finishes with the dictum 'Whatever Is, Is Right':

> All Nature is but Art, unknown to thee;
> All Chance, Direction which thou canst not see;
> All Discord, Harmony not understood;
> All partial Evil, universal Good:
> And spight of Pride, and in thy Reason's spight,
> One truth is clear; *Whatever Is, Is Right.*
>   (Epistle I, in this early edition ll. 276–81,
>   in later editions ll. 289–94)

The evil we experience in the world is only 'partial', and it is balanced against the overall 'universal good' that we, with our restricted human consciousness, are too limited to recognize behind God's grand design. Pope explains:

> But errs not Nature from this gracious end,
> From burning suns when livid deaths descend,
> When Earthquakes swallow, or when tempests sweep
> Towns to one grave, a Nation to the deep?
> Blame we for this the wise Almighty Cause?
> 'No ('tis reply'd) he acts by *gen'ral Laws*'.
>   (Epistle I, ll. 145–50, in later editions ll. 141–46)

The message is, we must not let the partial evil and destruction wrought even by comets, tempests and earthquakes hoodwink us into putting either God's general laws or the universal benevolence of his design into question.

For Voltaire the earthquake of Lisbon changed all this. Already through the subtitle to his *Poem on the Disaster of Lisbon, or Inquiry into the Maxim: 'Whatever Is, Is*

---

13 'Letter to Louis Bourguet (late 1712)', in *The Shorter Leibniz Texts*, pp. 207–08 (p. 208). The subsequent quotations from 'The elements of true piety' and 'Letter to André Morell (29 September 1698)', in *The Shorter Leibniz Texts*, pp. 192 and 197–98.

Right' (see Figure I.1) the French philosopher makes his intention explicit of putting Pope's maxim, derived from Leibniz's theodicy, to the test. And his conclusion is disastrous: how can a catastrophe of such proportion as the earthquake of Lisbon be reconciled with any notion of a harmonious equilibrium in which 'all partial evil' is offset by some larger 'universal good' that must forever remain indiscernible and unknown? How can anyone call a world the best of all possible choices when it involves, as part of its God-given universal laws, earthquakes that destroy the lives and livelihoods of thousands in an instant? With the Lisbon casualties in mind, Voltaire deploys his poem, written within weeks of the disaster, to question the 'will of God', a God who is claimed to be omnipotent and omnibenevolent yet undertook nothing to prevent the ruin that befell the blameless inhabitants of Lisbon; citing Pope verbatim, the poem's opening section thus comprises these lines:

> Come, ye philosophers, who cry, "All's well,"
> And contemplate this ruin of a world.
> Behold these shreds and cinders of your race,
> This child and mother heaped in common wreck,
> These scattered limbs beneath the marble shafts —
> A hundred thousand whom the earth devours,
> Who, torn and bloody, palpitating yet,
> Entombed beneath their hospitable roofs,
> In racking torment end their stricken lives.
> To those expiring murmurs of distress,
> To that appalling spectacle of woe,
> Will ye reply: "You do but illustrate
> The iron laws that chain the will of God"?
> Say ye, o'er that yet quivering mass of flesh:
> "God is avenged: the wage of sin is death"?
>
> [Philosophes trompés, qui criez, *tout est bien*,
> Accourez: contemplez ces ruines affreuses,
> Ces débris, ces lambeaux, ces cendres malheureuses,
> Ces femmes, ces enfans l'un sur l'autre entassés,
> Sous ces marbres rompus ces membres dispersés;
> Cent mille infortunés que la terre dévore,
> Qui sanglants, déchirés, et palpitans encore,
> Enterrés sous leurs toits terminent sans secours,
> Dans l'horreur des tourments, leurs lamentables jours.
> Aux cris demi-formés de leurs voix expirantes,
> Au spectacle effrayant de leurs cendres fumantes,
> Direz-vous, c'est l'effet des éternelles lois,
> Qui d'un Dieu libre et bon nécessitent le choix?
> Direz-vous, en voyant cet amas de victimes,
> Dieu s'est vengé, leur mort est le prix de leurs crimes?][14]

---

14 Voltaire, 'Poème sur le désastre de Lisbonne', critical edition by David Adams and Haydn T. Mason, in *Les Œuvres Completes de Voltaire*, vol. 45A (Oxford: Voltaire Foundation, 2009), pp. 269–358 (pp. 335–36, ll. 4–18); the subsequent passages pp. 345 (l. 175), 340 (l. 97) and 338 (ll. 59–62), again 338 (ll. 51–52), and 341–42 (ll. 121–28). As regards English rendition I have chosen to cite from

POEME
SUR LE
DESASTRE DE LISBONNE,
OU EXAMEN DE CET AXIOME,
TOUT EST BIEN.

O Malheureux mortels! ô Terre déplorable!
   O de tous les fléaux assemblage effroyable!
D'inutiles douleurs éternel entretien!
Philosophes trompés, qui criez, *Tout est bien*,
Accourez: contemplez ces ruïnes affreuses,
Ces débris, ces lambeaux, ces cendres malheureuses,
Ces femmes, ces enfans, l'un sur l'autre entassés,
Sous ces marbres rompus ces membres dispersés;
Cent mille infortunés que la Terre dévore,
Qui sanglants, déchirés, & palpitans encore,
Enterrés sous leurs toits terminent sans secours,
Dans l'horreur des tourments, leurs lamentables jours.
  Aux cris demi-formés de leurs voix expirantes,
Au spectacle effrayant de leurs cendres fumantes,
                                        Direz-

FIG. I.1. The opening page of the 1756 edition of Voltaire's *Poème sur le désastre de Lisbonne* with its subtitle 'Tout est bien' satirically echoing Pope's maxim 'Whatever Is, Is Right'.

No longer willing to accept Leibniz's and Pope's model of providential balance —
'T'is mockery to tell me all is well' ('Je ne conçois pas plus comment tout serait
bien') — Voltaire feels compelled to ask:

> "This misery", ye say, "is others' good" [...]
> Would it console the sad inhabitants
> Of these aflame and desolated shores
> To say to them: "Lay down your lives in peace;
> For the world's good your homes are sacrificed?"
>
> [Ce malheur, dites vous, est le bien d'un autre être. [...]
> Les tristes habitants de ces bords désolés,
> Dans l'horreur des tourments seraient-ils consolés,
> Si quelqu'un leur disait; *Tombez, mourez tranquilles,*
> *Pour le bonheur du monde on détruit vos asiles...*]

His questioning of a God who would allow such indiscriminate sacrificial wrong is blunt and unforgiving. 'Are not the means of the great artisan | Unlimited for shaping his designs?' ('L'éternel artisan n'a-t-il pas dans ses mains | Des moyens infinis tout prêts pour ses desseins?'), he queries, putting in question not just the notion of an all-powerful God, but also of a purely benevolent one:

> And as, with quaking voice,
> Mortal and pitiful, ye cry, "All's well,"
> The universe belies you, and your heart
> Refutes a hundred times your mind's conceit.
> All dead and living things are locked in strife.
> Confess it freely — evil stalks the land,
> Its secret principle unknown to us.
> Can it be from the author of all good?
>
> [ô mortel, et faible, et miserable!
> Vous criez, *tout est bien*, d'une voix lamentable.
> L'univers vous dément, et votre propre cœur
> Cent fois de votre esprit a réfuté l'erreur.
> Eléments, animaux, humains, tout est en guerre.
> Il le faut avouer, le *mal* est sur la terre:
> Son principe secret ne nous est point connu.
> De l'auteur de tout bien le mal est-il venu?]

Drafted within a few weeks of the earthquake in late 1755, the poem had by the end of 1756 reached some fourteen editions; it was accompanied in the same year by Voltaire's *Essay on general history and the customs and spirit of nations from Charles the Great to the present* (*Essai sur l'histoire générale et sur les mœurs et l'esprit des nations*

---

a hitherto unpublished translation by Joseph McCabe that I retrieved from the internet on 16 April 2016 (<https://en.wikisource.org/wiki/Toleration_and_other_essays/Poem_on_the_Lisbon_Disaster>) because it strikes me as superior to the poem's published translation by William F. Fleming in vol. 36 of *The Works of Voltaire. A Contemporary Version* (Akron: The Werner Company, 1906). Fleming sacrifices too much of the fine detail to his versification's need for rhyme; thus the first two lines of this cited passage lose the explicit mention of 'philosophers' as well as the direct allusion to Pope's maxim 'All is well' (Fleming's version reads: 'And lamentations which inspire my strain, | Prove that philosophy is false and vain').

depuis Charlemagne jusqu'à nos jours, published in Geneva in 1756) and followed in 1759 by the philosopher's second broadside against the philosophy of optimism, his satirical novel *Candide ou l'optimisme*.[15] Written in the aftermath of the earthquake of Lisbon, these texts together signal, according to the philosophers of history Karl Löwith and Odo Marquard, the crisis of theodicy and the collapse of the philosophy of optimism while at the same time announcing the birth of a genuinely modern philosophy of history in which nature, humankind and the movement of history are divested of any divine influence and left to their own devices.[16] As Löwith argues in his chapter on the French philosopher in *Meaning in History. The Theological Implications of the Philosophy of History* (1949), Voltaire draws a clear line between sacred and secular historiography; for Voltaire, God is no longer an active agency in the production of world history. The earthquake of Lisbon thus marks the watershed moment in European intellectual history when God and nature finally, and once and for all, part ways.

Such at least was the impression given by mid- to late twentieth-century intellectual historians studying the impact of the Lisbon earthquake on Enlightenment thought. Pursuing this line of argument, the literary historian Svend Erik Larsen for instance contends in an essay on Kant's response to the earthquake of Lisbon that in its immediate wake the German philosopher abandoned 'divine power' as the preferred interpretative paradigm through which to explain history's *telos*. The three essays that Kant wrote in 1756 within months of the Lisbon earthquake — entitled 'Of the causes of earthquakes on the occasion of the calamity that befell the western countries of Europe towards the end of last year', 'History and natural description of the most noteworthy occurrences of the earthquake that struck a large part of the Earth at the end of the year 1755' and 'Continued observations on the earthquakes that have been experienced for some time'[17] — show him taking an 'empirical turn' which leads not just to his rejection of any divine governance of world affairs, but also his stressing the importance of human freedom. Larsen notes: 'In the three texts, all references to divine teleology have vanished; instead Kant is trying his best to stay with material, causal explanations. Moreover, the quiet confidence in providence has been replaced by a concern with materially founded prognostic

---

15 An insightful secondary source in German is Harald Weinrich's essay 'Literaturgeschichte eines Weltereignisses: Das Erdbeben von Lissabon', in *Literatur für Leser. Essays und Aufsätze zur Literaturwissenschaft* (Stuttgart: Kohlhammer, 1971), pp. 64–76.

16 See Karl Löwith, *Meaning in History. The Theological Implications of the Philosophy of History* (Chicago: University of Chicago Press, 1949); and Odo Marquard, 'Die Krise des Optimismus und die Geburt der Geschichtsphilosophie', in *Das Erdbeben von Lissabon*, pp. 205–15.

17 'Von den Ursachen der Erderschütterungen, bei Gelegenheit des Unglücks, welches die westlichen Länder von Europa gegen das Ende des vorigen Jahres betroffen hat' (1756), in Immanuel Kant, *Sämmtliche Werke in chronologischer Reihenfolge*, ed. by G. Hartenstein (Leipzig: Leopold Voss, 1867), vol. 1, pp. 402–11; 'Geschichte und Naturbeschreibung der merkwürdigen Vorfälle des Erdbebens, welches an dem Ende des 1755sten Jahres einen grossen Theil der Erde erschüttert hat' (1756), in Immanuel Kant, *Sämmtliche Werke in chronologischer Reihenfolge*, vol. 1, pp. 414–45; and 'Fortgesetzte Betrachtung der seit einiger Zeit wahrgenommenen Erderschütterungen' (1756), in *Sämmtliche Werke in chronologischer Reihenfolge*, vol. 1, pp. 448–56. English translations are contained in Immanuel Kant, *Natural History*, ed. by Eric Watkins (Cambridge: Cambridge University Press, 2015), pp. 327–64.

procedures in order to avoid future catastrophes and an ethical obligation to try to come up with measures to prevent their effects';[18] Larsen concludes:

> Finally, out of the shadows behind the notion of harmonious nature allowing for human freedom as a continuous natural development in the best of all possible worlds he sketches the first modest attempts to understand human freedom as conditioned by the confrontation with an enigmatic and threatening nature. In short: not only is Kant's philosophical conception of nature and God in the process of chang[ing], but so is his way of writing, his value system and his focus of interest. [...] The occasion [i.e., the earthquake of Lisbon] is too mind-blowing and incomprehensible. The outcome is that Kant recontextualizes both his explanatory framework and his teleological orientation. [...] It is exactly the absence, and not the presence of the divine *telos* in nature, that makes it possible for another type of *telos* to emerge just as fundamental as any divine *telos*. Hence, the possibility of human freedom *is* for Kant the very *telos* of human life.

If the intention is to give the impression that based on the experience of the Lisbon earthquake Kant gave up divine causality as the force governing universal history, this would be wrong. What is crucial for the argument I aim to develop in *Sublime Conclusions* is that it confuses matters when we fail to take into account the full range of theophilosophical attitudes in competition during this period. For the impression often given — as is implied by Larsen above — is that belief in divine providence is, during this period, being supplanted by a purely secularist and natural scientific worldview, with the earthquake of Lisbon serving as a key moment and turning point in this development. However, as important as the earthquake of Lisbon may have been within the realm of philosophy, there is also a danger in presuming that one can transfer that impact onto other spheres of life. Thus Gerhard Lauer and Thorsten Unger rightly stress in their 'Introduction' to the essay anthology *The Earthquake of Lisbon and the Discourse of Disaster in the Eighteenth Century* (*Das Erdbeben von Lissabon und der Katastrophendiskurs im 18. Jahrhundert*):

> Within the horizon of Voltaire's *Poème* and its reception it has become customary to regard the destruction of Lisbon as a turning point of European intellectual history; as an event that makes palpable the cutting loose from the Enlightenment optimism of a Pope and Leibniz. But historically speaking this is a not unproblematic overstatement because it overlooks the fact not just that the established ways of interpreting the world remained unruffled but also that the sceptical questioning of a naive optimism had always been part and parcel of the Enlightenment itself; it also neglects that the essentially optimistic anthropology of the eighteenth century on the whole never really came to falter.
>
> [Im Horizont von Voltaires *Poème* und seiner Rezeption hat es sich außerdem eingebürgert, die Zerstörung Lissabons gesamteuropäisch als geistesgeschichtlichen Wendepunkt anzusehen; als Ereignis, an dem der Bruch mit dem Optimismus der Aufklärung à la Pope und Leibniz sinnfällig werde. Historisch ist das eine nicht unproblematische Überpointierung, weil sie verkennt, wie selbstverständlich tradierte Deutungsmuster der Katastrophe weiterliefen, skeptizistische Einwände gegen einen naiven Optimismus wesentlicher

---

18 Svend Erik Larsen, 'The Lisbon Earthquake and the Scientific Turn in Kant's Philosophy', *European Review*, 14 (2006), 359–67 (p. 362; the subsequent quotation pp. 362–64).

Bestandteil der Aufklärung selbst waren und die grundsätzlich optimistische Anthropologie des 18. Jahrhunderts keineswegs ins Wanken geraten ist.]¹⁹

Moreover, adopting a simple dualistic approach — Christian belief in God versus a secular natural scientific worldview — forces us to put deistic thinkers like Voltaire and Kant in the same category as such atheists as Paul-Henri Thiry d'Holbach and Denis Diderot who propounded a materialist worldview that did indeed do away with God. As the early chapters of my study will illustrate, the ability to imagine the death of humankind as a species — as Mary Shelley is the first to do in her novel *The Last Man* in 1826 — can only properly be understood against the backdrop of the competition between theistic, deistic and atheistic worldviews that pervaded European intellectual history between the seventeenth and the early nineteenth century. Even after the earthquake of Lisbon, Kant, for instance, as one of the foremost thinkers of his age, remained steadfastly true to the deistic belief that he had held before. Summing up his deistic position, Kant in *Critique of Pure Reason* will later declare: 'the *Deist* believes in God, but the *Theist* in a *living God*' ('der *Deist* glaube einen *Gott*, der *Theist* aber einen *lebendigen Gott* (summam intelligentiam)').²⁰

Kant is hence a good starting point if one wants to understand the complexities involved in the theophilosophical combat zone that was the eighteenth century. Kant effectively began his career not as a speculative philosopher but rather as a natural scientist who in 1755, at the age of 31 and in the year he gained his doctoral degree in Königsberg, published, as one of his earliest and least known works, a 'Cosmogony' (so the originally intended main title of the treatise) in which he set out to explain the development of our universe through God-given natural laws. The Kant of this pre-Critical period was no less commanding and original than he was during his later so-called Critical period; nor was, judged by the works he published before and after 1755, the early Kant any more or less deistic than was the Kant of *Religion within the Limits of Reason Alone*, published in 1793, by which time he views God as the moral essence of practical reason. Indeed, his 1755 treatise *Universal Natural History and Theory of the Heavens or Essay on the Constitution and the Mechanical Origin of the Whole Universe according to Newtonian Principles* (*Allgemeine Naturgeschichte und Theorie des Himmels, oder Versuch von der Verfassung und dem mechanischen Ursprung des ganzen Weltgebäudes nach Newtonischen Grundsätzen abgehandelt*), as he ultimately decided to title his pioneering work (see Figure I.2), must be considered the most advanced *scientific* manifesto of Enlightenment deism. While Kant describes our universe as having been created by God in His supreme wisdom, he does not argue simply *metaphysically* that following creation God took a step back to leave nature to its own devices, as many fellow deists held (in his 'Preface' Kant speaks of 'nature, which is left to itself'),²¹ but uses his work to

---

19 Gerhard Lauer and Thorsten Unger, 'Angesichts der Katastrophe. Das Erdbeben von Lissabon und der Katastrophendiskurs im 18. Jahrhundert', in *Das Erdbeben von Lissabon*, pp. 13–43 (p. 33).

20 Immanuel Kant, *Critique of Pure Reason*, trans. by Max Müller (London: MacMillan, 1881), Part 2, p. 543; *Kritik der reinen Vernunft*, in *Werke in sechs Bänden*, ed. by Wilhelm Weischedel (Darmstadt: Wissenschaftliche Buchgesellschaft, 1956–1964), vol. 2, p. 557.

21 Immanuel Kant, *Universal Natural History and Theory of the Heavens or Essay on the Constitution*

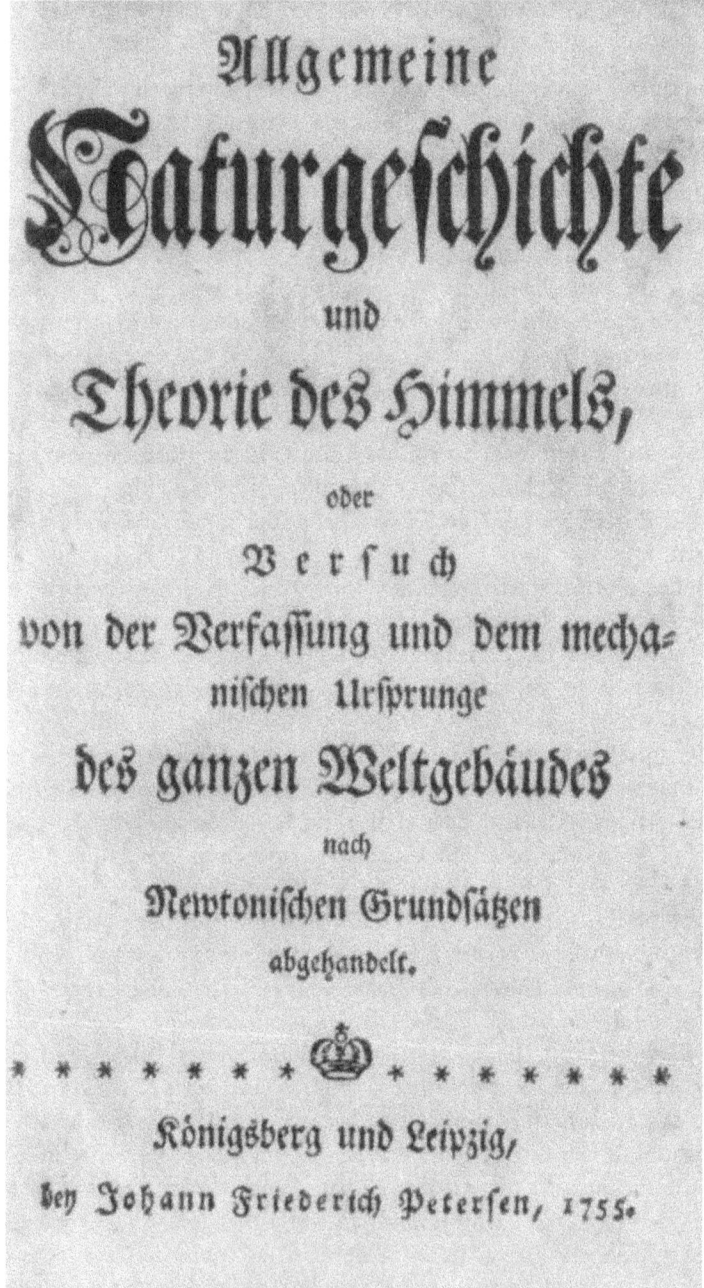

FIG. I.2. Title page of the 1755 first German edition of Immanuel Kant's *Universal Natural History and Theory of the Heavens or Essay on the Constitution and the Mechanical Origin of the Whole Universe according to Newtonian Principles*; in it the 31-year-old naturalist and budding philosopher grants that a Supreme Power created the world, but only as a chaos of matter which possessed independent developmental laws. In effect, Kant's early work of natural philosophy corresponds to an Enlightenment deist's scientific manifesto.

explain how this stepping back can be understood *physically* and in scientific terms. For Kant God is not Archbishop Ussher's Mosaic Old Testament divinity who created the universe in precisely the year 4004 B.C. with nature's fullness of species instantly in place (see Chapter One for more on Ussher's views); instead the German philosopher proposes a groundbreaking model of evolutionary development in which God created the universe as a chaos of matter which from its core proceeded over 'perhaps a thousand, perhaps a million centuries' ('tausend, vielleicht Millionen Jahrhunderte')[22] to accrete into such known physical bodies as the suns, planets and comets of our galaxy and solar system; in his own words, Kant speaks of 'the conjecture about the successive expansion of creation through the infinite spaces' ('sukzessive Ausbreitung der Schöpfung durch die unendlichen Räume').[23] Thus Kant effectively becomes the first natural philosopher to systematically explain through modified Newtonian mechanics and laws of gravitational pull the emergence of deep space and deep time. 'Modified' Newtonian mechanics because Kant explicitly rejects Newton's notion that God himself had, in the act of creation, thrust the completed planets into their eccentric rotational trajectories around our sun; God as the personification of perfection would himself not create things so imperfect — Kant speaks of 'imperfection and deviation' ('Unvollkommenheit und Abweichung') in this context.[24] In contrast to Newton Kant sees exclusively natural factors and laws at play in the gradual processual gestation of planets and comets; only this explains persuasively, and consistently, why their paths around our solar system's gravitational centre should be so imperfect.

---

and the Mechanical Origin of the Whole Universe according to Newtonian Principles (1755), trans. by Olaf Reinhardt, in *Natural History*, pp. 182–308 (p. 194). The extended passage reads in German: 'Von der andern Seite droht die Religion mit einer feierlichen Anklage über die Verwegenheit, da man der sich selbst überlassenen Natur solche Folgen beizumessen sich erkühnen darf, darin man mit Recht die unmittelbare Hand des höchsten Wesens gewahr wird, und besorgt in dem Vorwitze solcher Betrachtungen eine Schutzrede des Gottesleugners anzutreffen.' *Allgemeine Naturgeschichte und Theorie des Himmels, oder Versuch von der Verfassung und dem mechanischen Ursprunge des ganzen Weltgebäudes nach Newtonischen Grundsätzen abgehandelt*, in *Werke*, ed. Weischedel, vol. I, pp. 221–400 (p. 227).

22 *Universal Natural History*, p. 269 (*Allgemeine Naturgeschichte*, p. 339).

23 *Universal Natural History*, pp. 267–68 (*Allgemeine Naturgeschichte*, p. 336).

24 In *The Only Possible Argument for the Demonstration of the Existence of God* of 1763 he writes: 'Who, notwithstanding this, will have this structure immediately delivered into the hand of God, without attributing any thing to mechanical laws, is obliged to assign a reason, why he here finds necessary that which he does not easily grant in natural philosophy. [...] In fine, had God immediately distributed the projectile power and arranged their orbits, it is to be presumed that they would not bear the mark of imperfection and variation, which is to be met with in every production of nature'; in *Essays and Treatises on Moral, Political, Religious and Various Philosophical Subjects* (London: William Richardson, 1799), vol. 2, pp. 217–366 (pp. 335–36). 'Derjenige, welcher diesem ungeachtet dergleichen Bau unmittelbar in die Hand Gottes will übergeben wissen, ohne desfalls den mechanischen Gesetzen etwas zuzutrauen, ist genötigt, etwas anzuführen, weswegen er hier dasjenige notwendig findet, was er sonst in der Naturlehre nicht leichtlich zuläßt. [...] Wenn denn endlich Gott unmittelbar den Planeten die Wurfskraft erteilet und ihre Kreise gestellt hätte, so ist zu vermuten, daß sie nicht das Merkmal der Unvollkommenheit und Abweichung, welches bei jedem Produkt der Natur anzutreffen, an sich zeigen würden'. *Der einzig mögliche Beweisgrund zu einer Demonstration Gottes*, in *Werke*, ed. Weischedel, vol. I, pp. 617–738 (these passages p. 713).

Another integral part of the natural cycle is for the deist Kant that 'all finite things must pass and have an end' ('Alles, was endlich ist, [...] muß vergehen, und ein Ende haben').[25] This allows for nature to contain processes of construction and destruction fully independently of its maker. The theist's reservations are overruled already in Kant's 'Preface' as follows:

> The defender of religion is concerned that those harmonies that can be explained by a natural tendency of matter can be said to prove the independence of nature from divine providence. He admits it quite clearly: that if natural causes can be discovered for all the order in the universe that can be brought about by the most general and most essential properties of matter, then it is not necessary to invoke the highest governing power.
>
> [Der Verteidiger der Religion besorgt: daß diejenigen Übereinstimmungen, die sich aus einem natürlichen Hang der Materie erklären lassen, die Unabhängigkeit der Natur von der göttlichen Vorsehung beweisen dörften [sic]. Er gesteht es nicht undeutlich: daß, wenn man zu aller Ordnung des Weltbaues natürliche Gründe entdecken kann, die dieselbe aus den allgemeinsten und wesentlichen Eigenschaften der Materie zu Stande bringen können, so sei es unnötig, sich auf eine oberste Regierung zu berufen.][26]

Once matter and the laws of nature have been provided for, the process is autonomous and ongoing, with new worlds continually being created as old worlds expire. (Where Kant was mistaken, however, was that like Fontenelle, Pope, and many others, he held that most suns' planets — that is, not just those orbiting our sun but also other stars — were created for beings to live on them; he accordingly develops a theory about the disposition and character of these creatures, with humankind within our own solar system holding only a middling position in terms of physical and intellectual perfection. He even speculates where human beings might go once our own planet reaches the end of its natural life span.)[27]

Two sample passages from *Universal Natural History and Theory of the Heavens* may serve to illustrate Kant's brilliance. In his study's first chapter, entitled 'Of the Origin of the Structure of the World of the Planets generally and the Causes of their Motions', he describes the stirrings of our universe thus:

> I assume that when all matter of which the spheres that constitute our solar system, all the planets and comets, consist, was dissolved into its elementary basic material at the beginning of all things, it occupied the entire space of the universe in which these formal bodies now orbit. This state of nature, even if one considers it in and for itself without regard to any system, appears to be the simplest that could follow upon nothingness. At that time, nothing had formed yet. The arrangement of heavenly bodies distant from one another, their distance moderated by attraction, and their shape that derives from the

---

25 *Universal Natural History*, p. 269 (*Allgemeine Naturgeschichte*, p. 339).
26 *Universal Natural History*, p. 195 (*Allgemeine Naturgeschichte*, p. 229).
27 See in particular Part Three of *Universal Natural History*, pp. 295–306, in which humankind's middling position is discussed p. 301 (*Allgemeine Naturgeschichte*, p. 386) as well as our possible need to emigrate to another planet p. 307 (*Allgemeine Naturgeschichte*, p. 395), a necessity played out in the writer and astronomer Nicolas Camille Flammarion's futuristic novel *La Fin du monde* of 1894, to be discussed in Chapter Two.

equilibrium of their assembled matter, are a later state. Nature as it bordered directly on creation, was as raw, as unformed as possible. However, even in the essential properties of the elements that make up chaos, the characteristic of that perfection can be felt that they have from their origin, in that their essence is a consequence of the eternal idea of the divine reason.

[Ich nehme an: daß alle Materien, daraus die Kugeln, die zu unserer Sonnenwelt gehören, alle Planeten und Kometen bestehen, im Anfange aller Dinge in ihren elementarischen Grundstoff aufgelöst, den ganzen Raum des Weltgebäudes erfüllet haben, darin jetzo diese gebildete Körper herumlaufen. Dieser Zustand der Natur, wenn man ihn, auch ohne Absicht auf ein System, an und vor sich selbst betrachtet, scheinet nur der einfachste zu sein, der auf das Nichts folgen kann. Damals hatte sich noch nichts gebildet. Die Zusammensetzung von einander abstehender Himmelskörper, ihre nach den Anziehungen gemäßigte Entfernung; ihre Gestalt, die aus dem Gleichgewichte der versammelten Materie entspringt: sind ein späterer Zustand. Die Natur, die unmittelbar mit der Schöpfung grenzete, war so roh, so ungebildet als möglich. Allein auch in den wesentlichen Eigenschaften der Elemente, die das Chaos ausmachen, ist das Merkmal derjenigen Vollkommenheit zu spüren, die sie von ihrem Ursprunge her haben, indem ihr Wesen aus der ewigen Idee des göttlichen Verstandes eine Folge ist.][28]

Kant sees the universe as created by God as a chaos of widely scattered matter which ever since creation has been, by means of the laws of nature also created by God, gradually forming itself into the known universe. This premise allows him — and in this he deviates substantially from Newton — to claim that it was not God who physically created the known celestial bodies but the forces of nature God put into play. According to Kant 'Newton could not allow any material cause that would maintain the community of motions by extending it into the realm of the planetary system. He asserted that the direct hand of God had arranged this order without the application of the forces of nature' ('Newton, durch diesen Grund bewogen, konnte keine materialische Ursache verstatten, die durch ihre Erstreckung in dem Raume des Planetengebäudes die Gemeinschaft der Bewegungen unterhalten sollte. Er behauptete, die unmittelbare Hand Gottes habe diese Anordnung ohne die Anwendung der Kräfte der Natur ausgerichtet').[29] This distinction is crucial for Kant because it allows him to view God's freedom as limited by the 'forces of nature' God himself put in place; the universe we see before us today is thus created by the laws of nature, not the 'hand of God'. These laws also govern the processes of growth and decay — the scientific equivalents of the good and evil of Leibniz's theodicy; Kant hence explains, making specific reference to Pope's *Essay on Man*:

Considerable areas of the earth that we inhabit are buried again in the sea from which a favourable period had dragged them; but in other places, nature replaces the deficiency and brings forth other regions that had been concealed in the depths of the water to spread new riches of its fruitfulness over them. In the same way, worlds and world-orders pass away and are swallowed by the abyss of eternities; by contrast, creation is ever busy carrying out new formations

---

28 *Universal Natural History*, pp. 227–28 (*Allgemeine Naturgeschichte*, p. 275).
29 *Universal Natural History*, pp. 226–27 (*Allgemeine Naturgeschichte*, p. 274).

in other regions of the heavens and replacing what has gone with advantage. [...] However, we must not lament the end of a world structure as a true loss of nature. [...] Nature shows that it is just as bountiful, just as inexhaustible in the production of the most excellent of creatures as it is in that of those of low regard, and that even their end is a necessary gradation in the diversity of its suns, because their creation costs it nothing. The deleterious effects of infected air, earthquakes, floods eradicate whole peoples from the face of the earth, but it does not appear that nature has suffered any disadvantage through this. In a similar way, whole worlds and systems leave the scene after they have finished playing their roles. The infinity of creation is great enough for us to view a world or a Milky Way of worlds in comparison to it, just as we view a flower or an insect in comparison to the Earth. Meanwhile, so that nature will beautify eternity with changeable scenes, God remains busy in ceaseless creation to make the material for the formation of even greater worlds.

> Who sees with equal eye, as God of all,
> A hero perish or a sparrow fall,
> Atoms or systems into ruin hurl'd,
> And now a bubble burst, and now a world.
> POPE

Let us therefore accustom our eye to these frightening upheavals as being the ordinary ways of providence and regard them even with a kind of appreciation.

[Beträchtliche Stücke des Erdbodens, den wir bewohnen, werden wiederum in dem Meere begraben, aus dem sie ein günstiger Periodus hervorgezogen hatte; aber an anderen Orten ergänzet die Natur den Mangel, und bringet andere Gegenden hervor, die in der Tiefe des Wesens [the *Akademie Ausgabe* of Kant's works here has 'Wasser', as also reflected in the English translation; R. W.] verborgen waren, um neue Reichtümer ihrer Fruchtbarkeit über dieselbe auszubreiten. Auf die gleiche Art vergehen Welten und Weltordnungen, und werden von dem Abgrunde der Ewigkeiten verschlungen; dagegen ist die Schöpfung immerfort geschäftig, in andern Himmelsgegenden neue Bildungen zu verrichten, und den Abgang mit Vorteile zu ergänzen. [...] Wir dürfen aber den Untergang eines Weltgebäudes nicht als einen wahren Verlust der Natur bedauern. [...] Die Natur beweiset, daß sie eben so reich, eben so unerschöpflich, in Hervorbringung des Trefflichsten unter den Kreaturen, als des Geringschätzigsten, ist, und daß selbst deren Untergang eine notwendige Schattierung in der Mannigfaltigkeit ihrer Sonnen ist, weil die Erzeugung derselben ihr nichts kostet. Die schädlichsten Wirkungen der angesteckten Luft, die Erdbeben, die Überschwemmungen vertilgen ganze Völker von dem Erdboden; allein es scheint nicht, daß die Natur dadurch einigen Nachteil erlitten habe. Auf gleiche Weise verlassen ganze Welten und Systemwelten den Schauplatz, nachdem sie ihre Rolle ausgespielet haben. Die Unendlichkeit der Schöpfung ist groß genug, um eine Welt, oder eine Milchstraße von Welten, gegen sie anzusehen, wie man eine Blume, oder ein Insekt, in Vergleichung gegen die Erde, ansiehet. Indessen, daß die Natur mit veränderlichen Auftritten die Ewigkeit auszieret, bleibt Gott in einer unaufhörlichen Schöpfung geschäftigt, den Zeug zur Bildung noch größerer Welten zu formen. [Here follows the passage from Pope's *Essay on Man* in a German translation.] Laßt uns also unser Auge an diese erschreckliche Umstürzungen als an die gewöhnlichen Wege der Vorsehung gewöhnen, und sie sogar mit einer Art von Wohlgefallen ansehen.]³⁰

Kant approaches such 'frightening upheavals' as earthquakes with 'appreciation' ('Wohlgefallen') therefore because they are part and parcel of the eternal ebb and flow that defines the natural cycle of destruction and reconstruction. Yet despite his *implicit* championing of Leibniz's and Pope's notions of the best of all possible worlds, Kant carefully avoids *explicit* mention of Pope's phrase 'All is well'; he likewise engages critically with Leibniz's notion of our world being the best of all choices available to God. Because God and world are linked only obliquely rather than directly (with God being the originative First Cause of the world rather than the creator of its later stages and states of being, including the universe as we witness it today),³¹ God did not choose the best of all possible worlds but only the best laws of nature available to him. This in turn entails that the world's imperfections cannot be equated with God's imperfection, taking the wind out of the sails of Voltaire's refutation of Leibniz's theodicy following the Lisbon earthquake.³² For

---

30 *Universal Natural History*, pp. 269–70 (*Allgemeine Naturgeschichte*, pp. 338–40); in the English translation I substituted the retranslated lines from Brockes's version of Pope with those from Pope's English original of the *Essay on Man*.

31 In the last section of Part One of his *Critique of Pure Reason*, entitled 'Criticism of all theology, based on speculative principles of reason' ('Kritik aller Theologie aus spekulativen Prinzipien der Vernunft'), Kant distinguishes explicitly between God as 'a cause of the world only' ('bloß eine *Welturache*') and as a 'creator' ('*Welturheber*') or '*author* of the world', in Max Müller's translation. The deist believes in God as 'cause' ('*Ursache*'), the theist believes in him as 'creator' ('*Urheber*').

32 He states as much in the following somewhat convoluted passage of *The Only Possible Argument for the Demonstration of the Existence of God*, pp. 352–53: 'With such questions it is difficult and perhaps impossible to decide any thing from the contemplation of possible things only. But, when I weigh both problems in connexion with the Divine Being, and cognise that the preference of the choice, which the one world has before the other, may be gathered without the preference in the *judgment* of the same being that chuses, or even contrary to this judgment, a want in the agreement of this different active powers [*sic*] and a different reference of his efficacy, without a proportionate difference in the grounds, consequently a deformity in the most perfect Being, I conclude with great conviction That [*sic*] the proposed cases must be feigned and impossible. For according to all the preparations which have been seen I comprehend That there is much less ground, from presupposed possibilities, which cannot however be sufficiently ascertained, to conclude a necessary conduct of the most perfect Being (which is of such a nature, as to seem to lessen the conception of the greatest harmony in him) than from the cognised harmony, in which the possibilities of things must be with the Divine nature, from what is cognised to be the most suitable to this Being to conclude the possibility. I therefore presume that in the possibilities of all worlds there can be no such relations, as must contain a ground of the embarrassment in the rational choice of the Supreme Being; for this very Supreme Being containeth the last ground of all this possibility, in which, then, nothing else, than what harmonizes with its origin, can be met with.' 'Bei dergleichen Fragen ist es schwer und vielleicht unmöglich, aus der Betrachtung möglicher Dinge allein etwas zu entscheiden. Allein wenn ich beide Aufgaben in Verknüpfung mit dem göttlichen Wesen erwäge, und erkenne, daß der Vorzug der Wahl, der einer Welt vor der andern zu Teil wird, ohne den Vorzug in dem *Urteile* eben desselben Wesens welches wählt, oder gar wider dieses Urteil ein Mangel in der Übereinstimmung seiner verschiedenen tätigen Kräfte und eine verschiedene Beziehung seiner Wirksamkeit, ohne eine proportionierte Verschiedenheit in den Gründen, mithin einen Übelstand in dem vollkommensten Wesen abnehmen lasse, so schließe ich mit großer Überzeugung: daß die vorgelegten Fälle erdichtet und unmöglich sein müssen. Denn ich begreife nach den gesamten Vorbereitungen, die man gesehen

'all this shows', Kant emphasizes, 'that the first cause was tied to the mechanical rules of motion and did not act by free choice' ('alles zeigt, daß die erste Ursache an die mechanischen Regeln der Bewegung gebunden gewesen, und nicht durch freie Wahl gehandelt hat').[33] Because God has given nature free rein — albeit within the constraints of the mechanical and gravitational laws of nature that he established at the beginning of time and continues to maintain throughout time — the cycle of nature must encompass, as part of its divine essence, also the 'necessary shadings' ('notwendige Schattierung')[34] of decay and destruction alongside growth and construction.

In this way Kant, who devised his model of how the universe functions already before the earthquake struck Lisbon, provides the answer to Voltaire's quandary following the earthquake, namely how to retain a belief in God in plain sight of great evil and devastation on Earth. For Kant, God is not directly but only indirectly responsible: he has given his authority over to the laws of nature, and thus even God cannot change the way nature works. Taking his cue from Hume's essay 'Of Miracles', published seven years earlier in 1748, divine interventions are impossible, for they would oblige God to interfere with the natural processes he himself had set in motion at the moment of creation, yet to which he had also granted autonomy since then. Any miracle would hence require, in Hume's words, a volitional 'transgression of a law of nature'.[35] Like the deist Hume Kant holds 'that nature has brought forth [its] determinations without being interrupted in its free behaviour by any extraordinary compulsion' ('daß die Natur, ohne durch einen außerordentlichen Zwang in ihrem freien Betragen gestört zu sein, diese Bestimmungen hervorgebracht habe').[36] This did not necessitate the denial of the possible occurrence of natural calamities, for instance on the scale of the biblical Deluge, but it did necessitate giving them a purely natural explanation. Thus Kant granted in *Universal Natural History and Theory of the Heavens* that the Deluge had happened, but it stemmed not from God seeking to punish mankind for its sins, but rather from a ring of water particles that had formerly circled our planet in the manner of Saturn's existing rings; through disruptive gravitational forces (Kant

hat: daß man viel weniger Grund habe, aus vorausgesetzten Möglichkeiten, die man gleichwohl nicht genug bewähren kann, auf ein notwendiges Betragen des vollkommensten Wesens zu schließen (welches so beschaffen ist, daß es den Begriff der größten Harmonie in ihm zu schmälern scheinet), als aus der erkannten Harmonie, die die Möglichkeiten der Dinge mit der göttlichen Natur haben müssen, von demjenigen, was diesem Wesen am anständigsten zu sein erkannt wird, auf die Möglichkeit zu schließen. Ich werde also vermuten, daß in den Möglichkeiten aller Welten keine solche Verhältnisse sein können, die einen Grund der Verlegenheit der vernünftigen Wahl des höchsten Wesens enthalten müßten; denn eben dieses oberste Wesen enthält den letzten Grund aller dieser Möglichkeit, in welcher also niemalen etwas anders, als was mit ihrem Ursprung harmoniert, kann anzutreffen sein' (*Der einzig mögliche Beweisgrund zu einer Demonstration Gottes*, pp. 726–27).

33 *Universal Natural History*, p. 290 (*Allgemeine Naturgeschichte*, p. 370).

34 What Hastie translates as 'necessary shading' Reinhardt has translated as 'necessary gradation' in the quotation previously cited.

35 Hume had written: 'A miracle may be accurately defined [as] a transgression of a law of nature by a particular volition of the Deity'; *Hume on Religion*, ed. by Julian Baggini (London: The Philosophy Press, 2010), pp. 137–52 (p. 141).

36 *Universal Natural History*, p. 292 (*Allgemeine Naturgeschichte*, p. 373).

mentions the passing of a comet as one possible cause) the ring collapsed onto the Earth, causing a world-wide inundation. Today's rainbows remain a visual reminder of the immense rainbow early humans would have seen as a great ring circling our atmosphere. (Kant will later change his view as regards the details of this scientific explanation, but even then the principle of God's non-interference remains untouched.)[37] Against his theistic contemporaries, who would prefer to hold on to the Bible's miraculous account, he maintains:

> The similarity of the shape of this memorial sign with the event it signified could commend such a hypothesis to those who are devoted to the dominant tendency of bringing the miracles of revelation into the same system as the ordinary laws of nature. I consider it more advisable completely to forgo the fleeting applause such correspondences might arouse for the true pleasure that arises from the perception of regular connections when physical analogies support each other to designate physical truths.
>
> [Die Ähnlichkeit der Gestalt dieses Erinnerungszeichens mit der bezeichneten Begebenheit könnte eine solche Hypothese denenjenigen anpreisen, die der herrschenden Neigung ergeben sind, die Wunder der Offenbarung mit den ordentlichen Naturgesetzen in ein System zu bringen. Ich finde es vor ratsamer, den flüchtigen Beifall, den solche Übereinstimmungen erwecken können, dem wahren Vergnügen völlig aufzuopfern, welches aus der Wahrnehmung des regelmäßigen Zusammenhanges entspringet, wenn physische Analogien einander zur Bezeichnung physischer Wahrheiten unterstützen.][38]

As 'physical truths' all natural occurrences must, according to Kant, be accounted for through scientific means, never through supernatural ones.

And yet, true to his own deistic faith, Kant cannot and will not do away with the notion of a First Cause that miraculously created matter and nature's laws in the first place. This inconsistency in particular, deism's dilemma of wanting it both ways, a nature wholly independent of its maker as well as a God who created that nature at the outset, ultimately led, as I will show in Chapter Two, to deism's demise in the early nineteenth century. The challenge we as humans face is, from Kant's deistic perspective, first to recognize and accept that this is how God has created nature and then, second, to scientifically analyze nature's laws and ways of functioning — including its destructive and calamitous aspects — so as to allow ourselves better to respond to the disasters that are an unavoidable, but not preordained, consequence of the laws of nature. It was not in order to revise his theophilosophical position that Kant set out to write his three essays about the Lisbon earthquake in 1756, as Larsen seems to suggest, but rather to scientifically reflect on the actual physical causes that had brought on the earthquake as well as to identify and recommend reason-driven counter-measures through which one might avoid future loss of life especially in such earthquake-prone areas as Peru, Chile, Iceland and central Italy. Published just

---

37 In his *Physical Geography* lectures, given by Kant 49 times between 1756 and 1796 and published by his friend Friedrich Theodor Rink in 1802, the Flood becomes one of numerous inundations to have covered the continents on and off during the planet's development. See Immanuel Kant, *Physical Geography*, in *Natural Science*, pp. 434–679, especially p. 563.

38 *Universal Natural History*, pp. 258–59 (*Allgemeine Naturgeschichte*, p. 323).

months before the earthquake of Lisbon struck, Kant's 1755 *Cosmogony* offered an adequate *general* scientific explanation of why earthquakes must occur, but what it failed to provide — and indeed what it was never intended to provide — was an analysis of the *specific* geophysical reasons why earthquakes occur; it is these reasons that Kant felt prompted by the earthquake of Lisbon to investigate more closely in the three subsequent essays.

All three essays are premised on the observation — supported by numerous contemporary reports from geographical regions as far-flung as France, Bavaria, Naples, Iceland, Finland, the Kingdom of Fez (today's Morocco), the Indian Ocean islands of Banda and Amboina, the West Indies, Peru and Chile, as well as Portugal — that the ground we live on must be shot through with extensive subterranean vaults and caverns (three times deeper than the deepest man-made mines, Kant speculates) that reach even under the ocean beds, but which Kant recognizes as for the most part aligned with the direction of the world's great mountain ranges (something confirmed by today's knowledge of the Earth's tectonic plates and their stress zones). These cavities contain the surplus water from the deluge that once submerged the planet's surface in the dawn of history, but also the chemical and mineral elements that cause volcanic activity. When water combines with fire and air, subterranean explosions are the result; it is these explosions that rock the Earth's surface. Twentieth-century plate tectonics finally put paid to such speculation. My purpose in summarizing Kant's geophysical reflections on the origins of earthquakes is not to quibble with the time-bound details of his scientific ratiocination. Obviously Kant could not but operate within the Volcanic and Plutonic paradigms current in his day (and indeed we see him cleverly combining both in his own theorizing); obviously, too, much in the way of scientific knowledge that we take for granted today had to elude Kant and his eighteenth-century contemporaries. What I do want to highlight, by contrast, is how Kant deploys his detailed scientific argument among other things to counter Voltaire's dismay over the seeming cruelty tolerated, if not endorsed, by God when he 'allowed' the Lisbon earthquake to happen. In a key passage in the second and longest essay, 'History and natural description of the most noteworthy occurrences of the earthquake that struck a large part of the Earth at the end of the year 1755', Kant accordingly notes, mixing admonishment of people over their foolish ways with a caution not to confuse earthquakes with the workings of Providence:

> It is easy to guess that, if people build on ground that is filled with flammable matters, then sooner or later the whole glory of their buildings could be destroyed by earthquakes; but must we therefore become impatient with the ways of providence? Would it not be better to conclude that it was necessary for earthquakes to occur occasionally on the Earth, but it was not necessary for us to erect splendid houses on it? The inhabitants of Peru live in houses that are built with mortar only up to a low height and the rest consists of reeds. Man must learn to adapt to nature, but he wants nature to adapt to him.
>
> [Es lässt sich leicht rathen, dass, wenn Menschen auf einem Grunde bauen, der mit entzündbaren Materien angefüllt ist, über kurz oder lang die ganze Pracht ihrer Gebäude durch Erschütterungen über den Haufen fallen könne;

aber muss man denn darum über die Wege der Vorsehung ungeduldig werden? Wäre es nicht besser, so zu urtheilen: es war nöthig, dass Erdbeben bisweilen auf dem Erdboden geschehen; aber es war nicht nothwendig, dass wir prächtige Wohnplätze darüber erbauen. Die Einwohner in Peru wohnen in Häusern, die nur in geringer Höhe gemauert sind, und das Uebrige besteht aus Rohr. Der Mensch muss sich in die Natur schicken lernen; aber er will, dass sie sich in ihn schicken soll.][39]

In the same vein he had stressed in the introductory preamble to the scientific part of this essay:

> Even the terrible instruments by which disaster is visited on mankind, the shattering of countries, the fury of the sea shaken to its foundations, the fire-spewing mountains, invite man's contemplation, and are planted in nature by God as a proper consequence of fixed laws no less than other accustomed causes of discomfort which are thought to be more natural merely because they are more familiar.
>
> [Selbst die fürchterlichen Werkzeuge der Heimsuchung des menschlichen Geschlechts, die Erschütterungen der Länder, die Wuth des in seinem Grunde bewegten Meeres, die feuerspeienden Berge fordern den Menschen zur Betrachtung auf, und sind nicht weniger von Gott als eine richtige Folge aus beständigen Gesetzen in die Natur gepflanzt, als andere schon gewohnte Ursachen der Ungemächlichkeit, die man darum für natürlicher hält, weil man mit ihnen mehr bekannt ist.]

No different than in his 1755 *Universal Natural History and Theory of the Heavens*, Kant in the three 1756 essays on the earthquake of Lisbon sees God as the supreme architect of our universe and nature as a force independent of its maker. Man should not deceive himself to regard nature as created only for his benefit but should rather learn from nature's doings how better to take precautions. In short, *before as after* the Lisbon earthquake, Kant consistently regarded earthquakes — no less than any other manifestation of nature's destructive power — as integral to the functioning of nature as a whole; seeing the Lisbon earthquake as he did as governed by the laws of nature, Kant saw no reason in it to modify or change his views either on divine agency or natural law. But, most importantly, Kant stresses in 1763 in 'The Only Possible Argument for the Demonstration of the Existence of God' (as part of which he also recapitulates his cosmogonical findings put forward in *Universal Natural History and Theory of the Heavens*) that it would be folly to construe any direct connection between what happens in nature and the hand of divine Providence, and even more so to regard the activities of nature as a disciplinary instrument being wielded in response to man's moral conduct in this world; Kant writes:

> There are many powers in nature which have the faculty to destroy single men, states, or even the whole human race. Earthquakes, storms or tempests, comets &c. It is sufficiently founded in the constitution of nature according to a universal law that one of these shall now and then happen. But the vices and

---

39 'History and Natural Description of the Most Noteworthy Occurences of the Earthquake', p. 360 ('Geschichte und Naturbeschreibung der merkwürdigen Vorfälle des Erdbebens', p. 440); the subsequent quotation p. 340 (p. 415).

the moral corruption of the human species are no *natural* grounds at all that are in conjunction with the laws according to which it takes place. The crimes of a city have no influence on the hidden fire of the earth [...]. And when such a case happens, it is attributed to a natural law, which signifies that it is a misfortune, but not a punishment, the moral conduct of men can be no ground of an earthquake according to a natural law, because no connexion of causes and effects has here place.

[Es sind viele Kräfte in der Natur, die das Vermögen haben, einzelne Menschen, oder Staaten, oder das ganze menschliche Geschlecht zu verderben. Erdbeben, Sturmwinde, Meersbewegungen, Kometen etc. Es ist auch nach einem allgemeinen Gesetze genugsam in der Verfassung der Natur gegründet, daß einiges von diesen bisweilen geschieht. Allein unter den Gesetzen, wornach es geschieht, sind die Laster und das moralische Verderben der Menschengeschlechter gar keine *natürlichen* Gründe, die damit in Verbindung stünden. Die Missetaten einer Stadt haben keinen Einfluß auf das verborgene Feuer der Erde [...]. Und wenn sich ein solcher Fall ereignet, man mißt ihm aber einem natürlichen Gesetze bei, so will man damit sagen, daß es ein Unglück, nicht aber, daß es eine Strafe sei, indem das moralische Verhalten der Menschen kein Grund der Erdbeben nach einem natürlichen Gesetze sein kann, weil hier keine Verknüpfung von Ursachen und Wirkungen statt findet.][40]

Here Kant is not attacking deists like Voltaire who felt themselves prompted by the Lisbon earthquake to reject the notion of a benign and omnipotent God; rather, his target is their theological opposite, the theist for whom earthquakes represented a manifestation of God's discontent with and warning to his people.

In the heated religious climate of the mid-eighteenth century, when Protestant Pietism was at its high point and the counter-Enlightenment was picking up pace, devout Christians continued to interpret earthquakes as God serving notice to his people, prevailing upon the faithful to remain steadfast in their conviction and sinners to return to the virtuous path. Severe earthquakes like that of Lisbon in 1755, that is, those with a toll to human life, were habitually invoked by clerics as God dispensing punishment for mortal sins already committed. Prime examples are the British Protestant ministers John and Charles Wesley, the evangelical founder of Methodism and his younger sibling. Charles Wesley thus opens his 1750 tract *The Cause and Cure of Earthquakes. A Sermon preach'd from Psalm xlvi. 8* — the writing of which had been triggered by two milder earthquakes hitting London and southern England that year — with the unequivocal assertion: 'Of all the Judgments which the righteous GOD inflicts on Sinners here, the most dreadful and destructive is an Earthquake'.[41] Moreover, Wesley continues, earthquakes are portents of God's wrath to come when he expects the Last Judgment to be visited upon mankind; the above passage consequently continues: 'This he has lately brought on our Part of the Earth, and thereby alarmed our Fears, and bid us *prepare to meet our GOD!* The Shocks which have been felt in diverse Places since that which made this City

---

[40] *The Only Possible Argument for the Demonstration of the Existence of God*, pp. 278–79 (*Der einzig mögliche Beweisgrund zu einer Demonstration des Daseins Gottes*, pp. 667–68).

[41] Charles Wesley, *The Cause and Cure of Earthquakes. A Sermon preach'd from Psalm xlvi. 8* (London: n. pub.], 1750), p. 3.

tremble, may convince us that the Danger is not over, and ought to keep us still in Awe'.⁴² The following five sentences encapsulate the Wesleys' moral message:

> Sin is the Cause, Earthquakes the Effect of his Anger. [...] God warns you of the approaching Judgment, that ye may take Warning and escape it by timely Repentance. [...] The Lord was in the Earthquake, and put a solemn Question to thy Conscience, Art thou ready to die? [...] Repent *and* believe the Gospel. Believe on [sic] the Lord Jesus, and ye shall be saved.⁴³

In the same vein the Wesleys published numerous moralizing hymns in the wake of the Lisbon earthquake, in all of which they warn their reader to be prepared. A typical specimen is Charles Wesley's 'Hymn XVII', written and published in 1756, three strophes of which read (I have italicized Wesley's references to earthquakes):

> The Plague, and Dearth, and Din of War
> Our SAVIOUR's swift Approach declare,
> And bid our Hearts arise:
> *Earth's Basis shook* confirms our Hope,
> *Its Cities Fall* but lifts us up,
> To meet Thee in the Skies.
>
> Thy Tokens we with joy confess,
> The War proclaims the Prince of Peace,
> *The Earthquake speaks thy power,*
> The Famine all thy Fullness brings,
> The Plague presents thy healing Wings,
> And Nature's final Hour.
>
> Whatever Ill the World befall,
> A Pledge of endless Good we call,
> A Sign of JESUS near:
> His Chariot will not long delay:
> *We hear the rumbling Wheels,* and pray
> Triumphant LORD, appear.

John Wesley's hymn 'Rev. xvi, xvii, etc. Occasion'd by the Destruction of LISBON'⁴⁴ similarly presents the real earthquake as an ominous harbinger of the

---

42 Wesley is just one — albeit a prime — example of what T. D. Kendrick observed in *The Lisbon Earthquake*, an early study of the eighteenth-century response to the 1755 Lisbon earthquake and its 1750 English preludes; Kendrick writes: 'In that comfortable world it may have been the case that an earthquake was, except for the Day of Judgement, the most terrible thing that could happen to man [...]. No attempt at a scientific explanation had as yet made an earthquake in the general consciousness an understandable happening, like flood or a fire. [...] An earthquake remained therefore for the majority of people an event "instinct with deity", terrible because of the holiness of God. If it aroused pity, sympathy, and charity towards those who suffered in such a disaster, it aroused also a violently emotional theological reckoning, expressed in hysterical repentance and agitated speculation about man's relation to God and about God's purpose for this world. The sinner stood sharply rebuked, and terrified; the churches filled, and the parson had to chide and comfort his congregation. That was the result of [the] two light shocks of 1750'; Thomas D. Kendrick, *The Lisbon Earthquake* (London: Methuen, 1956), pp. 22–23.

43 *The Cause and Cure of Earthquakes*, pp. 4, 19 and twice 21.

44 'Rev. xvi, xvii, etc. Occasion'd by the Destruction of LISBON', in anon., *Hymns occasioned by the Earthquake, March 8, 1750. To which are added an Hymn upon the pouring out of the Seventh Vial, Rev.*

imminent apocalypse:

> The mighty Shock *seems now* begun,
> Beyond Example great,
> And lo! the World's Foundations groan
> As in their instant Fate!
> JEHOVAH shakes the shatter'd Ball,
> Sign of the general Doom!
> The Cities of the Nations fall,
> And *Babel's* Hour is come. (emphases by John Wesley)

The same year 1756 also saw the publication of John Wesley's homily *Serious Thoughts Occasioned by the Earthquake at Lisbon, to which is subjoin'd An Account of all the late Earthquakes there, and in other Places*. Going to no fewer than six editions that year alone, Wesley's *Serious Thoughts* usefully illustrates how cataclysmic events such as the Lisbon earthquake were instrumentalized by evangelical theists not just to indoctrinate their fellow believers and inoculate them against doubt, but also to berate and propagandize against their opponents. Thus Wesley sees in the Lisbon earthquake the hand of (the Protestants') God at work, meting out just punishment to Catholics for their reprehensible support of the Inquisition, a Catholic institution the Portuguese seat of which was headquartered in Lisbon. 'And what shall we say of the late Accounts from *Portugal*? That several thousand Houses, and many thousand Persons, are no more? That a fair City is now in ruinous Heaps? Is there indeed a GOD that judges the World?' he asks nearly as if to invoke Voltaire's argument, only to answer: 'And is He now making Inquisition for Blood? If so, it is not surprizing [sic] that He should begin there, where so much Blood has been poured on the Ground like Water; where so many brave Men have been murdered, in the most base and cowardly, as well as barbarous Manner, almost every Day, as well as every Night'; 'how long', he continues, in praise of God for having at last called down his ire on Catholics for their savagery against Protestants, 'has their Blood been crying from the Earth? Yea, how long has [...] the Scandal of all Religion, but even of human Nature, stood to insult both Heaven and Earth? And *shall I not visit for these Things, saith the LORD? shall not my Soul be avenged of such a City as this?*'[45]

However, the religious bigotry of Wesley's *Serious Thoughts* is only one reason for my interest in this partisan tract. The other is the disingenuous manner in which he first summons and — cursorily — debates the scientific argument concerning earthquakes and their causes only to swiftly overrule them as irrelevant. Like Kant in his 1756 essays on earthquakes (and indeed like the French *Encyclopedie* that, in its entry on earthquakes, '*Tremblemens de terre*', cites 'fire, air and water' ('*le feu, l'air*

---

xvi, xvii, etc. Occasioned by the destruction of Lisbon, Part 2, 2nd edn (Bristol: E. Farley, 1756), pp. 10–12, strophe 10. No author is given on the title page. Although I have seen this text attributed to John Wesley, his brother Charles was a by far more prolific writer of such religious hymns; it is likely that the author of this volume was Charles rather than John.

45 John Wesley, *Serious Thoughts Occasioned by the Earthquake at Lisbon, to which is subjoin'd An Account of all the late Earthquakes there, and in other Places*, 6th edn (London: [n. publ.], 1756), pp. 4–5.

& *l'eau*') as the three '*matieres [...] combustibles*' that cause earthquakes),⁴⁶ Wesley too speculates that only 'Fire, Water, or Air' can provide the possible natural causes for such subterranean phenomena.⁴⁷ But upon brief reflection he rejects all three as insufficient to produce the physical effects he himself had observed in Yorkshire. His perfunctory rejection of 'Fire' as the first of these natural options thus reads: 'It could not be Fire; for then some Mark of it must have appeared, either at the Time, or after it. But no such Mark does appear, nor ever did: Not so much as the least Smoke, either when the first or second Rock was removed, or in the whole Space between *Tuesday* and *Sunday*'. 'What then could be the Cause?' he inquires and answers, citing what he sees as the only plausible explanation:

> What, indeed but GOD, who arose to shake terribly the Earth: Who purposely chose such a Place, where there is so great a Concourse of Nobility and Gentry every Year [at the local races, as Wesley had explained earlier in his tract]; and wrought in such a Manner, that many might see it and fear, that all who travel one of the most frequented Roads in *England* might see it, almost whether they would or no, for many Miles together. [...] Nor can it well serve any Use, but to tell all that see it, *Who can stand before this great* GOD?

In short, Wesley concludes, 'it is not Chance which governs the World'; and Lisbon should serve as a warning to us all:

> Why should we not now, before *London* is as *Lisbon*, *Lima*, or *Catania*, acknowledge the Hand of the Almighty, arising to maintain his own Cause? Why, we have a general Answer always ready, to screen us from any such Conviction: "All these Things are purely natural Causes". But there are two Objections to this Answer: first, it is untrue; Secondly, it is uncomfortable.⁴⁸

To support his claim, he enlarges on both points in the following way:

> First, If by affirming, "All this is purely natural," you mean it is not providential, or that GOD has nothing to do with it, this is not true, that is, supposing the Bible to be true. For supposing this, you may descant ever so long on the natural Causes of Murrain, Winds, Thunder, Lightning, and yet you are altogether wide of the Mark, you prove nothing at all, unless you can prove, that GOD never works in or by natural Causes. [...] A second Objection to your Answer is, it is extremely uncomfortable. For if Things really be as you affirm, if all these afflictive Incidents entirely depend on the fortuitous Concourse and Agency of blind, material Causes, what Hope, what Help, what Resource is left, for the poor Sufferer by them?

Wesley not just seeks to eliminate Kant's careful reasoning based on natural law through argumentative sleight of hand (a reasoning that will be seen as stringent and adequate only by fellow religious believers for whom the Bible is the only

---

46 *Encyclopedie ou Dictionnaire Raisonné des Sciences, des Arts et des Métiers*, vol. 16, entry 'Tremblemens de Terre' (Neufchastel: Samuel Faulche, [n.d.]), pp. 580–83. This article is amended in the 1778 edition by two reports, one on Lisbon, the other on electricity as a further possible cause of earthquakes.

47 *Serious Thoughts Occasioned by the Earthquake at Lisbon*, p. 8; the subsequent passages pp. 8 and 10.

48 Ibid., p. 11; the subsequent quotation p. 12.

Fig. I.3. John Martin, *The Great Day of His Wrath*, 1852 (© Tate, London 2016), based on St. John's *Revelation* 6.12–17: 'And I beheld when he had opened the sixth seal, and, lo, there was a great earthquake; and the sun became black as sackcloth of hair, and the moon became as blood. [...] And the kings of the earth, and the great men, and the rich men [...], and every free man, hid themselves in the dens and in the rocks of the mountains; And said to the mountains and rocks, Fall on us, and hide us from the face of him that sitteth on the throne, and from the wrath of the Lamb; For the great day of his wrath is come; and who shall be able to stand?'

credible explanatory paradigm); he also summarily lumps together his opponents' competing philosophies of religion. Thus because they privilege natural law as the only acceptable explanatory paradigm for what happens in the natural world rather than God's ongoing miraculous intervention, Hume's and Kant's distinctly deistic stances find themselves lumped together with such manifestly materialistic and atheistic positions as those put forward by Julien Offray de La Mettrie before 1756 in his 1748 *Machine Man* (*L'homme machine*), and by Holbach after 1756 in his 1770 *System of Nature*. However, as I suggested earlier — and this is the core proposition I shall pursue in this book — it is precisely the competition between theism, deism and atheism that propels the gestation of the first secular Last Man narrative in the early nineteenth century.

For let us recall and be mindful of the fact that the Christian brand of terminal narrative — in other words, the pre-secular standard model of the terminal narrative that dominated European thought for so many centuries — was in actual fact no such thing. In terms of thinking about natural disasters, the two key cataclysmic events that underlie Christian doctrine are the Old Testament's narrative of the

Flood — which was to become one of the great stumbling blocks hampering the development of early geology (more about which in Chapter Four) — and the New Testament's narrative of Last Judgment, most vividly depicted in St. John the Divine's book of *Revelation* in which (in *Revelation* 6:12) the breaking of the sixth seal is followed by an earthquake that in turn precedes (as foreseen in *Revelation* 6:17) the 'great day of his wrath to come' — and which is so wonderfully and famously depicted by the Victorian artist John Martin in the 1852 painting of the same title (see Figure I.3). The Last Judgment may be prophesied to bring about the end of the world as we know it, yet humankind is predestined to live on nonetheless, with some of us suffering eternal woe in Hell, others everlasting bliss in Heaven; alternative accounts hold that we must face a liminal waiting period in limbo or linger through the millennium in expectation of God's final judgment. The Old Testament narrative of ending, the story of the Deluge and the survival of Noah and his family, bunked up in the Ark alongside the pairs of all animal creatures until the waters recede, is, although the larger part of humankind is destroyed, ultimately also a narrative of renewal and restoration. From Noah's sons and their wives a new humanity will proceed from which, for those who believe the tale, we all descend. Neither the narrative of the Last Judgment nor that of the biblical Flood are truly terminal narratives, however; they are what I above dubbed 'semi-terminal'. Humanity is wiped out only to resume existence after the cataclysm. Moreover, these are not just narratives of survival, in whatever physical or ethereal form; they are simultaneously narratives of punishment and reward by the hand of God. Certainly in its orthodox literalist manifestations, the Christian belief system cannot tolerate a truly terminal end for mankind; it cannot do without the eschatological promise of hope and resurrection, as John Wesley above makes so abundantly clear. For him, the notion of hopelessness alone is criterion enough to invalidate scientific explanation. As for the 'temporal' termination of species, their decline and extinction through natural means on our planet, the idea alone was sacrilege to Christian doctrine and was seen to threaten moral and social collapse since by contradicting the biblical account both of God creating all animal species and of Noah rescuing them in his Ark the notion of natural extinction — and especially the extinction of all descendants of Adam — put in question at once the authority and the supremacy of God as well as the Christian concept of salvation.

The argument surrounding the possibility of species extinction on which the Last Man narrative is premised played a crucial part in the gestation of modern secular science — especially geology, zoology, botany, (comparative) anatomy, anthropology, and paleontology — during the epistemic threshold era of 1775–1825. While it was a hurdle that needed overcoming, it also represented a potentially perilous terrain for naturalists to tread due to its profound religious implications; hence eighteenth-century naturalists and natural philosophers had to be no less on their guard as to how they formulated their ideas than in the following century Charles Darwin. Vis-à-vis Darwin the historian of science Thomas S. Kuhn once remarked:

When Darwin first published his theory of evolution by natural selection in 1859, what most bothered many professionals was neither the notion of species change nor the possible descent of man from apes. The evidence pointing to evolution, including the evolution of man, had been accumulating for decades, and the idea of evolution had been suggested and widely disseminated before. Though evolution, as such, did encounter resistance, particularly from some religious groups, it was by no means the greatest of the difficulties the Darwinians faced. That difficulty stemmed from an idea that was more nearly Darwin's own. All the well-known pre-Darwinian evolutionary theories — those of Lamarck, Chambers, Spencer, and the German *Naturphilosophen* — had taken evolution to be a goal-directed process. The 'idea' of man and of the contemporary flora and fauna was thought to have been present from the first creation of life, perhaps in the mind of God. That idea or plan had provided the direction and the guiding force to the entire evolutionary process. Each new stage of evolutionary development was a more perfect realization of a plan that had been present from the start. For many men the abolition of that teleological kind of evolution was the most significant and least palatable of Darwin's suggestions. The *Origin of Species* recognized no goal set either by God or by nature.[49]

Indeed, is this — 'the abolition of a teleological kind of evolution' — not the precise ramification of Mary Shelley's novel *The Last Man* in which only one sole man survives the universal plague which has condemned the human species to disappear once and for all? And is not Mary Shelley far more radical even than Darwin? After all, in his *On the Origin of Species* Darwin speaks of the extinction of species by and large as a corollary of the evolutionary transformation of species, not of some sudden cataclysmic disaster; he writes: 'The theory of natural selection is grounded on the belief that each new variety, and ultimately each new species, is produced and maintained by having some advantage over those with which it comes into competition; and the consequent extinction of less-favoured forms almost inevitably follows'.[50] Even where Darwin grants the possibility of 'sudden extermination', it remains firmly embedded within evolutionary gradualism; Darwin accordingly notes: 'With respect to the apparently sudden extermination of whole families or orders, as of Trilobites at the close of the palæozoic period and of Ammonites at the close of the secondary period, we must remember what has been already said on the probably wide intervals of time between our consecutive formations'.[51] Within Darwin's evolutionary theory 'sudden extermination' is only ever *the appearance thereof* due to a lack of evidence pertaining to the intermediate forms of life. And the species that do disappear over time are the forms that are 'less favoured' by evolution. In *The Last Man*, by contrast, humankind's extinction is sudden, swift, irreversible and non-evolutionary, allowing for no subsequent development or evolutionary transformation of the affected species. Shelley's novel is fundamentally

[49] *The Structure of Scientific Revolutions*, 2nd edn (Chicago: Chicago University Press, 1970), pp. 171–72.

[50] *On the Origin of Species by means of natural selection* (London: John Murray, 1856), p. 320. The edition I cite from is contained in Ernst Mayr's *A Facsimile of the First Edition* (Cambridge, MA, and London: Harvard University Press, 1984).

[51] Ibid., pp. 321–22.

anti-teleological as well as being dismissive of any possibility of hope or salvation for our kind; it debunks in particular any form of favouritism: mankind fares no better, and has no more right to survival, than any other species. Mary Shelley's mankind is not a species favoured by divine providence.

As I aim to show in *Sublime Conclusions* it was secular Enlightenment thought — by deists like Kant and Voltaire as well as, as we shall see momentarily, atheists like Denis Diderot — that paved the way for the imagining of the anti-teleological non-favourist terminal end of mankind as a species, a notion that stood in express opposition to the most engrained and unshakable principles of the Christian faith. Kant was among the eighteenth-century natural philosophers to allude to mankind's possible terminal end (as he imagined it through a comet strike) in 1763 in *The Only Possible Argument for the Demonstration of the Existence of God*, where he declared in the passage cited earlier 'There are many powers in nature which have the faculty to destroy single men, states, or even the whole human race. Earthquakes, storms or tempests, comets &c.' This is an early acknowledgement of the possibility that a nature let loose from divine control might turn hostile, if not deadly, to our species not just locally or regionally, but rather globally and as a whole. Despite the remark showing an appreciation of the lethal danger nature might pose to mankind, Kant shied away from pursuing the idea to its logical conclusion; instead, as I noted above, we find the German natural philosopher in the final part of *Universal Natural History and Theory of the Heavens* fancying mankind in some far-flung future emigrating to a younger planet — Saturn most probably, he speculates — once Earth's lifespan nears its end. This notion that man's terminal end will most likely be bound to the lifespan of his home planet is also central to French encyclopedist and atheist Denis Diderot's perspective; in a fictional dialogue entitled *D'Alembert's Dream* (and written probably in 1769, but never published during his lifetime due to the scandalous subject matter; it appeared posthumously in 1830), Diderot lets his friend Mademoiselle de l'Espinasse ponder the (as yet) unusual idea of 'a disappearing species' and has her ask: 'Who knows whether this is not the case with all animal species? Who knows whether everything is not tending to degenerate into the same great, inert, motionless sediment? [...] Let the present species of animals pass away, let the great, inert sediment go on working for millions more ages. It may well be that in order to renew species ten times longer is needed than their actual duration'.[52] In his *Conversation between D'Alembert and Diderot*, another fictional dialogue likewise published posthumously, Diderot speculates that in a very distant future our planet might find itself denuded of life; he muses there:

> If the sun is extinguished, what will happen? The plants will perish, the animals will perish, and you will have a deserted and silent earth. Light up that heavenly body again and at once you restore the indispensable cause of countless new forms of life; I wouldn't care to guarantee that as the ages roll on our present-day plants and animals will or will not recur among them.[53]

---

52 *Rameau's Nephew and D'Alembert's Dream*, ed. and trans. by Leonard Tancock (London: Penguin, 1966), p. 176.
53 *Rameau's Nephew*, p. 154.

The extinction of the sun will within decades develop into a veritable literary theme, manifesting itself in such wonderfully imaginative fictions as Byron's 1816 futuristic end-time poem 'Darkness' (which opens 'I had a dream, which was not all a dream. | The bright sun was extinguish'd, and the stars | Did wander darkling in the eternal space') and such telescopic science fiction novels of the far future as *La Fin du monde* by Nicolas Camille Flammarion (1894), *The Time Machine* by H. G. Wells (1895) and *Last and First Men: A Story of the Near and Far Future* by Olaf Stapledon (1930), all four of which will feature in later chapters. For the time being, however, mid- to late-eighteenth-century natural philosophers found it difficult, regardless of their degree of belief or non-belief, to contemplate a *sudden* end to humankind triggered by some colossal natural catastrophe.

This is where the true novelty of Mary Shelley's *The Last Man* lay. Granted, Shelley situated the action of her novel in a seemingly remote future between 2073 and 2100; and while for us this period may be fast approaching, for Shelley's contemporaries it was still some two and a half centuries distant. One may wish to call this a distant future, but as we all know time is relative, and by comparison with the distant futures some millions of years hence as conceived by Kant and Diderot, and as envisioned fictionally by Byron, Flammarion, Wells and Stapledon (among many others), hers is a palpably proximate future, measurable by a mere handful of human generations. What was always considered an imminent danger was the Last Judgment, of which the Lisbon and other earthquakes were a constant reminder, as the Wesleys could not emphasize enough in their sermonizing poems and treatises. But even poetic depictions of the Last Judgment such as Edward Young's 1713 *A Poem on the Last Day*, a discussion of which follows in Chapter One, as a rule shy away from citing precise dates for the event. For the philosophers Kant and Diderot the annihilation of mankind through natural means remains, in the second half of the eighteenth century, a literally 'remote' possibility; for such Christian zealots as the Wesleys it is distinctly on the horizon, and every earthquake is a portent thereof. That the theists' God might visit his final judgment on mankind was an ever more likely prospect, considering the levels of corruption, vice and unbelief (supposedly) at loose in our world; but that the deists' and atheists' nature might eradicate mankind *in toto* in the near future was — for the time being — beyond anyone's imagining. If for Kant it was nothing but a necessary moral fiction that God might some day visit the Last Judgment upon the progeny of Adam, for the theistic majority of Christian European populations during Kant's day it was more than just an imminent threat; for Christians Armageddon was as much prospect as promise, a promise of Christ's return as well as of mankind's redemption, as the various Christian poems and verse epics to be analyzed over the course of my study will testify, reaching from Young's *A Poem on the Last Day*, Jean-Baptiste Cousin de Grainville's 1805 prose epic *Le Dernier Homme* and Franz von Sonnenberg's 1806/1807 verse epic *Donatoa* (discussed in Chapters One and Two) to George Townsend's 1815 fragmentary verse epic *Armageddon* (discussed in Chapter Four) and the late twentieth-century evangelical prose revival of the nineteenth century's apocalyptic verse epic, Tim LaHaye and Jerry B. Jenkins's *Left Behind* novel cycle (discussed in my study's Conclusion). As I will detail in *Sublime Conclusions*, the Last Judgment continued well into the nineteenth century (as it still does in some Christian fundamentalist circles today) to serve the Christian world as the accepted narrative template for mankind's destruction, with earthquakes and other natural calamities functioning as the real-life harbingers of things soon to come.

From Apocalypse to Death of God

It is to this thematic and generic tradition that literary critics refer when they describe Mary Shelley's 1826 novel as a 'secularization of apocalypse'; a representative statement to this effect stems from the literary scholar Paul K. Alkon who observed in his important 1987 study on the *Origins of Futuristic Fiction*:

> Mary Shelley's story is a complete secularization of Apocalypse that reduces Revelation to a source of imagery decorating a work whose structure is more like that of a futuristic *Journal of the Plague Year*, told with romantic embellishments and given a bleak ending that foreshadows existentialist eschatologies of the sort now so much in vogue. [...] If her *Last Man* may be read as a kind of dialectic questioning of Revelation by the method of total secularization of apocalyptic form as well as doctrine — and certainly it may thus be interpreted — then so of course in varying degrees may the majority of subsequent futuristic fictions that tell of mankind's last days. In this as in other respects, Shelley's *Last Man* inaugurates a more viable structure for futuristic fiction than [Grainville's] *Le dernier homme* provides. But Shelley could only do so by turning away from conventional form as well as the doctrines of apocalypse.[54]

Taking my cue from Alkon's thesis (as well as similar studies on Mary Shelley's *The Last Man*), in my own Chapter Four I will seek not just to investigate her 'turning away from conventional form', her casting of the religious end-time theme into a secular novelistic form, but no less crucially also the factors that produced the impulse in her to take this momentous step. For a momentous step it was, momentous for her personally as also for European intellectual history because for a writer to describe the end of man in a near future as a terminal event, as Mary Shelley does in *The Last Man*, that writer had to presuppose the death of the Christian God. Thus the death of man — this being my central thesis in *Sublime Conclusions* — is premised on the death of God.

Put differently, before the Christian God was truly felt to be dead, European writers and philosophers remained incapable of imagining the sudden and immediate eradication of the human species separate from the Last Judgment. The German theoretician of historiography Rainer Rotermundt puts it in a nutshell in his book *Every Ending is a Beginning. Conceptions of the End of History* (*Jedes Ende ist ein Anfang. Auffassungen vom Ende der Geschichte*) when he first asks: 'What conditions must prevail for humans to imagine the imminent end of history?' ('Unter welchen Voraussetzungen läßt sich überhaupt ein immanentes Ende von Geschichte denken?'), and then answers:

---

54 *Origins of Futuristic Fiction* (Athens: University of Georgia Press, 1987), p. 190.

> clearly this is impossible as long as humans believe in a God of any kind. [...] The mere idea of an immanent end of history — in whatever shape or form — thus requires the "Death of God" in people's minds. Because only then is all superhuman power — in the literal sense — eliminated.
>
> [offensichtlich erscheint dies solange ausgeschlossen, wie Menschen an Götter — welcher Art auch immer — glauben. [...] Der bloße Gedanke an ein — wie immer näher bestimmtes — immanentes Ende der Geschichte setzt somit den "Tod Gottes" im Bewußtsein der Menschen voraus. Denn erst dann ist alle — im Wortsinne — übermenschliche Macht getilgt.]⁵⁵

For some, my early dating of the 'Death of God' will come as a surprise since we have become accustomed to associating it with the German philosopher Friedrich Nietzsche who in his 1882 *Gay Science* (*Fröhliche Wissenschaft*) famously has a madman utter 'God is dead. God remains dead. And we have killed him' ('Gott ist tot! Gott bleibt tot! Und wir haben ihn getötet'),⁵⁶ a sentiment reiterated in later works, above all *Thus spake Zarathustra* (see Chapter Three for more). In this work Nietzsche has Zarathustra, his prophet of the overman, proclaim: 'Now however this God hath died! Ye higher men, this God was your greatest danger. Only since he lay in the grave have ye again arisen' ('Nun aber starb dieser Gott! Ihr höheren Menschen, dieser Gott war eure größte Gefahr. Seit er im Grabe liegt, seid ihr erst wieder auferstanden').⁵⁷ God had to die for mankind to rise again, Nietzsche claims. In fact, as I will argue in *Sublime Conclusions*, God had to die for mankind to be able to die in the first place; and only when this end turns out to be not terminal, but rather semi-terminal in my vocabulary, will he be able 'to rise again'. By extension, then, I have to disagree in tenor if not in substance with Terry Eagleton who, in *Culture and the Death of God*, maintained:

> Perhaps it is with Nietzsche that the decisive break comes. He has a strong claim to being the first real atheist. Of course there had been unbelievers in abundance before him, but it is Nietzsche above all who confronts the terrifying, exhilarating consequences of the death of God. As long as God's shoes have been filled by reason, art, culture, *Geist*, imagination, the nation, humanity, the state, the people, society, morality or some other such specious surrogate, the Supreme Being is not quite dead. He may be mortally sick, but he has delegated his affairs to one envoy or another, part of whose task is to convince men and women that there is no cause for alarm, that business will be conducted as usual despite the absence of the proprietor [...]. When it comes to humanity doing the service for divinity, we have the curious situation of Man, panic-stricken at his own act of deicide, plugging the resultant gap with the nearest thing to hand, namely his own species. Man is a fetish filling the frightful abyss which is himself. He is a true image of the God he denies, so that

---

55 *Jedes Ende ist ein Anfang. Auffassungen vom Ende der Geschichte* (Darmstadt: Wissenschaftliche Buchgesellschaft, 1994), p. 3.

56 *The Gay Science*, trans. by Walter Kaufmann (New York: Random House / Vintage, 1974), p. 181. *Die Fröhliche Wissenschaft*, in *Werke*, ed. by Karl Schlechta, 5 vols (Frankfurt a.M.: Ullstein, 1979–1981), vol. 2, pp. 281–548 (p. 401).

57 *Thus spake Zarathustra*, trans. by Thomas Common (New York: Random House / The Modern Library, n.d.), p. 320. *Also sprach Zarathustra*, in *Werke*, ed. Schlechta, vol. 2, pp. 549–835 (p. 796).

only with his own disappearance from the earth can the Almighty truly be laid to rest. Only then can timorous, idolatrous Man pass beyond himself into that avatar of the future which is the *Übermensch*.[58]

Granted, Nietzsche may be the first to pronounce the death of God with such *explicit* philosophical unequivocalness, and I certainly agree that 'only with [Man's] disappearance from the Earth can the Almighty truly be laid to rest'. But I can imagine no better expression of someone 'confront[ing] the terrifying, exhilarating consequences of the death of God' than Mary Shelley through her novel *The Last Man* fifty years ahead of Nietzsche. After all, if 'only with [Man's] disappearance from the Earth can the Almighty truly be laid to rest', what better embodiment of this can there be than a narrative in which a solitary human survivor of a world-encompassing pandemic faces the terminal demise of his species. When Lionel Verney dies, God dies. Mary Shelley is the prime exemplification of the proposition that only once humans are able to imagine God as dead can they also imagine 'Man' — that is humankind as a species — as perishing, and once they can imagine 'Man' perishing can they then also, with Nietzsche's overman, his *Übermensch*, imagine him rising again. And it is Shelley in her novel — the first European narrative in which a lone survivor faces the terminal demise of his entire species — who lays the atheistic foundation, albeit philosophically *inexplicitly* in a literary guise, for our imagining both of man's terminal and of his semi-terminal end.

In 1878, in *Human, All Too Human*, Nietzsche notes, perhaps with more than just a pinch of self-reproach: 'No artist has as yet been equal to the task of depicting the *last* man, *that is the most simple yet simultaneously most complete* man' ('Der Darstellung des *letzten* Menschen, *das heißt des einfachsten und zugleich vollsten*, war bis jetzt kein Künstler gewachsen'; Nietzsche's emphases).[59] He was wrong, at least partially so. Unbeknownst to him, Mary Shelley had half a century earlier been equal to that task; but of course some will question whether her Last Man, her survivor Lionel Verney, would ever be able to measure up to the benchmarks the 'most simple' and 'the most complete' set by Nietzsche — Verney is, I grant, no overman. But Verney does have one thing in common with Nietzsche's overman: his atheism, for to be able to face the end of Man with such equanimity Verney's philosophical outlook must be in essence atheistic. Hence Verney sees no need for prayer or supplication to God; nor is the worldview invoked at the end of Shelley's novel one in which divine intervention would seem either imminent or forthcoming. Here neither salvation nor resurrection is in the offing.

As I will detail in Chapter Four, one can view Mary Shelley's novel as a literary extension of her father's and her husband's philosophical atheism. But as I will also show in that chapter, atheism alone did not suffice to inspire her to write that novel; other factors were needed. The objective of my study is thus not just to trace the atheistic derivation and lineage of the literary genre Mary Shelley inaugurated in 1826, but also to ask what enabled the author of *The Last Man* to come up with

---

58 *Culture and the Death of God* (New Haven and London: Yale University Press, 2014), pp. 151–52.

59 *Menschliches, Allzumenschliches. Ein Buch für freie Geister*, in *Werke*, ed. Schlechta, vol. 1, p. 806.

the extraordinary innovation of writing a novel about mankind's definitive and (relatively) proximate demise at the time that she did. No one before had had the audacity to date our demise, not to mention date it within a few generations, where even such staunchly atheistic philosophers as Holbach and Diderot had dared envision it to happen at best in an indefinitely far-off future when planet Earth or our Sun were coming to their natural end. To seek an answer to the question what motivated Mary Shelley requires us, as my brief indications above already suggest, to transcend the compass of literary history and to probe more deeply into the intersection of literature, philosophy, theology and the history of science in the half-century leading up to 1826, the precise half century that Michel Foucault identified in his 'Archaeology of the Human Sciences', *The Order of Things*, as the period in which the classical episteme came to be replaced by the modern episteme. This change-over happens between the *points extrêmes* 1775 and 1825, Foucault claims;[60] and with it comes the dawning of 'the finitude of human existence' ('la finitude de l'existence humaine'). Foucault enlarges: 'What is essential is that at the beginning of the nineteenth century a new arrangement of knowledge was constituted, which accommodated simultaneously the historicity of economics [...], the finitude of human existence [...], and the fulfilment of an end to History' ('L'essentiel, c'est qu'au début du XIXe siècle se soit constituée une disposition du savoir où figurent à la fois l'historicité de l'économie [...], la finitude de l'existence humaine [...] et l'échánce d'une fin de l'Histoire'). In short, Foucault infers, 'Man was constituted at the beginning of the nineteenth century in correlation with these historicities' ('L'homme s'est constitué au début du XIXe siècle en corrélation avec ces historicités'). More importantly even, he concludes:

> The great dream of an end to History is the utopia of causal systems of thought, just as the dream of the world's beginning was the utopia of the classifying systems of thought. This arrangement maintained its firm grip on thought for a long while; and Nietzsche, at the end of the nineteenth century, made it glow into brightness again for the last time by setting fire to it. He took the end of time and transformed it into the death of God and the odyssey of the last man; he took up anthropological finitude once again, but in order to use it as a basis for the prodigious leap of the superman...
>
> [La grande songerie d'un terme de l'Histoire, c'est l'utopie des pensées causales, comme le rêve des origines, c'était l'utopie des pensées classificatrices. Cette disposition a été longtemps contraignante; et à la fin du XIXe siècle, Nietzsche l'a fait une dernière fois scintiller en l'incendiant. Il a repris la fin des temps pour en faire la mort de Dieu et l'errance du dernier homme; il a repris la finitude anthropologique, mais pour faire jaillir le bond prodigieux du surhomme...]

Others may see it differently, but for me Mary Shelley put the plague to that arrangement half a century earlier. Published in 1826, thus winding up the epistemic shift's half century as it were, Mary Shelley's novel long before Nietzsche took 'the end of time and transformed it into the death of God and the odyssey

---

60 *The Order of Things*, p. 221; *Les Mots et les choses*, p. 233. The subsequent passages in English pp. 262, 262, 330 and 263, in French pp. 274, 274, 341 and 275.

of the last man', here named not 'superman' but — more down to earth — Lionel Verney. If Foucault rightly amplifies how 'man was constituted at the beginning of the nineteenth century', we might, with Mary Shelley, conclude that man was for the first time also killed off at the beginning of the nineteenth century. How it comes to this, and what it signals, is what I seek to explore in *Sublime Conclusions*. I begin in my first three chapters by preparing the ground through an exploration of the Last Man genre's Christian apocalyptic 'pre-texts' in Chapters One and Two as well as the Last Man theme's German Romantic precursors in the pivotal Chapter Three. Chapter Four moves to appraise the novelty of Mary Shelley's *The Last Man* in the light of both her husband Percy Bysshe Shelley's atheistic writings and her own novel *Frankenstein*, a novel that itself paved the way and set the precedent for the third paradigm behind speculative end-time literature, the narrative of humankind's self-annihilation. This is the subject of my fifth and final chapter which focuses on literary portrayals of Victor Frankenstein's descendants as they cope specifically with the twentieth century's discovery of the ultimate tool of mankind's self-eradication, the atomic bomb. The Conclusion will be devoted to recapping the three competing literary paradigms and their trajectories as well as amplifying on their likely interpretative ramifications. But to get there we must first let the Christian apocalypse, the topic of Chapters One and Two, unfold.

CHAPTER 1

Theism 1805: Franz von Sonnenberg and the Presence of God

> Much has been written [*gedichtet*] about the *first* human beings, perhaps it is time for someone to write about the two *last* human beings.
> GEORG CHRISTOPH LICHTENBERG, 1791[1]

> If God ever revealed himself on earth, or ever could, man must think: most naturally at the moment of Creation and at the moment of Destruction.
> FRANZ VON SONNENBERG, 1806[2]

A Tale of Two Writers

Two epics about the apocalypse by two writers from two nations, Germany and France; two men from the petty aristocracy of their countries, both devout Catholics troubled by Enlightenment philosophy, one wanting to become a missionary, the other becoming a priest; two biographies ending in two suicides just months apart in the same year — the very year in which Napoleon lost at Trafalgar but won at Austerlitz, consolidating French power in continental Europe: it is the year 1805. My story begins with one forgotten and one little known writer and their ambitious simultaneous projects, both put to paper in that fateful year, and both published posthumously, the French text in late 1805, its German companion piece in 1806 (Part I) and 1807 (Part II).

The latter is the virtually unknown German verse epic *Donatoa* in twelve cantos ('Gesänge') and close to 20,000 lines; since its publication it has been all but overlooked by modern scholarship, with only two pieces of secondary work on the author and his work appearing some sixty years apart in 1927 and 1989, the

---

[1] 'Man hat vieles über die *ersten* Menschen gedichtet, es sollte es auch einmal jemand mit den beiden *letzten* versuchen.' 'Aphorismen (Sudelbücher)', in *Aphorismen, Schriften, Briefe*, ed. by Wolfgang Promies (Gütersloh: Bertelsmann, [n.d.] (originally Munich: Carl Hanser)), p. 179 (Sudelbücher Heft J, no. 697).

[2] 'Preface' to *Donatoa*, 2 vols (Halle: Neue Societätsbuch- und Kunsthandlung, vol. I 1806, vol. II 1807, each in 2 parts), I.1, p. xi: 'Wenn sich die Gottheit jeh der Erde offenbart hat oder offenbaren kann, so denkt sich der Mensch doch: am natürlichsten bei ihrer Schöpfung und bei ihrem Untergange'.

first a short biographical survey by a Polish literary critic, the second a portion of a chapter in a book devoted to Goethe's assessment of and relationship to the younger generations of German-language writers who followed in his footsteps. The young author of *Donatoa*, who indeed had a brief encounter with Goethe in 1804, was Franz Anton Joseph Ignaz Maria von Sonnenberg (1779–1805), a minor aristocrat infused with an epic sensibility by his reading of Milton's *Paradise Lost* (1667) and Klopstock's *Messiah* (*Der Messias*, 1748–1773) during his adolescence. The French text, by contrast, is a prose poem in ten cantos, but one originally also conceived as a verse epic[3] and equally inspired by Milton and Klopstock, entitled *Le Dernier Homme*, 'The Last Man', written by the French priest Jean-Baptiste François Xavier Cousin de Grainville (1746–1805). Born some thirty years apart, Grainville in 1746, Sonnenberg in 1779, their lives exhibit very different trajectories, and yet, despite being Catholics for whom suicide should have been a mortal sin, both men chose the moment of completion of their apocalyptic works also as the moment to end their lives.

Sonnenberg's and Grainville's epics are unusual works. Although both end with humanity's demise in the Last Judgment — a common enough topic in seventeenth- and eighteenth-century literature[4] — in terms of narrative time and space they spend more time on the pitiful fortune of humanity leading up to the fateful Day of Reckoning than on the depiction of the apocalyptic events themselves. Indeed, their narratives seem to want to impart the very motive for the Coming of the Lord, a causality most of their predecessors in this genre had taken for granted. Aside from the Bible itself, with its many references and allusions to the Day of Judgment, the main literary blueprint for both authors was the writer Edward Young, the English country parson celebrated throughout the second half of the eighteenth century for his *The Complaint, or Night Thoughts on Life, Death and Immortality*, published in nine parts between 1742 and 1745. But it was not Young's *Night Thoughts* that afforded the primary stimulus for Grainville's and Sonnenberg's glum epics; rather, it was his lesser known first literary master stroke, *A Poem on the Last Day*, published in 1713 (see Figure 1.1). Translated less frequently than Young's *Night Thoughts*, but nonetheless circulating widely in Europe well into the nineteenth century

---

3 The editor of the second French edition of 1811 stresses that 'the published work was no more than a magnificent first draft that he had started to put into verse. The first canto was finished. I have had it in my hands'; in Jean-Baptiste François Xavier Cousin de Grainville, *The Last Man*, trans. by I. F. Clarke and M. Clarke (Middletown, CT: Wesleyan University Press, 2002), p. 138.

4 Among other treatments of this subject matter in English are the conclusion of John Dryden's 'Anne Killigrew', John Pomfret's Pindaric odes 'On the General Conflagration, and Ensuing Judgment' and 'Dies Novissima: Or, the Last Epiphany. A Pindaric Ode, on Christ's Second Appearance to judge the World', sections in Alexander Pope's 'The Messiah', and the conclusion of 'The Seasons' by James Thomson. None became so widely circulated as Young's *A Poem on the Last Day*, however. Another poem in this tradition written under the auspices of Edward Young was John Bulkeley's *The Last Day. A Poem*, whose first canto was published in 1717, with the complete 389-page work of twelve 'Books' appearing in 1720; Bulkeley cites Young as his model in the introduction to the 1717 edition. I have not, however, been able to trace any later editions of Bulkeley's work, nor any translation of this work into German or French. Paul Alkon, who brought my attention to this work, cites it besides Young's *A Poem on the Last Day* as another member of 'the tedious genre of last-day poems' (*Origins of Futuristic Fiction*, p. 168).

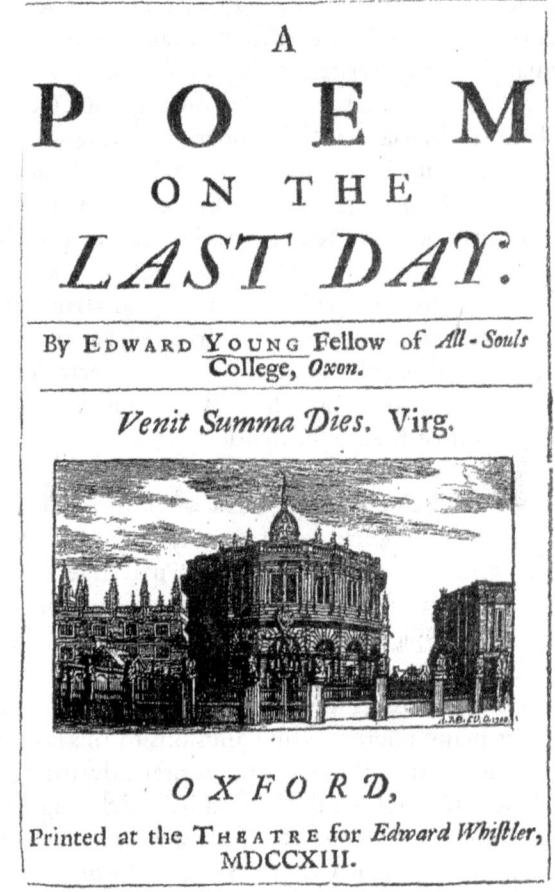

FIG. 1.1. Title page of the 1713 first edition of Edward Young's *A Poem on the Last Day*, a poem illustrating the way in which eighteenth-century Christians typically envisioned the commencement and unfolding of the Last Judgment.

(in 1856 George Eliot devoted a whole essay to Young's 'Worldliness and Other-Worldliness', in which she speaks of the poem's 'bombast of resurrection'[5]), *A Poem on the Last Day* has since been all but forgotten.[6] This is due in part to its stringently religious subject matter, a bleakly cautionary depiction of the apocalypse,[7] in part to a tedious and oftentimes over-wrought style (a graphic example of which reads: 'Now charnels rattle; scatter'd limbs, and all | The various bones, obsequious to

---

5 'Worldliness and Other-Worldliness: The Poet Young', in *The Works of George Eliot*, 12 vols (New York: P. F. Collier & Son, [n.d.]), vol. 11: *Miscellaneous Essays*, pp. 7–54 (p. 10).

6 See for instance John Louis Kind's study *Edward Young in Germany* (New York: Columbia University Press and London: Macmillan, 1906).

7 For reproductions of more works by Martin see William Feaver, *The Art of John Martin* (Oxford: Clarendon, 1975); and *John Martin. Apocalypse*, ed. by Martin Myrone (London: Tate Publishing, 2011).

the call, | Self-moved, advance; the neck perhaps to meet | The distant head; the distant legs, the feet. | Dreadful to view...'), a style that verges more towards comic bathos than grand pathos. Young's biographer Harold Forster accordingly observed: 'the subject was the Last Judgment, which was described in such naively apocalyptic terms as often to make it exquisitely bathetic to modern ears, earning it a place in that hilarious anthology of bad verse, *The Stuffed Owl*'.[8] Although the eighteenth-century critic Samuel Johnson once declared that 'many paragraphs [of this poem] are noble and few are mean, yet the whole is languid; the plan is too much extended and a succession of images divides and weakens the general conception',[9] the modern biographer offers the corrective that most of Young's contemporaries were far less exacting, 'finding the poem wholly admirable and duly paying tribute in commendatory verses'. To give a fairer taste of Young's original than the short passage cited above, an extended section of the poem's opening reads:

> While Others Sing the Fortune of the Great,
> Empire, and Arms, and all the Pomp of State,
> With Britains Heroe set their Souls on fire,
> And grow Immortal as His Deeds inspire;
> I draw a Deeper Scene, a Scene that yields
> A louder Trumpet, and more dreadful Fields;
> The World alarm'd, both Earth and Heaven o'erthrown,
> And gasping Natures last tremendous Groan;
> Death's antient Scepter broke, the Teeming Tomb,
> The Righteous Judge, and Man's Eternal Doom.
> 'Twixt Joy and Pain I view the bold Design,
> [...]
> Time shall be slain, all Nature be destroy'd,
> Nor leave an Atom in the Mighty Void.
> Sooner, or later, in some future Date,
> A dreadful Secret in the Book of Fate!
> This Hour, for ought all human Wisdom knows,
> Or when ten thousand Harvests more have rose,
> When Scenes are chang'd on this revolving Earth,
> Old Empires fall, and give new Empires birth:
> While Other *Bourbons* rule in other Lands,
> And (if Man's Sin forbid not) Other ANNES;
> While the still busie World is treading o'er
> The Paths they trod five thousand Years before,
> Thoughtless, as those who *Now* Life's Mazes run,
> Of Earth dissolv'd, or an extinguisht Sun;
> (Ye Sublunary Worlds awake, awake,
> Ye Rulers of the Nations hear and shake?)
> Thick Clouds of Darkness shall arise on Day,
> In sudden Night all Earth's Dominions lay;
> Impetuous Winds the scatter'd Forests rend,
> Eternal Mountains like their Cedars bend;

---

8 *Edward Young. The Poet of the Night Thoughts 1683–1765* (Alburgh Harleston: Erskine Press, 1986), p. 31.

9 Quoted by Forster, *Edward Young*, p. 32; the subsequent passage also p. 32.

> The Vallies yawn, the troubled Ocean roar,
> And break the Bondage of his wonted Shore;
> A Sanguine Stain the Silver Moon o'erspread,
> Darkness the Circle of the Sun invade;
> From inmost Heav'n incessant Thunders rowle,
> And the strong Echo bound from Pole to Pole.
>
> When loe! a Mighty Trump, One half conceal'd
> In Clouds, One half to mortal Eye reveal'd,
> Shall pour a dreadful Note: the piercing Call
> Shall rattle in the Centre of the Ball,
> Th' extended Circuit of Creation shake,
> The Living dye with fear, the Dead awake.[10]

Exemplifying the 'Standard Model' of Last Judgment poetry, Young's *A Poem on the Last Day* begins in its complex opening period — *in medias res* as it were — with a divine trumpet blast (l. 6) heralding the death of the living and the awakening of the dead. This is the focus also of the frontispiece to an 1813 edition of Young's works (see Figure 1.2) which displays the trumpet in the top right corner and the 'Living dy[ing] with fear' in the left lower foreground, between which two dead corpses can be seen arising from their graves. In his prefatory Augustan 'Dedication to the Queen', Young muses that 'there is no Subject more Exalted, and Affecting, than this which I have chosen; it's [*sic*] very first Mention Snatches away the Soul to the Borders of Eternity, Surrounds it with Wonders, Opens to it on every hand the most Surprizing Scenes of Awe, and Astonishment, and Terminates its view with nothing leß than the Fullneß of Glory, and the Throne of God'.[11]

Scholars invariably cite Young's *A Poem on the Last Day* alongside Milton's and Klopstock's verse epics as a key source for Sonnenberg's *Donatoa* and Grainville's *Le Dernier Homme*. It was the most widely circulated eighteenth-century British poem on this subject matter; the British Library's online catalogue alone records twenty-four editions in the one hundred years following its publication, and an extended search in continental online catalogues yields numerous German, French and Italian translations. Attesting its continuing popularity even a century after its first publication in 1713, a new French translation (*Le jugement dernier. Poème en trois chants, traduit d'anglais, en vers français*) was published as late as 1804 at the very moment when Grainville was putting pen to paper, with another 'imitation' (*Le jugement dernier. Poëme en trois chants, imité d'Young*) by the mathematician Jean-Louis Boucharlat appearing in January 1806, just one year after Grainville's suicide.[12]

However, it should perhaps not come as a surprise to find Young's poem coming to such renewed prominence especially in France at this moment in time. As we shall see later in this chapter and in Chapter Two, the French Revolution had not just plunged France into a prolonged period of social turmoil and military

---

10 Edward Young, *A Poem on the Last Day* (Oxford: Edward Whistler, 1713), pp. 1–7.

11 'Dedication' to *A Poem on the Last Day*, unpaginated.

12 *Le jugement dernier. Poème en trois chants, traduit d'anglais, en vers français*, trans. by M. Jolin (Orléans: Guyot, 1804); and *Le jugement dernier. Poëme en trois chants, imité d'Young* (Paris: Le Normant, 1806).

FIG. 1.2. The frontispiece of the second volume of the three-volume 1813 edition of *The Works of Edward Young* showing the trumpet top right announcing the arrival of the Day of Judgment and the dead arising from their graves.

conflict, but also French Catholicism into profound crisis. Having witnessed the 'Age of Enlightenment' veer off into near-apocalyptic *terreur*, the generation of Sonnenberg and Grainville found itself facing a fundamentally changed horizon of expectation for apocalyptic writing: for all those trying to hold on to traditional Christian values in the wake of the revolution's excesses, it was as if the guillotine and the dismantling of throne and altar in France had set off a train of events that was more than just the usual portent of the imminence of divine punishment, as embodied by the Lisbon earthquake half a century earlier. In painting a picture of a humanity careening towards its man-made catastrophic demise — although one ultimately controlled by the hidden hand of the Christian God, not by the revolutionary sceptics who rejected Christian faith — Sonnenberg and Grainville were both responding, as conformist petty aristocrats and conservative Catholics alike, to this heightened level of anxious expectation if not trepidation among the faithful. Remarkably, however, their depictions of divine intervention diverge as starkly from their predecessors' template, epitomized by Young's poem, as they do from one another. The question that hence arises is, why does apocalypse not equal apocalypse, and what does their differential reveal? And to what degree does the differential between Young's, Sonnenberg's and Grainville's representations of the apocalypse signal larger transformations at work — societal, political, philosophical and religious as well as aesthetic — between the early eighteenth and the early nineteenth century? These are some of the questions I shall seek to address, and hopefully answer, over the course of my first two chapters.

Epic Convergences

We know only the bare basics about each author in terms of verifiable biographical facts, and important facets of their lives remain obscured. What we do know is that both suffered from disenchantment with personal and political life — in Grainville's case his taking the Constitutional Oath as Catholic priest, thus becoming a *prêtre constitutionnel*, yet nonetheless unexpectedly finding himself incarcerated shortly thereafter, with no fixed parish curacy and hence no living to return to after his release; in Sonnenberg's case his thwarted courtship coupled with his alarm at Napoleon's victory over Austria in 1805, the surrender of Vienna on 13 November 1805 seemingly serving as the final trigger for his suicide one week later. Add to which their physical and mental exhaustion from writing such voluminous but simultaneously depressing works. Towards the end of their lives, both suffered from what we today would call a clinical depression, but for which their contemporaries used the words 'malaise' and 'melancholy'. This perhaps explains what some might describe as their morbid interest in the topic of their epics, the grand landscape of death and destruction that we have come to associate with depictions of the Last Judgment, but it also goes some way to explain why they might have opted to end their lives in the ways they did. Sonnenberg's friend and first biographer, Johann Gottfried Gruber, speaks first of his 'quiet melancholy' ('er versank in eine stille Melancholie'), then of the 'extreme fury of his fever' ('bald stieg sein Fieber zur höchsten Wuth') that ultimately precipitated his suicide and led him to throw himself from the window of his room in the small German university town of Jena on the evening of 22 November 1805.[13] Similarly, in the biographical entry for the 1817 *Biographie Universelle, ancienne et moderne*, we read that Grainville suffered a bout of melancholy ('une maladie mélancolique') that led to a severe fever accompanied by a delirium ('fièvre avec délire'), prompting him to throw himself into the freezing Somme canal during the night of 1 February 1805.[14]

These biographical parallels, as suggestive as they may be, are of course not alone what leads me to place their works at the beginning of this study. Crucially, it is the content of their works and the religious worldview they reveal. Grainville was

---

13 Johann Gottfried Gruber, 'Etwas über Franz von Sonnenbergs Leben und Charakter', appendix to *Donatoa*, II.2, pp. 465 and 467; this appendix was published in 1807 also as a stand-alone volume entitled *Etwas über Franz von Sonnenbergs Leben und Charakter* (Halle: Neue Societätsbuch- und Kunsthandlung).

14 *Biographie Universelle, ancienne et moderne* (Paris: L. G. Michaud, 1817), vol. 18, p. 272.

an ordained priest, and Sonnenberg's strict Jesuit education had moved him initially to want to become a missionary.[15] Both were steeped in Catholic dogma, and both responded critically to Enlightenment philosophy — indeed, in 1772, at the age of twenty-six, the brilliant young student Grainville submitted an award-winning treatise to the Academy of Besançon on the question 'What was the Influence of Philosophy on our Age' ('Discours qui a remporté le prix d'éloquence de l'Académie de Besançon sur ce sujet: Quelle a été l'influence de la philosophie sur ce siècle?'), in which he argued that throne and altar had been severely undermined by Enlightenment philosophy, a stock complaint among the representatives of the Counter-Enlightenment. But both also recognized that times were changing and that religion needed to adapt without giving up its core values. Coincidentally, from their early youth, both men had become fixated on the topic of the Last Judgment and the coming of the end, with both having conceived the plan for their later works already during their adolescence, at the ages of fifteen and sixteen respectively. Charles Nodier, the editor of the second French edition of *Le Dernier Homme*, wrote in 1811: 'M. de Grainville had conceived the idea for *The Last Man* at the age of sixteen. He was still working on it, to the exclusion of all else, when he died in terrible circumstances'.[16] And Sonnenberg, so Gruber claims, was given the homework assignment at school to compose a poem about the Last Judgment; Sonnenberg took on this task with uncommon enthusiasm, as his biographer vividly relates:

> Sonnenberg felt his whole being marvelously stirred; [...]. Before long he had produced a fairly long poem, which, despite the fact that his teacher considered it too quickly dashed off, and too long-winded and disjointed, nonetheless merited the palm. This was the moment that was to decide this fledgling youth's destiny. [...] In his fifteenth year he resolved to compose an epopee, devised the plan, and proceeded to execute it.
>
> [Wunderbar fühlte Sonnenberg sein ganzes Wesen dabei ergriffen; [...]. Bald hatte er ein ziemlich langes Gedicht zu Stande gebracht, das, ungeachtet es, nach des Lehrers Urtheil, zu sehr hingesprudelt, zu üppig und voll Sprünge war, doch den Preis vor allen übrigen erhielt. In diesem Augenblicke war des Jünglings gefährliches Schicksal bestimmt. [...] In seinem funfzehnten [sic] Jahre faßte er den Entschluß, eine Epopöie zu dichten, entwarf den Plan, eilte zur Ausführung.][17]

While the poem itself has not survived, some of its imagery will have gone into the writing of the fragmentary epic *The End of the World* (*Das Welt-Ende*), published in Vienna in 1801, which in turn was subsequently developed into the opening cantos of *Donatoa* itself.

Looking back to these early stages of his adolescence we need to remind ourselves that Sonnenberg turned fifteen in the very year 1794 in which the French

---

15 Gruber speaks of Sonnenberg's 'early and perhaps too eager schooling in the dogmas and doctrines of faith' ('frühzeitiger, vielleicht zu eifriger, Unterricht in den Dogmen und Glaubenslehren') and his 'fanatic zealotry' ('fanatische Schwärmerei'); 'Etwas über Franz von Sonnenbergs Leben und Charakter', pp. 230 and 231.
16 *The Last Man*, trans. by I. F. Clarke and M. Clarke, p. 138.
17 Gruber in *Donatoa*, II.2, pp. 239–41.

Revolution's phase of terror, *la Terreur*, peaked. Lasting eleven months from early September 1793 to late July 1794, some 40,000 people were executed across France during the Reign of Terror, more than 16,000 thereof ending their lives on the guillotine. Maximilien Robespierre, the leader of the radical Jacobin faction in the French National Convention which had instigated *la Terreur*, was at last himself deposed and guillotined on 28 July 1794 alongside some of his closest Jacobin associates. Following on the heels of the beheading of Louis XVI on 21 January and his wife Marie Antoinette on 16 October 1793, the murder of Marat on 13 July 1793 and the guillotining of Danton and Desmoulins on 5 April 1794, not to mention the resulting First Coalition War that was spreading across Europe (Battle of Valmy, 20 September 1792; Battle of Fleurus, 26 June 1794), these events meant more than ever that the topics of revolution and upheaval were in the air all across Europe. Thus large numbers of refugees, countless Catholic priests among them, had fled to Münster, where young Sonnenberg was growing up;[18] what space was left was soon filled with Prussian and Austrian troops preparing for war (Marie Antoinette had been the sister of the regent of Münster). In such turbulent times, even level-headed liberal-minded Christians were tempted to see the French Revolution as one of those very upheavals that scripture said would herald the advent of the Day of Judgment. 'The literal application of the apocalypse to historical events', writes Elinor Shaffer in an article on 'Secular Apocalypse: Prophets and Apocalyptics at the End of the Eighteenth century', 'became once again, as the French Revolution proceeded, almost irresistible. Enlightened scepticism and millennial enthusiasm seemed for a moment in the 1790s to inhabit the same individuals'.[19] Thus Goethe's Weimar friend Johann Gottfried Herder, an enlightened Protestant pastor, noted in a letter to his fellow curate Wilhelm Ludwig Gleim as early as 12 November 1792: 'What say you to the present times and the times to come? [...] Do we not live in strange times, and must we not almost believe in the apocalypse?' ('Was sagen Sie zu den Zeiten, die da sind, die kommen und kommen werden? [...] Leben wir nicht in besondern Zeiten und müssen fast an die Apokalypse glauben?').[20] In fact, and contrary to expectation as Darrin McMahon has pointed out in his fascinating study of the 'Enemies of the Enlightenment', people on *both* sides of the political and religious spectrum were describing the events as the result of providential action; 'God, of course', conservatives were claiming, 'willed France's punishment as ultimate orchestrator of the universe, but it was the *philosophes* who had summoned his wrath', whereas 'supporters of the Revolution, in France and abroad', were similarly

---

18 Timothy Tackett reports that 'an estimated 35,000 clergymen' departed for exile; 'The French Revolution and Religion to 1794', in *The Cambridge History of Christianity*, vol. 7: *Enlightenment, Reawakening, and Revolution*, ed. by Stewart J. Brown and Timothy Tackett (Cambridge: Cambridge University Press, 2008 (*Cambridge Histories Online*)), pp. 536–55 (p. 550).

19 'Secular Apocalypse: Prophets and Apocalyptics at the End of the Eighteenth Century', in *Apocalypse Theory and the Ends of the World*, ed. by Malcolm Bull (Oxford: Blackwell, 1995), pp. 137–58 (p. 139).

20 Wilhelm Ludwig Gleim, *Von und an Herder. Ungedruckte Briefe aus Herders Nachlaß*, ed. by Heinrich Düntzer and Ferdinand Gottfried von Herder, 3 vols (Leipzig: Dyk'sche Buchhandlung, 1861), vol. 1, p. 152. English translation cited from M. H. Abrams, *Natural Supernaturalism. Tradition and Revolution in Romantic Literature* (New York: W. W. Norton, 1971), p. 519.

presenting 'the rupture of 1789 as heralding a millennial transformation, a great rejuvenation of the French people, blessed and sanctified by God'.[21]

On the opposite side of the channel, too, many evangelical fanatics interpreted the French Revolution as a sign and rallying call that the Kingdom of God was a-coming. In fact, this kind of millenarianism became so widespread and virulent in Britain, with dissenters not just proclaiming that the millennium would 'arrive in their own lifetime, preceded by apocalyptic destruction', as the scholar Tim Fulford has put it, but some also going so far as to instigate civil unrest among their often lower-class audiences, so much so in fact that the government felt compelled to take action against them; as a consequence, the controversial publicist Gilbert Wakefield was put behind bars, the millenarian prophet Richard Brothers was confined to an asylum, and the clergyman and scientist Joseph Priestley was pressured into emigration to the United States. As a number of recent essays and books on English romanticism have shown, the works of Coleridge, Wordsworth, Blake, Shelley and Keats all show strong evidence of millenarian influence.[22]

Nor was Germany lacking in like-minded apocalyptic and evangelical doom-mongers, a telltale example of which is a contemporary Protestant German religious tract for which we know its date of publication (1792) and title, *The approaching End of the World, described through its Remarkable Events, since the Time of Creation* (*Das nahe Ende der Welt aus den merkwürdigen Begebenheiten derselben von ihrer Erschaffung an*), but neither its author nor publisher nor place of publication. Structured in the vein of the Irish Archbishop Ussher's influential 1650 *Annals of the Old Testament deduced from the first origin of the world* (*Annales veteris testamenti, a prima mundi origine deducti*, see Figure 1.3) as a tabulated history of the Earth and its human inhabitants reaching from the presumed point of creation around the year 4000 BC to an imagined Last Judgment in the year AD 2000, we read as part of the (partly historical, partly futuristic) section for the years of the Earth 5790 to 5793, that is in our counting AD 1790 to 1793 (my translation tries to capture the gist of the original's tone):

> How universal is not the State of Depravity, of all of Christendom! Oh, miserable Enlightenment at the End of this our eighteenth Century! [...] In all of this we have ample indication [...] that the Time is nearing, as foretold in Scripture and ushering in His Glory, in which God's Punishment of His Enemies, and All Those who pour scorn on His Word and the Grace He

---

21 *Enemies of the Enlightenment. The French Counter-Enlightenment and the Making of Modernity* (Oxford: Oxford University Press, 2001), pp. 56 and 57.

22 See Tim Fulford, 'Millenarianism and the Study of Romanticism', in *Romanticism and Millenarianism*, ed. by Tim Fulford (New York: Palgrave, 2002), pp. 1–22 (p. 2). Other worthwhile reading on this topic include John Beer's article 'Romantic Apocalypses' in the same volume, pp. 53–69; Elinor Shaffer's article 'Secular Apocalypse: Prophets and Apocalyptics at the End of the Eighteenth Century' (referenced above) and her book *'Kubla Khan' and 'The Fall of Jerusalem': The Mythological School in Literature and Biblical Criticism 1770–1880* (Cambridge: Cambridge University Press, 1975); and the substantial work in this area by Morton D. Paley, especially his 1999 monograph *Apocalypse and Millennium in English Romantic Poetry* (Oxford: Clarendon Press, 1999), but also his 1973 article 'William Blake, The Prince of the Hebrews, and The Woman Clothed with the Sun', in *William Blake: Essays in Honour of Sir Geoffrey Keynes*, ed. by Morton D. Paley and Michael Phillips (Oxford: Clarendon Press, 1973), pp. 260–93.

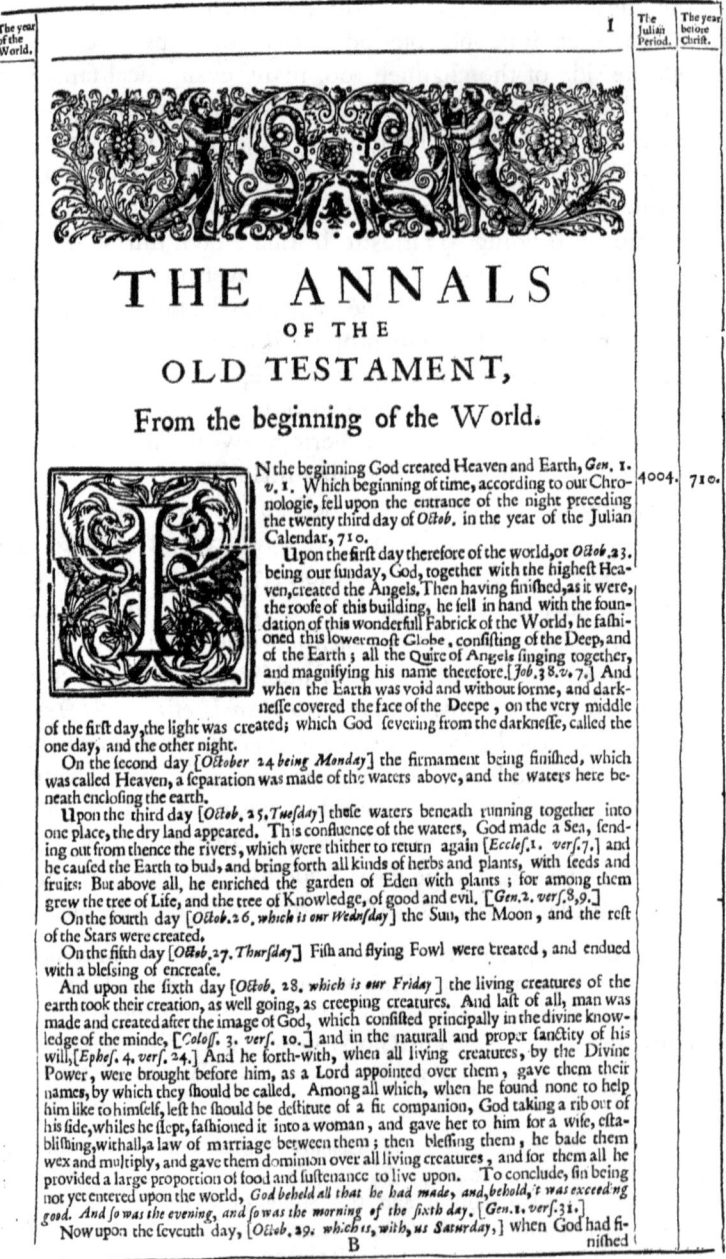

FIG. 1.3. First page of Archbishop James Ussher's 1650 *Annals of the Old Testament deduced from the first origin of the world*. Note the three marginal columns showing, on the left, 'The year of the World' and, in the two columns to the right, the corresponding years of 'The Julian Period' and 'The year before Christ'; note also, however, that the moment of Creation, falling according to Ussher on the night between 22 and 23 October 4004 BC, is wrongly placed in the column 'The Julian Period' instead of the column 'The year before Christ', where it actually belongs.

extends, will come to pass. But what do Those who mock our Times make of These Signs, of the approaching Calamities and End of the World. For them it is all a Matter of mere Mockery and Amusement; their occluded Reason takes all for Trickery and pious Fancy.

[Wie groß ist demnach nicht das allgemeine Verderben, der ganzen Christenheit! O betrübte Aufklärung am Schlusse dieses achtzehnten Jahrhunderts! [...] An all diesem haben wir überzeugende Merkmale genug [...], daß die Zeit vorhanden seye, in welcher die vorher verkündigte und vor seiner Herrlichkeit, vorhergehende Gerichte Gottes über seine Feinde, und Verächter seines Worts und seiner angebotenen Gnade einbrechen werden. Was sprechen aber die Spötter unserer Zeit von all diesen Merkmalen, von denen herannahenden Zorngerichten, und dem nahe kommenden Ende der Welt. Alles dient ihnen zur Verspottung und zum Gelächter, ihrer verfinsterten Vernunft nach sind es bloße Hirngespinste und fromme Träumereien.][23]

By 1818 (or 5818 in his biblical accounting — the anonymous author lists both dates side by side in his chronology) he predicts atheism will have taken hold to such a degree that 'people no longer listen to the Word of Jesus' ('niemand achtet mehr der Lehre Jesu'). By 1867 (5867) all religion will have disappeared, and humanity will have reverted to 'a state of frenzy, savagery and violence' ('Unbändigkeit, viehische Wildheit und Rohheit'); 'the Whole of Christendom', we read, 'save the minuscule and hidden Remnants of the Faithful, succumbs to a most despicable Godlessness and Freethinking, and all that once was hailed Divine is now laughed and scoffed at' ('Die ganze Christenheit, das kleine verborgene Häuflein der Glaubigen [sic] ausgenommen, verfällt in den aller abscheulichsten Unglauben und Freigeisterei, und alles, was ehemals göttlich geheißen, wird verlacht und verspottet'). In the 1950s (5950s) the Antichrist appears in Russia and the Pope declares himself divine, henceforth 'disputing the divinity of God Father and Son' ('Nun werden sie den Vater und Sohn läugnen'). Between the 1970s and 1990s and heralding the Day of Reckoning, the rivers of the world dry up and millions are killed in world-encompassing wars, earthquakes rift the highest mountains and send them hurtling into the depths of the world, and Rome and the (false) Pope are cast into Hell. Finally we reach the year 6000 of the Earth, our year AD 2000,

> in which Earth and Heaven expire, and the Son of God, Jesus Christ, reappears in all his Glory, accompanied by the Heavenly Hosts — and through the Trumpet Blasts all Living Souls and all the Dead are summoned to the Last Judgment, the Elect thereupon entering his Grace in Splendour and Jubilation, and the Godless and Traitors given over to Eternal Damnation and Anguish.
>
> [das Jahr 2000 erscheinet, darinn Himmel und Erden vergehen, und der Sohn Gottes, Jesus Christus, in aller seiner Herrlichkeit, und in Begleitung aller seiner himmlischen Heere wiederkommen — und durch den Schall der Posaunen alle Lebendige und Todte zum allgemeinen Weltgericht hervor rufen, die Auserwählten mit grosser Pracht und Freude in seine Herrlichkeit

---

23 Anon., *Das nahe Ende der Welt aus den merkwürdigen Begebenheiten derselben von ihrer Erschaffung an*, 1792 ([n.p.], [n.pub.]; Bayerische Staatsbibliothek, sign. H. misc. 92 m), pp. 205–06; the subsequent passages pp. 212, 216, 217, 220, and 224.

einführen[,] die Gottlosen und Verräther seiner Gnade aber zur ewigen Qual und Pein übergeben wird.]

This anonymous Protestant tract is indicative both of some of the continuities as well as some of the shifts in religious thinking taking place during this period, continuities and shifts we will also find reflected in Grainville's and Sonnenberg's religious epics. Precipitated by the French Revolution but also by a new sense of history, the anonymous author's perspective on the Last Judgment is markedly different from that of Edward Young in the early stages of the Enlightenment. Both seek to remind their readers to prepare for the Day of Reckoning but, in contrast to the anonymous German theologian,[24] Young gives neither a precise date for Judgment Day nor construes any concrete prehistory for it. No distinct events lead up to it and hence, ultimately, no specific reason is given why it should take place when it does take place (at least within the fictional setting of Young's poem); it simply happens. In the German clergyman's 'history' of the Earth, by contrast, we are given a detailed (albeit tabular) narrative that tells us of humankind's growing depravity and godlessness, its apostasy and atheism, if not neo-paganism. Indeed, as the author specifies, the earliest signs of the impending apocalypse are to be dated to 200 years before the millennial turning point, so his computation. Hardly accidentally, this timetable of course refers us to the decade following the French Revolution, which Christians like this anonymous author saw issuing from the excesses of rationalist freethinking and Enlightenment philosophy. This timeline chimes with fundamentalist Christian computations of the apocalypse still popular today, as was seen especially in the run-up to the millennial turning point of AD 2000, quickly extended, after nothing happened, to 2012 by the likes of the American radio evangelical Harold Camping. (As Ted Harrison's 2012 book *Apocalypse When? Why we want to believe there will be no tomorrow* illustrates entertainingly, there has been no letup in such prophetic predictions.)[25]

To predict the advent of the Last Judgment has always been a risky speculative enterprise. Already a generation prior to Edward Young, the English Anglican clergyman Thomas Burnet famously engaged with this challenge in his much-debated and immensely influential cosmogony *The Sacred Theory of the Earth. Containing an Account of the Original of the Earth, And of all the General Changes which it hath already undergone, or is to undergo, till the Consummation of all Things* (Part I of the English translation, 1684; Part II, 1690; the two parts of the original Latin version, *Telluris theoria sacra*, appeared in 1680 and 1689). Deliberating on the predictability, or rather, as he would have it, the unpredictability, of the apocalypse, Burnet examines the span of opinions and scriptural perspectives put forward; citing Jewish scripture first he observes: 'The Jews have a remarkable Prophecy which expresseth both the Whole, and the Parts of the World's Duration. The World, they say, will stand Six

---

24 I have of course no proof that this anonymous author was a theologian; for lack of any further information I am using this denomination conjecturally, assuming that the author of this religious treatise was no layman.

25 *Apocalypse When? Why we want to believe there will be no tomorrow* (London: Darton, Longman and Todd, 2012).

thousand Years: Two thousand before the Law, Two thousand under the Law, and Two thousand under the Messiah'.[26] Burnet sees it as 'receiv'd and approv'd' also by the Christian saint St. Barnabas 'that the Creation will be ended in Six thousand Years, as it was finish'd in six Days: Every Day according to the sacred and mystical Account, being a Thousand Years. Of the same Judgment is St. Irenaeus, both as to the Conclusion, and the Reason of it [...]. He saith, the History of the Creation in six Days, is a Narration as to what is past, and a Prophecy of what is to come. As the Work was said to be consummated in 6 Days, and the Sabbath to be the Seventh: So the Consummation of all Things will be in 6000 Years, and then the great Sabbatism to come on in the blessed Reign of Christ'. With the seventh day of 'the great Sabbatism' corresponding to the 1000-year Millennium, the lifetime of our world from its beginning in Creation to 'the End of the World' would amount to 7000 years, as Burnet makes explicit in an appendix to the 1726 edition:

> [The duration of our world] reaches, as you see, from one End of the World to the other; from the first Chaos to the last Day, and the Consummation of all Things. This probably, will run the length of seven thousand Years; which is a good competent Space of Time to exercise our Thoughts upon, and to observe the several Scenes which Nature and Providence bring into View within the Compass of so many Ages.[27]

Such general scriptural computations notwithstanding, Burnet cautions at the same time that 'the last Day and the Consummation of all Things' cannot be predicted with certainty because they rely not on nature's actions alone, but on divine providence — and divine providence cannot be predicted by man; he accordingly states:

> If I thought it possible to determine the Time of the Conflagration from the bare Intuition of natural Causes, I would not treat of it in this Place, but reserve it to the last; after we had brought into View all those Causes, weigh'd their Force, and examin'd how and when they would concur to produce this great Effect. But I am satisfied, that the Excitation and Concourse of those Causes does not depend upon Nature only; and tho' the Causes may be sufficient, when all united, yet the Union of them at such a Time, and in such a Manner, I look upon as the Effect of a particular Providence; and therefore no Foresight of ours, or Inspection into Nature, can discover to us the Time of this Conjuncture.[28]

In short, while no *precise* date for 'the last Day' can be given, an *approximate* one can, namely the time *around* 6000 years after 'the first Chaos' of Creation. The real imponderable is, obviously, the question when Creation occurred. And as one of the most learned and esteemed scholars of his age, Burnet would have been fully aware of the variance in scholarly conjectures as to when it might have

---

26 Thomas Burnet, *The Sacred Theory of the Earth, Containing an Account of the Original of the Earth, and of all the General Changes Which it hath already undergone, or is to undergo, till the Consummation of all Things* (London: J. Hooke, 1726), vol. 2, p. 47; the subsequent passages pp. 49 and 48.

27 'A Review of the Sacred Theory of the Earth and of its Proofs: Especially in Reference to Scripture', in *The Sacred Theory of the Earth*, vol. 2, pp. 321–400 (p. 323).

28 *The Sacred Theory of the Earth*, vol. 2, p. 35.

taken place, with the estimates put forward reaching from 3928 BC to 4103 BC, excluding Septuagint-based ones.[29] Thus the commencement of the Last Judgment was predicted for any year between AD 1897 and AD 2072, a window of time that provides considerable 'Latitude', as Burnet emphasizes:

> Thus we have gone through the Prophecies and Signs that concern the last Day and the last Fate of the World. And how little have we learned from them as to the Time of that great Revolution? Prophecies rise sometimes with an even gradual Light, as the Day riseth upon the Horizon: and sometimes break out suddenly like a Fire, and we are not aware of their Approach 'till we see them accomplish'd. Those that concern the End of the World, are of this latter Sort, to unobserving Men; but even to the most observing, there will still be a Latitude; we must not expect to calculate the coming of our Saviour, like an Eclipse, to Minutes and half Minutes.[30]

6000 years after Creation, give or take a little: even among those who like Burnet were trying to put the account of Genesis onto some form of scientific footing,[31] this remained the prevailing Christian worldview throughout the seventeenth and eighteenth centuries, and it remained so well into even the nineteenth and twentieth centuries — witness not just our German clergyman's 1792 tabularization of world history and such nineteenth-century Christian traditionalists as Sharon Turner (to whom I shall return in Chapter Four) who were trying to hold on to the literalist Mosaic timeframe even in the face of mounting scientific evidence to the contrary,[32] but also the pronouncements and publications of present-day Christian

---

29 For more on the fascinating range of dates for Renaissance computations of the Creation, see C. A. Patrides, 'Renaissance Estimates of the Year of Creation', *Huntingdon Library Quarterly*, 26 (1963), 315–22. On earlier Medieval computations of the apocalypse see James Palmer, 'The Ordering of Time', in *Abendländische Apokalyptik. Kompendium zur Genealogie der Endzeit*, ed. by Veronika Wieser, Christian Zolles, Catherine Feik, Martin Zolles and Leopold Schlöndorff (Berlin: Akademie Verlag, 2013), pp. 605–18.
30 *The Sacred Theory of the Earth*, vol. 2, p. 58.
31 See also Stephen Jay Gould, *Time's Arrow — Time's Cycle. Myth and Metaphor in the Discovery of Geological Time* (Cambridge, MA: Harvard University Press, 1987), Ch. 2, and Charles Taylor, *A Secular Age* (Cambridge, MA: Harvard University Press, 2007), pp. 332–35.
32 Turner's *The Sacred History of the World, as displayed in the Creation and subsequent events to the Deluge. Attempted to be philosophically considered in a series of letters to a son*, which was published in numerous British and American editions starting 1832 (the eighth edition was published 1848, a decade before Darwin's *On the Origin of Species*), is peppered with scientific footnotes that refer to the likes of Laplace, Herschel, Thomson, Dalton, Lyell, de la Mettrie, Werner, Wollaston, Humboldt, Saussure, Brongniart, Buckland, Cuvier, and countless other scholars, scientists and savants; and yet, despite all the scientific evidence mustered, Turner concludes: 'It was nearly 6,000 years ago, according to the chronology of the Hebrew Scriptures and their numerals, which, after much thought, I cannot but deem the true standard of the duration of this human existence, that it pleased the Almighty Sovereign of the Universe to determine on the Creation of the Earth which we inhabit, and upon the formation of those races of animated beings which appear upon it' (London: Longman, et al., vol. 1, 1833, p. 8); Turner adds in his preface: 'It is the great mistake of many eminent Philosophers on the Continent, that they systematically exclude the DEITY from all their reasonings on the formations and principles of things; and strive in vain to account for them rationally without Him. [...] If the British Empire keep its reasoning mind, firmly attached to the great Newtonian principle, of the Divine causation of all things, its men of science will always be in the foremost ranks of intellect, honour and celebrity' (pp. viii–ix).

evangelical fundamentalists in the United States like Tim LaHaye and Jerry B. Jenkins who, in their novel *Glorious Appearing: The End of Days* (2004), the final instalment of their twelve-volume *Left Behind* 'Tribulation' cycle, stage the return of Christ, the raising of the dead and the Last Judgment within this time-honoured biblical timeline (more about the *Left Behind* cycle in this volume's Conclusion).

Whereas Christian fundamentalists who still in our time tenaciously hold on to this kind of computation may represent a small remnant minority ('small' at least on the European side of the Atlantic, in the United States it figures in the millions, as the sales figures for the *Left Behind* novels suggest), the German clergyman's 1792 counter-Enlightenment view of the end-time and its possible unfolding would have been reflective of the sentiments circulating among a great part of the population in post-Revolution Europe, certainly within Protestant evangelical and Pietist circles in which millenarianism was generally more pronounced than among Catholics.[33] But even the French Catholic clergy, as decimated and beleaguered as it had become in the 1790s (more about which in the next chapter), was staging a comeback by 1801, the year in which Napoleon and the Pope entered into the Concordat, pursuant to which the Church in France regained much of the authority it had lost in the preceding decade. 1801 thus represented a signal date and a harbinger of the return to a restored 'Conservative Order', an *ancien régime* in new clothing, which was subsequently cemented after Napoleon's fall by the Congress of Vienna in 1815. Scholars like Stewart J. Brown, writing about 'Movements of Christian awakening in revolutionary Europe, 1790–1815', and Charles Taylor, writing in *A Secular Age* about the advent of modern Western secularism, have rightly pointed out that we would be mistaken to see Christian traditionalism as in abeyance either during the period leading up to the French Revolution or any time soon thereafter, despite the impression sometimes given in histories of philosophy of the seemingly unimpeded progress and triumph of rationalism, empiricism and (scientific) common sense over religion and superstition — otherwise called the history of secularization. Well into the nineteenth century, as we know from the reception of Darwin's work, religious conservatism and biblical literalism remained the order of the day across large swathes of society. Thus, if anything, among the population at large — as opposed to the elite community of educated *savants*, i.e., scholars, philosophers and scientists,[34] that broadly constituted the informal Republic of Letters — the Counter-Enlightenment remained far more ingrained and widespread than the new philosophy ever would be, spawning various brands of religious zealotry all across

---

33 See the entry 'Millennium and Millenarianism' by J. P. Kirst in the online *Catholic Encyclopedia (1913)*; accessed at <http://en.wikisource.org/wiki/Catholic_Encyclopedia_%281913%29/Millennium_and_Millenarianism> on 7 November 2012, and the highly informative article by Stewart J. Brown, 'Movements of Christian awakening in revolutionary Europe, 1790–1815', in *The Cambridge History of Christianity*, pp. 575–95.

34 'Scientist' here in the modern sense of the word, a sense that was just developing during this period; see Martin J. S. Rudwick, *Bursting the Limits of Time. The Reconstruction of Geohistory in the Age of Revolution* (Chicago and London: University of Chicago Press, 2005), especially pp. 639–41, who uses the modern science of geology as his prime example. I also used the term 'elite community': throughout his book *A Secular Age* Charles Taylor stresses that the development from theism to atheism was largely dependent on such elite communities.

Europe.³⁵ Brown provides the following concise summary of these movements' 'common characteristics':

> They opposed the scepticism and materialism prevalent in the later Enlightenment, and the rationalism and moderatism pervading the established churches. They viewed the French Revolution as a divine visitation, and they looked to a revival of Christianity as a means of averting or alleviating the judgement of God. But the revival movements were not simply reactions against the Revolution. They also shared some of the ideals of the Revolution, including an emphasis on elevating the condition of the common people. The evangelical work was directed largely to the middle and lower social orders, and emphasized the belief that every individual was of equal value before God. In a time of turbulence, it spread the message that God was on the side of the common people. [...] The movements were largely outside the established churches and indeed were frequently opposed by the authorities in church and state.³⁶

The Religious (Re)Turn

Two famous examples of this Christian resurgence in literature are in Germany the Protestant poet Friedrich von Hardenberg (1772–1801), better known by his penname Novalis, and in France the Catholic writer François-René de Chateaubriand (1768–1848). Chateaubriand's *The Genius of Christianity, or the Beauty of the Christian Religion (Le génie du christianisme ou beauté de la religion chrétienne)*, published in 1802, was directed as much against Voltaire and the French deistic *philosophes* as it opposed the established Church (for which reason the Vatican immediately placed it on its index of forbidden books), all the while expressing the nascent Romantic outlook. Chateaubriand's motivation is neatly summed up by his early American translator, the Doctor of Divinity Charles Wright, who writes in his 1856 'Preface':

> When this work made its appearance, in 1802, infidelity was the order of the day in France. [...] Churches and altars had been overthrown; the priests of God had been massacred, or driven into exile; asylums of virtue and learning had been profaned and laid waste; everything august and sacred had disappeared. [...] Men had become deluded with the idea that the Christian religion, or the Church, (for these terms are synonymous,) had been a serious obstacle in the way of human progress; that, having been invented in a barbarous age, its dogmas were absurd and its ceremonies ridiculous; that it tended to enslave the mind, opposed the arts and sciences, and was in general hostile to the liberty of man and the advancement of civilization. It was necessary, therefore, in order to refute these errors, to exhibit the intrinsic excellence and beauty of the Christian religion.³⁷

---

35 For an extended discussion of the 'Counter-Enlightenment', a term first coined by Sir Isaiah Berlin, see McMahon, *Enemies of the Enlightenment*.

36 'Movements of Christian awakening in revolutionary Europe, 1790–1815', p. 581.

37 François-René Chateaubriand, *The Genius of Christianity or the Spirit and Beauty of the Christian Religion*, trans. by Charles I. Wright (Philadelphia: J. B. Lippincott, and Baltimore: John Murphy, 1856), pp. 6–7.

Similarly Novalis; a member of the early Romantic Jena group and best known for the spiritual 'blue flower', the 'blaue Blume', of his posthumous 1802 novel *Heinrich von Ofterdingen*, he lamented in his stridently religious essay 'Christendom or Europe' ('Die Christenheit oder Europa', 1799) that religion had become debased and needed rejuvenating in order to recreate the Christian unity of spirit that defined the Middle Ages (epitomized of course most prominently by that spiritually loftiest of architectural styles, the Gothic).

Why was it though that among the Romantic generation even Protestants like Novalis were drawn specifically to Catholicism after their initially rebellious phase? The emissary of theoretical romanticism, Friedrich Schlegel, converted to Catholicism in 1808, the Romantic philosopher of nature Friedrich Schelling moved towards Catholicism after 1806. Likewise in England Coleridge and, somewhat more ambivalently, Wordsworth both returned to Anglican orthodoxy after 1800. The generic answer given by scholars ranging from the German sociologist Max Weber and the French historian Marcel Gauchet to the Canadian philosopher and social theorist Charles Taylor, namely that the 'disenchantment of the world' (*Entzauberung der Welt, désenchantement du monde*) that Enlightenment philosophy had spawned created a backlash of beleaguered spirituality, is insufficient in that it applies to both Catholics and Protestants alike.[38] A more convincing reason is the mystique which attaches to the Catholic Church and its rites and rituals, and which goes some way to explain why, outside of France, the religious reawakening was more palpable in Protestantism and Anglicanism (and particularly non-institutionally aligned Evangelicalism) than it was in Catholicism itself; in his short but instructive book on German romanticism the German scholar Eckart Kleßman amplifies as follows:

> [T]he Romantics reacted not just against the atheism that was promulgated by the French Revolution, but even more so against the Enlightenment which had reduced religion to a form of ethics devoid of all spirituality, a hollow rationalist exercise in virtue. This explains why the Protestant Novalis felt so detached from the supremacy of the word (of the Bible) as Luther had defined it. [...] This is key to understanding why Catholicism soon came to exert such a powerful hold over the Protestant Romantics; the reason is clear: Protestantism insisted on the holy asceticism of the word. [...] The Catholic Church by contrast appealed to them through the colourfulness of its rituals, the artfulness of its churches, its veneration of Mary and its adoration of saints and, last but not least, the reverence its age-old traditions inspired in them. The Protestant church could not provide the counterbalance to rationalism that the Romantics (and in particular the Protestants among them) sought, but Catholic rites could.[39]

The great mid-nineteenth-century German writer and master of satirical post-

---

38 Max Weber first formulated the concept 'disenchantment of the world' in the 1917 lecture 'Science as Vocation' ('Wissenschaft als Beruf'), now published in English in *The Sociology of Religion* (various editions); Gauchet's *Le Désenchantement du monde. Une histoire politique de la religion* was published in 1985; Taylor's *A Secular Age* appeared in 2007.

39 *Die deutsche Romantik* (Cologne: DuMont, 1981), pp. 42–43.

romanticism, Heinrich Heine, once wrote that the German Romantics were 'homesick for the Catholic Mother Church' — exhibiting 'Heimweh nach der katholischen Mutterkirche'[40] — and could no longer stomach the intellectual barrenness and pallid (un)spirituality of Protestantism.

Even if the religious sentiment that permeates his epic *Donatoa* allows us to position Franz von Sonnenberg within the post-Enlightenment (re)turn to religious traditionalism and spirituality outlined above, it would nonetheless be misleading to classify him either as a German Romantic or as an orthodox Catholic writer. Born 1779 into a petty-aristocratic family in the Roman Catholic diocese Münster (his father was on the bishop's staff), he belonged at best to the tail end of the Romantic cohort, but his Catholic education and life trajectory led him firmly on a path divergent to theirs.[41] Born just a couple of years later than his more fêted contemporaries, Sonnenberg never came to congregate with the leading German Romantics, notwithstanding the fact that it was in Jena that he spent the final months of his life, the very place that had been home to the Jena circle, the hub of early German Romantic theory. Congregating around the brothers Friedrich and August Wilhelm Schlegel, and including the writers Novalis, Ludwig Tieck, and Clemens Brentano, the philosophers Fichte and Schelling, and the Protestant theologian-cum-philosopher Friedrich Schleiermacher, the Jena circle became the seedbed of German and European romanticism especially through that most seminal of Romantic journals, the *Athenaeum*, which was edited by the two Schlegel brothers between 1798 and 1800; it is on the pages of the six issues of the *Athenaeum* that Novalis's *Pollen* (*Blütenstaub*, a selection of fragments) and *Hymns to the Night* (*Hymen an die Nacht*) and Friedrich Schlegel's *Fragments, Dialogue on Poetry* (*Gespräch über die Poesie*) and *On Goethe's Wilhelm Meister* (*Über Goethes Meister*) first saw the light of day. And it is here that readers first encountered the Romantic notions of 'fragment', 'Romantic irony', and 'progressive universal poesy'.

However, even if Sonnenberg had been attracted there perhaps by his admiration for Friedrich Schiller, who had taught in Jena in 1799, or should he have known of the university town's reputation as a powerhouse of early Romantic philosophy and speculation, by 1805 when he arrived in the town the Jena circle had long dissolved. Novalis had died in 1801, which was also the year in which Brentano had moved to Göttingen, Friedrich Schlegel had moved to Dresden in 1802, by 1805 his brother August Wilhelm Schlegel was travelling abroad with Madame de Staël, Fichte had lost his professorship in 1799 and was in the throes of moving to Erlangen, Schelling had long since taken up a post in Würzburg, and Schleiermacher had moved to Halle in 1804. In sum, by the time Sonnenberg arrived in Jena to live with the country clergyman Ludwig Schlosser in the small village of Drackendorf on the outskirts of the town, none of that illustrious and immensely influential circle

---

40 *Zur Geschichte der Religion und Philosophie in Deutschland* (1834), in *Sämtliche Schriften*, ed. by Klaus Briegleb, 12 vols (Munich: Hanser, 1976), vol. 5, pp. 505–641 (p. 619).

41 Sonnenberg's second biographer, the Polish literary critic Spiridion Wukadinović, was the first to draw the parallels that obtain between Sonnenberg and German Romantic philosophy on the one hand, and writers like Novalis on the other; see his *Franz von Sonnenberg* (Halle: Niemeyer, 1927), pp. viii, 157–58 and 245.

remained; clearly, Sonnenberg had missed that boat. And even if they had still been there, it remains doubtful whether Sonnenberg would have become involved in the Romantic goings on in Jena. After all, due to his austere religious upbringing in the diocese of Münster, Sonnenberg generally seems to have remained rather insulated from the more progressive intellectual trends of the period, as represented by the early Romantics; one can hardly imagine a meeting of minds. But he was aware of Goethe's and Schiller's works and indeed met both authors once in 1804 in Weimar where he also spent some days with that other Weimar literary luminary, Christoph Martin Wieland, the celebrated writer and translator of Shakespeare's works. However, Sonnenberg's comments on these encounters are suspiciously taciturn and reserved. Thus Sonnenberg wrote on 4 August 1804 in a letter to Princess Gallitzin: 'I should write something about Schiller, Goethe and Voß and Wieland, shouldn't I? But, my friend, you yourself have — studied their works, and I have little to add. So just for the sake of history: I spent some hours with Schiller and Goethe, to be sure some of the finest hours of my life, and with Wieland even some romantic days, and with Voß — consumed a pancake and a salad' ('Ueber Schiller, Goethe und Voß und Wieland sollte ich Ihnen doch auch etwas sagen, nicht wahr? Aber, Freundinn [sic], Sie haben sie ja — gelesen, und etwas neues weiß ich nicht hinzu[zu]setzen. Also bloß historisch. Ich habe mit Schiller und Goethe einige Stunden, gewiß einige der schönsten meines Lebens, und mit Wieland einige romantische Tage gelebt, und mit Voß — einen Pfannkuchen und Salat verzehrt').[42] In fact, the meeting with Schiller was brief because Schiller was ill, and Goethe felt irritated by the young man's apocalyptic topic and repulsed by his overly 'patriotic and messianic' attitude; nonetheless, after Sonnenberg's death, Goethe did send a copy of *Donatoa* to Charlotte von Stein.[43] With typical down-to-earth perspicacity Goethe describes Sonnenberg as exhibiting

> a physically heated disposition, although power of imagination could not be denied him, but one that seemed to gyrate in empty space. He was brimming with Klopstock's patriotism and messianism; these were the source of the figures and attitudes on which he held forth in wild and excessive manner, albeit in a kindly way. His main undertaking was a poem on Judgment Day, although, as will be appreciated, I did not find myself favourably disposed towards such apocalyptic goings-on. I tried to distract him since he, rejecting all caution, persisted in his strange ways. This is how he comported himself for some time in Jena, causing apprehension to many a good and reasonable companion and caring patron, until at long last — his madness ever deepening — he threw himself out of the window und put an end to his miserable life.
>
> [eine physisch glühende Natur, mit einer gewissen Einbildungskraft begabt, die aber ganz in hohlen Räumen sich erging. Klopstocks Patriotismus und Messianismus hatten ihn ganz erfüllt, ihm Gestalten und Gesinnungen geliefert, mit denen er denn nach wilder und wüster Weise gutherzig gebarte. Sein großes Geschäft war ein Gedicht vom jüngsten Tage, wo sich denn

---

[42] Cited in Wukadinović, p. 203; Sonnenberg knew Princess Gallitzin from the Münster Circle that she had established there.
[43] So related by Wukadinović, p. 162.

> wohl begreifen läßt, daß ich solchen apokalyptischen Ereignissen [...] keinen besondern Geschmack abgewinnen konnte. Ich suchte ihn abzulehnen, da er, jede Warnung ausschlagend, auf seinen seltsamen Wegen verharrte. So trieb er es in Jena eine Zeitlang zu Beängstigung guter, vernünftiger Gesellen und wohlwollender Gönner, bis er endlich bei immer vermehrtem Wahnsinn sich zum Fenster herausstürzte und seinem unglücklichen Leben dadurch ein Ende machte.][44]

As messianic as he might have come across at times, in other regards Sonnenberg could be quite level-headed. The comments that Gruber relays in the account he gives of Sonnenberg's life reveal a deep immersion in Kant's philosophy whose view that the material existence of God is beyond proof Sonnenberg accepts without compunction; he lauds the state of Prussia for appointing philosophers like Kant and Fichte to professorships; he even takes the side of the Enlightenment against the 'insect brood' ('Insektenbrut') of the 'Jesuit harpies' ('die Jesuitenharpie') under whose tutelage he himself had been educated.[45] Yet while 'theoretical philosophy' may have made substantive progress, he laments how 'practical philosophy' had made a step backwards since antiquity; in one of his few philosophical observations Sonnenberg remarks:

> One philosophical system is chasing the other in Germany today, but I can't say we have progressed much in two thousand years. I find nearly all of Kant in Aristotle, except where I can understand neither. It seems to me that there is a boundary to human reason beyond which it cannot reach, and if Kant has achieved anything new, it is in my opinion that he has resolved the quarrel of so many centuries by showing us once and for all what can be proven, and what not. — In theoretical philosophy we make progress, as in practical philosophy we have fallen back: and when I hear so much being parroted about the approaching emancipation of mankind I would prefer to declare the opposite, all those philosophical systems notwithstanding.
>
> [Ein philosophisches System verdrängt jetzt schnell in Teutschland das andere, und ich weiß nicht, ob wir seit zwei Jahrtausenden weiter gekommen sind. Ich finde fast den ganzen Kant im Aristoteles wieder, außer da, wo ich beide nicht verstehe. Es scheint mir dem menschlichen Verstande eine Gränzlinie gezogen zu seyn, über die er nicht hinauskann, und wenn Kant etwas Neues geleistet hat, so besteht es meines Erachtens darin, daß er den Streit so vieler Jahrhunderte gestillt, und endlich gezeigt hat, was sich denn eigentlich beweisen lasse, und was nicht. — In der theoretischen Philosophie schreiten wir voran, und in der praktischen zurück: und wenn ich so oft über die nahe Mündigkeit des Menschengeschlechts papageien höre; so möcht' ich, trotz der philosophischen Systeme, doch das Gegentheil behaupten.][46]

But as the biographer also stresses, Sonnenberg's intellectual horizon had been

---

44 This description is from Goethe's *Tages- und Jahreshefte* for 1795 (*sic*); written retrospectively from memory, Goethe confuses Sonnenberg's 1804 visit with that of a certain von Bielefeld in 1795. *Tages- und Jahres-Hefte*, ed. by H. Dünker, vol. 24 of *Goethes Werke. Historisch-kritische Ausgabe*, ed. by Joseph Kürschner (Stuttgart: Union Deutsche Verlagsanstalt, [n.d.]), vol. 1, p. 64.

45 *Donatoa*, II.2, pp. 331 and 340.

46 Ibid., pp. 300–01.

circumscribed, certainly well into late adolescence, far more by conformist religious scripture and such classics as Milton, Klopstock, Homer, Virgil, Petrarch and Tasso than by the writings of such 'enlightened' German philosophers as Kant, Fichte or Schelling, not to mention the pronouncements of the more extreme advocates of what Jonathan Israel has termed the 'Radical Enlightenment'.[47] As Gruber notes, Sonnenberg had become susceptible to mysticism and zealotry ('Schwärmerei') already at an early age and the pupil is reported to have prayed 'loudly and ardently' ('laut und brünstig') even during classes;[48] having decided to become a missionary, he began writing fervent religious verse inspired by Klopstock's poetry around the age of fifteen. Only then did he become acquainted with Klopstock's epic *Messiah*, the reading of which had become *de rigueur* among the German educated classes of this period, followed by Milton's *Paradise Lost*. However, both of these epics were the products of Protestants, which prompted this keen young Catholic to write a Catholic counter-piece. 'Forcefully a desire arose in my youthful soul', Sonnenberg later disclosed to Gruber looking back on this period, 'to become a poet of religion, and since the Catholics did not yet have one, the ambition sprang forth all the more fervently' ('Groß erhub sich einst in meiner Jünglingsseele der Gedanke, Dichter der Religion zu werden, und da die Katholiken noch keinen aufzuweisen haben, so sprang die Ehrbegierde mit allem ihrem Ungestüm in mein Herz').[49] But, as Gruber is also keen to underscore, trying to convey a favourable image of his deceased friend, Sonnenberg neither gave in to an unreflective orthodoxy, nor did he turn into a dogmatic zealot, although his work exhibits many hallmarks of an inflated religious enthusiasm; this notwithstanding, he seems to have been as critical of the institutional Church as he was of rationalist philosophy, both of which he considered soulless and out of touch with what he called the truth of nature. Between late adolescence and early manhood he is said to have drafted a (fragmentary and unpublished) essay on the nature of Christ, in which he portrays the Redeemer (rather sacrilegiously, at least as viewed from an orthodox Catholic perspective, and as Sonnenberg himself seems to have felt shortly before his suicide)[50] as the greatest human being, one who was at one with nature and life; he thus observes: 'Christ, whom I consider the greatest of all human beings, demolished the Mosaic thunder-belief and taught mankind the great and simple religion of Nature' ('Christus, den ich für das größte aller Menschenwesen halte, [...] stürzte [...] den mosaischen Donnerglauben, und lehrte die Menschheit die große, einfache Religion der Natur').[51] He goes on to speak of a 'Philosophy of Christ' ('Christusphilosophie') which he (proto-Romantically?) equates with a 'Philosophy of Life' ('Lebensphilosophie'), as opposed to the bland traditional 'school philosophy'

---

47 See his *Radical Enlightenment. Philosophy and the Making of Modernity 1650–1750* (Oxford: Oxford University Press, 2001, my paperback edition 2002).

48 So Gruber in *Donatoa*, II.2, pp. 227–31.

49 Quoted by Gruber in *Donatoa*, II.2, p. 247. Sonnenberg also uses the term 'Dichter der Religion' ('poet of religion') in the Preface to *Das Welt-Ende*, p. ii.

50 See Gruber's letter to Sonnenberg's teacher and friend Sprickmann, reproduced by Wukadinović, pp. 212–13.

51 *Donatoa*, II.2, pp. 264 and 266.

('Schulphilosophie') of books and dogmas, and of scribes and scholars, which he considered gangrenous to the core ('an der Herzensgicht krankend' are his German words).[52] 'Enraptured by [the value of] mother nature, and suffused by that feeling of warmth that bonds any noble being to humanity, Christ stepped into the world', Sonnenberg writes, 'to caution humankind that natural religion had been tarnished, and to return unto her her innate value and moral substance' ('Hingerissen von ihrem [der großen Mutter Natur] Werthe, und durchdrungen von jedem warmen Gefühle, das edle Wesen an die Menschheit knüpft, trat er [Christus] nun in die Welt, die Menschheit auf die entstellte Naturreligion aufmerksam zu machen, und ihr ihren angeborenen Werth und ihr moralisches Daseyn wiederzugeben').[53]

Sonnenberg's quasi-mystical notion of 'religion as nature' (one that perhaps reveals a Spinozist undertow) is clearly intended as his personal antidote to Kant's religion of reason, as are his later apocalyptic epics *The End of the World* and *Donatoa*; where Kant states explicitly that the apocalypse must be seen as a mere 'symbolic representation' or 'symbolic idea' ('symbolische Vorstellung')[54] through which man translates an internal moral concept into an imaginary narrative or image, Sonnenberg reverts to the more traditional 'classical' mode — albeit with an idiosyncratic spin, as we shall see momentarily — of depicting the apocalypse as a real-life and imminent religious certainty.

By the time Sonnenberg had turned twenty he had started writing the first version of his apocalyptic epopee *The End of the World*, the first part of which was completed in March 1800 in Münster and published under the title *Das Welt-Ende* in Vienna in 1801 (see Figure 1.4). No later parts appeared, leaving the work a fragment. With just 144 pages, and with the key human protagonists already in place, albeit under different names (Celimona will morph into Eliora, Selmina into Herkla, and Allfried into Heroal), *The End of the World* contains merely the opening scenes and external framework of what, a couple of years later, was to become a more fully developed epic. It was reviewed highly negatively in the widely circulated *Allgemeine Literatur-Zeitung* (22 June 1801); the anonymous reviewer upbraids Sonnenberg among other things for parroting Klopstock's style and objects to the utterly predictable nature of the action: 'Thus our interest in the action is doused. What happens has to happen. [...] the quintessence of these six cantos is: "Heaven and Hell! Do what I, Jehova, command"' ('Mithin fällt das Interesse der Handlung weg. Was geschieht, muß geschehen. [...] der Inbegriff aller sechs Gesänge ist: "Himmel und Hölle! Thut, was ich, Jehova, gebiet"').[55] Sonnenberg takes this criticism very much to heart — he later berates himself precisely for these

---

52 Gruber in *Donatoa*, II.2, pp. 264–67.

53 Ibid., pp. 265–66.

54 *Religion within the Boundaries of Mere Reason*, in *Religion and Rational Theology*, ed. and trans. by Allen W. Wood and George Di Giovanni (Cambridge: Cambridge University Press, 2001, first published 1996), pp. 39–215 (p. 161); *Die Religion innerhalb der Grenzen der blossen Vernunft*, in *Werke in sechs Bänden*, ed. Wilhelm Weischedel (Darmstadt: Wissenschaftliche Buchgesellschaft, 1960), vol. 4, pp. 647–879 (p. 800; see also p. 802). I will pick up on this once more later in this chapter as well as in Chapter Two.

55 Anon., review of Franz von Sonnenberg's *Das Welt-Ende* in *Allgemeine Literatur-Zeitung*, 22 June 1801.

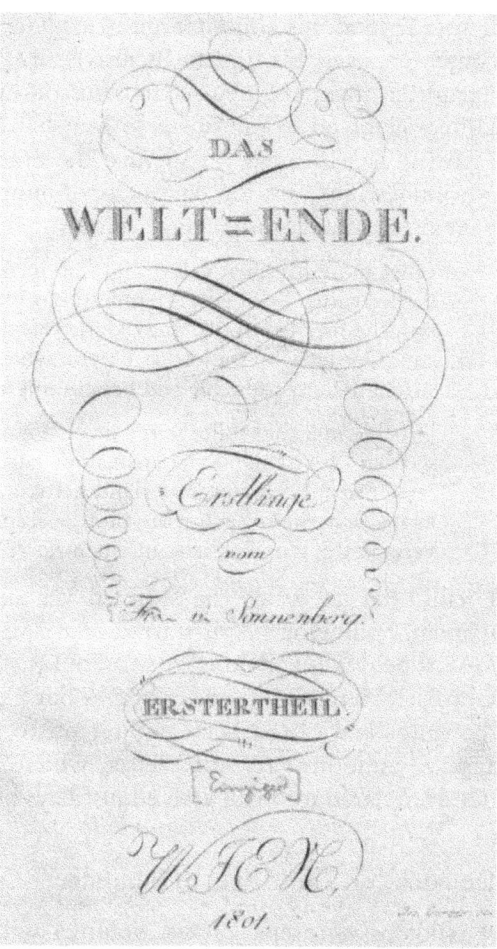

FIG. 1.4. Title page of Franz von Sonnenberg's *Das Welt-Ende*, published in Vienna in 1801. In its Preface the author writes: 'I conceived the plan to this poem in my fifteenth year. From earliest adolescence onwards the writings of the Prophets and the Apocalypse had been my favourite reading materials; in them I found myself cast into a desolate yet eerily appealing world, amid eternal creation and eternal destruction. The great picture of the end of the world had occupied my soul entirely, my fantasy revelled in it in ecstatic delight' ('Vorerinnerung', pp. 10–11).

shortcomings; but he also takes it on board in the 1804–1805 recasting of his epic, as especially the preface to *Donatoa* demonstrates. Reworking and considerably expanding both the framework and the psychological portrayal of the central characters, humans as well as angels, under considerable emotional strain, he completes the epic not without expense to his physical and mental health. If the depressing subject matter alone, coupled with the draining months of labour needed to compose an epic of this magnitude, might have sufficed to throw anyone of his religious susceptibility and increasingly delicate health into spiritual and physical paroxysms (which is how Gruber portrays his friend's condition in the lead-up to his suicide), Sonnenberg's breakdown was exacerbated by three additional setbacks to his hopes and aspirations. First, his pursuit of a permanent salaried position with the King of Prussia (Münster had in 1802 become the capital of the Prussian province of Westphalia) had been brusquely rejected, stripping him of any immediate chance of becoming financially independent of his parents; a painful exchange of letters with his mother in the last weeks of his life reminds him of this failure to secure a living. Second, his hopes for a unified 'Germany' (for Sonnenberg and many of his contemporaries this was an inclusive term which embraced all German-speaking territories, including Prussia and Austria) were dashed when the Austrian army in Ulm was forced to capitulate to Marshal Ney on 20 October 1805, allowing the French forces to move on Vienna: the French occupied the Austrian capital on 13 November 1805, just ten days before Sonnenberg committed suicide; Gruber gives a vivid picture of Sonnenberg's anguish:

> Once more his spirit was to light up in fiery enthusiasm. Germany engaged in battle against France. His tempestuous love for his fatherland burnt ever hotter now, he revelled in the idea that he was the last German. But then Ulm! — He gave Germany up for lost! [...] Upon which he, unfortunate wretch that he was, succumbed to a terrible and benumbing torpor.
>
> [Noch eimal aber sollte sein ganzes Wesen zu hohem Enthusiasmus entflammt werden. Teutschland trat in Kampf gegen Frankreich auf. Da entglühte alle seine Sturmliebe zum Vaterland heftiger, er schwelgte in dem Gedanken, der letzte Teutsche zu seyn. Ulm nun! — Teutschland gab er nun verloren! [...] Jetzt versank der Unglückliche in einen starren, schrecklichen Dumpfsinn.][56]

Finally, the last straw, he suffered yet another setback in his relationship with women. Following his ill-starred courtship of Lida Schücking in 1802 and 1803,[57] in 1805 he was equally unsuccessful in his courtship of Luise Herder, the late Johann Gottfried Herder's only daughter — but like Lida's father, Herder's widow rejected the suitor and carted her daughter off to the distant Freiberg to keep the lovers apart: the mother's rejection letter, which Sonnenberg, anticipating the worst, had not even dared to open, arrived just days before he committed suicide.[58]

Donatoa, or The Angel of Thunder

A religious verse epic in two volumes with twelve cantos ('Gesänge') and 19,800 verses, Franz von Sonnenberg's *Donatoa. Epopöie* (see Figure 1.5) tells the story of the final battle between Heaven and Hell over the hearts and minds of mankind. At the opening of Volume One we witness the 'Spirit of the Earth' ('Schutzgeist

---

56 Gruber in *Donatoa*, II.2, pp. 465–66.

57 Lida vacillated to agree to an engagement because she knew her father would reject the young man for want of a secure position, and because she vacillated Franz felt she did not love him unconditionally and broke off the relationship; in Gruber's biography Lida is called Fanny in order to anonymize the woman involved.

58 See Wukadinović, pp. 168–72 and pp. 218–19. It is thanks only to the research done by Wukadinović that the details of these two affairs have come to light; his 1927 biography *Franz von Sonnenberg* is simultaneously the only serious piece of modern literary criticism to date that engages with Sonnenberg's work. Wukadinović not only retraces the writer's development more fully and more objectively than Gruber, in the process filling in many of the gaps left by his predecessor, he also managed to track down a number of previously unknown letters by Sonnenberg that relate to his encounter with Schiller, Goethe and Wieland (related above), his two ill-fated love affairs, and his suicide, shedding light on some of the circumstances that Gruber knew about but consciously omitted from his biography in order not to damage the future prospects of the two young ladies involved.

FIG. 1.5. Title page of the 1806 first volume of Franz von Sonnenberg's *Donatoa. Epopöie*, a 20,000-verse apocalyptic epic depicting the battle for the world in the lead-up to the Last Judgment.

der Erde') complaining that humanity's end is approaching ('Humankind! your eve is nigh' — 'Menschengeschlecht! dein Abend ist da') and that it is no longer able to fulfil its role as humankind's guide and protector ('My Ward! Humanity!! . . . no longer can I guide this World' — 'Schutzkind! — Menschengeschlecht!!! . . . ich kann die Welt nicht mehr führen!').[59] The human race has degenerated and become greedy, egoistic and power hungry; its leaders wage endless war on one another; and worst of all, humankind no longer believes in the one true God ('O, how universal is the Iron Grip of Faithlessness on Humankind, and Lewdness and War' — 'Ach, wie allgegenwärtig schon drohte der Gottesläugnung Eiserne Zeit, die Menschheit in Wollust und Krieg'), revering its mortal leaders instead, the most powerful among them being a certain Abdul whom Satan has seduced into declaring himself divine:

> Satan spoke as if he were the Spirit, the Lord of the World:
> Be the Ruler of this Globe, I hand you the World,

---

59 *Donatoa*, I.1, pp. 8 and 9; the subsequent passages I.1, p. 110 and I.1, p. 187.

Take her as yours! But this Gift of the Gods is won through War only.
God is each unto himself...

[Satan sprach, als wär er der Geist, der Erdebeherrscher:
Sei der Herrscher der Welt, dir übergeb' ich die Erde,
Nimm sie als Dein! Doch Kriege nur holen das Göttergeschenk ab.
Gott ist jeder sich selbst...]

It is at this point that God calls upon his most powerful angel, Donatoa or the Angel of Death, who is also called the Thunderer (*Donner* is the German word for thunder, hence the epic's title *Donatoa*), to take stock of the state of the world. In light of the world's inveterate depravity Donatoa recommends that the Last Judgment commence. Here the Archangel Michael, speaking in the name of Christ the Redeemer ('der Mittler'), steps in to ask for one final reprieve; after much toing and froing Donatoa agrees to a stay of execution in order to give mankind an undeserved last chance. The action now shifts, towards the end of the second canto, back to the Earth where we encounter Michael's two elect, the last devout 'humans of love' ('Liebemenschen'[60]), who have been chosen to help humanity redeem itself by leading it out of its perilous state of infidelity and unbelief. The older of the two is Eliora, an aging sage who now turns missionary to win humankind back over to a path of Christian faith, thus returning it to God's loving grace. His younger companion and acolyte is Heroal ('*hero*-al'), who has fallen in love with Herkla, Eliora's daughter. By the end of the sixth canto, and thus at the precise mid-point of the epic, Eliora has to finally concede failure: he has criss-crossed the globe in vain without converting a single living soul back to Christianity and the belief in the one 'true' God. With humanity preferring to prance around the Golden Calves of their self-proclaimed godlike leaders, Eliora dies of disappointment and exhaustion.

At the opening of Volume Two, in a very Miltonic Canto Seven, the perspective shifts back to the Satanic legions whom the devil, reinvigorated by these events and seeing his time has come, has released from their captivity in Hell (a scene visualized two years after Sonnenberg's death by William Blake in his 1807 'Satan Calling up his Legions', a sketch for a new edition of Milton's *Paradise Lost*). They commence battle with the heavenly cherubs, but just when God's seraphs seem on the verge of succumbing to the overwhelming onslaught of the Grand Rebel's underworldly host, Donatoa himself enters the fray and engages in battle with the Lord of the Underworld, who is, of course, duly defeated and locked up in Hell along with his Satanic followers. However, in a separate plot-line, Satan's cunning acolyte Beelzebub has evaded capture by following Heroal and has successfully scuppered the young hero's attempts to save mankind through benevolent force (as if such existed). Beelzebub's machinations notwithstanding, Heroal (whom Sonnenberg had modelled on the Swiss national hero Wilhelm Tell)[61] has been able to convince some mountain tribes to rebel against the overlord Abdul's rule and

---

60 Ibid., I.1, p. 106.
61 At the very moment in time when Sonnenberg was finalizing the plans for his epic, Friedrich Schiller too was using Tell as the revolutionary prototype for his play *Wilhelm Tell*, staged for the first time in 1804 in Weimar.

wage war on the unbelievers with a small renegade but potent army. But through cunning and deception Beelzebub and his beloved, the Fury of War, succeed in turning some of Heroal's forces against him; when they defect to Abdul the battle is all but lost. At the last moment, however, Heroal's guardian angel Dälion helps his ward escape into a small valley where he encounters his beloved for one last time. Even now Heroal's and Herkla's love remains unconsummated and hence untainted (a reflection, to be sure, of Sonnenberg's two unhappy love affairs with Lida Schücking and Luise Herder; the twenty-two-year-old Sonnenberg complains in 1801 in the notes and glosses he left behind, some of which his biographer Gruber reproduces in the appendix to *Donatoa*, how he had never 'enjoyed the embrace of a woman' and had lived in complete sexual abstinence — 'noch nie hat mich ein weiblicher Arm umschlungen, nie noch hab' ich einen weiblichen Busen, nie mich selbst berührt').[62] When Abdul's scouts, guided by Beelzebub, approach Heroal and Herkla's final hideout, and their death seems imminent, true humanity and true belief in God amongst humans come to an end; thus once Heroal and Herkla, who have never doubted God for one instant, have been raised to heaven at the close of Canto Nine, God sees no option other than to let Judgment Day commence. Constituting the end of the 'human' portion of Sonnenberg's epic, and thus signalling the end of 'true humanity' (as if other humans were not worthy of the name), we read:

> As the Lovers both now floated to Heaven beyond
> The Star of Love to the Father of Love, the Earth convulsed
> With Tremors of Death — the Last Humans gone.
> Gripped by Tremors too Beelzebub and the Fury of War
> Fled Michael's Sword of Flame into the Abyss,
> Which now, with Angelic Majesty, Leli Alphaod sealed.
>
> [Als die Liebenden beiden itzt über dem Sterne der Liebe
> Aufwärts schwebten zum Vater der Liebe, gieng durch die Erde
> Schauder des Todes, es waren die letzten Menschen entschwunden.
> Aber auch Belzebub faßt' und des Krieges Furie Schauder,
> Und sie flohen vor Michaels flammendem Schwert in den Abgrund,
> Den [...] nun für ewig schloß die Hoheit Leli Alphaods.]

As William Blake contemporaneously put it in a description of his picture *The Last Judgment* (a picture painted in 1808 but subsequently lost): 'When Imagination, Art & Science & all Intellectual Gifts, all the Gifts of the Holy Ghost, are look'd upon as of no use & only Contention remains to Man, then the Last Judgement begins'.[63]

Sonnenberg cleverly devised his cosmos to allow him to present God as a purely benign 'Creator', a true 'Father of Love': it is accordingly neither God nor his son Jesus Christ who proceed to wreak death and destruction upon a faithless mankind in Canto Ten, but rather the supreme Angel of Death, Donatoa; in the eleventh canto Jehovah divulges to Donatoa: 'the Angel of Death | I first created. The Angel

---

62 *Donatoa*, II.2, p. 292; the subsequent passage II.1, pp. 259–60.
63 Blake, 'The Last Judgment', in *The Poems and Prophecies of William Blake* (London and Toronto: J. M. Dent, [n.d.]), pp. 357–72 (p. 371).

Fig. 1.6. William Blake, *The Day of Judgment* (courtesy of the William Blake Archive, Collection of Robert N. Essick), one of several pen and watercolour designs for the 1808 painting *A Vision of the Last Judgment*, a painting that was subsequently lost. The original allegorical design was commissioned in 1805 by Robert Hartley Cromwell to serve as one of twenty illustrations by Blake for the 1808 edition of Robert Blair's poem *The Grave*. (The book included only black and white engravings; Blake's watercolour originals, presumed lost for two centuries, were rediscovered only in 2003.) Blake claimed that he frequently had visions of the sort depicted in the image. Here he pictures Christ sitting on the Throne of Judgment holding the Book of Death amid the host of Heaven praising God; below him to his right the just can be seen ascending toward Heaven, to his left the damned are thrust into Hell, with Satan wrapped in a serpent in their midst.

of Death as the foremost among all beings! | Death was not what I begot [...]; God created, and what He once created | He does not kill, for God is Creator' ('den Engel des Todes | Schuf ich zuerst. Den Todesengel als höchstes der Wesen! | Tod war nicht mein Geschöpf | [...]; Gott schuf, und was Er schuf, | Tödtet nicht Er, denn Gott ist Schöpfer').[64] Moreover, whereas traditional representations of the Last Judgment effectively end with the destruction of mankind on planet Earth, often accompanied by some exhortation ever to be mindful of this day to come when one is engaged in present worldly actions — as in Young's *A Poem on the Last Day* — Sonnenberg opts for a more protracted and allegorical ending, one that might translate visually into something like William Blake's 1805 design *The Day of Judgment* (see Figure 1.6). In Blake's sketch humankind is relegated to the lower half of the picture: grace is bestowed on the righteous at bottom left (to Christ's right hand), death meted out to the faithless at bottom right (to Christ's left hand). The top half of Blake's illustration is devoted to an allegorical 'super-structure' that shows, above the trumpet blowing archangel in the middle foreground, Jesus as Redeemer on his Throne surrounded by the Heavenly Cherubim. Sonnenberg's epic, completed in the same year in which Blake created this design for a later painting, exhibits a similar allegorical quality not just in its Manichean structure, the battle between good and evil, but also in the way it concludes: in Canto Eleven, once Donatoa has accomplished the destruction of the temporal universe, we witness unexpectedly how God now consumes his heavenly host, including the surprised Donatoa himself, through all-embracing and all-devouring divine love. At the end of this penultimate canto, God rules supreme and alone. The epic ends, in its twelfth and final canto, with a *unio mystica*: God proceeds to resurrect the self-same world, beginning anew with the recreation of angels, good and evil, from Donatoa to Satan (whose final revolt is yet again overcome by the supremacy of God's Divine Love), but also elect humans such as Adam and Eve, and Heroal and Herkla, in an edenic picture of all-encompassing millennial harmony.[65] In a long concluding moralizing monologue Donatoa, who at this point seems to ventriloquize both for Jesus Christ as well as Sonnenberg himself, reminds the reader with a nearly Sartrean timbre that 'No other hell burned in you than that which you created for yourselves' ('Keine andere Höll' in euch entbrannt', als die

---

[64] *Donatoa*, II.2, p. 136.

[65] This is also the digest Sonnenberg himself gives of his epic's conclusion in a gloss reproduced by Gruber (*Donatoa*, II.2, pp. 443–44), where we read: 'The happiest hours of my life I spent doing this work. Images, ideas and feelings, which set my heart's natures all aquiver, welled up ablaze from the depth of my innermost being; and here all is dissolved into one grand harmony, the creation of Hell as well as of Heaven, God as He who condemns and God as He who confers bliss; all resolves itself through ideas that look up through me as if the Godhead had planted them directly inside me; here All is settled and resolves itself within a grand harmony: God is Love!' ('Die glückseligsten Stunden meines Lebens hab' ich gelebt unter dieser Arbeit. Bilder, Gedanken und Gefühle, denen alle Naturen meines Herzens erschauerten, drängten sich heiß aus jeder Tiefe meines Innern; und hier löst sich Alles in Eine große Harmonie auf, die Schöpfung der Hölle wie des Himmels, Gott als Verdammer und Gott als Beseeliger; Alles löst sich hier durch Ideen, die in mir emporblicken, als hätte sie die Gottheit in mir unmittelbar erschaffen; Alles löst und klärt sich hier in die große Harmonie auf: Gott ist die Liebe!')

ihr euch selbst schuft').[66] We read on, in the same didactic pitch:

> Yours the Fault alone if you did not grasp what was Good,
> Deaf to the Voice of God, you gave yourself to Blind Rage[,]
> Rebellion your Nature? Where was Your Spirit and Willpower.
> To transform warring Chaos into Harmonies?
> Unwilled Machines in the Eternal Clockwork of Creation
> Were ever worthless before God, and could never aspire to equal Him.
> Man driven to Sin, attracted to Vice,
> Manifoldly part of his Nature: But did not God plant also within him
> Judgment to discern what Good is from Bad,
> And the high Ideal of sublime Responsibility? [...]
> When the inner imperative cried out, why did you not follow?
> Creators of Evil, you disgraced yourselves to His Face,
> Creating your Hell for yourselves.
>
> [Euer die Schuld, wenn ihr das erkannte Gute nicht faßtet,
> Taub der Stimme Gottes dem blinden Wüthen euch hingabt
> Widerspruch Eure Natur? Wo war der Geist denn und Wille,
> Der das streitende Chaos zu Harmonien verbände?
> Willenlose Maschinen im ewigen Uhrwerk der Welten
> Waren auch werthlos vor Gott, und konnten nie ähnlich dem Gott seyn.
> Stark war im Menschen die Reizung zur Sünde, die Reize zu Lastern,
> Mannichfaltig in seiner Natur: doch gab ihm Gott nicht
> Einsicht, Gutes zu scheiden und Böses, und wirkte nicht mächtig
> In ihm das hohe Gesetz der erhabenen Pflicht? [...]
> Rufte das inn're Gesetz, warum nicht hörtet dem Ruf ihr?
> Selber Schöpfer des Bösen verwarfet ihr schmälig vor Gott euch,
> Eurer Hölle eigene Schöpfer!]

The message and warning are plain enough: throughout his epic Sonnenberg cautions his reader to remain faithful to God. Contrary to some of the central tenets of leading French *philosophes*, Sonnenberg tells his reader, humans are neither soulless machines lacking willpower ('willenlose Maschinen'), as the French rationalist physician Julien Offray de La Mettrie had pronounced in 1748 in *Man a Machine* (*L'homme machine*), nor is the world a mere clockwork based on necessity's law, as the German-French atheistic philosopher Paul-Henri Thiry d'Holbach argued in 1770 in his materialist treatise *The System of Nature* (*Système de la nature*), extending the standard clockwork metaphor for God's Creation. All beings are subject to God's divine will and wisdom — and all will meet their reckoning on Judgment Day.

Whereas in terms of style and expressiveness Sonnenberg's countless linguistic neologisms (appearing in such quantities as to make one uncertain whether all are intended or some mere spelling inconsistencies — as the five double-columned pages of 'Errata' that precede Canto One might suggest) clearly hark back to Klopstock's *Messiah*, in terms of plotline and agents of epic action *Donatoa* is equally clearly conceived as a counterpart to Milton's *Paradise Lost* (hence also the affinity between Sonnenberg's epic and Blake's illustrations). Both *Donatoa* and *Paradise*

---

66 *Donatoa*, II.2, p. 205; cp. Sartre's play *Huis clos*, in which hell is always 'the others'. The subsequent quotation pp. 210–11.

Lost contain twelve books or cantos (Milton's second edition had expanded the first edition's ten books to twelve) and two main narrative arcs, the human action on the ground on the one hand, the battle between the angelic and Satanic hosts, good and evil, on the other. Both show cherubs and guardian angels aiding their human wards through dreams and visions; both contain a figure powerful enough to defeat the angelic rebels and their Satanic leader, the Son of God in *Paradise lost*, the archangel Donatoa in Sonnenberg's epic; both render Satan's hubris and human vice as ultimately self-defeating; and both depict God as omnipresent and all-knowing as well as aloof from the Manichean battle raging below between the angelic and Satanic hordes.

We have to ask at this point why this text — in contrast for instance to the contemporaneous Romantic paintings of Philipp Otto Runge, Caspar David Friedrich or Blake himself, many of which are equally religious if not mystical in nature — came to be so utterly forgotten and why no modern history of German literature has deemed Sonnenberg's name and work worthy of mention. Indeed, I have yet to find a colleague in my field who has heard of the author, let alone read his work; I certainly had not until by sheer happenstance I came across a reference to *Donatoa* in a contemporaneous German book review, published in 1813, of the 1811 German translation of Grainville's *Le Dernier Homme*. As mentioned earlier, Sonnenberg is discussed only twice in twentieth-century German literary criticism, by Spiridion Wukadinović in his short 1927 monograph on Sonnenberg, and by Johannes Weber in his 1989 study *Goethe and Young Writers* (*Goethe und die Jungen*). Weber's assessment of *Donatoa* and its author is short and — hardly undeservedly, I have to admit — severe:

> To read Sonnenberg's work from beginning to end can be recommended only to those who do not fear for their sanity. To get an approximate impression of it imagine a film script for a disaster movie in the 'fantasy' genre with 150 instalments. Good and bad, the sublunary and the translunary are battling it out for survival. [...] We can leave it open from which Christian mystic or Early Father he came by such notions, but we can say for certain that he took his conceits deadly seriously. [...] As far as one can establish, Sonnenberg is a particularly grotesque example of erotic confusion and mystical aberration [...]. Without a doubt Sonnenberg represents an extreme pathological case, certainly as regards the ferocity of his emotions and the lethal trajectory of his biography. [...] Goethe was spot-on when, looking back retrospectively, he characterized this unfortunate young man as an object lesson and cautionary symptom of the 'energumenic' movement of young writers that arose in the wake of the 'enlightened' century.

> [Sonnenbergs Werk von A bis Z zu lesen, mag sich zutrauen, wem um seinen eigenen Kopf nicht bange ist. Um nur annähernd einen Begriff davon zu haben, stelle man sich ein Drehbuch für einen Katastrophenfilm im Genre der 'Fantasy' mit 150 Folgen vor. Gut und Böse, sublunar wie translunar, liegen im Endkampf. [...] Es sei dahingestellt, bei welchem Kirchenvater oder christlichen Mystiker Sonnenberg derlei aufgeschnappt haben mag. Jedenfalls war es ihm mit solchen Überspanntheiten todernst. [...] Aus unserer Kenntnis ist jedenfalls festzuhalten, daß Sonnenberg ein besonders traurig-groteskes

> Exempel von erotischer Verwirrung und mystischer Verirrung bildet [...]. Ohne Zweifel handelt es sich bei der Figur des Franz von Sonnenberg um einen pathologischen Extremfall, was die Furiosität seiner Affekte und den letalen Verlauf seiner Biographie betrifft. [...] Goethe hat durchaus eine glückliche Hand bewiesen, wenn er im Lebensrückblick diesen unglücklichen Jüngling als Exempel und Warnbild der 'energumenischen' Bewegung junger Dichter seit Ende des 'aufgeklärten' Jahrhunderts stilisierte.][67]

Donatoa's allegorical form of presentation, not to mention the epic's length (close to 20,000 lines of complex and frequently convoluted hexameters in twelve cantos with an equally convoluted plot line), clearly fuel this kind of negative appraisal, but the work's length and allegorical nature alone may not suffice as an explanation for its complete contemporary failure as well as later neglect.

The first and most obvious reason for its failure is the unabashed and uncompromising Christian zealotry that dominates the allegory to such a degree that it drains both allegory and storyline of aesthetic coherence and appeal. Successful allegory requires an element of ambiguity and elusiveness, but also a sense of compactness and graphicness, both of which are missing in Sonnenberg's epic. Blake's 1805 design *Day of Judgment* (referred to earlier, see also Figure 1.6), Runge's 1808 painting *The Morning* (*Der Morgen*), and Friedrich's 1810 painting *The Monk by the Sea* (*Der Mönch am Meer*, see Figure 3.1) — all produced within years of Sonnenberg's *Donatoa* — can each be considered allegorical in nature, albeit in very different ways, but what they have in common is that theirs is a visual medium, one that is taken in in a split second, even when the artwork requires thorough exploration and scrutiny, and perhaps also scholarly commentary, to effect a fuller understanding; thus Ifor Evans once observed, comparing Blake's poetry with his illustrations: 'The appeal to the eye is ever more immediate and consuming than verbal communication'.[68] Even for a pious Christian audience — one groomed to appreciate devout proselytizing, and one at which a text like *Donatoa* must have been targeted — reading Sonnenberg's epic would have been a most grueling and taxing enterprise as compared with an appreciation of any of the three paintings cited above.

And even if the Romantic generation fostered a (re)turn to the more spiritual dimensions of life and art, prizing emotion, intuition, spontaneity, naturalness, imagination and even religious contemplation over reason, utility and rationality, and even where their literature explored the more numinous, dream-like or fantastic facets of reality, their most celebrated works remained by and large a-religious and secular. Despite occasional religious overtones (as for instance most markedly in the works of Novalis or Chateaubriand), theirs was for the most part a secularized imagination — at times tinged even with an out-and-out pagan quality, one need only think of such famous novellas by Ludwig Tieck as *Blond Eckbert* (*Der blonde Eckbert*, 1797), *The Mountain of Runes* (*Der Runenberg*, 1802) or, much later, *The Old*

---

67 Johannes Weber, *Goethe und die Jungen: Über die Grenzen der Poesie und vom Vorrang des wirklichen Lebens* (Tübingen: Niemeyer, 1989), pp. 68–73 (pp. 70, 71, 68–69, 73 and again 73).

68 *A Short History of English Literature*, 3rd edn (Harmondsworth: Penguin, 1973 [1970]), p. 63. This is, of course, also the theme of Lessing's seminal *Laocoon* essay of 1766.

Book and the Trip into the Unknown (*Das alte Buch und die Reise ins Blaue hinein*, 1835) — that sought to avoid any appearance of religious affectation or bombast (and when they didn't, such works typically found themselves relegated to the second or third rank). With its angelic hosts, anaemic heroes and tortuous Manichean battle for the soul of mankind, Sonnenberg's epic was simply too devout, too moralizing, too lifeless and too affected, not to mention too long-winded, even for religious-minded audiences when it was first published, let alone for later more secularized generations of readers, critics and literary historians. Even in the year it appeared, the reviewer of the *Jenaische Allgemeine Literatur-Zeitung* deplored Sonnenberg's incapacity to credibly and realistically delineate the characters of his countless angels and spirits, observing:

> Does [he] believe that, because spirits possess no bodies, it must be impossible to render them concretely to our imagination? [...] Mr S. has indicated among his angels a certain hierarchy, but only in the manner that we accord a title to a person instead of showing his character through his actions. The author's whole spirit world appears like an idle ceremonial at court; one turns to the other, and he in turn to a third, without any one actually *doing* or affecting anything whatsoever.

> [Meint man, weil Geister keine Körper haben, so sey es auch unmöglich, sie mit bestimmten Umrissen vor der Phantasie erscheinen zu lassen? [...] Hr. S. hat zwar durch Andeutung verschiedener Kräfte seinen Engeln eine Rangordnung gegeben; aber nur so, wie man Personen Titel giebt, die ihren Charakter niemals durch entsprechende Handlungen zeigen. Seine ganze Geisterwelt erscheint wie ein unnützes Hofceremoniel; der eine wendet sich an den anderen, und dieser wieder an den dritten, ohne daß nur ein Einziger recht eigentlich *handelt* und wirkt.][69]

Second, Sonnenberg followed Milton by nearly one and a half centuries, Klopstock by half a century: he was an epigone. 1800 was the time of the religious verse epic no more. The trajectories of the epic and the novel pre- and post-1800 had become inverted: the novel was on its way in, the epic on its way out. Following on from what Ian Watt called the eighteenth-century *Rise of the Novel*, the nineteenth century was to become the 'Golden Age of the Novel': Austen, Cooper, Dickens, Collins, George Eliot, Melville, Hardy; Balzac, Stendhal, Flaubert, Zola; Goethe, Keller, Fontane, Mann, these were the future, the epic was the past. In Germany the last decade of the eighteenth century, i.e. the decade preceding Sonnenberg's *The End of the World* and *Donatoa*, saw the first true flowering of the up-and-coming genre: among the novels published during this decade are Goethe's *Wilhelm Meisters Lehrjahre* (1795–1796), Karl Philipp Moritz's *Anton Reiser* (1790), Jean Paul's four major novels *Die unsichtbare Loge* (1793), *Hesperus* (1795), *Siebenkäs* (1796–1797) and *Titan* (1800–1803), Ludwig Tieck's *William Lovell* (1795–1796) and *Franz Sternbalds Wanderungen* (1798), Friedrich Hölderlin's *Hyperion* (1797 and 1799), Friedrich Schlegel's *Lucinde* (1799) and Novalis's *Heinrich von Ofterdingen* (1799–1800); all of

---

69 Anon., review in *Jenaische Allgemeine Literatur-Zeitung*, no. 135, 9 June 1806, columns 465–72, this quote from columns 465–66.

these have since gone on to become classics of German literature.[70] By contrast, even as a trained scholar of German literature, I could name but one verse epic published since 1800 in German that made it into the top tier of German literature, namely the late Romantic Heinrich Heine's *Atta Troll* of 1843, which is, perhaps tellingly, a political satire. (*Donatoa*'s twentieth-century counterpart, but making it into the second tier only, would arguably be Theodor Däubler's *Das Nordlicht*, published in various versions starting 1910, which is equally massive in bulk, containing more than 30,000 lines, equally experimental and exuberant in linguistic form, and equally mystic and redemptive in outlook.)

Hegel was the first to clearly recognize the predicament the genre was in; he writes in his 1835–1838 *Lectures on Aesthetics* (*Vorlesungen über die Ästhetik*):

> If we try to discover really epic compositions in our own day we shall find ourselves in an atmosphere totally different from that of the genuine Epopaea [*epopaea* being a variant spelling of the word epopee, designating a traditional form of epic poetry, R.W.]. The general condition of our world to-day has assumed a form, which, in its prosaic character, is diametrically opposed to everything we found indispensable to the genuine Epos, while the revolutions, which have been imposed upon the actual social conditions of states and nations, are still too strongly riveted in our memory as actual experiences that they should be able to receive an epic type of art [treatment, R.W.]. Epic poetry has consequently taken refuge from the great national events in the narrow circle of the domestic life of individuals in the country and in the small town. [...] more particularly among us Germans, the Epic has become idyllic.

> [Suchen wir nun in neuester Zeit nach wahrhaft epischen Darstellungen, so haben wir uns nach einem anderen Kreise als dem der eigentlichen Epopöe umzusehen. Denn der ganze heutige Weltzustand hat eine Gestalt angenommen, welche in ihrer prosaischen Ordnung sich schnurstracks den Anforderungen entgegenstellt, welche wir für das echte Epos unerläßlich fanden, während die Umwälzungen, denen die wirklichen Verhältnisse der Staaten und Völker unterworfen gewesen sind, noch zu sehr als wirkliche Erlebnisse in der Erinnerung festhaften, um schon die epische Kunstform vertragen zu können. Die epische Poesie hat sich deshalb aus den großen Völkerereignissen in die Beschränktheit privater häuslicher Zustände auf dem Lande und in der kleinen Stadt geflüchtet. [...] Dadurch ist denn besonders bei uns Deutschen das Epos *idyllisch* geworden.][71]

Hegel's prime example, which he cites shortly after this passage, is Goethe's famous epic in hexameters *Hermann and Dorothea*, written and published in 1797. It is a work at the opposite end to *Donatoa*, short (certainly by comparison with Sonnenberg's multi-volume epic), realistic, and set in the immediate present, depicting an ill-starred love affair in an age of revolutionary upheaval. (Ironically, 'an ill-starred

---

70 For a brief but very informative discussion (in German) of the 'bourgeois epopaeia', i.e. the novel, see Gerhard Schulz, 'Bürgerliche Epopöen? Fragen zu einigen deutschen Romanen zwischen 1790 und 1800', in *Deutsche Literatur zur Zeit der Klassik*, ed. by Karl Otto Conrady (Stuttgart: Reclam, 1977), pp. 189–210.

71 G. W. F. Hegel, *The Philosophy of Fine Art*, trans. by F. P. B. Osmaston (London: G. Bell and Sons, 1920), vol. 4, p. 191; *Vorlesungen über die Ästhetik*, vol. 3: *Die Poesie*, ed. by Rüdiger Bubner (Stuttgart: Reclam, 1977), pp. 198–99.

love affair in an age of revolutionary upheaval' also applies to *Donatoa* to a degree, but the difference between the two texts is glaring.) But what Hegel is essentially arguing is that in the contemporary world there is no place for the traditional verse epic; and 'the religious Epopaea' ('die religiöse Kunstepopöe')[72] especially, which Hegel sees as a phenomenon primarily of the Reformation and post-Reformation periods, and which for him are epitomized by Milton's *Paradise Lost* and Klopstock's *Messiah*, has now, at the advent of the prosaic nineteenth century, truly and verily become obsolete. In short, anyone composing a traditional religious verse epic around 1800 had, according to Hegel, to be out of sync with his time.[73] Hegel's verdict has since been corroborated by literary history; the entry on 'Epic' in *The Princeton Encyclopedia of Poetry and Poetics* succinctly sums up the development:

> For [Voltaire] an epic is best defined [...] as 'a narration in verse of heroic adventures'. He ridicules, as do almost all eighteenth-century critics, the idea of using Greek and Roman mythological personages in modern literature. Judgment now is advocated as a check upon the marvelous, which must be handled with good taste as well as probability. [...] As in England, there is dispute whether Christian machinery is appropriate in epic. [...] With the development of romanticism in England, the concept of the epic as genre falls apart. [...] Long poems come under attack as straining patience; Coleridge (*Biographia Literaria*, 1817) and in America Edgar Allan Poe ('The Poetic Principle', 1845) deny their legitimacy altogether. At the end of the eighteenth century, Germany was the chief source of theoretical speculation on the nature of epic. [...] For Schiller, violent action, stimulating strong emotional response, is inappropriate to epic. And he also breaks with established tradition (from Aristotle onward) in contending that the marvelous is inappropriate to the clarity demanded of epic.[74]

By severely 'straining our patience', by liberally exploiting 'the marvellous', by heavy-handedly deploying 'Christian machinery', by not 'limiting [him]self to the depiction of domestic life', and by displaying 'violent action' throughout his epic and thereby 'stimulating strong emotional response', Sonnenberg seems to be committing every possible sin in the literary rule book. We will discover in Chapter Two how *Donatoa*'s French epic counterpart, Grainville's *Le Dernier Homme*, fared by comparison and what peculiar circumstances were required to ensure its survival.

Of course, the irony is that the epically marvellous has survived and is enjoying a veritable comeback even today, being relished daily by millions of readers, and I mean not in the shape of the Jehovah's Witnesses' widely circulated *Watchtower* pamphlets (with its monthly print run of some 45 million copies it is supposedly the magazine with the largest circulation in the world, although I am not sure how many of these give-away copies are actually read). Rather, the secular modern formula for the marvellous is embodied in such epic literary (and now silver screen) undertakings as

---

72 Ibid., p. 190 (*Vorlesungen über die Ästhetik*, p. 197).

73 Surely to the chagrin of Klopstock and his followers, Voltaire had already claimed mid-century that Milton was 'the last in Europe who wrote an epic'; quoted after Stafford, *The Last of the Race*, p. 33.

74 *The Princeton Encyclopedia of Poetry and Poetics*, ed. by Alex Preminger, 2nd enlarged edn (Princeton: Princeton University Press, 1974), pp. 245–46.

J. R. R. Tolkien's *Lord of the Rings* trilogy (with 150 million copies sold it represents the third best-ever selling work of literature according to Wikipedia's 'List of best-selling books') and J. K. Rowlings's *Harry Potter* series (450 million copies sold, as of June 2011), not to mention the more religiously inspired but equally popular Narnia chronicles by C. S. Lewis or the various brands of comic book (alias Hollywood) hero such as Superman or Spiderman. All of these tales with supernatural roots and characters subscribe to the same pattern as Sonnenberg's: it is the ever-thrilling saga of the good guys (wizards, lions, hobbits...) versus the bad guys (wizards, evil white queens, orcs...), the morally upright (the Gandalfs and Dumbledores) versus the greedy and power hungry (the Dark Lords and Voldemorts), the honest versus the debased and corrupt battling it out for supremacy, one with the aim to destroy the world along with humanity, the other to save it. The 'Christian machinery', however, is lacking in all of these; and all deploy either prose narrative or visual/film media. In short, they may qualify as epic in terms of scale, plot, action and dramatis personae, as well as marketing success, but, lacking the time-honoured and required metric shape, less so in terms of generic norm and aesthetic form.

Epic Divergences

But even in Sonnenberg's day, and notwithstanding the fact that the epic as a literary genre was clearly on the wane, there were alternatives. Even if such persuasive spokespersons as Edgar Allan Poe were soon to deride long poems more generally, considering them no longer viable (in his 1846 'The Philosophy of Composition' Poe self-servingly cited 'about one hundred lines' of verse as the maximum bearable),[75] lengthy epic-like poems remained immensely popular throughout the nineteenth century. In English literature Scott's and Byron's lyrics in particular come to mind — the six cantos of Scott's *The Lay of the Last Minstrel*, published in 1805, occupy some seventy pages, *Marmion*, begun in 1806 and published in 1808, more than one hundred; and the four cantos of Byron's partly autobiographical *Childe Harold's Pilgrimage*, published between 1812 and 1818, come in at some five thousand lines. But both Scott and Byron turn to past or contemporary history rather than

---

[75] Poe writes: 'It appears evident, then, that there is a distinct limit, as regards length, to all works of literary art — the limit of a single sitting — and that, although in certain classes of prose composition, such as *Robinson Crusoe* (demanding no unity), this limit may be advantageously overpassed, it can never properly be overpassed in a poem. Within this limit, the extent of a poem may be made to bear mathematical relation to its merit; in other words, to the excitement or elevation; again in other words, to the degree of the true poetical effect which it is capable of inducing; for it is clear that the brevity must be in direct ratio of the intensity of the intended effect: — this, with one proviso, that a certain degree of duration is absolutely requisite for the production of any effect at all. Holding in view these considerations, as well as that degree of excitement which I deemed not above the popular, while not below the critical, taste, I reached at once what I conceived the proper length for my intended poem, a length of about one hundred lines. It is, in fact, a hundred and eight.' 'The Philosophy of Composition', in *Complete Works of Edgar Allan Poe* (Valdemar Edition), 10 vols (New York: Fred de Fau, 1902), vol. 1, pp. 282–306 (pp. 291–92). The argument Poe contrives can, of course, hardly be taken seriously and is made self-servingly with a view to advocating his own poem 'The Raven'.

biblical or mythological/supernatural themes. And when Byron exceptionally does deploy Christian machinery, it tends to be refashioned for satirical purposes, as in 'The Vision of Judgment' (1821), which is peopled among others with the archangel Michael and Satan; thus in stanza thirty-four we see Byron explicitly lampooning contemporary theological debates about the historicity of the Bible and the factuality of (some of) its figures: 'And this is not a theologic tract, | To prove with Hebrew and with Arabic, | If Job be allegory or a fact, | But a true narrative; and thus I pick | From out the whole but such and such an act | As sets aside the slightest thought of trick. | 'Tis every tittle true, beyond suspicion, | And accurate as any other vision'.[76]

More important for our purpose here, though, is the path taken by William Wordsworth in *The Prelude*. Published in July 1850 in fourteen books with a total of some 7,900 lines, the poem was begun in 1798, the year of the *Lyrical Ballads*, with the first draft completed in 1805, the very year in which Sonnenberg completed *Donatoa*. Indeed, with some 8,500 lines of verse, the 1805 draft was longer than the completed poem published more than four decades later. And it was intended as the introductory poem to an even longer work (to be produced in part in collaboration with Coleridge who was himself purportedly so averse to the 'long poem', all the while praising Wordsworth for his 'excursions' into this terrain), the philosophical poem *The Recluse* which was meant to occupy some 33,000 lines, triple the length of Milton's *Paradise Lost*, whose epic Wordsworth and Coleridge were expressly aiming to surpass. As the literary historian M. H. Abrams put it in his superb study of Romantic literature, *Natural Supernaturalism*, Wordsworth was 'setting out to emulate his revered predecessor — and rival — by writing the equivalent for his own age of the great Protestant English epic', much as Sonnenberg had set out to do in the Catholic German context. Indeed, as Abrams points out, Wordsworth's 'long-standing plan' had been 'to write a traditional epic'.[77] One wonders in hindsight how Wordsworth's project of 1805 and resulting final version of 1850 might have fared had he gone ahead with his original plan. As it stands, the early twentieth-century Wordsworth scholar David Nichol Smith described his subject as 'our greatest nature poet',[78] and Ifor Evans has called *The Prelude* 'possibly the greatest poem of the modern period in English' — quite the opposite of Sonnenberg's virtually unknown *Donatoa*; Evans continues: being 'the record of a single mind honestly recording its own intimate experiences [...] in scale it is epical, and is composed in blank verse as was Milton's *Paradise Lost*, but instead of dealing with world events or the adventures of heroes, it outlines the development of one single, and from all outward considerations, unimportant personality'.[79]

---

76 *The Poems and Plays of Lord Byron*, 3 vols (London: J. M. Dent, [n.d.]), vol. 1, pp. 430–54 (p. 441).

77 *Natural Supernaturalism* (New York: W. W. Norton, 1971), pp. 22 and 21.

78 Cited after Ralph Pite, 'Wordsworth and the natural world', in *The Cambridge Companion to Wordsworth*, ed. by Stephen Gill (Cambridge: Cambridge University Press, 2003), pp. 180–95 (p. 180); Pite writes: 'In 1921, David Nichol Smith described Wordsworth as "our greatest nature poet" and it is a judgement many would still accept'.

79 *A Short History of English Literature*, p. 69.

As Abrams and Evans affirm, *The Prelude* possesses a distinctly epical quality, in design no less than magnitude, and yet the differential between Wordsworth's poem and Sonnenberg's contemporaneous epic could not be more pronounced — and indeed it is a differential that is symptomatic of the changes affecting the literary genre system during this period. The dramatis personae of Sonnenberg's epic are angelic legions on the one hand as opposed to the few select heroic humans on the other, but both groups remain equally allegorically abstract and ethereal; for this reason I have elsewhere called his characters Eliora, Heroal and Herkla anaemic. By contrast, the protagonist of Wordsworth's poem is the writer himself, a concrete real-life individual surveying the concrete world (and world history) that surrounds him; for this reason Abrams rightly calls *The Prelude* 'an autobiography of epic dimension', recognizing its 'radical novelty'.[80] Sonnenberg's is a detached third-person narrative that often verges on the didactic and moralizing, Wordsworth's poem is written in the first person and is descriptive, personal and introspective. Where the former sets out prophetically to show us the spectacle of Heaven and Hell locked in a cosmic struggle for Earth and its inhabitants, Wordsworth provides his reader with a more 'meditative history' of the poet as 'Prophet of Nature' (Book XIII, ll. 418 and 442), whose 'spirit', 'clothed in priestly robes', is engaged in 'holy services' before the 'Presences of Nature' (Book I, ll. 61–63 and 490). If Wordsworth portrays a spiritual battle at all, it is one of self-realization and personal identity formation in the modern world. As Abrams observes: 'the heights and depths of the mind are to replace heaven and hell, and the powers of the mind are to replace the divine protagonists, in Wordsworth's triple [...] successor to Milton's religious epic'[81] — and rival to Sonnenberg's. If in times of despair and loss of faith Sonnenberg's epic parades the sublimity of God's divine power as our only remaining solace and protection, Wordsworth invites us to experience the soothing embrace and sublimity of the natural world. Even where religion seeps into Wordsworth's narrative, it is invariably subordinate to Nature, as in the following passage from Book II:

> ...if in these times of fear
> This melancholy waste of hopes o'erthrown,
> If, 'mid indifference and apathy
> And wicked exultation, when good men
> On every side fall off, we know not how,
> To selfishness, disguised in gentle names
> Of peace and quiet and domestic love,
> Yet mingled not unwillingly with sneers
> On visionary minds: if, in this time
> Of dereliction and dismay, I yet
> Despair not of our nature, but retain
> A more than Roman confidence, a faith
> That fails not, in all sorrow my support,
> The blessing of my life; the gift is yours,
> Ye mountains! thine, O Nature! Thou hast fed
> My lofty speculations; and in thee,

---

80 *Natural Supernaturalism*, pp. 19 and 74.
81 Ibid., p. 25.

> For this uneasy heart of ours, I find
> A never-failing principle of joy
> And purest passion.
> (*The Prelude*, 1805–1806 version, Book II, ll. 448–66)[82]

Wordsworth's perspective on men 'falling off to selfishness 'mid indifference and apathy in this time of dereliction and dismay' is by far more sober, down to earth and introspectively philosophical than Sonnenberg's grandiloquent and excited over-dramatization of the demise of mankind. In effect, Wordsworth is adhering precisely to Hegel's prescription, cited above, to 'take refuge from the great national events and limit itself to the depiction of domestic life in the rural countryside and small towns', although 'grand events' will play their part in later sections of *The Prelude* in the shape of the French Revolution. It is perhaps apparent, nonetheless, that Sonnenberg's 'Roman [Catholic] confidence' in God is trumped in Wordsworth's poem by his '*more than Roman* [!] confidence' in nature. Joel Pace has accordingly observed: 'Wordsworth's verses celebrate the intrinsic value of the human mind as well as Nature. Many natural scenes are embalmed by imagination, which Wordsworth viewed as everlasting. In *The Prelude* Wordsworth transplants Nature from external reality to the landscape of the mind, which is "of fabric more divine"',[83] citing *The Prelude*'s last line. Here 'Nature' and 'Imagination' are what is divine: in Wordsworth's natural landscape of the mind there is no space for the Christian supernatural.

And yet the supernatural is hardly banished from Wordsworth's *Prelude*; indeed, as various scholars have shown, Wordsworth's poem on 'the growth of [his] own mind'[84] is suffused with allusions both to the apocalypse as well as the millennium — it is just that today's reader finds it difficult to grasp the import of the religious overtones and connotations nestled subtly below the surface language of this otherwise secularized epic. But in this poem of close to 8,000 lines we occasionally find tucked away passages of nature description that explicitly reference the apocalypse; thus, in Wordsworth's poem 'The Simplon Pass', composed 1799 and later integrated into the section of Book VI of *The Prelude* describing his descent from the Alps to Locarno, we read that

>   Brook and road
> Were fellow-travellers in this gloomy pass,
> And with them did we journey several hours
> At a slow step. The immeasurable height
> Of woods decaying, never to be decayed,
> The stationary blasts of waterfalls,
> And in the narrow rent at every turn
> Winds thwarting winds, bewildered and forlorn,

---

[82] *The Prelude. A Parallel Text*, ed. by J. C. Maxwell (London: Penguin, 1986 (Penguin Classics)), p. 96.

[83] Joel Pace, 'Wordsworth and America: Reception and Reform', in *The Cambridge Companion to Wordsworth*, ed. by Stephen Gill (Cambridge: Cambridge University Press, 2003), pp. 230–45 (p. 241).

[84] Wordsworth to Beaumont, 25 December 1804; cited by Abrams, *Natural Supernaturalism*, p. 492.

> The torrents shooting from the clear blue sky
> The rocks that muttered close upon our ears,
> Black drizzling crags that spake by the wayside
> As if a voice were in them, the sick sight
> And giddy prospect of the raving stream
> The unfettered clouds and regions of the Heavens,
> Tumult and peace, the darkness and the light —
> Were all like workings of one mind, the features
> Of the same face, blossoms upon one tree;
> Characters of the great Apocalypse
> The types and symbols of Eternity,
> Of first, and last, and midst, and without end.
> (*The Prelude*, 1805–1806 version, Book VI, ll. 553–72)

With 'such a book before our eyes' (Book VI, ll. 473–74) we are put in a position to envision behind Nature's 'types and symbols of Eternity' the divine 'one mind' that, at the end of time, will bisect his Creation into 'darkness and light', 'tumult and peace' — Hell and Heaven. Citing this passage, Elinor Shaffer has gone so far as to call 'Wordsworth's account of "Crossing the Alps" in Book VI of *The Prelude* [...] the major piece of English apocalyptic poetry in the Romantic period'.[85] Indeed, she adds, 'the language of apocalyptic is the true language of the time'.[86]

And yet, although a religious reading of such a passage might seem inescapable, it often becomes recognizable only when isolated from its larger 'natural' context; M. H. Abrams is right to observe in general:

> If we nonetheless remain unaware of the full extent to which characteristic concepts and patterns of Romantic philosophy and literature are a displaced and reconstituted theology, or else a secularized form of devotional experience, that is because we still live in what is essentially, although in derivative rather than direct manifestations, a Biblical culture, and readily mistake our hereditary ways of organizing experience for the conditions of reality and the universal forms of thought.[87]

While this may have held true for the 1960s when Abrams's book was conceived and written (it was published in 1971), the problem is compounded today by younger generations of readers being far less conversant with the Christian idiom and biblical themes than previous generations. When we thus read, in Book XIII, a clause like 'I remember well | That in life's every-day appearances | I seemed about this period to have sight | Of a new world' (ll. 368–71), not every reader will immediately grasp the millennial implication. And compared with many others, this is a relatively obvious passage. The following lines I had initially read as a merely descriptive image of nature's powerful hold on a child's imagination: 'A Child, I held unconscious intercourse | With the eternal Beauty, drinking in | A pure organic pleasure from the lines | Of curling mist, or from the level plain | Of waters colour'd by the steady clouds', only to learn from Paley's study on *Apocalypse and Millennium* that

---

85 'Secular Apocalypse', p. 150.
86 Ibid., p. 154.
87 *Natural Supernaturalism*, pp. 65–66.

this 'boy's perception of an Edenic nature in Cumbria' can also be read as a 'parallel to the millennial'.[88] And while Paley goes on to remind us that 'the apocalyptic elements here are contained within the framework of nature', and that 'throughout the poem apocalypse and millennium have alternated irregularly and in uneasy relationship', both statements of which might equally be applied to Sonnenberg's *Donatoa*, he also makes an observation that crucially sets Wordsworth off from his German counterpart; taking his cue from Abrams, Paley writes: 'Wordsworth's displacement of apocalypse and millennium is both a model for, and a prime example in, M. H. Abrams's powerful argument that, first sought in the political world and then in external nature, both come to exist internally as a secularized version of Milton's "Paradise within thee, happier far"'.[89] Wordsworth's apocalypse and millennium, in short, are not just much more thoroughly secularized than Sonnenberg's, but they are also psychologically internalized (as well as internally psychologized) and, in doing so, are made part of everyday life and personal history. The poet's biography harbours revelatory moments of apocalypse and millennium, expressed through everyday life's moments of crisis (such as his experience of Paris during the French Revolution, or his return to England at a time when his home country was preparing to go to war on revolutionary France) and repose (his childhood and adult experiences in the Lake District, or his narrative of the ascent to Mount Snowdon). Where Sonnenberg's epic conjures up an imagined artificial world, set in an indefinite future and in an invented landscape, with contrived actions and human agents of these actions (not to mention the hosts of angels and demons), Wordsworth's poem relates the personal biography of a real human being in the real world experiencing real historical events as they unfold before his eyes.

Interestingly, it is Sonnenberg's and Wordsworth's apotheosis less of 'Nature' than of 'Love' in the final sections of their works, occupying in *Donatoa* the eleventh and twelfth canto, in the 1805–1806 version of the *The Prelude* its Book XIII, that may present the most obvious parallel and commonality between them. 'Love' is also the concept that perhaps best establishes Sonnenberg's link with the Romantic generation, even where personal bonds specifically with members of the Jena group never came about. In writing about this keyword of European romanticism, Abrams notes how Schiller, Hegel and Percy Bysshe Shelley all wrote essays on the subject; indeed, Hegel's maxim 'genuine love excludes all opposition', cited by Abrams in a passage on the Romantics' notion of a 'unitive love', a *virtus unitiva*,[90] seems to sum up the creed of Sonnenberg's and Wordsworth's compositions, both 'centring all in love', as Wordsworth puts it in the 'Conclusion' of his *Prelude* (Book XIII, l. 384). And yet, in sentiment and moral they could hardly be more distinct. Where Sonnenberg's is a metaphysical love of and for God, the soul striving upwards to heaven, Wordsworth's is a nature-inspired 'intellectual' human love of and for man, a soul striving to appreciate what surrounds us in Nature, as the two following passages from *The Prelude* serve to illustrate:

---

88 *Apocalypse and Millennium*, p. 155.
89 Ibid., pp. 190 and 191.
90 *Natural Supernaturalism*, pp. 294–95.

> From love, for here
> Do we begin and end, all grandeur comes,
> All truth and beauty, from pervading love;
> That gone, we are as dust.
>   (Book XIII, ll. 149–52)
>
> Imagination having been our theme,
> So also hath that intellectual Love,
> For they are each in each, and cannot stand
> Dividually. — Here must thou be, O Man!
> Strength to thyself; no Helper hast thou here;
> Here keepest thou thy individual state:
> No other can divide with thee this work...
>   (Book XIII, ll. 185–91)

Wordsworth's much-commented-upon neologism 'dividually', conjoining the adverb 'individually' and the verb 'to divide', allows us to relate his observation regarding the quintessential unity and indivisibility of 'Imagination' and 'Love' to the opposition between 'I' and the 'other', or 'non-I' ('Here keepest thou thy individual state: | No other can divide with thee this work'). This division of 'I' and 'non-I', and its overcoming in what Fichte termed the 'absolute I' (*das absolute Ich*), was central to German idealistic philosophy around 1800, the core tenets of which were mediated to Wordsworth (who perhaps overstates his claim never to have read a line of German philosophy)[91] by Coleridge, who was indeed familiar with some of Fichte's and Schelling's work (in fact, Coleridge was in Göttingen around the very time when the so-called 'Atheism Row', the *Atheismusstreit*, surrounding Fichte's alleged atheism broke out in 1798–1799).[92] Fichte's 'absolute I' becomes Schelling's *Weltseele*, the soul of the world (*Von der Weltseele*, 1798), which combines identity and difference, subject and object, spirit and nature, the finite and the infinite, and the real and the ideal, all within one unified whole of 'Nature', much as Hegel some years later defines *Weltgeist*, the absolute spirit, as the identity of 'identity and non-identity' and 'general and individual' (*Philosophy of Spirit*, 1807). We would surely be overstating the case if we tried to argue that Wordsworth was in any way commenting directly either on German idealistic philosophy or German Romantic theory in *The Prelude*, even if 'Nature', 'Love', 'Man' and 'Imagination' loom large throughout his epic poem. But we do know from the documentary evidence given us by Gruber, little though it is, that Sonnenberg, like Coleridge, was informed about German philosophy's most recent developments, and commented accordingly on Kant, with whom he in part agreed, and Schelling, with whom he disagreed

---

91 If Wordsworth's knowledge of German philosophy was scant, he was by comparison well acquainted with contemporary German literature, including works by Klopstock, Schiller and Goethe, all of which, however, he reportedly read in English translation. On his way to Goslar he even visited Klopstock in Hamburg in autumn 1798; once in Goslar he preoccupied himself with reading Bürger's works, but it is in Goslar, too, that he devised the plan for *The Prelude*. For more on this topic see for instance Max Herzberg, 'Wordsworth and German Literature', *PMLA*, 40 (1925), 302–45.

92 I draw here from the illuminating article by Daniel Stempel, 'Revelation on Mount Snowdon: Wordsworth, Coleridge, and the Fichtean Imagination', *The Journal of Aesthetics and Art Criticism*, 29 (1971), 371–84.

profoundly and whose philosophy of nature he considered atheistic. One might contrast Wordsworth and Sonnenberg by observing that whereas the English Lake School poet came unconsciously to convey in poetry some of the import of German idealism's key philosophical maxims — at least that is the way Coleridge viewed it — the German writer composed his *Donatoa* as a conscious Christian antithesis of and riposte to idealism's 'absolute Ego' which seeks to deflate any notion of God in effect to a mere function of the mind. This Sonnenberg will not permit — consequently he makes sure that by the end of his epic, an end in which God annuls and neutralizes all contradiction and transmutes all antagonism into one unified and harmonious totality, the 'absolute Christian God' rules supreme, thereby religiously cancelling out even the possibility of any secular upstart's 'absolute Ego'.

In short, in writing *Donatoa* in 1804/1805, Sonnenberg succeeded neither in crafting a new epic style to compete with Klopstock, nor in creating with the figure of Donatoa the new mythology that Friedrich Schlegel had called for in his 'Speech on Mythology',[93] nor in leaving even the slightest of dents in German philosophy's new-found ego. Wordsworth, by contrast, very much succeeded in *The Prelude*, and specifically in the version of *The Prelude* completed in 1805, in creating a work of 'radical novelty';[94] so much so in fact that Abrams sees fit to call it 'a fully developed poetic equivalent of two portentous innovations in prose fiction, of which the earliest examples had appeared in Germany only a decade or so before Wordsworth began writing his poem', namely 'the Bildungsroman' and 'the Künstlerroman', the novel of education and the novel of the artist, the early prime examples of which were Karl Philipp Moritz's *Anton Reiser* (1785–1790), Goethe's *Wilhelm Meisters Lehrjahre* (1795–1796), Hölderlin's *Hyperion* (1797–1799), Ludwig Tieck's *Franz Sternbalds Wanderungen* (1798) and Novalis's *Heinrich von Ofterdingen* (1802). In the process Wordsworth succeeded in moving from the exteriority of the old epic style to the interiority of a new epic (and lyric) consciousness, that of Man and Nature mutually embedded; as Wordsworth put it in the opening lines of the 'Prospectus to *The Recluse*', his work is 'On Man, on Nature, and on Human Life, | Musing in solitude'.[95] 'Of genius, power, | Creation [...] I have been speaking' and, yes, of 'divinity', he confesses and calls himself 'a chosen son' (Book III, l. 82); and yet, despite seemingly raising himself to a Christ-like status with 'holy powers and faculties' (Book III, l. 83), and 'feeling [with a strangeness in my mind] that I was not for that hour' (Book III, ll. 79–80), all along his true 'theme has been | What passed within me' (Book III, ll. 171–74). His religious sentiments find themselves transferred into his inner being, turning him into that 'Prophet' and 'worshipper of Nature' that he calls himself in *The Prelude* and the last lines of 'Lines written a few miles above Tintern Abbey', rather than into a new Redeemer. In this way his work encapsulates the very shift from traditional (Christian) religion to modern (secular) subjectivity which the literary critic Geoffrey Hartman, in an important essay entitled 'Romanticism and Anti-Self-Consciousness', has diagnosed as crucial

---

93 Friedrich Schlegel's 'Speech on Mythology' ('Rede über die Mythologie') is a part of his *Gespräch über die Poesie* (*Dialogue on Poetry*) published in the journal *Athenäum* in 1800.
94 Abrams, *Natural Supernaturalism*, p. 74.
95 Ibid., p. 466.

to the Romantic sensibility; noting that in poems like Wordsworth's *The Prelude* 'the traditional scheme of Eden, Fall, and Redemption merges with the new triad of Nature, Self-Consciousness, and Imagination', Hartman goes on to observe:

> As soon as poetry is separated from imposed religious or communal ends it becomes as problematic as the individual himself. The question of how art is possible, though post-Romantic in its explicitness, has its origin here, for the artist is caught up in a serious paradox. His art is linked to the autonomous and individual: yet that same art, in the absence of an authoritative myth, must bear the entire weight of having to transcend or ritually limit these tendencies. No wonder the problem of the subjective, the isolated, the individual, grows particularly acute. Subjectivity — even solipsism — becomes the subject of poems which qua poetry seek to transmute it. This paradox seems to inhere in all seminal works of the Romantic period.[96]

Following Hartman, the two works written in 1805 by Sonnenberg and Wordsworth, *Donatoa* and *The Prelude*, thus represent the two poles of one of the main axes of nineteenth-century literature and art, and indeed of nineteenth-century culture and philosophy: it is the division, or carving up, long prepared by Enlightenment philosophy, of what was formerly a unified transcendent whole of Christian belief, in which God and nature (with a lower case 'n') were seen as a form of *unio mystica*, into two sovereign entities, God and Nature (the latter now emblazoned with a capital 'N', as in Wordsworth's *Prelude* and the scholarship pertaining to it). As we shall see in the subsequent chapters, it is the moment when (European) writers and philosophers recognize and declare 'Nature's' independence; this moment will be crucial for the larger argument that is to follow.

In Conversation with Sonnenberg

But let us return for a moment more to *Donatoa*. Imagine discussing the text with its author across the centuries: I am convinced Franz von Sonnenberg would emphatically disagree with my assessment of his work — he would perhaps concede that his choice of genre had been an unfortunate one, but he would consider my faulting him for 'heavy-handedly deploying "Christian machinery"' patently unfair. Why do I say this? In the first instance because Sonnenberg himself explicitly disapproved of using 'plain unadorned Christian machinery' in an epic. He writes expressly in the preface to *Donatoa*: 'To reproduce myth the way our forebears did, to create a mythological portrait of the end of the world merely in the vein of the Bible, or to avail oneself of plain unadorned Christian machinery — for all of this our times were too advanced' ('Den Mythos im Geist der Väter hervorzuheben, ein blos biblisch mythologisches Gemälde des Weltendes, nackte christianische Maschienerie darzustellen, war dem vorangeschrittenen Zeitalter zurük').[97] He had used the same expression 'Christian machinery' also in the preface to *The End of the World*. In both prefaces of 1801 and 1805 he makes the

---

[96] 'Romanticism and Anti-Self-Consciousness', in *Beyond Formalism. Literary Essays 1958–1970* (New Haven and London: Yale University Press, 1970), pp. 298–310 (p. 306).
[97] *Donatoa*, I.1, p. vii.

case for writing a religious epic (his precise term is *Religionsepopoe*)[98] for his era even against the strong anti-Christian sentiments on exhibit among the literati of his time, as well as against recent scientific discoveries indicating that the world might be destroyed by purely natural means rather than supernatural forces.[99] So how does his own disapproval of 'Christian machinery' chime with the character pool deployed in *Donatoa*? This includes, besides the key human agents Eliora, Heroal and Herkla, such otherworldly celestial figures as the archangels Donatoa, Michael and Leli Alphaod, the fallen angels Satan and Beelzebub, countless other angels good and bad, and the Fury of War — not to mention God himself as well as Jesus Christ, whom Sonnenberg in *Donatoa* curiously never calls Jesus or Christ but rather 'God-Human' or 'Reconciler' ('Gottmensch', 'Mittler'). Are they not 'Christian machinery'? To answer what might appear to us as a manifest contradiction, but clearly was not one for Sonnenberg, means better to understand the differential between then and now. While it goes to the heart of the matter that I intend to address in more detail in Chapter Two, it also warrants some preliminary discussion here.

'Well, no,' Sonnenberg himself would answer, 'the way I have presented them they are not Christian machinery'. He would argue that (and here I quote verbatim from that preface)

> by its very nature the tendency of this epic had to be religious. [...] But to avoid appearing like mere machinery, the supernatural beings have to be free, they should not give the impression that they are mere envoys of the Almighty, without their own will; they must be characters that intervene *of their own free accord* in the affairs of the world.
>
> [Die Tendenz dieser Epopoe mußte, ihrer Natur nach, religiös sein. [...] Um aber keine Maschinerie zu werden, müssen die Ueberirdischen frei, nicht als Boten der Allmacht, ohne eigenen Willen, erscheinen, sie müssen Charaktere werden, *frei* in den Weltgang eingreifen.][100] (Sonnenberg's emphasis)

---

98 'Vorerinnerung', in *Das Welt-Ende*, p. iii.

99 Thus in the 'Preface' to *Donatoa* he observes: 'Here the question arises: if a world can go under, how does she do this morally, how civilizationally, how physically? — To touch upon only some points here, some in more detail than others, depending on how obvious they are: There are traces of a sudden or successive ruin in an earlier era, traces of a preadamite creation. Might this not point to a metamorphosis of humankind, as with other species in nature — ? — The record of vanished stars, the star long observed by Keppler in Cassiopeia that disappeared after fluctuating in brightness: comets roll through our solar systems, striking, sooner or later perhaps, into the atmosphere of planets [...]. Does this not portend for our own planet!' ('Hier ergiebt sich denn die Frage: wenn eine Welt untergehn kann, wie geht sie sittlich, wie bürgerlich, und wie phisisch unter? — Einige Punkte näher berührend, andre nur flüchtig andeutend, je nachdem sie offener oder verhüllter daliegen, bemerk' ich nur hier: Spuren eines speziellen oder successiven Untergangs zeugen noch aus der Urzeit her, Spuren einer praeadamitischen Schöpfung. Kann nicht, wie mit andern Naturgeschlechtern, eine Metamorphose des Menschengeschlechts kommen — ? — Das Verzeichnis der verschwundenen Sterne, das lange von Keppler in der Kassiopea beobachtete Gestirn, das nach oftmaligem Lichtwechsel verschwand: Kometen rollen durch Sonnensisteme, treffend, vielleicht früh oder spät, die Atmosphären der Planeten [...]. Winkt nicht dieß auch auf unsern Planeten zurück!'; *Donatoa*, I.1, p. ix).

100 *Donatoa*, I.1, p. xii.

Here is the crux of the matter, then: whereas any epic with heavenly hosts and satanic hordes will inevitably strike the majority of today's readers as part of a Christian machinery — to what degree 'heavy-handed' will naturally depend on the individual reader and his or her religious or non-religious convictions — for Sonnenberg the concept of 'Christian machinery' implied deploying spirits with no will of their own. What he does, by contrast, is to create angelic figures that possess a psychology as independent as any human being's. He writes:

> As freely acting selves with a free will, these celestial beings are subject to finite laws and hence are fallible; they have to do battle as finite beings, the archangel no less than a human; finite in their reasoning, they cannot grasp the eternal consequences of their actions [...]. Any complication that arises, any association, any conversation with them must develop psychologically from the character, circumstances, emotions and milieus of the humans in their purview. [...] As mediators between God and human beings they can act only through those humans who attach themselves to them in spirit, willpower, nobility and holiness; this alone allows the supernatural to fuse with the natural, and thus the epic unites heaven and earth.
>
> [Die Ueberirdischen aber sind als freiwollende, freihandelnde Wesen, nach Gesetzen der Endlichkeit des Falls fähig; als Endliche müssen sie kämpfen, der Erzengel wie der Mensch; endlich in ihrer Vernunft, können sie nicht die unendliche Folgenreihe einer That überschauen [...]. Alle Verwicklungen und Vergesellschaftungen, alle Gespräche mit ihnen, müssen sich psychologisch aus den Charackteren, Situationen, Stimmungen und Umgebungen jener Menschen erklären lassen. [...] Als Mittler zwischen Gott und den Menschen können sie nur durch jene Erdenwesen, die sich ihnen zunächst anschließen in Geist, Kraft, Hoheit und Heiligkeit, auf die Menschheit wirken; so geht das Uebernatürliche ins Natürliche über, so werden Himmel und Erde in der Epopöe Eins.][101]

Sonnenberg accordingly portrays his angels and archangels as psychologically distinct from one another as any human individual is from the other; he sees his celestial troupe as autonomous entities and self-directed agents of action. And thus they are not to be equated with any form of celestial mechanics, but rather deserve to be treated no less as psychological characters than their earthly human counterparts. Look at Young's angels in *A Poem on the Last Day*, he would say; are they not will-less and soulless machines, doing merely God's bidding? Don't we read there sentences like 'But chiefly Thou Great Ruler! Lord of All! | Before whose Throne Archangels prostrate fall'?[102] And is there any action in the celestial realm? Do the angels have any independent role to play? No, he would say, adding: 'This has little to do with my understanding of apocalypse'.

But is this not splitting hairs? Is this a truly persuasive argument, we might ask. Are not the angels, good or evil, ultimately subject to the will of God? Do the archangelic Michaels and Donatoas really have any command over the events that unfold? Or, to put it more bluntly, is the Last Judgment plus the ensuing

---

101 Ibid., pp. xiii–xiv.
102 *A Poem on the Last Day*, p. 3.

harmony of Millennium even in Sonnenberg's world where angels have a say, and a purportedly independent role to play, not a foregone conclusion? Once within the Christian mould of an arc of action that ends in the Last Judgment and Millennium, the concept of free will becomes immaterial; in the end, no freedom of decision remains except for God's. As Fiona Stafford has put it in her fascinating survey of 'Last of the Race' figures in literature, 'while individual destinies were influenced by free will and conscience, [...] responsibility for the collective fate of mankind was effectively transferred to a higher authority'.[103] And is this not precisely what happens at the end of *Donatoa*? — even the supreme archangel Donatoa, the Angel of Thunder himself, this purveyor of death and destruction, is taken by surprise and consumed by God. At the (literal) end of the day, God's will alone is all that is left.

Nonetheless, to put Sonnenberg's argument into perspective, and to give him the credit he deserves, in *Donatoa* he goes well beyond the traditional mould of Christian representations of the Last Judgment. Let us recall: having grown up in an orthodox Catholic and, during his education, also Jesuit environment in the last decades of the eighteenth century, Sonnenberg did not doubt for one moment, neither as a young man asked by his teacher to compose a poem on the Last Judgment, nor as an adult now writing a multi-volume epic on the same topic, that the Christian apocalypse was a reality-to-come. It was going to happen, sooner or later: God would see to it. If one believed theistically in a Christian God during Sonnenberg's era, one by default believed as much in miracles and the existence of angels as one did in the Second Coming of Christ. It was part and parcel of the Christian belief system that was under attack by Enlightenment philosophy. (Note that I say 'theistically' here: I will come back to the relevance of the underlying concept of theism later.) But in one respect Sonnenberg was 'progressive', too, as was incidentally Edward Young, as opposed to Thomas Burnet and the German clergyman with his anonymous calendar of future events in the run-up to the Day of Judgment. Burnet and the anonymous German clergymen locate the commencement of the apocalypse around a specific preordained date, namely AD 2000, or 6000 years after the Creation of the world by God's hand. Young, by contrast, shows himself already influenced by sixteenth- and seventeenth-century deistic thinking which, in James Joyce's famous twentieth-century formulation, sees 'the God of the creation remain[ing] within or behind or beyond or above his handiwork, invisible, refined out of existence, indifferent, paring his fingernails'.[104] For Young the date of the Last Judgment is not set or predetermined by the sort of Mosaic biblical computation endorsed by more orthodox teaching; it is hence truly unpredictable and not — as Burnet saw it — unpredictable only within a margin that depended upon the timing of Creation. In *A Poem on the Last Day* we read accordingly:

---

[103] *The Last of the Race. The Growth of a Myth from Milton to Darwin* (Oxford: Oxford University Press, 1997, first published 1994), p. 35.

[104] *A Portrait of the Artist as a Young Man. Text, Criticism, and Notes*, ed. by Chester G. Anderson (New York: Viking Press, 1968), p. 215.

> Sooner, or later, in some future Date,
> A dreadful Secret in the Book of Fate,
> This Hour, for ought all human Wisdom knows,
> Or when ten thousand Harvests more have rose,
> When Scenes are chang'd on this revolving Earth,
> Old Empires fall, and give new Empires birth [...]
> Of Earth dissolv'd, or an extinguisht Sun.[105]

Let us be quite clear what Young is stating: not only is this 'future Date' 'a dreadful Secret', it might indeed be some 10,000 years or more away (from the year 1713, that is, hence commencing perhaps AD 12000). For his time, this is provocative stuff. It is un-Mosaic, un-biblical, and unorthodox, perhaps even surpassing the immediate source for this argument, the early British deist and nonconformist naturalist John Ray. In his 1692 *Miscellaneous Discourses Concerning the Dissolution and Changes of the World* Ray had argued much the same, and its third edition appeared in 1713, the year of Young's poem. It would have been a thesis Young was closely familiar with; indeed, the 'Earth dissolv'd' and 'extinguisht Sun' are two of the four 'probable Means of Cause of the World's Destruction' listed by Ray in his work; there we read (the wording of the first and third editions is virtually the same):

> The Fifth Question is, At what Period of Time shall the World be dissolved? I answer, This is absolutely uncertain and undeterminable. For, since this Dissolution shall be effected by the extraordinary Interposition of Providence, it cannot be to any Man known, unless extraordinarily revealed. And our Saviour tells us, That *of that Day and Hour knoweth no Man, no not Angels of Heaven, &. Matth. xxiv.36.* [...] But yet, notwithstanding this, many have ventured to foretell the Time of the End of the World, the Term prefixt being past, and the World still standing. [...] But the most famous Opinion, and which hath found most Patrons and Followers, even amongst the Learned and Pious, is that of the World's Duration for Six thousand Years. For the strengthening of which Conceit, they tell us, That as the World was created in six Days, and then followed the Sabbath, so shall it remain Six thousand Years, and then shall succeed the Eternal Sabbath. [...] The Tradition is [...] *Two thousand Years Vacuity: Two thousand Years of the Law: Two thousand Years the Days of the Messiah.* But they shoot far wide [...] So I leave this Question unresolved, concluding, that when that Day will come GOD only knows.

It is as if Young were poetically filling in the details of Ray's naturalist argument. Thus, for all its apparent Christian traditionalism, Young's *A Poem on the Last Day* surprisingly reveals an element of the emergent deistic thinking.

Likewise Sonnenberg: he too does away with temporal delimitations. Not only is there no specific timing attached to the events unfolding in *Donatoa*, more importantly the timing of the apocalypse is not determined by divine fiat but is dependent rather upon the state of human affairs on Earth. The apocalypse can commence only once humanity has succumbed to unbelief, paganism, atheism or, more generally, universal godlessness. It is only once Eliora, Heroal and Herkla as the last of the faithful have passed away that the apocalypse can ensue. That is to

---

105 *A Poem on the Last Day*, p. 5.

say, not God decides when the apocalypse can begin, but humanity itself does. This explains why for Sonnenberg the distinction between free will, freedom of choice and individuality on the one hand and necessity, predestination and determinate celestial mechanics on the other was so crucial: his angels, his Satan, his Beelzebub all act of their own free accord (although I grant that as a secular modern reader I find it very difficult to appreciate or recognize this), they are shown as in full possession of a free will rather than serving as mere puppets of the Almighty.[106]

The debate about necessity versus freedom, or (divine) predestination versus (human) free will, is of course an age-old philosophical and theological problem. But it was rekindled with particular intensity in a Christian theological context following Leibniz's publication in 1710 of his *Essays of Theodicy* (*Essais de theodicée*), whose full title announces exactly what these 'essays' are about: *Essays of Theodicy on the Goodness of God, the Freedom of Man and the Origin of Evil*.[107] Later in the century Kant will define theodicy as 'the defense [elsewhere he uses the word vindication] of the highest wisdom of the creator against the charge which reason brings against it for whatever is counterpurposive in the world' ('Unter einer Theodizee versteht man die Verteidigung der höchsten Weisheit des Welturhebers gegen die Anklage, welche die Vernunft aus dem Zweckwidrigen in der Welt gegen jene erhebt'),[108] and it was precisely the defence or 'vindication of divine providence' over which Sonnenberg is said constantly to have agonized. Sonnenberg's friend Gruber writes:

> Vindication of God against the (moral) evil in the world — Sonnenberg was obsessed with this problem which can leave no ethically and religiously educated person unmoved. In the freedom of will and the moral law that lie in us he at last found what he had been looking for in vain for so long. Both pointed to — a judgment in which must be resolved what is veiled in darkness, namely God's plan for humankind, the recognition of which must be that God appears as Love even where *we* deem it — contradiction.
>
> [Rechtfertigung der Gottheit gegen das (moralische) Uebel in der Welt, — dieses Problem, welches keinen sittlich und religiös gebildeten Menschen gleichgiltig lassen kann, beschäftigte unablässig Sonnenbergs Seele. In der Freiheit des Willens und dem moralischen Gesetze in uns fand er endlich, wonach er lange vergebens gesucht. Beide wiesen ihn auf ein — Gericht hin, in welchem sich auflösen müsse, was hier in Nacht gehüllt ist, der Plan der Gottheit mit dem menschlichen Geschlechte, nach dessen Erkenntniß die Gottheit auch da als Liebe erscheint, wo sie hier uns — Widerspruch dünkt.][109]

---

106 Wukadinović also notes the importance of this motif (p. 132).

107 A broad-ranging and intriguing study on this topic is Thomas McFarland's *Paradoxes of Freedom: the Romantic Mystique of a Transcendence* (Oxford: Oxford University Press, 1996). The latter sections of his Chapter Four in particular expand on what I can say here only in an abbreviated fashion, especially as regards Fichte's and Schelling's philosophical understanding and interpretation of the opposition between freedom and necessity.

108 'On the miscarriage of all philosophical trials in theodicy', in *Religion and Rational Theology*, pp. 24–37 (p. 24); 'Über das Misslingen aller philosophischen Versuche in der Theodizee', in *Werke*, ed. Weischedel, vol. 6, pp. 103–24 (p. 105).

109 *Donatoa*, II.2, pp. 447–48.

Gruber had picked up the word 'contradiction' ('Widerspruch') from notes his friend had left behind; in one of these notes, written one and a half years before his suicide, Sonnenberg had mulled over the theodicy issue, observing:

> Death must be great and sublime for any being that enjoys the presence of God, that finds peace of life in His presence, and awaits Him — with hope. Love must be the purpose of Creation, and the majority of beings must end blissfully happy, else God should not have created. For it would be more misery than bliss, and that is — contradiction, because — God is, God created. His goal must be achieved because God cannot undertake anything that fails. I dread death with trepidation, but the more I connect the thought of death with the highest of all thoughts, God, the more I feel myself composed.

> [Der Tod muß groß und erhaben und herrlich seyn für jedes Wesen, das sich des Daseyns Gottes freut, das in seinem Daseyn Ruhe des Lebens fühlt, und auf ihn — hofft. Liebe muß der Zweck der Schöpfung seyn, und der größte Theil der Wesen muß glückselig werden, sonst hätte Gott nicht erschaffen dürfen; denn es wäre mehr Elend als Seligkeit, und das ist — Widerspruch, weil — Gott ist, Gott schuf; sein Ziel muß erreicht werden, weil Gott als Gott nichts unternehmen kann, was mißlingt. Ich fürchtete mit Schauder den Tod, aber ich werde immer beruhigter, wenn ich den Gedanken Tod an den höchsten aller Gedanken Gott knüpfe.][110]

In his unmethodical deliberations on death, the purpose of being and human freedom Sonnenberg fuses aspects of Leibniz's 'theodicy' (i.e., the harmonious resolution of contradiction through God's superior perspective, but one unknown and inaccessible to man) and Kant's 'religion of reason' (in which God is in essence equated with human moral law and action, constituting, as many critics have observed, a psychological 'as if').[111] A travel notebook from the year 1800 — an extended excerpt of which Gruber reproduces in the appendix to *Donatoa* — bears out not just Sonnenberg's intense preoccupation with the dialectic of freedom and predetermination but shows also how the twenty-one-year-old is struggling to resolve for himself the theological conundrum arising from Kant's philosophy, namely how to retain belief in a God whose existence one will never be able to prove. Travelling by coach 'beyond Paderborn' ('Hinter Paderborn'), Sonnenberg becomes engaged in conversation with a Catholic priest ('Pater'); being educated men of the same faith their conversation soon begins to revolve around theological issues. Admiring nature's landscape passing by their coach window the priest begins by asking his young travel companion how anyone can deny the existence

---

110 Ibid., p. 400.

111 Mauthner speaks of Kant's 'Als-Ob-Philosophie' in his *Der Atheismus und seine Geschichte im Abendlande*, vol. 4, p. 32; on p. 66 of this volume he also speaks of Kant's 'fiction model as if a God existed' ('Fiktionenlehre als ob es einen Gott gäbe'), on p. 68 he reformulates Kant's moral imperative to read: 'Act as if God's existence had been proven' ('Handle so, als ob [die Existenz Gottes] bewiesen wäre'). Closer to today, the editors of Kant's writings on *Religion and Rational Theology* in English translation write: 'The most Kant will allow here is a "regulative use" of the concept, whereby we may talk and act "as if" God exists, if we have sufficient practical reasons for doing so, even though we remain totally ignorant of the *fact* of God's existence in any scientifically significant sense' (Allen W. Wood and George Di Giovanni, 'Introduction', in *Religion and Rational Theology*, p. xix).

of a divine being in view of such beauty; adopting the role of devil's advocate Sonnenberg answers: 'If you won't scold me for being an atheist I might dare to share with you my doubts' ('Wenn Sie mich nicht einen Atheisten schelten wollen, sagt' ich, so wagt' ich's wohl, Ihnen meine Zweifel zu äußern'), and then goes on to argue that from nature's causes and effects it is impossible to deduce the existence of anything outside of nature. 'From effects that we experience in nature', he thus tells his interlocutor,

> we can infer only necessary causes within that nature, but not causes beyond it. I therefore do not deny [the existence of] a being that is free and independent of nature, what I do deny is that we can prove his existence.
>
> [Von Wirkungen, die in der Natur sich zeigen, kann nur auf nothwendige Ursachen in ihr geschlossen werden, nicht auf Ursachen außerhalb der Natur. Ich läugne darum nicht das freie, von der Natur unabhängige Wesen, nur läugne ich jedem Beweise seines Daseyns die Richtigkeit ab.][112]

Not one to capitulate so easily the priest changes tack by pressing the point about every effect needing a cause, with the infinite regress of such causes and effects ultimately requiring a First Cause and Prime Mover that put the system in motion in the first place. This portion of their conversation Sonnenberg records as follows:

> He. What do you object to as regards this eternal order in nature, which surely cannot be the product of mere chance, but must be the product of a wise Creator?
> I. If we assume it is we who assign this regularity of order to nature the argument collapses [...].
> He. And the freedom of human will! — Since everything in nature must be either an effect or a cause, and therefore a necessary consequence — in what should they have their source? To be sure, nature cannot be this source because she would then be only a necessary effect, und there would be no freedom.
> I. If you can prove this freedom to me with apodictic certainty, then you would possess an unassailable axiom with which you could topple the system of the materialists. But for my part I question the freedom that is attributed to the human will.
>
> [Er. Was wenden Sie gegen die ewige Ordnung der Natur ein, die doch nicht das Werk eines Zufalles, sondern nur eines weisen Urhebers seyn kann? [...]
> Ich. Untersuchen wir, ob wir diese regelmäßige Ordnung nicht vielmehr in die Natur hineindenken, so sinkt auch dieser Pfeiler [...].
> Er. Aber die Freiheit des menschlichen Willens! — Da alles in der Natur Wirkung oder Ursache, mithin nothwendige Folge ist, — woher soll diese ihre Ursache haben? In der Natur kann sie nicht entspringen, weil sie dann nothwendige Folge, und nicht mehr Freiheit wäre.
> Ich. Wenn Sie diese Freiheit mit apodiktischer Gewißheit darthun können; so haben Sie für Ihren Beweis ein unumstößliches Axiom gefunden, und das System der Materialisten gestürzt. Ich aber zweifle an dieser dem menschlichen Willen angedichteten Freiheit.][113]

---

112 *Donatoa*, II.2, pp. 282–83.
113 Ibid., pp. 285–87.

However, having consciously adopted a sceptical theophilosophical counterposition during their tête-à-tête, Sonnenberg post festum attaches to his record of the conversation the following admission (and de facto disclaimer):

> Dear old man! Your principles were, with minor qualifications, the same as mine. I do not deny the existence of a loving omnipotence, a free primary essence; — indeed, I am convinced of his existence, but only morally so. Theoretical reason tells me that humans will never be able to prove his existence.
>
> [Guter Alter! Deine Grundsätze waren, nur mit einiger Einschränkung, auch die meinigen. Ich läugne nicht das Daseyn einer liebenden Allmacht, eines freien Urwesens; — ich bin von seinem Daseyn überzeugt, aber nur moralisch. Aus Gründen theoretischer Vernunft wird wohl von Menschen nie seine Existenz bewiesen werden können.][114]

Gruber reports how Sonnenberg throughout his final years struggled to defend man's freedom of will against the materialists' critique and denial of it. Sonnenberg 'fought a renewed battle within himself against materialism,' Gruber relates at one point, 'and an unspeakable anxiety took hold of him whenever he felt that the freedom of willpower and of the immortality of the soul were endangered; he felt outrage against this doctrine, as he did against Schelling's position which he deemed equally amoral and atheistic' ('er stritt nun einen neuen Kampf mit sich gegen den Materialismus, und eine unnennbare Unruhe ergriff ihn, wenn er Freiheit des Willens, Unsterblichkeit der Seele gefährdet glaubte; er empörte sich gegen diese Lehre wie gegen Schellings, die ihm eben so unmoralisch als atheistisch dünkte').[115]

Whilst Sonnenberg rejects the materialists' denial of God's existence, he accepts with Kant that his existence can never be proven. The formulation 'theoretical reason' ('theoretische Vernunft') here specifically refers to Kant's *Critique of Pure Reason* (*Kritik der reinen Vernunft*, 1781) in which the philosopher had made the case that the existence of God is unprovable, a position Sonnenberg showed himself well capable of adopting and defending, as his conversation with the priest illustrates. But even where Sonnenberg allows himself philosophically to subscribe to a Kantian line of reasoning, theologically he shows himself unwilling to abandon belief either in a free will answerable to a supreme being outside of us (as opposed to Kant's supreme being within us) or in the immortality of the soul. Kant was a deist for whom Christianity was just one form of (revealed) religion among others, with no claim to superiority; Sonnenberg by contrast remained a theist for whom the trinitarian Christian God was the one and only supreme being. As deist, Kant ruled out not just the divinity of Christian Revelation (for Kant the Bible was a product of human intellection) but also the possibility of any form of miraculous supernatural intervention, including the Last Judgment. (The only supernatural intervention Kant permitted was a supreme being's initial act of Creation.) As theist, Sonnenberg — despite yielding to the deists' argument about the logical

---

114 Ibid., p. 288.
115 Ibid., p. 461.

unprovability of God — continued to believe in a Day of Reckoning, even if he may have seen his (re)presentation of it in *The End of the World* and *Donatoa* as a purely speculative visualization of it.

For Kant the Last Judgment has a purely symbolic value as the Königsberg philosopher argues in his short but important essay 'The End of all Things' ('Das Ende aller Dinge'), which was published, at age 70, three years after his theodicy-essay in the *Berlinische Monatsschrift* in June 1794. The following passage from that essay may be dense, but it states unequivocally that (Christian) 'ideas' such as the end of all things (which is the theme of the essay) have no correlate in the real world and hence must be seen as 'speculative' conceits, although they may serve a practical purpose nonetheless by guiding our thinking about moral principles and the meaning of life (i.e., they may thereby 'acquire objective practical reality', as Kant expresses it). I quote more fully:

> Here we have to do (or are playing) merely with ideas created by reason itself, whose objects (if they have any) lie wholly beyond our field of vision; although they are transcendent for speculative cognition, they are not to be taken as empty, but with a practical intent they are made available to us by lawgiving reason itself, yet not in order to brood over their objects as to what they are in themselves and in their nature, but rather how we have to think of them in behalf of moral principles directed toward the final end of all things (through which, though otherwise they would be entirely empty, [they] acquire objective practical reality).
>
> [Da wir es hier bloß mit Ideen zu tun haben (oder damit spielen), die die Vernunft sich selbst schafft, wovon die Gegenstände (wenn sie deren haben) ganz über unsern Gesichtskreis hinausliegen, die indes, obzwar für das spekulative Erkenntnis überschwenglich, darum doch nicht in aller Beziehung für leer zu halten sind, sondern in praktischer Absicht uns von der gesetzgebenden Vernunft selbst an die Hand gegeben werden, nicht etwa um über ihre Gegenstände, was sie an sich und ihrer Natur nach sind, nachzugrübeln, sondern wie wir sie zum Behuf der moralischen, auf den Endzweck aller Dinge gerichteten, Grundsätze zu denken haben (wodurch sie, die sonst gänzlich leer wären, objektive praktische Realität bekommen).][116]

In the continuation to this passage Kant distinguishes three kinds of the end of all things, first 'the *natural* end of all things according to the order of divine wisdom's moral ends, which we therefore (with a practical intent) can *very well understand*'; second 'their *mystical* (supernatural) end in the order of efficient causes, of which we *understand nothing*'; and third 'the *contranatural* (perverse) end of all things, which comes from us when we *misunderstand* the final end' ('1) [...] das *natürliche* Ende aller Dinge, nach der Ordnung moralischer Zwecke göttlicher Weisheit, welches wir also (in praktischer Absicht) *wohl verstehen* können, 2) [...] das *mystische* (übernatürliche) Ende derselben, in der Ordnung der wirkenden Ursachen, von welchem wir *nichts verstehen*, 3) [...] das *widernatürliche* (verkehrte) Ende aller Dinge, welches

---

116 'The end of all things', in *Religion and Rational Theology*, pp. 221–31 (pp. 225–26; the subsequent passages p. 226 and again p. 226), 'Das Ende aller Dinge', in *Werke*, ed. Weischedel, vol. 6, pp. 173–90 (pp. 181–82; the subsequent passages p. 182 and pp. 182–83).

von uns selbst, dadurch daß wir den Endzweck *mißverstehen*, herbeigeführt wird'; Kant's emphases). His comments beg the question, of course, how one can, for all practical intents and purposes, distinguish between a 'mystical' and a 'contranatural' end; either way, Kant cautions his reader about the dangers of taking recourse to any 'nonnatural' ('nicht-natürliche')[117] notion, under which he rubricizes both 'mystical' and 'contranatural' representations of the end. As he explains in the middle sections of the essay, a person who 'broods' ('nachgrübeln') on the end may fall into mysticism and 'indulge in enthusiasm' ('schwärm[en]') 'rather than — as seems fitting for an intellectual inhabitant of a sensible world — to limit [himself] within the bounds of the latter' ('lieber [...] als sich, wie es einem intellektuellen Bewohner einer Sinnenwelt geziemt, innerhalb den Grenzen dieser eingeschränkt zu halten').[118] 'All this', Kant concludes,

> because people would like at last to have an *eternal tranquillity* in which to rejoice, constituting for them a supposedly blessed end of all things; but really this is a concept in which the understanding is simultaneously exhausted and all thinking itself has an end.
>
> [Alles lediglich darum, damit die Menschen sich endlich doch einer *ewigen Ruhe* zu erfreuen haben möchten, welche denn ihr vermeintes seliges Ende aller Dinge ausmacht; eigentlich ein Begriff, mit dem ihnen zugleich der Verstand ausgeht und alles Denken selbst ein Ende hat.]

As examples of such misdirected behaviour Kant cites Tibetan and Spinozist pantheists ('der *Pantheism* (der Tibetaner und andrer östlichen Völker); und der aus der metaphysischen Sublimierung desselben in der Folge erzeugte *Spinozism*') as cases in point; it is as if he were knowingly avoiding any direct reference to his Christian contemporaries, many of whom, perhaps most of whom, would have agreed that the Last Judgment was supernatural, but would have vehemently objected to it being described as 'mystical' ('mystisch') or 'perverse' ('widernatürlich verkehrt'). Christianity does come in for criticism elsewhere in the essay, but this criticism is formulated cautiously; Kant points out the moral discrepancy between the vociferous Christian advocacy of God's *all-embracing* love on the one hand and the widespread Christian conviction on the other that God will, in the end, mete out rewards to some and punishment to others 'as if the rewards are to be taken for the incentive of the actions' we carry out in our daily lives ('als sollten die Belohnungen für die Triebfedern der Handlungen genommen werden').[119] But as regards openly branding Christianity a 'non-natural' (mystical or contranatural) belief system, Kant in my opinion remains shrewdly evasive, and this for a reason. Kant's previous sovereign Frederick the Great, who had invited Voltaire to stay in Berlin in the early 1750s, had fostered an atmosphere of religious freethinking and non-conformism in Prussia; but this era of tolerance had come to an abrupt end with the accession to the Prussian throne of Frederick's nephew Frederick William

---

117 The term is used in a footnote appended to the cited passage.
118 'The end of all things', this and all subsequent passages p. 228 ('Das Ende aller Dinge', p. 185).
119 'The end of all things', p. 231 ('Das Ende aller Dinge', p. 189).

II in 1786. In stark contrast to his uncle, Frederick William was a religious fanatic who had converted to a mystical form of Christianity and become a member of the Rosicrucian Society in the 1780s. In 1788 Frederick William installed a resolutely anti-Enlightenment pastor and promulgator of traditional Christian orthodoxy, Johann Christoph Wöllner, as Minister of Education and Religious Affairs, making him Kant's immediate superior. As one of the editors of the new English translation of Kant's writings on religion, Allen W. Wood, notes in his introduction to the volume *Religion and Rational Theology*:

> Wöllner's aim was to halt the spread of undisciplined apostasy among the clergy and to compel both spiritual and secular teachers to return to orthodoxy at least in their public instruction, if not their private beliefs. [...] The religious edict [he had decreed in 1788] put many liberal pastors in the position of choosing between losing their livelihood and teaching what they regarded as a set of outdated superstitions. [...] Kant's friend and colleague, J. G. Hasse, was forced to choose between losing his post and recanting the contents of his treatise on 'neology'; he chose the latter and was generally regarded as having disgraced himself; for a time the fear was that the authorities would confront Kant with a similar choice.[120]

Wood sees Kant's essay 'The End of all Things' as a 'bitterly satirical essay targeting the religious projects of Wöllner' and his conservative ministers, and it was also 'the last straw': already under surveillance, Kant was now accused in an official letter signed by Wöllner on behalf of Frederick William II that he was (ab)using his philosophy to 'distort and disparage many of the cardinal and basic teachings of the Holy Scriptures and Christianity' ('zu Entstellung und Herabwürdigung von Grundlehren der Heiligen Schrift und des Christentums mißbraucht').[121] Thus the philosopher was henceforth prohibited from publishing anything further on the topic of religion. (Feeling himself released from this prohibition after Frederick William had died in 1797, Kant reproduced Wöllner's letter in 1798 in the Preface to *The Conflict of the Faculties*, as part of which Kant delineates the epistemological differential between philosophical and theological discourse.) To intimate — as Kant does in this essay — that the Christian belief in the Last Judgment might constitute an unnatural, and hence rationally untenable, mysticism was dangerous enough, but saying this unequivocally would have meant overstepping the mark, taking him beyond what the state and religious authorities at the time were willing to tolerate.

It is perhaps this that most obviously separates Sonnenberg from Kant. As I have indicated, Kant was a moderate deist; for his part Sonnenberg had, by the end of his life, become a moderate theist. For Kant God may exist, but he has limited his involvement in earthly affairs to the creation of the universe and the laws of nature at the beginning of time; as we saw in our discussion of his early scientific work *Universal Natural History and Theory of the Heavens or Essay on the Constitution and the Mechanical Origin of the Whole Universe according to Newtonian Principles*, published

---

120 *Religion and Rational Theology*, p. xvii.
121 Ibid., p. xx (*Werke*, ed. Weischedel, vol. 6, p. 268).

in 1755, Kant rejects Newton's conception of God as a constant active modifier of the shape of our universe. For Kant, ever since the moment of creation only natural factors and laws have been at play in the gestation of stars and planetary bodies; 'nature has brought [them] forth', he stresses, 'without being interrupted in its free behaviour by any extraordinary compulsion' ('daß die Natur [sie], ohne durch einen außerordentlichen Zwang in ihrem freien Betragen gestört zu sein, [...] hervorgebracht habe').[122] By subjecting nature to just such an 'extraordinary compulsion', the Last Judgment would constitute a 'contranatural' breach in the natural order of things; and inasmuch as it would violate the natural order of things it would constitute an inadmissible transgression of the laws and rules God himself had put in place. For Kant the Last Judgment is both a logical and metaphysical impossibility although it may serve as a practical (Christian) moral fiction.

Even where Sonnenberg accepts Kant's argument that we cannot prove the existence of God, as theist — albeit an enlightened one to degrees — he would never dismiss the possibility that God could reengage in the world's affairs at any time of his choosing. Even if God opts not to show himself before then, his supernatural authority, agency and power are never to be put in question. For Sonnenberg the Last Judgment is not a merely symbolic affair as it is for Kant, serving as a means of reflection on the practical moral responsibility of human beings in terms of the universal moral soundness and future legacy of their individual day-to-day actions; it is rather a concrete and tangible prospect, even if its realization is reserved for an indefinite future. Whereas for Kant the Last Judgment is a moral imperative (act 'as if' you *might* be judged by God), for Sonnenberg it constitutes a moral ultimatum (act 'as if' because you actually *will* be judged). *Donatoa* reminds us that we are given notice until the time cometh. While in effect Sonnenberg makes the case in *Donatoa* that man's freedom of will must also entail his freedom to defect altogether from a belief in God — as illustrated by the figures of Egol and Abdul and indeed all of mankind bar Eliora, Heroal and Herkla — the outcome of their choices and actions is a predictably negative one, resulting in man's loss of freedom after death by means of the Last Judgment because in life he lacked the necessary maturity to maintain belief in the principle of good, i.e. God. If man does not aspire actively and at all times to *moral* will, as do Eliora, Heroal and Herkla, man's freedom must ultimately be curtailed and lead to his destruction, as the demise of an atheistic humanity in *Donatoa* graphically exemplifies: because the non-believers, the faithless, the Egols and Abduls of this world fail to 'conquer the necessity of nature in them' — a phrasing Sonnenberg probably borrowed from Friedrich Schiller's essays[123] — and because they failed to follow the divine instincts bestowed on them by God ('did not God plant also within him | Judgment to discern what Good is from Bad, [...] When the inner imperative cried out, why did you not follow?') — a principle Sonnenberg loaned from Kant — we see them consigned, in Canto

---

[122] *Universal Natural History*, p. 292 (*Allgemeine Naturgeschichte*, p. 373).

[123] See especially his 'On the necessary limitations in the use of beautiful forms' ('Über die notwendigen Grenzen beim Gebrauch schöner Formen', published 1795 and again 1800) and 'On the moral utility of aesthetic manners' ('Über den moralischen Nutzen ästhetischer Sitten', published 1796).

Ten, to Hell and damnation. Sonnenberg's second biographer, Wukadinović, accordingly and correctly notes: 'In Canto Ten Donatoa's speech to the Angels of Death and Michael's parting oration become veritable philosophical discourses on the theodicy problem, [yet] in the end [...] his imagination soars to the lofty heights of a mysticism that only few readers will be able to follow with the appropriate devotion' ('Im zehnten Gesang werden Donatoas Rede an die Todesengel und Michaels Abschiedsrede an die Erde zu förmlichen philosophischen Abhandlungen über die Theodizee, und zuletzt entschwebt [...] [seine] Phantasie in die Höhen einer Mystik, der wohl nur die wenigsten Leser mit der geforderten Andacht zu folgen vermögen').[124]

Having said that, while Sonnenberg presents the Last Judgment in *Donatoa* as an end-time scenario with a distinct moral message, it is also a narrative fiction, a make-believe story about how the end might be imagined to unfold when the time comes. As Kant put it in one of the passages we cited above from 'The End of all Things', such stories must be considered mere 'ideas fabricated by reason' in order to 'play out' our (moralizing, perhaps demoralizing) mind-games. In this sense, narratives of the Last Judgment are always also narratives that allow us not just to imagine where we might find ourselves once we have departed this world and the shape in which this life after death might manifest itself, but also how we might be judged in death (by God or by posterity). They can, meanly and selfishly, also allow us to concoct scenarios in which others, whom we — for whatever conscious or unconscious reason — consider deserving of punishment, are infernally penalized for sins we consider reprehensible. An intriguing Christian fundamentalist case in point of how we might imagine such partisan chastisement through Last Judgment is Tim LaHaye and Jerry B. Jenkins's 2004 novel *Glorious Appearing. The End of Days*; I will expand on this aspect of their work in my Conclusion. Like LaHaye and Jenkins two hundred years after him, Sonnenberg singles out for eternal punishment all those who had fallen from belief in the Christian God. Outside of his mystical make-believe world, however, Sonnenberg was far less certain about the shape of things to come and how immortality might look; Gruber relates how, just as Sonnenberg began work on the concluding cantos of *Donatoa*, he noted:

> Is the thought: Destruction! something so terrible? Destruction does not exist! We shall be eternal as is nature! But what will we be? — Perhaps we will wander around in flowers, in the grass, in the dust. But whether with consciousness of our being; who can judge until the catastrophe of our aging universe closes in on us? — What will then be, who knows?
>
> [Liegt denn im Gedanken: Vernichtung! so viel Schreckliches? Vernichtung giebt's nicht! Wir werden ewig seyn wie die Natur! Aber was wir seyn werden? — Vielleicht wandern wir in Blumen, im Grase, im Staube herum. Ob mit dem Bewußtseyn unseres Daseyns; wer entscheidet's bis die Katastrophe des alternden Universums herannaht? — Was dann werden wird, wer weiß es?][125]

This is a rather unexpected statement from someone who is about to send all

---

124 Wukadinović, p. 159.
125 *Donatoa*, II.2, pp. 424–25.

unbelievers to Hell — the totality of humankind save the two last Christians, Heroal and Herkla (Eliora had died at the mid-point of the epic, as we recall). Not to mention that 'the catastrophe of our aging universe' can relate as much to the Christian belief in the Redeemer's Second Coming as to the natural historian Buffon's claim — widely popularized by Sonnenberg's time, as we shall see in the following chapter — that the cooling Earth is set eventually to die a gradual natural death in some distant future. 'What will then be, who knows?' — Sonnenberg's question (even if it is a rhetorical one) betrays a distinct hesitancy about what the looming afterlife will bring; nor does it smack of much 'Roman confidence' in things to come, to adopt Wordsworth's turn of phrase. This comment betrays little anxiety about, perhaps even little expectation of, a cataclysmic Last Judgment to wind up humankind's existence on Earth. The real paradox of Sonnenberg's life may be that his two epics *The End of the World* and *Donatoa* revolve entirely around a traditionalist Christian interpretation of the Last Judgment with rewards doled out to the devout and punishment meted out to sinners as befits their conduct in life, whereas personal comments made outside of those works plainly convey his reservations about the upholding of such a narrow Christian worldview. Indeed, the second concession Sonnenberg makes to Kant (and not just Kant) is that he has begun to doubt the divine power invested in Christ. As I mentioned earlier, Gruber cites various notes in which Sonnenberg describes Jesus as 'the greatest of all human beings [who] taught mankind the great and simple religion of Nature'. Christ is defined for Sonnenberg more by his humanity than by his divinity. In the crescendo of the final two cantos describing the Last Judgment Christ — who throughout *Donatoa* is, as I pointed out earlier, called 'God-Human' and 'Reconciler' — plays a mostly marginal role, sitting to the side of God's throne watching events as they unfold; it is not him but rather the Angel of Thunder Donatoa God calls upon when the Last Judgment commences to wield the sword of judgment and exact punishment and annihilation in the cleansing of our universe. In Sonnenberg's *Donatoa* it is the figure of Donatoa who fulfils the role of judge and slaughterer, not Christ; in LaHaye and Jenkins's doctrinaire Christian *Glorious Appearing*, by contrast, this role is conspicuously reserved for Jesus Christ personally. Where Sonnenberg seeks to ascribe a loving and caring quality to all of Christ's actions, in LaHaye and Jenkins's present-day fundamentalist evangelical rendering of the storyline of chastisement and salvation this benevolent side of Christ is reserved only for those who remained faithful to him; toward anyone who has fallen from faith, on the other hand, he is utterly unforgiving, hard-hearted and cruel.

However orthodox or dogmatic the plotline of *Donatoa* may appear to today's reader — including its battles of heavenly hosts and satanic hordes; its trite black-and-white characterization of the good and the bad; the stereotypically stalwart heroism of the few remaining Christian elect; the obsessive moral censure of human infidelity, vanity and arrogance; the visual prodigality of violence; and the insipid descriptions of God's all-encompassing love (things all still found two hundred years later in LaHaye and Jenkins's *Glorious Appearing*) — Sonnenberg's work also shows that Enlightenment thinking, secularized philosophy, and the new natural sciences were taking their toll on literary depictions of the apocalypse even at a time when religion seemed to be staging a comeback in the post-Revolutionary societies of Western Europe. Even where we see Sonnenberg objecting to such modern secular philosophies as La Mettrie's, Holbach's and Schelling's as materialist, atheistic and amoral, and even when he upholds his faith in God as well as belief in an afterlife and the immortality of the soul, *Donatoa* nonetheless shows signs that God is no longer fully in charge of his Creation — human freedom is beginning to impinge on and hollow out what had until then been seen as God's prerogative alone, namely his unconditional power and unconstrained freedom of action.

Reflecting on the connection between theodicy and idealistic philosophy as developed around 1800 by Kant, Schiller, Fichte and Schelling — the German thinkers and philosophers who exerted the most influence on Sonnenberg — the German philosopher Odo Marquard once observed how idealism, in its capacity as a 'philosophy of radical human freedom' ('Philosophie radikaler menschlicher Freiheit'), gave rise to the 'thesis of idealistic autonomy' ('idealistische Autonomiethese') which posits 'not God, but man himself, makes and directs human affairs' ('nicht Gott, sondern der Mensch selber macht und lenkt die Menschenwelt').[126] Marquard expands:

> It would seem that the thesis of idealistic autonomy is an expression of human self-aggrandizement and arrogance. [...] Clearly this autonomy condemns man to self-loneliness by preventing any true relationship with the Other; clearly it entails a revolt against God through its very disregard for the creatureness of man and his world. It would seem therefore that no theology can license this thesis of idealistic autonomy, and that no philosophy that takes theological concerns seriously will be prepared to accept it.
>
> [Offenbar ist [die idealistische Autonomiethese] der Ausdruck für 'Selbstherrlichkeit' und 'Vermessenheit' des Menschen; [...] offenbar doch verurteilt sie ihn zur 'Icheinsamkeit' durch Verweigerung eines echten Bezugs zum Du; offenbar doch bedeutet sie Auflehnung gegen Gott durch Mißachtung der Geschöpflichkeit des Menschen und seiner Welt. Es scheint also, daß keine Theologie diese idealistische Autonomiethese gelten lassen kann, und daß keine Philosophie, die Theologisches ernstzunehmen bereit ist, sie zu akzeptieren vermag.]

Marquard's comments on the twentieth-century debates surrounding the 'thesis of idealistic autonomy' go to show that Sonnenberg's religious reservations about and objections to Enlightenment philosophy are neither groundless — so long as one applies a theistic perspective to the end-time of humanity — nor irrelevant: it is merely a question of the quality and degree of one's (Christian) belief. But in a society faced with increasing stresses of secularization, as was the case in Sonnenberg's day, the peculiar and in many ways unfortunate combination of old-fashioned choice of subject matter and genre with a proselytizing tone and idiosyncratic style of writing that characterized Sonnenberg's work was bound to reduce *Donatoa*'s appeal even for a religiously-minded contemporaneous audience

---

126 Odo Marquard, 'Idealismus und Theodizee', in *Schwierigkeiten mit der Geschichtsphilosophie* (Frankfurt a.M.: Suhrkamp, 1982 [1973]), pp. 52–65 (this and the subsequent quotation p. 53).

— not to mention contemporary and later secular audiences. That *Donatoa*'s failure was not an exception, however, and that its author was not alone in miscalculating his epic's chances of success with a contemporary audience, is illustrated by the text's French companion piece, *Le Dernier Homme*, which like *Donatoa* was published posthumously following its author's suicide. In Grainville's epic, too, the focus is God's incapacity to act of his own accord; here likewise 'not God, but man himself, makes and directs human affairs'. How the Last Judgment plays out in *Le Dernier Homme*, and what both Sonnenberg's and Grainville's texts' larger literary and theophilosophical ramifications are, will be the subject of the following chapter.

CHAPTER 2

From Theism to Deism 1805: Jean-Baptiste Cousin de Grainville and the Absence of God

> We do love God, good people say,
> Because He's never in our way.
> JOHANN WOLFGANG GOETHE[1]

> 'The development of mankind', said I, 'appears to be laid out as a work for thousands of years.' 'Perhaps millions,' said Goethe — 'who knows? But let mankind last as long as it may, it will never lack obstacles to give it trouble, and never lack the pressure of necessity to develop its powers. Men will become more clever and more acute; but not better, happier, and stronger in action — or at least only at epochs. I foresee the time when God will have no more joy in them, but will break up everything for a renewed creation. I am certain that everything is planned to this end, and that the time and hour in the distant future for the occurrence of this renovating epoch are already fixed. But a long time will elapse first, and we may still for thousands and thousands of years amuse ourselves on this dear old surface.'
> ECKERMANN in conversation with Johann Wolfgang Goethe[2]

---

1 From 'Rhymed Sayings', in *Goethe's Poems*, trans. by Paul Dyrsen (New York: F. W. Christern, 1878), p. 358. The German reads: 'Warum uns Gott so wohl gefällt? Weil er sich uns nie in den Weg stellt.' *Goethe Gedichte 1800–1832*, ed. by Karl Eibl (Berlin: Deutscher Klassiker Verlag, 2010), p. 400.
2 *Conversations of Goethe with Eckermann*, ed. by J. K. Moorhead, trans. by John Oxenford (London: J. M. Dent, 1935), p. 275. '"Die Entwicklung der Menschheit", sagte ich, "scheint auf Jahrtausende angelegt." "Wer weiß," erwiderte Goethe, "vielleicht auf Millionen! Aber laß die Menschheit dauern so lange sie will, es wird ihr nie an Hindernissen fehlen, die ihr zu schaffen machen, und nie an allerlei Not, damit sie ihre Kräfte entwickele. Klüger und einsichtiger wird sie werden, aber besser, glücklicher und tatkräftiger nicht [...] Ich sehe die Zeit kommen, wo Gott keine Freude mehr an ihr hat, und er abermals alles zusammenschlagen muß zu einer verjüngten Schöpfung. Ich bin gewiß, es ist alles danach angelegt, und es steht in der fernen Zukunft schon Zeit und Stunde fest, wann diese Verjüngungsepoche eintritt. Aber bis dahin hat es sicher noch gute Weile, und wir können noch Jahrtausende und aber Jahrtausende auch auf dieser lieben alten Fläche, wie sie ist, allerlei Spaß haben."' Johann Peter Eckermann, *Gespräche mit Goethe in den letzten Jahren seines Lebens*, ed. by Fritz Bergemann, 2 vols (Frankfurt a.M.: Insel, 1981), vol. 2, pp. 647–48 (conversation of 23 October 1828).

From one 'End of the World' to the other

There was much talk in the previous chapter of Christian visions of mankind's demise — variously termed 'the Time of the Conflagration', 'the Consummation of all Things', the 'Apocalypse, 'the Second Coming' or 'the Last Judgment' — as we encountered them in the assorted seventeenth- to nineteenth-century literary texts and philosophical and theological treatises discussed in Chapter One. Yet so far there has been little mention of Last Men or Last Women, the exception naturally being the one couple, Heroal and Herkla, that Franz von Sonnenberg in *Donatoa* cast as his last Christian faithful on Earth. We recall the passage cited in Chapter One:

> As the Lovers both now floated to Heaven beyond
> The Star of Love to the Father of Love, the Earth convulsed
> With Tremors of Death, the Last Humans had gone...
>
> [Als die Liebenden beiden itzt über dem Sterne der Liebe
> Aufwärts schwebten zum Vater der Liebe, gieng durch die Erde
> Schauder des Todes, es waren die letzten Menschen entschwunden...][3]

But is the designation 'the Last Humans', 'die letzten Menschen', not a misnomer, or at least a sleight of (writer's) hand? Why should these two ill-starred lovers, as bloodless as they may appear to readers today, be called 'Last Humans' when, first, the 'enlightened' and 'emancipated' non-believers and unfaithful in *Donatoa* (Sonnenberg describes them as 'mündig', 'emancipated', referring explicitly to Kant's argument in 'What is Enlightenment?')[4] are, at least for a short remaining while, still alive in Canto X, even if only soon to be dispatched to Hell where they can expect to suffer eternal banishment and torment? And, second, will Heroal and Herkla not soon be found blissfully embarking on their thousand-year afterlife in a millennial Eden in Canto XII? Can we genuinely speak of Last Men and Women when it comes to representations of the Christian Last Judgment after which all human beings, whether they are good or evil, faithful or faithless, virtuous or sinful, are set to survive in one form (in Eden) or another (in the Inferno)? As W. Warren Wagar observed in his study *Terminal Visions*, 'the end in traditional cultures is the gateway to new life, whether the literal rebirth of cyclicalism or the beginning of eternal joy for God's elect', adding pithily: 'The end has no "sting" '.[5] By contrast, Wagar continues,

> in the linear model the end acquires a gravity that it cannot have in the cyclical.

---

3 *Donatoa*, II.1, pp. 259–60.

4 See *Donatoa*, II.2, p. 7, which describes an enlightened humanity unknowingly awaiting Donatoa's wrath and calling out to a heaven it no longer believes in:

> We are ALL and ONE, We ourselves are God, this to know,
> This alone is Truth, the Human Species is now emancipated,
> Owns the Crown itself now, knows at long last that it itself is God!
>
> [Wir sind Alles und Eins, Wir selbst sind Gott, dieß zu wissen,
> Dieß ist die Wahrheit allein, das Menschengeschlecht ist nun mündig,
> Hat die Krone nun selbst, weiß endlich jetzt selbst, daß es Gott ist!]

5 *Terminal Visions*, p. 35; the subsequent passage p. 43.

LE

DERNIER HOMME,

OUVRAGE POSTHUME;

PAR M. DE GRAINVILLE,

HOMME DE LETTRES.

TOME I.

A PARIS,

Chez DETERVILLE, Libraire, rue du Battoir, n° 16, quartier S. André-des-Arcs.

AN XIV — 1805.

FIG. 2.1. Jean-Baptiste Cousin de Grainville, *Le Dernier Homme*, title page of the posthumous 1805 first French edition, of which, purportedly, only thirty-six copies were ever sold.

The end is once-only, facilitating a once-only judgment of all creaturely being. Justice is done. There are many happenings in both cyclical and linear time, many of them identical or similar to other happenings. But in the linear paradigm the end comes only once.

The only question is, is the Christian vision of the Last Judgment cyclical or linear? On the surface it clearly seems linear: followed by an ethereal millennial future, in which the faithful enjoy a thousand-year reign of peace in Heaven under God's grace, the Last Judgment appears to be a 'once-only' event and hence a veritable 'last' Last Judgment. However, although the millennium is technically as well as theologically defined as lasting for a period of one thousand years, I have yet to encounter a narrative attempting to describe the end of the millennium or what happens thereafter; the focus of all literary portrayals is the Last Judgment and the commencement of the millennium rather than its conclusion. It is as if the millennial bliss in Heaven (or torment in Hell, if one is unfortunate anough to belong among the multitudes of dissenters, unfaithful, impious, heretics, heathens, infidels, atheists, schismatics, profaners, idolaters, unrighteous or apostates — or whatever name one prefers to grace them with) were eternal. The millennium seems to have no end; it is as if those who desire it want it to last literally forever.

This is certainly how Sonnenberg portrays it in his Christian verse epic *Donatoa*; and it is how Jean-Baptiste François Xavier Cousin de Grainville presents the end-time in *Donatoa*'s French counterpart *Le Dernier Homme* (*The Last Man*, see Figure 2.1), the subject of this chapter. Towards the end of *Le Dernier Homme* we are thus informed:

> All Heaven waited on this great event with impatience; and there came an instant, universal cry of joy. The reign of time had ended, and a vista of eternity opened up. At the same moment, however, howls of rage arose from Hell, and the sun and the stars were extinguished. The dark night of chaos covered the world; ...
>
> [Tout le ciel attendait avec impatience ce grand événement; ses voûtes retentissent aussitôt de cris d'allégresse. Le règne du temps est fini, les siècles éternels vont commencer; mais au même moment, les enfers jettent des cris de rage, le soleil et les étoiles s'éteignent. La sombre nuit du chaos couvre la terre, ...][6]

'The reign of time had ended' and a 'vista of eternity' opens up. It is precisely these two notions — how human beings look upon the end of time and how they conceive of eternity — to which Kant took objection on the opening pages of the essay 'The end of all things' that I discussed in Chapter One. Kant takes a sceptical deistic and naturalistic/scientific view of things, observing among other things:

> ... so the German language likes to call the last day [...] the *youngest day*. The last day thus still belongs to time, for on it something or other *happens* (and not to eternity, where nothing happens any more, because that would belong to the progress of time): namely, the settling of accounts for human beings, based on their conduct in their whole lifetime. It is a *judgment day*; thus the judgment of grace or damnation by the world's judge is therefore the real end of all things in time, and at the same time the beginning of the (blessed or cursed) eternity ...
>
> [... so hat unsre Sprache beliebt, den letzten Tag [...] den *jüngsten Tag* zu nennen. Der jüngste Tag gehört also annoch zur Zeit; denn es *geschieht* an ihm noch irgend etwas (nicht zur Ewigkeit, wo nichts mehr geschieht, weil das Zeitfortsetzung sein würde, Gehöriges): nämlich Ablegung der Rechnung der Menschen von ihrem Verhalten in ihrer ganzen Lebenszeit. Er ist ein Gerichtstag; das Begnadigungs- oder Verdammungs-Urteil des Weltrichters ist also das eigentliche Ende aller Dinge in der Zeit, und zugleich der Anfang der (seligen oder unseligen) Ewigkeit ...][7]

Even if the locution in parenthesis '(blessed or cursed)' can be read neutrally to refer to Heaven and Hell, it also hints at Kant's misgivings about eternity; elsewhere he is more explicit in his criticism of the eternalistic view of afterlife: the thought of eternity, Kant declares, 'has something horrifying about it because it leads us as it were to the edge of an abyss: for anyone who sinks into it no return is possible' ('Dieser Gedanke hat etwas Grausendes in sich: weil er gleichsam an den Rand eines Abgrunds führt, aus welchem für den, der darin versinkt, keine Wiederkehr möglich ist'). But, as Kant also goes on to point out, since all thinking about a millennial afterlife can be moral in purpose only because the attendant time concept lacks foundation in our physical world, 'the representaion of those last things which are supposed to come *after* the last day', he says, 'are to be regarded only as a way

---

6 *The Last Man*, trans. by I. F. & M. Clarke (Middletown, CT: Wesleyan University Press, 2002), p. 132; *Le Dernier Homme*, ed. by Anne Kupiec (Paris: Éditions Payot, 2010), p. 184.

7 'The end of all things', pp. 221–22, the subsequent passages pp. 221 and 222 ('Das Ende aller Dinge', p. 176; the subsequent passages pp. 175 and 176–77).

of making sensible this latter together with its moral consequences, which are otherwise not theoretically comprehensible to us' ('so muß die Vorstellung jener letzten Dinge, die *nach* dem jüngsten Tage kommen sollen, nur als eine Versinnlichung des letztern samt seinen moralischen, uns übrigens nicht theoretisch begreiflichen, Folgen angesehen werden'; Kant's emphasis). In short, depictions of millennial eternity are merely a 'making sensible' of things (for the purpose of moral instruction) that can have no basis in physical reality.

Although it is unlikely that Grainville knew Kant's 1794 essay as such, he would have been familiar with the deistic position that Kant's essay embodies; he certainly seems to respond in the final paragraph of *Le Dernier Homme* to Kant's concerns about the non-representability of such supernatural occurrences as the Last Judgment and the millennial eternity that follows — 'millennial eternity' being perhaps a fitting oxymoron to capture the Christian ambivalence about mankind's longest-term prospects. After being informed that the unfolding Last Judgment represents 'the dawn of eternity' ('c'était l'aurore de l'éternité'), the narrator, who wants to find out more about the future of humankind, relates:

> I desired to see the conclusion of these marvelous scenes, to know above all the fate of Omegarus, to see the resurrection of humankind, and God sitting in judgment on the multitude of human beings. But the Spirit of Futurity refused me. "Man will never be satisfied", he said. "If I were to show you the scenes you long to see, your curiosity would still not be satisfied. You would want to look beyond eternity, if there were anything more to discover. I wished only to let you witness the triumph of Omegarus, and to show you that, by obeying the commands of Heaven, he will one day cut short the reign of time and hasten the coming of eternity".
>
> "My mission is now accomplished", the Spirit of Futurity then informs his human listener, and concludes: "Tell men about this history of the last age of earth. Sacrifice to this glorious task your hopes of fortune and your ambitions; and I will make the hours of your labors the sweetest moments in your life".
>
> [Je désirais voir la suite de ces scènes admirables, et connaître surtout le sort d'Omégare; je voulais voir la résurrection des hommes s'achever, et Dieu juger cette grande multitude; mais l'esprit qui préside à l'avenir se refuse à mes vœux. "Ainsi," me dit-il, "l'homme sera toujours insaitable. Si j'exposais à tes regards les tableaux que tu demandes, tes désirs curieux ne seraient point assouvis: tu voudrais pénétrer au-delà de l'éternité, s'il y restait quelque chose à connaître. J'ai voulu seulement te rendre le témoin du triomphe d'Omégare, et t'apprendre comment, par son obéissance aux ordres du ciel, il doit un jour abréger le règne du temps, et hâter celui de l'éternité. Mes desseins sont remplis: révèle aux hommes cette histoire du dernier siècle de la terre; sacrifie à ce devoir glorieux que je t'impose, la fortune et les désirs de l'ambition. Je rendrai les heures de ton travail si douces, qu'elles seront les plus heureuses de ta vie."][8]

Thus ends Grainville's epic. The Spirit of Futurity may be right when he says 'If I were to show you the scenes you long to see, your curiosity would still not be satisfied. You would want to look beyond eternity, if there were anything more to discover'. But in formulating it in this way he is, cunningly but also prudently, able

---

8 *The Last Man*, trans. I. F. & M. Clarke, p. 135 (*Le Dernier Homme*, ed. Kupiec, p. 187).

to conceal the circumstance that the reason we may want to 'look beyond eternity' is that the lived reality of eternity would strike us, as Kant says, as 'horrifying', and bland and boring to boot. It is perhaps no surprise, then, that Grainville would want to deploy a narrative ruse in order to spare us the details. What could he write about life in eternity that would not either put us off the whole notion altogether or strike us as insipid, or both?

Either way, the unfolding of the Last Judgment is not Grainville's central concern in *Le Dernier Homme*; it occupies merely three of the work's ten cantos, as it occupies merely the last three cantos of *Donatoa*'s twelve. Both texts may end with the Last Judgment, and Sonnenberg's epic also with the millennium that follows, but their centre of attention lies not on the Day of Reckoning and its aftermath but rather on how humankind reached the point in the first place at which God or his minions felt necessitated to unleash the final apocalypse and call humankind to account.

With Grainville's work still so little known even among scholars of nineteenth-century French literature, and with it having fallen into 'the most profound oblivion in France', as Anne Kupiec, the editor of the 2010 French edition, admits[9] (it is far better known in English translation as a work of proto-science-fiction, more about which later in this chapter), it should prove helpful to provide a short outline of its contents before embarking on a more detailed analysis. Canto I of Grainville's narrative begins, as was customary with such fictions of futurity, by setting up a frame story: in Syria 'near the ruins of Palmyra' ('proches les ruines de Palmyre'), the anonymous present-day narrator-cum-traveler is invited by a mysterious torch-bearer to enter a 'solitary cavern' ('un antre solitaire') from which it is said that no previous visitor had ever returned alive. Deep in the cavern he is addressed by the 'Celestial Spirit' ('l'esprit céleste') who explains that he has invited the narrator in to witness in the cavern's magical mirrors the lifting of 'the veil which hides from mortal men the darkness of futurity' ('le voile qui dérobe aux mortels le sombre avenir'); 'I wish', the heavenly spirit declares, 'to make you a witness of the scene which will bring the world to a close. In these enchanted mirrors which surround you', he continues, 'the Last Man will appear before your eyes [...] and you will be witness to, and judge of, his actions' ('te rendre spectateur de la scène qui termina les destins de l'univers. Dans ces miroirs magiques qui t'environnent, le dernier homme va paraître à tes yeux [...] et tu seras le témoin et le juge de ses actions').[10] This 'Last Man' — he is named Omegarus and is the last remaining fertile male on the planet — is facing a stark choice: to procreate and in so doing condemn Adam, the 'Father of Men' ('le père des hommes'), to renewed centuries of torment, or to sacrifice his human love for his wife Syderia in order to fulfill God's will to terminate a corrupted and perpetually warfaring humankind and allow the Last Judgment to commence. Adam, whom the reader has been shown sitting at the gates of Hell watching endless generations of sinners being sentenced to perdition,

---

9 'L'énigme du *Dernier Homme*', in *Le Dernier Homme*, ed. by Anne Kupiec (Paris: Éditions Payot, 2010), pp. 205–69 (p. 244).

10 *The Last Man*, trans. I. F. & M. Clarke, p. 5 (*Le Dernier Homme*, ed. Kupiec, p. 46); the subsequent passages pp. 7, 23, 14, 15, 16, 17 and 69 (pp. 50, 67, 58, 59, 60, again 60, and 118–19).

aches to see Omegarus not repeat his own mistake and become yet another forefather ruefully condemned to sit at the gates of Hell in eternity to witness his progeny suffer everlasting damnation.

In Canto II the reader is made privy to Omegarus's tale, as he recounts it to his anonymous interlocutor, of the fortunes of humanity leading up to its current quandary. Descended from French royalty and 'the last son of our royal line' ('le dernier des enfants de nos souverains'; Grainville later indicates that the young man's family lineage can be traced back to Napoleon), Omegarus grows up as 'the only child in an aging and infertile Europe' ('le fils unique de la vieillesse des Européens et de leur fécondité'). On the day his parents are buried, Omegarus encounters the Guardian Spirit of the planet Earth, who is destined to die when humanity dies; warning Omegarus that 'the day of [Earth's] destruction is at hand' ('le jour de sa destruction est arrivé'), the Guardian Spirit reveals to Omegarus that one woman remains who is still fertile and with whom he can 'perpetuate the human race' ('perpétuer la race des humains') and thereby 'delay the moment of [...] annihilation' — not just for mankind but conveniently also for himself ('tu reculerais le moment de ma perte').

Following various narrative twists and turns, including sundry supernatural events, Omegarus by the conclusion of Canto V — the halfway point of the story — has succeeded in finding his future wife Syderia, the only remaining fertile maiden in the Americas. But moments after the local minister Ormus has blessed the couple's union, Ormus hears an inner voice telling him that the Almighty himself 'condemns this union' ('le ciel réprouve cet hymen'); he immediately proceeds to reverse the union by placing a curse on Omegarus should he insist on consummating his conjugal rights. Brazil's rulers meanwhile quickly move to secure the separation of the couple by throwing Syderia into prison and forcing Omegarus to return to Europe.

Book Two opens in Canto VI with Omegarus continuing his story: a mysterious stranger has orchestrated Syderia's miraculous escape from prison, and when at long last the two ill-stared lovers come together in a small temple 'the earth trembled with joy'; yet 'at the same moment, the sun grew dark', displaying ominous 'images of blood redden[ing] the skies' ('la terre en tressaille de joie', 'mais au même instant l'astre du jour s'est obscurci, des images sanglantes ont rougi la route du firmament').[11] Canto VII shows Omegarus's as yet nameless interlocutor telling him that God has ordained that he must leave Syderia for good; infuriated and distrustful of his interlocutor's intentions, Omegarus demands to know why. It is at this point that Adam sees himself forced to reveal his identity as well as the fact that all the miracles, apparitions and oracles, save those by the priest Ormus, were illusions brought upon men by the Spirit of the Earth, a 'faustian' and materialistic character intent on saving his own existence by prolonging mankind's.[12] This

11 Ibid., p. 89 (p. 137).
12 See Eva Horn, 'Die romantische Verdunklung. Weltuntergänge und die Geburt des letzten Menschen um 1800', in *Abendländische Apokalyptik. Kompendium zur Genealogie der Endzeit*, ed. by Veronika Wieser, Christian Zolles, Catherine Feik, Martin Zolles and Leopold Schlöndorff (Berlin: Akademie Verlag, 2013), pp. 101–24; the description of the Spirit of the Earth as 'faustisch' on p. 111.

revelation notwithstanding, Omegarus hesitates to renounce his love for Syderia; all of Adam's remonstrations are in vain until God himself grants Omegarus a vision of his future descendants: 'On a barren plain under a dark sky', we read, 'he saw his hideous progeny, misshapen in form and cruel in disposition, making perpetual war on one another' ('Il découvre dans une plaine aride, sous un ciel ténébreux, ses enfants d'une forme hideuse, aussi cruels que difformes, se faisant une guerre atroce et perpétuelle').[13] 'Recoiling in shock from these revolting images' Omegarus 'swears obedience to God rather than give life to such an infamous race' ('À ces images horribles, il recule épouvanté, il jure d'obéir à Dieu plutôt que de donner le jour à cette race infâme'). Now that God's will has been done and with the discontinuation of mankind secured, the Last Judgment can at last commence.

Canto VIII shows Omegarus wandering through a landscape covered by the ashes, dust and bones of mankind that have issued from all the world's graves within the space of three hours. The sun is eclipsed and darkness reigns. Among the ruins of what was once Paris our 'Last Man' comes across one remaining statue, that of Napoleon Bonaparte, and a house in which its last resident, a man called Tibes, had 'assembled the principal works of the human mind' ('les chefs-d'œuvre de la pensée humaine'),[14] which now have lost their purpose, prompting Omegarus to lament:

> So, these are the works [...] which men vainly have called immortal; and tomorrow, perhaps, they will be no more. Let the world vanish! I have no regrets for a dwelling that is falling to pieces; but I do weep over those books that the printing press has preserved, which are as fine now as they were when they were first published. Where, then, is the omniscience of a God who looks on the works of the human mind as nothing and consigns them to oblivion?
>
> [Les voilà donc, dit-il, ces ouvrages que l'homme appela si vainement immortels; demain peut-être ils n'existeront plus. Ah! que cet univers périsse, je ne regrette point une demeure qui tombe en ruines de toutes parts; mais je pleure sur ces écrits que l'impression rajeunissait sans cesse, et qui sont aussi beaux que si leurs auteurs venaient de les publier. Quelle est donc cette excellence d'un Dieu, qui regarde comme le néant les productions de l'esprit humain et les livre à la mort?]

His melancholy and grief are quashed, however, the moment he discovers a comment by that library's wise assembler, who had once written: 'Why should God, who will not save His own works [of creation] from destruction, preserve the works of man — man who is the crown of creation?' ('Pourquoi Dieu, qui ne sauvera point de la mort ses œuvres, épargnerait-il celle de l'homme? il est la seule beauté de la nature'). 'Struck by these great truths', we are now informed, 'Omegarus remained confounded by the vanity of human affairs. The pettiness of human beings terrified him. He [now] saw only God in the universe, letting his imagination paint a sublime picture of His greatness, of His dwelling place, and of the happiness He reserves for the just' ('Frappé de ces grandes vérités, [Omégare]

---

13 *The Last Man*, trans. I. F. & M. Clarke, this and the subsequent passage p. 100 (*Le Dernier Homme*, ed. Kupiec, p. 149).

14 Ibid., p. 107 (p. 157); the subsequent passages pp. 107, 108 and 108 (pp. 157, 158 and 158).

reste confondu de la vanité des choses humaines! la petitesse de l'homme l'effraie, il ne voit plus que Dieu dans l'univers; il se fait un tableau sublime de sa grandeur, du séjour qu'il habite et du bonheur qu'il réserve aux justes').

At the same time, Syderia too is going through similar trials and tribulations in Canto IX. Feeling deserted by her husband, she tries to detect his whereabouts and follows his footsteps in the ashes, but all in vain. Seeing the world crumbling around her, she is overcome by fatigue and reproaches God for his unjust and cruel treatment, but on second thought prays to the Almighty to ask for his protection. Omegarus himself is, at this very moment, praying to God to 'mitigate the sufferings of his wife' ('d'adoucir les peines de son épouse').[15] Hearing their simultaneous prayers, God 'was moved with pity for her fate' ('est ému de pitié sur son sort'), his angels descend and induce sleep, upon which she dreams of the Last Judgment unfolding, with Omegarus resurrected Christ-like surrounded by 'the just who stretched out their hands to him in thankfulness, for they perceived in his soul the sufferings he had accepted in order to hasten their day of glorification' ('il est entouré des justes qui, lisant dans son âme exposée à leurs yeux les peines qu'il a souffertes pour hâter le jour de leur gloire'). In her final vision Syderia sees herself ascending to Heaven with Omegarus, all the while 'the wicked trembled with rage to see the triumph of the just' ('Sydérie y monte à la suite d'Omégare, tandis que les méchants voient en frémissant ce triomphe des justes').

Canto X is a kind of postface: realizing that all his deceptions and 'siren voices of false promises' have been in vain, the alchemist-like Spirit of the Earth rises from his caverns in the planet's core in a last-stand pitch to keep Syderia alive, but to no avail. He cannot thwart God's providence and she is taken by Death, who then takes pursuit of the Spirit of the Earth himself. Fearing his time has come, the Spirit flees to his caverns and sets off a tremendous explosion, tearing the Earth apart and blowing it off its orbit. Meanwhile resurrection continues unabated until the 'human race [has become] extinct' ('le genre humain est éteint'). It is at this point — we have reached the text's final paragraph, cited above — that the frame narrator's request to see 'the conclusion of these marvelous scenes' is turned down by the Spirit of Futurity.

Religiously Squaring the Secular Circle

A number of things are remarkable about Grainville's text and its reception. Writ large across the narrative is its didactic and allegorical quality; and, as my summary surely illustrates, *Le Dernier Homme* is a deeply religious text with a stark and non-negotiable spiritual moral: be obedient to God and trust in his Providence, for the Last Judgment *is* coming (even if in some distant future). But if the motivation of the author and the moral of his text are so categorically and unambiguously religious, we have to ask why it is that scholars today see the overarching significance of Grainville's text as rooted in its secular aspect and quality. Thus Paul K. Alkon,

---

15 Ibid., p. 119 (p. 170); the subsequent passages pp. 119, 121, 122 and 125 (pp. 170, 172, 173 and 176)

who has arguably done most to reengage us with the work and investigate its historical underpinnings, observes in his important study on the *Origins of Futuristic Fiction* how 'Grainville's *Le Dernier Homme* in 1805 initiated the secularization of apocalypse',[16] noting that 'Grainville secularizes the Apocalypse *without* discarding its theological framework'. W. Warren Wagar, cited earlier and another specialist in this field, first registers a comparable ambivalence when he states: 'in Grainville's novel, the secular end, caused by the exhaustion of the soil and human sterility, gives way in the last pages to the terminal vision of Revelation', but then concludes: 'nearly all the imaginative force of *Le Dernier Homme* derives from its secular events, and from its detailed history of the future of the human race. It takes a long stride — although this surely was not Grainville's intention — toward secularism'.[17] The rear cover of the 2002 retranslation of *Le Dernier Homme* into English by I. F. and M. Clarke goes so far as to present the narrative as 'the first secular apocalypse story'. And Morton D. Paley, the premier scholar of Romantic poetry and millennialism, notes in his book review of that retranslation how Grainville manages, 'at one and the same time, to tell a story of the future as a record of secular progress and as a confirmation of the literal truth of *Genesis and Revelation*'; he closes by remarking:

> What strikes me most about Grainville's *The Last Man* is its seamless synthesis of Enlightenment optimism about the future, as expounded from one end of the eighteenth century to the other by the likes of the abbé de Saint-Pierre and the marquis de Condorcet, with the distinctly unscientific doctrine (by 1805) of the degeneration of nature, the cult of weepy sentimentality in early romanticism, and Christian apocalyptic. Closely interrogated, none of it fits together, all of it is nonsense, and yet somehow it succeeds. *The Last Man* is even a page-turner of sorts, holding the reader's interest closely from start to finish.[18]

In short, *Le Dernier Homme*'s ending in the Last Judgment notwithstanding, and despite its unmistakably Christian and epic machinery, it seems that Grainville has succeeded in producing a text that has enticed modern critics to interpret it for all intents and purposes as standing on the brink of the secular. But how can we reconcile this with the work's so obviously religious underpinnings? How can we religiously square this secular circle?

To answer these questions we need to look more closely at the work's early reception history as well as the author's biographical background. Both will supply clues to the reasons why this text generated, and still generates, such an 'enigma' and so many indeterminacies surrounding its interpretation. Indeed, enigma and indeterminacy are two words used by the editor of the recent French reedition of the work, Anne Kupiec; she entitles her highly illuminating afterword 'L'Énigme

---

16 *Origins of Futuristic Fiction*, p. 4; the subsequent passage p. 175.
17 *Terminal Visions*, p. 16.
18 'Jean-Baptiste François Xavier Cousin de Grainville. *The Last Man*', *Utopian Studies*, 1 (2003), 178–80 (pp. 178 and 180). In an earlier essay Paley observed: 'this fable may be read as a projection of post-Revolutionary despair expressed in terms of an only partially secularized eschatology. [...] It seems as if the French Revolution were being replayed in heaven, with the resurrection to come as the final enactment of Fraternité' ('*Le dernier homme*: The French Revolution as the Failure of Typology', *Mosaic: A Journal for the Interdisciplinary Study of Literature*, 24 (1991), 67–76 (pp. 70 and 71)).

du *Dernier Homme*' ('The Enigma of *The Last Man*'), and in her interpretation she goes on to speak of the text's peculiar strangeness ('étrangeté'), singularity ('singularité') and indeterminacy ('indétermination').[19] There are a number of questions that the available scholarship, right up to and including even Alkon's and Kupiec's most insightful and by and large persuasive interpretations, have not yet sufficiently addressed. Why, for instance, was this text not graced with more success when it was originally published? Thus the editor of the second French impression in 1811, Charles Nodier, bemoans 'the public apathy' and admits how 'the fate of this work astonished me. The first edition was launched in obscurity,' he writes, 'not a single reviewer, not a single man of letters deigned to advocate it in the face of public indifference' ('l'apathie [...]. La destinée de cet ouvrage m'étonna. Il s'en étoit écoulé très obscurément une première édition, sans qu'un seul journaliste, un seul homme de lettres daignât réclamer contre l'indifférence publique').[20] Purportedly only thirty-six copies of that first edition were ever sold.[21] The second edition may not have fared much better, but it did spawn a train of imitations written later in the century; these in turn prompted the republication of Grainville's text in its third French edition in 1859 (although we know little about its success). While there are genre-based and biographical arguments to be made in response to this enigma (and I will address these later in this chapter), it may prove helpful first to dwell for a moment on the imitations *Le Dernier Homme* inspired.

The first of these was by a member of the circle around Mme de Staël, namely the minor poet and translator baron Augustin-François Creuzé de Lesser, who in 1831 published a poem entitled *Le dernier homme, poème imité de Grainville* ('The Last Man. A poem in imitation of Grainville'); purportedly begun in 1814,[22] just years after the second edition of Grainville's *Le Dernier Homme* had been published, it presents a versification of Grainville's plot while expanding on it by describing a failed attempt to colonize another planet. Similarly, in 1858, the journalist and minor poet Paulin Gagne published a futuristic 'universal poem in twelve cantos' entitled *The 'Unitéide', or the Female Messiah* (*L'Unitéide, ou la Femme-Messie*), which was partially inspired by *Le Dernier Homme*. Paulin Gagne's wife Élise published yet another adaptation of Grainville's *Le Dernier Homme* just one year after her husband's in 1859. Entitled *Omegar, or the Last Man, a dramatic prose poem of the end of time in twelve cantos* (*Omégar, ou le Dernier homme, proso-poésie dramatique de la fin des temps en 12 chants*), it is located in the twenty-ninth century near Marseille and maintains the setting of the end of the world as well as the role of Omegar as the central God-fearing hero and 'personification of humanity',[23] but otherwise

---

19 'L'énigme du *Dernier Homme*', pp. 205, 268, and 281; see also p. 280.

20 'Preface to the Second Edition of *Le Dernier Homme*', in *The Last Man*, trans. by I. F. & M. Clarke, pp. 137–40 (p. 137); *Le Dernier Homme*, ed. by Charles Nodier (Paris: Deterville, 1811), p. v.

21 As per the entry on Grainville in the *Nouvelle Biographie Générale*, column 609. A German source even claims that only five copies were ever sold, see entry 'Grainville' in *Allgemeine Encyclopädie der Wissenschaften und Künste* (Leipzig: [n.pub.], [date unknown: the Göttingen State and University Library download states 1818, but the article relates information from the 1830s]), p. 309.

22 *Nouvelle Biographie Générale*, column 610.

23 Élise Gagne, 'Preface', *Omégar, ou le Dernier homme, proso-poésie dramatique de la fin des temps en 12 chants* (Paris: Didier, 1859), p. iii.

displays a vastly different cast of characters (Omegar's wife is now called Théolinde, and they have a daughter and an infant son); like Grainville's Adam, Paulin Gagne's Omegar supernaturally survives the passing of time, which forces him to witness the demise of his fellow beings across the centuries.

Later in the century, the French positivist scientist, astronomer and early science fiction writer Nicolas Camille Flammarion uses Grainville's *Le Dernier Homme*, or more likely Creuzé de Lesser's adaptation of it, as a matrix for his futuristic novel *La Fin du monde*; published both in French and in English translation (entitled *Omega: The Last Days of the World*) in 1894, it presents a history of the planet Earth from the 1950s to a distant future millions of years away. By the novel's final chapter the sun's ecliptic has shifted and the Earth has slowed its rotation, causing the planet to descend into a cold death. Human beings survive only in the equatorial zones by constructing gigantic glass living quarters designed to contain the sun's warmth. 'Toward the end', we read,

> only two groups of a few hundred human beings were left, occupying the last surviving centers of industry. From all the rest of the globe the human race had slowly but inexorably disappeared — dried up, exhausted, degenerated, from century to century, through the lack of an assimilable atmosphere and sufficient food. Its last remnants seemed to have lapsed back into barbarism [...]. Elsewhere the surface of the earth was a ruin, and even here only the last vestiges of a vanished greatness were to be seen. [...] All was over. The glories of the days gone by had forever vanished. If, in preceding centuries, some traveller, wandering in these solitudes, thought he had rediscovered the sites of Paris, Rome, or the brilliant capitals which had succeeded them, he was the victim of his own imagination; for these sites had not existed for millions of years, having been swept away by the waters of the sea.
>
> [Il ne restait plus que deux groupes de quelques centaines d'êtres humains, occupant les dernières capitales de l'industrie. Sur tout le reste du globe, la race humaine avait à peu près disparu, desséchée, épuisée, dégénerée, graduellement, inexorablement, de siècle en siècle, par manque d'atmosphère assimilable comme par manque d'alimentation suffisante. Ses derniers rejetons semblaient être revenus à la barbarie [...]. Partout ailleurs, à la surface de l'ancien monde terrestre, il'n'y avait que des ruines, et là aussi on ne retrouvait plus que les derniers vestiges des grandeurs évanouies. [...] Plus rien! Les gloires d'autrefois étaient pour jamais évanouies. Si quelque voyageur égaré dans les solitudes profondes avait cru, dans les siècles précédents, retrouver la place de Paris, de Rome, ou des brillantes capitals qui leur avaient succédé, il n'y eût eu là qu'une illusion de son imagination, car depuis des millions d'années cette place même n'existait plus, ayant été balayée par les eaux de la mer.][24]

It is in these latter stages of the Earth's existence that the thread of Grainville's plot is taken up explicitly, starting with Chapter Five of Part Two (in the English translation Chapter Four of Part Two), where we are told that humankind now

---

24 *Omega: The Last Days of the World*, trans. by Arthur Sherburn Hardy (New York: Cosmopolitan Publishing Co., 1894), pp. 240–41 and 243–44; *La Fin du monde* (Paris: Ernest Flammarion, 1894), pp. 314, 318 and 322–23; the subsequent passages pp. 242, 243, 246, 248 and 256, respectively, in the French original, pp. 319, 320, 324, 326 and 336.

survives only in two isolated pockets in glass cities, one located in an ocean valley of the Pacific Ocean, the other to the south of Ceylon in the Indian Ocean: 'In the first of these ancient cities of glass, the sole survivors were two old men, and the grandson of one of them, Omegar' ('Dans la première de ces antiques villes de cristal, les derniers survivants étaient deux vieillards et le petit-fils de l'un d'eux, Omégar'), in the second lives Eva with her mother and sister. Omegar soon finds his two companions 'stretched lifeless, side by side' ('étendus sans vie l'un près de l'autre'), whereupon he sets out, as 'the last heir of the human race' and 'last man' ('l'héritier du genre humain' and 'dernier homme'), to find the young woman Eva he had been dreaming of. For her part, the sixteen-year-old girl, whose mother and older sister had recently perished of consumption and cold, had likewise seen her future companion in her dreams and had called out to him for rescue. In his distant dwelling, Omegar hears her call and, 'yielding to a mysterious influence' ('subissant une mystérieuse influence'), he at once embarks in his 'electric air-ship' ('l'aéronef électrique') and is magically steered toward her ancient 'crystal palace' ('antique palais cristallin') in the Indian Ocean. Upon his arrival Eva's mother, awaking briefly from her state of death, reveals to the young couple that they are predestined to leave the exhausted Earth and create a new race on the planet of Jupiter (see Figure 2.2), to where they are soon supernaturally transported by the phantom of Cheops, the once Egyptian Pharaoh.

Despite this unexpectedly mystical turn at the end — the novel's narrative is in all other regards based on contemporary science — Flammarion's novel can in many ways be said to represent a late-nineteenth-century non-Christian counterpart to Grainville's early-nineteenth-century Christian epic. Notably however, both represent spiritual renderings of the same basic idea, the exhaustion and end of the world and the passing of mankind. To be sure, in Flammarion's novel there is no longer any Christian machinery, nor does Christian religion play any discernible role in the story's unfolding; quite to the contrary, the story is informed by an amusingly optimistic reliance on (Darwinian) evolutionary principles and scientific progress. But this seemingly secular and scientific plot-line is unexpectedly offset by the quite incongruous spiritualism on display at the novel's conclusion. Flammarion seems not to be able to cope with the prospect of a bleak finale in which mankind simply and depressingly comes to a natural end.[25] Unable to countenance such an end in nothingness, the author feels compelled to conjure up a cosmic force that 'presides over the universe and controls the destiny of worlds and their inhabitants' ('Nous croyons à une constitution intelligente de l'univers,

---

25 As his 1869 work *God in Nature* suggests, Flammarion sees some kind of divine force embedded pantheistically in nature; see in particular *Dieu dans la nature* (Paris: Didier, 1869), pp. iv–v. Published in 1894, the same year as Flammarion's *La Fin du monde*, Anatole France paints just the opposite picture in *Le Jardin d'Épicure* (Paris: Calmann-Levy, 1907); here nature is shown as acting disinterestedly and even in a 'hostile' fashion towards human beings: 'One day the last of them, beyond hatred or love, will expel the last human breath into the hostile air. And the Earth will continue to roll, bearing through silent space the ashes of humanity, the poems of Homer and the august remains of the marbles of Greece, clinging to her frozen flanks' (cited from W. Warren Wagar, 'The Rebellion of Nature', in *The End of the* World, ed. by Eric Rabkin, Martin Greenberg et al. (Carbondale: Southern Illinois Press, 1983), pp. 139–72 (p. 149)).

"'BEHOLD, WHERE WE SHALL BE TOMORROW!'"

FIG. 2.2. '"Behold, where we shall be tomorrow!"' — illustration in Nicolas Camille Flammarion's *Omega: The Last Days of the World* (1894) depicting the last couple Omegar and Eva with Eva's mother looking at Jupiter where humankind is destined to resettle after the death of planet Earth.

à une destinée des mondes et des êtres', the French original states),²⁶ and which can guarantee humankind's continuation and survival irrespective of our planet's physical demise. This 'intelligent order', we are informed on the closing pages of Flammarion's tale, marvelously teleports the two last humans to a fresh beginning on a new planetary home. No catastrophic life-annihilating apocalypse here, then, nor a bleak and dreary atheistic ending in unspiritual material nothingness; rather, a million-year gradual evolution of mankind and final spiritual passage of the Last Man and Last Woman into an otherworldy dimension. As Robert Galbreath notes: Flammarion 'presents a natural end succeeded by a transcendental end. The causal relationship is hazy, but he implies that human evolution progresses from the material to the spiritual plane of existence'.²⁷ Along the same lines, Arthur B. Evans has rightly spoken of Flammarion as a 'scientific popularizer and enthusiastic zealot of a kind of cosmic spiritualism', with *La Fin du monde* specifically cited as one of the texts Flammarion created with the intent to 'proselytize his own scientifico-religious beliefs',²⁸ beliefs delineated in his many scientific publications, including the 1866 treatise *Dieu dans la nature* (*God within Nature*). We may find it easy today to belittle Flammarion's crude blending of science and mysticism, but he was of course writing during the peak era of spiritualism, not to mention his being influenced by the French founding spiritualist Allan Kardec, whose funeral eulogy Flammarion gave in 1869 (stating in it that spiritualism is not a religion but 'a science of which we hardly yet know the ABC', 'une science dont nous connaissons à peine l'abc').²⁹

The works by Creuzé de Lesser, Paulin Gagne and Élise Gagne never feature in French literary histories; for all intents and purposes, their works have been forgotten — except of course as footnotes to the reception history of Grainville. And perhaps rightly so, one might add, for their works have no particular literary merit. Nor do Grainville's *Le Dernier Homme* or Flammarion's *La Fin du monde* register in histories of French literature; indeed, their literary merits are debatable.³⁰ But what

26 *Omega: The Last Days of the World*, p. 224 (*La Fin du monde*, p. 294).
27 Robert Galbreath, 'Ambiguous Apocalypse: Transcendental Versions of the End', in *The End of the World*, ed. Eric Rabkin et al., pp. 53–72 (p. 62).
28 Arthur B. Evans, 'Science Fiction in France: A Brief History', *Science Fiction Studies*, 16 (1989), 254–76 (p. 257).
29 'Discours de Camille Flammarion prononcé sur la tombe d'Allan Kardec', accessed via www.leon-denis.org on 14 October 2016.
30 As regards Grainville I have found only one exception among the French literary histories that I have consulted, namely Béatrice Didier's *Le XVIIIe siècle*, Part III *(1778–1820)* (Paris: B. Arthaud, 1976 = *Littérature Française*, ed. by Claude Pichois, vol. 11). However, even here ironies abound. While in her discussion of Grainville's *Le Dernier Homme* on p. 180 all is in order as regards Didier's analysis of the text, she assigns 1760 as Grainville's birth year; in her appended 'Dictionary of Authors' ('Dictionnaire des Auteurs') we are informed (p. 322): 'Grainville (Jean-Baptiste) [Lisieux, 1760–Lisieux, 1805]. Advocate, journalist (*Journal encyclopédique, Mercure, Journal littéraire*) and poet. He is the author of *Carnaval de Paphos* (1784), *Ismère et Tarsis* (1785), and *La Fatalité* (1791). Translator of Italian poets. He is chiefly remembered for his epopee, *Le Dernier Homme*.' ('Grainville (Jean-Baptiste) [Lisieux, 1760–Lisieux, 1805]. Avocat, journaliste (*Journal encyclopédique, Mercure, Journal littéraire*) et poète. Il est l'auteur du *Carnaval de Paphos* (1784), d'*Ismère et Tarsis* (1785), de *La Fatalité* (1791). Il a traduit des poètes italiens. Il est surtout connu par son épopée, *Le Dernier Homme*.') Didier is conflating two people, namely 'our' Jean-Baptiste Grainville (1746–1805) and Jean-Baptiste

sets them apart from de Lesser's and the Gagnes' works is that both Grainville's *The Last Man* and Flammarion's *The Last Days of the World* have established themselves as part of the history of science fiction. This is the rub: It is *not* for its literary or epical qualities, *nor* as regards any religious significance of its depiction of the Last Judgment that Grainville's text has been rescued from oblivion. Rather, Grainville's revival can be attributed exclusively and ironically to the fact that his prose epic has been taken for and interpreted as a work of early proto-science fiction; it has in effect been requisitioned by science fiction studies as a precursor to the modern genre. In the 'Preface' to its most recent English edition, which simultaneously presents the long overdue retranslation of the work into English, the editor I. F. Clarke labelled *Le Dernier Homme* as a 'seminal science fiction work',[31] with the rear cover of that new edition promoting the work as 'the first end-of-the-world story in future fiction'. Indeed, Clarke's edition of Grainville's work was published as part of the Wesleyan University Press's series 'Early Classics of Science Fiction' (with Arthur B. Evans serving as series editor) and stands there alongside Jules Verne's *Invasion of the Sea*, *The Mighty Orinoco* and *Mysterious Island* as well as Flammarion's *Lumen*. Paul K. Alkon, cited earlier, devotes a whole chapter of his *Origins of Futuristic Fiction* to Grainville's book; and in his *Science Fiction Before 1900. Imagination Discovers Technology*, another useful survey of early science fiction, Alkon says of Grainville's young hero Omegarus: 'Here we find the first of those many last men who populate science fiction. Grainville's *The Last Man* inaugurates a genre of stories recounting the end of human history'. But he also adds more cautiously: 'Grainville's *The Last Man* is most successful as a stimulus to more coherent variations of its theme by later writers'.[32] And as Fiona Stafford has detailed in her thematic study of *The Last of the Race*, among these 'more coherent variations' we find first and foremost Mary Shelley's *The Last Man*, the novel that truly and genuinely did kickstart the tradition of Last Men (and Last Women) narratives in 1826 (and to which my Chapter Four will be devoted).

But before moving deeper into this territory of the 'more coherent variations of this theme', we must pause to retrace *Le Dernier Homme*'s composition history and early reception itinerary more fully, for the work was not originally conceived as a prose epic. Grainville had actually set out to write a traditional verse epic, or epopee in the terminology of the time (Anne Kupiec is the only recent scholar to pick up on this term). He proceeded by first producing a rough prose draft of the work, dividing it into ten cantos (the number of cantos contained in the first edition of Milton's *Paradise Lost*), after which he began its versification, but only ever completed one canto. The 1811 editor Nodier accordingly informs us that 'the published work was no more than a magnificent first draft that he had started to put into verse', adding the footnote: 'The first canto was finished. I have had it in my hands'

Christophe Grainville, who was indeed born in Lisieux in 1760 and died there in 1805, and who was indeed 'advocat et poète', as his entry in the *Biographie Universelle, ancienne et moderne* of 1817 confirms on the pages (pp. 274–75) that immediately follow 'our' Grainville's entry (pp. 271–74).

31 I. F. Clarke, 'Preface', in *The Last Man*, trans. I. F. & M. Clarke, p. xi.

32 Paul K. Alkon, *Science Fiction Before 1900. Imagination Discovers Technology* (New York: Twayne, 1994), p. 62.

('l'ouvrage publié n'en étoit qu'une grande et superbe ébauche qu'il commençoit à mettre en vers. Le premier chant étoit achevé. Je l'ai eu entre les mains').[33] This first versified canto no longer exists, however. After the prose draft's original posthumous publication in French in 1805, by some serendipitous happenstance it came to be translated into English the following year; appearing in London in 1806 in an anonymized version (the name of neither author nor translator were given), Grainville's authorship remained unknown to English-speaking readers for over one and a half centuries, as I. F. and M. Clarke recap in the preface of their 2002 edition. Indeed, I. F. Clarke reminds us that in his own 1961 bibliography of futuristic fiction, *The Tale of the Future*, he had still cited the English edition of *The Last Man* as an anonymous 'British text by an unknown English author' and classified it under the rubric 'published in the United Kingdom between 1644 and 1960'.[34] It was only following an inquiry by a prominent French scholar of science fiction, Pierre Versins, who was at that time compiling the material for his wide-ranging and comprehensive *Encyclopédie de l'Utopie, des Voyages extraordinaires et de la Science-Fiction*, that Clarke realized that *The Last Man; or, Omegarus and Syderia: A Romance in Futurity* was in actual fact an unacknowledged English 'pirated version' of Grainville's French *Le Dernier Homme*. Initially assuming that this English translation would be a more or less faithful rendition of the French original, Clarke soon noticed that certain passages in the English version that made reference for instance to Edward Jenner's contemporary *Inquiry into the Causes and Effects of the Variolae Vaccinae* were not contained in the French edition. Proceeding to undertake a more systematic comparison, he and his wife found that the anonymous translator had rearranged the book to make the book more palatable to a British audience. The Grainville version follows the epic style: division into ten *Chants*, which are self-contained major sections of the narrative. In the English version, these are replaced by a division into twenty-one chapters, presumably designed to give *A Romance in Futurity* the appearance of the everyday London fiction to be found in the circulating libraries.

Put differently, the pirated 1806 English translation, calling itself a 'Romance', was making reference to itself as a form of novel. Mindful of Grainville's 'epic' structuring device, which the pirated English version effaces, it is both telling and significant that the Clarkes never once refer to Grainville's *Le Dernier Homme* as a novel either in the 'Preface' or the 'Introduction' to their new edition, speaking of it in terms only of 'story', 'text', 'book', 'an early example of future fiction', 'poème en prose' and 'the first Gothic romance of Heaven and Earth'. Many — if not most — previous Anglo-American critics, by contrast, had paid scant attention to this seemingly minor detail of genre attribution, persistently mischaracterizing the text as a novel. Thus the critic Warren Wagar talks explicitly of Grainville's novel, as do Fiona Stafford and Henry Majewski;[35] Alkon speaks more cautiously of Grainville's

---

[33] Charles Nodier, 'Preface to the Second Edition', *The Last Man*, trans. I. F. & M. Clarke, pp. 137–40 (p. 138) (*Le Dernier Homme*, 1811, p. vii).

[34] Ibid., p. xiv; the following passage p. xvi.

[35] Wagar, *Terminal Visions*, p. 16; Stafford, *The Last of the Race*, pp. 201 and 205; Majewski, 'Grainville's *Le dernier homme*', *Symposium: A Quarterly Journal in Modern Literatures*, 17 (1963), 114–22

'novelistic portrait of the phenomenology of apocalypse'[36] whereas today's favoured — and usually fairly reliable — online resource, the Wikipedia encyclopedia, informs us: '*Le Dernier Homme* is a French science fiction fantasy novel in the form of a prose poem'.[37] Most French critics, reading what might be called the original French 'prose-canto-version', for obvious reasons tend to be more cautious, as were the Clarkes; Pierre Versins in the above-cited encyclopedia thus calls it a 'prose poem' ('poème en prose'),[38] whereas Anne Kupiec, the editor of the new French edition, variedly calls it an epopee ('épopée'), work ('ouvrage' or 'œuvre'), book ('livre') or text ('texte'), but — revealingly — never once a novel. Attentive readers may have noticed that I, for the same reason, have refrained thus far from referring to the work as a novel.[39]

Why is this detail so important? Well, contemporary readers and reviewers of Grainville's 'novel' took such matters very seriously indeed; in fact, they were rather confused by the work's form and puzzled as to the genre under which it might best be classified. Most early nineteenth-century critics intuitively grasped its epic design, but then did not know how to categorize its prose form. Prose was not customary in the traditional epic genre in either of the three languages that we are dealing with in my study, French, English or German, and it was certainly not used in the religious epic genre, to which both *Donatoa* and *Le Dernier Homme* so clearly belonged and which was commonly divided into cantos, *Gesänge* or *chants*, as are *Donatoa* and *Le Dernier Homme*.

Let us take a closer look, then, at some of the contemporaneous responses in order to explore what they reveal about the text and the meanings Grainville's contemporaries would have attributed to it. As cited above, for instance, in preparing its 1811 second French edition, Nodier first calls *Le Dernier Homme* a 'rough draft' ('ébauche') and 'poem' ('poëme'),[40] but then goes on to label it 'a fantasy genre that was hitherto unknown' ('un genre de merveilleux encore unique'). 'Some readers saw it as a mere romance,' he adds, referring apparently to the English translation, 'and when considered in that light, it was at the mercy of readers incapable of judging it. Other readers must have seen in it the outline of a great epic poem — an epic which, as it stood, left much to be desired by exacting literary critics' ('[L]es uns n'y ont vu qu'un roman, et il est tombé dès-lors à la merci d'une classe de lecteurs incapable de le juger; les autres ont dû y apercevoir l'esquisse d'une belle épopée, mais qui, telle qu'elle étoit, laissoit trop à desirer à une critique sévère'). Twentieth- and twenty-first-century readers who neglect the importance attached

(pp. 116 and 122).

36 *Origins of Futuristic Fiction*, p. 167.

37 Retrieved 28 January 2013.

38 Pierre Versins, *Encyclopédie de l'Utopie des Voyages Extraordinaires et de la Science Fiction* (Lausanne: L'Age d'Homme, 1972), p. 238.

39 I have to amend this statement by adding that I, like other German critics, have also referred to *Le Dernier Homme* as a novel (*Roman*) in the past; I did so in my *Arcadia*-article of 2000, reprinted in the volume *Abendländische Apokalyptik* in 2013 (p. 85), as did Eva Horn in her essay in the same volume (pp. 109–11), cited earlier in this chapter.

40 Nodier, 'Preface to the Second Edition', pp. 138 and 139 (*Le Dernier Homme*, 1811, pp. vii and xi); the following quotes are all from this brief introduction.

to genre during the eighteenth and early nineteenth century do this, as Nodier rightly stresses, at their interpretive peril. For his part, Nodier commends Grainville for having been seized by 'an idea never before expressed' in poetry ('s'est saisi d'un sujet qui lui étoit échappé'), even if circumstance prevented him from completing the project as planned. And despite its shortcomings he extols the merits of the work to the reader: 'What would you say', he asks rhetorically,

> to a noble and sublime vision that would juxtapose the glorious days of the earth in its youth, as Milton described it, with the decadence and sickness of a dying world, the ill-fated loves of our last descendants with the delights of earthly paradise, and the end of all things with their beginning? [...] I am convinced, I repeat,

he pronounces,

> that if these facts had been known, M. de Grainville would have been assigned a place in literature which I hesitate to determine exactly, but which an enlightened sensibility would perhaps have placed not far below that of Klopstock.
>
> [Que penseriez-vous de la conception touchante et sublime qui opposeroit aux beaux jours de la terre naissante, comme Milton l'a décrite, la décadence et les infirmités d'un monde décrépit, les funestes amours de nos derniers descendans aux délices du paradis terrestre, et la fin de toutes choses à leur commencement? [...] je suis convaincu, dis-je, que M. de Grainville auroit été alors mis à sa place, que je n'ose pas déterminer, mais qu'une sensibilité éclairée ne fixeroit peut-être pas fort au-dessous de celle de Klopstock.]

Commendation indeed — albeit expressed with some telltale vacillation! I say this ironically, of course, because — what Nodier could not have foreseen — his claim backfires: alongside Milton's *Paradise Lost* Klopstock's *Messiah* was widely celebrated as one of the great epics produced since antiquity, and yet among university students and even scholars of German literature few today will venture to read Klopstock's *Messiah* beyond perhaps the opening canto. Indeed, even during Klopstock's lifetime many had not read the acclaimed work of this 'venerable father of German poetry', as Coleridge formulated it, admitting in the same breath that he had read only the first four books of Klopstock's epic, and this despite having made a pilgrimage to Hamburg in 1798 to visit the seventy-four-year-old poet (indeed, Coleridge had even expressed a desire to translate some of Klopstock's odes into English).[41] In short, Klopstock's *Messiah* must be one of the most unread 'classics' of German literature, then as now. Crucially, nonetheless, Klopstock's *Messiah* was one of the yardsticks Grainville's work was being measured against. Another yardstick, besides Milton as the most obvious contender, was Edward Young's *A Poem on the Last Day* that we encountered in Chapter One and which served as one of the chief models for Franz von Sonnenberg's *Weltende* and *Donatoa*. Young's continuing prominence even one hundred years after the initial publication of his Last Judgment poem is confirmed by one French critic who reviewed the 1811 second edition of *Le Dernier Homme*. Agreeing with the editor that the work exhibits 'great traits of originality',

---

41 Cited by Herzberg, 'Wordsworth and German Literature', this quote p. 304.

FIG. 2.3. Edward Young, *Le Jugement Dernier*, title page of the French translation of Young's 1713 *A Poem on the Last Day* published in Paris in 1804; this new translation may have served as inspiration for Grainville to write his version of the Last Judgment.

this reviewer goes on to compare Grainville's adaptation with earlier treatments of the same subject; specifically citing Edward Young — a new French translation of whose *A Poem on the Last Day* had just appeared in 1804 in time for Grainville to have seen it (see Figure 2.3) — we read: 'Grainville aspired to developing a new subject so much so that he sought to avoid rivalling Young as well as those other poets who have tried to depict the Last Judgment. [This explains why] [h]is work finishes at the very moment when the last human being breathes his last gasp' ('Il a eu si bien l'intention de traiter un sujet absolument neuf, qu'il n'a point voulu rivaliser Young, ni les autres poëtes qui ont essayé de peindre le *Jugement dernier*. Son ouvrage finit précisément lorsque le dernier des hommes rend le dernier soupir').[42] The reviewer also cannot desist from commenting disparagingly on the work's peculiar shape; admitting that he himself can make no sense of the term 'prose poem' ('I belong among those for whom the term *prose poem* has no meaning', 'Je suis de ceux pour qui le mot *poême en prose* n'a aucun sens'), he goes on to note:

---

42 D. T., review of *Le dernier Homme, ouvrage posthume*, in *Esprit des Journaux, français et étrangers*, vol. 5 (Mai 1811), pp. 84–102 (p. 88; the following quotations p. 87). In 1806 we encounter a further rendition of Young's poem by J. L. Boucharlat, *Le Jugement dernier, poëme en trois chants, imité d'Young* (Paris: Le Normant, 1806), underlining the degree to which Young was 'en vogue' in France between 1804 and 1806.

It is not without reason that I have designated *Le Dernier Homme* by this vague term 'work'. Still, it is important to make clear to which genre it belongs. To call it a novel would hardly be accurate; it deals with subjects far too grand to place it in this category. So it must be a poem, one might say. However much I am tempted to respond in the affirmative, I cannot bring myself to do so. [...] I prefer to follow the editor's advice who sees it as a 'great and superb rough draft'.

[Ce n'est pas sans intention que j'ai designé jusqu'ici le *Dernier Homme* par ce mot vague, ouvrage. Il faut cependant annoncer d'une manière plus positive de quel genre il est. Le titre de roman ne lui convient pas; il traite de sujets trop grands pour qu'on puisse le ranger dans cette classe. C'est donc un poëme, va-t-on dire? Quelque tenté que je sois de répondre affirmativement, je ne peux m'y résoudre. [...] Je me range donc à l'avis de l'éditeur, qui voit dans le *Dernier Homme* 'une grande et superbe ébauche'.]

Note how, due to the work's prose form, this reviewer cannot even contemplate calling it an epic, which was of course Grainville's intended form for his text, as Nodier was so keen to point out.

A much later French critic, Alfred Touroude, by contrast, writing in the middle of the nineteenth century and complaining about the French never having been able to compete with the great epics of Italy, England and Germany, citing specifically Dante's *Divine Comedy*, Milton's *Paradise Lost* and Klopstock's *Messiah*, sees Grainville's *Le Dernier Homme* as 'the only genuinely epic idea [having emanated] in France' ('la seule idée véritablement épique qui existe en France') — but only the idea, not the final product; he explains:

Milton has sung of the Fall of Man, Klopstock of the Redemption of Man, Dante of the Soul of Man, Grainville *has tried* [my emphasis] to sing of the Death of Man, the supreme flowering, the full bloom of man, the blending of life into immortality. [...] Of course, a modern epic poem must contain more than a glorification of a hero or heroism, it must be full of social and philosophical thought, like the ode, like the theatre, like the novel [...]. Well, I can confirm that *Le Dernier Homme* contains the shoot of a modern epic poem. [...] For me, then, the true achievement of Grainville is: to this day he is the only poet who, setting aside the poems of bygone days, has found a subject for an epic poem that is at once profound, original and modern. Would I go so far as to proclaim that, such as it is, *Le Dernier Homme* deserves pride of place beside the works of Dante or Milton, Homer or Klopstock? No. I would not dream of awarding the same accolade to a poem that is little more than a framework, a coarse draft, the mere fetus of a true poem. [...] it is nonetheless true that we owe to Grainville a poem that is a really good read, even if it remains a fragment...

[Milton a chanté la *Chute de l'homme*, Klopstock a chanté le *Rachat de l'homme*, Dante a chanté l'*Ame de l'homme*, Grainville a voulu chanter la *Mort de l'homme*, la floraison suprême, l'épanouissement de l'être humain, la fusion de l'être vivant dans l'être immortel. [...] donc, un poëme épique moderne doit contenir autre chose qu'une glorification d'un héros ou d'une héroïsme, il doit être plein d'une pensée sociale ou philosophique, comme l'ode, comme le théâtre, comme le roman [...]. Eh bien! le *Dernier homme* contient le germe d'un poëme épique moderne, je l'affirme. [...] Voilà, pour moi, la véritable gloire de Grainville: il est

> jusqu'à cette heure le seul poëte qui, oubliant les poëmes d'autrefois, ait trouvé un sujet de poëme épique, profond, original et moderne. Irai-je proclamer que, tel qu'il est, le *Dernier homme* doit prendre place à côté des œuvres de Dante ou de Milton, d'Homère ou de Klopstock? Non. Je n'ai jamais songé à pareille affirmation à propos d'un poëme qui n'est que la charpente, le gros œuvre, le fœtus d'un véritable poëme. [...] mais il n'en est pas moins vrai que nous devons à Grainville un poëme bon à lire, quoique incomplet...][43]

A 'really good read' prefigures the previously cited assessment of *Le Dernier Homme* two hundred years later as, in Paley's words, 'a page-turner of sorts, holding the reader's interest closely from start to finish'; it is also the view expressed by an anonymous German critic reviewing the first German translation in 1808. He praises, among other things, the vivid descriptions of the waning Earth, the airship's journey to South America, the characterization of Idamas and Syderia, the concluding vision of the dead arising from their graves and the commencement of the Last Judgment. Remarking how unsuitable he found the subtitle that the German translator had superfluously attached, 'a Romantic composition' ('eine romantische Dichtung': *Dichtung* is impossible to translate, meaning effectively a poetic work of any genre), he goes on to note: 'The whole piece is a grand nature poem about the end times and the termination of the Earth, pictured with bold imagination, and exhibiting vigour, a graceful language, and firm characters; yet, nonetheless, there is insufficient music in the rhythm to make it a powerful epic' ('Das Ganze ist ein großes Naturgedicht über die letzten Zeiten und das Ende der Erde, mit kühner Phantasie entworfen, mit Kraft und Leichtigkeit des Ausdrucks, in festen Charakteren durchgeführt, und nur die Musik des Rhythmus fehlt zu einem kräftigen Epos').[44] The anonymous reviewer of the 1811 German translation's second edition, writing in 1813, similarly praises Grainville's 'bold spirit' ('kühner Geist') and 'high oriental style' ('hoher orientalischer Stil') as well as its epical qualities, but likewise finds fault in precisely this aspect, asking: 'How much more is needed especially if we are to regard this poem as an epopee, in order to make it a finished product' ('Wie weit mehr würde erfodert [*sic*], um das Gedicht, zumal als Epopee betrachtet, gelungen zu nennen').[45]

What transpires from all these early responses is, on the one hand, that they commend Grainville for the force and genius of his visions, as well as for the novelty of plot and originality of design, but on the other that they are confused as to how to classify this text in generic terms: is it a poem, a prose poem, a romance, an epic/epopee, or merely a draft, all of these, or none of these? It is worth emphasizing the fact, however, that none of the contemporaneous French or German reviewers consider the text a novel, in stark contrast to the majority of their twentieth- and twenty-first-century successors. Why is this so, and what difference does this make?

---

43 Alfred Touroude, *Les Écrivains havrais* (Le Havre: Librairie de E. Touroude, 1865), pp. 106–07.

44 Anon., review of Grainville's *Der letzte Mensch. Eine romantische Dichtung* (1807), in *Jenaische Allgemeine Literatur-Zeitung*, no. 218 (September 1808), columns 516–19, this quotation column 516.

45 Anon., review of Grainville's *Der letzte Mensch* and *Omegar, der letzte Mensch*, in *Allgemeine Literatur-Zeitung* (December 1813), this and the previous quotation column 665.

Transcendental Homelessness in a Disenchanted World

To answer this question I want to turn to an early work of the Marxist critic Georg Lukács, written at a time when his thinking was still pre-Marxist and dominated by Hegelian idealism as well as a brand of intellectual history the Germans call *Geistesgeschichte* — in his later Marxist preface to the 1962 reprint, Lukács will describe his book as 'purely intuitive' ('bloß intuitiv'), 'overly abstract' ('höchst abstrakt') and 'far too general' (viel zu allgemein').[46] Published first in a German journal of aesthetics in 1916, it appeared in book form in 1920 under the somewhat lofty title *The Theory of the Novel. A historico-philosophical essay on the forms of great epic literature* (*Die Theorie des Romans. Ein geschichtsphilosophischer Versuch über die Formen der großen Epik*). *The Theory of the Novel* is, essentially, a comparative study of the classical epic and the modern novel (however broadly defined). It is a dense work that is difficult to read, not just because of its at times obscure philosophical vocabulary, but also because it still works within a relatively rigid system of genre demarcations. Moreover, for a study on the epic it is atypical in that it not once mentions Milton's *Paradise Lost* and Klopstock's *Messiah*, the great English and German epics of the seventeenth and eighteenth centuries. By and large, Lukács's concern is less historical than typological: his goal is not to deliver a comprehensive historical survey of the epic, hence its lack of reference to some of the most seminal representatives of that genre; rather, his goal is, as the subtitle stipulates, to provide a 'historico-*philosophical* essay on the forms of great epic literature' (my emphasis). His prime examples of the classical and medieval epic are Homer, Wolfram and Dante, who are opposed to the nineteenth-century novelists Goethe, Novalis, Balzac, Tolstoy and Dostoevsky, among others. The sixteenth, seventeenth and eighteenth centuries by contrast figure only marginally. Even if his material base is intentionally limited in this way, the results of his philosophical reflections still merit consideration today, and they are particularly germane to my discussion of Sonnenberg's *Donatoa* and Grainville's *Le Dernier Homme*.

The title and subtitle of Lukács's study call attention to the close ties between the modern novel and the traditional genre of the epic. Lukács in effect argues that the epic and its successor, the modern novel, have gone separate ways, and, perhaps more intruigingly, that they express different attitudes towards the world(s) they depict. Hegel had argued along similar lines, as we recall from our discussion in Chapter One. Hegel's thinking in this regard is suitably encapsulated in the following passage in his *Lectures on Aesthetics*:

> The *romances* and *ballads*, which we find both in the Middle Ages and modern times, are no doubt poetry of a kind, though it is impossible to define accurately their type; so far as their content is concerned they are in part epic. If we look at the form of their composition, however, they are for the most part lyrical, so that we have perforce to reckon them from different points of view to different types. The *romantic* novel, that Epopaea of *modern society*, opens a different field altogether. In this we possess, on the one hand, in all its completeness

---

46 *Theorie des Romans. Ein geschichtsphilosophischer Versuch über die Formen der großen Epik* (Darmstadt: Luchterhand, 1977), pp. 6–7.

and variety, an epic prodigality of interests, conditions, characters, and living relations, the extensive background in fact of an entire world. We have also the epic exposition of events. What fails us here is the *primitive* world-condition as poetically conceived, which is the source of the genuine Epos. The romance or novel in the modern sense pre-supposes a basis of reality already organized in its *prosaic form*, upon which it then attempts, in its own sphere, [...] both in its treatment of the vital character of events and the life of individuals and their destiny, to make good once more the banished claims of poetical vision.

[Poetischer freilich, doch ohne festen Gattungsunterschied, sind die *Romanzen* und *Balladen*, Produkte des Mittelalters und der modernen Zeit, dem Inhalte nach zum Teil episch, der Behandlung nach dagegen meist lyrisch, so daß man sie bald der einen, bald der anderen Gattung zurechnen möchte. Ganz anders verhält es sich dagegen mit dem *Roman*, der modernen *bürgerlichen* Epopöe. Hier tritt einerseits der Reichtum und Vielseitigkeit der Interessen, Zustände, Charaktere, Lebensverhältnisse, der breite Hintergrund einer totalen Welt sowie die epische Darstellung von Begebenheiten vollständig wieder ein. Was jedoch fehlt, ist der *ursprünglich* poetische Weltzustand, aus welchem das eigentliche Epos hervorgeht. Der Roman im modernen Sinne setzt eine bereits zur *Prosa* geordnete Wirklichkeit voraus, auf deren Boden er sodann in seinem Kreise [...] der Poesie [...] ihr verlorenes Recht wieder erringt.][47] (Hegel's emphases)

I want to emphasize two points here. First Hegel's stressing the fact that epic and novel are distinguished by their forms of composition, the former being *in essence* 'lyrical' (Hegel says 'for the most part' whereas I say 'in essence' — Hegel's cautious choice of words merely confirms how much he is struggling to encompass the great diversity of and shifts occurring within the countless genres and sub-genres that comprise literary history), the latter famously being defined by its 'prosaic form' as, in Lukács's words, '*bürgerliche* Epopöe' ('Epopaea of *modern society*', whereby Anna Bostock's English translation sacrifices the 'bourgeois' or 'bürgerlich' that is so distinct and memorable — and much-cited — in the German original). Second the novel's lack of a 'primitive world-condition' on which it is premised.

Hegel's demarcation of world-conditions here harks back to Friedrich Schiller's in part historical, in part psychological/anthropological differentiation between antiquity and modernity in his most important contribution to the theory of criticism, 'On Naïve and Sentimental Poetry' ('Über naive und sentimentalische Dichtung', 1795–1796). Schiller describes the Greeks as 'naïve' in their outlook on and relationship with the world, the moderns by contrast as 'sentimental' (the German term is 'sentimentalisch', which is linguistically distinct from 'sentimental'). That is, naïve poets (supposedly) live in inner harmony und unity with nature, and their works of art are produced spontaneously and in the absence of any critical self-reflection. Sentimental poets are self-conscious and sceptical of inspiration; and, crucially, they are apprehensive of the psychological abyss which dissociates their own age from antiquity, they feel their cultural and moral self cut off from the harmony of senses and from the union with nature that they ascribe to the writers

---

47 *The Philosophy of Fine Art*, trans. by F. P. B. Osmaston (London: G. Bell and Sons, 1920), vol. 4, p. 171; *Vorlesungen über die Ästhetik*, ed. by Rüdiger Bubner (Stuttgart: Reclam, 1971), vol. 3: *Die Poesie*, p. 177.

of antiquity. Schiller argues that it is impossible for the modern sentimental writer to recover that original sense of harmonious embeddedness within nature that he sees as characteristic of the antique writer; we shall never regain that state of naïve, or unconscious, communion with nature that for him is so enviably characteristic of Greek culture.[48] (Elsewhere in the same essay Schiller compares the Greek writer with a child and the modern writer with an adult who looks longingly on childhood without being able to return to it.)

Lukács takes his cue primarily from Schiller and Hegel, but leaves their core tenets with a pinch of Friedrich Schlegel's (notion of) irony (irony being the chief legacy of Schlegel's *Athenaeum*-fragments in which this key aesthetic concept of German romanticism was first advanced in 1798). Lukács then applies these combined aesthetic and philosophical principles to a historical analysis of the epic genre, broadly defined to encompass the traditional epopee and the modern nineteenth-century novel. Despite being members of the same epic genre, the epopee and the novel are, Lukács argues, existentially and philosophically fundamentally different literary forms of expression. He states:

> The [epopee] and the novel, these two major forms of great epic literature, differ from one another not by their authors' fundamental intentions but by the given historico-philosophical realities with which the authors were confronted. The novel is the epic of an age in which the extensive totality of life is no longer directly given, in which the immanence of meaning in life has become a problem, yet which still thinks in terms of totality.

> [Epopöe und Roman, die beiden Objektivationen der großen Epik, trennen sich nicht nach den gestaltenden Gesinnungen, sondern nach den geschichts-philosophischen Gegebenheiten, die sich zur Gestaltung vorfinden. Der Roman ist die Epopöe eines Zeitalters, für das die extensive Totalität des Lebens nicht mehr sinnfällig gegeben ist, für das die Lebensimmanenz des Sinnes zum Problem geworden ist, und das dennoch die Gesinnung zur Totalität hat.][49]

He continues by stressing that it is not crucial whether a text is written in verse or prose; what *is* crucial, however, is that

> the [epopee] gives form to a totality of life that is rounded from within [whereas] the novel seeks, by giving form, to uncover and construct the concealed totality of life. [...] All the fissures and rents which are inherent in the historical situation must be drawn into the form-giving process and cannot nor should be disguised by compositional means. Thus the fundamental form-determining

---

48 I should perhaps add here, however, that a careful reading of Schiller's 'On Naïve and Sentimental Poetry' will show how the distinction between antiquity and modernity begins as a historical and diachronical division between antiquity and modernity, but later, when he moves into his discussion of Goethe's *Wilhelm Meister*, is transformed into a non-historical typological/psychological one. This explains why, in the later parts of that essay, Goethe can be characterized as a modern naïve poet: he has a fundamentally different outlook on writing than Schiller. Put differently, the initial historical distinction/division between antiquity and modernity morphs into an anthropological/psychological distinction/division between Schiller and Goethe themselves.

49 *The Theory of the Novel. A historico-philosophical essay on the forms of great epic literature*, trans. by Anna Bostock (London: Merlin Press, 1978), p. 56, the following quotes pp. 60, 89, and 66 (twice); *Theorie des Romans*, p. 47, the following quotes pp. 51, 78, and 56–57 (twice).

intention of the novel is objectivised as the psychology of the novel's heroes: they are seekers. The simple fact of seeking implies that neither the goals nor the way leading to them can be directly given...

[Die Epopöe gestaltet eine von sich aus geschlossene Lebenstotalität, der Roman sucht gestaltend die verborgene Totalität des Lebens aufzudecken und aufzubauen. [...] Alle Risse und Abgründe, die die geschichtliche Situation in sich trägt, müssen in die Gestaltung einbezogen und können und sollen nicht mit Mitteln der Komposition verdeckt werden. So objektiviert sich die formbestimmende Grundgesinnung des Romans als Psychologie der Romanhelden: sie sind Suchende. Die einfache Tatsache des Suchens zeigt an, daß weder Ziele noch Wege unmittelbar gegeben sein können....]

I must admit here that I have made one change to the English translation of the previous two quotations, highlighted by the square brackets (which I will likewise apply in quotations later), but it is a crucial one, and it shows that the reader of the English translation is bound to be misled (and, more consequentially perhaps, also shows that the translator did not fully grasp Lukács's emphasis on genre). In the first line of these two passages, the English translator chose to render the German *Epopöe* as 'epic' instead of using the more precise term 'epopee'; however, one of the main points of Lukács's study is to contrast the functionally distinct sub-genres *Epopöe* (epopee) and *Roman* (novel), *both of which* are constituent elements of one and the same umbrella genre *Epos* (epic). Both epopee in English and *Epopöe* in German are rarely used today; they represent an archaic vocabulary that we tend to associate with eighteenth- and nineteenth-century genre theory and poetics, especially its division of literature into what Goethe and his contemporaries, following the conventional system of poetics, called the three basic forms (*Grundformen*) of literary discourse, the epic, the dramatic and the lyric (Goethe uses the adjectival derivatives *episch*, *dramatisch* and *lyrisch*). Drawing on this essentializing poetological tradition and its specialist vocabulary in German, Lukács's argument is precisely that the traditional *epopee* and the *novel*, as two distinct sub-genres of the epic, are deployed by writers to express fundamentally different worldviews. Only if we understand this can we also understand such key statements of Lukács's *Theory of the Novel* as:

> The novel tells of the adventure of interiority; the content of the novel is the story of the soul that goes to find itself, that seeks adventures in order to be proved and tested by them, and, by proving itself, to find its own essence. The inner security of the epic world excludes adventure in this essential sense: the heroes of the [epopee] live through a whole variety of adventures, but the fact that they will pass the test, both inwardly and outwardly, is never in doubt; the world-dominating gods must always triumph over the demons [...]. Hence the passivity of the epic hero that Goethe and Schiller insisted on: the adventures that fill and embellish his life are the form taken by the objective and extensive totality of the world; he himself is only the luminous centre around which this unfolded totality revolves, the inwardly most immobile point of the world's rhythmic movement. By contrast, the novel hero's passivity is not a necessity; it characterises the hero's relationship to his soul and to the outside world. The novel hero does not have to be passive: that is why his passivity has a specific psychological and sociological nature and represents a distinct type in the structural possibilities of the novel.

[Der Roman ist die Form des Abenteuers des Eigenwertes der Innerlichkeit; sein Inhalt ist die Geschichte der Seele, die da auszieht, um sich kennenzulernen [...]: die Helden der Epopöe durchlaufen eine bunte Reihe von Abenteuern, daß sie sie aber innerlich wie äußerlich bestehen werden, steht nie außer Frage; die weltbeherrschenden Götter müssen immer über die Dämonen [...] triumphieren. Daher die von Goethe und Schiller geforderte Passivität des epischen Helden: der Abenteuerreigen, der sein Leben ziert und erfüllt, ist die Gestaltung der objektiven und extensiven Totalität der Welt, er selbst ist nur der leuchtende Mittelpunkt, um den sich diese Entfaltung dreht, der innerlich unbewegliche Punkt der rhythmischen Bewegung der Welt. Die Passivität des Romanhelden ist aber keine formale Notwendigkeit, sondern bezeichnet das Verhältnis des Helden zu seiner Seele und sein Verhältnis zu seiner Umwelt. Er muß nicht passiv sein, darum hat jede Passivität bei ihm eine eigene psychologische und soziologische Qualität und bestimmt einen bestimmten Typus in den Aufbaumöglichkeiten des Romans.]

In line with this Lukács states elsewhere that 'the epic hero [that is, the hero of the epopee, R.W.] is, strictly speaking, never an individual. It is traditionally thought that one of the essential characteristics of the epic is the fact that its theme is not a personal destiny but the destiny of a community' ('der Held der Epopöe ist, strenggenommen, niemals ein Individuum. Es ist von alters her als Wesenszeichen des Epos betrachtet worden, daß sein Gegenstand kein persönliches Schicksal, sondern das einer Gemeinschaft ist'). The hero of the novel, by contrast, is 'the product of estrangement from the outside world. [...] The autonomous life of interiority is possible and necessary only when the distinctions between men have made an unbridgeable chasm; when the gods are silent' ('Das epische Individuum, der Held des Romans, entsteht aus dieser Fremdheit zur Außenwelt. [...] Das Eigenleben der Innerlichkeit ist nur dann möglich und notwendig, wenn das Unterscheidende zwischen den Menschen zur unüberbrückbaren Kluft geworden ist; wenn die Götter stumm sind'). The operative dichotomies that emerge are community versus individual, being without doubt versus being with doubt, inner security versus inner insecurity, objectivity of the world versus subjectivity of the world, and psychological exteriority versus psychological interiority.

There is one further and final aspect of Lukács's theory that requires our attention, namely the distinction he draws between man's relationship to the gods or God in the traditional epopee as opposed to the modern novel: 'the world-dominating gods must always triumph over the demons', he says with regard to the epopee, as we saw, whereas in the novel he claims that 'the gods are silent'. Plainly, in both Sonnenberg's *Donatoa* and Grainville's *Le Dernier Homme* the 'world-dominating gods' in the shape of the Christian Almighty and his angels of death triumph over the demons; here God does not remain silent. In fact, God's voice is not just heard, but is the last and ultimate pronouncement to end all things. In this regard, then, their heroes Heroal and Omegarus can hardly be considered modern subjects; nor do they exhibit the 'autonomous life of interiority' that Lukács sees as a prerequisite of the modern epic genre which in his view the novel represents. Sonnenberg's chief human protagonist Heroal no less than Grainville's chief human protagonist Omegarus are conceived more as the epopee's timeless heroes of yore, dependent on the power of a redeeming divinity, than as the independent agents of a modern novel who are psychologically embedded in prosaic time and real life. Lukács later repeats this point more forcefully when he declares that 'the novel is the [epopee] of a world that has been abandoned by God' ('Der Roman ist die Epopöe der gottverlassenen Welt'); it is a world characterized by 'the remoteness [and] absence of an effective God', by 'the God-forsakenness of the world' ('die Ferne und die Abwesenheit des wirkenden Gottes', 'das Gottverlassene der Welt').[50] This criterion alone would seem to destroy any chance that Grainville's *Le Dernier Homme* might qualify as a 'novel', its prose form notwithstanding. Nor does the work redeem itself by the use of irony, that other trademark of the modern novel. Clearly, irony does not lend itself easily to the serious treatment of a subject matter like the Christian Last Judgment. This would seem to be confirmed by Lukács's statement that 'the writer's irony is a negative mysticism to be found in times without a god' ('Die Ironie des Dichters ist die negative Mystik der gottlosen Zeiten'); and:

> For the novel, irony consists in this freedom of the writer in his relationship to God, the transcendental condition of the objectivity of form-giving. Irony, with intuitive double vision, can see where God is to be found in a world abandoned by God.
>
> [Für den Roman ist die Ironie diese Freiheit des Dichters Gott gegenüber, die transzendentale Bedingung der Objektivität der Gestaltung. Die Ironie, die das von Gott Erfüllte der von Gott verlassenen Welt in intuitiver Doppelsichtigkeit zu erblicken vermag,...][51]

Neither Sonnenberg's nor Grainville's worlds are abandoned by God — on the contrary, the whole point of their works is, I contend, to remind us that God's will governs all; he may not be present, but he will be in the future when the end of time approaches. In the modern novel, by contrast, and according to Lukács, God remains absent and without voice at all times.

But what kind of absence in our present is this? Is this the atheist's God who does not exist and hence cannot show himself, the world being left to its own devices? Or is it the deist's God, the *deus absconditus*, who has created the world like a clockmaker (this the traditional simile used by seventeenth-century deists, but also by early nineteenth-century theists like William Paley) only to absent himself from it and let it tick on in perpetuity, perhaps watching over us from afar but only ever as a detached observer who keeps out of our way, as Goethe so neatly suggested in the opening motto. This is the God as James Joyce conceived him in his early modernist novel *A Portrait of the Artist as a Young Man*, in which we are told that 'the God of the creation remains within or behind or beyond or above his handiwork, invisible, refined out of existence, indifferent, paring his fingernails'. But in Joyce's modern ironic cosmos this is also the role played by the artist — the full citation runs: '*The artist, like the God of the creation*, remains within or behind or beyond or above his handiwork, invisible, refined out of existence, indifferent, paring his

---

50 Ibid., pp. 88, 90 and again 90 (*Theorie des Romans*, pp. 77, 79 and again 79).
51 Ibid., pp. 90 and 92 (*Theorie des Romans*, pp. 79 and 81).

fingernails' (my emphasis).[52] Is Joyce suggesting that God no longer exists and has been supplanted by the artist? Or that the artist is simply emulating the role played by the deist's God and that both exist side by side? Formulated in reverse, M. H. Abrams equates God with an author like Joyce when he writes, in *Natural Supernaturalism*: 'The [Christian] plot of history has *a hidden author* who is also its director and the guarantor of things to come. God planned it all before it began, and He controls its details, under the seemingly casual or causal relations of events, by his invisible Providence' (again my emphasis).[53] Is not Joyce's *Ulysses* a book that is brimming with this kind of authorial 'invisible Providence'?

If the passage cited from Joyce's *A Portrait of the Artist as a Young Man* (published coincidentally in the same year — 1916 — as Lukács's *The Theory of the Novel*) remains suitably non-committal for a modernist novel founded on irony, Joyce's ironic narrator goes so far as to substitute Stephen's Catholic belief in and worship of the Virgin Mary in the early sections of the novel for the erotically charged worship of an anonymous girl on Sandymount Beach towards the end of its fourth and penultimate chapter, a chapter many with good reason consider the climax of Joyce's work. Amid 'the holy silence of [Stephen's] ecstasy' the girl senses the 'worship of his eyes', we read; and then: ' — Heavenly God! cried Stephen's soul, in an outburst of profane joy'.[54] Transferring the language of worship from the sacred Virgin Mary to this profane 'angel of mortal youth and beauty', as the girl is also described, Joyce enacts in his novel precisely the kind of irony Lukács is referring to. It is perhaps also a profane irony of sorts when the narrator/Stephen tersely but emphatically announces 'He was alone', signifying not just the artist's mental or physical solitude on this mundane Dublin Bay beach, but also his spiritual solitude, his forthcoming declaration of independence from the Christian faith in the final chapter. In this final chapter Stephen confides to his friend Davin: 'When the soul of a man is born in this country there are nets flung at it to hold it back from flight. You talk to me of nationality, language, religion. I shall try to fly by those nets'.[55] 'Too deep for me, Stevie', is Davin's baffled response. In his ironical use of myth — in *A Portrait of the Artist as a Young Man* Stephen Dedalus's name transforms the Irish lad simultaneously into a Christian Saint and the son of the mythical Greek architect Daedalus, in *Ulysses* Mr Leopold Bloom promenades through the streets of Dublin as a modern-day avatar of the Greek hero Odysseus, but in the 'Cyclops'-episode also as a reincarnation of Jesus Christ — Joyce shows himself to be a most scrupulous promulgator of Friedrich Schlegel's notion of Romantic irony.

I have used the opportunity here to digress on Joyce's early modernist novel because we can posit behind Stephen Dedalus's progression from faith in the Christian God to faith in art a much larger historical subtext. Mircea Eliade made the point in *Cosmos and History. The Myth of the Eternal Return* that men, when faced with a universe that seems to exhibit no obvious purpose, will begin to fear the

---

52 James Joyce, *A Portrait of the Artist as a Young Man*, ed. by Chester Anderson (New York: The Viking Press, 1969), p. 215.
53 *Natural Supernaturalism*, p. 36.
54 *A Portrait of the Artist*, this and the following quotes pp. 171–72.
55 Ibid., p. 203.

'terror of history', as he calls it. The invention of God, Eliade claims, provided early humans with a coping strategy, a compensatory device with which to counter the encroaching anxiety of nothingness. Shifting his attention to our own time, Eliade then observes:

> And in our day, when historical pressure no longer allows any escape, how can man tolerate the catastrophes and horrors of history — from collective deportations and massacres to atomic bombings — if beyond them he can glimpse no sign, no transhistorical meaning; if they are only the blind play of economical, social, or political forces, or, even worse, only the result of the 'liberties' that a minority takes and exercises directly on the stage of universal history? We know how, in the past, humanity has been able to endure the sufferings we have enumerated: they were regarded as a punishment inflicted by God, the syndrome of the decline of the 'age', and so on. And it was possible to accept them precisely because they had a metahistorical meaning, because, for the greater part of mankind, still clinging on to the traditional viewpoint, history did not have, and could not have, value in itself. Every hero repeated the archetypal gesture, every war rehearsed the struggle between good and evil, every fresh social injustice was identified with the sufferings of the Saviour.[56]

'By virtue of this view', Eliade continues, 'tens of millions of men were able, for century after century, to endure great historical pressures without despairing, without committing suicide or falling into that spiritual aridity that always brings with it a relativistic or nihilistic view of history'. History here is perceived as a vacuum, as a phenomenon devoid of meaning in itself. It requires either a belief in God or some similar supernatural power (the gods of the Greeks, pagan demons, a Redeemer), or a sense of cyclicality, or both, in order for us to feel that our life has not been in vain, that it has some purpose that transcends our merely transitory individual existence. Without God, Eliade is telling us, history is destined to turn into the 'nightmare' from which it is impossible to awake, as Stephen Dedalus so aptly tells his interlocutor Mr Deasy in the 'Nestor'-episode of *Ulysses*.

For his part Joyce resolved the struggle to fill the nihilistic void of history by making his 'heroes' Stephen Dedalus and Leopold Bloom into reincarnations of mythological figures, thus implicitly attributing to them a purpose and cyclico-historical gravity that reaches 'beyond that liminary situation' that 'there should be only nothingness', in Eliade's words. Eliade specifically cites Joyce and his contemporary T. S. Eliot as examples of authors whose works are 'saturated with nostalgia for the myth of eternal repetition and, in the last analysis, for the abolition of time'. If that were so, one would have to question whether a text like Joyce's *A Portrait of the Artist of the Young Man* could fairly be characterized as an 'expression of [...] transcendental homelessness', as which Lukács labels the modern novel.[57] And yet, the young girl that Joyce describes has not just been ascribed the function to reenchant the world and restore the fullness of awe that modern man purportedly lost when he abandoned God, but also symbolizes the very beauty and venerability of contemporary life and art itself.

---

56 *Cosmos and History. The Myth of the Eternal Return*, trans. by Willard R. Trask (New York: Harper & Bros., 1959), pp. 151–52, the following quotes pp. 160 and 153.
57 *The Theory of the Novel*, p. 41.

That human beings will always feel compelled to seek something beyond the futility and nothingness of history by, for example, reinvesting a phenomenon like art with a form of supernatural power or significance formerly only attributed to God, or religion in general, this also sums up the thrust of the argument Charles Taylor presents in his magisterial study *A Secular Age*. Formulated at the interstice of genre theory and aesthetics, Lukács's early twentieth-century reflections on the 'transcendental homelessness' of the modern novel, as opposed to the inner security exuded by the world of the traditional epopee, intersect one hundred years later with Taylor's work at the interstice of theology and philosophy. Taylor argues in his grand narrative of the interlaced ventures of the Christian faith and European philosophy that, once deism and, later, atheism have brought about the disenchantment of our world (thus creating that sense of existential homelessness that Lukács identifies as the hallmark of the novel), many of us develop a need to compensate for the resulting loss of spirituality; to achieve this, and in order to replenish our emptied or hollowed-out lives, we invest secular *Ersatz*-phenomena such as art, literature, and music with a quasi-religious solemnity. Accordingly, Taylor observes how

> people listen to concerts with an almost religious intensity. The analogy is not out of place. The performance has taken on something of a rite, and has kept it to this day. There is a sense that something great is being said in this music. This too helped create a kind of middle space, neither explicitly believing, but not atheistic either, a kind of undefined spirituality.[58]

Taylor will later speak of a 'neutral space' between belief and unbelief. We see this process of creating a neutral space between belief and unbelief at work in Joyce's depiction of Stephen Dedalus's maturing artistic spirituality, Stephen's conversion to which is portrayed in the very language we customarily associate with religious fervour. Let me cite the above-mentioned passage in *A Portrait* more fully where we see Stephen for the first time experiencing the exultation that comes with his new paganized *Ersatz*-religion and with the recognition of his new *Ersatz*-angels: 'his cheeks were aflame', we read,

> his body was aglow; his limbs were trembling. On and on and on and on he strode, far out over the sands, singing wildly to the sea, crying to greet the advent of the life that had cried out to him. Her image had passed into his soul for ever and no word had broken the holy silence of his ecstasy. Her eyes had called him and his soul had leaped at the call. To live, to err, to fall, to triumph, to recreate life out of life! A wild angel had appeared to him, the angel of mortal youth and beauty, an envoy from the fair court of life, to throw open before him in an instant of ecstasy the gates of all the ways of error and glory. [...] He closed his eyes in the languour of sleep. His eyelids trembled as if they felt the vast cyclic movement of the earth and her watchers, trembled as if they felt the strange light of some new world. [...] Evening had fallen when he woke and the sand and arid grasses of his bed glowed no longer. He rose slowly and, recalling the rapture of his sleep, sighed at its joy.[59]

---

58 *A Secular Age*, p. 360, the following quote p. 361.
59 *A Portrait of the Artist*, pp. 172–73.

Stephen's pseudo-religious rapture is a prime example of the condition that Taylor postulates as symptomatic of modern Western secularism. Describing how secular tourists tend to venerate the transcendent beauty of 'cathedrals, mosques and temples', Taylor likens their feelings to religious enthusiasm:

> But I don't believe that this is all there is to it, but there is also a certain admiration, wonder, mixed with some nostalgia, at these sites where the contact with the transcendent was/is so much firmer, surer. The existence of this middle space is a reflection of what I called above [...] the cross-pressure felt by the modern buffered identity, on the one hand drawn towards unbelief, while on the other, feeling the solicitations of the spiritual — be they in nature, in art, in some contact with religious faith, or in a sense of God which may break through the membrane.[60]

It is the sense of disenchantment unleashed by European humanist and Enlightenment philosophy — Taylor draws here obviously on the work of the German sociologist Max Weber, but also a later study by the French historian Marcel Gauchet — that led not just to such more immediate counter-movements as Wesleyanism, Pietism and Evangelicalism, but later also, especially in the increasingly scientific late nineteenth century, to various brands of parapsychology, spiritualism and mysticism. Taylor notes:

> Some people who opted for science over religion were later influenced by the sense of spiritual flatness which I mentioned above. They felt both sides of the cross-pressure. Indeed, this malaise seems to grow among educated élites in the late nineteenth century. They turned to various forms of spiritualism, para-scientific researches, para-psychology and the like.

It is precisely this kind of paraspiritual pseudo-mysticism that we saw in operation at the conclusion of Flammarion's late-nineteenth-century sci-fi novel *La Fin du monde*, written in the wake of Grainville's early-nineteenth-century *Le Dernier Homme*. His 'scientific' outlook induced Flammarion to move away from the almighty God of Christian tradition, a God who all-powerfully calls down the Last Judgment on his creation; and yet — as we saw — Flammarion could not fully give himself over to what Taylor sees as a form of materialism that was 'blind and indifferent to our fate'. In short, by opting for a 'transcendental end' rather than a 'natural' one, as Galbreath formulated it, Flammarion was reacting to and writing against the 'terror of history', 'the God-forsakenness of the world' and 'sense of malaise at the disenchanted world' that Eliade, Lukács and Taylor all diagnose as operative in post-religious thought. Taylor in his own words:

> I am not just referring to the way many people reacted against Deism, and even more against humanism, out of a strong sense of God, or the transcendent; the kind of reaction we see among Wesleyans, Pietists, later among Evangelicals. I am thinking much more of a wide sense of malaise at the disenchanted world, a sense of it as flat, empty, a multiform search for something within, or beyond it, which could compensate for the meaning lost with transcendence; and this not only as a feature of that time, but as one which continues into ours.[61]

60 *A Secular Age*, p. 360, the following passages pp. 364 and 363.
61 *A Secular Age*, p. 302.

Only by retaining a sense of transhistorical consequence and import, most commonly associated with religious faith of one form or another, Eliade seconds, those 'tens of millions of men were able to endure [...] without despairing, without committing suicide or falling into that spiritual aridity that always brings with it a relativistic or nihilistic view of history'.[62]

But what if one believes in a Christian God, this ostensible safety net against despair, and commits suicide nonetheless? What does it tell us that two practicing Catholics, Grainville in February 1805 in France and Sonnenberg in November 1805 in Germany, commit suicide expressly, it seems, against all principles of their creed? Had they lost their spiritual anchor, had they fallen into a state of 'spiritual aridity' or nihilistic relativism, as Eliade put it? Or had their formerly enchanted and God-fearing world become too disenchanted and God-denying, as Taylor might formulate it, for them to feel able to continue with their lives? Sonnenberg, we saw in Chapter One, had begun to doubt Christ's divinity, but he did not doubt God for one moment, even if he had accepted and taken to heart Kant's theoretical reasoning that God's existence could not be proven. From early 1804 onwards, Sonnenberg became increasingly depressed, one reflection of which was his debating in his mind what the future might hold after death. We recall how, in March 1804, he noted: 'But what will we be? — Perhaps we will wander around in flowers, in the grass, in the dust. But whether with consciousness of our being; who can judge until the catastrophe of our aging universe closes in on us?' These ruminations about death, the world and God go on for pages. Sonnenberg is digging himself ever deeper into a depression, it seems, for which, ultimately, suicide is the one resolution that would accelerate his becoming one with God. It is in this vein also, as we saw in Chapter One, that he recorded:

> Death must be great and sublime and wonderful for any being that trusts in the presence of God, that in his presence experiences the peace of life, and can set his hope in him. Love must be the purpose of Creation, and the majority of beings must be happy, else God should not have created; for there would be more misery than happiness. [...] I am frightfully scared of death, but I become calmer when I connect the thought of death to the highest of all thoughts, God.[63]

Grainville had fallen into a similar depression certainly during and probably also long before the writing of *Le Dernier Homme*; early biographical accounts, such as the one given by the author of the 1817 entry in the *Biographie universelle*, provide only scant detail: 'Having passed through every stage of misfortune, when writing his book no longer sustained his spirit,' we read,

> he finally fell into a melancholy sickness followed by a delirious fever. But since [...] in other respects he was not lacking in religious and domestic solace, it is very likely that it was not deliberate, but rather in a feverish fit that, on 1 February 1805 at two o'clock in the morning, engulfed by a most impetuous wind and a sharp chill, he threw himself into the Somme canal that passed close to his home and perished there.

---

62 *Cosmos and History*, p. 152.
63 *Donatoa* II.2, p. 400.

[Ayant passé par tous les degrés du malheur, lorsque l'activité de son esprit ne fut plus soutenue par la composition de son livre, il tomba dans une maladie mélancholique, qui fut suivie d'une fièvre avec délire. Mais [...] que d'ailleurs les consolations religieuses et domestiques ne lui manquaient pas[,] il est très vraisemblable que ce ne fut point volontairement, mais dans un de ses accès, que le 1er février 1805, à deux heures du matin, par le vent le plus impétueux, et le froid le plus vif, il se précipita dans le canal de la Somme, qui baignait sa maison, et y périt.][64]

Beyond this, unfortunately, we have no account of the last years of his life, no personal documents that date later than his 1794 marriage certificate, and no close acquaintance or biographer — like Sonnenberg's friend Gruber — who was able to shed light on his last months, weeks or days. In short, our biographical knowledge of Grainville is much more circumstantial than that of Sonnenberg, and hence our interpretation of his intentions must remain to a larger degree conjectural. This caveat notwithstanding, let us retrace what little we know of Grainville's life in order not just further to illuminate his suicide, but also the background to *Le Dernier Homme*, as well as to look into why the author might have given his work its specific shape.[65]

A Constitutional Priest's World in Turmoil

Jean-Baptiste François Xavier Cousin de Grainville was born 3 April 1746; the scholar Ross P. Grippen notes tersely but symptomatically: 'On the subject of his family we know nothing but that it was "an honourable family of the cloth"'.[66] One sister married a brother of the writer Bernard de Saint-Pierre (who later helped to get *Le Dernier Homme* published following the author's death); and one elder brother became bishop of Cahors in 1802 (which he remained until 1828). Grainville was trained at various institutions for a religious career, attending the Jesuit Collège Louis-le-Grand (which half a century earlier Voltaire had attended from the age of ten to seventeen) and the Séminaire de Saint-Sulpice, both in Paris, where he excelled at his studies. Already at the young age of sixteen, his editor Nodier later claimed, he conceived a plan to write an epic poem on the end of the world; but as the contributor of Grainville's entry to the *Biographie universelle, ancienne et moderne* of 1817 cautions, 'if the author really conceived his work at this age, as his editor suggests, then it can hardly have been more than a mere aperçu' ('Si l'auteur le conçut à seize ans, comme l'avance son éditeur, il n'en eut

---

64 Entry on 'Grainville', in *Biographie Universelle ancien et moderne*, vol. 18 (GO–GU) (Paris: L. G. Michaud, 1817), pp. 271–74 (p. 272). The source of this information, we are told in a footnote, were two citizens of Amiens, a Mr L. Jourdain and Mr Natalis La Morlière.

65 The main sources for the following biographical sketch were: Ross P. Grippen, *Jean Baptiste Cousin de Grainville: Le Dernier Homme. Edition présentée et commentée*, unpublished PhD dissertation University of Connecticut, 1979, whose work also contains a reprint in French of *Le Dernier Homme* and copies of some official documents from Le Havre, where Grainville was born; the entry on 'Grainville', in *Biographie universelle, ancienne et moderne*, pp. 271–74; Anne Kupiec's 'Postface' in her edition of *Le Dernier Homme*; and Paul Alkon's Grainville chapter in *Origins of Futuristic Fiction*.

66 *Jean Baptiste Cousin de Grainville*, p. 3.

probablement alors que l'aperçu').[67] At age twenty-six, Grainville won the prize for eloquence of the Academy of Besançon for an essay on what he argues was the 'cold' ('froid') and 'harmful ('pernicieuse') influence that philosophy has had in our century'.[68] His treatise illustrates as much his intellectual brilliance as his conservative disposition, as well as confirming his intimate knowledge not just of the discourses of contemporary (mostly) French philosophy and literature, but also of the natural sciences. What else we know about the years between 1762 and 1789 is that, after completing his theological studies, Grainville initially began his career as a priest, becoming vicar of the parish Saint-André-des-Arts in the heart of Paris, only at some point to turn away from his calling to become a playwright; it seems that in the lead-up to the French Revolution he produced a play entitled *Le Jugement de Paris* (of which no copy has survived) the staging of which at the Comédie Française, however, had to be postponed due to the outbreak of the Revolution.[69] Thus we find Grainville in the eye of the storm, and of European history in the making, when on 14 July 1789 the Paris citizenry storm the Bastille.

By little more than one year later, in October 1790, Grainville has returned to the priesthood. In January 1791 he pledges his Oath to the Civil Constitution of the Clergy,[70] whereupon in June 1791 he is elected priest of the parish Saint-Leu in Amiens in the Somme department; situated seventy-five miles north of Paris, the Saint-Leu parish at that time had some 8,000 parishioners. By taking the Oath he has become a constitutional priest (I will say more about this later), and by being elected curate of his church in June 1791 he has by default also taken on the secular function of a civil servant and town administrator, by and large indicating his compliance with the insurrectionist reorganization of Church and State and demonstrating his disregard for the Pope's 'Charitas' declaration of 13 April 1791, in which the Roman Pontiff had summoned Catholic priests to reject the Civil Constitution. (The historian Timothy Hackett notes how 'a clergyman's refusal to embrace the Constitution was viewed as evidence that he was an enemy and potential conspirator against the Revolution'.)[71] Perhaps preemptively to deflate

---

67 *Biographie universelle*, p. 272.

68 Abbé de Grainville, *Discours qui a remporté le prix d'éloquence, d l'Académie de Besançon, en l'année 1772, sur ce sujet: Quelle a été l'Influence de la Philosophie sur ce Siècle?* (Paris: Humblot, 1772). 'Froid' appears on pages 17 and 23, 'pernicieuse' appears on p. 21.

69 Anne Kupiec suggests in a footnote to her biographical survey (*Le Dernier Homme*, p. 214) that, as regards some of Grainville's early non-surviving work, there has been some confusion with Jean-Baptiste Christophe Grainville, who in turn is often mistakenly cited as the author of *Le Dernier Homme* (as we saw above with reference to Béatrice Didier's *Le XVIIIe siècle*).

70 How many Catholic French priests took this oath? John McManners formulates it thus: 'Out of 160 bishops, seven became jurors, only four being diocesans. Three of these were notorious for scepticism and easy living (Talleyrand, Loménie de Brienne and Jarente), and one, Lafont de Savine, Bishop of Viviers, was well-known for his enthusiastic eccentricities. Large numbers of lower clergy took the oath and large numbers refused it; amid a morass of incomplete and misleading statistics, the old-fashioned tug of war between clerical and anti-clerical historians never succeeded in hauling the totals further than a little way over the half-way line, on one side or another'; *The French Revolution and the Church* (Westport, CT: Greenwood Press, 1969), p. 48.

71 'The French Revolution and Religion to 1794' (Cambridge: Cambridge University Press, 2008, *Cambridge Histories Online*), pp. 536–55 (p. 548).

possible doubts about his support for the Revolution, Grainville co-founded the local branch of the 'Society of the Friends of the Constitution' ('Société des amis de la Constitution') in Amiens.[72] He also gives a 'Funeral Oration' to his parishioners on 30 August 1792 in which the 'citizen priest'[73] shows his resolve to wed religion and patriotism by paying tribute to the lives of those revolutionaries killed on 10 August when the Tuileries Palace was stormed, the Swiss Guards were massacred and the King thrown into prison. Thus far he has positioned himself cautiously on the side of the revolutionary movement, but without renouncing his Christian faith. In one vital regard, however, he now miscalculates the situation (at least according to the scholar Ross Grippen): while in his 'Funeral Oration' he sings the praise of the heroic citizens who had been killed in action and while he denounces Louis XVI for his tyranny and cruelty, he asks nonetheless that mercy be granted and the King's life be spared; the crucial passage reads:

> The people will reign. The blessings have waited for this moment to descend from heaven to earth. Commerce will acquire wings, industry will give birth to prodigious feats. All lands will be fertile, peoples will reunite to form a great federation, and wherever human beings venture they will find a brother and abundance. [...] What will be the fortune of the assassin of our Nation? Charles the First who was beheaded was less culpable than Louis XVI: will his execution be authorized by the National Convention? The terrible image of that troubles me. So, where does that pity for the murderer of my brothers stem from? Louis XVI! — look at the kind of people you have so abused! You have premeditated their ruin in such cold blood; you have made their blood flow in great torrents; and yet they still hesitate to condemn you, and are willing to shed tears over your destiny. [...] For us, *citoyens*, if you believe me, as soon as our enemies have been chased from our borders, you can drive this culprit out of our kingdom by the shortest possible route.

> [... le peuple va régner. Le bonheur attend ce moment pour descendre du ciel sur la terre. Le commerce aura des ailes; l'industrie enfantera des prodiges. Toutes les terres seront fertiles; les peuples se réuniront dans une fédération générale; et quelque part où les hommes porteront leurs pas, ils y trouveront un frère et l'abondance. [...] Quel sera le sort de l'assassin de la Nation? Charles Ier qui tomba sous la hache du bourreau fut moins coupable que Louis XVI: son supplice sera-t-il prononcé par la Convention Nationale? ... à cette image terrible, je sens que je me trouble. Eh! d'où me vient cette pitié pour le meurtrier de mes frères? Louis XVI! voyez de quel peuple vous avez abusé! Vous avez médité sa perte de sang-froid; vous avez fait couler son sang à grands flots; et il hésite encore à vous condamner, et il est prêt à verser des larmes sur votre sort. [...] Pour nous, citoyens, si vous m'en croyez, aussitôt que les ennemis seront chassés des frontières, vous conduirez, par le plus court chemin, ce grand coupable hors du royaume.][74]

In the midst of the debates surrounding the future of Louis XVI, now dubbed 'Citoyen Louis Capet', the Declaration of the French Republic on 22 September

---

72 See also Kupiec, 'Postface', *Le Dernier Homme*, p. 214.
73 For more on this topic see Hackett, 'The French Revolution and Religion to 1794'.
74 'Oraison Funèbre', in *Le Dernier Homme*, ed. Kupiec, pp. 189–204 (p. 202).

1792, and the outbreak of the revolutionary wars between France and her rival continental powers, Austria and Prussia in particular, to suggest sparing the King's life is asking one leniency too many and, for the more extreme wing of the Revolution, tantamount to treason. Whether his 'Funeral Oration' is indeed the reason for his fall from grace is less clear than the established fact that, by the beginning of the hot phase of the French Revolution, called the Reign of Terror, which lasted from 5 September 1793 to 28 July 1794, Grainville finds himself jailed in the Bicêtre prison of Amiens. Here, in September 1793, he is interrogated by a former acquaintance of his, André Dumont, the regicide *Montagnard* parlamentarian who is now, at this very moment, serving as the constitutional official for the Amiens region.[75] The most recent decree by the Convention had required that all Catholic priests demonstrate their allegiance to the Revolution not just by abjuring their Catholic faith but also, as an outward token of their renunciation, entering into a state of marriage. John McManners notes in *The French Revolution and the Church* that 'the de-Christianizers [...] seemed to have accepted this evidence as conclusive'. How many priests married?, he asks: 'We can only guess. [Abbé] Grégoire [the elected constitutional bishop of Blois], who would wish to limit the dimensions of what he regarded as a scandal, estimated that there were two thousand'.[76] Grainville and his immediate superior, bishop Desbois of Amiens, as well as some sixty further priests in the Amiens region, initially resist. In January 1794, Grainville is transferred to Abbeville where Dumont puts the choice to him either to marry or to face the guillotine. Faced with this stark choice, Grainville opts for life and agrees, at age 48, to marry his 32-year old orphaned cousin Jeanne Catherine Reynaud. Of course, Grainville is just one among thousands of such cases. The *Oxford History of the French Revolution* historian William Doyle notes that, by Spring 1794, of the estimated 130,000 French priests 'perhaps 20,000 [...] had been bullied into giving up their status, and 6,000 had given their renunciation the ultimate confirmation by marrying'.[77] 25,000–40,000 priests had emigrated, thereby avoiding being forced to abjure.[78] John McManners adds to this the observation that 'about two thousand [priests] were executed, perhaps as many as five thousand'; 'some of the clergy, orthodox and constitutional, married to save their lives. [...] better still, they might manage to find a partner who would agree to allow the marriage to remain unconsummated'.[79] This is in all likelihood the situation that obtained in the Grainville household.

These events all relate to what is now called the 'Dechristianization of France', essentially a process put in motion to rid France of Catholicism, a process that reached its climax in October 1793. A number of things are worth observing at this point: first, the leaders of the French Revolution were fundamentally split

---

75 See Kupiec, 'Postface', *Le Dernier Homme*, p. 215.
76 *The French Revolution and the Church*, pp. 111–12 and 115.
77 *The Oxford History of the French Revolution* (Oxford: Clarendon Press, 1989), p. 262. Citing estimates by Michel Vovelle, Emmet Kennedy gives the number as 6500; see his *A Cultural History of the French Revolution* (New Haven and London: Yale University Press, 1989), p. 341.
78 This number from Kennedy, *A Cultural History of the French Revolution*, p. 339.
79 *The French Revolution and the Church*, pp. 106 and 112.

as regards their views and policies toward religion. For most, dechristianization was not meant to imply the abolition of religion altogether.[80] While some, and above all the Hébertist faction around Jacques Hébert, the editor of the influential sans-culotte newspaper *Le Père Duchesne*, were staunch atheists and wanted to see religion wholly eradicated, others, including the leader of the Jacobin Montagnards himself, Maximilien Robespierre, were deistic in orientation and sought merely to replace the Christian denominations by a more neutral creed based on reason and natural religion, thus creating a 'civic religion'[81] in the spirit of Jean-Jacques Rousseau that retained a belief in God and immortality, but was not connected with any specific form of institutionalized religion. Thus during the years 1793 and 1794, in which dechristianization reached its peak, Paris and France saw the celebration and adulation of two competing deities. First, the Hébertists organised the so-called Festival of Reason, the *Fête de la Raison*, that was celebrated all across France on 10 November 1793 in the now renamed Temples of Reason, that is former Catholic churches and cathedrals stripped of all 'papal mummery'.[82] In the grandest of these festivities, in the now de-catholicized Notre-Dame Cathedral in Paris, an altar to reason substituted for the Christian altar and praise was sung to liberty and the goddess of reason, acted by a 'beautiful woman'.[83] On 23 November 1793 Robespierre lashed out against the Hébertists' overly radical practice of dechristianization in the National Convention and decried their atheism as aristocratic.[84] The Hébertist leaders Jacques Hébert, Antoine-François Momoro (the originator of the French republican creed 'liberté, égalité, fraternité'), Charles Philippe Ronsin and François-Nicolas Vincent were guillotined on 24 March 1794, effectively ending the Cult of Reason. This was soon to be replaced by the more moderate Cult of the Supreme Being, the *Culte de l'Être suprême*, celebrated for the first time on 8 June 1794. Established by Robespierre and organized by the classicist painter Jacques-Louis David (who is remembered in particular for his 1793 painting of the dying Marat), the Festival of the Supreme Being took place around an artificial mountain erected on the Champ de Mars (which we today associate with the Eiffel Tower, erected there for the 1889 Paris World's Fair to commemorate the centenary of the French Revolution);[85] the mountain was surmounted by an 'Altar of the Nation' and a 'Tree of Liberty' (nicely to be seen on Pierre-Antoine

---

80 Fritz Mauthner makes this point very clearly in his four-volume history of atheism, *Der Atheismus und seine Geschichte im Abendlande*, vol. 3, p. 114.

81 See Kennedy, *A Cultural History of the French Revolution*, p. 330.

82 Cited from a letter of the representative of the Gard and Lozère district to the Committee for Public Safety; see <http://revolution.fr.free.fr/chronologie_generale_1793.htm>, accessed 12 February 2013.

83 See Kennedy, *A Cultural History of the French Revolution*, p. 343.

84 Ibid., p. 344.

85 The Champs de Mars is cited in the Wikipedia entry 'Cult of the Supreme Being' (<https://en.wikipedia.org/wiki/Cult_of_the_Supreme_Being>, accessed 10 November 2016); in his book *A Cultural History of the French Revolution*, Emmet Kennedy cites the then National Gardens, today the Tuileries, as the site of this festival. However, the building seen on Demachy's painting of 1794 is clearly the École Militaire building, located at the south-east end of the Champ de Mars; the buildings were completed in the 1770s.

Demachy's contemporary painting *The Festival of the Supreme Being / Fête de l'Etre suprême* of 1794, held by the Carnavalet Museum in Paris and easily accessible on Wikimedia Commons).

The second point to note, which has a particular bearing on Grainville's biography, is the fact that by the end of the dechristianization of France the Catholic Church had effectively been stripped both of its spiritual authority and its secular wealth. And along with it Catholic priests had lost their livelihood — the newly secularized state was no longer willing or indeed financially able to pay clerics' salaries. And Catholic churches remained shut even after the end of the Reign of Terror and after the Jacobins' demise in 1794. Until the French Revolution and its policy of dechristianization, the Catholic Church had been the largest landowner in the country and freed from paying taxes, but now all its lands had been confiscated and secularized by the French state (in part of course in order to finance the continental wars the Revolution had unleashed). While throughout the eighteenth century the *philosophes* had attacked the Catholic Church for its immense wealth and the income it derived from the collection of tithes, as also for its material and ideological support of the King and the *ancien régime*, the Church had also been more or less the sole provider in France both of primary and secondary education and of hospitals. As historians like John McManners and Timothy Hackett have noted, the Church itself was (initially at least) divided about the merits of the Revolution; I cite once more from McManners's *The French Revolution and the Church*:

> There were clergy in France — and their numbers should not be underestimated — who were dedicated to the Revolution, equating the voice of God with the pronouncements of the representatives of the nation, setting the Constitution alongside the Bible as the token of a new order which Providence itself had conspired to bring to pass. There were many more who, without being so fanatical, were determined on reform, and were willing to take the oath to the new order without dwelling too much on its unsatisfactory stipulations in the matter of religion. After all, the King had swallowed everything: it was 'the Constitution accepted by the King'. It was assumed that the Pope would yield; he had had time to be fully informed, and no word of condemnation had been published from Rome.[86]

Thus the split, which soon escalated into a full-fledged schism, of the Catholic clergy into abjuring (constitutional) and non-abjuring (refractory) priests is reflective of a deeper divide among Catholic clerics at that time. But the pace of change was fast and perplexing: by 1794 even abjuring priests like Grainville had, despite their previous support for the revolutionary regime, been forced out of their positions. Doyle writes:

> During its last, fleeting endorsement of Jacobinism, on 18 September 1794, the Convention had carried the drift of the Revolution since 1790 to a logical conclusion when it finally renounced the constitutional Church. The Republic, it decreed, would no longer pay the cost or wages of any cult — not that it had been paying them in practice for a considerable time already. It meant the end of state recognition for the Supreme Being, a cult too closely identified with

---

86 *The French Revolution and the Church*, p. 51.

Robespierre. But above all it marked the abandonment of the Revolution's own creation, the constitutional Church. For the first time ever in France, Church and State were now formally separated.[87]

Whereas constitutional priests like Grainville were at least able to remain in France, refractory priests had either been forced underground, fled into exile or given up their priesthood. From October 1793 on, a new law decreed that any priest, constitutional or refractory, denounced for lack of *civisme* by six citizens would be subjected to deportation, and any priest previously sentenced to deportation but still found in France should be executed. Nonetheless, after the Reign of Terror attitudes towards religion and the Constitutional Catholic Church relaxed somewhat. In February 1795 the freedom of all cults to worship as they liked was proclaimed, which included Catholics. Doyle notes that, from this point on, 'religion was defined as a private affair, [although] local authorities were forbidden to lend it any recognition or support', bringing about 'a massive, swelling revival of everyday religious practice in France'.[88] So despite the continuing anti-clericalism, some bishops and clergy of the Constitutional Catholic Church were able to stay in office until Napoleon's Concordat with the Vatican in 1801. It seems that Grainville's church L'église de Saint-Leu in Amiens, too, was able to reopen as a Catholic church in 1796, and Grainville was encouraged to return to his post as constitutional priest by the constitutional bishop Desbois, who himself remained imprisoned because he continued to refuse to marry.[89] We don't know any biographical details of these years between 1796 and 1801, the latter being the year in which Bonaparte and the Pope signed the Concordat, reestablishing the Catholic Church in France; what we do know relates to the general history of the Catholic Church in France during this period. We know for instance that, by around 1795, 'out of 28,000 jurors, some 22,000 had either resigned or abdicated; many others had married, died, or retracted their oaths and decamped to the refractory side', as well as that 'the bishops held two National Councils in 1797 and 1801 to coordinate decisions about liturgy and politics, rid their church of married priests, and work towards filling [vacant] parishes and bishoprics'.[90] At the latest by 1802, when the Concordat came into effect, formerly ordained but now apostate priests like Grainville who had sworn the Constitutional Oath and who had married, even if under duress, found themselves disqualified from reentering the service of the reestablished Catholic Church in France, whose posts were filled with the refractory clergy who had remained faithful to the Roman Pontiff. The constitutionals thus (once more) lost their living: deprived of a living first by the Republican state authorities, who had outlawed even the Constitutional Catholic Church in 1794, now it was their own reinstated Catholic brethren who turned them away. Indeed, Grainville's own family may serve as an illustration of what Doyle has called French Catholicism's

---

87 *The Oxford History of the French Revolution*, pp. 287–88.
88 Ibid., pp. 288 and 385.
89 Kupiec, 'Postface', *Le Dernier Homme*, p. 216.
90 Suzanne Desan, 'The French Revolution and Religion, 1795–1815', *Cambridge Histories Online* (Cambridge: Cambridge University Press, 2008), pp. 556–74, 560 and 561.

'tragic schism',[91] for Grainville's brother Guillaume-Balthazar Cousin de Grainville had opted for the alternative, choosing in contrast to his brother not to pledge the oath to the Civil Constitution. Born 27 March 1745, and thus one year the elder, Guillaume-Balthazar had studied theology at the Sorbonne and had advanced to the position of Vicar General of Montpellier and chancellor of the town's university by the time the Revolution broke out; forced to give up these posts, he went into hiding until 1800 rather than emigrate. Following the Concordat the newly appointed archbishop of Rouen, Étienne Hubert de Cambacérès, appointed him Vicar General of Rouen in April 1802, shortly after which Napoleon appointed him bishop of Cahors in July 1802, a position he retained until his death in 1828.

Clearly, whereas Jean-Baptiste had, by 1802, become stuck between a rock (the newly established 'official' Roman Catholic Church) and a hard place (the French State under Napoleon which had now reined in the revolutionary excess and was abandoning the Constitutional Church), his brother had made the more felicitous and expedient decision. Even the pupils Jean-Baptiste Grainville had been teaching for some years to sustain a living began to stay away now that their education had once again come under the purview of the reinstated Catholic Church — to which Grainville of course no longer belonged. His death certificate, issued in Amiens and reproduced by Ross Grippen in the appendix to his dissertation, states unequivocally 'exprêtre et instituteur', *ex-priest* and teacher. Finding himself deprived of income and reduced to poverty, he took up the drafting of his epic, the prose version of which he produced within six months during 1804. The future publisher of *Le Dernier Homme*, Déterville, offered him 800 francs for the manuscript — we must assume that he thought he would receive a verse epic, but Grainville of course never got that far. Aged 58, with no prospects for the future, the writing of his work probably having overtaxed him physically no less than intellectually, he commited suicide on 1 February 1805 — I cited the circumstances of his death, as much (or as little) as we know them, earlier in this chapter.

Religiously Squaring the Secular Circle, continued

If literary scholarship of the past two hundred years and literary theory of the past one hundred has taught us anything, it is that textual meaning is never fully fathomable, retrievable, or ascribable, and that a text's interpretation as well as its value or relevance to successive generations of readers are by necessity subject to change over time. Hans-Georg Gadamer, one of the key German progenitors of twentieth-century philosophical hermeneutics, argues this very decidedly; he writes:

> The reality of the work of art and its significance are not to be limited to the original historical horizon in which the beholder is truly contemporaneous with the creator of the work of art. Engrained in the work of art, and an integral dimension of our experience of it, is a presence all its own and the fact that it reflects its historical origins only in a very limited way; the work of art

---

91 *The Oxford History of the French Revolution*, p. 397.

is an expression of a truth that by no means coincides with the intention of its originator.[92]

Grainville's *Le Dernier Homme* is a particularly instructive case in point. As I related earlier, many recent critics have cited Grainville's narrative as an early proto-text in the development of the modern genre of science fiction; due to its obvious futuristic qualities, it has been subsumed — maybe unfairly, but certainly understandably — under a generic rubric, science fiction, that only came into being long after the work itself was published. Alkon rightly observes, however, that 'tales of the future are not necessarily science fiction',[93] and for this reason he references *Le Dernier Homme* more cautiously as an example of 'futuristic fiction'. But this term too is a modern retroactive coinage. While either designation might be considered anachronistic, they nonetheless have the benefit not just of concentrating our attention on what made the text unique in its own time — providing a tale of humanity in the lead-up to the Last Judgment in an unspecified future — but more importantly perhaps of rendering the text more interesting for a late twentieth- and early twenty-first-century audience. To put it bluntly: if *Le Dernier Homme* had not been rediscovered as a proto-text of science fiction and as a likely precursor to one of science fiction's foundational futuristic novels, Mary Shelley's *The Last Man* of 1826, it would probably never have been rediscovered at all. Is not Franz von Sonnenberg's *Donatoa* the best proof? Equally apocalyptic and equally futuristic in character, spinning another version of the tale of humanity on the brink of Armageddon, it has been thoroughly forgotten. But, and this is the crucial point, it has been 'disremembered' not just because it is clearly identifiable as a religious apocalypse (after all, Grainville's *Le Dernier Homme* is precisely that as well), but primarily, it seems, because it was written as a verse epic, or what was then called an epopee. And because it was written in verse epic form, there was no way it could be confused with a prose novel, as happened with Grainville's prose draft of his planned verse epic. Nor could it be confused with modern science fiction, which tends to be premised on a secular content. By and large, most historians of the genre agree that religious depictions of the apocalypse, as futuristic as they may be, are to be excluded from the category of science fiction; in his *Encyclopédie de l'utopie, des voyages extraordinaires et de la science fiction*, Pierre Versins makes this quite explicit in his entry for 'Apocalypse', where he writes:

> Apocalypses: Neither they nor religious texts with a utopian bent, whatever their creed, are studied here. Indeed, religious belief is in essence irrational and belongs to a different kind of research than that undertaken here (see the entry for Fin du Monde/The End of the World).
>
> [Apocalypses: Nous ne les étudions pas, non plus que les textes religieux à tendances utopiques, à quelque foi qu'ils appartiennent. En effet, la croyance est d'essence irrationelle et appartient à une autre mode d'investigation que celui qui nous anime ici (voir Fin du Monde).][94]

---

92 'Ästhetik und Hermeneutik', in *Kleine Schriften II* (Tübingen: Mohr, 1979), pp. 1–8 (p. 1).
93 *Origins of Futuristic Fiction*, p. 12.
94 *Encyclopédie de l'utopie, des voyages extraordinaires et de la science fiction*, p. 56.

The irony of course is not just that Versins's entry 'The End of the World' nonetheless lists Grainville's religious apocalypse as a key text of science fiction, but also that his encyclopedia provides a separate independent entry for *Le Dernier Homme*. Must we conclude with Versins, then, that Grainville's text is *not* to be considered a religious text after all? Or is the issue of genre attribution more difficult than meets the eye?

Against the backdrop of Versins's definition — which, incidentally, I fully concur with — it seems quite remarkable just how often we find Grainville's *Le Dernier Homme* subsumed under the rubric of science fiction, its obvious religious character and features notwithstanding. I cited some such instances earlier in this chapter, among them the passage by I. F. Clarke where he labels *Le Dernier Homme* as a 'seminal science fiction work'. Clarke's phrasing is also taken up in the Wikipedia entry for Grainville's *Le Dernier Homme*, the beginning of which reads:

> *Le Dernier Homme* (English: *The Last Man*) is a French science fantasy novel [*sic!*] in the form of a prose poem. Written by Jean-Baptiste Cousin de Grainville and published in 1805, it was the first story of modern speculative fiction to depict the end of the world. Considered a seminal early work of science fantasy, specifically of the dying earth subgenre, it has been described by Gary K. Wolfe as 'A crucial document in the early history [...] of what became science fiction'. (Accessed 29 February 2012.)

The conclusion I have been moving towards is *not*, however, that this is all wrong, quite to the contrary. The Wikipedia entry by and large merely reflects today's consensus about this work. Put differently, regardless of the historical veracity of or flaws in this appraisal, this assessment is the outcome of the work's reception history in Gadamer's sense. But it is also, as I have likewise detailed, based on a crucial misreading and misclassification of the work as a novel. The upshot of this skewed genre designation — that is, reading *Le Dernier Homme* as a prose fiction in the prehistory of science fiction — is the extraordinary differential that arises between current and historical assessments of the work's merits.

To illustrate the initial response to *Le Dernier Homme* in the early nineteenth-century, and the way Grainville's contemporaries tried to make sense of this text, let us turn to the most extensive contemporaneous appraisal that I have been able to identify, namely an anonymous German critic's five-page review of the work's two German translations published in 1807 and 1811. The two-part review appeared in two consecutive December 1813 issues of the *Allgemeine Literatur-Zeitung*, one of the most influential German-language literary gazettes of that period. Indeed, it is through this reviewer's mention of Sonnenberg's *Donatoa* in his review of the French text, and his detailed comparison of the two works, that Sonnenberg's apocalyptic verse epic first came to my attention — I had not heard of him or his work before. The first part of the review is dedicated to providing a plot summary, as was customary at the time; in the second the reviewer proceeds to outline his opinion. He begins by focussing on three aspects of the work: its biographical background and the influence of the French Revolution; the author's national characteristics (a popular subject throughout the nineteenth century); and the work's genre. The reviewer specifically examines whether *Le Dernier Homme* can be considered a successful verse epic (poem/epopee) and commends the German publisher's decision not to retain the subtitle 'A Romantic Composition' ('Eine romantische Dichtung') in the second edition, a subtitle that was of course absent in the French original. We read:

> This work exudes a such peculiar and daring spirit that the impression is inevitable that the inspiration for it cannot derive from the native soil of French literature; it would be difficult to name a French poet with a comparable spirit, perhaps save Chateaubriand, by whom though this writer cannot have been influenced. [...] This, as well as perhaps the author's personal circumstances which are unknown to us, explains the unusual ebb and flow, the energy with which the images of death and destruction are recorded, these bleak melancholic shadows, which, wholly foreign to his nation, take up a large part of his canvas. His depictions — the most imposing aspect of his work — are mostly of a high oriental style, brimming with sensual intensity. [...] Even if the poem's meter lacks in external poesy, and at times the epical timbre finds itself reduced to a mere prose account, its expression — supported by a fitting prosody — nonetheless aspires to full poetic gravity, and seems even to have benefitted from its prose shape. In effect, however, this recommendation does not really say much. How much more would it require in order to bring this poem to perfection, especially if we regard it as an epopee. Of course, it is in the nature of its material that we must regard it as such; the indistinct appellation *a romantic composition*, which graced the first edition's title page, was clearly inappropriate and hence was rightly removed in the second edition.

> [Es herrscht in dem Werke des Vfs. ein so eigenthümlicher und grösstentheils kühner Geist, dass man leicht fühlt, die Anregung sey ihm nicht vom Boden seiner vaterländischen Literatur gekommen, auch möchte es schwer halten, einen Dichter seiner Nation von ähnlichem Geiste aufzufinden, *Chateaubriand*, nach dem sich der Vf. jedoch nicht bilden konnte, etwa ausgenommen. [...] Hieraus, und vielleicht aus individuellen uns unbekannten Verhältnissen des Dichters, während und nach der Revolution, erklärt sich dieser eigenthümliche Schwung, diese Energie, womit er die Bilder des Todes und der Zerstörung auffaßt, diese düstern melancholischen Schatten, die, dem Geiste seiner Nation fremd, auf einem grossen Theil seines Gemäldes ruhen. Seine Schilderungen — die glänzendste Seite seines Werks — sind meistens im hohen orientalischen Stil, voll sinnlichen Reichthums. [...] Obgleich das Gedicht der äussern Poesie des Sylbenmaaßes entbehrt, und der epische Ton sich deshalb oft zum Tone der Erzählung herabläßt, so erhebt doch der Ausdruck, von einem angemessenen prosaischen Numerus unterstützt, zum Theil mit voller poetischer Kraft, und scheint mitunter durch die Prosa sogar gewonnen zu haben. Mit diesem Lobe ist indes, genau genommen, noch nicht viel gesagt. Wie weit mehr würde erfodert, um das Gedicht, zumal als Epopee betrachtet, gelungen zu nennen. Es liegt zum Theil in der Natur des Stoffs, dass man es aus diesem Gesichtspunkte betrachten muss; die unbestimmte Benennung *romantische Dichtung*, welche das erste Titelblatt führte, war offenbar unpassend und ist mit Recht auf dem spätern unterdrückt worden.][95]

---

95 Anon., review of *Der letzte Mensch. Eine romantische Dichtung* and *Omegar, der letzte Mensch. Eine Dichtung. Allgemeine Literatur-Zeitung* (December 1813), issue 292, columns 657–62 and issue 293,

It is towards the end of his review that the anonymous reviewer moves to assess the religious qualities of the work, highlighting some of its perceived compositional strengths and weaknesses. In this section he observes:

> From the outset the fate of earth, as that of the aging population, seem inescapable. [...] The machinery is flawed. God acts neither consistently nor befitting the character of the most perfect Being. The droll speeches expose Death's allegorical provenance. The spirits of Christian mythology, angels and devils, the latter especially, appear only to provide spectators. Those who are most active are Adam and the peculiar Spirit of the Earth, who is entirely a product of the author's imagination, and who appears rather out of place among the other actors in the story.
>
> [Von Anfang herein erscheint das Loos der Erde, wie das Schicksal der Alten, unabwendbar. [...] Die Maschinerie ist unvollkommen. Gott handelt nicht auf das consequenteste, und dem Charakter des vollkommensten Wesens gemäß; der Tod verräth durch witzige Reden seine allegorische Abkunft. Die Geister der christlichen Mythologie, Engel und Teufel, erscheinen, zumal die letztern, nur, um Zuschauer abzugeben. Am thätigsten beweisen sich Adam und der sonderbare Erdgeist, der ganz das Erzeugniss des Dichters ist und unter den übrigen wirkenden Personen gar fremd erscheint.]

As in Sonnenberg's case, a key reference point in establishing an epic's faults and fortes is the scrutiny of the Christian machinery and its narrative function and internal (in)consistency. Particularly illuminating for our purposes is the section in which the reviewer sets out expressly to compare Sonnenberg's German and Grainville's French epic; he comes to what may strike some readers today as rather surprising conclusions — conclusions that reveal much about the literary (genre) system of the time. 'A German poet', he tells his reader,

> has recently used the same material in an epopee, not with unqualified approval; nonetheless, the French poet was at a disadvantage against the German, by virtue of the genius of his language, the lack of heroic meter and of the prosody in general. From this vantage point the German work is clearly the more important and the more poetically distinguished. Indeed what separates them is considerable, and already in laying the foundation for his material the author [Grainville] moves in an opposite direction. With *Sonnenberg* it is the moral decay of humankind, which results in the ruin of the earth. Once this has been established, the epic proceeds practically of its own accord; (we are not saying that S.'s design was the most efficacious;) [...] With Herr *von Grainville* the world goes under because she has aged, according to the natural course of things and the will of God; the moral conduct of humankind plays no role in this [...]. The question, which of these two poets motivated his action more persuasively, probably needs to be answered in favour of the German author; the path he took strikes us as the more natural and fertile and in harmony with the spirit of the epopee; the way the French poet approached his material seems more tragical and in the spirit of the classical tragedy.
>
> [Ein deutscher Dichter hat in unsern Tagen den gleichen Stoff in einer Epopee behandelt, nicht mit uneingeschränktem Beyfall, und wie sehr war

columns 665–68; this passage column 665, the subsequent passages columns 666 and 665–66.

> der französische Dichter gegen den deutschen gleichwohl im Nachtheil, durch das Genie seiner Sprache, den Mangel des heroischen Versmaaßes und des Sylbenmaaßes überhaupt. Von dieser Seite kündigt sich das deutsche Werk sogleich als das bedeutendere, poetisch vollendetere an. Ueberhaupt ist der Abstand beider groß, und in der ersten Begründung des Stoffes verfolgt das Genie der Verff. schon entgegengesetzte Richtungen. Bey *Sonnenberg* ist es das moralische Verderben der Menschheit, welches den Untergang der Erde nach sich zieht. Sobald dieß angenommen war, gestaltete sich gleichsam von selbst die Handlung des Epos; (wir behaupten nicht, daß S. sie aufs beste gestaltet habe;) [...] Bei Herrn *v. Grainville* geht die Erde unter, weil sie gealtert hat, dem natürlichen Laufe der Dinge und dem Willen Gottes gemäß; das moralische Verhalten der Menschen kommt dabey nicht in Betrachtung [...]. Die Frage, welcher von beiden Dichtern passender motiviert habe, möchte wohl zu Gunsten des deutschen entschieden werden müssen; der von ihm eingeschlagene Weg scheint uns natürlicher, fruchtbarer und dem Geiste der Epopee gemässer; bey der Art, wie der französische Dichter den Stoff aufgefasst hat, wirkt er gewissermassen tragisch, im Geiste der alten Tragödie.]

This characterization of the differential between the two works could be neither more apt nor more accurate. The reviewer correctly points out that Sonnenberg's epic centres on the opposition between moral and immoral action and, by extension, as I pointed out in Chapter One, belief and non-belief in the Christian God. By endeavouring to take the place of God, and to usurp his divine power, humanity has condemned itself to death and the Last Judgment. In Grainville's narrative, by contrast, it is nature's having run its course that portends the demise of humanity. It is above all a process not of moral but of natural decline that leads to Omégare's quandary as 'Last Man', his being forced to take the ultimate decision whether or not to sacrifice the lineage and life of humanity. Notably, it is, at least in the first instance, *not* in God's hands to take that final decision, this prerogative is Omégare's alone.

In short, what both texts have in common is, ultimately, that human beings are responsible for their species' destiny and downfall. The point at which the Last Judgment should commence is no longer determined per fiat from on high, whether this be by Christ, or God, or any of the archangels, but by human beings themselves. They are ascribed the power, fully independently of any supernatural force, to preside over their fate and initiate the beginning of the end. It is ultimately human choice, not human fate, that is decisive. To refer back once again to Joyce's acute formulation, God may not be 'refined out of existence, indifferent' or even 'paring his fingernails' in these two works, but Sonnenberg and Grainville have certainly forced God to remain veiled 'behind [and] beyond [and] above his handiwork, invisible', waiting for the moment when he can once more become engaged in the world's affairs. Only once human beings have chosen through free will to conclude the history of their race — as has Omégare in Grainville's *Le Dernier Homme* — or have opted out of their Christian faith — as have Abdul & Co. in Sonnenberg's *Donatoa* — can God take action to initiate the final trumpet blast that will usher in the Last Judgment. This shift of responsibility onto the human species' own shoulders — 'the final decision has been given over to man' ('Die letzte Entscheidung ist in die Brust eines Menschen gelegt'), Spiridion Wukadinović recognizes rightly in 1927[96] — represents Sonnenberg's and Grainville's chief innovation, and it is in this that they deviate most conspicuously from the conventional genus of Christian Last Judgment literature. Crucially too, their outward religious appearance notwithstanding, this is why both works can be credited with manifesting aspects of a deistic worldview. The first to acknowledge this fact was the mid-nineteenth-century French critic C. M. Le Roy de Bonneville, who lamented that *Le Dernier Homme* conveyed a regrettable 'air of Deism'; his words in full:

> In essence, although the fundamental philosophical idea that inspired Grainville was religious conviction, absolute submission to God, belief in life after death, resurrection, the Last Judgment, rewards for the faithful and punishment of the culpable, and although these factors throw into relief his spiritual and even Christian temperament, we believe he has not clearly arrived at an orthodox point of view, as had Dante, Milton and Klopstock. It is unfortunate, in our opinion, that he has completely lost from view the religious regeneration of man through Christ the Redeemer; it is regrettable that, in overgeneralizing the idea of God, he gave his work a certain air of Deism.
>
> [Au fond, bien que l'idée philosophique fondamentale qui a inspiré Grainville soit la conviction religieuse, la soumission absolue à Dieu, les croyances à la vie future, à la résurrection des corps, au jugement dernier, aux recompenses des justes et aux peines des coupables; bien que de cet ensemble ressorte une couleur spiritualiste et même chrétienne, nous pensons que l'auteur n'a point abordé nettement le point de vue catholique comme l'ont fait le Dante, Milton et Klopstock. Il est fâcheux, selon nous, qu'il ait entièrement perdu de vue la régénération religieuse de l'homme par le rédempteur; il est à regretter qu'il ait donné un certain reflet de Déisme à son ouvrage, en y généralisant trop l'idée de Dieu.][97]

Bonneville penned this with the benefit of hindsight: writing in 1863 he was able to compare Grainville's original 1805 tale of the last human beings in the run-up to the Last Judgment with the rechristianized versions offered by husband and wife Paulin and Élise Gagne in 1858 and 1859. Élise Gagne in particular had worked emphatically in her adaptation of *Le Dernier Homme* to correct Grainville's 'error' of faith and restore to the epic poem not just its Christian foundation and biblical credentials — she stresses in her 'Preface' how her work 'scrupulously conforms to the writings of the Evangelists and the Apocalypse'[98] (which in fact it doesn't) — but also to reinstate the Saviour to his rightful place as a key actor in the drama of the final chapters of world history (consequently, the Redeemer Jesus Christ is accorded a crucial role as the agent determining the events in Canto Ten of her versified drama).

---

96 *Franz von Sonnenberg*, p. 150.
97 C. M. Le Roy Bonneville, *Étude biographique et littéraire sur Cousin de Grainville* (Le Havre: Imprimerie Lepelletier, 1863), p. 31.
98 'Preface', p. ii.

From Theism to Deism and back

A deistic worldview in a text that outwardly appears to be intrinsically theistic? How do we square this purported deism of Grainville's *Le Dernier Homme* with the fact that his work concludes with the dead arising from their graves and the apocalypse commencing? It is this paradox that I wish to explore in the second half of this chapter. But why do I call it a paradox? To answer this question we need first to remind ourselves what deism was, what it stood for, and what Grainville's contemporaries would have associated with it.

Initiated first by English freethinkers, deism originated in the seventeenth century but was swiftly taken up, modified and spread further by French and German philosophers in the eighteenth century, above all Voltaire and Kant.[99] It was — as it still is today — a (religious) worldview generally premised on the notion that God created the world, but has since withdrawn from his Creation to let nature run its course. Stephen Toulmin and June Goodfield remind us in their book on *The Discovery of Time* how in the seventeenth and eighteenth centuries 'most people still assumed that God intervened in human affairs, but the influential group of Deists denied even that. They restricted God's role in the world to the initial Creation: in the beginning. He had set the cosmic machine working according to fixed laws, and from then on it had gone its own way'.[100] Charles Taylor's *A Secular Age*, a book I engage with variously in my study, is to a large extent about the transformation of modern deism, or 'Providential Deism', into what he terms 'exclusive humanism', whose impact on and relevance for contemporary twenty-first-century religious belief he examines in illuminating detail. Taylor recapitulates the associated 'anthropocentric shift'[101] rather succinctly as follows:

> The crucial feature here is a change in the understanding of God, and his relation to the world. That is, there is a drift away from orthodox Christian conceptions of God as an agent interacting with human beings and intervening in human history; and towards God as architect of a universe operating by unchanging laws, which human beings have to conform to or suffer the consequences. In a wider perspective, this can be seen as a move along a continuum from a view of the supreme being with powers analogous to what we know as agency and personality, and exercising them continually in relation to us, to a view of this being as related to us only through the law-governed structure he has created, and ending with a view of our condition as at grips with an indifferent universe, with God either indifferent or non-existent. From this perspective, Deism can be seen as a half-way house on the road to contemporary Atheism.

Charting the history of Christian belief from Early Modern humanism to the twentieth century, Taylor presents it as a gradated arc running from theism via

---

99 There are many surveys of deism; for my purpose particularly useful were Jonathan I. Israel's *Radical Enlightenment. Philosophy and the Making of Modernity 1650–1750* (Oxford: Oxford University Press, 2002, first published 2001), Part IV, and Peter Byrne's *Natural Religion and the Nature of Religion. The Legacy of Deism* (London: Routledge, 1991, first published 1989); in addition, in his *A Secular Age*, Charles Taylor uses the term as a key concept for the development of his argument.

100 *The Discovery of Time* (London: Hutchinson, 1965), pp. 86–87.

101 *A Secular Age*, p. 222, the subsequent quotes pp. 270 and 14.

deism to atheism. As a twenty-first-century Christian philosopher, the question that arises for Taylor is: 'How did we move from a condition where, in Christendom, people lived naïvely within a theistic construal, to one in which [...] unbelief has become for many the major default option?' It is specifically this path to 'unbelief', a path that has allowed Christian belief to become little more than one option among many, that Taylor sets out to describe in *A Secular Age*.

Whereas seventeenth-century deism may have set European Christianity off on an inexorable tangent towards unbelief, it is itself not yet atheistic in orientation, although many orthodox Christians viewed it as such at the time. Generally associated in English philosophy with the names of Herbert of Cherbury, John Locke, the third Earl of Shaftesbury, John Toland, Anthony Collins, Matthew Tindall, and David Hume, deism has a long and complex history, the convoluted twists and turns of which only partially need to interest us here. As a term it was first used in the French Protestant reformer Pierre Viret's *Instruction chrestienne* of 1564, and in English in Robert Burton's *Anatomy of Melancholy* of 1621.[102] But one of deism's ironies, and what is masked by the way the term is applied today, is that deism actually began as theism. The German 'Historical Dictionary of Philosophy' (*Historisches Wörterbuch der Philosophie*), an invaluable resource for anyone researching the history of philosophical concepts, informs us that the words theism and deism were originally used interchangeably as 'synonyms'; 'having come into circulation in late seventeenth-century England', we are told, '*Theism* initially is the polemical designation for deists who are accused of being opposed to a personal concept of God that includes Providence and supernatural agency, and who dispute Revelation. For this reason the term is used pejoratively into the early eighteenth century'.[103] Muddling matters further, as late as 1800 we find William Hamilton Reid maligning his deistic adversaries by writing, in *The Rise and Dissolution of the Infidel Societies*: 'Nor let the reader be surprised, that I have classed Atheists and Deists indiscriminately: for the common practice of Infidels, to cover themselves with the name of *Deists*, is a mere pretext, calculated to escape the more odious appellation of *Atheists*'.[104] Judging by Reid, deists and atheists are chips off the same block.

What is more, in his entry on 'Deism' in the Oxford University Press's 2003 *Encyclopedia of Enlightenment* Roger Lund warns us that, 'aside from [the activist deistic philosopher] Charles Blount, virtually no one accused of deism actually called himself a deist' at the time.[105] Certainly in the late seventeenth and early eighteenth century, even if one may have considered oneself a deist, one certainly preferred not to be identified as such, Hume being a prominent example. Ephraim Chambers stresses in 1728 in his *Cyclopaedia, or an Universal Dictionary of Arts and*

---

102 See Roger D. Lund, 'Deism', in *Encyclopedia of Enlightenment*, ed. by Alan Charles Kors, 4 vols (Oxford: Oxford University Press, 2003), vol. 1, pp. 335–40, especially p. 335.

103 *Historisches Wörterbuch der Philosophie*, ed. by Joachim Ritter (Basel and Stuttgart: Schwabe, 1998), vol. 10, column 1054.

104 Cited after Martin Priestman, *Romantic Atheism: Poetry and Freethought, 1780–1830* (Cambridge: Cambridge University Press, 1999), p. 39.

105 'Deism', p. 336.

Sciences:

> The Appellation *Deist* is more particularly given to such as are not altogether without Religion, but reject all Revelation as an imposition, and believe no more than what natural Light discovers to them; [...]. The Number of Deists is daily increasing. In England, a great Part of the Men of Speculation, and Letters, *are pretended to incline that Way*. And the like is observ'd in some of our Neighbour Nations, where Freedom of Speaking, Writing, and Thinking are indulged.[106] (my emphasis)

Some three decades on, in 1754, the French encyclopedist and atheist Denis Diderot distinguishes theism and deism thus:

> in the new usage, one does not attach to Theism the same idea as to Deism. The theist is he who is already convinced of the existence of God and the reality of good and bad morals, of the immortality of the soul, of the punishments and recompenses to come, but who waits, in order to acknowledge Revelation, that one prove it to him; he neither concedes nor denies it. The deist, by contrast, concurs with the theist merely with regard to the existence of God and the reality of good and bad morals, [but] denies Revelation, doubts the immortality of the soul, and of the punishments and recompenses to come.
>
> [dans le nouvel usage, on n'attache point au *théisme* la même idée qu'au *déisme*. Le *théiste* est celui qui est déjà convaincu de l'existence de Dieu, de la réalité du bien et du mal moral, de l'immortalité de l'âme, des peines et des récompenses à venir, mais qui attend, pour admettre la révélation, qu'on la lui démontre; il ne l'accorde ni ne la nie. Le *déiste*, au contraire, d'accord avec le *théiste*, seulement sur l'existence de Dieu et la réalité du bien et du mal moral, nie la révélation, doute de l'immortalité de l'âme, et des peines et des récompenses à venir.][107]

Another three decades on, in 1781, Kant attempts to distinguish the two concepts in his *Critique of Pure Reason* by attributing 'a natural theology' to the theist and 'a transcendental theology' to the deist; 'the *Deist* believes in *God*, but the *Theist* in a *living God*', he explains ('der *Deist* glaube einen *Gott*, der *Theist* aber einen *lebendigen Gott*').[108] Although intuitively we today might be inclined to reverse Kant's attributions, assuming theism to be more transcendental than deism, Kant's logic is coherent when seen within its context; Kant writes:

> If by *Theology* we understand the knowledge of the Original Being, it is derived either from reason only (theologia rationalis), or from revelation (revelata). The former thinks its object either by pure reason and through transcendental concepts only (ens originarium, realissimum, ens entium), and is then called *transcendental* theology, or by a concept, borrowed from the nature (of our soul), as the highest intelligence, and ought then to be called *natural* theology. Those who admit a transcendental theology [alone] are called *Deists*, those who [in addition] admit a natural theology *Theists*.

---

106 *Cyclopaedia, or an Universal Dictionary of Arts and Sciences*, 2 vols (London: [n.pub.], 1728), vol. I, p. 179.

107 'Observations sur l'instruction pastorale de M. L'évêque d'Auxerre', in *Œuvres Complètes*, I: *Philosophie*, vol. 1, ed. by J. Assézat (Paris: Garnier Frères, 1875), pp. 441–84 (p. 479).

108 *Critique of Pure Reason*, p. 543 (*Kritik der reinen Vernunft*, p. 557).

[Wenn ich unter Theologie die Erkenntnis des Urwesens verstehe, so ist sie entweder die aus bloßer Vernunft (theologia rationalis) oder aus Offenbarung (revelata). Die erstere denkt sich nun ihren Gegenstand entweder bloß durch reine Vernunft, vermittels lauter transzendentaler Begriffe (ens originarium, realissimum, ens entium), und heißt die *transzendentale* Theologie, oder durch einen Begriff, den sie aus der Natur (unserer Seele) entlehnt, als die höchste Intelligenz, und müßte die natürliche Theologie heißen. Der, so allein eine transzendentale Theologie einräumt, wird *Deist*, der, so auch eine natürliche Theologie annimmt, *Theist* genannt.][109]

To confuse matters, however, even for some of Kant's contemporaries 'natural religion' and 'natural theology' were considered bynames not for a theistic worldview, but rather for a deistic one in which the emphasis was placed on reading 'Nature' rather than the revealed Bible as the Book of God. Thomas Paine's *The Age of Reason, Being an Investigation of True and Fabulous Theology*, the first part of which was published to scandalous effect in 1794, best epitomizes this position, which included the sacralization of Nature, as it were, which went hand in hand with the desacralization of scripture; Paine writes:

> Deism, then, teaches us, without the possibility of being deceived, all that is necessary or proper to be known. The creation is the Bible of the Deist. He there reads, in the handwriting of the Creator himself, the certainty of his existence and the immutability of his power, and all other Bibles and Testaments are to him forgeries.

The confusing overlap regarding the role that nature was accorded in the definitions of theism and deism did not go unnoticed even at the time. The German lexicographer Johann Christoph Adelung's entry for 'Deist' in his *New High German Dictionary* (*Grammatisch-kritisches Wörterbuch der Hochdeutschen Mundart*), compiled and published between 1793–1801, begins by defining a deist as 'he who assumes the existence of a God, but not the validity of Revelation, and who pursues a natural religion', then continues in a Kantian vein 'the deist bases his belief wholly on speculative and abstract reasons; the theist by contrast defines the pure deistic concept of reason through his observation of the physical and moral world and makes it practical', only to conclude: 'Nonetheless, this distinction is purely arbitrary. Naturalist is a term that would apply to both' ('der zwar einen Gott, aber keine Offenbarung annimmt, sondern bloß der natürlichen Religion folget [...]. Der Deist gründet sich ganz auf speculative und abstracte Gründe; der Theist aber bestimmt den reinen deistischen Vernunftbegriff durch Betrachtung der physischen und moralischen Welt und macht ihn praktisch. Indessen ist dieser Unterschied bloß willkührlich. Naturalist ist eine allgemeine Benennung für beyde').[110] Indeed,

---

109 Ibid., pp. 541–42 (*Kritik der reinen Vernunft*, p. 556); the square brackets in the English rendering of this passage are my addition: the stress created through the words 'alone' ('allein') and 'in addition' ('auch') are important for this section's meaning (I also amended the italics to correspond with Kant's German original).

110 Johann Christoph Adelung, *Grammatisch-kritisches Wörterbuch der Hochdeutschen Mundart. Elektronische Volltext- und Faksimile-Edition nach der Ausgabe letzter Hand* (Leipzig: [n.pub.], 1793–1801), p. 1443 (accessed via <www.zeno.org/Adelung-1793>, 12 March 2013).

during the same decade that Adelung wrote this gloss in Germany, in England the Anglican theologian William Paley was requisitioning the very concept of 'natural theology' for a highly theistic Christian doctrine, albeit one based on the close observation of nature, as the title of his chief work *Natural Theology: or, Evidences of the Existence and Attributes of the Deity, Collected from the Appearance of Nature*, published in 1802, makes apparent. Paley's 1794 *A View of the Evidences of Christianity*, in which he laid the groundwork for his natural theology, was published in the same year as Paine published his anti-theistic and anti-Christian work which propounded the merits of a deistic natural religion, claiming: 'My own mind is my own church. All national institutions of churches, whether Jewish, Christian or Turkish, appear to me no other than human inventions set up to terrify and enslave mankind, and monopolize power and profit'.[111] Two hundred years later these historical oscillations and incongruities seem to have evaporated; theism today is generally and summarily defined as a belief in an active God, deism as belief in a passive one, as my edition of the *Oxford Dictionary of English* confirms: theism is here defined as 'belief in the existence of a god or gods, specifically of a creator who intervenes in the universe', deism as 'belief in the existence of a supreme being, specifically of a creator who does not intervene in the universe'.[112]

Clearly, the definitions of theism and deism shifted considerably between the early 1700s and the early 1800s. Regardless of the ebb and flow of the concept's meaning, Peter Byrne stresses in his 1989 study *Natural Religion and the Nature of Religion* that deism's 'importance lies in the way in which it opens up vital issues in the history of religion. It is concerned, among other things with the universality, comparability, and naturalness of religion and, through these things, with profound questions about the nature of history. To affirm the universality, comparability, and naturalness of religion is to place an obvious question-mark against the kind of traditional account of the place of Christianity in history'.[113] Deism thereby paved the way for modern secular Bible criticism and the historicization of scripture. But not just that, in putting an equally obvious question-mark against the possibility of miracles — as did Spinoza in his 1670 *Tractatus theologico-politicus* and in his wake David Hume in his 1748 chapter 'On Miracles' of *An Enquiry Concerning Human Understanding* — works by pantheistic and deistic philosophers also served to undermine traditional accounts of the role and essence of Christ. One of the prime objectives, if not *the* prime objective, of Spinoza's philosophy of religion was to critique precisely the imagined kind of belief in the supernatural that in his day characterized 'Revealed Religion' and the acceptance of miracles, and which Spinoza considered empirically untenable and hence philosophically insupportable; as Jonathan I. Israel observes,

---

111 *The Age of Reason, being an investigation of true and fabulous theology* (New York: Prometheus Books, [n.d.]), p. 8, the subsequent passage p. 184.

112 *Oxford Dictionary of English*, 2nd edn, ed. by Catherine Soanes and Angus Stevenson (Oxford: Oxford University Press, 2006), pp. 1828 and 458.

113 *Natural Religion and the Nature of Religion* (London: Routledge, 1989), p. 53.

TRACTATUS THEOLOGICO-POLITICUS

Continens

Differtationes aliquot,

Quibus oftenditur Libertatem Philofophandi non tantum falva Pietate, & Reipublicæ Pace poffe concedi : fed eandem nifi cum Pace Reipublicæ, ipfaque Pietate tolli non poffe.

Johan. Epift. I. Cap. IV. verf. XIII.

Per hoc cognofcimus quod in Deo manemus, & Deus manet in nobis, quod de Spiritu fuo dedit nobis.

HAMBURGI,

Apud *Henricum Künrath*. cIɔ Iɔ cLxx.

FIG. 2.4. Title page of the 1670 Latin 'first' edition of Spinoza's *Tractatus theologico-politicus*. Spinoza's publisher Rieuwertsz in Amsterdam used fictitious title pages to conceal the real number of editions issued in the 1670s, all given as published in Hamburg in 1670, 1672 or 1673. This edition, with the pagination misprint of p. 92 for p. 192 (Bamberger v), was probably published in 1678.

[n]o other element of Spinoza's philosophy provoked as much consternation and outrage in his own time as his sweeping denial of miracles and the supernatural. In fact, Spinoza stands completely alone among the major European thinkers before the mid-eighteenth century in ruling out miracles. [...] Between the rise of Christianity and the mid-eighteenth century then, only Spinoza categorically denies the possibility of miracles and supernatural occurrences wrought by magic.[114]

In Britain it was Hume to whom Spinoza passed the baton; taking his prompt from Spinoza's *Tractatus*, Hume in 'On Miracles' famously defined a miracle as 'a transgression of a law of nature by a particular volition of the Deity, or by the interposition of some invisible agent'.[115] In France it was the atheistic philosopher

---

114 *Radical Enlightenment*, p. 218.

115 'Of Miracles', in *Hume on Religion*, ed. by Julian Baggini (London: The Philosophy Press, 2010), pp. 137–58 (p. 141).

Baron Holbach, to whose circle Hume also belonged, who drew the obvious consequences, putting forward the, at the time, scandalous proposition that all New Testament accounts of Jesus's miracles and his resurrection must be man-made concoctions fabricated by his disciples in order to create the impression of Christ's divinity.[116] The radical questioning especially of the New Testament accounts of the life of Jesus culminated in the early nineteenth century in David Friedrich Strauß's controversial historicizing portrayal of the life of Jesus in his *Das Leben Jesu, kritisch bearbeitet* of 1835–1836 (translated into English as *Life of Jesus Critically Examined* by George Eliot in 1846). If one of deism's upshots is Christianity's loss of its privileged standing among religions, another is Christ's loss of standing as a trinitarian godlike being.

Religiously Squaring the Secular Circle, once more

Clearly, what emerges from this abbreviated history of theism and deism (I will return to atheism in the next chapters) is that they are separated by the role they attribute to the supernatural and miraculous in the progress of our world since its creation. Once God is viewed as a *deus absconditus*, and once miracles are taken to be against the law of nature and hence out of the question, the divinity of Christ for all intents and purposes also becomes defunct. To put it bluntly: the deist can no longer believe in Christ's godlike essence and attributes since the deistic belief system does not allow for any supernatural agency to impact on the course of history, human or planetary, aside from the initial act of 'Creation' itself. For a deist Christ is a mere mortal, a historical person who may have inspired his fellow beings to create a new religion based on his life, teaching and actions, but who otherwise lacked divine credentials (see Chapter Four for Percy Bysshe Shelley's views on Christ as precisely such a model human). Seen from a theist's perspective, by contrast, Christ's life is supernatural and miraculous from beginning to end, from conception to resurrection. This explains why the philosophical critique of miracles in deistic, pantheistic and atheistic philosophy was not just axiomatic to their undertaking, but also so eminently controversial and scandal-provoking, beginning with Spinoza's seminal treatise *Tractatus theologico-politicus* and running through the works of Hume and Holbach in the eighteenth century to those of Strauß, Feuerbach and Marx in the nineteenth.

A perfect illustration of the impact deism exerted on Christian thought is provided ironically by a German-Jewish poet and essayist, namely Heinrich Heine (1797–1856), who converted to Protestantism and a form of pantheism in mid-life only to turn back to a more full-fledged theism and belief in God and Revelation

---

[116] Holbach's 1770 critical analysis of Christ's resurrection here establishes a tradition of Bible criticism that reaches right into our present time; see Herman Philipse's rejection of the biblical account in surprisingly similar terms to Holbach's in his *God in the Age of Science? A Critique of Religious Reason* (Oxford: Oxford University Press, 2012), pp. 171–75 — a comparison of the two shows how little the terms of engagement have changed since the mid-eighteenth century. I should perhaps add as a postscript to this footnote that it remained a criminal offence up to 1813 in Britain to deny the divinity of Jesus.

shortly before his death.[117] Living in exile in Paris since 1831, Heine in 1834 published an extended prose essay for a French audience entitled *On Germany since Luther* (*De l'Allemagne depuis Luther*, an allusion of course to Madame de Staël's famous work *De l'Allemagne*), in which he summarizes the progress of German theology and philosophy from the Middle Ages to Hegel; in the second section of that work, which has the heading 'From Luther to Kant', we read:

> And since religion, as I have observed, sought assistance from philosophy, innumerable experiments were tried upon her by German *savants*. [...] At first they opened her veins, and all the superstitious blood was very slowly extracted; or, to speak without a simile, an attempt was made to take from Christianity its historical element, and only retain the moral portion. Thus they made of it a pure deism. Christ ceased to be an equal ruler with God; he was, so to speak, mediatised, and only found honourable recognition as a private person. His moral character was praised as being beyond all measure, and men could not find language to describe what an admirable person he was. As for his miracles, people explained them by natural causes, or, better still, kept as quiet as possible regarding them.
>
> [Seitdem nun, wie ich oben erzählt, die Religion Hülfe suchte bey der Philosophie, wurden von den deutschen Gelehrten, außer der neuen Einkleidung, noch unzählige Experimente mit ihr angestellt. [...] Zuerst wurde ihr zur Ader gelassen, alles abergläubische Blut wurde ihr langsam abgezapft; um mich bildlos auszudrücken: es wurde der Versuch gemacht, allen historischen Inhalt aus dem Christenthume herauszunehmen und nur den moralischen Teil zu bewahren. Hierdurch ward nun das Christenthum zu einem reinen Deismus. Christus hörte auf Mitregent Gottes zu seyn, er wurde gleichsam mediatisirt, und nur noch als Privatperson fand er anerkennende Verehrung. Seinen moralischen Charakter lobte man über alle Maßen. Man konnte nicht genug rühmen, welch ein braver Mensch er gewesen sey. Was die Wunder betrifft, die er verrichtet, so erklärte man sie physikalisch, oder man suchte so wenig Aufhebens als möglich davon zu machen.][118]

Later in this work Heine goes on to describe, with evident amusement, the dilemma faced by a Protestant theologian like Johann Gottfried Herder — the close friend of Goethe in Weimar — when he was training students of theology around the close of the eighteenth century:

> It is touching to read in the posthumous letters of Herder how the poor man had his own troubles and trials with the candidates of theology, who, after

---

117 Views on Heine's religious attitude diverge quite widely; two recent discussions of the bandwidth can be found in Bodo Morawe, 'Heine und Holbach. Zur Religionskritik der radikalen Aufklärung und über zwei zentrale Probleme der Büchner-Forschung', in *Georg Büchner Jahrbuch*, 11 (2005–2008) (Tübingen: Niemeyer, 2008), 237–65, and Jost Hermand, 'Auf einsamem Posten — Lessing und Heine', in *'Liebhaber der Theologie': Gotthold Ephraim Lessing — Philosoph — Historiker der Religion* (Frankfurt a.M.: Peter Lang, 2012), pp. 204–10.

118 'Germany', in *The Works of Heinrich Heine*, trans. by Charles Godfrey Leland (London: William Heinemann, 1892), vol. 5, pp. 1–384 (pp. 110–11); *Zur Geschichte der Religion und Philosophie in Deutschland*, in *Heinrich Heine. Historisch-kritische Gesamtausgabe der Werke*, ed. by Manfred Windfuhr (Hamburg: Hoffmann und Campe, 1979), vol. VIII.1, p. 67. The subsequent passage pp. 169–70 (pp. 98–99).

having studied in Jena, came before him in Weimar to undergo examination as Protestant preachers. He dared not ask them a question as to Christ the Son; he was only too glad when they would admit the existence of the Father.

[Es ist rührend, wenn man in Herders hinterlassenen Briefen liest, wie der arme Herder seine liebe Noth hatte mit den Candidaten der Theologie, die, nachdem sie in Jena studirt, zu ihm nach Weimar kamen, um als protestantische Prediger examinirt zu werden. Ueber Christus, den Sohn, wagte er im Examen sie gar nicht mehr zu befragen; er war froh genug, wenn man ihm nur die Existenz des Vaters zugestand.]

Heine's comments remind us of the fact that, in essence, any intellectual who aspired to deism during this period would be expected to avoid relating miracles as fact and depicting Christ as divine, or might try to circumvent the issue altogether, as we see in the anecdote Heine recounts about Herder's tutees.

Let us recall at this point the mid-nineteenth-century French critic Bonneville, cited earlier; his argument for Grainville being a deist was premised precisely on the fact that *Le Dernier Homme* omitted any mention of Jesus and seemed to lack the requisite Catholic unction. 'It is unfortunate, in my opinion,' Bonneville wrote, 'that [Grainville] has completely lost from view the religious regeneration of man through Christ the Redeemer; it is regrettable that, in overgeneralizing the idea of God, he gave his work a certain air of Deism'. The disappearance of Christ, but not of God, is similarly picked up on as a key issue by most twentieth-century interpreters of *Le Dernier Homme*. Morton D. Paley thus observes: 'The theodicy of this novel is, to say the least, problematic: the universe is presided over by a *dieu fainéant* [i.e., an idle God, R.W.], and Jesus (as Grippen emphasizes) is given no role at all'.[119] And Alkon likewise notes:

> Omegarus and Syderia live in a world without any trace of Christianity. [...] There are priests and oracles reminiscent of those in pagan antiquity. But there is no mention of Christ, no mention of the Bible, not even any allusion to specifically Christian precepts of morality.[120]

It is this trait first and foremost that prompted critics like Alkon to speak of the 'secularization of apocalypse', as we recall. And yet, all critics equally agree that *Le Dernier Homme* is an 'eminently religious' text, as Grainville's earliest biographer Louis Dubois observed when he wrote the 1817 Grainville entry for the *Biographie universelle* (an entry, incidentally, that Bonneville would have drawn on in writing his own biographical sketch in 1863); just one decade after Grainville's death Dubois noted:

> Those who have compared *Le Dernier Homme* with Klopstock's *Messias* have overlooked a crucial difference, namely that Grainville [...] cites no other figures from the Bible than Adam and Eve, that he takes nothing from Revelation but the concept of their culpability, that he not once refers to the Redeemer, and that the Last Judgment [...] is described only through Syderia's dream. It is

---

119 '*Le dernier homme*: The French Revolution', p. 74.
120 *Origins of Futuristic Fiction*, pp. 165–66. Grippen (pp. 59 and 75) and Kupiec (p. 262) similarly register this 'lack'.

regrettable that he has not given his work a more Christian hue and accorded more unction to his style. In effect this poem is not simply a moral romance: its subject, from source to end, is eminently religious.

[En comparant, au fond, le *Dernier Homme* avec la *Messiade* Klopstock, on n'a pas observé un point capital qui l'en fait différer extrêmement, c'est que l'auteur [...] n'a nommé d'autres personnages des livres saints qu'Adam et Eve, et n'a guère puisé dans la révélation que l'idée de leur faute; qu'il n'a pas désigné une seule fois le *Rédempteur*, et n'a dépeint le jugement dernier [...] que dans un songe de Sydérie. Il est à regretter qu'il n'ait pas donné à son plan une teinte plus prononcée de christianisme, comme plus d'onction à son style. Ce poème, en effet, n'est pas simplement un roman moral: le sujet, dans son principe et dans sa fin, est éminemment religieux.][121]

It is this ambivalence that constitutes not just this text's most remarkable trait — the oxymoron of its seemingly secularized religiosity — but also poses key hermeneutic questions, questions for which we need to supply the answers. First, what does this ambivalence tell us about Grainville's intentions and worldview, inasmuch as we can reconstruct them from the information available to us? And, second, will the answer to this question help us to resolve the paradox that has so nonplussed the critics of this text?

Alkon provides an answer that can usefully serve as a starting point by focusing our attention, rightly I believe, on the status and function of the apocalypse in Grainville's text. *Le Dernier Homme*, he maintains, 'goes a long way toward undermining conventional uses of eschatology by providing a phenomenology of the Apocalypse that calls into question the doctrines of Apocalypse'.[122] Grainville's 'method runs counter to the mainstream of apocalyptic writing', Alkon expands, in which, 'from the Renaissance through the eighteenth century and on into the Romantic period [...], prophecy as a mode of literature was usually taken as "a *no plot, no action* genre"'. Grainville, by contrast, by allowing three hours for the dead to arise from their graves,

> humanizes the time scale of the Apocalypse by choosing a duration that is both large enough and small enough to fit the time scale of daily life. It is neither instantaneous as in other versions of resurrection nor spread out over many days as it might well have been to achieve even greater scientific plausibility, given the many remains waiting throughout all history to be disgorged.

The effect of this expansion of the timeframe as regards the events surrounding the Last Judgment is that the text 'invites readers to ask how ordinary people *would* respond to a knock at their door during the world's last day'. The result is, in Alkon's view, that Grainville's

> mythology of apocalypse, along with his often effective portrayal of its phenomenology, serves the aesthetically valid epistemological purpose of raising questions *about* the Apocalypse. If difficult, those questions are by the same token interesting. They admit of a variety of answers, as in other fiction

---

121 Louis Dubois, entry 'Grainville', *Biographie universelle*, p. 274.
122 *Origins of Futuristic Fiction*, p. 174, the subsequent passages pp. 180, 170, 175 and 182 (all emphases are Alkon's).

> whose complexity challenges interpretation. However readers answer the questions, Grainville's book is all the more effective because it does raise such issues.

However, as much as I agree with Alkon's superb analysis, it falls short because he fails to pursue this line of reasoning further to address the specificity of Grainville's text in one crucial regard. This is the fact that *every* depiction of the Last Judgment ultimately 'invites readers to ask how ordinary people *would* respond to a knock at their door during the world's last day'. Indeed, is this not the programmatic function of each and every Last Judgment poem and epic like John Pomfret's *On the Conflagration, and Last Judgment* of 1699 or Edward Young's *A Poem on the Last Day* of 1713, which I cited in Chapter One?

Moreover, the key difference between Grainville's version of apocalypse and those of his predecessors in this sub-genre is less the duration of the apocalypse itself, the three hours that Alkon adduces for the dead to be summoned from their graves; to be sure, this is novel, but it is not Grainville's crucial innovation. Rather, it is the fact that the world, as well as its human population, has had time to run its course and is coming to the end of its natural life cycle following millennia of progress. We read in Canto III:

> Nothing can compare with the brilliance of their societies, the perfection of the arts, the scale of human virtue. For many centuries, these high standards were universal. Reading the history of those times, it is difficult to believe that such works were those of human beings; it seemed, rather, as if more perfect beings had come to live on earth. In genius and virtue they were giants. When earth had attained so high a degree of glory and of happiness, it began to experience the fate of humankind. Once they had arrived at the perfection of body and soul, the flame began to die within them. Chill old age and death followed.

> [Rien ne fut comparable à l'éclat des sociétés, à la perfection des arts, aux vertus de l'humanité. Cette grandeur fut commune à tous les pays, à plusieurs siècles. En lisant l'histoire de cet âge, on ne retrouve plus l'homme dans l'homme lui-même. Il semble que des êtres plus parfaits vinrent habiter le globe terrestre. Ils furent comme les géants du génie et de la vertu. La terre, parvenue à ce haut degré de gloire et de bonheur, éprouva le sort des hommes. Ont-ils atteint la perfection de l'esprit et du corps, le feu qui les animait s'affaiblit. Bientôt succèdent les glaces de la vieillesse et de la mort.][123]

This dense passage alludes to the adage of the 'dwarf standing on the shoulders of giants' which encapsulated the sentiment of the generation of the French Academy member and writer Charles Perrault around 1700 when, in the so-called *Querelle des anciens et des modernes*, he and his Académie colleague Nicolas Boileau-Despréaux debated the superiority of modernity over antiquity. Being smaller than the paragons of antiquity, but standing on their shoulders, the moderns could nonetheless see further, Perrault had argued, buttressing his claim with Newton's scientific discoveries and the architecture of the Palace of Versailles. It is, of course, also an all-too-human tale of hubris, of pride coming before a fall.

---

123 *The Last Man*, trans. I. F. & M. Clarke, p. 34 (*Le Dernier Homme*, ed. Kupiec, p. 79).

But first and foremost, perhaps, this extract formulates a critique of 'progress' and 'perfectibility'; born out of the civilizational optimism that blossomed in the wake of the French Revolution, the late-Enlightenment philosophy of progress and perfectibility was at the time epitomized by one key text of speculative historiography, written in hiding in 1794 and published posthumously in 1795, namely the Marquis de Condorcet's *Outlines of an Historical View of the Progress of the Human Mind* (*Esquisse d'un tableau historique des progrès de l'esprit humain*). Based on 'past experience [and] observations of the progress which the sciences and civilizations have hitherto made, and from the analysis of the march of the human understanding, and the development of its faculties', Condorcet concluded that 'nature has fixed no limits to our hopes' ('nous trouverons, dans l'expérience du passé, dans l'observation des progrès que les sciences, que la civilisation ont faits jusqu'ici, dans l'analyse de la marche de l'esprit humain et du développement de ses facultés [...] que la nature n'a mis aucun terme à nos espérances').[124] Following in the footsteps of Voltaire, the great preceptor of eighteenth-century French philosophy, and marking the beginning of the nineteenth-century grand narrative of progress and the 'indefinite perfectibility of the human race' ('perfectibilité indéfinie [...] de l'espèce humaine'), Condorcet asked, if only as a rhetorical ploy,

> whether the number of inhabitants in the universe at length exceeding the means of existence, there will not result a continual decay of happiness and population, and a progress towards barbarism, or at least a sort of oscillation between good and evil? Will not this oscillation, in societies arrived at this epoch, be a perennial source of periodical calamity and distress? In a word, do not these considerations point out the limit at which all farther improvement will become impossible, and consequently the perfectibility of man arrive at a period which in the immensity of ages it may attain, but which it can never pass?
>
> [cà l'augmentation du nombre des hommes surpassant celle de leurs moyens, il en résulteroit nécessairement, sinon une diminution continue de bien-être et de population, une marche vraiment rétrograde, du moins une sorte d'oscillation entre le bien et le mal? Cette oscillation dans les sociétés arrivées à ce terme, ne seroit-elle pas une cause toujours subsistante de misères en quelque sorte périodiques? Ne marqueroit-elle pas la limite où toute amélioration deviendroit impossible, et à la perfectibilité de l'espèce humaine, le terme qu'elle atteindroit dans l'immensité des siècles, sans pouvoir jamais le passer?]

Only to respond:

> There is, doubtless, no individual that does not perceive how very remote from us will be this period: but must it one day arrive? It is equally impossible to pronounce on either side respecting an event, which can only be realized at an epoch when the human species will necessarily have acquired a degree of knowledge, of which our short-sighted understandings can scarcely form an idea. And who shall presume to foretell to what perfection the art of converting

---

124 Nicolas Condorcet, *Outlines of an Historical View of the Progress of the Human Mind* (Philadelphia: Carey, Rice, Ormrod, 1796), pp. 252–53; *Esquisse d'un tableau historique des progrès de l'esprit humain* (Paris: Agasse, 1794), pp. 330–31. The subsequent passages pp. 272–73, 290 and 293 (pp. 357–58, 381 and 384).

the elements of life into substances fitted for our use, may, in a progression of ages, be brought?

[Il n'est personne qui ne voie sans doute combien ce temps est éloigné de nous; mais devons-nous y parvenir un jour? Il est également impossible de prononcer pour ou contre la réalité future d'un événement, qui ne se réaliseroit qu'à une époque où l'espèce humaine auroit nécessairement acquis des lumières dont nous pouvons à peine nous faire une idée. Et qui, en effet, oseroit deviner ce que l'art de convertir les élémens en substances propres à notre usage doit devenir un jour?]

Crucial for our purpose are the lack in the above of any mention of a divine power. For Condorcet human progress may not be endless in the strict sense, but its limits are not determinable, and certainly not foreseeable or predictable. In this vision of man's 'indefinite advancement' ('progrès indéfini'), and in the light of 'the eternal chain of the destiny of mankind' ('la chaîne éternelle des destinées humaines') that he sees governing the progress of history, no boundary seems set either by God or indeed by nature.

Writing in the wake of Condorcet, Grainville by contrast cannot subscribe to any such optimism. Opposed to any kind of open-ended view of historical progress, he delimits the course of history in his text, but — in crucial contradistinction to his fellow writer Franz von Sonnenberg — not just by having the Last Judgment terminate life on Earth because humankind has broken with God and jettisoned Christian fidelity as depicted in *Donatoa*, but rather by preempting the need for a *supernaturally* motivated apocalyptic demise by a *naturally* motivated process of material decline and exhaustion. By extending the internal narrative timeframe to the centuries leading up to the apocalypse, Grainville is able to offer his reader a no less realistic than pessimistic counter-vision to the optimistic grand narrative of ineluctible progress that was just beginning to take shape at the close of the eighteenth and opening of the nineteenth century.

However, we need to put the emerging doctrine of optimism and perfectibility — which is soon to culminate in Hegel's, Comte's, Marx's and Darwin's quite distinct brands of philosophy of history, dialectical, social, political and evolutionary — into perspective: the period also encompassed more pessimistic models of progress, which circulated in particular in Natural History (which itself was on the verge of developing into the history of nature and the modern disciplines of geology, biology and anthropology)[125] that saw our planet if not in decline per se, then certainly heading for a major catastrophe in an undefined distant future. Grainville alludes to this explicitly with the clause 'chill old age and death followed', a clause that neatly sums up the planetary theory of one of the leading naturalists of Grainville's age, namely Georges-Louis Leclerc Comte de Buffon.

Buffon's multi-volume work on natural history, *Histoire naturelle, générale et particulière* (1749–1788), was one of the most widely read works of science in late-

---

125 See Wolf Lepenies, *Das Ende der Naturgeschichte. Wandel kultureller Selbstverständlichkeiten in den Wissenschaften des 18. und 19. Jahrhunderts* (Frankfurt a.M.: Suhrkamp, 1978); and Martin Rudwick, *Bursting the Limits of Time*.

eighteenth and early-nineteenth-century Europe. Recognizing that our planet had 'originated as a hot body' but 'had been cooling ever since' — as Martin Rudwick succinctly condenses Buffon's geothermic hypothesis — Buffon's system 'required that eventually, with further diminution of the Earth's internal store of heat, the inexorable refrigeration shown by the present ice caps would extend over the whole globe and all life would be extinguished'.[126] Grainville's Scottish contemporary, the naturalist John Playfair, in the volume *Illustrations of the Huttonian Theory of the Earth* published in 1802, nicely sums up the state of opinion about Buffon's theory as contrasted with James Hutton's competing explanation of our planet's evolution:

> Buffon represents the cooling of our planet, and its loss of heat, as a process continually advancing, and which has no limit, but the final extinction of life and motion over all the surface, and through all the interior, of the earth. The death of nature herself is the distant but gloomy object that terminates our view, and reminds us of the wild fictions of the Scandinavian mythology, according to which, annihilation is at last to extend its empire even to the gods. This dismal and unphilosophic vision was unworthy of the genius of Buffon, and wonderfully ill suited to the elegance and extent of his understanding. It forms a complete contrast to the theory of Dr Hutton, where nothing is to be seen beyond the continuation of the present order; where no latent seed of evil threatens final destruction to the whole; and where the movements are so perfect, that they can never terminate of themselves. This is surely a view of the world more suited to the dignity of Nature and the wisdom of its Author.[127]

It is worth noting that neither Buffon nor Hutton find it necessary to take a 'Final Conflagration' into consideration through which our planet and its human residents might find their existence terminated. Martin Rudwick, the eminent historian of geology, remarks that, 'without being openly atheistic, Buffon had simply redefined the scope of the natural sciences in such a way that divine action was marginalized'; in like manner, he takes note of 'the deistic metaphysics and theology that underlay all Hutton's ideas about the earth'.[128] Hutton, in his initial article on the *Theory of the Earth* published in 1788 (and which was expanded in 1795 into his influential book of the same title), sees Earth's history as a constant process of recycling. In the volume *The Rise of Scientific Europe 1500–1800*, David Goodman and Colin Russell concisely recapitulate Hutton's theory as follows:

> In Hutton's account, geological time is directionless — it's not going anywhere: the earth has proceeded from no primeval state, and it will not culminate at some future final point. The steady-state of a habitable world can be projected backwards into the eternal vistas of the past, and can be confidently predicted,

---

126 *Bursting the Limits of Time*, pp. 142–43 and 147.

127 *Illustrations of the Huttonian Theory of the Earth* (Edinburgh: Cadell and Davies, 1802), pp. 485–86. Percy Bysshe Shelley in 1817 similarly speaks of 'Buffon's sublime but gloomy theory — that this globe which we inhabit will at some future period be changed into a mass of frost by the encroachment of the polar ice'; see his *History of a Six Weeks' Tour Through a Part of France, Switzerland, Germany, and Holland* (London: T. Hookham, jun., and C. and J. Ollier, 1817), pp. 161–62.

128 *Bursting the Limits of Time*, p. 160. Similarly, Rudwick says of Buffon that 'without being openly atheistic, Buffon had simply redefined the scope of the natural sciences in such a way that divine action was marginalized' (p. 141).

stretching into the equally endless vistas of the future. 'Time', he wrote, 'is to nature endless and as nothing'. And in one of the most memorable utterances in the history of geology [...] he concluded that the present landscape is built from the materials of former landscapes, which in turn are built from yet earlier landscapes, which in turn stretch back in endless succession. [...] Hutton wrote: [...] 'But if the succession of worlds is established in the system of nature, it is vain to look for anything higher in the origin of the earth. The result, therefore, of this physical enquiry is, that we find no vestige of a beginning, — no prospect of an end'.[129]

If Hutton's steady-state eternalism represents what we might call the optimistic vision of Earth's equilibrium and continuity, Buffon's theory of our planet's cold death represents its pessimistic counterpart. In *Le Dernier Homme* Grainville constructs yet another pessimistic vision of future events, and perhaps a no less likely one, namely the eventual exhaustion of the Earth's material resources and mankind's degeneration into sterility.

A decade later, Lord Byron — as some speculate perhaps inspired by the anonymous British translation of *Le Dernier Homme* — went on in his poem 'Darkness' to envision a further scenario of Earth's decline, one based on the assumption that the sun may one day lose its force. We may recall from my Introduction that Diderot had already in 1769 speculated in his fictional *Conversation between D'Alembert and Diderot* that the sun could one day expire, writing: 'If the sun is extinguished, what will happen? The plants will perish, the animals will perish, and you will have a deserted and silent earth'. Although that work was not published until 1830, it did not require Diderot's writings to be published for ideas of this kind to be picked up and circulate in society. Byron's 1816 dream vision provides a graphical illustration of the fact that by the early nineteenth century people had begun to grasp that the lifespan of our native sun or home planet might be limited for purely natural reasons; the poem's beginning and end read:

Darkness

> I had a dream, which was not all a dream.
> The bright sun was extinguish'd, and the stars
> Did wander darkling in the eternal space,
> Rayless, and pathless, and the icy earth
> Swung blind and blackening in the moonless air;
> Morn came and went — and came, and brought no day,
> And men forgot their passions in the dread
> Of this their desolation; and all hearts
> Were chill'd into a selfish prayer for light.
> [...]
>   The world was void,
> The populous and the powerful — was a lump,
> Seasonless, herbless, treeless, manless, lifeless —

---

[129] *The Rise of Scientific Europe 1500–1800*, ed. by David Goodman and Colin Russell (Sevenoaks: Hodder & Stoughton, 1991, for the Open University), p. 293. The original quote by Hutton can be found in his 'Theory of the Earth', in *Transactions of the Royal Society of Edinburgh*, vol. 1 (Edinburgh: Dickson, 1788), pp. 209–304 (p. 304).

> A lump of death — a chaos of hard clay.
> The rivers, lakes, and ocean all stood still,
> And nothing stirred within their silent depths;
> Ships sailorless lay rotting on the sea,
> And their masts fell down piecemeal: as they dropp'd
> They slept on the abyss without a surge —
> The waves were dead; the tides were in their grave,
> The moon their mistress had expir'd before;
> The winds were withered in the stagnant air,
> And the clouds perish'd; Darkness had no need
> Of aid from them — She was the Universe.

Byron took the inspiration for this 'apocalypse without millennium', as Morton D. Paley has described this poem,[130] not just from textual sources, but also from 'Nature'. While residing at Lake Geneva in Switzerland in the summer of 1816, Byron and his friends Polidori and Mary and Percy Bysshe Shelley experienced what has been dubbed the 'summer without sun'. It was by far the wettest summer in living memory; Mary in the 'Introduction' to the 1831 third edition of *Frankenstein* recalls it as having been a 'wet, ungenial summer' with 'incessant rain'.[131] Confining them 'for days to the house', the inclement weather gave the occasion for long evenings spent by the fireside reading and concocting ghost stories, resulting ultimately in the conception and drafting of Mary's first novel, *Frankenstein*.

The cause of the climatic anomaly was a natural disaster far removed in space and time, an outbreak of the volcano Mount Tambora on the Indonesian island of Sumbawa the previous year, on 10 April 1815. The largest on record in the past two millennia, Mount Tambora's eruption killed an estimated 71,000 people on the islands of Sumbawa and Lombok alone; the globe-encircling cloud of ash caused harvest failures across vast swathes of the northern hemisphere in 1816 and 1817, resulting in the worst famine in over a century.[132] The true cause of the changes in the weather patterns and the darkening of the sun was unknown to Europeans at the time; many speculated that they were brought about by sun spots, a phenomenon that only recently had been detected. *The London Chronicle* at the time reported as follows:

> The large spots which may now be seen upon the sun's disk have given rise to ridiculous apprehensions and absurd predictions. These spots are said to be the cause of the remarkable and wet weather we have had this Summer; and the increase of these spots is represented to announce a general removal of heat from the globe, the extinction of nature, and the end of the world.[133]

---

130 *Apocalypse and Millennium*, p. 66.

131 Mary Shelley, *Frankenstein. The 1818 Text*, ed. by J. Paul Hunter (New York and London: W. W. Norton, 1996), p. 170.

132 For more on this eruption see Clive Oppenheimer, 'Climatic, environmental and human consequences of the largest known historic eruption: Tambora volcano (Indonesia) 1815', *Progress in Physical Geography*, 27 (2003), 230–59 (p. 251), the subsequent passage p. 244.

133 Cited from Jeffrey Vail, '"the Bright Sun was Extinguish'd": The Bologna Prophecy and Byron's "Darkness"', *Wordsworth Circle*, 28 (Summer 1997), 183–92 (p. 184).

'A general removal of heat from the globe' and 'the extinction of nature' at 'the end of the world' was of course the very idea that lay at the heart of Buffon's geothermic hypothesis, as Byron well knew — and to which his reference to 'icy earth' is testimony. Whether we attribute Byron's poem alone to the tangible climatic effects experienced during that unusual summer or interpret it as an homage to Buffon, or both, one thing is clear: the author of 'Darkness' refrains from implicating God as the source of this destruction. Here 'Nature' rules supreme, and there is no suggestion either of Parousia or of Millennium.

Byron's poem is symptomatic of a crucial dilemma affecting the literature of his era (more specifically: our ability to interpret the literature of this period in religious terms). This dilemma derives from the fact that, because both the deist and the atheist reject the possibility of miracles, their works become indistinguishable in terms of how they represent the relationship between natural and supernatural phenomena. In deistic and atheistic literature the supernatural can have no tangible impact on reality. In theistic literature, by contrast, the supernatural is granted a separate and independent existence; it intrudes into and impinges on the natural world. The interplay Grainville conjures up between the two spheres of the natural and supernatural in *Le Dernier Homme* can leave us in no doubt as to the theism involved in his vision of the future; thus in Canto I the angel Ithuriel appears before Adam to pronounce that he has come to 'conduct [him] to earth where the Almighty has called [him] to implement the divine plan which He will disclose to [Adam] by supernatural means' ('Je vais te conduire sur la terre, où le Très-Haut t'appelle pour accomplir des desseins qu'il doit révéler à ton esprit, en y versant des lumières surnaturelles').[134] Passages like this underscore not just the theistic impulse behind Grainville's epic, but also signal the author's conscious counter-stance to the 'enlightened' discourse of contemporary philosophy. Grainville's educated reader would have easily recognized that by opening his story 'near the ruins of Palmyra' the author was making reference to a widely circulated 'key text of "revolutionary atheism"',[135] namely Comte de Volney's 1791 publication *The Ruins, or Meditation on the Revolutions of Empires* (*Les Ruines, ou Méditation sur les révolutions des empires*, see Figure 2.5). For Volney's book too opens with the narrator visiting the ruins of the ancient city of Palmyra in central Syria. Having sunk into a dreamlike trance he finds himself whisked out of his body into space by a spirit who parades before his eyes the ruins of history's procession of empires whose countless religions were once deemed as universally valid as Christianity's creed in his time. A good proportion of Volney's book serves to compare and contrast these religions; he has their priests engage in a grand debate about the superiority of their versions of belief, each spiritual leader accusing the others of mysticism, idolatry and pretentiousness, only to find themselves all rebutted by the 'Legislators' who have been listening to this cacophony of religious unreason. These legislators — Volney himself was not just a philosopher, historian and orientalist, but also an influential legislator, serving as member of the Estates-General and National Constituent Assembly during the

---

[134] *The Last Man*, trans. I. F. & M. Clarke, p. 8 (*Le Dernier Homme*, ed. Kupiec, p. 50).
[135] Priestman, *Romantic Atheism*, p. 22.

Fig. 2.5. Frontispiece from the first book edition of Comte de Volney's *Les Ruines, ou Méditation sur les révolutions des empires* of 1791. The caption reads: 'Here once flowered an opulent City; here was the seat of a once powerful Empire: Yes! these spaces now so deserted, once a teeming multitude animated their surroundings, &.'

French Revolution — at long last inform the 'general assembly of peoples and nations' how all religions had sunk into 'an inextricable labyrinth of contradictions' ('un labyrinthe inextricable de contradictions').[136] 'Whence it is obvious,' they conclude, 'that, in order to live in peace and harmony, we must [...] separate by an inviolable barrier, the world of fantastic beings from the world of realities: that is to say, all civil effect must be taken away from theological and religious opinions' ('D'où il faut conclure que, pour vivre en concorde et en paix, il faut consentir à [...] séparer d'une barrière inviolable le monde des êtres fantastiques du monde des réalités; c'est-à-dire, qu'il faut ôter tout effet civil aux opinions theologiques et religieuses'); 'the only way of restoring unanimity', they pronounce Solomonically, 'is by returning to nature, and taking the order of things which she has established for your director and guide' ('le seul moyen d'être d'accord est de revenir à la nature, et de prendre pour arbitre et régulateur l'ordre de choses qu'elle-même a posé'). In short, Volney appeals to his readers to turn away from religious factionalism, fanaticism, and intolerance and return to reason and nature.

Grainville harnesses the same narrative framework — an oriental location in Palmyra and a genie sharing with the narrator a vision of mankind's future — but deploys it not just to repudiate Volney's critique of religion, but also to remind his reader that, regardless of anything that *la fausse philosophie* might declare and regardless of how long it might take, the Almighty is waiting in the wings. It may be a question of centuries or millennia even, but no one can ultimately escape the 'divine plan' of the coming 'great revolution' ('des desseins [...] d'une grande révolution')[137] that awaits us all at the end of time. The French Revolution may have *changed* the course of history, but God's much grander revolution will *conclude* the course of history.[138]

I was initially inclined to think that Grainville's personal misfortunes during and after the French Revolution had induced the Catholic ex-priest to abandon theism for a modified deism in which the world progressed without divine intervention until the moment the planet Earth and its human inhabitants had exhausted themselves, at which point the Last Judgment could at last commence. But the more I thought about it I realized that the excessive number of miracles, prophecies come true, and other supernatural occurrences that riddle the plotline of *Le Dernier Homme* did not tally with a deist's worldview. Even leaving the end game of the Last Judgment aside, during which we witness 'the Almighty' himself come 'on clouds of gold and silver to pronounce the Last Judgment' ('Dieu [...] vient sur des nuages d'or et d'argent achever le jugement dernier'), the dead arise from their

---

136 Constantin François Chassebœuf, Comte de Volney, *The Ruins: Or A Survey of the Revolutions of Empires*, 2nd edn (London: J. Johnson, 1795), p. 214; *Les Ruines, ou Méditation sur les révolutions des empires* (Paris: Desenne, Vollard and Plassan, 1791), p. 214. The subsequent quotes, pp. 323 and 321 (pp. 328 and 326).

137 *The Last Man*, trans. I. F. & M. Clarke, p. 8 (*Le Dernier Homme*, ed. Kupiec, p. 50).

138 I do not have the space here to expand on the political ramifications of Grainville's *Le Dernier Homme*, but would like to refer my reader to two useful articles, Morton D. Paley's '*Le dernier homme*: The French Revolution as the Failure of Typology', cited earlier, and Katie Sainson's '"La Régénération de la France": Literary Accounts of Napoleonic Regeneration 1799–1805', *Nineteenth-Century French Studies*, 30 (Fall-Winter 2001–2002), 9–25.

graves and the 'legions of demons' of Hell ('des légions de démons') issue from their subterranean caverns,[139] it remains nigh on impossible to reconcile with a deist's 'naturalist' perspective the fact that Omegarus, the chief protagonist in the 'natural' plotline of the core narrative, is at liberty to commune with an immortal Adam, not to mention the countless miracles, wonders and enchantments effected by the Spirit of the Earth to extend his life. This overabundance in *Le Dernier Homme* of supernatural 'invisible agents' who arbitrarily 'transgress the laws of nature' in order to intervene in the progress of human history, to recall Hume's locution, demarcates the text clearly as theistic. The only genuinely deistic aspects of *Le Dernier Homme*, then, are first the fact that planet Earth and its human inhabitants are permitted to come to a naturally motivated end, as opposed to one enforced purely at random by an all-powerful God, and second the striking absence of Christ the Redeemer during the unfolding of the Last Judgment.

Where does all this leave us? What then is the hermeneutic question at the heart of Grainville's unusual prose epopee? And what kind of audience must we assume Grainville was trying to reach? The answer that comes most readily to mind would be a theistic one, a reader who believes in an active meddling God and does not doubt that the Last Judgment will occur. The novel question that Grainville raises, however, is *when and how* humankind and our planet will arrive at that point. The traditionalist Christian's answer was that given by Burnet, and in his wake by the likes of the anonymous German cleric I cited in Chapter One as well as many orthodox evangelicals today: 6000 years after Creation, give or take a little, depending on God's timing. Grainville's vision of the Last Judgment, by contrast, is tinged by deistic thought, as Alkon and other critics have correctly pointed out, inasmuch as the timing of the Last Judgment in *Le Dernier Homme* is not preordained by God, but rather established through a combination of natural and human factors. The initial catalyst is nature's exhaustion, the second catalyst is humankind losing its ability to procreate. It is at this moment in world history that a sole human being, Omegarus, is given the power to determine the fate of our species. Here Grainville accords with his German counterpart Sonnenberg: it is the human species that ultimately determines the onset of the Last Judgment. But whereas Sonnenberg leans more towards a theistic conclusion, Grainville leans more towards a deistic solution. Sonnenberg's deity acts per fiat in the midst of the majority of mankind continuing with their (faithless) lives on our globe — here the Almighty is a distinctly Christian God, assisted by his son Jesus Christ as 'Reconciler', who penalizes the unfaithful for their apostasy. Grainville's planet Earth by contrast is, as I detailed earlier, a deist's world populated by pagans that has come to the end of its life cycle; here Christ has no role to play in the drama of the end of time. The early nineteenth-century anonymous German reviewer I cited earlier clearly recognized this difference when he wrote: 'with Sonnenberg it is the moral deterioration of humankind that triggers the ruin of the world, and from this foundation all the action of this epic follows. [...] In Mr Grainville's case

---

139 *The Last Man*, trans. I. F. & M. Clarke, pp. 122 and 129 (*Le Dernier Homme*, ed. Kupiec, pp. 172 and 181).

the Earth comes to an end because of old age, as determined by the course of nature and God's will; it is not brought about by humankind's moral behaviour'.

But even all this should not tempt us to assume that Grainville is a deist — quite to the contrary. Granted, in *Le Dernier Homme* Grainville can be seen to address an audience that is aware of the progress made in the natural sciences and philosophy of his time; besides the references to Condorcet and Buffon discussed above, there are further allusions to Edward Jenner's medical advances and Thomas Malthus's at the time much debated theory about population growth and decline in his 1798 *An Essay on the Principle of Population*. Indeed, the decline of humanity's fortunes in *Le Dernier Homme* is rather reminiscent of Malthus's dire predictions for mankind's future: 'Famine seems to be the last, the most dreadful resource of nature', Malthus had claimed, explaining how

> [t]he power of population is so superior to the power of the earth to produce subsistence for man, that premature death must in some shape or other visit the human race. The vices of mankind are active and able ministers of depopulation. They are the precursors in the great army of destruction; and often finish the dreadful work themselves. But should they fail in this war of extermination, sickly seasons, epidemics, pestilence, and plague, advance in terrific array, and sweep off their thousands and ten thousands. Should success be still incomplete, gigantic inevitable famine stalks in the rear, and with one mighty blow, levels the population with the food of the world.[140]

And yet, even as Grainville alludes to these works of contemporary scholarship (we today would say science), the ex-priest seeks through the overall plot line of his narrative and its supernatural setting (e.g., the appearance of Adam in mankind's futurity, the machinations of the Spirit of the Earth, and the action's culmination in the Last Judgment) to remind his readers that, even in the face of such secular speculation about universal progress and human perfectibility, people must not lose sight of the more important spiritual dimension of any and all progress, namely that a time will come when God will summon his subjects to a final Day of Reckoning, a summons that will apply no less to the pagan infidels within his epopee than to the theists and deists among his intended audience.[141] His interpretation of progress and world history is inextricably entwined with the 'classical' vision of the Last Judgment viewed, in the words of the German apocalypse expert Eva Horn, as an *adventus*, as 'something always already decreed and approaching' ('als etwas immer schon Entschiedenes, auf uns Zukommendes').[142] This 'classical model' of the apocalypse, she explains, conceives of the end of the world as 'the emergence of a [final] truth which can become visible and thinkable only from the perspective of that end' ('als das Hervortreten einer Wahrheit, die erst vom Ende her sichtbar und denkbar werden wird'); Horn observes further: 'What the end yields is a particular insight into the state of mankind, an anthropological truth in the mode of the

---

140 *An Essay on the Principle of Population, as it affects the Future Improvement of Society* (London: J. Johnson, 1798), Ch. VII, pp. 139–40.

141 The population of the world of *Le Dernier Homme* is pagan, not Christian, as Alkon and others have rightly pointed out; see for instance Alkon, *Origins of Futuristic Fiction*, p. 166.

142 Horn, 'Die romantische Verdunklung', p. 101, the subsequent quote pp. 101–02.

futurum perfectum. From the end we can judge and assess what man *will have been*, and what he could have been' ('Was das Ende hervorbringt, ist eine Erkenntnis über den Menschen, eine anthropologische Wahrheit im Modus des *futurum perfectum*. Vom Ende aus lässt sich ermessen, was der Mensch *gewesen sein wird*, gewesen sein könnte'; Horn's emphases). In this sense any imagining of the apocalypse is not just 'hypothetical' ('Potentialis') or 'conditional' ('Konditionalis'), but always already also an eminently cautionary and proselytizing project aimed at the present.

Grainville's dilemma, however, was that he had fundamentally misjudged his audience. Even a theistic Catholic readership — we should remember that more than 95% of France's population at the time were Catholics (although I do not know how many of them were literate) — would have been puzzled, if not altogether put off, by the more than just unconventional fusion of mystical setting, preternatural plot and bombastic Christian ending, with all of this underpinned by a distinctly deistic core story. (Accordingly Élise Gagne, in her 1859 version of the tale, *Omégar, ou le Dernier Homme*, moved explicitly to strengthen the Christian underpinnings in her 'Preface' as well as in her storyline.) Even where Grainville's text is premised on a critique of progress and the Enlightenment, the storyline remains too unorthodox by far as well as too un-Christian, to satisfy the spiritual needs of a middle-class Catholic audience (middle-class in my opinion because his audience needed to be able to read and possess the means to purchase books at a time of acute economic crisis). A deistic or atheistic readership, on the other hand, would have rejected the author's obsession with and reliance upon miracles and the supernatural out of hand, as well as what many would have regarded as brazen Christian scare-mongering. There is far too much — and far too much unnecessary — supernatural machinery in *Le Dernier Homme*, Christian as well as non-Christian, for it successfully to cater to a modern enlightened taste. In short, Grainville had written himself out of an audience, Christian or sceptic. The supposedly at most forty copies sold of the first edition bear testimony to the contemporary audience's utter disinterest either in this topic or the manner of its presentation or, more probably, both.

The Last Judgment

Having come to this conclusion I must add, despite all that I have said, that Grainville's story of the last man has more merit and historical significance than meets the eye, not just because it has been (albeit in my view inaccurately) reclaimed as an early specimen in the tradition of futuristic science fiction. Writ large across *Le Dernier Homme* are two interconnected themes. First is the theme of obedience and disobedience to God. The 'First Man' Adam had in the infancy of time been disobedient (and *Le Dernier Homme* shows with grisly fascination what the consequences had been); would the 'Last Man' Omegarus dare to repeat that disobedience, or would he elect to heed God's will? Accordingly, the text's closing lines, cited earlier more fully, reiterate this key theme; bringing the story full circle and closing the frame narrative, the Spirit of Futurity says to the traveller deep in that 'solitary cavern near the ruins of Palmyra' (and we can safely assume that at this point the Spirit of Futurity's voice is identical with that of the author):

> I wished only to let you witness the triumph of Omegarus, and to show you that, by obeying the commands of Heaven, he [i.e., Omegarus] will one day cut short the reign of time and hasten the coming of eternity. My mission is accomplished. Tell men about this history of the last age of earth. Sacrifice to this glorious task your hopes of fortune and your ambitions, and I will make the hours of your labors the sweetest moments in your life.

By not submitting unquestioningly to God's commands, both Adam and Omegarus have made themselves guilty of a 'transgression'.[143] And thus the beginning of history, the A/*alpha* of humankind, is in danger of repeating itself at the end of history in the figure of Omegarus, the Ω/*omega* of humankind. But it is repetition with a difference: after copious trials and tribulations, Omegarus at long last yields to Adam's repeated entreaties not to repeat his original mistake by yet again challenging God's authority. At the moment Omegarus makes his decision he enters Syderia's dream in the form of a Christ-like apotheosis:

> Syderia saw Omegarus in that spot lit by the rays of the rising sun. He was surrounded by the just who stretched out their hands to him in thankfulness, for they perceived in his soul the sufferings he had accepted in order to hasten their day of glorification. At his side, Syderia saw the old man [Adam] she had seen the day before. His face was radiant; and his eyes shone with joy.
>
> [Sydérie voit Omégare aux lieux que le soleil éclaire de ses rayons naissants; il est entouré des justes qui, lisant dans son âme exposée a leurs yeux les peines qu'il a souffertes pour hâter le jour de leur gloire, tendent vers lui des mains reconnaissantes. Sydérie aperçoit à ses côtés ce vieillard qu'elle avait vu la veille; son front est radieux, la joie brille dans ses regards.][144]

Both passages also link into the second theme, the end of time and 'the coming of eternity', i.e. the Last Judgment. As noted above, *Le Dernier Homme* gives due notice to both its theistically and deistically inclined reader that no one will escape God's final reckoning, regardless of whether he (or she) believes in a theistic God who executes a precipitous intervention in human affairs (the kind Young and Sonnenberg present in their works), or in a deistic God who is content for history to run its course. What is clear in *Le Dernier Homme* is that the Last Judgment is inevitable and inescapable either way, and this in itself betokens the author's theistic worldview.

The true deist by contrast had long excised the apocalypse from the workings of the natural world and had relegated the Last Judgment to the realm of a symbolic language game. As mentioned in Chapter One Kant's 1793 *Religion within the Boundaries of Mere Reason* provides a good example; in it Kant states:

> This representation in a historical narrative of the future world, which is not itself history, is a beautiful ideal of the moral world-epoch brought about by the introduction of the true universal religion and *foreseen* in faith in its

---

143 The word 'transgression' is used only in the English translation (pp. 12 and 117), not in the French original (which uses 'faute').

144 *The Last Man*, trans. I. F. & M. Clarke, p. 121 (*Le Dernier Homme*, ed. Kupiec, p. 172).

completion — one which we do not *see directly* in the manner of an empirical completion but *have a glimpse of* in the continuous advance and approximation toward the highest possible good on earth (in this there is nothing mystical but everything proceeds naturally in a moral way), i.e. we can make preparation for it. The appearance of the Antichrist, the millennium, the announcement of the proximity of the end of the world, all take on their proper symbolic meaning before reason. And the last of them, represented (like the end of life, whether far or near) as an event which we cannot see in advance, expresses very well the necessity for us always to be ready for it, yet (if we ascribe to this symbol its intellectual meaning) in fact always to consider ourselves as actually the chosen citizens of a divine (ethical) state.

[Diese Vorstellung einer Geschichtserzählung der Nachwelt, die selbst keine Geschichte ist, ist ein schönes Ideal der durch Einführung der wahren allgemeinen Religion bewirkten moralischen, im Glauben *vorausgesehenen* Weltepoche, bis zu ihrer Vollendung, die wir nicht als empirische Vollendung *absehen*, sondern auf die wir nur im kontinuierlichen Fortschreiten und Annäherung zum höchsten auf Erden möglichen Guten (worin nichts Mystisches ist, sondern alles auf moralische Weise natürlich zugeht) *hinaussehen*, d.i. dazu Anstalt machen können. Die Erscheinung des Antichrists, des Chiliasm, die Ankündigung der Naheit des Weltendes können vor der Vernunft ihre gute symbolische Bedeutung annehmen, und die letztere, als ein (so wie das Lebensende, ob nahe oder fern) nicht vorher zu sehendes Ereignis vorgestellt, drückt sehr gut die Notwendigkeit aus, jederzeit darauf in Bereitschaft zu stehen, in der Tat aber (wenn man diesem Symbol den intellektuellen Sinn unterlegt) uns jederzeit wirklich als berufene Bürger eines göttlichen (ethischen) Staats anzusehen.][145] (Kant's emphases)

In a footnote appended to this passage Kant adds: 'A kingdom of God is here represented not according to a particular covenant ([it is] not a messianic kingdom) but according to a *moral* one (available to cognition through mere reason)' ('Hier wird nun ein Reich Gottes, nicht nach einem besonderen Bunde (kein messianisches), sondern ein moralisches (durch bloße Vernunft erkennbares) vorgestellt'). To mitigate what many would have perceived as his shockingly un-Christian interpretation of the last events, Kant closes his argument with a quote from the Bible, citing Luke 17:21–22: 'The Kingdom of God cometh not in visible form. [...] *For behold, the Kingdom of God is within you!*' ('Das Reich Gottes kommt nicht in sichtbarer Gestalt. [...] *Denn sehet, das Reich Gottes ist inwendig in euch!*'; Kant's emphasis).

If Kant sees nature's and humanity's end as tied in with his moral imperative, with the Kingdom to Come and the Last Judgment demoted to a purely symbolic status, how does Kant relate to that other fundamental tenet of deism, God as a first cause (albeit one that has since stepped back and away from intervening in history)? If, to adapt James Hutton's adage, there is 'no prospect of an end', does Kant at least hold on to 'a vestige of a beginning'? If we go back to Kant's 1755 *General Natural History and Theory of the Heavens*, the answer is clearly yes. In the 'Preface' to his contribution to the 'Theory of the Earth' genre, Kant explicitly

---

145 *Religion within the Boundaries of Mere Reason*, p. 162–63 (*Die Religion innerhalb der Grenzen der blossen Vernunft*, p. 802), the subsequent passage p. 163 (p. 803).

admits the existence of a 'most wise Author'. He writes: 'I am aware of the entire value of those proofs that are adduced from the beauty and perfect arrangement of the universe to confirm a most wise Author' ('Ich erkenne den ganzen Wert derjenigen Beweise, die man aus der Schönheit und vollkommenen Anordnung des Weltbaues zur Bestätigung eines höchstweisen Urhebers ziehet').[146] However, he is at pains to reconcile the notion of a 'wise Author' with the independence of the laws this divine 'Author' has created. Once the Book of Nature and Natural Law has been written and released into the world, no miraculous revision is possible. Kant accordingly notes:

> Matter, which is the original material of all things is thus bound by certain laws, and if it is left freely to these laws, it must necessarily bring forth beautiful combinations. It is not at liberty to deviate from this plan of perfection. Since, therefore, it is subject to a most wise purpose, it must necessarily have been placed into such harmonious connections by a first cause that ruled over it, and *a God exists precisely because nature cannot behave in any way other than in a regular and orderly manner, even in chaos.* (Kant's emphases)
>
> [Die Materie, die der Urstoff aller Dinge ist, ist also an gewisse Gesetze gebunden, welchen sie frei überlassen notwendig schöne Verbindungen hervorbringen muß. Sie hat keine Freiheit, von diesem Plane der Vollkommenheit abzuweichen. Da sie also sich einer höchst weisen Absicht unterworfen befindet, so muß sie notwendig in solche übereinstimmende Verhältnisse durch eine über sie herrschende erste Ursache versetzt worden sein, und *es ist ein Gott eben deswegen, weil die Natur auch selbst im Chaos nicht anders als regelmäßig und ordentlich verfahren kann.*]

If Kant prudently avoids going into more detail in this early treatise, and if the speculative pure and practical reasoning of his later 'Critical' period allows him to bypass the issue of God's direct agency altogether, discussing God as a 'concept' ('Begriff') and mere transcendental '*ideal*, though a *faultless* one' ('fehlerfreies Ideal') rather than a reality,[147] it is perhaps because he had registered the nagging inconsistency within deism, an inconsistency that, I contend, is also at the heart of Grainville's *Le Dernier Homme*. As Charles Taylor explains:

> What Deism in its various forms wanted to reject was seeing God as an agent intervening in history. He could be agent qua original Architect of the universe, but not as the author of myriad particular interventions, 'miraculous' or not, which were the stuff of popular piety and orthodox religion.[148]

Nor as the author, I would add, of that other particular intervention, the Last Judgment. Deists seemed most willing to concede a miraculous beginning, but far less willing to admit to the prospect of an equally miraculous end.[149] Put in a

---

146 *Universal Natural History*, p. 195 (*Allgemeine Naturgeschichte*, p. 228), the subsequent quotes pp. 195 and 199 (pp. 229 and 234–35).

147 *Critique of Pure Reason*, p. 393 (*Kritik der reinen Vernunft*, p. 563).

148 *A Secular Age*, p. 275.

149 Kant is in my opinion a prime example, as for instance the section 'The Ideal of Pure Reason' ('Das Ideal der reinen Vernunft') of his *Critique of Pure Reason* illustrates in terms of beginnings, and *Religion within the Boundaries of Mere Reason* and 'The End of all Things' in terms of the end.

nutshell: they wanted to have it both ways — an active and an inactive God at one and the same time. It is in this context that Franz von Sonnenberg makes an incisive observation in the 'Preface' to his *Donatoa*, concluding that who says Alpha must also say Omega, who says 'Beginning' must also say 'End': 'The physical ruin of the world through a blind clash of the elements', he writes,

> is an insult to any higher sense of religion in a human heart. If God ever has revealed Himself to the world, or ever could, man must think: most naturally this would occur *at the moment of Creation and the moment when the world terminates*. A belief in spirits above imposes itself when we look at the firmament; this belief is as deeply engrained in us as the belief in immortality. If the spirits above have ever approached our world, according to forces and laws concealed to us, and ever took control of the fate of humankind, then where more naturally so than *at its Creation and at its Dissolution*.
>
> [Phisischer Weltuntergang durch blinden Kampf der Elemente beleidigt die höhere Religion im Menschenherzen. Wenn sich die Gottheit jeh der Erde offenbart hat oder offenbaren kann, so denkt sich der Mensch doch: am natürlichsten *bei ihrer Schöpfung und bei ihrem Untergange*. Der Glaube an höhere Wesen drängt sich uns auf beim Blick an den Sternenhimmel; er ist so tief in uns gegründet, wie die Hoffnung der Unsterblichkeit. Wenn sich diese Höheren jeh der Erde nahten, jeh, nach uns verborgenen Kräften und Gesetzen, Einfluß auf die Menschenwelt äußerten; wo natürlicher, als *bei ihrer Schöpfung und bei ihrem Untergang!*][150] (my emphases)

The conclusion must be, in effect, that we either believe in theism — with an A *and* an O, with a beginning *and* an end (and perhaps also God's miraculous agency in between) — or we must take recourse to atheism, a belief system that consistently denies God's agency and existence at all times. (This will become the subject of Chapters Three and Four.)

Because of this irreconcilable internal inconsistency deism was, by 1800, beginning to lose traction. It was losing ground on the one hand against the resurgent (Romantic) theism discussed in Chapter One, and on the other against the ever burgeoning atheism heading for its nineteenth-century apexes, Ludwig Feuerbach's psychological materialism, Karl Marx's dialectical materialism and Nietzsche's philosophical nihilism. A sign of the times, and a harbinger of deism's looming exhaustion, were two publications by a German theist, the Leipzig theologian and philosopher Johann August Tittmann, and an English atheist, the poet Percy Bysshe Shelley. In his 1816 volume *On Supernaturalism, Rationalism and Atheism* (*Über Supranaturalismus, Rationalismus und Atheismus*), published at the same time as Byron wrote 'Darkness', Tittmann undertakes to bring down the edifice of deism by arguing very methodically and analytically that God either created the world *and* must therefore still be around, or he never existed in the first place; there can be no in-between, Tittmann reasons, no deism's having its cake and eating it. He writes:

> God either takes action directly, or he doesn't take action at all. [...] You cannot

---

150 'Einiges über den Gesichtspunkt dieses Gedichts', *Donatoa*, I.1, p. xi.

escape this abyss of rationalism by arguing that it is still possible to believe that God maintains the laws of Nature. For this empty phrase either means nothing, or it means that God is the reason that Nature endures with its laws. [...] But if one truly believes that God is the cause for the world to exist with its laws, then you must also assume that God is incessantly taking action. But since the principles of Rationalism do not allow for this, so one can also not claim that God truly maintains the world and its laws. [...] He is therefore dead for the world.

[Gott wirkt entweder unmittelbar, oder er wirkt gar nicht. [...] Diesem Abgrunde des sogenannten Rationalismus kann man nicht dadurch entfliehem, daß man sagt, man glaube doch, daß Gott die Gesetze der Natur erhalte. Denn auch diese Redensart sagt entweder gar nichts, oder sie sagt, daß Gott die Ursache sey, daß die Natur mit ihren Gesetzen fortdaure. [...] [D]enn eigentlich heißt es nichts weiter, als: die Welt erhält sich selbst durch ihre Gesetze, oder, die Gesetze, nicht Gott, erhalten die Welt. Meynt man aber wirklich, daß in Gott die Ursache liege, warum die Welt mit ihren Gesetzen fortdaure, so muß man ein fortwährendes Wirken Gottes annehmen [...]. Da dies aber laut der Prinzipien jenes Rationalismus nicht Statt haben kann, so kann man eigentlich auch nicht sagen, daß Gott die Welt mit ihren Gesetzen wirklich erhalte. [...] Er ist dann todt für die Welt.][151]

Tittmann consequently argues that,

if it contradicts Reason to believe in God's supernatural causality, then it contradicts Reason in principle to believe in *any* agency of God whatsoever; for no agency of God can be thought of as other than a supernatural causality, or this agency is truly nothing other than an agency of Nature.

[Wenn es also der Vernunft widerspricht, eine unmittelbare übernatürliche Causalität Gottes anzunehmen, so widerspricht es ihr überhaupt, an irgend eine Wirkung Gottes zu glauben; denn jede Wirkung Gottes muß als Folge einer übernatürlichen Causalität gedacht werden, oder sie ist eigentlich nichts, als Wirkung der Natur.]

In short, we are faced with the alternative *either* God *or* Nature. With the convenient but inconsistent deistic half-way house between the two excluded on the basis of his analytical method, everything that falls under the rubric of Rationalism (which includes the French *philosophes* and the British Free-Thinkers) must in essence be atheistic, Tittmann decrees; accordingly, the final paragraph of his book reads: 'Is this where Reason leads us? God forbid, and Reason too. But that is where those principles lead us which one mistakenly calls Rationalism, those principles, which applied consistently, leave Reason no other alternative than either to give them up, or to confess one's Atheism' ('Dahin also führte die Vernunft? Da sey Gott vor, und die Vernunft selbst. Aber jene Grundsätze führen dahin, welche man fälschlich Rationalismus nennt, jene Grundsätze, welche richtig angewendet, der Vernunft keine andere Wahl lassen, als sie entweder aufzugeben, oder sich zum Atheismus zu bekennen').

---

151 Johann August Tittmann, *Über Supranaturalismus, Rationalismus und Atheismus* (Leipzig: Fleischer, 1816), pp. 272–73, the subsequent passages pp. 275 and 287–88.

Two years before Tittmann's *Über Supranaturalismus, Rationalismus und Atheismus* appeared, Percy Bysshe Shelley was among those who had come to the same conclusion. In 1814 Shelley anonymously published a tract entitled *A Refutation of Deism: In a Dialogue* in which he too states equally unequivocally: 'The object of the following Dialogue is to prove that the system of Deism is untenable. It is attempted to shew that there is no alternative between Atheism and Christianity'.[152] But instead of turning to Christian theism Shelley chose to adopt atheism as his creed instead, which he considered the only logically consistent worldview. (See Chapter Four for an extended discussion of Shelley's *The Necessity of Atheism* of 1811 and his atheistic poem *Queen Mab* of 1813.) *A Refutation of Deism* is a most peculiar and duplicitous text in that, due to what Earl Wasserman has called its 'Humean artistry',[153] it takes some time even for an informed reader to get his bearings and figure out who is saying what and why. The text consists of a dialogue between a theist, Eusebes, and a deist, Theosophus, both of whom are opposed to atheism. As might be expected, the text opens with Eusebes and Theosophus each defending his own belief system and contesting the other's; thus Eusebes first challenges deism followed by Theosophus challenging theism. But the dialogue then resorts to a form of role inversion, in which Eusebes, for argument's sake and to pull the rug out from under his deist opponent's feet, adopts the position of an atheist — much supported by references to and footnote quotations of such recognized atheists, quasi-atheists, and deists as Lucretius, Spinoza, Holbach, Gibbon, Paine, Godwin and Southey (Eusebes is clearly well versed in anti-Christian literature) — in order to prove to Philosophus that there is no God, and that the deist must either accept the atheist's argument against the existence of God or make a conscious decision for God — he cannot have it both ways. Eusebes is of course expecting the deist to admit defeat, reject atheism and return to the fold. Ironically, and this is Shelley's ingenious ruse, this role reversal causes the theist Eusebes to formulate a stridently atheistic critique of both theism and deism that is virtually impregnable. In the end, Shelley has made a theist and a deist playact the demolition — or, in today's parlance, deconstruction — of all religious creed; as Kenneth Neill Cameron observed in his 1951 study *The Young Shelley. Genesis of a Radical*, which contains one of the most detailed discussions of Shelley's *A Refutation of Deism*, Shelley 'proceeds [...] by the highly ingenious method of a dialogue in which one speaker, a deist, annihilates the arguments of Christian theology, while another, a Christian, annihilates those of deism. [...] The two thus cancel each other out and nothing is left but atheism'.[154]

---

152 Percy Bysshe Shelley, *A Refutation of Deism: In a Dialogue*, in *The Works of Percy Bysshe Shelley*, ed. by Harry Buxton Forman, 8 vols (London: Reeves and Turner, 1880), vol. 6, pp. 29–80 (p. 33).

153 See Earl Wasserman, *Shelley. A Critical Reading* (Baltimore and London: Johns Hopkins University Press, 1971), p. 13. I found other useful discussions of *A Refutation of Deism* in Michael Henry Scrivener's *Radical Shelley. The Philosophical Anarchism and Utopian Thought of Percy Bysshe Shelley* (Princeton: Princeton University Press, 1982), pp. 77–83; and Paul Hamilton, 'Literature and Philosophy', in *The Cambridge Companion to Shelley*, ed. by Timothy Morton (Cambridge: Cambridge University Press, 2006), pp. 166–84, specifically pp. 171–78.

154 *The Young Shelley. Genesis of a Radical* (London: Victor Gollancz, 1951), p. 279.

As I will argue in Chapter Four, despite Shelley's adolescent and early adult pronouncements of his atheism, his poetic works, certainly those from 1817 on, seem to suggest that he could not completely relinquish his belief in some form of guiding spirituality in and behind nature and that, in effect, he returned towards a more pantheistically infused form of worldview later in life. Shelley might thus be considered a prime example of what Tittmann conveniently overlooks, namely that there was indeed an alternative between Christianity and atheism; however, it was not deism but rather pantheism, or some gradation thereof. Although orthodox Christian theologians and philosophers throughout the eighteenth century were keen to pigeon-hole and castigate pantheism as nothing more than a veneer for atheism, Spinozist pantheism far more than deism represented the true 'half-way house' between theism and atheism, to cite Taylor's expression once more, because in fusing theism and atheism it steers clear of deism's inconsistencies. It is precisely this that made Spinoza's philosophy so dangerous and threatening to Revealed Religion; in his study of the *Radical Enlightenment*, which can be read by and large as a reception history of Spinoza in Europe, Jonathan Israel accordingly declares:

> Spinoza's prime contribution to the evolution of early modern Naturalism, fatalism, and irreligion [...] was his ability to integrate within a single coherent or ostensibly coherent system, the chief elements of ancient, modern, and oriental 'atheism'. No one else in early modern times did this, or anything comparable, and it is primarily the unity, cohesion, and compelling power of his system, his ability to connect major elements of previous 'atheistic' thought into an unbroken chain of reasoning, rather than the novelty of force of any of his constituent concepts which explains his centrality in the evolution of the whole Radical Enlightenment.[155]

It is worth noting that Tittmann, writing as late as 1816, makes no reference whatsoever either generally to pantheism as a belief system (despite its manifesting itself quite prominently for instance in Goethe's poetry) or more specifically to Spinoza, perhaps out of fear that any such reference posed the danger of highlighting theism's own persisting limitations and inconsistencies.

Tittmann's contemporary Heinrich Heine, by contrast, himself vacillating during his lifetime between his native Jewish and adopted Protestant belief on the one hand and unbelief on the other, as I indicated earlier in this chapter, expounds amply on the subject in *On Germany since Luther*; he notes there (during a phase in the 1830s during which he leant more towards unbelief):

> I shall consequently indicate with the name pantheism not so much the system as the manner in which Spinoza regarded it. In this latter the unity of God may be assumed as well as in deism. But the God of the pantheists is in the world itself — not merely penetrated by his divinity. [...] No, the world is not steeped and impregnated in God, but is identical with God. [...] The God of the pantheists differs also from that of the deists, because he is himself in the world, while the latter is quite out of, or, what is the same, over it.
>
> [Ich werde in der Folge weniger das System als vielmehr die Anschauungsweise

---

[155] *Radical Enlightement*, p. 230.

des Spinoza mit dem Namen Pantheismus bezeichnen. Bey letzterem wird, eben
so gut wie bey dem Deismus, die Einheit Gottes angenommen. Aber der Gott
des Pantheisten ist in der Welt selbst, nicht indem er sie mit seiner Göttlichkeit
durchdringt [...]: nein, die Welt ist nicht bloß gottgetränkt, gottgeschwängert,
sondern sie ist identisch mit Gott. [...] Der Gott des Pantheisten unterscheidet
sich also von dem Gotte des Deisten dadurch, da er in der Welt selbst ist,
während letzterer ganz außer, oder was dasselbe ist, über der Welt ist.][156]

In effect, pantheism transmogrifies God into Nature, just as it elevates Nature to
the equivalent of God. As Spinoza's oft-repeated catchphrase *Deus sive Natura*, 'God
or Nature', implies, to know and understand God one must not study the scripture
of any revealed religion, but rather the 'mighty Volumes of visible Nature'[157] itself.
By equating God and Nature Spinoza was able to circumvent the inconsistency that
had come to plague deism when it retained the concept of a personal Creator God
at the beginning of time while rejecting his interference at all other times. Spinozist
pantheism with its fused unity of God and Nature, by contrast, allowed for an ever-
present God who as God was ever invisible, but simultaneously ever visible in the
shape of the 'eternal necessity of Nature'.[158]

This new pantheistic equation had one downside, however: when God becomes
Nature, and Nature is God, the boundary between pantheism and atheism, belief
and unbelief, inevitably becomes blurred to such a degree that it makes them all
but indistinguishable. The definition of 'Atheist' in Chambers's *Cyclopaedia* of 1728
makes for illuminating reading in this regard and is symptomatic of Spinoza's
standing and impact in the seventeenth and eighteenth centuries:

> ATHEIST, Atheus, a Person who denies the Deity; who does not believe the
> Existence of a God, nor a Providence; and who has no Religion, true nor false.
> See God, Providence, Religion. In general, a Man is said to be an Atheist who
> owns no Being superior to Nature, that is, to Men and the other sensible Beings
> in this World. See Nature. In this Sense, Spinosa may be said to be an Atheist;
> and it is an Impropriety to rank him, as the learned commonly do, among
> *Deists*; since he allows of no other God beside Nature.[159]

And as a modern historian of atheism, James Thrower, has put it equally illumi-
natingly:

> God, for [Spinoza], is no metaphysical or quasi-scientific postulate standing
> outside the natural order in the relationship of First Mover. He is the natural
> order. God and nature (*Deus sive Natura*) for him are identical. In this sense and
> in this sense only Spinoza is an atheist. He denies God's transcendence. For the
> rest his system begins, continues and ends in God.[160]

It should come as no surprise then to find that pantheistic brands of philosophy,

---

156 'Germany', pp. 88–89 (*Zur Geschichte der Religion und Philosophie*, ed. Windfuhr, p. 57).

157 This formula was used by Richard Bentley in his *The Folly and Unreasonableness of Atheism* (London: J. H. for H. Morlock, 1699, p. 2) to describe the 'impious Principles of these persons [who] preclude any argumentation from the Revealed Word of God'.

158 Benedict de Spinoza, *Ethics* (London: Penguin, 1996), p. 28.

159 Chambers, *Cyclopaedia*, vol. 1, p. 166.

160 *Western Atheism. A Short History* (Amherst: Prometheus Books, 2000), p. 89.

from Spinoza's own *Tractatus Theologico-Politicus* and *Ethics* down to Fichte's 'Absolute I' and Schelling's philosophy of nature, were uniformly condemned as atheistic by their Christian detractors. As one mid-nineteenth-century theologian wrote, responding in 1845 to the controversy surrounding David Friedrich Strauß's *Life of Jesus Critically Examined*:

> Pantheism, therefore, in making all things God (man, of course, included), destroys the very essence of our idea of Deity; for whether God is brought down to a level with his works, or his works are raised to rank with God, the result is the same; — all is God, there is no superior, still less a supreme being [...]. Religion has no beau-ideal, and therefore ceases to exist.[161]

Inasmuch as pantheism, deism and atheism have in common that they all deny an active existence to God (or other supernatural agencies) beyond Nature, they create a complication for literary interpretation. The textual surface of narratives by pantheists, deists and atheists will tend to look alike: in the natural immanent universe of pantheists, deists and atheists Gods and supernatural spirits may exist as a part of people's religious creeds and belief systems, but they can no longer bring about miracles that impinge on real life. In the (Christian) theists' transcendent universe, by contrast, gods, spirits and miracles constitute a 'real' alternative and often superior dimension of our natural world, as Sonnenberg's *Donatoa* and Grainville's *Le Dernier Homme* so amply illustrate; indeed, in the end, it is the realm of these supernatural beings that triumphs over the petty and transient reality of humankind. If during this period the literary worlds of pantheists, deists and atheists tend to be monadic in storyline, the literary worlds of theists are dualistic and dominated by the clash between a natural and supernatural reality; an upshot of this is that pantheistic, deistic and atheistic authors are far more interested than their theistic counterparts in exploring the development of their human protagonists towards autonomy and individuality. And this explains the intrinsic link between secularization, the rise of the novel and modern individualism, as Ian Watt underscored in *The Rise of the Novel*:

> We can say that the novel requires a world view which is centred on the social relationships between individual persons; and this involves secularization as well as individualism, because until the end of the seventeenth century the individual was not conceived as wholly autonomous, but as an element in a picture which depended on divine persons for its meaning, as well as on traditional institutions such as Church and Kingship for its secular patterns.[162]

It is for this reason, Watt continues, that it is Defoe and not Bunyan 'who is usually considered to be the first key figure in the rise of the novel'. Georg Lukács, whom Watt cites in this context, came to a similar conclusion, as we saw earlier; Lukács's focus was of course the transition from the classical epopee to the modern novel, and his prime example for this transition was Goethe's 1795/1796 *Wilhelm Meisters*

---

161 Rev. J. R. Beard, 'Strauss, Hegel, and their Opinions', in *Voices of the Church* (London: Simpkin, Marshall & Co., 1845), pp. 7–50 (p. 7).

162 Ian Watt, *The Rise of the Novel. Studies in Defoe, Richardson and Fielding* (Harmondsworth: Penguin, 1974, first published 1957), p. 94, the subsequent quote p. 93.

Lehrjahre (*Wilhelm Meister's Years of Apprenticeship*), a novel that by focussing on one individual's progress towards maturity and autonomy became the foundational text of the *Bildungsroman* tradition.

Precisely as Lukács and Watt stipulate, Sonnenberg and Grainville cannot conceive of their human protagonists 'as wholly autonomous', seeing them instead 'as an element in a picture which depended on divine persons for its meaning'. They were theists whose primary goal was to use literature to make an overtly religious statement about the dependency of human free will on divine judgment. Viewed from a secular vantage point, their paradox was that they sought to salvage the notion of human free will even in the face of the ultimate negation of free will, namely God's Day of Reckoning. By the early 1800s this line of reasoning had become as untenable and defunct as had the genre through which they had chosen to convey their message. None other than Walter Scott himself, the inaugurator of the modern historical novel, remarked in 1809, a handful of years after Sonnenberg and Grainville had penned their epics:

> The *epic* poem and the *romance of chivalry* transport us to the world of wonders, where supernatural agents are mixed with human characters, where the human characters themselves are prodigies, and where events are produced by causes widely and manifestly different from those which regulate the course of human affairs. With such a world we do not think of comparing our actual situation; to such characters we do not presume to assimilate ourselves or our neighbours; from such a concatenation of marvels we draw no conclusions with regard to our expectations in real life. But real life is the very thing which *novels* affect to imitate...[163]

The '*epic* poem and the *romance of chivalry*' lacked the very thing that, so Scott, constituted the subject of the modern novel, namely 'real life'.

One of the first novels that could be considered full of 'real life' — as opposed to the epopee's 'concatenation of marvels' — was, according to Lukács, Goethe's *Wilhelm Meister's Years of Apprenticeship*. A turning point in the history of the German novel, *Wilhelm Meister* established the genre of an individual's socialization in a secular world, a person's journey on his way to 'reconcile inner self and world' ('Versöhnung von Innerlichkeit und Welt'), as Lukács puts it;[164] in the protagonist's struggle to 'search and find' ('Suchen und Finden') his identity and place in the world, the hero of Goethe's novel simultaneously reveals the 'totality of the world' ('die Gesamtheit der Welt'). One peculiarity about this novel, however, and one that Lukács expresses his dissatisfaction about because it does not cohere with his definition of the new genre, is Goethe's use of the mysterious Society of the Tower, a kind of freemasonry group of friends who watch over the protagonist Wilhelm Meister's progression from late adolescence to his more mature early adulthood. Goethe uses the interactions between Wilhelm and the members of this Society to underscore the distinction between 'fate' and 'chance', *Schicksal* and

---

163 Walter Scott, review of Madame Cotting's *Amélie Mansfield*; excerpt cited from *Novelists on the Novel*, ed. by Miriam Allott (London and Henley: Routledge & Kegan Paul, 1965), p. 49.
164 *Theorie des Romans*, p. 117, the subsequent passage p. 119.

Zufall; it is important, Goethe aims to show, that an individual not confuse the two and misinterpret mere chance happenings as preternatural operations of fate. Put differently, on our path to adulthood we need to learn how to take control of our lives and avoid mistaking chance occurences for some numinous force or supernatural phenomenon governing our destiny, whether this be conceived as a God, a demon or a more depersonalized fate. Whereas fate for Sonnenberg and Grainville lay squarely in the hands of God, angelic apparitions and other kinds of spirits, operating in the service of the good or the bad, for Goethe fate is an aspect of everyday social life to be consciously negotiated by a self-determining enlightened human being. The modern novel is constituted as modern at the moment when its subject is shown taking control of its fate.

Thus, in a crucial passage in Book VII, Chapter 9, of *Wilhelm Meister's Years of Apprenticeship* Wilhelm ponders (upon being pushed by the Tower Society member Jarno into its 'Tower Room', the *Turmsaal*): 'Strange! [...] can chance occurrences have a connexion? Is what we call Destiny but Chance?' ('Sonderbar! [...] sollten zufällige Ereignisse einen Zusammenhang haben? Und das, was wir Schicksal nennen, sollte es bloß Zufall sein?').[165] The attentive reader is meant to recall at this point a passage some 450 pages earlier where, in Book I, a stranger (who is later identified as yet another Tower Society member) had approached Wilhelm in order to share with him the following advice:

> The fabric of our life is formed of necessity and chance; the reason of man takes its station between them, and may rule them both: it treats the necessary as the groundwork of its being; the accidental it can direct and guide and employ for its own purposes; and only while this principle of reason stands firm and inexpugnable, does man deserve to be named the god of this lower world. But woe to him who, from his youth, has used himself to search in necessity for something of arbitrary will; to ascribe to chance a sort of reason...!'
>
> [Das Gewebe dieser Welt ist aus Notwendigkeit und Zufall gebildet, die Vernunft des Menschen stellt sich zwischen beide, und weiß sie zu beherrschen, sie behandelt das Notwendige als den Grund ihres Daseins, das Zufällige weiß sie zu lenken, zu leiten und zu nutzen, und nur, indem sie fest und unerschütterlich steht, verdient der Mensch ein Gott der Erde genannt zu werden. Wehe dem, der sich von Jugend auf gewöhnt, in dem Notwendigen etwas Willkürliches finden zu wollen, der dem Zufälligen eine Art von Vernunft zuschreiben möchte...][166]

This is of course precisely the mistake Wilhelm has been making right up to Book VII, the penultimate book of *Wilhelm Meister's Years of Apprenticeship*. Despite the fact that Goethe clearly devised the Tower Society to represent a secular force in a world seemingly ruled by uncontrollable fate and chance, Lukács nonetheless feels that, by giving the Tower Society such a mystical air, Goethe had resorted to a mechanism that belonged properly to the archaic form of the epopee. He accordingly upbraids

---

[165] Johann Wolfgang Goethe, *Wilhelm Meister's Apprenticeship and Travels*, 2 vols, trans. by Thomas Carlyle (Boston: [n.pub.], 1876), vol. 2, p. 74; *Wilhelm Meisters Lehrjahre*, ed. by Wilhelm Voßkamp and Herbert Jaumann (Frankfurt a.M.: Deutscher Klassiker Verlag, 1992), p. 872.

[166] Ibid., vol. 1, p. 100 (*Wilhelm Meisters Lehrjahre*, pp. 423–24).

Goethe for making his novel appear as if it 'transcended' its native realistic form ('einem Transzendieren des Romans zur Epopöe', are Lukács's words) by taking on features of what Scott had called the epopee's 'concatenation of marvels'.

There is a certain irony in all of this. Here the Hegelian critic voices his discontent at Goethe's decision to take recourse to something that Lukács considers an inappropriately numinous force, one that belongs 'essentially' to the genre of the epopee rather than the novel. And yet, Lukács himself earlier in his Goethe-section cites a famous comment by the Romantic writer Novalis about *Wilhelm Meister* which would seem to suggest exactly the opposite, namely that Goethe's novel is (or at least came across to many a contemporaneous reader as) entirely secular in both outlook and design. Novalis wrote in that wonderful passage:

> *Wilhelm Meister's Apprenticeship Years* are, so to say, distinctly *prosaic* — and modern. All that is Romantic perishes — as does the poetry of nature, the miraculous — He deals exclusively with ordinary *human* things — nature and mysticism have disappeared. It is a poeticized bourgeois and domestic narrative. Anything miraculous in it is explicitly dealt with as poesy and enthusiasm. Artistic Atheism is the spirit of this book.
>
> [*Wilhelm Meisters Lehrjahre* sind gewissermaßen durchaus *prosaisch* — und modern. Das Romantische geht darin zu Grunde — auch die Naturpoesie, das Wunderbare — Er handelt bloß von gewöhnlichen *menschlichen* Dingen — die Natur und der Mystizismus sind ganz vergessen. Es ist eine poetisierte bürgerliche und häusliche Geschichte. Das Wunderbare darin wird ausdrücklich als Poesie und Schwärmerei behandelt. Künstlerischer Atheismus ist der Geist des Buchs.][167]

For Novalis *Wilhelm Meister* is utterly bourgeois and prosaic; it is void of mysticism and thoroughly a-miraculous and atheistic. Whether one agrees with Novalis's assessment or prefers to side with Lukács that Goethe's novel retains residues of a more 'transcendental' age, the common ground between them is nonetheless the differential between transcendence and self-sufficiency, hence Lukács's concept of the 'transcendental homelessness' of the modern novel. In the transcendental form of the epic, the epopee, the human protagonists of that world are securely embedded in a supernatural framework; in the untranscendental form of the epic, the novel, the human protagonists are left to their own devices and act outside of any supernatural framework. Hence Wilhelm's need to learn to control his own destiny by not relying on fate as emblem of some supernatural power; and hence Novalis's charge that atheism rules the world of Goethe's *Wilhelm Meister* novel.

If viewed through this Lukácsian lens Goethe's *Wilhelm Meister* appears as a key instance of a novel on the verge of modern atheism, yet imbued with vestiges of an earlier worldview, the same might be said to apply to Wordsworth's *The Prelude*, the consciousness of whose protagonist is still very much infused with an apocalyptic undertow all the while 'Nature' programmatically displaces the supernatural. In

---

[167] *Theorie des Romans*, p. 124; italics amended according to the reproduction of this quotation in *Goethes Wilhelm Meister. Zur Rezeptionsgeschichte der Lehr- und Wanderjahre*, ed. by Klaus F. Gille (Königstein: Athenäum, 1979), p. 60 (which in turn is based on the Kluckhohn/Samuel edition of Novalis's works).

his study of *Romantic Atheism* Martin Priestman accordingly makes the interesting observation that 'it is arguable that if *The Prelude* had been in circulation from 1804–05, it would have been taken as a very plain statement of pantheist infidelism, as well as of Jacobinism'.[168] Both texts serve as prime specimens within their respective genres, the novel and poetry, of the momentous shift from 'transcendence' to 'non-transcendence', or 'immanence', which according to Charles Taylor has become such a defining characteristic of Western modernity. And it is perhaps not coincidental that both texts present such innovative forms of interior self-(re)presentation; as noted in Chapter One, M. H. Abrams once made the observation that

> *The Prelude* is a fully developed poetic equivalent of two portentous innovations in prose fiction, of which the earliest examples had appeared in Germany only a decade or so before Wordsworth began writing his poem: the *Bildungsroman* (Wordsworth called *The Prelude* a poem on 'the growth of my own mind') and the *Künstlerroman* (Wordsworth also spoke of it as 'a poem on my own poetical education')...[169]

Goethe's *Wilhelm Meister* is, of course, the quintessential embodiment of both of these new forms and presages the Romantic novel as much it accelerates its emergence. As a revolution of thought Goethe's *Wilhelm Meister* was for Friedrich Schlegel as important as the French Revolution and Fichte's purportedly atheistic philosophy.[170] Conversely, what Abrams says about *The Prelude* very much also applies to Goethe's novel of identity formation:

> In other words, the Worsworthian theodicy of the private life (if we want to coin a term, we can call it a 'biodicy'), belongs to the distinctive Romantic genre of the *Bildungsgeschichte* [history of education], which translates the painful process of Christian conversion and redemption into a painful process of self-formation, crisis, and self-recognition, which culminates in a stage of self-coherence, self-awareness, and assured power that is its own reward.[171]

And inasmuch as Goethe's *Wilhelm Meisters Lehrjahre* and Wordsworth's *The Prelude* translate the Christian concepts of conversion and redemption into secular language, and theodicy into biodicy, both epitomize in literary form the rift between 'transcendence' and 'immanence' that came to demarcate belief and unbelief in the era of secularization. According to Taylor, 'immanence' has resulted from the sloughing off of religious belief during the Enlightenment and post-Enlightenment periods which have left the individual in the world reliant solely upon himself and bereft of any supernatural, or transcendent, spiritual support system; Taylor writes:

> The great invention of the West was that of an immanent order in Nature, whose working could be systematically understood and explained on its own

---

168 *Romantic Atheism*, p. 160.
169 *Natural Supernaturalism*, p. 74.
170 See his much-cited 'Critical Fragment 116': 'The French Revolution, Fichte's Theory of Science and Goethe's Meister are the greatest tendencies of our age' ('Die Französische Revolution, Fichtes Wissenschaftstheorie und Goethes Meister sind die größten Tendenzen des Zeitalters'); Friedrich Schlegel, *Kritische Schriften*, ed. by Wolfdietrich Rasch, 3rd edn (Munich: Carl Hanser, 1970), p. 48.
171 *Natural Supernaturalism*, p. 96.

terms, leaving open the question whether this whole order had a deeper significance; and whether, if it did, we should infer a transcendent Creator beyond it. This notion of the 'immanent' involved denying — or at least isolating and problematizing — any form of interpenetration between the things of Nature, on the one hand, and 'the supernatural' on the other, be this understood in terms of the one transcendent God, or of Gods or spirits, or magic forces, or whatever.[172]

Studying the same dynamic between transcendence and immanence some two decades earlier, but from the perspective of the history of speculative fiction and science fiction, Robert Galbreath has come to a rather surprising conclusion, namely that 'transcendence is basic to science fiction'; for Galbreath, reading speculative fiction can work to fill the existential void that Taylor sees as plaguing modern secular consciousness. However, the notions of 'transcendence and eschatology', writes Galbreath,

> no longer function in speculative fiction in quite the same manner as in formal theology or traditional metaphysics. In this regard, speculative fiction conforms to the general pattern in post-Newtonian thought of an immanentized transcendence or, as M. H. Abrams [...] has characterized it for the Romantic period, a natural supernaturalism. For those who cannot accept the transcendental in an ontological sense, yet who find the imaginative and emotional pull of transcendence still or even more powerful, the transcendental is displaced from the beyond and relocated within the cosmos, even within the human psyche. Thus immanentized or internalized, the transcendental is within nature, yet still beyond the known, still other (if not quite wholly), fully capable of eliciting awe, wonder, terror, but not truly a source of religious faith or an object of worship.[173]

What both Taylor and Galbreath are in a way suggesting, then, is that once people begin to agonize over their sense of 'transcendental homelessness', to use Lukács's term, they start looking for new homes in which to settle. If one of the literary vehicles of this search for a new home is the *Bildungsroman*, the novel of education with its focus on the individual's struggle to achieve autonomy, another is modern science fiction. But where the modern novel in the tradition of Goethe's *Wilhelm Meister* shows us the growth of one such individual — as does much modern poetry in the introspective tradition of Wordsworth's *The Prelude* — the eschatological religious epopee and much of science fiction function to show us the future history and prospects of humankind, or what Eva Horn has termed the *futurum perfectum*, the *will have been*, of our species. Indeed, the common denominator between the Christian apocalyptic epic and secular futuristic fiction (at least of the cataclysmic kind) is not just their interest in what happens in the future, but more specifically what happens 'at the end'; the main difference, by contrast, is how and to what purpose that end is brought about or, to take my cue from Galbreath, how transcendence is transacted.

---

172 *A Secular Age*, pp. 15–16.
173 'Ambiguous Apocalypse', p. 54.

In *Le Dernier Homme* humankind's entry into a state of transcendence may have been transacted by God, as is the custom within the genre of Last Judgment poetry and epics, but in Grainville's treatment of the theme this entry needed triggering by a human being struggling to reconcile the requirement of obedience to God with his desire for autonomy. The enhanced role attributed to human decision-making in Grainville's *Le Dernier Homme*, but also in Franz von Sonnenberg's *Donatoa*, resulted from the internecine battle within Christianity between theism and deism, so I have argued in this and the previous chapter. The larger theophilosophical story behind this development was of course, as I also hope to have shown, the increasing sense of abandonment of God — first God abandoning humans, then humans abandoning God. This is the background to and conjuncture for the emergent form of the modern secular novel which is characterized theophilosophically by the absence — whether pantheistically, deistically or atheistically defined — of the 'one transcendent God'. God's disappearance in turn dictates the disappearance of Christ; and hand in hand with their demise goes the waning also of the literary apparatus that was part and parcel of the belief system that they sustained, the supernatural Christian machinery with its heavenly hosts and satanic hordes. What takes their place is immanent Nature. The 'Dernier Homme' — and how he comes to be the last — is henceforth no longer at the mercy of supernatural forces; his destiny is forthwith determined by Nature alone. How this shift in dominion from God to Nature is registered by nineteenth-century writers, artists and philosophers, and how its ramifications graft themselves onto their work — the realization that the consequence of atheism is the death of God; the recognition that man's position in the universe has changed fundamentally, 'Man' no longer being central to God's Creation but just one among the myriad of Nature's creatures, all existentially on a par; hence the acknowledgment of humankind's singularity, but hence acknowledgment also of its fragility, if not frailty, as a species; and finally, hence also the proliferation among the Romantic generation of a sense of existential solitude and sublime lastness — will be the subject of the subsequent two chapters.

CHAPTER 3

From Theism to Atheism and Nihilism 1805: The German Romantics and the Death of God

With such sentiments I approach you, you oldest and most venerable monuments of time. Sitting on a high denuded summit and overlooking a vast landscape, I can tell myself: Here you rest on ground that reaches to the deepest recesses on earth, [...] these summits have created nothing living, nor devoured anything living, they are before all life and above all life. At this moment, just as the innermost forces of the earth pull and move and affect me most immediately, as it were, and just as the influences of heaven hover ever closer, I am inspired to reflect more profoundly on nature; and just as the human spirit enlivens everything, a simile comes to mind whose sublimity seems inescapable. So lonely, I tell myself while casting my eyes down this naked summit [...], so lonely must that man feel himself to be who is willing to open his soul to the oldest, profoundest and most primordial feelings of truth.

JOHANN WOLFGANG GOETHE (1784)[1]

But it seems that something has happened that has never happened before: though we know not just when, or why, or how, or where.
Men have left GOD not for other gods, they say, but for no God; and this has never happened before...

T. S. ELIOT (1934)[2]

---

[1] 'Mit diesen Gesinnungen nähere ich mich euch, ihr ältesten, würdigsten Denkmäler der Zeit. Auf einem hohen nackten Gipfel sitzend und eine weite Gegend überschauend, kann ich mir sagen: Hier ruhst du unmittelbar auf einem Grunde, der bis zu den tiefsten Orten der Erde hinreicht, [...] diese Gipfel haben nichts Lebendiges erzeugt und nichts Lebendiges verschlungen, sie sind vor allem Leben und über alles Leben. In diesem Augenblicke, da die innern anziehenden und bewegenden Kräfte der Erde gleichsam unmittelbar auf mich wirken, da die Einflüsse des Himmels mich näher umschweben, werde ich zu höheren Betrachtungen der Natur hinaufgestimmt, und wie der Menschengeist alles belebt so wird auch ein Gleichnis in mir rege, dessen Erhabenheit ich nicht widerstehen kann. So einsam, sage ich zu mir selber, indem ich diesen ganz nackten Gipfel hinab sehe [...], so einsam sage ich wird es dem Menschen zumute, der nur den ältsten, ersten, tiefsten Gefühlen der Wahrheit seine Seele eröffnen will'; 'Über den Granit', in *Goethes Werke*, ed. by Erich Trunz, vol. 13: *Naturwissenschaftliche Schriften*, ed. by Dorothea Kuhn (Hamburg: Wegner, 1953), pp. 253–58 (pp. 255–56).

[2] From 'Choruses from "The Rock"' (1934), in *Collected Poems 1909–1962* (London: Faber & Faber, 1974), p. 167.

Before I move, in Chapter Four, to a consideration of the first full-fledged Last Man novel in European literature, Mary Shelley's 1826 *The Last Man*, it is important to recognize that the death of mankind, on which all Last Man narratives are by definition premised, must also by definition presuppose the death of God. Belief in the existence of the Christian God, I contend, precludes any imagining of the death of mankind outside of the Last Judgment; so long as the God of Christianity reigns supreme, man must pass away to an afterlife either of bliss in Heaven or torment in Hell. From Edward Young's early eighteenth-century *A Poem on the Last Day* and Franz von Sonnenberg's and Jean-Baptiste Cousin de Grainville's early nineteenth-century epics of the Last Judgment to the Christian apocalypses of our own age, as instanced most theatrically in Tim LaHaye and Jerry B. Jenkins's twelve-volume ultra-evangelical *Left Behind* series of 1995–2004 (to which I shall return in my Conclusion), God is the guarantor of man's afterlife, whatever the judgment.

Thus, before man can imagine or envision his species being killed off, God himself must be killed off. Mankind's death is premised on God's death, this is the long and short of my story. Seen from this vantage point, the trajectory from Burnet's, Young's, Sonnenberg's and Grainville's visions of the divine 'Consummation of all Things' to the earliest fully developed non-Christian Last Man narrative is the result less of a gradual process of secularization than a sort of leap of faith — a leap of faith into unfaith, of belief into unbelief, of theism and even deism into atheism and nihilism. It is hence not until the passage of Christian theism to atheism in the early nineteenth century that writers feel able to exorcise the purely religious conceit of an end in apocalypse, dispatching it for an essentially secular imagining of humanity's natural extinction.

As a principled disbelief in a deity of any kind atheism is, of course, if not as old as philosophy itself, then certainly as old as metaphysics; in his *Introduction to Metaphysics* (*Einführung in die Metaphysik*) Martin Heidegger observes:

> [A]nyone for whom the Bible is divine revelation and truth already has the answer to the question 'Why are there beings at all instead of nothing?' before it is even asked: beings, with the exception of God Himself, are created by Him. God Himself 'is' as the uncreated Creator. One who holds on to such faith as a basis can, perhaps, emulate and participate in the asking of our question in a certain way, but he cannot authentically question *without giving himself up as a believer, with all the consequences of this step*. (my emphasis)

> [Wem z.B. die Bibel göttliche Offenbarung und Wahrheit ist, der hat vor allem Fragen der Frage: 'Warum ist überhaupt Seiendes und nicht vielmehr Nichts?' schon die Antwort: Das Seiende, soweit es nicht Gott selbst ist, ist durch diesen geschaffen. Gott selbst 'ist' als der ungeschaffene Schöpfer. Wer auf dem Boden solchen Glaubens steht, der kann zwar das Fragen unserer Frage in gewisser Weise nach- und mitvollziehen, aber er kann nicht eigentlich fragen, ohne sich selbst als einen Gläubigen aufzugeben mit allen Folgen dieses Schrittes.][3]

Atheism is this radical and unconditional questioning of existence *with all the*

---

[3] *Introduction to Metaphysics*, trans. by Gregory Fried and Richard Polt (New Haven and London: Yale University Press, 2000), pp. 7–8; *Einführung in die Metaphysik* (Frankfurt a.M.: Klostermann, 1983 = *Gesamtausgabe*, II. Abt., vol. 40), pp. 8–9.

consequences of this step, including the denial and demise of God; for this reason some claim that Descartes's radical doubt, the *dubito* that precedes his *cogito*, is the true starting point of modern philosophical atheism.[4] But atheism leads simultaneously and by necessity to nihilism, so I interpret Heidegger — or at least to an acceptance of the theoretical possibility of absolute nothingness. 'Why are there beings at all instead of nothing?', he tells us, 'is consequently the fundamental question of metaphysics' ('"Warum ist überhaupt Seiendes und nicht vielmehr Nichts?" ist daher die metaphysische Grundfrage').[5]

Nihilism, certainly the term if not also the concept, is an upshot not just of modern atheism, however; it is also a consequence of German idealism and romanticism, as I will argue in this chapter. Modern atheism from Spinoza onwards and modern nihilism, the earliest brand of which arose out of Fichte's philosophy, as we shall see later in this chapter, brought home the realization that, without God and without the afterlife that the belief in God guaranteed, man must experience himself as standing alone in the world, in life as in death. Georg Lukács's coinage 'transcendental homelessness' ('transzendentale Obdachlosigkeit') is a fitting expression for this modern feeling. The growing sense of transcendental homelessness that accompanied the rise of atheism and nihilism in the decades immediately following 1800 is in many ways the flipside of the Romantics' pursuit of genius and individualism. When the cult of individualism hypertrophies, as it does in Fichte's notion of the 'essentially narcissistic' Absolute I,[6] man's transcendental homelessness is one corollary. Transcendental homelessness and individualism are but two sides of the same coin. Together they form the precondition for the *horror vacui*, the horror of emptiness, that lurks just under the surface of the Romantics' yearning for loneliness. Existential *Angst* is the underbelly of transcendental solitude. At the peak of twentieth-century existentialism in the 1940s the German philosopher Otto Friedrich Bollnow once described this *Angst* as follows: 'All attribution to life of any meaning has sunk into hopeless uncertainty. Man is left with nothing to hold on to. Clutching at thin air he finds himself utterly and terribly isolated and alone' ('Alle Sinngebung des Lebens ist in hoffnungsloser Fragwürdigkeit versunken. Der Mensch hat nichts mehr, an das er sich halten könnte. Er greift ins Leere und findet sich in völliger schrecklicher Einsamkeit und Verlassenheit').[7] And it is, in turn,

---

4 See for instance Alexandre Koyré, *From the Closed World to the Infinite Universe* (Baltimore: Johns Hopkins University Press, 1957), especially p. 138: 'by his denial of both void space and of spiritual extension, Descartes practically excludes spirits, souls, and even God, from his world; he simply leaves no *place* for them in it. To the question "where?", [...] Descartes is obliged, by his principles, to answer: nowhere, nullibi. Thus, in spite of his having invented or perfected the magnificent *a priori* proof of the existence of God, [...] Descartes, by his teaching, leads to materialism and, by his exclusion of God from the world, to atheism. From now on, Descartes and the Cartesians are to be relentlessly criticized and to bear the derisive nickname of *nullibists*'.

5 *Introduction to Metaphysics*, p. 19 (*Einführung in die Metaphysik*, p. 20).

6 'Fichte's I, which grounds intelligibility in human reason, is, therefore,' writes Andrew Bowie, 'essentially narcissistic, only seeing what it itself produces'; Bowie, 'Romantic philosophy and religion', in *The Cambridge Companion to German Romanticism*, ed. by Nicolas Saul (Cambridge: Cambridge University Press, 2009), pp. 175–90 (p. 181).

7 *Existenzphilosophie* (Stuttgart: Kohlhammer, 1969, first edition 1942), p. 67.

Fig. 3.1. Caspar David Friedrich, *Der Mönch am Meer*, 1808–1810 (Nationalgalerie, Staatliche Museen zu Berlin; © bpk Nationalgalerie, SMB / Jörg P. Anders).

precisely this emphasis on isolation and loneliness, coupled with the recognition of humankind's frailty and finality, which gives rise to the idea of the Last Man. It should hence come as little surprise to find some of the earliest meditations on the finality of mankind as a species as well as on the death of God emanating from German Idealists and Romantics, the inventors of the absolute solitude of the absolute ego. To develop this context I shall begin this chapter with some reflections on a cluster of paintings that many today consider the very incarnation of romanticism's cult of loneliness.

The Monk by the Sea

In 1810 the German Romantic painter Caspar David Friedrich (1774–1840) exhibited a canvas at the Berlin Academy that critics later came to recognize as one of the quintessential expressions of romanticism's 'spirit of the era'. Entitled *The Monk by the Sea* (*Der Mönch am Meer*, Figure 3.1) and depicting a lone man gazing pensively into the limitless expanse of ocean and sky before him, the picture seems to incarnate romanticism's yearning for a mystical union between man and nature. The gulf between this canvas and earlier forms of landscape painting can be measured by comparing it with one of Friedrich's own pictures, *Coast with Fisherman* (*Meeresstrand mit Fischer*, 1807; Figure 3.2); painted just three years earlier, it uses virtually the same proportioning of space and yet leaves the viewer with a vastly different impression. Where the one appears symbolic, the other is

Fig. 3.2. Caspar David Friedrich, *Meeresstrand mit Fischer*, 1807 (Kunsthistorisches Museum, Vienna; © bpk / Hermann Buresch).

naturalistic; where one seems meditative and spiritual, with nature conjuring a veritable abyss of space and meaning, the other — in the manner typical of genre painting of the period — seems content to present a scene of everyday life devoid of any notable metaphysical quality.

In a major study of nineteenth-century art, Werner Hofmann, former curator of the Hamburger Kunsthalle art museum and a leading Austrian art historian, describes the significance of *The Monk by the Sea* as follows:

> Certainly a new road was opened here. The vast area of space in the background is no longer coterminous with the edge of the picture and appears to be of infinite extension. [...] One feels that this bare strip of beach continues without end, that it is in front of us, next to us, and behind us. [...] It is this element of endless uniformity that is the new pictorial medium, and it is this that imparts its peculiar solemnity to the work. The emphasis on the horizontal helps to drive home this note of monotony. [...] Here there is an endlessness that is a threat to man, it is something to which he is exposed and cannot adapt himself. The narrow bit of ground on which he is placed contracts to nothing, if compared with the devouring immensity of the sky. [...] There is about this picture something that suggests a monologue, a monologue that none but the speaker is there to hear; it is a symbol of the isolation of the creature that can no longer assert itself against nature, that no longer has any part in what happens in the natural world but stands as a mere observer at the edge of it. This picture is indeed an apocalypse.[8]

8 *Art in the Nineteenth Century*, trans. by Brian Battershaw (London: Faber & Faber, 1961), p. 73.

Hofmann reads the painting in essence as a symbol of man's dejection and forsakenness, of his loneliness and sense of isolation before an all-encompassing and all-overwhelming nature. The apocalypse here does not relate to the biblical vision of the Last Judgment, but is a secularized version of man's being without a God, as Hofmann later suggests:

> Never till then had any picture shown man so solitary, so helplessly exposed to the universe as was that monk by the sea. Around this isolated figure is 'the cold iron mask of formless eternity' (Jean Paul). There is no longer a [mantle] for created things, and the human creature stands shivering at the edge of an infinity which opens up beyond him, alien to all that pertains to man. [...] The poet whose vision most nearly reproduces this sense of a dreadful abyss in which man has been utterly forsaken by God, is Jean Paul. The [text] in question is his 'Rede des toten Christus vom Weltgebäude herab daß kein Gott sei' ('Declaration of the dead Christ from atop the World's Edifice that there is no God').[9]

As perceptive and astute as these comments may be, Hofmann, in striving to cast Friedrich as the herald of later more secular developments in nineteenth-century art history, has opted to ignore the degree to which Friedrich's art was rooted in his Christian belief. Not only were Friedrich's parents devout Pietists who exerted a profound and life-long influence on his thinking, he and some fellow-artists in the then Swedish-ruled protestant German Baltic town of Greifswald sought to create a progressive 'Altarkunst', a religiously inspired 'art of the altar'. Moreover, together with that other equally religious-minded German Romantic painter, Philipp Otto Runge, mentioned in Chapter One (a fine example of whose art is his allegorical painting *The Morning, Der Morgen*, of 1808), Friedrich was instrumental around 1805/1806 in creating the design for the chapel built for the poet-preacher Gotthard Kosegarten, whose celebrated sermons on the beach of Cap Arkona on the island of Rügen served as a real-life inspiration for *The Monk by the Sea*. Hence the mystical view of nature that we intuitively grasp as the foundation of Friedrich's art was vitally inspired by and infused with religious sentiment, as Norbert Wolf argues when he reminds us that Friedrich required of any painting an 'uplifting of the spirit' ('Erhebung des Geistes') and 'religious elevation' ('religiösen Aufschwung').[10]

In short, one can read Friedrich's mysticism of nature, as expressed not just in *The Monk by the Sea* but also many of his other paintings, from a more religious vantage point as a metaphysical expression of man's ultimate subservience to God. This is precisely the claim made by the art historian Kristina van Prooyen; '*The Monk by the Sea* was the most radical painting Friedrich created', she writes,

> because he completely abandoned rules of conventional landscape painting; there is no depth perception in the usual sense, and this creates a tension between the empty void of the sea and the endless sky. The narrow beach strip is sharply outlined against a cold, expansive sea that occupies the same

---

9 *Art in the Nineteenth Century*, p. 76 (I have modified the translation; in particular, Jean Paul's 'Rede des toten Christus' is *not* a poem, as the translation has it, but a prose text included in the larger novel by Jean Paul which will be discussed in more detail later in this chapter).

10 *Caspar David Friedrich 1774–1840. Der Maler der Stille* (Cologne: Taschen, 2007), p. 19.

amount of surface as the sand and yet seems larger and more distant. This visual paradox points to the metaphysical problem of the picture, which the rational intellect cannot immediately grasp, evoking the painfully awkward feeling of the viewer's own insignificance and reliance upon God for greater meaning. The unbroken line of the horizon, below which the monk is placed, suggests even more strongly the endlessness of nature and the smallness of man within it. Both monk and viewer are confronted by infinite space and are thus led to a self-conscious awareness of God.[11]

'By translating the outmoded dogmas of the Christian faith into a form that was relevant to the modern spectator', van Prooyen continues, 'Friedrich was able to create a poignantly spiritual work [...] that reflected the ideas of Romantic theology'. Little surprise then that one of Friedrich's contemporaries, the Romantic poet and critic August Wilhelm Schlegel (whose brother Friedrich Schlegel famously defined Romantic poetry as a 'progressive universal poetry'), likened Friedrich's vacant visions of nature to a veritable act of religious communion.[12] The seriousness of the subject matter and its formal representation is palpable. It is as if a conversation were taking place between minuscule man and God in all his divine grace and glory, incarnate in nature. Man, in his attempt to probe and penetrate the mysteries of nature, is shown as a solitary pensive figure cut off from his fellow beings.

Such figures in Friedrich's work seem to want to personify what his contemporary, the Romantic philosopher and theologian Friedrich Schleiermacher, says of religious sentiment; Schleiermacher observes at one point in his lectures to sceptics and unbelievers: 'The essence of religion is neither thought nor action, but perception and feeling. It wants to perceive the universe, in its images and actions it piously wants to listen in to the universe, it wants to be moved and filled by it in child-like passivity' ('Ihr Wesen ist weder Denken noch Handeln, sondern Anschauung und Gefühl. Anschauen will sie das Universum, in seinen eigenen Darstellungen und Handlungen will sie es andächtig belauschen, von seinen unmittelbaren Einflüssen will sie sich in kindlicher Passivität ergreifen und erfüllen lassen').[13] Those who speculate about the universe merely abstractly and in want of the necessary piety, and who hence overestimate man and falsely take him for God, will fail to see their 'limitations' ('Beschränktheit') and the 'contingency' ('Zufälligkeit') of their form; they will fail to acknowledge that they are destined some day silently to disappear in the vastness of being — 'geräuschloses Verschwinden seines ganzen Daseins im Unermeßlichen', is Schleiermacher's wording. It should come as no surprise, then, to find Prooyen arguing precisely that Caspar David Friedrich's art represents a transposition into painting of Schleiermacher's Romantic theology.

The tension between a religiously inspired spiritual mysticism, in which nature functions as a symbolic expression of God's all-embracing supremacy, and a more secular and earthly reverence for nature in all its grandeur and sublimity lies at the

---

11 'The Realm of the Spirit: Caspar David Friedrich's Artwork in the Context of Romantic Theology, with special reference to Friedrich Schleiermacher', *Journal of the Oxford University History Society* (Winter 2004), 1–16 (p. 12).

12 Wolf, *Caspar David Friedrich*, p. 21.

13 *Über Religion. Reden an die Gebildeten unter ihren Verächtern* (Stuttgart: Reclam, 1969), p. 35; the subsequent passages p. 36.

heart of Friedrich's Romantic paradox. I claimed in Chapter Two that pantheism, not deism, must be seen as the true half-way house between faith and apostasy, theism and atheism, in that in the pantheistic worldview God is simultaneously present and absent in nature. Friedrich's œuvre exudes precisely this pantheistic ambiguity: in *The Monk by the Sea* as in Friedrich's other paintings — and despite their frequent pictorial references to religion and its institutions, specifically in the shape of Gothic cathedrals, ruins of monasteries, mountain-top crosses, monks in silent meditation, or graveyards scattered throughout his landscapes — one is never quite sure whether, in what Norbert Wolf has called Friedrich's 'emblematic topography',[14] God is in or beyond nature.

In any event, when we see Friedrich's paintings on display today in some of the world's leading museums, we are prone to stand as awestruck and contemplative before them as the monk stands before the ocean and the sky. (With his blond shock of hair the monk purportedly resembled the artist Friedrich himself in appearance.) Are we not equally spellbound by the exquisite grandeur and sublime vastness of the spectacle of nature presented to us, pondering the precariousness of the monk's (and humanity's) position between earth, ocean and sky — or Earth and Heaven? But it goes without saying that, in his own day, Friedrich's paintings were not universally admired. The exaggerated gravitas and symbolic profundity paraded by this kind of painting went neither unnoticed nor uncriticized even during Friedrich's time. The German aristocrat Freiherr Friedrich Wilhelm Basilius von Ramdohr for instance had seen Friedrich's *Tetschen Altar* in December 1808 and, in a review published on 7 January 1809 in *Zeitung für die elegante Welt*, took offence at the conspicuousness of its religious message; with this kind of picture landscape painting was grovelling its way into churches, he nagged.[15] One of Friedrich's close associates, the Norwegian Romantic landscape painter Johan Christian Dahl, wrote in retrospect:

> Friedrich was never properly understood by his contemporaries, or at least only by a select few. Most saw in his works an unnaturally contrived mysticism. But that is not accurate. [...] His era saw in his paintings constructed ideas without truth of nature. For this reason many bought his paintings as a mere curiosity. [...] Artists and art critics saw in Friedrich only a kind of mystic because they themselves were chasing after mysticism. They could not see his faithful and conscientious study of nature; for Friedrich knew and felt strongly that one could not paint nature directly but only one's own emotions — but *they* had to be natural.[16]

Indeed, the degree of consternation and bewilderment, as well as ridicule, elicited by Friedrich's paintings is best brought home in a satirical gloss on *The Monk by the Sea* written by the German Romantic writer Clemens Brentano in collaboration with his friend Achim von Arnim.[17] The publication of Brentano's gloss by

14 Wolf, *Caspar David Friedrich*, p. 35.
15 See Wolf, *Caspar David Friedrich*, pp. 26–27.
16 Translated from the German version provided in *Caspar David Friedrich in Briefen und Bekenntnissen*, ed. by Sigrid Hinz (Berlin: Henschelverlag Kunst und Gesellschaft, 1968), p. 217.
17 The piece is often regarded as co-authored with Brentano's close friend and fellow writer Achim von Arnim, and it is to both that Kleist issued his apology for the unauthorized abridgement in the

Heinrich von Kleist in the 13 October 1810 issue of the *Berliner Abendblätter*, which Kleist edited, caused quite some consternation because Kleist had taken the liberty to substantially redact and shorten Brentano's text, in effect expunging the whole dialogue section as reproduced below. Brentano ended his collaboration with Kleist forthwith, and Kleist found himself forced to publish an apology, which he half-heartedly did in the 22 October issue of the *Abendblätter*, writing:

> The article by Messrs A. v. Arnim and C. Brentano on Friedrich's Seascape was originally cast in a dramatic form; limited space, however, compelled an abridgement, which liberty I was amicably permitted by A. v. A. Nevertheless the article, expressing as it now does a positive judgment, has been so altered in character that, while literally the work of those gentlemen, its spirit (and all responsibility for its final version) are mine alone.[18]

Read in whichever version, Brentano's extended original (which was published with delay sixteen years later in the journal *Iris*) or Kleist's abridgement of 1810, Brentano's response to Friedrich's painting remains one of the most remarkable documents of Friedrich's reception history as well as a key literary exhibit of German romanticism. Entitled 'Various Sentiments on a Seascape by Friedrich, on which is a Capuchin' ('Verschiedene Empfindungen vor einer Seelandschaft von Friedrich, worauf ein Kapuziner'), the text — here Brentano's original in translation[19] — warrants an extended citing, not least because it is delightfully witty:

> It is a magnificent thing to gaze off into a boundless watery waste, in infinite solitude by the sea, under a sullen sky; and this has to do with having travelled there, having to return, yearning to cross over, finding one cannot, and while missing all signs of life, nevertheless hearing its voice in the roar of the surf, the rush of the wind, the drift of the clouds, the lonely crying of birds: it has to do with an appeal from the heart, which nature herself rejects. All this however is not possible in front of the picture, and that which I should have found within the picture I found instead between the picture and myself, namely an appeal which the picture made to me, by not fulfilling mine to it, and so I myself became the Capuchin monk, the picture became the dune, but that across which I should have looked with longing, the sea, was absent completely. To come to terms with this strange feeling I listened carefully to the remarks of the various observers around me, and pass them on as appropriate to this picture, a backdrop in front of which there must always be activity, in that it allows of no repose.
>
> (A lady and gentleman approach, he apparently very witty.
> The lady looks in her programme)

Berliner Abendblätter on 22 October 1810; however, it was predominantly written by Brentano, and Kleist accordingly had placed a 'cb' under the version first published in the *Berliner Abendblätter*.

18 Cited in the appendix of Philip B. Miller's article 'Anxiety and Abstraction: Kleist and Brentano on Caspar David Friedrich', *Art Journal*, 33 (Spring 1974), 205–10; downloaded from <http://www.jstor.org/stable/pdfplus/775783.pdf?acceptTC=true> on 3 July 2012. The following quotations in English from Brentano's original version and Kleist's abridgement are from this source; I have taken the liberty to make minor changes where I saw fit.

19 In the interest of space I will not cite the full German original here but refer readers proficient in German to editions of Brentano's and Kleist's works; the German text is also easily accessible on the World Wide Web.

LADY. Number two. Landscape. Oils. How do you like it?
GENT. Infinitely deep and sublime.
LADY. You mean the sea. Yes, it must be very deep, and the monk is indeed very sublime.
GENT. No, Frau War Minister. I mean the sensibility of our incomparably great Friedrich.
LADY. Is it so old that he too could have seen it?
GENT. Ah, you misunderstand. I mean Friedrich the painter [not the Prussian King Friedrich der Große / Frederick the Great, R.W.]. Ossian's harp is audible in this picture. (They pass)

(Two young Ladies)

FIRST. Did you hear that, Louise? That is Ossian.
SECOND. No no! You misunderstand. That is the *ocean*.
FIRST. But he said he was playing a harp.
SECOND. I see no harp. It is really quite grisly to look at. (They pass)

(Two Connoisseurs)

FIRST. Grisly indeed. It's all completely grey, as this man paints only the driest subjects.
SECOND. You mean, this man paints wet things very drily.
FIRST. I'm sure he paints them just as well as he can. (They pass)

(A Tutoress with two *demoiselles*)

TUTORESS. That is the sea at Rügen.
FIRST DEMOISELLE. Where *Kosegarten* lives.
SECOND DEMOISELLE. Where the groceries come from.
TUTORESS. Why must he paint such a sad air? How beautiful if he had painted an amber fisher in the foreground. [Recall how Caspar David Friedrich in his painting *Coast with Fisherman* of 1807 (Figure 3.2) had positioned a 'fisher in the foreground', albeit not 'an amber' one; R.W.]
SECOND DEMOISELLE. I'd like to fish up a beautiful amber necklace of my own somewhere. (They pass)

(A young mother with two blond children and two gentlemen)

FIRST GENT. Magnificent! Only this man can express a soul in his landscape. What great individuality in this picture: the high truth, the solitude, the gloom of the melancholy sky. He certainly knows what he paints.
SECOND GENT. And paints what he knows, feeling and thinking and then painting.
FIRST CHILD. What is it?
FIRST GENT. It is the sea, my child, and a monk walking beside it and feeling very sad not to have a clever little boy like you.
SECOND CHILD. Why isn't he dancing around in front of it? Why doesn't he wag his head like the ones in the lantern shows? That would be even more beautiful.
FIRST CHILD. Is he like the monk that tells the weather outside our window?
SECOND GENT. Not exactly, my child, but he too tells the weather in a way. He is Oneness amid the All-Encompassing, the lonely centre in the lonely circle.

FIRST GENT. Yes, he is the heart and soul and consciousness of the whole picture in itself and of itself.

SECOND GENT. How divinely inspired the choice of that figure is, nor merely a relative measure for the vastness of the scene, he himself is the subject, he is the picture, and as he appears to be dreamily lost in the view as in a sorrowful reflection of his own isolation, the enclosing sea, void of ships, which binds him like an oath, and the barren dune, as joyless as his own life, seem to be symbolically drawing him out again, like some desolate, self-prophetic plant of the seashore.

FIRST GENT. Magnificent! To be sure. You are quite right. (To the Lady) But, my dear, you have said nothing at all.

LADY. Oh, I was feeling so at home with this picture, it is so touching, so genuine in its effect, but while you spoke it became just as obscure as when I went for a walk by the sea with our philosophical friends, hoping for nothing more than a fresh breeze and a sail, and for a glimpse of the sun and the thunder of the surf; but now it's all like one of my nightmares and longing for my homeland in my dreams. Let us go on. It is too sad. (They pass)

[...]

All this while a tall, mild-mannered gentleman had been listening with signs of impatience. I stepped accidentally on his toe, and as though I had thereby solicited his opinion, he answered: 'How fortunate it is that the pictures have no ears. They would have drawn their veils long ago. The public seem to suspect a lurking immorality, as though the pictures were pilloried here for some crime or other, which the viewers must guess at.' 'But what do you think of the picture?' 'It pleases me to see that there are still landscape painters who attend to the wonderful conjunctions of season and sky, which produce such gripping effects even in the most barren of regions. But of course I would much prefer for the painter to have not only the right feeling but the talent and training as well to reproduce it faithfully; and in this respect he stands as far behind certain Dutch painters of similar scenes as he surpasses them in the mood of his conception. It would not be difficult to mention a dozen pictures where sea and shore and monk are better painted. The monk from any distance looks like a brown smudge, and if I had wanted to paint one at all, I would have stretched him out in sleep, or placed him kneeling in all the humility of prayer or contemplation, so as not to obstruct the view of the spectators, on whom the sea obviously makes a stronger impression than that tiny figure. If someone then decided to look about for inhabitants of the shore, he could still have expressed such opinions as some people here, with presumptuous familiarity, so loudly imposed on everyone else.' These words so pleased me that I tagged along home with the gentleman and shall remain there indefinitely.

There has been much discussion of Kleist's abridgement and rewriting of Brentano's droll and diverting dialogue on the picture's effect; in essence, Kleist retains only the opening lines of Brentano's first paragraph and reworks the subsequent conversations into a much truncated prose version. Thus Brentano's one hundred and twenty-five lines are reduced to twenty-six, one fifth of the original's length (which makes Brentano's outrage all the more understandable). The middle section of Kleist's version in particular bears only a partial resemblance to the original; this passage reads:

Nothing could be sadder or more discomfited than just this position in the world: *the single spark of life in the vast realms of death*, the lonely centre in the lonely circle. The picture with its two or three mysterious objects lies before one like the Apocalypse, as though it were thinking Young's *Night Thoughts*, and since in its uniformity and boundlessness it has no foreground but the frame, the viewer feels *as though his eyelids had been cut off.* Yet the painter has doubtless opened a new path in the field of his art.

[Nichts kann trauriger und unbehaglicher sein, als diese Stellung in der Welt: *der einzige Lebensfunke im weiten Reiche des Todes*, der einsame Mittelpunct im einsamen Kreis. Das Bild liegt, mit seinen zwei oder drei geheimnisvollen Gegenständen, wie die Apokalypse da, als ob es Joungs Nachtgedanken hätte, und da es, in seiner Einförmigkeit und Uferlosigkeit, nichts, als den Rahm [sic], zum Vordergrund hat, so ist es, wenn man es betrachtet, *als ob Einem die Augenlider weggeschnitten wären*. Gleichwohl hat der Maler Zweifels ohne eine ganz neue Bahn im Felde seiner Kunst gebrochen.][20] (my emphases)

In discussing Kleist's version of the text, scholars have lavished considerable attention on the typically Kleistian metaphor 'the viewer feels as though his eyelids had been cut off'. But the remainder of this passage surely deserves no less attention, certainly from the perspective of our topic, 'Last Men'. I have rendered the most significant rephrasings in italics. To give credit where credit is due, Kleist retains some of the more incisive phrases and observations introduced by Brentano and his fictitious exhibit goers, but it is only through Kleist's compacting of the dialogue that the picture's apocalyptic dimension — which the art historian Hofmann in our era made indicative of the painting's core message — is brought to the fore.

Alone on the Mountain Top

Brentano's allusion to the melancholic tradition epitomized by the figure of Ossian (a layer strengthened by the explicit reference to Edward Young's still popular *Night Thoughts*, a reference retained by Kleist) positions Friedrich's painting *The Monk by the Sea* squarely within the larger thematic framework of the sublime, as the dialogue's opening lines make apparent: 'LADY. Number Two. Landscape. Oils. How do you like it? GENT. Infinitely deep and sublime'. Brentano's inspired phrase 'in infinite solitude by the sea' is also retained by Kleist unchanged, as is the locution 'the lonely centre in the lonely circle'; but significantly, he adds the words 'the single spark of life in the vast realms of death', giving it a much more sinister hue. By and large, then, three themes emerge from the intersection of Friedrich's painting and Brentano's satirical and Kleist's critical commentaries: the sublime, the apocalypse, and solitude.

Solitude is arguably the most visually tangible dimension of Friedrich's painting: the monk stands alone at the seafront, immersed in deep meditation about, in Friedrich's own words, 'the darkness of what the future holds'.[21] The apocalypse

---

20 'Empfindungen vor Friedrichs Seelandschaft', in Heinrich von Kleist, *Sämtliche Werke und Briefe*, 4 vols, ed. by Klaus Müller-Salget (Frankfurt a.M.: Deutscher Klassiker Verlag, 1990), vol. 3, pp. 543–44.
21 Only in the 1980s did some comments by Friedrich himself come to light which survived in a

and the sublime by contrast constitute the more subliminal and symbolic strata of Friedrich's art, much as they did, incidentally, in Wordsworth's *Prelude*, as we saw in Chapter One, in which the poet's surface solitude tied in with the poem's more obscured, but no less vital, references to the sublimity of nature and the apocalyptic undertow of recent history. Of course, if Friedrich's painting is apocalyptic at all — and this remains debatable — his is a very different painterly approach to the topic from what was customary or typical in his day. Morton D. Paley has devoted a whole book to manifestations of *The Apocalyptic Sublime* in paintings of this period, a mode inspired by and large (albeit not exclusively) by Edmund Burke's famous and highly influential disquisition on the sublime, *A Philosophical Enquiry into the Origin of our Ideas of the Sublime and Beautiful* of 1757. Paley notes:

> the sublime was now considered to lie in the perception of subjects that the mind could not entirely comprehend or contain; its chief source was power, its chief subject matter, terror, its identifying response, astonishment. While older views of the sublime continued to exist alongside the new, it was the Burkean idea that became intellectually dominant.[22]

And while 'its major practitioners' at the time included, 'each in his characteristic way, Benjamin West, P. J. de Loutherberg, William Blake, J. M. W. Turner, John Martin, Samuel Colman, and Francis Danby', Paley goes on to stress that 'no such development occurred outside of England, and the apocalyptic sublime is therefore a subject of exceptional interest in the study not only of British art but also of aesthetic taste, critical and popular, from the late eighteenth century through the Victorian period'. The 'typical' subject matters of this mode of painting were 'natural catastrophes', especially titillating portrayals of 'The Deluge', and ' "Gothic" supernatural subjects' (think John Henry Fuseli), but also landscape painting, in particular the kind where minuscule humans are eclipsed by the grandeur of nature, both graphically and emotionally. As Paley observes, 'what these landscapes have in common is the frightening imminence of the objects viewed from a perspective that virtually compels us to imagine ourselves as powerless'.

---

handwritten copy made of one of Friedrich's letters by Amalie von Beulwitz; Friedrich wrote: 'And even if you pondered from morn to eve, and from eve to midnight, you would still not comprehend, still not grasp, the unfathomable beyond. It is arrogant hubris alone that makes you believe you could become a torch for posterity, and decipher the night of our future state! What divine retribution will be, can be seen and sensed only through faith; to clearly know and to comprehend! As deep as the impression may be that your footprints leave on the desolate shore's sands, a mild wind blowing across them suffices to make your tracks disappear forever: foolish man full of vain conceit! ('Und sännest du auch vom Morgen bis zum Abend, vom Abend bis zur sinkenden Mitternacht; dennoch würdest du nicht ersinnen, nicht ergründen, das unerforschliche Jenseits! Mit übermüthigem Dünkel, erwegst du der Nachwelt ein Licht zu werden, zu enträtseln der Zukunft Dunkelheit! Was heilige Ahndung nur ist, nur im Glauben gesehen und erkannt; endlich klahr zu wissen und zu Verstehn! [sic] Tief zwar sind deine Fußstapfen am öden sandigen Strandte; doch ein leiser Wind weht darüber hin, und deine Spuhr wird nicht mehr gesehen: Thörichter Mensch voll eitlem Dünkel! —'); see Helmut Börsche-Supan, 'Berlin 1810. Bildende Kunst. Aufbruch unter dem Druck der Zeit', *Kleist-Jahrbuch* (1987), 52–75 (p. 75).

22 *The Apocalyptic Sublime* (New Haven and London: Yale University Press, 1986), p. 2; the subsequent passages pp. 1 and 3.

Especially in contrast with the obviously religious castings of the apocalyptic sublime, such as those by P. J. de Loutherberg or John Martin (see Figure I.3), which may or may not be intrinsically British (sublime landscape painting was no less a feature of continental and American art), Caspar David Friedrich goes his own unique way. For one, even where he uses overtly religious subject matter or paraphernalia (as most prominently in such paintings as his 1807/1808 *The Cross in the Mountains/Tetschen Altar* or his 1808–1810 *Abbey in an Oak Forest*), he eschews all explicitly apocalyptic connotations. Moreover, where Burke in *A Philosophical Enquiry into the Origin of our Ideas of the Sublime and Beautiful* observes, in Section VII on 'Vastness', that 'greatness of dimension is a powerful cause of the sublime', and that 'an hundred yards of even ground will never work such an effect as a tower an hundred yards high, or a rock or mountain of that altitude',[23] Friedrich's *The Monk by the Sea* goes to prove the opposite. And yet, when Burke writes, in Section VIII on 'Infinity', 'Infinity has a tendency to fill the mind with that sort of delightful horror, which is the most genuine effect, and truest test of the sublime', could there be any better test case than Friedrich's painting? Indeed, in an earlier section, Burke expands his observations by noting that 'hardly any thing can strike the mind with its greatness, which does not make some sort of approach towards infinity, which nothing can do whilst we are able to perceive its bounds'. It was precisely the 'boundlessness' of Friedrich's painting that had inspired Kleist to coin his celebrated metaphor; 'since in its uniformity and boundlessness it has no foreground but the frame,' Kleist had written, 'the viewer feels as though his eyelids had been cut off', eliminating any possibility to compass and thereby contain the expanse of reality one is looking at. The beholder intuitively follows the monk's gaze outwards into the endless space of nature and heaven, while the horizontal lines work to extend the vectors of beach, ocean and sky limitlessly beyond the confines of the frame.[24] Where the horizontal alignment of the foreground in Friedrich's 1807 *Coast with Fisherman* is compositionally quite similar to *The Monk by the Sea*, causing the space of the sky to appear equally boundless, the foreground detail of the earlier painting nonetheless provides ample signals suggesting the scene's internal and external boundedness and its integratedness into the 'real' world: there are boats on the ocean coming and going, there are various fishing implements on the verges of the path and in the distance which link us to the utilitarian activities of a world outside, and the central figure himself, the fisherman carrying his rod, clearly comes from a reality beyond the frame of the painting. The monk by the sea, by contrast, stands motionless and static on the beach, there is no path from where he might have come, there is no destination to where he might be going, there are no boats in the distance giving concrete depth and proportion to the dark blue sea. Even if in both paintings the sky opens up to the infinity of space, only in *The Monk by the Sea* are

23 *A Philosophical Enquiry into the Origin of our Ideas of the Sublime and Beautiful*, ed. by David Wombersly (London: Penguin, 2004), p. 114; the subsequent passage p. 106.
24 I should perhaps add at this point that in our own time Mark Rothko's paintings evoke very similar feelings of sublime limitlessness and puzzling, if not unsettling, infinitude; Rothko took much inspiration from Caspar David Friedrich, and many of his paintings descend directly from Friedrich's *The Monk by the Sea*. My thanks to Ingo Cornils for bringing this link to my attention.

FIG. 3.3. Caspar David Friedrich, *Wanderer über dem Nebelmeer*, around 1818 (© bpk / Hamburger Kunsthalle / Elke Walford).

we given the abysmal sense that the world beyond the frame is no different from what we see within it.

Even if the peculiarly roadless painting *The Monk by the Sea* 'opens a new road' for landscape painting, as the art historians Hofmann and van Prooyen agree, this is not meant to suggest that Friedrich is disconnected from his historical context; quite to the contrary, Friedrich builds on the existing tradition of landscape painting only to radicalize its compositional potential, in the process amplifying its representational and interpretational ambiguity. The companion piece to Friedrich's *The Monk by the Sea* is his *Wanderer above the Sea of Fog* (*Wanderer über dem Nebelmeer*, 1818; Figure 3.3). Equally famous, but abstaining from the overt religious connotation occasioned by the monk in *The Monk by the Sea* — or indeed the Moses-like figure in John Martin's watercolour painting *The Last Man* of the early 1830s — this painting epitomizes the Romantic fascination, if not obsession, with the sublimity of solitude. Despite its obviously secular appearance — some have interpreted it as a portrait of Goethe, others as a patriotic manifest, possibly commemorating Friedrich's contemporary, the Saxon chamberlain Friedrich Ernst von Brinken[25] — *Wanderer above the Sea of Fog* too has kindled religious interpretations, such as that by Friedrich's own student, the painter Carl Gustav Carus, who wrote in 1835:

> Step forward then to the mountain top and take in the long chains of hills ... and what feeling does this inspire? You feel a silent prayer in you, it is as if you dissolve in limitless space, your whole inner being experiences a silent ablution and purification, your self disappears, you are nothing, God is all.
>
> [Tritt denn hin auf den Gipfel des Gebirges, schau hin über die langen Hügelreihen ... und welches Gefühl ergreift Dich? Es ist eine stille Andacht in Dir, Du selbst verlierst dich im unbegrenzten Raume, Dein ganzes Wesen erfährt eine stille Läuterung und Reinigung, Dein Ich verschwindet, Du bist nichts, Gott ist alles.][26]

The first poet to 'step forward to the mountain top', as it were, was the Swiss naturalist and poet Albrecht von Haller who eulogized the sublimity of the Swiss Alpine landscape in his 1729 German poem 'The Alps' ('Die Alpen'), in which he drew, as he later states in a short preface to the poem, on the vivid memories of his 1728 trip into the Alps. In it Haller 'invokes the classical trope of the pastoral and extends it to the high peaks, introducing a discourse that had both immediately tangible and long-term paradigmatic effects', as Caroline Schaumann notes in the most detailed study in English of the poem to date.[27] Significantly, Haller also transferred the pastoral's rustic humble shepherd — a popular rococo motif — into this at once awe-inspiring and menacing mountain setting, creating the blueprint for the combination of beauty and terror that later came to underlie Burke's definition of the sublime. Unsurprisingly, the mountain shepherd is also a figure

---

25 See Werner Hofmann, *Caspar David Friedrich 1774–1840. Kunst um 1800* (Munich: Prestel and Hamburger Kunsthalle, 1974), p. 218.

26 Cited by Wolf, *Caspar David Friedrich*, p. 57.

27 'From Meadows to Mountaintops: Albrecht von Haller's "Die Alpen"', in *Heights of Reflection. Mountains in the German Imagination*, ed. by Sean Ireton and Caroline Schaumann (Rochester, NY: Camden House, 2012), pp. 57–75.

that Wordsworth revives, if in a romantically modified Lake District form, nearly a century later in *The Prelude*; composed a few years before Friedrich painted his lone monk on the beach, Wordsworth's poem relates:

> A rambling schoolboy, thus
> Have I beheld him [the shepherd], without knowing why
> Having felt his presence in his own domain,
> As of a lord and master, or a power,
> Or genius, under Nature, under God,
> Presiding; and severest solitude
> Seemed more commanding oft when he was there. [...]
> In size a giant, stalking through the fog,
> His sheep like Greenland bears; at other times
> When round some shady promontory turning,
> His form hath flashed upon me, glorified
> By the deep radiance of the setting sun:
> Or him have I descried in distant sky,
> A solitary object and sublime,
> Above all height! Like an aerial cross,
> As it is stationed on some spiry rock
> Of the Chartreuse, for worship. Thus was man
> Ennobled outwardly before my eyes,
> And thus my heart at first was introduced
> To an unconscious love and reverence
> Of human nature...
> (*The Prelude*, 1805–1806 version, Book VIII, ll. 390–414)

Elsewhere in *The Prelude* Wordsworth speaks of 'the self-sufficing power of Solitude' (Book II, l. 78). But where this 'self-sufficing power of Solitude' that enobles Friedrich's and Wordsworth's loners suggests autonomy and a kind of sheltered transcendence, theirs is only the positive and self-assured side of solitude's coin.

For the reverse connotation to an individual's loneliness and solitude is his isolation and diminution, both of which encapsulate solitude's more ominous and hostile flip side; the lone individual can thus stand as a symbol of grandeur as much as of fragility, of significance as much as of insignificance, and of sufficiency as much as of insufficiency in the face of an overwhelming external environment. Burke had for this reason remarked: 'But whilst we contemplate so vast an object, under the arm, as it were, of almighty power, and invested upon every side with omnipresence, we shrink into the minuteness of our own nature'.[28] But Burke also emphasized how both extremes, excessive minuteness no less than excessive vastness, could serve to inspire a sense of the sublime, observing '[as] the great extreme of dimension is sublime, so the last extreme of littleness is in some measure sublime likewise'. Friedrich's *The Monk by the Sea* is not just a prime instance of these two concurrent and competing aspects of the sublime as defined here by Burke, the painting exemplifies, too, how it is the *simultaneous* conjunction, and hence also *simultaneous* contrast, of both greatness (of Nature) *and* minuteness (of man before Nature) that comes to define the essence of sublime landscape painting in the late eighteenth

---

28 Burke, *A Philosophical Enquiry*, p. 111; the subsequent passage p. 114.

and early nineteenth century. And perhaps more even than the ocean it was great mountains that most perfectly epitomised this conjunction and contrast; mountains could as easily excite the highest sensations of rapture and exuberance as plunge one into the greatest depths of dejection and depression (as we shall see also in our discussion of Percy Bysshe Shelley's poem 'Mont Blanc' in Chapter Four). Nor is it a great stride to move from gloomy reflection of the 'minuteness of our own nature', as inspired by Friedrich's boundless sea- and mountainscapes, to contemplation of the great Nothing that surrounds us, as the German literary scholar Dieter Arendt observed in the most comprehensive study of German Romantic nihilism:

> But may the cross tower on the steep and solitary mountain peak, and may it serve as comforting symbol of orientation above the foggy desolation of pathless mountain slopes, yet it is no curb for the dread begot by the silence of crest and abyss. In the vast expanse our line of sight meets with no limit or barrier, and seized by dizziness it plunges without hold into Nothingness.
>
> [Aber ist [das Kreuz] auch über den weglosen Hängen in der nebligen Leere als Zeichen der Orientierung zugleich ein tröstendes Symbol, so spricht doch um so rückhaltloser das Grauen rings aus dem Schweigen der Höhen und Abgründe. Der Blick stößt in den Weiten kaum mehr auf Grenzen und Formen und vom Schwindel ergriffen stürzt er haltlos ins Nichts.][29]

Put differently, it was the simultaneity of conflicting sentiments that aroused the sense of awe and anxiety that the chief aestheticians of the late eighteenth century associated with the 'terror' (Burke) or 'Schrecken' (Kant) of the sublime.[30] This terror arises for the first time in European intellectual history, Arendt notes, when the idealistic spirit realizes it cannot but founder on the limitations set by objective reality; and it is embodied in German literary history by the figure of the Storm-and-Stress writer Jakob Michael Reinhold Lenz (1751–1792) and encapsulated in the moment when, so Arendt, his 'idealistic-pantheistic self-confidence, which is rooted in God, turns into fear of Nothingness' ('[seine] idealistisch-pantheistische gottnahe Selbstsicherheit schlägt um in Angst vor dem Nichts').[31] With his mental breakdown, which Georg Büchner made the subject of his much celebrated *Lenz*-novella in the 1830s, Lenz becomes, in Arendt's opinion, the 'prototypical representative of the age of idealism' ('Repräsentant der *gesamten* Epoche des Idealismus'). As we shall see later in this chapter, Lenz is the perfect illustration of what happens when the 'almighty power' invoked by Burke is banished, when belief in God loses its authority and can no longer provide sanctuary and shelter from the overpowering forces of Nature. This is the moment when pantheism succumbs to full-fledged atheism.

In the history of German philosophy this shift is perhaps best personified by the Spinozist philosopher Karl Heinrich Heydenreich (1764–1801). Heydenreich was among those who, in the 1790s, continued to reflect on the theological and

---

29 Dieter Arendt, *Der 'poetische Nihilismus' in der deutschen Romantik. Studien zum Verhältnis von Dichtung und Wirklichkeit in der Frühromantik* (Tübingen: Niemeyer, 1972), p. 170.

30 For Burke see Part II, Section 2, and Part IV, Section 8, of *A Philosophical Enquiry*, for Kant see §28 of his 1790 *Critique of Judgment*.

31 *Der 'poetische Nihilismus' in der deutschen Romantik*, p. 179; the subsequent quote p. 178.

philosophical ramifications of Spinoza's pantheism and the degree to which it might be considered atheistic. The result was Heydenreich's provocative 1796 *Letters on Atheism* (*Briefe über den Atheismus*), which contain a fictitious correspondence between an atheist and a theist, the scales of which tellingly fall in favour of the former. In his opening letter the anonymous atheist confesses that, Kant's reasoning in his *Religion within the Boundaries of Mere Reason* notwithstanding, he can no longer believe in God and God's Revelation. He is left with Nature simply and purely — and it is the resulting consciousness of man's solitude in Nature that instills in him a sense of sublime awe; we read:

> Alone I must confess that I think the opposite holds true and am convinced that the ability of a man to believe [in God] must be diminished to the same degree that his knowledge of Nature expands and his understanding of its power becomes more assured and more profound. That at least is the result of *my* experience. The more I have learnt of Nature the more she has led me back not to God but only ever to Nature herself. [...] Is it not the case that we subject Nature to the most farfetched fancies of last purposes and other purposes that are foreign to her? [...]. Show me a last purpose of Nature, indeed show me any purpose she might possess that has not been forced on her by our own fabulating mind.
>
> [Allein offenherzig muß ich gestehen, daß ich das Gegenteil für wahr halte, und überzeugt bin, die Fähigkeit eines Menschen zum Glauben werde in dem Maße eingeschränkt, in welchem er seine Erkenntnis der Natur ausbreitet, und seine Einsicht in ihre Kräfte fester und tiefer gründet. Wenigstens ist es das Resultat *meiner* Erfahrung. Die Natur hat mich, wenn ich schärfere Erforschungen über sie anstelle, nie zu Gott, sondern immer wieder auf sie selbst zurückgeführt. [...] Oder dringen wir nicht der Natur die phantastischen Hirngespinste von Endzwecken und Zwecken auf, die ihrem Reiche fremd sind, [...]. Zeigen Sie mir einen Endzweck der Natur, ja zeigen Sie mir nur einen Zweck in ihr, der nicht durch unsern dichtenden Geist untergeschoben wäre.]³²

He concludes, as if he were citing James Hutton's *Theory of the Earth* with the famous phrase 'no vestige of a beginning — no prospect of an end': 'I am struck by a sublime sensation whenever I think of this order which has no beginning and will never end' ('Mir verursacht es ein erhabnes Gefühl, diese Ordnung zu denken, welche nie anfieng und nie enden wird'). Heydenreich's atheist then proceeds to engage with the concept of immortality of the soul, that second cornerstone of Christian faith. Seventeenth- and eighteenth-century anti-atheistic discourse had argued resolutely first that atheists must be innately immoral since theirs is a world without laws and without the social and moral strictures that religion affords; and second that their worldview could not be but bleak and empty, depriving them not just of the sense of immortality but along with it of the spiritual succour that God, religion and a belief in the afterlife offer and that every human being purportedly needs. This assessment of atheism's perceived downside and deficiency persists until today; it is, as we saw in the previous chapter, at the heart of Charles Taylor's notion

---

32 Karl Heinrich Heydenreich, *Briefe über den Atheismus* (Leipzig: Gottfried Martini, 1796), pp. 8–10 of the main body (the 'Preface' is likewise paginated 4–10 in Roman numerals); the subsequent passage p. 10 of the main text.

of a compensatory 'middle space' of 'undefined spirituality', which atheism and the process of secularization have forced twentieth- and twenty-first century Europeans subconsciously to seek out in art and culture as *Ersatz*, or replacement, for the loss of religious nourishment.

What in our secularized world today is less widespread than it was two hundred years ago, however, is the sentiment that 'a human being whose spirit and heart are healthy must believe [i.e., in God]', and that he 'who feels compelled not to believe' must be 'truly sick in spirit and heart' ('Ein Mensch, dessen Geist und Herz gesund sind, muß Glauben haben; wer hingegen sich gezwungen fühlt, ungläubig zu seyn, ist wahrhaft krank, an Geist und Herz zugleich'), as Heydenreich claims in his 'Preface' in the adopted editor's voice of a believer, a 'protective artifice' that was intended simultaneously to shield Heydenreich from prosecution while allowing him to make the case for atheism all the more freely and forcefully in the subsequent anonymous letters.[33] Although he tells us under cover of the 'Preface' that atheism can only result in 'muddled reasoning' ('verwirrtes Räsonnement') and 'bad humour' ('verstimmter Gemüthszustand'), the atheist's arguments in the letters that follow are so much more compelling than anything the theist can muster, as Heydenreich himself frankly admits in the editor's 'Appendix' attached to the correspondence. The victor is unmistakably the atheist. In the volume's appendix, which is constituted by the editor's own fictitious 'letter to a friend', one can clearly make out Heydenreich's own voice when he first asks:

> Why, you ask, give accounts of Atheism in which it appears in a beautiful guise and through its seductive appearance allow it to blind people. Is it fair to people if one cloaks opinions, which must destroy their peace of mind, in a recommending and alluring mantle?

only to concede:

> Atheism acquires a certain character of nobleness, in as much as it coincides with morality and virtue, it appears exalted when we find it supporting the purity and strength of the moral disposition in men. This is when its aura of sublimity makes it all the more appealing.

> [Wozu, fragen Sie, daß man Darstellungen des Atheism giebt, bey denen er in einem schönen Lichte erscheint, und durch seine verführerische Außenseite viele Menschen blenden kann. Heißt es redlich gegen die Menschheit verfahren, wenn man Meynungen, welche die Ruhe der meisten Menschen zerstöhren müssen, in ein empfehlendes und einschmeichelndes Gewand kleidet? [...] Der Atheism gewinnt einen gewissen Charakter des Edeln, je nachdem er sich mit Sittlichkeit und Tugend verträgt, er erscheint gross, wenn wir in ihm eine Stütze der Reinheit und Stärke der moralischen Gesinnung eines Menschen zu treffen glauben. Dann ist er auch in der That wegen des Anscheins von Erhabenheit, den er mit sich führt, verführerisch.][34]

---

33 *Briefe über den Atheismus*, p. 9 of the 'Preface' ('Vorerinnerung'). 'Protective artifice' is an expression used by David Berman in *A History of Atheism in Britain: From Hobbes to Russell* (London, New York, Sydney: Croom Helm, 1988), p. 135. The locutions 'das verwirrte Räsonnement' and 'de[r] verstimmte[...] Gemüthszustand' that I cite later can be found on p. 4 of the 'Preface'.

34 *Briefe über den Atheismus*, pp. 162 and 164.

Nobleness, sublimity, and an acceptance of man's solitude and finality in death all come together in Heydenreich's shrewd version of atheism. Fritz Mauthner, who was the first to turn renewed attention to Heydenreich's philosophy in the early twentieth century, called his *Letters on Atheism* the 'most radical atheistic system' to predate Max Stirner and Arthur Schopenhauer.[35] What is of particular interest from our perspective are two things, first Heydenreich's rebuttal of the theists' claims that atheism inevitably leads the unbeliever into immorality, lawlessness, and despair, a claim that is upheld by Christian critics of atheism still today, as evidenced most recently by Rice Broocks' 2013 book *God's Not Dead. Evidence for God in an Age of Uncertainty* and the 2014 film based on Broocks' line of argument.[36] Of interest, second, is his quasi-Lucretian standpoint that there is sublimity in death and nothingness, and that the traceless annihilation of man is a natural given and nothing to be frightened of.

Heydenreich's view is hardly typical for his time (nor indeed for ours); just one year after Heydenreich published his 'pocketbook for thinking worshippers of God' ('Taschenbuch für denkende Gottesverehrer') the German poet Friedrich Hölderlin described 'nothingness' as an 'abyss that gapes at us from all around' ('Nichts, das, wie ein Abgrund, um uns her uns angähnt'),[37] reiterating a sentiment that was fast becoming a commonplace. And another quarter century later the Bishop of Chartres would admonish that 'not a single doctrine of Christianity is respected, not a single scrap of truth is left', warning how 'impiety [is rushing] headlong [toward] the frightful abyss of atheism'.[38]

Of course, Heydenreich was far less influential as an atheistic philosopher than the more illustrious of his atheistic predecessors, notably Holbach whose widely circulated *System of Nature* is today generally considered the 'first avowedly atheistic work'[39] and was already in Heydenreich's day viewed by many to be 'the Bible of Atheism', so Joseph Priestley in his *Letters to a Philosophical Unbeliever* in 1787.[40] What distinguished Heydenreich from his French precursor, however, was his

35 *Der Atheismus und seine Geschichte in Abendlande*, vol. 4, p. 47.
36 Broocks thus writes 'Man's search for meaning takes a tragic wrong turn without belief in God, leaving man with an existential philosophy of despair. In other words, how could meaningless, random processes produce conscious, rational creatures who are aware of meaning and purpose?'; *God's Not Dead. Evidence for God in an Age of Uncertainty* (Nashville and Dallas: Nelson, 2013), p. 119. The film — a surprise success in the United States, a flop in Britain — substantiates her thesis especially through the character of the atheistic college professor Jeffrey Radisson who at the end dies after being struck by a car in a random car accident. According to the film's Wikipedia entry, even an evangelical film critic, Michael Gerson, 'was highly critical of the film and its message, writing "The main problem with *God's Not Dead* is not its cosmology or ethics but its anthropology. It assumes that human beings are made out of cardboard. Academics are arrogant and cruel. Liberal bloggers are preening and snarky (well, maybe the movie has a point here). Unbelievers disbelieve because of personal demons. It is characterization by caricature"' (Wikipedia entry '*God's Not Dead* (film)', accessed 4 November 2014).
37 *Sämtliche Werke und Briefe*, ed. by Jochen Schmidt, 3 vols (Frankfurt a.M.: Deutscher Klassiker Verlag, 1992), vol. 3, p. 277 (letter to his brother of 2 November 1797).
38 *Mandement de Monseigneur l'évêque de Chartres sur le Jubilé*, in *Ami de la religion*, 47, no. 1212 (22 March 1826), 161, cited by McMahon, *Enemies*, p. 185.
39 Berman, *A History of Atheism in Britain*, p. 37.
40 *Letters to a Philosophical Unbeliever* (Birmingham: Pearson and Rollason, 1787), p. 160.

recognition that atheism was prone to create a spiritual void in the unbeliever, something Holbach did not seem willing even to contemplate. For the materialist Holbach the belief in Nature provided a quintessentially positive outlook on life — it is perhaps not so surprising therefore to see a theist like Priestley provocatively, but not without some justification, equating Holbach's philosophy with a religion of Nature; in *Letters to a Philosophical Unbeliever* we accordingly read:

> As this writer [i.e., Holbach, the author of *System of Nature*] ascribes every thing that exists to the energy of *nature*, he seems sometimes to annex the same ideas to that word, that others do to the word *God*; so that, from some passages in his work, one would imagine that he was an atheist in name only, and not in reality.[41]

Holbach's disquisition indeed exudes a sense of positivity that, via the optimism of the Condorcets and Godwins of the turn of the century, became transmuted into the nineteenth century's philosophy of progress and perfectibility. As the literary scholar A. J. Sambrook has noted,

> Holbach had no difficulty in detaching God from Newton's system and substituting Necessity, the movement of uncontrolled natural forces. Holbach, of course, retained a belief in human progress towards earthly perfection, and, indeed, made human betterment dependent upon the disappearence of God.[42]

But Sambrook is also right to observe that 'other writers took a gloomier view. Necessity's intentions regarding humankind were more enigmatic than God's, and the universe might be in a very perilous situation'. Heydenreich does not go this far; he nowhere resorts to the kind of negativity and nihilism that I will be presenting momentarily as the darker side of solitude's coin. Respectively, Heydenreich's interests lie elsewhere. His question in essence anticipates Charles Taylor's: how does the atheist fill the void left by the loss of faith? His fictitious atheist hence states expressly at one point:

> Thus the interesting question remains: on what is the impression founded that religious belief be an essential need of humankind, and that the majority, if deprived of religion, would never again enjoy peace of mind and a sense of concord?

> [So bleibt die interessante Frage übrig: woher der Schein entstehe, als ob religiöse Ueberzeugung ein wesentliches Bedürfnis für den Menschen sey, und warum die meisten wirklich ohne Religion keiner innren Ruhe und keiner Selbsteinigkeit geniessen.][43]

What Heydenreich's *Letters on Atheism* accentuate is the recognition that the ultimate incarnation of atheism's 'lack' — lack of God, lack of hope, lack of meaning — is the sense of 'Nothingness' that it can leave behind in the non-believer. Its positive emphasis on nature's immanent order and the here and now of life notwithstanding, atheism can instigate a feeling of existential vacuity regarding both the overarching purpose of life and what follows after the end of life. This at least is what atheism's

---

41 Ibid., p. 171.
42 'A Romantic Theme: The Last Man', *Forum for Modern Language Studies*, 2 (1966), 25–33 (p. 27).
43 *Briefe über den Atheismus*, p. 49.

detractors in the eighteenth century (and still today, as the example of Taylor demonstrates) invariably claimed must befall anyone who has the rug of faith pulled out from under his feet. In this spirit, Friedrich Hölderlin has his young idealistic freedom fighter Hyperion lament in the eponymous epistolary novel:

> We pity the dead as if they felt death, yet the dead have peace. But the pain, the pain that no pain equals, is the incessant feeling of utter annihilation when our life loses its meaning, when our heart bids itself 'Down! into the depths! there is nothing left of you' [...]. Oh, you wretches who feel all this, who even as I, cannot allow yourselves to speak of man's being here for a purpose, who, even as I, are so utterly in the clutch of the Nothing that governs us, so profoundly aware that we are born for nothing, that we love a nothing, believe in nothing, work ourselves to death for nothing only that little by little we may pass over into nothing — how can I help it if your knees collapse when you think of it seriously? Many a time have I, too, sunk into these bottomless thoughts...
>
> [Wir bedauern die Toten, als fühlten sie den Tod, und die Toten haben doch Frieden. Aber das, das ist der Schmerz, dem keiner gleichkömmt, das ist unaufhörliches Gefühl der gänzlichen Zernichtung, wenn unser Leben seine Bedeutung so verliert, wenn so das Herz sich sagt, du mußt hinunter und nichts bleibt übrig von dir; [...] O ihr Armen, die ihr das fühlt, die ihr auch nicht sprechen mögt von menschlicher Bestimmung, die ihr auch so durch und durch ergriffen seid vom Nichts, das über uns waltet, so gründlich einseht, daß wir geboren werden für Nichts, daß wir lieben ein Nichts, glauben an's Nichts, uns abarbeiten für Nichts, um mählich überzugehen in's Nichts — was kann ich dafür, daß euch die Knie brechen, wenn ihr's ernstlich bedenkt? Bin ich doch auch schon manchmal hingesunken in diesen Gedanken...][44]

Taking a stab at nihilism's 'dread thought' from a British evangelical angle some three decades later, the protestant reverend Robert Pollok censures the atheist thus in his 1827 apocalyptic epopee *The Course of Time*:

> The skeptic's route — the unbeliever's, who,
> Despising reason, revelation, God,
> And kicking 'gainst the pricks of conscience, rushed
> Deliriously upon the bossy shield
> Of the Omnipotent; and in his heart
> Purposed to deify the idol chance.
> And laboured hard — oh, labour worse than nought!
> And toiled with dark and crooked reasoning,
> To make the fair and lovely Earth which dwelt
> In sight of Heaven, a cold and fatherless,
> Forsaken thing, that wandered on, forlorn,
> Undestined, uncompassioned, unupheld:
> A vapour eddying in the whirl of chance,
> And soon to vanish everlastingly.
> He travailed sorely, and made many a tack,
> His sails oft shifting, to arrive — dread thought!
> Arrive at utter nothingness; and have

---

44 *Hyperion and Selected Poems*, ed. by Eric L. Santner (New York: Continuum, 1990 (German Library, vol. 22)), pp. 34 and 35; *Sämtliche Werke und Briefe*, vol. 2, pp. 53 and 54.

> Being no more — no feeling, memory,
> No lingering consciousness that e'er he was.[45]

Writing to his friend John Thelwall on 31 December 1796 — the year of the publication of Heydenreich's *Letters* — Samuel Taylor Coleridge put the same sentiment more pithily as follows: 'Well, true or false, Heaven is a less gloomy idea than Annihilation!'[46]

The Dutch atheistic philosopher Herman Philipse recently offered a unique acronym for this condition: 'According to traditional Christian theologians', he wrote in his 2012 study *God in the Age of Science? A Critique of Religious Reason*, 'each entity would immediately fall into nothingness unless God sustained it in being. We might call this the Principle of the Natural Collapse into Nothingness (PNCN)'.[47] The despondency or 'illness' of which a belief in PNCN was (and some may think still is) a prime symptom was so much to fear that the Spirit of the Earth in Grainville's *Le Dernier Homme* exclaims, just when he is facing Death's scythe:

> 'I am afraid to die, I who have seen men, those weaker creatures, face death and accept their end with courage. Death? It was not death, for they knew very well that they would outlive their mantle of clay. Death, it is not you I fear. It is nothingness that fills me with horror. All the human beings I have seen, all will rise again to eternal life. As for me, I shall be no more: I have no eternal life before me. A dreadful thought which I cannot bear. Oh God!' he groaned. 'Do with me as it pleases Thee. Cast me down to Hell. I would rather burn with the demons than suffer annihilation.' The Spirit did not have the strength to go on. The words died on his lips; his heart grew heavy; he staggered and fell. He suffered the most extreme agony.
>
> [J'ai peur de mourir, moi qui vis les hommes, ces êtres plus faibles que moi, braver la mort et la recevoir avec courage! La mort! ah! ce n'était pas elle; ils savaient bien qu'ils renaîtraient immortels; ils savaient bien que leurs âmes allaient survivre à l'argile de leurs corps. Ô mort! ce n'est pas toi que j'appréhende, j'ai horreur du néant. Tous ces hommes que j'ai vus revivre pendant des siècles d'une éternelle durée, et moi, je ne serai plus je ne serai jamais! Épouvantable idée que je ne puis souffrir! Ô Dieu! dit'il d'une voix gémissante, fais de mon être l'usage qu'il te plaira, jette-moi dans les enfers, j'aime mieux brûler aves les démons que d'être anéanti. Le génie n'a plus la force de proférer d'antres paroles, sa voix expire sur les lèvres; sa poitrine est oppressée, il chancelle et tombe. Son âme souffre les angoisses de l'agonie...][48]

From Grainville's anti-rationalist Christian perspective, the figure of the Spirit of the Earth is designed as the ultimate embodiment of an atheist who, seeing his end approach, becomes terror-stricken by the thought that nothing more is to come. As one comes to realize only at the end of *Le Dernier Homme*, it is the fear of meaningless annihilation that has all along been driving Grainville's Spirit of the

---

45 *The Course of Time. A Poem, in ten books*, 2 vols (Edinburgh: William Blackwood, and London: T. Cadell, 1827), vol. I, pp. 118–19.
46 *Letters*, 2 vols (London: William Heinemann, 1895), vol. I, p. 211.
47 *God in the Age of Science?*, p. 238.
48 *The Last Man*, trans. I. F. & M. Clarke, p. 130 (*Le Dernier Homme*, ed. Kupiec, pp. 181–82).

Earth to all his evil machinations, his multitude of callous trickeries, lies and ruses that are deployed in order to prolong his survival.

It is precisely this *angoisse de l'agonie* and *horreur du néant*, this agony and horror in the face of what Arthur Schopenhauer in his 1819 *The World as Will and Idea* called 'empty nothingness', 'das leere Nichts',[49] against which Heydenreich's atheist counters calmly yet resolutely:

> That death holds nothing terrifying for me, I have declared afore. From the very start I considered the annihilation of my whole being to be the common destiny of all life [...] and as surely as I expect only one thing, I also expect a limit where the unfathomable *something* of my nature returns to the *nothing* from which it came into being. *I want to perish*, this is the postulate of my reason, *perish as befits the course and design of Nature*. To be sure, this postulate does not *sound* as sublime as your advocacy of immortality; but if I am not mistaken, it *is* sublime nonetheless, and the free acceptance of our ultimate fate of annihilation represents the maximum strength that a human soul can attain.
>
> [Dass der Tod für mich nichts Schreckliches hat, habe ich bereits erklärt. Ich betrachtete schon frühzeitig diese Vernichtung meines ganzen Wesens, als das allgemeine Loos aller Lebenden. [...] und so gewiss ich nur *eines* verlange, verlange ich auch einen Grenzpunkt, wo das unbegreifliche *etwas* meines Wesens das *Nichts* wiederfindet, aus dem es zum Seyn übergieng. *Ich will untergehn*, so lautet das Postulat meiner Vernunft, *untergehn nach dem Laufe und der Ordnung der Natur*. Freylich *klingt* dieses Postulat nicht so erhaben, als eure Forderung der Unsterblichkeit; aber, wenn mich nicht Alles trügt, so *ist* es erhaben, und die freye Einwilligung in das Loos der Vernichtung ist das Maximum der Stärke einer menschlichen Seele.][50] (Heydenreich's emphases)

But where the apparent Lucretian serenity and calm materialist acceptance with which Heydenreich's atheist approaches the ultimate collapse of the universe and the existential abyss lurking behind nothingness may remind one of the figure of Friedrich's *Wanderer above the Sea of Fog*, most during this period would have considered the 'natural' response to atheism's PNCN to be the trepidation expressed by Hölderlin's Hyperion or the anxiety exhibited by Grainville's Spirit of the Earth.

What must be considered the textbook illustration of this kind of existential religious torment is the figure of the poet Lenz in Georg Büchner's novella *Lenz*, briefly alluded to earlier. Büchner (1813–1837) wrote his story in the mid-1830s, three decades after *Hyperion* and *Le Dernier Homme*, and four decades after the historical Lenz's death. In his haunting narrative, the German writer and revolutionary used Lenz's illness as a real-life medical case to illustrate the *angoisses de l'agonie* that can result from the clash of belief and unbelief in an overly sensitive intellect. Büchner had studied medicine in Strasbourg between 1831 and 1833, and it is here also that he gained access to some of Lenz's letters and the diary of the pietistic vicar Johann Friedrich Oberlin who had taken care of Lenz during the first weeks of his mental

---

49 *The World as Will and Idea*, trans. by R. B. Haldane and J. Kemp (London: Trübner & Co., 1883), vol. 1, p. 528 (Book 4, §71).
50 *Briefe über den Atheismus*, pp. 12 and 54 (his emphases).

breakdown in early 1778. Büchner took these materials — from which he cites liberally (a good portion of his story consists of verbatim quotations) — to create a stirring literary portrait of Lenz during this period of crisis; the resulting novella, written around 1835 but published posthumously only in 1839 (with the title chosen by Büchner's friend and posthumous editor Karl Gutzkow), shows Lenz suffering severest 'religious torment' ('religiöse Quälereien').[51] Grappling like the biblical 'Jacob' with the implications of his 'atheism', the young poet takes flight to nature to seek respite from his excruciating self-doubts. It is solitude in nature alone that seems to soothe his spiritual distress. But it is in nature too that his revolt against God comes to a head; here we see him standing Prometheus-like on a mountain top raging against God:

> Clouds raced across the moon, now blanketing everything in darkness, now revealing the melting, shadowy outline of the landscape in the moonlight. He rushed to and fro. His breast was bursting with the exultation of hell. The rushing wind was like a chorus of Titans; he felt as if he could thrust a gigantic fist into heaven and seize God by the scruff of the neck and drag Him bodily through the clouds, as if he could crunch the world to bits with his teeth and spit the pieces in their Creator's face; he cursed, he blasphemed. Thus he came to the crest of the mountains, and the uncertain light spread down into the depths below where lay the huge white masses of stone [...]. Lenz laughed out loud, he couldn't help it, and as he laughed the hand of atheism clutched at him and held him fast in a grip completely secure and steady and firm.
>
> [Wolken zogen rasch über den Mond; bald Alles im Finstern, bald zeigten sie die nebelhaft verschwindende Landschaft im Mondschein. Er rannte auf und ab. In seiner Brust war ein Triumph-Gesang der Hölle. Der Wind klang wie ein Titanenlied, es war ihm, als könne er eine ungeheure Faust hinauf in den Himmel ballen und Gott herbei reißen und zwischen seinen Wolken schleifen; als könnte er die Welt mit den Zähnen zermalmen und sie dem Schöpfer in's Gesicht speien; er schwur, er lästerte. So kam er auf die Höhe des Gebirges, und das ungewisse Licht dehnte sich hinunter, wo die weißen Steinmassen [...]. Lenz mußte laut lachen, und mit dem Lachen griff der Atheismus in ihn und faßte ihn ganz sicher und ruhig und fest.]

But this is merely the hubris before the fall; the passage, which many critics structurally consider the turning point of the story, continues:

> He no longer knew what had moved him so deeply earlier that day, he was frozen, he decided that sleep was what he wanted, and he strode cold and unshakeable through the ghostly darkness — everything seemed to him empty and hollow, he had to start running, and went to bed. The next morning a deep horror overcame him at the state he had been in the previous day; he stood now on the brink of an abyss, driven by an insane desire to keep on peering into it,

---

51 Georg Büchner, 'Lenz', in *Complete Plays, Lenz and Other Writings*, trans. by John Reddick (London: Penguin, 1993), pp. 139–64 (p. 155); *Sämtliche Werke, Briefe und Dokumente*, 2 vols, ed. by Henri Poschmann with Rosemarie Poschmann (Frankfurt a.M.: Deutscher Klassiker Verlag, 1992, reprint 2006), vol. 1: *Dichtungen*, pp. 223–50 (p. 241). 'Jacob' is cited p. 152 (*Dichtungen*, p. 238: 'er habe damit gerungen wie Jakob'). The subsequent quotes pp. 156, 156–57 and 160–62 (*Dichtungen*, pp. 242, 242 and 246–48).

reliving the same agony again and again. Then his fear grew more intense, his sin against the Holy Ghost stood starkly before him.

[Er wußte nicht mehr, was ihn vorhin so bewegt hatte, es fror ihn, er dachte, er wolle jetzt zu Bette gehn, und er ging kalt und unerschütterlich durch das unheimliche Dunkel — es war ihm Alles leer und hohl, er mußte laufen und ging zu Bette. Am folgenden Tag befiel ihn ein großes Grauen vor seinem gestrigen Zustand, er stand nun am Abgrund, wo eine wahnsinnige Lust ihn trieb, immer wieder hineinzuschauen, und sich diese Qual zu wiederholen. Dann steigerte sich seine Angst, die Sünde und der heilige Geist stand vor ihm.]

His state of catatonic despair grows ever more fierce, in due course culminating in abject madness:

Meanwhile his condition had grown ever more hopeless. The peace he had derived from the proximity of Oberlin and the tranquillity of the valley had gone completely; the world that he had wanted to enjoy was irredeemably fractured. He had no love, no hate, no hope, just a terrible emptiness and the frantic, agonizing urge to fill it. He had *nothing*. [...] When he was on his own, he felt such terrifying loneliness that he continually talked out loud to himself, then his fear redoubled and he imagined he was hearing the voice of a stranger. In conversation he often stumbled, seized by indescribable fear [...]. His nocturnal troubles intensified to the most terrible degree. Only with the greatest difficulty could he get to sleep, having first attempted to fill the dreadful emptiness. Then between sleep and waking, he fell into a terrifying state; he bumped against something hideous, horrific, madness seized hold of him. [...] He suffered these attacks in the daytime too, and they were then much worse, for the light had previously been his safeguard. He felt at such moments as if he alone existed, as if the world existed only in his imagination, as if there were nothing but him, as if he were Satan, damned in all eternity, alone on the rack of his imagination. He rehearsed his past life in a hectic frenzy and then gave his verdict: 'logical, logical'; the pronouncements of others were 'illogical, illogical'; it was the gaping abyss of incurable madness, a madness through all eternity.

[Sein Zustand war indessen immer trostloser geworden, alles was er an Ruhe aus der Nähe Oberlins und aus der Stille des Tals geschöpft hatte, war weg; die Welt, die er hatte nutzen wollen, hatte einen ungeheuern Riß, er hatte keinen Haß, keine Liebe, keine Hoffnung, eine schreckliche Leere und doch eine folternde Unruhe, sie auszufüllen. Er hatte *Nichts*. [...] Wenn er allein war, war es ihm so entsetzlich einsam, daß er beständig laut mit sich redete, rief, und dann erschrak er wieder und es war ihm, als hätte eine fremde Stimme mit ihm gesprochen. Im Gespräch stockte er oft, eine unbeschreibliche Angst befiel ihn [...]. Die Zufälle des Nachts steigerten sich auf's Schrecklichste. Nur mit der größten Mühe schlief er ein, während er zuvor die noch schreckliche Leere zu füllen versucht hatte. Dann geriet er zwischen Schlaf und Wachen in einen entsetzlichen Zustand; er stieß an etwas Grauenhaftes, Entsetzliches, der Wahnsinn packte ihn. [...] Auch bei Tage bekam er diese Zufälle, sie waren dann noch schrecklicher; denn sonst hatte ihn die Helle davor bewahrt. Es war ihm dann, als existiere er allein, als bestünde die Welt nur in seiner Einbildung, als sei nichts, als er, er sei das ewig Verdammte, der Satan; allein mit seinen folternden Vorstellungen. Er jagte mit rasender Schnelligkeit sein Leben durch und dann sagte er: konsequent, konsequent; wenn Jemand was sprach: inkonsequent, inkonsequent; es war die Kluft unrettbaren Wahnsinns, eines Wahnsinns durch die Ewigkeit.] (Büchner's emphasis)

Büchner's heart-rending portrayal of the poet's increasingly debilitating fits of anguish and mood swings, and his inexorable descent into mental illness, is to my knowledge the earliest attempt in European literature to depict the etiology of paranoid schizophrenia. It is perhaps not irrelevant to note — which is why I have cited from Büchner's novella at such length here — that part of the fascination with Lenz's (and of course also Büchner's) story stems from the intensity and veracity with which we are made witness to a person agonizing over his religious convictions and the rabid *Angst* and 'loss of spiritual concord', to adapt Heydenreich's expression, that atheism can ignite in a sufficiently susceptible mind.

The anxiety of Hölderlin's Hyperion, Grainville's Spirit of the Earth and Büchner's Lenz is in many ways an extension of the more general anxiety of existential meaninglessness which became a vital catchphrase in the battle over atheism during this era. This anxiety is centrally connected with that growing sense of disenchantment, transcendental homelessness and existential solitude associated with the process of secularization as diagnosed by Weber, Taylor, Lukács, Eliade and others, which was touched upon in the previous chapter. It is indeed an anxiety that has come to define the very foundation of modern literature itself according to J. Hillis Miller, who observed in his study on *The Disappearance of God* in nineteenth-century Victorian literature: 'One great theme of modern literature is the sense of isolation, of alienation, brought about by man's new situation. We are alienated from God; we have alienated ourselves from nature; we are alienated from our fellow men; and, finally, we are alienated from ourselves, the buried life we never seem able to reach. The result is a radical sense of inner nothingness'.[52] The crucial question raised by the juxtaposition of the pro-atheist Heydenreich and the anti-atheist Grainville is how we as humans respond to that challenge, positively or negatively.

The work of literature that for many readers in the nineteenth century most decidedly epitomized the fear of nothingness was the German Romantic writer Jean Paul's 'Speech of the dead Christ from atop the World's Edifice that there is no God' ('Rede des todten Christus vom Weltgebäude herab, daß kein Gott sei', see Figure 3.4), which Werner Hofmann had cited as a key intertextual reference point of Friedrich's *The Monk by the Sea*. Conceived in 1789 but only later embedded in the novel *Siebenkäs*, the first parts of which were being published at the very moment that Heydenreich's *Letters on Atheism* appeared in 1796, it is a text that has been aptly called the 'most powerful vision and one of the most famous expressions of Romantic agony' ('Jean Pauls gewaltigste Vision und eine der berühmtesten Dichtungen der sogenannten "Schwarzen Romantik"').[53] With Goethe's novel

---

52 *The Disappearance of God. Five Nineteenth-Century Writers* (Cambridge, MA: The Belknap Press and London: Oxford University Press, 1963), p. 8.

53 See Claudia Becker, 'Der Traum der Apokalypse — die Apokalypse ein Traum? Eschatologie und/oder Ästhetik im Ausgang von Jean Pauls "Rede des toten Christus"', in *Poesie der Apokalypse*

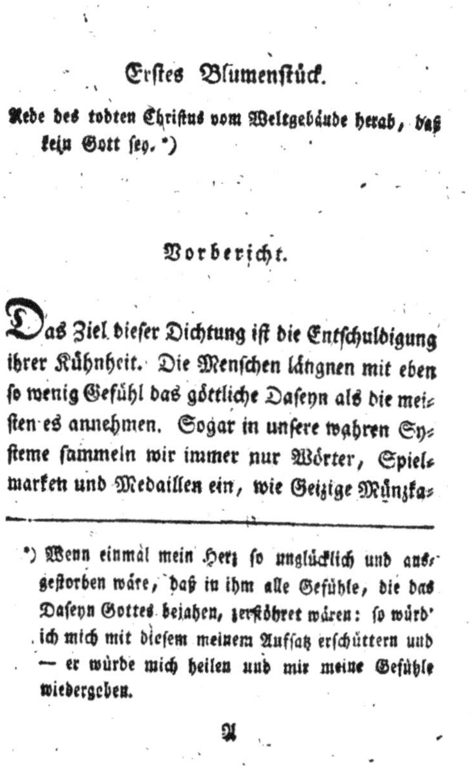

FIG. 3.4. The first page of the 'First Flower-Piece' in the 1796 first edition of Jean Paul's novel *Siebenkäs*. Note the footnote which reads (in Thomas Carlyle's translation): 'If ever my heart were to grow so wretched and so dead that all feelings in it which announce the being of God were extinct there, I would terrify myself with this sketch of mine; it would heal me, and give me my feelings back'.

Wilhelm Meister's Years of Apprenticeship, Schiller's aesthetic treatise 'On Naïve and Sentimental Poetry', and Ludwig Tieck's novel *William Lovell* all appearing in the same year, 1796 is truly an acme of German literary history. Prefiguring many motifs that later came to define European philosophical nihilism, and impacting directly on nihilism's chief advocate Friedrich Nietzsche, Jean Paul's 'Speech of the dead Christ' gained notoriety far beyond the borders of the German-speaking world through early translations by Madame de Staël in France (who incorporated a truncated version of it in Chapter 28 of the 'La Littérature et les arts' section of her celebrated *De l'Allemagne* in 1810) and Thomas Carlyle in Britain (who singled out precisely this and only this section of *Siebenkäs* for translation in his second essay on Jean Paul of 1830). Jean Paul's 'Speech of the dead Christ' begins (I cite Thomas Carlyle's translation):

> The purpose of this Fiction is the excuse of its boldness. Men deny the Divine Existence with as little feeling as the most assert it. [...] Of such sort, too, was my terror, at the poisonous stifling vapour which floats out round the heart of him who for the first time enters the school of Atheism. I could with less pain deny

(Würzburg: Königshausen & Neumann, 1991), pp. 129–44 (p. 130). Becker uses the term 'Schwarze Romantik'; in doing so she may also be referring to the German translation of Mario Praz's book *La carne, la morte e il diavolo nella letteratura romantica* which used 'Die Schwarze Romantik' as its subtitle, whereas the Oxford University Press English translation of Praz's seminal study used 'Romantic Agony' as its main title.

Immortality than Deity [...]; the whole spiritual Universe is dashed asunder by the hand of Atheism into numberless quick-silver-points of *Me's*, which glitter, run, waver, fly together or asunder, without unity or continuance. No one in Creation is so alone, as the denier of God.

[Das Ziel dieser Dichtung ist die Entschuldigung ihrer Kühnheit. Die Menschen leugnen mit ebensowenig Gefühl das göttliche Dasein, als die meisten es annehmen. [...] Ebenso erschrak ich über den giftigen Dampf, der dem Herzen dessen, der zum ersten Mal in das atheistische Lehrgebäude tritt, erstickend entgegenzieht. Ich will mit geringern Schmerzen die Unsterblichkeit als die Gottheit leugnen [...]; das ganze geistige Universum wird durch die Hand des Atheismus zersprengt und zerschlagen in zahlenlose quecksilberne Punkte von Ichs, welche blinken, rinnen, irren, zusammen- und auseinanderfliehen, ohne Einheit und Bestand. Niemand ist im All so sehr allein als ein Gottesleugner.][54]

Godlessness begets existential loneliness, this is the message that Jean Paul so emphatically conveys at the beginning of his novel.[55] The cited passage forms part of the authorial preface to the subsequent dream vision in which a dreamer is shown waking up in a graveyard at the onset of the Last Judgment; addressing the dead who have just risen from their graves, Christ preaches to them from a mountain top, proclaiming that God does not exist. We read, in a tone highly reminiscent of Nietzsche's Zarathustra:

Christ continued: 'I went through the Worlds, I mounted into the Suns, and flew with the Galaxies through the wastes of Heaven; but there is no God! I descended as far as Being casts its shadow, and looked down into the Abyss and cried, Father, where art thou? [...] and Eternity lay upon Chaos, eating it and ruminating it. Cry on, ye Dissonances; cry away the Shadows, for He is not!'

[Christus fuhr fort: 'Ich ging durch die Welten, ich stieg in die Sonnen und flog mit den Milchstraßen durch die Wüsten des Himmels; aber es ist kein Gott. Ich stieg herab, soweit das Sein seine Schatten wirft, und schauete in den Abgrund und rief: Vater, wo bist du? [...] und die Ewigkeit lag auf dem Chaos und zernagte es und wiederkäuete sich. — Schreiet fort, Mißtöne, zerschreiet die Schatten; denn er ist nicht!']

---

54 Thomas Carlyle, 'Jean Paul Friedrich Richter' (1830), in *Critical and Miscellaneous Essays*, 7 vols (London: Chapman and Hall, [n.d.]), vol. 3, p. 55; 'Die Rede des toten Christus', in *Siebenkäs*, in Jean Paul, *Werke*, 12 vols, ed. by Norbert Miller (Munich: Hanser, 1975), vol. 3, pp. 270–75 (p. 270). The subsequent passages pp. 56–57 (pp. 273–74). Ten years later, in 1805–1806, writing the educational treatise *Levana oder Erziehlehre* (*Levana, or a treatise on education*), Jean Paul reiterates the hypothesized connection between atheism and loneliness; he writes: 'Without God the ego remains lonely throughout eternity; but if it has a God, then it is more warmly, more deeply, and more strongly united than through friendship and love. Then I am no longer alone with my ego.' ('Ohne Gott ist das Ich einsam durch die Ewigkeiten hindurch; hat es aber seinen Gott, so ist es wärmer, inniger, fester vereiniget als durch Freundschaft und Liebe. Ich bin dann nicht mehr mit meinem Ich allein'); *Vorschule der Ästhetik / Levana*, in *Werke*, ed. Miller, vol. 9, p. 578.

55 Whereas the 'Speech of the dead Christ' section was originally positioned at the novel's opening, in later editions it was moved to the end of the second volume, removing some of the distinction this passage must have had for the original reader when the novel was first published in 1796.

'We are all orphans,' Christ then calls out, 'I and you: we are without Father!' The dream narrative continues:

> Then the Dissonances shrieked still louder, — the quivering walls of the Temple parted asunder; and the Temple and the Children sank down, and the whole Earth and the Sun sank after it, and the whole Universe sank with its immensity before us; and above, on the summit of immeasurable Nature, stood Christ, and gazed down into the Universe chequered with its thousand Suns, as into the Mine bored out of the Eternal Night, in which the Suns run like mine-lamps, and the Galaxies like silver veins. [...] then majestic as the Highest of the Finite, he raised his eyes towards the Nothingness, and towards the void Immensity, and said: 'Dead, dumb Nothingness! Cold, everlasting Necessity! Frantic Chance! [...] How is each so solitary in this wide grave of the All? I am alone with myself! O Father, O Father! where is thy infinite bosom, that I might rest on it?'

> ['Wir sind alle Waisen, ich und ihr, wir sind ohne Vater.' Da kreischten die Mißtöne heftiger — die zitternden Tempelmauern rückten auseinander — und der Tempel und die Kinder sanken unter — und die ganze Erde und die Sonne sanken nach — und das ganze Weltgebäude sank mit seiner Unermeßlichkeit vor uns vorbei — und oben am Gipfel der unermeßlichen Natur stand Christus und schauete in das mit tausend Sonnen durchbrochene Weltgebäude herab, gleichsam in das in die ewige Nacht gewühlte Bergwerk, in dem die Sonnen wie Grubenlichter und die Milchstraßen wie Silberadern gehen. [...] so hob er groß wie der höchste Endliche die Augen empor gegen das Nichts und gegen die leere Unermeßlichkeit und sagte: 'Starres, stummes Nichts! Kalte, ewige Notwendigkeit! Wahnsinniger Zufall! [...] Wie ist jeder so allein in der weiten Leichengruft des Alles! Ich bin nur neben mir — O Vater! o Vater! wo ist deine unendliche Brust, daß ich an ihr ruhe?']

Here the author of *Siebenkäs* and believer in a personal God lines up for censure the three pivotal anathemas associated with atheism, 'Nothingness', 'Necessity' and 'Chance', attributing to each what are deemed the most suitable adjectives: 'dead, dumb', 'cold, everlasting' and 'frantic'.

Jean Paul's compendium of critical epithets 'dead', 'dumb', and 'cold' would have served well as part of a Counter-Enlightenment attack on Holbach's *System of Nature*, and it is Holbach's kind of cold, 'hollow and deathlike' atheism — so it was perceived by many at the time, including Coleridge who describes the 'cave of Atheism' in his 1795 *Six Lectures on Revealed Religion* as 'unnaturally cold'[56] — against which Jean Paul felt compelled to warn his readership. Looking back on his adolescence and early adulthood in his autobiography *Poetry and Truth*, Goethe much later recalls the 'gloomy' and 'Cimmerian' impact that Holbach's materialist and atheistic philosophy had on him and his generation at the time of its pseudonymous publication in 1770:

> Prohibited books condemned to the flames, of which so much was heard at the time, produced no effect upon us. I mention as a typical instance, the *Système de la Nature*, which we looked into out of curiosity. We did not understand how such a book could be dangerous. It seemed to us so gloomy, so Cimmerian, so

---

56 Cited in Martin Priestman, *Romantic Atheism*, p. 152.

deathlike, that we found it difficult to endure its presence, and shuddered at it as at a spectre. [...] 'All had of necessity to be,' so said the book, 'and therefore there was no God.' But could not God also exist of necessity? we asked. [...] None of us had read the book through; for it had disappointed the expectation with which we opened it. It had announced a system of nature; and we had, therefore, hoped really to learn something of nature — of this idol of ours. [...] But how hollow and empty did we feel this melancholy, atheistic half-night to be, where earth vanished with all its creatures, heaven with all its stars.

[Verbotene, zum Feuer verdammte Bücher, welche damals großen Lärm machten, übten keine Wirkung auf uns. Ich gedenke statt aller des *Système de la nature*, das wir aus Neugier in die Hand nahmen. Wir begriffen nicht, wie ein solches Buch gefährlich sein könnte. Es kam uns so grau, so cimmerisch, so totenhaft vor, daß wir Mühe hatten, seine Gegenwart auszuhalten, daß wir davor wie vor einem Gespenste schauderten. [...] [uns] schien jenes Buch, als die rechte Quintessenz der Greisenheit, unschmackhaft, ja abgeschmackt. Alles sollte notwendig sein und deswegen kein Gott. Könnte es denn aber nicht auch notwendig einen Gott geben? fragten wir. [...] Allein wie hohl und leer ward uns in dieser tristen atheistischen Halbnacht zu Mute, in welcher die Erde mit allen ihren Gebilden, der Himmel mit allen seinen Gestirnen verschwand.]⁵⁷

And just as Goethe here emphasizes atheism's 'melancholy half-night', Jean Paul in the 'Speech of the dead Christ' speaks of its 'everlasting Midnight'; his dreamer conjures up a grim prediction of what an atheist should expect to suffer in afterlife: 'Ah, when the sorrow-laden lays himself [...] into the Earth, to sleep till a fairer Morning full of Truth, full of Virtue and Joy, — he awakens in a stormy Chaos, in the everlasting Midnight, — and there comes no Morning, and no soft healing hand, and no Infinite Father!' ('Wenn der Jammervolle sich mit wundem Rücken in die Erde legt, um einen schönern Morgen voll Wahrheit, voll Tugend und Freude entgegenzuschlummern: so erwacht er im stürmischen Chaos, in der ewigen Mitternacht — und es kommt kein Morgen und keine heilende Hand und kein unendlicher Vater!'). From this follows the adhortation: 'Mortal, beside me! If thou still livest, pray to *Him*; else hast thou lost him forever!' ('Sterblicher neben mir, wenn du noch lebest, so bete Ihn an: sonst hast du Ihn auf ewig verloren').⁵⁸ What also follows is the dreamer's profound expression of relief after he awakes from his nightmare: 'My soul wept for joy that I could still pray to God; and the joy, and the weeping, and the faith in him were my prayer' ('Meine Seele weinte vor Freude, daß sie wieder Gott anbeten konnte — und die Freude und das Weinen und der Glaube an ihn waren das Gebet'). Jean Paul's seemingly atheistic dream narrative is thus securely contained — in the double sense of that word — within a frame of faith.

57 Goethe, *Poetry and Truth*, pp. 38–40 (*Goethes Werke*, ed. Trunz, vol. 9, p. 490).
58 Carlyle, 'Jean Paul Friedrich Richter', p. 58 ('Die Rede des toten Christus', p. 275); the subsequent passage also p. 58 (p. 275). Jean Paul reuses this imagery of light and dark in §2 of *Vorschule der Ästhetik* (Pre-School of Aesthetics), the section on 'Poetic Nihilists', where he writes 'Where in a time God goes down like the sun, there darkness enters the world; he who despises the All [or: the Universe] has regard only for himself' ('Wo einer Zeit Gott, wie die Sonne, untergehet; da tritt bald darauf auch die Welt in das Dunkel; der Verächter des All achtet nichts weiter als sich'); *Vorschule der Ästhetik / Levana*, *Werke*, vol. 9, p. 31.

In a twist of fate peculiarly befitting of Romantic irony, Jean Paul's criticism of atheism and the dire warning he issued against it in the frame narrative of the 'Speech of the dead Christ' were doomed to escape the notice of the French reader — Mme de Staël's truncation of the narrative (respectively Charles de Villers's: it is widely believed that Mme de Staël's friend produced the version known in French as *Le Songe de Jean Paul*, 'The Dream of Jean Paul') expunged precisely the frame parts critical of atheism and positive about faith. 'Naturally these omissions', writes Byron R. Libhart in a study of the French reception of Jean Paul's text, 'gave the passage a character of hopeless finality, causing the French erroneously to think of it as a declaration of atheistic belief'.[59] As a consequence, subsequent generations of French writers and intellectuals (the French comparatist Claude Pichois specifically distinguishes three such generations) from Balzac, Baudelaire, Flaubert, Gautier, Hugo, Michelet, Musset, Nerval, Nodier (who edited the second edition of Grainville's *Le Dernier Homme*), Renan, Vigny and Villiers de l'Isle-Adam in the nineteenth century to Malraux in the twentieth saw Jean Paul as the first envoy of modern nihilism and, once Nietzsche stepped forward, as the German philosopher's immediate predecessor; as Pichois put it symptomatically in *L'Image de Jean-Paul Richter dans les lettres françaises*: 'Hence from Michelet to Malraux, a great part of French literature is dominated by the conception of the Death of God, by the obsession with the "horrendous void of God" for which to a great degree first Jean Paul and then Nietzsche are responsible' ('Si de Michelet à Malraux, une large région de la littérature française est dominée par la pensée de la mort de Dieu, par l'obsession du "vide épouvantable de Dieu", c'est en grande partie Jean-Paul puis Nietzsche qu'il faut en rendre responsables').[60] Whether this was what de Staël and de Villers had intended remains unclear; it was certainly not what Jean Paul had intended, as the Dutch scholar J. P. Vijn has argued in his study *Carlyle and Jean Paul*.[61] Similar misreadings have made their way into theological encyclopedias; thus the entry for 'Atheism' in *Religion Past & Present. The Encyclopedia of Theology and Religion* contains a section entitled 'Jean Paul and Nietzsche' in which we can read: 'Even before Nietzsche, the notion of the death of God had already led to a radicalization in the mood of atheism in Jean Paul's "Speech of the Dead Christ". Christ himself stands as witness and surety for atheism. [...] It remained for Nietzsche to radicalize atheism in a way that has not been outdone since'.[62] There is no mention here that Jean Paul stood on the opposite, i.e. non-atheistic, bank of the religious divide.[63] The German scholar Claudia Becker has nonetheless usefully

---

59 'Madame de Staël, Charles de Villers, and the death of God in Jean Paul's *Songe*', *Comparative Literature Studies*, 9 (1972), 141–51 (p. 142–43).

60 *L'Image de Jean-Paul Richter dans les lettres françaises* (Paris: Corti, 1963), p. 292.

61 *Carlyle and Jean Paul. Their Spiritual Optics* (Amsterdam: John Benjamins, 1982 (Utrecht Publications in General and Comparative Literature, vol. 18)), for instance p. 260.

62 Walter R. Dietz, 'Atheism', in *Religion Past & Present. The Encyclopedia of Theology and Religion*, ed. by Hans Dieter Betz, Don S. Browning et al. (Leiden and Boston: Brill, 2007), vol. I, pp. 477–82 (p. 479).

63 I might add as a cautionary note that Jean Paul's relationship to religion, and the Christian religion in particular, was not without complexities and internal tensions. In an article on Jean's Paul's theological views, Timothy J. Casey for instance argues that Jean Paul considered Christ

tried to bridge the gap between these conflicting interpretations by providing the following recap:

> The terminal visions in the works of Jean Paul [...] are poetic documents of the atmosphere of crisis around 1800, a time whose politico-social revolutions were driving the individual ever more into an insecure subjectivity; they are hence an expression of that 'transcendental homelessness' which had deprived the bourgeois citizen, feeling ever more disaffected, of any sense of metaphysical-religious comfort. [...] Nonetheless, this text does not belong unequivocally in the tradition of nihilism [...]. The 'Speech' is at once a 'poetic representation of apostasy' *and* a poetic profession of faith, in short a thoroughly ambivalent reflection on life and death, waking and dreaming, transience and eternity, scepticism and belief.

> [Die Endzeitvisionen im Œuvre Jean Pauls [...] sind poetische Dokumente des Krisenbewußtseins der Umbruchszeit um 1800, deren politisch-soziale Revolution(en) den einzelnen in seine ungesicherte Subjektivität getrieben hatte(n), und sind als solche Ausdruck jener 'transzendentalen Obdachlosigkeit', die dem sich selbst entfremdeten bürgerlichen Individuum auch keine metaphysisch-religiöse Geborgenheit mehr gewährte. [...] Gleichwohl läßt sich dieser Text nicht bruchlos in die nihilistische Tradition verorten [...]. Die *Rede* ist zugleich eine 'dichterische Gestaltung des Unglaubens' *und* ein poetisches Glaubensbekenntnis, mithin ein durchaus ambivalentes Denk-Stück über Leben und Tod, Wachen und Träumen, Vergänglichkeit und Ewigkeit, Skepsis und Glauben.][64]

The fact that Jean Paul's attempt to reaffirm faith in the face of apostasy later came to be misinterpreted precisely as the earliest instance of the very apostasy that the text was trying to discredit renders 'Speech of the Dead Christ' particularly emblematic of the battle of belief systems that so embodies this period in European intellectual history.

'God, or Nothing!'

If Jean Paul's 'Speech of the dead Christ' epitomizes the existential *Angst* and trepidation that unsettled believers in a personal God in the face of an atheism that was increasingly encroaching upon their religious domain in the late eighteenth century, other passages from later works show Jean Paul's continuing preoccupation with the topic of death, but now leavened with the ancillary connotation of 'lastness'. Written in December 1799 and published in March 1800, his 'Clavis Fichtiana seu Leibgeberiana' is not just a satirical take on Fichte's Absolute I, or what Jean Paul called 'this indeterminate indetermining, this logical afterbirth and absolute mother of if-subjectivity' ('dieses unbestimmt Unbestimmende, diese logische Nachgeburt und absolute Mutter der Ob-Subjektivität'),[65] but also a melancholic rumination on

---

a human only; see his 'Der tolle Mensch in der Pfarrhausstube. Jean Pauls Stellung zu der Gretchenfrage und seine Auseinandersetzung mit der Theologie', in *Die deutsche literarische Romantik und die Wissenschaften*, ed. by Nicholas Saul (Munich: iudicium, 1991), pp. 156–76.

64 'Der Traum der Apokalypse', p. 129–30.
65 'Clavis Fichtiana seu Leibgeberiana', in *Werke*, ed. Miller, vol. 6, pp. 1011–56 (p. 1015).

the turning of a century as symbolic of the end of an era; these are its concluding lines:

> Around me a broad fossilized humanity — In the dark uninhabited silence no love glows, no admiration, no prayer, no hope, no goal — Me so completely lonely, nowhere a pulse beat, no life, nothing around me without me nothing but nothing — In me the mute, blind, obscured Demogorgon who continues his labours, and I am him myself — Thus I come from eternity, and thus I enter into eternity —— And who is there to hear my lament and know me? — Me. — Who listens, and who knows me in eternity? — Me. —
>
> [Rund um mich eine weite versteinerte Menschheit — In der finstern unbewohnten Stille glüht keine Liebe, keine Bewunderung, kein Gebet, keine Hoffnung, kein Ziel — Ich so ganz allein, nirgends ein Pulsschlag, kein Leben, nichts um mich ohne mich nichts als nichts — In mir den stumm, blind, verhüllt fortarbeitenden Dämagorgon, und ich bin er selber — So komm' ich aus der Ewigkeit, so geh' ich in die Ewigkeit —— Und wer hört die Klage und kennt mich jetzt? — Ich. — Wer hört sie, und wer kennt mich nach Ewigkeit? — Ich. —][66]

Jean Paul's language exudes all the doom and gloom and dreariness of a deep-seated existential loneliness — it is as if he had been commissioned to create a literary template for Kant's philosophical declaration 'Deep solitude is sublime, but in a terrifying way' ('Tiefe Einsamkeit ist erhaben, aber auf eine schreckhafte Art').[67] The emphatic outcry 'Me so completely lonely, nowhere a pulse beat, no life, nothing around me without me nothing but nothing' connects this text with Jean Paul's tale 'The Strange Society of New Year's Eve', conceived and written around the same time as 'Clavis Fichtiana', but published a year later in 1801. Here we find the utterly and eternally lonely 'me' of 'Clavis Fichtiana' transformed into yet another incarnation of a man looking down on the earth from a summit, but this time converted into a vision of a Last Man:

> Some time in the future there will be a last human — he will stand on a mountain under the equator and look down upon the waters which cover the vast world — solid ice glistens at the poles. [...] Look up to Heaven, last man! On earth all life has disappeared — your great rivers rest dissolved in the ocean. [...] Listen further, in your amazement! In eternity a day will come [...] when Creation will wane ... God then still is; he stands bright in the night [...] —— Last man, do not brood over the long world before and after you; there is no age in the universe — eternity is young — sink into the wave when she comes, she will ebb, not you!
>
> [Es gibt einmal einen letzten Menschen — er wird auf einem Berg unter dem Äquator stehen und herabschauen auf die Wasser, welche die weite Erde überziehen — festes Eis glänzt an den Polen herauf. [...] Schau auf zum Himmel, letzter Mensch! Auf deiner Erde ist schon alles vergangen — deine großen Ströme ruhen aufgelöst im Meere. [...] Vernimm weiter, Erschrockener! In der Ewigkeit kommt ein Tag [...] wo es dämmert in der Schöpfung... Dann

---

66 Ibid., p. 1056.
67 'Beobachtungen über das Gefühl des Schönen und Erhabenen' (1764), in *Werke*, ed. Weischedel, vol. I, pp. 821–84 (p. 827).

> ist Gott noch; er steht licht in der Nacht [...] —— Letzter Mensch, denke nicht nach über die lange Welt vor und nach dir; im Universum gibts kein Alter — die Ewigkeit ist jung — sinke in die Welle, wenn sie kommt, sie versiegt, und nicht du!][68]

Again the tone may be reminiscent of Nietzsche, but again not so the thrust of the argument.[69] Jean Paul's and Nietzsche's worldviews could not be further apart. Jean Paul's swansong of humanity still presupposes an active God and a Last Judgment ('In eternity a day will come when Creation will wane ... God then still is'). For him the Death of God remains a Goya- or Fuseli-like nightmare from which we awake to find God still standing 'bright in the night', whereas for Nietzsche God is chimera only — and is hence, of course, truly dead. What's more, in Nietzsche's post-Romantic vision of God's demise it is men themselves who have killed the Almighty. Few passages in German philosophy have gained more notoriety than the opening lines of Section 125 of Nietzsche's *Gay Science* of 1882:

> *The madman.* — Have you not heard of that madman who lit a lantern in the bright morning hours, ran to the market place, and cried incessantly: 'I seek God! I seek God' — As many of those who were standing around just then did not believe in God, he provoked much laughter. Has he got lost? asked one. [...] Or is he hiding? Is he afraid of us? Has he gone on a voyage? emigrated? — Thus they yelled and laughed. The madman jumped into their midst and pierced them with his eyes. 'Whither is God?' he cried; 'I will tell you. *We have killed him* — you and I. All of us are his murderers. But how did we do this? [...] God is dead. God remains dead. And we have killed him.'

> [*Der tolle Mensch.* — Habt ihr nicht von jenem tollen Menschen gehört, der am hellen Vormittage eine Laterne anzündete, auf den Markt lief und unaufhörlich schrie: 'Ich suche Gott! Ich suche Gott!' — Da dort gerade viele von denen zusammenstanden, welche nicht an Gott glaubten, so erregte er ein großes Gelächter. Ist er denn verlorengegangen? sagte der eine. [...] Oder hält er sich versteckt? Fürchtet er sich vor uns? Ist er zu Schiff gegangen? ausgewandert? — so schrien sie und lachten sie durcheinander. Der tolle Mensch sprang mitten unter sie und durchbohrte sie mit seinen Blicken. 'Wohin ist Gott?' rief er, 'ich will es euch sagen! *Wir haben ihn getötet* — ihr und ich! Wir alle sind seine Mörder. Aber wie haben wir das gemacht? [...] Gott ist tot! Gott bleibt tot! Und wir haben ihn getötet!'][70] (Nietzsche's emphases)

Later, in the opening passage of *Gay Science*'s Section 343, programmatically entitled 'We Fearless Ones', Nietzsche expounds:

---

68 'Die wunderbare Gesellschaft in der Neujahrsnacht', in *Werke*, ed. Miller, vol. 8, pp. 1121–38 (pp. 1133–34).

69 Hendrik Birus was the first to flag up the direct connection between Nietzsche's notion of 'The Last Man' and Jean Paul's writings; see his 'Apokalypse der Apokalypsen. Nietzsches Versuch einer Destruktion aller Eschatologie', in *Das Ende. Figuren einer Denkform*, ed. by Karlheinz Stierle and Rainer Warning (Munich: Fink, 1996), pp. 33–58, especially pp. 38–40. Birus also points out, correctly, that Jean Paul's, Grainville's and Mary Shelley's 'last men' are the last of their species and as such condemned to die, whereas Nietzsche's last man is he who lives longest and the initiator of a new species.

70 *The Gay Science*, p. 181 (*Die Fröhliche Wissenschaft*, in *Werke*, vol. 2, pp. 400–01).

> *The meaning of our cheerfulness.* — The greatest recent event — that 'God is dead', that the belief in the Christian god has become unbelievable — is already beginning to cast its first shadows over Europe. [...] The event itself is far too great, too distant, too remote from the multitude's capacity for comprehension even for the tidings of it to be thought of as having *arrived* as yet. Much less may one suppose that many people know as yet *what* this event really means — and how much must collapse now that this faith has been undermined because it was built upon this faith, propped up by it, grown into it; for example, the whole of our European morality.
>
> [*Was es mit unsrer Heiterkeit auf sich hat.* — Das größte neuere Ereignis — daß 'Gott tot ist', daß der Glaube an den christlichen Gott unglaubwürdig geworden ist — beginnt seine Schatten über Europa zu werfen. [...] das Ereignis selbst ist viel zu groß, zu fern, zu abseits vom Fassungsvermögen vieler, als daß auch nur seine Kunde schon *angelangt* heißen dürfte; geschweige denn, daß viele bereits wüßten, *was* eigentlich sich damit begeben hat — und was alles, nachdem dieser Glaube untergraben ist, nunmehr einfallen muß, weil es auf ihm gebaut, an ihn gelehnt, in ihn hineingewachsen war: zum Beispiel unsre ganze europäische Moral.][71] (Nietzsche's emphases)

In observing this crisis of European morality and the collapse of (Christian) faith, Nietzsche symptomatically places himself as a visionary 'on the mountains, posted between today and tomorrow' ('auf den Bergen, zwischen Heute und Morgen').[72] The view from this mountain top is unobstructed and liberating — and it is the very antithesis of the prophet Moses standing lonely on the mountain top receiving the commandments in colloquy with God; the conclusion of the passage runs:

> Indeed, we philosophers and 'free spirits' feel, when we hear the news that 'the old god is dead', as if a new dawn shone on us [...]. At long last the horizon appears free to us again, even if it should not be bright; at long last our ships may venture out again, venture out to face any danger; all the daring of the lover of knowledge is permitted again; the sea, *our* sea, lies open again; perhaps there has never yet been such an 'open sea'.
>
> [In der Tat, wir Philosophen und 'freien Geister' fühlen uns bei der Nachricht, daß der 'alte Gott tot' ist, wie von einer neuen Morgenröte angestrahlt [...] endlich erscheint uns der Horizont wieder frei, gesetzt selbst, daß er nicht hell ist, endlich dürfen unsre Schiffe wieder ausfahren, auf jede Gefahr hin auslaufen, jedes Wagnis des Erkennenden ist wieder erlaubt, das Meer, *unser* Meer liegt wieder offen da, vielleicht gab es noch niemals ein so 'offnes Meer'.]

It has often been remarked that passages such as these link into Nietzsche's vision of the *Übermensch*, the new overman with his emphasis on a new and anti-Christian value system, which Nietzsche propounded in his *Thus spake Zarathustra* (*Also sprach Zarathustra*, 1883/1885) and elsewhere in his later writings. Symptomatically, Karl Löwith has called *Thus spake Zarathustra* 'an anti-Christian gospel and reversed Sermon on the Mount'.[73] We might add to this that it is also a ratification and rev-

---

[71] Ibid., p. 279, with a minor correction of mine (*Die Fröhliche Wissenschaft*, p. 479).
[72] *The Gay Science*, p. 279 (*Die Fröhliche Wissenschaft*, p. 479); the subsequent quote p. 280 (p. 480).
[73] *Nietzsche's Philosophy of the Eternal Recurrence of the Same*, trans. by J. Harvey Lomax (Berkeley: University of California Press, 1997), p. 184.

ersal at once of Jean Paul's 'Speech of the dead Christ from atop the World's Edifice that there is no God', a ratification insofar as Nietzsche repeats the pronouncement of the death of God as delivered by Christ in Jean Paul's dream narrative, but simultaneously a reversal insofar as Jean Paul revokes that selfsame pronouncement by reconfirming Christian faith in the dream's frame narrative. What Nietzsche and Jean Paul have in common, nonetheless, is their awareness of the spiritual agony and existential solitude that their mountain-top preachers must suffer.

Although we know that Nietzsche considered Jean Paul to be the prime contender for the position of 'favourite writer in my later life' ('Jean Paul wird einmal bei reiferen Jahren mein Lieblingsschriftsteller', he jotted in one of his notebooks)[74] and that he was particularly inspired by Jean Paul's 'Speech of the dead Christ', the more compelling predecessors of his madman are, arguably, not Jean Paul's several narrators, but rather the various eccentric characters presented in August Klingemann's *The Nightwatches of Bonaventura* (*Nachtwachen des Bonaventura*), a satire published under the pseudonym Bonaventura in 1805 (but dated 1804 on the first of the two separate title pages, see Figure 3.5). Written concurrently with Sonnenberg's *Donatoa* and Grainville's *Le Dernier Homme*, as well as Wordsworth's 1805/1806 version of *The Prelude*, this text, which today ranks among German literature's foremost contributions to the history of literary nihilism, must be considered their true antipode in spirit as well as temperament. The scholar Richard Brinkmann has called Klingemann's sardonic take on German society and mores around 1800 the 'summation of the reverse side of early romanticism' ('Summe der Kehrseite der Frühromantik') and the work's main character an 'unreserved representative of a desperate nihilism' ('rückhaltloser Vertreter eines hoffnungslosen Nihilismus').[75] Writing also on the subject of Romantic nihilism, another German literary scholar, Werner Kohlschmidt, has appointed *The Nightwatches of Bonaventura* a 'nihilistic Gesamtkunstwerk' ('nihilistisches Gesamtkunstwerk') and testimony to the author's 'overt atheism' ('offensichtlichen Atheismus').[76] But whereas Georg Büchner seems to have been thoroughly familiar with this text, and took considerable inspiration from it not just in *Lenz* but also *Danton's Death* (*Dantons Tod*) as well as his other works,[77] ironically it appears that Nietzsche never read it — I have yet to find evidence of him having encountered *The Nightwatches*, even despite the fact that his 'favourite writer' Jean Paul was one of the first to acknowledge that the then anonymous author of *The Nightwatches* had created a wonderfully parodical send-up of his own writing, as well as of Kant, Fichte, Schlegel, Novalis and Goethe, not to mention Shakespeare, whose 'mad' Hamlet and Ophelia play crucial roles in

---

74 'Autobiographisches aus den Jahren 1856–1869', in *Werke*, vol. 3, p. 772.

75 'Nachtwachen von Bonaventura. Kehrseite der Frühromantik?', in *Die deutsche Romantik*, ed. by Hans Steffen (Göttingen: Vandenhoeck & Ruprecht, 1970), pp. 134–58 (p. 137).

76 'Nihilismus der Romantik', in *Romantikforschung seit 1945*, ed. by Klaus Peter (Königstein: Anton Hain Meisenstein / Athenaeum, Hain, Scriptor, Hanstein, 1980), pp. 53–66 (pp. 63 and 64).

77 Walter Hinderer in his *Büchner Kommentar zum dichterischen Werk* (Munich: Winkler, 1977) sees Bonaventura's (Klingemann's) *Nachtwachen* as an ideational and literary nodal point ('Bezugsort') of *Lenz, Dantons Tod, Leonce und Lena* and *Woyzeck*, especially with regard to the motifs of boredom and existential anxiety.

FIG. 3.5. Second title page of the first edition of August Klingemann's *Nachtwachen*, published under the pseudonym Bonaventura. The volume was published as the seventh of eight annual instalments of a series of 'German Original Novels'; the series' title page for this volume states 1804, the novel's own title page 1805. That Jean Paul recommends the volume to a friend already on 14 January 1805 suggests that the volume indeed appeared in 1804; that the philosopher Schelling had also used the pseudonym Bonaventura three years earlier led many contemporary readers and later critics — including Jean Paul — to assume that Schelling had authored this work.

Klingemann's satirical hall of mirrors.[78]

It is all the more unfortunate that we have no documented response of Nietzsche to this 'novel' — if that is the appropriate genre designation for this quixotic charade in sixteen 'Night Watches' of a poet first turned madman, then turned night watchman — since the conceptual tenets underlying *The Nightwatches* certainly seem to anticipate many of Nietzsche's own philosophical precepts; especially the 'pessimistic-nihilistic outlook on life' ('pessimistisch-nihilistisches Lebensgefühl') that is commonly ascribed to Klingemann's 'bitter and bizarre' text,[79] combined with its stress on the madness that infests our world in innumerable guises, presages many of Nietzsche's statements on these matters; the following is a prime example: 'The main forms of pessimism', Nietzsche writes, are

---

78 For more on this aspect see Alice Kuzniar, 'The Bounds of the Infinite: Self-Reflection in Jean Paul's "Rede des todten Christus"', *German Quarterly*, 57 (1984), 183–96.

79 See the entry 'Pessimismus' in *Historisches Wörterbuch der Philosophie*, vol. 7: P–Q (1989), column 386–95, especially columns 386 and 387. 'bitter and bizarre' are words used by Gerald Gillespie in his 'Introduction' to his excellent bilingual edition of *Die Nachtwachen des Bonaventura / The Night Watches of Bonaventura* (Edinburgh: Edinburgh University Press, 1972), p. 1. Gillespie's English translation is referenced below as *The Night Watches of Bonaventura*; in the body of my chapter I use *Nightwatches* rather than *Night Watches*, following Gillespie's usage in the second edition of his translation.

> the pessimism of *sensibility* [...];
> the pessimism of *the »unfree will«* [...];
> the pessimism of *doubt* [...].

The attached psychological conditions can all be observed in the madhouse, albeit perhaps with a certain exaggeration. In particular 'nihilism' (the penetrating sense of — 'Nothingness').

> [*Die Hauptarten des Pessimismus*:
> der Pessimismus der *Sensibilität* [...];
> der Pessimismus des *»unfreien Willens«* [...];
> der Pessimismus des *Zweifels* [...].
>
> Die dazugehörigen psychologischen Zustände kann man allesamt im Irrenhause beobachten, wenn auch in einer gewissen Übertreibung. Insgleichen den 'Nihilismus' (das durchbohrende Gefühl des — 'Nichts').][80]

If exaggerated 'pessimism of doubt' and 'of the unfree will', in conjunction with a general pessimism of sensibility and a 'penetrating sense of Nothingness', are what can drive a person to bedlam, then Klingemann's mad narrator must surely represent the ultimate embodiment of this deranged genus of man. It is precisely these characteristics that have steered him to the madhouse, as we shall see momentarily; Gerald Gillespie has thus fittingly concluded with Shakespeare's despairing Macbeth that 'it would be no exaggeration to define the art of *The Nightwatches* as an attempt to portray life as "a tale told by an idiot, full of sound and fury, signifying nothing"'.[81]

Klingemann's first-person narrator, aptly called 'Kreuzgang' (that is 'cloister', but literally 'crossway' because his fortune-telling gipsy mother cast her child out in a casket at a crossroads), describes how he began his career as a poet who was so unsuccessful in his profession that his writings over time turned so cynical and irreverent of all authority, worldly and religious, that he, before long, was faced with 'more than fifty damage suits' ('mehr denn funfzig [sic] Injurienprozesse'),[82] upon which the town's officials saw no other alternative than to consign him to a madhouse. After his release he took the job of the town's night watchman, the only occupation that seemed still open to him; and it is the tale of this night watchman's pranks and observations, issued with scandalous irreverence, that we are witness to in Klingemann's outrageously cynical narrative. In one of its most blasphemous chapters we even encounter a 'Monolog of the Insane World Creator' himself, who, revealingly, is nothing but an idiot confined to a madhouse. The 'Ninth Night Watch' presents this lunatic's God-like musings on the state of Creation and humankind; in one key passage this 'Insane World Creator' muses:

> Then it [mankind] worshipped the sun, which I had ignited for it as illumination and which, compared with my study lamp, has the relation of a spark to the flame. Finally — and this was the worst — the speck fancied itself to be god

---

80 'Aus dem Nachlaß der Achtzigerjahre', in *Werke*, vol. 4, p. 253.
81 *The Night Watches of Bonaventura*, ed. Gillespie, p. 4.
82 *The Night Watches of Bonaventura*, ed. Gillespie, p. 119; August Klingemann, *Nachtwachen von Bonaventura*, ed. by Jost Schillemeit (Göttingen: Wallstein, 2012), p. 61.

and constructed systems in which it admired itself. What am I supposed to do with it now? — Allow it to hop about up here in eternity with its buffooneries? — Even in my case that won't do... [...] I also feel bad about utterly destroying it; for the mote does often dream so very pleasantly of immortality and thinks, just because it dreams such a thing, it must come true. — Where shall I begin? Truly, even my understanding comes to a stop here! Do I let the creature die and die again and each time erase the little spark of memory of itself so that it resurrect anew and wander about? That too, in the long run, will bore me, for the farce, repeated over and over again, must grow tiring! — Best above all is to delay the decision until it occurs to me to set a firm date for the Last Judgment, and come up with a clever idea.

[Dann betete [die arme Kreatur] die Sonne an, die ich ihr zur Erleuchtung anzündete und die, mit meiner Studierlampe verglichen, sich wie das Fünkchen zur Flamme verhält. Zuletzt — und das war das ärgste — dünkte sich das Stäubchen selbst Gott und bauete Systeme auf, worin es sich bewunderte. Was soll ich nur mit ihr anfangen? — Hier oben sie in der Ewigkeit mit ihren Possen herumhüpfen lassen? — Das geht bei mir selbst nicht an; denn da sie sich dort unten schon mehr als zuviel langweilt und sich oft vergeblich bemüht in der kurzen Sekunde ihrer Existenz die Zeit sich zu vertreiben, wie müßte sie sich bei mir in der Ewigkeit, vor der ich oft selbst erschrecke, langweilen! Sie ganz und gar zu vernichten thut mir auch leid; denn der Staub träumt doch oft gar so angenehm von der Unsterblichkeit, und meint, eben weil er so etwas träume, müsse es ihm werden. — [...] Am besten ich warte überhaupt mit der Entscheidung bis es mir einfällt einen jüngsten Tag festzusetzen und mir ein klügerer Gedanke beikommt. --][83]

The novel's narrative is far too dominated by the rambling nature of the night watchman's reflections and digressions, and far too intricate and meandering, to sensibly bear summarizing beyond what I have already said. Some earlier critics had taken its (seemingly) disorganized form to indicate its author's literary and stylistic incompetence; but critics today are more inclined to interpret its arabesque and anarchic form as a consciously and ironically enacted sleight of hand. As Brinkmann notes, 'everything in the *Nightwatches* is subjected to ironic distortion, not least romanticism, but also the narrator himself' ('Der Ironie verfällt in den *Nachtwachen* alles, nicht zuletzt die Romantik und schließlich der Erzähler selbst').[84] What is remarkable, either way, is how comprehensively this text's web of references and allusions relates to the range of issues that concern us here, the Last Judgment, the death of God, a belief or non-belief in the immortality of the soul and an afterlife, free will, solitude, the fear of Nothingness and imagining oneself a Last Man. Appropriately, the opening 'First Night Watch' sets the scene with the narrator Kreuzgang reflecting in the middle of the night how, calling out the hours on the town's streets, he would sometimes feel 'like a lone survivor after a universal plague or deluge', stressing 'the last comparison made me shudder' ('oder wie ein einzig Übriggebliebener nach einer allgemeinen Pest oder Sündfluth. Der

---

[83] *The Night Watches of Bonaventura*, ed. Gillespie, p. 151 (*Nachtwachen von Bonaventura*, ed. Schillemeit, p. 78).

[84] 'Nachtwachen von Bonaventura', p. 138.

letzte Vergleich machte mich schaudern').[85] Observing a sleepless poet high up in one of the delapidated attics he passes, he then ruminates how his calling out the hours must disturb this citizen's (and countless others') 'dreams of immortality which you dream up there' ('Träume von Unsterblichkeit, die du da oben in der Luft träumst'); his calling — in the double sense — is to remind people of 'time and transitoriness'. Passing a window, he next catches sight of a dying man, an unnamed 'excommunicated' freethinker (someone like Heydenreich perhaps, who had died in 1801), who, 'like Voltaire', 'is holding firm in his last hour', looking 'palely and calmly into empty nothingness, into which he intends to penetrate after an hour, in order to sleep forever the dreamless sleep' ('Der Mann war ein Freigeist von jeher, und er hält sich stark in seiner letzten Stunde, wie Voltaire. [...] er schaut blaß und ruhig in das leere Nichts, wohin er nach einer Stunde einzugehen gedenkt, um den traumlosen Schlaf auf immer zu schlafen'). The priest, meanwhile, who has come 'with raised crucifix' to reclaim this errant soul on his deathbed is frustrated by the freethinker's unexpected resolve and is forced to leave empty-handed:

> Firm and resolute, the sick man rejected the higher hope and thereby brought about a great moment. The priest thundered angrily into his soul and, like a desperate man, was now painting with tongues of fire and conjuring up all Tartarus into the final hour of the dying. The latter only smiled and shook his head. I was in this moment certain of his endurance; for only the finite being cannot think the thought of annihilation, while the immortal spirit does not tremble before it, who — a free being — can freely offer himself to it.
>
> [Der Kranke wieß die höhere Hoffnung fest und entschieden zurück, und führte dadurch einen großen Moment herbei. Der Pfaff donnerte ihm zornig in die Seele und mahlte [sic] jetzt mit Flammenzügen wie ein Verzweifelnder, und bannte den ganzen Tartarus herauf in die letzte Stunde des Sterbenden. Dieser lächelte nur und schüttelte den Kopf. Ich war in diesem Augenblicke einer Fortdauer gewiß: denn nur das endliche Wesen kann den Gedanken der Vernichtung nicht denken, während der unsterbliche Geist nicht vor ihr zittert, der sich, ein freies Wesen, ihr frei opfern kann.]

Powerless to rescue this obstinate heretic, the priest in his anger is consumed by a 'wild madness' ('wilder Wahnsinn') and forthwith flees the scene with foul curses on his lips, as if morphing into the devil himself. All this happens within just the first four pages!

Unsurprisingly, people were keen to know the identity of the author who had the audacity as well as the intellectual sagacity to verbalize such an acute dismemberment of contemporary mores, philosophy, and religion, not to mention its well-informed and barbed critique of Romantic idealism, specifically Fichte's system of *Wissenschaftslehre*. Everyone recognized that 'Bonaventura' had to be one of the period's cognoscenti, an insider to the world of (Romantic) literature and philosophy. The names of some of the most illustrious Romantic writers and philosophers were bandied about as possible offenders; in due course whole books came to be devoted to the subject. Was it Clemens Brentano, or E. T. A. Hoffmann,

---

85 *The Night Watches of Bonaventura*, ed. Gillespie, p. 29 (*Nachtwachen von Bonaventura*, ed. Schillemeit, p. 9); the subsequent quotes pp. 33–34, 97–99 and 101–03 (pp. 10–11, 48–49 and 51–52).

or one of the leading female writers, Caroline Schlegel-Schelling perhaps? Most contemporaries' and later critics' best guess was initially Schelling, the Romantic philosopher; by the 1820s many encyclopedias had even begun recording Schelling as the author based on the fact that he had used the same pseudonym, Bonaventura, to publish some poems in Schlegel's and Tieck's *Musenalmanach* poetry anthology in 1802. Accordingly, Jean Paul, one of the text's early readers, wrote to his friend Thierot on 14 January 1805: 'Do read the Night Watches of Bonaventura, that is Schelling. It is a superb imitation of my Giannozzo [i.e., 'Des Luftschiffers Giannozzo Seebuch', part of Jean Paul's 1801 novel *Titan*], but with rather too many reminiscences and taking too much liberty'.[86] All speculation notwithstanding, for one and a half centuries the identity of the author remained a mystery. Until two German scholars, Jost Schillemeit and Horst Fleig, and a Dutch scholar, Ruth Haag, uncovered new evidence that established, perhaps not conclusively once and for all, but certainly credibly, that the mysterious *anonymus* was August Klingemann (1777–1831), a Romantic novelist and playwright himself who had studied in Jena under Fichte, Schelling and August Wilhelm Schlegel.[87] At the time that he wrote *The Nightwatches*, Klingemann was an editor for the newspaper *Zeitung für die elegante Welt*, the very journal in which an excerpt from *The Nightwatches* was prepublished in July 1804 under the pseudonym Bonaventura.[88] After 1818 Klingemann became better known as director of the 'National Theatre' in Brunswick, in which capacity he was the first to stage Goethe's *Faust Part One*.

It is the Last Judgment, death and immortality, madness, and the notion of nothingness in particular to which Klingemann returns over and again in the *Nightwatches*, and to which he assigns a key role in ridiculing contemporary (im)morality and religious credulity. Among the most hilarious passages are two particularly illuminating scenes. First there is the incident in the sixth night watch in which Kreuzgang decides to take fate into his own hands by playing a crude and cruel joke on his fellow citizens: instead of proclaiming the midnight hour in the last hour of the century, he decides to proclaim the onset of the Last Judgment. Predictably, dismay and chaos ensue among the citizenry; we read:

> it occurred to me in the final hour of the century to portend the Last Judgment and to cry out eternity instead of time, over which many ecclesiastical and worldly gentlemen leapt in fright from their feathers and into perplexity, since

---

[86] Jean Paul, *Sämtliche Werke: Historisch-kritische Ausgabe*, ed. by Eduard Berend (Berlin: Akademie-Verlag, 1961), Abteilung III, vol. 5, p. 20.

[87] Despite Schillemeit's, Fleig's and Haag's efforts, speculation about the authorship of *Die Nachtwachen* has not come to a rest. Linde Katritzky for instance, in *A Guide to Bonaventura's 'Nightwatches'* (New York, Boston: Peter Lang, 1999), claims that only Lichtenberg can have been the author; see also her article 'Decoding Anonymous Texts: the Case of the *Nightwatches* of Bonaventura', *Monatshefte*, 95 (Fall 2003), 442–57. For more on this fascinating topic, and other possible authors, see Gerald Gillespie's comprehensive new 'Afterword' to the recent second edition of his translation of *The Nightwatches of Bonaventura* (Chicago and London: University of Chicago Press, 2014), pp. 127–45.

[88] This was part of Jost Schillemeit's circumstantial evidence that led him to propose Klingemann as author of the book; see his *Bonaventura. Der Verfasser der 'Nachtwachen'* (Munich: C. H. Beck, 1973), p. 25.

they were not prepared for anything so unexpected. The scene unfolded drolly enough at this false Last Judgment alarm, during which I played the sole calm onlooker, whereas all others had to serve me as passionate actors. Oh, you should have seen what a pushing and shoving arose among these poor human beings and how the nobility ran in fearful confusion and yet still sought to maintain their proper ranks before their Lord God. [...] For the first time, the proudest man in the state, with his crown in his hand, stood humble and almost crawling and exchanged polite hesitation over precedence with a tattered fellow, because the dawn of a general equality seemed possible to him.

[...indem es mir in der letzten Stunde des Säkulums einfiel mit dem jüngsten Tage vorzuspuken und statt der Zeit die Ewigkeit auszurufen, worüber viele geistliche und weltliche Herren erschrocken aus ihren Federn fuhren und ganz in Verlegenheit kamen, weil sie so unerwartet nicht darauf vorbereitet waren. Drollig genug machte sich die Szene bei diesem falschen jüngsten Tages Lerm, wobei ich den einzigen ruhigen Zuschauer abgab, indeß alle Anderen mir als leidenschaftliche Akteure dienen mußten. — O man hätte sehen sollen was das für ein Getreibe und Gedränge wurde unter den armen Menschenkindern und wie der Adel ängstlich durch einanderlief, und sich doch noch zu rangiren suchte vor seinem Herrgott; [...] Der stolzeste Mann im Staate stand zum erstenmale demüthig und fast kriechend mit der Krone in der Hand und komplimentierte mit einem zerlumpten Kerl um den Vorrang, weil ihm eine hereinbrechende allgemeine Gleichheit möglich schien.]

In an intriguing extension of the idea, Klingemann alias Kreuzgang, the enlightened fool, uses the opportunity to add an admonitory homily to his fellow citizens, singling out the clergy for particular reproof: 'Beloved fellow citizens!', he proclaims,

What indeed is of greater moment for us on the day of world judgment than a backward glance at the planet reeling under us which is about to collapse with its paradises and dungeons, with its crazy houses and scholars' republics; do let us for this reason in this final hour, when we are about to close off world history, review briefly and summarily what we have engaged in and carried out here since this earthly sphere rose forth from the chaos. [...] Tell me, with what kind of a face do you want to appear before our Lord God, you my brothers, princes, usurers, warriors, murderers, capitalists, thieves, state officials, jurists, theologians, philosophers, fools, and of whatever office or trade you may be; for today no one has a right to be missing from this general national convention, although I notice that several of you would like to get on your feet in order to take to your heels. [...] You theologians, who would so much like to be numbered among the divine household, yet while ogling and fawning upon the Almighty have instituted a miserable den of assassins here below and, instead of uniting men, have churned them apart in sects and, as malicious friends of the house, forever torn asunder the beautiful general estate of brotherhood and family.

[Theuerste Mitbürger! [...] Was liegt uns wohl am Weltgerichtstage näher als ein Rückblick auf den unter uns wankenden Planeten, der nun mit seinen Paradiesen und Kerkern mit seinen Narrenhäusern und Gelehrten Republiken zusammen stürzen soll; laßt uns deshalb in dieser letzten Stunde, da wir die Weltgeschichte abschließen wollen, nur kurz und summarisch überschauen, was wir, seit dieser

Erdball aus dem Chaos hervorgestiegen, auf ihm getrieben und ausgeführt haben. [...] Sagt mir, mit was für einer Mine wollt ihr bei unserm Herrgott erscheinen, ihr meine Brüder, Fürsten, Zinswucherer, Krieger, Mörder, Kapitalisten, Diebe, Staatsbeamten, Juristen, Theologen, Philosophen, Narren und welches Amtes und Gewerbes ihr sein mögt; denn es darf heute keiner in dieser allgemeinen Nationalversammlung ausbleiben, ob ich gleich merke, daß mehrere von euch sich gern auf die Beine machen möchten um Reisaus zu nehmen. [...] Ihr Theologen, die ihr so gern zur göttlichen Hofhaltung gezählt werden möchtet, und indem ihr mit dem Allerhöchsten liebäugelt und fuchsschwänzt, hier unten eine leidliche Mördergrube veranstaltet und den Menschen statt sie zu vereinigen in Sekten auseinander schleudert.]

Throughout all of this, Klingemann surely expects his contemporary reader to recognize the in-built allusions to Jean Paul's 'Clavis Fichtiana seu Leibgeberiana' and 'The Strange Society of New Year's Eve'; for our part, we can appreciate the differential between Klingemann's satire and Sonnenberg's *Donatoa* and Grainville's *Le Dernier Homme*, all published in the same year 1805 without knowledge of one another. It is surely a sign of the time, and of the decline of the Apocalypse and the ascent of atheism, that what the two Catholic writers took so seriously could become the subject of such burlesque ridicule.

The second scene is an excursus in the eighth night watch; it comprises an excerpt from the manuscript of a young poet who has just committed suicide. Entitled 'The Clown's Prologue to the Tragedy: Man' ('Prolog des Hanswurstes zu der Tragödie: der Mensch'), it takes up the theme of Nothingness that was introduced in the first night watch: 'Everything is Nothing and vomits itself up and gulps itself greedily down', the disillusioned and now deceased poet proposes,

and even this self-devouring is an insidious sham, as if there were something whereas, if the choking were once to cease, precisely the Nothing would quite plainly make its appearance and all would be terror-struck before it; by this cessation, fools understand 'eternity'; but it is the real Nothing and absolute death, since life on the contrary, only arises through a continual dying. If one were ready to take the like consideration seriously, it could easily lead to the madhouse; but I take it merely as Clown and thereby conduct the prologue up to the tragedy, in which the poet, of course, has taken it on a higher plane and even invented a God and an immortality in it, in order to make his personages more significant.

[Es ist Alles Nichts und würgt sich selbst auf und schlingt sich gierig hinunter, und eben dieses Selbstverschlingen ist die tückische Spiegelfechterei als gäbe es Etwas, da doch wenn das Würgen einmal inne halten wollte eben das Nichts recht deutlich zur Erscheinung käme, daß sie davor erschrecken müßten; Thoren verstehen unter diesem Innehalten die Ewigkeit, es ist aber das eigentliche Nichts und der absolute Tod, da das Leben im Gegentheile nur durch ein fortlaufendes Sterben entsteht. Wollte man dergleichen ernsthaft nehmen, so mögte es leicht zum Tollhause führen, ich aber nehme es blos als Hanswurst, und führe dadurch den Prolog bis zur Tragödie hin, in der es der Dichter freilich höher genommen und sogar einen Gott und eine Unsterblichkeit in sie hineinerfunden hat, um seinen Menschen bedeutender zu machen.][89]

---

89 *The Night Watches of Bonaventura*, ed. Gillespie, p. 141 (*Nachtwachen von Bonaventura*, ed.

If God and immortality appear here blasphemously as mere inventions to help us steer clear of the insane asylum, the same impious and nihilistic undertow resurfaces in the fourteenth night watch when the narrator, still interned in the madhouse, chances upon an actress who — as befits her character role — was driven insane by playing Ophelia. Their ill-starred relationship (she ends up committing suicide, again as befits her role) provides an opportunity for Kreuzgang to insert a fictitious correspondence between himself, naturally playing the role of Hamlet, and his beloved Ophelia; the following excerpt from one of these letters requires no further comment:

> To be or not to be! How simple I was at that time when I raised this question with my finger on my nose [...]. I should first have asked being itself about being; then afterwards something sensible could be ascertained about non-being too. At that time I was still carrying the theory of immortality from the university and proved it through every category. Yes, I truly feared death on account of immortality — and by heaven, rightly, if after this boring *comédie larmoyante* yet another was to follow.
>
> [Sein oder Nichtsein! Wie einfältig war ich damals, als ich mit dem Finger an der Nase diese Frage aufwarf [...]. Ich hätte das Sein erst um das Sein selbst befragen sollen, dann ließe sich nachher auch über das Nichtsein etwas Gescheutes ausmitteln. Ich brachte damals noch die Unsterblichkeitstheorie von der hohen Schule mit, und führte sie durch alle Kategorien. Ja, ich fürchtete wahrlich den Tod der Unsterblichkeit halber — und beim Himmel mit Recht, wenn hinter dieser langweiligen comedie larmoyante noch eine zweite folgen sollte.]

This delightful persiflage of Hamlet's famous monologue is, however, only the prelude to the grand finale in the sixteenth and last night watch, in which Kreuzgang, once more taking on the guise of Hamlet, revisits the graveyard where his alchemist father is buried. The stage is set by a dream in which he imagines a poet visiting the graveyard in order to write a 'Poem to Immortality'. The poem's words conjure up a vision of the Last Judgment, all with thunder and trumpet blasts and graves opening — think of the frontispiece to Edward Young's *A Poem on the Last Day* reproduced in Chapter One (Figure 1.2); but, alas, these dead will not arise. Having lost all faith in eternity, they are no longer willing to leave the peace and tranquility of their earthly entombments: 'They below all merely shook indignantly and turned from him onto their sides as so to sleep more tranquilly and show him the naked back of their heads' ('sie schüttelten nur alle unmuthig unten und wandten sich auf die andere Seite von ihm weg, um ruhiger schlafen und ihm die nackten Hinterköpfe zu zeigen'). 'What, is there then no God!' ('Wie, ist denn kein Gott!'), the bewildered poet exclaims, as if to impersonate Jean Paul's Christ atop the universe. 'And the echo gave him back the word "God" loudly and perceptibly' ('und das Echo gab ihm das Wort "Gott!" laut und vernehmlich zurück'), but nothing more. God remains just an echo. 'He stood there now quite naïve and chewed on his pen' ('Jetzt stand er ganz einfältig da und käuete an der Feder'), we are informed, and since nothing else happens, and since eternity itself

Schillemeit, pp. 72–73); the subsequent passages pp. 211 and 233 (pp. 115 and 128).

and with it all belief in God seem to have expired in the graveyard ('Immortality is recalcitrant', 'Die Unsterblichkeit ist widerspänstig', we are told facetiously), he resolves to pack up writing insipid poems and to write plays instead — if only because the honoraria are so much better.

Emulating Hamlet holding Yorick's skull, Kreuzgang later this night embarks on a truly Hamletesque monologue of his own about art and beauty, mortality and religious faith, and the philosophy of idealism — all this addressed to the lone worm he finds inhabiting his father's skull: 'For you nothing any longer is sacred, neither beauty nor ugliness, neither virtue nor vice', he remonstrates,

> you wind about everything, you Laokoon's serpent, and document your thorough sublimity on the whole human race. Where now is the eye which smiled so enchantingly? [...] What now is this palace which can enclose a whole world and a heaven; [...] this microcosm in which all that is great and splendid and everything terrible and fearsome reside together in embryo, which brought forth temples and gods, inquisitions and devils; this tail-piece of the creation — the human head! — shelter for a worm! — Oh, what is the world if that which it thought is nothing, and everything in it only transitory fantasy!
>
> [Dir ist nichts mehr heilig, weder Schönheit noch Häßlichkeit, weder Tugend noch Laster; alles umwindest du Laokoons Schlange, und beurkundest deine intensive Erhabenheit an dem ganzen Menschengeschlechte. Wo ist jetzt das Auge das so bezaubernd lächelte [...]. Was ist nun dieser Pallast, der eine ganze Welt und einen Himmel in sich schließt; [...] dieser Mikrokosmus, in dem alles was groß und herrlich, und alles Schreckliche und Furchtbare im Keime nebeneinander liegt, der Tempel gebar und Götter, Inquisitionen und Teufel; dieses Schwanzstück der Schöpfung — das Menschenhaupt! —— die Behausung eines Wurmes. — O was ist die Welt, wenn dasjenige was sie dachte nichts ist und alles darin nur vorüberfliegende Phantasie!]⁹⁰

All is Nothing, Kreuzgang concludes, a pronouncement that ushers in the work's concluding lines in which the words that the narrator addresses to his father's skeleton could as easily be directed at God the Father in atheism's 'demolished pantheon' ('zertrümmerten Pantheon'), as the narrator of *Nightwatches* terms it:

> 'Woe! What is this — are you too but a mask and deceive me? — I no longer see you, father, — where are you? At my touch all crumbles into ashes, and there is only a handful of dust lying yet on the ground, and a few satisfied worms creep secretly away [...]. I strew this handful of paternal dust into the air and it remains — Nothing!' On the grave beyond, the visionary is still standing and embracing Nothing! And the echo in the charnel-house cries for the last time *NOTHING!*
>
> ['Wehe! Was ist das — bist auch du nur eine Maske und betrügst mich? — Ich sehe dich nicht mehr Vater — wo bist du? — Bei der Berührung zerfällt alles in Asche, und nur auf dem Boden liegt noch eine Handvoll Staub, und ein paar genährte Würmer schleichen sich heimlich weg [...] Ich streiche diese Handvoll väterlichen Staub in die Luft und es bleibt — Nichts!' 'Drüben auf dem Grabe steht noch der Geisterseher und umarmt Nichts!' 'Und der Wiederhall im Gebeinhause ruft zum letztenmale — *Nichts!*' —]

90 Ibid., p. 243 (p. 133); the subsequent passages pp. 245, 247 and 135 (pp. 135, 136 and 69).

The absent God of deism has been converted into atheism's Nothingness, God is a mere echo of a racket that once was. All boils down to the opposition, proclaimed by the dead poet in his letter of farewell in the eighth night watch, 'God, or Nothing!' ('Gott, oder Nichts!').

Considering the thoroughly mocking tenor of Klingemann's narrative and the tongue-in-cheek way the various narrative voices engage with the notions of nothingness, death and immortality, I have to agree with the literary scholar Dorothee Sölle-Nipperdey, however, that the work's nihilism should not be considered 'existential', but rather 'programmatic' ('programmatisch, nicht existentiell').[91] The form, structure and style of the *Nightwatches* make it impossible to discern whether Klingemann's nihilism, as ostentatiously as it may seem articulated by the author's mouthpieces, is based on any genuine sense of existential anguish and despondency. Any sense of *angoisse de l'agonie* and *horror vacui* seems overridden by the 'abysmal laughter that highlights the gulf that has come to exist between man and his world' ('abgründiges Lachen [...], das den Riß aufhellt, der zwischen dem Menschen und seiner Umwelt entstanden ist'), as Sölle-Nipperdey put it. Contrary to Christ in 'Speech of the dead Christ', Klingemann's oddball spokesmen all seem to poke fun at the very gravity and seriousness that Jean Paul's text had accorded the vision of death and the anguish associated with man's entry into a state of nothingness. Here in the *Nightwatches* by contrast, a tale told by idiots, carnivalesque laughter rules supreme.

From 'Chimerism' to 'Nihilism', from Mad Men to Last Men

As we saw in Chapter Two as well as earlier in this chapter, opponents of atheism liked to put forward the view that once the unbeliever had peeled back all the layers of the onion of belief in God he would be left with a tearful Nothing, *nihil*. And this in turn would invariably lead not just to a person succumbing to depravity and immorality, but also to a general malady of the soul, as Novalis put it;[92] in the most extreme case atheism could lead to outright madness.

In his novella *Lenz* Büchner used the historical figure of the poet Lenz as precisely one such extreme case, as an example of someone being driven insane as a result of religious irresolution and the emptiness and concomitant *Angst* that can befall people in the face of 'Nothing'; Lenz felt 'no hope', we recall, 'just a terrible emptiness and the frantic, agonizing urge to fill it. He had *nothing*'. But an atheist did not need to be actually insane for people to ascribe madness to him; Heine in *On Germany since Luther* for instance attributes madness to Fichte alone for his attempt to declare God a mere chimera:

91 Dorothee Sölle-Nipperdey, *Untersuchungen zur Struktur der 'Nachtwachen von Bonaventura'* (Göttingen: Vandenhoeck & Ruprecht, 1959), p. 77, the subsequent quote p. 95.

92 Novalis, *Schriften. Die Werke Friedrich von Hardenbergs*, ed. by Paul Kluckhohn and Richard Samuel (Stuttgart: Kohlhammer, 1960), vol. 2, p. 19: 'Ein Atheist ist in den Augen der meisten ein Gegenstand des Abscheus, des Hasses, der Intoleranz; denn kaum ist einer für einen Atheisten bekannt, so meidet gewiß jeder seinen Umgang, sucht alles auf was diesen Seelenkranken noch mehr niederdrücken noch mehr verwirren kann ...' ('An atheist is in the eyes of most an object of disgust, hate, and intolerance; for, as soon as someone is known to be an atheist, people will avoid all association with him, and will seek out things to further press down on this sick soul...').

We who believe in a real God who reveals himself to our senses in infinite extension, and to our souls in infinite thoughts — we who honour and adore a visible God in Nature, and perceive His invisible voice in our own spirit — we are painfully repulsed by the coarse words with which Fichte declares, even ironically, that God is a mere cobweb of the brain. It is indeed doubtful whether Fichte is inspired by irony or mere madness when he disengages our dear God so absolutely from all material attributes, that he even denies his existence

[Wir, die wir an einen wirklichen Gott glauben, der unseren Sinnen in der unendlichen Ausdehnung, und unserem Geiste in dem unendlichen Gedanken sich offenbart, wir, die wir einen sichtbaren Gott verehren in der Natur und seine unsichtbare Stimme in unserer eigenen Seele vernehmen: wir werden widerwärtig berührt von den grellen Worten, womit Fichte unseren Gott für ein bloßes Hirngespinst erklärt und sogar ironisirt. Es ist zweifelhaft, in der That, ob es Ironie oder bloßer Wahnsinn ist, wenn Fichte den lieben Gott von allem sinnlichen Zusatze so rein befreyt, daß er ihm sogar die Existenz abspricht.]

But what atheists, and like-minded religious sceptics, from Heydenreich, Klingemann, and Büchner to Feuerbach, Marx and Nietzsche — in rough chronological order — were in fact arguing was that there was nothing inherently immoral, depraved, depressed or mad about an atheist's state of mind, nor that atheism must by necessity lead to a maddening existential void, but rather that atheism could as easily result in a positively sober and sane outlook on life and death and the human condition.

Likewise nihilism; no less than atheism it is defined as much by its detractors as it is by its proponents. In philosophical and theological encyclopedias, the German philosopher Friedrich Heinrich Jacobi (1743–1819) is generally credited with having introduced the term *Nihilismus* (nihilism) into philosophical discourse in 1799 in an 'open letter' to his philosopher colleague Fichte entitled *Jacobi an Fichte*. Jacobi was widely recognized among his contemporaries as a critic and opponent of unbelief and freethinking. In his missive Jacobi argues — in substance correctly — that whereas Kant metaphysically relegates God to the realm of the unknowable, God at least retains a nominal existence in moral law; Fichte by contrast denies God any existence outside of the transcendental ego, beyond which there is nothing or, in Latin, *nihil* — hence Jacobi's coinage of the term nihilism. The key passage in Jacobi's treatise reads:

> I therefore do not see why I, as a matter of taste, should not be allowed to prefer my philosophy of non-knowledge to the philosophical *knowledge of the nothing*, at least *in fugam vacui*. I have nothing confronting me, after all, except nothingness; and even *chimeras* are a good match for that. Truly, my dear Fichte, I would not be vexed if you, or anyone else, were to call *Chimerism* the view I oppose to the Idealism that I chide for *Nihilism*. — I have paraded my *not-knowing* in all my writings.

[... so sehe ich nicht ein, warum ich nicht, wäre es auch nur *in fugam vacui*, meine Philosophie des Nicht-Wißens, dem Philosophischen *Wißen des Nichts*, sollte aus Geschmack vorziehen dürfen. Ich habe ja nichts wider mich als das Nichts; und mit ihm können auch *Chimären* sich wohl noch meßen. Wahrlich, mein lieber Fichte, es soll mich nicht verdrießen, wenn Sie, oder wer es sey,

Chimärismus nennen wollen, was ich dem Idealismus, den ich *Nihilismus* schelte, entgegensetze — Mein *Nicht*-Wißen habe ich in allen meinen Schriften zur Schau getragen.]⁹³ (Jacobi's emphases)

Here as throughout his tract, Jacobi is arguing that it is one thing not to know whether God exists, which he whimsically calls his 'Chimerism' or 'Philosophy of Not-Knowing' — and which is, clearly, a concession to Kant. It is another matter altogether to submit to a 'Philosophy of Knowing [that there is only] Nothing' beyond the 'Absolute I' which, according to Jacobi, is the stance promoted by Fichte in his *Wissenschaftslehre*. In aggrandizing the transcendental 'I', and in refusing to appeal to any entity or measure outside of — not to mention superior to — human thought, the Fichtean brand of idealism seeks to negate everything beyond it. As Michael Allan Gillespie observes in *Nihilism before Nietzsche*: 'For Jacobi, idealism recognized no truth beyond consciousness and, therefore, lacked any objective standard against which to measure itself. It thus dissolved everything into subjectivity'.⁹⁴ Not God, but the projected 'Not-I', is the only horizon within which the 'I' can define itself as existence.

Jacobi was of course not alone in reading Fichte's system as atheistic: Friedrich Hegel had started teaching philosophy at Jena in 1801, just two years after Fichte had been forced to vacate his position there; in 1802 he published an early treatise on Kant, Jacobi and Fichte entitled *Believing and Knowing or the Philosophy of Reflection about Subjectivity* (*Glauben und Wissen oder die Reflexionsphilosophie der Subjektivität*) in which he argued that Fichte's philosophy had changed 'the feeling' on which religion was now based, and this was that 'Gott himself is dead' ('das Gefühl [...], worauf die Religion der neuen Zeit beruht, — das Gefühl: Gott selbst ist todt').⁹⁵ Some three decades later, in 1834, we find Heine similarly taking Fichte to task when he observes: 'The Idealism of Fichte is one of the most colossal errors which the mind of man ever hatched out. It is more godless and damnable than the coarsest materialism' ('Der Fichtesche Idealismus gehört zu den kolossalen Irrtümern, die jemals der menschliche Geist ausgeheckt. Er ist gottloser und verdammlicher als der plumpste Materialismus').⁹⁶

As a staunch defender of religion and of the belief in God, the alternative for Jacobi was thus a stark but non-negotiable one: either 'Nothingness or a God' ('das Nichts oder einen Gott'). He reasons:

> If [someone] chooses nothingness, he makes himself unto a God [...]. I repeat: God is, and is *outside me, a living, self-subsisting being*, or I am God. There is no third. Were I not to find God *outside* me, *before* me, and *above* me, so that I have to posit Him, the One Being on His Own, then I am myself this so called being, in virtue of my selfhood. [...] But as I do away with the delusion by coming

---

93 'Jacobi to Fichte', in *The Main Philosophical Writings and the Novel 'Allwill'*, trans. by George di Giovanni (Montreal and Kingston: McGill-Queen's University Press, 1994), pp. 497–536 (p. 519); *Jacobi an Fichte* (Hamburg: Perthes, 1799), p. 39.

94 *Nihilism before Nietzsche* (Chicago and London: University of Chicago Press, 1995), p. xvii.

95 *Glauben und Wissen oder die Reflexionsphilosophie der Subjektivität, in der Vollständigkeit ihrer Formen, als Kantische, Jacobische und Fichtesche Philosophie*, cited here from *Georg Wilhelm Friedrich Hegel's Werke* (Berlin: Duncker und Humblot, 1832), vol. I, pp. 3–157 (p. 157).

96 'Germany', pp. 179–80 ('*Zur Geschichte der Religion*', p. 622).

to an *understanding* of it, [...] I must also extirpate everything connected with it. I must extirpate from my soul the religion of love, of example; mock every impulse and outpouring from a *higher being*; ban *all* devotion, *all* adoration, from my heart.

[Das Nichts erwählend macht er sich zu Gott; [...]. Ich wiederhole: Gott ist, und ist *außer mir*, ein *lebendiges, für sich bestehendes Wesen*, oder Ich bin Gott. Es giebt kein drittes. Finde ich Gott nicht — so, daß ich ihn setzen muß: Ein Selbstseyn — *außer* mir, *vor* mir, *über* mir; so bin ich selbst, Kraft meiner Ichheit, *ganz und gar* was so genannt wird [...]. Indem ich ihn aber [...] vernichte, [...] muß ich auch alles was mit ihm zusammenhängt vertilgen; ich muß vertilgen aus meiner Seele die Religion der Liebe, des Beyspiels; muß verspotten jede Anregung und Eingebung eines Höheren; verbannen aus meinem Herzen jede Andacht, jede Anbetung.][97] (Jacobi's emphases)

Jacobi can hardly be called a heavyweight of German philosophy. But this friend of Jean Paul's and Goethe's (albeit in an at times uneasy relationship) did instigate the pantheism controversy in 1785 in which he charged Spinoza and by association Lessing with being atheists, as he also did Fichte in *Jacobi an Fichte* during the so-called *Atheismusstreit* (Atheism Row) of 1798–1799 surrounding Fichte's alleged atheism (and which led to Fichte's discharge from his professorship). But without Jacobi's coinage of the term *Nihilismus* what is generally known as Romantic nihilism would obviously have taken a very different trajectory, or may not have come into existence at all in this particular manifestation. Jean Paul's satirical 'Clavis Fichtiana' for instance is a direct offshoot of Jacobi's critique of Fichte (Jean Paul even sent Jacobi the manuscript of his Fichte-text for scrutiny before it was published), as are — perhaps more indirectly — Klingemann's *Nightwatches*. No surprise then to find Kreuzgang reporting mockingly from the madhouse:

The storm raged wildly about the madhouse. [...] It was for me as if I were standing close to the Nothing and cried into it [...]. Then I saw myself with me alone in the Nothing, only the late earth was still flickering far out in the distance, as an extinguishing spark — but it was only a thought of mine which was just ending. A single tone quavered gravely and earnestly through the void — it was chiming out, and eternity now set in. I had now ceased thinking everything else, and was thinking only myself! No object was to be found round about but the great dreadful I which drew only on itself...

[Es stürmte wild um das Tollhaus her [...]. Es war mir, als stände ich dicht am Nichts und riefe hinein. [...] Es dünkte mich, als entschliefe ich. Da sah ich mich selbst mit mir allein im Nichts, nur in der weiten Ferne verglimmte noch die letzte Erde, wie ein auslöschender Funken — aber es war nur ein Gedanke von mir, der eben endete. Ein einziger Ton bebte schwer und ernst durch die Öde — es war die ausschlagende Zeit, und die Ewigkeit trat jetzt ein. Ich hatte jetzt aufgehört alles andere zu denken, und dachte nur an mich selbst! Kein Gegenstand war ringsum aufzufinden, als das große schreckliche Ich, das an sich selbst zehrte...][98]

97 'Jacobi to Fichte', pp. 524–25 (*Jacobi an Fichte*, pp. 48–50).
98 *The Night Watches of Bonaventura*, ed. Gillespie, p. 213 (translation slightly modified) (*Nachtwachen von Bonaventura*, ed. Schillemeit, p. 116).

Ironically it was thus perhaps less Fichte himself, this chief proponent of philosophical idealism, who spawned the cult of Romantic nihilism than the anti-Fichte Jacobis, Jean Pauls and Klingemanns/Kreuzgangs in the early years of the new century.[99] It is they who helped to popularize a philosophy that, judging by Klingemann's satire, clearly was as inscrutable to readers then as it still seems to non-philosophers today.

What is more important from our perspective though is that nihilism, as modish as it may have quickly become, not just reinvigorated the existing fascination with and dread of 'nothingness', it also redirected the focus of that fascination toward the notions of absolute loneliness and absolute 'lastness'. Hence the outburst 'Me so completely lonely' of the narrator of Jean Paul's 'Clavis Fichtiana seu Leibgeberiana'; hence the desperation of the 'last human' in Jean Paul's 'Strange Society of New Year's Eve' when he finds himself 'stand[ing] on a mountain under the equator looking down upon the waters which cover the vast world'; hence also Kreuzgang's shuddering admission that he felt 'like a lone survivor after a universal plague or deluge'. To put it in a nutshell: all those later avatars of 'Last Men' and 'Last Women' in European literature, not to mention later science fiction and the Hollywood film industry, may just be an unintended consequence, as well as a kind of involuntary caricature, of Fichte's godless 'Absolute I'.

Naturally, most students of philosophy will associate not just the 'Death of God' but perhaps also the birth of this 'Last Man' with Nietzsche's philosophy rather than Fichte's. From his early to his late writings and notebooks, Nietzsche's work is shot through with references to last men and last times. The earliest instance is found in his unpublished notebooks, written around the time of his first major publication, the 1872 treatise *The Birth of Tragedy*. In a short fragment tellingly entitled 'Oedipus. Discussions of the last philosopher with himself. A fragment from the history of posterity' ('Oedipus. Reden des letzten Philosophen mit sich selbst. Ein Fragment aus der Geschichte der Nachwelt') and written between summer 1872 and early 1873, Nietzsche imagines himself to be both the last man and the last philosopher; we read:

> I call myself the last philosopher, for I am the last man. No one speaks with me but myself, and my voice comes to me like that of one who is dying. With you, my beloved voice, with you, the last breath of all memory of human joy, let me spend one last hour, through you I hoodwink away my loneliness and fib myself into multiplicity and love, for my heart refuses to believe that love is dead, it cannot tolerate the terror of the most lonely loneliness and forces me to speak as if I were two.

---

99 Looking at the origin of nihilism from the perspective of the history of philosophy, Michael Allan Gillespie comes to a similar conclusion; he observes in Chapter Three of his study *Nihilism before Nietzsche*: 'We see in the critique of idealism by Jacobi and Jean Paul the beginning of our modern concept of nihilism. [...] Nihilism [...] grows out of the notion of the infinite will that Fichte discovers in the thought of Descartes and Kant. Fichte, however, radicalizes this notion [...]. This radicalization leads thinking away from the bright dawn of Enlightenment that Descartes and Kant proclaimed, into the dark night of the noumenal I and the nihilism that so alarmed Jacobi and Jean Paul. Fichtean idealism in this way is the hidden source of the nihilism that becomes increasingly explicit in the nineteenth and early twentieth century' (pp. 66–67).

[Den letzten Philosophen nenne ich mich, denn ich bin der letzte Mensch. Niemand redet mit mir als ich selbst, und meine Stimme kommt wie die eines Sterbenden zu mir. Mit dir, geliebte Stimme, mit dir, dem letzten Erinnerungshauch alles Menschenglücks, laß mich nur eine Stunde noch verkehren, durch dich täusche ich mir die Einsamkeit hinweg und lüge mich in die Vielheit und Liebe hinein, denn mein Herz sträubt sich zu glauben, daß die Liebe todt sei, es erträgt den Schauder der einsamsten Einsamkeit nicht und zwingt mich zu reden, als ob ich Zwei wäre.][100]

A second reference to the end of humankind comes four years later in 'Richard Wagner in Bayreuth', the fourth piece of *Untimely Meditations* (*Unzeitgemäße Betrachtungen*), published in 1876; here Nietzsche observes:

> And when all of humanity must one day die — and who should doubt this! — what is assigned to him as the supreme task for the future is to grow together into unity and community in such a way that he can meet his imminent demise *as one* with *a sense for the tragic*. [...] There is only one hope and one guarantee for the future of humanity: it consists in his *retention of the sense for the tragic*.
>
> [Und wenn die ganze Menschheit einmal sterben muss — wer dürfte daran zweifeln! — so ist ihr als höchste Aufgabe für alle kommenden Zeiten das Ziel gestellt, so ins Eine und Gemeinsame zusammenzuwachsen, dass sie als *ein Ganzes* ihrem bevorstehenden Untergange mit einer *tragischen Gesinnung* entgegengehe [...]. Es gibt nur *eine* Hoffnung und *eine* Gewähr für die Zukunft des Menschlichen: sie liegt darin, *daß die tragische Gesinnung nicht* absterbe.][101] (Nietzsche's emphases)

Switching the perspective to that of his *Übermensch*, the overman, Nietzsche's Zarathustra a decade later proclaims the last man to be 'the most contemptible thing'. 'Alas!', we read in 'Zarathustra's Prologue',

> [t]here cometh the time when man will no longer give birth to any star. Alas! There cometh the time of the most despicable man, who can no longer despise himself. Lo! I show you *the last man*. [...] The earth hath then become small, and on it there hoppeth the last man who maketh everything small. His species is ineradicable like that of the ground-flea; the last man liveth longest.
>
> [Wehe! Es kommt die Zeit, wo der Mensch keinen Stern mehr gebären wird. Wehe! Es kommt die Zeit des verächtlichsten Menschen, der sich selber nicht mehr verstehen kann. Seht! Ich zeige euch *den letzten Menschen*. [...] Die Erde ist dann klein geworden, und auf ihr hüpft der lezte Mensch, der alles klein macht. Sein Geschlecht ist unaustilgbar wie der Erdfloh; der letzte Mensch lebt am längsten.][102]

---

100 'Oedipus. Reden des letzten Philosophen mit sich selbst. Ein Fragment aus der Geschichte der Nachwelt', in *Kritische Studienausgabe*, ed. by Giorgio Colli and Mazzino Montinari, vol. 7: *Nachgelassene Fragmente*, new edition (Munich: DTV/de Gruyter, 1999), pp. 460–61.

101 *Untimely Meditations*, trans. by R. J. Hollingdale (Cambridge: Cambridge University Press, 1997), p. 213 (Hollingdale does not translate the first section of this passage; that part of this translation is mine); 'Richard Wagner in Bayreuth', in *Werke*, ed. Schlechta, vol. 1, pp. 367–434 (p. 386).

102 *Thus spake Zarathustra* (1883–1885), trans. by Thomas Common (New York: Random House / The Modern Library, [n.d.]), p. 11; *Also Sprach Zarathustra*, in *Werke*, ed. Schlechta, vol. 2, pp. 275–835 (p. 561).

Clearly, with the species of the last man being 'ineradicable', we must interpret Zarathustra's pronouncement more metaphorically than literally. For Nietzsche's Zarathustra the last man is the conjectural antipode to the future *Übermensch*, or overman. Finally, in his 1878 *Human, All Too Human*, Nietzsche acknowledges, perhaps with more than just a pinch of self-reproach: 'No artist has as yet been equal to the task of depicting the *last* man, *that is the most simple yet simultaneously most complete* man' ('Der Darstellung des *letzten* Menschen, *das heißt des einfachsten und zugleich vollsten*, war bis jetzt kein Künstler gewachsen').[103]

Of course, as if seeking to prove Nietzsche wrong, authors ever since Jean Paul, Grainville and Klingeman have been devising ever more imaginative ways of 'depicting the *last* man' and, in the process, plotting the demise of the human species altogether. Indeed, since the turn of the eighteenth century, European literature has become increasingly obsessed with Last Men (however, how many of them Nietzsche would have been willing to accept as 'simple' or 'complete' is anyone's guess), from Mary Shelley's inaugural novel *The Last Man*, published some fifty years before Nietzsche's comment, to Cormac McCarthy's and Thomas Glavinic's recent works *The Road* and *Die Arbeit der Nacht*, published some 130 years after it.

Auspiciously, even before Grainville's 1805 *Le Dernier Homme* and Shelley's 1826 *The Last Man* — both of which Nietzsche did not know — the nineteenth century had begun with Jean Paul's 1801 tale 'The Strange Society of New Year's Eve', which Nietzsche probably did know; that century ended no less auspiciously with the burgeoning of a completely new genre, science fiction, along with its subgenre of end-time fiction. The year 1901 alone saw the publication of a short story by George C. Wallis entitled 'The Last Days of Earth. Being the Story of the Launching of the Red Sphere' (in which the sun has gone out and the last man and woman are spirited by spaceship to a nearby star), the novel *The Purple Cloud* by Matthew Phipps Shiel (in which a deadly purple cloud has seemingly wiped out all of mankind except for one tellingly named Adam Jeffson), and A. Lincoln Green's *The End of an Epoch. Being the Personal Narrative of Adam Godwin, the Survivor* (in which a scientifically-manufactured bacillus obliterates mankind, except for a new Adam and Evelyn), not to mention H. G. Wells's slightly earlier but immensely influential *The Time Machine*, published just one year after Camille Flammarion's *La Fin du monde* in 1895.

Flammarion's and Wells's more or less contemporaneous novels are instructive cases in point. Both take us on a journey to our planet's natural end in a very distant future. In *La Fin du monde* the 'apogee of the human race' ('l'apogée de l'humanité') is reached in eight million years time, after which humanity's decadence and decline set in; the sun and the Earth partake of this decline: the sun's heat is diminished, the Earth loses much of its ocean water, all vegetation and animal life is sentenced, just as Buffon predicted more than a century earlier, to a death by freezing. By the end of Flammarion's novel we have reached a point by which most latitudes had become 'totally uninhabitable for thousands of years, in spite of every effort to live in them'. Even in the equatorial zone 'no species of plants could exist'; and

---

[103] *Menschliches, Allzumenschliches. Ein Buch für freie Geister*, in *Werke*, ed. Schlechta, vol. 1, pp. 435–1008 (p. 806 = vol. 2, no. 177), Nietzsche's emphases.

> [i]n the latitudes of Paris, Nice, Rome, Napels, Algiers and Tunis, all protective atmospheric action had ceased, and the oblique rays of the sun had proved insufficient to warm the soil which was frozen to a great depth [like a rock of ice]. [...] Elsewhere the surface of the earth was a ruin, and even here only the last vestiges of a vanished greatness were to be seen.
>
> [Malgré leurs transformations séculaires, les espèces végétales ne pouvaient plus vivre, même dans cette zone équatoriale. Quant aux autres latitudes, depuis des milliers d'annés déjà elles étaient devenues complètement inhabitables, malgré tous les efforts réalisés pour s'y maintenir. Aux latitudes où vivent aujourd'hui Paris, Nice, Rome, Naples, Alger, Tunis, l'atmosphère ayant cessé de servir de serre protectrice, l'obliquité des rayons solaires ne pouvait plus rien échauffer et la terre restait gelée à toutes les profondeurs accessibles, comme un véritable rocher de glace. [...] Partout ailleurs, à la surface de l'ancien monde terrestre, il n'y avait que des ruines, et là aussi on ne retrouvait plus que derniers vestiges des grandeurs évanouies.][104]

The world's population has diminished and its last remnants 'have lapsed back into barbarism, vegetating like the Esquimaux of the north' ('Ses derniers rejetons semblaient être revenus à la barbarie, végétant comme des sauvages sur une terre d'Esquimaux'). In the end, even these scattered remnants must yield to the inexorable burdens placed on them by an 'implacable nature' ('l'implacabilité de la nature').

Wells extends the time scale even further: due to the depletion of the sun's energy some thirty or more million years hence virtually all life on Earth has come to an end; his 'Time Traveller' relates: 'I looked about me to see if any traces of animal life remained. A certain indefinable apprehension still kept me in the saddle of the machine. But I saw nothing moving, in earth or sky or sea. The green slime on the rocks alone testified that life was not extinct'. Soon thereafter

> the darkness grew apace; a cold wind began to blow in freshening gusts from the east, and the showering white flakes in the air increased in number. From the edge of the sea came a ripple and whisper. Beyond these lifeless sounds the world was silent. Silent? It would be hard to convey the stillness of it.[105]

Wells's end of the world is, of course, the inversion of the beginning of the world as related at the opening of the *Old Testament*: 'In the beginning God created the heaven and the earth', *Genesis* begins, 'and the earth was without form, and void; and darkness was upon the face of the deep. And the Spirit of God moved upon the face of the waters'. In Wells's futuristic vision, however, no God ripples the waters — 'Nature' is the only mover. If in the beginning there was God's word, as the Gospel of Saint John tells us, here all there is in the end is nature's silence. Where Flammarion's novel ends in a mystical apotheosis, as related in the previous chapter, Wells's classic of modern science fiction by contrast provides a profoundly secular if gloomy vision of a terminal decline into Nothingness. At the end of time, nature is left to its own devices, man has long vanished without trace, as have all other

---

104 *Omega; the Last Days of the World*, pp. 239–41, both subsequent quotes p. 241 (*La Fin du monde*, pp. 317–18 and twice p. 314).
105 *The Short Stories of H. G. Wells* (London: Ernest Benn, 1957), pp. 84–85.

advanced forms of life on Earth, and Wells makes sure that his tale holds out no hope of either redemption or new beginning, cyclical or otherwise.

If we consider Flammarion's pseudo-religious *La Fin du monde* of 1894 as the late-nineteenth-century counterpiece to Grainville's early-nineteenth-century *Le Dernier Homme* of 1805, we might similarly construe Wells's a-religious *The Time Machine* of 1895 as the late-nineteenth-century counterpiece to Byron's 1816 poem 'Darkness', which, as I laid out in the preceding chapter, was inspired in part by the atmospherical and meteorological anomalies brought about by the outbreak of the volcano Mount Tambora, in part by Buffon's *Histoire naturelle*. Here once more its closing lines:

> The waves were dead; the tides were in their grave,
> The moon their mistress had expir'd before;
> The winds were withered in the stagnant air,
> And the clouds perish'd; Darkness had no need
> Of aid from them — She was the Universe.

Here too the winds have withered and no 'Spirit of God moves upon the face of the waters', just as in Wells's vision of the dying Earth; here too the last lines provide no hope of redemption. Although Byron was not an atheist (critics tend to consider him a deist), the end-time of his poem nonetheless takes on a rather sinister if not nihilistic hue. Neither of its two last men is lifted unto Heaven, neither transported to Hell, they die simply and feebly of shock at experiencing one another's 'mutual hideousness'. Neither salvation nor torment awaits them, there is no resurrection, nor do trumpet blasts announce a Last Judgment or Second Coming. If Byron had indeed read the English translation of Grainville's *Le Dernier Homme*, as some interpreters have speculated, his poem certainly offers a deliberately gloomy deistic counterweight to Grainville's theistic vision and outlook.

Naturally, the appeal of 'lastness' was by no means a new phenomenon within European intellectual history; inspired in part by the excavations of the Roman ruins of Herculaneum under Charles Bourbon after 1738, the eighteenth and early nineteenth centuries exulted in stories of ruins and the decline and collapse of empires, not to mention last bards and last Mohicans and other varieties of last men. Volney's 1791 *Les Ruines, ou Méditation sur les révolutions des empires* that I cited in Chapter Two (see Figure 2.5 with its suggestive caption) was just one intermediary in a long line of similar publications. Interwoven with the melancholy of Edward Young's mid-eighteenth-century *Night Thoughts* and Macpherson's *Ossian*, and reinforced by the cult of the genius — often pictured as a lone and solitary figure — as well as the rise of modern individualism, this tradition of thought extended from John Dyer's *The Ruins of Rome* (1740), Robert Wood's *The Ruins of Palmyra* (1753) and *The Ruins of Balbec* (1757), and Thomas Major's *The Ruins of Paestum* (1768) in the mid-eighteenth century through Edward Gibbon's *The History of the Decline and Fall of the Roman Empire* (1776–1789), Louis Sébastien Mercier's dream of a dead Paris in *Le Tableau de Paris* (1781), and Volney's *Les Ruines* in the second half of the century to such works as Walter Scott's *The Lay of the Last Minstrel* (1805), Robert Southey's *Roderick, the Last of the Goths* (1814), James Fenimore Cooper's

The Last of the Mohicans (1826) and many of Byron's works in the opening decades of the nineteenth century.

Fiona Stafford has given a full and fascinating account of the English-language trajectory of this tradition in her study *The Last of the Race. The Growth of a Myth from Milton to Darwin*. She notes how

> the imaginative appeal of such remnants and chance survivals derives from something deeper than a mere nostalgic interest in the vanishing past. The same mysterious reverence is accorded to last works and last words, in the belief that they must have special significance, must somehow provide the definitive statement. It suggests a desire to find at the close of a life some revelation of purpose — an 'end' in both senses of the word. When an individual represents the end of a race, there is thus a sense of expectation, as if some explanation will be forthcoming to justify its disappearance and very often, the last survivor feels compelled to memorialize the vanished group.[106]

Stafford also relates how a genuinely modern (i.e. historical and evolutionary) conception of lastness was unable to develop as long as the Christian concept of temporality and divine intervention and salvation held sway, an analysis very much confirmed by the argument I have presented in my preceding chapters. 'It would be simplistic to suggest', Stafford writes,

> that the image of the last man emerges directly from the wreckage of traditional Christian eschatology, but there certainly appears to be a connection between the decline in Apocalyptic beliefs and the development of the myth [of the Last of the Race]. The very idea of a last man is impossible in a culture that adheres firmly to a sudden, divinely orchestrated ending of the entire race, while the disappearance of a particular family or social group is of little importance when the belief in universal resurrection and eternal life is beyond question.

Stafford is right to stress that the process is far more complex than meets the eye. In the previous chapters I have tried to sketch how the decline of the Christian eschatological paradigm was in part premised on the rise of deism, Enlightenment philosophy and the politics of the French Revolution, but also how that revolution in theology, philosophy and politics — and therewith the revolution in the broader Christian belief system of Western European societies of the time — was tied in with an equally seismic shift in aesthetic perception. In Chapter One we saw how Sonnenberg's religiously inspired epic revivalism was superseded by the turn to 'Nature', here represented by Wordsworth's *Prelude*. Similarly, in Chapter Two I related how the traditional quasi-religious literary genre of the epopee found itself unthroned by the modern secular equivalent of the epic, the novel and specifically the *Bildungsroman*, the novel of an individual's education and maturation. In this chapter I have foregrounded the use of the sublime and the Romantic cult of solitude against the backdrop of modern atheism and nihilism, the two dominant forms of nonbelief emerging during this period.

It is in this context that I would like to revisit some words by the German philosopher Odo Marquard that I cited in Chapter One. 'It would seem that

---

106 *The Last of the Race*, p. 3; the subsequent passage p. 18.

the thesis of idealistic autonomy is an expression of human self-aggrandizement and arrogance', he wrote; 'clearly this autonomy condemns man to self-seclusion ['Icheinsamkeit'] by preventing any true relationship with the Other; clearly it entails a revolt against God through its very disregard for the createdness of man and his world'. Put differently: the more 'man' sees himself as absolutely autonomous, and free from God, the more he is bound to experience himself as absolutely alone. Just as Jean Paul had decreed 'No one in Creation is so alone as the denier of God', Nietzsche followed suit by declaring, in Section 367 of *The Gay Science*, '[f]or the pious there is as yet no solitude; this invention was made only by us, the godless' ('denn für einen Frommen gibt es noch keine Einsamkeit — diese Erfindung haben erst wir gemacht, wir Gottlosen').[107] Fichte's philosophy of the Absolute I can thus be considered as the crucible of an absolute, and absolutely modern, sense of subject identity no less than of absolute *Icheinsamkeit*, self-loneliness. If Marquard is right, then German idealism, Kant and Fichte in particular, must be considered not just the well-spring of the modern positive spirit of the autonomy and creativity of the self — the Kantian manifestation of which is the conception of the self-sufficient 'original genius', promulgated in the *Critique of Judgment*, Kant's third critique of 1790, which segues into Fichte's late 1790s notion of the Absolute I — but also of the danger of man's hubris. The 'human self-aggrandizement' that is synonymous with man's 'revolt against God' occurs when, in the words of Klingemann's 'dead poet', 'Man [...] finally consider[s] himself as God or at least, like the idealists and world history, form[s] himself on such a mask' ('der Mensch sich zuletzt für Gott selbst halten oder zum mindesten wie die Idealisten und die Weltgeschichte, an einer solchen Maske formen soll').[108] But a mask is always an instrument of deceit, so Klingemann implies — and life and identity are shown to be as capricious as a carnival dance of masks, as Kreuzgang relates in the tenth night watch:

> And the masks turn in a mad swift dance around me — around me, who am called man — and I reel in the midst of their circle, dizzy from the sight and endeavouring in vain to embrace one of the masks and tear the disguise from its true countenance; [...] Who am I then, if the disguises should disappear? Give me a mirror, you carnival players, that I may once see myself — it's getting wearisome for me always to be looking at your changing faces. You shake — what? Does no *I* stand in the mirror, when I step before it — am I only the thought of a thought, the dream of a dream. [...] It is indeed terribly lonely in the ego, when I clasp you tight, you masks, and I try to look at myself — everything echoing sound without the disappeared note — nowhere substance, and yet I see — that must be the Nothing that I see! —
>
> [Und die Larven drehen sich im tollen raschen Tanze um mich her — um mich, der ich Mensch heiße — und ich taumle mitten im Kreise umher, schwindelnd von dem Anblicke und mich vergeblich bemühend eine der Masken zu umarmen und ihr die Larve vom wahren Antlitze wegzureißen. [...] Wer bin ich denn, wenn die Larven verschwinden sollten? Gebt mir einen Spiegel ihr Fastnachtsspieler, daß ich mich selbst einmal erblicke — es wird mir überdrüssig

---

107 Nietzsche, *The Gay Science*, p. 324 (*Die Fröhliche Wissenschaft*, p. 241).
108 *The Night Watches of Bonaventura*, ed. Gillespie, p. 141 (*Nachtwachen von Bonaventura*, ed. Schillemeit, p. 73); the subsequent quotes pp. 167–69 and 73 (pp. 88 and 33–34).

> nur immer eure wechselnden Gesichter anzuschauen. Ihr schüttelt — wie? steht kein *Ich* im Spiegel wenn ich davor trete — bin ich nur der Gedanke eines Gedanken, der Traum eines Traumes [...]. Das ist ja schrecklich einsam hier im Ich, wenn ich euch zuhalte ihr Masken, und ich mich selbst anschauen will — alles verhallender Schall ohne den verschwundenen Ton — nirgends Gegenstand, und ich sehe doch —— das ist wohl das Nichts das ich sehe!]

The realization that such human self-aggrandizement is but a signal of man's hubris — a fact that for contemporaries of Fichte like Klingemann forms the obvious corollary of Fichte's philosophy — simultaneously drives home the growing sense of fragility, tenuousness and finitude of man's condition. For Klingemann's narrator Kreuzgang Fichte's Absolute I is merely the expression of the proverbial pride that comes before the fall; we read:

> Take the matter from its lighter side; for it is amusing and worth the effort to attend this great tragicomedy, world history, as spectator up to its last act, and you can give yourself that quite unique pleasure finally, when at the end of all things, as sole survivor, you stand above the general deluge upon the last projecting mountain peak to hiss the entire production on your own hook, and then wild and angry, a second Prometheus, hurl yourself into the abyss.

> [Nimm die Sache von der leichten Seite, denn es ist doch spaßhaft und der Mühe werth, dieser großen Tragikomödie der Weltgeschichte bis zum letzten Akt als Zuschauer beizuwohnen, und du kannst dir zuletzt das ganz eigne Vergnügen machen, wenn du am Ende aller Dinge über der allgemeinen Sündflüth auf dem letzten hervorragenden Berggipfel als einzig Übriggebliebener stehst, das ganze Stück, auf deine eigene Hand, auszupfeifen und dich dann wild und zornig, ein zweiter Prometheus, in den Abgrund zu stürzen.]

Here man's Promethean spirit — such a popular topic in the decades around 1800, from Goethe's early Prometheus hymn of 1772–1774 to Percy Bysshe Shelley's 1820 verse drama *Prometheus Unbound* — literally comes to nothing, ending in an abysmal 'Nothing'. Does not this disappointed and disillusioned Promethean 'sole survivor' who, at least in Kreuzgang's version, hurls himself into the abyss stem from a landscape vastly different from that on display in Friedrich's *Wanderer above the Sea of Fog*?

A famous variation on the theme — a particular favourite of mine — is Percy Bysshe Shelley's poem 'Ozymandias'. Published pseudonymously in the 12 January 1818 issue of *The Examiner* (see Figure 3.6), the 'sole survivor' of this lost race is a petrified 'King of Kings', the scattered remnants of whose statue are all that is left on the 'boundless and bare' sands that 'stretch far away'. The motif of a traveller looking down on the ruins of 'a once opulent city' developed a distinct iconographical tradition in the eighteenth and nineteenth centuries, reaching from the already cited 1791 frontispiece in Volney's *Les Ruines, ou Méditation sur les Révolutions des Empires* that Grainville alludes to, through Shelley's poem, to Gustave Doré's 1872 engraving *The New Zealander* (Figure 3.7) and Octave Saumier's analogous *Paris en ruines* of 1899. In all of these a lone traveller is shown overlooking the once grand and mighty capital of a civilization now laid to waste before his eyes, as condensed in the caption to the Volney frontispiece previously cited: 'Here once flourished

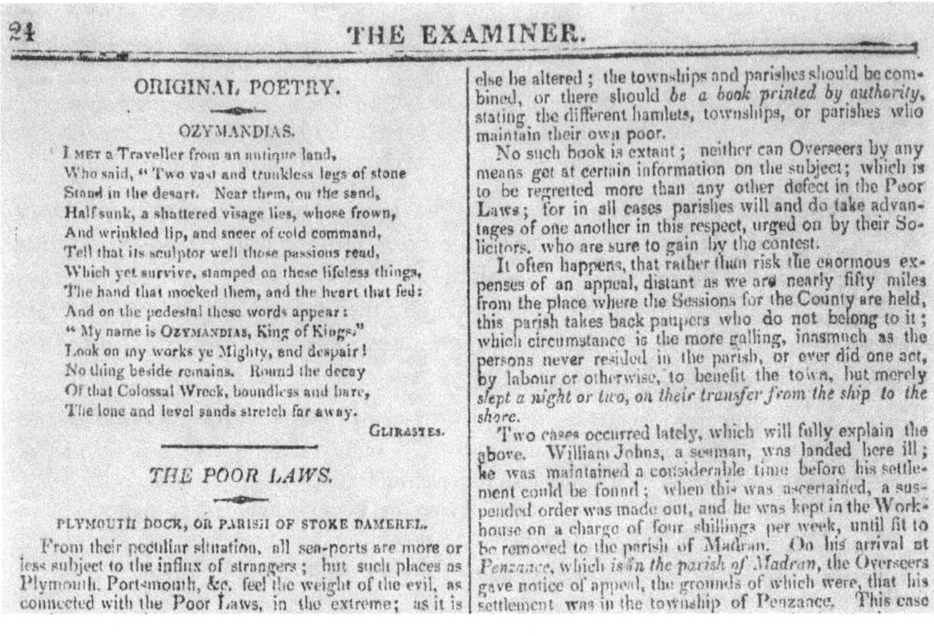

24 THE EXAMINER.

ORIGINAL POETRY.

OZYMANDIAS.

I MET a Traveller from an antique land,
Who said, "Two vast and trunkless legs of stone
Stand in the desart. Near them, on the sand,
Half sunk, a shattered visage lies, whose frown,
And wrinkled lip, and sneer of cold command,
Tell that its sculptor well those passions read,
Which yet survive, stamped on these lifeless things,
The hand that mocked them, and the heart that fed:
And on the pedestal these words appear:
"My name is OZYMANDIAS, King of Kings."
Look on my works ye Mighty, and despair!
No thing beside remains. Round the decay
Of that Colossal Wreck, boundless and bare,
The lone and level sands stretch far away.

GLIRASTES.

THE POOR LAWS.

PLYMOUTH DOCK, OR PARISH OF STOKE DAMEREL.

From their peculiar situation, all sea-ports are more or less subject to the influx of strangers; but such places as Plymouth, Portsmouth, &c. feel the weight of the evil, as connected with the Poor Laws, in the extreme; as it is else be altered; the townships and parishes should be combined, or there should *be a book printed by authority*, stating the different hamlets, townships, or parishes who maintain their own poor.

No such book is extant; neither can Overseers by any means get at certain information on the subject; which is to be regretted more than any other defect in the Poor Laws; for in all cases parishes will and do take advantages of one another in this respect, urged on by their Solicitors, who are sure to gain by the contest.

It often happens, that rather than risk the enormous expenses of an appeal, distant as we are nearly fifty miles from the place where the Sessions for the County are held, this parish takes back paupers who do not belong to it; which circumstance is the more galling, inasmuch as the persons never resided in the parish, or ever did one act, by labour or otherwise, to benefit the town, but merely *slept a night or two, on their transfer from the ship to the shore.*

Two cases occurred lately, which will fully explain the above. William Johns, a seaman, was landed here ill; he was maintained a considerable time before his settlement could be found; when this was ascertained, a suspended order was made out, and he was kept in the Workhouse on a charge of four shillings per week, until fit to be removed to the parish of Madran. On his arrival at *Penzance*, which *is in the parish of Madran*, the Overseers gave notice of appeal, the grounds of which were, that his settlement was in the township of Penzance. This case

FIG. 3.6. Percy Bysshe Shelley, 'Ozymandias', published pseudonymously under the name Glirastes on p. 24 of the 12 January 1818 issue of *The Examiner*, the top third of which is here reproduced.

an opulent City; here was the seat of a once powerful Empire: Yes! these spaces now so deserted, once a teeming multitude animated their surroundings, &'. The suggestive '&' at the end of this caption relates prima facie to the text of Volney's treatise (the passage is an abbreviated quote from Volume I, Chapter 2), but it is at the same an obvious invitation to the reader to enlarge upon the story with his or her own imagination.

Fiona Stafford has argued that the French Revolution in particular and Napoleon's rise to, and later his fall from, power gave further impetus to an already existing enthusiasm for the fall of empires and the last of their races. She notes:

> The last of the race is a myth of revolution: a form through which to express the conflicting emotions provoked by great change. We have already traced its steady growth in response to the various changes of the late eighteenth century, but in the wake of the French Revolution, it emerged as a dominant form. In the anticlimactic years of the early nineteenth century, the last of the race featured in works as diverse as Southey's *Thalaba*, of 1801, and Lady Morgan's *The Wild Irish Girl*, of 1806, while old favourites, such as Macpherson's *Ossian*, enjoyed a new popularity, boosted by Napoleon's admiration. By far the most successful poem of the first decade, however, was Walter Scott's *The Lay of the Last Minstrel*, of 1805, which made publishing history by selling almost 15,000 copies within the first five years of publication.[109]

The authors are all, Stafford underscores, deploying the theme of lastness to give

109 *The Last of the Race*, p. 162; the following quotes pp. 162 and 164.

Fig. 3.7. Gustave Doré, 'The New Zealander', detail of the last plate of Gustave Doré and Blanchard Jerrold's *London: A Pilgrimage* (1872), based on the following passage from Thomas Macaulay's 1840 review of Leopold von Ranke's *The Ecclesiastical and Political History of the Popes of Rome*: 'And she [the Catholic Church] may still exist in undiminished vigour when some traveller from New Zealand shall, in the midst of a vast solitude, take his stand on a broken arch of London Bridge to sketch the ruins of St. Paul's'.

some meaning to the seemingly random and hence 'meaningless flow of history'; thus Scott's 'Last Minstrel evokes both the myth of the Eternal Return and the "Terror of History"' — features readers in this period of upheaval could well relate to on both a personal and societal level.

For the most part the works named above deal with a mythical or distant historical past, or alternatively with a geographically distant present. The competing vision of the Last Man (and later, of course, also Last Woman) reflecting back on the past grandeur, or failure, of a humanity now deceased — or at least nearly so, as in Grainville's *Le Dernier Homme* — of course shifts the perspective squarely into a more or less distant future. As such it requires a radically different fictional framework, a narrative scaffold through which believably to project the narrative perspective, or vision, into a distant future that we under 'normal' human circumstances cannot know. We should recall for a moment that the genre of science fiction with its epic visions for example of a galactic futurity in outer space — a form of fictitious setting that we have grown thoroughly accustomed to in both the literary and the filmic medium — did not yet exist in the eighteenth and early nineteenth centuries. Louis Sébastian Mercier's immensely successful

L'An deux mille quatre cent quarante (*The Year 2440*), an example of proto-Science-Fiction first published in 1771 with countless reprints and translations into other languages, is arguably the most famous early instance of a utopian narrative located in a specified future some 700 years hence, a distant call from the millions of years called up by Flammarion's and Wells's works. In Mercier's day, 'deep time' was not yet a concept — the term was introduced, as the *Oxford English Dictionary* informs us, only in 1832 by Thomas Carlyle in an article in *Fraser's Magazine*. As compared with the prevalent 6000 years of the biblical record and the computations of the likes of Bishop Ussher and Thomas Burnet, even Buffon's moderate early estimates of the 75,000-year age of the planet Earth (successively increased in later editions of his *Histoire naturelle*) were nothing less than revolutionary. But even *The Year 2440*, despite its futuristic quality, hardly qualifies as science fiction in the modern sense: the author resorted to depicting the future not as an unmediated real-life futuristic reality, but rather as a mere vision of such a futuristic reality mediated through the prism of a dream; the subtitle *Rêve s'il en fut jamais* (*A dream if ever there was one*) is an index of Mercier's narrative ruse. The introductory 'Epistle to the Year Two Thousand Four Hundred and Forty' accordingly opens (in the version of the text's 1797 English translator, Harriot Augusta Freeman):

> Respectable and venerable year, destined to bring felicity to the inhabitants of this world, thou, alas! whom I have *only seen in a dream*, when thou shalt spring forth, from the bosom of eternity, those who shall see thy radiant glory, will trample my ashes, and those thirty generations, successively extinguished, and buried in the profound abyss of Death. Kings, who are this day seated on thrones, will then be no more, neither will any of their posterity remain...[110] (my emphasis)

It was one thing to tell stories of the historical or even a mythical past and of the last of the race in such bygone times — Walter Scott's *Waverley* of 1815, depicting events a mere 'Sixty Years Since' (as the subtitle states), is credited as being the first genuinely modern historical novel — but it was an altogether different challenge for writers in the eighteenth and early nineteenth century to explain how one can see into the future, how one can envision, and describe with literary means, historical events that have not yet occurred.[111] To overcome this obstacle, most authors deployed what they considered the most 'realistic' perspectivizing device available to them, namely that of a dream vision; such was Jean Paul's 1796 stratagem in 'Speech of the dead Christ', such was Byron's tactic in his 1816 poem 'Darkness', and such was Thomas Campbell's approach in his 1823 poem 'The Last Man'. Such was also the course taken by the anonymous author of a short story entitled 'The

---

[110] *Astræa's Return; or, The Halcyon Days of France in the Year 2440: A Dream*, trans. by Harriot Augusta Freeman (London: Chapman, 1797), p. xi.

[111] In his article 'Science fiction before the genre' in *The Cambridge Companion to Science Fiction* Brian Stableford observes: 'The more extreme versions of the fantastic voyage overlapped with the standard format of religious fantasy, the dream story. Whenever seventeenth- and eighteenth-century imaginary voyages found it convenient to cross interplanetary space their devices became phantasmagorical, and dreaming remained the only plausible means of gaining access to the future until the late nineteenth century' (p. 16).

Last Man' published in *Blackwood's Edinburgh Magazine* in March 1826 — the year in which Mary Shelley's novel was published — whose conclusion may stand as an example typical of the caricaturistic use this framework can also be put to:

> Desolation! Desolation! I knew that it was to be dreaded as a fearful and a terrible thing, and I had felt the sorrows of a lone and helpless spirit — but never, never had I conceived the full misery that is contained in that one awful word, until I stood on the brow of that hill, and looked on the wide and wasted world that lay stretched in one vast desert before me. Then despair and dread indeed laid hold of me — then dark visions of woe and of loneliness rose indistinctly before me [...]. I gave one wild shriek — one convulsive struggle — and — *awoke* ——and there stood my man John, with my shaving-jug. [...] By his entrance were these visions dispelled, else Lord knows how long I might have lingered out my existence in that dreary world, or what woes and unspeakable miseries had been in store for [me].[112]

Once the dream vision is dispelled, the imagined 'Last Man' with all his 'despair' and 'dread' finds himself thrust back into the perhaps no less 'dreary' and 'woeful' life of a gentleman of the Georgian era.

Grainville, by contrast, adopted what many will consider a more circuitous and therefore arguably less convincing form of narrative subterfuge — and less persuasive means to 'suspend disbelief', to adopt Coleridge's contemporary formula — namely placing the narrator in an extraordinary setting that no other mortal would have access to under 'normal' circumstances. Canto I of *Le Dernier Homme* thus reads:

> Near the ruins of Palmyra there is a solitary cavern, so greatly feared by the Syrians that they have named it the cavern of death. Men have never entered it without suffering immediate punishment for their temerity. The story is told of some reckless Frenchmen who dared to enter this place with weapons in their hands. The next day, at dawn, they were found slaughtered, and their limbs scattered upon the desert.
>
> [Proches les ruines de Palmyre, il est un antre solitaire si redouté des Syriens qu'ils l'ont appelé la caverne de la mort. Jamais les hommes n'y sont entrés sans recevoir aussitôt le châtiment de leur audace. On raconte que des Français intrépides osèrent y pénétrer les armes à la main, qu'ils y furent égorgés, et qu'au retour de l'aurore on trouva dans les déserts d'alentour leurs membres dispersés.][113]

Having set up this suitably exotic and perilous locale Grainville then singles his narrator out from all other human beings by having him summoned by 'a man bearing a torch' ('un homme armé d'un flambeau') to enter that cavern: 'I know not how he communicated his thoughts to me', we are told, 'but I understood that he was summoning me into the cavern. I felt myself drawn by a sudden and irresistible force; and in spite of the terror and the cries of the Syrians who tried to hold me back, I leapt into the cavern' ('J'ignore de quelle manière il me

---

112 Anon., 'The Last Man', *Blackwood's Edinburgh Magazine* (January–June 1826), 284–86 (p. 286).
113 *The Last Man*, trans. I. F. & M. Clarke, p. 3 (*Le Dernier Homme*, ed. Kupiec, p. 45); the subsequent passages pp. 3–4 (p. 46).

communiqua ses pensées; mais je compris qu'il m'appelait dans ce lieu. Je m'y sentis entraîné par une force irrésistible et soudaine. Et malgré la frayeur et les cris des Syriens qui voulurent m'arrêter, je m'élançai dans la caverne'). The narrator now follows its passages until he reaches the grand subterranean amphitheatre in which 'Time' can be seen chained to an adamantine pillar; because he is liberated from time's constraints, the cavern's 'Celestial Spirit' is miraculously free to share with his human interlocutor the vision of futurity which the subsequent narrative relays. Just as Grainville has liberated his narrator from the external constraints of the real world, and of real time, the framework's internal machinery of the Spirit and his cave of enchanted mirrors liberates the narrative from any further requirement of verisimilitude.

Whether Mary Shelley knew the English translation of Grainville's *Le Dernier Homme* or not when she began writing her novel of the same title remains a matter of debate among scholars of her work; she obviously knew Byron's poem 'Darkness', and she may have been familiar with the slew of imitations and lampoons of Byron's poem that followed in short succession between 1816 and 1826, including Thomas Campbell's poem 'The Last Man' of 1823, Thomas Hood's satirical ballad 'The Last Man' of 1826, and the short story in *Blackwood's Magazine* mentioned above. Indeed, when Campbell was accused by one reviewer of his volume *Theodoric, a Domestic Tale: with Other Poems* (which included his Last Man poem) that he had 'borrowed' from Byron, Campbell responded angrily with an 'Open Letter' in *The Times* in which he insisted that, on the contrary, it was Byron who had plagiarized his idea; he himself, he avers, had brought the possibilities inherent in this topic to Byron's attention in a conversation they had had some 'fifteen or it may be some more years ago', but Campbell had not gotten to writing his own poem sooner.[114] Whatever knowledge Mary Shelley had of these pre-texts, the subject matter was clearly in the air when she put pen to paper in the mid-1820s. Indeed, the 'prefatory fiction' of her novel is rather reminiscent of *Le Dernier Homme*'s, as I will detail in the following chapter.[115] Such correspondences notwithstanding, hers is truly the first futuristic Last-Man novel of European literature — I place the stress here of course on the term *novel*. Her predecessors one and all in this subject matter had used either verse (poetry or the epopee) as their generic vehicle, or, when prose was engaged, the Last Man allusions were either peripheral to the main storyline, as in Jean Paul's novel *Siebenkäs* and Klingemann's Romantic satire *Nightwatches*, or remained underdeveloped, as in Jean Paul's tale 'The Strange Society of New Year's Eve' and the anonymous satirical prose sketch 'The Last Man' in *Blackwood's Magazine*.

---

114 There are a number of useful discussions of these Last Man poems and Byron's impact; among them are Morton D. Paley, 'Envisioning Lastness: Byron's "Darkness", Campbell's "The Last Man", and the Critical Aftermath', *Romanticism*, 1 (1995), 1–14; R. J. Dingley, '"I had a Dream...". Byron's "Darkness"', *The Byron Journal* (1981), 20–33; A. J. Sambrook, 'A Romantic Theme: The Last Man', *Forum for Modern Language Studies*, 2 (1966), 25–33; and Fiona Stafford, *The Last of the Race*, pp. 160–231.

115 I take the phrase 'prefatory fiction' from Sophie Thomas's article 'The Ends of the Fragment, the Problem of the Preface: Proliferation and Finality in *The Last Man*', in *Mary Shelley's Fictions. From 'Frankenstein' to 'Falkner'*, ed. by Michael Eberle-Sinatra (Basingstoke: MacMillan, 2000), pp. 22–38 (p. 22).

While the exception to this rule may have been Grainville's *Le Dernier Homme*, as I hope to have shown in my previous chapter Grainville never intended his work as a novel in the first place; what many have described as an early prototype of the secular futuristic novel was in actual fact a mere Christian apocalyptic epopee in prose veneer. Against this backdrop Mary Shelley's *The Last Man*, the subject of the following chapter, represents a truly new beginning; it prefigures on the one hand the post-religious kind of futuristic fiction that revels so much in portraying mankind as forever poised on the brink of cataclysmic annihilation, on the other it presages the arrival on the literary scene of atheism as a worldview. Indeed, as I shall endeavour to show in the subsequent chapter, we must consider atheism as axiomatic to the Last Man genre. It is for this reason that my chapter on Mary Shelley's *The Last Man* must begin not with the novel's author herself, but rather with her husband Percy Bysshe Shelley, the first major British poet to publicly profess his atheism.

CHAPTER 4

Atheism, Science and Religion 1811/1826: The Shelleys and the Death of Man

> Science doesn't make it impossible to believe in God. It just makes it possible not to believe in God.
> STEVEN WEINBERG (1999)[1]

> The death of a species is so remarkable an event in natural history that it deserves commemoration.
> CHARLES LYELL (1835)[2]

On the Threshold

In his immensely influential *The Order of Things* (*Les Mots et les choses*), published 1966, the French philosopher, social theorist, psychoanalyst and literary critic Michel Foucault introduced to the field of literary study a powerful new conceptual tool, the term *episteme*. Foucault's notion of episteme comprised what might be considered the unconscious epistemological grammar of discourse and representation that limits and shapes what can be thought and formulated in a given culture at a given time. While in *The Order of Things* Foucault distinguished three stages in the episteme of European thought, the pre-classical, the classical, and the modern, he lavished particular attention on the two epistemic shifts that separated them; he notes in the preface to his study:

> [T]his archaeological inquiry has revealed two great discontinuities in the *episteme* of Western culture: the first inaugurates the Classical age (roughly halfway through the seventeenth century) and the second, at the beginning of the nineteenth century, marks the beginning of the modern age.
>
> [[C]ette enquête archéologique a montré deux grandes discontinuités dans l'*épistémè* de la culture occidentale: celle qui inaugure l'âge classique (vers le milieu du XVIIe siècle) et celle qui, au début du XIXe marque le seuil de notre modernité.][3]

---

1 'A Designer Universe?', *New York Review of Books*, 21 October 1999; cited from Lawrence M. Krauss, 'Religion vs. Science?', in *The Religion and Science Debate. Why Does It Continue?*, ed. by Harold W. Attridge (New Haven and London: Yale University Press, 2009), pp. 125–53 (p. 125).
2 *Principles of Geology, Being an Attempt to Explain the Former Changes of the Earth's Surface, by Reference to Causes Now in Operation*, 3rd edn, 4 vols (London: Murray, 1834–1835), vol. 3, pp. 60–61.
3 *The Order of Things*, p. xxii (*Les Mots et les choses*, p. 13).

This second shift, he explains in the foreword to the 1970 English edition, occurred 'within a few years around 1800',[4] with 'the outer limits [being] the years 1775 and 1825'; it is at this turn of the eighteenth to the nineteenth century that 'the great hiatus' ('la grande rupture') occurs 'in the modern *episteme*'. The years around 1800 are, of course, also the very years to which I have devoted so much attention in the first two chapters of my study. Indeed, in a passage I cited earlier in my study Foucault sees man as 'constituted at the beginning of the nineteenth century'.

The primary reason why 'man was constituted' during precisely this period was because, in Foucault's view, the role and function of language had changed both radically and abruptly. Up until the classical period, language had remained 'translucent' ('translucide');[5] when people spoke they saw through language to the thing represented by that language. Once the Western *episteme* entered its modern stage, however, language turned opaque, and representation became a thing or process to be doubted and questioned. The epistemic shift that took place between the classical and modern stages created a revolution in self-perception which for Foucault becomes foundational of our modern condition; he observes:

> As long as that language was spoken in Western culture it was not possible for human existence to be called into question on its own account, since it contained the nexus of representation and being [...]. As long as Classical discourse lasted, no interrogation as to the mode of being implied by the *cogito* could be articulated. [...] But the essential consequence is that Classical language, as the *common discourse* of representation and things, as the place within which nature and human nature intersect, absolutely excludes anything that could be a 'science of man'.
>
> [Tant que ce langage-là a parlé dans la culture occidentale, il n'était pas possible que l'existence humaine fût mise en question pour elle-même, car se qui se nouait en lui, c'était la représentation et l'être. [...] Mais tant qu'a duré le discours classique, une interrogation sur le mode d'être impliqué par le Cogito ne pouvait pas être articulée. [...] Mais la conséquence essentielle, c'est que le langage classique comme *discours commun* de la représentation et des choses, comme lieu à l'intérieur duquel nature et nature humaine s'entrecroisent, exclut absolument quelque chose qui serait 'science de l'homme'.]

Foucault concludes that

> when natural history becomes biology, when the analysis of wealth becomes economics, when, above all, reflection upon language becomes philology, and Classical *discourse*, in which being and representation found their common locus, is eclipsed, then, in the profound upheaval of such an archaeological mutation, man appears in his ambiguous position as an object of knowledge and as a subject that knows.
>
> [Lorsque l'histoire naturelle devient biologie, lorsque l'analyse des richesses devient économie, lorsque surtout la refléxion sur le langage se fait philologie et que s'efface ce *discours* classique où l'être et la représentation trouvaient leur lieu commun, alors, dans le mouvement profond d'une telle mutation

---

4 Ibid., p. xii; the subsequent quotes pp. 221 and 325 (*Les Mots et les choses*, pp. 233 and 336).
5 Ibid., p. 311 (p. 322); the subsequent two passages pp. 311–12 (pp. 322–23).

archéologique, l'homme apparaît avec sa position ambiguë d'objet pour un savoir et de sujet qui connaît.]

However, some philosophers and historians of science have taken issue with what they consider Foucault's too monolithic a conception of epistemes and his unwarranted stress on the 'profound upheavals' and 'great discontinuities' that occur between stages. Thus the Harvard University evolutionary biologist and historian of his science, Ernst Mayr, notes in 1982 in his *The Growth of Biological Thought*:

> Some historians of science like to distinguish different periods, each with a single dominant paradigm (Kuhn), episteme (Foucault) or research tradition. This interpretation does not fit the situation in biology. Ever since the later seventeenth century, one finds more and more often that even within a given biological discipline or specialization, two seemingly incompatible paradigms may exist side by side, like preformation and epigenesis, mechanism and vitalism, iatrophysics and iatrochemistry, deism and natural theology, or catastrophism and uniformitarianism, to mention only a few of the numerous polarities. [...] Foucault's ideal, to paint the progress of science (and its milieu) as a series of consecutive *epistemes*, is clearly not encountered in the real world.[6]

Similarly, a leading German philosopher and theoretician of romanticism, Manfred Frank, objects that 'nothing suggests that the step from the self-reflexivity of the idea to the self-reflexive relationship with the *subject* of the idea is the unexplainable, unreconstructable and abrupt "emergence" as which Foucault does not tire to portray it' ('Nichts deutet darauf hin, daß es sich um eine unerklärliche, unnachvollziehbare und abrupte "Emergenz" handelt, als die Foucault nicht müde wird sie hinzustellen').[7]

Their disagreement over discontinuity versus processuality notwithstanding, Frank concurs with Foucault, albeit with differing philosophical emphases, that the years between 1775 and 1825 constitute an unprecedented turning point in European intellectual history, a 'threshold era' ('Schwellenzeit' — Manfred Frank), a 'threshold period' ('Schwellenepoche' — Hans Blumenberg and Hans Robert Jauß), or 'saddle era' ('Sattelzeit' — Reinhart Koselleck), as German philosophers, discourse theoreticians and historians of science have variously called it.[8] This

---

6 *The Growth of Biological Thought. Diversity, Evolution, and Inheritance* (Cambridge, MA: Belknap Press, 1982), p. 113.

7 *Das Sagbare und das Unsagbare. Studien zur deutsch-französischen Hermeneutik und Texttheorie* (Frankfurt a.M.: Suhrkamp, 1989), p. 396.

8 Frank speaks of 'Schwellenzeit' in *Das Sagbare und das Unsagbare*, p. 395. For Blumenberg see his *Aspekte der Epochenschwelle* (Frankfurt a.M.: Suhrkamp, 1976), for Koselleck the volume *Epochenschwelle und Epochenbewußtsein*, ed. by Reinhart Herzog and Reinhart Koselleck (Munich: Fink, 1987), and his introduction to *Geschichtliche Grundbegriffe* (vol. 1, Stuttgart: Klett-Cotta, 1979), for Jauß his *Die Epochenschwelle von 1912* (Heidelberg: Winter, 1986). See also the volume *Epochenschwellen und Epochenstrukturen im Diskurs der Literatur- und Sprachhistorie*, ed. by Hans-Ulrich Gumbrecht and Ursula Link-Heer (Frankfurt a.M.: Suhrkamp, 1985). It should perhaps be added that in his later essay '"Neuzeit". Remarks on the Semantics of Modern Concepts of Movement' (in *Futures Past. On the Semantics of Historical Time*, trans. by Keith Tribe (New York: Columbia University Press, 2004), pp. 222–54) Koselleck defines this 'epochal threshold' ('Epochenschwelle') slightly more broadly as occupying the years 1770 to 1830 (p. 247).

is also the precise period that another German scholar, the sociologist, political scientist and historian of science Wolf Lepenies, identified as the crucial phase in the history of the emerging modern sciences of biology, zoology and anthropology; more specifically, according to Lepenies, it is the century during which 'Natural History' — the classical study of nature epitomized by the Swedish botanist Carl Linné's *Systema Naturae* (1735–1768) with its essentially synchronic and God-given taxonomy of species — is once and for all transformed into the 'history of nature' with its first culmination point, Charles Darwin's radically diachronic and Nature-driven theory of evolution, presented in 1859 in *On the Origin of Species*.

The supplanting of (God-given) 'Natural History' by the (Nature-driven) 'history of nature' — a complex process that Lepenies contracts into the concurrent processes of what he calls temporalization and denaturalization[9] — parallels the simultaneous rift, described by the German philosopher of historiography Reinhart Koselleck, taking place in the discipline of history (inasmuch as it existed as a discipline before the nineteenth century). During the eighteenth century, Koselleck relates, the plural usage of history in German, *Historien* (literally 'histories'), is gradually replaced by the 'modern' singular term *Geschichte* ('history'), whose first use as a 'collective singular' is documented in Adelung's dictionary of the German language in 1775.[10] If, just for argument's sake, we take Koselleck's and Frank's 1775 as the beginning of this momentous half century of revolution and transformation in the sciences as much as the world of politics, Foucault's 1800 as its apex, and Foucault's and Frank's 1825 to denote its end, then we might well be justified in using Mary Shelley's 1826 novel *The Last Man*, the book to which we turn later in this chapter, as the hinge text of a radically new era that has moved beyond the threshold. Of course, as the preceding paragraphs have surely borne out, my argument — which revolves around the shift in consciousness and conviction that characterizes the move from theism via deism and pantheism to atheism, from an active God via a silent or absent God to the death of God and his supplanting by an unmoved Nature, or from Burnet, Young, Sonnenberg, Jacobi, Grainville and Jean Paul via Spinoza, Kant, Paine, Goethe and Wordsworth to Holbach, Heydenreich, Fichte and Klingemann, and from there on to Percy Bysshe and Mary Shelley, both of whom will preoccupy us on the next pages — is not a new one. There have been many tellings of it from a wide spectrum of varying disciplinary perspectives, some of which we have already encountered; Foucault's epistemic approach is one, Charles Taylor's historico-theological story another, Ernst Mayr's survey of 'The Growth of Biological Thought' a third, Wolf Lepenies's account of the transformation of Natural History into the history of nature a fourth. (Some months after I had first drafted these lines, Terry Eagleton added yet another version of this narrative in his *Culture and the Death of God*, published in early 2014.) Thus my narrative cannot but be a variation on a theme, a retelling of a story in many ways already familiar

---

9 See for instance *Das Ende der Naturgeschichte. Wandel kultureller Selbstverständlichkeiten in den Wissenschaften des 18. und 19. Jahrhunderts* (Frankfurt a.M.: Suhrkamp, 1978), p. 121.

10 See his 'Historia Magistra Vitae: The Dissolution of the Topos into the Perspective of a Modernized Historical Process', in *Futures Past*, pp. 26–42.

in European intellectual history and the history of secularization. And yet, every retelling offers its own emphases and rewards. In the previous chapters I combined, in a transdisciplinary fashion, literary and art history with philosophy and theology; this chapter needs to move the emerging sciences more to the fore. But before I do this I must return to literature for a short while: my narrative needs to begin with the first stirrings of overt atheism in English literary history.

The Necessity of Atheism

Less than a decade after Klingemann put those telltale final words 'God, or Nothing!' into the mouth of his suicidal poet, a factual real-life poet took up that fictitious poet's battle cry. Few outside the confines of specialist scholarship will know that Percy Bysshe Shelley (1792–1822) wrote a number of prose essays and poems, only some of which were published during his lifetime, in which he openly promoted atheism, albeit a brand of atheism unique to him. It is thus not the author of *Prometheus Unbound* and *A Defence of Poetry* who will be my focus and central concern here, nor even the reform-minded political radical and follower of William Godwin who sought to abolish marriage and introduce vegetarianism, but rather Shelley as a critic of religion. The texts that will hence play key roles in the first sections of this chapter are, in roughly chronological order, Shelley's early anonymous pamphlet *The Necessity of Atheism* of 1811; the atheistic poem *Queen Mab* of February 1813 with its extended philosophical 'Notes' section; the prose dialogue *A Refutation of Deism*, published anonymously in 1814 (and referred to already in Chapter Two); the undated essay fragment 'On a Future State'; the essay fragment 'Essay on Christianity', written as far as we know between late 1816 and 1817;[11] and the poem 'Mont Blanc' of the summer of 1816. All of these belong to what one might call Shelley's middle period of intellectual and poetical maturation. Even before this phase the adolescent Shelley had preoccupied himself with atheism: the villain Zastrozzi of his first — and very premature — literary publication, the Gothic novel *Zastrozzi. A Romance*, is characterized as an atheist, signalling the onset of religious doubt; written in 1809 at Eton College, the novel was published in June 1810 when Shelley was barely eighteen and just entering University College, Oxford. It was during his first year at Oxford that his rationalist scepticism turned into full-fledged atheism; at University College he wrote, in a pseudo-scientific vein, the five-page tract *The Necessity of Atheism* in which he undertook to disprove, logico-empirically as it were, the possibility of the existence of God. The tract's concluding paragraphs read:

> From this it is evident that having no proofs from any of the three sources of conviction: the mind cannot believe the existence of a God, it is also evident that as belief is a passion of the mind, no degree of criminality can be attached to disbelief, they only are reprehensible who willingly neglect to remove the false medium thro' which their mind views the subject.

---

[11] This dating, 'written between late 1816 and 1817: some time after returning from Switzerland in 1816 and before the completion of *Laon and Cythna* in 1817', is given by Michael Henry Scrivener in *Radical Shelley*, p. 89.

> It is almost unnecessary to observe, that the general knowledge of the deficiency of such proof, cannot be prejudicial to society: Truth has always been found to promote the best interests of mankind. — Every reflecting mind must allow that there is no proof of the existence of a Deity. Q. E. D.[12]

Despite 'taking great care to remain anonymous', as the Shelley-biographer Richard Holmes underscores,[13] Shelley was soon caught out and expelled from the university in March 1811, with a public prosecution looming for blasphemous libel.[14] In a January 1812 letter to William Godwin, the father of Shelley's future second wife, Mary Wollstonecraft Shelley (née Mary Wollstonecraft Godwin), the nineteen-year-old himself sums up the affair as follows:

> In the meantime I became in the popular sense of the word 'God' an Atheist. I printed a pamphlet avowing my opinion, and it's [sic] occasion. I distributed this anonymously to men of thought and learning wishing that Reason should decide on the case at issue. It was never my intention to deny it. Mr Copelstone at Oxford among others had the pamphlet; he shewed it to the master and the fellows of University College, and *I* was sent for: I was informed that in case I denied the publication no more would be said. — I refused, and was expelled.[15]

Needless to say, as obstinate and impulsive as this refusal may have been, his expulsion only served to reinforce his freethinking and anti-Christian sentiments. In his 'Memoir of Shelley' published some ten years after Shelley's death, Thomas Medwin relates: 'Shelley looked upon the refusal of the examining masters to accept his challenge in the schools, as a proof that his logic was incontrovertible, and gloried in what he considered a persecution'.[16] Mary Shelley similarly observed in 1839: 'Various disappointments tortured, but could not tame, his soul. The more enmity he met, the more earnestly he became attached to his peculiar views, and hostile to those of the men who persecuted him'.[17]

---

12 Percy Bysshe Shelley, *The Necessity of Atheism*, in *The Works of Percy Bysshe Shelley in Verse and Prose*, ed. by Harry Buxton Forman, 8 vols (London: Reeves and Turner, 1880), vol. 5, pp. 305–09 (p. 309). It is perhaps worth noting here that Georg Büchner, whose *Lenz* we discussed in Chapter Three, similarly writes in his commentary on Spinoza's *Ethics*: 'The proof by the way that demonstrates God's existence through his essence is based merely on logical necessity; he says *if I think God* I must think him as existing, but what entitles me to think God' ('Der Beweis übrigens welcher aus dem Wesen Gottes, sein Dasein demonstriert, stützt sich nur auf eine logische Notwendigkeit, er sagt, *wenn ich mir Gott denke muß ich ihn mir als seiend denken*, aber was berechtigt mich denn Gott zu denken?'); 'Spinoza', in Georg Büchner, *Sämtliche Werke, Briefe und Dokumente*, vol. 2: *Schriften, Briefe, Dokumente* (Frankfurt a.M.: Deutscher Klassiker Verlag, 1999, reprint 2006), pp. 280–352 (p. 291).

13 *Shelley, the Pursuit* (London: Weidenfels and Nicolson, 1974), p. 51. Martin Priestman, in *Romantic Atheism*, reminds us of the limited options open to self-proclaimed atheists like Shelley during this period: 'The four possible strategies were: to publish and be damned; to write but not to publish; to publish under a pseudonym; and to write with enough of an air of disinterested scholarship to avoid prosecution' (p. 184).

14 Holmes, *Shelley, the Pursuit*, p. 59.

15 Letter of 10 January 1812; cited from Percy Bysshe Shelley, *Poems and Prose*, ed. by Timothy Webb and George E. Donaldson (London: J. M. Dent, 1995), p. 456.

16 *The Shelley Papers. Memoir of Percy Bysshe Shelley* (London: Whittaker, Treacher, Co., 1833), p. 14.

17 Mary Shelley, 'Note on *Queen Mab*', in *The Poetical Works of Percy Bysshe Shelley*, 4 vols, ed. by Mary Shelley (London: Edward Moxon, 1839), vol. 1, pp. 96–106 (p. 100).

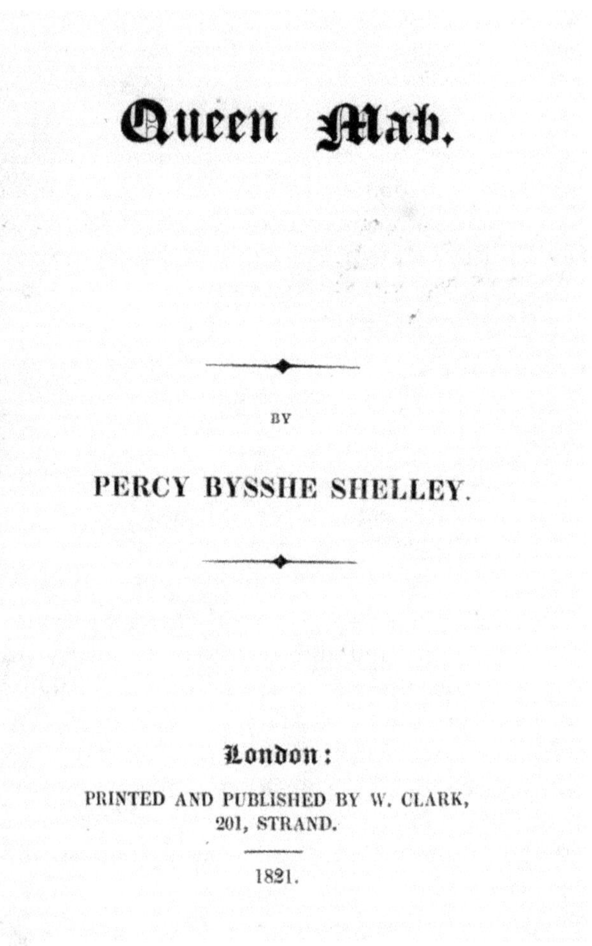

Queen Mab.

BY

PERCY BYSSHE SHELLEY.

London:

PRINTED AND PUBLISHED BY W. CLARK,
201, STRAND.

1821.

FIG. 4.1. Percy Bysshe Shelley, *Queen Mab*, title page of the 1821 pirated 'London' edition; the first edition of 1813 was printed and circulated only privately. The publisher of the pirated edition, William Clark, was prosecuted by the 'Society for the Suppression of Vice' and claimed to have served four months in prison. The 'New York' edition, published as a response to the pirated 'London' edition in November or December 1821 and edited in all likelihood by George Cannon (using the pseudonym 'Reverend Erasmus Perkins'), was actually produced by William Benbow in London. The camouflage was adopted in order to avoid prosecution. This edition contains a 'Preface' by 'A Pantheist' (i.e., Cannon alias Perkins) and a letter by Shelley, distancing himself from Clark's edition.

The upshot of this was that, within the next two years, Shelley felt compelled to compose an explicitly atheistic poem entitled *Queen Mab* (see Figure 4.1), which included a philosophical 'Notes' section running to 117 pages, comprising roughly half the volume. This is how Richard Holmes sums up this work: 'Politics conducted by propaganda; polemics, visions, prophecies and philosophical disquisitions [...]. Essentially subversive in intent, vigorously polemic in attack, and revolutionary in content and implication'; the Shelley-scholar Kenneth Neill Cameron calls it, 'taken together with the Notes [...], the most revolutionary document of the age in England', and one that became 'known as "The Chartist's Bible"'.[18] Shelley himself put it like this in 1821, when the poem was published without his consent: '*Queen Mab*, a poem written by me when very young, in the most furious style, with long notes against Jesus Christ, and God the Father, and the king, and bishops, and marriage, and the devil knows what'.[19]

18 Holmes, *Shelley. The Pursuit*, pp. 157 and 201; Cameron, *The Young Shelley*, pp. 273 and 274.

19 Letter of 16 June 1821 to John Gisborne; *The Letters of Percy Bysshe Shelley*, 2 vols, ed. by Frederick L. Jones (Oxford: Clarendon Press, 1964), vol. 2, pp. 300–01.

Consisting of an extended dialogue between a 'Fairy Queen' named Mab and the spirit of a sleeping maiden called Ianthe, the poem recounts how Queen Mab carries off the young woman's spirit in her celestial chariot in order to present to the 'slumbering maid' a vision of the universe and its past, present and future. During the course of their journey through the universe and at the opening of Section VII, Ianthe's spirit relates how, as an infant, she was taken by her mother to witness the burning of an atheist at the stake, a man who, her mother says, had claimed 'There is no God'; hearing her account, the Fairy Queen immediately proceeds to back up the unfortunate atheist's assertion by likewise proclaiming that

> There is no God!
> Nature confirms the faith his death-groan sealed:
> Let heaven and earth, let man's revolving race,
> His ceaseless generations tell their tale;
> Let every part depending on the chain
> That links it to the whole, point to the hand
> That grasps its term! let every seed that falls
> In silent eloquence unfold its store
> Of argument: infinity within,
> Infinity without, belie creation;
> The exterminable spirit it contains
> Is nature's only God...[20]

This passage is significant because it is to the opening statement 'There is no God!' that Shelley attached perhaps the most provocative note that this work contains, one that comprises a lengthy polemic against the existence of God, including a verbatim reproduction of *The Necessity of Atheism*. This basic atheistic message is buttressed by extended quotations from the works of Francis Bacon, Spinoza and Holbach, especially the latter's so-called Bible of atheism, *The System of Nature*.[21]

Even if one argues that the words 'There is no God!' in *Queen Mab* are attributable to a 'Fairy Queen' and thus to an imaginary figure, the seventeen 'Notes' sections of this 'philosophical poem' — so the poem's subtitle — can be ascribed to none other than the author himself. And these 'Notes' sections contain not just lengthy quotations from the works of various alleged atheists, but also unequivocal expressions of Shelley's own atheistic creed, including the following appendage to *The Necessity of Atheism*: 'God is an hypothesis, and, as such, stands in need of proof: the *onus probandi* rests on the theist'[22] (an appendage, incidentally, that may owe its existence to Shelley's familiarity with the catchphrase about God famously attributed to the astronomer Laplace in conversation with Napoleon, 'Je n'avais pas besoin de cette hypothèse-là' — 'I had no need of that hypothesis').

20 *Queen Mab*, in *The Works of Percy Bysshe Shelley*, ed. Forman, vol. 4, pp. 379–536 (p. 437).
21 It is worth noting that Holbach's 'Bible of Atheism' was at this time still being published pseudonymously in Britain, with publishers continuing to face prosecution — the 1817, 1820 and 1834 British reissues thus all continue to cite Mirabaud as the author; it is only the 1835 New York edition that for the first time used Holbach's real name. For his citations from *Système de la Nature* — inserted initially in their French original, but in later editions replaced by an English translation — Shelley in *Queen Mab* hence provided the work's title, but not the author's name which he would have known was fictious.
22 *Queen Mab*, p. 495; the subsequent quotes pp. 489–90, 490 and 488.

In the context especially of Britain at this time, this is stark and confrontational language: it is not the atheist's responsibility to disprove the existence of God, but rather the theist's obligation to prove it, something Shelley knew was impossible (of course, it is equally impossible to disprove his existence). In the preceding 'Note' Shelley had written, in the 'Necessitarian' vein of Holbach and Godwin:

> But the doctrine of Necessity teaches us that in no case could any event have happened otherwise than it did happen; and that, if God is the author of good, he is also author of evil that, if he is entitled to our gratitude for the one, he is entitled to our hatred for the other; that, admitting the existence of this hypothetic being, he is also subjected to the dominion of an immutable necessity. [...] The doctrine of Necessity tends to introduce a great change into the established notions of morality, and utterly to destroy religion. Reward and punishment must be considered, by the Necessitarian, merely as motives which he would employ in order to procure the adoption or abandonment of any given line of conduct.

In 1817, four years after its initial circulation in 250 privately printed copies, Shelley is still worried that *Queen Mab* may yet result in his imprisonment as 'an atheist & a republican'.[23] To make matters worse, a further four years later a London printer, William Clark, published an unauthorized pirated edition, the so-called 'London' edition of *Queen Mab*, in which the author's name appeared unmasked on the title page. In order to distance himself from this publication, Shelley, residing at the time in Pisa, immediately wrote to the editors of the London Sunday weekly *The Examiner*, the leading radical newspaper published by John and Leigh Hunt, to request the publication of the following disclaimer:

> Sir, — Having heard that a poem, entitled *Queen Mab*, has been surreptitiously published in London, and that legal proceedings have been instituted against the publisher, I request the favour of your insertion of the following explanation of the affair as it relates to me. A poem, entitled *Queen Mab*, was written by me at the age of eighteen, I dare say in a sufficiently intemperate spirit — but even then was not intended for publication, and a few copies only were struck off, to be distributed among my personal friends. I have not seen this production for several years: I doubt not but that it is perfectly worthless in point of literary composition; and that in all that concerns moral and political speculation, as well as in the subtler discriminations of metaphysical and religious doctrine, it is still more crude and immature. I am a devoted enemy to religious, political, and domestic oppression; and I regret this publication, not so much from literary vanity, as because I fear it is better fitted to injure than to serve the cause of freedom. I have directed my solicitor to apply to Chancery for an injunction to restrain the sale; but after the precedent of Mr. Southey's *Wat Tyler* (a poem, written, I believe, at the same age, and with the same unreflecting enthusiasm), with little hopes of success. Whilst I exonerate myself from all share in having divulged opinions hostile to existing sanctions, under the form, whatever it may be, which they assume in this poem, it is scarcely necessary for me to protest against the system of inculcating the truth of Christianity and the excellence of Monarchy, however true or however excellent they may be, by such equivocal

---

23 See his 11 January 1817 letter to Mary; *The Letters of Percy Bysshe Shelley*, ed. Jones, vol. 1, p. 527.

arguments as confiscation, and imprisonment, and invective, and slander, and the insolent violation of the most sacred ties of nature and society.

This disclaimer, which appeared in *The Examiner* on 16 July 1821, was added later that year to the 'Preface' of the 1821 New York edition of *Queen Mab* (an edition actually printed in London; see commentary to Figure 4.1). Clearly, Shelley is making the most of this incident and trying to turn it to his advantage, as he himself remarks in a personal letter to his friend John Gisborne dated 16 June 1821:

> A droll circumstance has occurred. *Queen Mab*, a poem written by me when very young, in the most furious style, with long notes against Jesus Christ, and God the Father, and the King, and bishops, and marriage, and the devil knows what, is just published by one of the low booksellers in the Strand, against my wish and consent, and all the people are at loggerheads about it. [...] You may imagine how much I am amused. For the sake of a dignified appearance, however, and really because I wish to protest against all the bad poetry in it, I have given orders to say that it is all done against my desire, and have directed my attorney to apply to Chancery for an injunction, which he will not get.[24]

Since he does not expect an injunction to be granted, Shelley is in effect now free to circulate this work and the atheistic views contained therein, regardless of their poetic merits or failings. In contrast to the prose essays *The Necessity of Atheism* and *A Refutation of Deism*, which have led a rather secluded existence among Shelley's writings, for obvious reasons not being incorporated in major editions of his 'poetical' works, *Queen Mab* was incorporated because it was a poem, albeit 'A Philosophical Poem, with Notes'; indeed, in the nineteenth century it went on to enjoy a certain measure of popularity from the late 1820s, with numerous official and nearly as many pirated editions reaching out to an Owenite and Chartist working class readership, making it, as Cameron observes in *The Young Shelley. Genesis of a Radical*, 'an important weapon in the arsenal of British working-class radicalism'.[25] As the German Shelley-specialist Susanne Schmid has uncovered, it was even read by Friedrich Engels, who possessed one of the German pirate editions and who seems to have wanted to publish some translations into German of Shelley's work, a project that in the end did not materialize.[26]

There has been endless debate about whether Shelley's self-professed atheism was genuine, a useful summary of which has been given by David Berman in a chapter of his 1988 *History of Atheism in Britain*. Whereas Berman insists that the poet was indeed an atheist, certainly in the early years 1811–1814,[27] many Shelley-scholars

---

24 Here cited from *The Works of Percy Bysshe Shelley*, ed. Forman, vol. 8, p. 250.
25 *The Young Shelley*, p. 274.
26 *Shelley's German Afterlives 1814–2000* (New York: Palgrave/Macmillan, 2007), p. 28
27 Berman writes: 'My conclusion is that in the period 1811–1814 Shelley was an atheist. He was so because, firstly, he called himself an atheist, not merely in the *Necessity,* but also in letters written at that time. Secondly, he also denies the existence of God in both published works and private letters. And, thirdly, far from having an idiosyncratic understanding of the words "atheist" and "God", he has an unusually firm grasp of their ordinary meanings. Fourthly, he also presents a reasoned case against the existence of God, perhaps as powerful a case as has ever been presented in such a short work'; *A History of Atheism in Britain*, p. 143.

have either sidestepped the issue[28] or have preferred to call him a sceptic or an agnostic, among them Cameron, M. H. Abrams, Carlos Baker, Neville Rogers and David Lee Clark. Along these lines Alister McGrath observed, in his 2004 book *The Twilight of Atheism. The Rise and Fall of Disbelief in the Modern World*:

> Shelley argues [in *The Necessity of Atheism*] that, since compelling evidence for the existence of God is lacking, there is no intellectual obligation to believe in God. The essay actually makes a case for a practical agnosticism — or perhaps a skeptical empiricism — rather than atheism, in that Shelley's argument leads only to the conclusion that an informed mind cannot reach a reliable conclusion on the existence of God on the basis of the available evidence.[29]

Berman by contrast believes that 'Shelley's claim to be considered a pioneer atheist is unassailable [although it] has in fact been assailed by nearly all Shelley scholars. For various reasons they resist the conclusion that Shelley was an atheist, a denier or disbeliever in God's existence'.[30]

I agree with Berman that certainly up to around 1815 Shelley was more stridently atheistic than in his later years, as I will illustrate later. There are justifiable reasons, however, why scholars were at such loggerheads over this issue: first, many of Shelley's key pronouncements are suffused with ambiguity and ambivalence (this being by and large the guiding argument put forward by Earl Wasserman in his 1971 study *Shelley. A Critical Reading*); second, while Shelley later seems indeed to have shied away from the more extreme necessitarianism of his younger years to adopt a more pantheistically flavoured spiritualism towards the end of his life (this the argument of Michael Henry Scrivener in his 1982 *Radical Shelley*),[31] it is neither easy to pin down when this shift occurred nor to discern the degree to which Shelley's thinking mellowed; and finally, third, some of the contexts within which he embeds his key pronouncements appear self-contradictory — in all likelihood intentionally so. To cite just one example: whereas the 'Fairy's' declaration 'There is no God!' in *Queen Mab* seems quite straightforward and unambiguous, the note attached to this line appears to backpedal: 'This negation must be understood solely to affect a creative Deity. The hypothesis of a pervading Spirit co-eternal with the universe remains unshaken'.[32] Shelley is clearly implying that the 'creative Deity',

---

28 In 1951, Cameron in *The Young Shelley* observed: 'Shelley's critics do not seem to know what to do about his anti-religious works except to apologize for them as evidence of youthful metaphysical dissipation' (p. 274); Shelley-scholarship has of course changed significantly since those New Critical days.

29 See his *The Twilight of Atheism. The Rise and Fall of Disbelief in the Modern World* (London: Rider, 2004), p. 122.

30 *A History of Atheism in Britain*, p. 136.

31 Scrivener observes, for instance: 'A turning-point comes with *Alastor* [1816], which signifies a transition from a radical rationalism to a new, "romantic" synthesis. With *Alastor*, Rousseauistic and Wordsworthian pantheism enters the mainstream of Shelley's public wiriting. Many poems in the Esdaile Notebook also bear evidence of pantheism, so that clearly it was something Shelley wrote about before *Alastor*. Just how much before is hard to tell, because of the uncertain dating of most of the Esdaile poems'; *Radical Shelley*, p. 78.

32 *The Poetical Works of Percy Bysshe Shelley*, ed. by William Michael Rossetti, 3 vols (London: John Stark, 1885), vol. 1, p. 229.

as which both theistic Christians and deists define their God, is opposed to some form of non-creative all-pervading Spirit-God within nature. Is this proof of his atheism, or not rather proof of a personal form of pantheism? It is as if Shelley is trying to hedge his bets. Whether his prevarication is philosophically inspired or politically motivated in order to avoid legal prosecution may remain debatable; what is clear is that such ambiguities in his pronouncements have resulted in competing interpretations of Shelley's religious attitude, although I doubt anyone would dispute that his worldview was stridently anti-Christian.

It is perhaps also worth adding here that the ambiguity embedded in Shelley's *Queen Mab* and its notes was picked up and commented upon as early as the year of its first unauthorized publication in London in 1821. William Clark, the publisher of that edition who was indicted and brought to trial for printing the volume, in the same year published a seventy-page tract entitled *Reply to the Anti-Matrimonial Hypothesis and Supposed Atheism of Percy Byssche [sic] Shelley, as laid down in Queen Mab*, in which its anonymous author questioned Shelley's ostensible atheism. The writer draws attention to the fact that the way in which Shelley deploys the notions of 'Necessity' and 'Spirit' is, fundamentally, not far removed from the way Christians deploy their concept of God; he observes:

> The declaration, that there is *no God*, is contradictory to the idea of the *inexterminable spirit*, being *Nature's only God!* But is it not grossly foolish, to shock in this manner the nerves of his ordinary readers — to lead them to imagine he is denying the *existence* of a God, when he is only denying the *mode* of his existence.[33]

He goes on to add, 'whether this power be called First Cause, or God, or Necessity, matters not to the fact', and concludes, not without some justification:

> The grand secret is merely an exchange of nomenclature. We are not to call the vivifying and superintending principle of creation by the name of God, because impostors have belied his character, and villains have abused his attributes; but we are to get rid of all difficulty and doubt by hailing 'Necessity' as the '*Mother of the world!*' [...] Nor do I see ought of distinction between necessity and predestination; save that one is applied to a sectarian definition of the Christian faith, and the other is the general principle applied to the whole phenomena of nature. [...] Allow Mr. Shelley to designate his ruling power by the term Necessity, and his theology remains as sound as that of other men. He is not an atheist.[34]

---

33 Anon., *Reply to the Anti-Matrimonial Hypothesis and Supposed Atheism of Percy Byssche Shelley, as laid down in Queen Mab* (London: Clark, 1821), pp. 59–60, the following quotation p. 61. It is worth pointing out that the author of this treatise uses the word 'inexterminable' here; although this seems to make more sense in the context of the relevant line, all editions of Shelley's works show 'exterminable'.

34 *Reply to the Anti-Matrimonial Hypothesis*, pp. 50 and 54. It is striking that this treatise appeared in the same publishing house so soon after the publication of *Queen Mab* itself. Indeed, the first time I came across this *Reply* was in a book in which it had been bound together with Shelley's *Queen Mab*. It is possible that it was quickly hobbled together in an attempt to play down and depreciate Shelley's atheism in order (obviously unsuccessfully) for Clark to evade prosecution and imprisonment. I should perhaps also add at this point that in their considerations of the poem 'Mont

Tellingly, nearly ten years earlier, at the turn of the year 1812/1813, Shelley himself represented a conversation he had had with the poet Southey at his and Coleridge's residence Greta Hall in Keswick as follows in a letter to his friend and then soul-mate Elizabeth Hitchener:

> I have lately had some conversation with Southey which has elicited my true opinions of God. He says I ought not to call myself an atheist, since in reality I believe that the universe is God. I tell him that I believe that 'God' is another signification of 'the universe'. I then explain: I think reason and analogy seem to countenance the opinion that life is infinite; that, as the soul which now animates this frame was once the vivifying principle of the infinitely lowest link in the chain of existence, so it is ultimately destined to attain to the highest; that everything is animation [...], and in consequence, being infinite, we can never arrive at its termination. [...] Southey agrees in my idea of Deity — the mass of infinite intelligence. [...] [PS] Southey says I am not an atheist, but a pantheist.[35]

Indeed, Cameron observes in his superbly detailed treatment of Shelley's atheism, materialism and necessitarianism in *Queen Mab* and *A Refutation of Deism* in *The Young Shelley. Genesis of a Radical* how Shelley 'departs from [Holbach's] strict materialism in his dualistic conception of Necessity as a spiritual force pervading matter but not identical with it', concluding: 'But [Shelley] does not conceive of this force as creative and hence denies that it can be considered a Deity; in fact he is always at pains to deny creation and to insist on the eternity of all things, both spirit and matter'.[36] Shelley himself, in *The Necessity of Atheism*, had put it thus: 'it is easier to suppose that the Universe has existed from all eternity, than to conceive a being capable of creating it'.[37] Shelley is clearly no theist, nor is he a deist, denying creation as he did. But how to describe what he subscribed to, whether as a full-fledged atheism, a modified pantheism, or some idiosyncratic variant of scepticism, is not so easily answered, even if one considers only his early works *The Necessity of Atheism*, *Queen Mab* and *A Refutation of Deism*. The situation is further complicated by the fact, moreover, that Shelley later expanded his philosophical interests, exploring in particular Berkeleyan idealism and Platonism, which substantially altered his outlook on such religious issues as the possibility of an afterlife of the spirit; at the time that he wrote *Queen Mab*, however, Shelley was not yet a Platonist, Cameron stresses.[38]

Blanc' various Shelley-scholars have underlined what they see as the quasi-religious manner in which 'Power' is presented in it. Earl S. Wasserman in *The Subtler Language. Critical Readings of Neoclassic and Romantic Poems* (Baltimore: Johns Hopkins University Press, 1950) thus comes to the conclusion that, emanating from a 'quasi-religious experience' (p. 238), 'Mont Blanc' is 'in effect [...] a religious poem, and the Power is Shelley's transcendent deity' (p. 232); Spencer Hall similarly, in 1953, spoke of Shelley's 'approximation of theological grace' in the poem, albeit an approximation with a secular thrust ('Shelley's "Mont Blanc"', *Studies in Philology*, 70 (April 1973), 199–221 (p. 201)).

35 Quoted from *The Complete Works of Percy Bysshe Shelley*, ed. by Nathan Haskell Dole (Laurel Edition) (London and Boston: Virtue & Company, 1906), vol. 8, pp. 11–12 and 14.
36 *The Young Shelley*, pp. 254–55.
37 *The Works of Percy Bysshe Shelley*, ed. Forman, vol. 5, p. 307.
38 See *The Young Shelley*, p. 256; Cameron makes the perhaps valid point that 'the roots of Shelley's

Regardless of whom one sides with, Berman in *A History of Atheism in Britain* offers a number of useful observations that can help us better to appreciate the context of atheism within which Shelley was operating in the early nineteenth century. First, Berman notes that even in Germany at that time with its generally more advanced discourse in theology and philosophy, authors remained surprisingly hesitant publicly to avow their atheistic predilection; he writes:

> German society was prepared to tolerate (reluctantly, of course) *indirect* expressions of atheism, but not open professions [...]. Thus one finds almost no direct published denials of God's existence, or open avowals of atheism, even in such allegedly strong-minded German atheists as Schopenhauer and Marx.[39]

Second, he observes how 'the first such published avowal of speculative atheism', as rare as such avowals may have been, appeared in 1770s France — specifically in the shape of Holbach's *The System of Nature*. However, Berman overlooks one crucial fact, one that underscores Shelley's truly exceptional role in the history of atheism (at least as far as I can discern). Although Holbach and Diderot are generally considered 'the first explicit and self-confessedly atheist philosophers',[40] the works in which they propounded their atheism actually appeared either anonymously, pseudonymously or posthumously. For decades Holbach's *System of Nature* was published in France, Germany and Britain pseudonymously under the name Mirabaud, meaning legally the work could not be attributed to Holbach. Accordingly, Shelley writes to William Godwin on 3 June 1812: 'I have just finished reading *La Système de la Nature* par M. Mirabaud. Do you know the real author, — it appears to me a work of uncommon powers'. Godwin's response leads Shelley to suspect Helvétius as the author; he writes to Godwin on 29 July 1812: 'I have read *La Système de la Nature*. I suspect this to be Helvétius's by your charges against it. It is a book of uncommon powers yet too obnoxious to accusations of sensuality & selfishness'.[41] Diderot's *D'Alembert's Dream*, the most direct expression of his atheistic thought, circulated only clandestinely during the author's lifetime and was first published after his death in 1830. Similarly, the first such avowal in Britain came in 1782 in the shape of William Hammon's *An Answer to Dr Priestley's Letters of a Philosophical Unbeliever*,[42] yet the name of William Hammon is, one generally suspects, a mere pseudonym and cover for the as yet unidentified anonymous author. Likewise in Germany, Heydenreich, as we saw in the previous chapter, was careful to use what Berman has called a 'protective artifice' in the tradition of his philosophical predecessors, making himself the mere editor of unattributable atheistic letters. Shelley himself resorted to a similar artifice when he attached his name neither to *The Necessity of Atheism*, nor to *A Refutation of Deism*. But he did

---

future partial acceptance of Berkeleian idealism' are already present in *Queen Mab* and *A Refutation of Deism*, and hence 'it is wrong to consider him as having passed through an intermediary state of consistent Holbachian materialism' (pp. 286–87).

39 *A History of Atheism in Britain*, p. ix.
40 Gavin Hyman, 'Atheism in Modern History', in *The Cambridge Companion to Atheism*, ed. by Michael Martin (Cambridge: Cambridge University Press, 2007), pp. 27–46 (p. 30).
41 *The Letters of Percy Bysshe Shelley*, ed. Jones, vol. I, pp. 303 and 315.
42 See Berman, *A History of Atheism in Britain*, p. 3.

attach his name to the first edition of *Queen Mab*, approximately 70 copies of which he disseminated privately in and after 1813 (180 remained unused at the time of his death)[43] and which later led to its being reprinted in 1821 under his name, even if without his express permission. Consequently and as regards Berman's statement that 'Shelley was only the second open avower of speculative atheism in Britain', in light of the anonymity respectively pseudonymity of his predecessors' works and the public mention of Shelley's name both in the 1821 unauthorized London edition of *Queen Mab* and the authorized New York imprint of the same year it might be more accurate to designate Shelley the *first* openly avowed British atheist — despite the fact that, if only for legal protection, Shelley put on a deliberate show to distance himself from that publication.

The Science behind Religion

The passage from *Queen Mab* that I cited earlier is significant for a second reason. It provides an early instance of one of Shelley's key aesthetic formulations, encapsulated in the expression the 'silent eloquence' of nature, as well as a key reference to Shelley's scientific worldview. This scientific worldview is the explicit subject of a note appended to 'Section I' of *Queen Mab* in which we read:

> The plurality of worlds, — the indefinite immensity of the universe is a most awful subject of contemplation. [...] The nearest of the fixed stars is inconceivably distant from the earth, and they are probably proportionably distant from each other. By a calculation of the velocity of light, Sirius is supposed to be at least 54,224,000,000,000 miles from the earth. That which appears only like a thin and silvery cloud streaking the heaven, is in effect composed of innumerable clusters of suns, each shining with its own light, and illuminating numbers of planets that revolve around them. Millions and millions of suns are ranged around us, all attended by innumerable worlds, yet calm, regular, and harmonious, all keeping the paths of immutable necessity.[44]

'The plurality of worlds' is an instantly recognizable catchphrase for Shelley's educated audience for whom it would have been an obvious allusion to the seventeenth-century deist Bernard le Bovier de Fontenelle's celebrated and widely circulated 1686 *Entretiens sur la pluralité des mondes* (*Conversations on the Plurality of Worlds*). The French writer and secretary of the Academy of Sciences had postulated in his popularizing work of science that the universe was in perpetual motion and flux, and that even as we live out our lives on planet Earth new suns are being born and are dying all around us; indeed, Fontenelle suggests, ours is just one populated planet among countless others — for what other purpose can so many stars have, he reflects, but to provide light for planets revolving around them, and what purpose can so many planets — and even our own moon — have but to provide the means of life for their inhabitants.

As its title indicates, Fontenelle's *Entretiens* is a dialogue; it is a dialogue conducted

---

[43] See Harry Buxton Forman, *The Shelley Library. An Essay in Bibliography* (London: Reeves and Turner for the Shelley Society, 1886), p. 36.
[44] *Queen Mab*, p. 466.

over five evenings (in 1687 Fontenelle added a sixth evening, which is not yet contained in the 1687 English translation by 'Sir W. D. Knight' cited below) between a scientifically informed *savant* and his female interlocutor, a marchioness, about the structure and nature of our universe. Staggered by her educator's conclusions, the woman expresses her awe at their ramifications, but also her apprehension about our species' consequent insignificance and the danger of our being reduced to a meaningless speck in the universe, a mere nothing:

> But, says she, why there's the Universe so big that I am lost in it, I know not where I am, I'm nothing. What, shall all be divided into *Vortices* confusedly thrown one among another? Shall every Star be the Center of a *Vortex* as big perhaps as that wherein we are? Shall all the immense space that comprehends our *Sun* and our Planets be no more than a little Spot of the Universe? This confounds, perplexes and astonishes me. [...] You offer me, said she, a kind of Perspective so long, that my eye cannot reach the end of it. I clearly see the Inhabitants of the Earth, and afterward you shew me those of the *Moon* and the other Planets of our *Vortex*, truly clearly enough, but less than those of the *Earth*, and after them come the Inhabitants of the Planets of other *Vortices*. I protest to you they are wholly drown'd, and with all that I can do to see them, they are still almost wholly discernable. And in effect, are they not almost annihilated by the expression you are fain to make use of in speaking of them, you are fain to call them *the Inhabitants of one of the Planets of one of those infinite Vortices*. You must confess that you hardly know how to disingage us our selves, to whom the same expression agrees, from the midst of so many Worlds. For my share, I begin to see the Earth so fearfully little, that from hence forward I shall have no value for any thing in it.[45]

These valid concerns notwithstanding, her interlocutor seeks to counter the marchioness's disquiet and anxiety by providing a more composed and serene view of this infinite post-Copernican universe:

> And, said I, for my share, I am wholly at ease. Were Heaven no more than that blue Vault where the Stars are nail'd, the Universe would seem small and narrow to me, and I should find my self straighten'd and oppress'd. But now that this Vault is of infinite more extent and profundity, in dividing it into a thousand thousand *Vortices*, methinks I breath with more liberty, and am in a more open Air; and most assuredly the Universe has wholly another Magnificence. Nature spar'd nothing in making it, but made a profusion of her Riches wholly worthy of her. Nothing can be represented so beautiful as that prodigious number of *Vortices* in the Center whereof is seated the *Sun* turning the Planets about him. The Inhabitants of a Planet of one of those infinite *Vortices*, see on all sides the luminous centers of those *Vortices* which surround them, but they see not the Planets, which having but a feeble light borrowed from their *Sun*, do not propagate it beyond their World.

As these passages illustrate, Fontenelle was among the earliest Enlightenment thinkers to open up the universe to an infinity of (deep) space and (deep) time.

---

45 Bernard le Bovier de Fontenelle, *A Discourse of the Plurality of Worlds written in French by the most ingenious author of the Dialogues of the Dead; and translated into English by Sir W. D. Knight* (Dublin: William Norman, 1687), this and the subsequent quote pp. 71–72.

And the more the universe became extended in space and time, the more profound 'Nature' was felt to be and divine in its own right, depriving God of both a teleological and ontological space within which to exist. In his germinal study *The Legitimacy of the Modern Age* the German philosopher Hans Blumenberg speaks of an 'eschatology without God' ('Eschatologie ohne Gott'); he notes: 'The world of the Middle Ages was finite, but its God was infinite. In Modernity *the world takes on this attribute of God; infinity becomes secularized*' ('Die Welt des Mittelalters sei endlich, ihr Gott aber unendlich gewesen; in der Neuzeit *übernimmt die Welt dieses Attribut Gottes; die Unendlichkeit wird säkularisiert*', Blumenberg's emphasis).[46]

Kant followed suit in a more scientific vein in the mid-eighteenth century with his *General Natural History and Theory of the Heavens*, of which Stephen Toulmin and June Goodfield write in *The Discovery of Time*:

> Kant's 1755 *General History of Nature and Theory of the Heavens* was the first systematic attempt to give an evolutionary account of cosmic history: in it, he spoke of the whole Order of Nature, not as something completed at the time of the original Creation, but as something *still coming into existence*. [...] Kant's cosmology clearly owed more to Fontenelle's *Plurality of Worlds* than it did to the Old Testament. In the balance between Biblical interpretation and physical science, the scale was at last beginning to tilt decisely in favour of physics.[47]

One upshot of this new state of affairs is Kant's recognition of the middling role of our human species within the universal chain of beings; Kant speculates how the inhabitants of planets orbiting at a further remove from our sun must be physically more perfected that those living closer to it:

> The inhabitants of the Earth and of Venus could not exchange their domiciles without the destruction of both. [...] The material of which the inhabitants of different planets, indeed even the animals and plants on them, are formed must altogether be of a lighter and finer type and the elasticity of the fibers together with the advantageous arrangement of their build be more perfect, the further they are away from the sun. [...] Human nature, which occupies as it were the middle rung on the ladder of beings, sees itself as being between the two extreme limits of perfection, equally distant from both ends. If the idea of the most sublime classes of rational creatures that inhabit Jupiter or Saturn arouses [our] jealousy and humiliates [us] by the knowledge of [our] own baseness, then [we] can be satisfied again and comforted by the sight of the low stages on the planets Venus and Mercury, which are lowered far below the perfection of human nature.
>
> [Die Einwohner der Erde und der Venus können ohne ihr beiderseitiges Verderben ihre Wohnplätze gegeneinander nicht vertauschen. [...] Der Stoff, woraus die Einwohner verschiedener Planeten, ja so gar die Tiere und Gewächse auf denselben, gebildet sein, muß überhaupt um desto leichterer und feinerer Art, und die Elastizität der Fasern, samt der vorteilhaften Anlage ihres Baues, um desto vollkommener sein, nach dem Maße als sie weiter von der Sonne abstehen. [...] Die menschliche Natur, welche in der Leiter der Wesen gleichsam

---

46 *Die Legitimität der Neuzeit* (Frankfurt a.M.: Suhrkamp, 1996), p. 22 (my translation).

47 Stephen Toulmin and June Goodfield, *The Discovery of Time* (London: Hutchinson, 1965), pp. 130 and 133.

die mittelste Sprosse inne hat, siehet sich zwischen den zwei äußersten Grenzen der Vollkommenheit mitten inne, von deren beiden Enden sie gleich entfernet ist. Wenn die Vorstellung der erhabensten Klassen vernünftiger Kreaturen, die den Jupiter oder den Saturn bewohnen, ihre Eifersucht reizet, und sie durch die Erkenntnis ihrer eigenen Niedrigkeit demütiget: so kann der Anblick der niedrigeren Stufen sie wiederum zufrieden sprechen und beruhigen, die in den Planeten Venus und Merkur weit unter der Vollkommenheit der menschlichen Natur erniedrigt sein.][48]

Regardless of the — as we now know — scientific inaccuracy of Fontenelle's and Kant's (and many others', including Shelley's)[49] belief in the other planets of our solar system being inhabited, it is crucial to recognize that both philosophers imply that humankind has lost its privileged position as the 'Crown' and acme of God's creation. Mankind is no longer the annointed species for which the world and the universe surrounding it were exclusively created. Fontenelle's and Kant's works are symptomatic for the degree to which the new post-Baconian, post-Cartesian and post-Newtonian science emerging during this period is transforming 'Nature' into the only force that can create and take life, with God relegated to a speculative realm beyond the physical universe. It is at this point in European intellectual history that religious faith and scientific knowledge, believing and knowing finally part ways, with revealed (Christian) religion giving way to various forms of natural religion. (We may recall from Chapter Three that *Believing and Knowing or the Philosophy of Reflection about Subjectivity — Glauben und Wissen oder die Reflexionsphilosophie der Subjektivität* — was the title of an early treatise on Kant, Jacobi and Fichte by Hegel, published in 1802.)

More than a century after Fontenelle's 'Plurality of Worlds' (the reference to which Shelley places so conspicuously at the beginning of his note), and more than half a century after Kant's *Universal History of Nature and Theory of the Heavens* (a book Shelley would not have known since even in German it was not widely disseminated during Kant's lifetime, nor was it translated into English until 1900),[50] and indeed more than two centuries after Francis Bacon (cited by Shelley in *Queen Mab*) first 'replaced the name "God" by the name "Nature"',[51] these issues

---

48 *Universal Natural History*, pp. 300–01 (*Allgemeine Naturgeschichte*, pp. 385–87). I have amended Olaf Reinhardt's translation in line with my own reading and understanding of Kant's text.

49 In Shelley's undated fragmentary satirical essay 'On the Devil, and Devils' we thus read: 'The sphere of the operations of the Devil is difficult to determine. The late inventions and improvements in telescopes have considerably enlarged the notions of men respecting the bounds of the universe. It is discovered that the Earth is comparatively a small globe, in a system consisting of a multitude of others, which roll round the sun; and there is no reason to suppose but that all these are inhabited by organized and intelligent beings'; *The Works of Percy Bysshe Shelley*, ed. Forman, vol. 6, pp. 381–406 (p. 396). See also *Prometheus Unbound*, I.163–65, where we read: 'Then, see those million worlds which burn and roll / Around us: their inhabitants beheld / My spherèd light wane in wide Heaven...'.

50 The first and only partial translation was contained in the volume *Kant's Cosmogony. As in his Essay on the Retardation of the Rotation of the Earth and his Natural History and Theory of the Heavens*, ed. and trans. by W. Hastie (Glasgow: James Maclehose and Sons, 1900); there have since been three further translations by Stanley Jaki (1981), Ian Johnston (2009) and Olaf Reinhardt (2012).

51 I have not discussed Bacon at length in my study, but should perhaps use this opportunity to

remained hotly debated in the nineteenth century. When Shelley writes '[m]illions and millions of suns are ranged around us, all attended by innumerable worlds, yet calm, regular, and harmonious, all keeping the paths of immutable necessity', he is of course not just reminding us of his endorsement of the philosophical notion of the harmony and necessity of the universe derived from Spinoza, Holbach and Godwin, but simultaneously documenting his familiarity with contemporary science, here specifically astronomy and cosmology. This preoccupation with science remained a constant in Shelley's life.

Already in the various notes to *Queen Mab* the fledgling poet and intellectual is keen to parade not just his extensive reading in the Greek and Latin classics and the seventeenth- and eighteenth-century *philosophes*, but also his modern scientific credentials. Among others he cites Laplace's *Système du monde*, whose 'harmonics' and celestial mechanics are also implied in the quotation above; the detailed scientific entry on 'Man' in Abraham Rees's *Cyclopaedia or, Universal Dictionary of Arts, Sciences, and Literature*; the equally fact-filled entry on 'Light' from William Nicholson's 1809 *British Encyclopedia or Dictionary of Arts and Sciences*, which is the source of most of the details about stars in the quotation above (although the distance of Sirius is miscited, Nicholson giving the distance as two trillion English miles; however, the distance given by Shelley is closer to fact than Nicholson's, although I have as yet not been able to identify his source); and William Herschel's *'nebulae'* (by 1809 Herschel had discovered some 2,000 nebulae, so the information supplied in the edition of Nicholson's *Cyclopedia* used by Shelley). He similarly cites various recent medical and anatomical tracts and treatises, among them William Lambe's 'Report on Cancer' (i.e., *Reports on the Effects of a Peculiar Regimen on Scirrhous Tumours and Cancerous Ulcers*, 1809); Pierre Jean Cabanis's *Rapports du physique et du moral de l'homme* (*On the Relations between the Physical and Moral Aspects of Man*, 1802); Georges Cuvier's *Leçons d'Anatomie Comparée* (*Lessons on Comparative Anatomy*), specifically Volume III of 1805; John Frank Newton's *The Return to Nature or, A Defence of the Vegetable Regimen* of 1811; and 'Trotter on the Nervous Temperament' (i.e., Thomas Trotter, *A View of the Nervous Temperament*, 1807).

link the developments I have been discussing with his name; the citation here stems from Karl Popper who, in his article 'Science: Problems, Aims, Responsibilities', provides the following useful account of Bacon's importance: 'The movement inaugurated by Bacon was a religious or semi-religious movement, and Bacon was the prophet of the secularized religion of science. He replaced the name "God" by the name "Nature", but he left almost everything else unchanged. Theology, the science of God, was replaced by the science of Nature. The laws of God were replaced by the laws of Nature. God's power was replaced by the forces of Nature. And at a later date, God's design and God's judgments were replaced by scientific determinism, and the book of fate by the predictability of Nature. In short, God's omnipotence and omniscience were replaced by the omnipotence of nature and by the virtual omniscience of natural science. It was also in this period that the phrase "*deus sive natura*" — which may perhaps be translated as "God, or what is the same, nature" — was almost casually used by the physicist and philosopher Spinoza. [...] Bacon was the prophet, the great inspirer of the new religion of science, but he was not a scientist. Yet the inspiration and the influence of his new theology of nature were at least as great and as lasting as those of his contemporary Galileo, who might be described as the true founder of modern experimental science'; cited from Karl Popper, *The Myth of the Framework. In Defence of Science and Rationality* (London: Routledge, 1994), pp. 82–111 (pp. 82–83).

A decade on and just months before his death, in April 1822, a dealer in foreign books in Paris sent Shelley a consignment of books to Italy that was accompanied by the following letter:

> Sir,
> We have the honor to acknowledge the receipt of your letter 2d inst. and to inform you of our having forwarded on the 17th inst. the work of 'Laplace essai sur les probabilités', of 'Cuvier' the only two volumes as yet published, and 'Dabuisson's Géognosie' which is considered the best work of its kind. [...] Herschel's Work notwithstanding all the enquiries we made could not be procured.[52]

Laplace's *Essai philosophique sur les probabilités* (*Philosophical Essay on Probabilities*) was published 1814, but Shelley also knew his earlier work well, writing to his close friend Thomas Jefferson Hogg in 1813: 'I am now studying Laplace, *Système du Monde*, and am determined not to relax until I have attained considerable proficiency in the physical sciences'.[53] The two volumes of Cuvier mentioned here probably refer to the first two volumes of Cuvier's *Recueil des éloges historiques* (*A Miscellany of Historical Eulogies*, published in 1819, with the third volume published in 1827) rather than his *Recherches sur les ossemens fossiles* (*Studies on Fossil Bones*),[54] the first three volumes of which had been printed by Deterville, the publisher of Grainville's *Le Dernier Homme*, in 1812. The reference to 'Dabuisson's *Géognosie*' relates to the geognost Jean François d'Aubuisson de Voisins's *Traité de Géognosie* (*Treatise on Geognosy*), published in Strasbourg and Paris in 1819; this thousand-page two-volume work by the close friend and collaborator of the German Neptunist geologist Abraham Gottlob Werner contained an up-to-date compendium of current geological and mineralogical knowledge. By ordering these works in French Shelley was clearly trying to keep himself *au courant* with the most recent scientific findings in these disciplines coming out of the world's then capital of science, Paris. (That Herschel's work could not be obtained should come as no surprise, incidentally; the editor of Shelley's letters, Frederick L. Jones, observes that Herschel did not publish books but only papers in the scientific journal *Philosophical Transactions*.)[55]

Shelley's life-long interest in the natural and medical sciences has been much commented on by scholars as an important background to his work. From it emerged his belief in the immanence of the natural world which in so many ways mirrors that of a modern secular scientist. In this context it is worth reminding ourselves of the passage by Charles Taylor I cited in Chapter Two in which he

---

52 *The Letters of Percy Bysshe Shelley*, ed. Jones, vol. 2, p. 458 (Appendix V): Letter No. 2: A. & W. Galignani to Shelley, Librairie Française et Etrangère, Paris, 25 April 1822.

53 *The Letters of Percy Bysshe Shelley*, ed. Jones, vol. 1, p. 380.

54 William D. Brewer in his study *The Shelley–Byron Conversation* (Gainesville: The University of Florida Press, 1994) mistakenly speaks of the 'first two volumes of Cuvier's *Recherches*...' (p. 34) 'sent for and received' by Shelley. The letter here specifically states 'of "Cuvier" the only two volumes as yet published'; however, all four volumes of the *Recherches* had been published before 1822, namely 1812. This statement can apply only to the *Recueil des éloges historiques*, of which only the first two volumes had appeared by 1822.

55 *The Letters of Percy Bysshe Shelley*, ed. Jones, vol. 1, p. 380.

speaks of the shift toward immanence that underlay the turn from religion to science taking place between the seventeenth and nineteenth century. If it was the deist Hume and the atheist Holbach in the 1740s to 1770s who in theory — taking the scientific tenets of Bacon and Newton to their logical conclusion — buttressed the denial of 'any form of interpenetration between the things of Nature, on the one hand, and "the supernatural" on the other, be this understood in terms of the one transcendent God, or of Gods or spirits, or magic forces, or whatever' (as Taylor phrased it), it was not until a generation later that science in practice — the science that Shelley after 1810 was responding to — began parting company with religion to a degree that would in due course make it the secular reserve as which many see it today. This trajectory of divergence would, by the late nineteenth century, inspire secularists like John William Draper, a founder of the New York University School of Medicine, and Andrew Dickson White, the co-founder of Cornell University, to posit an inborn 'Conflict' or 'Warfare' between religion and science (see Draper's 1874 *History of the Conflict between Religion and Science* and White's 1896 *A History of the Warfare of Science with Theology in Christendom*). This position found its ultimate expression in the twentieth century's 'Secularization Paradigm' according to which the progress of modernity is linked ineluctably to the decline of religion. And yet, if for much of the twentieth century many saw secularization as an inevitable and unstoppable process, the recent global resurgence of religious fundamentalisms has occasioned not just the emergence of the term 'post-secularism' but also a major reconsideration of the relationship between science and religion. Christian scholars and scientists in particular — and I am speaking here not of the kind of fundamentalist evangelicals who still today advocate a Mosaic chronology and literalist reading of the Bible, or a watered down version thereof — have, over recent decades, been increasingly making the case that religion and science are not axiomatically at loggerheads. The theistic philosopher and Greek orthodox natural theologian Richard Swinburne, who served as Nolloth Professor of the Philosophy of the Christian Religion at the University of Oxford from 1985 to 2002, the University of Notre Dame analytic philosopher Alvin Plantinga, the philosopher of religion William Lane Craig, the University of Notre Dame historian Brad S. Gregory, and Rodney Holder, the astrophysics-trained former course director at the Faraday Institute at St Edmund's College, Cambridge — to name just some of the leading Christian academic spokespersons — all hold by and large, in Gregory's words, that 'all scientific findings and all *possible* scientific findings are compatible with the mysterious, providential influence of God throughout the natural world as understood in traditional Christian theology'; he continues: 'the natural world investigated by science is nothing other than God's creation, and all scientific findings and theories disclose incrementally more and more about its intricate workings. The findings of science remain exactly the same, whether in particle physics, evolutionary biology, or anything else, but they are taken as the data for theological reflection'.[56]

56 Brad S. Gregory, 'No Room for God? History, Science, Metaphysics, and the Study of Religion', *History and Theory*, 47 (December 2008), 495–519, these quotations pp. 509 and 508. Although we

Most notably Craig and Holder have engaged in such scientific theological reflection, using Big Bang cosmology and the notion (and perceived necessity) of divine fine-tuning as the newest testing ground for the existence of God and proof of his natural dominion over the laws of physics. Craig notes in a 1990s 'debate' with the atheist Quentin Smith about the validity of the so-called Hartle-Hawking (HH) cosmological model and its efficacy as a proof, or disproof, of some god-like force, and the Christian God specifically:

> This, the HH model is in no wise incompatible with God's freely creating the universe [...]. There is no reason, apart from an anti-theological bias, to prefer the exorbitant ontology of the Many Worlds Interpretation over a theistic version of the Copenhagen Interpretation, which supplies a mathematically consistent picture of creation and enjoys the advantage of simplicity.[57]

Holder deploys a comparable technical-scientific argument in his 2013 book *Big Bang Big God. A Universe Designed for Life?* to argue that only a divinely fine-tuned cosmos can provide 'meaning and purpose' for our human existence; he concludes his volume with the words: 'My argument has been that the fine-tuning is best explained by Christian theism. It is an argument from nature to God, an exercise in "natural theology".'[58]

---

might be justified to some degree in calling Gregory's, Craig's, and Holder's interventions in the scientific debate about the origins of our universe a successful twenty-first-century attempt at the 'resynthesization' of science and theology, it strikes me nonetheless as baffling how these Christian scientists avoid addressing the crucial dilemma identified already by the German playwright, essayist and polemicist Gotthold Ephraim Lessing in his late eighteenth-century foundational critique of religion; rather than putting religion per se in doubt (Lessing was a deist), in his famous 'Ring Parable' in *Nathan the Wise* (1779) Lessing posed a question that was ultimately as unanswerable as unavoidable, namely which belief system should take priority, the Christian, the Muslim or the Jewish faith. God the Father may exist, Lessing tells us, but which is the true religion of his choice is altogether a different matter: no one can tell which of the three sons' rings in the parable is the true original. This issue seems non-existent for Craig, Gregory and Holder; once they have established that science cannot disprove the existence God ('The question about the possibility of miracles', writes Gregory, 'is therefore a function of whether such a God is real — a question the answer to which [...] lies by definition beyond the investigative methods of science'; 'No Room for God?', p. 510), and once they have proven that only an entity as omnipotent as God can have created our universe, each and all end up hailing the *Christian* God as *the one and only god* who could have effected this miracle; see as one specific instance Rodney Holder, *Big Bang Big God. A Universe Designed for Life?* (Oxford: Lion Hudson, 2013), p. 178.

57 William Lane Craig, 'Hartle-Hawking Cosmology and Atheism', *Analysis*, 57 (October 1997), 291–95 (p. 294). For the larger context and other debates between Craig and his various atheistic counterparts see: William Lane Craig, '"What Place, Then, for a Creator?" Hawking on God and Creation', *The British Journal for the Philosophy of Sciences*, 41 (December 1990), 473–91; Quentin Smith, 'Atheism, Theism and Big Bang Cosmology', *Australasian Journal of Philosophy*, 69 (1991), 48–66; David B. Myers, 'Exclusivism, Eternal Damnation, and the Problem of Evil: A Critique of Craig's Molinist Soteriological Theodicy', *Religious Studies*, 39 (December 2003), 407–19; William Lane Craig, 'Response to David Myers', *Religious Studies*, 39 (December 2003), 421–26; David B. Myers, 'Rejoinder to William Lane Craig', *Religious Studies*, 39 (December 2003), 427–30; William Lane Craig and Walter Sinnott-Armstrong, *God? A Debate between a Christian and an Atheist* (Oxford: Oxford University Press, 2004).

58 *Big Bang Big God*, pp. 8 and 177. Craig for his part claims that his *Kalam* cosmological argument functions as 'a successful piece of natural theology'; see his 'A Swift and Simple Refutation of the

There is in my opinion no qualitative distinction between Craig's and Holder's late twentieth-century and early twenty-first-century approach to the relationship of faith and science and that of the seventeenth-, eighteenth- and early nineteenth-century clergymen and Christian naturalists who felt it necessary to adapt their Christian worldview successively to Newtonian physics, Buffonian natural history, Laplacian cosmology or even Darwinian evolutionary theory, whether that of Erasmus Darwin, Charles Darwin's grandfather to whom Percy Shelley refers in his 'Preface' to the 1818 first edition of Mary's novel *Frankenstein*, or that of Charles Darwin himself. Then as now natural theologians sought to use the most recent scientific findings to enhance their appreciation of the *Wisdom of God Manifested in the Works of Creation* (1691), so the title of a famous study by the Christian parson, physico-theological naturalist, and empirical taxonomist John Ray, a precursor to the English Anglican apologist William Paley, whose work I touched upon briefly in Chapter Two and who was the foremost natural theologian of Shelley's time.

Paley intended his theistic 'Natural Theology' to compete with the Enlightenment's more denomination-neutral deistic 'religion of reason', as exemplified by Kant's concept of *Vernunftreligion* (religion of reason) and Paine's book *The Age of Reason*. However, where their 'religion of reason' does away with God as an explanatory trope for the physical world we live in today, retaining him only as the numinous 'Creator' and First Cause at the very beginning of time, Paley's version of 'Natural Theology' sees a personal God not just as the ultimate *causa prima* of all things, but also — literally — as a personal agent, as 'someone' responsible for the micro-design of our planet, in the past *as well as in the present* (as do Paley's direct heirs Craig, Holder and Gregory in our own time). Paley's most celebrated and at the time immensely influential works were *A View of the Evidences of Christianity*, published in 1794 with numerous editions during the following century, and *Natural Theology: or, Evidences of the Existence and Attributes of the Deity, Collected from the Appearance of Nature*, published in 1802, again with equally numerous later editions. Paley famously used the first two chapters of the latter work to expand the deists's clockmaker simile into his own theistic watchmaker analogy: his argument throughout *Natural Theology* is premised on the divine logicality and necessity of all that has been created by a God conceived as 'supreme intelligent Author',[59] an author indeed who continues to be engaged in micro-managing his creation on a daily basis. Yet whatever else Paley's theological objectives might have been, it is certainly not amiss to regard his Natural Theology as an attempt to reconcile the Christian belief system, as well as the notion of a Creation of the universe through a personal God, with the unprecedented expansion of knowledge that science was generating during his time. Paley then and Craig and Holder now are thus attempting to achieve precisely what the materialist philosopher Holbach had argued should be impossible, or unworkable, namely the fusing of (Christian) religion and modern science. Natural Theology of the kind promoted

---

Kalam Cosmological Argument?', *Religious Studies*, 35 (March 1999), 69–72 (p. 69).

59 *Natural Theology; or, Evidences of the Existence and Attributes of The Deity* (Philadelphia: John Morgan, 1802), p. 395.

by Paley, Craig and Holder aims of course not just to confirm with the means of science how marvelously complex and unfathomable the world *really* is, a fact spotlighted by the purported 'magnificence of [God's] operations'; it does so with the aim specifically also to furnish the 'meaning and purpose' that pure scientific materialism allegedly cannot supply. Hence Gregory's distinction between 'science' (which he considers open to a belief in a Christian God) and a pejoratively qualified 'ideological scientism', which Gregory claims is nothing more than 'an ideological imperialism masquerading as an intellectual inevitability' and whose 'secularized academy' practitioner (disapprovingly called 'scientistic ideologue') 'ignores the compatibility of a traditional Christian view of God with scientific findings'.[60] (That his own position might be no less 'ideological' than that of the academy practitioners he so takes to task is conveniently ignored.) Two hundred years earlier Paley similarly engaged expressly, and no less judgmentally, with what he sets up as the atheists' 'fixed' materialistic notion of natural necessity, which he opposed to a more malleable and accommodating divine necessity. In Chapter XII of *Natural Theology*, entitled 'Comparative Anatomy', a subject close also to Shelley's heart, Paley thus expounds:

> Whenever we find a general plan pursued, yet with such variations in it, as are, in each case, required by the particular exigency of the subject to which it is applied, we possess, in such plan and such adaptation, the strongest evidence, that can be afforded, of intelligence and design; an evidence, which the most completely excludes every other hypothesis. If the general plan proceeded from any fixed necessity in the nature of things, how could it accommodate itself to the various wants and uses which it had to serve, under different circumstances, and on different occasions?[61]

One leading contemporary English proponent of this hypothesis of a 'plan proceed[ing] from [a] fixed necessity in the nature of things' was Erasmus Darwin, Charles Darwin's grandfather mentioned above, who had died in 1802, the year in which Paley published his *Natural Theology*. Rather than cite Darwin directly I would like to use instead a satirical passage contained in Klingemann's 1805 *Nightwatches*, discussed in Chapter Three, in order to convey a flavour not just of how Erasmus Darwin's work was being received by his contemporaries, but also how his work was deployed to ridicule contemporary mores; Klingemann's narrator Kreuzgang observes in his 'Prologue' on the 'Tragedy that is Humankind':

> Dr Darwin, whom I present here as my representative and attorney, maintains namely that Man as man owes his existence to a species of ape on the Mediterranean Sea and that the latter, merely by learning so to make use of their thumb muscle that thumb and fingertips touched, gradually acquired refined feelings, made the transition from this to concepts in following generations and finally donned the costume of judicious men, as we still see them now marching about daily in their court and other uniforms. The whole matter has a lot to recommend it; for after millennia we still now and again find striking approximations and affinities in this regard; indeed, I believe I have

60 'No Room for God?', pp. 509, 500, 499, 515 and 517.
61 *Natural Theology*, p. 150; the following two quotations pp. 287 and 288.

observed that many respective and esteemed persons still have not yet learned how to make proper use of their thumb muscle, as, for example, a number of writers and people who presume to guide the pen; should I not be mistaken in this, then that speaks very much for Darwin. On the other hand, we also find a number of feelings and agilities in the ape which obviously slipped from us during the *salto mortale* to man; thus, for example, an ape mother even today loves her children more than many a prince's mother.

[Doktor Darwin, den ich hier als meinen Stellvertreter und Anwald aufführe, behauptet nämlich, daß der Mensch als Mensch einer Affenart am mittelländischen Meere sein Dasein verdanke, und daß diese blos dadurch daß sie sich ihres Daumenmuskels so bediente lernte, daß Daumen und Fingerspitzen sich berührten, sich allmählig ein verfeinertes Gefühl verschaffte, von diesem in den folgenden Generationen zu Begriffen überging und sich zulezt zu verständigen Menschen einkleidete, wie wir sie jezt noch täglich in Hof- und anderen Uniformen einherschreiten sehen. Das Ganze hat sehr viel für sich; finden wir doch nach Jahrtausenden noch hin und wieder auffallende Annäherungen und Verwandschaften in dieser Rüksicht, ja ich glaube bemerkt zu haben, daß manche respektive und geschäzte Personen sich ihres Daumenmuskels noch jezt nicht gehörig bedienen lernten, wie z. B. manche Schriftsteller und Leute die die Feder führen wollen; sollte ich darin nicht irren, so spricht das sehr für Darwin. Auf der andern Seite finden wir auch manche Gefühle und Geschicklichkeiten in dem Affen, die uns offenbar bei dem salto mortale zum Menschen entfallen sind, so liebt z. B. eine Affenmutter noch heutiges Tages ihre Kinder mehr als manche Fürstenmutter.][62]

Interestingly, when Paley cites Erasmus Darwin's evolutionary hypothesis he hesitates to describe it as out-and-out atheistic; he reflects rather:

Although I have introduced the mention of this theory into this place, I am unwilling to give to it the name of an atheistic scheme, for two reasons: first, because, so far as I am able to understand it, the original propensities and the numberless varieties of them, (so different, in this respect, from the laws of mechanical nature, which are few and simple,) are, in the plan itself, attributed to the ordination and appointment of an intelligent and designing Creator: secondly, because, likewise, that large postulatum, which is all along assumed and presupposed, the faculty in living bodies of producing other bodies organized like themselves, seems to be referred to the same cause; at least is not attempted to be accounted for by any other. In one important respect, however, the theory before us coincides with atheistic systems, viz. in that, in the formation of plants and animals, in the structure and use of their parts, it does away final causes. Instead of the parts of a plant or animal, or the particular structure of the parts, having been intended for the action or the use to which we see them applied; according to this theory, they have themselves grown out of that action, sprung from that use. The theory therefore dispenses with that which we insist upon, the necessity, in each particular case, of an intelligent, designing mind, for the contriving and determining of the forms which organized bodies bear.[63]

---

62 *The Night Watches of Bonaventura*, ed. Gillespie, p. 137 (*Nachtwachen des Bonaventura*, ed. Schillemeit, p. 70; all spellings as in source).
63 *Natural Theology*, pp. 321–22.

In short, Paley tells us, the deist believes in a Creator God and hence cannot be designated an atheist, but his God is one who has stepped back and away from his creation, leaving the world to its own devices, which is nature's necessity (see also my related discussion in Chapter Two). Paley by contrast sees God as persistently engaged in micro-managing the universe he has created (in this his *Natural Theology* serves neatly as an early nineteenth-century blueprint of present-day designer fundamentalism). However, especially in his earlier *A View of the Evidences of Christianity*, Paley takes this one step further; in the 'Conclusion' to this tract he offers the following extension of his argument (an extension to which we also find Craig, Holder and Gregory resorting in our own time):

> Let the constant recurrence to our observation, of contrivance, design, and wisdom in the works of nature, once fix upon our minds the belief of a God, and after that all is easy. In the counsels of a being, possessed of the power and disposition, which the Creator of the universe must possess, it is not improbable that there should be a future state; it is not improbable that we should be acquainted with it. A future state rectifies every thing.[64]

Using a rhetorical sleight of hand ('after that all is easy'), Paley takes the liberty to reintroduce not just Christian Revelation into the workings of nature ('the counsels of [...] the Creator') but also a future state of rewards and punishments ('a future state rectifies every thing').

This is where Shelley drew the line. Shelley was thoroughly familiar with both of Paley's treatises and engaged with them directly and critically especially in the footnote apparatus to *A Refutation of Deism*. Here, as elsewhere in his religious essays, Shelley specifically rejects any endorsement of 'a future state' in which 'rewards' are doled out to the faithful and 'punishments' meted out to all others. Even granting that Shelley may not have been as pronounced an atheist as his early writings seem to suggest, one thing is certain: he militantly rejected any belief system that advocated a supernatural agency seeking retribution for sins committed during our life-time, including especially the sin of religious infidelity. The Shelley-scholar Desmond King-Hele once summed it up thus: Shelley 'reserves his fiercest fire for two targets, power-seeking priests and the concept of a revengeful anthropomorphic God'.[65] Identifying neither with the natural theologian nor the theologian of reason, but rather with 'the natural philosopher' as which he casts himself, Shelley states unambiguously in his undated essay 'On a Future State' (with a stress on the opening 'if'):

> If it be proved that the world is ruled by a Divine Power, no inference necessarily can be drawn from that circumstance in favour of a future state. It has been asserted, indeed, that as goodness and justice are to be numbered among the attributes of the Deity, he will undoubtedly compensate the virtuous

---

64 *A View of the Evidences of Christianity* (Boston: I. Thomas and E. T. Andrews, 1803), pp. 317–18. Engaging with David Hume's seminal views on miracles set forth in the famous Chapter X 'Of Miracles' of his *Enquiries Concerning the Human Understanding*, Paley states even more pithily in his 'Preparatory Considerations': 'In a word, once believe that there is a God, and miracles are not incredible' (*A View of the Evidences of Christianity*, p. 13).

65 *Shelley. His Thought and Work* (London: Macmillan, 1960), p. 34.

> who suffer during life, and that he will make every sensitive being, who does not deserve punishment, happy for ever. But this view of the subject, which it would be tedious as well as superfluous to develope [sic] and expose, satisfies no person, and cuts the knot which we now seek to untie. Moreover, should it be proved, on the other hand, that the mysterious principle which regulates the proceedings of the universe, is neither intelligent nor sensitive, yet it is not an inconsistency to suppose at the same time, that the animating power survives the body which it has animated, by laws as independent of any supernatural agent as those through which it first became united with it. Nor, if a future state be clearly proved, does it follow that it will be a state of punishment or reward.[66]

Shelley leaves no doubt that for him no Christian God exists who metes out rewards and punishments; at the same time, in another essay fragment entitled 'On Life', he is prepared to admit that a purely materialist view of the universe is unsatisfactory, conceding:

> How vain is it to think that words can penetrate the mystery of our being! [...] For what are we? Whence do we come? and whither do we go? Is birth the commencement, is death the conclusion of our being? What is birth and death? [...] The shocking absurdities of the popular philosophy of mind and matter, its fatal consequences in morals, and their violent dogmatism concerning the source of all things, had early conducted me to materialism. This materialism is a seducing system to young and superficial minds. [...] But I was discontented with such a view of things as it afforded; man is a being of high aspirations, 'looking both before and after', whose 'thoughts wander through eternity', disclaiming alliance with transience and decay; incapable of imaging to himself annihilation; existing but in the future and the past; being, not what he is, but what he has been and shall be. Whatever may be his true and final destination, there is a spirit within him at enmity with nothingness and dissolution.[67]

Although here as elsewhere in his religious essays Shelley leaves open what the precise nature of such a future state might be,[68] the implication is clear, namely that 'the mysterious principle which regulates the proceedings of the universe' would indeed seem to allow some form of life force, call it mind, spirit or soul, to

---

66 *The Works of Percy Bysshe Shelley*, ed. Forman, vol. 6, pp. 271–80 (pp. 274–75).
67 *The Works of Percy Bysshe Shelley*, ed. Forman, vol. 6, pp. 255–63 (pp. 259–60).
68 See also the following passage from an early letter of Shelley's to Elizabeth Hitchener of 24 November 1811 in which Shelley is clearly contemplating the existence of some form of animated universal soul: 'You talk of a future state [...]. It seems to me that everything lives again. What is the soul? Look at yonder flower. The blast of the north sweeps it from the earth; it withers beneath the breath of the destroyer. Yet that flower hath a soul: for what is soul but that which makes an organized being to be what it is, without which it would not be so? On this hypothesis must not that (the soul) without which a flower cannot be a flower exist, when the earthly flower hath perished? Yet where does it exist — in what state of being? Have not flowers also some end which nature destines their being able to answer? [...] I will say, then, that all nature is animated; that microscopic vision, as it has discovered to us millions of animated beings whose pursuits and passions are as eagerly followed as our own, so might it, if extended, find that nature itself was but a mass of organized animation. [...] Perhaps the animative intellect of all this is in constant rotation of change: perhaps a future state is no other than a different mode of terrestrial existence to which we have fitted ourselves in *this* mode' (*The Complete Works of Percy Bysshe Shelley*, ed. Dole, vol. 8, pp. 5–6).

recirculate after death.[69] The after-life condition of Nothingness that the German atheist Heydenreich seemed happy to reconcile himself with was unacceptable to Shelley. Mary Shelley for her part always assumed that her husband believed in some form of afterlife (as she did herself), yet she too is clear that his belief was not Christian in outlook. She writes, in the 'Preface' to her 1840 edition of Percy Shelley's *Essays, Letters from Abroad, Translations and Fragments*:

> In this portion of his Essay he gives us only that view of a future state which is to be derived from reasoning and analogy. It is not to be supposed that a mind so full of vast ideas concerning the universe [...] should be content with a mere logical view of that which even in religion is a mystery and wonder. [...] he assuredly believed that hereafter, as now, he would form a portion of that whole.[70]

She adds, expressing her own heartfelt hope that she would one day be reunited with her spouse in afterlife:

> To me, death appears to be the gate of life; but my hopes of a hereafter would be pale and drooping, did I not expect to find that most perfect and beloved specimen of humanity on the other shore; and my belief is that spiritual improvement in this life prepares the way to a higher existence.

If Percy Shelley might have agreed with Paley that some form of supreme power, or 'great Being', afforded the possibility of an afterlife, he certainly disagreed with the Natural Theologian on the shape this afterlife will take. Despite his avowed endeavour to take contemporary science into account, Paley never relinquished his belief in Christian Revelation: 'The true Theist', he professed in the 'Conclusion' to *Natural Theology*,

> will be the first to listen to *any* credible communication of divine knowledge. Nothing he has learnt from Natural Theology, will diminish his desire of further instruction [...]. His inward veneration of this great Being will incline him to attend with the utmost seriousness, not only to all that can be discovered concerning him by researches into nature, but to all that is taught by revelation. Which gives reasonable proof of having proceeded from him. But, above every other article of revealed religion, does the anterior belief of a Deity, bear with the strongest force, upon that grand point, which gives indeed interest and importance to all the rest — the resurrection of the human dead.[71]

---

69 That Shelley's crucial 'dilemma' and 'polarized impulse' (p. 11) was his being pulled in two directions, with his rationalism demanding the rejection of a Christian God alongside any notion of reward or punishment after death, whereas he emotionally did not want to give up faith in some form of spiritual immortality, is at the heart also of Earl S. Wasserman's argument in his *Shelley. A Critical Reading* (1971). Wasserman concludes: 'Shelley's two aspirations, then, are unrelated and have different roots. On the one side, he has rational confidence in a Spirit of Nature that, operating in the same manner on nature and man, can impel them interminably toward perfection; on the other, he aspires to a perfect eternal afterlife, sanctioned not by divine revelation and a transcendent deity but only by his feelings and wishes' (p. 4).

70 Mary Shelley, 'Preface', in Percy Bysshe Shelley, *Essays, Letters from Abroad, Translations and Fragments*, 2 vols (London: Edward Moxon, 1840), vol. 1, p. xiii; the following quotation vol. 1, p. xiv.

71 *Natural Theology*, p. 398.

In short, Paley envisions a concept of Natural Theology in which our planetary and human existence not just begins by divine fiat, but also ends by divine fiat in the Last Judgment as revealed by Scripture. Shelley by contrast gave himself over to a belief in a natural power that transcends all institutional and scriptural religion. (I will return to this later in this chapter.) Nonetheless, any disagreement over First Cause and Last Judgment notwithstanding, what Paley and Shelley had in common is that both sought to premise their arguments on the most advanced science of their day.

And yet, as Paley's case amply illustrates, even the best empirical science of its day will never be able to put off Christian apologists from conjuring up visions of apocalypse that are as wildly inventive as they are unempirical. This holds no less true for the early decades of the nineteenth century than it does for our own present. There is thus little of substance that differentiates Tim LaHaye and Jerry B. Jenkins's Christian fundamentalist *Left Behind* cycle of 1995 to 2004 from the Anglican reverend George Townsend's 1815 Christian epic of the Last Judgment; entitled *Armageddon* and written around the same time that Shelley was drafting his essay fragment 'On a Future State', Townsend's 'Poem in Twelve Books', of which only eight were ever published, was likewise left in a fragmentary state. Although Shelley and Townsend never knew one another's works (as far as we know), we do know that, by coincidence, Shelley's elder friend Byron had either seen parts of Townsend's work-in-progress or had heard details of it; he certainly comments on it in a letter to R. C. Dallas dated 27 August 1811 in which he remarks:

> There is a sucking epic poet at Granta, a Mr. Townsend, *protégé* of the late Cumberland. Did you ever hear of him and his *Armageddon*? I think his plan (the man I don't know) borders on the sublime: though, perhaps, the anticipation of the 'Last Day' (according to you Nazarenes) is a little too daring: at least, it looks like telling the Lord what he is to do, and might remind an ill-natured person of the line, 'And fools rush in where angels fear to tread'. But I don't mean to cavil, only other folks will, and he may bring all the lambs of Jacob Behmen [sic] about his ears. However, I hope he will bring it to a conclusion, though Milton is in his way.[72]

Unlike Franz von Sonnenberg's *Donatoa* and Jean-Baptiste Cousin de Grainville's *Le Dernier Homme*, Townsend's *Armageddon* does not detail the human pre-history leading up to the Last Judgment; it provides no rationale why the Last Judgment is unleashed, picking up like Edward Young's *A Poem on the Last Day* in medias res 'with a commission to the Angels to bear up the Inhabitants of Earth, and of the surrounding stars, to Armageddon, the seat of Judgment', as Book One's summary of the 'Argument' informs us.[73] I mention Townsend here less because his epic happens to fall neatly into the first paradigm of theistic apocalyptic epics discussed in Chapters One and Two than because it is the perfect literary complement of and counterpart to Paley's Natural Theology. Both Paley in his expository treatise

---

72 *The Works of Lord Byron*, new, revised, and enlarged edition: *Letters and Journals*, ed. by Rowland E. Prothero (London: John Murray, 1922), vol. 2, p. 9.

73 George Townsend, *Armageddon. A Poem in Twelve Books. The First Eight Books* (London: J. Hatchard, 1815), p. 4; the subsequent quotes pp. xiii, xvi–xvii, xvii–xviii and xx–xxiii.

and Townsend in literary form were responding to religion's predicament in the face of modern science not by rejecting science but by engaging with it. Townsend introduces science as a key frame of reference for his traditionalist religious epic already in the introduction to his work. Indeed, it is as if his statements on religion were intended as an explicit reciprocation to Shelley's unpublished essays on religion; thus Townsend notes:

> An opinion has of late years been silently gaining ground among many, who profess themselves the admirers of Science and Philosophy, that the Stars are boundless in their extent, and eternal in their duration; and the discoveries of the telescope have been supposed to support this opinion: but if the glorified body of the Messiah still exists in some remote part of the Universe, distinct from the stars, it is certain that the heavenly bodies cannot be continued to infinity; and if they are bounded on one side, they may be bounded on another. The hypothesis, therefore, that I have ventured to adopt from this supposition, is, that the whole space filled with Stars is inclosed by Heaven above, and by Hell beneath, and incircled from East to West, by the place appointed for the judgment of Mankind, the scene of the last contest between the powers of good and evil; to this ideal circumference I have appropriated the name of Armageddon.

A couple of pages later he reflects, taking issue with the likes of Fontenelle and Kant, as well as unbeknownst to him Shelley:

> When the mind was lost in the wide field of being, thus opening to its contemplation, another consideration forcibly arrested attention. He, who is the infinite Soul, and Lord of the Universe, having made nothing in vain, we may reasonably suppose, has not created the innumerable systems around us, to spangle the blue skies with barren grandeur: may we not therefore conjecture that every star and every planet are filled with beings, as much the objects of the love of the Deity, as the human race? God sees at one view, and governs by one exertion of his Power, the Zodiacs of other Clusters, and the Equators of other Systems: for what purpose then have the inhabitants of the Earth, an inferior planet to one of those stars, been so highly distinguished by Omnipotence, that for them the Messiah, the Creator, and Preserver of the World, should have become incarnate. Why is Man thus honored by the Deity? Why so elevated in the scale of Creation?'

For Townsend the answer to this question is reproachfully clear, whereas for Shelley it was not; Townsend's solution to the riddle does not speak for mankind:

> The cause assigned to solve this Phenomenon must be consistent both with reason, and Christianity: and I have ventured to suppose, that this planet is the only spot among the works of God degraded by moral evil; and that Revelation and an Atonement were necessary for Man alone. If he only, of all the Beings that crowd the world of stars, has sinned; how conspicuous is the divine Mercy; — how great the goodness of his Maker; — how well suited to his wants and infirmities the system of Christianity; — and how truly does Revelation promote the real happiness of the human race, wherever its holy influence has been imparted.

Of all the populations of all the worlds in the universe, only planet Earth's mankind has fallen foul of God's will, Townsend moralizes, a logic Shelley would have found not just objectionable, but also irrationally conceited.

Equally objectionable Shelley would have found the way in which Townsend characterizes time as subordinate to the Christian Deity's 'Eternity'; Townsend claims:

> After the Creation of Heaven, Hell, and Chaos, the defection that had been foreseen took place, and the followers of evil were consigned to the darkness prepared for them. In my endeavour to answer the question, what was the object of the Deity in thus creating the stars, I have adhered to the traditions of the Jews, and the inferences apparently deducible from Scripture: I hope I am sanctioned by these Guides in supposing, not only that the Earth, but the whole number of the Suns around it, were created and filled with Beings, to be received, after sufficient probation, into the presence of their Maker, in the room of the offending Angels [...]. When the object of the creation of the World of Stars is accomplished, there is no necessity for their continued existence: the Stars may be extinguished in utter darkness [...]. The splendor of the starry Heavens is eclipsed; and all the Suns, and constellations, inclosed by the wide circle of Armageddon rush together in inextricable confusion, forming a mass of fire on the central World, till nothing remain of the glories of the firmament: the beings who are saved rest in happiness; the condemned continue with the powers of evil, who are vanquished by Omnipotence, without hope or consolation; Chaos is commanded to resume its first seat, forming an impassable gulph between the realms of happiness and misery; the dispensations of Providence, that decreed the wonderful formation, preservation, and destruction of the stars, are completed, and Time is lost in Eternity.

'Time is lost in Eternity' is an apt condensation of the Christian view of what the apocalypse ultimately accomplishes, a view reiterated nearly verbatim by Grainville towards the end of *Le Dernier Homme* when he envisions how the Last Judgment will terminate 'the reign of time' by allowing a 'vista of eternity' to open up ('Le règne du temps est fini, les siècles éternels vont commencer'). As I mentioned in Chapter Two, it was precisely the Christian proclivity to subordinate physical natural time to religion's transcendent notion of a timeless eternity that Kant took such objection to in his 1794 essay 'The end of the world'. For Kant there can be no stepping outside of natural time, hence eternity is 'theoretically not comprehensible'; he writes: 'the representation of those last things which are supposed to come *after* the last day are to be regarded only as a way of making sensible this latter together with its moral consequences, which are otherwise not theoretically comprehensible to us' ('so muß die Vorstellung jener letzten Dinge, die *nach* dem jüngsten Tage kommen sollen, nur als eine Versinnlichung des letztern samt seinen moralischen, uns übrigens nicht theoretisch begreiflichen, Folgen angesehen werden').[74] But Shelley would not have needed to know Kant's 'The end of the world' to develop similar ideas, for the counter-Christian arguments that Kant's essay articulates were not unique to the German philosopher and were fast gaining ground among cognoscenti. For his part, Shelley simply upends the Christian privileging of eternity (Heaven) over time

---

74 'The end of all things', p. 222 ('Das Ende aller Dinge', pp. 176–77).

(Earth); in Act 3, Scene 1 of *Prometheus Unbound* Shelley forces the 'omnipotent' God Jupiter (alias the Christian God Almighty) to yield to Demogorgon, the spirit of Nature's time whose name is 'Eternity' (III.1, l. 52).

For Townsend time has been created by God and can hence be unmade by God and replaced by eternity; for Shelley time itself is eternal and can be neither created nor undone. Shelley's and Townsend's examples rightly remind us, as Martin Rudwick observes in a different context, that in conceptualizing and contrasting such notions as time and eternity it was 'not a case of "Religion versus Science"', or even God versus Nature, but rather a case 'of one religious view of the world [pitted] against another'; Rudwick explains:

> If some Christian (and Jewish) theists believed they had a stake in the short timescale, because it helped guarantee the doctrine of creation, deists and atheists often felt an equal stake in the doctrine of the uncreated eternity of the world. For many deists, eternity seemed appropriate to an almost impersonal 'Supreme Being', who (or which) presided over a perfect cosmos that ran forever in accordance with its own timeless natural laws. For atheists — a much more elusive breed in the eighteenth century — an eternal cosmos could seem the best guarantee of the absence of a creative design of any kind.[75]

The word 'eternity' was one of those distinctive semantic vessels employed on both sides of the discursive divide during this period; yet depending on where one stood it was invested with widely divergent connotations, with theist, deist and atheist each incommensurably projecting their particular brand of worldview onto it. For the one side eternity was a promise held out by an eternally existing God who had the power to rescind finite time and grant heavenly permanence to the human soul, for the other it signalled a promise of an infinite world eternally existing independent of God. Yet in his recent 2014 study *Earth's Deep History. How It Was Discovered and Why It Matters* Martin Rudwick also cautions that the 'apparent modernity' of this non-Christian brand of eternalism is 'deceptive and deeply misleading'; in fact, he stresses, 'a "young Earth" and an eternal one, which were the only two alternatives considered in the seventeenth century, were *equally un-modern*. Both assumed that human beings have always been and will always be essential to the universe'.[76] Whereas Christians believed that humans were the acme of God's Creation and placed on planet Earth on the sixth day, eternalists 'assumed that there had never been a time when the world was without human or at least rational life',[77] Rudwick observes and emphasizes that 'strong "ideological" issues were at stake on *both sides* of the argument'.[78] But what non-Christian 'eternalism did offer', Rudwick also informs us, was 'a radical alternative to what was then the culturally dominant picture of a probably brief and certainly finite universe', and it is this view, both with regard to the longevity and infinity of the universe as well as

---

75 *Bursting the Limits of Time*, p. 118.
76 *Earth's Deep History. How It Was Discovered and Why It Matters* (Chicago and London: The University of Chicago Press, 2014), pp. 27–28.
77 *Bursting the Limits of Time*, p. 118
78 *Earth's Deep History*, p. 28; the subsequent passage also p. 28.

to the longevity of mankind, to which Shelley seems to have subscribed.[79] We will see shortly how this eternalist worldview sedimented itself in his poetry, specifically in his poem 'Mont Blanc'.

Genesis, Geology and Deep Time

But what my discussion has also shown is that in the early-nineteenth-century 'debate', if that is the right word, the battle lines drawn were far less clear-cut than they were later made out to be; it was certainly not a divide between scientists-as-atheists and churchmen-as-theists. Indeed, we find as many scientists holding on to their Christian values and beliefs, when necessary modulating the biblical chronology to accord with modern scientific findings, as we find clergymen turning towards modern science to help them better to understand the nature of God's Creation. The Reverend William Buckland, professor of geology and mineralogy at the University of Oxford, and William Conybeare, vicar and founder of the Bristol Philosophical Institution, are perhaps the best-known examples of British Anglican churchmen doing what would become groundbreaking geological fossil research in order to prove the account given in Genesis of Noah's flood, but allowing for a more liberal and less literal reading of the Bible. As prominent early members of the British Geological Society in London in the 1820s, Buckland discovered and classified the first Megalosaurus fossil and Conybeare numerous forms of marine reptile fossils, including the Plesiosaurus. In 1820 Buckland tellingly published his 1819 inaugural lecture under the title *Vindiciae Geologiae; or the Connexion of Geology with Religion explained*; in 1836, in the 'Preface' to his equally tellingly entitled book *Geology and Mineralogy Considered with Reference to Natural Theology*, he responds thus to the debate raging between Cuvierians and Lamarckians:

> The second [subject of my book] relates to Theories which have been entertained respecting the Origins of the World; and the derivation of existing systems of organic Life, by an eternal succession, from preceding individuals of the same species; or by gradual transmutation of one species into another. I have endeavoured to show, that to all these Theories the phenomena of Geology are decidedly opposed.[80]

Using the fossil record to dismiss the competing theories promulgated both by 'atheists and polytheists', Buckland maintains with Paley that the complexity of the myriads of life forms found on our planet can only be a testament to the unrivalled and enduring 'intelligence and power' of God. The third subject of his book, he writes,

> extends into the Organic Remains of a former World the same kind of investigation, which Paley has pursued with so much success in his examination of the evidences of Design [...]. The myriads of petrified Remains which are disclosed by the researches of Geology all tend to prove, that our Planet has

---

79 So also Kenneth Neill Cameron, *The Young Shelley*, p. 248.
80 *Geology and Mineralogy Considered with Reference to Natural Theology* (London: William Pickering, 1836), p. vii; the following quotation pp. vii–viii.

been occupied in times preceding the Creation of the Human Race, by extinct species of Animals and Vegetables, made up, like living Organic Bodies, of 'Clusters of Contrivances', which demonstrate the exercise of stupendous Intelligence and Power. They further show that these extinct forms of Organic Life were so closely allied, by Unity in the principles of their construction, to Classes, Orders, and Families, which make up the existing Animal and Vegetable Kingdoms, that they not only afford an argument of surpassing force, against the doctrines of the Atheist and the Polytheist; but supply a chain of connected evidence, amounting to demonstration, of the continuous Being, and of many of the highest Attributes of the One Living and True God.

Because Buckland engaged directly in science as one of the leading geologists and palaeontologists of his day, his example perhaps more so than Paley's instantiates the degree of concord rather than discord that could be achieved between religion and science. Religion was not by definition a retardant to scientific progress, as Holbach had always insisted, quite to the contrary. Thinkers on *both* sides of the religious divide were equally interested in achieving a fuller understanding of the universe; whether the world existed by purely natural means — however conceived — or whether it had been created through an act of divine *fiat*, early nineteenth-century Christian scientists like Buckland and Conybeare ultimately pursued their goal with no less scientific rigour than their supposedly more heathen counterparts.

In their 2006 critical study of *Nineteenth-Century Religion and Literature*, Mark Knight and Emma Mason hence rightly propose, as one of their 'central arguments', that the nineteenth century is characterized by 'a continual slippage between the sacred and the secular'. Observing how '[t]heological debate was almost inseparable from philosophical, scientific, medical, historical, and political thought',[81] Knight and Mason are right to remind us that the interdependency and 'interlocked and reciprocally influential' nature of the secular and the sacred are easily overlooked when we look back on the period from a twenty-first-century European vantage point with its long-established scientific institutions and in many ways flourishing secularized everyday life. In the introduction to his Gifford Lectures, given at the University of Edinburgh in 1973–1974, Owen Chadwick, a former Regius Professor of Modern History in Cambridge and specialist in nineteenth-century British Christianity, likewise reminds us

> not [to] confuse secularization with the perpetual task of adjusting religious understanding of the world to new knowledge about the world. Older historians of the European intellect, like Lecky or J. B. Bury, doubted what I have just said. To them the progress of truth consisted in the light of science invading dark chambers inhabited by mysticism, until at last no darkness should be left. What I have called religious restatement they saw as a shrinking [of] religion into an ever smaller corner of the intellectual world. I doubt that way of stating the matter. But the underlying point — namely, that secularization and Christian restatement are connected — cannot be denied.[82]

---

81 *Nineteenth-Century Religion and Literature* (Oxford: Oxford University Press, 2006), p. 3.
82 *The Secularization of the European Mind in the Nineteenth Century* (The Gifford Lectures in the University of Edinburgh for 1973–1974) (Cambridge: Cambridge University Press, 1975), p. 15.

It seems, however, that both sides were equally involved in this process of restatement; just as the forces of secularization compelled Christian theologians and scientists to adapt their belief to the new scientific realities, the ideologies of the secularists were often molded — so the theory of secularization goes that is perhaps best represented by the philosophers of history Ernst Troeltsch and Karl Löwith — on the very (Christian) models that they sought to overturn, transforming the Christian notion of a providential-eschatological culmination of history into the — hardly less speculative — universalized idea of historical progress moving inexorably, albeit in some versions dialectically, towards the ideal of perfection, be it Hegel's absolute idea or Marx's state of communism. Thus for the German philosopher Odo Marquard the long history of philosophy is reduced to a form of 'indirect theology'.[83] Hans Blumenberg on the other hand cautions us nonetheless not to underestimate and undercut the autonomy and hence 'legitimacy' of the modern secular *Weltanschauung* by tracing its roots all too insistently and exclusively back to a Christian understanding of providence, thereby demoting our modern scientific worldview to an 'eschatology without God' ('Eschatologie ohne Gott').[84] Whether we regard secularization as a process of decline whereby religion in general and Christianity more specifically incrementally lose the authority to determine what and how we should believe and how we should conduct our lives, or as the process of separation of religious and public life, or as a transposition of transcendent religious beliefs into immanent philosophical or political ideologies, or finally as a desacralization and disenchantment of the world (or of course as all of the above),[85] secularization always entails 'restatement' in one form or another, both for believers as well as for those who reject religious belief.

The high degree to which such 'restatement' and the process of secularization are constitutively conjoined is also at the heart of the argument made in the earliest in-depth study of religion and geology in the first half of the nineteenth century; in his pioneering 1951 *Genesis and Geology. A Study in the Relation of Scientific Thought, Natural Theology, and Social Opinion in Great Britain, 1790–1850*, Charles Coulston Gillispie explores the at times fractious, at times cordial, but always fruitful relationship between theologians and naturalists working at the forefront of the scientific domain we today call geology. Surveying the genesis of geology Gillispie underscores how naturalists working in this area were, with only few exceptions, Christian in outlook, aiming in one way or another to square geology and Genesis. It was not a battle between science and religion, quite the reverse; Gillispie writes:

> The role of divine Providence in the course of nature was the central issue, to which the question of the relationship of scriptural history to natural history, while important, was subsidiary. The interpretative problems were not produced by the demands of theology against science. Instead, the fundamental

---

83 The words are Blumenberg's in his discussion of Marquard's concept of the philosophy of history; see *Die Legitimität der Neuzeit*, p. 68.

84 Blumenberg, *Die Legitimität der Neuzeit*, p. 22.

85 Some of this language is culled from Larry Shiner's six definitions of secularization in his article 'The Meanings of Secularization', in *International Yearbook for the Sociology of Religion*, 3 (1967), 51–62.

and continuing difficulty lay in the persistence of a quasi-theological frame of mind within science. From the publication of Hutton's *Theory of the Earth* in 1795, every interpretation which marked a definite step forward for the descriptive sciences touched off the same pattern of religious apprehension and disagreement among natural scientists. And after each successive retreat, providential empiricists took up positions on new ground, which their own researches were simultaneously cutting out from under them. [...] But it was never a black-and-white picture. The providentialists were themselves respectable and productive scientists. [...] The doctrine of final cause was attacked by no one.[86]

Certainly in the British Isles, albeit less so within continental science, the shift from natural philosophy to science during the first half of the nineteenth century — and hence from the traditional synchronic brand of Natural History to our modern diachronic conception of the history of nature — was not coterminous with a detachment from religion, scriptural or otherwise. From Priestley and Paley to Buckland and Conybeare, and even to Lyell and Darwin, God's act of Creation — what Gillispie here terms 'the doctrine of final cause' — was rarely put in doubt, and most definitely not explicitly. The question these scientists were all asking, whether from the evangelical Christian end of the scientific spectrum or from its more secular end, was how one got from Creation to the present shape of the Earth. Had God created once and let the world freewheel on in some uniformitarian drift, 'continuing its repetitive cycle of similar "worlds" from and to eternity',[87] with 'no vestige of a beginning, — no prospect of an end', as Hutton, Playfair and Lyell all held? Or had he continued to involve himself in the shaping of global geology via a sequence of such miraculous interventions as the Deluge and the wiping out of failed (now fossilized) species as well as the creation of new species, in particular, as most Christian scientists continued to believe, humankind some six thousand years ago? Of course, if that was the case, as Christian scientists assumed, then we also have sufficient cause to believe in the Supreme Lawgiver's power to give his son Christ to humankind in order to atone for their sins, which in turn justified a belief in the Second Coming and the Last Judgment. It ultimately all boiled down to the question of Divine Providence and design. As Buckland wrote in *Vindiciae Geologicae*:

> The evidences afforded by the sister sciences exhibit indeed the most admirable proofs of design and intelligence originally exerted at the Creation: but many who admit these proofs still doubt the continued superintendence of that Intelligence, maintaining that the system of the Universe is carried on by the force of the laws originally impressed on matter, without the necessity of fresh interference or continued supervision on the part of the Creator. Such an opinion [...] nowhere meets with a more direct and palpable refutation, than is afforded by the subservience of the present structure of the earth's surface to final causes; for that structure is evidently the result of many and

---

[86] Charles Coulson Gillispie, *Genesis and Geology: A Study in the Relation of Scientific Thought, Natural Theology, and Social Opinion in Great Britain, 1790–1850* (Cambridge, MA, and London: Harvard University Press, 1996 [first edition 1951]), pp. 220–21 and 226
[87] The formulation is Rudwick's from his *Earth's Deep History*, p. 104.

> violent convulsions subsequent to its original formation. When therefore we perceive that the secondary causes producing these convulsions have operated at successive periods, not blindly and at random, but with a direction to beneficial ends, we see at once the proofs of an overruling Intelligence continuing to superintend, direct, modify, and control the operations of the agents which he originally ordained.[88]

Buckland's referencing of Paley's Natural Theology and his notions of 'design' and divine intelligence serves to remind us that, just as Christian scientists like Buckland and Conybeare were seeking to adjust the findings of modern science to their vision of Natural Theology in that perpetual process of 'restatement' that Chadwick described, the poet Percy Shelley was using that selfsame scientific evidence to question the very fundamentals on which the edifice of Natural Theology was erected. As such, Paley (and his many heirs) and Shelley epitomize two exemplary but opposing responses to modern science.

The pace at which science was progressing was nowhere so palpable as in the field of geology, a discipline even whose name was still in flux, with Wernerians preferring to call it geognosy. It is here that the issues of temporalization, or *Verzeitlichung*, and 'the crisis of chronology' ('die Krise der Chronologie'), as Lepenies calls them in his history of Natural History during this period, cited at the beginning of this chapter, most tangibly came to a head. Initially, the fossil discoveries made by eighteenth-century Natural Historians were simply integrated into the Procrustes-bed of the Mosaic timescale; thus Camerarius argued in 1712 that God had created fossils in order to give the inside of the planet an appearance comparable to its outside.[89] By the early nineteenth century these makeshift explanatory models had lost credibility; it was becoming increasingly apparent that, as Lepenies writes, 'Cosmology and Genesis' could no longer be reconciled. But even then this divorce was a gradual process, and it was not until Charles Darwin in the mid- to late nineteenth century that a persuasive explanatory paradigm not just for evolution, but through evolution also for the existence of fossils was put forward.

The debate between those who advocated a traditionalist Christian and static view of Natural History, subjecting all natural processes to a Mosaic timeline and a fixed range of species, and those who were beginning to acknowledge Earth's deep history and even the possibility of historically shifting species was carried well beyond the confines of specialized science into the realms of pedagogy and everyday life by such Victorian popularizers of science as the British historian and contemporary of Percy Shelley's, Sharon Turner. Remembered mostly for his four-volume *History of the Anglo-Saxons*, which appeared 1799–1805, Turner was also a fervent Christian educator, who in 1832, a decade after Shelley's death, published an educational volume entitled *The Sacred History of the World, as displayed in the Creation and subsequent events to the Deluge, attempted to be philosophically considered, in a series of letters to a son*.

---

88 As cited by Gillispie, *Genesis and Geology*, pp. 105–06.
89 So described by Lepenies in *Das Ende der Naturgeschichte*, p. 42; the subsequent formulation p. 43.

Harking back in its title on the one hand to Thomas Burnet's *Sacred Theory of the Earth*, but on the other simultaneously placing itself in opposition to the more modern 'historical' genre promulgated by more secular eighteenth-century naturalists such as Buffon in his *Histoire et théorie de la terre* of 1749, Kant in his *Allgemeine Naturgeschichte und Theorie des Himmels* of 1755, and Hutton in his *Theory of the Earth* of 1788, Turner's orthodox Christian 'Sacred History' is remarkable for the way in which it allows us to observe how a scientifically knowledgeable Christian theist sought to engage the most up-to-date science in order to uphold and preserve the very worldview whose edifice this science was in the process of toppling. Indeed, Turner turns science's inability to provide a sufficiently convincing explanation of how the world evolved against itself so as to buttress his literalist reading of Genesis. Citing Paley's *Natural Theology* as his prime inspiration, Turner's goal is spelled out in the title and introduction, namely to propose a series of philosophically argued letters to 'the youthful inquirer' about God's design of the universe; 'philosophically', however, here means deploying a Creationist argument to combat the purportedly misguided teaching of contemporary science. The book was so successful (it appeared simultaneously in Britain and the United States in 1832 and had gone into eight editions by 1848) that Turner added a second volume in 1834 and a third in 1838.

The author starts by reclaiming for 'divine philosophy' its status as a form of 'reasoned' science: 'Divine philosophy', he writes,

> should be regarded as a science, and be treated as the physical sciences are; the facts which relate to it should be carefully searched for, and as carefully reasoned upon. We shall then find that it is truly a science, and the most exhilarating of all that we can select to be the subject of our pursuit. It has really all the characters of a science, and will be seen to be so, and will become more visibly such, in proportion as it is studied in this aspect, and in the same mode, and with the same caution, assiduity and judgment with which our analytical or chemical investigations are conducted.[90]

Turner's larger objective was *not* to fully reconcile religion and science from a Christian perspective, however — even if this is the impression he is keen to impart to his adolescent reader; rather, he is merely outwardly adopting a scientific guise in order more convincingly to disprove science's anti-scriptural claims. The method Turner adopts is to pepper his 'Letters' with detailed footnotes citing and discussing the most recent works by natural historians, geologists, botanists and zoologists, physicists and astronomers, pointing out their contradictions and inconsistencies, all of which he tells his adolescent audience can only be resolved by resorting to an explanatory model based on God's providence and design. Indeed, the impressive footnote apparatus documents nothing less than the current state of affairs in early nineteenth-century science, illustrating Turner's immense erudition if nothing else. The first footnote to Letter XIX in Volume Two, published in 1834, for instance

---

90 Sharon Turner, *The Sacred History of the World, as displayed in the Creation and subsequent events to the Deluge, attempted to be philosophically considered in a series of letters to a son*, vol. 2 (London: Longman, et al., 1834), Letter I, p. 9.

engages with the most recent theorems regarding geology, the age of planet Earth and the duration of humankind put forward by Cuvier (Turner cites his 'Fossil Bones, 4th edit. Engl. 1834'), the mineralogist Alexandre Brongniart (whose *Tableau des Terrains*, published 1829, Turner cites), and the entomologist and geologist Nérée Boubée (whose *Géologie populaire*, published 1833, is discussed in some detail). But all these books are contorted through Turner's Mosaic prism. Exploiting science's lacunae in order to corroborate the biblical account, Boubée is thus taken to task as follows for trying to extend the age of the Earth to 300,000 years:

> It has been inferred by some that there was no antediluvian race, because no fossil human bones of that antiquity have yet come to light; but their absence does not disprove the existence of mankind between the Creation and the Deluge; it only indicates that they were not living in those sites, where these strata have been examined, as there are now many parts of Asia, Africa and even America, without them. [...] No authenticated facts in geology carry the present mode and state of human society, beyond that period at which the Jewish history places the Deluge, from which the subsequent propagation of mankind began. [The appended footnote reads: 'Baron Cuvier's ideas coincide with this view. [...] Cuv. Foss. Bones, p. 78.'] Geology and this history are, therefore, not at variance on this great point. [...] If it were not on print before our eyes, could we have supposed, that in this sceptical age, men of science, men of knowledge and reasoning, and who desire to be respected also for their judgment, should seriously teach and write that our earth has been existing, not as Moses indicates, 6,000 years only; but 300,000.[91]

I have chosen this excerpt from the sections on geology because more than any other of the emerging sciences geology, together with evolutionary biology, was predestined to become the chief battleground in the clash between belief systems. The modern study of geology is premised on the notion of deep time, with planet Earth requiring — as we know today — billions of years to advance to its current state, with complex life forms on Earth — the subject of evolutionary biology — requiring many hundreds of millions of years to evolve (life on Earth is estimated to have begun some 3.5 billion years ago). But the notion of deep time has a surprisingly short lifespan, having come about as a concept in its modern sense only in the mid-eighteenth century, with the term itself being brought into circulation in English only in 1832 by Thomas Carlyle. Buffon was one of the first *savants* to have publicly advocated a much greater age of the Earth than the 6000 years endorsed by the Christian scriptural literalists; in a table published 1775, he puts the duration needed for the Earth to cool to its then current temperature at 74,832 years; he later increased this number to three, then to ten million years.[92] Unbeknownst to his fellow natural philosophers, Kant in 1755 had already spoken of millions of years for our planet to evolve; 'perhaps a number of millions of years and centuries has passed before the sphere of formed nature in which we find ourselves has grown to the perfection that now attends it' ('es ist vielleicht eine Reihe von Millionen

---

91 *The Sacred History of the World*, vol. 2, Letter XIX, pp. 351–54.
92 See Rudwick, *Bursting the Limits of Time*, pp. 128–29, where we also find a facsimile reproduction of Buffon's 1775 table.

Jahren und Jahrhunderten verflossen, ehe die Sphäre der gebildeten Natur, darin wir uns befinden, zu der Vollkommenheit gediehen ist, die ihr jetzt beiwohnet') are his words.[93] In the first 1788 version of his 'Theory of the Earth', Hutton for his part observed:

> Now, if we are to take the written history of man for the rule by which we should judge of the time when the species first began, that period would be but little removed from the present state of things. The Mosaic history places this beginning of man at no great distance; and there has not been found, in natural history, any document by which a high antiquity might be attributed to the human race. But this is not the case with regard to the inferior species of animals, particularly those which inhabit the ocean and its shores. We find in natural history monuments which prove that those animals had long existed; and we thus procure a measure for the computation of a period of time extremely remote, though far from being precisely ascertained.[94]

In contrast to Hutton, however, who supported an eternalistic 'uniformitarian' and 'steady-state model of the earth' that entailed an 'imperceptibly slow and unceasing displacement of continents and oceans around the globe',[95] Cuvier argued that only 'sudden and violent causes [could have] produced the [geological] formations we observe' today. Cuvier assumed that a number of convulsive geological upheavals or revolutions had occurred in our planet's history, propelling areas previously submerged under the oceans to the surface whilst simultaneously inundating other portions of our globe's surface. This theory helped to explain not just why beds of fossil shells could be found high in the Swiss Alps, but also allowed for the possibility that the most recent of these revolutions might have been the biblical Flood, which due to its recent occurrence became the only geological upheaval to impress itself on mankind's cultural memory. The fact that according to Cuvier a whole sequence of floods, with a regular alternation between seawater and freshwater periods, had occurred over the course of geological history did not deter Christian apologists like Cuvier's British editor Robert Jameson or Sharon Turner from (rightly, albeit with certain geohistorical qualifications) seeking in it *specific* confirmation that a deluge of biblical proportions had been a real historical event, but (wrongly) deducing from this the *general* validity and truth of Genesis and the Old Testament.

Cuvier is also credited with being the first geologist to provide a theoretical grounding for the notion that species could become extinct. Due to the catastrophic convulsions of our planet's surface 'whole races' must have been 'destroyed forever', Cuvier surmises, 'leaving only a few relics which the naturalist can scarcely recognize'.[96] Although this argument challenged the view of those Christian geologists who continued to hold that all species that God brought to life when he originally created the world must still exist in some corner of our globe, albeit perhaps still undetected by European scientists, Cuvier was, as Rudwick points

---

93 *Universal Natural History*, p. 266 (*Allgemeine Naturgeschichte und Theorie des Himmels*, p. 334).
94 'Theory of the Earth', in *Transactions of the Royal Society of Edinburgh*, vol. 1 (Edinburgh: J. Dickson, 1788), pp. 209–304 (p. 217).
95 Rudwick, *Bursting the Limits of Time*, p. 452; the following quotation also p. 452.
96 Cited from Gillispie, *Genesis and Geology*, p. 100.

out, by no means bent on fundamentally contesting the biblical account of Genesis, quite to the contrary; he merely claimed that '"geologically", fossil fish had preceded fossil mammals', some of which had been wiped out through the series of abrupt violent geological upheavals he assumed to have taken place. Because humans were missing from the fossil record, they must be considered 'the last and newest creatures', a species that had succeeded in surviving at least the last cataclysm which theistic interpreters of Cuvier's work like Jameson and Turner considered coincidental with the biblical Deluge. In other words, Rudwick continues, 'the fossil record conformed in broad outline to the Creation story in Genesis, provided one assumed that the biblical "days" were long stretches of time'.[97] Cuvier was in this regard a non-literal interpreter of the Mosaic account; he was not putting the Bible fundamentally in question, but rather was merely deploying science to set the record straight.

In line with the biblical account Cuvier also maintained the fixity of species, contrary to Cuvier's colleague Jean-Baptiste Lamarck, the French naturalist who was by that time advocating his theory of the spontaneous generation and subsequent transmutation of species. Rudwick explains: 'On the politically sensitive question of the timescale of geohistory, [Cuvier] steered a sober middle course between two extremes. He emphatically rejected the traditional short timescale of a few millennia, which was enjoying a popular revival in the wake of Napoleon's new pact with the Catholic church', and which, as Rudwick relates elsewhere, was epitomized by Chateaubriand's brand of biblical literalism in his *Génie du christianisme*, as it was in Britain by the likes of Turner. 'But he also rejected', Rudwick continues,

> the eternalism that Lamarck was continuing to propound, which was being exploited by the anti-religious party for equally ideological purposes. Cuvier's middle way was to claim, more scientifically, a vast but finite timescale for geohistory as a whole, but also to follow de Luc and Dolomieu in dating its most recent catastrophe to the dawn of human history, implicitly confirming the Flood story in Genesis and thereby linking geohistory to its human epilogue.[98]

Cuvier thus writes in his *Essay on the Theory of the Earth* (in Robert Jameson's 1817 translation):

> If the species have changed, as they [the Lamarckians] assume, we ought to find traces of this gradual modification. [...] and yet no such discovery has ever been made. Since the bowels of the earth have not preserved monuments of this strange genealogy, we have a right to conclude, That [sic] the ancient and now extinct species were as permanent in their forms and characters as those which exist at present; or at least, That [sic] the catastrophe which destroyed them did not leave sufficient time for the production of the changes that are alleged to have taken place.[99]

Many species of animals perished in this most recent of Earth's catastrophes, others

---

[97] Rudwick, *Bursting the Limits of Time*, p. 447.
[98] Ibid., pp. 647–48.
[99] *Essay on the Theory of the Earth*, ed. by Robert Jameson (Edinburgh: Blackwood, 1817), p. 115.

had perished in preceding revolutions, Cuvier believed, and it is for the fossils of these animal types that we accordingly find no correspondence among today's living species. Amazingly, the historian of biology Ernst Mayr remarks,

> neither Cuvier nor the great British geologists (including Lyell) of the first half of the nineteenth century drew the conclusion from this evidence, which to us seems so inescapable, that there was a continuing evolutionary change of these faunas. Instead, they maintained for another fifty years either that each fossil fauna was wiped out by a catastrophe, to be replaced through special creation by an entirely new fauna, or else that the extinction was more piecemeal, the replacement nevertheless being due to individual special creations. Origins rather than evolution remained the explanatory concept.[100]

Whereas Cuvier was mistaken about evolutionism and continued to advocate the immutability of species, albeit conceding that some species had become extinct due to our planet's geological revolutions, Lamarck for his part was mistaken in that he did not accept that species could become extinct, assuming instead a gradual adaptation of life forms over time. In Cuvier's opinion, however, even any slow transmutation must change a creature's anatomy away from its original viable state, ultimately making it unfit to survive.[101] Conversely, Lamarck, like many of his contemporaries, 'rejected the possibility of extinction as contrary to the fundamental character of nature's economy and could not conceive how it could ever happen naturally without human intervention', as Rudwick explains in *Bursting the Limits of Time*.[102] In *Earth's Deep History*, Rudwick reminds us that at that time

> the only well-documented cases of extinction, such as the famous flightless dodo on the Indian Ocean islands of Mauritius, were those due to recent *human* agency. And such doubts about the reality of extinction in nature were strongly reinforced by the gut feeling, as it were, that neither the caring providential God of Judeo-Christian theism, nor the almost impersonal Supreme Being of Enlightenment deism, would or could have allowed any created species to go extinct, the exception being due to the actions of sinful or at least careless human beings.[103]

And because, as Rudwick goes on to observe, Lamarck's

> work on mollusks convinced him, against his expectations, that not all fossil shells had exact 'analogues' among living species [...], so transmutation [...] became the only explanation of the *non*-identity of past and present that Lamarck could accept. [...] For if every organism was continually changing in

---

100 *The Growth of Biological Thought*, p. 320. I should perhaps add here that Michel Foucault, in the Cuvier-section of his *The Order of Things*, cited at the outset of this chapter, sees Cuvier in a rather different light; he makes the interesting observation that Cuvier's concept of comparative anatomy, despite the 'fixity' underlying it, is premised nonetheless on a notion of 'living historicity' rather than the stability of species that Foucault ascribes to the leading taxonomy of the Classical episteme, Linnaeus's *Systema Naturae*; see *The Order of Things*, pp. 263–79, especially p. 276.

101 See Rudwick, *Earth's Deep History*, p. 112; this point is also stressed by Gottfried Hofbauer, *Die geologische Revolution. Wie die Entdeckung der Erdgeschichte unser Denken veränderte* (Darmstadt: WBG, 2015), pp. 49 and 52.

102 *Bursting the Limits of Time*, pp. 390–91.

103 *Earth's Deep History*, p. 104.

form, albeit insensibly slowly, the apparent differences between fossil and living species could be due to the passage of time and change of environment; the supposedly 'lost' species could simply have changed in appearance. [...] This turned Cuvier's argument on its head: the greater the contrast between fossils and living forms, the more — according to Lamarck — it proved the ubiquity of transmutation in the organic world and the vast scale of time, rather than any catastrophic extinction.[104]

Despite their differences, Lamarck's and Cuvier's models of course had one very crucial premise in common, namely a reliance upon a modern concept of deep time — deep time alone could explain how the natural world could arrive at the shape it presents to us today, whether by way of natural transmutation or as a result of a sequence of catastrophic revolutions. Regardless of whether the world had come into existence by natural means or by divine fiat, fossils were recognized as holding a key role in determining how life had developed. And for that reason, Rudwick concludes, 'the question of extinction [became] central to any attempt to understand the deep past. This is why fossil bones, in particular, became such a focus of attention among naturalists in the years around 1800'.[105]

Interestingly, although the more conservative Christian literalists persisted in advocating an exclusively Mosaic explanation of our planet's genesis — among them even geologists like Granville Penn (*A Comparative Estimate of the Mineral and Mosaical Geologies*, 1822), George Bugg (*Scriptural Geology. Geological Phenomena Consistent Only with the Literal Interpretation of the Sacred Scriptures*, 1826–1827) and Andrew Ure (*New System of Geology, in which the Great Revolutions of the Earth and Animated Nature are reconciled at once to Modern Science and Sacred History*, 1829) — Rudwick remarks that for many Christian *savants* the extended timescale was no more problematic or troubling than for their atheistic contemporaries, not least because the more progressive biblical scholars themselves 'had recognized the ambiguity of the key word "day" in the Genesis narrative'; for these more open-minded and less literal Christian believers 'world history might be of much greater length than a few millennia without affecting the authority of the biblical text'.[106] So it is not surprising, Rudwick notes,

> that those who in the later eighteenth century began to take a very long timescale for granted were not criticized by church authorities, except occasionally and in very specific local circumstances (contrary to modern myths of universal conflict, repression, and persecution). What mattered far more, from a religious point of view, was that the finite 'createdness' of the whole universe should continue to be affirmed, against those who claimed it was eternal and therefore uncreated.

Nonetheless, even as people were beginning to absorb this novel notion of deep time into their personal belief systems, it remained a rather unsettling concept; the French geologist Nicolas Desmarest accordingly observed in 1803: 'The depth of the abyss of time [*l'abîme des tem[p]s*] into which our mind is [...] obliged to plunge seems

---

[104] *Bursting the Limits of Time*, pp. 390–91.
[105] *Earth's Deep History*, p. 104.
[106] Ibid., this and the following quote p. 100.

so immense, so little in accord with our way of thinking, that it is not surprising that most people are little inclined to believe in these revolutions, although they are confirmed by many monuments',[107] 'monuments' here meaning not just the various geological strata of deposits but also the fossilized remains of species within those deposits that *savants* like Cuvier had finally come to accept as extinct, including such newly discovered but clearly no longer extant species as the so-called Maastricht lizard or the ptero-dactyle. Deep time, deep space, the growing fossil record detailing the layering of Earth's history, including the possibility if not probability of the extinction of species, and the accelerating revolutions not just of civil society but also even of our planetary surface, were setting in motion a tectonic shift on a massive scale of the ways in which the world needed to be conceptualized — or rather reconceptualized — beyond the time-honoured modes of religious and philosophical understanding. As Reinhart Koselleck writes in an essay dealing with the concept and notion of modernity ('Neuzeit'):

> As long as one believed oneself to be living in the final epoch, the only new aspect of contemporaneity could be doomsday ['*der Jüngste Tag*', 'the Last Judgment'], putting an end to all previous time. '*Et ob hoc sancti saepe hoc tempus novissimum et finem saeculorum nominant.*' (*Because of this, holy men often call this age the last and the end of all ages.*) It was only when Christian eschatology shed its constant expectation of the imminent arrival of doomsday that a temporality could be revealed that would be open for the new and without limit. Until then, it had been a question of whether the End of the World would occur earlier than anticipated; now, calculations concerning the timing of doomsday shifted gradually into a receding distance, to a point where it was no longer a matter of controversy.
>
> [Solange man sich im letzten Zeitalter glaubte, konnte das wirklich Neue der Zeit nur der Jüngste Tag sein, der aller bisherigen Zeit ein Ende setzte. *Et ob hoc sancti saepe hoc tempus novissimum et finem saeculorum nominant*. Erst nachdem die christliche Enderwartung ihre stete Gegenwärtigkeit verlor, konnte eine Zeit erschlossen werden, die unbegrenzt und für das Neue offen wurde. Ging es bislang um die Frage, ob das Weltende allenfalls früher als vorgesehen oder erwartet eintreffen würde, so verschoben allmählich die Berechnungen den Jüngsten Tag in immer weitere Ferne, bis er gar nicht mehr zur Debatte stand.][108]

Of course, the progress of science was putting enormous pressure not just on theologians and philosophers, but also on the public at large. Anyone among the educated classes who took a serious interest in such sciences as geology, chemistry, biology, anthropology or zoology that were emerging from what was once Natural History must have felt compelled to rethink the relationship between religion, scripture and Revelation on the one hand and philosophy and science on the other. The need for 'restatement' that Owen Chadwick identified as key to the reformulation of the Christian way of thought in the nineteenth century was

---

107 Nicolas Desmarest, *Géographie physique*, vol. 2 (1803), pp. 536–37, cited by Rudwick in *Bursting the Limits of Time*, pp. 450–51.

108 Reinhart Koselleck, '"Neuzeit". Remarks on the Semantics of Modern Concepts of Movement', in *Futures Past*, pp. 222–54 (p. 232); *Vergangene Zukunft*, p. 315.

taking its toll on *all* members of society regardless of religious creed. And Percy Bysshe Shelley is a particularly instructive case in point because he is one of the few documentable atheists during this period in Britain. Shelley's religious writings — most of which, owing to their atheistic inclinations, were not published during his lifetime, and even once published were often neglected by scholars — show how a critically-minded member of the intelligentsia responded when faced with the rapid expansion of knowledge that the new sciences were affording. For him the case was clear-cut: Christianity was failing to deliver convincing answers to the questions raised by science and the empirical factual revelations supplied by such innovations as microscope and telescope, the two optical instruments which arguably best epitomize modern man's expanded access to the hitherto concealed microcosmic and macrocosmic dimensions of our universe.

A Mountain of Doubt: Mont Blanc's 'Silent Eloquence'

In the previous sections of this chapter a picture should have emerged of a gifted and enquiring young intellectual — Percy Bysshe Shelley — growing up in an era of unprecedented scientific expansion and religious reconfiguration, an era that grew out of as much as it followed on from the political turmoil and social upheaval brought on by Enlightenment philosophy, the French Revolution and the ensuing European wars which coincided with much of Shelley's life span. But as in the political and social arenas, progress in the domain of science too was neither uniform nor orderly: especially in geology, the science which at that time was beginning to model our modern notion of 'deep time', the leading scientists of Shelley's day were locked in at times fierce debate. Most prominently, of course, there was the disagreement between the Neptunists (including Werner in Germany and Jean-André de Luc in Switzerland and Britain) and the Vulcanists (most prominently James Hutton and John Playfair in Britain) — or between 'champions of water and fire as causal agents'[109] — over their competing models of how to explain geohistory in general and the formation of basalt in particular; Gillispie observes in *Genesis and Geology* that the polemic between Neptunists and Vulcanists reached its apogee in British publications precisely around 1812–1815, the very period in which Shelley intensified his scientific studies and embarked on his writing career.[110] As regards the scientific debate between Lamarckians and Cuvierians, whose theories clashed fundamentally as to how to interpret fossilized 'monuments' and what they told us about deep history and the development of our species, their quarrel was not to be resolved for another half century until the publication of Charles Darwin's work on evolution and natural selection.

Percy Shelley is such a useful case in point because he showcases how such rivalries about deep time and deep space provided laymen like him interested in

---

109 Rudwick, *Bursting the Limits of Time*, p. 94.

110 I am indebted to Nigel Leask for this reference; see his article 'Mont Blanc's Mysterious Voice: Shelley and Huttonian Earth Science', in *The Third Culture: Literature and Science*, ed. by Elinor Shaffer (Berlin and New York: de Gruyter, 1998), pp. 182–203, especially p. 193.

scientific matters a certain latitude to engage creatively with their philosophical and religious ramifications. An illuminating instance is the note attached to 'Section I' of *Queen Mab* that I cited earlier in this chapter in which we saw an awe-struck Shelley ruminating in the vein of Fontenelle on the plurality of worlds and the immensity of space; following its opening locution, 'The plurality of worlds, — the indefinite immensity of the universe is a most awful subject of contemplation [...]. The nearest of the fixed stars is inconceivably distant from the Earth', I omitted a section in my original quotation; this section contains a passage that delves directly into a critique of religion. It reads:

> He who rightly feels its mystery and grandeur, is in no danger of seduction from the falsehoods of religious systems, or of deifying the principle of the universe. It is impossible to believe that the Spirit that pervades this infinite machine, begat a son upon the body of a Jewish woman; or is angered at the consequences of that necessity, which is a synonym of itself. All that miserable tale of the Devil, and Eve, and an Intercessor, with the childish mummeries of the God of the Jews, is irreconcileable [sic] with the knowledge of the stars.[111]

It is only after this brief religious digression that Shelley embarked on those further scientific meditations on astronomy that I cited above. For him as for the majority of intellectuals of his age science and philosophy were intrinsically linked with religion. If the universe is truly unlimited in time and space, as Hutton, Herschel and Laplace were claiming in as many different ways, why should our solitary planet, not to mention our feeble species inhabiting it, be so unique and exceptional that a God, indeed any god, would want to reveal himself to us, Shelley asks. And if the human species is just one among innumerable intelligent forms of life, as Fontenelle, Kant, Diderot and many others were arguing, why should one (continue to) believe that the God of Christianity saw our own species as fit to be considered elect? And besides, as the materialist philosopher Holbach had intimated, what historical proof was there anyway for the divinity of the human 'intercessor' Jesus Christ? In the third 'Note' to Section VII of *Queen Mab*, Shelley — following in the footsteps of Holbach's *Histoire Critique de Jésus-Christ*, an anonymous work accessible to Shelley in the shape either of its 1799 translation into English (published under the work's French subtitle as *Ecce Homo*) or this translation's more recent 1813 reprint[112] — describes Christ in secular terms as 'a man of pure life, who desired to rescue his countrymen from the tyranny of their barbarous and degrading superstitions'; he continues:

> Jesus was sacrificed to the honour of that God with whom he was afterwards confounded. It is of importance, therefore, to distinguish between the pretended character of this being as the Son of God and the Saviour of the world, and his real character as a man, who, for a vain attempt to reform the world, paid the forfeit of his life to that overbearing tyranny which has since so long desolated the universe in his name. Whilst the one is a hypocritical demon, who announces himself as the God of compassion and peace, even whilst he

---

111 *Queen Mab*, p. 466.
112 That Shelley was influenced by Holbach's *Histoire Critique de Jésus-Christ* is also the opinion of Cameron in *The Young Shelley*, pp. 259 and 397.

> stretches forth his blood-red hand with the sword of discord to waste the earth [...]; the other stands in the foremost list of those true heroes, who have died in the glorious martyrdom of liberty [...]. The vulgar, ever in extremes, became persuaded that the crucifixion of Jesus was a supernatural event.[113]

Clearly, here as in his fragmentary 'Essay on Christianity', Shelley seeks to model Christ as 'first and foremost an ethical paragon',[114] as a mere mortal who, in Shelley's own words in the above quotation, becomes a martyr for freedom in his 'vain attempt to reform the world'. Moreover, taking his various cues from the likes of Holbach, but also poets such as the early Southey and Coleridge, Shelley recognizes in Christ not just a visionary human, but also a visionary philosopher and poet.[115] 'It is important to observe', he remarks,

> that the author of the Christian system had a conception widely differing from the gross imaginations of the vulgar relatively to the ruling Power of the universe. He everywhere represents this Power as something mysteriously and illimitably pervading the frame of things. [...] Jesus Christ has said no more than the most excellent philosophers have felt and expressed that virtue is its own reward. It is true that such an expression as he has used was prompted by the energy of genius, and was the overflowing enthusiasm of a poet; but it is not the less literally true [because] clearly repugnant to the mistaken conceptions of the multitude. God, it has been asserted, was contemplated by Jesus Christ as every poet and every philosopher must have contemplated that mysterious principle. He considered that venerable word to express the overruling Spirit of the collective energy of the moral and material world.[116]

It goes without saying that it was not just Jesus Christ who 'considered that venerable word [i.e., God] to express the overruling Spirit of the collective energy of the moral and material world', but Shelley too. It likewise goes without saying that in the same measure as the divine prophet Jesus Christ is here reduced to a worldly philosopher and poet, the worldly poet Percy Bysshe Shelley elevates himself to a prophet of all that is divine in nature; in *A Defence of Poetry*, poetry is accordingly defined as 'indeed something divine'.[117] And finally, it goes without saying, too, that Shelley is here conjuring up a vision of Jesus in his own image, a vision of a revolutionary who challenged orthodoxies and had to suffer the consequences for his refusal to compromise with authority.[118]

---

113 *Queen Mab*, pp. 507–08.

114 Scrivener, *Radical Shelley*, p. 95.

115 I should perhaps add here though that Shelley's assessment of Christ fluctuated considerably, as Cameron notes in *The Young Shelley*; at times his judgment is noticeably more 'sardonic and hostile' (p. 259). For Southey and Coleridge, see Martin Priestman, *Romantic Atheism*, p. 129.

116 'Essay on Christianity', in *The Works of Percy Bysshe Shelley*, ed. Forman, vol. 6, pp. 338–74 (pp. 341–43).

117 *A Defence of Poetry*, in *The Works of Percy Bysshe Shelley*, ed. Forman, vol. 7, pp. 97–144 (p. 136).

118 Some of these wordings I have taken from Timothy Webb, who in *Shelley. A Voice not Understood* (Manchester: Manchester University Press, 1977) rightly writes: 'Christ, then, was an important figure in Shelley's poetic world. On the one hand, he was a revolutionary hero who had challenged the prevailing orthodoxies and who had suffered death for his refusal to compromise with authority. In this way he provided Shelley with a powerful symbol both for the defiant revolutionary

The theme of an 'overruling Spirit of the collective energy of the moral and material world' or of a 'Power as something mysteriously and illimitably pervading the frame of things', as articulated in his 'Essay on Christianity', is not just at the heart of Shelley's religious essays. It is also at the core of his mid-period and late poetry, and arguably nowhere more so than in the two transitional poems 'Hymn to Intellectual Beauty' and 'Mont Blanc' which he conceived during the time that he was working on his various unpublished essays on religion, metaphysics and life. This period, comprising roughly the years 1815 and 1816, also encompassed the phase of his life in which he lived on Lake Geneva, touring its vicinity with Mary and her stepsister Claire as well as Lord Byron, Claire's lover at the time. If in his 'Essay on Christianity' we thus read 'There is a Power by which we are surrounded, like the atmosphere in which some motionless lyre is suspended, which visits with its breath our silent chords at will',[119] we find this echoed in the opening lines of 'Hymn to Intellectual Beauty', the earlier of these two poems, where we read:

> The awful shadow of some unseen Power
> Floats tho' unseen amongst us, — visiting
> This various world with as inconstant wing
> As summer winds that creep from flower to flower...[120]

As Cameron remarks in his discussion of 'Hymn to Intellectual Beauty' and 'Mont Blanc' in *Shelley. The Golden Years*, Shelley 'never defined this power — and indeed did not believe that its nature was known — but contented himself with equating it with "the collective energy of the moral and material world"'.[121] Harold Bloom, in his 1959 study *Shelley's Mythmaking*, sees in 'Mont Blanc' 'the beginning of Shelley's mature mythopoeia: his first statement (allied [...] with its complement in the almost simultaneously composed "Hymn to Intellectual Beauty") of what can be termed, almost precisely, a primal vision; that is, a strictly poetic attempt to compete with religion and philosophy as a coherent presenter of ultimate realities'.[122]

This 'poetic attempt to compete with religion' manifests itself in Shelley's many semantic redefinitions of religious signal words and their meanings. We encountered this above in his use of the term and concept 'Eternity'. Similarly, in 'Hymn to Intellectual Beauty' Shelley deploys the adjective 'awful' not to designate something terrible or unpleasant, as we commonly apply that term today, but rather in its more archaic sense of 'awe-ful', full of awe, indicating something inspiring reverential wonder or fear and closely related to the 'mystery and grandeur' of the sublime. In deliberate opposition to his contemporaries Shelley did not associate awe with the Christian God;[123] rather, awe is for him vested in the 'Power' that

---

and for the virtuous man who is seemingly defeated in this life by enemies who do not recognise his worth. [...] On the other hand, Christ was also important for being a profound moral teacher, who expressed his meaning with the imagistic force of a great poet' (p. 170).

119 'Essay on Christianity', pp. 343–44.
120 'Hymn to Intellectual Beauty', in *The Works of Percy Bysshe Shelley*, ed. Forman, vol. 1, pp. 371–75 (p. 371).
121 *Shelley. The Golden Years* (Cambridge, MA: Harvard University Press, 1974), p. 237.
122 *Shelley's Mythmaking* (Ithaca: Cornell University Press, 1959), p. 24.
123 In Anna Laetitia Barbauld's 1773 'An Address to the Deity', we read the following lines:

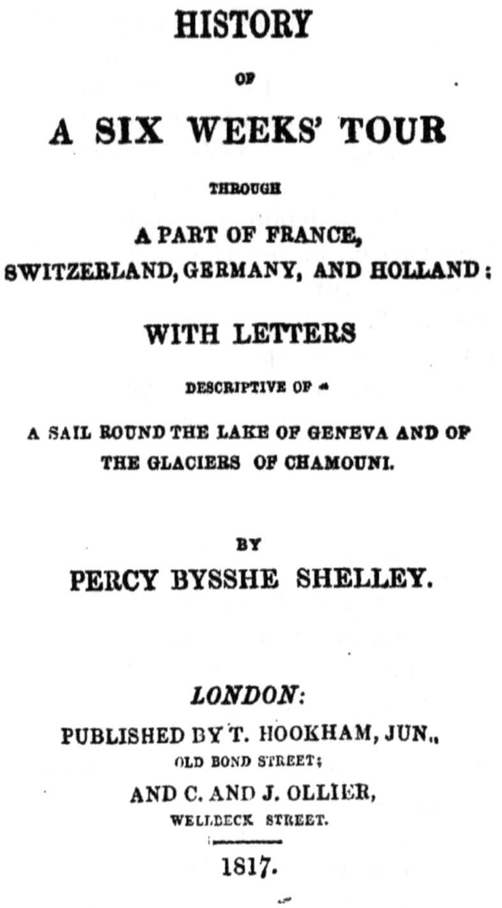
HISTORY

OF

A SIX WEEKS' TOUR

THROUGH

A PART OF FRANCE,
SWITZERLAND, GERMANY, AND HOLLAND:

WITH LETTERS

DESCRIPTIVE OF

A SAIL ROUND THE LAKE OF GENEVA AND OF
THE GLACIERS OF CHAMOUNI.

BY

PERCY BYSSHE SHELLEY.

LONDON:
PUBLISHED BY T. HOOKHAM, JUN.,
OLD BOND STREET;
AND C. AND J. OLLIER,
WELBECK STREET.

1817.

FIG. 4.2. Title page of *History of a Six Weeks' Tour through a part of France, Switzerland, Germany, and Holland, with Letters*; based on Percy Shelley's letter to his friend Thomas Love Peacock and Mary Shelley's diaries, this 1817 travelogue also contains the first printing of Percy Shelley's poem 'Mont Blanc'.

resides within 'Nature', of which the mountain 'Mont Blanc' is its grandest and most mysterious emblem, teaching us 'awful doubt'. (This will be discussed more fully below.)

As Mary relates, 'Hymn to Intellectual Beauty' was composed when Shelley was out sailing on Lake Geneva with Byron in June 1816.[124] 'Mont Blanc' was

'While GOD is seen in all, and all in GOD. / I read his awful name, emblazon'd high / With golden letters on th' illumin'd sky / Nor less the mystic characters I see / Wrought in each flower, inscrib'd on every tree...'; *Poems*, 3rd edn (London: Joseph Johnson, 1773), pp. 128–29. Viewing the majesty of Mount Snowdon in Book XIII of *The Prelude*, Wordsworth tellingly transfers the epithet 'awful' onto Nature: 'The perfect image of a mighty mind, / Of one that feeds upon infinity, / That is exalted by an under-presence, / The sense of God, or whatsoe'er is dim / Or vast in its own being — above all, / One function of such mind had Nature there / Exhibited by putting forth, and that / With circumstance most awful and sublime: / That domination which she often times / Exerts upon the outward face of things.' (*The Prelude*, XIII, ll. 69–78)

124 See her 'Note on Poems of 1816', in *The Poetical Works of Percy Bysshe Shelley*, ed. Mary Shelley, vol. 2, p. 235.

conceived one month later, on or around 23 July 1816.[125] Published in 1817 as an appendix to Percy and Mary's travelogue *History of a Six Weeks' Tour through a part of France, Switzerland, Germany, and Holland, with Letters* (see Figure 4.2), 'Mont Blanc' registers and reflects Shelley's reaction to his first encounter with Europe's highest and most massive mountain during their tour to the region around Chamonix during that eventful summer of 1816. Mont Blanc appeared to him as a kind of divine apparition, or as nature's secular Revelation, as the relevant section in *History of a Six Weeks' Tour* relates: 'Mont Blanc was before us,' the letter dated 22 July 1816 tells us (a letter which is based verbatim on the actual letter Percy sent to his friend Thomas Love Peacock), describing their three-day trip into the 'valley of Chamouni',

> but it was covered with cloud; its base, furrowed with dreadful gaps, was seen above. Pinnacles of snow intolerably bright, part of the chain connected with Mont Blanc, shone through the clouds at intervals on high. I never knew — I never imagined what mountains were before. The immensity of these aerial summits excited, when they suddenly burst upon the sight, a sentiment of extatic [sic] wonder, not unallied to madness. And remember this was all one scene, it all pressed home to our regard and our imagination. Though it embraced a vast extent of space, the snowy pyramids which shot into the bright blue sky seemed to overhang our path. [...] — all was as much our own, as if we had been the creators of such impressions in the minds of others as now occupied our own. Nature was the poet, whose harmony held our spirits more breathless than that of the divinest.[126]

Elsewhere in their travelogue, we read of the mountain's 'awful grace', its 'sublime' appearance, and its 'untameable, inaccessible solitude'. With its awe-inspiring 'grandeur' and 'untameable solitude' Mont Blanc came to represent for Shelley a form of materialized 'Necessity' — in the letter to Peacock he describes the glaciers of Boisson and Montanvert as 'palaces of death & frost, sculptured in this their terrible magnificence by the unsparing hand of necessity'; 'one would think', he adds, 'that Mont Blanc was a living being & that the frozen blood forever circulated slowly thro' his stony veins'.[127] However, if Mont Blanc's necessity is here portrayed as literally cold and in a metaphysical sense everlasting, as well as menacing in its 'terrible magnificence', it is nonetheless not to be confused with the kind of 'cold, everlasting Necessity' that Jean Paul had invoked in his 'Speech of the dead Christ from atop the World's Edifice that there is no God', discussed in the previous chapter. As something 'unsparing' and 'adamantine'[128] Shelley's necessity may be merciless and severe, but, as embodied in this magnificent if terrible mountain, it is

---

125 Percy and Mary Shelley actually date it mistakenly to 23 June 1816 — such is the date given in *History of a Six Weeks' Tour Through a Part of France, Switzerland, Germany, and Holland, with Letters*, p. 183), in which the poem was first published, and Mary Shelley's second volume of the 1839 *The Poetical Works of Percy Bysshe Shelley* (p. 239); however, as scholars later noticed, the Shelleys did not begin their trip to Chamonix and Mont Blanc until 21 July 1816. (Although based on their joint diary and letters, *History of a Six Weeks' Tour* was tellingly published under Percy Shelley's name alone.)
126 *History of a Six Weeks' Tour*, pp. 151–52; the subsequent passages pp. 155, 50, 144 and 168.
127 *The Letters of Percy Bysshe Shelley*, ed. Jones, vol. 1, pp. 499–500.
128 In *History of a Six Weeks' Tour* Shelley substitutes 'adamantine' for 'unsparing', p. 162.

also something neutral and impartial, standing literally above the fray of the world, as we shall see momentarily.

The poem — 144 lines divided into five sections[129] — famously opens by setting up a dichotomy between nature and man, matter and mind, eternity and the present moment, light and darkness, and despair ('gloom') and delight ('splendour'); this opening simultaneously, if more obliquely, also evokes a sense of how the ecstatic experience of Mont Blanc's 'untameable wildness and inaccessible solemnity' has put the poet in touch with an enhanced sense of the universe's eternity and infinity. These are the poem's first five lines:

> The everlasting universe of things
> Flows through the mind, and rolls its rapid waves,
> Now dark — now glittering — now reflecting gloom —
> Now lending splendour, where from secret springs
> The source of human thought its tribute brings...

Encapsulating the poem's overall message, which is to underscore how interdependent and reliant upon one another nature and the (poet's) mind are, the word 'everlasting' — besides the word 'awful' another signal term in Shelley's poetry — here relates to the contemporary scientific notion of a universe that has lasted forever, has not been created by a Creator God, and will not end in a Last Judgment. Let us recall here Shelley's formulation in *The Necessity of Atheism*, cited earlier: 'it is easier to suppose that the Universe has existed from all eternity, than to conceive a being capable of creating it'.[130] This is consonant, of course, with James Hutton's uniformitarian conception of the universe, John Playfair's summary of which I cited in Chapter Two and repeat here: 'the theory of Dr Hutton, where nothing is to be seen beyond the continuation of the present order; where no latent seed of evil threatens final destruction to the whole; and where the movements are so perfect, that they can never terminate of themselves. This is surely a view of the world more suited to the dignity of Nature and the wisdom of its Author'. It was obvious to Hutton's contemporaries, Rudwick observes, that this 'eternalism denied that the cosmos had an ultimately divine foundation'.[131] And it should be as obvious to us that Hutton's classically inspired deism[132] represented a view of the universe that was perfectly suited to Shelley's own understanding of the world, as indeed Nigel Leask has argued.[133]

---

129 Cited here from its original version in *History of a Six Weeks' Tour*, pp. 175–83.
130 *The Works of Percy Bysshe Shelley*, ed. Forman, vol. 5, p. 307.
131 *Bursting the Limits of Time*, p. 334.
132 Since we have so frequently referred to Hutton's celebrated phrase 'no vestige of a beginning, — no prospect of an end', it is perhaps worth pointing out that this phrase is derived from a 'heathen' source, namely Pythagorean philosopher Ocellus Lucanus's work *On the Nature of the Universe*, which was published in English translation in 1831; the key passage there reads: 'But if the universe was generated, it was generated together with all things; and if it should be corrupted, it would be corrupted together with all things. This, however, is impossible. The universe, therefore, is without a beginning, and without an end; nor is it possible that it can have any other mode of subsistence'; Ocellus Lucanus, *On the Nature of the Universe*, trans. by Thomas Taylor (London: John Bohn, Henry Sohn, and Thomas Rodd, 1831), p. 2.
133 'Mont Blanc's Mysterious Voice', pp. 198–203, especially p. 202 where he observes: 'In

This notion of an 'everlasting' eternity of time in Section I intersects in Section III of the poem with a view of the infinity of space that Shelley had derived from Herschel and Laplace; inspired by the most modern science, Shelley casts the mountain Mont Blanc as Nature's symbol on earth for both dimensions of infinity, space and time:

> Far, far above, piercing *the infinite sky*,
> Mont Blanc appears, — still, snowy, and serene –
> Its subject mountains their unearthly forms
> Pile around it, ice and rock [...] — how hideously
> Its shapes are heaped around! rude, bare, and high,
> Ghastly, and scarred, and riven. — Is this the scene
> Where the old Earthquake-dæmon taught her young
> Ruin? Were these their toys? or did a sea
> Of fire, envelope once this silent snow?
> None can reply — *all seems eternal now*!
> (ll. 60–63 and 69–75; my emphases)

And yet, although 'none can reply', nature and the mountain do have a 'voice' — a voice 'naturally' brought to eloquent expression through the poet's 'interpretation' of it, as suggested at the close of Section III:

> The wilderness has a mysterious tongue
> Which teaches awful doubt, or faith so mild,
> So solemn, so serene, that man may be
> But for such faith with nature reconciled;
> Thou hast a voice, great Mountain, to repeal
> Large codes of fraud and woe; not understood
> By all, but which the wise, and great, and good
> Interpret, or make felt, or deeply feel.
> (ll. 76–83; my emphases)

These famous and much-interpreted lines are not easy to untangle; critics have argued especially about the meaning of the 'cryptic and tortuous'[134] phrase 'but for such faith', with the majority of interpreters now opting for the equivalent of 'In such a faith' or 'With such a faith', this reading being based on a recently discovered manuscript variant, the so-called Scrope Davies fair copy.[135] My preferred interpretation of this difficult passage is that Shelley seeks to convey to us how the experience of the 'great Mountain' compels us to reconsider our metaphysical assumptions about the origins of the universe and hence the existence of God. Such 'awful' yet 'serene' monuments of Nature as Mont Blanc demand that the Christian 'codes of fraud' and indoctrination, and the socio-political 'codes of woe' and

---

"Mont Blanc", Shelley builds upon the foundation of Hutton's theory of an earth-machine working inexorably in deep time in order to establish a philosophical aesthetics of the natural sublime. This becomes the basis for an anti-catastrophist politics of reconstruction, challenging the prevalent post-Napoleonic castigation of revolution and revolutionary doctrines of perfectibility'.

134 So Michael O'Neill, 'Shelley's Lyric Art', in *Shelley's Poetry and Prose. A Norton Critical Edition*, ed. by Donald H. Reiman and Neil Fraistat (New York and London: W. W. Norton, 2002), pp. 616–26 (p. 617).

135 See *Shelley's Poetry and Prose. A Norton Critical Edition*, p. 99, footnote 4.

inequality that are associated with them, be critically put in question; they teach us a new 'solemn', 'serene' and 'mild' faith, one which reconciles us with Nature rather than separating us from it.[136] And it is philosophers-cum-poets, 'the wise, and great, and good' in particular, who through their poetic imagination and expressive craft are able to 'interpret, or make felt, or deeply feel' the true essence of the universe that surrounds us. Nigel Leask puts a more prosaic spin on this when he writes: 'The poem's difficult task is to win back the interpretation of the natural sublime from myth-making poets, pious tourists and geological catastrophists'.[137]

In *A Defence of Poetry*, written in 1821, a year before his fatal sailing accident off the Italian coast, Shelley observes: 'Poetry [...] arrests the vanishing apparitions which haunt the interlunations of life, and veiling them, or in language or in form, sends them forth among mankind, bearing sweet news of kindred joy to those

---

136 Arguably, Shelley is deploying the word 'mild' in 'Mont Blanc' in the vein of Humphry Davy as a sort of anti-Christian key word denoting a natural philosophy devoid of God, as in Davy's 1799 poem 'Ode to St Michael's Mount, in Cornwall' with its lines:

> Whilst Superstition rules the vulgar soul,
> Forbids the energies of man to rise,
> Rais'd far above her low, her mean controul
> Aspiring Genius seeks her native skies.
> She loves the silent solitary hours,
> She loves the stillness of the starry night,
> When o'er the brightening view Selene pours
> The soft effulgence of her pensive light.
> Tis then disturb'd not by the glare of day
> To mild tranquility alone resign'd,
> Reason extends her animating sway
> O'er the calm empire of the peaceful mind. [...]
> To them no wakeful moon-beam shines in vain
> On the dark bosom of the trackless wood,
> Sheds its mild radiance o'er the desart plain,
> Or softly glides along the chrystal flood.
> Yet not alone delight the soft and fair
> Alike the grander scenes of Nature move,
> Yet not alone her beauties claim their care,
> The great, sublime, and terrible, they love. [...]
> To scan the laws of Nature, to explore
> The tranquil reign of mild Philosophy,
> Or on Newtonian wings sublime to soar,
> Thro' the bright regions of the starry sky. [...]

In a similar vein, Cameron notes as regards Shelley's use of the specific combination 'mild faith' in *Shelley. The Golden Years* how the poet 'clearly favors the kind of "mild faith" that can come from a contemplation of nature, in implied contrast to the superstitious "faith" of religion. He has faith that the "Spirit of Nature" or the power, working outside and through mankind, will help to restore the balance between nature and society and, in the process, will destroy social and other evils. The concept is similar to that in the conclusion of the *Hymn to Intellectual Beauty*. After being declared himself in favor of this kind of faith — "So solemn, so serene" — Shelley would hardly have reversed himself in the next line and denounced it as an evil that man should get rid of. The "faith", furthermore, is specifically a faith in the "voice" of the mountain of the following lines, the "voice" of the power; it is the good "faith" that will destroy the evil "faith" of the church' (pp. 249–50).

137 'Mont Blanc's Mysterious Voice', p. 196.

with whom their sisters abide — abide, because there is no portal of expression from the caverns of the spirit which they inhabit into the universe of things', which is of course the very 'universe of things' with which the poem 'Mont Blanc' opens.[138] It is the poet, not the scientist, who has privileged access to that universe, as a Promethean Shelley declares self-servingly elsewhere in *A Defence of Poetry*; 'Poetry', he writes,

> is at once the centre and circumference of knowledge; it is that which comprehends all science, and that to which all science must be referred. It is at the same time the root and blossom of all other systems of thought; it is that from which all spring, and that which adorns all; and that which, if blighted, denies the fruit and the seed, and withholds from the barren world the tree of life. [...] What were virtue, love, patriotism, friendship, — what were the scenery of this beautiful universe which we inhabit; what were our consolations on this side of the grave — and what were our aspirations beyond it, if poetry did not ascend to bring light and fire from those eternal regions where the owl-winged faculty of calculation dare not ever soar?

Written five years before *A Defence of Poetry*, the fifth and final section of 'Mont Blanc', which I quote here in full, anticipates key aspects of Shelley's later philosophy of poetry:

> V.
>
> Mont Blanc yet gleams on high: — the power is there,
> The *still* and solemn power of many sights,
> And many sounds, and much of life and death.
> In the calm darkness of the moonless nights,
> In the lone glare of day, the snows descend
> Upon that Mountain; none beholds them there,
> Nor when the flakes burn in the sinking sun,
> Or the star-beams dart through them: — Winds contend
> *Silently* there, and heap the snow with breath
> Rapid and strong, but *silently*! Its home
> The *voiceless* lightning in these solitudes
> Keeps innocently, and like vapour broods
> Over the snow. The *secret* strength of things
> Which governs thought, and to the infinite dome
> Of heaven is as a law, inhabits thee!
> And what were thou, and earth, and stars, and sea,
> If to the human mind's imaginings
> *Silence* and solitude were vacancy?
>   (ll. 127–41; my emphases)

In these remarkable final lines of 'Mont Blanc' Shelley has included copious references to silence, secrecy and voicelessness, as highlighted in the italicized passages; the calculated repetition of this central trope impresses upon us that Mont Blanc, as Nature incarnate and embodiment of Nature's power, remains 'necessarily' silent — it is given expression only through the human mind. (And, as Michael O'Neill

---

138 *A Defence of Poetry*, p. 139; the subsequent passage pp. 136–37.

has poignantly observed, affording yet another layer to this dimension of the poem, 'the "power" worshipped is also a power which Shelley is creating as he writes').[139] In the traditional dualism of matter and mind, matter has no say in things. It is the human mind alone that possesses a voice expressed through language. The achievement of Shelley's accomplished concluding fifth part of his poem is to disclose the secret, break the silence, and make heard the voice that inhabits Nature. The law of the universe, as well as of the mountain ('thou'), the earth, the stars and the sea, comes to enunciation through the 'human mind's imaginings', mediated of course through the poet's language, which interprets the 'silence and solitude' of the mountain, thereby serving to fill the 'vacancy' and give it expression. Put differently, the 'silence and solitude' of Nature's monuments are vacant, or hollow and meaningless, only so long as the 'human mind's imaginings' remain unable to ascribe significance to them; as soon as the mind furnishes them with significance, however, as does Shelley programmatically through his poem 'Mont Blanc', any vacancy in Nature's distinctive silence and solitude dissolves.[140]

It is well possible that, by placing such stress on the term 'vacancy' in the last line of his poem, Shelley was responding directly to Wordsworth, who in 'The Prospectus to *The Recluse*', published just two years earlier as part of the 1814 preface to *The Excursion*, had included the following lines (ll. 28–41):

> For I must tread on shadowy ground, must sink
> Deep — and, aloft ascending, breathe in worlds
> To which the heaven of heavens is but a veil.
> All strength — all terror, single or in bands
> That ever was put forth by personal form —
> Jehovah — with his thunder, and the choir
> Of shouting Angels, and the empyreal thrones —
> I pass them unalarmed. Not Chaos, not
> The darkerst pit of lowest Erebus,
> Nor aught of blinder vacancy, scooped out
> By help of dreams — can breed such fear and awe
> As fall upon us often when we look

---

139 'Shelley's Lyric Art', p. 617.

140 While this wording is my own, I make no claim for the novelty of my interpretation; in one of the best readings of the poem Earl S. Wasserman similarly writes: 'What the mountain's voice tells us is the inaccessible Power and its amoral necessary laws. Thereby it teaches us the skeptical doubt that divulges how little of total Being is revealed to us by our senses and conscious mind; or it teaches such a faith in the necessary beneficent Power and its laws — a faith that, unlike "Christian" faith, is mild, solemn, serene ... [...]. For the vision of Power is, in one sense, also a vision of nothingness — silence, stillness, and emptiness. But it is, ironically, the emptiness which is the absolute of potential fullness [...]. Nature's silence and solitude are indeed a "vacancy"; the emptiness of the Power is infinite plenitude. The first is what appears to the senses; the second is apprehended by the trance-like and apparently vacant imaginings. [...] Were reality only the discontinuous external world or even the world that is born, dies, and revives, it would be meaningless, futile. Meaning lies in the mind's visionary apprehension of a single eternal, immutable, and amoral Power which lies behind the seemingly absurd mutability and recurrent emptiness, and of whose necessary laws the activities of the world are a manifestation' (*Shelley. A Critical Reading*, pp. 236–37). I have also drawn valuable insight from Wasserman's interpretation of 'Mont Blanc' in *The Subtler Language*, cited earlier in this chapter.

> Into our Minds, into the Mind of Man —
> My haunt, and the main region of my song.

Shelley treads the same Dante-like path as Wordsworth past God and his angelic hosts, and through Hell, into the 'Mind of Man', which for both poets is the 'main region of [their] song'. And yet, if Shelley was leaning toward any form of idealism — broadly defined for this purpose as man taking his human intellect as the force that shapes, if not creates, the universe — it was not an idealism of the Fichtean ilk. Where Fichte, at least as his philosophy was received by his contemporaries, dissolved God and Nature into the unified Absolute I, reducing everything outside of it to a paltry non-essential reflection of the mind — what Jean Paul disapprovingly coined Fichte's 'if-subjectivity' — Shelley takes a dualistic position, seeing Nature and Mind as both co-essential and co-dependent, each in need of and premised on its Other.[141] The mountain with its forbidding glaciers and 'snows' and 'winds' and 'solitudes' is thus the creative source not just of the material 'dark, deep Ravine of Arve [...] | Where Power in likeness of the Arve comes down | From the ice gulphs that gird his secret throne' (ll. 12–16), but also of the metaphorical and imaginative river of thought, 'where from secret springs | The source of human thought its tribute brings | Of waters' (ll. 4–6). God here is absent — Shelley, too, passing him 'unalarmed', to repeat Wordsworth's locution above. Instead, God is supplanted by the thought-infusing 'everlasting universe of things', summoned in the poem's opening line. Nature's awe-inspiring physical landscape is transposed into a sublime meta-physical mindscape of the poet's making. Neither can exist without the other. It is the 'unremitting interchange' between matter, 'the clear universe of things around' (l. 40), and mind that Shelley proclaims as the poem's central theme and message. 'And when I gaze on thee', the River Arve's 'Dizzy Ravine!' is addressed,

> I seem as in a trance sublime and strange
> To muse on my own separate phantasy,
> My own, my human mind, which passively
> Now renders and receives fast influencings,
> Holding an unremitting interchange
> With the clear universe of things around...
> (ll. 34–40)

This 'interchange' is hence also a form of translation, the translation of Nature's tongue and the Mountain's voice into a poetic idiom that aims to make the inaccessible and 'unutterable'[142] perhaps not *logically* intelligible but certainly *affectively* graspable and far less distant. When Shelley encountered the mountain for the first time, Mont Blanc seems intuitively, if not to say epiphanically, to have struck him

---

141 In his analysis of Shelley's essay 'On Life', Kenneth Neill Cameron in *Shelley: The Golden Years* likewise speaks of Shelley's 'dualistic assumption' during this middle period immediately preceding the composition of 'Mont Blanc' (p. 157); later in this book, however, he is no longer so certain, questioning whether Shelley was still a dualist at the time of composing 'Mont Blanc' — 'it is difficult to say', he concludes (p. 246).

142 *History of a Six Weeks' Tour*, p. 155.

as a potent visual and material symbol for the very forces of 'Nature' he had been trying to fathom philosophically and scientifically ever since writing *The Necessity of Atheism* and *Queen Mab*; god-like in their 'inaccessibility' and 'omnipotence',[143] Shelley considers them far more detached — in a positive way — than the Christian Almighty, possessing a neutrality and disinterestedness towards people of all faiths and religious dispositions and yet being more awe-inspiring and sublime than Holbach's and Godwin's pure and abstract 'cold Necessity', to recite Jean Paul's words.

Of course, no less than Mont Blanc came to represent for Shelley a symbol of the potency of Nature, for the true Christian believer mountains were — and remain until today, as the example of Alvin Plantinga shows, for whom mountain panoramas serve still in the year 2000 to 'warrant' the Christian's 'belief that God must be great to have created [such a] magnificent heavenly host'[144] — an equally compelling reminder of and testimony to the power of God. We recall the symbolic function, religious and secular, of the many mountaintops that we encountered in the previous chapter, in the paintings by Caspar David Friedrich and texts by Albrecht von Haller, Jean Paul, Georg Büchner and Friedrich Nietzsche. As Sean Ireton and Caroline Schaumann point out in their illuminating introduction to the volume *Heights of Reflection*, a compendium of essays on German literary representations of mountains from the Middle Ages to Thomas Mann, W. G. Sebald and Christoph Ransmayr, this preoccupation with mountains as a symbolic reservoir of the glory of God or the dominion of Nature dates back to the earliest beginnings of our literary and religious tradition; in the Judeo-Christian tradition, the Bible is the prime instance, as Ireton and Schaumann note:

> With specific respect to mountains, the Judeo-Christian tradition — somewhat paradoxically — tends to accord a privileged status to such desolate and elevated territory. In the Old Testament, Noah's ark came to rest on Mount Ararat; Abraham bore Isaac to a mountaintop for sacrifice; Moses received the Ten Commandments on Mount Sinai; and Elijah triumphed over the followers of Baal on Mount Carmel. As for the New Testament, one need only mention a few critical stations in the life and teaching of Jesus: the Mount of Temptation, the Sermon on the Mount, the Mount of Transfiguration, the Mount of Olives, and Golgotha. All of these physical heights function as symbolic sites of spirituality, sacrifice, and transcendence.[145]

In *Theory of the Earth* Thomas Burnet, the seventeenth-century Anglican clergyman whose influential work we have already variously touched upon, picks up on this tradition. He dedicates Chapter XI of the first volume of his work expressly to a study of mountains, entitling it 'Concerning the Mountains of the Earth, their Greatness and irregular Form, their Situation, Causes, and Origin'; the

---

143 'Inaccessibility' relates to the adjective used in *History of a Six Weeks' Tour* cited above; 'some unknown omnipotence' appears on l. 53 of the poem itself.

144 *Warranted Christian Belief* (New York and Oxford: Oxford University Press, 2000), p. 173.

145 'Introduction: The Meaning of Mountains: Geology, History, Culture', in *Heights of Reflection. Mountains in the German Imagination from the Middle Ages to the Twenty-First Century* (Rochester, NY, and Woodbridge: Camden House, 2012), pp. 1–19 (p. 3).

chapter begins:

> We have been in the Hollows of the Earth, and the Chambers of the Deep, amongst the Damps and Streams of those lower Regions; let us now go air our selves on the Top of the Mountains, where we shall have a more free and large Horizon, and quite another Face of Things will present it self to our Observation. The greatest Objects of Nature are, methinks, the most pleasing to behold; and next to the great Concave of the Heavens, and those boundless Regions where the Stars inhabit, there is nothing that I look upon with more Pleasure than the wide Sea and the Mountains of the Earth. There is something august and stately in the Air of these things, that inspires the Mind with great Thoughts and Passions; we do naturally, upon such Occasions, think of God and his Greatness: And whatsoever hath but the Shadow and Appearance of INFINITE, as all Things have that are too big for our Comprehension, they fill and over-bear the Mind with their Excess, and cast it into a pleasing kind of Stupor and Admiration.[146]

As Burnet confesses, he too had 'crossed the *Alps*' and experienced at first hand the capacity of these 'wild, vast, and indigested Heaps of Stones' to infuse a sense of awe in the face of God's majesty and plenitude — indeed, his words are not that far removed from Shelley's own 'sentiment of extatic wonder, not unallied to madness'.

As Nigel Leask has pointed out, by the late eighteenth century — and still well before Shelley's time — extolling the Alpine mountain-scape, and eulogizing the grandeur and sublimity of mountain peaks and icy glaciers in hymns addressed to them, had become a favourite pastime of (not just) English travellers touring Switzerland 'in search of the pious edification afforded by Alpine sublimity'.[147] He cites Helen Maria Williams as a prime example, whose two-volume *A Tour in Switzerland* was published in 1798 and can be considered the British tourists' Baedeker of the time, probably also known to Shelley; in Chapter XXII Williams recounts:

> While my fellow travellers amused themselves by wandering over that world of ice, a difficult and dangerous enterprize, I sat down on the border of the Glacier, to enjoy the new and magnificent vision around me. On the right, rocks and mountains of ice, arose in dread and sublime perspective [...]. I employed the hours of meditation in throwing together the new images with which the Alpine scenery had filled my mind, into the form of an hymn, to the author of nature; and no spot can surely be more congenial to devotional feelings, than that theatre where the divinity has displayed the most stupendous of his earthly works.[148]

At the end of her chapter she encloses her 'Hymn written among the Alps', the opening and closing stanzas of which read:

---

146 Burnet, *Theory of the Earth*, vol. 1, pp. 188–89, the following quotations p. 190.
147 'Mont Blanc's Mysterious Voice', p. 184.
148 *A Tour in Switzerland; or, A View of the Government and Manners of those Cantons with Comparative Sketches of the Present State of Paris*, 2 vols (London: G. G. and J. Robinson, 1798), vol. 2, Ch. 22, pp. 8–10; the subsequent strophes pp. 16 and 19.

> Creation's God! with thought elate
> Thy hand divine I see;
> Impressed on scenes where all is great,
> Where all is full of thee! [...]
>
> In every scene, where every hour
> Sheds some terrific grace,
> In nature's vast, overwhelming power,
> THEE, THEE, my GOD, I trace!

A German encomium to Mont Blanc, published some years earlier in 1791, is Danish-German writer Friederike Brun's ode 'Chamounix beym Sonnenaufgang' ('Chamounix at Sunrise'), whose title and structure are replicated a decade later by Coleridge in his 'Hymn before Sunrise in the Vale of Chamouni' (more on which below).[149]

Shelley's composition of 'Mont Blanc' is, then, as much a response to theology and natural philosophy as it is a rejoinder to contemporary poetry, of which Brun's 'Chamounix beym Sonnenaufgang' and Williams's 'Hymn written among the Alps' are only the tip of the proverbial iceberg. Indeed, if the close of Shelley's 'Preface' to *History of a Six Weeks' Tour* resonates with the religious pitch of Burnet's prose, and if Percy's and Mary's travelogue *History of a Six Weeks' Tour* represents their own rendering of 'A Tour in Switzerland', there are further echoes in this work that a cultured contemporary audience would have immediately recognised, in particular the allusion to Wordsworth and Coleridge's definition of 'all good poetry' as 'the spontaneous overflow of powerful feelings' in the 'Preface' to (the second edition

---

[149] 'Chamounix beym Sonnenaufgange', in *Gedichte*, ed. by Friedrich Matthißon (Zurich: Orell, Geßner, Füßli and Co, 1791), p. 1:

> Chamounix beym Sonnenaufgange
> (im Mai 1791)
>
> Aus tiefem Schatten des schweigenden Tannenhains
> Erblick' ich bebend dich, Scheitel der Ewigkeit,
> Blendender Gipfel, von dessen Höhe
> Ahndend mein Geist ins Unendliche schwebet!
> Wer senkte den Pfeiler tief in der Erde Schooß,
> Der, seit Jahrtausenden, fest deine Masse stützt?
> Wer thürmte hoch in des Aethers Wölbung
> Mächtig und kühn dein umstrahltes Antlitz?
> Wer goß euch hoch aus des ewigen Winters Reich,
> O Zackenströme, mit Donnergetös' herab?
> Und wer gebietet laut mit der Allmacht Stimme:
> 'Hier sollen ruhen die starrenden Wogen!'
> Wer zeichnet dort dem Morgensterne die Bahn,
> Wer kränzt mit Blüthen des ewigen Frostes Saum?
> Wem tönt in schrecklichen Harmonieen,
> Wilder *Arveiron*, dein Wogengetümmel?
> Jehovah! Jehovah! kracht's im berstenden Eis;
> Lavinendonner rollen's die Kluft hinab;
> Jehovah! rauscht's in den hellen Wipfeln,
> Flüstert's an rieselnden Silberbächen.

of the) *Lyrical Ballads*. Shelley's remarks on the composition of 'Mont Blanc' overtly rehearses their vocabulary:

> 'Mont Blanc' [...] was composed under the immediate impression of the deep and *powerful feelings* excited by the objects which it attempts to describe; and as an undisciplined *overflowing* of the soul, rests its claim to approbation on an attempt to imitate the untameable wildness and inaccessible solemnity from which those feelings sprang.[150] (my emphases)

If this paratext — which is of course not part of the poem itself, but a passage that accompanied only the poem's original 1817 printing — can be read as Shelley's riposte to Wordsworth and Coleridge's definition of the Romantic sensibility, the text of 'Mont Blanc' itself enters into an analogous dialogue with their poetry, as Shelley-scholars have variously pointed out.

First we may recall how Wordsworth's 'Simplon Pass', cited in full in Chapter One, uses a similar range of topoi and signal words, including 'decaying woods', 'blasts of waterfalls', 'torrents', 'rocks', 'crags' and 'giddy prospects', as well as the opposition of matter and 'one mind', only to end on a dramatic and foreboding apocalyptic note with distinctly biblical overtones:

> Characters of the great Apocalypse
> The types and symbols of Eternity,
> Of first, and last, and midst, and without end.

Where Wordsworth's 'Simplon Pass' expressly invokes eternity through the medium of the apocalypse, and hence through the Christian imagery of salvation and its prefiguring of nature's limitations and man's demise, Shelley translates his precursor's sacred vocabulary into his own secular idiom; in 'Mont Blanc' — as in 'Hymn to Intellectual Beauty' and 'Ode to Heaven' — 'Eternity' and 'Heaven' signify not divine realms or states of being or undoing, but rather Nature's godless domain. In Shelley's Heaven there may be 'Power' and 'Strength', but it is no longer the realm of (the Christian) God. In 'Ode to Heaven' we accordingly read how Nature's Heaven remains even when the 'unremaining gods' and the 'generations' of humans who venerate them have long passed or 'rolled away':

> Even thy name is as a god,
> Heaven! for thou art the abode
> Of that power which is the glass
> Wherein man his nature sees.
> Generations as they pass
> Worship thee with bended knees.
> Their unremaining gods and they
> Like a river roll away;
> Thou remainest such alway.[151]

---

150 *History of a Six Weeks' Tour*, p. vi.
151 'Ode to Heaven', in *The Poetical Works of Percy Bysshe Shelley*, ed. Mary Shelley, vol. 2, pp. 415–17, this stanza p. 416. I noticed that some newer editions spell 'god' with a capital 'G', 'God'; I think Shelley consciously opted to use the more neutral lower case spelling 'god', as Mary uses in her edition.

Nature alone is infinite ('measureless') and everlasting ('thou remainest'), in marked contrast with the transient gods and the generations of religious faithful who believe in them.

The programmatically 'antireligious nature'[152] of 'Mont Blanc' can be inferred also from a second comparison, namely its intertextual differential with poems Wordsworth and Coleridge had written and published more than a decade earlier. We know that Shelley and Byron were reading both Wordsworth and Coleridge during their outings on Lake Geneva,[153] and Shelley had originally planned, while composing 'Mont Blanc' in July 1816, to subtitle 'Mont Blanc' 'Scene — Pont Pellisier in the vale of Servox'; this at least is what appears in the Scrope Davies Notebook. But for the published final version Shelley chose on second thought to substitute that subtitle, replacing it by 'Lines Written in the Vale of Chamouni'. Shelley knew that this caption would immediately call up for his audience both Wordsworth's poem 'Lines Written a Few Miles Above Tintern Abbey' (with its stress on nature's 'power' to infuse the mind with 'elevated thoughts') and, perhaps more importantly for our argument, Coleridge's 1802 'Hymn before Sunrise in the Vale of Chamouni'. Much as Shelley's 'poetic reply' to it,[154] Coleridge's 'Hymn before Sunrise' is a paean to the mountain, beginning in a very similar vein with the following lines:

> Hast thou a charm to stay the morning-star
> In his steep course? So long he seems to pause
> On thy bald awful head, O sovran Blanc,
> The Arve and Arveiron at thy base
> Rave ceaselessly; but thou, most awful Form!
> Risest from forth thy silent sea of pines,
> How silently! Around thee and above
> Deep is the air and dark, substantial, black,
> An ebon mass: methinks thou piercest it,
> As with a wedge! But when I look again,
> It is thine own calm home, thy crystal shrine,
> Thy habitation from eternity!
> O dread and silent Mount!

Here too the mountain rises awe-fully and eternally from its base, releasing the rivers Arve and Arveiron unto their ceaseless raving oceanwards; note how ingeniously the verb 'rave' is contained within the rivers' names, note too how silence is deployed as a key term to embody Mont Blanc's rugged and dreadful appearance. And yet, in a religious sense Shelley's 'Mont Blanc' is the very antithesis of Coleridge's poem. 'Whatever the genetic history,' remarks Harold Bloom, whether 'Coleridge and his "Hymn" were in Shelley's thoughts' or not 'when he stood in the vale of Chamouni, and when he composed "Mont Blanc", the two poems are in violent contrast, with Shelley's meditation replying to Coleridge's orthodox transport'.[155]

---

152 Cameron, *Shelley. The Golden Years*, p. 244.
153 See William D. Brewer, *The Shelley–Byron Conversation*, pp. 23–27.
154 Leask, 'Mont Blanc's Mysterious Voice', p. 185.
155 *Shelley's Mythmaking*, p. 12.

For Coleridge, the mountain represents merely a natural expedient through which to effectively recognize and worship the power invested in the Christian God Almighty. His poem's opening section thus continues and closes:

> I gazed upon thee,
> Till thou, still present to the bodily sense,
> Didst vanish from my thought: entranced in prayer
> I worshipped the Invisible alone.

Following the mid-sections of the poem, which sing — in 'fundamentalist raptures', as Kenneth Neill Cameron has put it[156] — the praise of the Christian God as the Creator of all things, the poem concludes thus, exhibiting phrases that we find echoed nearly verbatim in Shelley's counter-piece:

> Thou too, hoar Mount! with thy sky-pointing peaks,
> Oft from whose feet the avalanche, unheard,
> Shoots downward, glittering through the pure serene
> Into the depth of clouds, that veil thy breast —
> Thou too again, stupendous Mountain! thou
> That as I raise my head, awhile bowed low
> In adoration, upward from thy base
> Slow travelling with dim eyes suffused with tears,
> Solemnly seemest, like a vapoury cloud,
> To rise before me — Rise, O ever rise,
> Rise like a cloud of incense from the Earth!
> Thou kingly Spirit throned among the hills,
> Thou dread ambassador from Earth to Heaven,
> Great Hierarch! tell thou the silent sky,
> And tell the stars, and tell yon rising sun
> Earth, with her thousand voices, praises God.

Brun's, Williams's and Coleridge's manner of fusing, and in Shelley's view confusing, the genuine majesty of the mountain Mont Blanc with the fallacious majesty of the Christian God was the tradition that Shelley was seeking with his own poem to debunk. Leask notes:

> Although the mountain had formerly represented a potent symbol for the revolutionary followers of Rousseau (including the young William Wordsworth, who cast it as a symbol of the revolutionary sublime in his poem 'Descriptive Sketches' of 1793, and as a monument to revolutionary disappointment in Book 6 of the 1805 *Prelude*), by 1816 its cultural significance was predominately fideistic and legitimist, emblem of catastrophist natural order vindicating the workings of an all-powerful and vengeful Creator. [...] It is tempting in this light to read 'Mont Blanc' as an explosive assertion of revolutionary sublimity against Coleridgean piety....[157]

Just as the mountain Mont Blanc incarnated a dual symbolism, political on the one hand and religious on the other, Shelley's eponymous poem likewise embodied a twofold rebellious temper. Despite Shelley's rejection of Wordsworth's return to

---

156 *Shelley. The Golden Years*, p. 250.
157 'Mont Blanc's Mysterious Voice', p. 185.

political conservativism and the bosom of the Church, a rejection expressed most immediately in Shelley's poem 'To Wordsworth', written to voice his disappointment after reading the parts of *The Excursion* that Wordsworth had published in 1814, it is perhaps unsurprising that Shelley remains in spirit 'far closer to Wordsworth than Coleridge', as Martin Priestman has observed in *Romantic Atheism*.[158] This closeness derives from the fact that even in his later poetry Wordsworth retained a distinctly pantheistic air, not unlike Shelley's poetry. As Priestman goes on to remind us, extolling 'spiritual elevation in natural surroundings' without explicitly referencing God as the 'Prime Cause' would have been interpreted by many at this time as an unambiguous 'sign of infidelism'; in this regard both Wordsworth's early 'Lines Written a Few Miles Above Tintern Abbey' as well as *The Prelude* contrast as starkly with Coleridge's 'Hymn before Sunrise in the Vale of Chamouni' (which, in its last line, undisguisedly 'praises God' with a 'thousand voices') as does Shelley's rejoinder 'Mont Blanc. Lines Written in the Vale of Chamouni'.

The Monster of Mont Blanc

Needless to say, Mont Blanc was, during Shelley's day, not just the celebrated subject of hymns and travelogues. Indeed, his wife and intellectual companion Mary Wollstonecraft Shelley famously made dramatic use of the mountain as a backdrop to her Gothic fantasy, the 1818 novel *Frankenstein; or, The Modern Prometheus*. The opening chapters of Volume Two relate Victor Frankenstein's autonarrative of his visit with his family in Geneva and environs; like Byron and Shelley, Frankenstein passes 'many hours' sailing on Lac Leman, and, to allay the family's anguish about the monster's vile murder of William and the wrongful execution of Justine Moritz for that murder, Frankenstein's father proposes 'an excursion to the valley of Chamounix' to allow the scenery 'so wonderful and sublime' to afford them some spiritual solace.[159] The source and valley of the Arveiron, Frankenstein admits, thus provided 'the greatest consolation that [he] was capable of receiving. They elevated [him] from all littleness of feeling'. One day he decides to strike out alone to visit the 'summit of Montanvert', a popular tourist destination even then, and one that offered magnificent views across the Mer de Glace glacier, the Arve valley and Mont Blanc; we read:

> I remembered the effect that the view of the tremendous and ever-moving glacier had produced upon my mind when I first saw it. It had then filled me with a sublime ecstacy that gave wings to the soul, and allowed it to soar from the obscure world to light and joy. The sight of the awful and majestic in nature had indeed always the effect of solemnizing my mind, and causing me to forget the passing cares of life.

Continuing on his path past scenes 'terrifically desolate' he eventually reaches the 'top of the ascent' beyond Montanvert; Frankenstein recounts:

---

158 *Romantic Atheism*, p. 234; the subsequent quote p. 180.
159 Mary Shelley, *Frankenstein. The 1818 Text*, ed. by J. Paul Hunter (New York and London: W. W. Norton, 1996), p. 62; the subsequent passages pp. 63, 63–64 and 65.

> From the side where I now stood Montanvert was exactly opposite, at the distance of a league; and above it rose Mont Blanc in awful majesty. I remained in a recess of the rock, gazing on this wonderful and stupendous scene. [...] My heart, which was before sorrowful, now swelled with something like joy; I exclaimed — 'Wandering spirits, if indeed ye wander, and do not rest in your narrow beds, allow me this faint happiness, or take me, as your companion, away from the joys of life.

But the 'wandering spirit' he encounters at this literal 'summit' and climax of the novel is not one which grants happiness and the joys of life, quite to the contrary — it is the monster Frankenstein himself has created; by appearing 'with superhuman speed', 'bounding over the crevices of the ice', it is he who not just destroys the sublime mountaintop idyll but also forces Victor out of his lofty trance back into the cold embrace of reality. This reality consists of the monster's sobering tale of initial destitution and forlornness, but then gradual socialization into the world of men, spun out over the seven chapters of the novel that form the major part of the first edition's second volume, all of which is thus staged on this summit in the Swiss Alps in full view of Mont Blanc.

The opening exchange of words between the Promethean human scientist who has sought to assume the power of God and the new Adam he has created deserves some scrutiny. Encountering the monster, Victor Frankenstein exclaims:

> 'Devil! [...] do you dare approach me? And do not you fear the fierce vengeance of my arm wreaked on your miserable head? Begone, vile insect! or rather stay, that I may trample you to dust! And, oh, that I could, with the extinction of your miserable existence, restore those victims whom you have so diabolically murdered!'[160]

To this the 'daemon' replies:

> 'I expected this reception. [...] All men hate the wretched; how then must I be hated, who am miserable beyond all living things! Yet you, my creator, detest and spurn me, thy creature, to whom thou art bound by ties only dissoluble by the annihilation of one of us.'

Their dialogue is, poignantly, a reprise *in nuce* of traditional depictions of the biblical clash between God and the fallen angel Lucifer, not least among them Milton's *Paradise Lost* and *Paradise Regained*. In their interpretation of *Frankenstein* in their groundbreaking 1979 study *The Madwoman in the Attic*, a feminist rereading of literature by nineteenth-century women writers, Sandra M. Gilbert and Susan Gubar put forward a case for reading Mary Shelley's novel as a deliberate female rejoinder to Milton's classic male epic. Noting that Mary, a 'puzzled but studious Miltonist',[161] read and indeed reread *Paradise Lost* during the years 1815, 1816 and 1817, before and during the writing of *Frankenstein*, this novel represents its author's 'retelling' of Milton's 'story of the fall not so much to protest against it as to

---

160 This and the next passage ibid., p. 65.
161 *The Madwoman in the Attic. The Woman Writer and the Nineteenth-Century Literary Imagination* (New Haven and London: Yale University Press, 1984), p. 225; the subsequent quotes and passages pp. 224–25, 230, 232 and 233.

clarify its meaning' from an early nineteenth-century female writer's perspective. *Frankenstein*, they contend, is

> ultimately a mock *Paradise Lost* in which both Victor and his monster, together with a number of secondary characters, play all the neo-biblical parts over and over again — all except, it seems at first, the part of Eve. Not just the striking omission of any obvious Eve-figure from this 'woman's book' about Milton, but also the barely concealed sexual component of the story as well as our earlier analysis of Milton's bogey should tell us, however, that for Mary Shelley the part of Eve *is* all the parts.

Victor Frankenstein in particular, being described in Volume One, Chapter Three, as 'emaciated with confinement' and suffering 'days and nights of incredible labour' during the period when he pieced together his monster, is shown effectively first to have given birth to the creature — 'Victor Frankenstein has a baby', Gilbert and Gubar recap pithily — but then to have cast it off after 'labour'. But while 'Victor Frankenstein's self-defining procreation dramatically also transforms him into an Eve-figure', so Gilbert and Gubar, both he and the monster he has conceived comport themselves at one stage or another in the narrative like 'God'. Indeed, the passage from *Paradise Lost* that Mary included as the epigraph to her novel is intended to equate Frankenstein and his progeny with God and his offspring Adam: 'Did I request thee, Maker, from my clay | To mould me man? Did I solicit thee | From darkness to promote me? — '.

Perhaps less predictably, but unsurprising nonetheless in this context, it is Milton's *Paradise Lost* that belongs among the first texts the monster comes to read in his unnaturally accelerated socialization; in the seventh chapter of Volume Two, Mary puts the following words into his mouth, words which mirror not just her own response to Milton but also, as Gilbert and Gubar contend, create a parallel between his and her position in the world of men:

> But *Paradise Lost* excited different and far deeper emotions. I read it, as I had the other volumes which had fallen into my hands, as a true history. It moved every feeling of wonder and awe, that the picture of an omnipotent God warring with his creatures was capable of exciting. I often referred the several situations, as their similarity struck me, to my own. Like Adam, I was created apparently united by no link to any other being in existence; but his state was far different from mine in every other respect. He had come forth from the hands of God *a perfect creature* [...]: but I was wretched, helpless, and alone. Many times I considered Satan as the fitter emblem of my condition; for often, like him, when I viewed the bliss of my protectors, the bitter gall of envy rose within me.[162] (my emphasis)

The monster is both Satan, ejected from Heaven, and Adam, ejected from Paradise. Foreshadowing the fate of Lionel Verney, the 'Last Man' of Mary Shelley's later novel, the monster goes on to declaim:

> And sometimes I allowed my thoughts, unchecked by reason, to ramble in the fields of Paradise, and dared to fancy amiable and lovely creatures sympathizing

---

162 *Frankenstein. The 1818 Text*, p. 87; the subsequent passages pp. 88, 155 and 61.

with my feelings, and cheering my gloom; their angelic countenances breathed
smiles of consolation. But it was all a dream: no Eve soothed my sorrows, or
shared my thoughts. I remembered Adam's supplication to his Creator; but
where was mine? *he had abandoned me*, and, in the bitterness of my heart, I
cursed him. (my emphasis)

Of course, the monster is mistaken. First, he implies that Adam and his issue are a 'perfect' creation in contrast to which he cannot but appear as monstrous. But it is Adam who, in disobeying his divine father's command, commits the original sin, exposing his and his race's fateful imperfection; and it is in consequence of this imperfection, leading in the following generation to Cain's murder of his brother Abel, that Adam's progeny across the centuries is condemned to become as vile and murderous a creature as the monster himself was soon to become owing to his hatred of his creator, the scientist Victor Frankenstein. Thus in the final paragraphs of the novel the creature confesses to Walton:

> I have murdered the lovely and the helpless; I have strangled the innocent as
> they slept, and grasped to death his throat who never injured me or any other
> living thing. I have devoted my creator, the select specimen of all that is worthy
> of love and admiration among men, to misery; I have pursued him even to that
> irremediable ruin.

It is Victor's cousin Elizabeth who, in light of the monster's crimes against humanity, but unaware who the perpetrator of these crimes had been, presciently relates: 'men appear to me as monsters thirsting for each other's blood'. Gilbert and Gubar accordingly observe correctly how all three main characters of the novel, Walton, Frankenstein and the monster, 'like Shelley herself, appear to be trying to understand their presence in a fallen world, and trying at the same time to define the nature of the lost paradise that must have existed before the fall'.[163]

The monster is mistaken also in another way. He claims by implication that whereas he was abandoned by his creator, Victor Frankenstein, Adam was never abandoned by his. But of course, from a deist's point of view this is precisely what God has done — following the act of Creation he has left the world to its own devices, withdrawing callously to merely watch on as mankind took to murdering one another in social conflict and religious strife. There is some truth to Gilbert and Gubar's observation that 'not only do Frankenstein and his monster both in one way or another enact the story of Prometheus, each is at one time or another like God'; but due to their Miltonic and feminist focus, they stop short of probing more deeply the religious ramifications of Mary's complex role modelling for her key characters. It is this substratum of the novel *Frankenstein* that I want to explore in more detail before we finally turn our attention to the novel *The Last Man*.

Gilbert and Gubar point out correctly that the first three texts read by the monster, in Volume Two, Chapter Seven, are Plutarch's *Lives*, *The Sorrows of Young Werther* and Milton's *Paradise Lost*. What they fail to mention is the fact that this is not the first book the monster has come across. Two chapters earlier, and before he has learnt to read, the monster can be found listening in to a domestic scene of

---

163 *The Madwoman in the Attic*, p. 225; the subsequent passage p. 230.

an unusual nature; having sought refuge in a shack that abuts an isolated cottage, the monster is able to eavesdrop on a well-born family living in seclusion from good society. One day, the young man Felix brings home his mysterious fiancé, a beautiful young woman of Arabian birth; Safie, as she is called, is as yet unable to communicate in Felix's and his sister Agatha's native tongue. Proceeding to teach her their language, Felix unwittingly allows the monster to 'make use of the same instructions to the same end'.[164] The creature relates, instancing his considerable intelligence:

> My days were spent in close attention, that I might more speedily master the language; and I may boast that I improved more rapidly than the Arabian, who understood very little, and conversed in broken accents, whilst I comprehended and could imitate almost every word that was spoken. While I improved in speech, I also learnt the science of letters, as it was taught to the stranger; and this opened before me a wide field for wonder and delight.

The book from which Felix instructs Safie, and hence also the monster, in the ways and defects of the world is one we have encountered before in our exploration of the advent of atheism; it is none other than 'Volney's *Ruins of Empires*', a book we discussed in the context of Grainville's *Le Dernier Homme* in Chapter Two. This is how the monster describes the effect this experience has on him:

> I should not have understood the purport of this book, had not Felix, in reading it, given very minute explanations. He had chosen this work, he said, because the declamatory style was framed in imitation of the eastern authors. Through this work I obtained a cursory knowledge of history, and a view of the several empires at present existing in this world; it gave me an insight into the manners, governments, and religions of the different nations of the earth. [...] I heard of the discovery of the American hemisphere, and wept with Safie over the hapless fate of its original inhabitants. These wonderful narrations inspired me with strange feelings. Was man, indeed, at once so powerful, so virtuous, and magnificent, yet so vicious and base? He appeared at one time a mere scion of the evil principle, and at another as all that can be conceived of noble and godlike.

To fully 'understand the purport of this book' and the monster's observations we have to remember that Volney's work was widely received as 'a key text of "revolutionary atheism"', as I have already cited Martin Priestman calling it. And yet it is striking that Mary Shelley alias the monster makes no explicit mention of atheism here. Nonetheless, the author's educated contemporary reader would have been sufficiently informed to recognise the significance of this reading material for the development of a mind so pliant and so susceptible as the monster's.

Although Volney's atheism is very much implied in the monster's account, direct reference to it is withheld; so let us fill in that gap. On the final pages of the second and last volume of *The Ruins of Empires*, thus forming the work's ultimate climax, we are shown the Solomonic 'Legislators' addressing the following questions to the peoples of the world (taking Lessing's *Nathan the Wise* to a higher level):

---

164 *Frankenstein. The 1818 Text*, p. 79; the subsequent two passages pp. 79–80.

'Is sugar sweet, and gall bitter?' — 'Yes.' 'Do you love pleasure, and hate pain?' — 'Yes.' 'Respecting these objects and a multiplicity of others of a similar nature, you have then but one opinion. Now tell us, is there an abyss in the centre of the earth, and are there inhabitants in the moon?' At this question, a general noise was heard, and every nation gave a different answer. Some replied in the affirmative, others in the negative; some said it was probable, others said it was an idle and ridiculous question, and others that it was a subject worthy of enquiry; in short, there prevailed among them a total disagreement. After a short interval, the legislators having restored silence: 'Nations,' said they, how is this to be accounted for? We proposed to you certain questions, and you were all of one opinion without distinction of race or sect: fair or black, disciples of Mahomet or of Moses, worshippers of Bedou or of Jesus, you all gave the same answer. We now propose another question, and you all differ! whence this unanimity in one case, and this discordance in the other.' And the groupe of simple and untaught men replied: 'The reason is obvious. Respecting the first questions, we see and feel the objects; we speak of them from sensation: respecting the second, they are above the reach of our senses, we have no guide but conjecture.' 'You have solved the problem,' said the legislators; 'and the following truth is thus by your own concession established: Whenever objects are present and can be judged of by your sense, you invariably agree in opinion; and you differ in sentiment only when they are absent, and out of your reach. From this truth flows another equally clear and deserving of notice. Since you agree respecting what you with certainty know, it follows, that when you disagree, it is because you do not know, do not understand, are not sure of the object in question: or in other words, that you dispute, quarrel and fight among yourselves, for what is uncertain, for that of which you doubt. But is this wise; is this the part of rational and intelligent beings? And is it not evident, that it is not truth for which you contend; that it is not her cause you are jealous of maintaining, but the cause of your own passions and prejudices; that it is not the object as it really exists that you wish to verify, but the object as it appears to you; that it is not the evidence of the thing that you are anxious should prevail, but your personal opinion, your mode of seeing and judging? There is a power that you want to exercise, an interest that you want to maintain, a prerogative that you want to assume; in short, the whole is a struggle of vanity.'[165]

All belief in God is therefore, so Volney's implication, a mere prejudice sourced by vanity; various religions believe in their various gods 'because [they] do not know, do not understand [and] are not sure of the object in question'. God is something one can ultimately only subject to 'doubt', a term that returns us to the very premise from which Descartes more than one hundred years before Volney had set out. But whereas Descartes in his *Meditationes de prima philosophia* — rather unconvincingly from our perspective today — harnesses doubt in order to substantiate the existence of God, Volney harnesses that same doubt to explode the certitude of religious belief.

It is this atheistic message that also underlies Mary Shelley's *Frankenstein*.[166] It is difficult to judge the precise degree to which she subscribed to atheism herself, and

---

165 *The Ruins*, pp. 318–21.
166 Indeed, Brian Aldiss perceptively calls the novel 'dark and atheistic' in his history of science fiction, *Billion Year Spree* (London: Weidenfeld & Nicolson, 1973), p. 199.

later in her life, following Percy's death, she may have returned to some form of religious spirituality. But during her most formative adolescent and early adulthood years Mary was certainly under the sway of the atheistic worldview propagated by the two most important men in her life, her father William Godwin and her husband Percy Shelley. Where Gilbert and Gubar remind us that the novel's above-cited epigraph stems from Milton's *Paradise Lost*, it is surely no less significant that the novel was, on the page following its title and epigraph, 'respectfully inscribed' 'To William Godwin, Author of *Political Justice, Caleb Williams*, etc.' If one reads the novel between the lines, one finds ample evidence to suggest that *Frankenstein* exhibits as much an atheistic agenda as it does a feminist one. Take for instance the last lines of the previous quotation from her novel and reread them as a comment not alone on mankind but also on God: 'Was [God], indeed, at once so powerful, so virtuous, and magnificent, yet so vicious and base? He appeared at one time a mere scion of the evil principle, and at another as all that can be conceived of noble and godlike'. These lines rehearse arguments Percy Shelley had put forward in *Queen Mab* in which he expressly critiques the Christian conception of a benevolent God; he notes there how '[t]he doctrine of Necessity [...] teaches us, that in no case could any event have happened otherwise than it did happen, and that, if God is the author of good, he is also the author of evil; that, if he is entitled to our gratitude for the one, he is entitled to our hatred for the other'.[167] In *Frankenstein* Mary Shelley seems to ventriloquize Percy's 'hatred' of God onto the monstrous second Adam who cries out 'in agony': 'Hateful day when I received life! [...] Accursed Creator! Why did you form a monster so hideous that even now you turned from me in disgust?'[168]

We know far less about Mary Shelley's religious attitude than we do about her husband's; she did not write much expressly about religion, and the statements she did produce remain largely inconclusive. And even in Percy Shelley's case, despite the plethora of pronouncements on atheism, Christianity and God in his numerous publications and essay fragments, critics' opinions have diverged more than one might expect, as we saw earlier. Was he an atheist, an agnostic or some kind of spiritual sceptic? And to what degree did he change his opinion on religion and the afterlife after 1817? Whatever the answer we might give from today's perspective, Shelley throughout his life certainly liked to present himself — often with a dash of daring, and always defiantly, especially towards his father — as an atheist, whatever he may have understood this atheism to entail. And he remained adamantly anti-Christian until his untimely death. For her part, Mary was as much a companion of her husband in body — bearing him five children, only one of whom, Percy Florence Shelley, survived — as she was in spirit and intellect. Although she had a mind of her own, as we shall see later when we discuss *The Last Man*, she was strongly influenced by her husband during his lifetime. Thus in the 'Introduction' to the 1831 third edition of *Frankenstein* she recollects: 'Travelling, and the cares of a family, occupied my time; and study, in the way of reading, or improving my

---

167 *Queen Mab*, pp. 488–90.
168 *Frankenstein. The 1818 Text*, p. 88.

ideas in communication with [Percy's] far more cultivated mind, was all of literary employment that engaged my attention'.[169]

We are fortunate that Mary Shelley's journals have survived in which she lists, in scrupulous detail, all of her and most of her husband's reading in the years preceding and during the period of composition of *Frankenstein*. Indeed, many of the books they read at home were read aloud by Percy to his wife, and conversations would have inevitably followed. Likewise, Mary was an attentive listener of — and occasional contributor to — her husband's conversations with his friends; recalling the events of summer 1816 on Lake Geneva, Mary in 1831 notes: 'Many and long were the conversations between Lord Byron and Shelley, to which I was a devout but nearly [*sic*] silent listener'. And it was not just 'ghost stories' that preoccupied them there, but also the most recent scientific discoveries and theories; she continues:

> During one of these, various philosophical doctrines were discussed, and among others the nature of the principle of life, and whether there was any probability of its ever being discovered and communicated. They talked of the experiments of Dr. [Erasmus] Darwin, (I speak not of what the Doctor really did, or said that he did, but, as more to my purpose, of what was then spoken of as having been done by him,) who preserved a piece of vermicelli in a glass case, till by some extraordinary means it began to move with voluntary motion. Not thus, after all, would life be given. Perhaps a corpse would be re-animated, galvanism had given token of such things: perhaps the component part of a creature might be manufactured, brought together, and endued with vital warmth.

Through her own readings as much as through intellectual osmosis, Mary was fully au fait with the most advanced science of her day. The Shelley-scholar Anne K. Mellor thus observes in a chapter on the science background of *Frankenstein*:

> While no scientist herself [...], Mary Shelley nonetheless had a sound grasp of the concepts and implications of some of the most important scientific work of her day. In her novel, she distinguished between that scientific research which attempts to describe accurately the functionings of the physical universe and that which attempts to *control* or *change* the universe through human intervention. Implicitly she celebrates the former, which she associates most closely with the work of Erasmus Darwin, while she calls attention to the dangers inherent in the latter, found in the work of [Humphry] Davy and [Luigi] Galvani.[170]

As Mellor relates, Mary notes in her diary for 29 October 1816: 'Read Davy's Chemistry with Shelley', a reading she continued for some days while Percy pursued his study of Montaigne and Don Quixote, sometimes reading from them aloud.[171] Lest we overlook this, let us remind ourselves that at this time in September 1816 Mary had just turned nineteen!

Two years earlier, having just eloped with Percy to France in July 1814, Mary records having read, among many other titles, her father's *Political Justice* and Percy's

---

169 Ibid., p. 170; the two subsequent quotations pp. 171 and 171–72.

170 Anne K. Mellor, *Mary Shelley: Her Life, Her Fiction, Her Monsters* (New York & London: Routledge, 1989), p. 90.

171 Mary Shelley, *The Journals of Mary Shelley 1814–1844*, ed. by Paula R. Feldman and Diana Scott-Kilvert, 2 vols (Oxford: Clarendon Press, 1987), vol. 2, p. 143.

Queen Mab, rather weighty reading for a sixteen-year-old in any period considering the degree to which both works are steeped in contemporary materialist discourse and an unorthodox atheistic worldview; in that year and the following year 1815 she reads, besides Goethe's *Sorrows of Werter* (her spelling) and Milton's *Paradise Lost* and *Paradise Regained*, her mother's *Posthumous Works*, Gibbon's *History of the Decline and Fall of the Roman Empire* (a work notorious for its author's criticism of Christianity as 'a new species of tyranny' especially in Chapters XV and XVI), Fontenelle's *'Plurality of the Worlds'* (as she cites the title), Madame de Staël's *'De l'Alemagne'* (again, as she cites it), Voltaire's *Candide*, *La Bible Expliquée* and his *Micromégas*, Swift's *Tale of a Tub*, Coleridge's *Poems*, Wordsworth's *Excursion*, and the '1st vol. of [Holbach's] *Système de la Nature*', the last of which of course was that era's Bible of atheism. Her list of Percy's readings for 1815 includes '2 vols of Plutarch in Italian' — which together with Milton's *Paradise Lost* and Goethe's *Werther* make up the triumvirate of texts read by the monster. Mary's reading list for 1816 covers works by Locke, Voltaire, Rousseau, Montesquieu, more Gibbon and more of her mother's work, specifically her *Rights of Women*, as well as the above-cited 'Introduction to Davy's Chemistry'; her literary quota comprises works by Byron, Cicero, Cervantes, Moritz, Richardson, Schiller, Scott, Swift, Wieland, and again Milton, as well as countless Gothic novels, constituting in the words of Gilbert and Gubar 'a program of study in English, French, and German literature that would do credit to a modern graduate student'.[172] Percy meanwhile was studying Aeschylus's *Prometheus*, Plutarch, Tacitus and Lucretius's *'De Naturâ'*, as she gives the title, as well as Locke's essays and Godwin's *Political Justice*. Clearly, many of the authors they are reading together during these years are, if not explicitly anti-religious, then certainly decidedly anti-Christian, with such pagan proponents of a materialistic worldview as Lucretius standing side-by-side with some of the leading Enlightenment critics of religion.

That Percy and Mary were, by and large, like-minded in their opposition to any form of organized religion, at least during Percy Shelley's lifetime, is testified by two biographical 'events', if that is the right term. The first relates to an intriguing episode during Mary's and Percy's stay in Chamonix in the summer of 1816 accompanied by Mary's stepsister (Jane) Claire Clairmont. The details of the story are related by Gavin de Beer in an article tellingly entitled 'An "Atheist" in the Alps'.[173] Based on de Beer's discoveries, the Shelley-biographer Richard Holmes went on to summarize the sequence of events as follows:

> In the hotel register at Chamonix, and in another at Montanvert, and possibly in a third on the return journey down the Arve valley, [Percy] made a celebrated entry in Greek. Under the 'Occupation' column, he inscribed the deliberately provocative tag: [...] Democrat, Philanthropist and Atheist. Under the destination column, for him and the two girls, he wrote succinctly 'L'Enfer' [French for 'Hell', R.W.]. Only by considering the reputation Chamonix [which stood for Mont Blanc, R.W.] had among the travelling English at this time, as a natural temple of the Lord and a proof of the Deity by design, is it possible

172 *The Madwoman in the Attic*, p. 224.
173 'An "Atheist" in the Alps', *Keats–Shelley Memorial Bulletin*, 9 (1958), 1–15.

to realize the spirit in which Shelley wrote these entries, and the astounding fury with which they were greeted. [...] Yet when Byron himself came came across one of Shelley's three entries with [his friend] Hobhouse in September, he immediately felt obliged to cross it out as indelibly as possible for Shelley's own protection.[174]

In his resumé Holmes does not do full justice to de Beer's findings. Originally scholars had assumed that Percy Shelley had made only one such entry in a visitors' album kept at the hut on the Montanvert elevation (that is, the very location where Victor Frankenstein reencountered the monster of his making) and that it was this entry that all subsequent travellers were referring to and which Byron had erased. But as de Beer has convincingly documented, the varying accounts of Shelley's and Byron's contemporaries as well as the surviving documentary evidence show that Shelley had made no fewer than four album entries, all with different wordings, yet all professing his atheism. It was as if Shelley was trying to flaunt his atheistic creed as ostentatiously and provocatively as possible in a place that, for British travellers in the early nineteenth century, had taken on symbolic significance as nature's temple to the Christian Creator God; as one such British traveller, Thomas Raffles, deplored in 1817: 'Yet, amid these scenes — surrounded by the sublimest demonstrations of the eternal power and Godhead of the Almighty, a wretch has had the hardihood to avow and record his atheism'.[175] However, as de Beer reveals, it was not the Montanvert entry that Byron could have erased because he actually never visited the Montanvert lodge; the entry Byron *had* come across and sections of which he *had* erased was the one Shelley had written into the register of an inn on the road from Chamonix to Geneva, so de Beer surmises. Moreover, Byron had erased the entry, or parts of it, in order not to protect Shelley but rather himself and Claire Clairmont, who was now carrying Byron's child; he wanted neither Claire to be associated with atheism nor himself through his connection with her. Perhaps the most crucial piece of documentary evidence that de Beer was able to uncover was an original leaf from one of these albums dated 23 July 1816 which someone had later torn out and bound together with a copy of Shelley's *The Revolt of Islam*, and which, by the late nineteenth century, had come into the possession of Lord Crewe. This is the entry described by Holmes above, with the destination given as 'Hell' alongside the Greek words for 'I am a lover of mankind, democrat, and atheist'; and this entry is also the one which shows Claire's name scratched through, de Beer writes, so as 'to be decipherable only to anyone knowing what to look for'.[176] Whereas this entry designates only Shelley himself as an atheist, the destination of 'Hell' (*Enfer*) is placed beside both his name and Mary's (although, curiously, 'Hell' does not appear next to Claire's cancelled out name in the subsequent line).

Another entry is perhaps even more significant in our context; it is the one described by Humphrey Senhouse in his diary who was doing the Mont Blanc tour with the poet Robert Southey and Edward Nash in 1817. On 26 June of that year,

---

174 *Shelley, the Pursuit*, p. 342.
175 'An "Atheist" in the Alps', p. 7; the subsequent quote p. 8.
176 Ibid., p. 9.

just one year after Shelley had visited the area, they ascended to the Montanvert lodge; Senhouse's diary entry reads:

> A blank book is kept here in which travellers enter their names, many have indulged their Genius in recording their travelling achievements, in Scraps of Poetry &c. &c. Amongst other entries were the following:
> Mr Percy Bysche [sic] Shelley
> Madame son Epouse [French for: Madame his wife, R.W.]
> Theossteique la soeur [a gallicized version of the Greek word θεοστυγη, hating god or hated of god, followed by the French words for 'the sister', here concealing Claire Clairmont, R.W.]¹⁷⁷

Crucially, in the column to the right Shelley had placed the Greek words Εκαστοι αθεοι, 'atheists one and all', indicating that all three saw themselves, certainly at this moment in time, as atheistic freethinkers and infidels.¹⁷⁸

The second 'event' is a short manuscript fragment Mary wrote in late 1821 or early 1822 and which was published for the first time only one hundred and sixty years later in a short article by Emily Sunstein in the *Keats-Shelley Memorial Bulletin* for 1981. Sunstein relates how around this time Percy was challenged by Byron, who always remained hostile towards Shelley's manifest atheism, to produce a rebuttal of a Christian treatise Byron had recently come across, namely Charles Leslie's late seventeenth-century *A Short and Easy Method with the Deists*. Byron had ordered Leslie's book from the publisher and bookseller John Murray in London on 9 October 1821 just as he was preparing to leave Ravenna to join the Shelleys in Pisa. Thomas Medwin, Shelley's cousin and later biographer who also became a close friend of Byron's, had just moved in with the Shelleys in Pisa in the autumn of 1820 and witnessed Byron broaching the challenge; these are purportedly Byron's words (as recollected by Medwin in his 1824 *Conversations of Lord Byron*):

> 'Here is a little book somebody has sent me about Christianity, that has made me very uncomfortable: the reasoning seems to me very strong, the proofs are very staggering. I don't think you can answer it, Shelley; at least I am sure I can't, and what is more, I don't wish it.'¹⁷⁹

Shelley immediately set himself to drafting a response which survives in the form of two untitled fragments which as the Shelley scholar Claude Brew has argued

---

177 Ibid., p. 5.

178 It is perhaps of more than just biographical interest to add here that, one year later in 1817, Shelley was denied legal custody of his children by Harriet for his 'atheism', 'republicanism' and 'infidelism'. On 11 January 1816 [wrongly for 1817], Percy writes to Mary: 'They have filed a bill, to say that I published *Queen Mab*, that I avow myself to be an atheist & a republican; with some other imputations of an infamous nature. This by Chancery law I must *deny* or *admit* upon oath, & then it seems that it rests in the *mere* discretion of the Chancel[l]or to decide whether those are fit grounds for refusing me my children. They [the Westbrookes] cannot have them at any rate; my father or *my* nearest relations are the persons whom the Chancellor will intrust with them if they must be denied to me. It is therefore sheer revenge. [...] because I am an infidel'; *The Letters of Percy Bysshe Shelley*, ed. Jones, vol. 1, p. 527.

179 Medwin, *Conversations of Lord Byron*, second edition 1824, as cited by Emily Sunstein in 'Shelley's Answer to Leslie's *Short and Easy Method with the Deists* and Mary Shelley's Answer, "The Necessity of a Belief in the Heathen Mythology to a Christian"', in *Keats-Shelley Memorial Bulletin*, 32 (1981), 49–54 (p. 49).

must have been part of this projected but soon abandoned essay on the subject of miracles and Christian doctrine.[180] The fragments rehearse a number of arguments familiar to us from Shelley's other writings on religion in general and Christianity in particular. Replying directly to Byron, the first fragment begins: 'At your request I shall endeavour to state, in the form of remarks on Leslie's short Method with the Deists, a few of the most obvious reasons for considering that system of opinions most erroneously called the Christian religion [...] as false', and continues later:

> According to the theory of every religion, the universe is governed by an intelligent Power infinitely benevolent and wise; had a Being of this character interested itself in instructing and benefiting mankind it is probable it would have devised means less inadequate to such an end than the system of doctrines so tardy[,] so inefficacious and so partial as the Christian religion.[181]

Mary too felt inspired to produce a response and began drafting an essay of her own that would have carried the heading 'The Necessity of a Belief in the Heathen Mythology to a Christian'. What we have is not a fully worked out product but a draft outline of thoughts and ideas which would have been worked into a fully fledged essay that was intended to serve as an 'Examination of the proofs of the Xtian religion'; but like Percy's, her essay too was soon abandoned. What we are left with is a sketch that contains an assortment of notes, only some short passages of which I shall cite here; her plan seems to have been to compare 'heathen', specifically Greek, and Christian belief systems in order to demonstrate that the Christian notion of divine revelation is neither more consistent nor more credible than the Greek notion of divine revelation, and hence that no superiority can or should be granted to Christianity which bases itself on Jewish pronouncements no older than those of the ancient Greek philosophers and poets. She opens by noting: 'If two facts are related not contradictory of equal probability and with equal evidence, if we believe one we must believe the other. 1st — There is as good proof of the Heathen Mythology as of the Christian religion. 2^{ly} that they not contradict one another con. if a man believes in one he must believe in both'. She goes on to observe,

> the revelation of God as Jupiter to the Greeks [may be] a more successful revelation than that as Jehovah to the Jews. Power wisdom beauty & obedience of the Greeks — greater & of longer continuance — than those of the Jews. Jehovahs promises worse kept than Jupiters. [...] If the revelations of God to the Jews on Mt. Sinai had been more peculiar & impressive than some of those to the Greeks they wd [would] not immediately after have worshipped a calf. [...] The only public revelation that Jehovah ever made of himself was on Mt. Sinai — Every other depended upon the testimony of a very few & usually of a single individual — [182]

---

180 See his 'A New Shelley Text: Essay on Miracles and Christian Doctrine', in *The Keats-Shelley Memorial Bulletin*, 28 (1977), 10–28; Brew argues that the essay fragments formerly known as 'On the Christian Religion' and 'On Miracles' were part of one essay, which he gives the title 'Essay on Miracles and Christian Doctrine'.
181 Ibid., pp. 22 and 23.
182 Sunstein, 'Shelley's Answer to Leslie's *Short and Easy Method with the Deists*', pp. 52–53.

The background to these truncated notes is that Leslie's argument in *A Short and Easy Method with the Deists* had revolved around the claim that if a number of people confirmed independently of one another the accounts given in the Bible, including the miracles described in it, then these accounts must be considered true. In her counter-argument Mary was planning to argue, it seems, that if that were the case one would, by that measure, have to dismiss Moses's account as untenable (by virtue of it being based 'upon the testimony [...] of a single individual'). When she elsewhere asks 'whether as God revealed himself as the Almighty to the Patriarchs & as Jehovah to the Jews he did not reveal himself as Jupiter to the Greeks', we are reminded of Percy Shelley's equally irreverent equation of the Christian God and Jupiter in his *Prometheus Unbound*, which he had completed two years earlier in late 1819. By reducing the Christian religion to the same status as (Greek) mythology, Mary like Percy is seeking to put Christianity's claim to primacy in question.

At least during Percy's lifetime, it seems, Mary was by and large of a similar mind as her husband in religious matters. It should come as little surprise, therefore, to find her freethinking showing through in an early work like *Frankenstein*, written towards the end of the Shelleys' most active antireligious phase. I gave examples above illustrating how the main protagonists of that novel, Victor Frankenstein and the monster he had birthed, can be read also as a caricature of the biblical account of God's creation of Adam. Shelley thus attributes to Frankenstein 'the capacity of bestowing animation', of injecting 'a spark of being into a lifeless thing' in order to fashion 'a human being' in his own likeness. But his is a 'workshop of filthy creation'.[183] When Frankenstein tells Walton '[a] new species would bless me as its creator and source; many happy and excellent natures would owe their being to me', his hubris is God's hubris, too. The 'new species' degenerates, because of its creator's neglect, into a vile miscreant and murdering monster — not unlike God's own creation in his likeness, some might say. Mary Shelley's critique of modern science and the 'Modern Prometheus' segues plainly into a critique of any power that aspires to be not just almighty, but also purportedly — to use Percy Shelley's words in his rejoinder to Leslie, cited above — 'infinitely benevolent and wise', but actually being the opposite. In the second chapter of Volume One of the novel, Mary thus has Frankenstein cite one of the lectures of his chemistry professor, M. Waldmann at Ingolstadt, which concludes:

> The ancient teachers of this science [...] promise impossibilities, and performed nothing. The modern masters promise very little; they know that metals cannot be transmuted, and that the elixir of life is a chimera. But these philosophers, whose hands seem only made to dabble in dirt, and their eyes to pour over the microscope or crucible, have indeed performed miracles. They penetrate into the recesses of nature, and shew how she works in her hiding places. They ascent into the heavens; they have discovered how the blood circulates, and the nature of the air we breathe. They have acquired new and almost unlimited powers; they can command the thunders of heaven, mimic the earthquake, and even mock the invisible world with its own shadows.

---

183 *Frankenstein. The 1818 Text*, pp. 31–34; the subsequent passages pp. 32, 27–28 and 172.

If *Frankenstein* illustrates anything, it is that such haughty ambition can only backfire, much as God's Creation has backfired. Yet, subconsciously aware perhaps of the atheistic acerbity implied by her novel, and possibly in an attempt to mitigate its antireligious thrust, Mary adds in the 'Introduction' to the 1831 third edition of the novel, as if on second thought: 'Frightful must it be; for supremely frightful would be the effect of any human endeavour to mock the stupendous mechanism of the Creator of the world'. But even this is ambiguous, for who is mocking the stupendous mechanism? Is it Frankenstein by creating his monster, or is it Mary by creating her tale? Is her tale not frightful, one must ask involuntarily, because God's own creation had turned out to be no better than Frankenstein's?

That Mary felt compelled to add this comment to her 1831 'Introduction' may have come as a result of the negative reviews that the first edition of her novel had incurred. As those reviews illustrate, contemporary readers were very much attuned to the religious double entendre that the narrative masked. Nearly all reviewers remark upon the 'impious' nature of the story. Some see it as a deplorable outgrowth of what they called the Godwinian School of novel writing, recoiling from its 'strong tendency towards materialism', so the reviewer for *The Literary Panorama and National Register* in its June 1818 issue. Mr Godwin's disciples, complained the reviewer for the January 1818 issue of the *Quarterly Review*, 'are a kind of *out pensioners of Bedlam*, and like "Mad Bess" or "Mad Tom", are occasionally visited with paroxysms of genius and fits of expression, which makes sober-minded people wonder and shudder'.[184] And like the reviewer of *The Belle Assemblée, or Bell's Court and Fashionable Magazine*, who wishes 'almost [to] pronounce it to be *impious*', the *Edinburgh Magazine* too takes offense at the author's irreligious attitude; he begins:

> Here is one of the productions of the modern school in its highest style of caricature and exaggeration. It is formed on the Godwinian manner, and has all the faults, but many likewise of the beauties of that model. In dark and gloomy views of nature and of man, bordering too closely on impiety, — in the most outrageous improbability, — in sacrificing every thing to effect, — it even goes beyond its great [Godwinian] prototype...

He concludes:

> We are accustomed, happily, to look upon the creation of a living and intelligent being as a work that is fitted only to inspire a religious emotion, and there is an impropriety, to say no worse, in placing it in any other light. It might, indeed, be the author's view to shew that the powers of man have been wisely limited, and that misery would follow their extension, — but still the expression 'Creator', applied to a mere human being, gives us the same sort of shock with the phrase, 'the Man Almighty', and others of the same kind, in Mr Southey's 'Curse of Kehama'. All these *monstrous* conceptions are the consequences of the wild and irregular theories of the age; though we do not at all mean to infer that the authors who give in to such freedoms have done so with any bad intentions. (my emphasis)

---

184 Both cited from <http://www.rc.umd.edu/editions/mws/lastman/index.html>, accessed on 11 July 2013.

In the light of the novel's 'monstrous' tendencies towards religious 'caricature', 'materialism', 'impropriety' and impiousness, it is no wonder that some reviewers like Walter Scott felt that *Frankenstein* could not have been written by anyone other than Percy Shelley himself.[185] It is highly unlikely that Scott knew of Shelley's *A Refutation of Deism* which had appeared in 1815 in a rather obscure new periodical entitled *Theological Inquirer* published by George Cannon, whose visit at their home Mary records in her journal for January 1815,[186] but should Scott or indeed any other reviewer have been aware of it, they would surely not have overlooked the poignancy in relation to Mary's novel of the statement made there by the deist Theosophus — 'the atheist is a monster among men'.[187]

Of First Monsters and Last Men

Victor Frankenstein's atheism-inculcated monster is not just Mary Shelley's first literary creation, the novel is also widely acclaimed as — in the words of the science fiction writer Brian Stableford — 'the *archetypal* science fiction novel'.[188] In his *Billion Year Spree. The History of Science Fiction*, another distinguished writer of science fiction, Brian Aldiss, opened his historical survey with a discussion of the work that he considers the first authentic novel of modern science fiction, written by 'the first science fiction writer' — the novel is of course *Frankenstein*, the writer Mary Shelley.[189] *Frankenstein* is, W. Warren Wagar remarks in the same vein in his 1982 study on *Terminal Visions. The Literature of Last Things*, 'a pioneering effort to bring man and the science and technology of his modern world into significant confrontation'.[190] But critics on the whole concur that Mary Shelley was a literary pioneer in two regards — Wagar accordingly continues by noting that, 'if the earlier work [*Frankenstein*] founded the genre of science fiction [...], *The Last Man* has an even stronger claim to consideration as the first major example of secular eschatology in literature'. In his 1987 *Origins of Futuristic Fiction* Paul Alkon enlarges on Wagar's assessment:

> Mary Shelley's story is a complete secularization of Apocalypse that reduces revelation to a source of imagery decorating a work whose structure is more like that of a futuristic *Journal of the Plague Year*, told with romantic embellishments and given a bleak ending that foreshadows existentialist eschatologies of the sort now so much in vogue. [...] If her *Last Man* may be read as a kind of dialectic questioning of Revelation by the method of total secularization of apocalyptic form as well as doctrine — and certainly it may thus be interpreted — then so

---

185 'It is said to be written by Mr Percy Bysshe Shelley, who, if we are rightly informed, is son-in-law to Mr Godwin', Scott wrote in his review of *Frankenstein* in *Blackwood's Edinburgh Magazine*, 20 March–1 April 1818; downloaded and cited here from <http://www.rc.umd.edu/editions/mws/lastman/index.html>, accessed 11 July 2013.
186 *The Journals of Mary Shelley 1814–1844*, vol. 1, p. 62.
187 *The Works of Percy Bysshe Shelley*, ed. Forman, vol. 6, p. 59.
188 Brian Stableford, citing Brian Aldiss, in 'Man-Made Catastrophes', in *The End of the World*, ed. by Eric Rabkin, Martin Greenberg et al. (Carbondale: Southern Illinois Press, 1983), pp. 97–138 (p. 102).
189 *Billion Year Spree*, pp. 8 and 21.
190 *Terminal Visions*, p. 13; the subsequent quote also p. 13.

of course in varying degrees may the majority of subsequent futuristic fictions that tell of mankind's last days. In this as in other respects, Shelley's *Last Man* inaugurates a more viable structure for futuristic fiction than *Le dernier homme* provides. But Shelley could only do so by turning away from conventional form as well as the doctrines of apocalypse.[191]

By and large critics agree that Mary Shelley's claim to originality rests on this 'turning away from conventional form as well as the doctrines of apocalypse'. It is this turning point that I wish to illuminate in more detail in the final section of this chapter. But in order to gauge the degree of this work's novelty we need first to remind ourselves of its plotline and conclusion.

Set between the years 2073 and 2100 *The Last Man* (see Figure 4.3) is a tale told from the perspective of one Lionel Verney, a republican leader in a post-monarchical England who is set to become the last man to survive a world-encompassing seven-year plague pandemic. After the peaceful deposition of the royal family, Britain has become a republic.[192] Verney himself is an orphaned and penniless shepherd whose father had been friend and confidant of the old king. His lonely and brutish life among the Cumbrian hills is transformed when he meets Adrian Windsor, the quondam heir to the throne. At the age of sixteen Lionel is elevated to a life of culture, scholarship and intellectual pursuit; he later weds Adrian's sister Idris against the wishes of their domineering and ambitious mother, the Duchess of Windsor. Lionel's own sister Perdita marries the equally ambitious Lord Raymond. The happy group settles at Windsor Castle until Raymond is prompted to re-enter political life. In so doing he forms an illicit relationship with the Greek noblewoman and patriot Evadne, former beloved of Adrian, destitute since the death of her father. When he is rejected by Perdita, the Byron-look-alike Raymond escapes his shame by joining the Greeks in their war for independence. In 2092 the plague breaks out in Egypt and reaches Constantinople just as the city is being beleaguered by the Greeks; 'this enemy to the human race', we read, 'had begun in June to raise its serpent-head on the shores of the Nile; parts of Asia, not usually subject to this evil, were infected. It was in Constantinople, [...] the strong hold [*sic*] of the Moslems' which was to be 'rescued from slavery and barbarism, and restored to a people illustrious for genius, civilization, and a spirit of liberty'.[193] The fall of the city opens the way for the plague to spread across Europe. In the second volume we see Raymond killed within the city's walls. His death is followed by that of his wife whose suicide leaves Clara, their only daughter, an orphan. During the ensuing years the plague depopulates the East, Europe and America; by the time it reaches the British Isles it has become apparent that humanity is in the process of being completely eradicated. As the plague crosses the channel, the traditional social order in England breaks down: 'Poor and rich were equal now, or rather the poor were the superior', we are told, 'since they entered on [the necessary] tasks with alacrity and experience, while ignorance, inaptitude, and habits of repose, rendered

---

191 *Origins of Futuristic Fiction*, pp. 188 and 190.
192 I have adapted portions of this summary from Jane Blumberg's *Mary Shelley's Early Novels. 'This Child of Imagination and Misery'* (Basingstoke: MacMillan Palgrave, 1992), pp. 118–19.
193 *The Last Man*, pp. 127–28; the subsequent passages pp. 223 (similarly 230) and 233.

them fatiguing to the luxurious'. By the time we reach the third and last volume of Shelley's horrendous tale of sickness and suffering, London is reduced to a mere thousand souls. 'Man existed by twos and threes', we read, 'man, the individual who might sleep, and wake, and perform the animal functions; but man, in himself weak, yet more powerful in congregated numbers than wind or ocean; man, the queller of the elements, the lord of created nature, the peer of demi-gods, existed no longer'. In 2096 the few hundred remaining survivors decide that, in order to escape the plague, they must flee the damp British climate; eighty survivors reach Dijon in a France eerily vacated of its population, fifty reach Geneva. By the time they cross the Alps into the drier clime of Italy only four are left, the girls Clara and Evelyn, and the two male protagonists Adrian and Lionel. Then Evelyn dies of typhus; shortly thereafter Adrian and Clara drown in a storm while trying to cross by boat to Greece. The 'sole survivor of [his] species', Lionel Verney, who has rescued himself to the Italian shore, makes for Rome where, portentously, he looks down as the last human being on millennia of human history, manifested in Rome's countless 'truncated columns' and 'broken capitals' 'which once made part of the palace of the Caesars'.[194] 'The voice of dead time, in still vibrations', he contemplates, 'is breathed from these dumb things, animated and glorified as they were by man', reminding one of the overbearing 'king of kings' Ozymandias in Percy Shelley's eponymous poem. While 'the world was empty [and] mankind was dead', only poetry, 'stamped on these lifeless things', seems able to survive. 'The sight of the poetry eternized [sic] in these statues', Verney goes on to reflect, 'took the sting from the thought, arraying it only in poetic ideality'.[195] Hence he resolves 'to write a book', should a 'saved pair of lovers' somewhere on this world one day pass this way; the passage runs:

> I also will write a book — for whom to read? — to whom dedicated? And then with silly flourish (what so capricious and childish as despair?) I wrote,
>
> DEDICATION
> TO THE ILLUSTRIOUS DEAD.
> SHADOWS, ARISE, AND READ YOUR FALL!
> BEHOLD THE HISTORY OF THE
> LAST MAN.
>
> Yet, will not this world be re-peopled, and the children of a saved pair of lovers, in some to me unknown and unattainable seclusion, wandering to these prodigious relics of the ante-pestilential race, seek to learn how beings so wondrous in their achievements, with imagination infinite, and powers godlike, had departed from their home to an unknown country?

In the meantime, with neither God's Last Judgment nor a new Eve for himself in sight, Lionel has no other option but to resign himself to his fate: 'I had, from the moment I had reasoned on the subject, instituted myself the subject to fate, and the servant of necessity, the visible laws of the invisible God'.

---

[194] Ibid., pp. 336, again 336, 335 and 337.

[195] It has often been pointed out that it is probably no mere coincidence that the appellation of Shelley's protagonist, Verney, which is after all not a particularly common name in English, is reminiscent of Voltaire's country seat in Switzerland, Ferney.

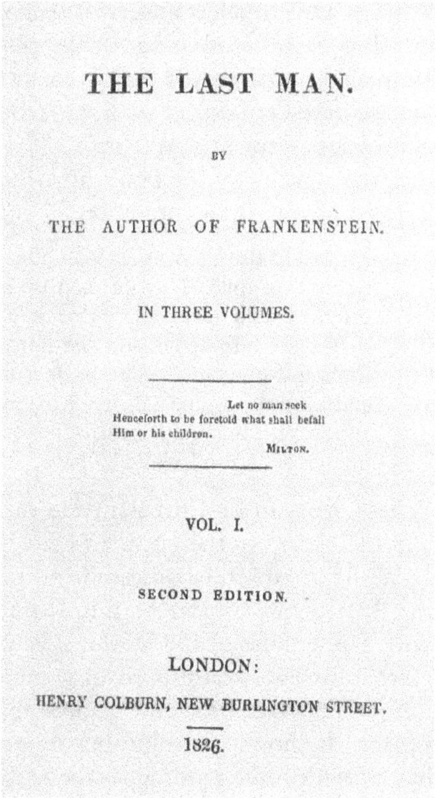

FIG. 4.3. Title page of the 1826 anonymously published first British edition of Mary Shelley's *The Last Man*.

'Invisible God' and 'the servant of necessity' — do these two key phrases not recall the deists' invisible God on the one hand and Holbach's and Godwin's materialism on the other? 'All had of necessity to be', Goethe had complained after reading Holbach's *Système de la nature* as we saw in Chapter Three, 'and therefore no God'. Through to its end, *The Last Man* is eerily drained of any signs of God's presence or compassion. For its part, religion is portrayed primarily as a form of pretense and deceit, most prominently in the figure of the 'impostor-prophet' the small band of survivors encounter on their way through France in Volume Three:

> The principal circumstances that disturbed our tranquility during this interval, originated in the vicinity of the impostor-prophet and his followers. They continued to reside at Paris; but missionaries from among them often visited Versailles — and such was the power of assertations, however false, yet vehemently iterated, over the ready credulity of the ignorant and fearful, that they seldom failed in drawing over to their party some from among our numbers. [...] But [the preacher] was instigated by ambition, he desired to rule over these last stragglers from the fold of death; his projects went so far, as to cause him to calculate that, if, from these crushed remains, a few survived, so that a new race should spring up, he, by holding the reins of belief, might be remembered by the post-pestilential race as a patriarch, a prophet, nay a deity.[196]

---

196 *The Last Man*, p. 281; the subsequent passage p. 335.

Morton D. Paley has observed regarding this false prophet, whose fraternity will perish no less than all others: 'The episode of the preacher, like the earlier one of the maniac, seems designed to show that one can neither have one's eschatological cake nor eat it: the religious paradigm is shown to be irrelevant even when the conditions it prophesies are brought forth'.[197] This irrelevance of religion is underscored in the final episode of the book, in which we see Verney visiting a Vatican uncannily vacated of any divine presence:

> I haunted the Vatican, and stood surrounded by marble forms, and the eternal fruition of love. They looked on me with unsympathizing complacency, and often in wild accents I reproached them for their supreme indifference — for they were human shapes, the human form divine was manifest in each fairest limb and lineament. The perfect moulding brought with it the idea of colour and motion; often, half in bitter mockery, half in self-delusion, I clasped their icy proportions, and, coming between Cupid and his Psyche's lips, pressed the unconceiving marble.

Whether pagan or Christian, the marble saints and gods are 'unconceiving', 'icy' and indifferent to the last man's fate.

With humankind eradicated and Lionel Verney finding himself the sole survivor, the 'Last Man' reflects: 'I am in Rome! I behold, and as it were, familiarly converse with the wonder of the world, sovereign mistress of the imagination, majestic and eternal survivor of millions of generations of extinct men.' This short passage is a unique illustration of how a mere few words can take on deep interpretive significance. It shows on a number of levels how Mary is using her book to position herself within the argumentative latticework of contemporary science and religion. Not only does it hark back to keywords and concepts we became familiar with from our discussion of Percy Shelley's religious writings and the interpretation of his poem 'Mont Blanc', it also shows how Mary is translating her husband's and her father's theories into her own sceptical idiom. Three points are worth highlighting.

First, feminist scholars in particular have rightly stressed that Mary used her novel to formulate a female counter-argument to Godwin's and Percy's philosophies. Mellor thus observes:

> Inherent in Godwin's and Percy Shelley's political ideology were more extreme utopian concepts that Mary Shelley's novel specifically calls into question. Adrian repeats the visionary ideas that Godwin had propounded in *Political Justice* (1793) and that Percy Shelley had endorsed in *Prometheus Unbound*: the conviction that the improved powers of the rational mind could conquer disease and even death. As Godwin argued, 'We are sick and we die [...] because we consent to suffer these accidents'. When the rational mind has reached its full powers, Godwin claimed, 'there will be no disease, no anguish, no melancholy and no resentment'. At that point, he speculated, man 'will perhaps be immortal'. [...] But Mary Shelley shows that the powers of the human mind are feeble in comparison to those of all-controlling nature.[198]

---

197 'Mary Shelley's *The Last Man*: Apocalypse Without Millennium', in *The Other Mary Shelley*, ed. by Audrey A. Fisch, Anne K. Mellor and Esther H. Schor (Oxford: Oxford University Press, 1993), pp. 107–23 (p. 118).
198 *Mary Shelley: Her Life, Her Fiction, Her Monsters*, pp. 161–62; the following quotation p. 168.

She shows also that not just man as an individual is mortal, but also mankind as a species. Mellor goes on to note:

> But Mary Shelley explicitly denies a religious interpretation of her plague. The illiterate who insists that the plague is God's punishment for human sin and that he and his followers constitute an 'Elect' that will be saved is explicitly condemned as an 'Imposter' [sic] whose deceived followers perish along with everyone else. [...] Mary Shelley's novel recognizes only one controlling Power — not Percy Shelley's Necessity, but Mutability. Mary Shelley's skepticism thus cuts through the fabric, not only of her own ideology of the egalitarian family and a sacred mother nature, but of *all* ideologies.

In her study of Mary Shelley's early novels, Jane Blumberg similarly declares that Verney's conclusions 'represent a kind of proto-existentialism and at the same time depart from the political and philosophical systems that preoccupied Godwin and Percy Bysshe Shelley'; she contends: 'Of all her novels, *The Last Man* is perhaps Shelley's most political; [...] it attempts to realize and debunk the variety of Utopian ideas imagined by her circle [and] exemplified first in *Queen Mab* and later modified and developed in *Prometheus Unbound*'.[199] Mary Shelley uses the novel 'as a platform for arguing against some of the ideals of her husband, and against revolution and political idealism in particular. [...] The monsterlike holocaust that descends upon the Greek revolution in *The Last Man* is a graphic fictional rebuttal of Percy's political views'.[200] This rebuttal of Percy's Godwinian ideals is aptly illustrated by a dialogue between the characters Adrian and Ryland shortly after the plague has reared its head in Volume Two; the spring of 2093 has arrived with particular splendour this year and 'delight awoke in every heart, delight and exultation; for there was peace through all the world; [...] and man died not that year by the hand of man', we are told. Adrian, who all critics agree is the novel's stand-in for Mary's husband, then addresses his friend Ryland thus, expressing all the ideals that Percy held high:

> 'Let this last but twelve months [...] and earth will become a Paradise. The energies of man were before directed to the destruction of his species: they now aim at its liberation and preservation. Man cannot repose, and his restless aspirations will now bring forth good instead of evil. The favoured countries of the south will throw off the iron yoke of servitude; poverty will quit us, and with that sickness. What may not the forces, never before united, of liberty and peace achieve in this dwelling of man?'[201]

To which the more sceptical Ryland responds:

> 'Dreaming, for ever dreaming, Windsor!' said Ryland, the old adversary of Raymond, and candidate for the Protectorate at the ensuing election. 'Be

---

199 *Mary Shelley's Early Novels*, pp. 117 and 134; the following quotation p. 139.

200 It is of course not just feminist scholars who recognize Mary's antagonism to the prevailing male 'Romantic mythologies'; Morton D. Paley observes in his article '*The Last Man*: Apocalypse Without Millennium': 'Ultimately, *The Last Man* is a repudiation of what might simplistically be termed the Romantic ethos as represented, for example, in the poetics and politics of Percy Bysshe Shelley' (p. 111; 'romantic mythologies' appears on the same page).

201 *The Last Man*, this and the subsequent quotation p. 159.

assured that earth is not, nor ever can be heaven, while the seeds of hell are natives of her soil. When the seasons have become equal, when the air breeds no disorders, when its surface is no longer liable to blights and droughts, then sickness will cease; when men's passions are dead, poverty will depart. When love is no longer akin to hate, then brotherhood will exist: we are very far from that state at present.'

Of course, the irony that Mary introduces into her novel is that both are wrong; 'Paradise' is neither a short-term nor a long-term prospect because men are not masters over their own destiny; there are forces in this world that they cannot control.

But whereas these passages bear out Mellor's and Blumberg's conclusion that Mary was sceptical to the utmost of the utopian promise held out by Godwin and espoused also by Percy, the short segment I cited earlier also betrays, secondly, that she had nonetheless also come to internalize some of their atheistic views of religion and science, even as she sought to modify them in order to reflect her personal outlook. Thus the turn of phrase that the world is the 'sovereign mistress of the imagination' harks back directly to the poetics of the imagination that Percy Shelley had formulated in 'Mont Blanc' and elsewhere in his work; the word 'eternal' in 'majestic and eternal survivor' conjures up Percy's belief in James Hutton's eternalism, which, as Rudwick informed us, 'denied that the cosmos had an ultimately divine foundation'.[202] (I earlier also cited the passage in *A Refutation of Deism* in which Shelley had claimed that 'until it is clearly proved that the Universe was created, we may reasonably suppose that it has endured from all eternity'.)[203] And when she speaks of 'millions of generations of [...] men' Mary is echoing Percy's 'ceaseless generations' of 'man's revolving race', as he had put it in *Queen Mab*. Verney as Mary Shelley's *alter ego* and mouthpiece is clearly embracing Percy Shelley's notion of 'eternal nature's law'[204] alongside with nature's indifference to mankind's fate on planet Earth; but Verney alias Mary does not endorse Percy's and Godwin's vision of a humanity that will ultimately succeed in transcending 'transience and decay' in the future. Indeed, Mary is much more down to earth, and pessimistic even, in formulating her own counter-vision of a human species destined to suffer the very annihilation and dissolution that Percy so abhorred.

Third, and finally, the locution 'millions of generations of *extinct* men' connotes the latest theories not just of deep time that were emerging from the new geological and biological sciences, but also the inference that species could become extinct — but in this regard, too, Mary is putting her own unique stamp on this highly contested scientific finding. If it is true that, as the German historian Lucian Hölscher has observed, it is 'only since the discovery of the endless expansion of space and time that a notion of the long-term progress of humankind could emerge; since then humans have begun to conceive utopias and projections of a long-term future for mankind' ('Erst seit der Entdeckung der unendlichen Ausdehnung von

---

202 *Bursting the Limits of Time*, p. 334.
203 *The Works of Percy Bysshe Shelley*, ed. Forman, vol. 6, p. 65.
204 *Queen Mab*, p. 397.

Raum und Zeit konnte es die Vorstellung eines langfristigen Fortschritts der Menschheit geben. Seither entwirft sich die Menschheit in Utopien und Prognosen eine langfristige Zukunft')[205] — Godwin being a prime example — then we must add to Hölscher's observation the corrective that it is also only since the discovery of deep space and deep time that writers have permitted themselves to envision an annihilation of mankind that supersedes the Christian vision of a terminal Last Judgment. We could hence amend Hölscher's statement to read: 'since then humans have also begun to conceive utopias and projections of a long-term future *in which mankind has no future at all because he is made to die out*'. And Mary Shelley is the first European novelist explicitly to do so. The opening lines of Volume Three of *The Last Man* thus expressly 'undramatically and even banally'[206] renounce any coming of the Last Judgment:

> Hear you not the rushing sound of the coming tempest? Do you not behold the clouds open, and destruction lurid and dire pour down on the blasted earth? See you not the thunderbolt fall, and are deafened by the shout of heaven that follows its descent? Feel you not the earth quake and open with agonizing groans, while the air is pregnant with shrieks and wailings, — all announcing the last days of man?
>
> No! none of these things accompanied our fall! [...] Once man was a favourite of the Creator, as the royal psalmist sang, 'God had made him a little lower than the angels, and had crowned him with glory and honour. God made him to have dominion over the works of his hands, and put all things under his feet.' Once it was so; now is man lord of the creation? Look at him — ha! I see plague! She has invested his form, is incarnate in his flesh, has entwined herself with his being, and blinds his heaven-seeking eyes. Lie down, O man, on the flower-strown earth [...], all you can ever possess of it is the small cell which the dead require.[207]

Of course, Mary Shelley was not the first writer to put the Day of Reckoning in question, as we have already seen. There were forerunners to *The Last Man*, first and foremost among them Klingemann's *Nightwatches of Bonaventura* examined in the previous chapter; Byron's 1816 poem 'Darkness', discussed variously throughout this study; and Thomas Campbell's 1823 poem 'The Last Man', Thomas Hood's 1826 satirical ballad 'The Last Man', and the March 1826 short story 'The Last Man' in *Blackwood's Magazine*, all three of which I briefly mentioned at the close of the previous chapter. But Mary Shelley's novel is of a fundamentally different order. Her vision of the end is serious and set in a near future, theirs either satirical (Hood's poem and the anonymous *Blackwood's Magazine* story) or set in a future world in which nature is expiring due to exhaustion, as in Campbell's and Byron's poems. Campbell's poem begins:

---

205 Cited in 'Abendrot — Gutwetterbot', an interview with Lucian Hölscher, *Spektrum der Wissenschaft*, January 2011, p. 25.

206 I have adapted this formulation from Robert Lance Snyder's highly instructive analysis of 'Apocalypse and Indeterminacy in Mary Shelley's *The Last Man*', in *Studies in Romanticism*, 17 (Fall 1978), 435–52 (p. 441).

207 *The Last Man*, pp. 229–30.

> I saw a vision in my sleep,
> That gave my spirit strength to sweep
> Adown the gulf of Time!
> I saw the last of human mould
> That shall Creation's death behold,
> As Adam saw her prime!
>
> The Sun's eye had a sickly glare,
> The Earth with age was wan,
> The skeletons of nations were
> Around that lonely man!
> Some had expired in fight — the brands
> Still rusted in their bony hands;
> In plague and famine some!
> Earth's cities had no sound nor tread;
> And ships were drifting with the dead
> To shores where all was dumb!
>
> Yet, prophet-like, that lone one stood,
> With dauntless words [...][208]

This is the deist's vision of the world and 'the eclipse of Nature', as Campbell calls it later in his poem. There is neither divine reckoning here nor any form of celestial retribution, nor does humankind become extinct before its time. In both Byron's and Campbell's poems, the history of nature on Earth and the history of man on Earth are coterminous. Only when the sun and planet Earth come to the end of their lifespans, when 'with age [they are] wan', is humankind too forced to encounter its natural demise. But whatever Mary Shelley believed, her story is neither Christian nor deistic in outlook. The life of humankind is not just terminated by a global pandemic, it is taken in the midst of humanity's very bloom on planet Earth. Rather than being allowed to run its natural course, the life of the human species is cut short as if unnaturally, but — so the irony of this novel — by quintessentially natural means. Its annihilation seems not even to be motivated by any particular villainy or sin of mankind. The plague is no different from any other disease at any other time — this time it just happens to be more encompassing, more deadly and more unsparing. The plague may thus be nature's instrument, but it happens as if by caprice: all other life forms on planet Earth remain unaffected, after all.[209] It is just one species that is extinguished, and this seems by mere chance or happenstance to be the human species. In Mary Shelley's novel, 'beautiful nature' — which at the beginning of Volume Two once afforded such 'enthusiastic

---

[208] Thomas Campbell, 'The Last Man', *The Complete Poetical Works* (Boston: Phillips, Sampson and Co., 1854), pp. 199–201 (p. 199).

[209] Morton D. Paley observes in '*The Last Man*: Apocalypse Without Millennium': 'In contrast to the universe of Cousin de Grainville, Mary Shelley's has no sovereign God and no supernatural agency. However, although eschatology has been secularized to a great degree, there remains ghosts of a former paradigm and any rational explanation of the destruction of humankind is conspicuously absent — the plague that kills everyone in the world save four people and then stops remains at least as arbitrary as Calvinist predestination' (p. 110).

pleasure' to all who beheld her[210] — is the one and only force that determines life and death, and in this world there is no longer any place for an active God. 'Nature asserted *her* ascendancy' (my emphasis), Verney tells us — and we can add, from today's interpretive vantage point, she has asserted her female ascendancy especially also over the male Christian God.[211]

This paradigm shift from (the Christian) God to Nature was long in the making, as I detailed in the earlier parts of this study. By the time Mary Shelley began to conceive and write *The Last Man* in 1824, that is at the very waning of the threshold period 1775–1825 identified by Foucault in *The Order of Things*, she had studied many of the seminal works written by deists and atheists during and before that half century, including key texts by William Drummond, Fontenelle, Gibbon, Holbach, Hume, Paine and Voltaire, not to mention their antique predecessor Lucretius, the pagan philosopher of nature; together with her father's *Political Justice*, her mother's *Rights of Women* and her husband's *Queen Mab* with its explicitly atheistic 'Notes' this constitutes a veritable early nineteenth-century armoury of deistic and atheistic tracts. Beyond these, she and Percy took an active interest in the work of such contemporary scientists as the British chemist Davy and the Italian physicist Galvani, as we saw above in the context of her researching the scientific underpinnings for her novel *Frankenstein*; in December 1814 Percy and Mary attended one of the Garnerin brothers' London lectures on electricity, gasses and 'Phantasmagoria' (that is, optical illusions). And like her husband, her interest extended also to the new science of geology, Mary reading Buffon's 'theorie du terre' in 1817, and Percy ordering, as we saw, Cuvier's work from Italy via a Paris bookseller in early 1822. It is hardly surprising therefore to find both Percy and Mary taking an interest in fossils, too, with Mary at age seventeen jotting into her journal on 7 March 1815 the entry: 'Breakfast with Hogg — go to British Museum — see all the fine things — ores, fossils, statues divine &c &c'.[212]

During the second and third decades of the nineteenth century, when Percy and Mary Shelley wrote their poetry, essays and novels, one could easily keep abreast of current advances in the sciences even without having to resort to any overly burdensome reading programme of primary sources; journals like the *Edinburgh Review* and the *Quarterly Review*, both of which the Shelleys read on a regular basis (as documented by Mary's reading lists in her journals), were easily accessible and contained a wealth of informative digests, often accompanied — with varying political emphases (the *Quarterly* was more conservative and Christian in orientation) — by extended original quotations and commentary, of contemporary publications in the sciences (including the volumes of the *Transactions of the Geological Society*), politics, law, medicine, economics, literature and literary criticism as well as of scientific travel accounts like those by Archibald Campbell, Lewis and Clarke or Mungo Park, whose 1799 *Travels in the Interior Districts of Africa* Mary read in

---

210 *The Last Man*, p. 128, the subsequent passage p. 319.
211 In his article 'Of Gender, Plague, and Apocalypse: Mary Shelley's *Last Man*', Steven Goldsmith argues that the plague in *The Last Man* serves as 'Shelley's meticulously plotted revenge against patriarchy'; in *The Yale Journal of Criticism*, 4 (Fall 1990), 129–73 (p. 154).
212 *The Journals of Mary Shelley 1814–1844*, vol. I, p. 73.

1814 and again in 1816. Thus Mary would have been aware, not just through her and Percy's first-hand knowledge of Buffon's and Cuvier's work, but also through these journals' abstracts of the transactions of the various philosophical and scientific societies that leading geologists were now convinced that many of the fossil species they were finding had become extinct in earlier epochs of our planet's ever lengthening history. Thus *The Edinburgh Review* ran a long review of the first edition of the Italian geologist Giovanni Battista Brocchi's 1814 study of fossil shells, *Conchiologia Fossile Subapennina con Osservazioni Geologiche sugli Apennini e sul Suolo adiacente*, in its February 1816 issue; it was this study that inspired Charles Lyell some years later to articulate the following observation on the extinction of species:

> Now we might coincide in opinion with the Italian naturalist, as to the gradual extinction of species one after another, by the operation of regular and constant causes, without admitting an inherent principle of deterioration in their physiological attributes. We might concede 'that many species are on the decline, and that the day is not far distant when they will cease to exist'.[213]

Mary would have been even more keenly aware of the fact that her husband had made specific reference to these debates surrounding the Earth's long prehistory, fossils and the extinction of species in his *Prometheus Unbound* (written 1818 and 1819), especially Act IV, lines 296–318:

> The wrecks besides of many a city vast,
> Whose population which the earth grew over
> Was mortal, but not human; see, they lie,
> Their monstrous works, and uncouth skeletons,
> Their statues, homes and fanes; prodigious shapes
> Huddled in grey annihilation, split,
> Jammed in the hard, black deep; and over these,
> The anatomies of unknown wingèd things,
> And fishes which were isles of living scale,
> And serpents, bony chains, twisted around
> The iron crags, or within heaps of dust
> To which the tortuous strength of their last pangs
> Had crushed the iron crags; and over these
> The jaggèd alligator, and the might
> Of earth-convulsing behemoth, which once
> Were monarch beasts [...]: till the blue globe
> Wrapt deluge round it like a cloke, and they
> Yelled, gasped, and were abolished; or some God
> Whose throne was in a comet, past, and cried,
> Be not![214]

William D. Brewer remarks in his study *The Shelley-Byron Conversation* that these lines are

> consistent with a nonevolutionary theory of extinction, such as the one dev-

---

213 Lyell, *Principles of Geology*, vol. 2, p. 129.
214 'Prometheus Unbound', Act IV, ll. 296–318; here cited from *Shelley's Poetry and Prose*, ed. Reiman and Fraistat, p. 278.

eloped by Cuvier. And as Cameron argues, Panthea's speech as a whole is 'based on Cuvier's famed catastrophe theory, which posited neither a divine creation nor an evolutionary progression but a series of natural creations and destructions'. [...] And in both [Byron's] *Cain* and [Shelley's] *Prometheus Unbound* there seems to be the suggestion that mankind, like the inhabitants of the dead civilizations described by Parkinson, could be annihilated by future geological revolutions.[215]

The name Parkinson here refers to the Christian natural philosopher James Parkinson, to whose traditionalist *Organic Remains of a Former World. An Examination of the Mineralized Remains of the Vegetables and Animals of the Antediluvian World; centrally termed extraneous fossils* (1804–1811) Percy Shelley had been introduced by his friend Elizabeth Hitchener already at the end of 1811.[216] Parkinson is manifestly opposed to both Hutton's notion of unitarianism and Lamarck's and Brocchi's notion of a gradual change in the planet's surface formations and species; he writes:

> The phenomena particularised in the latter part of this volume, yield some important knowledge respecting the structure of the planet which we inhabit. These facts would also supply, if it were needed, the strongest proof of the error of those who believe, that there had always been a succession something similar to what is continually observed; and that the human species have had, and will have, a uniform and infinite existence. With almost equal force will these phenomena oppose that system also, which considers the form and structure of the surface of this planet, as resulting from a regularly recurring series of similar mutations. The loss of whole species or genera, and the later creation of others, as is assumed in this work, are circumstances which strongly militate against both these hypotheses. It must, however, be acknowledged whether a single species has been thus lost.[217]

What is essential about this account is the degree to which it substantiates how even a biblical literalist like Parkinson was by this time at the end of the first decade of the nineteenth century finding himself necessitated to accommodate the newest fossil findings within his traditionalist Christian belief system; while accepting the concept of deep time, in his *Organic Remains of a Former World* Parkinson resorts to equating the long timespan of Cuvierian geohistory 'with the "successive" days of the Creation story in Genesis'.[218] This peculiar amalgam is graphically visualized by the frontispiece of his work which shows Noah's Ark foregrounded by a beach with fossil shells (see Figure 4.4); the Deluge has wiped out countless species whose remains now litter the shores onto which the Ark will soon disembark the remaining extant species Noah has rescued.

---

215 *The Shelley-Byron Conversation*, p. 32. See also Lloyd N. Jeffrey, 'Cuvierian Catastrophism in Shelley's *Prometheus Unbound* and *Mont Blanc*', *The South Central Bulletin*, 38 (Winter 1978), 146–52.

216 See Cameron, *The Young Shelley*, p. 394; also see his letters to Hitchener of 26 December 1811 in which he admits 'never [to have] heard of Parkinson', but that he will send for the volume, and the letter of 14 February 1812 in which he now acknowledges that he has a copy of it.

217 *Organic Remains of a Former World. An Examination of the Mineralized Remains of the Vegetables and Animals of the Antediluvian World generally termed Extraneous Fossils*, 3 vols (London: Sherwood, Neely and Jones, 1811), vol. 3, pp. xii–xiii.

218 Rudwick, *Bursting the Limits of Time*, p. 497.

In short, by the time Mary started conceiving *The Last Man* in the early 1820s, little doubt remained, certainly among the more progressive geologists of the period, but even also among Christian scriptural geologists and *cognoscenti* like Jean-André de Luc, James Parkinson, William Buckland, William Conybeare, William Whewell, Adam Sedgwick and Granville Penn that many of the fossils that were being uncovered indeed stemmed from now extinct animal species. Of course, that species could die out through large-scale geological catastrophes is one thing, but that the cause of extinction might be a merely mundane natural epidemic gone global was altogether another thing. Moreover, that *animal species* could become extinct was perhaps imaginable, but was it possible that *Homo sapiens*, Creation's crowning glory, might become extinct before its prime? This seemed unthinkable. After all, in the Christian view of Creation the human species was generally accorded a privileged place, and a domineering one to boot, a view that culminated in the axiomatic anthropomorphism which, as Lynn Barber has pointed out, was 'such a conspicuous feature of Victorian natural history writing'.[219] With the eternalism of a Hutton, Lamarck and Percy Shelley for its part premised — in Hutton's words — on the 'wisdom, system, and consistency'[220] of nature, it in effect — in Rudwick's words — equally 'denied the reality of extinction'.[221] Hutton conceded, Rudwick details,

> that there was no fossil evidence of *human* life before the times of recorded human history, but he treated plant and animal fossils as surrogates or proxies for that missing evidence. In his deistic system of intelligent design, any 'world' with lots of non-human life would have been pointless, unless in reality humans were also present to fulfill its ultimate purpose.[222]

To imagine in a work of fiction the complete annihilation of the human species, nipped in the bud by a natural pandemic, after which all other species continued as if *Homo sapiens* had never existed, thus marked a radical break with both dominant strands of thinking in the domain of Natural History; even Cuvier with his catastrophe theory had not dared venture down the path of humankind's extinction, rescuing the human species through the cataclysm of the last revolution — which was widely equated with the biblical Deluge — to the present day.[223] In this context Lionel Verney's above-cited phrase 'survivor of millions of generations of extinct men' takes on a double edge, indicating first that he may be the last in a long succession of generations of human beings, all of whom are now deceased, but also second that, assuming his eventual death as the sole lone survivor, humanity would have died out as a species altogether.

---

219 *The Heyday of Natural History 1820–1870* (London: Jonathan Cape, 1980), pp. 77–78.
220 Hutton, 'Theory of the Earth', p. 304.
221 *Bursting the Limits of Time*, p. 452.
222 *Earth's Deep History*, p. 72.
223 Lloyd N. Jeffrey notes, 'Cuvier believed, following the scholarship of his day, that man had not existed on the earth for more than about five thousand years. It is not true, as is often supposed, that Cuvier visualized a "special creation" succeeding every destructive cataclysm. What he did propose was that, after each geological convulsion, the earth was repeopled from the remaining human population'; 'Cuvierian Catastrophism in Shelley's *Prometheus Unbound* and *Mont Blanc*', p. 149.

FIG. 4.4. James Parkinson, frontispiece of *Organic Remains of a Former World. An examination of the Mineralized Remains of the Vegetables and Animals of the Antidiluvian World* (1804). Note the outline of Noah's Ark positioned precariously on a mountain above the waters of the Deluge; the rainbow in the background symbolically touches the Ark, the foreground shows fossil shells on a beach.

My argument thus far has been to build a case that the unique combination of atheism and modern science, especially geology, supplies not just the foundation but indeed the necessary prerequisite for Mary Shelley's narrative of a sole 'Last Man' surviving a lethal pandemic. But atheism and modern geology were not the final trigger for the novel's inception. The immediate impulse came, as is so often the case in literary inspiration, from a different source, namely personal circumstance. *The Last Man* is what scholars call a *roman à clef*,[224] with its central figures corresponding to real-life persons in Mary's close-knit circle: Adrian thus stands for her husband Percy Shelley, Lord Raymond for Lord Byron and Lionel Verney for Mary Shelley herself.[225] Ever since Percy's unexpected passing away in his sailing accident we find Mary's journal filled with expressions of her most disconsolate grief and despair. She gave up writing the third book of her journal on 8 July 1822, the day Percy Shelley and Edward William were found drowned on the Italian coast. The fourth book is begun with a delay of three months: she titles it her 'Journal of Sorrow', adding 'Begun 1822 | But for my Child it could not End too soon'.[226] This gloomy remark is symptomatic of the journal's overall tone and temper. Mary feels bereft and left alone; she records in the new journal's very first entry, dated 2 October 1822:

> On the Eighth of July I finished my journal. This is a curious coincidence — The date still remains, the fatal 8th — a monument to shew that all ended then. And I begin again? — oh. never! But several motives induce me, when the day has gone down, and all is silent around me, steeped in sleep, to pen, as occasion wills, my reflexions & feelings. First; I have now no friend. [...] Now I am alone! Oh, how alone!

During the subsequent months and years she declaims over and again her 'sense of eternal & infinite misery' and how 'all is to me dead', deploring her 'utter solitude', 'irreperable misery', and 'vacant days'. But it is not just the loss of her husband Percy that affects her so; her lament is also that of a mother who has lost all but one of her children. Her first child Clara died just weeks after its birth in March 1815; her second child William died of malaria in 1819; her third child Clara Evelina died in September 1818; and while her fourth child Percy Florence survived, her fifth child died of a miscarriage in June 1822 just weeks before Percy Shelley's death. Thus she writes on 7 October 1822:

> My William, Clara, Allegra [Claire Clairmont's child with Byron, who had died in early 1822, R.W.] are all talked of — They lived then — They breathed

---

[224] So Mellor in *Mary Shelley: Her Life, Her Fiction, Her Monsters*, p. 148, so also more recently Graham Allen, *Mary Shelley* (Basingstoke: Palgrave, MacMillan (*Critical Issues* series), 2008), p. 90.

[225] Muriel Spark in *Child of Light. A Reassessment of Mary Wollstonecraft Shelley* (Hadleigh: Tower Bridge Publications, 1951) sees Verney's 'solitary wanderings' as 'symboli[zing] Mary Shelley's own destiny' (p. 161). However, Mellor points out that the equation of Verney and Mary is too simple; the author of *The Last Man* deposited aspects of herself also in the characters of Perdita and Idris (*Mary Shelley: Her Life, Her Fiction, Her Monsters*, p. 153), as well as Lionel Verney, who all figure as 'self-projections' of one sort or another.

[226] *The Journals of Mary Shelley 1814–1844*, vol. 2, p. 428; the subsequent passages pp. 429, 433, 440 (repeated 441), 443 and 436.

this air & their voices struck on my sense, their feet trod the earth beside me — & their hands were warm with blood & life when clasped in mine. Where are they all? [...] They are all gone & I live — if it be life to be as I am.[227]

Her feelings of 'extreme melancholy' and solitude continue into 1824; on 30 January she writes: 'I never prayed so heartily for death as now'; and on 14 May she notes how her 'mind is as gloomy as this odious sky — without human friends I must attach myself to natural objects'. It is at this time, in May 1824, that Mary begins to conceive and write her novel *The Last Man*. With her mind preoccupied by the new undertaking, she records in her journal on 14 May: 'The last man! Yes I may well describe that solitary being's feelings, feeling myself as the last relic of a beloved race, my companions, extinct before me — '. It was on the next day that she learned of the death of Byron at Missolonghi, the friend she called Albe, the lover of Claire and the father of Allegra; but Byron was, as Mary well knew, the author also of the 'mystery' drama 'Heaven and Earth', containing Byron's dark and melancholic vision of a vanishing mankind being inundated by the waters of the Deluge, and whose last words — uttered by Noah's son Japhet — are 'Why, when all perish, why must I remain?'[228] Just as Byron's Japhet laments the loss of the woman he loves to the rising waves, Mary records on 15 May:

> This then was the 'coming event' that cast its shadow on my last night's miserable thoughts. Byron has become one of the people of the grave — that innumerable conclave to which the beings I best loved belong. [...]
> Albe — the dear capricious fascinating Albe has left this desart world
> What do I do here? Why am I doomed to live on seeing all expire before me? [...] At the age of twenty six I am in the condition of an aged person — all my old friends are gone [...]. Each day I repeat with bitterer feelings 'Life is the desart and the solitude'...

It is melancholy reflections like these, along with the utter despair and despondency that she felt during the years following the death of her closest loved ones, that trigger the extraordinary idea to invent a tale of a lone survivor bereft of all human companionship. Hers are no idealized 'solitudes sublime', as in Wordsworth's *Prelude* (Book IV, l. 484), her solitudes are composed of real-life anguish and depression — a factual rather than an imaginary epitome of Romantic *Weltschmerz*. If the sublime is quintessentially about the smallness of man in the face of an overpowering force of nature, then what could be more sublime, and more humbling, than the image of a singular and lonely Last Man staring out at the vast space that is nature, now emptied of all human presence bar himself. At the exact mid-point of *The Last Man*, in Chapter Five of Volume Two, Verney — in the knowledge of the fate that would befall him (we must recall that Verney decides to pen his story retrospectively at the end of the novel) — had accordingly declared:

> In the face of all this we call ourselves lords of the creation, wielders of the elements, masters of life and death, and we allege in excuse of this arrogance,

---

227 Ibid., p. 435; the subsequent quotations pp. 474–76, 476–77 and 478.
228 'Heaven and Earth. A Mystery', in *The Poems and Plays of Lord Byron*, 3 vols (London: J. M. Dent, [n.d.]), vol. 2, pp. 405–29 (p. 429).

> that though the individual is destroyed, man continues for ever. Thus, losing our identity, that of which we are chiefly conscious, we glory in the continuity of our species, and learn to regard death without terror. But when any whole nation becomes the victim of the destructive powers of exterior agents, then indeed man shrinks into insignificance, he feels his tenure of life insecure, his inheritance on earth cut off.[229]

In construing a world in which only one human being survives a deadly plague, Mary Shelley radicalizes, and in doing so simultaneously deflates, the Romantic fantasy of both absolute solitude and absolute individuality, exposing them as the delusional figments that they had always been. Absolute solitude and absolute individuality, her novel declares prosaically but resolutely, can be achieved only at the expense of the complete annihilation of humanity — save the last man to enjoy that solitude.

However, there can be no enjoyment in and of this solitude because, as Mary Shelley does not fail to remind us, Verney's position is not that of Robinson Crusoe, who was the first ever fictional character to be subjected to this kind of extreme existential solitude in a novel. As Paul Alkon notes in his study of *Science Fiction Before 1900*:

> Before Daniel Defoe published *Robinson Crusoe* in 1719, no one, not even those who sent their travelers out to the moon and beyond, had imagined anything like Crusoe's long solitude. It is from this unusual perspective that Defoe invites readers to contemplate afresh every aspect of their civilization from its religion to its chairs, tables, and ways of making bread.[230]

In the penultimate chapter of her novel, written one hundred years after Defoe's, Mary Shelley underscores just how different the situation is into which she has placed her protagonist; in a passage I have cited more fully in my Introduction, she lets Verney reflect:

> For a moment I compared myself to that monarch of the waste — Robinson Crusoe. [...] Yet he was far happier than I: for he could hope, nor hope in vain — the destined vessel at last arrived, to bear him to countrymen and kindred, where the events of his solitude became a fire-side tale. To none could I ever relate the story of my adversity; no hope had I.[231]

And this in turn deprives the survivor of the very essence of that which makes him human — or indeed *her*. Verney is after all, as all scholars who have written about *The Last Man* have remarked, Mary's primary self-projection in this novel.[232] In this very vein the 1826 contemporary reviewer of *The Literary Gazette* asks: 'Why not *the last Woman?*', but then adds rudely, 'she would have known better how to paint her distress at having nobody left to talk to: we are sure the tale would have been

---

229 *The Last Man*, p. 167.
230 *Science Fiction Before 1900*, p. 23.
231 *The Last Man*, p. 326.
232 W. Warren Wagar observes in *Terminal Visions*: Lionel Verney 'is also a masculine version of Mary herself. The last man was in fact a woman' (p. 14).

more interesting'.²³³ As regards 'having nobody left to talk to', the atheistic German philosopher and critic of Christianity and another contemporary of Mary Shelley's, Ludwig Feuerbach, notes more to the point in *The Essence of Christianity*, published fifteen years after *The Last Man* in 1841:

> Without other men, the world would be for me not only dead and empty, but meaningless. Only through his fellow does man become clear to himself and self-conscious; but only when I am clear to myself, does the world become clear to me. A man existing absolutely alone, would lose himself without any sense of his individuality in the ocean of Nature; he would neither comprehend himself as man, nor Nature as Nature. The *first* object of man is man.
>
> [Ohne den Andern wäre die Welt für mich nicht nur tot und leer, sondern auch sinn- und verstandlos. Nur an dem Andern wird der Mensch sich klar und selbstbewußt; aber erst, wenn ich mir selbst klar, wird mir die Welt klar. Ein ganz für sich allein existierender Mensch würde sich selbstlos und unterschiedslos in dem Ozean der Natur verlieren; er würde weder sich als Menschen, noch die Natur als Natur erfassen. Der *erste* Gegenstand des Menschen ist der Mensch.]²³⁴ (emphasis by Feuerbach)

As if to accord with the German philosopher, Verney's narrative appropriately ends with him setting sail on the Mediterranean, the very 'ocean of Nature' conjured up by Feuerbach, 'in search of a partner for their solitude'.²³⁵ Should that partner never be found, the inevitable result will be the end of humankind.

Recent criticism has viewed this end as one necessarily based on an anti-Christian agenda. As William Lomax has noted, Mary's intention in this 'most pessimistic of Romantic novels' is 'to *reverse* the Christian narrative of creation by "decreating" the human race [...], thereby subverting the Christian *telos* and philosophical world system'.²³⁶ Similarly, Mellor has remarked:

> Once all human perceivers are dead, history ends. The death of the last man is the death of consciousness [...]. This is Mary Shelley's sweeping critique of the Romantic poetic ideology. [...] Mary Shelley posits no overarching mind of God, no eternal Power, no transcendental subject to guarantee the truth or endurance of mental things.²³⁷

Interestingly, although contemporary reviewers of the book were generally rather hostile in their estimations of it (one reviewer described the novel as 'a dedicated failure' and the 'offspring of a diseased imagination, and of a most polluted taste',²³⁸

---

233 Review of *The Last Man* in *The Literary Gazette and Journal of Belles Lettres, Arts, Sciences, &c.*, no. 473 (18 February 1826), 102–03 (p. 103).

234 Ludwig Feuerbach, *The Essence of Christianity* [1841] (based on text of second edition of 1843), trans. by Marian Evans [George Eliot] (London: John Chapman, 1854), p. 81; *Das Wesen des Christentums* (Stuttgart: Reclam, 1969), p. 146.

235 *The Last Man*, p. 341.

236 William Lomax, 'Epic Reversal in Mary Shelley's *The Last Man*: Romantic Irony and the Roots of Science Fiction', in *Contours of the Fantastic: Selected Essays from the Eighth International Conference on the Fantastic in the Arts*, ed. by Michele K. Langford (New York: Greenwood Press, 1990), pp. 7–17 (p. 7).

237 *Mary Shelley: Her Life, Her Fiction, Her Monsters*, p. 159.

238 Review of *The Last Man* in *The Monthly Review, Or Literary Journal*, New Series 1, March 1826,

another spoke of the novel's 'monstrous fable',[239] whereas the reviewer for *The Panoramic Miscellany* carped: 'With respect to the work before us, we are free to declare — that we have rarely met with an instance in which a subject so promising was more lamely or incompetently treated. We looked for the sublime, and we met with the frivolous; for the pathetic, and we encountered the inane; for the terrific, and we stumbled on the ridiculous'),[240] in contrast to *Frankenstein* none of the contemporary reviewers of *The Last Man* took any particular notice of what today's critics, myself included, see as the novel's distinctly anti-Christian message (although it was banned in June 1826 throughout the Habsburg Empire because the works by both Shelleys were considered anti-Catholic by the Austrian authorities).[241] As regards the novel's religious implications, Wagar has remarked:

> The end is not a gateway to a new world, nor a judgment, but simply an end, produced by the cold necessity of natural causes. *The Last Man* is thus a more or less pure example of secular eschatology. [...] mother earth is beheld murdering her own children. Of the anthropomorphic God and the life after death in which Shelley, paradoxically, believed, there is hardly a word. They are not expressly excluded; but she does not need them in her story, even though its subject is the end of all human life on earth. *The Last Man* will probably never rank as a first-rate work of imaginative literature, and will probably always be overshadowed by *Frankenstein*. But its writing is an event of high significance in the history of secular eschatology, and in the history of the secularization of Western consciousness itself. No such book could have been produced in earlier centuries, or at any rate before the last few decades of the eighteenth.[242]

In a similar vein, Morton D. Paley has observed:

> this Last Man [...] made his appearance in relatively modern times. There is no suggestion of any such being in the Bible, where the unique, elected individual — Moses, Noah, Jesus — who figures in stories of redemption is always seen in relation to a community. The Last Judgment is collective and admits of no exceptions. Likewise in secular literature up to the end of the eighteenth century there may be plagues and other disasters, but never general destruction with a sole survivor. The Last Man entered print no less than two centuries ago, early in the period we now call Romantic...[243]

Indeed, I have been making the case that no such book could have been written before the first decades of the nineteenth century when the new science of geology was beginning to provide evidence of the possibility of the extinction of species so compelling that even believers in a strictly Mosaic worldview felt forced to admit

---

pp. 333–35; cited from <http://www.rc.umd.edu/reference/chronologies/mschronology/reviews/mrrev.html>, accessed 8 July 2014.

239 Review of *The Last Man* in *The Literary Gazette, and Journal of Belles Lettres, Arts, Sciences, &c.*, 18 February 1826, 102–03 (p. 102).

240 Review of *The Last Man* in *The Panoramic Miscellany, or Monthly Magazine and Review of Literature*, March 1826, 380–86.

241 See Susanne Schmid, *Shelley's German Afterlives 1814–2000*, p. 27; thanks also to Susanne Schmid for additional information communicated to me in August 2014.

242 *Terminal Visions*, pp. 15–16.

243 'Envisioning Lastness', p. 1.

that fossil 'monuments' cannot but be traces of such lost species within God's Creation.

If Grainville's *Le Dernier Homme* is the prototypical text — half incomplete novel, half unfinished epic, as we detailed in Chapter Two — representing the first paradigm of humankind's demise, the divine (in Europe specifically Christian) paradigm in which the destruction of man is effected by God yet mitigated by resurrection after death, Mary Shelley's novel is the archetype of the second paradigm, Nature's paradigm. Shelley's novel shows that, no sooner than Enlightenment philosophy had succeeded in hollowing out the Christian belief system, traditional Natural Philosophy and Natural History — premised as they mostly were on divine causation and the shallow Mosaic timeframe — became untenable. Once humans had conceived of the 'Death of God', they could also conceive of, and subsequently play out in their imagination, the 'Death of Humankind'. Hence, to return to my earlier conundrum, the birth of mankind that according to Foucault was predicated on the death of God ironically (or maybe not so ironically) coincides with the death of mankind, respectively the emergence of the notion that if God is mortal humanity must be mortal too. Terry Eagleton was the first to recognize this correlation as far as I can see, albeit without specific reference to Mary Shelley: 'There can be no obsequies for the Almighty', he writes poignantly in his recent *Culture and the Death of God*, 'without a funeral ceremony for humanity as well', adding 'The death of God must herald the death of Man, in the sense of the craven, guilt-ridden, dependent creature who bears that name at present'.[244] And now that this extinct God can no longer be held responsible for the death of humankind by way of that quintessential Christian mode of annihilation, the Final Judgment, this capacity for extinction is transferred to a far less numinous but scientifically far more verifiable force, Nature. But, as Shelley's novel also illustrates, Nature is far less forgiving than God. Unlike the Almighty God of Christian scripture, Nature holds out no consolation: there is no promise of resurrection and no admission into paradise, and perhaps no entry even into any form of afterlife. Nature is all there is. And the end is truly the end for humankind. We recall here our discussion in Chapter Three of the German atheist Heydenreich's positive incantation of nature's nothingness as opposed to his contemporaries' perception of it as a terrifying existential abyss. And where both Nietzsche (in his 'Overman' figure, as Eagleton points out) and Foucault postulate a death of man that only serves to portend or herald his rebirth in some superior form, Mary Shelley is the true radical by seemingly following Heydenreich in his more drastic conclusion. Underscoring the revolutionary significance of her work, humankind in *The Last Man* dies without any hope of continuation; unlike Sonnenberg's *Donatoa* and Grainville's *Le Dernier Homme* with their salvational Last Judgment or even Flammarion's *La Fin du Monde* with its transplanetary transplanting of humankind, her tale licenses no such cycling higher to any new shape or place of being; Verney's end represents a definitive end and true annihilation of his species.

244 *Culture and the Death of God*, p. 159.

Having said that, I have to stress that to the best of our knowledge Mary Shelley was not a full-fledged atheist herself. She and Percy steadfastly, as I have indicated, held on to a belief in some form of afterlife or recycling within Nature. What I am arguing is that her exposure to William Godwin's and Percy Shelley's atheism provided her with the philosophical instruments and (anti-)theological underpinnings that made possible the construal of a plotline which, because it presupposed the death of God, also allowed her to envision the death of man. Even where on its surface *The Last Man* contains references to God, they remain only token gestures; the novel's ending allows only one conclusion: the God who reigns in this world is — in the vein of deism — either indifferent or powerless or does not wish to interfere, or — in the vein of atheism — he simply does not exist. Whichever it is, the power to determine over life or death is given over to Nature alone. And should a species ever disappear — as mankind is destined to do in *The Last Man* — Nature herself will continue unmoved; as Jane Blumberg rightly observed,

> [i]n Shelley's ironic vision, man's demise has no effect on nature; she retains her implacable beauty. Nature mocks; after all man's vanity, he emphatically does *not* control his world. Nature's beauty of spring are the flowers of the field, as well as the corpses of men. The plague is hers, just as the burgeoning buds of spring are hers. The physical world remains plentiful and healthy, the seasons persist and the spring and summer still bring forth their bounty. Life goes on without its supposed master.[245]

In formulating a plotline in which not just the male God is made impotent, as it were, but also the promise of mankind's eternal perfectibility is shown to be illusory because mankind becomes extinct before the end of the third millennium, Mary can be seen to reject both the Christian worldview prevailing in this period as well as Godwin's and Percy's alternative atheistic worldview, which itself was premised on the belief in mankind's progressive amelioration in perpetuity. Just years before Mary conceived her novel, Godwin had written in the conclusion of his 1820 anti-Malthus polemic *Of Population. An Enquiry Concerning the Power of Increase in the Numbers of Mankind being an Answer to Mr. Malthus's Essay on that Subject*:

> Look upon this picture and on this, the faithful representment of two worlds! One is the world I was born in [...]; the other is the world of Mr. Malthus. In the Old World [...] there was something exhilarating and cheerful. We felt that there was room for a generous ambition to unfold itself. If we were under the cloud or the grief of calamity, we had still something to console us. We might animate our courage with reflections on the nature of man, and support our constancy by recollecting the unlimited power we possess to remedy our evils, and better our condition. [...] Mr. Malthus blots all this out with one stroke of his pen. [...] He tells us that our ills are remediless [...]. We are fallen into the hands of a remorseless stepmother, Nature: it is in vain that we struggle against her laws; the murderous principle of multiplication will be for ever at work. [...] He forbids us to augur well of the general weal, for all is despair. [...] I can liken Mr. Malthus's world to nothing but a city under severe visitation of a pestilence.

---

245 *Mary Shelley's Early Novels*, pp. 121–22.

All philanthropy and benevolence are at an end. To serve our fellow-citizens is a hopeless undertaking.[246]

By inventing her own method of 'blotting all out with one stroke of her pen', Mary opposes both Malthus and Godwin: she devises a 'remorseless stepmother Nature' that allows for neither a positive nor a negative outcome of mankind's long-term propagation. Her secular vision of a 'severe visitation of a pestilence', which results in mankind's total annihilation bar one, takes *The Last Man* beyond all existing belief systems and worldviews — Christian, Godwinian, Malthusian or otherwise — into hitherto uncharted imaginative terrain. As William Lomax has pointed out,

> with the collapse of the great mythic system of Christianity, new metaphors and new myths had to be found. They are necessarily located in other worlds and future times, for those are the only places new myths can settle; the dead past is the home of the old myth. Thus out of Romantic pessimism and its artistic demolition of the past, science fiction arose. It is the dramatization of the search for new myths that characterizes science fiction. *The Last Man* has had little direct influence on subsequent literature, but it was an early efflorescence in English literature of a cultural consciousness that later crystallized in modern science fiction. The term *anti-epic* means, then, not the destruction of epic, but the transformation of epic.[247]

Lomax's formulation 'new myths' unwittingly harks back to a key aesthetic tenet of German idealism and German romanticism, the perceived need to generate a 'new mythology' in order to move beyond the past (antique) and present (Christian) mythologies and belief systems. This demand for a 'new mythology' was formulated first by Hegel, Hölderlin and Schelling in Tübingen in their so-called 'draft' or 'sketch' ('Entwurf'), subtitled by later editors 'The oldest system programme of German idealism' ('Das älteste Systemprogramm des deutschen Idealismus') — but who of the three actually drafted the text remains a matter of some debate; what we know is that the existing fragment was handwritten by Hegel probably in the summer of 1796. Soon thereafter the expression reappears in Friedrich Schlegel's 'Dialogue on Poetry' ('Gespräch über die Poesie'), a seminal text of German romanticism published in the Jena circle's famous *Athenaeum* journal in 1800.

As vaguely defined as this 'new mythology' was in both the 'Entwurf' and Schlegel's 'Gespräch', it would be rather far-fetched to assume that science fiction is what they had in mind when they proclaimed the need for some form of new mythology. But Lomax's point is well taken: Mary Shelley's novels *Frankenstein* and

---

246 *Of Population. An Enquiry Concerning the Power of Increase in the Numbers of Mankind being an Answer to Mr. Malthus's Essay on that Subject* (London: Longman et al., 1820), pp. 619–20. As Lauren Cameron notes, comparing Mary Shelley's novel on the one hand with the various 'Last Man' texts written in the 1810s and 1820s, on the other with Percy Shelley's and Godwin's philosophies: 'Shelley's work differs from others, however, in the future setting of the events, the natural origin of that destruction, the lack of a melioristic Christian framework, and the pro-social, anti-solipsistic concerns implicit in the book's ethical imperative'; 'Mary Shelley's Malthusian Objections in *The Last Man*', *Nineteenth-Century Literature*, 67 (2012), 177–203 (p. 179).

247 'Epic Reversal in Mary Shelley's *The Last Man*', pp. 14–15.

The Last Man, these two foundational texts of the modern genre of science fiction, both of which simultaneously qualify as defining texts of British romanticism, and both of which are inspired by a new atheistic counter-creed, spawn nothing less than a new kind of literary mythology. Surely one can imagine few better examples of genuinely modern, post-Enlightenment myths than Frankenstein's monster and the notion of a last man on planet Earth. The historian of science fiction Paul K. Alkon seconds this observation when he writes, in 1994:

> Science fiction might indeed be defined as the narrative use of science to create myths allowing novel points of view to the imagination — adding, to be sure, the caveat that such a definition is normative rather than descriptive since not all science fiction succeeds in creating such myths, much less in creating myths so powerful as those established by the genre's masterpieces from *Frankenstein* through *Nineteen Eighty-Four* and beyond.[248]

Mary Shelley's novels *Frankenstein* and *The Last Man* provide two of the most germinal models — the mythic paradigms, as it were — for future novelists and screenwriters to imagine the consequences of that cosmic void left behind after the demise of God. In the galaxy of science fiction God is, if he is permitted to exist at all, relegated to realms beyond the limits of outer space. There is, to re-cite the French science fiction expert Pierre Versins I quoted in Chapter Two, a certain secular rationality inherent in modern science fiction that by necessity transcends religion's 'irrationality'.[249] Where religion does enter into the realm of science fiction, it usually appears, as Versins suggests, as a form of irrationality that no longer befits a technological age; such at least is the supposition behind such literary examples of twentieth-century science fiction as Aldous Huxley's *Ape and Essence* (1948), George Stewart's *Earth Abides* (1949), Arno Schmidt's *Schwarze Spiegel* (*Dark Mirrors*, 1951), Nevil Shute's *On the Beach* (1957), or Günter Grass's *Die Rättin* (*The Rat*, 1986), to mention here only some of the English and German works of literature I will be returning to for closer inspection in the final chapter.

Interestingly, it is not just science fiction that Mary Shelley's *The Last Man* prefigures, Mellor submits, but also twentieth-century existentialism and nihilism as well as deconstruction; she observes:

> *The Last Man* thus opens the way to twentieth-century existentialism and nihilism. Like Camus's *The Plague*, it asserts that all meaning resides, not in an indifferent universe, but in human relationships and language-systems which are inherently temporal and doomed to end. Further, *The Last Man* initiates the modern tradition of literary deconstruction. It is the first work to demonstrate that all cultural ideologies rest on nonreferential tropes [...]. But as the author of the first fictional example of nihilism, Mary Shelley expresses the emotional desolation that such philosophical conviction brings as has no writer since. That this experience of emotional and intellectual despair was first voiced by a woman is, I think, no accident.[250]

---

248 *Science Fiction Before 1900*, p. 7.
249 *Encyclopédie de l'utopie, des voyages extraordinaires et de la science fiction*, p. 56.
250 *Mary Shelley: Her Life, Her Fiction, Her Monsters*, p. 169.

In a similar vein, Barbara Johnson observes how 'the story of *The Last Man* is in the last analysis the story of modern Western man torn between mourning and deconstruction'; the conclusion she draws is that, 'in a certain sense, one can say that modern literature begins with this end of man, at the moment when the last man leaves Rome without knowing what language to speak to it'.[251] One can quibble about the finer points of these assessments[252] (for instance by suggesting that Mary's nihilistic 'conclusion' — if nihilistic is the appropriate term[253] — was anticipated by Klingemann in his *Nightwatches*, discussed in Chapter Three), but there can be little disagreement that, in addition to her powerfully envisioning in *The Last Man* a godless cosmos in which man is at the mercy of Nature alone, her novel succeeds also in simultaneously deflating the Romantics' myth of the sublimity of solitude — epitomized so compellingly by Caspar David Friedrich's paintings — and debunking (or 'deconstructing', to adopt Mellor's expression) the Christian apocalypse as a false myth expressive at best of mankind's vain hope in some form of redemptive immortality, at worst — in Percy Shelley's reading — as a brutal instrument unfairly and vindictively adopted by God to take revenge on human beings for their immorality and infidelity.

Of course, Christian faith in the coming of the Last Judgment did not end there and then, as can be witnessed by the legion of Christian fundamentalists who continue today to believe in the imminence of Armageddon; nor was the artistic Christian imagining of the apocalypse ever drained of its fascination by secular science, as corroborated by the unrelenting production of apocalyptic epics and paintings with a clearly Christian intent, some of which I cited earlier in this study, among them Robert Pollok's *The Course of Time* (1827), Augustin-François Creuzé de Lesser's *Le dernier homme, poème imité de Grainville* (1831), Paulin Gagne's *L'Unitéide, ou la Femme-*

---

[251] 'The Last Man', in *The Other Mary Shelley*, pp. 258–66 (p. 265).

[252] Thus Graham Allen notes in his *Critical Issues* study on Mary Shelley, with specific reference to Mellor: 'Deconstruction does not get rid of our ideas of reason, Enlightenment, right, justice, democracy, fraternity; rather, it attempts to imagine them stripped of the totalization and universalization which has historically tried to fix them as eternal monuments of truth. The target of the most persuasive forms of deconstructive philosophy, which generally means the work of Derrida himself, is the very hidden metaphysics we have seen Shelley critiquing in the apparently rationalist, Enlightenment discourse of her immediate circle. The recurrent analogy made between *The Last Man* and deconstruction is only useful if we recognize the possibility that Shelley's novel, far from simply undermining human ideological systems, uses her story of the plague to re-establish her commitment to reformist, democratic ideas, but stripped of their traditional masculinist, totalizing authority'; *Mary Shelley*, p. 107.

[253] In one of the earliest comparative treatments of this subject matter, Werner von Koppenfels accordingly observes: 'In its pessimism the imaginary visualization of the global catastrophe possesses a nihilistic streak; this is because, in the extreme, it sees itself as apocalypse without metaphysics and as an unveiling of nothingness. Viewed from its outermost exploratory vantage point the writer's imagination presents the universe as subject to the total and final absence of God and human abandonment' ('Diese imaginäre Vergegenwärtigung der Weltkatastrophe trägt in ihrem Pessimismus [...] nihilistische Züge, denn sie versteht sich im Extremfall als Apokalypse ohne Metaphysik, als Entschleierung des Nichts. Von ihrem äußersten Explorationspunkte aus präsentiert die Dichterphantasie das Universum im Zustand totaler, endgültiger Gottferne und menschlicher Verlassenheit'); '"Le coucher du soleil romantique" — Die Imagination des Weltendes aus dem Geist der visionären Romantik', *Poetica*, 17 (1985), 255–98 (p. 257).

FIG. 4.5. Film Poster of the 2009 Hollywood blockbuster *2012*, directed by Roland Emmerich (© 2009 Columbia Pictures Industries, Inc.; All Rights Reserved. Courtesy of Columbia Pictures), which 'updates' the Biblical legend of Noah's Ark. When increased solar radiation heats up the earth's planetary core, causing the earth's tectonic plates and crust to destabilize, Christian fundamentalists believe their apocalyptic prophecies are coming true. Meanwhile, the world's governments build four gigantic arks which they load with humans and animal species in order 'to ensure the continuity of the species'.

The poster image (presenting an image not contained as such in the film) shows a Tibetan monk watching his Himalayan monastery drown under huge tsunami waves; note the structural affinity with Caspar David Friedrich's 1818 *Wanderer above the Sea of Fog*, reproduced as Fig. 3.3 of this volume.

Messie (1858), Élise Gagne's *Omégar, ou le Dernier homme* (1859), John Martin's various Victorian adaptations of the topic in his paintings, including his awe-inspiring *The Great Day of His Wrath* (see Figure I.3) which was the centrepiece of the 2011–2012 Tate Britain exhibition in London (appropriately entitled 'John Martin: Apocalypse'), and most recently Tim LaHaye and Jerry B. Jenkins's evangelical end-time *Left behind* series that I have mentioned on and off and to which I will be returning in my Conclusion. More generally though, audiences today prefer what could be called the secularized adaptations of and sequels to religion's apocalyptic storylines (the Deluge on the one hand, the Last Judgment on the other) as presented by such twentieth-century disaster films as *Armageddon* (Michael Bay, 1998), *Deep Impact* (Mimi Leder, 1998), and *2012* (Roland Emmerich, 2009; see Figure 4.5); or *Children of Men* (Alfonso Cuarón, 2006, based on P. D. James's 1992 novel in which, like in Grainville's *Le Dernier Homme*, mankind has lost its ability to procreate); or *The Road* (John Hillcoat, 2009, based on Cormac McCarthy's 2006 novel in which father and son roam through a barren and ashen world not unlike that depicted in Canto VIII and IX of *Le Dernier Homme*). Similarly, Mary Shelley's death by plague motif has been effectively requisitioned by the silver screen in such films as *Outbreak* (Wolfgang Peterson, 1995), *I am Legend* (Francis Lawrence, 2007, based on the 1971 Boris Segal movie *The Omega Man* — note the use of the term 'omega' — which in turn was based on Robert Matheson's 1954 horror novel *I am Legend*) and, most recently, *Contagion* (Steven Soderbergh, 2011).

Whatever we make of this development and whether we love or loathe today's creative revisionings of such apocalyptic subject matters and scenarios, one thing remains indisputable: it is Mary Shelley who with her novel *The Last Man* established the secular alternative to the religious paradigm of the apocalypse, one that would develop by the late twentieth century into one of the most widely deployed representational templates for mankind's destiny; it is Mary Shelley who provided the blueprint for writers and filmmakers to visualize in a non-religious vein the (impending) annihilation of mankind through natural (or sometimes also unnatural) forces. Klingemann touches on the idea in his *Nightwatches* but fails to exploit its full potential, whereas Grainville in *Le Dernier Homme* — despite some concessions to deism — retains the traditional eschatological framework alongside all the accoutrements of Christian machinery.

What was required for the new template to come into existence was a quantum leap from the Christian paradigm with its faith in the Last Judgment to the secular paradigm and its belief in Nature's power; in the new secular paradigm Nature alone is ascribed the power to determine the destiny of species. With her lone last man Lionel Verney — a figure not imaginable within a Christian framework — Mary Shelley makes this leap. And it was atheism and a secular scientific worldview that laid the foundation for this leap to happen; atheism and science provided the vital ingredients: First, the loss of the sense of human singularity and exceptionalism — from the late seventeenth century onwards, man could no longer arrogantly regard himself as the uniquely God-given focus of the universe; specifically the envisioning of multiple inhabited worlds in the footsteps of Cyrano de Bergerac, Fontenelle,

Kant and others impelled even Christian theologians like Goethe's Weimar friend Johann Gottfried Herder to acknowledge that 'we are not in the centre but rather in a throng' ('wir sind nicht im Mittelpunkt, sondern im Gedränge') and 'just a small fraction of the whole' ('denn wir sind offenbar mit unsrer ganzen Erde nur ein kleiner Bruch des Ganzen').[254] Second, the recognition that the extinction of species is not just possible but has indeed been a routine and recurring feature of the natural history of life on our planet — once one can imagine the finitude of animal existence (as proven by fossil 'monuments', as they were then called), one can also begin to imagine what Foucault called 'the finitude of human existence'. Third, the realization that there are natural forces at work on our planet even today (that is, Mary Shelley's time) that could in fact lead to the extinction of species — in Mary Shelley's case most scholars cite her knowledge of the widespread cholera epidemics surfacing during her lifetime, but she was also versed in the literature on the plague, imaginative and scientific. (We know she had studied Ovid's descriptions of the plague in his *Metamorphoses*, 'Defoe on the Plague' — so her diary entry — and John Wilson's 1816 *City of the Plague*; but she may also have been aware of recent research into the causes of epidemics and viruses which had become a subject of hot scientific debate by her day — one 1822 issue of the *Quarterly Review* contained a summary and critique of six contemporary treatises on 'the Laws and Phenomena of Pestilence'.)[255] Fourth, Mary's understanding, derived from Percy's philosophy of life, that these natural forces were, unlike the Christian God, entirely neutral and disinterested. Fifth, Mary's disillusionment vis-à-vis her father's and husband's notion of infinite human perfectibility — *The Last Man* serves as a (female) corrective to overly optimistic (male) assessments of mankind's capabilities and an unrestrained belief in human progress. Sixth, that God was certainly absent (as in a deistic worldview) and possibly non-existent (as in her husband's early atheistic worldview) — we recall Georg Lukács's trenchant observation, cited in Chapter Two, that 'the novel is the epopee of a world that has been abandoned by God'. And finally, seventh, that Mary Shelley's emotional state of absolute despair and personal isolation following the death of her children, her husband and Lord Byron precipitated a novel that resolutely works to demystify and debunk the Romantic yearning for an absolute — and absolutely sublime — solitude of an absolute ego.

All things considered this is an extraordinary confluence of factors. One should note, however, that for the most part *The Last Man* is *not* a novel of the last man as such, but rather a novel of how one man came to become the last man; the actual story of Lionel Verney as 'the Last Man' begins in earnest only at the end of Mary Shelley's novel, occupying merely the final two chapters of a twenty-nine-chapter book. Thus ironically, while Mary Shelley's *The Last Man* established the template for the near endless procession of last man narratives in the twentieth and twenty-first centuries, supplying as Paul Alkon notes 'a more viable structure for futuristic

---

[254] *Ideen zur Philosophie der Geschichte der Menschheit*, in *Werke*, ed. by Martin Bollacher et al., 10 vols (Frankfurt a.M.: Deutscher Klassiker Verlag, 1989), vol. 6, pp. 26 and 29.

[255] See *The Journals of Mary Shelley 1814–1844*, vol. 1, pp. 75 and 99; see also *Quarterly Review*, vol. 27 (April and July 1822), 524–53.

fiction than *Le Dernier Homme*',[256] it does not make the best use of the template's potential, being characterized among other things, in the words of Muriel Spark, by 'weak characterisation, [a] want of humour, and heaviness of style'.[257] His and his narrative's shortcomings notwithstanding, Lionel Verney remains the defining matrix for every later last man; thus *The Last Man* looks ahead, writes Robert Lance Snyder,

> to a host of subsequent novels which explore these anxieties in more detail. One thinks, for example, of Samuel Butler's *Erewhon* (1872), Fergus Hume's *The Years of Miracle* (1891), H. G. Wells' *The Time Machine* (1895), M. P. Shiel's *The Purple Cloud* (1901), and Jack London's *The Scarlet Plague* (1912), all of which challenge the idea of a future homologous to either the present or the immediate past.[258]

It also looks ahead to those last man figures of the later twentieth century whom we will be encountering in our fifth and final chapter, the narrators of such 'cataclysmic' works as Stewart's *Earth Abides* and Schmidt's *Dark Mirrors*, mentioned earlier, or Nevil Shute's *On the Beach* (1957), Mordecai Roshwald's *Level 7* (1959), Jens Rehn's *Die Kinder des Saturn* (*The Children of Saturn*, 1959), Guido Morselli's *Dissipatio humani generis* (1977), and Cormac McCarthy's *The Road* (2006), as well as such rare last woman narrators as the protagonists of Marlen Haushofer's *Die Wand* (*The Wall*, 1968) and David Markson's *Wittgenstein's Mistress* (1988). Each in his or her own way accomplishes what the Austrian apocalypse expert Eva Horn has described as the unifying feature and function of the last man or last woman figure: 'it is in the figure of the Last Man', she writes,

> that the future becomes a staging ground for imagined scenarios in which man plumbs the range of his existential possibilities and questions his core values and developmental abilities, but also his limits and weaknesses.
>
> [An der Figur des letzten Menschen wird Zukunft zur Szenerie von Gedankenexperimenten, in denen der Mensch seinen eigenen Möglichkeitsspielraum auslotet, seinen innersten Kern befragt, seine Entwicklungsmöglichkeiten, aber auch seine Grenzen und Unvermögen.][259]

Mary Shelley's *The Last Man* conforms faithfully to these stipulations. In doing so, the novel heralds the advent of a long and growing tradition of secular storytelling in which the storywriters take pleasure in threatening us — both as an individual and as a species — with eradication and erasure, but without the involvement of any supernatural divinity or promise of afterlife. With Mary Shelley's *The Last Man* the religious verse epopee cedes primacy to the secular prose novel, and traditional Christian apocalypticism and scriptural catastrophism segue into a more modern scientifically authenticated form of catastrophism. Steven Goldsmith formulates it thus: 'put simply, *The Last Man* dramatizes the incompatibility of the

---

256 *Futuristic Fiction*, p. 190.
257 *Child of Light*, p. 160.
258 'Apocalypse and Indeterminacy in Mary Shelley's *The Last Man*', p. 451.
259 'Die romantische Verdunkelung. Weltuntergänge und die Geburt des letzten Menschen', p. 103.

terms *apocalypse* and *novel*'. But Goldsmith also adds: 'unless, that is, *apocalypse* is so thoroughly revalued as to take on a different meaning, which is precisely what happens'.[260] Indeed, in both religious and 'revalued' guise the imagination of apocalypse remains all around us today due especially — but not exclusively — to our post-1945 nuclear state of being, as I will detail in my discussion of the third paradigm in Chapter Five and my Conclusion.

In the first four chapters of *Sublime Conclusions* I introduced the two earliest paradigms of how writers envisioned the ways in which man's end might be staged, how his annihilation could be accomplished, the causal agents of which were either God or Nature. In the final chapter I will be looking at the third and final paradigm, mankind's own, in which *Homo faber* becomes through technological ingenuity and dexterity the agent and cause of his own downfall and destruction. Remarkably, one can argue that Mary Shelley was the instigator of this paradigm, too; her novel *Frankenstein* inaugurates the tradition of storytelling in which man invents some technological contraption over which he later loses control and which goes on to jeopardize his existence. In *Frankenstein* the monster may not actually kill Victor Frankenstein, but the chase to the arctic regions serves to exhaust the inventor's energy, leading to the scientist's untimely death, thereby establishing the matrix for this third paradigm. Thus Mary appropriately has her protagonist and inventor Victor reflect, in Volume Three, Book Six of *Frankenstein*, on the 'monster whom I had created, the miserable daemon whom I had sent abroad into the world for my destruction'.[261] As Brian Stableford has rightly concluded:

> There are actually very few nineteenth-century stories which invite description as tales of man-made catastrophe, though there is a certain touch of foreboding in many stories of personal tragedy. It is not too difficult today to read Mary Shelley's *Frankenstein* (1818) as a kind of parable in which the unlucky scientist represents modern man in his totality, threatened with destruction at the hands of the monsters of his own creation. This interpretation certainly helped Brian Aldiss to find in *Frankenstein* not only the first but also the *archetypal* science fiction novel.[262]

But it is not alone modern man who is threatened by monsters of his own creation, but God too. God's invention in his own likeness has turned against his maker and now monstrously seeks to overthrow and usurp the all-powerful father-figure. In looking to eradicate his own creator, Frankenstein's monster, this 'homme machine', becomes a metaphor for Promethean Enlightenment man; as the German comparatist Werner von Koppenfels once fittingly observed in regard to Frankenstein's creature, thereby establishing an unexpected bridge between Frankenstein's monster and *The Last Man*'s Lionel Verney: 'Utopia turns into dystopia, the creature destroys his own maker as well as himself, and the First Man becomes Last Man' ('Die Utopie schlägt um in Dystopie, das Geschöpf vernichtet

---

260 'Of Gender, Plague, and Apocalypse', p. 131.
261 *Frankenstein. The 1818 Text*, p. 138.
262 'Man-Made Catastrophes', p. 102.

seinen Schöpfer und sich selbst, der Erste Mensch wird zum Letzten Menschen').[263] An equally intriguing bridge between the novels is the fact that in *The Last Man*'s third-last chapter (that is, Chapter Eight of Volume Three) the plague disappears once and for all at the very location where the monster appears in *Frankenstein*, namely in the 'vale of Chamounix', which as we recall Percy so extolled in his poem 'Mont Blanc'; we thus read in *The Last Man*, as if to rehearse or recast the sense of awe that inspired her husband's poem:

> Yellow lightning played around the vast dome of Mont Blanc, silent as the snow-clad rock they illuminated; all was bare, wild, and sublime [...]. Now the riving and fall of icy rocks clave the air; now the thunder of the avalanche burst on our ears. In countries whose features are of less magnitude, nature betrays her living powers in the foliage of the trees, in the growth of herbage, in the soft purling of meandering streams; here, endowed with giant attributes, the torrent, the thunder-storm, and the flow of massive waters, display her activity. Such the church-yard, such the requiem, such the eternal congregation, that waited in our companion's funeral. [...] From this moment I saw plague no more. She abdicated her throne, and despoiled herself of her imperial sceptre among the ice rocks that surrounded us. She left solitude and silence co-heirs of her kingdom.[264]

While 'solitude and silence' may be all that attends the end of man on Earth, the story of the end of man itself of course does not end here, as I have already indicated; quite to the contrary, Mary Shelley's *The Last Man* is just the beginning in a long succession of works fictionalizing the decline and ruin of man. Lionel Verney stands not alone. He is the first last man of many last men (and last women) who have since been conjured up by creative writers (as well as scriptwriters) to cater to the — should I say monstrous? — tastes of modern secular audiences who seem addicted to stories of end-time catastrophe and our species' existential vulnerability.

---

263 '"Le coucher du soleil romantique"', p. 265.
264 *The Last Man*, p. 310.

CHAPTER 5

'The Earth Void of Man': Variations on a Theme 1945 and Beyond

> *This is the way the world ends*
> *This is the way the world ends*
> *This is the way the world ends*
> *Not with a bang but a whimper.*
> T. S. ELIOT, *The Hollow Men* (1925)[1]

> To the manifold sources of collectively perceived absurdity, the bomb contributes a pervasive sense of the final madness.
> ROBERT JAY LIFTON, *The Future of Immortality* (1987)[2]

The 'Dialectic of Enlightenment'

We have come a long way from Franz von Sonnenberg, the German author of the 1806 Christian apocalyptic epic *Donatoa*, to Mary Shelley, the British author of the 1826 first ever terminal pandemic novel *The Last Man*: although the two authors were born just two decades apart, 1779 and 1797 respectively, their works, likewise separated by just two decades, seem generationally and ideologically light years apart. Their ways of conceptualizing our cosmos could hardly be more different, the former counting on the Christian God not just to watch over the destiny of humankind, but also to reside in judgment over every one of us in a cataclysmic Day of Reckoning, the latter doing away with God as an explanatory paradigm and turning to Nature as a more disinterested and impartial arbiter of our fate. Their works stand for competing paradigms and belief systems; one relies on supernatural powers to govern the ebb and flow of human history, the other looks to natural forces alone to determine our place in the world. Yet no less than the Christian God, Nature can be an unpredictably fickle sovereign, Mary Shelley poignantly reminds us. But unlike Nature, God — or, rather, the picture of God in the image of man, as the early nineteenth-century German philosopher Ludwig Feuerbach saw it — privileges humankind; the human species alone is elect among all creatures,

---

1 *Collected Poems 1909–1962*, p. 82.
2 *The Future of Immortality*, p. 144.

all monotheistic religions tell us. Who does not recall in this context the cynical final post-Darwinian commandment in George Orwell's *Animal Farm*: 'All animals are equal, but some are more equal than others'? But take that anthropocentric vision of God away and one is left with Nature, a Nature that truly sees all species as equal and makes no distinction among them. And if one species can die out and become extinct, as early nineteenth-century geologists had come to recognize by the 1820s, so can any other of its manifold creatures — humankind not excepted. This recognition sets the stage for the storyline of Mary Shelley's *The Last Man*; in her novel she once and for all divests us as a species of the illusion, religiously harboured for so long, of our favoured position in this universe. I cite once more the passage that opens Volume Three of her novel:

> Once man was a favourite of the Creator, as the royal psalmist sang, 'God had made him a little lower than the angels, and had crowned him with glory and honour. God made him to have dominion over the works of his hands, and put all things under his feet'. Once it was so; now is man lord of the creation? Look at him — ha! I see plague! She has invested his form, is incarnate in his flesh, has entwined herself with his being, and blinds his heaven-seeking eyes. Lie down, O man, on the flower-strown earth; give up all claim to your inheritance, all you can ever possess of it is the small cell which the dead require.[3]

This is a thoroughly anti-Christian point of view, and even if Mary Shelley may not have considered herself an atheist, the worldview her novel promulgates, and the worldview she derived from her father and husband, is thoroughly atheistic in disposition, as I hope to have illustrated in the previous chapter. 'In its refusal to place humanity at the centre of the universe, its questioning of our privileged position in relation to nature', writes Kari E. Lokke in *The Cambridge Companion to Mary Shelley*, '*The Last Man* constitutes a profound and prophetic challenge to Western humanism'; she continues:

> the extremity of [Mary Shelley's] particular form of apocalypse bears comparison with twentieth-century existentialist, absurdist, and nihilist reactions to two World Wars, the Holocaust, and the atomic bomb, such as Camus's *La Peste* or Ionesco's *Les Chaises*, thus revealing *The Last Man*, like *Frankenstein*, as an uncannily prescient novel.[4]

The Last Man is a challenge in that it succeeds in bringing the human spirit back down to earth — and indeed *under* the earth, as the quotation above testifies as well as the one that will follow momentarily — from its lofty religious flight of fantasy, making believe that there was a supernatural Creator who could single out one species in order to grant it the capacity to defy Nature's limitations and survive death in eternity. In Mary Shelley's novel it is not God who serves notice to humankind as a species and holds us to account, but Nature. And Nature does not care about religion, nor does it care about material wealth or morality: it treats everyone alike. 'We were all equal now', the 'Last Man' Verney thus relates after

---

[3] *The Last Man*, pp. 229–30.
[4] '*The Last Man*', in *The Cambridge Companion to Mary Shelley*, ed. by Esther Schor (Cambridge: Cambridge University Press, 2003), pp. 116–34 (p. 116).

the plague has struck, and continues:

> magnificent dwellings, luxurious carpets, and beds of down, were afforded to all. Carriages and horses, gardens, pictures, statues, and princely libraries, there were enough of these even to superfluity; and there was nothing to prevent each from assuming possession of his share. We were all equal now; but near at hand was an equality still more levelling, a state where beauty and strength, and wisdom, would be as vain as riches and birth. The grave yawned beneath us all...[5]

If it was Mary Shelley's core achievement that she introduced atheism — not to mention a radical vision of social egalitarianism — conceptually into the modern novel through the all-encompassing, unsparing and indifferent 'Plague' of her novel, visualizing the complete and irreversible eradication of the human species through Nature, it was no less an achievement that her novel *Frankenstein* presaged the third and final paradigm of catastrophism, mankind's demise not through God, nor through Nature, but through Man's own machinations. Victor Frankenstein's monster is as 'prescient' a metaphor as Nature's plague, a blueprint *in nuce*, as it were, for man's soon-to-develop ability to eradicate himself through his own technology. In creating this monster of man's design, scholars by and large agree not just that Mary Shelley led the way towards the creation of the modern-day genre of science fiction — with its stress on fictionalizing the power and potential of science alongside its hazards and risks — but that in doing so she was arguably also the first to show up the perils of science's hubris. Anne K. Mellor thus notes:

> Even more important is Mary Shelley's implicit warning against the possible dangers inherent in the technological developments of modern science. Although we have not yet discovered Frankenstein's procedure for reanimating corpses, recent research in biochemistry — the discovery of DNA, the technique of gene-splicing, and the development of extra-uterine fertilization — has brought us to the point where human beings are able to manipulate life-forms in ways previously reserved only to nature and chance. The replacement of natural childbirth by the mechanical eugenic control systems and baby-breeders envisioned in Aldous Huxley's *Brave New World* or Marge Piercy's *Woman on the Edge of Time* is now only a matter of time and social will. Worse by far, of course, is the contemporary proliferation of nuclear weapons systems resulting from the Los Alamos Project and the political decision to drop atomic bombs on Hiroshima and Nagasaki in 1945. As Jonathan Schell has so powerfully reminded us in *The Fate of the Earth*, as such docudramas as *The Day After* (1983) and *Threads* (1984) have starkly portrayed, a morally irresponsible scientific development has released a monster that can destroy human civilization itself. As Frankenstein's monster proclaims, 'Remember that I have power; [...] I can make you so wretched that the light of day will be hateful to you' [...]. Mary Shelley's tale of horror is no fantastical ghost story, but rather a profound insight into the probable consequences of 'objective' — gendered — or morally insensitive scientific and technological research.[6]

Indeed, the science fiction scholars David Dowling and H. Bruce Franklin have both

---

[5] *The Last Man*, pp. 230–31.
[6] *Mary Shelley: Her Life, Her Fiction, Her Monsters*, p. 114.

called Victor Frankenstein the 'locus classicus' of the predicament and dilemma of the scientist who has developed and now wields the power to annihilate the human species; Dowling writes, with specific reference to the subject of this chapter, the unlocking of nuclear fusion: 'The actual performance of atomic scientists since 1945 has been, by and large, a playing out of the archetypal positions defined by [such] early stories' as Shelley's *Frankenstein*.[7]

As such, Shelley's *Frankenstein* provides a cautionary prefiguration of what Max Horkheimer and Theodor W. Adorno have famously called the 'Dialectic of Enlightenment' in their 1944 philosophical study of that title; the 'dialectic' they describe shows how modern enlightened man — epitomized by Victor Frankenstein — is prone to turn the very knowledge that science has afforded him against himself in the form of terror and tyranny. Whenever Enlightenment thought fails self-critically to take into account its self-destructive potential, Horkheimer and Adorno argue, it will regress into renewed barbarism, the prime example of which is, for them, twentieth-century fascism and its racist ideology which put the technologies of enlightenment to the most inhuman use history has ever witnessed, perverting the very definition of enlightenment. They write in their 'Preface': 'The aporia which faced us in our work thus proved to be the first matter we had to investigate: the self-destruction of enlightenment. [...] If enlightenment does not assimilate reflection on this regressive moment, it seals its own fate' ('Die Aporie, der wir uns bei unserer Arbeit gegenüber fanden, erwies sich somit als der erste Gegenstand, den wir zu untersuchen hatten: die Selbstzerstörung der Aufklärung').[8] In their opening essay, entitled 'The Concept of Enlightenment', they enlarge as follows:

> Enlightenment, understood in the widest sense as the advance of thought, has always aimed at liberating human beings from fear and installing them as masters. Yet the wholly enlightened earth is radiant with triumphant calamity. Enlightenment's program was the disenchantment of the world. It wanted to dispel myths, to overthrow fantasy with knowledge. [...] Myth becomes enlightenment and nature mere objectivity. Human beings purchase the increase in their power with estrangement from that over which it is exerted.
>
> [Seit je hat Aufklärung im umfassendsten Sinn fortschreitenden Denkens das Ziel verfolgt, von den Menschen die Furcht zu nehmen und sie als Herren einzusetzen. Aber die vollends aufgeklärte Erde strahlt im Zeichen triumphalen Unheils. Das Programm der Aufklärung war die Entzauberung der Welt. Sie wollte die Mythen auflösen und Einbildung durch Wissen stürzen. [...] Der Mythos geht in die Aufklärung über und die Natur in bloße Objektivität. Die Menschen bezahlen die Vermehrung ihrer Macht mit der Entfremdung von dem, worüber sie die Macht ausüben.]

---

7 'The Atomic Scientist: Machine or Moralist?', *Science-Fiction Studies*, 13 (1986), 139–47 (pp. 141 and 145); see also H. Bruce Franklin, 'Strange Scenarios: Science Fiction, the Theory of Alienation, and the Nuclear Gods', *Science-Fiction Studies*, 13 (1986), 117–28 (p. 117).

8 Max Horkheimer and Theodor W. Adorno, *Dialectic of Enlightenment. Philosophical Fragments*, ed. by Gunzelin Schmid Noerr, trans. by Edmund Jephcott (Stanford: Stanford University Press, 2002), p. xvi. *Dialektik der Aufklärung. Philosophische Fragmente* (Frankfurt a.M.: Fischer, 1993), p. 3. The subsequent quote pp. 1 and 6 (pp. 9 and 15).

We do not have to concur with Horkheimer and Adorno's censure of the Enlightenment to recognize that Victor Frankenstein, as someone who has employed technological reason to overcome myth and magic, but whose creativity has led to nothing but calamity, can be read as the quintessential embodiment not just of 'the modern Prometheus', as the subtitle of Shelley's novel specifies, but also as a prefigurement of the kind of instrumental reason that Horkheimer and Adorno indict in their work; Frankenstein too has purchased the increase in his power as a scientist at the cost of estrangement both from his fellow citizens as well as from that which he created, as we saw in Chapter Four. Frankenstein is the earliest personification in European literature of the obsessed scientist who, in trying to instrumentalize Nature in order to escape from the monsters of the past, succeeds only in engineering a more modern monster, one of no less evil — and no less mythical — magnitude. Instead then of 'installing them as masters', enlightenment serves instead to install human beings as (makers of) monsters. It is only after the event, only long after he has unleashed his monster on the world, that Frankenstein comes to reflect on the folly of his monomaniacal ambition; he concedes in the concluding chapter of *Frankenstein*, comparing himself with Milton's fallen Satan:

> [L]ike the archangel who aspired to omnipotence, I am chained in an eternal hell. My imagination was vivid, yet my powers of analysis and application executed the creation of a man. Even now I cannot recollect, without passion, my reveries while the work was incomplete. I trod heaven in my thoughts, now exulting in my powers, now burning with the idea of their effects. From my infancy I was imbued with high hopes and a lofty ambition; but how am I sunk! [...] I must pursue and destroy the being to whom I gave existence; then my lot on earth will be fulfilled, and I may die.[9]

Only by destroying the fruit of his enlightened scientific endeavours does he feel that he can make amends for his hubris and presumption. (One wishes that today's nuclear powers — including those aspiring to become one — would take this painfully acquired insight to heart.)

Whatever the monster's destiny, whether he survives the Arctic cold or fulfills his promise to end his life, by the end of the novel there is indication that the lesson of the dangers of scientific obsession has been learnt not just by Victor Frankenstein, but also by the second scientist in this novel, the Arctic explorer Robert Walton, the master of the vessel onto which Victor Frankenstein had rescued himself in pursuit of the monster. In the same concluding chapter Walton is described as having begun to reflect on the risks inherent in his own scientific venture; he writes in a letter to his sister:

> My beloved Sister, — I write to you encompassed by peril and ignorant whether I am ever doomed to see again dear England, and the dearer friends that inhabit it. I am surrounded by mountains of ice which admit of no escape and threaten every moment to crush my vessel. The brave fellows whom I have persuaded to be my companions look towards me for aid; but I have none to bestow. There is something terribly appalling in our situation, yet my courage and hopes do

---

9 *Frankenstein. The 1818 Text*, pp. 147–48.

not desert me. Yet it is terrible to reflect that the lives of all these men are endangered through me. If we are lost, my mad schemes are the cause.[10]

His scheme is not just a scheme, it is a 'mad' scheme, and it constitutes a danger for all who are involved in it. It is noteworthy, however, that Mary Shelley introduced the two last sentences of this paragraph only into the book's third edition in 1831; in the 1818 edition by contrast this paragraph of Walton's letter reads (following 'desert me'): 'We may survive, and if we do not, I will repeat the lessons of my Seneca, and die with a good heart'.[11] The more optimistic 1818 version of the novel is thus about repeating lessons, whereas the 1831 version is clearly about *not* repeating them; it is about learning from history what to avoid rather than what to emulate. It seems as if in the intervening years Mary Shelley had become much more attuned to, and indeed more sceptical of, the very dangers of modern science that she herself had so presciently sketched out with her tale of Promethean hubris.

Perhaps unsurprisingly, Horkheimer and Adorno too pick up on this issue in their *Dialectic of Enlightenment*. In one of the 'Notes and Sketches' ('Aufzeichnungen und Entwürfe') appended at the end of their study, entitled 'On the Critique of the Philosophy of History' ('Zur Kritik der Geschichtsphilosophie'), they begin by discussing what some decades later was to be coined the Anthropocene,[12] the most recent epoch of world history, an epoch in which, driven by his faculty of reason, man has succeeded in turning himself into a 'global geophysical force', and one resulting in various waves of extinction. 'The cerebral organ, human intelligence', Horkheimer and Adorno write,

> is firmly established enough to constitute a regular epoch of the earth's history. In this epoch, the human species, including its machines, chemicals, and organizational powers — for why should they not be seen as a part of it as teeth are a part of the bear, since they serve the same purpose and merely function better? — is the last word in adaptation. Humans have not only eradicated their immediate predecessors but have eradicated them more thoroughly than almost any other recent species, not excluding the carnivorous saurians. In face of this it seems somewhat whimsical to try to construe world history, as did Hegel, in terms of such categories as freedom and justice.
>
> [Das Gehirnorgan, die menschliche Intelligenz, ist handfest genug, um eine reguläre Epoche der Erdgeschichte zu bilden. Die Menschengattung einschließlich ihrer Maschinen, Chemikalien, Organisationskräfte — und warum sollte man diese nicht zu ihr zählen wie die Zähne zum Bären, da sie doch dem gleichen Zweck dienen und nur besser funktionieren — ist in dieser Epoche le dernier cri der Anpassung. Die Menschen haben ihre unmittelbaren Vorgänger nicht nur überholt, sondern schon so gründlich ausgerottet wie wohl kaum je eine modernere species die andere, die fleischfressenden Saurier nicht ausgeschlossen. Demgegenüber scheint es eine Art Schrulle zu sein,

---

10 *Frankenstein. or The Modern Prometheus*, ed. by Siv Jansson (Ware: Wordsworth Classics, 1999), p. 162.
11 *Frankenstein. The 1818 Text*, p. 148.
12 A useful and compact survey of the concept is contained in Will Steffen, Paul J. Crutzen and John R. McNeill's article 'The Anthropocene: Are Humans Now Overwhelming the Great Forces of Nature?', *Ambio*, 36 (December 2007), 614–21.

> die Weltgeschichte, wie Hegel es getan hat, im Hinblick auf Kategorien wie Freiheit und Gerechtigkeit konstruieren zu wollen.]¹³

Horkheimer and Adorno are quick to recognize that it is only a small step from the eradication of his 'immediate predecessors' to man also eradicating himself. They remark how 'reason's ruse consists in making humans into beasts with an ever-wider reach' ('[die] List [der Vernunft] besteht darin, die Menschen zu immer weiter reichenden Bestien zu machen'), culminating in the possibility of mankind's self-eradication; and they hence observe how

> the human capacity for destruction promises to become so great that — once this species has exhausted itself — a *tabula rasa* will have been created. Either the human species will tear itself to pieces or it will take all the earth's fauna and flora down with it, and if the earth is still young enough, the whole procedure — to vary a famous dictum — will have to start again on a much lower level.
>
> [Seine Vernichtungsfähigkeit verspricht so groß zu werden, daß — wenn diese Art sich einmal erschöpft hat — tabula rasa gemacht ist. Entweder zerfleischt sie sich selbst, oder sie reißt die gesamte Fauna und Flora der Erde mit hinab, und wenn die Erde dann noch jung genug ist, muß — um ein berühmtes Wort zu variieren — auf einer viel tieferen Stufe die ganze chose noch einmal anfangen.]

Equally unsurprisingly, this subject — mankind's 'start[ing] again on a much lower level' following some cataclysmic disaster, natural, nuclear or otherwise — is one of the most popular and entertaining ingredients of twentieth-century science fiction, being a part of the entertainment industry that Horkheimer and Adorno as Frankfurt School cultural critics were already in the early 1940s so keen to denigrate. (The fifth chapter of their seminal study is evocatively entitled 'The Culture Industry: Enlightenment as Mass Deception', 'Kulturindustrie, Aufklärung als Massenbetrug'.) Our perspective on the 'Culture Industry' and its means and mechanisms of 'Mass Deception' has of course changed significantly since their time; many today no longer look upon mass entertainment with the same sense of disdain and disapproval. But regardless of whether one adores or abhors the 'Culture Industry' kind of apocalyptic end-of-time fiction that makes up such a successful part of contemporary science fiction, on paper or its silver-screen next of kin, it is clear not just that these formats are here to stay, but also that they convey perhaps a more positively vital message than Horkheimer and Adorno in their time would have cared to admit. These formats pander not just to (part of) the public's craving for nerve-tingling sensationalism — the mass deception that Horkheimer and Adorno reject — but can also serve firstly quite openly to expose, but then more subliminally and secondly, also to inure us to the dangers we humans face today. Thus, in a much-acclaimed article entitled 'The Imagination of Disaster' and published in the journal *Commentary* in 1965, the cultural critic Susan Sontag argued that contemporary man lives 'under continual threat of two equally fearful, but seemingly opposed destinies: unremitting banality and inconceivable terror'. 'It

---

13 *Dialectic of Enlightenment*, p. 184, the subsequent passage p. 186 (*Dialektik der Aufklärung*, pp. 234 and 235–36).

is fantasy,' she continued,

> served out in large rations by the popular arts, which allows most people to cope with these twin specters. For one job that fantasy can do is to lift us out of the unbearably humdrum and to distract us from terrors, real or anticipated — by an escape into exotic dangerous situations which have last-minute happy endings. But another one of the things that fantasy can do is to normalize what is psychologically unbearable, thereby inuring us to it. In the one case, fantasy beautifies the world. In the other, it neutralizes it. The fantasy to be discovered in science fiction films does both jobs. These films reflect world-wide anxieties, and they serve to allay them.[14]

Significantly, at the end of her article Sontag went on to reflect how mid-twentieth-century humankind had reached a turning point of sorts, indeed more precisely a point of no return; she writes:

> it is not enough to note that science fiction allegories are one of the new myths about — that is, ways of accommodating to and negating — the perennial human anxiety about death. (Myths of heaven and hell, and of ghosts, had the same function.) Again, there is a historically specifiable twist which intensifies the anxiety, or better, the trauma suffered by everyone in the middle of the twentieth century when it became clear that from now on to the end of human history, every person would spend his individual life not only under the threat of individual death, which is certain, but of something almost unsupportable psychologically — collective incineration and extinction which could come any time, virtually without warning.

In her concluding paragraph, finally, she gave this new sentiment a name — it is 'the expectation of apocalypse'.

The difference between, on the one hand, Franz von Sonnenberg's rendering of the 'myth of heaven and hell' in *Donatoa* and Mary Shelley's vision, in *The Last Man*, of a plague-induced natural apocalypse and, on the other hand, the kind of 'collective incineration and extinction' that Sontag is referring to here, namely the possibility of a nuclear holocaust, is that the two early-nineteenth-century authors depict what from a secular point of view would be considered either an impossible event or a highly improbable one. Sonnenberg's and Shelley's scenarios could be imagined, as their texts bear out, but were unlikely ever to come to pass during the writers' lifetimes (and probably won't in ours either); they were fictions of fantasy. Sontag's vision of nuclear disaster, by contrast, was, in the light of the Cuban Missile Crisis and the precipitous escalation of the Cold War, looming as a distinct possibility by the mid-1960s — how near or distant, no one could foretell. Ironically, as I write this at year's end 2014 during a renewed and highly contagious Ebola outbreak in West Africa, nearly two centuries after *The Last Man* was published, many of my fellow citizens would be more inclined to accept the possibility of a world-encompassing plague than the likelihood of a nuclear Armageddon, under whose threat we daily continue to strut and fret our hours upon the stage of life. In the light of the current Ebola strain's unprecedented infectiousness and mortality

---

[14] 'The Imagination of Disaster', *Commentary* (October 1965), 42–48 (p. 42); the subsequent passage p. 48.

rate — and the difficulties faced in containing this virus — Mary Shelley's warning has suddenly and uncomfortably taken on a new urgency, more so than other threats we face save perhaps a man-made ecological disaster, which, however, most would consider far less imminent. And yet, no less frightening than Nature's uncontrollability — something we have become accustomed to as a species ever since *Homo sapiens* came into being — must be the uncontrollability of what the twentieth-century Swiss writer Max Frisch fictionalized as *Homo faber*, namely 'man the maker' himself, a being who in Frisch's novel is shown as having lost his sense of natural connectedness, and who believes he can dominate and even overcome Nature through his advances in technology. But in the process, Frisch submits, *Homo faber* has forgotten that human rationality is only the flipside of human irrationality, and that the tools he has created can be employed rationally to eradicate not just Nature's presumed insufficiency, but indeed also irrationally man's own existence.

It was none other than Sigmund Freud who, more than a decade before (!) the first atomic bomb was detonated above Hiroshima, stated prophetically in the final paragraph of *Civilization and Its Discontents* (written 1929, published 1930):

> The fateful question for the human species seems to me to be whether and to what extent their cultural development will succeed in mastering the disturbance of their communal life by the human instinct of aggression and self-destruction. It may be that in this respect precisely the present time deserves a special interest. Men have gained control over the forces of nature to such an extent that with their help they would have no difficulty in exterminating one another to the last man. They know this, and hence comes a large part of their current unrest, their unhappiness and their mood of anxiety. And now it is to be expected that the other of the two 'Heavenly Powers', eternal Eros, will make an effort to assert himself in the struggle with his equally immortal adversary. But who can foresee with what success and with what result.
>
> [Die Schicksalsfrage der Menschenart scheint mir zu sein, ob und in welchem Maße es ihrer Kulturentwicklung gelingen wird, der Störung des Zusammenlebens durch den menschlichen Aggressions- und Selbstvernichtungstrieb Herr zu werden. In diesem Bezug verdient vielleicht gerade die gegenwärtige Zeit ein besonderes Interesse. Die Menschen haben es jetzt in der Beherrschung der Naturkräfte so weit gebracht, daß sie es mit deren Hilfe leicht haben, einander bis auf den letzten Mann auszurotten. Sie wissen das, daher ein gut Stück ihrer gegenwärtigen Unruhe, ihres Unglücks, ihrer Angststimmung. Und nun ist zu erwarten, daß die andere der beiden 'himmlischen Mächte', der ewige Eros, eine Anstrengung machen wird, um sich im Kampf mit seinem ebenso unsterblichen Gegner zu behaupten. Aber wer kann den Erfolg und Ausgang voraussehen?][15]

The irony is of course that Freud's warning was so soon to be overtaken by the Nazis' unleashing on Europe and the world the Second World War and their creating in the midst of it a technological machinery as well as a matching technocratic mindset to

---

15 Sigmund Freud, *Civilization and Its Discontents* (1930), trans. by James Strachey (New York: W. W. Norton, 1962), p. 92. *Das Unbehagen in der Kultur*, in *Abriß der Psychoanalyse/Das Unbehagen in der Kultur* (Frankfurt a.M.: Fischer, 1979), pp. 128–29.

murder millions of human beings. Theirs was precisely the 'new kind of barbarism' that Horkheimer and Adorno had identified and indicted on the opening page of *Dialectic of Enlightenment*, a new barbarism into which these two Frankfurt School philosophers, more pessimistically perhaps than their teacher Freud, saw humanity 'sinking into [...] instead of [it] entering a truly human state' ('in eine neue Art von Barbarei [...] anstatt in einen wahrhaft menschlichen Zustand einzutreten').[16] In the battle between the two 'Heavenly Powers', Eros and Thanatos, Thanatos seemed ever more to be gaining the upper hand.

Through Enlightenment to the Death of God

Dialectic of Enlightenment was first published less than a year before the end of the Second World War and the detonation of the first nuclear bombs, initially for test purposes on 16 July 1945 in the Alamogordo Desert of New Mexico, then with devastating consequences on 6 and 8 August 1945 over the Japanese cities Hiroshima and Nagasaki. 1945 thus marks a critical juncture in global history; from our point of view, in fact, it was a fourfold juncture. First, it was the year in which the Second World War came to a close, putting an end to Hitler's reign of terror and six years of global slaughter on an unprecedented scale. Second, it was the year in which the magnitude of the genocide became apparent that the Nazis had visited upon the Jewish people and all those they considered 'unworthy' of life (their German expression was 'unwertes Leben', an expression since anathematized in the German language); indeed, the authors of *Dialectic of Enlightenment* were themselves not yet aware of the full enormity of Nazism's barbarity when they conceived and published their study in 1944. Third, it was the year in which humanity for the first time more generally experienced the life-negating potential of nuclear energy; with the dropping of the atomic bombs on Hiroshima and Nagasaki mankind came to the realization that it had mastered a technology of ultimate self-destruction. And, finally fourth, and to compound this third point, the Allies' victory over fascism in 1945 marks the juncture at which the victors start turning their arsenals against one another. With the emerging two global powers, the United States and the Soviet Union, entering a half century of ideological antagonism and Cold War, the stage is now set for the nuclear arms race between capitalism and communism.

Horkheimer and Adorno's *Dialectic of Enlightenment* was a book about fascism and the lapse of enlightenment into barbarity and racial hatred; although its underlying argument was the turning of scientific and technological reason against itself, their study was not about the atomic bomb, or at most only marginally so. (By 1944 it was generally assumed on the allied side that a nuclear bomb was being developed by a circle of Nazi nuclear scientists around Werner Heisenberg and Carl Friedrich von Weizsäcker at the *Kaiser-Wilhelm-Institut für Physik* in Berlin, an institute directed by Albert Einstein until his forced emigration from Germany in 1933.) Of course, global nuclear genocide — or what the German social philosopher and essayist Günther Anders aptly termed 'globocide', *Globozid*,[17] and the American

---

16 *Dialectic of Enlightenment*, p. xiv (*Dialektik der Aufklärung*, p. 1).
17 *Die Antiquiertheit des Menschen*, vol. 2: *Über die Zerstörung des Lebens im Zeitalter der dritten*

psychiatrist Robert Jay Lifton no less aptly 'self-genocide'[18] — would constitute nothing less than the ultimate pinnacle and perversion of the 'Dialectic of Enlightenment', with the philosophy of 'progress' leading potentially to the total annihilation of mankind along with the science that made this progress possible in the first place. With exceptional quickness of perception Albert Camus noted just two days after 'Hiroshima' in his famous *Combat*-editorial of 8 August 1945: 'mechanical civilization has just reached its final degree of savagery. We are going to have to choose, in a future that is more or less imminent, between collective suicide and the intelligent use of scientific conquests' ('la civilisation mécanique vient de parvenir à son dernier degré de sauvagerie. Il va falloir choisir, dans un avenir plus ou moins proche, entre le suicide collectif ou l'utilisation intelligente des conquêtes scientifiques').[19]

And yet, although the genocidal infernos of the Holocaust and Hiroshima are distinctly dissimilar historical events, they do have three things in common. First, both have come to epitomise the impossibility of the linguistic representation of horrors of such magnitude. Writing about Hiroshima and Nagasaki, David Dowling has put it thus:

> Writers have been able to extrapolate and caricature the conditions leading up to a nuclear conflict, but when it comes to writing after 1945 about the actual disaster, the imagination is fettered by two things: the inconceivable magnitude of the horror, and the two historical experiences of Hiroshima and Nagasaki. The memory of the Japanese holocaust acts as a brake and a stimulus to the apocalyptic imagination; the attempt to write about *that* experience commands us to be faithful to the dead and the living survivors, and also exposes the limits of our language and our imaginations.[20]

Discussing the condition of psychic numbing that the survivors of the nuclear attacks experienced, which is captured in Japanese by the term 'hibakusha', Dowling pinpoints the dilemma we face in the aftermath of these events as follows: 'To avoid the reality of the bombings', he writes, 'is to attempt to escape from the nightmare of history into a dangerous neverland of ignorance; yet to attempt to understand it is to risk debasing or trivialising it'. It is precisely this quandary that Adorno was, famously, to diagnose in 1951 regarding the Holocaust when he claimed that to write poetry after Auschwitz cannot but be barbaric because it would only serve to aestheticize the torture and agony of the victims, a claim, of course, that did not remain without its detractors, as the works of many Holocaust poets have shown, writing even in the language of the perpetrators, as did H. G. Adler, Paul Celan and Nelly Sachs, among others.

Second, Auschwitz and Hiroshima once again put in question what Aldous Huxley has called the 'religion of Inevitable Progress'.[21] Insofar as the savagery of

industriellen Revolution (Munich: C. H. Beck, 1995, first published 1980), p. 410.
   18 'The New Psychology of Human Survival', in *The Future of Immortality and Other Essays for a Nuclear Age* (New York: Basic Books, 1987), pp. 111–35 (p. 113).
   19 *Combat*, 8 August 1945, editorial; text retrieved from <https://www.matisse.lettres.free.fr/artdeblamer/tcombat.htm> on 8 June 2015.
   20 *Fictions of Nuclear Disaster* (Houndsmills, Basingstoke: MacMillan Press, 1987), p. 47.
   21 *The Perennial Philosophy* (London: Chatto & Windus, 1946), p. 93.

the First World War had not already curbed the nineteenth century's all too naïve overconfidence in progress and positivity, the Holocaust certainly 'explodes as myth the popular belief in steady, irreversible progress', as Ronald Aronson remarked in an article in the 1988 essay collection *Echoes from the Holocaust*.[22] Yet although this is the case, and although Horkheimer and Adorno's analyses in *Dialectic of Enlightenment* plainly put before us how 'progress creates disaster', their conclusions have by and large gone unheeded by those in power; as Aronson is quick to add, *Dialectic of Enlightenment* goes 'against the grain of official optimism and self-celebration that has survived Auschwitz as well as Hiroshima, Chernobyl as well as Vietnam'. In today's world it might be a truism to state that scientific progress has led to ever greater slaughter also because science has progressively provided ever more efficient technologies to effect it, and yet we humans seem never to want to learn the lesson from our experience and mend our ways.

And third, just as in the eighteenth century Voltaire and many of his contemporaries felt forced to question their Christian belief in the face of the Lisbon earthquake in 1755, which inflicted so much misery and suffering upon that city's population on a day of religious celebration, even steadfast theologians began to wonder in the aftermath of the Second World War, Auschwitz and Hiroshima whether their belief in the existence of an omnipotent beneficent God could be maintained in the face of the twentieth-century's far higher toll of lives destroyed. The estimates of those killed by the earthquake of 1 November 1755, striking on All Souls' Day during Mass, range between 10,000 and 60,000; between 1939 and 1945 no fewer than thirty three million people were killed or murdered in Europe alone (including the Soviet Union), among them some six million Jews, and among these some 1.5 million Jewish children. How could an omnibenevolent all-powerful God allow evil on this scale to happen, including even to the most innocent of human beings? Just as the earthquake of Lisbon reopened the theodicy question for eighteenth-century savants like Voltaire, the totalitarian terror of Stalinism and Fascism, the killing fields of the Second World War, the Holocaust and the bombings of Hiroshima and Nagasaki recharged that question for twentieth-century Jewish and Christian philosophers and theologians, among them Yosef Achituv, Günther Anders, Hannah Arendt, Martin Buber, Arthur A. Cohen, Roy Eckardt, Emil Fackenheim, Peter H. Hare, Warren Zev Harvey, Hans Jonas, Emmanuel Levinas, Franklin Littell, Johann Baptist Metz, Alexander Mitscherlich, Jürgen Moltmann, Jonathan Sacks, Dorothee Sölle, Joseph B. Soloveitchik and Edith and Michael Wyschogrod.

From my perspective as a literary historian the structure of responses to the slaughters of the twentieth century seems uncannily to replicate that of the eighteenth-century responses to the Lisbon earthquake. Then as now the majority of theists steadfastly held on to their religious faith even in the face of such overwhelming and seemingly incomprehensible levels of suffering and killing. But theists are theists for a reason — as the history of mankind has shown, religious faith

---

22 'The Holocaust and Human Progress', in *Echoes from the Holocaust. Philosophical Reflections on a Dark Time*, ed. by Alan Rosenberg and Gerald E. Myers (Philadelphia: Temple University Press, 1988), pp. 223–44 (p. 224); the subsequent quote pp. 231–32.

provides for many ways to vindicate the existence of evil and suffering in our world without necessitating the denial of God. Religion and faith have been confronted and weighed down by natural catastrophes, wars, genocide, murder and other forms of violence and victimhood ever since the advent of human consciousness, and neither religion in general (as a belief in a god or gods) nor specific historical forms of religious faith (such as in our day Christianity, Judaism, and Islam, to name only those that have played a defining role in recent European history) have crumbled under that burden. Even if the order and magnitude of evil and violence witnessed between 1933 and 1945 outstripped anything experienced in earlier centuries, most religious believers still did not feel swayed to abandon their faith. Faith is true faith only when, in the face of adversity, it is troubled yet not abandoned. Abandonment of faith is thus not the inexorable outcome of the twentieth century's unparalleled scale of inhumanity, even if some critics of religion expected this to be the case. What might be expected, by contrast, is that human beings — believers *and* non-believers alike — feel moved to reexamine the fundamentals of their religious faiths or secular worldviews, as the case may be, in the light of the scale of evil that was meted out by so many human beings — for whatever personal or professional gain, and for whatever racial, ideological or psychological motive — against so many other human beings. What are the lessons to be learnt today from the fact that such large-scale oppression and slaughter was able to occur from within the midst of what one had assumed were 'civilized' societies, not just for civil society at large and its institutions, but also for every individual person's religious, philosophical, moral and ethical understanding of what it means to be human in our day and age?

Having said that, while everyone without exception must feel affected by and called upon to mull over these events and their ramifications, the occurrence of such evil nonetheless remains something that — theologically and philosophically speaking — raises questions that religious believers, in particular Jews and Christians as victims and perpetrators of the Holocaust, or as their descendants, must find more difficult to answer than persons without religious belief; this is because non-believers are not necessitated, as believers are, to reconcile their faith in (the existence of) an all-powerful and all-beneficent God with events those of faith would not expect their God to condone — this being of course the very starting point of the notion of theodicy, conceived as 'the vindication of divine providence' in view of the existence of evil, as we saw already in Chapter One. In the eighteenth century Voltaire wrote *Candide* to satirize Leibniz's answer to this quandary and to lampoon his notion of ours being 'the best of all possible worlds', despite the best part of a capital city's population being wiped out by an earthquake.²³ Nonetheless, although the Lisbon earthquake spurred Voltaire to question theism's notion of an all-powerful all-beneficent God, in the end it did not persuade him to jettison belief in God altogether; rather than turn to atheism Voltaire embraced deism instead, viewing God henceforth not as inexistent but rather as merely disengaged from and perhaps also indifferent to the world's day-to-day business. Similarly in the twentieth-century, God's perceived non-agency moved some theologians to reconceive their faith along lines that resemble Voltaire's eighteenth-century deistic solution to the theodicy predicament. A particularly instructive case in point on the Jewish side is Hans Jonas, a German-born philosopher of religion who had studied under the Christian theologian Rudolf Bultmann and the existentialist philosopher Martin Heidegger but had managed to escape Nazi persecution by emigrating to Palestine in 1933, from where he moved on to Canada in 1949 and, a decade later, the United States. In an essay entitled 'The Concept of God After Auschwitz: A Jewish Voice', Jonas expressly draws a connection between Lisbon and Auschwitz, but he also usefully underscores the difference between these two historical events. Lisbon, he reminds us, was of nature's making whereas Auschwitz was of man's. It is, Jonas asserts, 'the fact and success of deliberate evil rather than the inflictions of blind, natural causality — [...] (Auschwitz rather than the earthquake of Lisbon) — with which Jewish theology has to contend at this hour'.²⁴ 'After Auschwitz', Jonas consequently goes on to assert, 'we must rethink the concept of God entrusted to us from the past'. 'Rethink the concept of God', he says deliberately but with care, not abandon it altogether. Jonas feels necessitated to seek a more convincing explanation for God's non-interventionism, inertia and seeming indifference than he felt had been provided by previous Jewish theologians. In this process of rethinking the concept of God in the face of 'the specter of Auschwitz' and seeking an explanation — and a credible theological rationalization — of events, Jonas harks back to the kabbalistic notion of *tzimtzum*, 'the cosmogonic center concept of the Lurianic Kabbalah' which denotes the 'contraction, withdrawal, self-limitation' of the divine being. In seeing God as withdrawing himself from the world through 'self-limitation', Jonas feels he can salvage 'the idea of a God who for a time — the time of the ongoing world process — has divested himself of any power to interfere with the physical course of things'. In effect, by deploying the kabbalistic concept of

---

23 There was of course justification for Leibniz's rationale. As the German philosopher Hans Blumenberg makes clear in his study *Die Legitimität der Neuzeit*, Leibniz was merely trying to *integrate into* God's 'Creation' what Augustine saw as *distinct from* divine purpose; in effect signalling his having moved beyond older medieval conceptions of nature, Leibniz regarded natural catastrophes no longer as divine punishment or retribution for human sins. Blumenberg writes: 'An essential characteristic of Leibniz's argumentation, by which he is distinguished from Augustinus, is the integration of the bad aspects of the Creation. Even the God who is to be vindicated by His works can Himself generate physically bad things to the extent that they are unavoidable in the accomplishment of the optimal overall goal'; *The Legitimacy of the Modern Age*, trans. by Robert M. Wallace (Cambridge, MA: The MIT Press, 1983), p. 55 (*Die Legitimität der Neuzeit*, p. 65).

24 'The Concept of God after Auschwitz', in *Echoes from the Holocaust. Philosophical Reflections on a Dark Time*, ed. by Alan Rosenberg and Gerald E. Myers (Philadelphia: Temple University Press, 1988), pp. 292–305 (p. 302); the following quotes pp. 292, 295, 301, 301, 303, and 302.

tzimtzum Jonas comes to formulate a position that approximates the Christian deists' notion of a *deus absconditus*, despite this notion of a hidden God being in essence 'a profoundly un-Jewish conception', as Jonas himself concedes.

Among Anglo-American Christian theologians struggling to come to terms with God's inaction both generally in our world as well as specifically during the Holocaust were the advocates of the so-called 'Death of God Theology' (which also went by the names 'radical theology', 'new theology' and 'negative theology') that arose in the early to mid-1960s. Death of God Theology is a remarkable amalgam: whereas outwardly it presented itself as atheistic (but which in actual fact it never was, as I will illustrate below), inwardly it exhibited both deistic and theistic features, conceding on the one hand God's current state of absence in our world while on the other predicting Christ's return in the future, albeit — if I understand correctly — not as a reckoning Redeemer but rather in a spiritual internalized form. This peculiar theological potpourri requires some elaboration and is best elucidated through some direct quotations lifted from key works of the movement's leading proponents, the Protestant religious scholars Thomas J. J. Altizer and William Hamilton. Altizer's and Hamilton's atheistic starting point was Friedrich Nietzsche; early in one of Death of God Theology's most programmatic essays, 'Theology and the Death of God', published in the 1966 volume *Radical Theology and The Death of God*, Altizer asserted 'we shall simply assume the truth of Nietzsche's proclamation of the death of God, a truth which has thus far been ignored or set aside by contemporary theology. This means that we shall understand the death of God as a historical event: God has died in *our* time, in *our* history, in *our* existence'. He continues:

> Nietzsche's proclamation of the death of God shattered the transcendence of Being. No longer is there a metaphysical hierarchy or order which can give meaning or value to existing beings (*Seiendes*); [...] for to exist in our time is to exist in what Sartre calls a 'hole in Being', a 'hole' created by the death of God. However, the proclamation of the death of God — or, more deeply, the *willing* of the death of God — is dialectical: a No-saying to God (the transcendence of *Sein*) makes possible a Yes-saying to human existence (*Dasein*, total existence in the *here* and *now*). Absolute transcendence is transformed into absolute immanence; being *here* and *now* (the post-Christian existential 'now') draws into itself all those powers which were once bestowed upon the Beyond.[25]

Altizer's resolute existentialist declaration of independence from God, his express 'No-saying to God' and 'Yes-saying to human existence', is deceptive: if God has 'died in *our* time', he must until recently have been alive. This is explicitly confirmed by Altizer and Hamilton in the 'Preface' to their book.[26] Hamilton enlarges on this in an interview conducted in the mid-1960s; asked whether radical theologians like himself would 'call themselves agnostics, or atheists, or antitheists', he responds:

---

25 'Theology and the Death of God', in Thomas J. J. Altizer and William Hamilton, *Radical Theology and The Death of God* (Harmondsworth: Penguin, 1966), pp. 102–17 (pp. 102 and 105).

26 See *Radical Theology and The Death of God* (Indianapolis: Bobbs-Merrill, 1966), pp. ix–xiii (especially p. x).

'Atheist' would be the closest. Agnostic suggests maybe, and 'death of God' is not a maybe theology. Antitheism suggests an aggressiveness about others' views that the radicals don't have. But if they are atheists, they are atheists with a difference. Perhaps the difference can be put this way. Traditional atheism believes that there is now no God and that there never has been, beliefs in God of the past being deception, ignorance, fear. Radical theology believes that there was once a time (Bible, sixteenth century, for example) when having a god was appropriate, possible, even necessary. But now is not such a time. There was once, and is not now.[27]

Hamilton usefully amplifies later in the interview by introducing two themes, first *'The Bonhoeffer theme'*, which he describes thus: 'Here I would put my development of Bonhoeffer's idea of man come of age, the end of religion, the breakdown of the idea of God as problem-solver and need-meeter. God is not needed, even on the boundary or in the depths, to do things the world cannot do'. The second theme, which Hamilton titles *'The Dostoevsky–Camus theme'*, relates directly to the issue of theodicy; he writes: 'The problem of suffering as written about by such writers, and as lived out in the twentieth century, has put an end, I think, to classical doctrines of Providence, and thus to the very centre of the biblical doctrine of God. A God to whom could be ascribed the death of the six million Jews in our time would be a monster'.

If this gives the impression that Altizer and Hamilton are advocating an existentialist atheism derived primarily from Nietzsche, Sartre and Camus, alongside such non-dogmatic Christian theologians as Bonhoeffer, other pronouncements provide a corrective. In 'The Significance of the New Theology' Altizer thus remarks in 1967:

> Now the Christian God is unsayable, his name for the first time unnameable, and those who truly try to speak in his name are inevitably drawn to the language of absence, eclipse, and silence. No longer does the theologian attempt to speak of faith to the world, for he is mute in face of the contemporary challenge of faith, and is rapidly losing the power to speak.[28]

Hamilton similarly insists that 'the "death of God" does not imply the disappearance of the mystery, richness, complexity of life' (as Charles Taylor claims it must for the atheistic non-believer, see Chapter Two and elsewhere in this study), it merely implies 'that God can no longer be a word, a name, or a concept appropriate to explain these things'.[29] The tenth and final 'meaning' of the expression 'death of God', as enumerated in the 1966 'Preface', hence entails, 'finally, that our language about God is always inadequate and imperfect'.[30] The proposition here is in both cases less that God is dead than merely that Christian theologians like William

---

27 'Questions and Answers on the Radical Theology', in *The Death of God Debate*, ed. by Jackson Lee Ice and John J. Carey (Philadelphia: The Westminster Press, 1967), pp. 213–41 (p. 214); the subsequent passages both p. 217.
28 'The Significance of the New Theology', in *The Death of God Debate*, ed. by Jackson Lee Ice and John J. Carey (Philadelphia: The Westminster Press, 1967), pp. 242–55 (p. 243).
29 'Questions and Answers on the Radical Theology', p. 217.
30 *Radical Theology and The Death of God*, p. xi.

Hamilton have lost the ability to speak credibly about God.

In all of their pronouncements one notices considerable caution about the way in which Altizer and Hamilton formulate their positions regarding Christian belief today; from what I have cited, for instance, we might already — and rightly — sense that their language indicates not that they have actually given up on God, nor that they truly believe in his non-existence, as would the fully-fledged atheist with whom they boast affinity, but rather that they admit merely to lack an 'authentic'[31] language with which convincingly to explain to a contemporary Christian audience the existence of a God who never shows himself to the world. As Jacques Derrida rightly put it in his reflections on 'Negative Theology' in his groundbreaking 1968 essay 'Différance', negative theologians are 'always hastening to recall that God is refused the predicate of existence, only in order to acknowledge His superior, inconceivable, and ineffable mode of being'.[32] What emerges from close analysis of Altizer's and Hamilton's key statements is that, while they admit that God may for all intents and purposes have disappeared from our world and may seem to be as good as dead, he is actually lying in wait in the figure of Christ. This is the message behind the seventh of their ten meanings of the expression 'death of God', which states 'that men do not today experience God except as hidden, absent, silent. We live, so to speak, in the time of the death of God, though that time will doubtless pass'.[33] The crucial final flourish 'though that time will doubtless pass' reveals that theirs truly is a 'theology', albeit a 'death of God' *version of theology* rather than a genuine form of philosophical atheism; what they put forward is thus indeed, as they state in their 1966 'Preface', 'an attempt to set an atheistic point of view *within the spectrum of Christian possibilities*' — I here stress the preposition 'within'.[34]

---

31 See for the application of this term Thomas J. J. Altizer, *The Gospel of Christian Atheism* (Philadelphia: The Westminster Press, 1966), p. 103.

32 'Différance', in *Margins of Philosophy*, trans. by Alan Bass (Chicago: University of Chicago Press, 1982), pp. 1–27 (p. 6); for more on Derrida and Negative Theology, and for Derrida's extended reflections on Negative Theology, see *Derrida and Negative Theology*, ed. by Harold Coward and Toby Foshay (Albany: State University of New York Press, 1992).

33 Altizer and Hamilton, *Radical Theology and The Death of God*, pp. x–xi.

34 Ibid., p. ix. The main — and perhaps even only — German advocate of Death Of God Theology in the 1960s, the literary scholar and theologian Dorothee Sölle (who, revealingly, was the author of the dissertation on Klingemann's atheistic *Nightwatches of Bonaventura* that we cited in Chapter Three; and who, equally revealingly, was never accepted into the Church establishment but was forced into non-theological teaching and political activism), underscores this point as well; in her 1966 article 'Believing in God atheistically' she writes: 'In short, the issue of theology today can only be described as "believing in God atheistically". This paradox locution articulates that faith is here understood as a manner of living that does without the supernatural, transcendent notion of a heavenly being, without the reassurance and the consolation that such a notion can afford: a kind of life, in other words, that now lacks the metaphysical advantage we used to have over the non-Christian, but that still holds on to the interest of Jesus through practice. To see faith as practice in this sense has a long Christian tradition' ('In einem Sinne gefasst, ließe sich die Problematik gegenwärtiger Theologie beschreiben als ein "atheistisch an Gott glauben". Der paradoxe Ausdruck will sagen, dass Glauben hier als eine Art Leben verstanden wird, das ohne die supranaturale, überweltliche Vorstellung eines himmlischen Wesens auskommt, ohne die Beruhigung und den Trost, den eine solche Vorstellung schenken kann: eine Art Leben also ohne metaphysischen Vorteil vor den nicht-Christen, in dem trotzdem an der Sache Jesu in der Welt festgehalten wird. Den

Their positioning themselves *within* rather than atheistically *outside* of 'the spectrum of Christian possibilities' is made more explicit in Altizer's book *The Gospel of Christian Atheism*, published also in 1966; he writes there in a section entitled 'The death of God':

> What can it mean to speak of the death of God? Indeed, how is it even possible to speak of the death of God, particularly at a time when the name of God would seem to be unsayable? First, we must recognize that the proclamation of the death of God is a Christian confession of faith. For to know that God is dead is to know the God who died in Jesus Christ, the God who passed through what Blake symbolically named as 'Self-Annihilation' or Hegel dialectically conceived as the negation of negation. Only the Christian can truly speak of the death of God, because the Christian alone knows the God who negates himself in his own revelatory and redemptive acts.[35]

There is little here that justifies the application of the term atheism to their venture. Clearly, as Altizer and Hamilton conceive it, Death of God Theology is premised not on the traditional notion of 'God' as an omnipotent being, positioned somewhere *beyond our world* and *beyond our reach*, but rather on the specifically Christological notion of God-who-became-man *in our world* and *within our reach*, who died on the Cross, and whose return we must now await. Hence their stress on the 'centrality of Jesus',[36] hence also their emphasis on the notion of 'waiting for God'. Hamilton defines and defends his understanding of 'waiting' thus:

> Waiting here refers to the whole experience I have called 'the death of God', including the attack on religion and the search for a means by which God, not needed, may be enjoyed. [...] Thus we wait, we try out new words, we pray for God to return, and we seem willing to descend into the darkness of unfaith and doubt that something may emerge on the other side. [...] We turn from the problems of faith to the reality of love. [...] There is something more than our phrase 'waiting for God' that keeps this from sheer atheistic humanism. Not only our waiting but our worldly work is Christian too, for our way to our neighbour is not only mapped out by the secular social and psychological and literary disciplines, it is mapped out as well by Jesus Christ and his way to his neighbour. Our ethical existence is partly a time of waiting for God and partly an actual Christology.[37]

Glauben in diesem Sinne als Praxis zu nehmen, entspricht durchaus [d]er christlichen Tradition...'; 'Atheistisch an Gott glauben', in *Gesammelte Werke*, ed. by Ursula Baltz-Otto and Fulbert Steffensky, vol. 3: *Stellvertretung* (Stuttgart: Krenz, 2006), pp. 217–33 (p. 219).

35 *The Gospel of Christian Atheism*, p. 102.

36 William Hamilton, 'The Death of God Theologies Today', in *Radical Theology and The Death of God*, pp. 36–62 (p. 57).

37 'The Death of God Theologies Today', pp. 58–60. For Dorothee Sölle too the redefinition of Christology is key to the new Christian understanding of divinity; for her Christology must be understood as a form of anthropology, a question of human beings relating to one another in the name of Christ, whether Jesus be human or divine. In her own words: 'Theology after "The Death of God" can conduct Christology only as anthropology because God can only occur between human beings' ('Theologie nach dem "Tod Gottes" wird [...] Christologie als Anthropologie betreiben, weil Gott sich zwischen Menschen ereignen kann...'); 'Theologie nach dem Tod Gottes' (first published in 1964), in *Gesammelte Werke*, vol. 3, pp. 195–217, this quotation 216.

What Death of God Theology ultimately hinges on is how this 'waiting for God' is to be understood. For Altizer more than for Hamilton God was transposed into the figure of Christ-as-man whose spirit will unfold over time in human history (or so I interpret Altizer's Hegelian dialectical position in *The Gospel of Christian Atheism* — although this aspect is in my view presented with a gratuitous measure of mystical obtuseness). What remains ambiguous throughout, however, is why, if God has died in recent history or perhaps even never existed at all as the all-powerful benevolent being from which they clearly are trying to distance themselves, they see it as so important to stress that God has sublated himself in Christ (to adopt the Hegelian notion of 'Aufhebung' on which Altizer's position is thoroughly premised). To put it rigorously: either Christ is just a man, a historical person with exclusively human qualities, as David Friedrich Strauß already reasoned in his 1835–1836 demythologizing *Life of Jesus Critically Examined*, in which case Christianity becomes hollowed out; effectively, it becomes defunct as a system of religion based on divine agency (which is why Strauß's book created such an uproar and controversy in his day, leading also to Strauß being suspended from his teaching position at the University of Tübingen). Or Christ continues in some way to possess a divine nature, in which case *Death of God* Theology nullifies its name. However, with a dead God and a living Christ Death of God Theology seems to want to have it both ways.

Predictably, the Christological quandary which forces Christian theologians to perform veritable metaphysical somersaults in order to rescue their religious faith in the face of a God who no longer appears to exist,[38] evaporates in Jewish theology as becomes apparent when one compares Christian Death of God Theology with its Jewish counterpart. In 1966, the same year as Altizer and Hamilton published *Radical Theology and The Death of God*, Richard L. Rubenstein, a Jewish theologian and trained rabbi who served as Director of the B'nai B'rith Hillel Foundation from 1958 to 1970, published a book programmatically entitled *After Auschwitz. Radical Theology and Contemporary Judaism*. In the 'Introduction' to his book Rubenstein openly acknowledges the assistance he received from Altizer and Hamilton in firming up his argument, all the while confessing that he initially 'experienced something of a crisis upon reading Hamilton's article "The Death of

---

[38] Another intriguing example of such metaphysical somersaults is the unorthodox German Catholic theologian Hans Küng, professor of dogmatics and ecumenical theology at the University of Tübingen. Towards the end of his 800-plus page 1978 book *Does God exist? Answering the Question of God's Existence in Modernity* (*Existiert Gott? Antwort auf die Gottesfrage der Neuzeit*) — which contains an insightful and well-informed history of the development of theism and atheism in European thought — he notes: 'Yes, in the face of (Jesus on) the Cross we can lose all faith: it is this one has to think of when one propagates the slogan "God is dead. But Jesus is alive". For if God is dead, then Jesus too comes to an end. In which case Jesus would have nothing of import, nothing essential to tell us. [...] Inversely, what this also suggests is, if Jesus is at an end, then God too is at an end' (*Existiert Gott?*, 6th edn (Munich: Piper, 2010), p. 740). After reiterating this reasonable — throughout his study Küng appeals to the importance of *rational* reflection — criticism of Death of God Theology he goes on, in the two hundred pages of Sections F and G of his study, to reclaim Christian belief and maintain faith in both God and Jesus Christ with more or less the same arguments as Altizer, albeit using less mystical language.

God Theologies Today" in *The Christian Scholar* for the spring of 1965', adding: 'I learned to my surprise that Hamilton regarded my writing as an example of death of God theology'.[39] His 'surprise' originates from the fact that 'for Jews, because of our alienation from the symbolism of the cross, it is impossible to use the words "God is dead"'; nonetheless, Rubenstein continues,

> we must use these words of alien origin and connotation. We share the same cultural universe as the contemporary Christian thinker; we experience the radical secularity of our time as do they. We have been deeply influenced by Freud, Sartre, Hegel, Dostoevsky, Melville, and Kierkegaard. Above all, we have been moved by Nietzsche. [...] After Nietzsche, it is impossible to avoid his language to express the total absence of God from our experience.

Rubenstein admits forthrightly in the 'Preface' to his book that it was the implications of Auschwitz for belief more even than his reading of Nietzsche, Dostoevsky or Sartre that had turned him away from God; he declares: 'Our images of God, man, and the moral order have been permanently impaired. No Jewish theology will possess even a remote degree of relevance to contemporary Jewish life if it ignores the question of God and the death camps. That is *the question* for Jewish theology in our times'. More pointedly he adds elsewhere: 'I am amazed at the silence of contemporary Jewish theologians on this most crucial and agonizing of all Jewish issues. How can Jews believe in an omnipotent, beneficent God after Auschwitz?'[40] While Jewish theology may not have been as silent as Rubenstein here makes out (as thoroughly documented in the 2007 volume *Wrestling with God. Jewish Theological Responses during and after the Holocaust*, edited by Steven T. Katz, Shlomo Biderman and Gershon Greenberg), his book nonetheless brought the issue to the fore, triggering considerable debate (not just) within Jewish theology, with some of Rubenstein's most vehement critics branding him a blasphemer (unfairly) and an atheist (fairly, although with some qualifications: Rubenstein throughout held on to religion as a social anchor). The religious scholar Zachary Braiterman sums up Rubenstein's contribution thus:

> [Rubenstein] attacked belief in the God of History, the notions of covenant and election, the hallowed texts of Jewish tradition, and the scandal of theodicy. Rubenstein's argument was simple: to posit a just and omnipotent God covenanted to Israel *and active in its affairs* could only mean that God justly willed the murder of six million Jewish people. Rubenstein therefore proclaimed 'the death of God' and turned to what he called 'the tragic fatalities of the God of nature'. No Jewish theologian had ever attacked the God and tradition of covenant and election with such categorical rage.[41] (Braiterman's emphasis)

It was only after the publication of Rubenstein's *After Auschwitz* in 1966 that the

---

39 Rubenstein, *After Auschwitz. Radical Theology and Contemporary Judaism* (Indianapolis: Bobbs-Merrill, 1966), pp. x and 244; the subsequent quotes p. 245 and p. x.

40 'Symposium on Jewish Belief', in *Wrestling with God. Jewish Theological Responses during and after the Holocaust*, ed. by Steven T. Katz, Shlomo Biderman and Gershon Greenberg (Oxford: Oxford University Press, 2007), pp. 415–16 (p. 415).

41 '"Hitler's Accomplice?": The Tragic Theology of Richard Rubenstein', *Modern Judaism* 17 (1997), 75–89 (p. 75).

question came to be addressed whether Auschwitz, as a radical *novum* and unparalleled *tremendum* (in George M. Kren's and Arthur Allen Cohen's respective coinages), also represents 'a theological point of no return'.[42] As much as the Holocaust was — in the words of Cohen — a 'traumatic event'[43] that defies explanation and understanding, the question had to be asked, and it was asked, whether it denoted something theologically fundamentally unique or whether it was just yet another manifestation of anti-Jewish butchery in a long succession in history of genocidal assaults on and persecutions of Jews, perhaps quantitatively larger and more brutal than earlier incidents, but not in essence qualitatively new, as such examples illustrate as 'the destruction of the Temple, the Crusader massacres, the Chmelniki pogroms, and widespread massacres in the Ukraine following World War I', which Braiterman enumerates in *(God) After Auschwitz*.[44] Thus Braiterman asks, 'even if the Holocaust was *historically* unique, does it truly represent a *theologically* unique evil?' Should 'the death of thousands, tens of thousands, hundreds of thousands […] trouble religious faith' less than the death of millions? After all, 'no less than the Holocaust, these events call into question the notion of a good and powerful God, acting in history, and watching over Israel with special care. The Holocaust, it would seem, does not substantially change the problem'. The rabbinical teacher and professor of philosophy Eliezer Berkovits reiterates this point as follows:

> The enormity of the number of martyrs of our generation — six million — is not essential to the doubt. As far as our faith in an absolutely just and merciful God is concerned, the suffering of a single innocent child poses no less a problem than the undeserved suffering of millions. As far as one's faith in a personal God is concerned, there is no difference between six, five, four million victims or one million. […] The German crime of the ghettos and concentration camps stands out in all human history as the most abominable, the most sickening, and the most inhuman. But justice and injustice, guilt and innocence are matters of degree only for man. When one questions the acts of an absolute God, whose every attribute, too, is absolute by definition, the innocent suffering of a single person is as incomprehensible as that of millions. […] Once the problem of evil is understood in its valid dimensions, the specific case of the Holocaust is not seen to be essentially different from the old problem of theodicy.[45]

Regardless of the position we ourselves take and how we respond to the inordinate magnitude of evil that the Holocaust represents, the observations by Braiterman and Berkovits (and one could add similar pronounements by scores of other theologians, philosophers and religious scholars, not to mention historians and poets) underscore the degree to which Auschwitz today serves as theodicy's prism for the twentieth century, its Lisbon moment, as it were.

---

42 See George M. Kren, 'The Holocaust: Moral Theory and immoral Acts', in *Echoes from the Holocaust. Philosophical Reflections on a Dark Time*, pp. 245–61; and Arthur A. Cohen, *The Tremendum. A Theological Interpretation of the Holocaust* (New York: Crossroad, 1981).
43 I cite this expression here from the excerpt 'Thinking the Tremendum' in *A Holocaust Reader*, ed. by Michael L. Morgan (New York and Oxford: Oxford University Press, 2001), pp. 183–96 (p. 184).
44 *(God) After Auschwitz*, this and the following quotation p. 13.
45 'Faith after the Holocaust', in *Wrestling with God*, pp. 463–85 (p. 481).

Let us return for a moment to Hans Jonas's distinction between the suffering inflicted by nature (as through the Lisbon earthquake) as opposed to the evil inflicted by man on man (as at Auschwitz) which, in philosophical discussions of theodicy, equates with the distinction between *malum physicum* (the woe brought about by nature's agency) and *malum morale* (the evil wrought by human free will).[46] We can superimpose these two types of *malum* onto the three paradigms at the core of my argument: whereas in the eighteenth century the earthquake of Lisbon symbolically marked the transition between the first and the second paradigm, between the agency of God and the agency of Nature, the Holocaust in the twentieth can be rendered doubly as a point of transition. For secularists it demarcates the transition between the second and third paradigm, death incurred through the violence of (a godless) Nature (*malum physicum*) being supplanted by — as well as complemented by — death incurred through the (godless) violence of Man (*malum morale*). For believers and theologians, by contrast, it serves to delineate the shift from the first to the third paradigm, from a world governed by God being put in jeopardy by a world governed by Man.

However, worse even than the *actual* evil man has already inflicted on man in the first half of the twentieth century is the *potential* evil man can now, in the wake of Hiroshima and Nagasaki, inflict on man in the future. In the context of the Christian 'death of God' debate we earlier cited William Hamilton's 'idea', derived from the German theologian Dietrich Bonhoeffer, of 'man come of age'. Man's coming of age signals also his ability to annihilate himself as a species and end his existence on planet Earth (not to mention the existence of other species). Although 'the death of God', or even our 'waiting for God', may mean that man has at long last come into his own, and can hence do away with divine agency in his life, it may be more accurate to invert cause and effect, and thus to state: because our capacity to annihilate ourselves has given us the God-like privilege and power of total annihilation, the death of God in theology may just turn out to be the prelude to the death of man in reality.

It is hard not to notice how Death-of-God-Theology's notion of endlessly 'waiting for God' was parodied *avant la lettre*, as it were, by Samuel Beckett in *Waiting for Godot*. Written in 1952, a decade before the theological movement itself came into existence, Beckett's play at one point shows us the slave-like character Lucky, ordered by his master Pozzo to 'Think!', launching into an incoherent *Finnegans-Wake*-like torrent of gibberish, the beginning of which suggestively reads:

> Given the existence as uttered forth in the public works of Puncher and Wattmann of a personal God quaquaquaqua with white beard quaquaquaqua outside time without extension who from the heights of divine apathia divine athambia divine aphasia loves us dearly with some exceptions for reasons unknown but time will tell and suffers like the divine Miranda with those who for reasons unknown but time will tell are plunged in torment plunged in fire flames if that continues and who can doubt it will fire the firmament that is to

---

46 For more on this see Klaus von Stosch, *Theodizee* (Paderborn: Schöningh, 2013), and, specifically in the context of a discussion of Hans Jonas, Martin Hailer, *Religionsphilosophie* (Göttingen: Vandenhoeck & Ruprecht, 2014), pp. 114–18.

say blast to hell to heaven so blue...[47]

Understandably, many have taken Beckett's play to be not just about our endlessly frustrated 'waiting for God[ot]', but also, as is intimated at the end of this passage by 'blast to hell to heaven so blue', about the imminence of a nuclear holocaust. *Waiting for Godot* as well as Beckett's later plays *Endgame* (1957) and *Happy Days* (1961) are replete with internal textual pointers showing them to be 'metaphors of [a] nuclear abyss', as Melinda Jo Guttman has put it, through which humankind would reduce itself through nuclear incineration to a madcap nucleus of insane last men and women, as all three plays suggest.[48] Regardless of whether we are 'waiting for God' or 'waiting for Godot', ultimately we are waiting to find out how mankind's appearance on the stage of life will pan out. And, as I have been arguing over the course of this study, the cause of or means to this end can be threefold: God, Nature and Man, with the likelihood growing that it will be Man himself, rather than God or Nature, who through nuclear weaponry — or some other lethal technology of his own devising — will be the ultimate cause of his terminal demise. What Beckett metaphorically calls 'waiting for Godot' Robert Jay Lifton hence more literally translates into 'waiting for the bomb'.[49]

Of course, waiting for the bomb has its own absurd logic and dynamic, as Lifton, who has spent most of his academic career studying the psychological impact of the twentieth-century's two worst kinds of genocide, the death camps of Auschwitz and the bombings of Hiroshima and Nagasaki, explains; in analysing what he calls the 'debased millennialism' of extremist secular 'world-destructionists' as well as of apocalyptic evangelical Armageddonists in the 'border area of theology and psychopathology', the American psychiatrist thus observes:

> Those we may call the world-destructionists (or Armageddonists) are not always clear on exactly *who* would be committing the ultimate act of annihilation (it is sometimes man, sometimes God). Yet that does not so much matter to them because ultimately God would be responsible: he, and he alone would be carrying out his promise, as prophesied in Revelation and other biblical texts. However dubious the theology, it conjoins nuclear holocaust with the evangelical Christian impulse toward world cleansing in the name of achieving the ultimate spiritual moment (the Second Coming or the Kingdom of God). Integral to that world cleansing is *self*-cleansing. What takes on greatest moral urgency for the Armageddonist is not the prevention of nuclear holocaust but the individual's spiritual preparation for his or her transport (via the 'Rapture') to a higher state. [...] Though I speak of an absurd psychic extreme, one should not underestimate the broader appeal of end-time ideology as a perverse vision of hope.

In the Armageddonist's 'perverse vision of hope' — man fulfilling God's will

---

[47] *Warten auf Godot — En attendant Godot — Waiting for Godot* (Frankfurt a.M.: Suhrkamp, 1971), p. 110.

[48] See Melinda Jo Guttmann, 'Préface', in *Les Cahiers du GRIF*, 41–42 (1989, special issue on 'L'imaginaire du nucléaire'), 11–22, p. 14. A useful analysis of Beckett's work in a nuclear context can also be found in Eva Horn's *Zukunft als Katastrophe* (Frankfurt a.M.: Fischer, 2014), pp. 224–32.

[49] *The Future of Immortality*, p. 138; the subsequent quotations pp. 5 and 6.

through the means of nuclear warfare — the old paradigm of God and the new paradigm of Man fuse into one. The prospect that human beings might relish the thought and indeed, worse, might want to accelerate the onset or initiate the outbreak of nuclear Armageddon for parochial religious reasons will drive moral revulsion, if not terror, into the minds of most people, both (non-fundamentalist) religious faithful and secularists, who are not obsessed with the abstruse logic of extreme end-time millennialism. But even among religiously unaffected minds there can be a danger, as Lifton worries, that ideological obsession or pathological illness can take one over the brink (as witnessed 2015 by the German Wings pilot who committed suicide with his planeload of passengers and colleagues in the French Alps); Lifton argues that 'there is a real sense in which we can speak of "secular Armageddonists", who, like their religious counterparts, renounce responsibility for the holocaust they anticipate and, in some cases, press toward bringing about'. Elsewhere he uses the characters from Stanley Kubrick's film *Dr. Strangelove* as instructive filmic cases in point:

> There is, on the one hand, the impulse to 'press the button' and 'get the thing over with', even the orgiastic excitement of the wild forces let loose — destroying everything in order to feel alive. But the other side of the Strangelove image, what I take to be its wisdom, is the insistence that we confront the radical absurdity or 'madness' of the world destruction we are contemplating. [...] We must imagine something close to nuclear extinction in order to prevent it. We must extend our psychological and moral imaginations in order to hold off precisely what we begin to imagine.[50]

The first to formulate this new 'nuclear' moral imperative was the stridently atheistic German-Jewish philosopher Günther Anders, who had been arguing untiringly ever since the late 1950s that, in the words of Lifton, 'we must extend our psychological and moral imaginations in order to hold off precisely what we begin to imagine'. Anders's role as the principal analyst and Cassandra of our absurd 'nuclear condition', exposing the acuteND dangers that inhere in the godlike 'apocalyptic powers' we acquired in 1945, has not received due credit in Anglo-American criticism, primarily due I believe to only a fraction of his work having appeared in English translation. Because this leading nuclear critic's line of reasoning is crucial for my own argument, however, I would like to devote a good part of the following section to presenting his core statements and reflections on the subject.

The Dialectic of the Nuclear Age

In a joint article entitled 'The Holocaust as a Test of Philosophy', published in 1988, the psychologist Paul Marcus and the philosopher Alan Rosenberg give emphasis to the same linkage I have been drawing attention to in the introductory sections of this chapter: 'Finally, as philosophers, above all else,' they write, 'we must still face the awful possibility that we will, one day, be drawn into another genocidal

---

50 'The Image of "The End of the World": A Psychohistorical View', in *Visions of Apocalypse*, ed. Saul Friedländer et al., pp. 151–67 (p. 165).

Holocaust. Indeed, the nuclear threat, laced with the same perilous confidence in technology, may be understood as the genocide to end all genocides'.[51] As I indicated earlier, in his study of our genocidal condition and its 'logic of madness', Robert Jay Lifton has spoken of our species' looming 'self-genocide', adding: 'In 1945, a new image came into the world, an image of extinguishing ourselves as a species by our own hand, with our own technology. This "imagery of extinction" derived primarily from the atomic bombing of Hiroshima and Nagasaki and from the Nazi Holocaust in Europe'.[52] Hiroshima means that it is no longer *either* God *or* Nature who alone possess the power to annihilate humankind; now Man himself through devices of his own invention, through the progeny of Frankenstein's monster, can kill off his own species if and when he so wills it. 6 August 1945 is the datum, the point from which my third paradigm, the paradigm of Man, becomes not just fictively imaginable but also factually realizable. And it is Günther Anders, the Jewish-German anthropologist, philosopher and essayist cited above, who personifies this paradigm's prime theoretician. Others before and alongside him had written about the dangers inherent in nuclear technology, and especially nuclear weaponry — among them the British philosopher, logician, political activist and 1950 Nobel Prize Laureate for Literature Bertrand Russell, the French-German theologian and philosopher and 1952 Nobel Peace Prize Laureate Albert Schweitzer, the German philosopher Karl Jaspers, the German nuclear scientist Carl Friedrich von Weizsäcker, the Austrian publicist Robert Jungk, and the American science journalist Jonathan Schell. In particular Schell's *The Fate of the Earth* of 1982 — published initially in three parts in *The New Yorker* in 1981 — found widespread resonance in the anglophone world; his study is indisputably far more scientifically detailed than any of Anders's writings, but Anders is the observer who outlined the philosophical ramifications of our nuclear condition most starkly and programmatically.

Since Anders is little known in the anglophone world and yet is such an interesting figure within twentieth-century German intellectual history, it is worth taking a moment to provide some background here. Born into a German-Jewish family as Günther Siegmund Stern in what was then Breslau, Germany, today Wroclaw, Poland, in 1902, and a cousin of Walter Benjamin, Anders studied philosophy under Edmund Husserl in Freiburg, where he graduated with a PhD in 1923. He met his first wife Hannah Arendt in Marburg in 1925 where both attended seminars by Martin Heidegger. For a short while they lived in Heidelberg, then Frankfurt, where he hoped to launch a university career. Based on a lecture he gave at Frankfurt that was attended by Theodor W. Adorno and Max Horkheimer, Adorno came to suspect him (wrongly, as Adorno was later to admit) of a Heideggerian leaning and an un-Marxist attitude; this induced Adorno to thwart Anders's attempt to submit a thesis for a *Habilitation* at Frankfurt university, the German academic prerequisite for a university professorship. Finding himself forced

---

51 'The Holocaust as a Test of Philosophy', in *Echoes from the Holocaust. Philosophical Reflections on a Dark Time*, ed. Rosenberg and Myers, pp. 201–22 (p. 218).

52 *The Future of Immortality*, pp. 120 and 141.

into a journalistic career, Anders (and Arendt) moved to Berlin where from 1930 he worked for the newspaper *Berliner Börsen-Kurier*; this is also the period during which he adopted his pen-name Günther Anders ('anders' being the German word for 'different') under which all of his later publications were to appear. In short succession Anders and then Arendt fled Germany after Hitler came to power in 1933, both emigrating first to Paris in 1933, then to the United States in 1936, but separating in 1937. Anders returned to Europe in 1950 where he settled in Vienna with his second wife and became recognized, among other things, as a political activist who co-initiated the anti-nuclear civil rights movement and served as one of the jurors of the 1966–1967 International Vietnam War Crimes Tribunal (also known as the Russell–Sartre Tribunal). Familiar to an English-speaking audience primarily through his 1951 essay on Kafka and his correspondence with the Hiroshima-pilot Claude Eatherly, the only books of his to appear in English translation (*Kafka*, 1960; *Burning Conscience: The Case of the Hiroshima Pilot Claude Eatherly*, 1961), he was known in German-speaking countries as a prolific essayist and writer of scholarly books on contemporary philosophical anthropology and such topical post-World-War-II issues as what it means to live in a technological age and how we should respond to the nuclear threat faced by humanity in the wake of Hiroshima. Despite his prominence in these areas his key philosophical works *The Obsolescence of Mankind* (*Die Antiquiertheit des Menschen*, vol. 1, 1956; vol. 2, 1980) and *End-Time and End of Time* (*Endzeit und Zeitenende*, 1972, a collection of essays written between 1958 and 1967) remain for the large part untranslated. It is in the latter, which was republished in German in 1981 under the title *The Nuclear Threat* (*Die atomare Drohung*), that Anders most forcefully states his case. Fortunately for the English-language reader, the key sixth chapter in this volume, entitled 'Thesen zum Atomzeitalter' ('Theses for the Atomic Age'), appeared in translation in the Spring 1962 issue of *The Massachusetts Review*, as did some extracts entitled 'Reflections on the H Bomb' that condense the important fourth section of the first volume of *The Obsolescence of Mankind*; taken together with *Burning Conscience*, which includes the ten-page tract 'Commandments in the Atomic Age', the English reader has access to some of Anders's most salient and thought-provoking pronouncements, and I shall cite from them liberally below as I will from some of the untranslated German sources.

The thrust of Anders's reasoning is that the atomic bomb symbolically demarcates the point of transition from what he calls the second to the third industrial age. However, it was only in the late 1950s after the publication of the first volume of *The Obsolescence of Mankind* that Anders recognized the need for this distinction, a recognition precipitated by the explosion of the first hydrogen bomb which Matthew Grant in an article on 'Nuclear War on British Screens from 1945 to the Early 1960s' describes as the true 'thermonuclear moment'; 'before 1954,' Grant writes, 'atomic bombs could be depicted as enormous, dangerous, but ultimately manageable', in conspicuous contrast to the newer and far more powerful technology.[53] The

---

53 'Images of Survival, Stories of Destruction: Nuclear War on British Screens from 1945 to the Early 1960s', *Journal of British Cinema and Television*, 10 (2013), 7–26 (p. 14).

advance in Anders's thinking manifests itself in the change of subtitles between the first and second volume of *The Obsolescence of Mankind*, the first volume of which was subtitled 'On the Soul in the Age of the Second Industrial Revolution' ('Über die Seele im Zeitalter der zweiten industriellen Revolution'), the second 'On the Destruction of Life in the Age of the Third Industrial Revolution' ('Über die Zerstörung des Lebens im Zeitalter der dritten industriellen Revolution'). While both are preoccupied with formulating a 'philosophical anthropology in the age of technocracy' ('eine philosophische Anthropologie im Zeitalter der Technokratie'), as he calls it retrospectively in the 'Preface' to the later volume,[54] Anders clearly had come to recognize that the shift in the human condition that he had been describing in his earlier book had become far more pronounced and axiomatic than even he himself had at first appreciated, hence the switch to the notion of a 'Third Industrial Revolution' in the later work. But it is not the digital era of personal computers, the internet and digital consumerism that Anders had in his sights, as some might imagine, for these were still in their infancy in 1980. (And it is arguable, in any case, that Anders would have seen the computer age merely as an extension of the second industrial revolution's technologification of mass consumer culture and hence as a quantitative radicalization rather than a genuinely qualitative revolution.) His focus rests squarely on what, for him, had become a far more fundamental and far more menacing concern. In the wake of the development of the hydrogen bomb Anders realized that the world had moved qualitatively beyond any of the worries raised by the technologies of the second industrial revolution; mankind, Anders now believed, had entered a phase that would end all history and suspend any and every philosophy of progress, technological, political, social or moral. Although most of the essays anthologized in *End-Time and End of Time* (1972) and the second volume of *The Obsolescence of Mankind* (1980) were written in the late 1950s and the 1960s, the diagnosis Anders put forward in them holds true no less today than it did at the time, even if it has since been swept under the carpet as a disillusioned Anders saw it towards the end of his life.

In the 'Preface' and 'Introduction' to the second volume of *The Obsolescence of Mankind* Anders puts his revised reasoning in a nutshell; it is technology, he now declares, that 'has become the subject of history' ('Technik ist nun zum Subjekt der Geschichte geworden').[55] The German phrase 'Subjekt der Geschichte' is less ambiguous than the dual meaning of the English transcription conveys; it asserts that technology has taken over the role of active agent of history, suggesting that the human race has lost control of the technology — viz. Frankenstein's monster — that it has created and that this monster has made itself the supreme 'subject' and driving force of history. Humankind, conversely, finds itself reduced to a mere plaything or pawn of technology's regime. Subject and object have become inverted. We have been 'dethroned' by technology without us even having realized what has happened, Anders contends; 'wir werden "maschinell infantilisiert"', he states elsewhere, deploying Freudian phraseology: the machinery we have engineered

---

54 *Die Antiquiertheit des Menschen*, vol. 2, p. 9.
55 Ibid.; the subsequent passages pp. 279 and 254.

is turning us back into infants, our unbridled consumerism has made us regress into an 'industrial oral phase' ('industrielle Oralphase'). In the second industrial revolution we as humankind learnt to manufacture a technology that, by serving us, was meant to accelerate progress and eradicate inequality, as envisaged by Godwin and Shelley and their nineteenth-century heirs — a utopian dream already put in question by Mary Shelley in *The Last Man*, as we saw in the previous chapter. However, as Horkheimer and Adorno recognized, and as Anders passionately and persuasively elaborates, our technological advances have also enabled us to amplify the killing power of our arsenals and devise tools of mass destruction beyond all imagining (some of the worst among which were incontestably the poison gasses of the First World War and the Zyklon B employed by the SS in the extermination camps during the Second World War), resulting ultimately in the corruption and perversion of the very Enlightenment ideals that saw in science and technology an instrument of human emancipation and betterment. But with those technological advances culminating first in the atomic bomb and then in the hydrogen bomb, the whole notion of progress finds itself reduced to tatters (if not to say ashes — that may yet come).

In 'Reflections on the H Bomb', the English translation and compilation of select passages from the first volume of *The Obsolescence of Mankind*, Anders reflects how 'all history can be divided into three chapters, each subject to a different caption: (1) All men are mortal, (2) All men are exterminable, and (3) Mankind as a whole is exterminable'.[56] The first proposition expresses a truth every human being has been forced to acknowledge ever since the dawn of humanity; it refers to our recognition that we are all, as individuals, mortal. The second proposition pertains to a fact that the Nazis not only recognized, but also ruthlessly exploited, namely that modern mass technology can be turned into a means of mass murder. But even the Nazis, Anders submits, neither planned nor could have carried out the mass murder of *all* of humankind; this would have had to involve what Lifton designated 'auto-genocide', and this is not what the Nazis had in mind. The situation that arises with the atomic bomb of 1945 and its successor, the hydrogen bomb, is thus of a different order: 'What is exterminable today', Anders concludes in their wake, 'is not "merely" all men' as a plurality of individuals, but 'mankind as a whole', as a singular species; he elaborates in his diary on 19 March 1979: 'For the atomic threat jeopardizes the existence of mankind as a whole — something one cannot say of the extermination camps. Whereas nuclear weapons are quite literally "apocalyptic", such camps were, and are, "apocalyptic" only in a metaphorical sense' ('Denn die atomare Gefahr bedroht den Bestand der Menschheit als ganzer — was man von den Vernichtungslagern nicht behaupten kann. Während die atomaren Waffen im wörtlichsten Sinne "apokalyptisch" sind, waren oder sind die Lager "apokalyptisch" nur im metaphorischen Sinne').[57] It is for this reason that not Auschwitz but rather Hiroshima signifies for Anders the beginning of a new era; 6 August 1945, he

---

56 'Reflections on the H Bomb', *Dissent*, 3 (Spring 1956), 146–55 (p. 148).
57 *Tagesnotizen. Aufzeichnungen 1941–1979*, ed. by Volker Hage (Frankfurt a.M.: Suhrkamp, 2006), p. 175.

underscores in an interview in 1979, is 'day zero of a new age: the day from which on humanity was irrevocably endowed with the power to annihilate itself' ('daß der 6. August den Tag Null einer neuen Zeitrechnung darstellte: den Tag, von dem an die Menschheit unrevozierbar fähig war, sich selbst auszurotten').[58]

Anthropologically speaking, this turning point in history is simultaneously a point of no return, as Anders emphasizes. '*The era of transitioning eras has ended with 1945*', he stresses and continues:

> we now live in a period that is no longer one merely transient era preceding countless others, but rather an age of respite in which our being is, in perpetuity, nothing but a 'just-still-being'. [...] The period we inhabit will be, whether it ends or endures, the *last* because the peril to which we are exposed thanks to our spectacular discovery [the atomic bomb] can never end — except through the end itself.
>
> [*Die Epoche der Epochenwechsel ist seit 1945 vorüber*. Nunmehr leben wir in einem Zeitalter, das nicht mehr eine vorübergehende Epoche vor anderen ist, sondern eine 'Frist', während derer unser Sein pausenlos nichts anderes mehr ist als ein 'Gerade-noch-sein'. [...] Unser Zeitalter ist und bleibt, ob es nun endet oder weiterwährt, das *letzte*, weil die Gefahr, in die wir uns durch unser spektakuläres Produkt gebracht haben, [...] niemals aufhören kann — es sei denn durch das Ende selbst.][59] (Anders's emphases)

And should this end ever come to pass, that is, should humankind ever succeed in eradicating itself through the monstrous machinery of nuclear technology, the human species will have simultaneously succeeded not just in destroying its historical present, but also its historical past and its as yet dormant and provisional future. In 'Commandments in the Atomic Age', published in German in 1957, in English in 1961, Anders reasons that we have become 'more mortal' than previous generations of mankind,

> 'more mortal' because our temporality means not only that we are mortal, not only that we are 'killable'. That 'custom' has always existed. But that we, as *mankind*, are 'killable'. And 'mankind' doesn't mean only today's mankind, not only mankind spread over the provinces of our globe; but also mankind spread over the provinces of time. For if the mankind of today is killed, then that which *has* been, dies with it; and the mankind to come too.

In 'Theses for the Atomic Age' Anders therefore extends the notion of a 'League of Nations' into a 'League of Generations', declaring 'the distinction between the generations of today and of tomorrow [...] meaningless'. We must consider our

---

58 'Wenn ich verzweifelt bin, was geht's mich an?' (interview with Mathias Greffrath 1979), in *Günther Anders antwortet. Interviews & Erklärungen* (Berlin: Bittermann, 1987, Edition Tiamat: Critica Diabolis 13), pp. 19–53 (p. 42).

59 *Die Antiquiertheit des Menschen*, vol. 2, p. 20. I should add that the word 'respite' is used for 'Frist' in the English translation of 'Theses for the Atomic Age' (*The Massachusetts Review*, 3 (Spring 1962), 493–505) authorized by Anders. Interestingly, Thomas Mann similarly noted in his diary on 14 August 1945, eight after days after Hiroshima and five days after Nagasaki were bombed, 'the atomic bomb, it would seem, means the end of "world history"' ('Denn die Atom-Bombe bedeutet gewissermaßen das Ende der "Weltgeschichte"'); Thomas Mann, *Tagebücher 1944–1.4.1946*, ed. by Inge Jens (Frankfurt a.M.: Fischer, 1968), p. 241.

grandchildren 'neighbours in time', Anders argues; thus

> by setting fire to *our* house, we cannot help but make the flames leap over into the cities of the future, and the not-yet-built homes of the not-yet-born generations will fall to ashes together with our homes. Even our ancestors are full-fledged members of this League: for by dying we would make them die, too — a second time, so to speak; and after this second death everything would be as if they had never been.[60]

Invoking 'the unborn generations [that] will never experience their cancellation by us', Jonathan Schell, the leading American critic of our nuclear predicament, would two decades later, in *The Fate of the Earth* in 1982, similarly speak of humanity's 'greater space — the only space fit for human habitation — of past, present, and future'.[61] The newly, if rather haphazardly, acquired apocalyptic and transgenerational kind of temporality overturns all moral foundations of our existence. 'Thus the basic moral question of former times must be radically reformulated', Anders argues; 'instead of asking "*How* should we live?", we must now ask "*Will* we live?"'[62]

With this new apocalyptic temporality and as an accessory to this new power comes man's elevation — or perhaps better, self-aggrandizement — also to God-like status. In the important 1966 essay 'The Obsolescence of Malice' ('Die Antiquiertheit der Bosheit'), which was later incorporated within the second volume of *The Obsolescence of Mankind*, Anders observes how 'we have made ourselves, by means of the tools we have created (and not just the atomic ones), the equals of gods, if not the equal of God' ('wir uns mit Hilfe der von uns selbst geschaffenen Geräte (und nicht etwa nur der atomaren) göttergleich, sogar *gottgleich*, gemacht haben').[63] He uses this essay to reflect, always from his atheistic anthropological perspective, on the religious ramifications of mankind's new situation; the heading of the essay's fourth section is consequently titled 'A Theology of the Atomic Situation' ('Theologie der atomaren Situation'). Man has, for Anders, stolen the march on both God and Nature; humankind has become nothing less than master of the apocalypse. Anders remarks in 'Reflections on the H Bomb', which picks up on and rephrases some of the key points of 'The Obsolescence of Malice':

> If there is anything that modern man regards as infinite, it is no longer God; nor is it nature, let alone morality or culture; it is his own power. *Creatio ex nihilo*, which was once the mark of omnipotence, has been supplanted by its opposite, *potestas annihilationis* or *reductio ad nihil*; and this power to destroy, to reduce to nothingness lies in our own hands. The Promethean dream of omnipotence has at long last come true, though in an unexpected form. Since we are in a position to inflict absolute destruction on each other, we have apocalyptic powers.[64]

The explosion of the atomic bomb has not just fundamentally transformed our

---

60 'Theses for the Atomic Age', pp. 494–95.
61 *The Fate of the Earth* (New York: Avon Books, 1982), pp. 169 and 172.
62 'Theses for the Atomic Age', p. 493.
63 *Die Antiquiertheit des Menschen*, vol. 2, p. 404.
64 'Reflections on the H Bomb', pp. 146–47.

relationship with the world and with God, but it has also inverted the significance of the apocalypse. Anders notes:

> Our end of time differs fundamentally from the way it is understood by Christians, for whom it embodied a Day of Reckoning that, although not *created* by humankind, was *rooted in* human *guilt*. Moreover — and this must sound sacrilegious — our time-worn talk of the end of the world must now, measured against today's real and actual threat, appear like mere metaphorical prattle. This all the more so as early Christianity's expectation of Judgment Day [...] has been comprehensively debunked by reality. The universe never took notice of the threat that was foretold, and world history has carried on unperturbed until today. Christianity has never really recovered from the shock that the feverishly expected end of the world, that is, the *Parousia*, never came to pass, not even in the year 1000. [Nor, we might today add, in the year 2000; R.W.] [...] In other words, although it rarely cloaks itself in the solemn mantle of religious vocabulary, today's threat of apocalypse is incomparably more serious than earlier threats ever were. More serious precisely because we now have the means to actually produce it, and these means are daily on the increase (if it even makes sense to speak of an 'increase').
>
> [Unsere Endzeit unterscheidet sich grundsätzlich von der im Christentum gemeinten, [als] die ja in dessen Augen der jüngste Tag, obwohl vom Menschen *verschuldet*, so doch *nicht* als von ihm *hergestellt* gegolten hatte. Dazu kommt — und das muß natürlich sakrilegisch klingen — daß uns die damalige Rede vom Weltende nunmehr, nun vor der Folie der realen Bedrohung, als eine nur noch metaphorische vorkommt. Dies um so mehr, als sich das frühe Christentum mit seiner Erwartung des 'jüngsten Tages' [...] vor der Wirklichkeit blamiert hat. Das Universum hat von der Bedrohung, die man ihm nach- bzw. vorhersagte, keine Notiz genommen, die Weltgeschichte ist bis heute weitergegangen. Von jenem Staunen darüber, daß das von ihm zitternd erwartete Weltende, bzw. die Parousie, nicht eintrat, auch im Jahre 1000 noch nicht eintreten wollte, hat sich ja das Christentum bis heute noch nicht ganz erholt. [...] In anderen Worten: die heutige apokalyptische Gefahr ist, obwohl sie kaum je im feierlichen Gewand einer religiösen Sprache auftritt, ungleich ernster, als es frühere Apokalypse-Gefahren je gewesen sind. Ernster eben deshalb, weil nun Mittel zu deren Herstellung seit zwei Jahrzehnten bereitliegen und sich täglich (sofern von 'Steigerung' zu reden überhaupt noch einen Sinn hat) noch steigern.][65]

Nuclear technology has, in effect, rendered man 'almighty'. The dilemma is that while he may have acquired the *'Allmacht'*, the god-like omnipotence, to induce apocalypse, the ill-fated *'Zauberlehrling'* and novice in things nuclear — the sorcerer's apprentice of Goethe's famous poem (see Figure 5.1) to whom Anders alludes in 'The Obsolescence of Malice'[66] — has not yet fully learnt to master the forces he has unleashed. As Hans Blumenberg put it in a very early 1946 essay on

---

65 *Die Antiquiertheit des Menschen*, vol. 2, pp. 407–08.

66 He writes there: 'For we can call it almighty that we (or, more precisely, our broomsticks: the technology we have summoned) can annihilate the complete human species' ('Denn als "Allmacht" dürfen wir es ja wirklich bezeichnen, daß wir (oder richtiger: unsere "Besenstiele": die von uns gerufenen Geräte) die gesamte Menschheit und Menschenwelt auslöschen können'); *Die Antiquiertheit des Menschen*, vol. 2, p. 404.

'THE EARTH VOID OF MAN' 389

FIG. 5.1. Illustration to Goethe's poem 'Der Zauberlehrling' picturing the sorcerer's apprentice, from vol. 1 of *Goethes Werke*, ed. Heinrich Düntzer (Stuttgart and Leipzig: Deutsche Verlagsanstalt, 1882). Ferdinand Barth's etching shows the novice who, having bewitched the broomstick with the expectation that it would clean the house, fails miserably to control the spirit he has called. In her diaries Susan Sontag once called this the 'old vision of scientist (Prospero, etc.) as a dotty magician only partly in control of the forces in which he dabbles' (*Diaries 1964–1980*, p. 14).

'The Morality of the Atom' ('Atommoral — Ein Gegenstück zur Atomenergie'): 'It is as if we are watching a "Zauberlehrling" who has conjured up spirits even the magus knows not effectively how to control'.[67] And, to make things worse, nor has the nuclear novice acquired enough imagination to take in the magnitude and monstrosity of his acts. Like the forces on the loose in Goethe's poem, man's new-gained omnipotence will inexorably one day turn on its master to drown and destroy him. *Allmacht*, omnipotence, is only the — deceptively alluring — flip side of *Ohnmacht*, impotence, Anders reminds us, certainly if one does not learn to control the powers one has unchained; accordingly, he observes,

> omnipotence has become truly dangerous only after we have got hold of it. Before then, all manifestations of omnipotence, whether regarded as natural or supernatural (this distinction, too, has become unimportant), have been relatively benign: in each instance the threat was partial, only particular things were destroyed — 'merely' people, cities, empires, or cultures — but we were always spared if that 'we' denotes mankind.

Unfortunately, man is a by far less benign, and a by far less indifferent, master of the forces he now imprudently brandishes than God or Nature ever were. Consequently, Anders believes, 'there is little hope that we, cosmic parvenus, usurpers of the apocalypse, will be as merciful as the forces responsible for former cataclysms were out of compassion or indifference, or by accident'.[68] Sadly, as the pessimist that he so often suggests he is, he personally feels compelled to conclude that 'there is no hope at all: the actual masters of the infinite are no more imaginatively or emotionally equal to this possession of theirs than their prospective victims, i.e., ourselves'. Verily, has not the prospect of nuclear Armageddon turned our Promethean dream of omnipotence into a Promethean nightmare?

This is the crux for Anders, a key point he reiterates over and again in his essays about the nuclear predicament and the impending catastrophe we humans currently face. Anders time and again lays emphasis on the fact that, while we humans may have developed a technology of apocalyptic proportions and potential, we have not developed the corresponding imaginative faculty; we are not 'imaginatively or emotionally' able to grasp what our technology is truly capable of doing, and this ultimately, he warns, will seal our fate. From the first volume of *The Obsolescence of Mankind* on through to the 1980s, he speaks of a 'Promethean *Gefälle*' — which translates as differential or gradient — between 'our two faculties, between our *actions* and our *imagination*'.[69] Elsewhere he speaks of the 'gulf between our emotional capacity and our destructive powers'[70] which restricts our ability to foresee and hence

---

67 'Atommoral — Ein Gegenstück zur Atomenergie', in *Schriften zur Technik*, ed. by Alexander Schmitz and Bernd Stiegler (Frankfurt a.M.: Suhrkamp, 2015), pp. 7–16 (p. 9).

68 'Reflections on the H Bomb', p. 147; the subsequent quotation also p. 74.

69 'Commandments in the Atomic Age', p. 12. First published in German in the *Frankfurter Allgemeine Zeitung* (13 July 1957), they are here cited from the English translation contained in Günther Anders and Claude Eatherly, *Burning Conscience. The Case of the Hiroshima Pilot Claude Eatherly*, 'Preface' by Bertrand Russell, 'Foreword' by Robert Jungk (New York: Monthly Review Press, 1961), pp. 11–20 (p. 12).

70 'Reflections on the H Bomb', p. 154.

comprehend the consequences of our actions, thereby reducing our apprehension about surrounding ourselves with such perilous tools of mass destruction. We are lacking 'apocalyptic mentality' ('die apokalyptische Mentalität'),[71] not of the religious sort, but of the secular, political, technological order. This is what Anders crucially terms our blindness towards apocalypse ('Apokalypseblindheit'). In the above-cited 1979 interview he tells his interlocutor:

---

[71] *Die atomare Drohung* (Munich: C. H. Beck, 1983), p. 111.

What came together was the chapter in *The Obsolescence of Mankind* about the 'Roots of our Apocalypse-Blindness', and about the discrepancy between what we can produce and what we can imagine. Indeed I still believe today that by describing this discrepancy I have characterized the *conditio humana* not just of our age but of all following ages, inasmuch as they may be granted to us.

[Was da zustande kam, war das Kapitel in der *Antiquiertheit des Menschen* über die 'Wurzeln unserer Apokalypseblindheit', und über die Diskrepanz zwischen dem, was wir herstellen und was wir vorstellen können. In der Tat glaube ich auch heute noch, daß ich mit der Betonung dieser Diskrepanz die conditio humana unseres Zeitalters und aller folgenden Zeitalter, sofern uns noch solche vergönnt sein sollten, charakterisiert habe.]

And there is only one conclusion to be drawn from this circumstance, he continues:

The prime postulate today is: expand your imagination so that you know what you are doing. This is all the more important because our imagination cannot keep up with what we can produce; how harmless the *Zyklon-B*-flasks look — I saw them in Auschwitz — with which millions were annihilated! And how cosy a nuclear reactor looks with its cupola!

[Das erste heutige Postulat lautet: Erweitere deine Vorstellungskraft, damit du weißt, was du tust. Das ist übrigens um so nötiger, als die Wahrnehmung dem, was wir herstellen, auch nicht gewachsen ist — wie harmlos sehen doch die Zyklon-B-Behälter aus — ich sah sie in Auschwitz —, mit denen Millionen vertilgt wurden! Und wie gemütlich schaut ein Atomreaktor mit seinem Kuppeldach aus!][72]

In 'Reflections on the H Bomb' he enlarges as follows:

If all is not to be lost we must first and foremost develop our moral imagination: this is the crucial task facing us. We must strive to increase the capacity and elasticity of our intellectual and emotional faculties, to match the incalculable increase of our productive and destructive powers. Only where these two aspects of man's nature are properly balanced can there be responsibility, and moral action and counteraction.[73]

The aim of this 'spiritual exercise' must be to reduce if not to bridge the gulf between our faculties. In 'Theses for the Atomic Age' he advises: 'If we do not wish to lag behind the effects of our products [...] we have to try to widen our horizon of responsibility until it equals that horizon within which we can destroy everybody and be destroyed by everybody — in short, till it becomes global'.[74] If we don't, the inevitable result will be humanity's global suicide, or globocide ('Globozid').

What makes our nuclear *conditio humana* so precarious, however, is that nuclear mass murder is so different from earlier forms of mass murder. Set in motion by the personal push of impersonal buttons, its means of delivery — nuclear missiles fired from continental silos or ocean-bound submarines, or bombs dropped

---

72 *Günther Anders antwortet*, p. 43.
73 'Reflections on the H Bomb', pp. 153–54.
74 'Theses for the Atomic Age', p. 495.

from invisibly great heights — creates a distance, unbridgeable by any feat of the imagination, between the location of agency and the site of effect. And when the buttons are pushed, all of humankind may be destroyed, not 'merely' a fraction of the world's population.

Anders accepts nonetheless in the 1979 diary entry cited earlier that 'despite the fact that the world will not go down because of Auschwitz, but rather because of Hiroshima, Auschwitz was morally incomparably more despicable than Hiroshima'; he explains:

> I stress this because, from sifting through my notes, the suspicion arises that I approached Auschwitz with the prejudice that what counts for one form of mass murder must also count for the other. That is wrong. Compared with the perpetrators of Auschwitz — and there were untold thousands of them — the pilots above Japan were angels. [...] The two Air-Force-pilots who released the bombs above those two unfortunate cities neither humiliated nor tortured the hundreds of thousands of their victims for days and years, as was custom in Auschwitz, nor did they even see them; no, they could not even imagine.

In 'Reflections on the H Bomb' Anders adds how 'the chain of events leading up to the explosion is composed of so many intermediate steps and partial actions, none of which is the crucial one, that in the end no one can be regarded as the agent. Everyone has a good conscience, because no conscience was required at any point'.[75] The second difference between Auschwitz and Hiroshima is magnitude; we are dealing with (local) genocide versus (potentially total) globocide, as Anders points out in 'The Obsolescence of Malice'.[76] Anders's new post-Kantian moral imperative, formulated cynically but none the less fittingly in 'The Obsolescence of Malice' in 1966, could have as its model Eichmann's justification of his actions during his Jerusalem trials (and compacted by Anders's first wife Hannah Arendt into what she termed Eichmann's 'thoughtlessness'); it reads: 'You should not consider the consequences of your actions, even if they are within reach of your conscious reasoning, no, especially when and because they are within reach of reason' ('Du sollst die Konsequenzen deines Tuns, auch wenn diese deinem Denken zugänglich sind, nein gerade wenn und weil sie deiner Ratio zugänglich sein könnten, nicht bedenken!').[77] The more complex and the more lethal the technology, it seems, Anders is telling us, the greater becomes our ability, and our willingness, to shunt and shun responsibility. And this, in the end, may serve to kill us all.

What is required, this deliberate peddler of doom and gloom advises us, are means to educate and inform ourselves, and to make ourselves more conscious of the burden we — as humanity in a bomb-riddled world — carry not just for ourselves but also for past and future generations of our species. As *'homines fabri'* — as the tool- and weapon-making creatures that we are — 'we must at least try to imagine nothingness' ('Wir müssen es mindestens versuchen, das Nichts auch vorzustellen').[78] 'For us, who are "not yet non-existing" in this Age of Respite,'

---

75 'Reflections on the H Bomb', p. 149; the subsequent passage p. 150.
76 See *Die Antiquiertheit des Menschen*, vol. 2, p. 410.
77 *Die Antiquiertheit des Menschen*, vol. 2, p. 401.
78 *Die atomare Drohung*, p. 96.

Anders declares,

> there is but one answer: although at any moment The Time of the End could turn into The End of Time, we must do everything in our power to make The End Time endless. Since we believe in the possibility of The End of Time, we are Apocalyptics, but since we fight against this man-made Apocalypse, we are — and this has never existed before — 'Anti-Apocalyptics'.[79]

This certainly holds true for the political activist Günther Anders; but most people, Anders laments, either underestimate the danger we are in, or do not care what happens, or indeed have stopped worrying about it altogether — all with potentially disastrous consequences for our common future, Anders claims. We are no longer just blind to the looming apocalypse, but have also, ominously, become indifferent to what stands before our eyes. And, as the nuclear critic Daniel L. Zins lamented in 1990 at what many thought would be the end of the Cold War, and the end of nuclear stockpiles, this applied not just to the proverbial man on the street, but also to the most highly educated in our society; Zins writes, with his colleagues in American departments of English studies in mind: 'Our age was "invented" in the summer of 1945, but as I read postwar literary criticism and the past decade's voluminous debate over the canon, I am struck by how thoroughly oblivious our profession seems to be to this fact'.[80] In the 'Preface' to the second edition of *Endzeit und Zeitenende*, dated February 1981, Anders put it thus:

> The reflections I present in this book cannot become obsolete because their subject, the danger of total catastrophe, continues to exist in perpetuity. This danger continues to exist not just because we cannot unlearn the techniques of self-annihilation, but also because we have gotten used to this threat, in fact alarmingly so. We are no longer alarmed. The expression 'to live with the bomb' has become boring. We are not just apocalypse blinkered (which is how I characterized our condition thirty years ago), but — since we now supposedly claim to know what is at stake — apocalypse blunted.

> [Die in diesem Buche präsentierten Überlegungen können nicht inaktuell werden, weil deren Gegenstand: die Gefahr der Totalkatastrophe, pausenlos weiterbesteht. Sie besteht aber nicht nur deshalb weiter, weil wir die Methoden der Selbstauslöschung nicht mehr verlernen können, sondern auch deshalb, weil wir uns an die Tatsache der Bedrohung aufs erschreckendste gewöhnt haben, also überhaupt nicht mehr erschrecken: Die Redensart 'mit der Bombe leben' ist uns bereits langweilig geworden. Nicht nur 'apokalypseblind' sind wir (wie ich unseren Zustand vor dreißig Jahren genannt hatte), sondern, da wir nun ja zu wissen behaupten, was auf dem Spiel steht, 'apokalypsestumpf'.][81]

Looking at it from a psychiatrist's perspective, Robert Jay Lifton has dubbed our nuclear predicament a 'double life'; he writes:

> On the one hand, we know that a series of bombs could be dropped that, within moments, would destroy us — all of us and everything we have known, loved,

---

[79] 'Theses for the Atomic Age', p. 493.
[80] 'Exploding the Canon: Nuclear Criticism in the English Department', in *Papers on Language and Literature*, 26 (1990), 13–40 (p. 14).
[81] 'Vorwort zur zweiten Auflage', *Die atomare Drohung*, pp. ix–x (p. ix).

or touched — and on the other hand, we go about our lives with business as usual, as though no such threat existed. To some extent we have to do that; we have to get through the day and take care of our daily tasks. But we routinize and mute our situation at great peril. Ours is not so much an age of anxiety as an age of numbing. Our fundamental impairment lies in the gap between knowledge and feeling.[82]

Picking up on the same point as Anders and Lifton regarding this 'gulf between our emotional capacity and our destructive powers', Jacques Derrida came to a very similar conclusion in his much-cited 1984 article 'No apocalypse, not now (full speed ahead, seven missiles, seven missives)'. In it Derrida too scrutinizes the 'nuclear question', observing similar to Anders and Lifton how 'between the Trojan War and nuclear war, technical preparation has progressed prodigiously, but the psychagogic and discursive schemas, the mental structures and the structures of intersubjective calculus in game theory have not budged'; an abyss has opened up, Derrida declares, between technology and discourse, between — in his words — 'the hyperbolic refinement, the technological sophistication of *missility* or missivity, and the rusticity of the sophistic ruses that are elaborated in the politico-military headquarters' (his emphasis).[83] Because of the ever-widening gap between our 'knowing' and our 'acting', Derrida concludes, 'we have to re-think the relations between [...] constative speech acts and performative speech acts', much as Anders had concluded that we can bridge the gulf 'between our emotional capacity and our destructive powers', between our two faculties of *action* and *imagination*', only by widening our 'moral fantasy'.[84] Derrida's pronouncements generally have much in common with Anders's argument although the German philosopher is not once acknowledged, and it seems as if Derrida was unaware of his predecessor's work in this area. In nearly the same language as his German counterpart Derrida at one point observes that we are 'suicidal sleepwalkers' who are 'blind and deaf, *alongside the unheard-of*' (Derrida's emphasis), and his reasoning similarly echoes Anders's when he declares that 'the nuclear age is not an epoch, it is the absolute épochè'.[85] Anders and Derrida both stress the cross-generational consequences of a nuclear war for human culture, history and memory, essentially wiping out, so Anders, not just the present but also humanity's past and the future; Derrida similarly observes:

> If [...] nuclear war is equivalent to the total destruction of the archive, if not of the human habitat, it becomes the absolute referent, the horizon and the condition of all the others. An individual death, a destruction affecting only a part of society, of tradition, of culture may always give rise to a symbolic work of mourning, with memory, compensation, internalization, idealization, displacement, and so on. Culture and memory limit the 'reality' of individual death to this extent, they soften or deaden it in the realm of the 'symbolic'. [...] The only referent that is absolutely real is thus of the scope or dimension of an

---

[82] *The Future of Immortality*, p. 145.
[83] 'No Apocalypse, not now (full speed ahead, seven missiles, seven missives)', *Diacritics*, 14 (Summer 1984), 20–31 (p. 24); the subsequent passages pp. 21 and 23.
[84] 'Commandments in the Atomic Age', pp. 12 and 13.
[85] 'No Apocalypse', p. 27; the subsequent passages pp. 28 and 30.

absolute nuclear catastrophe that would irreversibly destroy the entire archive and all symbolic capacity, would destroy the 'movement of survival', what I call 'survivance', at the very heart of life.

'No apocalypse, not now' appeared in the American theory journal *Diacritics* under the rubric 'nuclear criticism', the topic to which the special colloquium issue of *Diacritics* was devoted in which Derrida's article appeared. Derrida explicitly picks up on this rubric in his final 'seventh missile': '"Nuclear criticism", like Kantian criticism,' he says, 'is thought about the limits of experience as a thought of finitude'. This apt characterization unquestionably holds no less for Derrida's essay than it does for Anders's manifold contributions to 'nuclear criticism' across the decades. What unites both philosophers, whether or not they knew of each others' works, is their focus on what Derrida calls the 'essential rhetoricity'[86] of 'the nuclear question', the fact that, again in the French philosopher's words, the '"Reality", let's say the encompassing institution of the nuclear age, is constructed by the fable, on the basis of an event that has never happened (except in fantasy...)'; 'the anticipation of nuclear war (dreaded as the fantasy, or phantasm, of a remainderless destruction)', Derrida continues, 'installs humanity — and through all sorts of relays even defines the essence of modern humanity — in its rhetorical condition'. It is only through language, through discourse, through fables about a non-existing event, that the 'reality' of all-out nuclear war as well as the reality of our 'just-still-being' (Anders) can be apprehended, in the double sense of this word as both 'anticipate with fear' and 'understand'. Speaking of the four-part U.S. television miniseries *Holocaust*, broadcast by NBC in 1978, Anders enlarges: 'We must never ever forget the lesson: Only through *fictio* can the *factum*, only through individual cases can the innumerable [cases] be brought home and made unforgettable. And this is what this film has achieved' ('Die Lehre darf nicht wieder verlernt werden: Nur durch fictio kann das factum, nur durch Einzelfälle das Unabzählbare deutlich und unvergeßlich gemacht werden. Und das ist in dem Film geschehen').[87] Derrida describes the function of such fictionalizing as a 'translating [of] the unknown into a known', as a 'metaphoriz[ing], allegoriz[ing], domesticat[ing] [of] the terror, to circumvent (with the help of circumlocutions: turns of phrase, tropes and strophes) the inescapable catastrophe, the undeviating precipitation toward a remainderless cataclysm'.[88]

If, as Adorno and Horkheimer held in *Dialectic of Enlightenment*, 'human beings purchase the increase in their power with estrangement from that over which it is exerted', and if enlightenment was intended to 'dispel myths [and] to overthrow fantasy with knowledge', it is perhaps worth contemplating whether we have foolishly privileged, and in the process overestimated, the power and utility of the knowledge we have accumulated. If that is the case, we should perhaps try, instead of turning the table and 'dispelling' or 'overthrowing' knowledge through fantasy — that might be to throw out the baby with the bathwater — to seek to moderate

---

86 Ibid., p. 24; the subsequent quotes pp. 23 and 24.
87 *Tagesnotizen*, p. 158.
88 'No Apocalypse', p. 21.

and mitigate through fantasy some of knowledge's arrogance, overconfidence and Frankensteinian 'MAD schemes', bearing in mind that during the Cold War the abbreviation MAD was used to designate the policy of 'Mutual Assured Destruction'. If knowledge and fact — and knowledge of fact — cannot achieve this, then perhaps *fictio* can, in Anders's words, 'reach out to millions of our contemporaries' ('Millionen von Zeitgenossen erreichen') and 'really shock those millions' ('diese Millionen auch wirklich [...] *erschrecken*') into imagining and acting.[89]

Indeed, while the main instruments to achieve this shock-effect may be 'radio and television', as he specifies in his late work *Heresies* (*Ketzereien*, 1982), the most strident expression of atheism I have come across in twentieth-century philosophy, another useful tool to reach out to these millions could be, Anders concedes in *The Obsolescence of Mankind*, precisely one of those genres of modern mass consumer culture that he, like Adorno and Horkheimer, is otherwise so disdainful of, namely science fiction. Due to its visionary perspective on the technological future of mankind, science fiction has managed to become a genre that has beaten even philosophy to the goal post, as Anders admits:

> Naturally, some of our contemporaries very well know about this 'turn of events' because the new situation is part and parcel of their daily business. I speak of all those science-fiction authors and the cartoonists of interstellar incidents, as well as the producers of futurist films — in other words all those vulgar prophets of our end time who pictured all this decades before we philosophers managed to catch up with them.
>
> [Einige unserer Zeitgenossen wissen freilich sehr genau über den 'Umschlag' bescheid, und zwar deshalb, weil sie die neue Situation zur Voraussetzung bzw. zum Gegenstande ihrer *Geschäfte* gemacht haben. Ich spreche von den Science-Fiction-Autoren, den Zeichnern der, interstellare Ereignisse darstellenden, cartoons, den Produzenten der futurologischen Filme — in anderen Worten: von den uns Philosophen um Jahrzehnte vorauslaufenden Vulgärpropheten unserer Endzeit.][90]

However, Anders sees what Derrida calls the 'metaphoriz[ing], allegoriz[ing] and domesticat[ion] [of] terror' in an even more sinister light than his French successor; he worries in various parts of *The Obsolescence of Mankind* that works of science fiction are being deployed merely as 'heralds' ('Herolde') and 'fifth columns' ('fünfte Kolonnen' and 'Vorhut') of the total technologification of our world that he sees being prepared for us by scientists in their laboratories in the service of the mighty. As entertainment commodities the narratives of science fiction are, in Anders's perspective, instruments of a 'conformist system' ('konformistisches System') that strives to blind us to the true predicament of our species. Indeed, to describe what he calls science fiction's 'tendentiously avantgardistic art of technology' ('avantgardistische Tendenzkunst der Technik') Anders deploys the loaded German term 'gleichgeschaltet', a term that is normally used highly pejoratively to designate

---

89 Anders, *Ketzereien*, p. 209.
90 *Die Antiquiertheit des Menschen*, vol. 2, pp. 279–80; the following passages and quotations are taken from pp. 136–39 and 287–88.

the Nazis' cracking down on Germany's political and educational institutions in the 1930s and bludgeoning them into ideological conformity. The entertainment that science fiction procures, he states as categorically as acerbically, similarly functions as 'terror' because it 'disarms' us ('Weil *Unterhaltung Terror* ist' and 'weil sie uns total *entwaffnet*'; his emphases). Superman is the epitome of this instrumentalization of science fiction in the service of a 'brazen lie' ('Lebenslüge'); the figure of Superman serves to give back to us the sense of power over technology that we have already long lost, the illusory sense that we are still the 'subject of history' and have the 'almightiness' ('Allmacht') to control our own destiny. But these figures and metaphorizations of our own 'omnipotence' ('Omnipotenz') have been overused to such a degree that we have lost all sense of how powerless (his word is 'Ohnmacht') we have truly become. Dealing nearly exclusively in 'the most obsolete forms and hackneyed idioms' ('obsoleteste Formen und ausgeleiertste Idiome'), science fiction is able to attain a degree of popularization higher than any other literary genre, and it is this faculty that makes it an ideal instrument through which to perpetuate the 'master lie of survival' ('Herren- und Überlebenslüge'), the lie that we might be able to survive nuclear self-annihilation. It is a 'master lie', so Anders, because *owning* the '*absolute* monster weapons' ('*absolute* [...] Monsterwaffen'; his emphasis)[91] means, ultimately, *using* these weapons; if we believe, or allow ourselves to be (mis)led to believe, that we can escape this fate we are merely deceiving ourselves.

With which we seem to have come full circle to Susan Sontag's essay 'The Imagination of Disaster' of 1965, cited at the outset of this chapter, in which she reflects on the feats and faults of science fiction as a genre. It appears that, like Derrida, Sontag did not know of Anders's 'nuclear criticism'. (Whereas she notes in her diaries for 1960 that she had read Anders's *Kafka*-essay, her personal diary for the period in which she conceived 'The Imagination of Disaster', the year 1964, contains no further mention of Anders's work.)[92] Anders, Derrida and Sontag all concur that the nuclear apocalypse is outdone only by our blindness and bluntedness towards it, and all three warn of the danger of diminishing and hence domesticating the terror through incessant rhetorical replication. Thus Sontag warned, as we recall, of fiction's faculty to fuel that blindness and to intensify the bluntedness. 'It is fantasy', she argued, which 'distracts us from terrors, real or anticipated, by an escape into exotic dangerous situations which have last-minute happy endings', effectively 'normaliz[ing] what is psychologically unbearable'. For his part, Derrida warns that our 'fabulous specularization' of the threat will lead to the 'anticipatory assimilation of that unanticipatable entirely-other'; 'the growing multiplication of the discourse — indeed, of the literature — on this subject', he observes,

> may constitute a process of fearful domestication [...]. For the moment, today, one may say that a non-localizable nuclear war has not occurred; it has existence only through what is said of it, only where it is talked about.

---

91 *Ketzereien*, a compilation of pp. 315 and 317.
92 The reference to Anders's *Kafka* can be found in Susan Sontag, *Reborn. Early Diaries 1947–1963*, ed. by David Rieff (London: Penguin, 2009), p. 255. Her diary entries for 'The Imagination of Disaster' were made in 1964; see Susan Sontag, *As Consciousness is Harnessed to Flesh. Diaries 1964–1980*, ed. by David Rieff (London: Penguin, 2013), p. 14.

> Some might call it a fable, then, a pure invention; in the sense in which it is said that a myth, an image, a fiction, a utopia, a rhetorical figure, a fantasy, a phantasm, are inventions. It may also be called a speculation, even a fabulous specularization.[93]

In *Fictions of Nuclear Disaster* David Dowling likewise speaks of the 'de-sensitizing' that inevitably results from the overdiscursification of catastrophe; he notes: 'Of course, the danger of mind-numbing familiarity must always be stressed. Like violence on television, a ceaseless bombardment of nuclear disaster stories which give the reader no framework, no "angle" beyond a sado-masochistic thrill or nihilism, may accustom the reader, at least in his dim imagination, to annihilation'.[94] He concludes by citing the following excerpt from the poem 'Tomorrow Loses Its Excitement' by the Australian poet Philip Neilsen:

> Returning from another pleasant Armageddon
> we are veterans already.
> Visiting all our friends, reading newspapers,
> we start to enjoy
> this living-room Angst. . . .
> We dig the grave with the shovels we made.

True; but what is the alternative? Should we *not* write about it, in highbrow literature or in popular science fiction? Should we avoid the topic on the silver screen? Should newspapers stop reporting on the dangers of a nuclear catastrophe? Would that serve to make us less 'inured' and the subject less 'domesticated'? We truly sit between a rock and a hard place: depict the nuclear apocalypse and it will, over time and through discursive reiteration, become 'boring' (Anders), 'domesticated' (Derrida), and 'normalized' (Sontag), making us 'blunted' and 'blind' (Anders) to its fateful consequences and horrendous magnitude. Yet through not depicting it we would lose all possibility to expand our horizons and to 'translat[e] the unknown into a known', thereby learning to imagine what nuclear 'Annihilism' — Anders uses this neologism in 1981 — might really mean. And in any case, would an interdiction not merely kindle a similar debate to that which followed Adorno's much contested statement that to write poetry after Auschwitz could not but be barbaric because it would either have to aestheticize its subject or it would fail to capture the magnitude of suffering and destruction inflicted on the victims? The German apocalypse specialist Klaus Vondung has this to say about precisely this quandary:

> Can a nuclear inferno that would annihilate all of mankind be represented appropriately, such that the unimaginable and what it really means, namely the irrevocable end of human history, is given due treatment? Does not every aesthetic representation per se generate pleasure, even if it is only the thrill-like pleasure of the sort we experience when we read a report like [the German journalist and writer Anton Andreas] Guha's *Diary from the Third World War*? Is not aesthetic pleasure fundamentally misplaced when we consider the ultimate demise of all physical life and mental being? There is no normative answer to

---

93 'No Apocalypse', p. 23.
94 *Fictions of Nuclear Disaster*, p. 216.

these questions. It is writers who give answers, and each responds in his or her own way. It is our task as critics to ascertain how convincing they are. The most radical response was [the German writer] Wolfgang Hildesheimer's. He simply stopped writing, not just about the possible end of the world, but altogether because he considered the 'abysmal end' not just a possibility but an actual certainty. With the result that he saw 'no future for literature': 'I at least am at a loss for words', he says. But Hildesheimer is the exception.

[Kann ein nukleares Inferno, das der Menschheit das Ende bereiten würde, adäquat wiedergegeben werden, d. h. so, daß das eigentlich Unvorstellbare und dessen Bedeutung, nämlich Abschluß der Menschheitsgeschichte zu sein, angemessen repräsentiert ist? Erzeugt nicht jede künstlerische Gestaltung per se ästhetisches Vergnügen, und sei es nur das Vergnügen der Spannung, das selbst ein so brutal-realistischer Report wie Guhas *Tagebuch aus dem 3. Weltkrieg* hervorruft; und ist ästhetisches Vergnügen angesichts des finalen Ernstfalls alles Seins und Denkens nicht grundsätzlich deplaziert? Auf diese Fragen gibt es keine normative Antwort. Die Schriftsteller sind es, die die Antworten geben, jeder auf seine Weise: unsere Sache ist es zu prüfen, wie überzeugend sie ausfallen. Die radikalste Antwort gab Wolfgang Hildesheimer. Er hörte auf zu schreiben, nicht nur über den möglichen Untergang, sondern überhaupt, denn er erachtet das 'schreckliche Ende' nicht nur als Möglichkeit, sondern als Gewißheit, und dies hat zur Folge, daß er auch 'keine Zukunft für die Literatur' mehr sieht: 'Jedenfalls mir hat es die Worte verschlagen'. Doch Hildesheimer ist ein Ausnahmefall.][95]

Yes indeed, Hildesheimer is the exception, and who is to say whether this is our gain or loss. If we follow Adorno we cannot write after Auschwitz, nor can we write, if we follow Hildesheimer, in the run up to the impending nuclear Holocaust. Suffice it to say that most writers took another path, both in terms of nuclear self-eradication as in terms of the Holocaust. The 1972 German Nobel Prize Laureate for Literature Heinrich Böll once reflected in a lecture given at Frankfurt University:

In this city Theodor W. Adorno once formulated a profound insight: one cannot write poems after Auschwitz. I would like to modulate this statement: one cannot breathe after Auschwitz, nor eat, love or read — whenever you breathe, or merely light a cigarette, you have already decided to survive, to write, to eat, to love.

[Es ist in dieser Stadt von Theodor W. Adorno ein großes Wort gesagt worden: man kann nach Auschwitz keine Gedichte mehr schreiben. Ich moduliere das Wort: man kann nach Auschwitz nicht mehr atmen, essen, lieben, lesen — wer den ersten Atemzug getan hat, sich nur eine Zigarette ansteckt, hat sich entschlossen, zu überleben, zu lesen, zu schreiben, zu essen, zu lieben.][96]

But write writers did regardless; this is what writers do, it is their vocation, and no dictum or prohibition is going to stop them — and few will want to follow in Hildesheimer's footsteps. The Swiss writer Peter Bichsel, also lecturing at Frankfurt University some years after Böll, for his part responded to Adorno's challenge by

---

95 *Die Apokalypse in Deutschland* (Munich: DTV, 1988), p. 433.
96 Cited from *Lyrik nach Auschwitz?*, ed. by Petra Kiedaisch (Stuttgart: Reclam, 1995), p. 90.

drawing a connection precisely with the nuclear *conditio humana* that Anders had described:

> The question 'Can one continue to write poems after Auschwitz?' is, and always has been, a pertinent one. Can one write poetry when threatened by the atomic bomb, or by the cynicism of politicians and their neutron bomb? Can one write poetry under the conditions of unemployment and starvation? The question could always be answered with a Yes or a No. There are more important things to do in this world than to palaver over literature. At best, one can write poetry despite all this. But the question is justified nonetheless. Strictly speaking, it is about the very irresponsibility of storytelling. Is one permitted to do anything irresponsible in a time so much in need of responsibility?
>
> [Die Frage 'Kann man nach Auschwitz noch Gedichte schreiben?' war immer angebracht. Kann man es unter der Bedrohung durch die Atombombe, dem Zynismus der Politiker und ihrer Neutronenbombe, kann man es unter den Bedingungen von Arbeitslosigkeit und Hunger? Die Frage konnte immer mit gutem Recht mit Ja oder mit Nein beantwortet werden. Es gibt bestimmt auf dieser Welt Wichtigeres zu tun, als über Literatur zu schwatzen. Man kann es höchstens trotzdem tun. Aber die Frage ist berechtigt. Es ist im Grunde genommen die Frage nach der Verantwortungslosigkeit des Geschichtenerzählens. Kann man Verantwortungsloses tun in dieser Zeit, die Verantwortung nötig hätte?][97]

Could we not, however, with equal validity invert this question? Would it not be irresponsible, such inversion might run, *not* to tell stories, especially if what we are charged with to describe is something that has never before existed and hence requires critical 'translat[ion] [of] the unknown into a known', to repeat Derrida's phrase? And to continue with Derrida, he also observes:

> Unlike the other wars, which have all been preceded by wars of more or less the same type in human memory (and gunpowder did not mark a radical break in this respect), nuclear war has no precedent. It has never occurred, itself; it is a non-event. The explosion of American bombs in 1945 ended a 'classical', conventional war; it did not set off a nuclear war. The terrifying reality of the nuclear conflict can only be the signified referent, never the real referent (present or past) of a discourse or a text.[98]

As Dowling rightly notes in his study of *Fictions of Nuclear Disaster* it is science fiction especially, in its capacity as such a 'signified referent', that allows us 'to locate the experience of nuclear disaster by surrounding the inexpressible with verbal strategies'.[99]

In the most wide-ranging and also most incisive recent contribution to the field of Last Man studies, Eva Horn's 2014 *Future as Catastrophe* (*Zukunft als Katastrophe*), the author underscores precisely this capacity of narratives of catastrophe to offer 'verbal strategies', as Dowling puts it, through which we can translate what might come to pass in the future into concrete visual scenarios; she writes:

---

97 *Der Leser. Das Erzählen. Frankfurter Poetik-Vorlesungen*, 3rd edn (Darmstadt and Neuwied: Luchterhand, 1983), pp. 9–10.
98 'No Apocalypse', p. 23.
99 *Fictions of Nuclear Disaster*, pp. 13–14.

> To show the future as having taken place is precisely what these fictions accomplish. They place something imaginary *before our eyes* in such a way that it can be experienced as a present situation, fixed and credible like a 'memory of what is to come'. But they also do more: They make transparent both the conditions that make such a vision of the future possible and the preconditions that would allow us to understand this future and identify any action that is required of us in the present. This clear-sighted reflexivity sets the better texts and films [...] off from those purely alarmist scenarios that simply invoke or, citing the ever ominous 'case of emergency', decree what must be done.
>
> [Die Zukunft als gegeben schildern: genau dies leisten Fiktionen. Sie stellen etwas Imaginäres so *vor Augen*, dass es als gegenwärtige Situation erfahrbar wird, fixiert und überzeugend wie eine 'Erinnerung an die Zukunft'. Aber sie tun noch etwas anderes: Sie machen auch durchsichtig, unter welchen Bedingungen dieser Blick auf die Zukunft möglich wird, was also die Voraussetzungen einer Erkenntnis der Zukunft und damit auch die Voraussetzungen eines Handelns in der Gegenwart wären. Diese klarsichtige Reflexivität unterscheidet die besseren Texte und Filme, die wir betrachtet haben, von rein alarmistischen Szenarien, die Handlungsgebote vortragen oder mit Hinweis auf den ominösen 'Ernstfall' rechtfertigen.][100]

But as the debate surrounding Adorno's dictum revealed, even the most sophisticated of 'signified referents' always also carries the danger to arouse 'complicity with the abhorrent', as Susan Sontag deplored in her discussion of the power that science fiction films exert over their audiences; adding:

> Here, 'thinking about the unthinkable' [...] becomes, however inadvertently, itself a somewhat questionable act from a moral point of view. The films perpetuate clichés about identity, volition, power, knowledge, happiness, social consensus, guilt responsibility which are, to say the least, not serviceable in our present extremity.[101]

In a similar vein Richard Klein, the editor of the *Diacritics* issue in which Derrida's article was published, asked in his introductory 'Proposal for a *Diacritics* Colloquium on Nuclear Criticism':

> To what extent do all the current versions of apocalypse now merely feed the vice of the hypocritical reader, the deep-seated boredom of an alienated public that dreams of debris, of swallowing the world with a yawn? To what degree do the stereotypes of nuclear destruction, like the proliferative figure of the mushroom cloud, aim to make us forget by their mechanical repetition the reality they are supposed to designate?[102]

Horn, too, is very aware of this pitfall; and yet she feels nonetheless that the critical function transported perhaps not by all, but certainly by many such narratives of catastrophe must override this kind of objection. She writes:

> On the one hand fictions of catastrophe can be consumed as a kind of preoccupation with catastrophe that *releases* oneself from taking any further

---

100 *Zukunft als Katastrophe*, pp. 386–87.
101 'The Imagination of the Disaster', p. 42.
102 *Diacritics*, 14 (Summer 1984), 2–3 (p. 3).

action. On the other hand they can be understood as highly forcible alarmist narratives that, by reminding us of the coming disaster, demand an urgency of action that suspends all further reflection or objection. [...] Many of the materials we discussed speak for the latter function: Fictions of catastrophe pick up on the most acute anxieties of an epoch and see themselves as a pressing intervention or 'cautionary tale'.

[Einerseits lassen sich [Katastrophenfiktionen] als Formen einer Beschäftigung mit der Katastrophe konsumieren, die von jeder weiterführenden Konsequenz gerade *entlastet*. Andererseits [werden sie] als hochgradig wirksame, alarmistische Narrative verstanden [...], die im Verweis auf das kommende Desaster eine Dringlichkeit des Handelns fordern, die alle weiteren Reflexionen und Bedenken suspendiert. [...] Mit Blick auf das Material, das wir betrachtet haben, spricht vieles für die [zweite], mobilisierende Funktion: Katastrophenfiktionen greifen die jeweils akutesten Befürchtungen einer Epoche auf und sehen sich dabei als dringliche Intervention oder 'cautionary tale'.][103] (Horn's emphasis)

Citing the nuclear critic Herman Kahn (a chief nuclear war strategist at the RAND Corporation who in his influential 1960 book *On Thermonuclear War* outlined the options and likely consequences of nuclear warfare), Horn also speaks of these fictions' ability to serve as hypothetical 'scenarios' and 'aids to the imagination'.[104]

This being so, the issue would then seem less *whether* we narrate such stories — we hardly seem to have an option — than *how* we narrate them. This was also Peter Schwenger's conclusion in a short 'Forum' debate in the journal *PMLA* which had published his article 'Circling Ground Zero' in its March 1991 issue. Clair James had responded to Schwenger's article by objecting:

His solution presents narrative as a way of learning what cannot be expressed, of experiencing knowledge outside rational thought. Schwenger's logic seems to be that (a) nuclear destruction is unthinkable; (b) narrative can show what it cannot tell and we cannot think; and (c) therefore, by allowing us to think (extrarationally) about the (rationally) unthinkable, narrative can show us how to avoid nuclear war. This argument is fatally flawed and, considering the deadly seriousness of the topic, the flaw might prove fatal. [...] Imagining the end of the world shows no more imagination than, and is in fact very similar to, the work of Pentagon planners who invent scenarios for nuclear war in order to make it possible. These fictions offer no path for avoiding nuclear holocaust. [...] What I want to see is antinarrative that leads away from the experiential knowledge of nuclear war.[105]

Schwenger counters this criticism by observing:

I will merely say that a narrative [...] may of course contribute to nuclear war: there are many narratives of nuclear war as orgasmic release, as punishment and purification, as survival, even as victory. However, narratives need not be written in such a manner. The question is *how* literature is to be written to enable us to go through the changes needed. And this is my concern as well

---

103 *Zukunft als Katastrophe*, p. 381. (In order better to integrate it syntactically into my argument I have shifted the order of the sections within this statement, but without changing their meaning.)
104 *Zukunft als Katastrophe*, pp. 382 and 385; see pp. 91–95 for Horn's discussion of Kahn's work.
105 'Narrative against Nuclear War?', in 'Forum', *PMLA*, 106 (October 1991), 1175–76.

as James's.[106]

That such stories have been narrated is beyond debate, everyone agrees; the question then is *how* they must be written. So let us look in the following at some of those narratives of nuclear Armageddon in order to probe how they hold up in the light of such criticism, and whether and how they succeed in negotiating — or perhaps how they fail to negotiate, as the case may be — the Scylla of necessary and serious forewarning and the Charybdis of clichéd indifference-inducing entertainment.

Man-Made Apocalypses, from H. G. Wells to Pat Frank

The reader will recall from my discussion of Mary Shelley's *Frankenstein* that mankind's self-destruction through his own haughty ingenuity had become a prime constituent of science fiction long before 1945, the year in which this self-destruction for the first time became a factual prospect rather than a merely fictional possibility. Since 1818 when *Frankenstein* was first published, novelists had imaginatively concocted all kinds of scientific experiments that had rebounded on their inventors, creating a plethora of cataclysmic plotlines, some quite plausible, others less so, but each enthralling in its own way. One of the earliest such stories was A. Lincoln Green's 1901 *The End of an Epoch. Being the Personal Narrative of Adam Godwin, the Survivor*, in which a scientist develops a bacillus that wipes out most of the world's population, a subject particularly popular with Hollywood scriptwriters today. Published a few years later, E. M. Forster's 1909 short story 'The Machine Stops' portrays the humankind of an unspecified future some thousands of years hence reduced to subsisting in a beehive-like global super-machine in which human beings live out their carefree existence in minute cells with access neither to the world outside nor to other human beings, not even their own children; but with mankind now become so decadent and corporally reliant upon the godlike 'Machine' that no one is left even to service the very apparatus their forebears had once designed for their species' ease of existence, the Machine at long last begins to malfunction, subjecting everyone within its honeycomb structure to an excruciatingly distressing and physically painful end. In 1920 the Czech author Karel Čapek envisions, in his futuristic play *R.U.R.*, 'Rossum's Universal Robots' (this being the first use of the word 'robot'), a group of scientists 'playing at God' and producing millions of robots by means of which man is meant to lead a carefree life. But after realizing that they are being cruelly exploited, the man-made robots decide to dislodge and eradicate not just their human creators, the handful of leading scientists at Rossum's robot factory, but mankind as a whole. Alas, after robots worldwide have successfully wiped out mankind, save one last and lone scientist at the factory, the head of construction Alquist, the realization dawns on the robots — whose lifespan is limited, yet who are incapable of procreating — that they have destroyed the means of their own survival. Luckily, however, as it appears in the play's final scene, one of the now deceased scientists had secretly

---

106 Peter Schwenger, 'Reply', in 'Forum', *PMLA*, 106 (October 1991), 1176–77 (p. 1176).

created an experimental pair of robots with sexual organs, Primus and Helena; in an act mirroring God's bond with Adam and Eve, Alquist sends the pair out into the world in order for them to become the forebears of a new generation of human(oid) beings — surprisingly at the last moment turning what appeared to be a terminal text into a semi-terminal one (of sorts).

It was also Čapek who in 1924 wrote the novel *Krakatit* — alluding in its title to the volcano Krakatau — in which Prokop, a crazed scientist, discovers in the wake of Rutherford what he calls the 'Alphaexplosion', a form of nuclear fission through which explosions on a world-encompassing scale can be triggered. Which is to say, humanity's demise through nuclear technology had become the subject of fiction well before even the commencement of the top-secret Manhattan Project in 1942; perhaps in fact it was a case of life following fiction. Ever since Wilhelm Roentgen's discovery of electromagnetic X-rays in 1895 (for which he received the first ever Nobel Prize for Physics in 1901), Henri Becquerel's discovery of radioactivity in uranium in 1896, and the Curies' isolation of the radioactive isotopes polonium and radium (for which they, together with Becquerel, also received the Nobel Prize for Physics in 1903), writers of fiction had set out imaginatively to pick up on these physicists' research and enlarge upon the ramifications these advances in physics and chemistry might have for the human species. Čapek's *R.U.R.* and *Krakatit* stand beside Robert Cromie's 1895 *The Crack of Doom*, Roy Norton's 1907 *The Vanishing Fleets*, Hollis Godfrey's 1908 *The Man Who Ended War*, Pierrepont Noyes's 1927 *The Pallid Giant* and Harold Nicolson's 1932 *Public Faces* as fictions in which their authors show, in the words of Brian Stableford in the article cited in the previous chapter, 'a developing awareness of the *vulnerability* of society to the destructive power of new inventions';[107] Stableford expands:

> In 1895 [...] Roentgen discovered X-rays and Becquerel described the property of 'radioactivity' in uranium. Both discoveries were widely publicised, and the following year saw publication by Marconi of his work on wireless telegraphy. So dawned, in the popular imagination, the age of miraculous rays and no-longer-unsplittable atoms. These discoveries provided an imaginative *carte blanche* for technological fantasies of all kinds, including stories involving weapons of miraculous potency. It was the notions of death-rays and disintegrator-rays which fed the new apocalyptic imagination, together with the less popular but more prophetic notion of atomic bombs. By 1900 it was a great deal easier to imagine that the power to annihilate mankind might one day rest in human hands than it had been in 1894, and it was this expansion of imaginative power which made the year 1900 a genuine *fin de siècle*.

This 'genuine *fin de siècle*' turns into a veritable *fin du monde* or End of the World scenario as soon as the possible magnitude of slaughter, brought on by the technologies of mass warfare introduced during the First World War, becomes apparent. Taking stock of the research he conducted for his 1982 study *Terminal Visions. The Literature of Last Things* W. Warren Wagar thus observes in his later article 'The Rebellion of Nature':

---

107 'Man-Made Catastrophes', this quote p. 106, the following quote p. 107.

> In an inventory of two hundred and fifty literary doomsdays, the present writer has found a two-to-one ratio of man-made to natural catastrophes in stories written since the outbreak of World War I. Before 1914, the ratio is just the opposite: one-to-two. Man's fears of himself have obviously multiplied in this century of total wars and total states, of genocide and ecocide.[108]

Ironically, already one year before the outbreak of the First World War H. G. Wells created in fiction what only forty years later, at the conclusion of the Second World War, would become gruesome reality; written in 1913 and published in early 1914, H. G. Wells's *The World Set Free. A Story of Mankind* is the first novel ever to render a picture of nuclear warfare and the destruction through air-bound nuclear weaponry of whole cities and populations. Looking presciently into a future set in the mid-twentieth century, Wells's novel begins with a nuclear scientist named Holsten discovering the power of nuclear energy in the early decades of the twentieth century. The first chapter opens thus:

> The problem which was already being mooted by such scientific men as Ramsay, Rutherford, and Soddy, in the very beginning of the twentieth century, the problem of inducing radio-activity in the heavier elements and so tapping the internal energy of atoms, was solved by a wonderful combination of induction, intuition, and luck by Holsten so soon as the year 1933. From the first detection of radio-activity to its first subjugation to human purpose measured little more than a quarter of a century. For twenty years after that, indeed, minor difficulties prevented any striking practical application of his success, but the essential thing was done, this new boundary in the march of human progress was crossed, in that year. He set up atomic disintegration in a minute particle of bismuth; it exploded with great violence into a heavy gas of extreme radio-activity, which disintegrated in its turn in the course of seven days, and it was only after another year's work that he was able to show practically that the last result of this rapid release of energy was gold. But the thing was done — at the cost of a blistered chest and an injured finger, and from the moment when the invisible speck of bismuth flashed into riving and rending energy, Holsten knew that he had opened a way for mankind, however narrow and dark it might still be, to worlds of limitless power.[109]

'However narrow and dark it might be' — the ominous tone is a portent of things to come: by mid-century Holsten was 'destined to see atomic energy dominating every source of power'. 'By 1954', we read, 'a gigantic replacement of industrial methods and machinery was in progress all about the habitable globe', including ships, planes and helicopters driven by 'atomic engines'. But just as the steam engine in the nineteenth century had put millions of labourers out of work and inspired rebellion, this new source of energy also quickly reveals its downside:

> The coal mines were manifestly doomed to closure at no very distant date, the vast amount of capital invested in oil was becoming unsellable, millions of coal miners, steel workers upon the old lines, vast swarms of unskilled or under-skilled labourers in innumerable occupations, were being flung out of

---

108 'The Rebellion of Nature', p. 141.
109 H. G. Wells, *The World Set Free. A Story of Mankind* (New York: Dutton, 1914), pp. 40–41; the subsequent passages pp. 50, 52, 52–53, and 54–56.

> employment by the superior efficiency of the new machinery, the rapid fall in the cost of transit was destroying high land values at every centre of population, the value of existing house property had become problematical, gold was undergoing headlong depreciation, all the securities upon which the credit of the world rested were slipping and sliding, banks were tottering, the stock exchanges were scenes of feverish panic; — this was the reverse of the spectacle, these were the black and monstrous under-consequences of the Leap into the Air. [...] There was an enormous increase also in violent crime throughout the world. The thing had come upon an unprepared humanity; it seemed as though human society was to be smashed by its own magnificent gains. For there had been no foresight of these things.

Nor had there been any foresight of the dangers of nuclear warfare. War breaks out in the heart of Europe, with 'Central European Powers suddenly attacking the Slav confederation, with France and England going to the help of the Slavs'.[110] The Central European Powers use their new atomic 'aeroplanes' to drop an atomic bomb on Paris, the effects of which, as witnessed by a young Parisian woman employed in the offices of the 'War Control', are described in harrowing detail (considering that in 1914 when the book was published no one had ever beheld a nuclear explosion):

> She found she was lying face downward on a bank of mould and that a little rivulet of hot water was running over one foot. She tried to raise herself and found her leg was very painful. She was not clear whether it was night or day nor where she was; she made a second effort, wincing and groaning, and turned over and got into a sitting position and looked about her. Everything seemed very silent. She was, in fact, in the midst of a vast uproar, but she did not realise this because her hearing had been destroyed. At first she could not join on what she saw to any previous experience. She seemed to be in a strange world, a soundless, ruinous world, a world of heaped broken things. And it was lit — and somehow this was more familiar to her mind than any other fact about her — by a flickering, purplish-crimson light. Then close to her, rising above a confusion of debris, she recognised the Trocadero; it was changed, something had gone from it, but its outline was unmistakable. It stood out against a streaming, whirling uprush of red-lit steam. [...] She drew herself a little way up the slope of earth on which she lay, and examined her surroundings with an increasing understanding [...]. Near at hand and reflected exactly in the water was the upper part of a familiar-looking stone pillar. On the side of her away from the water the heaped ruins rose steeply in a confused slope up to a glaring crest. Above and reflecting this glare towered pillowed masses of steam rolling swiftly upward to the zenith. It was from this crest that the livid glow that lit the world about her proceeded, and slowly her mind connected this mound with the vanished buildings of the War Control.

The French respond immediately by throwing nuclear bombs on Berlin; the consequences are no less disastrous:

> The bomb flashed blinding scarlet in mid-air, and fell, a descending column of blaze eddying spirally in the midst of a whirlwind. Both the aeroplanes were

---

110 Ibid., p. 87; the subsequent passages pp. 102–03, 113, and 114–17.

> tossed like shuttlecocks, hurled high and sideways and the steersman, with gleaming eyes and set teeth, fought in great banking curves for a balance. The gaunt man clung tight with hand and knees; his nostrils dilated, his teeth biting his lips. He was firmly strapped.... When he could look down again it was like looking down upon the crater of a small volcano. In the open garden before the Imperial castle a shuddering star of evil splendour spurted and poured up smoke and flame towards them like an accusation. They were too high to distinguish people clearly, or mark the bomb's effect upon the building until suddenly the facade tottered and crumbled before the flare as sugar dissolves in water.

Already in 1913, when he wrote this novel, Wells was clearly well aware of the half-life of nuclear particles and the resulting hazard of nuclear radiation; he distinguishes the way this new type of bomb functions from its conventional predecessors as follows (substituting the fictional substance Carolinum for the real thing, uranium or plutonium):

> Never before in the history of warfare had there been a continuing explosive; indeed, up to the middle of the twentieth century the only explosives known were combustibles whose explosiveness was due entirely to their instantaneousness; and these atomic bombs which science burst upon the world that night were strange even to the men who used them. Those used by the Allies were lumps of pure Carolinum, painted on the outside with unoxidised cydonator inducive enclosed hermetically in a case of membranium. A little celluloid stud between the handles by which the bomb was lifted was arranged so as to be easily torn off and admit air to the inducive, which at once became active and set up radio-activity in the outer layer of the Carolinum sphere. This liberated fresh inducive, and so in a few minutes the whole bomb was a blazing continual explosion. The Central European bombs were the same, except that they were larger and had a more complicated arrangement for animating the inducive. Always before in the development of warfare the shells and rockets fired had been but momentarily explosive, they had gone off in an instant once for all, and if there was nothing living or valuable within reach of the concussion and the flying fragments then they were spent and over. But Carolinum, which belonged to the beta group of Hyslop's so-called 'suspended degenerator' elements, once its degenerative process had been induced, continued a furious radiation of energy and nothing could arrest it. Of all Hyslop's artificial elements, Carolinum was the most heavily stored with energy and the most dangerous to make and handle. To this day it remains the most potent degenerator known. What the earlier twentieth-century chemists called its half period was seventeen days; that is to say, it poured out half of the huge store of energy in its great molecules in the space of seventeen days, the next seventeen days' emission was a half of that first period's outpouring, and so on. As with all radio-active substances this Carolinum, though every seventeen days its power is halved, though constantly it diminishes towards the imperceptible, is never entirely exhausted, and to this day the battle-fields and bomb fields of that frantic time in human history are sprinkled with radiant matter, and so centres of inconvenient rays. [...] Such was the crowning triumph of military science, the ultimate explosive that was to give the 'decisive touch' to war....

By early 1959, the world's capitals and major population centres are [burning]; we read:

> For the whole world was flaring then into a monstrous phase of destruction. Power after Power about the armed globe sought to anticipate attack by aggression. They went to war in a delirium of panic, in order to use their bombs first. China and Japan had assailed Russia and destroyed Moscow, the United States had attacked Japan, India was in anarchistic revolt with Delhi a pit of fire spouting death and flame; the redoubtable King of the Balkans was mobilising. It must have seemed plain at last to every one in those days that the world was slipping headlong to anarchy. By the spring of 1959 from nearly two hundred centres, and every week added to their number, roared the unquenchable crimson conflagrations of the atomic bombs [...]. Most of the capital cities of the world were burning; millions of people had already perished, and over great areas government was at an end.[111]

Only two avenues remained for humankind, either bombing itself back to primitivism or finding a way to unite and coexist peacefully. The latter is the outcome Wells paints in his novel; he writes:

> The old tendencies of human nature, suspicion, jealousy, particularism, and belligerency, were incompatible with the monstrous destructive power of the new appliances the inhuman logic of science had produced. The equilibrium could be restored only by civilisation destroying itself down to a level at which modern apparatus could no longer be produced, or by human nature adapting itself in its institutions to the new conditions. It was for the latter alternative that the assembly existed. Sooner or later this choice would have confronted mankind. The sudden development of atomic science did but precipitate and render rapid and dramatic a clash between the new and the customary that had been gathering since ever the first flint was chipped or the first fire built together.

Wells's novel may not have been the most successful of his writings, but it did carry a both prophetic and educational message, if only humans wanted to hear it. Wells issues in 1913, one year before the outbreak of the First World War, a warning that has, by and large, remained unheeded by governments and is now, at the beginning of the twenty-first century, coming home to roost; we read, a third of the way into Wells's *Story of Mankind*, presaging Anders's and Derrida's diagnosis of the gulf between our emotional capacity and our destructive powers:

> Certainly it seems now that nothing could have been more obvious to the people of the earlier twentieth century than the rapidity with which war was becoming impossible. And as certainly they did not see it. They did not see it until the atomic bombs burst in their fumbling hands. Yet the broad facts must have glared upon any intelligent mind. All through the nineteenth and twentieth centuries the amount of energy that men were able to command was continually increasing. Applied to warfare that meant that the power to inflict a blow, the power to destroy, was continually increasing. There was no increase whatever in the ability to escape. Every sort of passive defence, armour, fortifications, and so forth, was being outmastered by this tremendous

---

111 Ibid., p. 152; the subsequent passages pp. 210–11 and 117–18.

increase on the destructive side. Destruction was becoming so facile that any little body of malcontents could use it; it was revolutionising the problems of police and internal rule. Before the last war began it was a matter of common knowledge that a man could carry about in a handbag an amount of latent energy sufficient to wreck half a city. These facts were before the minds of everybody; the children in the streets knew them. And yet the world still, as the Americans used to phrase it, 'fooled around' with the paraphernalia and pretensions of war.

It is only after the inevitable — but in Wells's view predictable and hence preventable — has happened, namely the outbreak of a nuclear Armageddon, that the politicians and leaders of the world pull together to create a global government that can, by *unified* force, ensure that an end is put to mass warfare once and for all. Even if Wells's *The World Set Free. A Story of Mankind* contains remarkably prescient portrayals of the material devastation and human toll that would befall mankind in the event of a nuclear world war — a prognosis borne out by the bombings of Hiroshima and Nagasaki thirty years later — the novel's focus lies squarely on its political message, namely that humankind should already now in 1913/1914, and literally only months before the 1914 declarations of war, begin to contemplate the ruinous effects with which this kind of modern technology would some day engulf our planet, and that only a global and unified federation of nations led by rational and sane leaders could ensure a lasting peace for our planet. Of course, in the end one can ask whether it is reassuring — as it was surely intended to be — or not somewhat disappointing that Wells opts for a positive political outcome of his story of nuclear warfare, resorting, in Sontag's terminology, to a rather clichéd 'happy ending'. Such criticism aside, what Wells achieves with *The World Set Free* is nonetheless remarkable; in the words of W. Warren Wagar, the novel 'contains what is quite obviously one of the most incredible *coups de maître* in the history of scientific and technological forecasting. Its atomic bombs exploded in imagination more than a quarter of a century before the discovery of nuclear fission in experiments with uranium and before Einstein's letter to President Roosevelt'.[112] Indeed, as Peter Schwenger has pointed out in an article on nuclear fiction, one of the physicists who went on to collaborate on the Manhattan Project, and who was the first to conceive of a nuclear chain reaction in 1933, Leo Szilard, admitted to being inspired in his research by his reading of Wells's novel.[113]

While Wells and other early twentieth-century writers such as Hollis Godfrey (in *The Man Who Ended War*, 1908), Arthur Train and Robert Williams Wood (in *The Man Who Rocked the Earth*, 1915), John Ulrich Giesy (in *All For His Country*, 1915) and Harold Nicolson (in *Public Faces*, 1932) were the first to imagine the development of nuclear weaponry and the dangers inherent in it, they tended to paint this technology in a positive light as a convenient tool to improve the lot of man through the development of innovative technologies, but also to enforce global peace. Unsurprisingly, their unfounded 'optimism' later often comes in for criticism; looking '100 Years Hence' in one of his *Hearst Essays*, Aldous Huxley on 25 June

---

112 *Terminal Visions*, pp. 119–20.
113 See Schwenger, 'Writing the Unthinkable', *Critical Inquiry*, 13 (Fall 1986), 33–48 (p. 33).

1934 thus rails against what he calls 'the Wellsian paradise'. Huxley observes:

> A hundred years hence what will our descendants be doing and thinking? According to the most pessimistic school of prophets, they won't be doing or thinking anything — for the excellent reason that they won't be there. The final war-to-end-war will have been a complete success: It will have ended the human race. Less extravagant pessimists foresee only partial destruction and a return to primitive barbarism. [...] But not all of our prophets are Jeremiahs. There are some to whom the future looks not black, but brilliant pink. They admit that there may be a few wars, a generation or two of confusion. But, after that, men will have learnt their lesson and all will go well. A hundred years hence our descendants will be living in a Wellsian paradise.[114]

Seventeen years later, now in full knowledge of the — no longer just fictional — scale of destruction nuclear weaponry can inflict upon human populations, Bertrand Russell picks up on Huxley's triad of alternatives in his 1951 article 'The Future of Man', compacting the three options as follows:

> Before the end of the present century, unless something quite unforeseeable occurs, one of three possibilities will have been realized. These three are: —
> 1. The end of human life, perhaps of all life on our planet.
> 2. A reversion to barbarism after a catastrophic diminution of the population of the globe.
> 3. A unification of the world under a single government, possessing a monopoly of all the major weapons of war.[115]

Huxley in turn picks up on Russell's statement in one of his 1959 Santa Barbara lectures; 'what are our short-range prospects?', Huxley now asks, and answers:

> Let us begin with the military and political prospects immediately confronting us. These were discussed a few years ago by Bertrand Russell, and it seems to me that his conclusions are extremely realistic and sensible. He says that there are three possibilities. First of all, if we get into a nuclear war, there is the possibility of the complete extinction of the species — and perhaps of all life upon earth if the nuclear war is sufficiently prolonged and waged with sufficiently deadly weapons. This is improbable, however, in the present state of technology. The second possibility is that the nuclear war would result in a return to barbarism. Under the present circumstances, this second alternative seems to have a good deal of probability [...]. If there were to be, for any reason, high mortality among the specially trained personnel on whom we depend for the functioning of the system, then it seems extremely probable that the whole industrial system would break down — it would be virtually impossible to run without one or another part of it — and the result would probably be a return of barbarism. [...] It would be very difficult for any people which had been reduced to a primitive level to rebuild a complex civilization on the basis of the rather impoverished resources left, particularly in those countries which have been highly developed up to now. [...] The third alternative which Lord Russell looks forward to is the creation of a single world state, which could

---

114 *Aldous Huxley's Hearst Essays*, ed. by James Sexton (New York and London: Garland, 1994), p. 281.

115 'The Future of Man', *The Atlantic*, 1 March 1951, unpaginated version downloaded 30 March 2015 from <http://www.theatlantic.com/magazine/archive/1951/03/the-future-of-man/305193>.

occur in one of two ways: by force, as the result of one power being victorious in a nuclear war [...], or under the threat of force.[116]

Coincidentally, or perhaps not so coincidentally, Huxley's and Russell's three scenarios map out exactly the three main paths taken by writers of science fiction in the wake of 1945 in their varied attempts to imagine a future nuclear Third World War and its aftermath. Wells's utopian 'paradise' of *The World Set Free* clearly falls into the last of these categories, and it is the one favoured and promulgated also by Bertrand Russell himself, whereas Huxley's novel *Ape and Essence*, to which I will return later, falls into the second grouping. The bleakest of them all, however, is certainly the first, involving — in the vein of Mary Shelley's *The Last Man*, but translated from nature's paradigm into the nuclear paradigm of man's self-annihilation — 'the complete' and thus irrevocable 'extinction of the species'. Even if Huxley and Russell consider this the most improbable of their three scenarios, and even if it may prove the most depressing to conjure up, writers of science fiction have not shirked their responsibility to tackle even this gravest of possibilities. The two earliest and also most graphic novelistic attempts to envision 'the complete extinction of the species' in the wake of Hiroshima are without doubt Nevil Shute's 1957 *On the Beach* and Mordecai Roshwald's 1959 *Level 7*, two classics of post-1945 nuclear science fiction.

Shute derived the title *On the Beach* from Part IV of T. S. Eliot's poem 'The Hollow Men', which the author cites in the epigraph to his novel and whose famous concluding lines I cite in this chapter's first motto. *On the Beach* is precisely about 'the way the world ends' for humankind. And the 'last men and women' here too end first with a bang and then with a whimper. In fact, they are not destined to remain last men and women for long: a devastating 'bang' that has taken the shape of a thirty-seven-day nuclear war on the northern hemisphere has released a massive cloud of radioactive dust which has already killed off all life north of the equator and is now gradually yet mercilessly drifting south on nature's trade winds. Although no one in south Australia, where the action of this novel unfolds, was responsible for the nuclear war, not a soul will escape — with radioactivity inexorably creeping down the globe into the southern latitudes the contamination certainly of all mammalian and avian life, and perhaps of all animal life on Earth, is not just inevitable, its arrival can be predicted by Australian meteorologists more or less to the day: with the novel's action setting in — futuristically, we should recall — around December 1962, one year after the nuclear holocaust in the north, the inhabitants of Falmouth near Melbourne in Australia's southernmost province of Victoria are expecting the cloud to reach them by September 1963. One of the three chief male protagonists, Dwight Towers, the captain of an American submarine 'stranded' in Australia since the outbreak of hostilities, conjectures as follows about the approaching radioactive fallout:

> 'Finally, of course, it'll get to the same level all around the world.'
> 'They're still saying that it's going to get here in September.'

---

[116] 'The World's Future', in *The Human Situation. Lectures at Santa Barbara, 1959*, ed. by Piero Ferrucci (London: HarperCollins / Flamingo, 1994), pp. 93–94.

> 'I would say that's right. It's coming very evenly, all around the world. All places in the same latitude seem to be getting it just about the same time. [...] If it goes on the way it's going now, Cape Town will go out a little before Sydney, about the same time as Montevideo. There'll be nothing left then in Africa and South America. Melbourne is the most southerly major city in the world, so we'll be near to the last.' He paused for a moment in thought. 'New Zealand, most of it, may last a little longer, and, of course, Tasmania. A fortnight or three weeks, perhaps.'[117]

Some weeks later, with humanity's demise inching ever closer, he contemplates:

> Very soon, perhaps in a month's time, there would be no one here, no living creatures but the cats and dogs that had been granted a short reprieve. Soon they too would be gone; summers and winters would pass by and these houses and streets would know them. Presently, as time passed, the radioactivity would pass also; with a cobalt half-life of about five years these streets and houses would be habitable again in twenty years at the latest, and probably sooner than that. The human race was to be wiped out and the world made clean again for wiser occupants...

Focusing on its three male and two female protagonists (the American captain Dwight Towers, his Australian navy liaison officer Peter Holmes, and the scientist John Osborne on the male side, Peter Holmes's wife Mary and Moira Davidson, an attractive single woman, on the female side), the novel follows how the denizens of southern Australia prepare for their untimely albeit foreseeable death during the last months of their lives. Some drink themselves to death, others pursue such hobbyhorses as car racing with suicidal recklessness, but the majority decide at one point or another simply to continue their habitual routines in an attempt to uphold decorum and face death in as dignified a fashion as possible, either at home in bed or enjoying a final glass of port in their favourite rocker. The manner of death is described in blood-curdling detail: radiation sickness resembles cholera, a chemist enlightens Peter Holmes; nausea is the first symptom, then come vomiting and diarrhoea, followed by bloody stools. 'All the symptoms increase in intensity', the chemist informs him; 'there may be slight recovery, but if so it would be very temporary. Finally death occurs from sheer exhaustion. [...] In the very end, infection or leukaemia may be the actual cause of death. The blood-forming tissues are destroyed, you see, by the loss of body salts in the fluids. It might go one way or the other'. The only way to avoid this grim end is to commit suicide, for which the health system has opportunely planned to provide the means free of charge; at the very end, those who wish can spare themselves the worst by taking the government prescribed dose of lethal tablets.

Shute's novel is in many ways a highly realistic work of fiction, and it provides a depressingly cautionary tale about the menace of the nuclear world we now live in, comprising a categorical refutation of the notion of survivability and of many a government's disingenuous claim that their population could withstand radiation death given adequate civil preparation and protection. In 1959 the novel was turned

---

117 *On the Beach* (Toronto: Random House, 1974), p. 115; the subsequent passages pp. 239, 134 and 278.

into an equally depressing film with Gregory Peck and Ava Gardner in the lead roles playing Dwight Towers and his new-found soul mate Moira Davidson, and Fred Astaire playing the scientist John Osborne, renamed Julian Osborn for the film. While Moira's taking of the lethal tablet is omitted in the 1959 film version's final sequence, the text is less equivocal, describing Moira's — and hence the novel's — 'whimper' of last moments thus:

> She could not see detail but she knew that Dwight was there upon the bridge, taking his ship out on her last cruise. [...] Presently she could see the submarine no longer; it had vanished in the mist. She looked at her little wrist watch; it showed one minute past ten. Her childhood religion came back to her in those last minutes; one ought to do something about that, she thought. A little alcoholically she murmured the Lord's Prayer. Then she took out the red carton from her bag, and opened the vial, and held the tablets in her hand. Another spasm shook her, and she smiled faintly. 'Foxed you this time,' she said. She took the cork out of the bottle. It was ten past ten. She said earnestly, 'Dwight, if you're on your way already, wait for me.' Then she put the tablets in her mouth and swallowed them down with a mouthful of brandy, sitting behind the wheel of her big car.

In 2000 *On the Beach* was readapted for a three-hour long television mini-series featuring Armand Assante and Rachel Ward in the lead roles and appropriately updated to the year 2006 in order to retain its futuristic quality.

The title phrase 'On the Beach' refers of course not just intertextually to Eliot's 'The Hollow Men', but also to the naval phrase 'on the beach', meaning 'retired from active service'. Here the implication is obviously not alone that the American submarine captain Dwight Towers and his Australian naval colleagues are forced by circumstance into retirement from their professional duties, but also that humankind itself is retiring from active service on this planet. In *Fictions of Nuclear Disaster* Dowling observes how 'the sense of remorseless doom which powers [Shute's] novel is accentuated by its powerfully symbolic setting "on the beach"',[118] noting that, 'like Orwell's *1984*, [*On the Beach*] has become an imaginative landmark in modern consciousness'. But there are also weaknesses, Dowling contends, remarking (not without justification):

> The trouble with Shute's world is that *everyone* seems to be as sensible and stiff-upper-lipped as his military heroes. [...] The thinness at the heart of the novel was exposed in the 1959 film version, which prompted one critic to call it 'a sentimental sort of radical romance, in which the customers are spared any scenes of realistic horror, and are asked instead to accept the movie notion of what is really horrible about the end of the world: boy (Gregory Peck) does not get girl (Ava Gardner)'.

In all fairness, however, Dowling grants also that 'Shute's reticence may have been a wiser decision than the attempt to realise Armageddon with its problems of scale and language', something I will return to when I come to discuss Tim LaHaye and Jerry B. Jenkins's bizarre Christian fundamentalist *Left Behind* cycle, which in its

---

118 *Fictions of Nuclear Disaster*, pp. 66–67; the subsequent passages pp. 66, 68 and 68.

twelfth and final volume does indeed 'attempt to realise Armageddon', but only at the expense of ending — in my view unavoidably — in heavy-handed histrionics and grotesque hyperbole.

The year in which Shute published his novel, 1957, was the year that also saw Albert Schweitzer issue his 'Declaration of Conscience', in which, as the Nobel Prize Laureate put it in a subsequent appeal, broadcast the following year, 'I raised my voice, together with others, to draw attention to the great danger of radioactive poisoning of the air and the earth, following tests with atom (uranium) bombs and hydrogen bombs'.[119] Transmitted worldwide from Oslo, Norway, on 24 April 1957 under the auspices of the Nobel Peace Prize Committee, Schweitzer in this speech warned less of a nuclear war per se — this was to follow in the later broadcast of 1958 — than of the long-term effects of radiation caused by the nuclear test programmes being conducted at the time by the United States, the Soviet Union and Great Britain. He asks, 'Why do they not come to an agreement?' to stop these tests; he answers:

> The real reason is that in their own countries there is no public opinion asking for it. Nor is there any such public opinion in other countries with the exception of Japan. This opinion has been forced upon the Japanese people because, little by little, they will be hit in a most terrible way by the evil consequences of all the tests. An agreement of this kind presupposes reliability and trust. There must be guarantees preventing the agreement from being signed by anyone intending to win important tactical advantages foreseen only by him. Public opinion in all nations concerned must inspire and accept the agreement. When public opinion has been created in the countries concerned and among all nations — an opinion informed of the dangers involved in going on with the tests and led by the reason which this information imposes —, then the statesmen may reach an agreement to stop the experiments.

Schweitzer's 1957 and 1958 radio broadcasts are just two of a series of similar pronouncements by the international scientific community warning against the dangers inherent in the nuclear arms race. It had been preceded by the so-called Russell–Einstein Manifesto of 9 July 1955, in which eleven prominent signatories headed by Bertrand Russell and Albert Einstein — the latter putting his name to the document just days before his death on 18 April 1955 — called for an international conference at which scientists would assess the dangers posed to the survival of the human race by nuclear weapons; the cosignatories included Max Born, Frédéric Joliot-Curie, Linus Pauling, Joseph Rotblat and Hideki Yukawa. (Although the conference was ultimately delayed in coming about, the Russell–Einstein Manifesto in due course became the founding charter of the Pugwash Conference series on Science and World Affairs.) In Germany eighteen nuclear scientists, the so-called 'Göttinger Achtzehn', including Carl Friedrich von Weizsäcker and the three Nobel Laureates Max Born, Otto Hahn and Werner Heisenberg, signed a declaration on 12 April 1957 expressing their 'deep concern' over the German Chancellor Konrad Adenauer's plan to equip the West German army with so-called tactical

---

119 Albert Schweitzer, *Peace or Atomic War?* (New York: Henry Holt, 1958), p. 9.

nuclear weapons; by pointing out that 'tactical' nuclear weapons — smaller atomic bombs as opposed to the more recently developed and far more powerful 'strategic' hydrogen bombs — are nuclear weapons nonetheless, possessing no less destructive power than the bomb dropped on Hiroshima, the Göttinger Eighteen prepared the ground for West Germany's rejection of nuclear weapons, a stance that Germans continue to take for granted as I write these lines in March 2015. In West Germany's then communist counterpart, the German Democratic Republic, fourteen East German nuclear scientists quickly followed suit on 14 April 1957, similarly demanding a stop to nuclear tests and the arms race. In January 1958 the American biochemist and 1954 Nobel Prize Laureate for Chemistry, Linus Pauling, handed the Secretary General of the United Nations a declaration signed by some 10,000 scientists worldwide warning of the hazards of nuclear radiation. In February 1958 the 'Campaign for Nuclear Disarmament' (CND) was launched in Great Britain, opposing the government policy of nuclear deterrence and branding the possession of nuclear weaponry as immoral. In March 1958 in Munich, thirty-four German writers, academics and intellectuals — among them Ingeborg Bachmann, Günther Eich, Erich Kästner, Wolfgang Koeppen, Vicco von Bülow (known as Loriot), Hans Werner Richter and Gerhard Szczesny — formed a 'Committee against Nuclear Arms' ('Komitee gegen Atomrüstung'). On 28, 29 and 30 April 1958, Albert Schweitzer himself broadcast from Oslo the further appeal I alluded to earlier (which was published that same year under the title *Peace or Atomic War?*) in which he now warned about the dangers of nuclear warfare, calling upon the three nuclear powers of his day, the United States, the Soviet Union and Great Britain (France joined them only in February 1960, China in 1964) to disarm and do away with their nuclear stockpiles. All across the globe similar resolutions, pronouncements, declarations and manifestos began snowballing; the 'public opinion' that Schweitzer had found lacking in 1957 had by the early 1960s finally been roused.

The statements and proclamations cited above were of course an index of the mounting pressure to end the nuclear arms race. It is difficult to say in hindsight what ultimately goaded politicians into taking action (the first treaty for instance, named the 'Partial Test Ban Treaty', was signed by John F. Kennedy and Nikita Khrushchev in 1963); what we can say is that the efforts to mobilize popular support for disarmament were immeasurably reinforced by novels like *On the Beach*. This novel and its film adaptation in particular remind us how effective a vehicle for political action science fiction can be, not least because novel and film add an emotive and identificational dimension to political tract and scientific fact. We can connect with these (fictional) people 'on the beach', live with them through their existential trauma and, in the end, experience grief at their death. It is hard not to shed a tear for Moira Davidson as she ends her life, in the book perhaps even more so than in the film because in the novel she is shown actually taking the lethal tablet; it is equally impossible not to feel for Dwight Towers when he scuttles his submarine and goes down with it and his crew off the coast of Australia (despite this not being shown either in the novel or its film adaptation). Allowing the reader psychologically to identify and empathize fully and deeply with a character is the prerogative of fiction, and this is what permits it so uniquely to go under the skin; it is certainly one of the ways in which literature trumps scientific description and political statement. Thus Shute's novel, which was published in four instalments in the London weekly periodical *Sunday Graphic* in April 1957, was the ideal graphic accompaniment to the declarations and statements by the intellectuals and scientists listed above. What better vehicle was there than a novel like *On the Beach* to convey what Russell had cautioned against in his 1951 article 'The Future of Man', in which he observed that

> it is thought by many sober men of science that radioactive clouds, drifting round the world, may disintegrate living tissue everywhere. Although the last survivor may proclaim himself universal Emperor, his reign will be brief and his subjects will all be corpses. With his death the uneasy episode of life will end, and the peaceful rocks will revolve unchanged until the sun explodes.

And can one imagine a better way to substantiate Schweitzer's warnings than Shute's novel? Schweitzer had declared in his April 1958 radio broadcast:

> Today there is little difference between a local war and a global war. [...] In an atomic war there would be neither conqueror nor vanquished. During such a bombardment both sides would suffer the same fate. A continuous destruction would take place and no armistice nor peace proposals could bring it to an end. [...] Those who conduct an atomic war for freedom will die, or end their lives miserably. Instead of freedom they will find destruction. Radioactive clouds resulting from a war between East and West would imperil humanity everywhere.[120]

Nevil Shute may have been the first writer to seriously and realistically engage with 'the possibility of the *complete* extinction of the [human] species' through nuclear warfare, but he was not alone. Among the writers of futuristic novels who followed suit were in America Mordecai Roshwald with *Level 7* (1959) and in Germany Jens Rehn with *The Children of Saturn* (*Die Kinder des Saturn*, 1959), Anton Andreas Guha with *The End: Diary of the Third World War* (*Ende: Tagebuch aus dem dritten Weltkrieg*, 1983), and Günter Grass with *The Rat* (*Die Rättin*, 1986). Roshwald and Grass take up the same premise as Shute, a premise that was underscored by Albert Schweitzer in his 1958 broadcast, namely that a mere 'accident' could lead to the outbreak of hostilities between the Superpowers. Schweitzer thus 'specularizes' in *Peace or Atomic War?*, to adopt Derrida's coinage, how 'unknown events in the Middle East could endanger the peace of the world [...]. The risk of an atomic war is being increased by the fact that no warning would be given in starting such a war, which could originate in some mere incident'. This is precisely the starting-point of Shute's novel. And indeed, as Paul Brians observes in *Nuclear Holocausts: Atomic War in Fiction*, a study of narratives of nuclear war, accident is the premise on which the plots of most nuclear war novels hinge, terminal or semi-terminal; the accidental scenario allows writers to avoid ascribing concrete intent or guilt to any one side or party in their fictional conflicts. Brians writes:

---

120 *Peace or Atomic War?*, pp. 25–27; the subsequent passage p. 29.

> A peculiar feature of the age of nuclear combat is the possibility of accidental war. Wars have in the past been begun on the basis of trivial incidents, misunderstandings, and errors in judgment; but the notion that civilization might be ended or life on Earth be destroyed through a technical malfunction or an error in judgment presents an absurdity of such enormous dimensions that it can scarcely be grasped. The resultant air of futility about much nuclear war fiction is convincing in ways that similar views of conventional war could not be. Even those few writers who try to establish that atomic war might be purposeful or beneficent seem led by its internal logic to depict it as absurd.[121]

The accidental scenario is of course not at all far-fetched — Schweitzer in *Peace or Atomic War?* for instance cites just one of many real-life instances in which such an accidental ignition nearly became reality: 'Attention was drawn to this danger by the American general Curtis Le May', Schweitzer writes,

> when the world was recently on the brink of such a situation. The radar stations of the U.S. Air Force and U.S. Coastal Command reported that an invasion of unidentified bombers was on the way. Upon this warning the General, who was in command of the strategic bomber force, decided to order a reprisal bombardment to commence. However, realizing the enormity of his responsibility, he then hesitated. Shortly afterward it was discovered that the radar stations had made a technical error.[122]

'What would have happened', Schweitzer asks, 'if a less balanced general had been in his place?' By and large — and fortunately — such incidents have remained limited to non-hostile situations in which, for instance, an American B-47-bomber equipped with nuclear bombs crashed, or lost its lethal cargo, or a Soviet submarine disappeared at sea (or the inverse: both Americans and Soviets have 'lost' armed nuclear submarines). Such 'incidents' have documentably happened in 1956, 1957, 1958, 1959, 1961, 1963, and 1965, to enumerate the known episodes of just one decade. Jonathan Schell cites three further such instances in his 1982 *The Fate of the Earth*.[123] Perhaps the closest call yet occurred in 1995; called the Norwegian rocket incident, or Black Brant scare, a scientific rocket was launched from Norway on 25 January 1995, but its initial trajectory happened to resemble that of a submarine-launched Trident nuclear missile; while the Russian government had been informed according to protocol, the information had by mistake not been passed on to the military, and Boris Yeltsin, then Russian President, was forced to decide whether to launch a retaliatory nuclear strike. Following this event, notification and disclosure protocols were reassessed and redesigned. In all these cases, by chance or good fortune, escalation was avoided, but the potential for such an 'incident' to go awry and 'explode' beyond control is always given, and Mordecai Roshwald shrewdly exploits this possibility to create the setting for his bleak depiction of 'complete extinction' in his novel *Level 7*.[124]

---

121 *Nuclear Holocausts: Atomic War in Fiction* (1987), unpaginated internet download from <http://public.wsu.edu/~brians/nuclear/>, accessed 17 November 2014.
  122 *Peace or Atomic War?*, p. 29; the subsequent quote pp. 29–30.
  123 *The Fate of the Earth*, pp. 26–27.
  124 The following page references in parentheses refer to Mordecai Roshwald, *Level 7* (London:

Situated in an unspecified but recognizably proximate future, *Level 7* visualizes the 'Mutual Assured Destruction' which the Cold War was making ever more conceivable and which Robert McNamara, the 1961–68 U.S. Secretary of Defense under John F. Kennedy and Lyndon B. Johnson, only a few years later championed as the optimal defense strategy. Refracted through the diary of a so-called 'Push-Button' (PB) officer in his country's deepest underground bunker, Level 7 is the designation for a top-secret military installation located 4,400 feet under ground; housing the 'offensive branch of the military machine of our country and its allies',[125] as the narrator informs us, Level 7's sole *reason d'être* is to house and safeguard the four officers assigned the crucial task, in the event of a nuclear war, of pressing the buttons that will release their country's nuclear armoury from its underground silos. Each officer has been screened for his psychological probity and sanity, and all have now been secreted away from life above ground to the presumed safety of Level 7 and its select community of 500 military personnel whose exclusive function it is to secure the functioning of the subterranean nuclear command centre. Cut off from the surface, this shielded community has been given the resources to survive any all-out nuclear attack as well as the resulting irradiation of the planet's surface for up to 500 years (!). Not only have all occupants of Level 7 been assigned numbers rather than names in order to maintain a depersonalized anonymity, they have been spirited away to this hidden military sanctum without knowledge of their families and friends above: for all intents and purposes, the inhabitants of Level 7 are dead, having disappeared overnight without trace. 'You need not worry about your friends and relatives outside', the bunker's occupants are informed on the intercom system shortly after their arrival; 'they will be notified that you have been killed in a painless accident and that you left no remains. We regret this, but your disappearance must remain absolutely secret'. The announcer adds: 'Needless to say, there is no way back available to you; but it will please you to know that neither is there any way for radioactive pollution, should any occur, to find its way down here: the system was hermetically sealed as soon as the last of you arrived this morning'.

The novel's protagonist is one of the four Push-Button-officers; and the novel's content is the diary he starts writing soon after his and his community's subterranean sequestration deep under earth. Beginning on April 27 and closing half a year later on October 12 of the action's unspecified year, officer PB X–127's diary shows him reflecting back initially on the many months of psychological training that preceded his and his co-workers' confinement, then on his experiences entering and acclimatizing himself to life on Level 7, and finally on the months leading up to and following the outbreak of hostilities — interspersed with descriptions of his intensifying bouts of soul searching and, eventually, depression. PB X–127's narrative also provides particulars of the other six levels of nuclear bomb shelters and the population groups that are intended to inhabit them in the event of war as well as a description of the 'gadget' that he has been trained to control; it is the

---

The New English Library, 1962).

125 Roshwald, *Level 7*, p. 14; the subsequent two quotations also p. 14.

ultimate game console war machine and described thus:

> On the gadget are three rows of four buttons. The front row, nearest the operator, covers enemy Zone A; the middle row Zone B; and the third row Zone C, the most distant. Each set of buttons controls a different type of destructive weapon — all of them long-range atomic rockets, of course. [...] Each of the twelve buttons would release several thousands of otherwise electronically controlled and guided missiles, every one of them aimed at a pre-determined target. They would hit the enemy within anything from fifteen minutes to an hour from when the button was pushed. [...] It is not certain whether Buttons 4 would actually be used. Some people have said they might prove dangerous even to the country using them.[126]

Of course, as is predictable, hardly half a year passes before hostilities erupt and PB X–127 is given the order to push the buttons, *all* the buttons, including 'Buttons 4': the diary relates the brief period of all-out nuclear warfare and the global destruction that ensues. But only once the 'entire surface of the earth' has been 'laid in ruins' does it turn out that no one on either side had actually given the orders. The enemy's first twelve rockets had escaped by accident, and this set off computerized retaliatory automatisms on both sides, requiring no human authorization. The diarist records on June 11:

> Perhaps the whole thing would never have happened if those twelve enemy rockets had not escaped their controls. It was just an accident, a sort of joke played on us all by — well, I do not know whose joke it was. The gods? Fortune? The devil? It really does not matter. It is all over now. [...] A child could have done it. An imbecile. A trained monkey!

Indeed, in his unquestioning willingness to press the buttons once instructed by the automated intercom system, PB X–127 had shown himself to be no better than such a trained monkey. When he retrospectively asks 'Has humanity been destroyed by its own ingenuity?', one cannot but agree; but one may also want to add that ingenuity alone was perhaps not sufficient: it required human conceit, conformity and subservience in addition, as evidenced by officer PB X–127's absolute and unhesitating obedience. He realizes this only too late, echoing the lesson we have been taught by Günther Anders:

> But the moment those guided missiles appeared — especially those devilish ground-to-ground intercontinental rockets — civilisation was doomed. No more glory for men, no more brave combats in the air, no more bombing of cities and installations by men who knew what they were about. But dehumanized war, automatic war, and its inevitable result: the end of civilisation. [...] I could not kill with a club or a bayonet or a knife, let alone with my bare hands. But pushing a button — that was a different matter. It has become so easy to destroy and kill. With a push-button a child, an innocent baby, could do it. In a sense, I suppose, the idea that the present disaster happened because war became dehumanized may have something in it.

After the briefest of wars is over — 'the whole war lasted two hours and fifty-eight

---

126 Ibid., pp. 19–20; the subsequent passages pp. 106, 102, 129, 97, 124, and 107.

minutes', we are told — Level 7's ban on communications with the outside world is, for reasons left unexplained, lifted and the bunker's denizens are once again able to communicate with people in other bunkers at higher levels. It soon transpires, however, that no one in the civilian Level 1 shelters survived the nuclear onslaught of 'A–Day ("A" for Atomic War)', whereas the more fortunate survivors of the civilian Levels 2 and 3 bunkers do not begin dying of radioactive fallout until some weeks after the event. By September even the Levels 4 and 5 populations of VIPs and top administrators, scientists, politicians and ex-generals have also been wiped out by radiation, whereas the military levels 6 at 3000 feet and 7 at 4400 feet under ground seem to be holding fast; their small populations are, together with the enemy's counterparts in their lowest bunkers, the last men and women on planet Earth — a couple of thousand at best.

Only once the scale and extent of destruction has sunk in does the diarist recognize the true moral of his story; he spells it out in his June 15 entry: 'self-defence with thermonuclear weapons means *total* destruction'. And it is this total destruction that Roshwald pictures in *Level 7* without his nameless protagonist ever once leaving his underground vault. 'This morning', the diarist notes on September 22, two and a half months after 'A-Day',

> we picked up a radio message from the enemy suggesting that we should conclude a peace treaty. It also informed us that the entire civilian population over there, including the government and its various officials, is gone. They were all killed at one time or another by blast, fire or, finally, radiation. All that is left is the military level — about a thousand people, self-sufficient for centuries. [...] So the enemy's lot is similar to ours.[127]

By September 24 contact with Level 6 goes dead, but it is not clear what has caused the death of this level's inhabitants. On September 27 the peace treaty with the enemy — although they are not named, the antagonistic world powers of Roshwald's novel clearly resemble the United States and the Soviet Union — is agreed; we read: 'We, our former enemy and ourselves, wanted to be masters of mankind. Each of us wanted to rule the whole world, or to save it (both formulas amount to the same thing now). And the result: both sides have been diminished to a few hundred cave-dwellers'.

At this point in his novel Roshwald introduces an interesting irony (one, however, that will not be to every reader's liking): he could let the survivors of these lowest levels either be driven crazy in the tedium of a Beckettian loneliness and monotony, or he could have them too die of war-induced radiation, which, contrary to the builders' designs, could have been depicted as seeping into their underground vault, causing its inhabitants to die of the nuclear menace they themselves had unleashed. But Roshwald prefers a different twist: the energy source of Level 7 is a nuclear reactor, and it is this reactor that begins to malfunction and leak radioactivity, over a short span of time killing off all occupants of the hermetically sealed bunker. Something similar seems to have happened on the enemy side; by October 3, PB X–127 notes, the former enemy has fallen silent, and on October 4 the diarist

---

[127] Ibid., pp. 131–32; the subsequent passages pp. 134–35, 137, 141, 141 again, and 142.

records: 'The ex-enemy has been given up for dead. We *are* alone now, literally and absolutely alone'. The diarist PB Officer X–127 holds out longest; he reports in his entry dated October 11, the day before his diary breaks off: 'Nobody! I did not see a living person today. For all I know I may now be the last man alive on earth. And I shall be the last to die. A distinction in the midst of extinction!'. In his dying hours Lionel Verney's nuclear counterpart recognizes two ironies, observing first: 'Perhaps God intends it as a sort of joke. "You killed with bombs," He says. "You will be killed by peaceful radiation"'; and then: 'I am dying, and the world is dying with me. I am the last man on earth, the sole survivor specimen of homo sapiens. *Sapiens* indeed'. It was mankind's preeminent distinction among all creatures, his (technological) brain power, his *sapientia* and enlightenment, that ultimately led to his downfall and undoing, confirming once again Adorno and Horkheimer's 'Dialetic of Enlightenment'.

Even if the novel's storyline is 'weakened by its all-too-visible didactic impulses',[128] as one recent reviewer of the 2004 reprint of this novel argued perhaps not without justification, *Level 7* remains a 'powerful [...] reminder of Cold War history and nuclear anxiety'; it is, in Dowling's words, 'one of the best "shelter" fictions'.[129] However skeptical one wants to be as regards *Level 7*'s aesthetic merits and entertainment value, its moral is not to be taken lightly, especially the two facets of his yarn that, first, he uses an accident as the immediate cause of war and, second, the button is pressed by a nameless military bureaucrat ensconced in a subterranean bunker far removed from the killing fields. Roshwald's Officer PB X–127 is, in short, the perfect embodiment of Günther Anders's thesis that the notions of 'enemy' ('Feind'), 'enmity' ('Feindschaft') and 'hatred' ('Hassen') have been made obsolete by nuclear warfare. Just as our fictional PB X–127 writes in his diary that he 'could not kill with a club or a bayonet or a knife', Anders writes in a diary entry for 1958:

> But not just the term 'enemy' is obsolete but rather all that is connected with 'enmity'. That he who presses the button thousands of miles from his targets and obliterates them can feel neither hate nor the rage of heated battle seems obvious [...]. The future distant murder war will be the most hateless war history has ever witnessed. [...] The more terrible the deed the easier it gets. It is easier to press the button with which, somewhere 'in the boondocks of Turkey', hundreds of thousands will be killed than to stab your fellow man between the ribs.

> [Aber nicht nur der Begriff 'Feind' ist antiquiert, vielmehr alles, was psychologisch mit 'Feindschaft' zu tun hat. Daß derjenige, der vermittels eines Knopfdrucks, Tausende von Meilen von seinen Zielobjekten entfernt, diese Objekte vertilgt, weder Haß noch die durch Kampf sich steigernde Kampfwut empfinden kann, also haßlos bleibt, das liegt ja auf der Hand [...]. Der kommende Fernmord-Krieg wird der haßloseste Krieg sein, den es in der Geschichte jemals gegeben hat. [...] Je furchtbarer eine Tat, um so leichter wird

---

128 C. M., 'A Nuclear No Exit' (review of the 2004 University of Wisconsin Press reprint of *Level 7*), *Science Fiction Studies*, 33 (2006), 198–202 (p. 201).
129 *Fictions of Nuclear Disaster*, p. 63.

sie. Zum Knopfdruck, mit dem man irgendwo, 'weit hinten in der Türkei', Hunderttausende umbringt, entschließt man sich ungleich rascher als dazu, seinem Nebenmann das Messer zwischen die Rippen zu stoßen.]

Anders concludes:

> Because they are no longer really master of their actions but blindly conform to the conditions set by their contraptions when they press the buttons, and because it is impossible for the person who presses the button to see or imagine those hundreds of thousands whom he is murdering with the flick of his hand, all personal feeling wilts, not just the feeling of love but also the feeling of hate. Their hatelessness, this especially, is the mark of their dehumanization.
>
> [Da sie, nicht eigentlich mehr handelnd, blindlings dem Gang ihrer Erfindungen und den Anforderungen ihrer Apparate gehorchen und nur noch Knöpfe drücken; und da es unmöglich ist, als Knopfdrücker die Hunderttausende, die man durch solche Handgriffe umbringt, vor sich zu sehen oder vorzustellen, ist jedes mögliche Fühlen in ihnen abgedrosselt; nicht nur ihr Lieben, sondern eben auch ihr Hassen. Ihre Haßlosigkeit, selbst diese, ist ein Zeichen der Dehumanisierung.][130]

This dehumanization is the result of the anonymization of warfare in the 'Age of the Third Industrial Revolution'; in 'Reflections on the H Bomb' Anders hence adds to his observations:

> The chain of events leading up to the explosion is composed of so many intermediate steps and partial actions, none of which is the crucial one, that in the end no one can be regarded as the agent. [...] 'responsibility has been displaced on to an object'. The consequences of this 'action' are so great that the agent cannot possibly grasp them before, during, or after his action.[131]

As if he had been explicitly tasked with personifying the German philosopher's suppositions, the American fiction writer has portrayed Officer PB X–127 as certainly beyond grasping the effects of his actions before and during the crisis, nor does he feel any enmity for his enemy counterpart. However, Roshwald does not leave it at that; after the fact and once the irreversible damage has been done, he shows PB X–127 as coming around in hindsight to the realization of what he has done. This constitutes, one might argue, the moral message that Roshwald wants his novel to convey (even if it is 'all-too-visibly didactic', as the above-cited reviewer bemoaned): don't let yourself be lured into becoming a brainwashed PB X–127, and act on your feelings and humanity *before* it is too late. Naturally, and perhaps unavoidably, this may be the necessary pitfall of all literature of this ilk: that in warning against the hazards of nuclear warfare it cannot but fall into the trap of — more or less overt and not always very subtle — moralizing.

Both Shute's *On the Beach* and Roshwald's *Level 7* provide fictional substantiations of Schweitzer's suggestion that nuclear Armageddon is more likely to be caused by accident than any purposeful intentionality taking the shape of, for instance, ideological or superpower antagonism. They are complemented in this respect by

---

130 *Tagesnotizen*, pp. 128–30.
131 'Reflections on the H Bomb', pp. 149–51.

another novel published in 1959 as if in direct response to Schweitzer's declarations; the American novelist Pat Frank's sci-fi novel *Alas, Babylon* is premised on the plotline that a gung-ho American F-11-F fighter pilot's failed intercept of a Soviet jet over the Mediterranean leads to all-out nuclear war. Instead of hitting the Soviet IL-33 as intended, the American's heat-seeking Sidewinder missile inadvertently slams into a Soviet military base in Latakia, Syria; within days, and without further warning, the Soviets retaliate with a full-fledged nuclear attack on the United States. Frank's story focuses on the — suggestively named — former Army Reserve Officer Randy Bragg, who opens the novel living a rather aimless life in his — equally suggestively named — hometown of Fort Repose in Central Florida. But his life is soon turned on its head when the nuclear Soviet submarine rockets begin hitting Miami, Tampa, St. Petersburg, Orlando and other major conurbations in Florida as well as neighbouring military installations, the SAC base at Homestead and MacDill Air Force Base. Situated some 75 miles away from the centres of destruction, Bragg's rural backwater is miraculously spared immediate incineration. Having equally miraculously dodged both nuclear irradiation and contamination, Fort Repose's inhabitants find themselves cut off from the rest of the United States in what has become — like the other former population centres of the United States that have taken direct hits — a prohibited radiation zone. Despite the devastation surrounding them, they survive on an irradiation-free inland atoll, as it were — Frank's goal was not to show how everyone perishes in the nuclear fallout, but how the 'last men and women' in this small township try to put their lives together again once technological civilization has been wiped out.

But as so often — and Pat Frank too, like so many of his fellow storytellers in this genre, falls into this trap, as predictable and avoidable as it may be — the author cannot refrain from including a goodly quantum of moral instruction and finger wagging. Thus those worst affected by radiation sickness are people who are materialistic and covetous, hoarding and wearing lethally contaminated jewelry smuggled in from the radioactive areas adjacent to unaffected Fort Repose; their greed all too deservedly, but also rather stereotypically, rebounds on them when they turn out to be the only ones in the community to die of radiation poisoning. With 'the fallout [seemingly] confined to military targets', and radiation appearing 'in a moral guise', as Dowling observes, contamination is depicted as more social and moral in nature than nuclear.[132]

Which in itself is hardly anything novel: narratives of world's end, we have seen over and again in this study, from Franz von Sonnenberg's and Jean-Baptiste Cousin de Grainville's early nineteenth-century apocalyptic epics of divine wrath to the mid-twentieth-century novels of nuclear extinction discussed above, are nearly always deployed by their authors to comment on and critique the mores and morals of their contemporary society; they are also deployed to stir people into action, whether this be *Donatoa*'s or *Le Dernier Homme*'s call to return to true faith in God and the Christian creed or Shute's, Roshwald's and Frank's warning to do whatever is necessary to prevent nuclear Armageddon. What all these narratives have in

---

132 *Fictions of Nuclear Disaster*, p. 91.

common is that they contain exhortatory trumpet calls, moral and political. What separates them is that the religiously inspired epics programmatically welcome the apocalypse and see it as a means to accomplish first a cleansing and then deliverance within a transcendent realm; narratives of nuclear extinction by contrast abhor the impending apocalypse and counsel against it, they see it, if not explicitly then at least by implication, as leading to either an end in natural immanence and nothingness (Shute and Roshwald) or, because humans survive in sufficient numbers, immediate social demolition followed by gradual civilizational reorganization (Frank).

As Jeffrey L. Porter observes in one of the few substantive treatments of *Alas, Babylon*, Frank's 'survivalist narrative [...] dictates that catastrophe must be viewed as an opportunity, not as a disaster', so much so in this case that 'everyone begins to thrive in ways never experienced before'.[133] Randy especially, the former 'do-nothing liberal' miraculously metamorphoses into the 'symbolic father' providing his 'friends and family with military-styled leadership'. 'No doubt', Porter muses, 'Frank does not mean to say that a nuclear war will improve the moral fiber of individuals, although he comes close to implying as much', but his 'charming image of nuclear survival' does come worryingly close to giving the reader the 'illusion that middle-class life can, with a little sweat and ample ingenuity, transcend the psychosis of nuclear catastrophe'. The novel troublingly for a narrative of nuclear annihilation takes on qualities of the pastoral, with 'the characters in this story carry[ing] on as though at summer camp'. Perhaps more worrying than Frank's pandering to clichéd audience taste and conventional morals is his somewhat disingenuous downplaying and trivializing of the real hazards of radiation poisoning, all too well established by this time, as we know from Schweitzer's contemporaneous appeals and Shute's *On the Beach*. David Dowling notes how 'some of the earlier post-nuclear fictions are remarkable for their optimism, based in an ignorance of the effects of radiation'; an instance of such disingenuousness occurs when in conversation with the local doctor Randy asks: 'Are we getting any radiation, do you think?', to which the doctor responds: 'Some, undoubtedly. But I don't think a dangerous dose'.[134]

Yet even if, as Porter rightly argues, 'Frank's novel does its best to tame the fear of annihilation', his objective is nonetheless also 'to imagine the unimaginable', the express words used by Randy Bragg, the novel's leading character.[135] It can thus be read as a novelistic rendering — albeit a problematic one — of Derrida's demand to 'translate the unknown into a known', or as a fictional enactment of Anders's mandate to decrease the gulf between our two faculties of *action* and *imagination* by widening our 'moral fantasy'. Whether Frank's approach is the most efficacious way to achieve this of course remains debatable; Porter thus deplores how

> Frank's novel emphasizes the optimistic side of nuclear war while underplaying its grislier possibilities. We see no refugee camps filled with sick and dying people, no bombed out cities with charred corpses, no sign of madness or

---

[133] Jeffrey L. Porter, 'Narrating the End: Fables of Survival in the Nuclear Age', *Journal of American Culture*, 16 (December 1993), 41–47 (p. 42); the following quotes pp. 42–44.

[134] Pat Frank, *Alas, Babylon* (New York: HarperCollins, 1993), p. 134.

[135] Ibid., p. 19.

despair (as we do, say, in Hersey's *Hiroshima*). Instead, we see happy survivors surrounded by clean water, blue sky and green trees, and amply supplied with fruit, pecans, and catfish.[136]

But Porter also rightly emphasizes the in-built dilemma of all such survivalist novels as *Alas, Babylon*, a dilemma that issues from the limited range of plotline options that are available to authors of post-apocalyptic narratives; Porter observes: 'If Frank wished to build a "viable society" on the ruins of the old, he would have to play down the problem of fallout and play up the practice of survival in military terms, and this he does, in effect creating a compelling novel on behalf of civil defense'. The paradoxical outcome is, in the end, that despite his probable intention to write against nuclear war — if that is what his intention was — 'Frank's tale of survival is essentially sympathetic to the idea of nuclear war', hence Porter's inference that 'Frank's novel reaches preposterous conclusions about surviving the Bomb'. This is the ultimate impasse of the majority of semi-terminal survivalist plots: whenever these narratives show the survivors successfully managing the aftermath, frequently presented in the guise of a primitivist return to nature, it seems to suggest that the nuclear inferno may well be worth enduring.

Such reservations notwithstanding, it would be unfair to suggest that in their time such survivalist novels as *Alas, Babylon* were meant as anything other than a warning against the hazards of nuclear warfare. After all, Frank's novel succeeds in translating into narrative action some of the philosophical concerns articulated by Anders, among them the notion that we have become blunted to the apocalypse. Thus at one point Randy Bragg declares: 'That business in the Mediterranean? It's happened before. I guess that's one of the dangerous things about it. We get shockproof. We've been conditioned. Standing on the brink of war has become normal posture';[137] talking about her children Randy's sister-in-law Helen similarly observes: 'Yes, you see, all their lives, ever since they've known anything, they've lived under the shadow of war — atomic war. For them the abnormal has become the normal. All their lives they have heard nothing else, and they expect it', to which Randy's pithy retort is: 'They're conditioned'. Invoking Anders's notion of the obsolescence of enmity and enemy, and of the dangers inherent in the anonymity of intercontinental warfare, Bragg reflects elsewhere: 'It seemed incongruous to call The Day a war — Russo-American, East-West, or World War III — because the war, really was over in a single day. Furthermore, nobody in the Western hemisphere ever saw the face of a human enemy'.

It is clear that Shute, Roshwald, and Frank, not to mention the many other authors who deployed the World War III nuclear plot or, like George Orwell in *1984*, related to it as a contextual background for their futuristic tales, intended their novels to serve as warnings, as cautionary tales about the present, future or, as in Orwell's case, (the future's) past dangers of nuclear warfare. Thus in *1984* we are told in the political tract by the fictional character Emmanuel Goldstein (fictional, in this instance, perhaps even within the novel's storyline), a tract entitled

---

136 'Narrating the End', p. 45; the subsequent quotes pp. 45 and 46.
137 *Alas, Babylon*, p. 58; the subsequent passages pp. 84 and 123.

'The Theory and Practice of Oligarchical Collectivism' and clandestinely read by Winston Smith, that following 'the ravages of the atomic war of the nineteen-fifties' the world had become 'more primitive than it was fifty years ago'; the tract goes on to amplify:

> Although the Party, according to its habit, claims the invention for itself, atomic bombs first appeared as early as the nineteen-forties, and were first used on a large scale about ten years later. At that time some hundreds of bombs were dropped on industrial centres, chiefly in European Russia, Western Europe, and North America. The effect was to convince the ruling groups of all countries that a few more atomic bombs would mean an end of organized society, and hence of their own power. Thereafter, although no formal agreement was ever made or hinted at, no more bombs were dropped. All three powers merely continue to produce atomic bombs and store them up against the decisive opportunity which they all believe will come sooner or later. And meanwhile the art of war has remained almost stationary for thirty or forty years.[138]

Orwell's 1948 novel of post-World War III political reorganization can be read as a cynical dystopian counter-narrative to Wells's *The World Set Free. A Story of Mankind*; caustically upending Wells's grand optimism about the future, in which all mankind lives happily ever after in freedom and peaceful coexistence, in *1984* the populations of the three remaining world powers — inasmuch as they exist at all (we can't be sure) — live unhappily ever after in a state of perpetual conventional warfare, and the only freedom known to them is slavery and thought control.

Their and their novels' diverging outlooks notwithstanding, what unites Wells and Orwell across the decades, pre-World War I and post-World War II, is that both saw themselves as actively taking a stand in current political affairs; each in his way is 'try[ing] to intervene' — to adopt Günther Anders's phrasing — by 'reach[ing] out to millions of [their] contemporaries' and attempting 'to really shock those millions' if not into taking immediate action, then at least into changing their attitude over time. This applies in the same way to Shute, Roshwald, and Frank. Instead of utilizing 'radio and television', however, as Anders had proposed, they chose as their instrument the literary medium and, when a novel lent itself to a successful adaptation, the medium of film — as was the case with Shute's *On the Beach* which indeed managed to reach out to 'millions'. Not just did Shute's novel come to figure prominently in the Anglophone world on required reading lists of schools and colleges, the storyline proved, as we saw, eminently popularizable also in the visual medium perhaps precisely because it pandered to aesthetic cliché. As star-studded Hollywood melodrama Stanley Kramer's adaptation was well received right up to the power-wielding echelons of society, with its premiere attended by such high-ranking officials and statespersons as Mayor Robert F. Wagner, Jr., in New York, the Soviet Ambassador to the United Kingdom in London, the members of the Japanese Royal Family in Tokyo, and King Gustav VI in Stockholm.[139]

---

138 *1984* (Harmondsworth: Penguin, 1977), pp. 153 and 157.

139 Thanks to Wikipedia for this and other film-related information cited here (entry 'On the Beach (1959 film), <https://en.wikipedia.org/wiki/On_the_Beach_(1959_film)>, and entry '*On the Beach* (2000 film)', <https://en.wikipedia.org/wiki/On_the_Beach_(2000_film)>, both accessed 10

Of course, such markers of success don't really tell us much about the scale of impact these novels and their film adaptations elicited or what the readers and cinema goers truly thought. To what degree did books and films like these contribute to the galvanization of public opinion during this phase of the Cold War in the late 1950s and early 1960s? Whether they managed to effect a change of heart or mind either at the time or over the long term is impossible to assess; at best we can give an educated answer. And this educated answer comes not from the medium of literature but from film, and not from the first high point of the nuclear debate in the late 1950s but rather from the second hot phase of Cold War tension in the early 1980s. It is not a novel but a film made for television that provides the data.

The (Political and Aesthetic) Fallout of Nuclear War

It was during the early Reagan years — a period in which the Cold War rivalry was approaching yet another boiling point with Soviet SS-20s and American Cruise and Pershing II missiles either already deployed or in the process of being deployed — that an American film director, Nicholas Meyer, known for two *Star Trek* movie instalments, *Star Trek II* and *Star Trek IV*, decided to engage in the nuclear debate when he agreed to direct an ABC television movie about the effects of a thermonuclear war. Depicting an all-out attack on the United States the film, entitled *The Day After*, aired on American television screens during prime time on 20 November 1983. Replicating the three-part plot matrix adopted by Pat Frank in *Alas, Babylon*, *The Day After* begins with a peaceful prelude set in the American heartland in urban Kansas City, Missouri, and provincial university town Lawrence, Kansas. The initial scenes are peopled with an array of individualized characters representing hard-working Main Street USA conducting their everyday lives, the doctor Russell Oakes (played by one of the few known actors, Jason Robards) and his wife and daughter, the farmer Jim Dahlberg (played by John Collum) and his family, young lovers, a black soldier and his wife, a medical student: people, in short, an American audience could easily identify with. The deceptive calm of this opening with its mundane civil society setting is blown apart in the film's nightmarish mid-section by the havoc and destruction wrought once the nuclear bombs begin hitting their targets, with some of the characters we have just familiarized ourselves with being brutally incinerated and disappearing from the plot — at times with vivid use of special effects, although none of the bodies seen being vaporized are directly identifiable as a named character. The movie ends with the depiction of the fallout of the attack and its consequences for the survivors, the panic, chaos and disorientation that ensues among them, the run of the countless injured on the one remaining hospital, the exasperation and exhaustion of the few remaining doctors and medics, or the lone farmer and his family trying to save themselves from the radioactive fallout in their isolated farm's tornado shelter. Likewise echoing the storyline of Frank's *Alas, Babylon*, the film overlays its opening sequences with a staccato of radio and television news bulletins

October 2016).

reporting on the rapidly escalating tensions between the superpowers, centering in *The Day After* on the most emblematic of pretexts for Cold War confrontation, divided Berlin; building on long-established and readily recognizable markers of superpower rivalry, devices like this contribute to the film's poignant sense of realism and remind us, in one scholar's words, that these individuals' 'private narratives and lives are highly vulnerable to public narratives that impose themselves dramatically from outside'.[140]

Even before it aired on ABC the movie caused considerable debate. It was pre-screened to journalists, critics and select officials in Washington, including the Joint Chiefs of Staff, with Ronald Reagan, former Hollywood star turned President and avid movie enthusiast, watching an advance screening at Camp David already on 10 November, ten days before the television premiere; he recorded in his diary:

> In the morning at Camp David. I ran the tape of the movie ABC is running on the air Nov. 20. It's called *The Day After*. It has Lawrence, Kansas wiped out in a nuclear war with Russia. It is powerfully done — all $7 mil. worth. It's very effective & left me greatly depressed. So far they haven't sold any of the 25 spot ads scheduled & I can see why. Whether it will be of any help to the 'anti nukes' or not, I can't say. My own reaction was one of our having to do all we can to have a deterrent & to see there is never a nuclear war.[141]

Not only was ABC struggling to find advertisers willing to pay for the 'spot ads', as a surprisingly well informed Reagan reveals. Because of the producers' considerable anxiety about the psychological shock the film might spawn among its viewers, the network took a range of measures to mitigate any overreaction: half a million 'viewer's guides' were distributed in advance to prepare the public for the film's grim subject matter, parents were cautioned not to let children watch it on their own, telephone help hotlines were installed on the evening of the broadcast, and the following advisory accompanied the airing: 'Although based on scientific fact, this film is fiction. Because the graphic depiction of the effects of a nuclear war may not be suitable for younger viewers, parental discretion is advised'.[142] In addition — and to capitalize on the opportunity as much as possible — ABC also laid on, in the slot immediately following the movie, a live debate hosted by the network's popular *Nightline* anchor Ted Koppel, the heavyweight panelists of which were the outspoken advocate of nuclear disarmament Carl Sagan, former Secretary of State Henry Kissinger, the writer and Holocaust survivor Elie Wiesel, General Brent Scowcroft, conservative commentator William F. Buckley and former Secretary of Defense Robert McNamara, champion of the American government's 'Mutual Assured Destruction' policy.

Due to this pre- and post-airing promotional 'hullabaloo', as one critic has called

---

140 Daniel Cordle, ' "That's going to happen to us. It is": *Threads* and the Imagination of Nuclear Disaster', *Journal of British Cinema and Television*, 10 (2013), 71–92 (p. 84).

141 *The Reagan Diaries*, ed. by Douglas Brinkley (New York: Harper Collins, 2007), p. 185.

142 Cited by Susan Boyd-Bowman, '*The Day After*: Representations of the Nuclear Holocaust', *Screen*, 25 (August-September 1984), 71–97 (p. 83).

«Handkerchief over face will keep you from inhaling radioactive mist from water burst.»

«Crawl under desk, out of line of windows, to avoid heat flash burns, falling plaster.»

«A good scrubbing after blast will remove radioactive particles clinging to skin.»

FIG. 5.2. Illustrations taken from the pamphlet *Atomic Bombing. How To Protect Yourself*, circulated by the U.S. Government Science Service in 1950. Other illustrations contained such captions as: 'Dash into a doorway. If wheeling a carriage [pram], cover yourself and baby with blanket'; 'Crouch behind a tree. Turn away from the blast and cover exposed skin'; 'Uninjured persons who may have come in contact with radioactive materials should thoroughly scrub themselves'.

it,[143] the movie succeeded in reaching a far larger audience than originally targeted, an estimated one hundred million viewers. It thus became 'the biggest media event of 1983'[144] and was, at the time, 'the second most-watched program in American television history'.[145] In Britain it was aired by ITV three weeks after its American showing, attracting an audience of seventeen million, although purportedly only 5.4 million watched the movie in its two-hour entirety; here, however, the film met with a vastly different reaction, with critics 'whining almost in unison', in one scholar's words, that the film 'was a particularly tasteless example of the American penchant for soap opera'. The negative British response ultimately led to the British director Mick Jackson producing *The Day After*'s British pendant, *Threads*, a neorealist and quasi-documentary film set in the British industrial heartland in Sheffield which aired in 1984.[146]

Although ABC sought to market *The Day After* as factual, and thus supposedly as apolitical and non-partisan, any film about a nuclear holocaust was bound to be perceived by conservatives as anti-nuclear propaganda and hence as an intrinsically partisan endeavour to challenge the Reagan government's nuclear agenda. It did not help to have the film's director Nicholas Meyer reputedly admitting to journalists that 'ABC is spending millions of dollars to go on the air and call Ronald Reagan a liar',[147] the point being that the official line of Western governments had for decades been to claim — contrary even to what they themselves knew to be true — that a nuclear war was survivable by a majority of their populations so long as they took the appropriate civil defence precautions (such as ducking under a table, or taking a shower, or covering one's head and eyes when the bombs struck, as recommended in some nuclear emergency pamphlets; see Figure 5.2).[148] Nor did it help that Brandon Stoddard, the president of ABC Motion Pictures and producer of *Roots*, who was the driving force behind the production of *The Day After*, is said to have stated: 'we wanted to do a movie about [...] what [the] lives [of ordinary Americans] would be like after a nuclear war, not what it would be like in the President's bunker'.[149] The question it all boiled down to was, writes the scholar Susan Boyd-Bowman in a study of the film, whether Meyer and ABC had delivered '"fiction based on fact" (as they claimed), or disarmament propaganda (as their hawkish critics claimed)' or indeed merely 'a pretentious disaster movie' (with British *Guardian*-critic Nancy Banks-Smith, for instance, calling it 'as cliché-ridden a film as ever insulted its subject').[150]

Of course, the film's conservative critics had a point; as Boyd-Bowman rightly

---

143 Deron Overpeck, '"Remember! it's Only a Movie!" Expectations and Receptions of *The Day After* (1983)', *Historical Journal of Film, Radio and Television*, 32 (2012), 267–92 (p. 280).

144 Boyd-Bowman, '*The Day After*', p. 71.

145 See Stanley Feldman and Lee Sigelman, 'The Political Impact of Prime-Time Television: *The Day After*', *The Journal of Politics*, 47 (June 1985), 556–78 (p. 556).

146 Boyd-Bowman, '*The Day After*', p. 72.

147 Overpeck, '"Remember! it's Only a Movie!"', p. 273.

148 The pamphlet's texts and illustrations were taken from the volume *Der Montag, der die Welt veränderte. Lesebuch des Atomzeitalters*, ed. by Claus Biegert (Reinbek: Rowohlt, 1996), pp. 72–80.

149 Cited by Overpeck, '"Remember! it's Only a Movie!"', p. 272.

150 '*The Day After*', p. 74; the subsequent quote p. 76.

observes, the 'first issue' about 'making a film on the subject of the effects of nuclear war' is whether it can be considered 'tantamount to advocating nuclear disarmament'. This was certainly the opinion voiced by supporters of nuclear disarmament when the airing of *The Day After* was announced; activists and spokespersons for the American National Nuclear Weapons Freeze Campaign thus declared: 'This show presents an unprecedented opportunity to reach tens of millions of people uninvolved in the nuclear issue' and offers 'an occasion for not only educating millions of Americans about the consequences of nuclear war, but also encouraging [them] to act now to prevent this nuclear devastation from ever happening'.[151] Meyer himself once said about his decision to take on the unusual task of directing this made-for-TV movie, 'I think I was the fourth director to be offered it. I tried to think of all the reasons why I couldn't, shouldn't do it. We all live in terror of nuclear annihilation, but we don't like to think about it'.[152] Directing *The Day After* now gave him the opportunity to make his contemporaries think about 'the unthinkable' by, as he himself put it, 'clobber[ing] sixty million people over the head' (sixty million being the audience ABC had originally expected its film to attract).[153] Meyer had clearly — albeit unknowingly, I assume — found a way to live up to Anders's summons; he had deployed the medium of television successfully to 'reach out to millions of [his] contemporaries' and 'really shock' them.

Shock millions the film may have done, and it certainly stimulated debate, but was it actually 'effective'? (Meyer at one point admitted: 'it wasn't intended to be a good movie; it was intended to be effective'.)[154] Did it change people's attitudes and spur them on to civic action? Put differently, did *The Day After* in any way fulfill Anders's hopes about the deployment of modern media in the service of political change? Various scholars have looked into this and have come up with answers that are as surprising as they are sobering. To put it crudely, the film may have gone off like a bomb, but the actual political fallout was negligible. From the evidence they have gathered and analyzed, all scholars are in agreement that opinions were, by and large, hardly changed by the film; instead, existing positions were reinforced. Citing William Adams, the director of a *Washington Post* poll, Stanley Feldman and Lee Sigelman thus observe in an article on 'The Political Impact of Prime-Time Television: *The Day After*' which was published soon after the film's release: '*The Day After* failed to change existing views on the horror of nuclear war, the need for mutual arms control, and the strategy of deterrence', adding:

> Viewers did not, on this evidence, react to *The Day After* in a strongly emotional

---

151 Cited in Overpeck, '"Remember! it's Only a Movie!"', p. 277.

152 Simon Braund, 'How Ronald Reagan Learned to Start Worrying and Stop Loving the Bomb', *Empire*, 257 (2010), 134–38 (unpaginated ProQuest internet download: <http://0-search.proquest.com.catalogue.libraries.london.ac.uk/docview/868609671/fulltext/849DE0593C144DC0PQ/1?accountid=14565>).

153 Meyer quoted by Mark Gerzon, 'Watching the World End', *The Times*, 7 November 1983 (cited by Boyd-Bowman, '*The Day After*', p. 73).

154 Cited by Braund, 'How Ronald Reagan Learned to Start Worrying and Stop Loving the Bomb'.

fashion; the movie did not infuriate them, nor, notwithstanding some of the more extreme predictions that were made about its potentially traumatizing impact, did it drop them into an abyss of despair. It did, however, cause them to become somewhat more worried about America's nuclear defenses than they had been before watching.[155]

Based on closer analysis of the poll's data, they do, however, record a distinct educational disparity: 'Having watched the movie', they remark, 'those with little education became more supportive of higher defense spending, but those with high levels of education became more likely to endorse defense spending cutbacks'. Barrie Gunter and M. Svennevig likewise note that the effect of such films as *The Day After* and *Threads* was 'generally to strengthen attitudes among self-selected samples of viewers who were already cautious or anti-nuclear to make them somewhat more cautious'.[156] After seeing *The Day After* viewers were for instance more likely to downgrade their chances of survival after an attack, with 54.4% now believing that 'almost no one' would survive as compared to 48.7% before viewing the film and 81.5% considering it 'very unlikely' that 'there would be adequate medical care', as compared with 74.1% previously.[157] Yet despite these shifts in viewer attitudes before and after, political opinions as such hardly changed. As regards two families representing opposing points of view who were followed on PBS's influential *MacNeil/Lehrer Newshour*, Deron Overpeck notes in his 2012 article '"Remember! it's Only a Movie!" Expectations and Receptions of *The Day After* (1983)': 'Their responses to [the journalists'] questions demonstrate that the film [merely] galvanized their previous beliefs'. Overpeck also tells of 'a poll conducted by George Washington University' which 'determined that the level of support for the nuclear freeze movement remained the same after the film was broadcast'; he concludes:

> *The Day After* neither compelled vast numbers of people to march on Congress to demand a nuclear weapons freeze nor drove them panicked into the streets [...]. Instead those viewers either interpreted the film through their previously held political perspectives or understood that it was a work of fiction. [...] *The Day After* did not by itself inspire public action; it was caught up in an already contentious public debate and used by the participants to further their own goals. The film-makers catered to both sides [...]. *The Day After* did not change the terms of the nuclear debate; the nuclear debate shaped *The Day After* and the popular response to it.[158]

Overpeck goes on to remark that, even though Reagan found the film distressing, he continued nonetheless 'to insist on the placement of Pershing II and Tomahawk missiles in Europe, believing they were necessary to prod the Soviets back to the negotiating table'; in short, Overpeck infers, 'the film had no immediately noticeable impact on Reagan's foreign policy'. This is borne out by Reagan's own reaction to *The Day After*. In his diaries he notes on 18 November, two days before

---

155 'The Political Impact of Prime-Time Television', pp. 557 and 574; the following quote p. 574.
156 Cited by Cordle, '"That's going to happen to us. It is"', p. 77.
157 'The Political Impact of Prime-Time Television', p. 564.
158 '"Remember! it's Only a Movie!"', p. 283; the subsequent passage p. 282.

the film is aired:

> George Schultz & I had a talk mainly about setting up a little in house group of experts on the Soviet U. to help us in setting up some channels. I feel the Soviets are so defense minded, so paranoid about being attacked that without being in any way soft on them we ought to tell them no one here has any

intention of doing anything like that. What the h--l have they got that anyone would want. George is going on ABC right after its big Nuclear bomb film Sunday night. We know it's 'anti-nuke' propaganda but we're going to take it over & say it shows why we must keep on doing what we're doing.[159]

Although *The Day After* demonstrably boosted the argument for deterrence, as Matthew Grant has observed, it equally demonstrably contributed to Reagan's realization that any nuclear war would have catastrophic consequences not just for his own country, but also for the planet as a whole. What the film showed was in all likelihood borne out by a briefing and report Reagan received that same 18 November 1983; the above-cited diary entry concludes as follows: 'A most sobering experience with Cap. W. & Gen. Vessey in the situation room — a briefing on our complete plan in the event of a nuclear attack. The Chiefs have been working on it for 2 yrs. in reply to my request in October 1981'. In his 1990 autobiography *An American Life* Reagan comments specifically on these remarks, observing: 'There are many aspects of the report, which I'd requested of the Pentagon two years earlier, that remain so secret even now that I cannot even begin to discuss them. But, simply put, it was a scenario for a sequence of events that could lead to the end of civilization as we knew it'.[160] The subsequent pages of his autobiography are devoted largely to his lengthy dealings with the Soviet leaders during the remainder of this decade, at first the General Secretaries Andropov and Chernenko as well as Foreign Minister Gromyko, and later Gorbachev, about how to reach some kind of nuclear deal to scale back the arms race. These discussions ultimately resulted in two Strategic Arms Reduction Treaties being concluded in 1991 and 1993, START I reducing and limiting offensive arms to 6000 nuclear warheads and 1600 intercontinental ballistic missiles — ICBMs — and bombers, START II banning the use of multiple independently targetable reentry vehicles — MIRVs — in ICBMs. (START II, however, was never ratified by the United States and hence never entered into effect.)

If we take the film *The Day After* as symptomatic for the power of fictional depictions, in film or literature, to imprint on the beholder's eye the consequences of nuclear warfare in mind-numbing detail, it is also symptomatic for the fact that this tells us little about how audiences will ultimately weigh the significance of what they have beheld. As Grant says, a film like *The Day After*, or books like Shute's *On the Beach* and Roshwald's *Level 7*, can boost the case for disarmament just as much as they can advance the case for its opposite, deterrence. This is confirmed by Reagan's diaries and autobiography, an outcome that would not have provided much reassurance for Günther Anders who had staked so much on the media's ability not just to reach out to millions but also to change opinion and foster political action for change.

Yet, while the direct political fallout may have been wanting — not least because arms negotiations are always in the hands of those in power (which is why one would wish that those in positions of political and military nuclear authority would be required by law to view such films or read such novels so as to develop

---

159 *The Reagan Diaries*, p. 199.
160 *An American Life* (London: Random Century Group, 1990), pp. 585–86.

their imagination in this regard) — the aesthetic fallout was, I would like to argue nonetheless, considerable. As Grant notes with regard to filmic expressions of the nuclear theme, including *The Day After*:

> The inability of existing screen representations to change minds of viewers also helps to explain why those who produced later depictions of nuclear war, from *The War Game* to *Threads*, placed the horrors of survival, the pain and trauma of those left alive and broken by nuclear attack, at the centre of their work. Survival would turn out to be much more shocking than total annihilation.[161]

In fact 'total annihilation', or in Bertrand Russell's words 'complete extinction', turns out to be a storyline that does not warrant rehearsing too often. After all, what more literary (or filmic) mileage could be gotten out of a plotline that ended with everyone's death, with no continuation, no sequel, no afterlife, no hope for renewal possible? For this reason the nuclear plot of 'complete extinction' had, ironically, exhausted itself hardly had it begun. There is thus a sad paradox at play here: once we have beheld the end of mankind in novel form — viz. Shute's and Roshwald's stark imaginings of the complete eradication of our species — our interest in repeating that depressing reading experience quickly wanes. How many times can we bear to experience an end that allows for no regeneration, an end that is truly the end? After all (let us remind ourselves), the essence of the traditional concept of the apocalypse ever since its inception was an end that was *not* truly the end, especially — but not only — in the Christian tradition of apocalyptic thought inaugurated by Saint John's Revelation. Klaus Vondung, the German scholar whose book on *The Apocalypse in Germany* I cited earlier in this chapter and elsewhere in this study, notes that the apocalypse traditionally meant 'the total and final eradication of humankind, the end of the world' ('totalen und endgültigen [...] Untergang der Menschheit, das Ende der Welt'), but that this eradication was simultaneously perceived as a necessary period of transit ('Durchgangsphase') to a 'new Earth' ('einer "neuen Erde"'), a 'new Jerusalem' ('einem "neuen Jerusalem"'); and this notion of a new Earth, Vondung goes on,

> defined the apocalypse well into the twentieth century, even when it had long moved beyond its religious roots: The old, imperfect and corrupt world must be destroyed in order for a new perfect world to be established. It was always this notion of a new world on which the apocalypse was founded; the apocalypse was a vision of deliverance and salvation.
>
> [Und dieser Gedanke bestimmte auch die Apokalypse bis in unser Jahrhundert, auch wenn sie sich von ihrem religiösen Ursprung entfernt hat: Die alte, unvollkommene und verdorbene Welt muß zerstört werden, damit eine neue, vollkommene aufgerichtet werden kann. Stets kam es der Apokalypse letztlich auf diese neue Welt an; die Apokalypse war eine Erlösungsvision.]

But, building on Günther Anders's nuclear criticism, Vondung then formulates a crucial insight; he writes:

---

161 'Images of Survival, Stories of Destruction, *Journal of British Cinema and Television*, 10 (2013), 7–26 (p. 25).

It is only today, because of 'the threat of a man-made apocalypse', as Günther Anders called our 'ability to annihilate ourselves', that deliverance and salvation have become eclipsed. If we speak nonetheless of the apocalypse of a nuclear war, then we are in fact dealing with a 'cropped' apocalypse. We therefore today really only mean the first half of the traditional concept of apocalypse; the other half, the establishment of a new and perfect world that formerly afforded meaning and purpose to the annihilation of our world, has evaporated.

[Erst heute, unter der Drohung der 'von uns selbst gemachten Apokalypse', wie Günther Anders die 'Möglichkeit unseren Selbstauslöschung' nannte, ist Erlösung nicht mehr im Blick. Wenn wir dennoch von der Apokalypse eines Atomkriegs sprechen, so haben wir es mit einer 'kupierten' Apokalypse zu tun. Wir können nur die erste Hälfte der herkömmlichen apokalyptischen Vision meinen; die zweite Hälfte, die Errichtung der neuen, vollkommenen Welt, die früher dem Untergang Sinn und Ziel verlieh, hat sich verflüchtigt.][162]

But this is true only to a point — after all, what I am arguing here is precisely that the continuation after the nuclear apocalypse does have meaning and purpose; it is just that the continuation of life on our planet and the survival of mankind that so piques our interest are no longer supernatural occurrences but natural ones, they are no longer otherworldly phenomena but worldly ones. The continuation of life as portrayed in the semi-terminal class of Last Man narratives no longer entails a vision of deliverance and salvation in some transcendent heavenly sphere but rather, typically, a vision of prolonged suffering, perseverance and reconstruction on Earth. It is the material and spiritual tenacity and creativity shown by last men and women in our world, not beyond our world, that transfixes us; we are captivated by the ways in which writers (and filmmakers) imagine how we come through as human species despite whatever befalls us, how we endure even in the face of utmost hardship and privation. In *Fictions of Nuclear Disaster* Dowling cites the following rather fitting observation by the protagonist of John Griffith's 1965 novel *The Survivors*: 'We've survived the holocaust and all the dangers it brought. It remains to be seen if we can survive ourselves'.[163] The protracted adventure of survival after the cataclysm is, all told, simply more engrossing and absorbing — not least because it gives fiction writers more latitude for plot and character development — than the short-lived agony of what would befall us during the nuclear onslaught itself (not to mention the eternal if blissful monotony of what I imagine Christianity's millennial afterlife to entail). Gertrude Stein once put it rather curtly when asked, in 1946, to respond to the question what she thought of the atomic bomb; she answered: 'Sure it will destroy a lot and kill a lot, but it's the living that are interesting not the way of killing them, because if there were not a lot left living how could there be any interest in destruction'.[164] Survival is thus not just 'more shocking than total annihilation', as Grant put it, it is — more positively speaking — in many ways also aesthetically more appealing and satisfying because it provides so much more scope and latitude for the creative imagination.

---

162 *Die Apokalypse in Deutschland*, pp. 11-12.
163 *Fictions of Nuclear Disaster*, p. 63.
164 'Reflection on the atomic bomb', in *Les Cahiers du GRIF*, 41-42 (1989), 149.

This comes close to the essence of what is now termed 'the nuclear sublime'; Frances Ferguson thus notes in an article on this subject, 'the trick with the sublime, of course, is that we live to tell the tale of our encounters with it [...] because it never proves to be quite as deadly in experience as it had in thought', and continues:

> In that sense, the notion of the sublime is continuous with the notion of nuclear holocaust: to think the sublime would be to think the unthinkable and to exist in one's own nonexistence. And just as the sublime continually fails in its promise in eighteenth- and nineteenth-century aesthetics because its threat cannot deliver a consciousness of individual identity that seems more than a temporary delusion, so the effort to think the nuclear sublime in terms of its absoluteness dwindles from the effort to imagine total annihilation to something very much like calculations of exactly how horrible daily life would be after a significant nuclear explosion.[165]

This focus on the here and now (of life on our planet in our time) certainly helps to explain science fiction's seeming obsession with Russell's second and third options, the 'return to barbarism' and the attempt to rebuild civilization on the one hand or, on the other, 'the creation of a single world state', the latter of which 'could occur in one of two ways: by force, as the result of one power being victorious in a nuclear war [...], or under the threat of force', the widely acclaimed early post-1945 example of which was Orwell's earlier mentioned *1984* with its population under Big Brother's permanent dictatorial mind-control. What follows the nuclear bomb blasts is, as I suggested above, far more gripping than what happens when the bombs fall; hence narratives of survival and Last Men and Women outlasting a nuclear holocaust abound, whereas stories of complete nuclear extinction are remarkably limited in number. As W. Warren Wagar once remarked, 'the end of the world is seldom the end. [...] Ends that lead to fresh beginnings and further ends appear regularly in science fiction, reflecting some of the most characteristic anxieties and ideological paradigms of late industrial culture'.[166] No surprise then to read in a prominent encyclopedia of science fiction:

> The aftermath of holocaust may be the most popular theme in sf; this encyclopedia mentions at least 400 examples at novel length. The genre is as old as sf itself: a convenient starting point is Mary Shelley's second sf novel *The Last Man* (1826). [...] The novel in which the post-holocaust story takes on its distinctive modern form is Richard Jefferies's *After London* (1885), in which the author's strategy is to set the novel thousands of years after the catastrophe has taken place [...]. Ever since Jefferies's time the post-holocaust story has tended to follow this pattern; for every book whose hero lived through the holocaust itself [...] there are several whose story begins long after the disaster is over but while its effects are still making themselves felt. Though such stories continue to fascinate, there has been surprisingly little variation in the basic plot: disaster is, in the average scenario, seen as being followed by savage barbarism and a bitter struggle for survival, with rape and murder commonplace; such an era is often succeeded by a rigidly hierarchical feudalism...

---

[165] 'The Nuclear Sublime', *Diacritics*, 14 (Summer 1984), 4–10 (pp. 6–7).
[166] 'Round Trips to Doomsday', in *The End of the World*, ed. by Eric Rabkin, Martin Greenberg et al. (Carbondale: Southern Illinois Press, 1983), pp. 73–96 (p. 73).

While holocaust is here (perhaps too) liberally defined to include natural calamities or ecological cataclysms such as those portrayed by Mary Shelley and Richard Jefferies, but also, in the twentieth and twenty-first centuries famously by George R. Stewart in *Earth Abides* (1949) and equally impressively, if more recently, by Emily St. John Mandel in *Station Eleven* (2014) — testimony to the enduring appeal of Nature's paradigm — the point is valid nonetheless: life's continuation in the aftermath of the event seems more engrossing than the extinction of life in and through the event itself. The entry cited above continues:

> After the Hiroshima bombing, a new period began in which, unsurprisingly, the post-holocaust story came to seem less fantastic; it also became more popular, and developed a distinctively apocalyptic atmosphere, a heavy emphasis on a supposed anti-technological bias among the survivors, and a concentration on the results of nuclear power in general and radiation in particular. The mood was darker in that imagined catastrophes were now primarily man-made. [...] Paramount among such books is Walter M. Miller's *A Canticle for Leibowitz* (1960), an ironic black comedy about the ways in which a post-holocaust civilization's history recapitulates the errors of its predecessor. [...] Life after the holocaust is a theme that continues to grip the imagination. The idea of destroying our crowded, bureaucratic world and then rebuilding afresh offers an exciting psychic freedom. The rusting symbols of a technological past protruding into a more primitive, natural, future landscape are among the most potent of sf's icons.[167]

The degree to which the theme of disaster, broadly speaking, continues to flourish is made manifest by the two lists provided by Wikipedia cited in my Introduction. Under the heading 'List of apocalyptic and post-apocalyptic fiction' Wikipedia on 24 July 2015 logged over 960 titles which were itemized under thirteen genre categories: Comic (42), Film (263), Game (125), Novel (338), Novella (1), Play (4), Poem (4), Radio (5), Song (6), (Short) Story (53), TV (118), (Animated) Web Series (1) and Other (6); the brackets give the numbers for each category. The titles were also classified under the following thematic categories: Alien invasion, disease, dying sun, ecological catastrophe, future collapse, human decline, impact event, monsters, social collapse, supernatural (religious and supernatural) apocalypse, technology, and war. Under the heading of, more specifically, 'List of nuclear holocaust fiction', Wikipedia itemized no fewer than 370 titles under 9 rubrics: Film (68), TV Programmes (23) and TV Episodes (13), Novels (98), Short Stories (15), Short Story Collections (3), Comics (10), Animation Shorts (2), Music (112), and Games (27). Already in 1982 W. Warren Wagar had tallied in the bibliography of primary sources used in *Terminal Visions. The Literature of Last Things*, his key study of literary end-time narratives, 'three hundred novels, stories, plays and poems'. With so many versions of and variations on the theme of apocalypse and post-catastrophe survival or non-survival — and I am sure any of my readers would easily be able to add to the lists referenced above — and with so much scholarship already written on the subject — I have cited liberally for instance from the studies

---

167 *The Encyclopedia of Science Fiction*, ed. by John Clute and Peter Nicholls (New York: St. Martin's Press, 1993), pp. 581–84.

by Paul Brians, David Dowling and W. Warren Wagar — there seems little point in rehearsing here what has already been said. Nor would there be much gain in trying to enumerate, not to mention discuss, all the works of speculative or futuristic fiction that have deployed the nuclear plot, as I call it here, in order to portray either the end or, as in most narratives, the continuing survival of mankind after a nuclear war. My interests lie elsewhere.

God's (Not So) Grand Finale

My approach has centred by and large on the interface between philosophy, theology and literature (including science fiction), availing itself also of occasional incursions into art history and the history of science. Extending the theological sub-theme around which the five chapters of this study have pivoted, I want to use the remainder of this fifth and final chapter to probe more deeply into the role that the theme of the death of God plays in nuclear fiction, a theme already touched upon in parts of my discussion above. My contention throughout this study has been that, outside of the religious sphere, the death of Man is premised on the death of God; we cannot imagine, so my narrative runs, the annihilation of Man in the presence of God. So how does the death of God actually play out in secular nuclear Last Man narratives? And how are religion and belief presented in fictions of Last Men and Women? Let us begin with the post-1945 novels of nuclear apocalypse we discussed above.

In Nevil Shute's *On the Beach* religion plays a peculiarly peripheral and subdued role. Despite the end inching ever closer, we are told only as if in passing that churches are filled to the brim, but no one seriously questions God's purpose in ending the life of mankind. Any genuinely deep-seated psychological despair seems absent, and no mass hysteria ensues. Dwight Towers acts as if he were soon to be reunited with his family in the United States, Peter Holmes and his wife Mary are shown making plans for the planting of their garden. There is a distinct air of 'collective denial', as one critic has put it.[168] Another speaks of Shute's text being 'a study of the numbing phenomenon' that can set in when people become overwhelmed by the feeling that they are no longer in control of their own fates but are simultaneously unable to change that situation.[169] A popular motif of many end-of-time narratives in such situations is the radicalization of belief and the formation of religious sects, but in *On the Beach* there is no mention of such zealots or religious fanatics, quite to the contrary; people seem to be loath to philosophizing on any purpose of life or afterlife. The novel is — considering its end-time topic — remarkably thin on philosophy or theology, the narrator no less 'sedulously avoiding any serious topic of conversation'[170] than the characters he is describing. To be sure, there are moments of religious reflection. For instance we are told that to match the population's mood

---

[168] John J. Pierce, *Great Themes of Science Fiction. A Study in Imagination and Evolution* (New York and Westport, CT: Greenwood Press, 1987), p. 149.
[169] Schwenger, 'Writing the Unthinkable', p. 44.
[170] *On the Beach*, p. 32; the subsequent quotes pp. 150, again 150, 150–51 and 56.

the National Gallery in Melbourne has put on an exhibition of religious pictures, 'oil paintings, mostly in a modernistic style', and we are shown Moira Davidson and Dwight Towers standing in front of the prizewinner's entry, depicting 'the sorrowing Christ on a background of the destruction of a great city'. The following dialogue between them ensues, starting with Moira:

> 'I think that one's got something', she said. 'For once I believe that I'd agree with the judges.'
> He said, 'I hate it like hell.'
> 'What don't you like about it?'
> He stared at it. 'Everything. To me it's just phoney. No pilot in his senses would be flying as low as that with thermo-nuclear bombs going off all around. He'd get burned up. [...] If that's meant to be the R.C.A. building, he's put Brooklyn Bridge on the New Jersey side, and the Empire State in the middle of Central Park.'
> She glanced at the catalogue. 'It doesn't say that it's New York.'
> 'Wherever it's meant to be, it's phoney,' he replied. [...]
> 'Don't you see anything of the religious angle here?' she asked. It was funny to her, because he went to church a lot and she had thought this exhibition would appeal to him. He took her arm. 'I'm not a religious man', he said.

In short, the whole exhibition is painted as a more 'phoney' than serious effort to deliver the spiritual solace people might be in need of — and it provides a cheap opportunity to upbraid modern art to boot. The only serious mention of God occurs earlier in the novel when Moira visits Dwight on his nuclear submarine. She begins by asking 'Can you visualize it, Dwight?' 'Visualize what?', he asks. 'All those cities, all those fields and farms, with nobody, and nothing left alive. Just nothing there. I simply can't take it in. [...] I don't suppose there'll ever be a movie made of them as they are now'. He replies, ever the realist:

> 'It wouldn't be possible. A cameraman couldn't live, as far as I can see. I guess nobody will ever know what the Northern Hemisphere looks like now, excepting God.' He paused. 'I think that's a good thing. You don't want to remember how a person looked when he was dead. [...]'
> 'It's too big,' she repeated. 'I can't take it in.'
> 'It's too big for me, too,' he replied. 'I can't really believe in it, just can't get used to the idea. I suppose it's lack of imagination.'

Despite the idea being too big for them, no anger or despair, religious, atheistic or otherwise, sets in; no existential doubt or deep-rooted psychological apprehension seems to trouble them, nor any thought of what might come after death. God and religion are token notions; God is at best some form of deistic presence looking down on his Creation with as much equanimity as possessed by the people that populate Shute's novel. This passage ties in neatly, incidentally, with Anders's contemporaneous lament that it is our very lack of imagination that will bring about our downfall as human species; clearly Shute has resolved with his novel to address and remedy that lack, but probing philosophical or religious reflection seems equally clearly irrelevant to that task.

In Pat Frank's *Alas, Babylon*, which is — lest we forget this rather inconspicuous fact — set in part of the American Bible belt, religion is accorded a similarly muted role, even if the title of the book is derived from the Revelation of St. John 18:10 in which the Apostle envisions a voice proclaiming the downfall of Babylon; we read there:

> [18:8] Therefore shall her plagues come in one day, death, and mourning, and famine; and she shall be utterly burned with fire. [...]
>
> [18:9] And the kings of the earth, who have committed fornication and lived deliciously with her, shall bewail her, and lament for her, when they shall see the smoke of her burning.
>
> [18:10] Standing afar off for the fear of her torment, saying, Alas, alas, that great city Babylon, that mighty city! For in one hour is thy judgment come.

It would be too facile, and perhaps also unfair to the author, to describe Frank's chief objective as, quasi-biblically, to admonish us to lead better lives in order to avoid corruption and resultant nuclear Armageddon. Despite the obvious biblical allusion contained in its title, Frank is careful not to let his novel appear religiously motivated or devotionally underpinned. The cataclysm is not brought on by God, nor is God invoked other than through a few unobtrusive references. The most interesting such instance is one in which we are referred once again to the theodicy question: in light of the fact that 'Helen's little girl' Peyton was blinded by looking directly at the nuclear mushroom, Fort Repose's doctor Daniel Gunn exclaims 'Oh, God! Why? Why to that child?'; this passage concludes:

> He looked and sounded like a rebellious Old Testament prophet. He looked and sounded half-mad. The worst thing that Randy could imagine, at that moment, was that Dan Gunn should lose his mental equilibrium. Randy said, 'God had nothing to do with it. This was strictly man-made.'[171]

Institutional religion by contrast does play a role in the plotline, but it moves to the fore only well into the second half of the novel when Frank describes the social reorganization that begins to take shape in the aftermath of the nuclear attack. We see Randy, a liberal who generally seems quite divorced from religious matters, encountering a notice posted at the town's square announcing interdenominational 'Easter Services'; 'all citizens of Fort Repose, of whatever faith, are invited to attend', he reads, with the notice signed by the reverends of the First Methodist Church, the Church of St. Paul's, the Timucuan County Baptist Church and the Afro-Repose Baptist Church (the reverend of the Episcopal Church, we are told, is missing due to his having been in Jacksonville on the day when the bombs struck). Nuclear war has miraculously succeeded not just in dispelling religious rivalry but also in overcoming the racial divide: the nuclear holocaust is the occasion that unites all faiths and races, making all men truly equal — so Frank's subliminal message. The notice also signifies the moment when Randy experiences a religious epiphany of sorts; the narrator comments:

> Randy wasn't much of a churchgoer. He had contributed to the church regu-

---

171 *Alas, Babylon*, p. 103; the subsequent passages pp. 190, 190–91, 225, 197, 215, 296, 307 and 310.

larly, but not of his time or himself. Now, reading this notice, he felt an unexpected thrill. Since The Day, he had lived in the imperative present, not daring to plan beyond the next meal of the next day. This bit of paper tacked on peeling white paint abruptly enlarged his perspective, as if, stumbling through a black tunnel, he saw, or thought he saw, a chink of light. If Man retained his faith in God, he might also retain faith in Man. He remembered words which for four months he had not heard, read, or uttered, the most beautiful words in the language, faith and hope. He had missed these words as he had missed other things. If possible, he would go to the service.

Indeed, more than just attending, Randy and Elizabeth McGovern are wed on Easter Sunday during sunrise service in Marines Park.

But Randy's — and the narrative's — more immediate concern is his and his fellow beings' survival. Four months into the new era Randy observes how mankind has been bombed back into a state of 'neolithic' primitivism (in keeping with Bertrand Russell's 'second possibility', 'the return to barbarism'); he comments, 'in four months [...] we've regressed four thousand years. More maybe. Four thousand years ago the Egyptians and Chinese were more civilized than [neighbouring] Pistolville is right now'. Faith in God and religion may be able to furnish a modicum of psychological hope and social cohesion, but humankind's physical salvation lies in the hands of Darwinian nature and natural selection. It is nature that is the true source of comfort, reassurance and even mercy, at least if we believe the novel's physician; thus when Helen and Randy express their concerns about the effects of radiation fallout, Doctor Gunn replies:

> 'Certainly some human genetic damage can be expected', Dan said. 'What will happen to the birth rate is anybody's guess. And yet, this is only nature's way of protecting the race. Nature is proving Darwin's law of natural selection. The defective bee, unable to cope with its environment, is rejected by nature before birth. I think this will be true of man. It is said that nature is cruel. I don't think so. Nature is just, and even merciful. By natural selection, nature will attempt to undo what man has done.'

No surprise then to find, by late October of year one after The Day, Gunn reporting to Randy that he has just delivered the first healthy baby. 'So what's so wonderful about delivering a baby?', Randy asks. Gunn replies: 'You see, this was the first live baby, full term. I had two other pregnancies that ended prematurely. Nature's way of protecting the race, I think, although you can't reach any statistical conclusion on the basis of three pregnancies. Anyway, now we know that there's going to be a human race'. Humanity's afterlife on Earth is secured, it seems. And it is secured despite 'Hell Day or Hydrogen Day or The Day' by the mercy of Nature rather than the grace of God. But Frank adds a final irony at novel's end when it transpires that the human race was hardly endangered at all, with many countries having escaped the nuclear holocaust and radiation fallout. No nuclear cloud inches its way down planet Earth's latitudes, as in Shute's *On the Beach*; here in *Alas, Babylon* the United States, with a population now estimated as no larger than formerly that of France, has hence been demoted to a minor power, with 'Thailand and Indonesia [...] contributing rice' to keep Americans alive and Venezuela supplying the oil to alleviate the fuel shortage.

In Shute's and Frank's novels, religion is social and conventional, not metaphysical. It is the collective glue that holds society together; it may represent a bond in people's lives, but it is one lacking in spiritual gravity and significance, despite their waiting for death as in *On the Beach*, or their (Darwinian) battle for survival as in *Alas, Babylon*. In the Death-of-God-theologian William Hamilton's words, these novels may be about the 'experience of the absence of God' but the characters in them hardly despair for it; or, in Thomas J. J. Altizer's words, God is in these narratives at best a 'language of absence, eclipse, and silence', at worst he is an irrelevance whose existence, or non-existence, is without practical import.

In Roshwald's *Level 7*, by contrast, religion does not exist even as a social convention: Level 7 has neither chapel nor (military) chaplain, there is no religious meditation room, and marriage is by bureaucratic and personal consent, but not sanctified by any kind of religious rite. Nonetheless, it is maybe precisely because Level 7 lacks an institutionalized religious practice that Officer PB X–127 gradually turns to metaphysics and religious reflection. Just days before he will be commanded to press the buttons that will spell disaster for millions of people on Earth, he mulls over the metaphysical ramifications of his position:

> I feel like an omniscient being, severed from contact with other human beings, but knowing all about what is going to happen. If God exists — in heaven, or in the centre of the earth — He must feel the same way. In seclusion He watches the impending disaster which is about to overtake the ant-like human beings. Watches with interest, but also with detachment.[172]

But the similarity of their situations brings home to him also God's quandary, his existential loneliness: 'But perhaps [God] envies [human beings] sometimes', PB X–127 muses; '[t]here they are, all the ants, running about, enjoying each other's company, planning, analysing, discussing, believing, criticising. And there He is — alone. Wiser, more powerful, but alone'. Two days later he confides to his diary:

> Shall I be like God before He created the world, sitting lonely in an empty universe? How cruel men were to create a God who is self-sufficient living a solitary life throughout eternity. Why have they condemned God, why have they condemned me, to such a lonely prison?

The lone (last) being is ever the prisoner of his fate, whether he is man or God. In search of a suitable linguistic equivalent for God's quandary, which is also his own, he comes up with a parable:

> The god wants to make a bargain with a butterfly for a day — but outside the caves, up there — and he offers the butterfly in return an eternal existence — down here. What do you say to that, butterfly? Will you agree to the bargain? It's a good one: eternity for one day of flying among the flowers.

But the butterfly rejects the offer. 'What is it saying?', PB X–127 asks:

> It says it will not exchange one day of happiness for eternal misery! Damnable butterfly! The audacity to refuse a god's bargain! To defy a god! To defy God!

---

172 *Level 7*, p. 90; the subsequent passages pp. 90, 92, 92–93, 93 and 141.

> I shall curse you, butterfly, you colourful hedonist, I shall curse you till the end of your days! It says something. It dares to answer! What is it? 'I do not mind your curses, O God, for my day is short.' It flies away. Butterfly! Butterfly! Listen to me, don't go away! Stay with me, I won't curse you. But stay here with me. Wait! Please stay!

If there is a God, PB X–127 is conveying to us by means of his parable, his position is hardly enviable. We need no Mephistophelian pact to come to the conclusion that living in utter solitude as Last Man or lone God is no better than living in Hell. But it also tells us that just to imagine being the Last Man, or a lone God, can drive one to insanity: accordingly we read in PB X–127's diary one week later that he just returned 'from the psychological department' where he spent the last week — 'apparently I was going mad'.

At the end of the novel and on the penultimate day of his life, October 11, PB X–127 enters into his diary:

> It is strangely ironical that we, PBX Command, should be killed by a gadget making a peaceful use of atomic energy. It does not seem fair. Divine justice, I always thought, was eye for eye, tooth for tooth. It should be bomb for bomb. Instead we are being killed by a piece of faulty machinery. Not really a warrior's death. Perhaps God intends it as a sort of joke. 'You killed with bombs', He says. 'You will be killed by peaceful radiation.' Or maybe He is a Christian God, and Christian charity inspires his acts: 'You killed with atomic missiles,' He says, 'but I shall help you over to the other side with a reactor.' What am I talking about? God? Reactor?

Of course, God can only make jokes if he exists; the only divine justice — and irony — here seems to be that, with PB X-127 breathing the last gasp of mankind, it has become irrelevant whether God, playing mad jokes and parroting the 'Insane World Creator' of Klingemann's mad narrator in *The Nightwatches of Bonaventura*, exists or not. Whether we call it divine justice, providence, destiny, fate, charity, chance, accident, irony, or mockery, it all makes no difference now that mankind is about to expire: if God is but a figment of man's imagination or fancy, as some philosophers have held, God must die when the Last Man stops thinking.

God plays a role in another regard, too. Roshwald's novel is deliberately studded with references and allusions to the philosopher Leibniz and his notion — very much contested, as we have already seen — of the best of all possible worlds. Indeed, in a final twist of irony Level 7 is described by its occupants as the 'best of all possible worlds'.[173] PB X–127 relates:

> X–107 is doing his best to get me out of my depression. He uses a peculiar method: discussing various arrangements on Level 7 and trying to find a rational explanation and a justification for each. [...] After these discussions we usually arrive at the conclusion that arrangements on Level 7 have been made in the best of all possible ways. Any alternative arrangements which we think up turn out, on examination, to be less perfect. The logical conclusion would seem to be that Level 7 is the best of all possible levels, the best of all possible worlds.

---

173 Ibid., p. 31 (but also frequently thereafter); the subsequent passages pp. 31, 39 and 59.

This Leibnizian leitmotif, which includes such statements as 'it was necessary for [PB X–107] to believe in the inevitability of the arrangements on Level 7, because only in that way could he console himself for their disadvantages', of course revisits the dilemma of theodicy that we have encountered at various points in this study, first and foremost in the context of the earthquake of Lisbon. Here, in Roshwald's novel, it is of course no longer some invisible God or uncontrollable Nature but a man-made military-technological command structure that brings on the calamity, making humans themselves into a god unto their own — but a god who ultimately succeeds only in destroying himself, with no prospect of survival or salvation. In Roshwald's twentieth-century nuclear anti-theodicy there can be no question of balancing good and evil in the best of all possible worlds: by the end of the novel, there is no longer a (human) world, bad, good, better or best. God has been converted into the devil-like Strontium 90 of the fairy tale written by another occupant of Level 7 as reading material for the future generations of Level–7 children that should have survived beyond 'A-Day' if only fate had been more favourable; the fairy tale reads (in excerpt):

> Once upon a time, many years ago, there lived on Level 7 a little child called Ch–777. He was a nice little boy. 'Tell me,' he used to say, 'please tell me what goes on up there.' And when his parents heard him ask that they were frightened, for they did not want even to speak of the hell up there. [...] The higher you went up from Level 7, they said, the closer you came to Him whose name must not be mentioned. He could not be seen, and He could not be heard, and He could not be touched, and He could not be smelled, but up there His power was infinite. [...] His real name [...] was (she said in a whisper) Strontium 90.

Perhaps unsurprisingly, Shute and Frank were more successful in reaching out to a mass audience than Roshwald; *On the Beach* and *Alas, Babylon* were not just well received in their time, but went on to become oft-cited 'classics' within the genre of science fiction. Roshwald's novel by contrast is perhaps exceptional in that it seeks to include, especially in its latter sections, a degree of philosophical reflection that is less typical for the genre. What is typical for science fiction is that we often find it opposed to highbrow literature; as a form of popular fiction it is taken by many to pander to the tastes of a broad and — and in some critics' opinion — unsophisticated audience, providing purportedly shallow entertainment rather than deep intellectual stimulation, hence Anders's deprecatory comments about science fiction authors cited earlier. I do not dispute that such distinctions as lowbrow versus highbrow, popular versus elitist, and the like, may have some appeal, as simplistic as they are. But since the advent of Postmodernism such facile distinctions have by and large lost their usefulness. One of science fiction's most vocal advocates — as signalled by the first of the two mottos to this chapter — was Leslie Fiedler who instigated the turn to Postmodernism in the late 1960s. In his seminal 1969 article 'Cross the Border — Close the Gap' he is among the first to dismantle and debunk the dated dissection of culture into low and high, entertainment and elite art, writing:

> Reversing the process typical of Modernism [...] Post-Modernism provides an example of a young, mass audience urging certain aging, reluctant critics onward toward the abandonment of their former elite status in return for a freedom the prospect of which more terrifies than elates them. In fact, Post-Modernism implies the closing of the gap between critic and audience, too, if by critic one understands 'leader of taste' and by audience 'follower'. But most importantly of all, it implies the closing of the gap between artist and audience, or at any rate, between professional and amateur in the realm of art.[174]

This closing of the gap has a near-Nietzschean and apocalyptic ring to it, as he goes on:

> We have, however, entered quite another time, apocalyptic, antirational, blatantly romantic and sentimental; an age dedicated to joyous misology and prophetic irresponsibility; one, at any rate, distrustful of self-protective irony and too great self-awareness. If criticism is to survive at all, therefore, which is to say, if criticism is to remain or become useful, viable, relevant, it must be radically altered from the models provided by Croce or Leavis or Eliot or Erich Auerbach.

While those old 'models', to which Anders still subscribed as did Adorno and Horkheimer in their writings about the culture industry, have long been ditched in what one might term 'high criticism and literary theory', market practice has in many ways held on to this questionable divide. Science fiction is thus subject to an in-built dilemma. While the bulk of its titles may be classified as popular entertainment without much claim to literary artistry, there are richly literary texts among science fiction's canon; by the same token, among its mass audience's most avid readers are many who would consider themselves highbrow intellectuals, myself included. But in terms of marketing practice little has changed since Fiedler's day: in most bookstores I have visited over the decades, I have never once encountered what I consider highbrow science fiction — such truly sophisticated (and difficult to read) works as Günter Grass's *The Rat* (*Die Rättin*) or Arno Schmidt's *School for Atheists* (*Die Schule der Atheisten*) — on the bookshelves designated 'Science Fiction' or 'Fantasy Fiction', or whatever equivalent category the bookstore proprietor might favour.[175] Despite criticism's postmodern rebellion texts by such authors continue to be considered too intellectual and too heavy, if not to say too overwrought, to gratify the middling expectations ascribed to the average

---

174 'Cross the Border — Close the Gap', p. 287; the subsequent quote pp. 271–72.

175 Just weeks after having written this passage, I found a similar lament regarding Arno Schmidt voiced by Kai U. Jürgens in his article '"Wir sind hier nich [*sic*] modern!" Arno Schmidts *Schule der Atheisten* als Science-Fiction-Roman', in *Bargfelder Bote*, 393–94 (October 2015), 15–25; tellingly, to set the tone Jürgens begins his article with a quotation drawn from an article by Dietmar Dath in the 11 January 2014 edition of the *Frankfurter Allgemeine Zeitung* that reads (in my translation): 'Is it even known that Schmidt was the greatest ever ['der größte je vorhandene'] German-language science fiction author, a creator of worlds equal to Robert A. Heinlein, a doubter of worlds equal to Philip K. Dicks, and a spoofer of worlds equal to Kurt Vonnegut — and a better stylist than all three of them put together' (p. 15).

reader of science fiction — inasmuch as such an 'average' reader exists. Indeed, Wikipedia's 960-title comprehensive listing of 'apocalyptic and post-apocalyptic fiction' features neither David Markson nor Günter Grass nor Arno Schmidt, not to mention Jens Rehn whom we mentioned earlier and who is a near-inconnu even in his home country. In Wikipedia's shorter list of 'nuclear holocaust fiction' at least we can find two of the four post-nuclear-holocaust narratives written by Schmidt (*Schwarze Spiegel/Dark Mirrors* and *Die Schule der Atheisten/School for Atheists*; but not listed are his novels *Die Gelehrtenrepublik/Republica Intelligentsia* and *Kaff auch Mare Crisium/Boondocks–Moondocks*). Nor is there any mention of Grass and Rehn, both of whose novels can be classified as 'nuclear holocaust fiction'. Of course, my reader will surely want to interject, these are German authors and German-language texts; what can one expect of English-language encyclopedias? But language seems not to be the issue: Robert Merle's French *Malevil* has an entry in both Wikipedia listings, yet Schmidt's and Grass's German works are no less available in English translation than Merle's novel. And Markson's *Wittgenstein's Mistress* was written in English and published in the United States. What Markson's, Grass's and Schmidt's works have in common, however, is that they offer intellectually demanding and artistically elaborate (if not to say convoluted in the case of Grass's *The Rat* and Schmidt's *School for Atheists*) visions of humankind's demise and post-apocalypse afterlife. Although they are not totally devoid of the absorbing yarn that characterizes the more popular specimens of science fiction, their texts are difficult reads, even for the most astute and proficient of learned readers in their source language, and their yarn is more of a challenge to fathom than many readers will like. What makes them of especial interest for our particular purpose, however, is that they tend to engage more with philosophical and theological topics. Their closest English-language counterpart in this respect as well as in terms of technical artistry and intellectualism is Aldous Huxley's *Ape and Essence*. It is with this text that I shall continue my discussion before closing with an analysis of three of the above-mentioned German texts, one each by Rehn, Schmidt, and Grass.

While Wikipedia's long-list 'of apocalyptic and post-apocalyptic fiction' itemizes hundreds of science fiction texts, surely few among them were intended to cultivate as profound a philosophical and theological reflection as Huxley's 1948 novel *Ape and Essence*. Presenting himself in the 1930s essay cited above as one of the 'less extravagant pessimists' who 'foresee only partial destruction and a return to primitive barbarism' even before the first nuclear bombs exploded, *Ape and Essence* — set in a post-World-War-III California bombed back into a state of civilizational crudeness — shows how what is left of the United States has regressed to a form of religious autocracy and Devil-worship. Although the novel in many ways comes across as a more farcical than realistic take on nuclear Armageddon, there is a serious message embedded in its madness, namely to conjure up a vision — as cynical and exaggerated as it may be — of the metaphysical and spiritual damage nuclear warfare would be certain to inflict on the survivors. The novel's futuristic 'nuclear core' is contained in a present-day narrative casing: Beginning on the day of Gandhi's assassination in 1947, *Ape and Essence* presents the story of a nameless first-person narrator and Hollywood hack-writer who later that year happens to chance upon a mysterious film script itself also entitled 'Ape and Essence' which had been rejected by a Hollywood film studio. The narrator and his colleague Bob Briggs are keen to find out more about this script's enigmatic author, a certain William Tallis; after locating his presumed whereabouts on a ranch in the outback of the Californian desert, they arrive there only to find that Tallis had died six weeks earlier. With the scriptwriter's intentions thus condemned to remain shrouded in mystery, the second part of the novel gives us '"The Script" [...] as I found it, without change and without comment', as the narrator informs us.[176] Occupying one hundred and thirty pages, some five sixths of the novel overall, the script relates the initially rather mannered tale of a ship of scientists from New Zealand who visit California in the year 2108, a century or so after the northern hemisphere had been obliterated by a nuclear Third World War. New Zealand, we are told caustically, survived 'not [...] for any humanitarian reason, but simply because, like Equatorial Africa, it was too remote to be worth anybody's while to obliterate';[177] so now, one century later, the 'members of the New Zealand Re-Discovery Expedition to North America' make their way across the Pacific to discover whether any life remains on the North American continent all the while their African counterparts start 'working their way down the Nile and across the Mediterranean' to explore what remains of Europe. And indeed, as the New Zealanders find out to their surprise, some Californians had managed to survive the nuclear holocaust; not only that, their progeny have since succeeded in creating a new kind of society, an inverted one of sorts, yet one that shows itself to be unexpectedly hostile to the visitors from afar. With the exception of the biologist Dr. Alfred Poole, all of the scientists who venture onto Californian soil are either killed or driven back to their ship. Poole, however, who has attached himself to a young Californian female savage named Loola, remains behind; and what he discovers is a brutish society that has reverted to a perverted form of religious belief, worshipping not God but rather Satan in the guise of Belial. In a tone of retrospective propheticism, the Arch-Vicar of the tribe gives Poole his assessment of the evolution of man in the lead-up to 'the Thing', the name they have given to the Third World War:

> 'And remember this [...]: even without synthetic glanders, even without the atomic bomb, Belial could have achieved all His purposes. A little more slowly, perhaps, but just as surely, men would have destroyed themselves by destroying the world they lived in. They couldn't escape. He had them skewered on both His horns. If they managed to wriggle off the horn of total war, they would find themselves impaled on starvation. And if they were starving, they would be tempted to resort to war. And just in case they should try to find a peaceful and rational way out of their dilemma, He had another subtler horn of self-destruction all ready for them. From the very beginning of the industrial revolution He foresaw that men would be made so overwhelmingly bumptious by the miracles of their own technology that they would soon lose all sense of reality. And that's precisely what happened. These wretched

---

176 *Ape and Essence* (London: Vintage, 2005), p. 23.
177 Ibid., p. 28; both subsequent passages also p. 28.

slaves of wheels and ledgers began to congratulate themselves on being the Conquerors of Nature. Conquerors of Nature, indeed! In actual fact, of course, they had merely upset the equilibrium of Nature and were about to suffer the consequences. Just consider what they were up to during the century and a half before the Thing. Fouling the rivers, killing off the wild animals, destroying the forests, washing the topsoil into the sea, burning up an ocean of petroleum, squandering the minerals it had taken the whole of geological time to deposit. An orgy of criminal imbecility. And they called it Progress.'[178]

'Technological progress', the Arch-Vicar goes on to declare, 'provides people with the instruments of ever more indiscriminate destruction, while the myth of political and moral progress serves as the excuse for using those means to the very limit'.

From the perspective of a post-World-War-III society that continues to suffer from radiation-induced physical malformations even one hundred years after the conflict, the history of mankind, culminating in the twentieth-century nuclear holocaust, cannot be explained by any positive theistic model of divine intervention; only a Satanic rewriting of religion can account for how a combination of economic irrationalism and nationalistic bigotry could lead mankind to self-destruct against all metaphysical and practical reason: 'I tell you, my dear sir, [...] the longer you study modern history, the more evidence you find of Belial's Guiding Hand', the Arch-Vicar lectures, adding: 'Progress! I tell you, that was too rare an invention to have been the product of any merely human mind — too fiendishly ironical! There had to be Outside Help for that. There had to be the Grace of Belial'. But progress alone was not sufficient, nationalism needed to be added to the mix in order to produce the deadly concoction that would lead to nuclear self-eradication, the Arch-Vicar underscores; 'Progress and Nationalism — those were the two great ideas he put into their heads',

> Progress — the theory that you can get something for nothing; [...] the theory that you alone understand the meaning of history; [...] the theory that, in the teeth of all experience, you can foresee all the consequences of your present actions; the theory that Utopia lies just ahead... [...] And then there was Nationalism — the theory that the state you happen to be subject to is the only true god, and that all other states are false gods. [...] The fact that such theories came, at a given moment of history, to be universally accepted is the best proof of Belial's existence...

'The lunatic dreams'[179] of 'Progress' and 'Nationalism' are the two wellsprings of Satanic evil that ultimately, according to Huxley's avatar, the Arch-Vicar of this new devil-worshipping race, led to the Third World War and the annihilation of (most of) mankind. 'Each is intrinsically absurd and each leads to courses of action that are demonstrably fatal', the Arch-Vicar catechizes, 'and yet the whole of civilized humanity decides, almost suddenly, to accept these notions or guides to conflict. Why? And at Whose suggestion, Whose prompting, Whose inspiration? There can only be one answer.' 'You mean, you think it was . . . it was the Devil?', Dr. Poole asks back; the Arch-Vicar's response is unequivocal: 'Who else desires the

---

178 Ibid., pp. 92–93; the subsequent five citations are all from pages 93 and 94.
179 Ibid., p. 97; the subsequent passages pp. 95 and 98.

degradation and destruction of the human race?' No wonder then that the survivors have decided to redirect their religious zeal to the worship of the Devil instead of God. God is dead and the Devil alive: 'The more one thinks about the workings of His Providence, the more unfathomably marvellous it seems', the Arch-Vicar concludes.

The novel was not well received. The scholar Sanford E. Marovitz has remarked how *Ape and Essence* was 'received poorly by many readers, even devotees of Huxley's earlier work', with reviewers 'frequently recoil[ing] from the horrid forecast of the book'.[180] Even the renowned science fiction author and critic I. F. Clarke observed that *Brave New World* seemed to him 'almost idyllic in comparison with the often unrestrained savageness of *Ape and Essence*'.[181] The critic Rudolf B. Schmerl similarly judged the two novels' relative merits thus:

> Contrasted with *Brave New World*, *Ape and Essence* is an almost incredibly bad novel. It has none of the earlier fantasy's careful construction; its symbolism is labored, crude, and spoiled by the unnecessary explanations of the narrator; its originality of form seems to be indifference to form itself rather than indication of interest in experimentation with it.[182]

Others point out that *Ape and Essence* is confusing not just in terms of its aesthetic form, but also in that Huxley leaves it — perhaps intentionally — unclear whether his primary intention is to warn of the hazard of the nuclear arms race or to criticize humankind for its political, economic, ecological and humanitarian failings. After all, in the post-Hiroshima 'Foreword' that he wrote for the 1946 edition of *Brave New World* Huxley seems to downplay the danger of complete annihilation through nuclear warfare, writing: 'Assuming [...] that we are capable of learning as much from Hiroshima as our forefathers learned from Magdeburg, we may look forward to a period, not indeed of peace, but of limited and only partially ruinous warfare'.[183] (Magdeburg was a city destroyed during the Thirty Years War, the implication being, as Huxley details in his argument, that for a certain period following the 'unimaginable horrors of the Thirty Years War [...] politicians and generals of Europe consciously resisted the temptation to use their military resources to the limits of destructiveness'.) Instead, Huxley asserts,

> during that period it may be assumed that nuclear energy will be harnessed to industrial uses. The result, pretty obviously, will be a series of economic and social changes unprecedented in rapidity and completeness. All the existing patterns of human life will be disrupted and new patterns will have to be improvised to conform with the nonhuman fact of atomic power.

But here too a certain equivocalness remains, with Huxley also noting: 'It is probable

---

[180] 'Aldous Huxley and the Nuclear Age: *Ape and Essence* in Context', *Journal of Modern Literature*, 18 (Winter 1992), 115–25 (p. 116); the second half of Marovitz's quotation is a citation lifted from an article by Donald Watt.

[181] *Voices Prophesying War* (London: Oxford University Press, 1966), p. 196.

[182] 'The Two Future Worlds of Aldous Huxley', *PMLA*, 77 (June 1962), 328–34 (p. 334).

[183] 'Author's Foreword (to the 1946 edition)', in *Brave New World* (New York, London, Toronto: Alfred A. Knopf / Everyman's Library, 2013), pp. 223–32 (p. 228); the subsequent quotes pp. 228, 229 and 231.

that all the world's governments will be more or less completely totalitarian even before the harnessing of atomic energy; that they will be totalitarian during and after the harnessing seems almost certain', with the result that, while in *Brave New World* 'I projected it six hundred years into the future, today it seems quite possible that the horror may be upon us within a single century. That is, if we refrain from blowing ourselves to smithereens in the interval', thus creating the apocalypse that nuclear warfare makes possible, as Huxley observed in the 1959 lecture he gave in Santa Barbara (the lecture we cited earlier in this chapter in which he discusses Bertrand Russell's three options of humankind's 'short-range prospects'):

> The tempered optimism is the most prominent view of the future, but another interesting fact is that with the coming of the hydrogen bomb human technology has re-introduced into the thinking of the West the old eschatological idea of the end of the world. The sudden and catastrophic ending of the world about which the Apocalyptic literature talks — a notion we had come to regard as untenable and absurd — has become once more a real possibility. Again, whether there shall be an indefinite future or whether there shall not is up to us.[184]

Clearly Huxley's concerns in *Brave New World* and *Ape and Essence* are first and foremost political. But what is often overlooked, or perhaps conveniently skirted, is that *Ape and Essence* is as much also about theology and the dangers of religious fanaticism. Critics have rightly stressed the interlocking and complementary nature of Huxley's literary and non-literary writings in any given period. The 1940s when Huxley wrote *Ape and Essence* are no exception; we just cited the 1946 'Foreword' to *Brave New World* as one such instance. Another 1946 publication was Huxley's *The Perennial Philosophy*, a treatise half-compendium, half-commentary on key concepts of Western and Eastern philosophy and religion. Here Huxley picks up explicitly on some of the philosophical and metaphysical issues that lie at the heart of *Ape and Essence*. Huxley asks in this philosophical work for instance whether we can imagine circumstances through which the 'passions' of 'anger and hatred, pride, cruelty and fear' might ever be stirred to such a degree that they would make people willing and able 'to sacramentalize actions whose psychological by-products are [...] completely God-eclipsing', thereby creating a 'distorted notion of the universe'.[185] This is precisely what happens in *Ape and Essence*'s post-World-War-III California where the survivors' anger about 'the Thing' has eclipsed all belief in a benign divinity, allowing the 'Grace of God' to be usurped by the 'Grace of Belial'. In this new society, Belial reigns supreme because the small colony of Californian degenerates has lost all trust in a God who was either not willing or not able to prevent the total annihilation of mankind. In a very modern guise *Ape and Essence* thus reopens the question of theodicy which we have encountered so often in this study: how can a benign and all-powerful God sanction the degree of material destruction, physical suffering and psychological torment that is brought on the world by a man-made holocaust such as nuclear war. The post-World-War-III Californian survivors of *Ape and Essence* have only one answer: since such a benign

---

184 'The World's Future', in *The Human Situation. Lectures at Santa Barbara*, pp. 86–101 (p. 91).
185 *The Perennial Philosophy*, pp. 312–13.

God cannot have been in command — or else He would have thwarted the nuclear confrontation — it can only be a Satan (or, as the colony calls him, Belial) who controls our existence. What follows 'logically', as it were, from this premise is that only Satan can be the true object of our veneration and worship, so the reasoning of the Californian Arch-Vicar and his confrères.

Similarly, Chapter 24 of *The Perennial Philosophy* covers 'Ritual, Symbol, Sacrament', concepts about which the members of the post-apocalyptic Californian community in *Ape and Essence* seem singularly obsessed. At times *Ape and Essence* reads like an illustration to Huxley's observation in *The Perennial Philosophy* that 'very large numbers of men and women have an ineradicable desire for rites and ceremonies'.[186] It likewise illustrates how 'a great deal of ritualistic religion is not spirituality', but rather 'occultism' and a form of 'idolatry' that can lead the believer 'away from deliverance' rather than towards it. Huxley adds: 'There is another disadvantage inherent in any system of organized sacramentalism, and that is that it gives to the priestly caste a power which is all too natural for them to abuse. [...] The possession of such power is a standing temptation to use it for individual satisfaction and corporate aggrandizement'. If critics are right to concur that *Ape and Essence* is testament to Huxley's disillusionment with nationalism and global politics, we must add that it is also testament to Huxley's disillusionment with organized religion and his growing apprehension about the instrumentalization of God and religion that he sees as an intrinsic aspect of Christianity's 'organized sacramentalism'. Perhaps somewhat ironically, Huxley comes back to reflect some two decades later on the fact that what he describes in *Ape and Essence*, namely the 'maniacal aberration' of collective persecution for religious purposes, is structurally not that dissimilar from the non-religious forms of persecution that dominate in our own technocratic age; he thus writes in his 1963 essay on *Literature and Science* about religious believers:

> Only too frequently, it is true, they took their theories too seriously, mistook poetical fancies for established truths, picturesque metaphors for reality, the verbiage of philosophizing *littérateurs* for the word of God. When this happened, disasters inevitably followed. Obeying the dictates of an unrealistic anthropology and world-view, they embarked upon courses of personal and collective insanity — frightful self-torture and the equally frightful persecution of heretics; the repudiation of instinctual life and the sadistic torturing of wretched women accused of witchcraft; puritanism and the launching of crusades, the waging of hideously savage wars of religion. The notions *we* take too seriously are not the same as those which drove our fathers into their maniacal aberrations. But, though the causes differ, the results, at least on the collective level, are identical. Their unrealistic theories of man's nature and the nature of the world made it mandatory for them to bully, persecute and kill — always in the name of God. We too kill, persecute and bully, but not in order to propitiate Allah or to gratify the Holy Trinity. Our collective paranoia is organized in the name of the idolatrously worshipped Nation or the Divine Party. The misused notions, the overhauled words and phrases are new; but the resultant slaughters and oppressions are dismally familiar.[187]

---

186 *The Perennial Philosophy*, p. 308; the subsequent quotes pp. 307, 308 and 309–10.
187 A further irony about this passage is that, with me writing some 50 years later in 2015, it is sad

If Huxley's *Ape and Essence* demonstrates anything, it is that twentieth-century secular novels of nuclear apocalypse don't lag behind their epical precursors in terms of religious symbolism and import. The bleakest post-Hiroshima confirmation thereof is provided less by *Ape and Essence*, however, than by the German writer Jens Rehn's apocalyptic novel *The Children of Saturn* (*Die Kinder des Saturn*, as yet untranslated into English). Published in the same year as Roshwald's *Level 7* and Frank's *Alas, Babylon*, *The Children of Saturn* is another representative of 'shelter fiction', and like *Level 7* it is presented in diary form. Rehn's sadly neglected novel (it enjoyed only one further reprint in 1975) provides a chilling outlook of unparalleled hopelessness and despair by ending with humankind's complete extinction through physical deterioration resulting from nuclear fallout. At the opening of the novel, only three persons have survived the Third World War, a doctor and a young couple, the pregnant Eskimo woman Maljutka and her partner Bruce; they had taken shelter in a disused underground mine shaft in an unspecified location on the North American continent, presumably close to the Canadian coast, but the locale is nowhere stated explicitly. Anticipating a nuclear holocaust, the doctor had had the foresight to create an underground bunker equipped with everything needed for survival. But months into their involuntary exile deep below the earth's surface in what is at one point evocatively called their 'Noah's ship of concrete' ('Noah-Betonschiff'),[188] the men's bodies begin to mutate; radiation sickness is taking its toll despite the bunker's subterranean isolation. The doctor's brain goes into decline all the while his sick and aging body miraculously starts to recover and restore itself to full health. The physically powerful but less intellectual Bruce, by contrast, begins to turn intellectual all the while his body starts to rot literally on the bone. The woman Maljutka, meanwhile, seems to remain unchanged and unaffected. When they return to the surface months later, all they find is a landscape in ruins:

> Inland the denuded mountain range in the South, between its foothills and the river's estuary the horizontal line, the flat plain of the city without silhouette. In the town centre the churches and administrative high-rises, [...] between them the rays of the motorways, interrupted only by the urban sprawl of suburbia. Now swept empty, a void plain on which nothing could be seen except its boundary with the sky, a straight line carefully drawn with a ruler. [Bruce] was not surprised, nor was he shocked. He knew this is how it would be. He had had time enough to intuit, to ponder and, finally, to know. But hope? He smiled with an immovable countenance.
>
> [Landeinwärts der kahle Höhenzug im Süden, zwischen seinem Ausläufer und der Flußmündung der glatte Strich, die platte Ebene der Stadt ohne Schattenriß. Im Zentrum die Kirchen und Verwaltungshochhäuser [...] zwischen ihnen die Strahlen der Ausfallstraßen, unterbrochen nur von den modernen Hochsiedlungen der Vororte. Jetzt eine ausgeräumte, gefegte Ebene, auf der

to have to note that some religious faithful around the globe have once again returned to 'kill[ing], persecut[ing] and bully[ing] [...] in order to propitiate Allah' and other divinities, religious and political; indeed, as Huxley says, 'the resultant slaughters and oppressions are dismally familiar'.

188 Jens Rehn, *Die Kinder des Saturn* (Darmstadt: Luchterhand, 1959), p. 112; as indicated it was republished in 1975 in the series 'Science-Fiction Classics' by the publisher Heyne. The subsequent passages pp. 33 and 7.

nichts zu sehen war als nur ihre Grenze gegen den Himmel, ein sorgfältiger Linealstrich. [Bruce] wunderte sich nicht und erschrak auch nicht. Er hatte gewußt, daß es so sein würde. Ihm war genügend Zeit gegeben worden, um es zu ahnen, zu bedenken und schließlich zu wissen. Doch die Hoffnung? Er lächelte, ohne daß sich sein Gesicht bewegte.]

At the end of the novel Maljutka's health proves to be illusory; she dies in childbirth just after delivering a stillborn mutated baby, half fish, half bird. The doctor, now reduced to a healthy but brainless automaton, finds Bruce dead, what remains of his body putrefying on the rock he always sat on in deep thought, sitting like Rodin's 'Thinker' pondering his fate. Towards the book's conclusion we see the doctor in his increasing mental derangement planting the cherries, pineapples, vegetables, ham and gulash that he has taken from the bunker's store of tinned foods; in the end, finding his companions dead, the dimwitted Last Man that he has become departs for some unknown destination.

Like Huxley's *Ape and Essence*, Rehn's gruesome depiction of the final months of this trinity of last men and woman is methodically shot through with religious imagery and symbolism. Whereas the text alludes variously to the biblical motif of Noah's Ark, with which the mine shaft is explicitly identified, it is not this that dominates the novel's religious scaffold, but rather the one-page semi-paratextual 'Preamble' ('Vorspann'), an English approximation of which might read:

THE WORD
I   Our LORD GOD then looked upon Earth and, lo!, she was corrupted. For all Flesh had corrupted His Path on Earth.
II And the Elect thereupon spoke unto one another, saw the Signs and went forth to build a Vessel of Stone,
III and they made Chambers therein, sealed them from within and from without, and buried the Vessel deep below the Earth;
IV also together gathered they all Manner of Provender and Implement, so as to sustain them in said Vessel when the Time arriveth.
V   And that Time arrivéd, and all Flesh that was quick and animate was laid waste, all Fish and Worm and all Manner of Beast,
VI and all Men.
VII The Earth was set aflame with all its Flowers and Trees up unto Heaven, one hundred Fathoms high and low,
VIII and Nothing lived on Earth but those Men in the Vessel of Stone, whom the LORD GOD graced with Mercy,
IX and so also their Provender and Implement.
X   And the LORD GOD saw that he
XI had done well.

[DAS WORT
I   Da sahe GOTT, der HERR auff Erden, und siehe sie war verderbet. Denn alles Fleisch hatte seinen Weg verderbet auff Erden.
II Und die Ausgewählten sprachen untereinander, deuteten die Zeichen und gingen hin, einen Kasten zu machen aus Stein,
III und sie macheten Kammern darein, verpichteten ihn innen und außwendig, und den Kasten vergruben sie tief inner der Erden;
IV auch sammelten sie allerley Speys und Gerätschaft, auff daß es ihnen wohl

	ergehe in dem Kasten zu der Zeit.
V	Und die Zeit kam, und alles Fleisch ging unter, alles, was da kreucht und fleucht, alle Fische, Wurm und Getier,
VI	und auch alle Menschen.
VII	Die Erde verbrennete sammt allen Blumen und Bäumen bis in den Himmel, an die hundert Klafter hoch und tief,
VIII	und lebete nichts mehr auff Erden als nur die Menschen in dem Kasten aus Stein, mit denen GOTT, der HERR sich erbarmet hatte,
IX	sammt ihrer Speys und Gerät.
X	Und GOTT, der HERR sahe, daß er wohl
XI	getan hatte.]

Here too, like in Roshwald's *Level 7*, theological ironies abound. The two principal ones are, first — inasmuch as this 'Preamble' supplies the central exegetical framework for the narrative overall — that it is 'God' himself who, 'graced with Mercy', deploys the nuclear conflagration through which he has decided to punish a Babylonian humankind for its corruption and descent into sin; the obvious inversion of the Old Testament Creation parable is underscored by the closing eleventh pronouncement that 'he had done well'. And second that, contrary to the promise of survival connoted by the biblical motif of Noah's Ark, these three surviving but mutating adults as well as their offspring, the stillborn monster, are *not* rescued by their underground stone Ark. Quite the inverse, they are destined to die a death of frightful decay no less agonizing, and perhaps even more protracted, than what their fellow humans must have suffered above when the nuclear holocaust was unleashed. However much he is invoked as a powerful presence in the novel's 'Preamble', in the core narrative itself God is conspicuous through his absence; he represents at best a silent presence who has opted not to intervene in mankind's demise, at worst an existential void. What is more, the suggestive juxtaposition of 'Preamble' and core narrative creates a vision of God as a cruel and callous avenger whose grace and mercy it is to destroy even the elect. In the end, no one is spared, no one survives. There is no deliverance, no salvation, and no expectation of Last Judgment. Nor is there a Noah who could procreate a new and better mankind. The biblical narrative of the divinely elect Last Man Noah and his kin who are called upon to repopulate the Earth after the Deluge is comprehensively dismantled, debunked and subverted.

This ability to repopulate the Earth after a nuclear deluge is, as has emerged variously over the course of this study, one of the dividing lines between true narratives of the end and narratives of survival and continuation, or what I have called terminal and semi-terminal narratives. Mary Shelley's *The Last Man* was unique not just because it was the first text in European literary history to annihilate the human species (through a global natural pandemic, as we recall), but also because, with Verney being the only human being left alive at the novel's conclusion, the reader is given no indication how mankind might yet manage to procreate and survive. Of course, Verney might yet locate his Eve somewhere on the Mediterranean coast, but the novel's conclusion does not hold out much promise in this regard. Naturally, the survival of mankind hinges on the existence of at least one pair of a species, a male and a female, and their ability to reproduce and multiply: this was the idea behind Noah's Ark, of which Verney's small vessel — 'the tiny bark, freighted with Verney' (and his dog), as the novel's last line tells us — is but an atrophied and dysfunctional miniature. The *sine qua non* of both Sonnenberg's and Grainville's epics of the end, *Donatoa* and *Le Dernier Homme*, is precisely the ability, or indeed inability, to reproduce (as it is in P. D. James's 1992 novel *The Children of Men* and its subsequent 2006 film adaptation by Alfonso Cuarón). The trigger for the trumpet call that would set in motion the Day of Reckoning was, in both *Donatoa* and *Le Dernier Homme*, either the infertility of the Last Man and Last Woman, entailing their inability to propagate their species, or their conscious decision no longer to do so. This is also the theme on which Arno Schmidt's early nuclear post-apocalyptic narrative hinges, *Dark Mirrors* (*Schwarze Spiegel*), published in 1951.

Without knowledge of one another two human beings, one man and one woman, have survived the 1950s nuclear Armageddon. The story commences on 1 May 1960, five years after World War III was fought with hydrogen bombs that have reduced Europe to a largely radioactive wasteland. (The first U.S. test of a hydrogen bomb took place in 1952, incidentally, one year after *Dark Mirrors* was published!) At the narrative's opening, we encounter the male protagonist, a cross between James Fenimore Cooper's Leatherstocking character Natty Bumppo and Daniel Defoe's Robinson Crusoe, scouting through North Germany's Luneburg Heath on his bicycle in search of the ideal location for a new fixed domicile. However, his movements are restricted to the few remaining non-radioactive corridors through the otherwise depeopled heartland of Europe. He is a misanthropic loner who relishes his unanticipated solitude: 'Natty was right: forests are the most beautiful! And I was only in my early forties; if everything went well (?) I could ramble the earth void of man for a long while yet: I needed No One!' ('Natty hatte schon recht: Wälder sind das Schönste! Und ich war erst Anfang Vierzig; wenn Alles gut ging (?) konnte ich noch lange über die menschenleere Erde schweifen: ich brauchte Niemanden!').[189] Conveniently for him, not just mankind has been decimated but also most kinds of insects, especially the annoying kinds. Ironically, Jonathan Schell observed in 1982 in *The Fate of the Earth* — whose Part One was suggestively titled 'A Republic of Insects and Grass' — that it is precisely the pesky phylophagous species that possess very high tolerances toward nuclear contamination and 'so could be expected to survive disproportionately, and then to multiply greatly in the aftermath of an attack'.[190] In Schmidt's tale, by contrast, it is the more likeable animal species, such as foxes, deer, horses, cows, wild pigs and birds, that have

---

189 Arno Schmidt, *Dark Mirrors*, in *Nobodaddy's Children*, vol. 2 of *Collected Early Fiction 1949–1964*, trans. by John E. Wood (Normal, IL: Dalkey Archives Press, 1995), pp. 177–236 (p. 189); German quotations are from *Schwarze Spiegel*, *Bargfelder Ausgabe* I.1 (Zurich: Haffmans, 1987), pp. 199–260 (p. 211). The subsequent passages pp. 179–80, 198 and 220–21 (*Schwarze Spiegel*, pp. 201–02, 221 and 244).

190 Schell, *The Fate of the Earth*, p. 63.

— equally conveniently for the narrator — survived, although no explanation is given for this biologically rather haphazard and most improbable state of affairs. Having said that, Schmidt did not intend his text to give a realistic depiction of the outcome of nuclear warfare; rather, the narrative is used as a kind of mind-game ('Gedankenspiel') through which the author can play out some of his personal literary likes and dislikes (such as for instance his passion for James Fenimore Cooper's writings, some of which Schmidt later went on to translate into German), intellectual obsessions (the celebration of solitude, cultural cynicism, misanthropy and atheism) and political fixations (for instance his staunch anti-militarism). What follows is the opening sequence, composed in the distinctive narrative style that is so characteristic of much of Schmidt's early writings, reproducing the original's arrangement and punctuation:

> (1. 5. 1960)
> *Lights ?* (I raised myself on the pedals) — : — Nowhere. (So, same as always for the past five years).
> *But* : the laconic moon along the crumbled road (grass and quitch have crept from the shoulders, breaking up the blacktop and leaving only two yards of pavement in the middle: that's enough for me !)
> *Push on* : staring from the juniper, the peaked silver mask — so onward —
> *Man's life* : means two score years of dodging and doubling. And if by reason of the toss (I'm tossing often these days !), they be two score and five; yet is their strength only fifteen years of war and a mere three inflations.
> *Backpedal* : (and it squeaked with the stop; have to oil it all tomorrow). By way of precaution, I aimed my carbine's mouth at the greasy wreck: the windows thickly dusted; only after I hit it with the butt did the car door open a little. Backseat empty; a skeletal lady at the wheel (so, same as always for the past five years !); well: enjoy your bliss ! But it would be dark soon too, and I still didn't trust creatureliness: whether ferny ambush or mocking birds: I was ready with ten rounds in the automatic: so pump onward. [...]
> *As always* : the empty husks of houses. Atom bombs and bacteria had done thorough work. Automatically, my fingers kept pressing the dynamo–flashlight. In one room, a corpse: stench intensity of twelve men: so at least in death a Siegfried (rare, by the way, for it still to stink; was all so long ago now). On the second floor lay almost a dozen skeletons, men and women (you can tell by the pelvic bones). So then, six men (and/or boys); five women and girls. [...] Good, really, that it had All come to an end; and I spat it out: The End ! Uncoupled the trailer and dragged it behind me across the threshold (first room on the right; why make a fuss).

> [*(1. 5. 1960)*
> *Lichter ?* (ich hob mich auf den Pedalen) — : — Nirgends. (Also wie immer seit den fünf Jahren).
> *Aber* : der lakonische Mond längs der zerbröckelten Straße (von den Rändern her haben Gras und Quecken die Teerdecke aufgebrochen, so daß nur in der Mitte noch zwei Meter Fahrbahn bleiben : das genügt ja für mich !)
> *Weiter treten* : starrt die spitze Silberlarve aus m Wacholder — also weiter —
> *Des Menschen Leben* : das heißt vierzig Jahre Haken schlagen. Und wenn es hoch

> kommt (oft kommt es einem hoch ! !) sind es fünfundvierzig; und wenn es köstlich gewesen ist, dann war nur fünfzehn Jahre Krieg und bloß dreimal Inflation.
> *Rücktritt* : (und es quietschte beim Halten; morgen muß ich mal Alles durchölen). Ich richtete den Karabinermund vorsichtshalber gegen das schmierige Wrack : die Fenster dick verstaubt; erst als ich mit dem Kolben darauf schlug, ging die Wagentür ein wenig auf. Hinten leer; eine Skelettdame am Steuerrad (also wie immer seit den fünf Jahren !); nun : wünsche Glückseligkeiten ! Aber es wurde auch gleich dunkel, und ich traute dem Kreatorium immer noch nicht: ob Farnhinterhalt, ob Vogelspötterei : ich war bereit mit zehn Schuß im Vollautomatischen : also weiter trampeln. [...]
> *Wie immer* : die leeren Schalen der Häuser. Atombomben und Bakterien hatten ganze Arbeit geleistet. Meine Finger preßten mechanisch, unaufhörlich, an der Dynamotaschenlampe. In einer Kammer ein Toter : sein Gestank hatte Zwölfmännerstärke : also wenigstens im Tode Siegfried (nebenbei selten, daß es noch roch; war ja alles schon zu lange her). Im ersten Stock lagen fast ein Dutzend Gerippe, Männer und Frauen (an den Beckenknochen kann mans unterscheiden). Also sechs Männer (bzw. Knaben); fünf Frauen und Mädchen. [...] Bloß gut, daß Alles zu Ende war; und ich spuckte aus : Ende ! Koppelte den Anhänger los und zerrte ihn mir nach über die Schwellen (gleich rechts rein; wozu Umstände).][191]

Our new Robinson then proceeds to reconnoitre the area, collect provisions and identify a site to erect a new home. Like Mary Shelley's Lionel Verney at the conclusion of *The Last Man*, Schmidt's nameless narrator-cum-diarist wonders 'whether there was anyone left besides me?' 'Hardly probable', he tells himself, 'maybe somewhere on the southern tips of the continents, that presumably got the least of it' ('Ob außer mir überhaupt noch jemand übrig war? Wohl kaum; vielleicht irgendwo auf den Südzipfeln der Kontinente, die vermutlich am wenigsten abgekriegt hatten'). He is mistaken. Two years into the storyline a gun-toting woman appears on her iron steed, a loner like the protagonist himself, having travelled through the few remaining non-radioactive regions of Eastern Europe and Russia. The few survivors she had come across are now deceased, but her mixed experiences have made her wary of further human encounters. Thus the initial coming together of Last Man and Last Woman is marred by violence, each believing their adversary must be bent on taking the other's life. (This motif of the violent encounter of Last Man and Last Woman is taken up also by a 2015 futuristic short film entitled *The Last Man*, written and directed by Gavin Rothery and accessible on YouTube; the film ends with the stalemate reached when it comes to a stand-off with Last Man and Last Woman each watching the other through the cross hairs of their automatic rifles.) But once they have negotiated this crisis in true pathfinder-like manner and gotten to know one another, Schmidt's adversaries start comparing notes:

> *In summary* : 'From our autopsy, then, we know that all of Central Europe is void of humans — ' She nodded. 'And in adjoining regions there can't be any groups of people worth mention.' [...]

---

[191] *Dark Mirrors*, pp. 179–80 (*Schwarze Spiegel*, p. 201–02); the subsequent passages pp. 220–21, 221, 187, 188, 202, 188, 223, 181 and 201 (pp.: 244, 244–45, 210, again 210, 224, 210, 247, 203 and 224).

'THE EARTH VOID OF MAN' 461

FIG. 5.3. Karl Staudinger's cover graphics for the first edition of Arno Schmidt's *Leviathan*, published in 1949, depicting on the front cover (here the right hand half) a monstrous demon leaving a trail of destruction. The rear cover (here the left hand half) shows the damned on their march towards death, the tune to which is being trumpeted by an angel-like spectre hovering in the sky above. (This reproduction is based on the 1985 Fischer Verlag reprint, courtesy of the S. Fischer Verlag, Frankfurt am Main.)

> '*So what's left really*' she said pensively, and I nodded in approval : straight to the point ! 'In my opinion,' I declared icily, 'the situation is as follows: Asia, Europe (or better, Asiopa) — ; likewise North America — ' I brushed my hand across the blue and yellow northern hemisphere, and she pinched her lips together in agreement. 'South Africa got it too; likewise the industrial centers of Australia and South America.' 'My theory is: that, separated by very large spaces, here and there a few isolated individuals are still nomadizing about. Perhaps at the southernmost points of the continents there are — ' (automatically I resorted to catchwords I'd thought out) — 'still small communities left. — The individuals, unaccustomed to the harsh life and raw disease, will quickly die out.' She took melancholy and cozy breaths : by lamp-light it sounded like a book. 'Eventually those aforesaid tiny groups may pave the way for a repopulated earth; but that will take — well — let's hope a thousand years.' 'And that's all to the good !' I concluded defiantly.
>
> [*Resümieren* : »Wir wissen also durch Autopsie, daß ganz Mitteleuropa menschenleer ist — « Sie nickte. »Auch in den angrenzenden Gebieten können keine nennenswerten Gruppen mehr sitzen [...].«
> »*Was bleibt eigentlich*« sagte sie tiefsinnig, und ich nickte anerkennend: genau zur Sache! »Meiner Ansicht nach«, erklärte ich kalt, »wird die Lage folgende sein: Asien, Europa (Asiopa besser) — ; ebenso Nordamerika — « ich wischte mit

> der Hand über die blaue und gelbe Nordhalbkugel, und sie kniff zustimmend die Lippen ein. »Südafrika hats auch erwischt; ebenso die Industriezentren Australiens und Südamerikas.« »Meine Theorie ist: daß, getrennt durch sehr große Räume, hier und da noch ein paar Einzelindividuen nomadisieren. — Vielleicht sind auf den Südzipfeln der Kontinente — « (ich verfiel unwillkürlich in oft gedachtes Formelhaftes) — »noch kleine Gemeinden übrig. — Die Einzelnen werden, des rauhen Lebens und der Wildkrankheiten ungewohnt, wahrscheinlich rasch aussterben.« Sie atmete schwermütig und behaglich: bei Lampenlicht klangs wie ein Buch. »Von den erwähnten Kleinstgruppen aus kann sich ja eventuell eine Wiederbevölkerung der Erde anbahnen; aber das dauert — na — hoffentlich tausend Jahre.« »Und es ist gut so!« schloß ich herausfordernd.]

Why 'all to the good'? Obviously because mankind was not worth preserving in the first place; in this vein, the narrator holds forth misanthropically:

> *Reasons ?:* 'Lisa ! !' : 'Just recall to mind what humanity looked like ! Culture ! ? : one in a thousand passed culture on; one in a hundred thousand created culture ! : Morality ? : Hahaha ! : Let every man prove his conscience and say he wasn't ripe for hanging long ago !' She nodded, convinced at once. 'Boxing, soccer, the lottery: how those legs did run ! — Very big when it came to weapons !' — 'What were a boy's ideals: auto-racer, general, world-champion sprinter. A girl's: film star, »creator« of fashion. The men's: harem owner and manager. The woman's : car, electric kitchen, to be addressed as »milady«. [...] — ' I ran out of air.

> [*Begründung ?:* »Lisa ! !«: »Rufen Sie sich doch das Bild der Menschheit zurück! Kultur ! ? : ein Kulturträger war jeder Tausendste; ein Kulturerzeuger jeder Hunderttausendste ! : Moralität ? Hahaha ! : Sehe jeder in sein Gewissen und sage er sei nicht längst hängensreif !« Sie nickte sofort überzeugt. »Boxen, Fußball, Toto: da rannten die Beine ! — In Waffen ganz groß ! « — »Was waren die Ideale eines Jungen : Rennfahrer, General, Sprinterweltmeister. Eines Mädchens : Filmstar, Mode»schöpferin«. Der Männer : Haremsbesitzer und Direktor. Der Frau : Auto, Elektroküche, der Titel »gnädige Frau«. [...] Die Luft ging mir aus.]

Schmidt's narrator is not at all sad to see humankind evaporate into nothingness; neither is he scared by the prospect of being alone. As the protagonist puts it, a veritable leitmotif of his narrative: 'long live solitude' ('es lebe die Einsamkeit'), adding 'ah, it was indeed good that they were all gone' ('ach, es war doch gut, daß Alle weg waren'). Elsewhere he enlarges: 'good thing it's all been swept away! (And when I'm gone someday, the last blot will have disappeared: the experiment, man the stench, will have come to an end!) Such contemplations put me in a cheerful mood again' ('es ist doch gut, daß mit all dem aufgeräumt wurde! (und wenn ich erst weg bin, wird der letzte Schandfleck verschwunden sein: das Experiment Mensch, das stinkige, hat aufgehört!) Solche Betrachtungen stimmten mich wieder fröhlich'). Schmidt's text thus comprises a prime instance of what one critic has called the 'egotistical sublime', a condition in which an individual delights in mankind's demise because it rids him 'of the claustrophobic burden of the existence of others'.[192]

Nor does the narrator exhibit any particular attachment to religion or God. Feeling the urge to defecate, Schmidt's narrator looks around for some toilet paper:

> Is there no paper in this house; I broke into the desk drawers, set them cracking; a stamped leather portfolio, a Parcheesi game — (takes two — mocking me), and I grew visibly vexed; finally a book: Rilke, Stories of God, just what I expected; and I ripped the requisite number of pages out of the giltsmithy prose: the very title outraged me; refined bunk.
>
> [Ist denn kein Papier im Hause; ich erbrach die Schreibtischfächer, daß es knallte; eine lederne geprägte Mappe, ein Mensch ärger Dich nicht (wie zum Hohn), und ich wurde zusehends ungehalten; endlich ein Buch: Rilke, Geschichten vom lieben Gott, du kommst mir gerade recht; und ich riß der Goldschmiedsprosa sogleich die benötigte Anzahl Blätter heraus: schon der Titel empörte mich; feinsinniges Geschwafel.]

Symptomatically, stories of God no longer have a place in this world. Yet God does have a role to play in Schmidt's vision of a nuclear Armageddon, namely an inverted negative one. As in Huxley's *Ape and Essence*, in which veneration for God has been supplanted by the worship of Belial, God in *Dark Mirrors* is the Creator turned Destructor: 'And who's at fault?', the narrator asks at one point in his diary-like stream of consciousness, only to respond: 'Why, the primo motore of it all, of course, the creator, whom I have named Leviathan' ('"*Schuld daran?*" — "Ist freilich der Primo Motore des Ganzen, der Schöpfer, den ich den Leviathan genannt [...] habe"'). In the Bible Leviathan is an all-devouring serpent-like demon through whose Hellmouth the damned are destined to pass into Hell on Judgment Day; on an allegorical plane, Leviathan also serves as a symbol of Satan. In *Dark Mirrors* Schmidt extends this equation; here man has turned himself into a Leviathan. 'In the end', the narrator thus muses, 'I'll be alone with the Leviathan (or even be him myself)' ('am Ende werde ich allein mit dem Leviathan sein (oder gar er selbst)'). The resulting twin equation God = Leviathan = Man suggests what Anders was to articulate more pointedly some years later: Humankind has become godlike in its capacity to execute the Apocalypse — and in the process this human Leviathan has succeeded merely in executing and devouring himself, piling up mountains of murdered as a result, as the following passage illustrates (in which Schmidt leaves intentionally unclear, I would argue, whether the 'hill of corpses' relates to the bodies of concentration camp inmates murdered by the SS or heaps of corpses resulting from nuclear incineration, or both):

> At the barrier, where a hill of corpses was piled, I turned around, and walked back down the promenade : for this, then, man had been given reason.
> *I was so hate-full*, that I raised my rifle, aimed it towards heaven : and through his Leviathan's maw gaped ten thousand nebulae : I'd like to pounce on the dog!
>
> [Vor der Sperre — wo ein Leichenberg haufte, drehte ich um, und ging den Korso wieder zurück : dazu also hatte der Mensch die Vernunft erhalten.

---

[192] Schwenger, 'Writing the Unthinkable', p. 38.

> *Ich war so haß-voll*, daß ich die Flinte ansetzte, in den Himmel hielt : und klaffte sein Leviathansmaul über zehntausend Spiralnebel : ich spränge den Hund an!]

That heaven, Leviathan and God are, for Schmidt, a demonic trinity is confirmed by a reading of Schmidt's earlier story *Leviathan or The Best of Worlds*. Appearing in Schmidt's earliest published book *Leviathan* in 1949 (see Figure 5.3),[193] the story relates the last two days — again in diary-like manner — in the life of a German *Wehrmachts*-officer and a group of refugees fleeing from the Red Army's advance on the eastern border of Germany in a train to which is attached a so-called *Schwellenreißer*, a 'tie-buster' designed to tear up the sleepers (in American 'ties'; the text was rendered into English by the American translator John E. Woods) behind the train as it moves along the tracks. The sleeper-buster is a Leviathan-like symbol of Nazi Germany tearing itself apart — as much as it is being torn apart by the Red Army's shelling — as it moves forward through time and space.

On a philosophical and theological level the story is also about guilt and the theodicy problem, as the ironic subtitle 'or The Best of Worlds' indicates. It is about belief in a God — respectively the inability to continue believing in a God — who has been transformed by the Second World War and the Holocaust into a demon who in destroying the world simultaneously destroys himself. Two quotations from this text will help to illustrate Schmidt's take. The first shows the evacuees coming under Soviet shelling and a child being ripped apart, which prompts the narrator to pour scorn on Alexander Pope's adage 'Whatever Is, Is Right', a maxim we already encountered in my Introduction:

> Immediately we ran in a crouch back behind the embankment : the ground there was red; red, oh. [...] And one of the children had been ripped almost totally apart by two giant fragments, neck and shoulders, everything. Its mother was still holding the head, staring in wonder at the greasy scarlet puddle. The pastor comforted the weeping woman; he suggested : 'The Lord hath given; the Lord hath taken away —' and may he rot in hell, the coward and Byzantine added : 'Blessed be the name of the Lord !' (And gazed proudly at us poor lost heathens, shameless lackey's soul !) — That guiltless child — Let him tell his ancient corny joke about original sin to people who still have bibs on their overalls : Hasn't it ever occurred to them all that God could be the guilty party ? Have they never heard of Kant and Schopenhauer, and Gauss and Riemann, Darwin, Goethe, Wieland ? [...] Whatever is, is right [...]. — Scum.
>
> [Wir rannten sofort geduckt hinter der Böschung zurück: da war der Boden rot; rot, ach. [...] Und eins der Kinder war fast völlig zerrissen von zwei Riesensplittern, Hals und Schultern, alles. Die Mutter hielt noch immer den Kopf und sah wie verwundert in die fette karminene Lache. [...] Der Pfarrer tröstete die weinende Frau; er meinte: „Der Herr hat's gegeben; der Herr hat's genommen —" und, hol's der Teufel, der Feigling und Byzantiner setzte hinzu:

---

[193] Arno Schmidt, *Leviathan or The Best of Worlds*, in *Collected Novellas*, vol. 1 of *Collected Early Fiction 1949–1964*, trans. by John E. Woods (Normal, IL: Dalkey Archives Press, 1994), pp. 25–44; German quotations from *Leviathan* in *Leviathan* (Frankfurt a.M.: Fischer, 1985 = reprint of the first edition 1949), pp. 43–76. I would like to thank the Fischer Verlag in Frankfurt am Main for permission to reproduce Karl Staudinger's cover graphics to the *Leviathan* volume.

„Der Name des Herrn sei gelobt!" (Und sah dabei stolz auf uns arme verlorene Heiden, die schamlose Lakaienseele! — Das schuldlose Kind — Seine 2000 Jahre alten Kalauer von der Erbsünde kann er doch nur einem erzählen, der keine Krempe mehr am Hut hat: Haben diese Leute denn nie daran gedacht, daß Gott der Schuldige sein könnte? Haben Sie denn nie von Kant und Schopenhauer gehört, und Gauß und Riemann, Darwin, Goethe, Wieland? [...] Whatever is, is right: [...]. — Pack.]

The second passage reads:

> Nietzsche's joke of physics about eternal return : what a shallow mind that sometimes was ! (That his Leviathan of Power was limited and 'thus' [...] would itself have to die one day, seems never to have occured to him.) — Religion with their 'creations' and 'incarnate gods' (despite which they all then make the mistake of letting their God go right on as before without any change). [...] This past month, in Pirna, I saw a concentration camp on the march : Jewish women and their children, all frightfully emaciated, with unearthly large, dark eyes, beside them cursing, red-cheeked SS executioners mounted and wearing heavy gray-green coats, woe !) — The old man thrust forward; he asked in a shrill voice : 'What ? The Leviathan is going to die too ? ! — ' [...] (At one point, way off, heavy earthquake rumbling. A long time. Like some huge bombing attack. Dresden ? God out for a stroll on bomb carpets).

> [Meinetwegen auch Nietzsches Physikalischer Witz von der ewigen Wiederkunft: was das manchmal für ein flacher Kopf war! (Daß sein Macht-Leviathan begrenzt und „also" [...] selbst sterblich sein müßte, hat er wohl gar nicht gedacht). — Die Religionen mit ihren „Schöpfungen" und „menschengewordenen Göttern" (obwohl sie alle dann den Fehler begehen, ihren Gott trotzdem unverändert weiterbestehen zu lassen). [...] Ich habe diesen Monat in Pirna ein KZ auf dem Marsch gesehen: Judenfrauen und ihre Kinder, alle fürchterlich abgezehrt, mit unirdisch großen dunklen Augen, daneben fluchende rotbackige berittene SS-Henker, in schweren graugrünen Mänteln, wehe!) — Der Alte warf sich vor; er fragte schrill: „Wie? Auch der Leviathan stirbt?! —" [...] (Einmal ganz fern schweres erdbebengleiches Rollen. Lange. Wie ein Riesenluftangriff. Dresden? Gott spaziert auf Bombenteppichen.)][194]

The senseless killings of innocent civilians, the Shoah and the bombing of Dresden fuse in these two passages to spotlight the age-old theodicy dilemma: How can any god dare to stroll on such carpets of mass destruction? Here, as in Huxley's *Ape and Essence*, Heaven and Hell, God and Satan (alias Belial alias Leviathan), become interchangeable. '[P]iles of bones, rib cages don't bother me nowadays,' we read in *Dark Mirrors*, 'may not heaven be nothing but an invention of the devil to torment us, the damned, all the more?' ('Knochenhaufen, Rippenkörbe stören mich nicht mehr: sollte der Himmel nicht bloß eine Fiktion des Teufels sein, uns arme Verdammte noch mehr zu quälen?').[195] Speaking about this God–Devil–Leviathan figure, the narrator of *Leviathan* tries to console his dying fellow traveller, the old man on the train carriage, with what is meant to serve as words of solace: 'His power is immense, but limited. And so too, then, his span of life' ('Seine Macht

---

194 Ibid., pp. 34 and 42 (*Leviathan*, pp. 58–59 and 71–72).
195 *Dark Mirrors*, p. 201 (*Schwarze Spiegel*, p. 224).

ist riesig, aber begrenzt. Daher auch seine Lebensdauer').[196] If the Jewish-German philosopher Hans Jonas confidently uses God's limitation of power to excuse him for his inability to intervene in the course of history, including the unfolding of the Holocaust, Schmidt's narrator concludes less optimistically that, since even such beings as God or Leviathan cannot escape the movement of time, they must themselves be either dying or already dead. 'Good', the old man concludes, his last dying word expressing his relief that even Gods who wield such great power are no less condemned to die than the lesser subjects over whose fortunes they preside. The death of Man is balanced in Schmidt's fictional world against the reassurance that God too has, equally deservedly, met his end. 'Kant. Schopenhauer [...] how do you picture it: that spot where space comes to an end?' the narrator at one point asks, upon which his interlocutor, a pastor, answers: 'God is infinite — '. The narrator responds coldly: 'You're mistaken as well; there was once a demon of fundamentally cruel and diabolical nature, but he too no longer exists' ('"Kant. Schopenhauer, [...] wie stellen Sie sich das vor: die Stelle, wo der Raum ein Ende hat?" Auch der Pfarrer ließ sich von dem gestirnten Himmel über sich ergreifen: "Gott", gab er an, "ist unendlich — ." Ich disputiere nie mit Frommen, ich sprach auch jetzt in Richtung unseres Sonderzuges: "Auch Sie irren sich; es gab einen Dämon von wesentlich grausamem, teuflischem Charakter, aber auch er existiert jetzt nicht mehr"'). I stress the word 'too' ('auch'): the narrator's message to the pastor and his fellow travellers is that, like the demon Leviathan, God no longer exists.

If God alias Leviathan is dead in Schmidt's Second-World-War and Third-World-War narratives, and if at the end of *Leviathan* the narrator dies together with his fellow refugees, will humankind in *Black Mirrors* at least be allowed to survive the nuclear Armageddon of the Third World War? The answer is not obvious. On the one hand the story relates the encounter of a Last Man and a Last Woman — a potential Adam and Eve. But we recall from Chapter Two how in Grainville's *Le Dernier Homme* the Last Man protagonist Omégare was faced with the option to extend the lifespan of humankind by allowing Syderia to deliver their child, or to let humanity die out by sacrificing Syderia and thereby calling down the Day of Reckoning; following some unexpected twists and turns it was of course eventually the latter that transpired in Grainville's epic. Schmidt adds to this denouement an unexpected twist. While our Last Man and Last Woman in *Dark Mirrors* have no qualms about making love, neither wishes to propagate their species; both agree that the 'experiment, man the stench', is not worth preserving. But revealingly, here it is not our misanthropic male recluse and alter ego of the author who is the decision maker and who shies away from procreation; rather, it is the symbolic Eve, Lisa (an inversion of the name of Schmidt's wife Alice), who won't allow herself to be redomesticated and to serve as a birthing machine of a new humanity. She is the one who makes the decision and subsequently also takes the initiative; one morning Lisa thus proclaims: '"*Tomorrow I'm leaving* : just in time, before I get too fat and sassy. You're too strong for me." [...] "I have to" ! She declared with determination, "here

---

196 *Leviathan or The Best of Worlds*, p. 44 (*Leviathan*, p. 75); the subsequent passages pp. 31, 34–35 and 36 (pp. 52, 58–59 and 61).

with you — I don't know — I'm getting heavier and more classical"' ('»*Morgen fahre ich ab*: es ist gerade noch Zeit, ehe ich ganz behäbig werde. Du bist mir zu stark. [...] »Ich muß!« erklärte sie entschlossen, »ich werde bei Dir — ich weiß nicht — dicker und klassischer«').[197] In Schmidt's take on the end-time narrative it is the woman who takes control, leaving the man behind at home, alone and at a loss for words: Lisa has the last spoken word in this narrative when she sends the narrator back into the house searching for matches, all the while she takes off by bicycle. Among the final entries in the Last Man's account are: '*Gone*: She was gone! Of course! [...] Stupid face. [...] In my right hand a box of matches. [...] *Toward morning cloudworks arose* (and rain showers). Fresh yellow smoke wafted towards me: my stove! So I left the wood and pushed onto the house: the last human being' ('*Fort*: Sie war fort! Natürlich! [...] Blödes Gesicht. [...] In der Rechten ein Paket Streichhölzer. [...] *Gegen Morgen kam Gewölk auf* (und Regenschauer. Frischer gelber Rauch wehte mich an: mein Ofen! So verließ ich den Wald und schob mich ans Haus: der letzte Mensch'). While technically this is, of course, incorrect since Lisa is still alive, what we can say is that no new Adam and Eve are on the horizon. Lisa may or may not return, but either way the two last beings in this story seem disinclined to propagate a species whose most lasting achievement has been to exterminate itself in three world wars within one century. The story leaves humankind without issue (much as Arno and Alice Schmidt themselves, who had no children). And, ironically it must be noted, it is the man, not the woman, who settles down to house and hearth in this tale of nuclear frontier romanticism.

My final example is Günter Grass's novel *Die Rättin* (*The Rat*), published in 1986. *The Rat* is cast essentially as a dream book about the demise of mankind through nuclear apocalypse; it opens with the narrator, an avatar of the author himself, dreaming of being given a female rat for Christmas (the German word *Rättin* designates a feminine animal, a gender ascription lost in the English translation's title). Usurping the position of Christ in the manger, this female rat enters into dialogue with her human interlocutor, telling him about her species' knotty history, a history that is inseparable from the lifecycle of her race's host, humankind. The rat relates in Grass's baroquely convoluted and multi-layered novel how, in the certain knowledge that mankind's nuclear self-destruction was imminent, her species decided — aided by their knowledge of Hiroshima and Nagasaki — to take cover in subterranean safe havens they had pre-prepared for this eventuality; how before they left the sinking ship, as it were (a ship associated throughout the novel with Noah's Ark), they tried to 'enlighten' and warn their human counterparts about the impending peril; how they came out in millions and flooded the famous squares and boulevards of the world's capital cities, Brussels, London, Moscow, Rome, Sydney, Tokyo, Washington; how human statesmen and politicians failed to understand and heed the rats' warnings; and how the human race perished in the nuclear holocaust bar the narrator who — in his dream — survives in a spaceship circling the Earth. She relates also how only human children read the signs correctly, but

---

[197] *Dark Mirrors*, p. 235 (*Schwarze Spiegel*, p. 259); the final quotation from this text p. 236 (p. 260).

their intuition was ignored: 'Only a few of the letters to the press, those written by children, tell the truth', we are told by the narrator; 'I think the rats are afraid', he continues,

> because people aren't afraid enough any more. — In my opinion the rats are trying to say goodbye to people before everything comes to an end. — My little sister, who has seen the rat processions on TV, says: First God abandoned us, and now even the rats are clearing out.
>
> [Nur einige von Kindern geschriebene Leserbriefe sprechen wahr: Ich glaube, die Ratten haben Angst, weil die Menschen nicht genug Angst haben. — Ich nehme an, daß die Ratten, bevor alles zu Ende geht, von uns Menschen Abschied nehmen wollen. — Meine kleine Schwester, die die Rattenumzüge im Fernsehen gesehen hat, sagt: Zuerst hat uns der liebe Gott verlassen, und jetzt hauen auch noch die Ratten ab.][198]

The narrator's dream rat further reports how, far back in history, humans had once before tried to eradicate her species. When Noah took the world's animal species onto his Ark he refused to allow rats on board; but the rats survived nonetheless, she informs us, by burying themselves into Mount Ararat until the waters had receded. At that time they learnt the technique of survival, blocking all entry and exit points with the fattened bodies of aged fellow rats, a technique they now intend to deploy once again to save them from nuclear annihilation. And to cap her story she admits to the narrator in his dream that it may be the rats themselves who may have caused humankind's extinction, not by devouring mankind's food resources nor by reintroducing the plague, but this time by gnawing through the military hardware's computer wiring and thereby accidentally — or perhaps not so accidentally — setting off the superpowers' MAD — Mutual Assured Destruction — software. In the dream world of Grass's novel, God is dead. He hovers above humankind as their illusory God, a mythical God who, in the novel's first chapter, punishes the equally mythical Noah by allowing the rats to survive.

For those who are familiar with Grass's habit to interlace his texts with all kinds of intertextual references it will come as no surprise to find him in this dream novel picking up, in its very first chapter, on one of the German literary tradition's most famous Romantic dream texts, one we encountered earlier in this study, Jean Paul's 'Declaration of the dead Christ from atop the World's Edifice that there is no God'. We may recall from our prior discussion of it in Chapter Three that Jean Paul's nightmarish vision of Christ standing on a mountain top overseeing the advent of the Last Judgment and declaring the Death of God was intended as an invective against atheists who question the existence of God, among them, in Jean Paul's and his friend Jacobi's view, the philosopher Fichte. Grass's reworking of Jean Paul's matrix is as ironic as it is profane: in *The Rat* it is the dream-She-rat who proclaims the end of mankind from atop a mountain of man-made garbage ('Müllgebirge') on which she stands; all that remains of the human species which has just committed

---

[198] Günter Grass, *The Rat*, trans. by Ralph Manheim (London: Secker & Warburg, 1987), pp. 57–58; *Die Rättin* (Reinbek: Rowohlt, 1988, first published 1986), p. 76; the subsequent passage pp. 6–7 (pp. 11–13).

nuclear suicide are the mountains of rubbish it has left behind. We read:

> Yea verily, ye have ceased to be, I hear her proclaim. As resoundingly as the dead Christ speaking from the top of the world, the She-rat speaks from atop the garbage mountain: If it were not for us, nothing would bear witness to you humans. It's we who inventory what the human race has left behind. Vast plains infested with garbage, beaches strewn with garbage, valleys clogged with garbage. [...] How crumpled is his fallen progress. And I saw what I dreamed, saw gelatin shimmying and tapes on the move, saw truckloads of scrap and foil buffeted by storms, saw poison seeping from barrels. And I saw the She-rat on top of the garbage mountain, proclaiming that man is no more.
>
> [Wahrlich, ihr seid nicht mehr! höre ich sie verkünden. Wie einst der tote Christus vom Weltgebäude herab, spricht weithallend die Rättin vom Müllgebirge: Nichts spräche von euch, gäbe es uns nicht. Was vom Menschengeschlecht geblieben, zählen wir zum Gedächtnis auf. Vom Müll befallen, breiten sich Ebenen, strändelang Müll, Täler, in denen der Müll sich staut. [...] Seht, wie zerknautscht sein Fortschritt zu Fall kam! Und ich sah, was mir träumte, sah Gelee bibbern und Filmbänder unterwegs, sah rollenden Schrott und Folien von Stürmen bewegt; sah Gift aus Fässern suppen; und ich sah sie, die vom Müllberg herab verkündete, daß der Mensch nicht mehr sei.]

Grass's impious she-rat inverts Jean Paul's Christian nightmare, turning it into a depressing dreamscape of unenlightened mankind's irrationalism and suicidal decline: the Mount of Olives appears transmogrified into endless mounds of garbage; the male Jesus of the Christian tradition appears transfigured into an irreverent speaking female rat; the dead awaking in their graves morph into poison seeping from barrels in the wastelands of human refuse; the Last Judgment mutates into the nuclear holocaust; and not only is God dead but also mankind: the only human survivor is the lone narrator, ensconced in his dreamscape's spaceship, circling a radioactively contaminated planet Earth. In the end the only thing left for the narrator is to acknowledge that 'my dream exposes reality' ('mein Traum [...] entblößt die Wirklichkeit').[199]

The thesis I have put forward in *Sublime Conclusions* — for which the science fiction novels (and films) discussed in this chapter provide the textbook cases in point — is that science fiction as a modern literary genre could only ever have arisen as a consequence of the Death of God. Look at the worlds of Jules Verne, H. G. Wells, Olaf Stapledon, Stanislaw Lem, Arthur C. Clarke, Isaac Asimov, or Philip Pullman, to name only a sampling, their universes are all premised on the disappearance of God. God is no longer a force to be reckoned with, and religion, when it is depicted as still existing, is demoted to a ritual or mythical practice of some residual primitive way of thinking; or God is simply made fun of, as in Douglas Adams's endlessly riotous *The Hitch Hiker's Guide to the Galaxy* (which of course pokes fun at everything in our universe, not just God but also last men and women).[200] Alternatively, we find God cynically inverted into or collapsed with

---

199 *Die Rättin*, p. 219.
200 A wonderfully droll example of this is the following excerpt from *The Hitch Hiker's Guide to the Galaxy*; it concerns the invention of the 'Babel fish' which has since gone on to rematerialize

SUBLIME (?) CONCLUSIONS

> The human will to believe that the End of the World is not the end
> of the world is as powerful as the hope or the fear of the End.
> ELINOR SHAFFER (1995)[1]

> I have published these words in order to prevent them from
> becoming true.
> GÜNTHER ANDERS (1962)[2]

Christ's Second Coming

In this study's five chapters we have explored a wide array of texts in the broad semiotic sense, mostly epics and novels, but also poems, plays and films alongside the occasional painting, film poster and book illustration as well as academic essays and monographs that all revolve around the subject of the end that might befall man should some form of lethal species-consuming disaster ever come to pass. I grouped these texts into three paradigms of mankind's demise with three causes propelling this end: first, God's active intervention in the world's affairs; second, Nature's cataclysms; and third, Man's violent self-eradication through the fruits of his own technological advances. In Christian theology, God's end-time intervention occurs through Last Judgment and apocalypse. The most common forms of catastrophic intervention attributed to Nature are viral plagues and pandemics; devastating tsunamis and floods; tectonic upheavals; cosmic collisions; and the 'natural' waxing and waning of the sun and our solar system. The most common forms of catastrophe attributed to Man are a nuclear Third World War; a nuclear winter following in its wake; chemical and biological warfare; genetic engineering; and man-made climate change.

These three paradigms may have arisen consecutively in time, as I have shown, hence my sequencing of this book's chapters; but now that these paradigms have come into being they coexist contemporaneously as competing modes and models of how one can envision humankind's demise. To be sure, the literary genre of the religious apocalyptic verse epic is no longer en vogue and has been outstripped by the secular paradigms of Nature and Man; but we would be mistaken nonetheless to assume that the religious apocalyptic plot has been abandoned altogether. As we shall see momentarily, the apocalyptic epic of yore has been given a facelift; translated into novelistic form, its prose issue is no less metaphysically speculative

---

1 'Secular Apocalypse: Prophets and Apocalyptics at the End of the Eighteenth Century', (p. 137).
2 'Theses for the Atomic Age', p. 505.

than was its verse progenitor. In short, all three paradigms continue to prosper; and it is these paradigms that provide the moulds and matrices through which creative artists shape their visions of Last Men and — less frequently — Last Women.

In Chapter Five I covered in outline what I called the third paradigm of man's nuclear self-eradication, labeled variously humankind's 'collective suicide' (Albert Camus), 'globocide' (Günther Anders) or 'auto-genocide' (Robert Jay Lifton). In the preceding four chapters, by contrast, we explored the paradigms of religious — in our case specifically Christian — eschatology on the one hand (Chapters One and Two) and, on the other, of secularized nature (Chapters Three and Four) as they developed between the seventeenth and early nineteenth century. In my Conclusion I wish to share some final thoughts on the three paradigms' trajectories, transformations and possible ramifications.

Let us then return first to the Christian eschatological paradigm; as we recall, the textual exemplars of this paradigm that I presented were, in chronological order, Edward Young's *A Poem on the Last Day* (1713), Jean Paul's prose narrative 'Speech of the dead Christ from atop the World's Edifice that there is no God' (conceived 1789, but later embedded in the 1796 novel *Siebenkäs*), and the apocalyptic epics *Le Dernier Homme* (1805) by Jean-Baptiste Cousin de Grainville, *Donatoa* (1806–1807) by Franz von Sonnenberg, and *Armageddon* (1815) by George Townsend; briefer mention was also made of Robert Pollok's *The Course of Time* (1827), Augustin-François Creuzé de Lesser's *Le dernier homme, poème imité de Grainville* (1831), Paulin Gagne's *L'Unitéide, ou la Femme-Messie* (1858), and Élise Gagne's *Omégar, ou le Dernier homme* (1859). As a literary historian who, due to my secular socialization, had for the greater part of my academic career steered clear of the topic 'literature and religion' I was taken by surprise to find that the literary treatment of the Last Judgment was not something that had 'passed its expiry date' in the nineteenth century, as I had initially — and perhaps too naïvely — assumed. Quite to the contrary I found that the Christian eschatological paradigm had staged a rather successful literary comeback through its 'translation' or 'transposition' from verse epic into the contemporary genres of novel and film. What is more, this reversal of literary fortune started only quite recently, little more than two decades ago in the mid-1990s. But one caveat is needed: we are not talking about a mainstream phenomenon; both the creators of these products and their target audience are firmly entrenched in Christian evangelical circles, for the most part in the United States. In previous chapters we encountered the work of such Christian apologists as William Lane Craig, Rodney Holder, Alvin Plantinga, Richard Swinburne and Charles Taylor, whose Christian philosophizing confirmed the degree to which mainstream Christian theologians today are seeking to regain the initiative in our 'Secular Age', as Taylor calls it, by synchronizing as far as possible Christian belief and the findings of modern science. Reflecting on religion's resurgence in their 2006 study on *Nineteenth-Century Religion and Literature*, Mark Knight and Emma Mason have observed:

> Rather than applying secularization theory in an indiscriminate and dogmatic fashion to insist upon the historic inevitability of religious decline, it is more

constructive, and more accurate, to think about the ways in which Christianity adapted its form and message to engage with widespread cultural change. Not only does this help uncover a strong religious presence beyond the period when it was supposed to have fallen into dramatic decline; it resists the monolithic assumption of secularization theory that religion cannot have a place in the modern world.[3]

'To engage with widespread cultural change' by adapting Christianity's 'form and message' is precisely what Craig, Holder, Plantinga, Swinburne and Taylor have all sought to do by (re)connecting with the natural sciences through exchange and debate. But not all Christians have been willing to go down this mainstream path; rather than give in to ostensibly secular science, some Christian evangelical ministers went on the offensive instead. By tailoring novels and films — the two most popular genres of a largely secular entertainment industry — to meet their flock's evangelical needs, they found ways to requisition for their purposes the very media of popular culture that they had spurned for so long because they had previously considered them fundamentally at variance with their Christian values. Instigating what one critic has called Christian fundamentalism's 'unprecedented capitulation to pop culture, which the godly Right had until recently held in well-nigh Adornian contempt',[4] the fundamentalist Christian minister Tim LaHaye and his collaborator Jerry B. Jenkins began publishing a series of novels in the mid-1990s that encapsulated their evangelical vision of an impending apocalypse as well as the events that would usher it in. The resulting *Left Behind* cycle — one of the major success stories within an industry that Joe L. Kincheloe and Shirley R. Steinberg have called 'Christotainment'[5] — eventually grew to twelve volumes that, together, sold over forty million copies, with several of its novels reaching top rankings on the *New York Times* best seller list. The cycle's narrative plot covers the seven years that stretch from the beginning of 'The Rapture' — an era that is marked by the sudden and unexplained disappearance of evangelical Christian believers who are miraculously transported to heaven — to the conclusion of the Last Judgment and the capture of Satan and his being cast into Hell by Jesus Christ. The original series was later expanded by an additional four volumes, three of which form the prequel depicting the events preceding 'the Rapture', the fourth — entitled *Kingdom Come: The Final Victory* (2007) — forming the sequel and relating the thousand-year Millennium between the Second Coming and the establishment of the New Jerusalem, shortly before which we witness the 'Final Victory' of God over a reawakened Satan and his forces.

Capitalizing on the success of the series, the *Left Behind* novels were subsequently complemented by graphic novels, music CDs, audio dramatizations for Christian radio programmes, various spin-off series including one for teenagers (*Left Behind: The Kids*, with forty short novels authored by Jerry Jenkins, Tim LaHaye and Chris

---

3 *Nineteenth-Century Religion and Literature*, p. 153.
4 Christian Thorne, 'The Revolutionary Energy of the Outmoded', *October*, 104 (2003), 97–114 (p. 98).
5 For more on this topic see the volume they edited, *Christotainment: Selling Jesus through Popular Culture* (Boulder, CO, and Oxford: Westview Press, 2009).

Fabry), a video game with three sequels, and four movies (*Left Behind: The Movie*, 2000; *Left Behind II: Tribulation Force*, 2002; *Left Behind: World at War*, 2005; and *Left Behind: The Movie*, a 2014 remake of the first film featuring Nicolas Cage in the lead role playing Rayford Steele, one of the 'Tribulation Force' heroes).[6] In short, the success of the *Left Behind* series as a business venture was epical. By catering to the millions of American fundamentalist evangelical Christians who believe, as the authors themselves do, that the Second Coming of Christ is imminent, LaHaye and Jenkins were able to access a sizeable target group, one that concurs with the authors that the U.S. government, the education system, the liberal media, the Catholic Church, the Pope, liberal universities such as Harvard and Yale, the ACLU, and organisations like the Rockefeller and Carnegie Foundations are all conspiring to undermine America's Christian values and bring the Antichrist to power.

The original series climaxes with its twelfth and final instalment, entitled *Glorious Appearing: The End of Days*. Published in 2004, it depicts the gathering storm, with Satan's forces of evil — the millions of 'Carpathia's Global Community Unity Army' soldiers who have amassed in the Holy Land — moving to attack the last stronghold of the 'remnant' Christian faithful assembled in their mountaintop compound in Petra. The faithful are close to despair, for Christ's promised return seven years after the new covenant is becoming unnervingly overdue; but, as stalwart evangelical Christians should, most heroically hold on to their trust in prophecy nonetheless: 'They think Jesus is late?', the 'Tribulation Force' hero Rayford Steele suspects of some of his compatriots in Petra, only to be reminded by fellow-fighter Leah Rose that 'God's ways are not our ways. He's on His own clock'.[7] Elsewhere the narrator informs the reader that

> God had proved faithful and true to His Word. Every prophecy had been fulfilled. While there had to be those who wondered why the Lord tarried even now and whether there was any sense or logic to allowing Antichrist to reach the very boundary of the city of refuge, Rayford found himself simply trusting. God had His plans, His ways, His strategy. Only when Rayford stopped questioning God had he finally come to grips with the confusing, sometimes maddening, ways of God — which the Scriptures said were 'not our ways'.

And, true to His word, just as the last stronghold of the faithful comes under attack and when all seems lost, Christ descends from heaven as a brilliant light in order to engage the enemy's forces in battle:

> But as [Carpathia's] petrified, lethargic soldiers slowly turned back to the matter at hand, the brilliant multicolored cloud cover parted and rolled back like a scroll from horizon to horizon. Rayford found himself on his knees on the ground, hands and head lifted. Heaven opened and there, on a white horse,

---

6 The source of some of this information is Wikipedia (entry 'Left Behind', <https://en.wikipedia.org/wiki/Left_Behind>, and entry 'Left Behind (2014 film)', <https://en.wikipedia.org/wiki/Left_Behind_(2014_film)>, both last accessed 10 April 2017); I cannot vouch for this information's correctness.

7 Tim LaHaye and Jerry B. Jenkins, *Glorious Appearing. The End of Days* (Carol Stream, IL: Tyndale House, 2004, my imprint 2010), p. 47; the subsequent passages pp. 194, 202–04, 146, 244, 149, again 149, and again 244.

> sat Jesus, the Christ, the Son of the living God. [...] Jesus' eyes shone with a conviction like a flame of fire, and He held His majestic head high. He wore a robe down to the feet so brilliantly white it was incandescent and bore writing, something in a language wholly unfamiliar to Rayford and something else he easily understood. On His robe at the thigh a name was written: KING OF KINGS AND LORD OF LORDS. [...] The armies of heaven, clothed in fine linen, white and clean, followed Him on white horses. [...] 'I am the Alpha and the Omega,' Jesus said, 'the First and the Last, the Beginning and the End, the Almighty. [...] And with those very first words, tens of thousands of Unity Army soldiers fell dead, simply dropping where they stood, their bodies ripped open, blood pooling in great masses.

The ensuing gruesome slaughter of the unbelievers of this world — that is, more precisely, of all those who do not believe in LaHaye's and Jenkins's particular evangelical brand of Christianity — is presented as 'the greatest show on earth', the best viewing position of which the good guys have from their 'front-row seats'. 'What a show!', an evangelical character muses in awe in Illinois, 'the awful and terrible wrath of the Lord on display for the whole world!'. At the same time, watching the 'electrical extravaganza' of Christ's pitiless retribution thousands of miles away in the environs of Jerusalem, the 'Tribulation Force' pilot Montgomery Cleburn ('Mac') McCullum quips to his fellow-fighter for Christ, Rayford Steele: 'And why wouldn't I want a front-row seat for that?'. This is what is unfolding before their eyes:

> The great army was in pandemonium, tens of thousands at a time screaming in terror and pain and dying in the open air. Their blood poured from them in great waves, combining to make a river that quickly became a swamp. [...] It seemed to Rayford that the entire Unity Army within his field of vision was dead or dying, and the blood continued to rise. Millions of birds flocked into the area and feasted on the remains.[8]

No quarter is given to those who followed the Antichrist. As one might expect from this manner of black-and-white portrayal, even in full sight of the Saviour on his brilliant white steed Satan's followers remain steadfastly true to their cause, proving just how corrupt and evil they are; we are accordingly informed:

> Survivors remained only in scattered spots, but instead of trying to find cover or protecting their heads or even falling to their knees and begging for mercy, they lifted their faces to the sky, shouting, apparently railing against God, flashing obscene gestures at Jesus and his army. Soon they were crushed under the monstrous hailstones.

Christ's eleventh-hour — but nonetheless faithfully expected — charge of the light brigade and triumph over Satan's armies is promptly followed by the Last Judgment, at the end of which the members of the 'Tribulation Force' who were 'left behind' to wage the final battle against Satan's minions (hence the series' title), now find themselves happily reunited with their loved ones who were 'raptured' in the preceding volumes. For the faithful a happy end ensues, whereas the less fortunate

---

[8] Ibid., pp. 249–50; the subsequent passages pp. 254, 307 and 243.

followers of Satan and his deputy Carpathia are 'cast alive' into hell's 'lake of fire'. 'For believers who loved Him [i.e., Christ] and who loved the truth,' we are told, 'His rule would be a marvelous change from the last seven years and, indeed, the millennia before that. But for people interested only in their own gain, still thumbing their noses at God, Jesus' rule would be most uncomfortable'.

When I last mentioned the *Left Behind* series in Chapter Five I suggested that any such Christian portrayal of the apocalypse and Last Judgment in the late twentieth- or early twenty-first-century must appear grotesquely regressive in terms of literary characterization and histrionic in terms of plot; indeed, to anyone not wedded to an evangelical worldview the inflated melodrama of the volume's storyline comes across as utterly contrived, with the true Christian faithful predictably being compensated for the tyranny and cruelty that they have suffered at the hands of Satan and his sycophants, whereas unbelievers are indiscriminately killed off by a Christ who displays neither pity nor mercy for those Satan has duped and corrupted. The degree of resentment and gratification one can detect behind the brutality with which Christ is shown punishing Satan's followers is no less disturbing than it is revealing; we are, as Saul Friedländer has expressed it, witness to an especially spiteful and vindictive kind of 'jubilation at the end of those others who do not belong among the Chosen'.[9] For a non-evangelical audience, the conclusion to the *Left Behind* cycle reads like an overplayed exercise in evangelical self-congratulation and self-affirmation. Indeed, as a whole 'the Christian fundamentalist action thriller', as the critic Christian Thorne has called the 'Rapture Novel' genre,[10] serves to reassure the like-minded that their struggle against what they perceive as our society's secular depravity and self-indulgence as well as its members' sexual and moral debauchery was not embarked upon in vain; the up-hill battle is not just a worthy cause but also one nearing its soon-to-come conclusion in Christ's 'Glorious Appearing'. The message runs: we told you unbelievers all along, but you did not listen, so now you can deservedly go to hell. Of course, ironically, few of those at whom this message is aimed will ever read this novel; its true target audience is the evangelical in-group of all those who already believe. That the narrative comes with a goodly measure of religious bombast and interpretive caprice whose callous one-upmanship only the fundamentalist Christian will be disposed to overlook should hence take no one by surprise.

Nor can it come as a surprise that the *Left Behind* authors came in for considerable criticism for their work's many theological absurdities or for subscribing to a highly dishonest kind of 'pick-and-choose' biblical literalism[11] as well as a bigoted stylization

---

9 'Introduction', in *Visions of Apocalypse. End or Rebirth?*, ed. by Saul Friedländer, Gerald Molton, Leo Marx and Eugene Skolnikoff (New York and London: Holmes & Meier, 1985), pp. 3–17 (p. 10). The *Left Behind* series has 'inspired' various sustained critical treatments, among them those by Glenn Shuck, *Marks of the Beast. The Left Behind Novels and the Struggle for Evangelical Identity* (New York: New York University Press, 2004), and Robert M. Price, *The Paperback Apocalypse* (Amherst: Prometheus Books, 2007).

10 'The Revolutionary Energy of the Outmoded', p. 98.

11 So the critic Barbara Rossing, author of *The Rapture Exposed* (Boulder, CO, and Oxford: Westview Press, 2004), in a YouTube clip entitled 'Debunking the Rapture', accessed online on 16 October 2015; she rebukes those who promulgate such notions as the 'Rapture' — which she argues

of the forces of good and evil, a stylization that not just projects religious and social prejudice and intolerance but also emphatically encourages them. A prime example is the villain Leon Fortunato who plays the right hand of Lucifer's dictatorial worldly agent Nicolae Jetty Carpathia (the 'self-appointed Global Community potentate' and one-time Secretary General of the United Nations); underscoring LaHaye's and Jenkins's well-broadcast anti-gay sentiment, Fortunato is depicted in slapstick manner as a conceited gay buffoon who is at one point caricatured as follows: 'Leon was in his most resplendent, gaudiest, Day-Glo getup, including a purple felt fez with multiple hangy-downs and a cranberry vestment with gold collar'.[12] Likewise, if stylistically more subtle, Satan's and Carpathia's personal pronouns 'he', 'him' and 'his' are invariably given in lower case, as contrasted with Christ's and God's upper case 'He', 'Him' and 'His', deploying spelling to subliminally reinforce the black-and-white message that the good are intrinsically superior to their adversaries. That 'the names of the rugged male protagonists sound like those of porn stars (Dirk Burton, Rayfold Steele, and Buck Williams)' and that the character portrayals advocate 'the thorough remasculinization of Christianity along with a world purified of the corrupting influences of the feminine' — with good women angelically transported to heaven and bad women enjoying themselves incubus-like with the Devil on Earth — underscores all the more the chauvinist bias of their work, as one critic has remarked.[13] More worrying still is the politico-ideological premise behind their narrative worldview, a worldview that promotes, in the words of one professor of religious studies, David Carlson, dangerously 'extreme views' on current affairs such as the Near-East conflict between Israel and its Palestinian neighbours or the bringing down of the World Trade Center twin towers in 2001. Carlson cites as a case in point the 'skewed view of the Christian faith that, all in the name of Christ', emerges from statements such as those by the evangelical webmaster of the *Rapture Ready* website, Todd Strandberg, who 'welcomes war and disaster, while dismissing peace efforts in the Middle East and elsewhere', and who expressed his 'joy' over the fact that 9/11 was yet another sign of the nearing of the end.[14] In his 'Introduction' to the volume *Visions of Apocalypse. End or Rebirth?*, Saul Friedländer at one point cites James Rhodes's 1980 *The Hitler Movement* to emphasize the dangers that are intrinsic to such a blinkered and self-serving evangelical fanaticism; he writes:

is nowhere found in the Bible but was cooked up in the nineteenth century — for 'teaching people to be scared', instilling a 'sense of fear' especially in children, and generally thrusting 'spiritual abuse' upon a credulous audience.

12 *Glorious Appearing*, pp. 48–49.

13 Joyce Janca-Aji, 'The Dark Dreamlife of Postmodern Theology. *Delicatessen*, *The City of Lost Children* and *Alien Resurrection*', in *Religion and Science Fiction*, ed. by James F. McGrath (Eugene, OR: Pickwick Publications, 2011), pp. 9–31 (these quotations p. 27). Janca-Aji is in turn citing in part from the article by Christian Thorne that I quoted earlier and in which Thorne observes that '*Left Behind* has almost no use for women at all. They all either disappear in the novel's opening pages or get left behind and metamorphose into the whores of anti-Christ' (p. 99).

14 David Carlson, '*Left Behind* and the Corruption of Biblical Interpretation', originally published in 2003, here accessed online at OrthodoxyToday.org on 16 October 2015.

Rhodes stresses the similarity [between modern and traditional apocalyptic beliefs and imagery] by pointing out that Nazi ideological imagery, like that of the traditional apocalypticists, approximated the following sequence: disaster, revelation of the way to salvation, discovery of the fundamental forces of Evil and of the imminence of a final attack by those forces, discovery of one's own election to fight the ultimate battle against the evil forces — all leading to a vision of the subsequent millennium (the Thousand-Year Reich).[15]

Moreover, both brands of extremist self-staging, the political and the religious, ultimately rely on 'a messianic figure, a saviour, the leader of the ultimate battle' whose 'revelation is laid down in a Gospel-like text'.

This description of course perfectly fits the schema that LaHaye and Jenkins resorted to when they set up the storyline of their *Left Behind* cycle. While they themselves parade the Bible as their immediate source — the epilogue's commentary at the end of *Glorious Appearing* is as shot through with quotes from the Bible as is the novel's narrative itself — the authors also drew on a number of non-scriptural sources, although these are not explicitly identified. The two most important of these are, first, the concept of millennial dispensationalism, a concept that was introduced by two nineteenth-century clergymen, the British Bible teacher John Nelson Darby and, in Darby's wake, the American minister and Bible editor Cyrus I. Scofield; and, second, the books by the Christian Zionist preacher Harold (Hal) Lee Lindsey, who with Carole C. Carlson co-authored the evangelical best seller *The Late, Great Planet Earth*, a pseudo-documentary prophecy of the coming apocalypse. Published in 1970 *The Late, Great Planet Earth* was followed in the next three decades by a slew of titles ranging from *Satan is Alive and Well on Planet Earth* (1972), *Promise* (1974), *Terminal Generation* (1976), *The 1980s: Countdown to Armageddon* (1981), *The Rapture* (1983) and *There's a New World Coming: A Prophetic Odyssey* (1984) to, in the 1990s, *Planet Earth 2000 A.D.: Will Mankind Survive?* (1994), *Final Battle* (1995), *Amazing Grace* (1995) and *Planet Earth, the Final Chapter* (1998), all of whose titles read like headline abbreviations of the plotline behind LaHaye and Jenkins's *Left Behind* sequence. The red thread of Lindsey's work is that we are living in the era of the Antichrist and that the biblical prophecies of Armageddon and the end of time are proving themselves true in our very day, the signs being all around us for everyone to see: global famines, regional wars, the arms race, and ominous planetary constellations engulfing our world as well as the European Community replicating the Roman Empire as purportedly foretold in the Bible. What was predicted in ancient prophecy is 'what is happening right now', states the second narrator in the film adaptation of *The Late, Great Planet Earth*; giving himself the air of a scientific researcher, he goes on to cite nuclear war as the possible means of these prophecies' fulfilment, with the hailstones and meteors of ancient prophecy soon to rain down on us in the shape of atomic bombs and Intercontinental Ballistic Missiles — all this highly effectively visually underlaid with nuclear mushroom clouds and images from Hiroshima. Although Lindsey makes no reference to them, any of the several apocalyptic verse epics we encountered over the course of this study, as well as the

---

15 'Introduction' to *Visions of Apocalypse. End or Rebirth?*, this and the subsequent quotation p. 7.

anonymous Protestant German cleric's 1792 end-time chronology *The approaching End of the World, described through its Remarkable Events, since the Time of Creation*, could have served as the blueprint for *The Late, Great Planet Earth*; in their time Sonnenberg's *Donatoa*, Grainville's *Le Dernier Homme*, Townsend's *Armageddon* and Pollok's *The Course of Time* all aimed to impress the same end-time message on their readers as does Lindsey on his late twentieth-century Christian fundamentalist audience. There is a sad irony, but perhaps little surprise, in the fact that Lindsey by far outdoes his predecessors in terms of success, sales and circulation.[16]

What this also reminds us of, naturally, is that the storyline of *Glorious Appearing* is not a new one. Having said that, LaHaye and Jenkins have of course gone to great lengths to cater to the tastes and belief horizons of a contemporary evangelical audience by updating the plot and modernizing the character cast. What remains in place, by contrast, is the role of biblical location and ancient prophecy; we thus read in a 2011 epilogue added to a new imprint of the cycle's first instalment, *Left Behind. A Novel of the Earth's Last Days*:

> two significant pieces of prophecy that play into the *Left Behind* series are the role of Russia ('Rosh' in the Bible) as an enemy of Israel and the future importance of Babylon. [...] Babylon is where Satan located his headquarters and began his centuries-old battle against God for the souls of men. [...] Babylon will again become Satan's headquarters for a short time [...]. Even now, in our lifetime, Babylon is being prepared for its final appearance on the stage of human history. [...] Another recent story out of Taiwan noted that a Taiwanese tour agency is starting to take people to Iraq to tour — among other things — the city of Babylon as it is being rebuilt. As Iraq becomes increasingly stable and secure, direct foreign investment is going to flood in, and Iraq will become the wealthiest country on the planet.[17]

(As things currently stand in the Middle East, however — I write this in summer 2015 — the Antichrist's taking over of the world may not be quite as imminent as LaHaye and Jenkins make it out to be.) Readers familiar with the *Left Behind* series may also agree that in terms of style and rhetoric it is a rather crude product; the authors clearly wrote their novels not with any literary ambition in mind but rather to achieve a particular effect, namely to broadcast their brand of evangelical eschatological message. The irreconcilability of aesthetic merit and utilitarian message is not a new dilemma; it has always been intrinsic especially to didactic literary genres to which religious end-time literature of this kind belongs. The dilemma is compounded once the Christian eschatological apocalyptic narrative — which is by definition a narrative of futurity — has to compete, starting in the nineteenth century, with secular science fiction's futuristic narratives of the end of our world, a selection of which I have discussed in this study. Essentially, religious

---

16 Alone for its anti-Protestant and anti-evangelical sentiment it is less likely that the earliest 'translation' of the verse epic apocalypse into a prose format, Robert Hugh Benson's 1907 novel *Lord of the World*, served as an influence on Lindsey; Benson's novel recounts the takeover of the world by the Antichrist figure Felsenburgh in the twenty-first century, a takeover that culminates in the last line of the novel in the end of our world and the likely advent of Armageddon.

17 Tim LaHaye and Jerry B. Jenkins, *Left Behind. A Novel of the Earth's Last Days* (Carol Stream, IL: Tyndale House, 2011), pp. 479, 481, 482 and 485.

apocalyptic texts are, as measured by the standards of modern natural science, anti-realistic, whereas the ethos of modern science fiction is by and large realistic, its futuristic setting notwithstanding; futuristic and speculative both may be, but science fiction writers generally aspire to portray the world of the future based on a scientific understanding of natural law that excludes supernatural agency. As the noted theoretician of science fiction Darko Suvin observed in his 1979 *Metamorphoses of Science Fiction: On the Poetics and History of a Literary Genre*: 'It is intrinsically or by definition impossible for SF to acknowledge any metaphysical agency, in the literal sense of an agency going beyond *physis* (nature). Whenever it does so, it is not SF, but a metaphysical or (to translate the Greek into Latin) a supernatural fantasy-tale'.[18] It is precisely for this reason that the Christian eschatological epic has not aged well: it appeals to modern expectations neither in terms of content nor of form. By the end of the eighteenth century the era of the religious verse epic had, for all intents and purposes, come to an end, as I elaborated in Chapters One and Two; the nineteenth-century authors Sonnenberg, Grainville, Townsend and Pollok were fighting a lost cause. As emerged from our discussion of Percy Bysshe Shelley's poem 'Mont Blanc' in Chapter Four, Shelley's atheistic critique of key tenets of Christian doctrine was symptomatic of the increased scrutiny Christian theology was coming under as it tried (or tried not) to square its eschatological view of the universe with the findings of modern science.

The reasons for the Christian verse epic becoming unpalatable — as corroborated by Sonnenberg's and Grainville's dwindling audience — related not just to the perceived unrealism of the verse epic's didactic eschatological message; they were also aesthetic. For it may have been the very success and matchlessness of Milton's religious verse epic that led to the genre's downfall in the first place; with *Paradise Lost* having become the yardstick used to measure the quality of later verse epics even well beyond the British borders, few works managed to live up to the benchmark set by Milton. The perfect illustration of this fact is the following observation made around 1827 by an anonymous reviewer of Pollok's eschatological verse epic *The Course of Time*; this reviewer wrote:

> The end of the world, the resurrection, and the judgment, follow in succession and close the scene. How all this is filled up, and how relieved, we have no intention of stating: we have answered our object, if we have laid enough before the reader to enable him to perceive that, to fill up such a plan as it should be filled, requires not only a man earnest in his religious views, but one of profound thought, and of almost unmatched poetic powers. The first two qualifications we believe we may grant in full to our author; but we cannot, in sincerity, say so much for him in the last requisite. We doubt whether the mere poetic excellencies of the work are such as to make it deeply interesting to any but truly religious minds; and to render its sound evangelical sentiment palatable with the world at large, would require in its poetry all the magnificence of Milton himself. It is a pity that any, in their zeal for religion, should have compared our author with him, the sublime character of whose mind has not been equalled since the days of the prophets. Simply as a poet,

---

18 *Metamorphoses of Science Fiction: On the Poetics and History of a Literary Genre* (New Haven and London: Yale University Press, 1979), p. 66.

Mr. Pollok is neither a Cowper nor a Young.[19]

Nor are LaHaye and Jenkins. As this reviewer's remarks make plain, the problems facing the eschatological genre of writing remain in principle the same today as they were two hundred (or more) years ago. I am sure this nineteenth-century reviewer would agree that changing the narrative form from traditional verse epic to modern prose alone should not suffice to exempt the authors of the *Left Behind* novels from the requirement 'to render its sound evangelical sentiment palatable with the world at large', something that 'would require in its [prose] all the magnificence of Milton himself'.

Another obstacle this kind of writing faces outside of its predisposed in-group target audience stems from the circumstance that its Christian eschatological end-time subject matter cannot be divorced from the constraints set by its religious antecedents. We recall from Chapter One the anonymous *Allgemeine Literatur-Zeitung*'s reviewer of Sonnenberg's *Das Weltende* (the abandoned first version of *Donatoa*) already lamenting in 1801 that, due to the predictable nature of events, 'predetermined as they are by scripture' ('aus der *Schrift* genommen, und durch die *Schrift* voraus bestimmt'), 'our interest in the action is doused' because 'what happens has to happen'. While LaHaye and Jenkins may have more or less satisfactorily risen to the challenge of psychologizing their Christian characters' actions — something that Sonnenberg and Grainville, too, had taken great pains to achieve in their verse epics — they too fail to deliver in terms of (un)predictability of action; they likewise follow in the footsteps of the traditional religious apocalyptic epic in regard to the biased way in which they present their heroes' worldly antagonists. In short, LaHaye and Jenkins subscribe to precisely the kind of jaded black-and-white characterization and tediously predictable 'last-minute happy ending' that not just Susan Sontag in our own time attacked as 'perpetuat[ing] clichés', but also Sonnenberg's anonymous reviewer already in 1801 saw as ill-judged, inflated and ineffectual; writing two centuries even before the authors of the *Left Behind* series put pen to paper, this reviewer complained: 'even the most profligate fantasy will not be sufficient to portray the unchanging seraphic and devilish natures with the requisite variety' ('selbst die schwelgerischte Phantasie reicht nicht hin, grosse Mannigfaltigkeit in die unwandelbaren seraphischen und teuflischen Naturen zu legen'),[20] a warning left unheeded by LaHaye and Jenkins. Already in Sonnenberg's day the implausible rescue and, in a sense, 'rapture' of Heroal and Herkla at the close of *Donatoa* would have been considered sublime only by the most orthodox of religious-minded readers; but to 'rapture' and rescue the faithful today, two centuries later, as well as dispatch millions of unbelievers uniformly to Hell without specific individual justification (except that they had fallen under Satan's spell), must be viewed from a purely generic vantage point as anachronistic, unrealistic and deficient in motivation. And yet 'rapture' and rescue the Christian faithful LaHaye

---

[19] Anon., 'Critical Observations [from *The Spirit of the Pilgrims*]', in Robert Pollok, *The Course of Time, with Critical Observations of Various Authors on the Genius and Writings of the Poet*, ed. by James R. Boyd (New York and Chicago: A. S. Barnes, 1871), pp. 28–34 (pp. 28–29).

[20] Anon., review in *Allgemeine Literatur-Zeitung*, 22 June 1801, columns 633–36 (column 633).

and Jenkins do, as well as send their adversaries wholesale and indiscriminately to burn in Hellfire. Little surprise then that the *Left Behind* novels read like a prose parody of the religious apocalyptic epic of yore, penned in malicious jest by an atheist seeking to poke fun at the genre of evangelical end-time fantasies. Were it not for the captive target audience, the millions of Bible-literalist evangelical Christians in the United States who seek to obtain religious solace and spiritual refuge from this kind of writing, *Glorious Appearing* would surely have experienced the same fate as Sonnenberg's *Donatoa* and Grainville's *Le Dernier Homme* in their day. The *Left Behind* novels offer their in-group target audience, in Susan Sontag's words, an 'escape into [an] exotic dangerous situation', in this instance the battle for survival of the dwindling troupe of the Christian faithful who, against all odds, heroically dare to stand up to the evil armies of the Antichrist. The only irony is (and the characters all know this): with the 'happy end' being scripturally pre-ordained, the outcome is weighted in their favour. Although the final battle is presented as a nail-bitingly perilous culmination and moment of truth, by its very nature any Christian eschatological plotline that leads up to Christ's Second Coming and the Last Judgment cannot but have a predictably comforting outcome for the reader–cum–true–believer. How comforting is best measured by the *Left Behind* cycle's and its accoutrements' immense marketing success which, it must be said, constitutes a truly miraculous reversal of fortune for religious apocalyptic storytelling and testifies to the lasting allure of this kind of speculative religious esotericism. Here we have *Donatoa* all over again in the guise of contemporary evangelical make-believe: the embattled Christian remnant, in *Donatoa* a mere three faithful, here counts in the tens of main characters and thousands of like-minded confederates around the globe, but the basic storyline has remained essentially the same; it is one of triumph and redemption for all those who, against persistent harassment and brutal maltreatment, remained faithful to their (Christian) God. As such, the twelve cantos of Sonnenberg's *Donatoa* (as well as of Milton's *Paradise Lost* and Townsend's *Armageddon*) find themselves successfully translated — if success here is not measured by aesthetic standards, but by merely commercial ones — into the twelve novels of the *Left Behind* cycle. The message is clear: the religious verse epic may have been 'left behind', but the evangelical Christian apocalyptic mindset clearly has not.

Nature's Final Reckoning

In his 'Foreword' to the second edition of *Brave New World* Aldous Huxley once remarked, 'whatever its artistic or philosophical qualities, a book about the future can interest us only if its prophecies look as though they might come true'.[21] If there is anything my observations in the previous section have illustrated, it must be less that the *Left Behind* series can be of no interest than that the validity of Huxley's statement is contingent upon what an individual believes can come true, and what not. For the evangelical Christian reader who fully subscribes to the worldview

---

21 'Author's Foreword (to the 1946 edition)', p. 225.

presented by LaHaye and Jenkins in their *Left Behind* cycle, the fact that Christ will return to Earth in an apocalyptic Second Coming is a certainty; debatable is at best when and how this will occur.[22] This when and how is the subject of the first paradigm of Last Man narratives.

For non-believers, however, this is one prophecy that will never come true. And yet believers and non-believers alike all agree that mankind's existence on planet Earth must come to an end sooner or later; they also have in common that none of them know when this end will come about. The causes we have learnt to associate with the end are threefold; they can be divine, natural or man-induced. The end can be gradual or sudden, all-inclusive (that is, 'terminal' in my phrasing) or selective ('semi-terminal'), and it can take place within our time, in an undefined near future or in a far-flung future millions or even billions of years hence. Such is the case in Olaf Stapledon's path-breaking 1930 science-fiction novel *Last and First Men: A Story of the Near and Far Future*, in which mankind is portrayed as incrementally mutating over millions of millennia into a species that, by the time we reach the year two billion A.D., lives up to 250,000 years 'on average', has had to leave its home planet and emigrate to Neptune via Venus (because Earth's moon developed a collision course with its sister planet), and is now, having survived so many catastrophes and vicissitudes, facing extinction due to the dying sun's rays intensifying and making life on any planet in our solar system unsustainable. Stapledon's Last Man may be removed in time by two billion years, giving us some respite as a species, but last he is nonetheless. The message of Stapledon's novel is clear: the end may not be nigh, but it is inevitable.

When and especially how the end through non-divine means will come about is the subject of the second and third paradigms of Last Man narratives, the second attributing the cause of our end to natural agency, the third to human agency. The plot revolving around a lethal global plague was the first blueprint of nature's paradigm; since Mary Shelley introduced it, it has come to constitute a staple of the genre of futuristic fiction. Stapledon too makes use of this matrix: about mid-story, in Chapter IX of *Last and First Men*, the author lets his end-time narrator — a narrator who retrospectively relates the billion-year history of the spectacular rises and equally spectacular declines of eighteen distinct species of human beings (our own species of *Homo sapiens* being merely the first in this long line), as well as of the complete transformation of our planet's continents across those hundreds of millions of years — also recount how in the Third Dark Ages humankind as well as virtually all other animal species were all but killed off by a lethal virus. Published some two hundred years after Shelley's *The Last Man*, the most recent literary avatar of mankind's annihilation through a global pandemic is Canadian writer Emily St. John Mandel's 2014 novel *Station Eleven* — winner of the 2015 Arthur C. Clarke Award — that will be discussed in more detail below. Interestingly, but

---

22 Robert Jay Lifton notes in 'The Image of "The End of the World"': 'Christian millennial images can, at least at times, be included on the side of the continuum of the relatively acceptable interpretation. That is true as long as the theological structure of meaning, the eschatology involving something like Armageddon, is generally believed' (p. 151). I am not sure I fully agree with Lifton on this score: the question his remarks beg is 'acceptable' to whom?

unsurprisingly, most novelists writing within this matrix have chosen to pick up where Mary Shelley's novel left off, preferring instead to focus on the process and progress of survival; they show us not, or not just, what came before and led to annihilation, but rather what came after, what happened to those who were left after disaster struck; we detected the same tendency in novels of nuclear warfare, as we saw in Chapter Five. As opposed to authors like Mary Shelley who preclude perpetuation of the species *tout court*, the writers who go down the alternate path quickly move on to the regeneration of mankind that transpires after the crisis has subsided. This is the matrix followed by what many would consider the two most classic pandemic novels to succeed Mary Shelley's *The Last Man*, namely Jack London's *The Scarlet Plague*, first published in the *London Magazine* in 1912, and George R. Stewart's *Earth Abides*, published in 1949. Their texts exhibit a dual focus: first, they describe the ravages of the plague and the rapid dissolution of human society, which typically results in a violent battle of all against all in the fight for diminishing resources; they then, second, depict the slow recovery of mankind as the isolated survivors — the solitary Lionel Verneys, as it were — at some point discover they are not alone after all and gradually congregate into motley bands of human beings who begin to form new communities. This process takes time; thus to achieve the necessary temporal extension, the narrators of *The Scarlet Plague* and *Earth Abides* trace the lives of the key protagonists of their narratives until old age, concluding the novel many decades after the plague came and went. At the beginning of London's *The Scarlet Plague* we accordingly encounter the 87-year-old James Howard Smith, the tale's protagonist and former professor of English literature at the University of California at Berkeley, in conversation with his grandchildren who have by this time, six decades after the scarlet plague hit the Bay Area, turned into 'true savages', 'skin-clad and barbaric', as Smith laments.[23] Likewise, the protagonist of *Earth Abides*, Isherwood Williams (or Ish for short), formerly a graduate student of ecology doing solitary fieldwork in the mountains when the virus broke out, is pictured at the close of the novel as surrounded by some of his great-grandchildren. As the last of his generation to die Ish calls himself 'The Last American', for his great-grandchildren, Americans though they may be, no longer have any notion what the term 'United States' means and what it once stood for; the few score members of 'The Tribe' have reverted to a 'primitive' state of hunting with bows and arrows, wearing under their 'tawny lion-skins' blue jeans that they have salvaged from the civilizational debris of a now mythical people they call the 'Old Ones'.[24]

Structurally, that is in terms of their internal sequencing, *The Scarlet Plague* and *Earth Abides* both represent continuations of Mary Shelley's storyline: whereas Lionel Verney remains alone *at the end* of his narrative, James Howard Smith and Isherwood Williams remain alone *at the beginning* of theirs.[25] *The Last Man* is about

23 *The Scarlet Plague* (London: Hesperus Press / Modern Voices, 2008), pp. 8 and 63.
24 As described in Part Three, Chapter Two, of George R. Stewart's *Earth Abides* (New York: Ballantine Books, 1983, first published 1949), p. 321.
25 Echoing the conclusion of Mary Shelley's *The Last Man* but commingling it with a reference to Defoe's *Robinson Crusoe*, early in *Earth Abides* Ish is described thus: 'He was like a sailor in his own

Verney's life before the catastrophe, it ends when all but Verney have died; *The Scarlet Plague* and *Earth Abides* are about life after the catastrophe, they begin when all but their heroes have died (at least until we eventually find out that there are other survivors). *The Last Man* shows us society falling apart, it is a story of cruel terminal decline; *The Scarlet Plague* and *Earth Abides* show the survivors in the process of rebuilding their lives and reestablishing society, theirs are stories of adaptation and anticipation. While Smith's and Ish's communities have, by the time of their passing decades after the nadir, turned 'back to nature' and a 'primitive' state of being, there is no question that the human species as a whole has withstood the crisis and is now moving forward afresh — and perhaps civilizationally refreshed — on a trajectory of gradual recovery. Reduplicating the old Indian ways of life in the American West, Smith's and Ish's offspring are physically redynamized and are reintegrated more naturally into their environment, hunting confidently once again with bow and arrow; thus Ish 'could not help thinking', we read in the final chapter of *Earth Abides*, 'that men had lost that old dominance and the arrogance with which they had once viewed the animals, and were now acting more or less as equals with them'.[26] Stewart's book ends as I see it on a more positive note than London's, with Ish pondering how, while 'he was the last of the old', his great-grandchildren were 'in the cycle of mankind [...] many thousands of years younger than [him]' — 'they were the first of the new'. London gives his portrait of the future a more sinister and pessimistic inflection; as his protagonist, the once college professor of English, sees it, his grandson Hare-Lip is no better than a brute 'savage with the dark and clouded mind of a savage', he is a 'primitive' being who is deeply 'sunk in black superstition'.[27] Looking back over his life and survival, Smith concludes: 'I am the last man who was alive in the days of the plague and who knows the wonders of that far-off time. We, who mastered the planet — its earth, and sea, and sky — and who were as very gods, now live in primitive savagery along the watercourses of this California country'. Yet although Smith remarks to his grandson much as Ish does in *Earth Abides*: 'But we are increasing rapidly — your sister, Hare-Lip, already has four children. We are increasing rapidly and making ready for a new climb toward civilization', we are clearly meant to take this comment in London's novel as cynical: after all, civilization represents for Smith 'the eternal types — the priest, the soldier, and the king' as well as the 'gunpowder [that] enabled us to kill surely and at long distances', not the best ambassadors of our social order. And in due course, Smith concludes, 'the gunpowder will come. Nothing can stop it — the same old story over and over. Man will increase, and men will fight'.

In fact, there is nothing nostalgic about the main protagonist's perspective in either London's or Stewart's novel, for Ish too reflects in the penultimate chapter of *Earth Abides*:

---

boat stocked and ready for emergencies, and he also felt the deep desperation of the solitary survivor of a ship-wreck, alone in all the vastness' (p. 44).

26 *Earth Abides*, p. 333; the subsequent passages pp. 335, 326 and 59.
27 *The Scarlet Plague*, pp. 61 and 60, the subsequent passages pp. 58–59 and 61–62.

> The Great Disaster! Ish had not thought of those words for a long time. Now they seemed to have lost meaning. Those people who had died then would now be dead anyway, from mere passage of time. Now it seemed to make little difference whether they had all died in one year, or slowly over many years. And as for the loss of civilization — about that too he had long doubted.

If the authors of these novels of natural eradication exhibit a proclivity to remind their readers of humankind's fragility on planet Earth, they also like to show how nature, having been rid of humankind's propensity to encroach on and destroy the natural habitats it depends on, can get along quite well without man. It is man who needs nature, not nature that needs man; this is the *basso continuo* in the majority of these novels. Thus in many of these tales — the earliest among them being to my knowledge Richard Jefferies's 1885 novel *After London or Wild England*, in which London's population was, long before the story sets in, killed by the deadly chemicals amassed in the city, embodying 'the very essence of corruption'[28] — nature is shown as making a swift recovery from mankind's irresponsible tyranny over the planet's fauna and flora and its reckless exploitation of the world's natural resources. Stewart for instance in *Earth Abides* has the narrator go about describing nature's revival with quasi-scientific ostentation, buttressing his narrative with inserts in a more impersonal voice offering italicized projections about the future, as in the passage cited below. The context here is that Ish, after finding himself alone in California, has decided to crisscross the United States in search of other survivors; on his way he encounters a small family of blacks trying to eke out an existence with traditional farming methods in the vicinity of Memphis. 'As he drove on', we are told,

> he began to think that the Negroes had really solved the situation better than he. He was living as a scavenger upon what was left of civilization; they, at least, were still living creatively close to the land and in a stable situation, still raising most of what they needed.
>
> *Of half a million species of insects only a few dozen were appreciably affected by the demise of man, and the only ones actually threatened with extinction were the three species of the human louse. [...] At the funeral of* Homo sapiens *there will be few mourners.* Canis familiaris *as an individual will perhaps send up a few howls, but as a species, remembering all the kicks and curses, he will soon be comforted and run off to join his wild fellows.* Homo sapiens, *however, may take comfort from the thought that at his funeral there will be three wholly sincere mourners.*

Notwithstanding these few 'wholly sincere mourners' — that is, mourners only should any of these 'three species of the human louse' manage to survive their host's death — nature is invariably shown to be far more resilient than the human species it sustains. Indeed, in many tales we are given to understand that it is in fact a good thing that the cancer of humanity has been, if not removed altogether from nature, then at least reduced to a more sustainable level. Man's diminution is nothing to pine over, but rather something rejuvenating within the larger scheme of things, giving mankind a second chance within another cycle of natural development to do things better.

---

28 Richard Jefferies, *After London or Wild England* (Cirencester: The Echo Library, 2005), p. 128.

As we saw with London and Stewart, whose novels' post-catastrophe communities have reverted to an autochthonous way of life (calling themselves accordingly a 'tribe'), a favourite pastime of the authors of pandemic novels is to remind their readers what would transpire should mankind be reduced to a level where human civilization as well as the technologies that uphold it have fallen irretrievably apart. Mandel, whose 2014 novel *Station Eleven* is the latest literary reworking of the plague matrix, follows in her predecessors' footsteps when she writes:

> No more diving into pools of chlorinated water lit green from below. No more ball games played out under floodlights. [...] No more trains running under the surface of cities on the dazzling power of the electric third rail. No more cities. No more films [...]. No more screens shining in the half-light as people raise their phones above the crowd to take photographs of concert stages. [...] No more pharmaceuticals. No more certainty of surviving a scratch on one's hand [...], a dog bite. [...] No more towns glimpsed from the sky through airplane windows. [...] No more airplanes, no more requests to put your tray table in its upright and locked position — but no, this wasn't true, there were still airplanes here and there. They stood dormant on runways and in hangars. They collected snow on their wings.[29]

When the plague hits, Western civilization stalls and humankind's evolutionary clock is turned back, in *Station Eleven* as in *The Scarlet Plague* and *Earth Abides*.

Harking back ironically to our Romantic obsession with ruins, Mandel envisages how survivors might bestow upon the relics of our past civilizational grandeur and technological dexterity an emotional consequence that we might otherwise consider abnormal. To illustrate this point she introduces the character Clark Thompson, a man who, be it to hold in check the withdrawal symptoms he might not otherwise be able to escape, be it to keep at bay the ghosts of the past, has started a 'Museum of Civilization' in the — now defunct — Severn City airport terminal, exhibiting among other things 'the laptops, the iPhones, the radio from an administrative desk, the electric toaster from an airport-staff lounge, the turntable and vinyl records that some optimistic scavenger had carried back from Severn City' — all of which were 'taken-for-granted miracles' that in this post-pandemic day and age no longer have any 'practical use, but that people want to preserve' anyway. In like manner the protagonist of Margaret Atwood's 2003 novel *Oryx and Crake*, a man who was once called Jimmy but is now known among the tribe as Snowman, and who is 'the last *Homo sapiens*'[30] from the time before the (man-made) 'contagion' wiped out his fellow beings (the members of the tribe that he shepherds by contrast are genetically spliced humans resulting from biological engineering), tries to imagine explaining the cultural significance of 'Toast' and 'toaster' to the children of this artificial tribe:

> 'What is toast?' says Snowman to himself, once they've run off. *Toast is when you take a piece of bread — What is bread? Bread is when you take some flour — What is*

---

29 *Station Eleven* (London: Macmillan / Picador, 2014), p. 31; the subsequent passages pp. 232, 233, 258, 262 and 311.

30 *Oryx and Crake* (London: Little, Brown Book Group / Virago Press, 2010), p. 263, the subsequent quotation p. 112.

flour? We'll skip that part, it's too complicated. Bread is something you can eat, made from a ground-up plant and shaped like a stone. You cook it . . . Please, why do you cook it? Why don't you just eat the plant? Never mind that part. [...] *So, the toaster turns the slice of bread black on both sides with smoke coming out, and then this 'toaster' shoots the slice up into the air, and it falls onto the floor . . .* 'Forget it', says Snowman. 'Let's try again.' *Toast was a pointless invention from the Dark Ages. Toast was an implement of torture that caused all those subjected to it to regurgitate in verbal form the sins and crimes of their past lives. Toast was a ritual item devoured by fetishists in the belief that it would enhance their kinetic and sexual powers. Toast cannot be explained by any rational means. Toast is me. I am toast.* (Atwood's emphases)

In whichever way he might choose to explain what 'toast' is, whether it be realistic or cynical, the tribe would not know the difference. The protagonists of *The Scarlet Plague* and *Earth Abides* made similar experiences — Smith's and Ish's grandchildren and great-grandchildren have stopped taking their ancestors' mumbo-jumbo seriously, although they cannot deny them a certain mystique. And given time, the same problem could emerge for Kirsten Raymonde, the key female protagonist in Mandel's *Station Eleven*; how will she even start to explain to her as yet unborn descendants the functioning of the laptops and iPhones in Severn City Airport's 'Museum of Civilization', not to mention the dysfunctional aircraft standing unused on the tarmac? Already now, by 'Year Fifteen' after the onset of the pandemic, the children being taught in the new school in what was once 'Concourse C' are confused:

> They were told about the Internet, how it was everywhere and connected everything, how it was us. They were shown maps and globes, the lines of the borders that the Internet had transcended. This is the yellow mass of land in the shape of a mitten, this pin here on the wall is Severn City. That was Chicago. That was Detroit. The children understood dots on maps — *here* — but even the teenagers were confused by the lines. There had been countries, and borders. It was hard to explain.

But the survivors congregated in the concourse buildings of Severn City Airport are the lucky ones: their society is destined to reestablish itself faster than the tribes in London's and Stewart's novels. For, using a telescope positioned on the airport tower, they detect one night a distant village or town on the southern horizon that is 'lit up with electricity', the means through which the Museum's now unoperational gadgets might one day come back to life again.

Nothing might seem more 'natural' for the protagonists of post-catastrophe narratives than the obvious pastime of watching and commenting upon the social disintegration and the struggle for survival that inevitably result from whatever apocalyptic calamity has befallen them — except perhaps to wallow nostalgically in cultural memories and personal reminiscences, and to lament over the waning of their former world. In the book's penultimate chapter the narrator of *Earth Abides* describes how Ish revisits the university campus where he had once studied; we are told:

> Though [Ish] was still tired, he stood up curiously, and made out the shape of the Library a hundred yards or so distant. The trees around it had burned, but

> the building itself was still intact. Nearly all of its volumes, the whole record of mankind, would probably be still available. *Available for whom?* Ish did not try to answer the question that rose so spontaneously in his mind. In some way, the rules of the game had changed. He would not say whether they had changed for better or worse. In any case, the Library — its preservation or destruction — seemed to make very little difference in his thoughts now. Perhaps, this was the wisdom of old age. Perhaps, it was only despair and resignation.[31] (Stewart's emphasis)

Protagonists are also frequently shown meditating, more or less melancholically as befits the individual's mental constitution and situation, upon the decline of their descendants' linguistic abilities — as do Smith in *The Scarlet Plague* and Ish in *Earth Abides*, as does also Jimmy the Snowman in Atwood's *Oryx and Crake*. Describing the grandchildren of the once college professor Smith, the narrator of *The Scarlet Plague* observes at one point:

> their speech [...] was truly a gabble. They spoke in monosyllables and short jerky sentences that was more a gibberish than a language. And yet, through it ran hints of grammatical construction, and appeared vestiges of the conjugation of some superior culture. Even the speech of Granser [that is, Smith himself, the 'grandsire' of the children, R.W.] was so corrupt that were it put down literally it would be almost so much nonsense to the reader. This, however, was when he talked with the boys. When he got into the full swing of babbling to himself, it slowly purged itself into pure English. The sentences grew longer and were enunciated with a rhythm and ease that was reminiscent of the lecture platform.[32]

Another perennial theme is the turning to religion and trust in God by small groups of fanaticized faithful. We recall from Chapter Four how the historical prototype of nature's paradigm, Mary Shelley's *The Last Man*, featured an 'impostor-prophet and his followers'; likewise in Mandel's *Station Eleven*, written after 9/11 and the intensifying religious radicalization of today's world, we are shown the actor Arthur Leander's son, who survived the virus as a young boy, developing in adulthood into a fanatical preacher who rules with an iron fist with the aid of a gang of violent hoodlums. He is described as holding 'sway over the town of St. Deborah by the Water, ruling with a combination of charisma, violence, and cherry-picked verses from the Book of Revelation'.[33] He sees everyone's suffering as 'part of a greater plan'. But his vision of a world religiously reborn is not destined to gain the upper hand: the novel climaxes with a battle between three members of the 'Travelling Symphony', a troupe of travelling actors who stage Shakespeare's plays in the surviving communities, and the prophet and his thugs. It is one of the prophet's own followers, a young boy, who saves the day for Kirsten Raymonde and her companions by first shooting the prophet and then committing suicide by shooting himself. The boy had intuitively grasped that Kirsten's artistic way of life was more worth protecting than the heartless and inhuman religious zealotry of the prophet.

---

31 *Earth Abides*, p. 327.
32 *The Scarlet Plague*, p. 14.
33 *Station Eleven*, p. 280.

Religious fanaticism is similarly pivotal to the plotline of one of the most gripping of all late twentieth-century disaster novels, *Lucifer's Hammer* by Larry Niven and Jerry Pournelle, which depicts the collision of planet Earth with a comet from deep within our solar system. The approaching comet is immediately hailed by religious fanatics such as the Californian Christian TV evangelist Henry Armitage as 'the Hammer of God' sent to 'punish the decadent and the willful'.[34] After the comet's impact, with earthquakes, tsunamis, and inclement weather having devastated vast swathes of our planetary surface, the novel culminates in its final chapters in a show-down between the New Brotherhood Army that Armitage, now turned self-proclaimed prophet of God, has assembled and the secularists trying to reestablish a humane society amidst the destruction wrought by the comet. Niven and Pournelle give their novel an unexpected topical twist in that the followers of this new prophet of God see themselves as latter-day Luddites whom God has called upon to return mankind to nature and an ecological way of life by turning the civilizational clock back to the time before the industrial revolution. One character, Hugo Beck, who has escaped from his imprisonment by Armitage's militant henchmen, has managed to cross safely to the side of Senator Jellison's farm, the safe haven of the 'good guys'; Beck describes the ideology of the self-proclaimed prophet thus:

> His name was Henry Armitage, and we were in the hands of the Angels of the Lord. He kept talking, sometimes just talk like anybody, sometimes in a singsong voice with a lot of 'my brethren' and 'ye people of God, hear and believe'. We'd all been spared, he said. We'd lived through the end of the world, and we had a purpose in this life. We had to complete the Lord's work. The Hammer of God had fallen, and the people of God had a holy mission. The part I really listened to was when he told us we could join up or we could die. If we joined we'd get to shoot the ones who didn't join [...]. The work of Hammerfall is not finished, God never intended to make an end of mankind. It is God's intent that civilization be destroyed, so that man can live again as God intended. In the sweat of his brow he shall eat his bread. No longer shall he pollute the earth and the sea and the air with the garbage of industrial civilization that leads him further and further from God's way.

Of course, here too clichés abound; part of the story's appeal derives from the simple — not to say simplistic — black-and-white characterizations of good and bad guys as well as the obligatory 'last-minute happy ending' with its victory of the supposedly good over the purportedly evil, although the means deployed by Senator Jellison's motley forces are no better, and no less brutal, than those deployed by their adversaries.[35]

Obviously, with Niven and Pournelle's *Lucifer's Hammer* we have begun to shift ground. Their novel is about the destruction of mankind not through a plague but through other natural causes, in this instance an errant comet. The plague may have been the first means through which a writer sought 'realistically' to imagine nature

---

34 Larry Niven and Jerry Pournelle, *Lucifer's Hammer* (New York: Random House / Ballantine Books, 1983, first published 1977), p. 80, the subsequent quotation pp. 516–18.

35 One also cannot but wonder what sort of (subliminal?) message is meant to be conveyed by the equation between the evangelical hate-preacher with his bands of violent thugs and the ecological movement.

wiping out mankind, give or take the one or more surviving loners; but, once that matrix has been established, it becomes easy to imagine other natural means capable of destroying *Homo sapiens*. The list of nature's auxiliaries is long. Plagues were soon followed by comets, of which Niven and Pournelle's *Lucifer's Hammer* is only one of the later manifestations; the earliest narrative of a collision — or a threatened collision — between Earth and a comet (or asteroid) that I am aware of is Edgar Allan Poe's 1839 tale 'The Conversation of Eiros and Charmion', later narratives reach from Flammarion's 1894 *Omega: The Last Days of the World* (discussed in Chapter Two) and Werner Scheff's 1917 *The Ark* (*Die Arche*) to such recent movies as *Armageddon* and *Deep Impact* (both 1998). An extension of the comet theme is interstellar bodies — comets, planets or stars — hurtling into our solar system from outer space and colliding with Earth, as nearly happens in H. G. Wells's 1899 short story 'The Star' and actually does happen in Philip Wylie and Edwin Balmer's 1933 *When Worlds Collide*. Other themes include solar radiation storms (of which J. G. Ballard's 1962 *The Drowned World* is perhaps the best-known example), geophysical upheavals such as volcanic eruptions or plate tectonic movements that cause gigantic tsunami floods (an instance of which we cited in Chapter Four with Roland Emmerich's 2009 Hollywood blockbuster *2012*), the infertility of men (as in Grainville's 1805 *Le Dernier Homme* and P. D. James's 1992 novel *The Children of Men*), a new Ice Age (as in Douglas Orgill and John Gribbin's 1979 *The Sixth Winter*), or the eventual extinction of our sun and the resulting cold death of planet Earth (as in Flammarion's 1894 *La Fin du monde*, H. G. Wells's 1895 novel *The Time Machine* and George Wallis's 1901 story 'The Last Days of Earth').

A compact yet detailed survey of such naturally induced end-time scenarios can be found in the article 'The Rebellion of Nature' by W. Warren Wagar, the leading authority in the field whose work I frequently cite in this study; this article contains some of the most astute observations on the subject. Towards the end of his essay Wagar asks why this particular subject matter should have gained such popularity; 'the tale of natural catastrophe is a cheap thrill,' he explains, 'a form of escapism that does not cost us the feelings of guilt often stirred by visions of future wars or man-made ecological disasters.' 'Another answer to the question of the abundance of tales of natural catastrophe is', he continues,

> that visions of catastrophe meet a spectrum of psychological needs of writers and readers alike that no other imaginary events can quite fill. This answer is certainly true, if not the whole truth. The end of the world enables us, for example, to project in our imaginations a time when all our enemies, all the sources of our current distress and feelings of powerlessness, are removed, and we have survived. Such a situation is not exactly depressing.[36]

Wagar also accurately spotlights the close connection between natural catastrophism and secularism; I too focused on this connection in Chapter Four, where I noted that in Mary Shelley's *The Last Man* nature was depicted as an indifferent and neutral arbiter of fate, one that in contrast to the Christian God gives priority to no species. Wagar observes in the same vein that nature's paradigm results from 'the

---

36 'The Rebellion of Nature', pp. 168–69; the subsequent quote pp. 170–71.

erosion of the systems of belief and value'; he adds:

> In such tales, nature is not a symbol of divinity, or a garden for man to tend, or a cosmos proclaiming the coherence of creation, or even a storehouse of punishments provisioned by God to keep wayward man in line. In a universe with no known transcendental purpose or sanction, nature simply exists, indifferent to man, capable by the grinding operation of its laws of wiping him out in the wink of an eye, or in the fullness of time. As for God, the alleged creator of this obscene wilderness, there is nothing at all to say. Secular man does not believe in such things as God, who rarely appears or even rates a veiled allusion in eschatological fiction. The secular universe is a theater of absurdity and rebellion.

Although Wagar's argument here coincides with my own, I would like to remind ourselves nonetheless that even science fiction's concept of natural catastrophism has a trajectory that reaches back to religious scripture, at least in terms of the underlying premise: for the time-honoured blueprint is, of course, the Noachian Deluge and its destruction of all of mankind barring those legendary few survivors in Noah's Ark (the most recent visual adaptation thereof being the 2014 Hollywood blockbuser *Noah* directed by Darren Aronofsky and starring Russell Crowe, Emma Watson and Anthony Hopkins). And even the biblical portrayal of the Flood is not the oldest known depiction of a natural cataclysm of this kind but has its predecessors in older Mesopotamian and Sumerian writings, in particular the epics of Ziusudra and Gilgamesh. Naturally, deities were considered the driving force behind such natural disasters, but it was through natural rather than supernatural means that the divinity effected the destruction, cleansing and renewal of mankind. But let us remind ourselves also that the biblical Deluge provided not just the chief archetype within the Christian tradition for how to picture the physical destruction of mankind through natural means (as opposed to supernatural agency in the Last Judgment) — as well as a model of how to picture mankind's miraculous survival due to the ingenuity of a single pioneering engineer/shipbuilder, emulated on a grander scale even than in the film *Noah* by the film *2012* — but also that, as a topic of intense scientific scrutiny in the early nineteenth century, the recognition that major floods had actually occurred in Earth's planetary development became instrumental in fostering the gestation of modern anthropology and geology. Let us remember, too, that the shift from a biblical sacred history of our planet's 'Creation' through the Christian God, as represented for instance by James Parkinson's *Organic Remains of a Former World. An Examination of the Mineralized Remains of the Vegetables and Animals of the Antediluvian World* of 1804/1811 or Sharon Turner's *The Sacred History of the World, as displayed in the Creation and subsequent events to the Deluge* of 1832, to Cuvier's modern scientific confirmation that the continents of our planet had indeed been inundated at various stages in Earth's catastrophe-ridden history (with the attendant recognition that species could indeed become extinct) occurred in the first decades of the nineteenth century, inspiring the conception of Mary Shelley's novels *Frankenstein* and *The Last Man*. The lesson to be extracted from Cuvier's findings was and remains clear (again in Wagar's words): 'Any writer of fiction could draw the obvious moral: nature was not the anthropomorphic

Fig. C.1. John Martin, *The Opening of the Seventh Seal*, mezzotint, published 1837 as part of Richard Westall and John Martin's *Illustrations of the New Testament*. (This reproduction courtesy of the Yale Center for British Art, Paul Mellon Collection.)

mother of romantic myth or the mighty whirling mechanism of Newtonian physics, but a stage of endless slaughter and catastrophe'.[37] Earth's nature no longer embodies the supposedly benign basis for life, placed there by a benevolent and all-powerful creator god, but a hostile and menacing environment in which the vast uncontrollable energies within our universe, our solar system and our own planet's fiery inner core coalesce and disperse, marry and divorce, with no regard for the puny — and in the larger scheme of things irrelevant — creatures living atop this tiny speck of matter in the infinity of space. H. G. Wells aptly put it in perspective in his story 'The Star' when he let Martian astronomers wonder what had befallen their neighbours' planet after its near-collision with a comet-like star from outer space. Taking parts of the moon with it, which has now diminished in size, the star has plunged into the sun, causing it to emit more heat; the resulting change of climate on Earth has forced the humans who survive to move to the north and south poles. But the 'only difference' the Martian astronomers can actually see with their astronomical instruments is 'a shrinkage of the white discoloration (supposed to be frozen water) round either pole', which only goes to show, the story

---

37 Ibid., p. 145.

Fig. C.2. John Martin, *The Last Man* (courtesy of the Walker Art Gallery, Liverpool), oil painting exhibited 1850. This painting was Martin's third portrayal of a Last Man, following his 1826 *An Ideal Design of the Last Man* and his watercolour *The Last Man*, dated to 1833.

concludes, 'how small the vastest of human catastrophes may seem, at a distance of a few million miles' from our planet'.[38]

To graphically encapsulate this feeling of puniness and irrelevance of human affairs in the larger scheme of things was, of course, the specific objective of those genres of late eighteenth-century and early to mid-nineteenth-century pictorial art that sought to capture the sublime in portrayals of imposing landscapes, natural catastrophes, and Gothic supernatural subjects, including what Morton D. Paley has called 'the apocalyptic sublime'. A particularly popular subject within the apocalyptic sublime was, according to Paley, 'the Deluge' because it was able to 'form a bridge between natural catastrophe and [religious] apocalypse by showing divine forces virtually breaking through nature'.[39] Representative Victorian instances can be found in William Turner's and John Martin's decidedly dissimilar works. Often based on biblical themes and iconographical traditions, the apocalyptic sublime competed in its day with the natural sublime, with paintings on both sides at times exhibiting remarkably similar structural designs. Thus Caspar David Friedrich's tri-partite horizontal arrangement in *The Monk by the Sea*, with the vast scope of earth, sea and sky enfolding the minute human figure in the foreground (depicting a monk but otherwise lacking express indication of any supernatural intrusion) is

---

38 H. G. Wells, 'The Star', in *The Short Stories of H. G. Wells* (London: Ernest Benn, 1957), pp. 644–55 (p. 655).
39 *The Apocalyptic Sublime*, p. 2.

replicated compositionally by John Martin in his dramatic 1837 *The Opening of the Seventh Seal* (see Figure C.1), which shows a minuscule St. John the Divine standing on a promontory facing the open ocean witnessing the divine lightning bolts being cast from Heaven. This mezzotint illustration in turn relates structurally to Martin's 1837 *The Angel with the Book* and, inversely, his 1833 watercolour *The Last Man* as well as his 1849/1850 oil painting *The Last Man* (see Figure C.2), all of which exude a sensuously intense religious mood. Competing with them for popularity was the genre of secular landscape painting that presented its subject matter in purely naturalistic terms, usually positioning minuscule human beings within or close to such awe-inspiring natural settings as volcanic eruptions, ocean storms, or craggy Alpine peaks towering over thundering waterfalls and roaring ravines, two literary visualizations of which that we encountered earlier in our study were the 'Simplon Pass' section of Wordsworth's *The Prelude* and Percy Bysshe Shelley's 'Mont Blanc'.

Regardless of whether they were biblically or religiously motivated, freely imagined or inspired by authentic natural scenery, renderings of the sublime invariably showed nature as a site of awe-inducing superhuman forces operating beyond our intellectual grasp. In this sense too the sublime was the upshot of modern science and its new secularized understanding of the forces presiding over natural history; Wagar puts it in a nutshell when he writes: 'The world-model of Newtonian science had stressed mathematical order, harmony, uniformity, and stability. Much of the newer science found a place for struggle and disaster'.[40] Cuvier's theory about the violent 'revolutions' that had rocked our planet's surface during its several developmental stages and the resulting extinction of countless early animal species was at its time a prominent example of this 'newer science', hastening the realization not just among geologists (as we saw in Chapter Four) that, again in Wagar's words, 'anything that had happened before could happen again, here and now'. Wagar continues:

> Yet it is arguable that none of the theories and discoveries of science between, say, 1750 and 1900, would have caused more than brief alarm if not for one other event: the event that Friedrich Nietzsche billed in *The Joyful Wisdom* as the death of God. The steady decay of Jewish and Christian faith after the middle of the eighteenth century deprived nature of her divine origins and purposes. Natural disasters could no longer be viewed in any literal sense as 'acts of God', as punishments or tests of man imposed by an ultimately loving Father for his own ultimately good ends. Except for those whose faith remained intact or who subscribed to any of the various idealist or vitalist cosmologies that in effect turned nature herself into a god, the disasters of the natural order were simply disasters, the blind and brutal doings of an intrinsically pointless universe.

The development can hardly be summed up more concisely, and by and large it accords with what I have argued over the course of this study. But one has to query Wagar's final words nonetheless, for here I beg to differ. Must we consider a universe governed by what we take to be natural laws as necessarily 'intrinsically

---

40 'The Rebellion of Nature', p. 144; the subsequent passages pp. 143 and 145.

pointless'? Is 'the secular universe', as Wagar put it in the quotation cited earlier, really 'a theater of absurdity and rebellion'? (I should note, in all fairness, that these words may not reflect Wagar's own opinion, but rather what he is presenting as the general consensus.) It is a widespread Christian supposition — evidenced in the works for instance of Mircea Eliade, Hans Küng[41] and Charles Taylor (see also Chapter Two of my study where I engage with Eliade's and Taylor's arguments) — that a world without God must appear to the non-believer as a meaningless void that either results in a feeling of forlornness, despair and terror about history, as Eliade contends, or needs to be filled through some form of substitute for religion, in Taylor's case modernity's buffered identity through which the non-believer searches 'for something within, or beyond it, which could compensate for the meaning lost with transcendence'; through his buffered identity modern secular man protects himself from the 'wide sense of malaise at the disenchanted world', so Taylor.[42] Indeed, in *A Secular Age* Taylor distinguishes 'three forms which the malaise of immanence may take: (1) the sense of the fragility of meaning, the search for an over-arching significance; (2) the felt flatness of our attempts to solemnize the crucial moments of passage in our lives; and (3) the utter flatness, emptiness of the ordinary'. The opposition he constructs — which has a long pedigree — is that only belief in God provides unqualified fullness of meaning, whereas unbelief equates with a *lack* of meaning, a lack and emptiness that need compensating and filling through some form of substitute activity; as we saw earlier, Taylor cites art,

---

41 I have so far mentioned the German Catholic theologian Hans Küng only in passing; he belongs among those who have engaged in sophisticated debate with atheism, specifically for instance in his book *Existiert Gott?* (*Does God Exist?*) that I cited briefly in Chapter Five. But even Küng, whose knowledge of atheistic philosophy is second to none, falls into the same trap as Taylor in assuming that atheists must, in the end, lack a meaning for life. He writes: 'After all that I have said the conclusion must be obvious: a tie between belief in God and atheism is out of the question. Man cannot appear to be simply indifferent to the decision whether to believe in God or not. He is already biased: in principle he wants to understand himself and the world, wants to find an answer to the questions posed ['Fraglichkeit'] by reality, wants to know what determines reality, is looking for a first cause, a principal foundation and a final goal of reality, wants to know the ultimate origin ['Ursprung'], the ultimate meaning ['Ursinn'] and the ultimate value ['Urwert'] of things. This is from where religion originates. But here too Man remains — within limits — *free*. He can say No. He can ignore or even repress with all his skepticism any and all budding trust in a final cause, foundation and goal. He can, perhaps even honestly and truthfully, admit that he cannot know: agnosticism with a tendency toward atheism; or he can champion a thorough Nothingness, a lack of foundation and goal, a lack of meaning and value in a reality that is fundamentally questionable: atheism with a tendency toward nihilism. But just as basic trust is in no way irrational, trust in God is likewise in no way irrational' (*Existiert Gott?*, pp. 629–30). He goes on to argue, via a number of intricate steps, not just that trust in God is as rational as trust in commonsensical reason, but that we access true trust only by moving towards God because only God can (purportedly) provide a true foundation for our trust in 'identity, meaning and value of reality'. That the same might be said of an atheist or agnostic in moving toward whatever he or she perceives as the truth and value of reality is completely overlooked. It is taken for granted that atheists and agnostics must innately suffer the lack of identity, meaning and value that Küng — and alongside him Taylor — sees only the believer as able to escape.

42 *A Secular Age*, p. 302; the subsequent quote p. 309.

literature, music and also the sublimity of nature herself as prime examples of such substitutes in our secularized Western societies.

What is problematic about Taylor's handling of this discursive opposition is that he deploys it in order to promote and validate one of the sides over the other. The default condition for him is belief in God; meaningfulness in life and a gratifying understanding of the universe are achieved only through such a belief. To seek meaningfulness in or through nature or the arts, or any other form of 'substitute', is an ancillary process, one that fills the gap left by the more originative or primal religious belief once that is given up. Substitutes are thus subordinate and inferior. It is not made clear — at least not to me — why religious belief, Christian or otherwise, must be defined as fullness and presence, against which the atheist's, agnostic's or secular humanist's worldview cannot but be regarded as a mere lack or absence. (Hans Blumenberg once noted in a related context that the use of metaphors like 'emptiness', 'Leere', reveal more about the *person* deploying such terms than the *argument* he or she is making.)[43] As Taylor grants with his notion of 'a "neutral space" between belief and unbelief' which can be filled by the above-mentioned *Ersatz*-phenomena, meaning — no less than meaninglessness — can be found in many places, and it can take many shapes and forms. Why should religious belief be more immediate and more fulfilling than any other form of belief, irrespective of whether this is defined as faith in the god-like Nature of Pantheism; or belief in a spirit world; or the veneration of the beauty and marvels of nature as constituent parts of science's secular universe; or love of art, literature, and music; or appreciation of history and ancestry; or dedication to linguistic, ethnic and political community; or devotion to family, partners and friends; or enthusiasm for sport and personal hobby horses, not to mention any combination thereof? The jettisoning of the religious supernatural as part of a secular worldview does not demand, as I see Taylor and many fellow-Christian apologists implying, the simultaneous jettisoning of all interest in the immaterial or spiritual, whether or not this embraces aspects of the supernatural or transcendent.[44] On the concluding pages of *Mehr Licht in Deutschland* (*Light in Germany*), his 2009 study of the German Enlightenment, Terence James Reed writes:

---

43 See his essay 'Abgesang auf Weltbewohner. Über die Tröstlichkeit von Weltmodellen', in *Die Vollzähligkeit der Sterne* (Frankfurt a.M.: Suhrkamp, 1997), pp. 384–99.

44 The supernatural of fantasy fiction, Middle Earth and Harry Potter surely has as much attraction for believers as for non-believers; but this is equally surely a dimension most readers do not 'believe' in as such. Another interesting point to be made here is perhaps also that Taylor sees belief in the religious supernatural as something eminently and unqualifiedly positive and, together with Eliade, as something providing a fullness of sense and meaning that serves to ward off the terror of history. But as the Algerian writer Boualem Sansal pointed out in an interview with the German newspaper *Frankfurter Allgemeine Zeitung* in November 2015 religion may well satiate especially young people's yearnings for fullness of meaning in life; however, among young Muslim adolescents living in the Parisian banlieues or in similar circumstances elsewhere, the fullness they seek and find often lies in the religious fundamentalism and terror of the so-called IS terrorist organization; see 'Die Anschläge werden nicht aufhören. Ein Gespräch mit Boualem Sansal', *FAZ*, 18 November 2015 (feuilleton section), p. 9.

> Non-belief [...] itself is a positive belief, a conviction drawn from the experience of life and reflection; this down-to-earth conviction is no less powerful and valid than any transcendental idea. To upbraid someone for not believing is, as Schopenhauer observed, a case of false pretence because it paints belief as a norm from which one is deviating. But the burden of proof lies the other way round.
>
> [Schließlich ist der Unglaube [...] selber ein positiver Glaube, eine aus Lebenserfahrung und Reflexion gewonnene Überzeugung, die in ihrer Bodenhaftung mindestens ebenso stark und gültig ist wie jede transzendente Vorstellung. Der Vorwurf des Unglaubens enthält, wie Schopenhauer bemerkt, bereits eine Erschleichung, weil er den Glauben als die Norm vorspiegelt, von der abgewichen werde. Die Beweislast liegt umgekehrt.]⁴⁵

Reed's last sentence restates the conclusion to which Percy Bysshe Shelley had come two centuries earlier in the final appendage to his *The Necessity of Atheism*, cited in Chapter Four, where the Romantic poet argued 'God is an hypothesis, and, as such, stands in need of proof: the *onus probandi* rests on the theist'. In contrast to this notion of 'positive belief' as posited by Reed, Taylor insists on calling the atheist's world a 'waste land', with the non-believer being spiritually shut out from what Taylor calls 'further discovery'.⁴⁶

Taylor paints a very bleak picture indeed; the way he describes the barren world of the atheist reminds one of Albert Camus's existentialist description of modern man's state of absurdity and what the French existentialist, in *The Myth of Sisyphus. An Essay on the Absurd* (*Le mythe de Sisyphe. Essai sur l'absurde*), called absurd man's battle against 'the bottomless void that nothing can fill' ('le vide sans fond que rien ne peut combler').⁴⁷ Indeed, in Part 5 of *A Secular Age*, Taylor draws specifically on Camus as a spokesperson for exactly the kind of arid modern secular humanism whose deficiencies Taylor himself is seeking to lay bare. It was this aridity that for Camus touched off absurd man's floundering between the desire to live and the urge to commit suicide in the face of the 'world's lack of meaning' ('la non-signification du monde') and the certainty only of death. But instead of committing suicide, and in effect capitulating to this quandary, absurd man for Camus must rebel by taking a positive 'leap' ('saut') into the ultimate meaninglessness of life, a leap that may appear to some as no different from the leap of the religious believer into faith. But whereas for the latter it is a leap into the spiritually imagined fullness of meaning (Camus would stress the word imagined and the fact that it is an irrational choice), for absurd man it is a conscious and rational leap into accepting the unattainability of meaning and the nothingness that follows death. Camus notes: 'I don't know

---

45 *Mehr Licht in Deutschland. Eine kleine Geschichte der Aufklärung* (Munich: C. H. Beck, 2009), p. 215 (my translation; this passage is not contained in the 2015 English translation/version of his book, *Light in Germany. Scenes from an Unknown Enlightenment*).

46 *A Secular Age*, pp. 769–70.

47 Cited here from Albert Camus, 'An Absurd Reasoning (1942)', in *The Existentialist Reader. An Anthology of Key Texts*, ed. by Paul S. MacDonald (Edinburgh: Edinburgh University Press, 2000), pp. 144–83 (p. 170); *Le Mythe de Sisyphe. Essai sur l'absurde. Nouvelle édition augmentée d'une étude sur Franz Kafka* (Paris: Les Éditions Gallimard, 1942), p. 61. The subsequent quotations pp. 171, 166, 175, 176 and 180 (*Le Mythe de Sisyphe*, pp. 62, 52, 73, 76 and 84).

whether this world has a meaning that transcends it. But I know that I do not know that meaning and that it is impossible for me just now to know it' ('Je ne sais pas si ce monde a un sens qui le dépasse. Mais je sais que je ne connais pas ce sens et qu'il m'est impossible pour le moment de le connaître'). The consequence for Camus is that, whereas 'it was previously a question of finding whether or not life had to have a meaning to be lived[,] it now becomes clear on the contrary that it will be lived all the better if it has no meaning', because living this experience consciously and without reliance on God means making the best of our 'particular fate' and 'accepting it fully'; only 'living to the highest [...] keep[s] the absurd alive' ('Il s'agissait précédemment de savoir si la vie devait avoir un sens pour être vécue. Il apparaît ici au contraire qu'elle sera d'autant mieux vécue qu'elle n'aura pas de sens. Vivre une expérience, un destin, c'est l'accepter pleinement. [...] Vivre, c'est faire vivre l'absurde. [...] ce qui compte n'est pas de vivre le mieux mais de vivre le plus').

Taylor is right to conclude that for Camus the state of the absurd is what defines the condition of secular man facing a meaningless world. But is he right implicitly to equate Camus's mid-twentieth-century existentialist notion of absurdity with the situation non-believers are presented with at the beginning also of the twenty-first century? And was Camus's analysis 'right' in the first place, if 'right' is the appropriate word — was it not perhaps born out of a specific time and context, namely the conjunction of philosophical existentialism and the German occupation of France with all the intellectual strictures, deprivations and anxieties that this entailed? And must *every* non-believer necessarily feel stricken by a sense of the absurdity of his (or her) existence in a God-denuded secular world; must the existential absurdity that Camus felt in the early 1940s and the existential *Angst* described by Eliade in the late 1940s be identical with what an atheist might feel today in a different time and under different circumstances? In the 1940s existentialism peaked as a philosophy expressing what the German existentialist philosopher Otto Friedrich Bollnow called a sense of 'constrictedness and the uncanny' ('Beengung und [...] Unheimlichkeit');[48] picking up on Karl Jaspers's existentialist notion and conception of the 'threshold situation' ('Grenzsituation') in which man is existentially entrapped by the very nature of his being in the world, Bollnow defines the existential quandary of modern man as follows — notably without reference to Camus and *The Myth of Sisyphus*:

> In this sense threshold situations are situations in which man is led to the limits of his being. They are encountered in the experience that reality does not cohere into one harmonious and meaningful unity but that reality appears shot through with contradiction, a contradiction that reflection cannot overcome and that seems fundamentally irresolvable. [...] It is in such threshold situations that man experiences the finitude of his existence most acutely because they constitute the impregnable barrier that keeps us from a harmonious understanding of the world and human existence.

---

48 *Existenzphilosophie*, p. 58, the subsequent quotation p. 63 (my translations); on 'Grenzsituation' especially pp. 61–64.

[In diesem Sinn sind also Grenzsituationen solche Situationen, in denen der Mensch an die Grenze seines Daseins geführt wird. Sie werden überall in der Erfahrung erlebt, daß sich die Wirklichkeit nicht zum harmonischen und sinnerfüllten Ganzen zusammenschließt, sondern daß Widersprüche in ihr auftreten, die sich nicht durch das Denken schließen lassen oder auch nur als grundsätzlich behebbar erscheinen. [...] In diesen Grenzsituationen wird also in der schneidendsten Form die Endlichkeit des menschlichen Daseins erfahren, denn sie bezeichnen die harte Schranke, die jede harmonische Auffassung der Welt und des menschlichen Lebens unmöglich macht.]

As Odo Marquard stressed in his university 'Lectures on the Philosophy of Existentialism' — given 1974 to 1978, but published for the first time in 2013[49] — such key existentialist issues as modern man's existential unease in the knowledge of his 'living towards death' ('Sein zum Tode'), as Martin Heidegger calls it in *Being and Time* (§53), his radical contingency of being, the limitations placed on his freedom of choice, or his natural anxiety in the face of an inscrutable world (which congeals into Camus's notion of the absurd) define mankind's existence in our post-existentialist world as much as ever; but there is no inherent reason why our dealing with these issues today must lead to the nihilism that was so often ascribed to the existentialists' and specifically Sartre's worldview when he claimed in 1946, citing Dostoevsky in 'The Humanism of Existentialism' ('L'existentialisme est un humanisme'), that 'everything is permissible if God does not exist, and as a result man is forlorn, because neither within him nor without does he find anything to cling to' ('En effet, tout est permis si Dieu n'existe pas, et par conséquent l'homme est délaissé, parce qu'il ne trouve ni en lui, ni hors de lui une possibilité de s'accrocher').[50] Marquard cites Christian theologians above all as decrying existentialism's nihilism yet points up the amusing irony that the Christian Death of God Theology of the 1960s was itself intrinsically existentialist in nature, calling it 'a veiled existentialism' ('ein verkappter Existenzialismus').[51]

Likewise, is Taylor 'right' when he contrasts transcendence (and hence also the religious meaningfulness of the world, as he sees it) with immanence and materiality, which for him a belief in nature alone embodies? In his view, any belief in an immanent and material nature must be drained of the fullness of meaning that only a belief in God can guarantee. But do not believers in God also partake of and take pleasure in the immanence of the natural world, just as many non-believers find ways of creating for themselves non-religious forms of spirituality that are not reliant on a belief in God? (The Innsbruck University empirical psychologist Tatjana Schnell specializes on this topic and runs various research projects at her institution to survey the depth and breadth precisely of such non-religious forms of spirituality.)[52] I am sure Taylor would not deny any of this, and *A Secular Age* makes

---

49 *Der Einzelne. Vorlesungen zur Existenzphilosophie* (Stuttgart: Reclam, 2013).

50 Jean-Paul Sartre, 'The Humanism of Existentialism', in *Essays in Existentialism*, ed. by Wade Baskin (Secaucus, NJ: The Citadel Press, 1965), pp. 31–68 (p. 41); *L'existentialisme est un humanisme* (Paris: Nagel, 1947), p. 36.

51 *Der Einzelne*, p. 13.

52 One article that presents the results of her research in this area is 'Spirituality with and without Religion — Differential Relationships with Personality' (2012).

substantive concessions in this direction. My point is that not all non-believers will feel necessitated to succumb to, or to have to wrestle with, the feelings of absurdity, terror or meaninglessness in the face of the world that Camus and Eliade and, in their wake, Taylor ascribe to them. Karl Heinrich Heydenreich in the late eighteenth century was, as I detailed in Chapter Three, an early example of an atheist who had made his peace with the supposedly blank nothingness of death; he did not allow himself to fall prey to the 'nostalgia for unity' that Camus considers characteristic of the absurd man.[53] Heydenreich's experience was that 'the more [he] learnt of Nature the more she led [him] back not to God but only ever to Nature herself'. He let his fictional atheist aver how he felt 'struck by a sublime sensation' whenever he thought of 'this order which has no beginning and will never end' (in obvious allusion to Hutton's eternalist view of our universe having 'no vestige of a beginning, — no prospect of an end'). The appreciation of nature's order, he added, instilled in him so much 'pleasure' ('Wollust') and gratification that he was 'able to overcome the "dread" ("Schrecken") which the limits of existence hold for most people'; in the face of death he takes 'solace' ('Trost') from the fact that of all creatures only humankind is endowed with the 'spirit' ('Geist') and intellect to recognize and value nature's design.[54] I repeat one of the passages cited in Chapter Three in which Heydenreich contrasts his atheistic creed about the natural nothingness that follows death with the Christian's belief in a supernatural afterlife:

> That death holds nothing terrifying for me, I have declared afore. From the very start I considered the annihilation of my whole being to be the common destiny of all life [...] and as surely as I expect only one thing, I also expect a limit where the unfathomable *something* of my nature returns to the *nothing* from which it came into being. *I want to perish*, this is the postulate of my reason, *perish as befits the course and design of Nature*. To be sure, this postulate does not *sound* as sublime as your advocacy of immortality; but if I am not mistaken, it *is* sublime nonetheless, and the free acceptance of our ultimate fate of annihilation represents the maximum strength that a human soul can attain.

Although from what I gather Heydenreich seems to have led a somewhat unsettled private life, the passage cited above from his *Letters on Atheism* suggests nonetheless that he may have suffered neither from the 'angoisses de l'agonie', the 'agony of anguish' vis-à-vis the existential void looming after death that Grainville attributes to his atheistic Spirit of the Earth, nor from the paradox of the absurd invoked by Camus. In a similar vein we saw in Chapter Four how Percy Bysshe Shelley attributed a new kind of secular transcendence to Mont Blanc as (in a quite literal way) the highest symbol of nature's eternal and infinite universe. In a section of his history of atheism, *The Twilight of Atheism. The Rise and Fall of Disbelief in the Modern World*, entitled 'Nature: Affirming the Transcendent without God', Alister McGrath, himself an observant Christian, writes of the contemporaries of Mary Shelley's father William Godwin, who was one of the earliest British atheists to make his non-belief public:

---

53 See his 'An Absurd Reasoning (1942)', p. 174.
54 Heydenreich, *Briefe über den Atheismus*, p. 10.

Yet the explicit atheism of Godwin and others left them with nothing to which they could meaningfully anchor their sense of transcendence. If God was being irreversibly relegated to the margins of British culture, to be replaced by the more predictable and unimaginative enterprise of merely attending church, they would have to find something else to which to attach their longing for the transcendent. They found what they were looking for in nature herself.[55]

According to McGrath 'Nature' made possible the 'reenchantment' of the world that had been disenchanted just one century earlier; it allowed the non-believer 'to regard the beauty of the natural order as a thoroughly satisfying alternative to God', a process that 'began in earnest from about 1790'. Published in 1796, Heydenreich's *Letters on Atheism* strike me as an early corroboration of this.

A few decades later Mary Ann Evans, better known of course under her pen name George Eliot, moved to elevate humanity and human 'sympathy' to the metaphysical centre of her atheistic creed; aside from Spinoza's *Ethics*, Eliot also translated two key early-nineteenth-century works of secular/atheistic German Bible criticism, both of which were highly controversial during their day, David Friedrich Strauß's 1835 *The Life of Jesus* (*Das Leben Jesus*, published in Eliot's translation in 1846) and Ludwig Feuerbach's 1841 *The Essence of Christianity* (*Das Wesen des Christentums*, published in Eliot's translation in 1854). As McGrath notes:

> Eliot, like many others, [...] turned to a 'religion of human sympathy' in place of this rather dark and dismal conception of God. Similar patterns of alienation from conventional religion are found throughout her novels, from *Adam Bede* through to *Middlemarch*. The moral aspect of faith could, she believed, be maintained without the metaphysical basis of Christianity. We can be good without God. Indeed, belief in the Christian God can be a significant obstacle to the achievement of 'individual and social happiness'.

For Eliot, influenced by Strauß and his British counterpart Charles Hennell (whose 1838 *An Inquiry concerning the Origin of Christianity* she was equally familiar with), the New Testament narrative of Christ was about a mortal human being in possession of exemplary morals but without a claim to divinity. As a consequence, the Christian religion was, for her as for her philosophical and theological antecedents, based on the deification of a worldly human individual; yet despite its in Eliot's view false theological premises, Christianity had nonetheless succeeded in creating an effective moral value system.

Karl Heinrich Heydenreich, Percy Bysshe Shelley and Mary Ann Evans are thus three instances of early atheists who put the question to us why the metaphysics and, by extension, the transcendence and morality of religion should be considered superior to the metaphysics, transcendence and morality of the non-believer, through whichever means he or she chooses to source and practice them. In his history of atheism McGrath, too, grants that 'one of the most interesting features of British literary culture throughout the nineteenth century is that a growing interest in atheism did not entail abandoning belief in the transcendent'. One could make the point, I believe, that by the mid-twentieth century, in the depths of the

---

55 *The Twilight of Atheism*, p. 116; the subsequent quotations pp. 117, 131 and 121.

Second World War when the world looked a much bleaker place to live and when the nineteenth century's secularized and optimistic 'religion of Inevitable Progress' (Aldous Huxley) in all its manifestations, Hegelian, Marxist or scientific, was in the process of bankrupting itself in a manner more traumatizing even than the First World War had led to, it might seem only 'natural' for a philosopher like Albert Camus to proclaim the inherent absurdity of existence.[56] Camus's premise was indeed that the universe and world history, as well as the individual's role therein, must be regarded as 'intrinsically pointless'. Abbreviating Sartre's existentialist critique of religion, Mc Grath observes: 'we are haunted by the specter of cosmic meaninglessness, which we find unbearable. In consequence, we invent God so as to explain the unexplainable'.[57] But although Camus and Sartre felt 'haunted by the specter of cosmic meaninglessness', 'invent God' is precisely what they did not do in order 'to explain the unexplainable'. Quite to the contrary, Camus, rather than try to *explain* the unexplainable, resorted to the notion of the 'absurd' in order to *contain* the unexplainable, a formula that allowed him not just to describe man's predicament as he saw it for his age, but also to put forward ways of dealing with this predicament without recourse to religious belief. Camus's creed — nicely summed up in Wagar's above-cited phrase 'the secular universe is a theater of absurdity and rebellion' — is secularly humanist through and through.

Living with a 'Sense for the Tragic'

Camus wrote *The Myth of Sisyphus* between 1939 and 1941; it was published in 1942, three years before the atom bombs fell on Hiroshima and Nagasaki. If Günther Anders was right to proclaim that 1945 demarcates not just a new epoch in human history, but its *final* epoch *tout court*, an epoch that changes the fundamentals of our existence, perhaps this should compel us to reflect for a moment whether this new form of temporality also changes the role we must attribute to the absurd for post-1945 mankind. With today's hindsight one might ask whether the true condition of absurdity might lie not in the modern psychological conflict that Camus diagnosed between our longing for unity and meaning in a natural environment that seems devoid of all rational sense and logical coherence; but rather whether it might reside instead in the state of affairs that has emerged since 1945, with man since that juncture having succeeded in putting himself not just in a position to annihilate himself in one fell swoop by means of the nuclear or chemical or biotechnological fruits of his rational intellect, or less suddenly and more incrementally by the destruction of the planet's very biosphere that secures his life's sustenance, but at the same time acting as if he were in denial about or not responsible for what he is doing. It is exactly this that Robert Jay Lifton laments. In Chapter Five I cited his observation, formulated in the context of a discussion of Stanley Kubrick's 1964 black comedy *Dr. Strangelove or: How I learned to Stop Worrying and Love the Bomb*, that

---

56 See also Chapters Four and Five for more on the critique of modernity and its dialectic of progress, especially in the shape of Horkheimer and Adorno's *Dialectic of Enlightenment*.
57 *The Twilight of Atheism*, p. 156.

through his film Kubrick exhorts us to 'confront *the radical absurdity* or "madness" of the world destruction we are contemplating' (my emphasis); elsewhere in *The Future of Immortality* Lifton repeats this sentiment: 'It is a fact of the greatest absurdity', he points out, 'that we human beings threaten to exterminate ourselves with our own genocidal technology. One must never lose that sense of the absurdity, the madness, the insanity of it'.[58] Already on the opening pages of his volume Lifton had observed how

> a sense of absurdity pervades and sometimes informs contemporary experience. That sense, which surely predates nuclear threat, is radically intensified by the specter of species self-annihilation. [...] Most absurd of all is the worldwide refusal to accept the true lessons of Chernobyl: our universal vulnerability to nuclear technology, especially to the weapons, and our shared fate in connection with the human future.

He concludes: 'Inevitably, there is a dangerous psychic edge to contemporary absurdity, which I would locate in a longing for the nuclear "end", as well as in the resigned acceptance of that end'.

Indeed, in the light of the non-occurrence of nuclear self-annihilation some might argue that ecological self-destruction is a more insidious danger to human existence on our planet even than that posed by the (as yet) unused stockpiles of nuclear weaponry. Critics of this ilk feel we are submitting all too thoughtlessly to a 'resigned acceptance of our end', at least in terms of life as we know it, by not taking swift and substantial enough an action to reduce the causes of global warming and avert its worst consequences. (After I had written these lines in this chapter's first draft the Paris climate change conference of December 2015 came to what many consider a successful conclusion: of course it remains to be seen whether the parliaments and people of the treaty's signatory nations will be willing both to ratify and then actually implement the recommendations — as I read and correct the proofs in July 2017 the new President of the United States, Donald Trump, has already announced his intention to withdraw from this treaty.) In a book with the suggestive title *Our Final Century: Will the Human Race Survive the Twenty-First Century?* (published in the United States equally tellingly as *Our Final Hour: A Scientist's Warning. How Terror, Error, and Environmental Disaster Threaten Humankind's Future in this Century — on Earth and Beyond*) the British astrophysicist and Astronomer Royal Sir Martin Rees predicted in 2003 that we stand an approximately fifty-fifty chance within this century that we will obliterate our own species through either the malicious or accidental deployment of man-made mass-destructive technology or the unchecked pollution of our biosphere. In a similar vein, the British environmentalist and creator of the Gaia-thesis, James Lovelock, suggested in *The Vanishing Face of Gaia* in 2009 that we may have moved beyond the tipping point at which a terrestrial climate catastrophe can no longer be averted. The American climate specialist Jason E. Box, professor of glaciology in Copenhagen, conjured up an apt image in a recent interview with the German newspaper *Süddeutsche Zeitung* when he told his interlocutors: 'Our species is quite

---

58 *The Future of Immortality*, p. 137; the subsequent quotations pp. 4 and 5.

intelligent, in technological matters and so forth. But we are not wise. We have run over the precipice like those characters in comics who now find themselves hanging in the air with no ground under their feet, but are not yet falling'.[59] Even were such predictions to be exaggerated, as conservative critics have argued against all of the above, or merely intended to goad us into action, the dangers are nonetheless real; there is no disputing the fact, whichever way one looks at it, that since the mid-twentieth century we have, against all better evidence and judgment, persisted in living on the brink, as Günther Anders argued in nuclear terms.

Regardless of how imminent or far-fetched either of these scenarios, nuclear or ecological self-annihilation, may be, a number of recent publications and television documentaries have already begun imagining a world without humans. What would happen if we were suddenly to disappear, this was the question asked by the American journalist Alan Weisman in his 2007 non-fiction best seller and thought experiment *The World Without Us*. Weisman's book in turn inspired two documentaries produced for television, the first for Canadian TV entitled *Aftermath: Population Zero*, the second for U.S. TV entitled *Life After People*. Shown on the National Geographic Channel in 2008, the aim of the two-hour Canadian film was to play through, from science's perspective, the likely consequences of man's disappearance from planet Earth. The overly constructed premise notwithstanding — the producers resorted to the implausible scenario that all human beings would evaporate into nothingness all of a sudden and all at one and the same time — the after-effects of mankind's disappearance are brought home persuasively and starkly. Aside from the cars suddenly spinning out of control on motorways and airplanes dropping from the skies in the film's surreal opening, the longer term perspective gives a more realistic picture, showing how only a few years later roads would start to deteriorate and become overgrown, metal would succumb to corrosion, roofs on houses would start to collapse, buildings would gradually crumble, cultivated fields would return to native prairies, and so forth. The same hypothetical scenario of a sudden removal of humankind was also at the heart of the twenty episodes of the U.S. TV-series *Life After People* which ran for two seasons in 2009 and 2010 on the History Channel in the United States and on Channel 4 in the United Kingdom. Created by David de Vries, each episode had a particular scientific focus, and each spotlighted what might happen to the world's major cities over the course of time, and what had actually happened to places that had already been abandoned by their human residents in the past, such as in the first episode Japan's Hashima Island that was abandoned in 1974, in the third episode Cambodia's Angkor Wat abandoned in the fifteenth century, or in the fifteenth episode the Italian ghost town Balestrino whose original town centre was abandoned in 1953 due to hydrogeological instability.

This scenario of a sudden and unexplained evaporation of mankind into nonbeing, as it were, has been used as the narrative premise also for a number of novels in

---

59 Jason E. Box in 'Die Wahrheit bekommt uns nicht gut', an interview with Hans Joachim Schellnhuber, Alice Bows-Larkin and Jason E. Box, in *Süddeutsche Zeitung* (Magazin), 22 January 2016, 22–28 (p. 27).

recent decades, starting in the 1970s with the Italian writer Guido Morselli's *Dissipatio H. G.* (1977) in whose city of Chrysopolis and environs all humans — bar one, the narrative's protagonist — have tracelessly disappeared out of the blue in the middle of the night; the protagonist is shown trying to cope physically and mentally with the state of utter solitude to which he finds himself reduced. The same fate awaits the protagonist Anton L. in the German writer Herbert Rosendorfer's *Grand Solo for Anton* (*Großes Solo für Anton*, 1979; English translation 2006), the protagonist Jonas in the Vienna of Thomas Glavinic's *The Work of Night* (*Die Arbeit der Nacht*, 2006) and the protagonist Lorenz in Jürgen Domian's novel *The Day When the Sun Disappeared* (*Der Tag, an dem die Sonne verschwand*, 2008). A different case altogether is David Markson's 1988 first-person experimental novel *Wittgenstein's Mistress* in which the reader encounters an unreliable rambling female narrator and aspiring novelist who seems to have woken up one morning to find herself all alone in the world; keeping us in doubt throughout as to the reality-status of what is related, the novel is replete with passages in the vein of what follows:

> Or certainly not when your ordinary novel is basically expected to be about people too, obviously.
> And which is to say about certainly a good number more people than just one, also. [...]
> So that as I say, there went my novel practically even before I had a chance to start thinking about a novel.
> Unless on third thought it just might change matters if I were to make it an absolutely autobiographical novel?
> Hm.
> Because what I am also suddenly now thinking about is that it could be an absolutely autobiographical novel that would not start until after I was alone, obviously.
> And so that obviously there could be no way whatsoever that it could be expected to have more than one person in it after all. [...]
> Which is to say a novel about somebody who woke up one Wednesday or Thursday to discover that there was apparently not one other person left in the world.
> Well, or not even one seagull, either.
> Except for various vegetables and flowers, conversely.
> Certainly that would be an interesting beginning, at any rate. Or at least for a certain type of novel.
> Just imagine how the heroine would feel, however, and how full of anxiety she would be. And with every bit of that being real anxiety in this instance, too, as opposed to various illusions.[60]

By the end of the novel's 240 pages we have a surfeit of information but not an inkling who the narrator *really* is and what truth claim we can attach to any part of her sprawling interior monologue. Nominally at least the novel gives the appearance of being a Last Woman narrative (the narrator throughout speaks of herself as a woman), but strictly speaking even this must remain uncertain.

---

60 *Wittgenstein's Mistress* (Normal, IL: Dalkey Archive Press, 1988), pp. 229–30.

However we look at these novels, because they avoid mention of the actual cause of man's disappearance they all move conceptually beyond the three paradigms that underlie the argument I have been making in my study. A similar borderline case, but one worth highlighting nonetheless if only because it clearly marks itself out as a Last Woman narrative, is Austrian writer Marlen Haushofer's remarkable 1968 novel *The Wall* (*Die Wand*; English translation 1990). Having retreated for a solitary break to an isolated hunting lodge in the mountains, the recently widowed narrator finds herself trapped one morning by a gigantic transparent wall that has appeared overnight, enclosing her as well as the resident animals within a section of mountainous territory; in the outside world beyond the wall all living beings, humans and animals alike, can be seen to have been struck dead as if frozen in place when the glass-like wall was erected, by whose power we never find out. What we do find out later in the novel is that one other human being, a potential Adam, has also survived behind 'the Wall', a man, however, whom the female protagonist finds herself forced to kill in self-defense, and in so doing prevents the generation of a new mankind. *The Wall* is thus a rare terminal Last Woman narrative, but one in which not the cause (a transparent wall) but the agency of the disaster (where does the wall come from? why is the region around the hunting lodge spared?) remains opaque and unclassifiable.

A similarly unclassifiable best seller that avoids specific mention of the cause of catastrophe, but whose storyline hovers on the cusp between the nuclear and the natural paradigm, is Cormac McCarthy's semi-terminal *The Road*, published in 2006 and quickly followed in 2009 by the Hollywood blockbuster version directed by John Hillcoat and starring Viggo Mortensen and Kodi Smit-McPhee. On first reading *The Road* seems to depict the environmental and physical effects brought on by a nuclear winter, yet nowhere does radiation or nuclear fallout actually feature as a hazard the protagonists must confront on their journey through the bleak and surreal landscape in which McCarthy has set his narrative. The novel's background setting thus vacillates, intentionally one must assume, between nuclear winter and a man-made global ecological catastrophe, the precise nature of which is never revealed. What we are told is that the northern United States, the place of action, has been reduced to a 'country where firestorms had passed', in which all clocks had stopped at 1:17 following 'a long shear of light and then a series of low concussions', where the 'wreckage of buildings [could be found] strewn over the landscape', where the countryside and roads were covered in layers of ash inches deep, and where human bodies lay like 'mummied figures', save the few miserable survivors.[61] Due to food being in short supply — fields are empty of crops, rivers empty of fish — and the remaining stocks of canned foods becoming ever more scarce and hard to come by, some of the survivors have banded together to scour the countryside for human beings to devour instead. It is these cannibals that the main protagonists, a father and his son, keep trying to elude while moving 'like pilgrims' through this 'barren, silent, godless' world. They once encounter an old man and the following dialogue ensues, commenting acerbically not just on the

---

61 *The Road* (London: Pan Macmillan / Picador, 2007), pp. 202, 54, 293, 23 and 204, the subsequent quotation pp. 1 and 2.

tradition of Last Man fiction but also on the New Testament story of Jesus Christ born as a God unto men:

> The man watched him. How would you know if you were the last man on earth? he said.
> I dont guess you would know it. You'd just be it.
> Nobody would know it.
> It wouldnt make any difference. When you die it's the same as if everybody else did too.
> I guess God would know it. Is that it?
> There is no God.
> No?
> There is no God and we are his prophets. [...]
> I never thought to see a child again. I didn't know that would happen.
> What if I said that he's a god?
> The old man shook his head. I'm past all that now. Have been for years. Where men cant live gods fare no better. It's better to be alone. So I hope that's not true what you said because to be on the road with the last god would be a terrible thing so I hope it's not true. Things will be better when everybody's gone. [...] When we're all gone at last then there'll be nobody here but death and his days will be numbered too.[62]

'Where men cant live gods fare no better', the old man says — God's existence is premised on mankind's existence. This question 'Will God survive the death of man?' is not a new one; the old man's maxim harks back to a sentiment expressed more than three centuries earlier by the German Franciscan priest and mystic poet Angelus Silesius (1624–1677), who in his collection of mystic poetry *The Cherubinean Journeyman* (*Cherubinischer Wandersmann*, 1675) had published the couplet: 'I know, deprived of me, God could not live a wink. | He must give up the ghost if into naught I sink' ('Ich weiß, daß ohne mich Gott nicht ein Nu kann leben, | Werd ich zu nicht, er muß von Noth den Geist aufgeben').[63] Of course, Silesius — who converted to Roman Catholicism in 1653 — asks the question from the perspective of a Christian mystic; and he asks too from the perspective of a devout individual deeply immersed in his personal relationship with God rather than from the broader perspective of the human species as a whole. Nonetheless, as Silesius's early-twentieth-century English translator Paul Carus points out, his 'God-conception, if expressed in a dry dogmatic formula, appears pure atheism'.[64] A twenty-first-century 'pure atheistic' reformulation of this 'dry dogmatic formula' reads: 'The last god will expire with the last man' — so articulated by the French atheistic philosopher Michel Onfray in his *Atheistic Manifesto*, published in French in 2005, in English translation 2007.[65]

Although McCarthy uses his figure of the old man to invoke this question, he

62 *The Road*, pp. 180–81, 183 and 184.
63 *Des Angelus Silesius Cherubinischer Wandersmann*, ed. by Wilhelm Bölsche (Jena and Leipzig: Eugen Diederichs, 1905), p. 2 (I.8); the translation is by Paul Carus and taken from *Angelus Silesius. A Selection from the Rhymes of a German Mystic* (Chicago: Open Court Publishing, 1909), p. 15.
64 'Introduction', in *Angelus Silesius. A Selection*, p. xxiii.
65 *Atheistic Manifesto. The Case Against Christianity, Judaism, and Islam* (New York: Arcade Publishing, 2011), p. 13.

uses the final pages of his novel to steer clear from the maxim's dire consequence. Resisting the temptation to end his storyline on a depressing note — which would have been fully in character with the story up to this point — McCarthy opts instead to give *The Road* a more optimistic and upbeat conclusion. Not only is the boy, following his father's dismal death, found and taken in by a man, a woman and their two children (a boy and a girl), the nuclear family as it were; and not only do the trout that the boy sees standing in the amber current of the mountain streams symbolize nature's impending reawakening in the novel's very last paragraph — with their 'vermiculate patterns' the fishes' backs symbolize 'maps of the world in its becoming'. But with this boy a new mankind is now in the offing, for he can function as a new Adam to the young girl, the new Eve. Perhaps it is for this very reason that the boy is described as 'carrying the fire' inside him; for the boy's biological father, he is the 'warrant' that God may not yet have disappeared. Indeed, religion will have a part to play in the boy's future, it seems, for the substitute mother is God-fearing and speaks to the boy 'sometimes about God' and considers him 'the breath of God'.[66]

In one way or another all of these authors meditate in novelistic form on issues that were 'once the preserve of theology and metaphysics', to pick up again on Dowling's phrase, cited at the end of Chapter Five. Whether humankind expires in a nuclear inferno or owing to some natural virus (or any other cause), whether there are survivors or not, whether the circumstances of mankind's disappearance strike us as 'realistic' — however we define realism in this context — or constructed and artificial, authors have always used such scenarios to mull over, as well as pass judgment on, our way of life and the values and belief systems we hold dear. To be sure, futuristic science fiction novels are typically taken to be intellectually less demanding and also less probing than highbrow literature, not to mention philosophical, theological or scientific treatises. But they do have one major advantage: they give us a view of our present from the vantage point of a future yet to come, and they do this in such a palpably concrete way that we can identify with and put ourselves in the position of the human actors in this drama. As Eva Horn argues in *Zukunft als Katastrophe*, futuristic fiction outdoes journalistic and academic forms of discourse because of its distinctive combination of narrative content with an unusual grammatical tense: in Last Man futuristic fiction, Horn reasons, 'man looks back upon himself, but from a vantage point after the end; it is a reflection in the future perfect tense: all will once have been' ('Der Mensch schaut auf sich selbst zurück, aber nach seinem eigenen Ende, eine Reflexion im Futur II: Es wird einmal gewesen sein').[67] By giving us a picture of (fictionally) 'real' people forced

---

66 *The Road*, pp. 3 and 306–07. Religion and belief in God represent the bracket that binds beginning and end of the novel together. Thus at the novel's opening we read: '[The father] knew only that the child was his warrant. He said: If he is not the word of God God never spoke' (p. 3); at the novel's close we are told: 'The woman when she saw him put her arms around him and held him. Oh, she said, I am so glad to see you. She would talk to him sometimes about God. He tried to talk to God but the best thing was to talk to his father and he did talk to him and he didn't forget. The woman said that was all right. She said that the breath of God was his breath yet though it pass from man to man through all of time' (p. 306).

67 *Zukunft als Katastrophe*, p. 11; the subsequent passages pp. 32 and 21.

suddenly and unexpectedly into action by an imaginary catastrophe in the future, fictions of disaster are able to perspectivize the full gamut of human qualities and behaviours, as well as strengths and weaknesses, from an internally personalized subjective perspective rather than externally and scientifically from a supposedly objectivized scholarly distance. Such fictional perspectivizations of the future provide unparalleled experimental access, as it were, to the inner mental and moral life of *Homo sapiens*; Horn observes:

> In this scenario fictional literature throws the spotlight on that which science cannot: the question of the robustness of social ties in a crisis, of the strength or weakness of an individual, of the ethical decisions that must be made in an emergency, of the practices and things that are left to humans once nature has come to an end. Fiction captures the interior view of catastrophe as no scientific scenario can.
>
> [In diesem Szenario aber wendet Literatur den Blick auf genau das, was Wissenschaft nicht in den Blick nehmen kann: die Frage nach der Belastbarkeit sozialer Bindungen in der Krise, nach der Stärke oder Schwäche des Einzelnen, nach ethischen Entscheidungen, die im Ernstfall getroffen werden, nach den Praktiken und den Dingen, die dem Menschen nach dem Ende der Natur noch bleiben. Fiktion ermöglicht so einen Innenblick auf die Katastrophe, den kein wissenschaftliches Szenario entwerfen kann.]

One of the aims of Horn's book is to ask why Western audiences exhibit such an insatiable 'desire for catastrophe that no one wants to admit' ('uneingestehbares Begehren nach Katastrophe'), and why we seem endlessly to enjoy day-dreaming ourselves into such cataclysmic scenarios of end times and Last Men and Last Women. She cites 'epistemic' reasons for our evidently boundless obsession with such stories about the end: they 'come with the claim to reveal or uncover something that is buried just under the surface of our present-day', she contends, and explains:

> For this reason they exhibit a literally apocalyptic — that is, revelatory — stance: they capture something 'real' about what it means to be human, about our character, our civilization, our social interaction. Disasters illuminate our social being under conditions of extreme adversity, from cooperation and self-sacrifice to the ruthless will to survive. The catastrophe 'tests' human beings, their strength and ability to act under duress, the resilience of their relationships and social institutions. It shows what 'really' defines human beings once the cocoon of an intact civilization is removed. Catastrophes generate their own anthropology of disaster: they show humans as heroic or egoistic, vulnerable or robust, panicky or rational. Situations are generated that demand decisions [...], decisions between friend and foe, decisions too about who may survive and who must be sacrificed.
>
> [Darum eignet ihnen stets eine im Wortsinn *apokalyptische* — also enthüllende — Geste: Sie zeigen ein 'Reales' des Menschen, seines Wesens, seiner Zivilisation, seines Sozialen. So leuchten Desaster Spielarten des Sozialen unter verschärften Bedingungen aus, von der gegenseitigen Hilfe oder Selbstaufopferung bis zum rücksichtslosen Überlebenswillen. Die Katastrophe 'testet' den Menschen, seine Stärke und Belastbarkeit, die Haltbarkeit seiner Bindungen und die Krisenfestigkeit seiner sozialen Institutionen. Sie zeigt, was

> ihn jenseits der Cocons einer intakten Zivilisation 'tatsächlich' ausmacht. So entwerfen Katastrophen ihre eigene Anthropologie des Desasters: Sie zeigen den Menschen als heroisch oder egoistisch, verletzlich oder belastbar, panisch oder rational. Es werden Entscheidungssituationen entworfen [...], Entscheidungen zwischen Freund und Feind, Entscheidungen aber auch darüber, wer überleben darf und wer geopfert werden muss.][68]

Horn later enlarges: 'These situations involve limited options, the pressure of time, and extreme danger — they are "emergency situations" in the true sense, situations that force people to take exceptional actions and decisions' ('Sie sind Situationen begrenzter Handlungsmöglichkeiten, großen Zeitdrucks, höchster Gefahr — eben "Ernstfälle", die einen besonderen Handlungs- und Entscheidungszwang entfalten'). Such emergency situations, she goes on, follow 'a logic of exceptionality in which new rules become operational' ('Logik der Ausnahme, in der andere Regeln gelten'); 'the moment of disaster suspends the binding character of our normal ethical values and political agreements' ('der Moment des Untergangs suspendiert die Verbindlichkeit unserer normalen ethischen Werte und politischen Grundkonsense'), on occasion requiring 'tragic decisions' ('tragische Entscheidungen'). Such narratives can thus come to function as 'exercises in a politics of emergency' ('Einübungen in eine Politik des Ernstfalls').

The way Horn formulates this one must expect fictions of future catastrophe to represent far better vehicles of existentialist exploration than anything ever thought up or put to paper by Camus or Sartre. By placing their protagonists into 'threshold situations' ('Grenzsituationen'), 'situations in which man is led to the limits of his being' (so Bollnow in the footsteps of Jaspers, as cited above), Sartre and Camus — and, for that matter, most novelists with a serious message about the vagaries and vicissitudes of life — tried to prepare their readers for analogous eventualities in their lives or, if not that, then to give readers insight into an Other's struggle with life and the decisions they may be forced to make when faced with comparable crisis situations. What readers actually experience is of course different from the threshold situations experienced by fictional protagonists, but the reader has at least been given the opportunity to reflect on these situations and the dilemmas they might pose were they to arise in real life. But does this hold equally true for futuristic fictions of catastrophe, and specifically for ones of such global magnitude in which the key player — the deplorable victim of mass extinction — is not an individual but the human species as a whole? Thus when Horn writes: 'In the exceptional circumstance, when everything collapses, the "true essence" of our existence is revealed — such is the assumption' ('in der Ausnahme, im Zusammenbruch offenbart sich, so die unterliegende Vorstellung, ein 'wahres Wesen' unserer Existenz'),[69] one feels prompted to respond by asking whether a '"true essence" of our existence' really exists or whether it is not rather just another figment of our, or an author's, imagination. In the same vein she also ascribes special 'epistemic' significance to these narratives, as in the following passage:

---

68 Ibid., pp. 25–26; the words following the omission bracket are taken from a parallel statement on p. 192. The subsequent passages pp. 221–23.

69 Ibid., p. 26; the subsequent passage p. 25.

> Indeed depictions of the future *as catastrophe* enjoy a special epistemic status that sets them distinctly apart from other forms of projecting the future, such as utopias, promises, plans or hopes: the future as catastrophe cries out for prevention, and for preventive action. [...] catastrophic futures possess an urgency that tolerates no delay.
>
> [Dabei haben die Entwürfe einer Zukunft *als Katastrophe* einen besonderen epistemischen Status, der sie von anderen Formen des Zukunftsentwurfs wie Utopien, Versprechen, Plänen oder Hoffnungen scharf unterscheidet: Zukunft als Katastrophe schreit nach ihrer Verhinderung, nach einem präventiven Eingreifen. [...] katastrophische Zukünfte reklamieren für sich eine Dringlichkeit, die eben nicht einfach abgewartet werden kann.]

No doubt, Horn's assessment is well-intentioned, and I can't imagine anyone wanting not to agree with the thrust of her argument. I am convinced no one — at least no one of sane mind — wants such a catastrophe actually to occur, however much pleasure we might derive from reading about them or seeing them play out in literary or filmic form. But there is a difference — call it epistemic or not — between the urgency of, say, scientific predictions about man-made global warming and a novelist's futuristic 'prediction' of the outbreak of a global plague or a comet-strike on Earth, regardless of how realistically or grippingly that prediction may be related in the storyline. In the one instance we know it is happening right now in the 'real' world, in the other it is just a hypothetical mind-game playing itself out in an invented 'unreal' world. The former scenario is fact, the latter fiction. Put differently, one should be cautious not to overestimate the use to which readers will either be able to put such fictionalizations of extremity or will actually want to react to them in real life. After all, few readers can in reality expect to face the protagonist's quandary not least because, even if such a catastrophe — a comet striking Earth, a global virus wiping out our fellow beings, a nuclear world war incinerating the world's population — were in actual fact to occur, the reality would hit us in ways that no fiction could ever prepare us for; and we know that, consciously or subliminally. For that reason literary or filmic fictionalizations of end-time scenarios rarely (if ever) provoke us to take urgent and immediate action. No one (to my knowledge) runs out of the cinema after watching subterranean shelter fiction films like *La Jetée* or *12 Monkeys* (which itself was based on Chris Marker's *La Jetée*) or *Deep Impact* looking for the underground caves through which they might save themselves or their family members; and rare is the reader of novels and viewer of films like *On the Beach* or *The Rat* who then camps out in the parliament square of his or her respective country to protest against its nuclear arsenal. Nor do I see many people today scrambling to reduce their carbon footprint by radically trimming down on their use of cars or travel by plane following the 2015 Paris climate change conference. Once we stand up from our easy chair or the cinema seat, life for most just seems to go on. And, as my discussion in Chapter Five showed, even as uncompromising and depressing a film as *The Day After* allowed for vastly divergent responses regarding nuclear disarmament; we found that people's responses were not always what one might have expected them to be. In short, even when fictional texts or films do serve as an existential testing ground or provide impetus for action, this often happens in a mediated or deferred way.

Horn's conclusions are nonetheless highly cogent and to the point; I disagree with her argument not in substance, but only as regards some nuances of wording. For obvious reasons our studies revolve around many of the same texts; specifically Grainville's *Le Dernier Homme*, Byron's poem 'Darkness', Shelley's *The Last Man*, Shute's *On the Beach*, McCarthy's *The Road*, Kubrick's film *Dr. Strangelove*, Martin's *The Last Man* paintings and Beckett's play *Endgame* feature centrally in both of our analyses. And indeed, how could it be otherwise with these works forming the indispensable touchstones of any study of Last Man end-time narratives? Another such key study, Fiona Stafford's *The Last of the Race. The Growth of a Myth from Milton to Darwin*, similarly examines Byron's 'Darkness', Grainville's *Le Dernier Homme* and Shelley's *The Last Man*; but Stafford approaches the subject from a different angle, conceiving it more broadly in terms of 'the myth of lastness' as it plays out in the two centuries between Thomas Burnet and Charles Darwin. This necessarily directs her focus onto such figures as Daniel Defoe's lone shipwreck survivor Robinson Crusoe (1719), last oak trees (William Cowper's 1791 poem 'Yardley Oak'), last bards and last minstrels (James Macpherson's 1765 two-volume faux translation of *The Works of Ossian* and Walter Scott's 1805 poem 'The Lay of the Last minstrel'), last Goths (Robert Southey's 1814 poem 'Roderick, the Last of the Goths') and last Mohicans (James Fenimore Cooper's 1826 novel *The Last of the Mohicans*). Whereas Stafford's survey ends in the late nineteenth-century with H. G. Wells's 1895 *The Time Machine*, Horn in *Zukunft als Katastrophe* preoccupies herself by and large with the same time frame that I have chosen, beginning with Burnet and ending in the present day, albeit of course with varying historical and methodological emphases; most importantly in this regard, her approach is for the most part political, sociological and psychological in orientation, whereas my study focuses more on the philosophical and theological backgrounds to and ramifications of Last Man narratives.

I would like to conclude this discussion of Horn's parallel undertaking by citing the final paragraph of her book; her study ends, not without some pathos, with the words:

> The most lucid [among these narratives of catastrophe] therefore provide a *tragic* vision of this future: it is a vision that sees in catastrophe not just the destruction of assets and values, but also the ultimate destruction of a human nature that has dispossessed itself of its own essentials. A vision that will have known that we did not stop this future from coming about.
>
> [Die luzidesten unter ihnen werfen daher einen *tragischen* Blick auf diese Zukunft: Es ist ein Blick, der in der Katastrophe nicht nur die Zerstörung von Gütern und Werten liest, sondern die grundlegende Zerstörung einer menschlichen Natur, die sich ihre eigene Grundlage entzogen hat. Ein Blick, der gewusst haben wird, dass wir diese Zukunft nicht verhindert haben.][70] (Horn's emphasis)

As Horn rightly notes, in looking to the future these narratives of catastrophe —

---

70 Ibid., pp. 386–87.

a genre to which all Last Man narratives by definition belong — simultaneously reflect back from that future onto an inner-fictional past which is our real present (or at least the present of the time when the respective piece of literature was written). We saw this instanced earlier in our discussion of London's 1912 *The Scarlet Plague*, Stewart's 1949 *Earth Abides* and Mandel's 2014 *Station Eleven*, all of which use a future world-encompassing epidemic to formulate a critique of the authors' own present. Although Horn does not refer to Nietzsche in the context of her argument, the turn of phrase 'with a *tragic* vision' ('mit *tragischem* Blick') picks up where, in his *Untimely Meditations*, the German philosopher can be found cogitating in 1876, one and a half centuries earlier, about man's impending end; Nietzsche wrote there, in a passage I cited in Chapter Three:

> And when all of humanity must die one day — and who should doubt this! — what is assigned to him as the highest task for the future is to grow together into Unity and Community such that he can meet his imminent demise *as One* with *a sense for the tragic*. [...] There is only One Hope and One Safeguard for the future of humanity: it consists in his *retention of the sense for the tragic*.

To be sure, Nietzsche did not have science fiction in mind when he wrote these lines; but what better medium could there be through which to foster the 'retention of the sense for the tragic' than such grim foretellings of a future calamity as Mordecai Roshwald's *Level 7* or Jens Rehn's *The Children of Saturn*? But surely there is a difference between Nietzsche's and our understanding of the sense for the tragic, with the 'progress' of science having fundamentally changed the equation since Nietzsche's day. What could be more tragic, and indeed more absurd, than the complete self-extirpation of mankind as a living and thinking species? Yet even if Nietzsche could have had little inkling to what great powers of destruction and self-destruction mankind would graduate within one hundred years of the writing of his *Untimely Meditations*, his declaration 'There is only One Hope and One Safeguard for the future of humanity: it consists in his *retention of the sense for the tragic*' is perhaps more valid today than it ever was. While we may not rush in chorus onto the streets voicing our concern and protest after reading novels like *On the Beach*, *Level 7* or *The Rat*, or viewing films like *The Day After*, *Threads* or *Dr. Strangelove*, it is arguable — and this is Eva Horn's point — that readers may use the experience of such fictions to develop and keep alive their personal 'sense for the tragic'. And, in the light of the fact that these narratives all have a bearing on the destiny of humankind as a whole, this keeping alive a 'sense for the tragic' accordingly also entails a fostering of a sense of community about the destiny that the human species shares, a sense of our 'Unity', as Nietzsche put it. Reading or viewing these narratives may represent an isolated individual experience, but it is an experience that works to remind us of our common purpose. Indeed, even at a time when segregation reigned in the United States, novelists like George Stewart in *Earth Abides* and Pat Frank in *Alas, Babylon* employed their novels to pedagogic effect to stress the cross-racial dimension of our collective fate — Isherwood Williams's partner and mother of their children, Em, who is also one of mankind's new Eves, is a black woman (albeit one with a light skin complexion); Ish declares:

'Maybe a thousand years from now people can afford the luxury of wondering and worrying about that kind of thing again'.[71] Mary Shelley did the same in *The Last Man* albeit not in terms of racial equality but rather in terms of social equality, underscoring that before Nature we are in fact all equal regardless of rank and social position or — as we would say today — gender, sexual orientation, religion, age, and ethnic, racial or national identity.

Expecting the Worst, Hoping for the Better

The expressions 'our shared destiny' and 'our collective fate' that I have just used clearly relate not just to the notion and concept of future per se, but also to our expectation, often held more intuitively than consciously, that there actually will be a future for the human species beyond the death that we as individuals must all face. Whereas we know from experience that an individual's future is limited, it is as if we expect to take for granted that our species will enjoy an unlimited future. *Ex negativo* — counting on the probability that what they depict will *not* come true — hope in the future, or what Kant has called 'the hope of what is to come', 'die Hoffnung des Künftigen',[72] is what lies at the heart of every Last Man and Last Woman narrative.[73] Indeed, most if not all of their authors created their texts specifically to coax the reader into reflecting on the present as a prelude to the very future that they depict and that they wish will never become the present. In that sense, these texts are designed, albeit some more deliberately than others, to help us retain 'the sense for the tragic' which may in turn prod us to safeguard the foundations of life, foundations without which our species would lose its capacity to 'grow together into Unity and Community'.

A secular philosopher who doggedly pursued not just the idea that humankind must 'grow together into Unity and Community' but also that this communal future must be considered indivisible from our all-too-human 'hope of what is to come' was the Jewish-German messianic Marxist Ernst Bloch, an intimate friend of Georg Lukács during their Heidelberg period. Just as the early Lukács was drawn to a Romantic messianic spiritualism (echoes of which we still find in *The Theory of the Novel*), Bloch in his work too moves 'to conjoin socialism with the messianic spirit of the Bible, Marx with the Apocalypse', as J. P. Stern put it in his 1987 critical review of the 1986 English translation of Bloch's magnum opus *The Principle of*

---

71 *Earth Abides*, p. 118.

72 *Universal Natural History*, p. 299 (*Allgemeine Naturgeschichte und Theorie des Himmels*, p. 383). See also, written some forty years later, Kant's 'Verkündigung des nahen Abschlusses eines Traktats zum Ewigen Frieden in der Philosophie' (December 1796), *Werke*, ed. Weischedel, vol. 3: *Schriften zur Metaphysik und Logik* (Darmstadt: Wissenschaftliche Buchgesellschaft, 1959), pp. 403–16 (p. 412).

73 Ingo Cornils concludes his discussion of Carl Amery's 1975 *Der Untergang der Stadt Passau* by stating: 'There is an apparent paradox when a writer who is so concerned about the survival of the planet so obviously enjoys sending it to ruins, but on closer reflection the paradox disappears: only if you believe that history can be changed is there any hope for the future'; the article then closes with the observation: 'Using the "lighter touch" of Science Fiction, the "image of the future which takes shape in the minds of the readers" remains one of hope'. 'Alles kaputt? Visions of the End in West German and Austrian Science Fiction', pp. 73 and 76.

Hope (published in German in 1959).⁷⁴ According to Bloch the ultimate goal of human progress must be the utopian 'Kingdom of Freedom' ('Reich der Freiheit')⁷⁵ in which all men lead 'an unalienated life' ('Dasein ohne Entfremdung').⁷⁶ But while this goal may appear akin to religion's hope for and expectation of an end in millennial transcendence, for Bloch 'The Principle of Hope' must be underpinned materialistically rather than supernaturally; 'if [man] is to maintain his grip on the only enduring *Summum bonum* of human finality,' he stresses in his late work *Atheism in Christianity* (*Atheismus im Christentum*), published in 1968 at age 83, he 'must be able to see the Kingdom of heavenly freedom as his *geo*-graphical Utopia too' ('aber das unter dem Himmel als Reich unserer Freiheit utopisch Intendierte muß ebenso unsre *geo*-graphische Utopie sein, wenn der Mensch das auf die Dauer einzig haltende und orientierende Summum bonum seiner Zweckreihen halten will').⁷⁷ For Bloch the *other-worldly* 'transcendence' of religion — he also calls it the 'chimera of transcendence' ('Schimäre Transzendenz') — is superseded by what he calls the *this-worldly* 'transcendere' of the concrete '*geo*-graphical' steps we must take within the 'immanent' historical-dialectical world process which will allow us eventually to overcome, i.e. 'transcend', our existing inequalities.⁷⁸ Atheism's 'forward-look has replaced [religion's] upward-look', Bloch maintains, observing how 'a-theism' (his spelling) now allows us to view the 'gravitational center of an as yet unrealized At-all, which men used to call God, [...] as the Utopian Omega of the fulfilled Moment, the Eschaton of our immanence' ('So hat der Blick nach vornhin den nach Oben abgelöst. [...] ... Anziehungspunkt eines ausstehenden Überhaupt in der prozeßhaften *Sinnperspektive* — früher auf einen Gott bezogen. A-theistisch aber bezogen auf das utopische Omega: erfüllter Augenblick, Eschaton unserer Immanenz').⁷⁹ It is worth pointing out in this context, however, that Bloch contrasts two kinds of atheism, setting off his own positive kind, which is premised on 'the Principle of Hope', from a negative nihilistic kind that 'has no implication' ('ohne Implikationen') and 'no contact with the freedom movement among men and its fundamental stake in the realm of hope' ('ohne Begegnung mit der menschlichen Freiheits-Bewegung sowohl wie mit ihrem Hoffnungs-Fundus').⁸⁰

What it all comes down to is, ultimately, that only a processual dialectical real-life progression towards utopia can constitute history's proper 'fulfilment' for

---

74 J. P. Stern, 'Marxism on Stilts', *The New Republic*, 9 March 1987, 38–42 (p. 38). As regards Lukács's *Theory of the Novel*, Michael Löwy has observed: 'Although *The Theory of the Novel* did not speak of the Messiah, its last chapter (dealing with Tolstoy and Dostoevsky) was illuminated by utopian hope, presented, in a typical romantic way, as the restoration of the epic form — which corresponded to an age of absolute harmony between individual and community, man and universe' ('1910: Ernst Bloch and Georg Lukács meet in Heidelberg', p. 289).

75 Ernst Bloch, *Atheism in Christianity* (London: Verso, 2009), p. 249; *Atheismus im Christentum* (Frankfurt a.M.: Suhrkamp, 2009, page identical with the 1968 edition), p. 346.

76 *Atheismus im Christentum*, p. 326; this passage is not contained in the English translation.

77 *Atheism in Christianity*, p. 225 (*Atheismus im Christentum*, p. 317); the subsequent formulation p. 223 (p. 315).

78 See especially *Atheism in Christianity*, p. 223 (*Atheismus im Christentum*, p. 316).

79 Ibid., p. 249 (*Atheismus im Christentum*, p. 346).

80 Ibid., p. 223 (*Atheismus im Christentum*, p. 316).

Bloch; any divine intervention in the shape for instance of a counter-processual, i.e. sudden, supernatural Christian Last Judgment would, by contrast, 'frustrate' ('vereiteln') the immanent dialectical advance of humankind in history.[81] Of course, as an atheist Bloch does not believe in the possibility of supernatural intervention; he thus states: 'the *transcendere* without transcendence, the subject–object of a well-founded hope [...] is what lives on when the opium, the fool's paradise of the Other-world, has been burnt away to ashes. That remains as a call, signalling the way to the fulfilled This-world of a new earth' ('...das Transcendere ohne Transzendenz: das Subjekt-Objekt fundierter Hoffnung [...] bleibt, nachdem das ganze Opium, auch Narrenparadies des Jenseits verbrannt ist, [...] als Aufruf wie Anweisung zum vollen Diesseits oder zur neuen Erde'). With religion's millennial utopia discounted as impossible in Bloch's view, the only kind of utopia that can come about is that of the Marxist. As he states in *Atheism in Christianity*: 'Atheism-with-concrete-Utopia is at one and the same time the annihilation of religion and the realization of its heretical hope, now set on human feet' ('Atheismus mit konkreter Utopie ist im gleichen gründlichen Akt die Vernichtung der Religion wie die häretische Hoffnung der Religion, auf menschliche Füße gestellt').[82]

Strangely, despite having derived much of his Marxist messianic message and teleology from Christian thought Bloch shows himself unwilling to admit that Christians might be justified in considering their millennial expectation of resurrection and salvation in the future as a no less valid 'fulfilment of utopia' than the Marxist's.[83] Bloch's Marxist conception of the hope of utopian fulfilment through immanent history might differ substantively from a Christian's transcendent

---

[81] In *Das Prinzip Hoffnung* Bloch speaks of the 'alternative between absolute Nothing and absolute All: the absolute Nothing is the sealed frustration of utopia; the absolute All [...] is the sealed fulfilment of utopia' ('Alternative zwischen absolutem Nichts und absolutem Alles: das absolute Nichts ist die besiegelte Vereitelung der Utopie; das absolute Alles [...] ist die besiegelte Erfüllung der Utopie'). Ernst Bloch, *Principle of Hope*, trans. by Neville Plaice, Stephen Plaice and Paul Knight (Oxford: Basil Blackwell, 1986), pp. 312–13 (Bloch's emphases); I am citing the German from *Atheismus im Christentum*, pp. 326–27.

[82] Ibid., p. 225 (*Atheismus im Christentum*, p. 317).

[83] It is perhaps worthwhile noting here that Joseph Ratzinger (the later Pope Benedict XVI) has written extensively about the Last Judgment and resurrection as salvation. In his *Eschatology. Death and Eternal Life* (Washington, D.C.: Catholic University of America Press, 1988 and 2007, first German edition 1977), for instance, he describes the Last Judgment, or Parousia, as a kind of *unio mystica* of a deceased person with Christ in a timeless sphere; he writes: 'The person who dies steps outside time. He enters upon "the end of the world", which is not the final day of the cosmic calendar but is, rather, something alien to the diurnal round of this world's time. [...] when a person, by his dying, enters into non-time, into the end of the world, he also enters, by the same token, into Christ's return and the resurrection of the dead' (pp. 251–52). However, although sections of Pope Benedict's book read as if his conclusions applied universally to all human beings, it is clearly stated in certain passages that resurrection happens only to Christians; we thus read: 'Even now, in our decision as between faith and non-faith, judgment falls. Naturally, this does not simply wipe out the final judgment. [...] Christ inflicts pure perdition on no one. In himself he is sheer salvation. Anyone who is with him has entered the space of deliverance and salvation. Perdition is not imposed by him, but comes to be wherever a person distances himself from Christ' (p. 205). In the end it comes down to a question of free choice as depicted by Sonnenberg in *Donatoa*: a Christian can expect salvation, non-Christians cannot.

conception of a utopian end in the Grace of God, but hope in a utopian fulfilment it nonetheless represents for both. This — call it lack or lapse in Bloch's conception of utopia — is precisely what prompted the German Christian theologian Jürgen Moltmann in 1964 to counter Bloch's philosophy of hope with a 'Theology of Hope'. Moltmann's book of that title, *Theology of Hope*, subtitled *On the Ground and the Implications of a Christian Eschatology* (*Theologie der Hoffnung. Untersuchungen zur Begründung und zu den Konsequenzen einer christlichen Eschatologie*, English translation published in 1967), was later supplemented by an *Ethics of Hope* (*Ethik der Hoffnung*, 2010), both of which Moltmann intended as programmatic Christian responses to and rebuttals of Bloch's atheistic *Principle of Hope*.[84] In dialogue with fellow-theologians Moltmann later expressed his disappointment over the fact that Christian theologians had had to wait for an atheistic Marxist philosopher to remind them of what is quintessential about Christian belief, namely the hope in and expectation of utopian salvation.[85]

Both Moltmann's Christian theology of hope and Bloch's Marxist philosophy of hope are premised on a promise of future fulfilment, harmony and happiness, or what Bloch called the '*Definitivum of an all-fulfilling All*' ('das *Definitivum eines allerfüllenden Alles*') as opposed to nihilism's 'hypothetically possible *Definitivum of a Nothing*' ('hypothetisch möglichen *Definitivum eines Nichts*').[86] The German scholar Bernd U. Schipper thus rightly sees Christian 'apocalyptic anxieties' ('apokalyptische Ängste') and Marxist 'chiliastic hopes' ('chiliastische Hoffnungen')

---

84 I cannot refrain from adding here, however, that A. Roy Eckardt sees Moltmann's Christian 'Theology of Hope' as fundamentally dishonest, founding Christian hope on the suffering of Christ in the face of the suffering of the thousands of children burnt alive by Nazis during the Holocaust; see his 'Christians and Jews. Along a Theological Frontier', in *A Holocaust Reader. Responses to the Nazi Extermination* (Oxford: Oxford University Press, 2001), pp. 138–57.

85 See *Wie ich mich geändert habe*, p. 25; Moltmann observes there: 'In 1960 I discovered Ernst Bloch's *The Principle of Hope*. I read it in its GDR-edition during a holiday in Switzerland and was so taken by it that I missed out on the beauty of the mountains. My spontaneous impression was: Why did Christian theology let its own quintessential subject matter Hope slip by? After all, Bloch himself refers to "*Exodus* and the messianic sections of the Bible" [...]. And what has happened to the fundamentally Christian spirit of hope in [and anticipation of] God's empire to come in today's established Christianity? With my *Theology of Hope* of 1964 I wanted not to succeed Bloch, nor did I want to baptize his *Principle of Hope*, as Barth suspected; rather, I wanted to carry out a parallel action in Christian theology based on Christianity's own principles' ('1960 "entdeckte" ich *Ernst Bloch: Das Prinzip Hoffnung*. Ich las es in der DDR-Ausgabe während eines Urlaubs in der Schweiz und war so fasziniert, daß ich nichts mehr von der Schönheit der Berge sah. Mein spontaner Eindruck war: Warum hat sich die christliche Theologie ihr ureigenstes Thema Hoffnung entgehen lassen? Berief sich Bloch doch auf den "Exodus und die messianischen Partien der Bibel" [...]. Und wo ist der urchristliche Geist der Hoffnung auf das Reich Gottes in der heutigen etablierten Christenheit geblieben? Mit meiner "Theologie der Hoffnung" 1964 wollte ich Bloch nicht "beerben". Ich wollte sein "Prinzip Hoffnung" auch nicht "taufen", wie Barth in Basel argwöhnte. Ich wollte vielmehr eine Parallelhandlung in der christlichen Theologie aufgrund ihrer eigenen Voraussetzungen unternehmen').

86 These formulations are from *Das Prinzip Hoffnung*, but are cited by Bloch in *Atheismus im Christentum*, pp. 326–27 (however, because they are quotes from *Das Prinzip Hoffnung* the English translators have excised them from their English translation of *Atheism in Christianity* (cp. pp. 232–33); the English wording can be found in Ernst Bloch, *Principle of Hope*, trans. by Neville Plaice, Stephen Plaice and Paul Knight (Oxford: Basil Blackwell, 1986), pp. 312–13 (Bloch's emphases).

as 'genetically related' ('genetisch aufeinander bezogen'), forming 'two sides of the same coin' ('zwei Seiten einer Medaille). 'One has to distinguish between a religious and a non-religious secular form of chiliasm', Schipper observes, and continues:

> secular and religious utopia are on the same level, their only difference being that the latter embeds utopia in an apocalyptic frame. [...] The [utopian] projection of an ideal counter-vision to the present state of being — which simultaneously comprises a critique of this state and a normative claim [to truth] — coincides structurally with apocalyptic visions. Utopian projections are — and this is the core of my argument — religious visions in a secular mantle in which, in terms of the subject of this ideal state, God has been replaced by man who has become conscious of himself. [...] In terms of their philosophy of history utopia and apocalypse thus both present themselves as visions of the future with a distinct truth claim. [...] Both are looking for change, and in this sense the classical apocalypse narrative acts as a utopian vision in that it contains, for the in-group, i.e., the faithful, the promise of a Golden Age.

> [Man wird somit zwischen einer religiösen Form des Chiliasmus und einer nicht religiösen, säkularen Form unterscheiden müssen — oder anders formuliert: Die säkulare Utopie steht auf einer Stufe mit der religiösen, welche jedoch als Utopie in einen apokalyptischen Gesamtrahmen integriert ist. [...] Die Vorstellung eines idealen Gegenentwurfs zur erlebten Gegenwart, verbunden mit einer Kritik daran und einem normativen Anspruch, lässt sich auf struktureller Ebene apokalyptischen Entwürfen an die Seite stellen. Es sind — und dies ist meine These — gleichsam religiöse Entwürfe im säkularen Gewande, bei denen nun in Bezug auf das Subjekt des idealen Zustandes an die Stelle Gottes der Mensch tritt, der sich seiner selbst bewußt ist. [...] Utopie und Apokalypse erscheinen beide als geschichtsphilosophische Entwürfe mit einem klaren Deutungsanspruch. [...] Beide zielen auf eine Veränderung, denn darin ist die klassische Apokalypse eine Utopie, dass sie für die Ingroup, in klassischer Terminologie, die Gläubigen, ein goldenes Zeitalter verheißt.][87]

What the 'Principle of Hope' and the 'Theology of Hope' have in common, then, is that in life or in death they look to the future for some form of salvation or liberation from current misery or injustice.

What they less obviously also have in common is that both Bloch's Marxist utopia and Moltmann's Christian-utopian millennium regard the future as grounded upon the continuing existence of a community of beings, irrespective of whether this community is situated in life's this-worldly immanence (as Bloch in the name of Marxism sees it) or in death's other-worldly millennium following upon the Last Judgment (as Moltmann in the name of Christian salvation theology sees it). The continuity of human existence in whatever shape or form is simply taken for granted. But it is this that Last Man narratives powerfully put in question. In fact, one could go so far as to claim that in this sense apocalyptic Last Man narratives are truly 'revelatory', for as the German scholar Hartmut Böhme has reminded us (as have many others, including Eva Horn in one of the passages from her book that I cited

---

[87] 'Zwischen apokalyptischen Ängsten und chiliastischen Hoffnungen. Die religiöse Dimension moderner Utopien', in *Utopie und Apokalypse in der Moderne*, ed. by Reto Sorg and Stefan Bodo Würffel (Munich: Fink, 2010), pp. 47–61, the cited passages pp. 47, 52, 57 and 59.

earlier) the term 'apocalypse' denotes, etymologically speaking, not 'catastrophe' but rather 'revelation' (being derived as it is from the Greek *apokaluptein*, to uncover or reveal, hence the title 'The Revelation of St John'). Accordingly, Böhme notes, 'the apocalypse is not a metaphysics of catastrophe [...], it is a theology of hope which interprets history not through a "logic of disintegration" (Adorno) but in the light of salvation' ('die Apokalypse [ist] keine Metaphysik der Katastrophe [...], sondern eine Theologie der Hoffnung, welche die Geschichte nicht in der "Logik des Zerfalls" (Adorno), sondern im Licht des Heils rekonstruiert').[88]

But take man out of the equation, and his future as well as any notion of hope — Marxist or Christian — must dissolve with him into nothingness; conversely, as Camus recognized, 'a man devoid of hope and conscious of being so has ceased to belong to the future' ('un homme sans espoir et conscient de l'être n'appartient plus à l'avenir').[89] Of course, the fundamental question raised by terminal Last Man narratives is whether there will be a humanity to populate that future in the first place. The urgency of this question is brought home to us over and again by the authors of such narratives; Shelley in *The Last Man*, Shute in *On the Beach*, Roshwald in *Level 7*, Rehn in *The Children of Saturn* and, to include the most significant film in this sub-genre, Kubrick in *Dr. Strangelove*, all portray worlds in which, once their protagonists have died, the human species will have come to an end. But it is not just humankind that disappears: all human plans and hopes and expectations — as well as all religious faith and human anticipation of afterlife — will have perished too. And even the less 'terminal' storylines, those of novels like Jefferies' *After London or Wild England*, London's *The Scarlet Plague*, Huxley's *Ape and Essence*, Stewart's *Earth Abides*, Miller's *A Canticle for Leibowitz*, Frank's *Alas, Babylon*, Niven's and Pournelle's *Lucifer's Hammer*, Atwood's *Oryx and Crake* or Mandel's *Station Eleven*, in all of which a vestige of the human species survives the catastrophe and is shown trying to rebuild an existence, remind us of our species' fragility and mortality as well as of the voidance of community and continuity that would await us if mankind came to a sudden tragic end. If as Nietzsche says our 'highest task for the future' is to use the 'retention of the sense for the tragic' in order 'to grow together into Unity and Community', these Last Man novels, terminal as well as semi-terminal, serve to underscore that, in order for mankind to be able to do just that, we must ensure above all else that there is a community of people in the first place who we can rely on to continue to exist. All philosophies and all religions take far too much for granted that humanity will continue to exist into the future,[90] irrespective of whether they express this in terms of an other-worldly afterlife (as instanced by Moltmann for Christianity) or in terms of a this-worldly historical progression

---

88 'Vergangenheit und Gegenwart der Apokalypse', in *Freiburger literaturpsychologische Gespräche*, vol. 8: *Untergangsphantasien*, ed. by Johannes Cremerius, Wolfram Mauser, Carl Pietzcker and Frederick Wyatt (Würzburg: Königshausen + Neumann, 1989), pp. 9–26 (p. 17).

89 'An Absurd Reasoning (1942)', p. 166 (*Le Mythe de Sisyphe*, p. 50).

90 Thus Jane I. Smith, a co-author of the 'Afterlife' entry in the Thomson–Gale *Encyclopedia of Religion*, observes: 'Despite the variations in conceptions of what the afterlife may entail, a belief that human beings will continue to exist in some form after the experience they term death is a universal phenomenon'; 'Afterlife: An Overview', in *Encyclopedia of Religion*, editor in chief Lindsay Jones, 2nd edn, vol. 1 (Detroit: New York, Thomson Gale, 2005), pp. 128–35 (p. 135).

in time (as instanced by Bloch for Marxism) or in terms even of a cyclical return, as did Nietzsche as well as his antecedent Giambattista Vico and his heir Oswald Spengler. Where the latter believe in the cyclicality of history and the variation of the same, Hegelians and Marxists believe in dialectical progress towards an ideal end point, Christians believe in a sudden intervention and break in time when the Day of Judgment commences, and atheistic secularists and humanists believe in the 'advance' of mankind within the framework of time's natural movement towards the future (leaving aside whether this 'advance' is valued positively, negatively or neutrally). Embodying Bloch's 'absolute In-Vain of the historical process', all these philosophies and theologies would retroactively come to nought — as indeed would everything we care about as human beings — the moment mankind vanishes from this planet. (I could emphasize the word 'care' here in order to remind ourselves that Heidegger's existentialist concept of *Dasein*, i.e. our 'Being' in this world with temporal consciousness, is defined through our condition of existential *Sorge*, 'Care' or 'Worry': 'Temporality reveals itself as the meaning of authentic care' and 'Care is Being-towards-death', Heidegger writes in *Being and Time* — 'Zeitlichkeit enthüllt sich als der Sinn der eigentlichen Sorge. [...] Die Sorge ist Sein zum Tode'.)[91] This is the core message Last Man narratives relay: all we hope for and all we care about would be lost were humankind ever to be wiped out — people, family, friends; love, hate, compassion, sympathy, joy, grief, envy, regret, anticipation, amusement, exhilaration, tedium, disinterest, indeed every manner of feeling; all relationships and interactions imaginable between humans; all our creative faculties, artistic and technological; the wealth of human languages and cultures; all philosophies, all religions, all ideologies; all our memories of the past as well as all our aspirations and hopes for the future — the list could of course go on forever.

The Joke of Anthropocentrism

Just as clearly as terminal Last Man narratives put mankind's continued existence in the future categorically in doubt (even if only within a fictional compass), with our current state of knowledge about nature's hazards as well as about the menace posed by our own technological capabilities we know that such visions of a 'near' future eradication of humankind ('near' however defined) through a world-encompassing pandemic, a fatal comet strike or an all-out nuclear war are 'real possibilities' the world may have in store for us, as Huxley warned in 1959. The void these narratives place before our mind's eye is not the vacuum left following the death of God which, as Charles Taylor describes it in *A Secular Age*, the unbeliever supposedly feels pressed to offset through substitute buffers; rather, it is the substitute-less barrenness that opens up whenever we try to visualize a universe wholly devoid of human sentience and imagination. In manifest contrast to semi-terminal Last Man narratives, terminal narratives hold out no such comfort or buffer (except perhaps that in reading them we can prove to ourselves that we still exist, more about which later).

To compound matters, the literary scholar Ursula K. Heise is not alone in

[91] *Being and Time*, pp. 374 and 378 (*Sein und Zeit*, pp. 326 and 329), both in §65.

reminding us that 99 per cent of all species that have lived on Earth during the last four and a half billion years are already extinct today, suggesting that it would be arrogant for us to assume that our own species might be the only one exempt from such a fate. In her 2010 study *After Nature. The Extinction of Species and Modern Culture* (*Nach der Natur. Das Artensterben und die moderne Kultur*) she cites the distinction made by biologists and ecologists between an anthropocentric and a biocentric perspective.[92] The biocentric perspective looks holistically at the survival of all of nature's species, of which humankind is only one, and indeed one whose existence is not necessary for life on our planet to continue (quite the opposite in fact, since we are in the process of destroying nature's equilibrium by artificially speeding up the processes of natural extinction). The anthropocentric perspective by contrast places humankind in the centre: from this perspective all hinges on our existence. Heise emphasizes that we need to see the human species as just one of nature's myriad species; doing so helps us to recognize and acknowledge not just that the differences of race or ethnic belonging, gender and sexual orientation, nationality, religion and political orientation, and so forth, that lure so many members of our species into strife, murder and war fade into irrelevance, but also that our continued existence depends on the prolonged existence also of the ecosystem within which we are embedded; she observes:

> The extinction of species forces man to reflect once more on himself as a species, as a post-human creature embedded within a structure of ecological systems in which his privileged position is far less important than his being interdependent upon other species. [...] To think of humankind as a species also means to relegate all those differences as well as the inequalities between people that have dominated the history of mankind to the background, whether these differences be those between industrialized and developing nations, between classes, nations, races, and genders, or between those who subscribe to differing religious creeds.
>
> [Das Sterben der Arten zwingt den Menschen, sich selbst erneut als Art zu denken, als posthumanes Menschentier innerhalb ökologischer Systeme, in denen seine Sonderstellung weniger wichtig ist als seine Vernetzung mit anderen Arten. [...] Den Menschen als Art zu denken heißt auch, all jene Unterschiede und die Ungleichheit zwischen Menschen (ob nun zwischen Industrie- und Entwicklungsländern, zwischen Klassen, Nationen, Rassen, Geschlechtern oder den Anhängern unterschiedlicher Religionen) in den Hintergrund zu rücken, die die Geschichte der Menschheit geprägt haben.]

It is exactly this that terminal Last Man narratives achieve. At the same time that they serve to remind us of the foolish and unnecessary pettiness and indeed irresponsibility of our squabbling among ourselves, their storylines refocus our perspective by calling to our attention mankind's tenuous and fragile position on this planet. Mary Shelley recognized our predicament already in 1826 when she let her lone survivor Lionel Verney declaim at the mid-point of the first ever secular Last Man narrative:

---

92 *Nach der Natur. Das Artensterben und die moderne Kultur* (Frankfurt a.M.: Suhrkamp, 2010), pp. 20–21; the subsequent passage pp. 149 and 161.

> In the face of all this we call ourselves lords of the creation, wielders of the elements, masters of life and death, and we allege in excuse of this arrogance, that though the individual is destroyed, man continues for ever. Thus, losing our identity, that of which we are chiefly conscious, we glory in the continuity of our species, and learn to regard death without terror. But when any whole nation becomes the victim of the destructive powers of exterior agents, then indeed man shrinks into insignificance, he feels his tenure of life insecure, his inheritance on earth cut off.

And in *The Last Man* Shelley shows us the eradication not just of 'any whole nation', but indeed of the whole of humankind.

Yet, where the truly terminal visions deny hope, the semi-terminal visions — those Last Man narratives that provide for an Adam and an Eve and consequently the chance of a regenerated human community, such as *La Fin du monde*, *The Scarlet Plague*, *Earth Abides*, *Lucifer's Hammer*, *Oryx and Crake*, *Station Eleven* and their countless siblings — reinstate it; their narratives encourage us to hope that humankind might just manage to escape the obliteration that is awaiting us, whatever course or shape it might take. Whether this is a realistic hope or not is another question. Of course, what terminal and semi-terminal narratives have in common is that they all seek to reinforce the message that it would mean risking suicide for us not to safeguard our natural habitat for the benefit of future generations through every means possible, ensuring, as Mary Shelley calls it above, 'the continuity of our species'.

But human beings are known to commit suicide as individuals, so why not also as a species? In a work entitled *Responsibility for Future Generations* (*Verantwortung für zukünftige Generationen*, 1988), the German philosopher and ethicist Dieter Birnbacher takes up Nietzsche's and Bloch's concerns about the future of humanity. Taking his cue from Hobbes, Spinoza, Hume, Kant and Nietzsche, Birnbacher sees man as the only species in possession of a self-conscious orientation toward past and future, an orientation that enables us to look beyond our purely immediate needs in order to assess and anticipate those of the future, both for ourselves as well as for our offspring.[93] But Birnbacher also cautions how

> our assessment as such will not necessarily result in action. We cannot take for granted that the person who is aware of the long-term consequences of his actions and who may even assess them correctly, will actually do what this assessment would seem rationally to require of him. Who recognizes the long-term evil consequences of his actions, yet nonetheless gives in to the temptation of short-term gain, does not necessarily demonstrate that he was not sufficiently informed about the consequences of his actions. However adequate one's perception and assessment of the future may be, they are in themselves not sufficient to ensure that one will actually take responsibility for the future.
>
> [Eine Bewertung treibt noch nicht in die Aktion. Es versteht sich nicht von selbst, daß derjenige, der sich der langfristigen Folgen seines Tuns bewußt ist und sie angemessen bewertet, auch tut, was diese Bewertung rationalerweise

---

[93] *Verantwortung für zukünftige Generationen* (Stuttgart: Reclam, 1988), pp. 175–76 and 179–80; the subsequent quotations pp. 187, 188 and 189.

von ihm verlangt. Wer sich der langfristigen üblen Folgen seines Tuns bewußt ist, dennoch aber der Versuchung eines kurzfristig erreichbaren Nutzens erliegt, gibt dadurch nicht notwendig zu erkennen, daß er sich über die Folgen seines Tuns nicht hinreichend klar geworden ist. Eine noch so adäquate Zukunftswahrnehmung und eine noch so adäquate Zukunftsbewertung reichen allein nicht hin, damit Zukunftsverantwortung tatsächlich übernommen wird.]

Birnbacher cites various reasons for such non-action or wrong action; most obvious, he argues, is the fact that the further we look into the future, the more abstract the affected populations become, even when we are dealing with our own imagined progeny. And even when we are dealing with our own contemporaries, he observes, pure love of humanity does not always inspire people to take the action that would seem reasonable and vital to our existence. He cites three factors that tend to influence our decision-making in this regard: first our doubt about whether we as individuals can actually influence an outcome in a distant future; second the presumed similarity or dissimilarity with ourselves of those who will be affected; and third their relative closeness to us in time (he speaks of 'die [vermeinte] *Beeinflußbarkeit* der Zukunft, die [vermeinte] *Ähnlichkeit* der Betroffenen sowie deren *zeitliche Nähe*', all emphases are Birnbacher's). He observes in this context that most people tend to see their great-grandchildren, even those not yet born, as closer to themselves than members of a geographically distant ethnic and cultural grouping alive on the planet at the same time as they are. Finally, the more we believe that a catastrophe is inescapable, the less we are inclined to take action, believing fatalistically that action would be nothing but a waste of our time and energy. It seems, both in terms of climate change and nuclear weaponry, that Birnbacher's conclusions do not bode well for the future.

Over the course of this book's five chapters we have dealt at great length with fictional narratives about our end and disappearance, or tenuous survival, as a species due to some cataclysmic event occurring in the near or distant future. But let me stress again, should this not be apparent from what I have already argued: The end of *our* world is not the end of *the* world, minuscule and short-lived beings that we are, and certainly the end of *our planet* would not be the end of *the universe* that surrounds us. Yet in imagining *our* end we as human beings — being the self-centered creatures that we are — like to imagine it involving the end of being and time altogether (to obliquely quote Heidegger whose notion of *Dasein*, literally 'being here', in *Being and Time* is indissolubly tied in with our human consciousness of temporality). Perhaps this is because we like to think that the *particular* end of our *specific* kind of temporal (and hence historical) consciousness of being would entail the *general* end of *all* being. The much-vaunted 'End of History' is, of course, pure anthropocentrism — and wishful thinking to boot. It is in this vein that the narrator of Italian writer Guido Morselli's *Dissipatio H. G.*, the sole being left after all his fellow beings have seemingly evaporated into nothingness overnight, reflects:

> The end of the world? One of those jokes of anthropocentrism: to describe the end of our species as implying the death of all fauna and flora, as the end of the world as such. [...] There is no eschatology that does not consider the continuity

of humankind as essential for the continuity of all matter. One is happy to
grant that things came into existence *before* we did, but not that they might end
after we do. [...] My goodness, you sages and bigheads, you take yourselves too
seriously. The planet was never as alive as today now that that particular species
of bipeds has stopped treading her surface.

[La fine del mondo? Uno degli scherzi dell'antropocentrismo: descrivere la fine
della specie come implicante la morte della natura vegetale e animale, la fine
stessa della Terra. [...] Non esiste escatologia che non consideri la permanenza
dell'uomo come essenziale alla permanenza delle cose. Si ammette che le
cose possano cominciare *prima*, ma *non* che possano finire *dopo* di noi. [...]
Andiamo, sapienti e presuntuosi, vi davate troppa importanza. Il mondo non
è mai stato così vivo, come oggi che una certa razza di bipedi ha smesso di
frequentarlo.][94]

The idea of a world with neither human life nor historical consciousness seems as unbearable as it seems unfathomable. As Robert Jay Lifton notes from the perspective of a 'secular psychiatrist', as he labels himself, it is for this reason that the (possibility of) nuclear self-eradication of humankind strikes most human beings as particularly unsettling and worrisome; its *meaningless* inevitability (if inevitable it is) stands opposed to what Lifton calls religion's eschatologically '*meaningful* inevitability' (my emphases). Lifton contends:

If some people view nuclear holocaust as inevitable, they do so with resignation
or hopelessness — as opposed to the meaningful inevitability of an eschatology
or the submission to irresistible forces of nature. [...] Nuclear nothingness has
no such redeeming virtue. It is just that — *literal* nothingness, an end to human
existence and to the existence of most other animal species and to plant species
as well.[95]

One can of course imagine alternative non-religious responses beyond 'resignation or hopelessness', for instance the short-lived satisfaction of the vain doomsayer or the cynical pleasure of the uncompromising misanthrope (Arno Schmidt attributes this stance to some of his protagonists) or the stoic acceptance of the hard-nosed realist. But I assume most of us, whether religiously inclined or not, will neither gloat over nor jubilate at mankind's self-annihilation through nuclear Armageddon, should we ever be unfortunate enough to witness it. As Lifton remarks, 'the mind [...] rebels against such a stark image'; he continues:

Human language and imagination [...] tend to be bound to the flow of life,
and of continuing human events. [...] That kind of imagination and experience
takes place within a context of larger flow and ongoing events, a context of
expectation that life will somehow resume or continue. Freud touched on
this mental struggle in his famous statement that we cannot imagine our own
death but are only present as spectators. But (though Freud did not say this) we
do regularly imagine a human world that continues without us as individuals
(which is why we take out life insurance, prepare wills, and in other ways
provide for people and projects that will outlive us). In that post-self world, the

---

94 *Dissipatio H.G.*, 4th edn (Milano: Adelphi Edizioni, 1980), p. 56.
95 *The Future of Immortality*, pp. 149 and 156; he calls himself a 'secular psychiatrist' in the opening essay of *The Future of Immortality* (p. 11).

self's influence and contributions, however modest, continue to reverberate. That is very different from there being no human world at all — and precious little world of anything else. The latter is what defies our imaginative capacity — so much so that literal nothingness may be a contradiction in terms.[96]

Even beyond our death as an individual, Lifton submits, we count on human community to persist and carry on without us, as we count on our 'continuing to reverberate' as a part of humankind's storehouse of memories and archives for a certain duration; but take this expectation and hope away and we would feel robbed of our sense of connection and community: we would feel untethered, unchained from the 'great chain of life' into which we were born. As Push-Button-Officer PB X–127 in Roshwald's *Level 7* confesses on the last pages of his diary,

> it is lonely here. I wish I had someone to talk to. Even a dying soldier deserted on the battle-field cannot have felt as lonely as I feel. He had his comrades to think of, his family — people he was dying for, or thought he was dying for. But I have nobody to die for. Nobody to think of. They are all dead. [...] I wonder if it makes any difference to have family and friends around you. I wish I had. I would give anything to have some people around me! [...] I am dying, and humanity dies with me. I am the dying humanity.[97]

Through his protagonist PB X–127 Roshwald is making an important point. It is one thing to imagine our own death as an individual in the knowledge not just that there are people who will remember us and 'carry the fire', as McCarthy has his father and son call it in *The Road*; it is another thing altogether to imagine the total and irrevocable disappearance of all of humankind, including all of mankind's culture and civilization alongside the full panoply of its cultural archives in addition to everyone's memories. Part of our humanity as sentient emotional and historical beings is that we want and expect our species to survive even beyond the people we know, the 'family and friends' who PB X–127 wishes could share his dying hours. For, as Lifton observes, 'in a postnuclear world, one can hardly be certain of living on in one's children or their children; in one's creation or human influences; in some form of lasting spirituality [...]; or in eternal nature, which we know to be susceptible to our weapons and pollutions. The radical uncertainty of these four modes may indeed play a large part in our present hunger for direct experiences of transcendence'.[98] He later adds: 'The protean or postmodern question is perhaps, How does one maintain a sense of vitality and life-continuity in the face of the threat of extinction, and in the face of the breakdown of all the symbols by which our lives are organized?'

One way we maintain such a 'sense of vitality and life-continuity in the face of the threat of extinction' is, according to Lifton, first to recognize that as particularized selves we are embedded within a larger communal and collective *species self* and then, second and as a consequence thereof, to respond accordingly in order to safeguard this *species self*. Under the evocative chapter heading 'The

---

96 Ibid., pp. 156–57.
97 *Level 7*, p. 142.
98 'The Image of "The End of the World"', p. 164; the subsequent passages pp. 262 and 134.

New Psychology of Human Survival', Lifton argues that it is precisely our being endangered by nuclear annihilation that propels the emergence of our awareness of such a '*species self*, of a self-concept inseparable from all other human selves in sharing with them the ultimate questions of life and death'. It is this sense of *species self*, he adds, writing in 1987, that stirred him to 'take [a] stand against both American and Soviet nuclear-arms buildup and against actions by either country [...] that threaten the peace and increase the danger of nuclear holocaust'. He reasoned at that time:

> Within that sense of species self, I must struggle to balance these commitments and *make the best ethical and political choices I am able* — with that species self *keeping me mindful of the human beings involved in stands on survival and justice*. This broadening and deepening of an inclusive sense of human self is one of the most fundamental sources of *hope* available to us.[99] (*human beings* italicized by Lifton, otherwise my emphases)

It is as if Lifton were, one hundred years after Nietzsche, reiterating for a nuclear age the German philosopher's demand for the 'retention of the sense for the tragic' and the need for it to be based on concrete 'Safeguards' as well as the more abstract affect of 'Hope'; such safeguards for Lifton include the actions we take today to ensure our survival tomorrow, as underscored by the italics I added to the passage cited above.

A kind of resigned antithesis to Lifton's essay 'The New Psychology of Human Survival' is the German writer Wolfgang Hildesheimer's causerie 'Does hope still have a future?' ('Hat die Hoffnung noch eine Zukunft?'), published in the *Frankfurter Allgemeine Zeitung* in December 1986 at the very moment Lifton was preparing *The Future of Immortality and Other Essays for a Nuclear Age* for publication. Hildesheimer answers that question with 'a categorical and devastating NO'; anyone 'who denies this, lives in and through repression' ('Die Antwort ist [...] ein kategorisches und vernichtendes NEIN. Wer das leugnet, lebt in und von Verdrängung'), Hildesheimer declares.[100] As we recall from Chapter Five, Hildesheimer's own response to our nuclear dilemma was to proclaim that he would stop writing literature, and so he did in 1984. And yet two years later, even Hildesheimer felt compelled in this follow-up pronouncement to relativize his initial response; he now answers the question 'How can we live without hope?' ('Wie man ohne Hoffnung leben kann?') thus:

> Answer: the individual impulse to live cannot be quenched by the terror of the future, but rather is nurtured by it. Moreover: a modicum of hope is hidden in each of us, never plumbed by conscious thought. (As much as I have searched, I cannot find hope in *my own* innermost consciousness.) Spero, ergo sum? [I hope, therefore I am?] The opposite it seems applies: the fact that I am still alive must mean that somewhere inside me something still hopes. Sum, ergo spero. [I am, hence I (must) hope].
>
> [Antwort: der individuelle Lebensimpuls wird von dem Schrecken der Zukunft nicht gelöscht, eher gefördert. Zudem: ein minimales Quantum an Hoffnung

---

99 *The Future of Immortality*, p. 134.

100 'Hat die Hoffnung noch eine Zukunft?', in *Gesammelte Werke in sieben Bänden*, ed. by Christiaan Lucas Hart Nibbrig and Volker Jehle, vol. 7: *Vermischte Schriften* (Frankfurt a.M.: Suhrkamp, 1991), pp. 739–40 (p. 739); the subsequent quote p. 740.

versteckt sich in jedem, vom Denken nicht erreicht. (In *meinem* Inneren ist sie als Bewußtes unauffindbar, ich habe viel gesucht.) Spero, ergo sum? Eher umgekehrt: die Tatsache, daß ich noch am Leben bin, muß wohl bedeuten, daß es irgendwo in mir noch hofft. Sum, ergo spero.] (Hildesheimer's emphasis)

As one of the most resolute skeptics, and as one of the most doubtful pessimists, even Hildesheimer has to admit that in being we cannot do without 'a modicum of hope'. To be is to hope, he acknowledges by shrewdly reformulating Descartes's famous philosophical dictum 'Cogito ergo sum'.

The Peekaboo Principle

As will have become apparent on the preceding pages, Last Man narratives — even the terminal ones — cater to our, shall we call it, 'existential need' for hope as they are premised on the promise that, in one form or another, our species will continue long beyond our death as an individual. W. Warren Wagar observed astutely in an essay fittingly entitled 'Round Trips to Doomsday' that 'in science fiction, as in mythology and cosmology, the end of the world is seldom the end. It may usher in the millennium, set stages for the romantic exploits of last men and women, or inaugurate a new cycle of rise and fall. Whatever the aftermath, fictions of the end-time feed our hopes for fresh beginnings'.[101] From his psychologist's perspective Robert Jay Lifton agrees, noting that, 'indeed, a sense of, or even desire for, the end of the world is part of a general human psychological potential [...] and can be strongly evoked by combinations of inner terror and desperate need for regenerative hope'.[102] And what better exemplifies this combination of terror — Burke's 'ruling principle of the sublime' — and need for hope than the Last Man narratives we encountered on the pages of this study?

The combination of terror and hope may constitute a key psychological motive for our desire to read end-time narratives in that it arouses a censored kind of pleasure, as suggested by Sigmund Freud in his writings on that concept. Indeed, Freud's psychoanalytic writings offer some useful instruments to dissect and better understand the conflicting impulses that draw us as readers and viewers to literary and filmic end-time narratives, allowing us to enjoy what should 'normally' be repulsive. Freud's dualism of death and life instincts provides an obvious starting point, particularly illuminating pronouncements of which are contained in some of his later writings, specifically *Beyond the Pleasure Principle* (*Jenseits des Lustprinzips*, 1920), *The Ego and the Id* (*Das Ich und das Es*, 1923), *Civilization and Its Discontents* (*Das Unbehagen in der Kultur*, 1930) and *An Outline of Psycho-Analysis* (*Abriß der Psychoanalyse*, 1938). However, one can easily be confused by the fact that the description, demarcation and even nomenclature of these two instincts shifted considerably over time — for instance Freud recognized in the 1920s that his early opposition of ego instincts and sexual instincts did not correlate with his later opposition of death and life instincts, forcing him to recast his understanding of

---

101 'Round Trips to Doomsday', p. 96.
102 *The Future of Immortality*, p. 6.

how the ego instincts worked; he also regularly admitted that this dualism was far more speculative than his earlier psychoanalytic concepts and hypotheses (at the beginning of the fourth section of *Beyond the Pleasure Principle* he speaks of the 'often far-fetched' nature of his 'speculation', the 'weitausholende Spekulation'). What complicates the matter further is that Freud used the term death instincts, 'Todestriebe', and destruction instincts, 'Destruktionstriebe', synonymously whereas especially in English-language psychoanalytic scholarship they are additionally called Thanatos; although Freud himself never used this third term in his published writings, according to Ernest Jones he did use it in conversation.[103] Leaving such complications aside, what Freud's definitions of death and life instincts, Thanatos and Eros, all have in common — and what makes them particularly germane to our argument — is that the former seeks to 'undo connections and so to destroy things' ('Zusammenhänge aufzulösen und so die Dinge zu zerstören') in order to make 'what is living' ('das Lebende') regress to a lifeless inorganic state of primordial unity ('Einheiten aufzulösen [um sie] in den uranfänglichen, anorganischen Zustand zurückzuführen').[104] The latter by contrast endeavours 'to establish ever greater unities and to preserve them thus' ('immer größere Einheiten herzustellen und so zu erhalten'), it 'aims at complicating life and at the same time, of course, at preserving it' ('das Leben durch immer weitergreifende Zusammenfassung der in Partikel zersprengten lebenden Substanz zu komplizieren, natürlich es dabei zu erhalten').[105] 'Affirmation — as a substitute for uniting — ', he sums up in a short piece entitled 'Negation' in 1925, 'belongs to Eros; negation — the successor to expulsion — belongs to the instinct of destruction' ('Die Bejahung — als Ersatz der Vereinigung — gehört dem Eros an, die Verneinung — Nachfolge der Ausstoßung — dem Destruktionstrieb').[106] In *Civilization and Its Discontents* Freud in 1930 sees the dualism of death and life instincts and the correlative pairing of negation and affirmation as presiding dialectically over the civilizational evolution of our species; he writes:

> I may now add that civilization is a process in the service of Eros, whose purpose is to combine single human individuals, and after that families, then races, peoples and nations, into one great unity, the unity of mankind. Why

---

103 See Jean Laplanche and J.-B. Pontalis, *Das Vokabular der Psychoanalyse*, vol. 2 (Frankfurt a.M.: Suhrkamp, 1977), p. 494 (entry 'Thanatos').

104 A compilation of passages from Sigmund Freud, *An Outline of Psycho-Analysis*, in *The Standard Edition of the Complete Psychological Works of Sigmund Freud*, trans. by James Strachey in collaboration with Anna Freud, vol. 23 (London: The Hogarth Press and the Institute of Psycho-Analysis, 1964; other volumes of the *Standard Edition* have different dates), pp. 139–207 (p. 148); *Civilization and Its Discontents*, in *Standard Edition*, vol. 21, pp. 57–145 (pp. 118–19); *The Ego and the Id*, in *Standard Edition*, vol. 19, pp. 1–66 (p. 40). The corresponding German passages are from *Das Unbehagen in der Kultur*, in *Gesammelte Schriften*, vol. 12 (Vienna: Internationaler Psychoanalytischer Verlag, 1934), pp. 27–114 (p. 86) and *Das Ich und das Es*, in *Gesammelte Schriften*, vol. 6 (Leipzig, Vienna, Zurich: Internationaler Psychoanalytischer Verlag, 1925), pp. 351–405 (p. 385).

105 A compilation from *An Outline of Psycho-Analysis*, p. 148, and *The Ego and the Id*, p. 40. *Abriß der Psychoanalyse*, in *Abriß der Psychoanalyse / Das Unbehagen in der Kultur* (Frankfurt a.M.: Fischer, 1979), p. 12, and *Das Ich und das Es*, p. 385.

106 'Negation', in *Standard Edition*, vol. 19, pp. 233–39 (p. 239); 'Negation', in *Gesammelte Schriften*, vol. 11 (Leipzig, Wien, Zürich: Internationaler Psychoanalytischer Verlag, 1928), pp. 3–7 (p. 7).

this has to happen, we do not know; the work of Eros is precisely this. These collections of men are to be libidinally bound to one another. [...] But man's natural aggressive instinct, the hostility of each against all and of all against each, opposes this programme of civilization. This aggressive instinct is the derivative and the main representative of the death instinct which we have found alongside of Eros and which shares world-dominion with it. And now, I think, the meaning of the evolution of civilization is no longer obscure to us. It must present the struggle between Eros and Death, between the instinct of life and the instinct of destruction, as it works itself out in the human species. This struggle is what all life essentially consists of...

[Wir fügen hinzu, [die Kultur] sei ein Prozeß im Dienste des Eros, der vereinzelte menschliche Individuen, später Familien, dann Stämme, Völker, Nationen zu einer großen Einheit, der Menschheit, zusammenfassen wolle. Warum das geschehen müsse, wissen wir nicht; das sei eben das Werk des Eros. Diese Menschenmengen sollen libidinös aneinander gebunden werden [...]. Diesem Programm der Kultur widersetzt sich aber der natürliche Aggressionstrieb der Menschen, die Feindseligkeit eines gegen alle und aller gegen einen. Dieser Aggressionstrieb ist der Abkömmling und Hauptvertreter des Todestriebes, den wir neben dem Eros gefunden haben, der sich mit ihm in die Weltherrschaft teilt. Und nun, meine ich, ist uns der Sinn der Kulturentwicklung nicht mehr dunkel. Sie muß uns den Kampf zwischen Eros und Tod, Lebenstrieb und Destruktionstrieb zeigen, wie er sich an der Menschenart vollzieht. Dieser Kampf ist der wesentliche Inhalt des Lebens überhaupt...][107]

We need not subscribe to every facet of Freud's psychoanalytic theory in order to appreciate the connection that can be drawn between the death and life instincts and Last Man narratives. The 'struggle between Eros and Death, between the instinct of life and the instinct of destruction' is battled out in each and every Last Man storyline. Thanatos with its 'impetus toward dissolution'[108] reigns in those narratives in which mankind is irreversibly wiped from the surface of our planet and no hope for regeneration remains, from Mary Shelley's *The Last Man* to Nevil Shute's *On the Beach* and Mordecai Roshwald's *Level 7*. Where mankind survives, by contrast, it might be said that Eros takes the upper hand; here we are typically shown the remaining 'single human individuals' combining first to form 'families' and then, albeit usually in the future beyond the storyline's narrative framework, to rebuild the 'races, peoples and nations' that catastrophe — nuclear, biotechnological, robotical, ecological, cosmical — had torn apart and dissolved, with the ultimate goal being to recreate the 'one great unity, the unity of mankind', as Freud put it. In *The Ego and the Id* Freud tellingly also remarked how 'for purposes of discharge the instinct of destruction is habitually brought into the service of Eros' ('der *Destruktionstrieb* [ist] regelmäßig zu Zwecken der Abfuhr in den Dienst des Eros gestellt'),[109] reminding us not just that the two conflicting instincts are but two complementary aspects of one larger unconscious dynamic, but also

---

107 *Civilization and Its Discontents*, p. 122; *Das Unbehagen in der Kultur*, p. 89.
108 So described in *International Dictionary of Psychoanalysis*, editor-in-chief Alain de Mijolla (Detroit, New York, San Francisco: Thomson Gale, 2005), p. 371.
109 *The Ego and the Id*, p. 41 (*Das Ich und das Es*, p. 386).

why we can — at least from the psychoanalyst's vantage point — take pleasure in something that would at first glance seem so appalling and objectionable as well as, literally, contrary to our whole existence. This is picked up upon tongue-in-cheek in the sexual imagery of the closing scenes of Kubrick's film *Dr. Strangelove*, as Eva Horn astutely observes when she writes: 'The ultimate logic of MAD (Mutual Assured destruction), so Kubrick's film tells us, is a (self-)destructive instinct, an instinct that, in its banality and productivity, cannot be differentiated from our sex drive' ('Die *Ultima Ratio* der MAD, so macht Kubrick deutlich, ist ein (Selbst-)Vernichtungstrieb, ein Trieb, der gerade in seiner Banalität und Produktivität nicht zu unterscheiden ist vom Trieb nach Sex').[110] Put differently, with Major Kong's nuclear bomb joy ride, which heralds the world-encompassing nuclear holocaust that is about to happen (and which is represented vividly in the film's closing 'nuclear sublime'[111] montage sequence of atomic mushroom clouds), the film *Dr. Strangelove* stages the definitive sexual climax and Freudian 'discharge' ('Abfuhr'), the latter in a most literal sense; Kong's orgasmic holler on his phallic projectile thus represents, so Horn, a 'secret fantasy of concurrent and communal death' ('eine heimliche Phantasie vom gleichzeitigen und gemeinsamen Sterben'), a communal death of one and all that 'evokes a unity and equality that humanity possesses only in its collective demise' ('im gemeinsamen Sterben aller ist eine Einheit und Gleichheit heraufbeschworen, die die Menschheit nur im gemeinsamen Untergang haben kann'). The film thus tells us that the only unity realizable any time soon is Freud's regressive 'primordial unity', a unity that is achievable, but only through deployment of the ultimate instrument of self-eradication available to our death instinct, nuclear weaponry. *Dr. Strangelove* hence relates, as graphically as chillingly, how one irrational and abnormal individual's death drive — typified in this film by U.S. Air Force Brigadier General Jack D. Ripper — can suffice to set the terminal demise of the whole of mankind in motion; one singular madman's crazy impulses can, if in our technological age he is placed in the right position, set off the destruction of his whole species.

Having said that, even as cynical and pessimistic a film as *Dr. Strangelove* has its proverbial silver lining. While the film may indulge our inborn death instinct and in so doing cater to our 'Pleasure Principle' (the 'Lustprinzip' of Freud's early

---

110 *Zukunft als Katastrophe*, p. 104, the subsequent passages p. 107.

111 If we can call a nuclear mushroom cloud sublime, it is not because what led to it was the order given by a human being, nor because the bomb was ridden rodeo-like by a zealous stratobomber pilot, nor because it was set in motion by some Doomsday Machine, all three scenarios of which figure in Kubrick's film, the final sequence of which signals the end of life on planet Earth. Sublimity here lies not in the fact that the American U.S. Air Force Brigadier General Jack D. Ripper's mad scheme or the Soviets' retaliatory Doomsday Machine has actually gone off according to plan, rather it lies in the fact that these mushroom clouds once again symbolize the awe-inspiring force of Nature. For more on the nuclear or atomic sublime see Peter B. Hales, 'The Atomic Sublime', *American Studies*, 32 (1991), 5–31, and Karin Harrasser, 'Das atomare Sublime und die standardisierte Katastrophe', in *Atombilder. Ikonographie des Atoms in Wissenschaft und Öffentlichkeit des 20. Jahrhunderts*, ed. by Charlotte Bigg and Jochen Hennig (Göttingen: Wallstein, 2009), pp. 168–76. Harrasser in particular highlights the multiple layers of sexual connotations behind Kubrick's *Dr. Strangelove*, but also the degree to which Kubrick was miming and satirizing the nuclear sexism of such propaganda materials as the U.S. Army Airforce's 1964 film *Special Delivery*.

metapsychological writings), it — perhaps even more subliminally — concurrently gratifies our life instinct, or instinct of self-preservation. If the film may appear at first glance to humour only our longing for 'negation' and 'dissolution' (much as the novels *The Last Man*, *On the Beach* and *Level 7* might also seem to do), the simple fact that we are actually engaging with these narratives while sitting popcorn-munching in front of cinema's silver screen (or sipping a glass of sherry at home with book in hand) is as unfailing as reassuring a reminder that we are still alive and going about our daily business, as well as enjoying our daily entertainment amidst a community of other human beings doing the same all around us. In this sense, all narratives of definitive end times, whether these end times appear in the shape of mankind's consummation through divine apocalypse, death by natural cataclysm or ruin by nuclear conflagration, or any variation thereupon, are, inasmuch as their authors expect them to be viewed (or read) once they have been released (or published), expressions of hope that there will in fact be a spectator (or reader) and, through him or her, a living human being to appreciate the scriptwriter's and director's (or author's) genius and dexterity, as well as his or her wisdom and warning. Reading novels and viewing films are based on an unstated contract, a tacit understanding that the book or film has been written by a living human being for its posterior (and on occasion even posthumous) appreciation by other living human beings. Even if end-time novels are brute reminders that this contract may one day no longer hold (should what they describe become equally brute reality), as long as we are actively engaged in reading or viewing such novels and films — or indeed my own book about them — we can rest assured that the contract is still in force — we are the living physical confutation of what the novels and films we are reading or viewing fictionally enact. Is there not a (sublime?) poignancy about the irony at work in all of these narratives of ends and conclusions, sublime or not so sublime, apocalyptic and not so apocalyptic, that so long as we are still able to read them — or indeed about them — that that end has not yet come?

 Although Freud acknowledged the speculative nature of his dualism of death and life instincts, what he never put in doubt was the crucial role played by childhood memories and experiences, deposited in our unconscious during the first years of our life, in the formation of the adult psyche. In the second chapter of the work in which Freud first introduced the dualism of death and life instincts, *Beyond the Pleasure Principle*, he also related the story of his one-and-a-half-year-old infant grandson playing what in the lexicon of psychoanalysis is now dubbed the 'Fort–Da' game. Similar to the English 'peekaboo' game, a child or an adult hides an object or himself, saying in German 'Fort' ('Gone!'), only to reappear (or make the object reappear) exclaiming an elated 'Da' ('There!', or 'Here I am again!'). As Freud relates it, his grandson would repeatedly thrust 'a wooden reel with a piece of string tied round it [...] over the edge of his curtained cot', a game through which the child learnt to 'allow his mother to go away without protesting'; 'he compensated himself for this, as it were, by himself staging the disappearance and return of the objects within his reach'.[112] The dynamic is, for Freud, imbued with considerable

---

112 Freud discussed the game in the second section of *Beyond the Pleasure Principle*, trans. by James

significance for the development of the infantile psyche (and hence also for the adult psyche); through the pleasure obtained from repeatedly making something or someone first disappear and then reappear we are trained already during our infancy to handle the loss or absence of objects that we cherish or of human beings we feel close to. The entry on 'Fort–Da' in the *International Dictionary of Psychoanalysis* provides a useful account of this game, suggesting how it might also transfer over to our context of Last Man narratives; we are told that

> it is thus the *fort* game that is the more problematical, in that the subject obtains from the disappearance of the other or of himself an unconscious gratification which runs counter to the most fundamental prohibitions. In view of his belief in the omnipotence of thoughts, the child cannot conceive of death or disappearance otherwise than as the outcome of a wish; he can form an idea of these concepts solely through seeing or losing sight of objects [or people; R.W.], so he links these to the deployment of visual desire, thereby transforming trauma into pleasure, albeit a forbidden pleasure.[113]

By allowing us to delight in the unconscious wish of mankind's (self-)extermination, Freudian psychoanalysis suggests, Last Man narratives create a bad conscience about our relishing such a 'forbidden pleasure'. They pander to both our unconscious sadistic and masochistic desires, sadistic because in our fantasy we are subjecting everyone around us to an excruciating death, masochistic because we ourselves will suffer too. (As Freud notes in the sixth section of *Beyond the Pleasure Principle* the death and life instincts are closely connected with the dynamism of sadism and masochism.) This bad conscience is of course offset by the pleasure we take in these narratives, at least in the semi-terminal ones, because, in identifying with the protagonist, we can fantasize ourselves into the role of survivor and hero of catastrophe. This dynamic of identification was elucidated by Freud in his short but seminal 1908 essay 'Creative Writers and Day-Dreaming' ('Der Dichter und das Phantasieren'), in which he observed that 'every child at play behaves like a creative writer, in that he creates a world of his own, or, rather re-arranges the things of his world in a new way which pleases him'; shifting his focus to the creative writer and his audience, Freud then continues:

> The creative writer does the same as the child at play. He creates a world of phantasy which he takes very seriously — that is, which he invests with large amounts of emotion [...]. The unreality of the writer's imaginative world, however, has very important consequences for the technique of his art; for many things which, if they were real, could give no enjoyment, can do so in the play of phantasy, and many excitements which, in themselves, are actually distressing, can become a source of pleasure for the hearers and spectators at the performance of a writer's work.
>
> [Jedes spielende Kind benimmt sich wie ein Dichter, indem es sich eine eigene Welt erschafft oder, richtiger gesagt, die Dinge seiner Welt in eine neue, ihm

---

Strachey, *Standard Edition*, vol. 18, pp. 14–17, the quoted passages p. 15 (*Jenseits des Lustprinzips, Gesammelte Schriften*, vol. 6, pp. 199–203, with the quoted passages pp. 200–01).

113 *International Dictionary of Psychoanalysis*, ed. Alain de Mijolla, entry 'Fort-Da', pp. 599–600 (p. 600).

gefällige Ordnung versetzt. [...] Der Dichter tut nun dasselbe wie das spielende Kind; er erschafft eine Phantasiewelt, die er sehr ernst nimmt, d.h. mit großen Affektbeträgen ausstattet [...]. Aus der Unwirklichkeit der dichterischen Welt ergeben sich aber sehr wichtige Folgen für die künstlerische Technik, denn vieles, was als real nicht Genuß bereiten könnte, kann dies doch im Spiele der Phantasie, viele an sich eigentlich peinliche Erregungen können für den Hörer und Zuschauer des Dichters zur Quelle der Lust werden.][114]

What in reality would be utterly distressing, Freud tells us, can in fiction produce feelings of elation and satisfaction for author and reader alike by releasing 'pleasure arising from deeper psychical sources' ('Entbindung größerer Lust aus tiefer reichenden psychischen Quellen'), by allowing us to 'overcom[e] the feeling of repulsion' ('Überwindung [der] Abstoßung') and 'to enjoy our own day-dreams without self-reproach or shame' ('unsere eigene Phantasien [...] ohne jeden Vorwurf und ohne Schämen zu genießen'), and thereby transforming potential trauma into pleasure and liberating 'tensions in our minds' ('Befreiung von Spannungen').[115]

The relevance of Freud's observations for the analysis of Last Man narratives must be obvious. But there is another, and far less obvious, side to the 'Fort–Da' dynamic; it relates to what I would like to call the Peekaboo Principle, using the English term to designate a different version of the game than the one Freud describes, but one I am more familiar with. What Freud does not discuss in *Beyond the Pleasure Principle*, but what I have always found crucial about this game whenever I have played it with children, is that the game creates the most fun when it is played by two people (typically an infant or young child and an adult) rather than just the child alone, as Freud, in *Beyond the Pleasure Principle*, outlines the game his grandson played. It is the feigned surprise of the knowing adult, exclaiming 'Da!' ('Oh, there you are!') when the child suddenly appears out of nowhere — so it believes — that the child particularly relishes. Or, if the roles are reversed, it is the being surprised by the adult, who had hidden him- or herself in a wardrobe or behind a door, seemingly reappearing out of nowhere exclaiming 'There!', 'Da!', that the child delights in above all. It is the mutual enjoyment gained by the disappearance/reappearance bluff that makes this game so much fun to play with small children. Although the version of the game I know may make it less amenable to Freud's psychoanalytical introspection, focused as it was on the subliminal dimension of the early childhood psychic apparatus, it brings out better than Freud's version an important aspect of our psychic functioning, namely the joy and excitement, the bond and commonality, we experience as human beings in being together with other human beings when we play such games, whether they be psychoanalytically significant or not.

Put differently, the best part of the game is not the 'Gone!', the 'Fort!', the act of disappearing by hiding oneself (although that can be fun too), but the 'There!', the 'Da!', the sudden reappearing and reuniting with the fellow player. The strength of this effect (or indeed affect, be the phenomenon psychological, be it anthropological)

---

[114] Sigmund Freud, 'Creative Writers and Day-Dreaming', trans. by James Strachey, *Standard Edition*, vol. 9, pp. 142–53 (pp. 143–44); 'Der Dichter und das Phantasieren', *Gesammelte Werke*, vol. 7, pp. 213–23 (pp. 213–14).

[115] 'Creative Writers and Day-Dreaming', p. 153 ('Der Dichter und das Phantasieren', p. 223).

derives as much from the appreciation that there is someone else there to share this joy and excitement with us as from the recognition that we are not alone in this world, that we are not the Last Man or Last Woman on Earth looking like Mary Shelley's Lionel Verney in 'vague lament' down upon the ruins of Rome pondering 'the voice of dead time'; 'the generations I had conjured up to my fancy', Verney reflects in silent contemplation, feeling enveloped in 'seven-fold barriers of loneliness', 'contrasted more strongly with the end of all — the single point in which, as a pyramid, the mighty fabric of society had ended, while I, on the giddy height, saw vacant space around me'.[116] The phrases 'end of all' and the 'vacant space around me', written by Mary Shelley in 1825 or 1826, three or four years after her husband had drowned off the Italian coast, echo her own despair at having lost her partner and companion; we recall from Chapter Four how Mary bemoaned the resulting 'vacant days' and how she felt that 'all is to me dead' after Percy's death. Recollecting 'the fatal eighth' of July in her journal entry on 2 October 1822, she laments: 'I have now no friend. [...] Now I am alone! Oh, how alone!' Calling her journal 'a monument to shew [sic] that all ended then', she asks herself 'And I begin again?,' only to answer, ' — oh. never!'[117] On 7 October she complains 'They are all gone & I live — if it be life to be as I am. But it is not — I am in the valley of the shadow of death'. Over the next weeks and months her diary shows her sinking ever deeper into a state of 'melancholy' and 'self depression' coupled with feelings of 'irreperable [sic] misery', 'sorrow' and 'excessive agony'. Over and again she invokes her 'despair', 'anguish' and sense of 'utter solitude' and 'annihilation'. Like Mary left alone never to begin again, Verney at the end of *The Last Man* accuses nature of looking on mankind 'with *unsympathizing complacency*' and '*supreme indifference*'; his sentiment clearly replicates Percy Bysshe Shelley's reverence for Mont Blanc's 'unsparing' 'voiceless' grandeur and 'untameable, inaccessible solitude'. But it is simultaneously a mirror image of Mary's state of mind after her husband's sudden and unexpected disappearance — 'Shelley! You have left me deserted and alone!', she writes on 17 March 1823, and on 31 May 'I am deserted by you'.[118] Knowing there would be no 'Da' moment with her partner, a 'Here I am again!', in this world, Mary Shelley could not keep herself from agonizing over the 'Fort', the 'Gone'; admitting to herself that she is no 'materialist', she holds on to the hope that she will see Percy again in the next world. 'But I have faith — a firm & true knowledge', she confides to her journal on 19 December 1822, 'that I go to him'; two months later, on 17 February 1823, she notes: 'And we shall again meet — shall we not?'

Inasmuch as Mary Shelley's *The Last Man* is a novel born from the author's sense of anguish and abandonment following the loss of the person closest to her in life (or indeed persons, if we include Byron and the children she has lost), it can be

---

116 *The Last Man*, pp. 336–37.

117 *The Journals of Mary Shelley 1814–1844*, vol. 2, p. 429; the subsequent references in the following order, pp. 435, 462 ('melancholy', also p. 463), p. 441, p. 443 ('irreperable [sic] misery'), p. 446 ('sorrow'), p. 465 ('excessive agony'), 'despair' (pp. 435, 438, 443 and 446), 'anguish' (pp. 448, 449 and 467), 'utter solitude' (pp. 440, 441 and 451), and 'annihilation' (pp. 438 and 448).

118 Ibid., pp. 459 and 465; the final passages pp. 453, 446 and again 453.

argued that this first terminal novel in European literature to depict mankind's extinction by natural means might never have seen the light of day without Percy's tragic boating accident. The strength of Mary Shelley's sense of loss and dejection underscores the power of the Peekaboo Principle and what it teaches us: that it is neither God nor nature but only other human beings who will look on us and play games with us with *sympathizing compassion* and *supreme involvement*, to invert Shelley's formulations. It teaches us too that without 'the Other' the game of life would not just be only half the fun, but that in actual fact it would be no fun at all.

And — is not the final conclusion unavoidable? — from this perspective modern literature's genre of Last Man narratives might just represent the Peekaboo Principle's most graphic and most potent illustration. But, of course, Mary Shelley's *The Last Man*, the first specimen and formative model of this genre, gives us, for reasons outlined above, only the pessimistic half of the game, the terminal 'Fort', the 'Gone', which in her projection of the end is effected by nature's plague; her novel does away with Christianity's millennial vision of mankind's return after the Last Judgment, it is wanting the 'Here I am again!' As are those equally downbeat later nuclear incarnations of her narrative, Nevil Shute's *On the Beach*, Mordecai Roshwald's *Level 7*, Jens Rehn's *The Children of Saturn*, Anton Andreas Guha's *The End: Diary of the Third World War*, and Günter Grass's *The Rat* in which not nature but mankind is the cause of mankind's extinction. Most narratives within the genre, however, are more upbeat, as we saw in the previous chapters; they prefer to invoke the Peekaboo Principle's more optimistic side. Thus such narratives as Jack London's *The Scarlet Plague*, H. G. Wells's *The World Set Free*, Aldous Huxley's *Ape and Essence*, George R. Stewart's *Earth Abides*, Pat Frank's *Alas, Babylon*, Margaret Atwood's *Oryx and Crake*, Emily St. John Mandel's *Station Eleven* or even Cormac McCarthy's *The Road*, as grisly and depressing as they may initially present the catastrophe and mankind's entry into post-cataclysmic mayhem, all end in the promise of hope and the assurance of a rekindled future for mankind and its survival as a species, whatever shape that survival might assume. It seems that an end in absolute nothingness, that extinction without any prospect of rebirth or resurrection, remains as hard to digest today as it was for Goethe more than two centuries ago; we recall how, in the autobiographical reminiscence about his response to Holbach's ostensibly 'gloomy' and 'Cimmerian' *System of Nature*, Goethe expressed his fear that the 'earth might vanish with all its creatures', leaving no trace — as well as leaving us with no promise of afterlife or hope of continuance in any form. Like many of his contemporaries, theists, deists and pantheists alike, Goethe felt a need to reject what he felt to be the cold emptiness of the atheist's view of afterlife — we recall in the same vein Jean Paul's verdict 'No one in Creation is so alone, as the denier of God' and his condemnation of atheistic philosophy's 'Dead, dumb Nothingness!' and 'Cold, everlasting Necessity!' Indeed, the dominance of semi-terminal narratives over their terminal siblings seems to suggest that the notion of an end in utter nothingness remains as haunting and disagreeable as ever; it is a possibility few of us like to contemplate, even in our 'Secular Age'. And yet, it is the very atheism that precipitated the death of God that also created the stimulus, as its 'natural' corollary, as it were, for someone to imagine the death of man in all its dire consequences. *At* the conclusion of my study — and perhaps also *as* the (sublime?) conclusion of my study — I would like to return to the words of the atheistic philosopher Ludwig Feuerbach that I cited in Chapter Four; in *The Essence of Christianity*, published in 1841, he wrote: 'Without other men the world would be for me not only dead and empty, but meaningless. Only through his fellow does man become clear to himself and self-conscious; but only when I am clear to myself, does the world become clear to me'. In short, it is not the death of God that makes us truly feel 'alone' in the universe, as Jean Paul believed, nor must the death of God rob us of all meaningfulness in life, as Charles Taylor stipulates. Rather, what would make life meaningless, and what would make us feel infinitely alone, is, as Feuerbach suggests and as Last Man narratives corroborate in imaginary form, the death of all our fellow beings, the death of man as a species.

BIBLIOGRAPHY

ABRAMS, M. H., *Natural Supernaturalism. Tradition and Revolution in Romantic Literature* (New York: W. W. Norton, 1971).
ADAMS, DOUGLAS, *The Hitch Hiker's Guide to the Galaxy. A Trilogy in Five Parts* (London: William Heinemann, 1995, first edition 1979).
ADELUNG, JOHANN CHRISTOPH, *Grammatisch-kritisches Wörterbuch der Hochdeutschen Mundart. Elektronische Volltext- und Faksimile-Edition nach der Ausgabe letzter Hand* (Leipzig: [n.pub.], 1793–1801), retrieved from <www.zeno.org/Adelung-1793>, accessed 12 March 2013.
ADORNO, THEODOR W., 'Jargon der Eigentlichkeit', in *Negative Dialektik. Jargon der Eigentlichkeit = Gesammelte Schriften*, vol. 6, ed. by Rolf Tiedemann et al. (Frankfurt a.M.: Suhrkamp, 2003), pp. 413–523.
—— *The Jargon of Authenticity*, trans. by Knut Tarnowski and Frederic Will (Evanston: Northwestern University Press, 1973).
ALDISS, BRIAN, *Billion Year Spree* (London: Weidenfeld & Nicolson, 1973).
ALKON, PAUL K., *Origins of Futuristic Fiction* (Athens: University of Georgia Press, 1987).
—— *Science Fiction Before 1900. Imagination Discovers Technology* (New York: Twayne, 1994).
ALLEN, GRAHAM, *Mary Shelley* (Basingstoke: Palgrave, MacMillan (*Critical Issues* series), 2008).
ALLOTT, MIRIAM, ed., *Novelists on the Novel* (London and Henley: Routledge & Kegan Paul, 1965).
ALTIZER, THOMAS J. J., *The Gospel of Christian Atheism* (Philadelphia: The Westminster Press, 1966).
—— 'The Significance of the New Theology', in *The Death of God Debate*, ed. by Jackson Lee Ice and John J. Carey (Philadelphia: The Westminster Press, 1967), pp. 242–55.
—— 'Theology and the Death of God', in Thomas J. J. Altizer and William Hamilton, *Radical Theology and The Death of God* (Harmondsworth: Penguin, 1966), pp. 102–17.
ALTIZER, THOMAS J. J., and WILLIAM HAMILTON, *Radical Theology and The Death of God* (Harmondsworth: Penguin, 1966).
AMÉRY, JEAN, 'Jargon der Dialektik', in *Werke*, vol. 6: *Aufsätze zur Philosophie*, ed. by Gerhard Scheit (Stuttgart: Klett-Cotta, 2004), pp. 265–96.
ANDERS, GÜNTHER, *Die Antiquiertheit des Menschen*, vol. 2: *Über die Zerstörung des Lebens im Zeitalter der dritten industriellen Revolution* (Munich: C. H. Beck, 1995, first published 1980).
—— *Die atomare Drohung* (Munich: C. H. Beck, 1983).
—— 'Commandments in the Atomic Age' (first published in German in the *Frankfurter Allgemeine Zeitung*, 13 July 1957), in Günther Anders and Claude Eatherly, *Burning Conscience. The Case of the Hiroshima Pilot Claude Eatherly*, pp. 11–20.
—— *Ketzereien* (Munich: C. H. Beck, 1996 [first edition 1982]).
—— 'Reflections on the H Bomb', *Dissent*, 3 (Spring 1956), 146–55.
—— *Tagesnotizen. Aufzeichnungen 1941–1979*, ed. by Volker Hage (Frankfurt a.M.: Suhrkamp, 2006).
—— 'Theses for the Atomic Age', *The Massachusetts Review*, 3 (Spring 1962), 493–505.

—— 'Wenn ich verzweifelt bin, was geht's mich an?' (interview with Mathias Greffrath 1979), in *Günther Anders antwortet. Interviews & Erklärungen* (Berlin: Bittermann, 1987, Edition Tiamat: Critica Diabolis 13), pp 19–53.

——, and Claude Eatherly, *Burning Conscience. The Case of the Hiroshima Pilot Claude Eatherly*, 'Preface' by Bertrand Russell, 'Foreword' by Robert Jungk (New York: Monthly Review Press, 1961).

ANGELUS SILESIUS, *Angelus Silesius. A Selection from the Rhymes of a German Mystic*, trans. by Paul Carus (Chicago: Open Court Publishing, 1909).

—— *Des Angelus Silesius Cherubinischer Wandersmann*, ed. by Wilhelm Bölsche (Jena and Leipzig: Eugen Diederichs, 1905).

ANON., 'Critical Observations [from *The Spirit of the Pilgrims*]', in Robert Pollok, *The Course of Time, with Critical Observations of Various Authors on the Genius and Writings of the Poet*, ed. by James R. Boyd (New York and Chicago: A. S. Barnes, 1871), pp. 28–34.

ANON., entry 'Grainville', in *Allgemeine Encyclopädie der Wissenschaften und Künste* (Leipzig: [n.pub.], [n.d.]), p. 309.

ANON., entry 'Grainville', in *Biographie Universelle ancien et moderne*, vol. 18 (GO–GU) (Paris: L. G. Michaud, 1817), pp. 271–74.

ANON., entry 'Grainville', in *Nouvelle Biographie Générale depuis les temps les plus reculés jusqu'a nos jours*, ed. by M. le Hoefer (Paris: Firmin Didot Frères, 1857), vol. 21 (Goertz–Grevile), columns 608–10.

ANON., 'The Last Man', *Blackwood's Edinburgh Magazine* (January–June 1826), 284–86.

ANON., *Das nahe Ende der Welt aus den merkwürdigen Begebenheiten derselben von ihrer Erschaffung an* ([n.p.]: [n.pub.], 1792, Bayerische Staatsbibliothek, sign. H. misc. 92 m).

ANON., *Reply to the Anti-Matrimonial Hypothesis and Supposed Atheism of Percy Byssche [sic] Shelley, as laid down in Queen Mab* (London: W. Clark, 1821).

ANON., review of Franz von Sonnenberg's *Das Welt-Ende* in *Allgemeine Literatur-Zeitung*, 22 June 1801, columns 633–36.

ANON., review of Franz von Sonnenberg's *Donatoa* in *Jenaische Allgemeine Literatur-Zeitung*, 135, 9 June 1806, columns 465–72.

ANON., review of Jean-Baptiste François Xavier Cousin de Grainville's *Der letzte Mensch. Eine romantische Dichtung* (1807), in *Jenaische Allgemeine Literatur-Zeitung*, no. 218, September 1808, columns 516–19.

ANON., review of Jean-Baptiste François Xavier Cousin de Grainville's *Der letzte Mensch* (1807) and *Omegar, der letzte Mensch* (1811), in *Allgemeine Literatur-Zeitung*, nos. 292 and 293, December 1813, columns 657–62, and 665–68.

ANON., review of Mary Shelley's *Frankenstein*, in *The Literary Panorama and National Register*, June 1818, cited from <http://www.rc.umd.edu/editions/mws/lastman/index.html>, accessed on 11 July 2013.

ANON., review of Mary Shelley's *Frankenstein*, in *Quarterly Review* (January 1818), cited from <http://www.rc.umd.edu/editions/mws/lastman/index.html>, accessed on 11 July 2013.

ANON., review of Mary Shelley's *The Last Man*, in *The Literary Gazette and Journal of Belles Lettres, Arts, Sciences, &c.*, no. 473, 18 February 1826, 102–03.

ANON., review of Mary Shelley's *The Last Man*, in *The Monthly Review, Or Literary Journal*, New Series 1, March 1826, 333–35, cited from <http://www.rc.umd.edu/reference/chronologies/mschronology/reviews/mrrev.html>, accessed 8 July 2014.

ANON., review of Mary Shelley's *The Last Man*, in *The Panoramic Miscellany, or Monthly Magazine and Review of Literature*, March 1826, 380–86.

ANON., 'Article XI', *Quarterly Review*, vol. 27 (April and July 1822), 524–53.

ARENDT, DIETER, *Der 'poetische Nihilismus' in der deutschen Romantik. Studien zum Verhältnis von Dichtung und Wirklichkeit in der Frühromantik* (Tübingen: Niemeyer, 1972).

ARONSON, RONALD, 'The Holocaust and Human Progress', in *Echoes from the Holocaust. Philosophical Reflections on a Dark Time*, ed. by Alan Rosenberg and Gerald E. Myers (Philadelphia: Temple University Press, 1988), pp. 223–44.

ATWOOD, MARGARET, *Oryx and Crake* (London: Little, Brown Book Group / Virago Press, 2010).

BARBAULD, ANNA LAETITIA, *Poems*, 3rd edn (London: Joseph Johnson, 1773).

BARBER, LYNN, *The Heyday of Natural History 1820–1870* (London: Jonathan Cape, 1980).

BEARD, J. R., 'Strauss, Hegel, and their Opinions', in *Voices of the Church* (London: Simpkin, Marshall & Co., 1845), pp. 7–50.

BECKER, CLAUDIA, 'Der Traum der Apokalypse — die Apokalypse ein Traum? Eschatologie und/oder Ästhetik im Ausgang von Jean Pauls "Rede des toten Christus"', in *Poesie der Apokalypse* (Würzburg: Königshausen & Neumann, 1991), pp. 129–44.

BECKETT, SAMUEL, *Warten auf Godot — En attendant Godot — Waiting for Godot* (Frankfurt a.M.: Suhrkamp, 1971).

BEER, JOHN, 'Romantic Apocalypses', in *Romanticism and Millenarianism*, ed. by Tim Fulford (New York: Palgrave, 2002), pp. 53–69.

BENTLEY, RICHARD, *The Folly and Unreasonableness of Atheism* (London: J. H. for H. Morlock, 1699).

BERKOVITS, ELIEZER, 'Faith after the Holocaust', in *Wrestling with God. Jewish Theological Responses during and after the Holocaust*, ed. by Steven T. Katz, Shlomo Biderman and Gershon Greenberg (Oxford: Oxford University Press, 2007), pp. 463–85.

BERMAN, DAVID, *A History of Atheism in Britain: From Hobbes to Russell* (London, New York, Sydney: Croom Helm, 1988).

BICHSEL, PETER, *Der Leser. Das Erzählen. Frankfurter Poetik-Vorlesungen*, 3rd edn (Darmstadt and Neuwied: Luchterhand, 1983).

BIEGERT, CLAUS, ed., *Der Montag, der die Welt veränderte. Lesebuch des Atomzeitalters* (Reinbek: Rowohlt, 1996).

Biographie Universelle, ancienne et moderne (Paris: L. G. Michaud, 1817).

BIRNBACHER, DIETER, *Verantwortung für zukünftige Generationen* (Stuttgart: Reclam, 1988).

BIRUS, HENDRIK, 'Apokalypse der Apokalypsen. Nietzsches Versuch einer Destruktion aller Eschatologie', in *Das Ende. Figuren einer Denkform*, ed. by Karlheinz Stierle and Rainer Warning (Munich: Fink, 1996), pp. 33–58.

BLAKE, WILLIAM, 'The Last Judgment', in *The Poems and Prophecies of William Blake* (London and Toronto: J. M. Dent, [n.d.]), pp. 357–72.

BLOCH, ERNST, *Atheismus im Christentum* (Frankfurt a.M.: Suhrkamp, 2009).

—— *Atheism in Christianity* (London: Verso, 2009).

—— *Principle of Hope*, trans. by Neville Plaice, Stephen Plaice and Paul Knight (Oxford: Basil Blackwell, 1986).

BLOOM, HAROLD, *Shelley's Mythmaking* (Ithaca: Cornell University Press, 1959).

BLUMBERG, JANE, *Mary Shelley's Early Novels. 'This Child of Imagination and Misery'* (Basingstoke: MacMillan Palgrave, 1992).

BLUMENBERG, HANS, 'Abgesang auf Weltbewohner. Über die Tröstlichkeit von Weltmodellen', in *Die Vollzähligkeit der Sterne* (Frankfurt a.M.: Suhrkamp, 1997), pp. 384–99.

—— *Aspekte der Epochenschwelle* (Frankfurt a.M.: Suhrkamp, 1976).

—— 'Atommoral — Ein Gegenstück zur Atomenergie', in *Schriften zur Technik*, ed. by Alexander Schmitz and Bernd Stiegler (Frankfurt a.M.: Suhrkamp, 2015), pp. 7–16.

—— *The Legitimacy of the Modern Age*, trans. by Robert M. Wallace (Cambridge, MA: The MIT Press, 1983).

—— *Die Legitimität der Neuzeit* (Frankfurt a.M.: Suhrkamp, 1996).

BÖHME, HARTMUT, 'Vergangenheit und Gegenwart der Apokalypse', in *Freiburger literaturpsychologische Gespräche*, vol. 8: *Untergangsphantasien*, ed. by Johannes Cremerius, Wolfram

Mauser, Carl Pietzcker and Frederick Wyatt (Würzburg: Königshausen + Neumann, 1989), pp. 9–26.

BOLLNOW, OTTO FRIEDRICH, *Existenzphilosophie* (Stuttgart: Kohlhammer, 1969, first edition 1942).

BONNEVILLE, C. M. LE ROY, *Étude biographique et littéraire sur Cousin de Grainville* (Le Havre: Imprimerie Lepelletier, 1863).

BÖRSCHE-SUPAN, HELMUT, 'Berlin 1810. Bildende Kunst. Aufbruch unter dem Druck der Zeit, in *Kleist-Jahrbuch* (1987), 52–75.

BOUCHARLAT, JEAN-LOUIS, *Le jugement dernier. Poëme en trois chants, imité d'Young* (Paris: Le Normant, 1806).

BOWIE, ANDREW, 'Romantic philosophy and religion', in *The Cambridge Companion to German Romanticism*, ed. by Nicolas Saul (Cambridge: Cambridge University Press, 2009), pp. 175–90.

BOX, JASON E., 'Die Wahrheit bekommt uns nicht gut' (an interview with Hans Joachim Schellnhuber, Alice Bows-Larkin and Jason E. Box), in *Süddeutsche Zeitung* (Magazin), 22 January 2016, 22–28.

BOYD-BOWMAN, SUSAN, '*The Day After*: Representations of the Nuclear Holocaust', *Screen*, 25 (August-September 1984), 71–97.

BRAITERMAN, ZACHARY, '"Hitler's Accomplice?": The Tragic Theology of Richard Rubenstein', *Modern Judaism* 17 (1997), 75–89.

BRAUND, SIMON, 'How Ronald Reagan Learned to Start Worrying and Stop Loving the Bomb', *Empire*, 257 (2010), 134–38.

BREW, CLAUDE, 'A New Shelley Text: Essay on Miracles and Christian Doctrine', in *The Keats-Shelley Memorial Bulletin*, 28 (1977), 10–28.

BREWER, WILLIAM D., *The Shelley–Byron Conversation* (Gainesville: The University of Florida Press, 1994).

BRIANS, PAUL, *Nuclear Holocausts: Atomic War in Fiction* (1987), unpaginated internet download from <http://public.wsu.edu/~brians/nuclear/>, accessed 17 November 2014.

BRINKMANN, RICHARD, 'Nachtwachen von Bonaventura. Kehrseite der Frühromantik?', in *Die deutsche Romantik*, ed. by Hans Steffen (Göttingen: Vandenhoeck & Ruprecht, 1970), pp. 134–58.

BROOCKS, RICE, *God's Not Dead. Evidence for God in an Age of Uncertainty* (Nashville, Dallas: Thomas Nelson, 2013).

BROWN, STEWART J., 'Movements of Christian awakening in revolutionary Europe, 1790–1815', in *The Cambridge History of Christianity*, vol. 7: *Enlightenment, Reawakening, and Revolution*, ed. by Stewart J. Brown and Timothy Tackett (Cambridge: Cambridge University Press, 2008 (*Cambridge Histories Online*)), pp. 575–95.

BRUN, FRIEDERIKE, 'Chamounix beym Sonnenaufgange', in *Gedichte*, ed. by Friedrich Matthißon (Zurich: Orell, Geßner, Füßli and Co, 1791), p. 1.

BÜCHNER, GEORG, 'Lenz', in *Complete Plays, Lenz and Other Writings*, trans. by John Reddick (London: Penguin, 1993), pp. 139–64.

—— *Sämtliche Werke, Briefe und Dokumente*, 2 vols, ed. by Henri Poschmann with Rosemarie Poschmann (Frankfurt a.M.: Deutscher Klassiker Verlag, 1992, reprint 2006).

—— 'Spinoza', in *Sämtliche Werke, Briefe und Dokumente*, vol. 2: *Schriften, Briefe, Dokumente*, ed. by Henri Poschmann with Rosemarie Poschmann (Frankfurt a.M.: Deutscher Klassiker Verlag, 1999, reprint 2006), pp. 280–352.

BUCKLAND, WILLIAM, *Geology and Mineralogy Considered with Reference to Natural Theology* (London: William Pickering, 1836).

BULKELEY, JOHN, *The Last Day. A Poem* (London: J. Stagg, J. Roberts and E. Berrington, 1720).

BURKE, EDMUND, *A Philosophical Enquiry into the Origin of our Ideas of the Sublime and Beautiful*, ed. by David Wombersly (London: Penguin, 2004).
BURNET, THOMAS, *The Sacred Theory of the Earth, Containing an Account of the Original of the Earth, and of all the General Changes Which it hath already undergone, or is to undergo, till the Consummation of all Things*, 2 vols (London: J. Hooke, 1726).
BYRNE, PETER, *Natural Religion and the Nature of Religion. The Legacy of Deism* (London and New York: Routledge, 1989).
BYRON, GORDON LORD, 'Heaven and Earth. A Mystery', in *The Poems and Plays of Lord Byron*, 3 vols (London: J. M. Dent, [n.d.]), vol. 2, pp. 405–29.
—— *The Poems and Plays of Lord Byron*, 3 vols (London: J. M. Dent, [n.d.]).
—— *The Works of Lord Byron*, new, revised, and enlarged edn: *Letters and Journals*, ed. by Rowland E. Prothero, 6 vols (London: John Murray, 1922).
CAMERON, KENNETH NEILL, *Shelley. The Golden Years* (Cambridge, MA: Harvard University Press, 1974).
—— *The Young Shelley. Genesis of a Radical* (London: Victor Gollancz, 1951).
CAMERON, LAUREN, 'Mary Shelley's Malthusian Objections in *The Last Man*', *Nineteenth-Century Literature*, 67 (2012), 177–203.
CAMPBELL, THOMAS, 'The Last Man', in *The Complete Poetical Works* (Boston: Phillips, Sampson and Co., 1854), pp. 199–201.
CAMUS, ALBERT, 'An Absurd Reasoning (1942)', in *The Existentialist Reader. An Anthology of Key Texts*, ed. by Paul S. MacDonald (Edinburgh: Edinburgh University Press, 2000), pp. 144–83.
—— *Le Mythe de Sisyphe. Essai sur l'absurde. Nouvelle édition augmentée d'une étude sur Franz Kafka* (Paris: Les Éditions Gallimard, 1942).
—— ['Humanity's Last Chance'], editorial in *Combat*, 8 August 1945; retrieved from <www.matisse.lettres.free.fr/artdeblamer/tcombat.htm> on 8 June 2015.
CARLSON, DAVID, '*Left Behind* and the Corruption of Biblical Interpretation', originally published in 2003, accessed online at OrthodoxyToday.org on 16 October 2015.
CARLYLE, THOMAS, *Critical and Miscellaneous Essays*, 7 vols (London: Chapman and Hall, [n.d.]).
CASEY, TIMOTHY J., 'Der tolle Mensch in der Pfarrhausstube. Jean Pauls Stellung zu der Gretchenfrage und seine Auseinandersetzung mit der Theologie', in *Die deutsche literarische Romantik und die Wissenschaften*, ed. by Nicholas Saul (Munich: iudicium, 1991), pp. 156–76.
CHADWICK, OWEN, *The Secularization of the European Mind in the Nineteenth Century* (The Gifford Lectures in the University of Edinburgh for 1973–1974) (Cambridge: Cambridge University Press, 1975).
CHAMBERS, EPHRAIM, *Cyclopaedia, or an Universal Dictionary of Arts and Sciences*, 2 vols (London: [n.pub.], 1728).
CHATEAUBRIAND, FRANÇOIS-AUGUSTE, *The Genius of Christianity or the Spirit and Beauty of the Christian Religion*, trans. by Charles I. Wright (Philadelphia: J. B. Lippincott, and Baltimore: John Murphy, 1856).
CLARKE, I. F., *Voices Prophesying War* (London: Oxford University Press, 1966).
CLUTE, JOHN, and PETER NICHOLLS, eds, *The Encyclopedia of Science Fiction* (New York: St. Martin's Press, 1993).
COHEN, ARTHUR ALLEN, 'Thinking the Tremendum', in *A Holocaust Reader*, ed. by Michael L. Morgan (New York and Oxford: Oxford University Press, 2001), pp. 183–96.
COLERIGDE, SAMUEL TAYLOR, *Letters*, 2 vols (London: William Heinemann, 1895).
CONDORCET, JEAN-ANTOINE NICOLAS DE CARITAT, *Esquisse d'un tableau historique des progrès de l'esprit humain* (Paris: Agasse, 1794).

—— *Outlines of an Historical View of the Progress of the Human Mind* (Philadelphia: Carey, Rice, Ormrod, 1796).
CORDLE, DANIEL, '"That's going to happen to us. It is": *Threads* and the Imagination of Nuclear Disaster', *Journal of British Cinema and Television*, 10 (2013), 71–92.
CORNILS, INGO, 'Alles kaputt? Visions of the End in West German and Austrian Science Fiction', in *Twentieth-Century Literary Criticism*, vol. 218, ed. by Thomas L. Schoenberg and Lawrence J. Trudeau (Detroit: Gale, 2009), pp. 67–77.
COWARD, HAROLD, and TOBY FOSHAY, eds, *Derrida and Negative Theology* (Albany: State University of New York Press, 1992).
CRAIG, WILLIAM LANE, 'Hartle-Hawking Cosmology and Atheism', *Analysis*, 57 (October 1997), 291–95.
—— 'Response to David Myers', *Religious Studies*, 39 (December 2003), 421–26.
—— 'A Swift and Simple Refutation of the *Kalam* Cosmological Argument?', *Religious Studies*, 35 (March 1999), 69–72.
—— '"What Place, Then, for a Creator?" Hawking on God and Creation', *The British Journal for the Philosophy of Sciences*, 41 (December 1990), 473–91.
——, and Walter Sinnott-Armstrong, *God? A Debate between a Christian and an Atheist* (Oxford: Oxford University Press, 2004).
CUVIER, GEORGES, *Essay on the Theory of the Earth*, ed. by Robert Jameson (Edinburgh: William Blackwood, 1817).
DARWIN, CHARLES, *On the Origin of Species by means of natural selection* (London: John Murray, 1856), in *A Facsimile of the First Edition*, ed. by Ernst Mayr (Cambridge, MA. and London: Harvard University Press, 1984).
DE BEER, GAVIN, 'An "Atheist" in the Alps', *Keats–Shelley Memorial Bulletin* 9 (1958), 1–15.
DERRIDA, JACQUES, 'Différance', in *Margins of Philosophy*, trans. by Alan Bass (Chicago: University of Chicago Press, 1982), pp. 1–27.
—— 'No Apocalypse, not now (full speed ahead, seven missiles, seven missives)', *Diacritics*, 14 (Summer 1984), 20–31.
DESAN, SUZANNE, 'The French Revolution and Religion, 1795–1815' (Cambridge: Cambridge University Press, 2008, *Cambridge Histories Online*), pp. 556–74.
DIDEROT, DENIS, 'Observations sur l'instruction pastorale de M. L'évêque d'Auxerre', in *Œuvres Complètes*, I: *Philosophie*, vol. 1, ed. J. Assézat. Paris: Garnier Frères, 1875, pp. 441–84.
—— *Rameau's Nephew and D'Alembert's Dream*, ed. and trans. by Leonard Tancock (London: Penguin, 1966).
DIDIER, BÉATRICE, *Le XVIIIe siècle*, Part III *(1778–1820)* (Paris: B. Arthaud, 1976 = *Littérature Française*, ed. by Claude Pichois, vol. 11).
DIETZ, WALTER R., 'Atheism', in *Religion Past & Present. The Encyclopedia of Theology and Religion*, ed. by Hans Dieter Betz, Don S. Browning et al. (Leiden and Boston: Brill, 2007), vol. 1, pp. 477–82.
DINGLEY, R. J., '"I had a Dream...". Byron's "Darkness"', *The Byron Journal* (1981), 20–33.
DOWLING, DAVID, 'The Atomic Scientist: Machine or Moralist?', *Science-Fiction Studies*, 13 (1986), 139–47.
—— *Fictions of Nuclear Disaster* (Houndsmills, Basingstoke: MacMillan Press, 1987).
DOYLE, WILLIAM, *The Oxford History of the French Revolution* (Oxford: Clarendon Press, 1989).
DUBOIS, LOUIS, 'Grainville', in *Biographie Universelle ancien et moderne*, vol. 18 (GO–GU) (Paris: L. G. Michaud, 1817), pp. 271–74.
EAGLETON, TERRY, *Culture and the Death of God* (New Haven and London: Yale University Press, 2014).
ECKARDT, A. ROY, 'Christians and Jews. Along a Theological Frontier', in *A Holocaust Reader. Responses to the Nazi Extermination*, ed. by Michael L. Morgan (Oxford: Oxford University Press, 2001), pp. 138–57.

ECKERMANN, JOHANN PETER, *Gespräche mit Goethe in den letzten Jahren seines Lebens*, ed. by Fritz Bergemann, 2 vols (Frankfurt a.M.: Insel, 1981).
ELIADE, MIRCEA, *Cosmos and History. The Myth of the Eternal Return*, trans. by Willard R. Trask (New York: Harper & Bros., 1959).
ELIOT, GEORGE, 'Worldliness and Other-Worldliness: The Poet Young', in *The Works of George Eliot*, 12 vols (New York: P. F. Collier & Son, [n.d.]), vol. 11: *Miscellaneous Essays*, pp. 7–54.
ELIOT, T. S., *Collected Poems 1909–1962* (London: Faber & Faber, 1974).
Encyclopedie ou Dictionnaire Raisonné des Sciences, des Arts et des Métiers (Neufchastel: Samuel Faulche, [n.d.]).
EVANS, ARTHUR B., 'Science Fiction in France: A Brief History', *Science Fiction Studies*, 16 (1989), 254–76.
EVANS, IFOR, *A Short History of English Literature*, 3rd edn (Harmondsworth: Penguin, 1973, first published 1970).
FEAVER, WILLIAM, *The Art of John Martin* (Oxford: Clarendon, 1975).
FELDMAN, STANLEY, and LEE SIGELMAN, 'The Political Impact of Prime-Time Television: The Day After', *The Journal of Politics*, 47 (June 1985), 556–78.
FERGUSON, FRANCES, 'The Nuclear Sublime', *Diacritics*, 14 (Summer 1984), 4–10.
FEUERBACH, LUDWIG, *The Essence of Christianity* (1841, based on text of second edition of 1843), trans. by Marian Evans [George Eliot] (London: John Chapman, 1854).
―― *Das Wesen des Christentums* (Stuttgart: Reclam, 1969).
FIEDLER, LESLIE, 'Cross the Border — Close the Gap' (1970), in *A Fiedler Reader* (New York: Stein and Day, 1977), pp. 270–94.
FLAMMARION, NICOLAS CAMILLE, *Dieu dans la nature* (Paris: Didier, 1869).
―― 'Discours de Camille Flammarion prononcé sur la tombe d'Allan Kardec', accessed on 14 October 2016 via www.leon-denis.org.
―― *La Fin du monde* (Paris: Ernest Flammarion, 1894).
―― *Omega: The Last Days of the World*, trans. by Arthur Sherburn Hardy (New York: Cosmopolitan Publishing Co., 1894).
FONTENELLE, BERNARD LE BOVIER DE, *A Discourse of the Plurality of Worlds written in French by the most ingenious author of the Dialogues of the Dead; and translated into English by Sir W. D. Knight* (Dublin: William Norman, 1687).
FORMAN, HARRY BUXTON, *The Shelley Library. An Essay in Bibliography* (London: Reeves and Turner (for the Shelley Society), 1886).
FORSTER, HAROLD, *Edward Young. The Poet of the Night Thoughts 1683–1765* (Alburgh Harleston: Erskine Press, 1986).
FOUCAULT, MICHEL, *Les Mots et les choses. Une archéologie des sciences humaines* (Paris: Gallimard, 1966).
―― *The Order of Things. An Archaeology of the Human Sciences* (New York: Random House / Vintage, 1973).
FRANCE, ANATOLE, *Le Jardin d'Épicure* (Paris: Calmann-Levy, 1907).
FRANK, MANFRED, *Das Sagbare und das Unsagbare. Studien zur deutsch-französischen Hermeneutik und Texttheorie* (Frankfurt a.M.: Suhrkamp, 1989).
FRANK, PAT, *Alas, Babylon* (New York: HarperCollins, 1993).
FRANKLIN, H. BRUCE, 'Strange Scenarios: Science Fiction, the Theory of Alienation, and the Nuclear Gods', *Science-Fiction Studies*, 13 (1986), 117–28.
FRANZEN, JONATHAN, 'Rage against the machine', *Guardian*, 14 September 2013, *Review* section pp. 2–4.
FREUD, SIGMUND, *Abriß der Psychoanalyse / Das Unbehagen in der Kultur* (Frankfurt a.M.: Fischer, 1979).

―― *Beyond the Pleasure Principle*, in *The Standard Edition*, vol. 18, pp. 1–64.
―― *Civilization and Its Discontents* (1930), trans. by James Strachey (New York: W. W. Norton, 1962).
―― *Civilization and Its Discontents*, in *The Standard Edition*, vol. 21, pp. 57–145.
―― 'Creative Writers and Day-Dreaming', in *The Standard Edition*, vol. 9, pp. 142–53.
―― 'Der Dichter und das Phantasieren', in *Gesammelte Werke*, vol. 7, ed. by Anna Freud (Frankfurt a.M.: S. Fischer, 1969), pp. 213–23.
―― *The Ego and the Id*, in *The Standard Edition*, vol. 19, pp. 1–66.
―― *Gesammelte Schriften*, 12 vols (Vienna: Internationaler Psychoanalytischer Verlag, varying dates).
―― *Das Ich und das Es*, in *Gesammelte Schriften*, vol. 6, pp. 351–405.
―― *Jenseits des Lustprinzips*, in *Gesammelte Schriften*, vol. 6, pp. 189–257.
―― 'Negation', in *The Standard Edition*, vol. 19, pp. 233–39.
―― 'Negation', in *Gesammelte Schriften*, vol. 11, pp. 3–7.
―― *An Outline of Psycho-Analysis*, in *The Standard Edition*, vol. 23, pp. 139–207.
―― *The Standard Edition of the Complete Psychological Works of Sigmund Freud*, trans. by James Strachey in collaboration with Anna Freud (London: The Hogarth Press and the Institute of Psycho-Analysis, varying dates).
―― *Das Unbehagen in der Kultur*, in *Gesammelte Schriften*, vol. 12, pp. 27–114.
FRIEDLÄNDER, SAUL, 'Introduction', in *Visions of Apocalypse. End or Rebirth?*, ed. by Saul Friedländer, Gerald Molton, Leo Marx and Eugene Skolnikoff (New York and London: Holmes & Meier, 1985), pp. 3–17.
――, and others, eds, *Visions of Apocalypse. End or Rebirth?* (New York and London: Holmes & Meier, 1985).
FULFORD, TIM, 'Millenarianism and the Study of Romanticism', in *Romanticism and Millenarianism*, ed. by Tim Fulford (New York: Palgrave, 2002), pp. 1–22.
GADAMER, HANS-GEORG, 'Ästhetik und Hermeneutik', in *Kleine Schriften II* (Tübingen: J. C. B. Mohr, 1979), pp. 1–8.
GAGNE, ÉLISE, *Omégar, ou le Dernier homme, proso-poésie dramatique de la fin des temps en 12 chants* (Paris: Didier, 1859).
GALBREATH, ROBERT, 'Ambiguous Apocalypse: Transcendental Versions of the End', in *The End of the World*, ed. by Eric Rabkin, Martin Greenberg et al. (Carbondale: Southern Illinois Press, 1983), pp. 53–72.
GEORGI, MATTHIAS, 'Das Erdbeben von Lissabon in der englischen Publizistik', in *Das Erdbeben von Lissabon und der Katastrophendiskurs im 18. Jahrhundert*, ed. by Gerhard Lauer and Thorsten Unger (Göttingen: Wallstein, 2008), pp. 96–109.
GILBERT, SANDRA M., and SUSAN GUBAR, *The Madwoman in the Attic. The Woman Writer and the Nineteenth-Century Literary Imagination* (New Haven and London: Yale University Press, 1984).
GILLE, KLAUS F., *Goethes Wilhelm Meister. Zur Rezeptionsgeschichte der Lehr- und Wanderjahre* (Königstein: Athenäum, 1979).
GILLESPIE, GERALD, ed., *Die Nachtwachen des Bonaventura / The Night Watches of Bonaventura* (Edinburgh: Edinburgh University Press, 1972).
――, ed., *The Nightwatches of Bonaventura* (Chicago and London: University of Chicago Press, 2014).
GILLESPIE, MICHAEL ALLAN, *Nihilism before Nietzsche* (Chicago and London: University of Chicago Press, 1995).
GILLISPIE, CHARLES COULSON, *Genesis and Geology: A Study in the Relation of Scientific Thought, Natural Theology, and Social Opinion in Great Britain, 1790–1850* (Cambridge, MA, and London: Harvard University Press, 1996 [first edition 1951]).

GLEIM, WILHELM LUDWIG, *Von und an Herder. Ungedruckte Briefe aus Herders Nachlaß*, ed. by Heinrich Düntzer and Ferdinand Gottfried von Herder, 3 vols (Leipzig: Dyk'sche Buchhandlung, 1861).

GODWIN, WILLIAM, *Of Population. An Enquiry Concerning the Power of Increase in the Numbers of Mankind being an Answer to Mr. Malthus's Essay on that Subject* (London: Longman et al., 1820).

GOETHE, JOHANN WOLFGANG, *Conversations of Goethe with Eckermann*, ed. by J. K. Moorhead, trans. by John Oxenford (London: J. M. Dent, 1935).

—— *Dichtung und Wahrheit*, in *Hamburger Ausgabe*, ed. by Erich Trunz (Hamburg: Wegner, 1955), vol. 9.

—— *From My Life. Poetry and Truth*, trans. by Robert R. Heitner, in *Goethe's Collected Works*, ed. by Thomas P. Saine and Jeffrey L. Sammons (New York: Suhrkamp, 1987), vol. 4.

—— *Goethe's Poems*, trans. by Paul Dyrsen (New York: F. W. Christern, 1878).

—— *Tages- und Jahres-Hefte*, ed. by H. Dünker, vol. 24 of *Goethes Werke. Historisch-kritische Ausgabe*, ed. by Joseph Kürschner (Stuttgart: Union Deutsche Verlagsanstalt, [n.d.]).

—— 'Über den Granit', in *Goethes Werke*, ed. by Erich Trunz, vol. 13: *Naturwissenschaftliche Schriften*, ed. by Dorothea Kuhn (Hamburg: Wegner, 1953), pp. 253–58.

—— 'Warum uns Gott so wohl gefällt? Weil er sich uns nie in den Weg stellt,' in *Goethe Gedichte 1800–1832*, ed. by Karl Eibl (Berlin: Deutscher Klassiker Verlag, 2010), p. 400.

—— *Wilhelm Meister's Apprenticeship and Travels*, 2 vols, trans. by Thomas Carlyle (Boston: [n.pub.], 1876).

—— *Wilhelm Meisters Lehrjahre*, ed. by Wilhelm Voßkamp and Herbert Jaumann (Frankfurt a.M.: Deutscher Klassiker Verlag, 1992).

GOLDSMITH, STEVEN, 'Of Gender, Plague, and Apocalypse: Mary Shelley's *Last Man*', *The Yale Journal of Criticism*, 4 (Fall 1990), 129–73.

GOODMAN, DAVID, and COLIN RUSSELL, eds, *The Rise of Scientific Europe 1500–1800* (Sevenoaks: Hodder & Stoughton, 1991, for the Open University).

GOULD, STEPHEN JAY, *Time's Arrow — Time's Cycle. Myth and Metaphor in the Discovery of Geological Time* (Cambridge, MA: Harvard University Press, 1987).

GRAINVILLE, JEAN-BAPTISTE FRANÇOIS XAVIER COUSIN DE, *Le Dernier Homme*, ed. by Anne Kupiec (Paris: Éditions Payot, 2010).

—— *Discours qui a remporté le prix d'éloquence, à l'Académie de Besançon, en l'année 1772, sur ce sujet: Quelle a été l'Influence de la Philosophie sur ce Siècle?* (Paris: Humblot, 1772).

—— *The Last Man*, trans. by I. F. Clarke and M. Clarke (Middletown, CT: Wesleyan University Press, 2002).

GRANT, MATTHEW, 'Images of Survival, Stories of Destruction: Nuclear War on British Screens from 1945 to the Early 1960s', *Journal of British Cinema and Television*, 10 (2013), 7–26.

GRASS, GÜNTER, *The Rat*, trans. by Ralph Manheim (London: Secker & Warburg, 1987).

—— *Die Rättin* (Reinbek: Rowohlt, 1988, first published 1986).

GREGORY, BRAD S., 'No Room for God? History, Science, Metaphysics, and the Study of Religion', *History and Theory*, 47 (December 2008), 495–519.

GRIPPEN, ROSS P., *Jean Baptiste Cousin de Grainville: Le Dernier Homme. Edition présentée et commentée* (unpublished PhD dissertation University of Connecticut, 1979).

GRUBER, JOHANN GOTTFRIED, *Etwas über Franz von Sonnenbergs Leben und Charakter* (Halle: Neue Societätsbuch- und Kunsthandlung, 1807).

GUMBRECHT, HANS-ULRICH, and URSULA LINK-HEER, eds, *Epochenschwellen und Epochenstrukturen im Diskurs der Literatur- und Sprachhistorie* (Frankfurt a.M.: Suhrkamp, 1985).

GUTTMANN, MELINDA JO, 'Préface', in *Les Cahiers du GRIF*, 41–42 (1989, special issue on 'L'imaginaire du nucléaire'), 11–22.

HACKETT, TIMOTHY, 'The French Revolution and religion to 1794' (Cambridge: Cambridge University Press, 2008, *Cambridge Histories Online*), pp. 536–55.
HAILER, MARTIN, *Religionsphilosophie* (Göttingen: Vandenhoeck & Ruprecht, 2014).
HALES, PETER B., 'The Atomic Sublime', *American Studies*, 32 (1991), 5–31.
HALL, SPENCER, 'Shelley's "Mont Blanc"', *Studies in Philology*, 70 (April 1973), 199–221.
HAMACHER, BERND, 'Strategien narrativen Katastrophenmanagements. Goethe und die "Erfindung" des Erdbebens von Lissabon', in *Das Erdbeben von Lissabon und der Katastrophendiskurs im 18. Jahrhundert*, ed. by Gerhard Lauer and Thorsten Unger (Göttingen: Wallstein, 2008), pp. 162–72.
HAMILTON, PAUL, 'Literature and Philosophy', in *The Cambridge Companion to Shelley*, ed. by Timothy Morton (Cambridge: Cambridge University Press, 2006), pp. 166–84.
HAMILTON, WILLIAM, 'The Death of God Theologies Today', in Thomas J. J. Altizer and William Hamilton, *Radical Theology and The Death of God* (Harmondsworth: Penguin, 1966), pp. 36–62.
—— 'Questions and Answers on the Radical Theology', in *The Death of God Debate*, ed. by Jackson Lee Ice and John J. Carey (Philadelphia: The Westminster Press, 1967), pp. 213–41.
HARRASSER, KARIN, 'Das atomare Sublime und die standardisierte Katastrophe', in *Atombilder. Ikonographie des Atoms in Wissenschaft und Öffentlichkeit des 20. Jahrhunderts*, ed. by Charlotte Bigg and Jochen Hennig (Göttingen: Wallstein, 2009), pp. 168–76.
HARRISON, TED, *Apocalypse When? Why we want to believe there will be no tomorrow* (London: Darton, Longman and Todd, 2012).
HARTMAN, GEOFFREY, 'Romanticism and Anti-Self-Consciousness', in *Beyond Formalism. Literary Essays 1958–1970* (New Haven and London: Yale University Press, 1970), pp. 298–310.
HASTIE, W., ed., *Kant's Cosmogony. As in his Essay on the Retardation of the Rotation of the Earth and his Natural History and Theory of the Heavens* (Glasgow: James Maclehose and Sons, 1900).
HEGEL, GEORG WILHELM FRIEDRICH, *Glauben und Wissen oder die Reflexionsphilosophie der Subjektivität, in der Vollständigkeit ihrer Formen, als Kantische, Jacobische und Fichtesche Philosophie*, in *Georg Wilhelm Friedrich Hegel's Werke* (Berlin: Duncker und Humblot, 1832), vol. 1, pp. 3–157.
—— *The Philosophy of Fine Art*, 4 vols, trans. by F. P. B. Osmaston (London: G. Bell and Sons, 1920).
—— *Vorlesungen über die Ästhetik*, 3 vols, ed. by Rüdiger Bubner (Stuttgart: Reclam, 1977).
HEIDEGGER, MARTIN, *Being and Time*, trans. by John Macquarrie and Edward Robinson (Oxford: Blackwell, 2001).
—— *Einführung in die Metaphysik* (Frankfurt a.M.: Klostermann, 1983 = *Gesamtausgabe*, II. Abt., vol. 40).
—— *Introduction to Metaphysics*, trans. by Gregory Fried and Richard Polt (New Haven and London: Yale University Press, 2000).
—— *Sein und Zeit*, 12th edn (Tübingen: Niemeyer, 1972, first published 1927).
HEINE, HEINRICH, 'Germany', in *The Works of Heinrich Heine*, trans. by Charles Godfrey Leland (London: William Heinemann, 1892), vol. 5, pp. 1–384.
—— *Zur Geschichte der Religion und Philosophie in Deutschland* (1834), in *Historisch-kritische Gesamtausgabe der Werke*, vol. VIII.1, ed. by Manfred Windfuhr (Hamburg: Hoffmann und Campe, 1979).
—— *Zur Geschichte der Religion und Philosophie in Deutschland* (1834), in *Sämtliche Schriften*, ed. by Klaus Briegleb, 12 vols (Munich: Hanser, 1976), vol. 5, pp. 505–641.
HEISE, URSULA K., *Nach der Natur. Das Artensterben und die moderne Kultur* (Frankfurt a.M.: Suhrkamp, 2010).

HERDER, JOHANN GOTTFRIED, *Ideen zur Philosophie der Geschichte der Menschheit*, in *Werke*, ed. by Martin Bollacher et al., 10 vols (Frankfurt a.M.: Deutscher Klassikerverlag, 1989), vol. 6.

HERMAND, JOST, 'Auf einsamem Posten — Lessing und Heine', in *'Liebhaber der Theologie': Gotthold Ephraim Lessing — Philosoph — Historiker der Religion* (Frankfurt a.M.: Peter Lang, 2012), pp. 204–10.

HERZBERG, MAX, 'Wordsworth and German Literature', *PMLA*, 40 (1925), 302–45.

HERZOG, REINHART, and REINHART KOSELLECK, eds, *Epochenschwelle und Epochenbewußtsein*, (Munich: Wilhelm Fink, 1987).

HEYDENREICH, KARL HEINRICH, *Briefe über den Atheismus* (Leipzig: Martini, 1796).

HILDESHEIMER, WOLFGANG, 'Hat die Hoffnung noch eine Zukunft?', in *Gesammelte Werke in sieben Bänden*, ed. by Christiaan Lucas Hart Nibbrig and Volker Jehle, vol. 7: *Vermischte Schriften* (Frankfurt a.M.: Suhrkamp, 1991), pp. 739–40.

HINDERER, WALTER, *Büchner Kommentar zum dichterischen Werk* (Munich: Winkler, 1977).

HINZ, SIGRID, ed., *Caspar David Friedrich in Briefen und Bekenntnissen* (Berlin: Henschelverlag Kunst und Gesellschaft, 1968).

HOFBAUER, GOTTFRIED, *Die geologische Revolution. Wie die Entdeckung der Erdgeschichte unser Denken veränderte* (Darmstadt: WBG, 2015).

HOFMANN, WERNER, *Art in the Nineteenth Century*, trans. by Brian Battershaw (London: Faber & Faber, 1961).

—— *Caspar David Friedrich 1774–1840. Kunst um 1800* (Munich: Prestel and Hamburger Kunsthalle, 1974).

HOLBACH, PAUL-HENRI THIRY [under pseudonym M. Boulanger], *Le Christianisme devoilé ou examen des principes et des effets de la religion chrétienne* (London [?]: [n.pub.], 1766).

—— *Christianity Unveiled; being an Examination of the Principles and Effects of the Christian Religion*, trans. by W. M. Johnson (1804), Ch. 8, 'Mysteries and Dogmas of Christianity', in *The Deist, or, Moral Philosopher. Being an Impartial Inquiry after Moral and Theological Truths Selected from the Writings of the Most Celebrated Authors in Ancient and Modern Times*, vol. 2 (London: R. Carlile, 1819), pp. 11–125.

—— *The System of Nature; or, Laws of the Moral and Physical World*, transl. by H. D. Robinson (New York: G. W & A. J. Matsell, 1835).

—— [under pseudonym M. Mirabaud], *Systême de la Nature ou Des loix du monde Physique & du monde Moral* (London [?]: [n.pub.], 1775).

HOLDER, RODNEY, *Big Bang Big God. A Universe Designed for Life?* (Oxford: Lion Hudson, 2013).

HÖLDERLIN, FRIEDRICH, *Hyperion and Selected Poems*, ed. by Eric L. Santner (New York: Continuum, 1990 (German Library, vol. 22)).

—— *Sämtliche Werke und Briefe*, ed. by Jochen Schmidt, 3 vols (Frankfurt a.M.: Deutscher Klassiker Verlag, 1992).

HOLMES, RICHARD, *Shelley, the Pursuit* (London: Weidenfels and Nicolson, 1974).

HÖLSCHER, LUCIAN, 'Abendrot — Gutwetterbot', an interview with Lucian Hölscher, *Spektrum der Wissenschaft*, January 2011, p. 25.

HORKHEIMER, MAX, and THEODOR W. ADORNO, *Dialectic of Enlightenment. Philosophical Fragments*, ed. by Gunzelin Schmid Noerr, trans. by Edmund Jephcott (Stanford: Stanford University Press, 2002).

—— *Dialektik der Aufklärung. Philosophische Fragmente* (Frankfurt a.M.: Fischer, 1993).

HORN, EVA, 'Die romantische Verdunklung. Weltuntergänge und die Geburt des letzten Menschen um 1800', in *Abendländische Apokalyptik. Kompendium zur Genealogie der Endzeit*, ed. by Veronika Wieser, Christian Zolles, Catherine Feik, Martin Zolles and Leopold Schlöndorff (Berlin: Akademie Verlag, 2013), pp. 101–24.

—— *Zukunft als Katastrophe* (Frankfurt a.M.: Fischer, 2014).

HUME, DAVID, *Hume on Religion*, ed. by Julian Baggini (London: The Philosophy Press, 2010).
HUTTON, JAMES, 'Theory of the Earth', in *Transactions of the Royal Society of Edinburgh*, vol. 1 (Edinburgh: J. Dickson, 1788), pp. 209–304.
HUXLEY, ALDOUS, *Aldous Huxley's Hearst Essays*, ed. by James Sexton (New York and London: Garland, 1994).
—— *Ape and Essence* (London: Vintage, 2005).
—— 'Author's Foreword (to the 1946 edition)', in *Brave New World* (New York, London, Toronto: Alfred A. Knopf / Everyman's Library, 2013), pp. 223–32.
—— *Brave New World* (New York, London, Toronto: Alfred A. Knopf / Everyman's Library, 2013).
—— 'The World's Future', in *The Human Situation. Lectures at Santa Barbara, 1959*, ed. by Piero Ferrucci (London: HarperCollins / Flamingo, 1994), pp. 93–94.
—— *The Human Situation. Lectures at Santa Barbara, 1959*, ed. by Piero Ferrucci (London: HarperCollins / Flamingo, 1994).
—— *The Perennial Philosophy* (London: Chatto & Windus, 1946).
HYMAN, GAVIN, 'Atheism in Modern History', in *The Cambridge Companion to Atheism*, ed. by Michael Martin (Cambridge: Cambridge University Press, 2007), pp. 27–46.
IRETON, SEAN, and CAROLINE SCHAUMANN, 'Introduction: The Meaning of Mountains: Geology, History, Culture', in *Heights of Reflection. Mountains in the German Imagination from the Middle Ages to the Twenty-First Century* (Rochester, NY, and Woodbridge: Camden House, 2012), pp. 1–19.
IRRLITZ, GERD, *Kant Handbuch. Leben und Werk*, 2nd edn (Stuttgart: Metzler, 2010).
ISRAEL, JONATHAN, *Radical Enlightenment. Philosophy and the Making of Modernity 1650–1750* (Oxford: Oxford University Press, 2001).
JACOBI, FRIEDRICH HEINRICH, *Jacobi an Fichte* (Hamburg: Perthes, 1799).
—— 'Jacobi to Fichte', in *The Main Philosophical Writings and the Novel 'Allwill'*, trans. by George di Giovanni (Montreal and Kingston: McGill-Queen's University Press, 1994), pp. 497–536.
JAMES, CLAIR, 'Narrative against Nuclear War?', in 'Forum', *PMLA*, 106 (October 1991), 1175–76.
JAMESON, FREDRIC, FRANZ ROTTENSTEINER, and JAMES BLISH, 'Change, SF, and Marxism: Open or Closed Universes?', *Science Fiction Studies*, 1 (Fall 1974), 269–75.
JANCA-AJI, JOYCE, 'The Dark Dreamlife of Postmodern Theology. *Delicatessen*, *The City of Lost Children* and *Alien Resurrection*', in *Religion and Science Fiction*, ed. by James F. McGrath (Eugene, OR: Pickwick Publications, 2011), pp. 9–31.
JASPERS, KARL, *Kleine Schule des philosophischen Denkens* (Munich and Zurich: Piper, 2014, first edition 1965).
JAUSS, HANS ROBERT, *Die Epochenschwelle von 1912* (Heidelberg: Winter, 1986).
JEAN PAUL (Jean Paul Friedrich Richter), 'Clavis Fichtiana seu Leibgeberiana', in *Werke*, ed. Miller, vol. 6, pp. 1011–56.
—— *Sämtliche Werke: Historisch-kritische Ausgabe*, ed. by Eduard Berend, Abt. III, vol. 5 (Berlin: Akademie-Verlag, 1961).
—— *Siebenkäs*, in *Werke*, ed. Miller, vol. 3, pp. 7–576.
—— *Vorschule der Ästhetik / Levana*, in *Werke*, ed. Miller, vol. 9, pp. 7–639.
—— *Werke*, ed. by Norbert Miller, 12 vols (Munich: Hanser, 1975).
—— 'Die wunderbare Gesellschaft in der Neujahrsnacht', in *Werke*, ed. Miller, vol. 8, pp. 1121–38.
JEFFERIES, RICHARD, *After London or Wild England* (Cirencester: The Echo Library, 2005).
JEFFREY, LLOYD N., 'Cuvierian Catastrophism in Shelley's *Prometheus Unbound* and *Mont Blanc*', *The South Central Bulletin*, 38 (Winter 1978), 146–52.

JOHNSON, BARBARA, 'The Last Man', in *The Other Mary Shelley*, ed. by Audrey A. Fisch, Anne K. Mellor and Esther H. Schor (Oxford: Oxford University Press, 1993), pp. 258–66.
JONAS, HANS, 'The Concept of God after Auschwitz', in *Echoes from the Holocaust. Philosophical Reflections on a Dark Time*, ed. by Alan Rosenberg and Gerald E. Myers (Philadelphia: Temple University Press, 1988), pp. 292–305.
JONES, FREDERICK L., *The Letters of Percy Bysshe Shelley*, 2 vols (Oxford: Clarendon Press, 1964).
JOYCE, JAMES, *A Portrait of the Artist as a Young Man. Text, Criticism, and Notes*, ed. by Chester G. Anderson (New York: Viking Press, 1968).
JÜRGENS, KAI U., '"Wir sind hier nich modern!" Arno Schmidts *Schule der Atheisten* als Science-Fiction-Roman', *Bargfelder Bote*, 393–94 (October 2015), 15–25.
KANT, IMMANUEL, *Allgemeine Naturgeschichte und Theorie des Himmels, oder Versuch von der Verfassung und dem mechanischen Ursprunge des ganzen Weltgebäudes nach Newtonischen Grundsätzen abgehandelt*, in *Werke*, ed. Weischedel, vol. 1, pp. 221–400.
—— 'Beobachtungen über das Gefühl des Schönen und Erhabenen' (1764), in *Werke*, ed. Weischedel, vol. 1, pp. 821–84.
—— *Critique of Pure Reason*, trans. by Max Müller (London: MacMillan, 1881).
—— *Der einzig mögliche Beweisgrund zu einer Demonstration Gottes*, in *Werke*, ed. Weischedel, vol. 1, pp. 617–738.
—— 'The end of all things', in *Religion and Rational Theology*, pp. 221–31.
—— 'Das Ende aller Dinge', in *Werke*, ed. Weischedel, vol. 6, pp. 173–90.
—— *Essays and Treatises on Moral, Political, Religious and Various Philosophical Subjects*, 2 vols (London: William Richardson, 1799).
—— 'Fortgesetzte Betrachtung der seit einiger Zeit wahrgenommenen Erderschütterungen' (1756), in Immanuel Kant, *Sämmtliche Werke in chronologischer Reihenfolge*, ed. by G. Hartenstein (Leipzig: Voss, 1867), pp. 448–56.
—— 'Geschichte und Naturbeschreibung der merkwürdigen Vorfälle des Erdbebens, welches an dem Ende des 1755sten Jahres einen grossen Theil der Erde erschüttert hat' (1756), in Immanuel Kant, *Sämmtliche Werke in chronologischer Reihenfolge*, ed. by G. Hartenstein (Leipzig: Voss, 1867), pp. 414–45.
—— *Kritik der reinen Vernunft*, in *Werke*, ed. Weischedel, vol. 2.
—— *Natural Science*, ed. by Eric Watkins (Cambridge: Cambridge University Press, 2015).
—— *The Only Possible Argument for the Demonstration of the Existence of God*, in *Essays and Treatises on Moral, Political, Religious and Various Philosophical Subjects* (London: William Richardson, 1799), vol. 2, pp. 217–366.
—— 'On the miscarriage of all philosophical trials in theodicy', in *Religion and Rational Theology*, pp. 24–37.
—— *Religion and Rational Theology*, ed. and transl. by Allen W. Wood and George Di Giovanni (Cambridge: Cambridge University Press, 2001, first published 1996).
—— 'Die Religion innerhalb der Grenzen der blossen Vernunft', in *Werke*, ed. Weischedel, vol. 4, pp. 647–879.
—— *Religion within the Boundaries of Mere Reason*, in *Religion and Rational Theology*, pp. 39–215.
—— 'Über das Misslingen aller philosophischen Versuche in der Theodizee', in *Werke*, ed. Weischedel, vol. 6, pp. 103–24.
—— *Universal Natural History and Theory of the Heavens or Essay on the Constitution and the Mechanical Origin of the Whole Universe according to Newtonian Principles*, trans. by Olaf Reinhardt, in *Natural History*, pp. 182–308.
—— 'Verkündigung des nahen Abschlusses eines Traktats zum Ewigen Frieden in der Philosophie' (December 1796), *Werke*, ed. Weischedel, vol. 3, pp. 403–16.

—— 'Von den Ursachen der Erderschütterungen, bei Gelegenheit des Unglücks, welches die westlichen Länder von Europa gegen das Ende des vorigen Jahres betroffen hat' (1756), in Immanuel Kant, *Sämmtliche Werke in chronologischer Reihenfolge*, ed. by G. Hartenstein (Leipzig: Voss, 1867), vol. 1, pp. 402–11.

—— *Werke in sechs Bänden*, ed. by Wilhelm Weischedel, 6 vols (Darmstadt: Wissenschaftliche Buchgesellschaft, 1956–1964).

KATRITZKY, LINDE, 'Decoding Anonymous Texts: the Case of the *Nightwatches* of Bonaventura', *Monatshefte*, 95 (Fall 2003), 442–57.

—— *A Guide to Bonaventura's 'Nightwatches'* (New York, Boston: Peter Lang, 1999).

KENDRICK, THOMAS D., *The Lisbon Earthquake* (London: Methuen, 1956).

KENNEDY, EMMET, *A Cultural History of the French Revolution* (New Haven and London: Yale University Press, 1989).

KIEDAISCH, PETRA, ed., *Lyrik nach Auschwitz?* (Stuttgart: Reclam, 1995).

KINCHELOE, JOE L., and SHIRLEY R. STEINBERG, *Christotainment: Selling Jesus through Popular Culture* (Boulder, CO, and Oxford: Westview Press, 2009).

KIND, JOHN LOUIS, *Edward Young in Germany* (New York: Columbia University Press and London: Macmillan, 1906).

KING-HELE, DESMOND, *Shelley. His Thought and Work* (London: Macmillan, 1960).

KIRST, J. P., 'Millennium and Millenarianism', in *Catholic Encyclopedia* (1913), accessed at <http://en.wikisource.org/wiki/Catholic_Encyclopedia_%281913%29/Millennium_and_Millenarianism> on 7 November 2012.

KLEIN, RICHARD, 'Proposal for a *Diacritics* Colloquium on Nuclear Criticism', *Diacritics*, 14 (Summer 1984), 2–3.

KLEIST, HEINRICH VON, 'Empfindungen vor Friedrichs Seelandschaft', in *Sämtliche Werke und Briefe in vier Bänden*, 4 vols, ed. by Klaus Müller-Salget (Frankfurt a.M.: Deutscher Klassiker Verlag, 1990), vol. 3, pp. 543–44.

KLESSMANN, ECKART, *Die deutsche Romantik* (Cologne: DuMont, 1981).

KLINGEMANN, AUGUST, *Nachtwachen von Bonaventura*, ed. by Jost Schillemeit (Göttingen: Wallstein, 2012).

KNIGHT, MARK, and EMMA MASON, *Nineteenth-Century Religion and Literature* (Oxford: Oxford University Press, 2006).

KOEPPEN, WOLFGANG, *Nach Russland und anderswohin. Empfindsame Reisen* (Stuttgart: Goverts, 1958).

KOHLSCHMIDT, WERNER, 'Nihilismus der Romantik', in *Romantikforschung seit 1945*, ed. by Klaus Peter (Königstein: Anton Hain Meisenstein / Athenaeum, Hain, Scriptor, Hanstein, 1980), pp. 53–66.

KOPPENFELS, WERNER VON, '"Le coucher du soleil romantique" — Die Imagination des Weltendes aus dem Geist der visionären Romantik', *Poetica*, 17 (1985), 255–98.

KOSELLECK, REINHART, *Futures Past. On the Semantics of Historical Time*, trans. and intro. by Keith Tribe (New York: Columbia University Press, 2004).

—— *Geschichtliche Grundbegriffe* (Stuttgart: Klett-Cotta, 1979).

—— 'Historia Magistra Vitae: The Dissolution of the Topos into the Perspective of a Modernized Historical Process', in *Futures Past*, pp. 26–42.

—— '"Neuzeit". Remarks on the Semantics of Modern Concepts of Movement', in *Futures Past*, pp. 222–54.

—— *Vergangene Zukunft. Zur Semantik geschichtlicher Zeiten* (Frankfurt a.M.: Suhrkamp, 1985, first published 1979).

KOYRÉ, ALEXANDRE, *From the Closed World to the Infinite Universe* (Baltimore: Johns Hopkins University Press, 1957).

KRAUSS, LAWRENCE M., 'Religion vs. Science?', in *The Religion and Science Debate. Why Does It Continue?*, ed. by Harold W. Attridge (New Haven and London: Yale University Press, 2009), pp. 125–53.

KREN, GEORGE M., 'The Holocaust: Moral Theory and Immoral Acts', in *Echoes from the Holocaust. Philosophical Reflections on a Dark Time*, ed. by Alan Rosenberg and Gerald E. Myers (Philadelphia: Temple University Press, 1988), pp. 245–61.

KUHN, THOMAS S., *The Structure of Scientific Revolutions*, 2nd edn (Chicago: Chicago University Press, 1970).

KÜNG, HANS, *Existiert Gott? Antwort auf die Gottesfrage der Neuzeit*, 6th edn (Munich: Piper, 2010).

KUPIEC, ANNE, 'L'énigme du *Dernier Homme*', in Jean-Baptiste François Xavier Cousin de Grainville, *Le Dernier Homme*, ed. by Anne Kupiec (Paris: Éditions Payot, 2010), pp. 205–69.

KUZNIAR, ALICE, 'The Bounds of the Infinite: Self-Reflection in Jean Paul's "Rede des todten Christus"', *German Quarterly*, 57 (1984), 183–96.

LAHAYE, TIM, and JERRY B. JENKINS, *Glorious Appearing. The End of Days* (Carol Stream, IL: Tyndale House, 2004, my imprint 2010).

—— *Left Behind. A Novel of the Earth's Last Days* (Carol Stream, IL: Tyndale House, 2011).

LAPLANCHE, JEAN, and J.-B. PONTALIS, *Das Vokabular der Psychoanalyse*, 2 vols (Frankfurt a.M.: Suhrkamp, 1977).

LARSEN, SVEND ERIK, 'The Lisbon Earthquake and the Scientific Turn in Kant's Philosophy', *European Review*, 14 (2006), 359–67.

LAUER, GERHARD, and THORSTEN UNGER, 'Angesichts der Katastrophe. Das Erdbeben von Lissabon und der Katastrophendiskurs im 18. Jahrhundert', in *Das Erdbeben von Lissabon und der Katastrophendiskurs im 18. Jahrhundert*, ed. by Gerhard Lauer and Thorsten Unger (Göttingen: Wallstein, 2008), pp. 13–43.

——, eds, *Das Erdbeben von Lissabon und der Katastrophendiskurs im 18. Jahrhundert* (Göttingen: Wallstein, 2008).

LEASK, NIGEL, 'Mont Blanc's Mysterious Voice: Shelley and Huttonian Earth Science', in *The Third Culture: Literature and Science*, ed. by Elinor Shaffer (Berlin and New York: de Gruyter, 1998), pp. 182–203.

LEIBNIZ, GOTTFRIED WILHELM, *The Shorter Leibniz Texts. A Collection of New Translations*, ed. by Lloyd Strickland (London: Continuum, 2006).

LEPENIES, WOLF, *Das Ende der Naturgeschichte. Wandel kultureller Selbstverständlichkeiten in den Wissenschaften des 18. und 19. Jahrhunderts* (Frankfurt a.M.: Suhrkamp, 1978).

LIBHART, BYRON R., 'Madame de Staël, Charles de Villers, and the Death of God in Jean Paul's *Songe*', *Comparative Literature Studies*, 9 (1972), 141–51.

LICHTENBERG, GEORG CHRISTOPH, *Aphorismen, Schriften, Briefe*, ed. by Wolfgang Promies (Gütersloh: Bertelsmann, [n.d.], originally Munich: Hanser).

LIFTON, ROBERT JAY, *The Future of Immortality and Other Essays for a Nuclear Age* (New York: Basic Books, 1987).

—— 'The Image of "The End of the World": A Psychohistorical View', in *Visions of Apocalypse. End or Rebirth?*, ed. by Saul Friedländer, Gerald Molton, Leo Marx and Eugene Skolnikoff (New York and London: Holmes & Meier, 1985), pp. 151–67.

—— 'The New Psychology of Human Survival', in *The Future of Immortality and Other Essays for a Nuclear Age* (New York: Basic Books, 1987), pp. 111–35.

LOKKE, KARI E., '*The Last Man*', in *The Cambridge Companion to Mary Shelley*, ed. by Esther Schor (Cambridge: Cambridge University Press, 2003), pp. 116–34.

LOMAX, WILLIAM, 'Epic Reversal in Mary Shelley's *The Last Man*: Romantic Irony and the Roots of Science Fiction', in *Contours of the Fantastic: Selected Essays from the Eighth International Conference on the Fantastic in the Arts*, ed. by Michele K. Langford (New York: Greenwood Press, 1990), pp. 7–17.

LONDON, JACK, *The Scarlet Plague* (London: Hesperus Press / Modern Voices, 2008).

LÖWITH, KARL, *Meaning in History. The Theological Implications of the Philosophy of History* (Chicago: University of Chicago Press, 1949).

―― *Nietzsche's Philosophy of the Eternal Recurrence of the Same*, trans. by J. Harvey Lomax (Berkeley: University of California Press, 1997).

Löwy, Michael, '1910: Ernst Bloch and Georg Lukács meet in Heidelberg', in *Yale Companion to Jewish Writing and Thought in German Culture 1096–1996*, ed. by Sander L. Gilman and Jack Zipes (New Haven and London: Yale University Press, 1997), pp. 287–92.

Lucanus, Ocellus, *On the Nature of the Universe*, trans. by Thomas Taylor (London: John Bohn, Henry Sohn, and Thomas Rodd, 1831).

Lukács, Georg, *Theorie des Romans. Ein geschichtsphilosophischer Versuch über die Formen der großen Epik* (Darmstadt: Luchterhand, 1977).

―― *The Theory of the Novel. A historico-philosophical essay on the forms of great epic literature*, trans. by Anna Bostock (London: Merlin Press, 1978).

Lund, Roger D., 'Deism', in *Encyclopedia of Enlightenment*, ed. by Alan Charles Kors, 4 vols (Oxford: Oxford University Press, 2003), vol. 1, pp. 335–40.

Lyell, Charles, *Principles of Geology, Being an Attempt to Explain the Former Changes of the Earth's Surface, by Reference to Causes Now in Operation*, 4 vols, 3rd edn (London: John Murray, 1835).

M., C., 'A Nuclear No Exit' (review of the 2004 University of Wisconsin Press reprint of Mordecai Roshwald's *Level 7*), *Science Fiction Studies*, 33 (2006), 198–202.

Majewski, Henry, 'Grainville's *Le dernier homme*', *Symposium: A Quarterly Journal in Modern Literatures*, 17 (1963), 114–22.

Malthus, Thomas, *An Essay on the Principle of Population, as it affects the Future Improvement of Society* (London: J. Johnson, 1798).

Mandel, Emily St. John, *Station Eleven* (London: Macmillan / Picador, 2014).

Mann, Thomas, *Tagebücher 1944–1.4.1946*, ed. by Inge Jens (Frankfurt a.M.: Fischer, 1968).

Marcus, Paul, and Alan Rosenberg, 'The Holocaust as a Test of Philosophy', in *Echoes from the Holocaust. Philosophical Reflections on a Dark Time*, ed. by Alan Rosenberg and Gerald E. Myers (Philadelphia: Temple University Press, 1988), pp. 201–22.

Markson, David, *Wittgenstein's Mistress* (Normal, IL: Dalkey Archive Press, 1988).

Marovitz, Sanford E., 'Aldous Huxley and the Nuclear Age: *Ape and Essence* in Context', *Journal of Modern Literature*, 18 (Winter 1992), 115–25.

Marquard, Odo, *Der Einzelne. Vorlesungen zur Existenzphilosophie* (Stuttgart: Reclam, 2013).

―― 'Idealismus und Theodizee', in *Schwierigkeiten mit der Geschichtsphilosophie* (Frankfurt a.M.: Suhrkamp, 1982, first published 1973), pp. 52–65.

―― 'Die Krise des Optimismus und die Geburt der Geschichtsphilosophie', in *Das Erdbeben von Lissabon und der Katastrophendiskurs im 18. Jahrhundert*, ed. by Gerhard Lauer and Thorsten Unger (Göttingen: Wallstein, 2008), pp. 205–15.

Mauthner, Fritz, *Der Atheismus und seine Geschichte in Abendlande*, 4 vols (Stuttgart and Berlin: Deutsche Verlags-Anstalt, 1922).

Mayr, Ernst, *The Growth of Biological Thought. Diversity, Evolution, and Inheritance* (Cambridge, MA: Belknap Press, 1982).

McCarthy, Cormac, *The Road* (London: Pan Macmillan / Picador, 2007).

McFarland, Thomas, *Paradoxes of Freedom: the Romantic Mystique of a Transcendence* (Oxford: Oxford University Press, 1996).

McGrath, Alister, *The Twilight of Atheism. The Rise and Fall of Disbelief in the Modern World* (London: Rider, 2004).

McMahon, Darrin, *Enemies of the Enlightenment. The French Counter-Enlightenment and the Making of Modernity* (Oxford: Oxford University Press, 2001).

McManners, John, *The French Revolution and the Church* (Westport, CT: Greenwood Press, 1969).

MEDWIN, THOMAS, *The Shelley Papers. Memoir of Percy Bysshe Shelley* (London: Whittaker, Treacher, Co., 1833).

MELLOR, ANNE K., *Mary Shelley: Her Life, Her Fiction, Her Monsters* (New York & London: Routledge, 1989).

MERCIER, LOUIS SÉBASTIAN, *Astræa's Return; or, The Halcyon Days of France in the Year 2440: A Dream*, trans. by Harriot Augusta Freeman (London: T. Chapman, 1797).

MIJOLLA, ALAIN DE (editor-in-chief), ed., *International Dictionary of Psychoanalysis* (Detroit, New York, San Francisco: Thomson Gale, 2005).

MILLER, J. HILLIS, *The Disappearance of God. Five Nineteenth-Century Writers* (Cambridge, MA: The Belknap Press and London: Oxford University Press, 1963).

MILLER, PHILIP B., 'Anxiety and Abstraction: Kleist and Brentano on Caspar David Friedrich', *Art Journal*, 33 (Spring 1974), 205–10.

MOLTMANN, JÜRGEN, ed., *Wie ich mich geändert habe* (Gütersloh: Chr. Kaiser/Gütersloher Verlagshaus, 1997).

MORAWE, BODO, 'Heine und Holbach. Zur Religionskritik der radikalen Aufklärung und über zwei zentrale Probleme der Büchner-Forschung', in *Georg Büchner Jahrbuch*, 11 (2005–2008) (Tübingen: Niemeyer, 2008), 237–65.

MORSELLI, GUIDO, *Dissipatio H.G.*, 4th edn (Milano: Adelphi Edizioni, 1980).

MYERS, DAVID B., 'Exclusivism, Eternal Damnation, and the Problem of Evil: A Critique of Craig's Molinist Soteriological Theodicy', *Religious Studies*, 39 (December 2003), 407–19.

—— 'Rejoinder to William Lane Craig', *Religious Studies*, 39 (December 2003), 427–30.

MYRONE, MARTIN, ed., *John Martin. Apocalypse* (London: Tate Publishing, 2011).

NIETZSCHE, FRIEDRICH, *Also sprach Zarathustra*, in *Werke*, ed. Schlechta, vol. 2, pp. 549–835.

—— 'Autobiographisches aus den Jahren 1856–1869', in *Werke*, ed. Schlechta, vol. 3, pp. 715–862.

—— *Die Fröhliche Wissenschaft*, in *Werke*, ed. Schlechta, vol. 2, pp. 281–548.

—— *The Gay Science*, trans. by Walter Kaufmann (New York: Random House / Vintage, 1974).

—— *Kritische Studienausgabe*, ed. by Giorgio Colli and Mazzino Montinari (Munich: DTV/de Gruyter, 1999).

—— *Menschliches, Allzumenschliches. Ein Buch für freie Geister*, in *Werke*, ed. Schlechta, vol. 1, pp. 435–1008.

—— 'Oedipus. Reden des letzten Philosophen mit sich selbst. Ein Fragment aus der Geschichte der Nachwelt', in *Kritische Studienausgabe*, ed. by Giorgio Colli and Mazzino Montinari, vol. 7: *Nachgelassene Fragmente*, new edition (Munich: DTV/de Gruyter, 1999), pp. 460–61.

—— 'Richard Wagner in Bayreuth', in *Werke*, ed. Schlechta, vol. 1, pp. 367–434.

—— *Thus spake Zarathustra*, trans. by Thomas Common (New York: Random House / The Modern Library, n.d.).

—— *Untimely Meditations*, trans. by R. J. Hollingdale (Cambridge: Cambridge University Press, 1997).

—— *Unzeitgemäße Betrachtungen*, in *Werke*, ed. Schlechta, vol. 1, pp. 153–434.

—— *Werke*, ed. by Karl Schlechta, 5 vols (Frankfurt a.M.: Ullstein, 1979–1981, based on the 1969 6th reprint of the Carl Hanser edition).

NIVEN, LARRY, and JERRY POURNELLE, *Lucifer's Hammer* (New York: Random House / Ballantine Books, 1983, first published 1977).

NODIER, CHARLES, 'Preface to the Second Edition of *Le Dernier Homme*', in Jean-Baptiste Grainville, *The Last Man*, trans. by I. F. & M. Clarke (Middletown, CT: Wesleyan University Press, 2002), pp. 137–40.

NOVALIS, *Schriften. Die Werke Friedrich von Hardenbergs*, ed. by Paul Kluckhohn and Richard Samuel (Stuttgart: Kohlhammer, 1960).
O'NEILL, MICHAEL, 'Shelley's Lyric Art', in *Shelley's Poetry and Prose. A Norton Critical Edition*, ed. by Donald H. Reiman and Neil Fraistat (New York and London: W. W. Norton, 2002), pp. 616–26.
ONFRAY, MICHEL, *Atheistic Manifesto. The Case Against Christianity, Judaism, and Islam* (New York: Arcade Publishing, 2011).
OPPENHEIMER, CLIVE, 'Climatic, environmental and human consequences of the largest known historic eruption: Tambora volcano (Indonesia) 1815', *Progress in Physical Geography*, 27 (2003), 230–59.
ORWELL, GEORGE, *1984* (Harmondsworth: Penguin, 1977).
OVERPECK, DERON, '"Remember! it's Only a Movie!" Expectations and Receptions of *The Day After* (1983)', *Historical Journal of Film, Radio and Television*, 32 (2012), 267–92.
Oxford Dictionary of English, 2nd edn, ed. by Catherine Soanes and Angus Stevenson (Oxford: Oxford University Press, 2006).
PACE, JOEL, 'Wordsworth and America: Reception and Reform', in *The Cambridge Companion to Wordsworth*, ed. by Stephen Gill (Cambridge: Cambridge University Press, 2003), pp. 230–45.
PAINE, THOMAS, PAINE, *The Age of Reason, being an investigation of true and fabulous theology* (New York: Prometheus Books, [n.d.], Part I first published 1794).
PALEY, MORTON D., *Apocalypse and Millennium in English Romantic Poetry* (Oxford: Clarendon Press, 1999).
—— *The Apocalyptic Sublime* (New Haven and London: Yale University Press, 1986).
—— '*Le dernier homme*: The French Revolution as the Failure of Typology', *Mosaic: A Journal for the Interdisciplinary Study of Literature*, 24 (1991), 67–76.
—— 'Envisioning Lastness: Byron's "Darkness", Campbell's "The Last Man", and the Critical Aftermath', *Romanticism*, 1 (1995), 1–14.
—— 'Jean-Baptiste François Xavier Cousin de Grainville. *The Last Man*', *Utopian Studies*, 1 (2003), 178–80.
—— 'Mary Shelley's *The Last Man*: Apocalypse Without Millennium', in *The Other Mary Shelley*, ed. by Audrey A. Fisch, Anne K. Mellor and Esther H. Schor (Oxford: Oxford University Press, 1993), pp. 107–23.
—— 'William Blake, The Prince of the Hebrews, and The Woman Clothed with the Sun', in *William Blake: Essays in Honour of Sir Geoffrey Keynes*, ed. by Morton D. Paley and Michael Phillips (Oxford: Clarendon Press, 1973), pp. 260–93.
PALEY, WILLIAM, *Natural Theology; or, Evidences of the Existence and Attributes of The Deity* (Philadelphia: John Morgan, 1802).
—— *A View of the Evidences of Christianity* (Boston: I. Thomas and E. T. Andrews, 1803).
PALMER, JAMES, 'The Ordering of Time', in *Abendländische Apokalyptik. Kompendium zur Genealogie der Endzeit*, ed. by Veronika Wieser, Christian Zolles, Catherine Feik, Martin Zolles and Leopold Schlöndorff (Berlin: Akademie Verlag, 2013), pp. 605–18.
PARKINSON, JAMES, *Organic Remains of a Former World. An Examination of the Mineralized Remains of the Vegetables and Animals of the Antediluvian World generally termed Extraneous Fossils*, 3 vols (London: Sherwood, Neely and Jones, 1811).
PATRIDES, C. A., 'Renaissance Estimates of the Year of Creation', *Huntingdon Library Quarterly*, 26 (1963), 315–22.
PHILIPSE, HERMAN, *God in the Age of Science? A Critique of Religious Reason* (Oxford: Oxford University Press, 2012).
PICHOIS, CLAUDE, *L'Image de Jean-Paul Richter dans les lettres françaises* (Paris: Corti, 1963).
PIERCE, JOHN J., *Great Themes of Science Fiction. A Study in Imagination and Evolution* (New York and Westport, CT: Greenwood Press, 1987).

PITE, RALPH, 'Wordsworth and the natural world', in *The Cambridge Companion to Wordsworth*, ed. by Stephen Gill (Cambridge: Cambridge University Press, 2003), pp. 180–95.
PLANTINGA, ALVIN, *Warranted Christian Belief* (New York and Oxford: Oxford University Press, 2000).
PLAYFAIR, JOHN, *Illustrations of the Huttonian Theory of the Earth* (Edinburgh: Cadell and Davies, 1802).
POE, EDGAR ALLAN, 'The Philosophy of Composition', in *Complete Works of Edgar Allan Poe* (Valdemar Edition), 10 vols (New York: Fred de Fau, 1902), vol. 1, pp. 282–306.
POLLOK, ROBERT, *The Course of Time. A Poem, in ten books*, 2 vols (Edinburgh: William Blackwood, and London: T. Cadell, 1827).
POPPER, KARL, *The Myth of the Framework. In Defence of Science and Rationality* (London: Routledge, 1994).
PORTER, JEFFREY L., 'Narrating the End: Fables of Survival in the Nuclear Age', *Journal of American Culture*, 16 (December 1993), 41–47.
PREMINGER, ALEX, *The Princeton Encyclopedia of Poetry and Poetics*, 2nd enlarged edn (Princeton: Princeton University Press, 1974).
PRICE, ROBERT M., *The Paperback Apocalypse* (Amherst: Prometheus Books, 2007).
PRIESTLEY, JOSEPH, *Letters to a Philosophical Unbeliever* (Birmingham: Pearson and Rollason, 1787).
PRIESTMAN, MARTIN, *Romantic Atheism. Poetry and Freethought, 1780–1830* (Cambridge: Cambridge University Press, 1999).
RATZINGER, CARDINAL JOSEPH (later Pope Benedict XVI), *Eschatology. Death and Eternal Life*, trans. by Michael Waldstein (Washington, D.C.: Catholic University of America Press, 1988 and 2007, first German edition 1977).
REAGAN, RONALD, *An American Life* (London: Random Century Group, 1990).
—— *The Reagan Diaries*, ed. by Douglas Brinkley (New York: HarperCollins, 2007).
REED, TERENCE JAMES, *Mehr Licht in Deutschland. Eine kleine Geschichte der Aufklärung* (Munich: C. H. Beck, 2009).
REHN, JENS, *Die Kinder des Saturn* (Darmstadt: Luchterhand, 1959).
REIMAN, DONALD H., and NEIL FRAISTAT, eds, *Shelley's Poetry and Prose. A Norton Critical Edition* (New York and London: W. W. Norton, 2002).
RITTER, JOACHIM, ed., *Historisches Wörterbuch der Philosophie*, vol. 10 (Basel and Stuttgart: Schwabe, 1998).
ROSENBERG, ALAN, and GERALD E. MYERS, eds, *Echoes from the Holocaust. Philosophical Reflections on a Dark Time* (Philadelphia: Temple University Press, 1988).
ROSHWALD, MORDECAI, *Level 7* (London: The New English Library, 1962).
ROSSING, BARBARA, *The Rapture Exposed* (Boulder, CO, and Oxford: Westview Press, 2004).
ROTERMUNDT, RAINER, *Jedes Ende ist ein Anfang. Auffassungen vom Ende der Geschichte* (Darmstadt: Wissenschaftliche Buchgesellschaft, 1994).
RUBENSTEIN, RICHARD L., *After Auschwitz. Radical Theology and Contemporary Judaism* (Indianapolis: Bobbs-Merrill, 1966).
—— 'Symposium on Jewish Belief', in *Wrestling with God. Jewish Theological Responses during and after the Holocaust*, ed. Steven T. Katz, Shlomo Biderman and Gershon Greenberg (Oxford: Oxford University Press, 2007), pp. 415–16.
RUDWICK, MARTIN J. S., *Bursting the Limits of Time. The Reconstruction of Geohistory in the Age of Revolution* (Chicago and London: University of Chicago Press, 2005).
—— *Earth's Deep History. How It Was Discovered and Why It Matters* (Chicago and London: The University of Chicago Press, 2014).
RUSSELL, BERTRAND, 'The Future of Man', *The Atlantic*, 1 March 1951 retrieved from

<http://www.theatlantic.com/magazine/archive/1951/03/the-future-of-man/305193>, 30 March 2015.
SAINSON, KATIE, '"La Régénération de la France": Literary Accounts of Napoleonic Regeneration 1799–1805', *Nineteenth-Century French Studies*, 30 (Fall-Winter 2001–2002), 9–25.
SAMBROOK, A. J., 'A Romantic Theme: The Last Man', *Forum for Modern Language Studies*, 2 (1966), 25–33.
SANSAL, BOUALEM, 'Die Anschläge werden nicht aufhören. Ein Gespräch mit Boualem Sansal', *Frankfurter Allgemeine Zeitung*, 18 November 2015 (feuilleton section), p. 9.
SARTRE, JEAN-PAUL, 'The Humanism of Existentialism', in *Essays in Existentialism*, ed. by Wade Baskin (Secaucus, NJ: The Citadel Press, 1965), pp. 31–68.
—— *L'existentialisme est un humanisme* (Paris: Nagel, 1947).
SCHAUMANN, CAROLINE, 'From Meadows to Mountaintops: Albrecht von Haller's "Die Alpen"', in *Heights of Reflection. Mountains in the German Imagination*, ed. by Sean Ireton and Caroline Schaumann (Rochester, NY: Camden House, 2012), pp. 57–75.
SCHELL, JONATHAN, *The Fate of the Earth* (New York: Avon Books, 1982).
SCHILLEMEIT, JOST, *Bonaventura. Der Verfasser der 'Nachtwachen'* (Munich: C. H. Beck, 1973).
SCHILLER, FRIEDRICH, *Theoretische Schriften*, ed. by Rolf-Peter Janz (Frankfurt a.M.: Deutscher Klassiker Verlag, 2008).
SCHIPPER, BERND U., 'Zwischen apokalyptischen Ängsten und chiliastischen Hoffnungen. Die religiöse Dimension moderner Utopien', in *Utopie und Apokalypse in der Moderne*, ed. by Reto Sorg and Stefan Bodo Würffel (Munich: Fink, 2010), pp. 47–61.
SCHLEGEL, FRIEDRICH, *Kritische Schriften*, ed. by Wolfdietrich Rasch, 3rd edn (Munich: Hanser, 1970).
SCHLEIERMACHER, FRIEDRICH, *Über Religion. Reden an die Gebildeten unter ihren Verächtern* (Stuttgart: Reclam, 1969).
SCHMERL, RUDOLF B., 'The Two Future Worlds of Aldous Huxley', *PMLA*, 77 (June 1962), 328–34.
SCHMID, SUSANNE, *Shelley's German Afterlives 1814–2000* (New York: Palgrave/Macmillan, 2007).
SCHMIDT, ARNO, 'Dark Mirrors', in *Nobodaddy's Children*, vol. 2 of *Collected Early Fiction 1949–1964*, trans. by John E. Woods (Normal, IL: Dalkey Archives Press, 1995), pp. 177–236.
—— 'Leviathan', in *Leviathan* (Frankfurt a.M.: Fischer, 1985 = reprint of the first edition 1949), pp. 43–76.
—— 'Leviathan or The Best of Worlds', in *Collected Novellas*, vol. 1 of *Collected Early Fiction 1949–1964*, trans. by John E. Woods (Normal, IL: Dalkey Archives Press, 1994), pp. 25–44.
—— 'Schwarze Spiegel', *Bargfelder Ausgabe* I.1 (Zurich: Haffmans, 1987), pp. 199–260.
SCHNELL, TATJANA, 'Spirituality with and without Religion — Differential Relationships with Personality', *Archive for the Psychology of Religion*, 34 (2012), 33–61.
SCHOPENHAUER, ARTHUR, *The World as Will and Idea*, trans. by R. B. Haldane and J. Kemp (London: Trübner & Co., 1883).
SCHULZ, GERHARD, 'Bürgerliche Epopöen? Fragen zu einigen deutschen Romanen zwischen 1790 und 1800', in *Deutsche Literatur zur Zeit der Klassik*, ed. by Karl Otto Conrady (Stuttgart: Reclam, 1977), pp. 189–210.
SCHWEITZER, ALBERT, *Peace or Atomic War?* (New York: Henry Holt, 1958).
SCHWENGER, PETER, 'Reply', in 'Forum', *PMLA*, 106 (October 1991), 1176–77.
—— 'Writing the Unthinkable', *Critical Inquiry*, 13 (Fall 1986), 33–48.
SCOTT, SIR WALTER, review of Mary Shelley's *Frankenstein* in *Blackwood's Edinburgh Magazine*

(20 March–1 April 1818), cited from <http://www.rc.umd.edu/editions/mws/lastman/index.html>, accessed 11 July 2013.

SCRIVENER, MICHAEL HENRY, *Radical Shelley. The Philosophical Anarchism and Utopian Thought of Percy Bysshe Shelley* (Princeton: Princeton University Press, 1982).

SHAFFER, ELINOR, *'Kubla Khan' and 'The Fall of Jerusalem': The Mythological School in Literature and Biblical Criticism 1770–1880* (Cambridge: Cambridge University Press, 1975).

—— 'Secular Apocalypse: Prophets and Apocalyptics at the End of the Eighteenth Century', in *Apocalypse Theory and the Ends of the World*, ed. by Malcolm Bull (Oxford: Blackwell, 1995), pp. 137–58.

SHELLEY, MARY, *Frankenstein. The 1818 Text*, ed. by J. Paul Hunter (New York and London: W. W. Norton, 1996).

—— *Frankenstein, or The Modern Prometheus*, ed. by Siv Jansson (Ware: Wordsworth Classics, 1999).

—— *The Journals of Mary Shelley 1814–1844*, ed. by Paula R. Feldman and Diana Scott-Kilvert, 2 vols (Oxford: Clarendon Press, 1987).

—— *The Last Man*, ed. by Hugh J. Luke, intro. by Anne K. Mellor (Lincoln and London: University of Nebraska Press, 1965).

—— 'Note on Poems of 1816', in *The Poetical Works of Percy Bysshe Shelley*, 4 vols, ed. by Mary Shelley (London: Edward Moxon, 1839), vol. 2, p. 235.

—— 'Note on *Queen Mab*', in *The Poetical Works of Percy Bysshe Shelley*, 4 vols, ed. by Mary Shelley (London: Edward Moxon, 1839), vol. 1, pp. 96–106.

——, ed., [Percy Bysshe Shelley] *Essays, Letters from Abroad, Translations and Fragments*, 2 vols (London: Edward Moxon, 1840).

——, ed., *The Poetical Works of Percy Bysshe Shelley*, 4 vols (London: Edward Moxon, 1839).

SHELLEY, PERCY BYSSHE, *The Complete Works of Percy Bysshe Shelley*, ed. by Nathan Haskell Dole (Laurel Edition), 8 vols (London and Boston: Virtue & Company, 1906).

—— 'Daemon of the World. A Fragment', in *The Works of Percy Bysshe Shelley*, ed. Forman, vol. 1, pp. 59–70.

—— *A Defence of Poetry*, in *The Works of Percy Bysshe Shelley*, ed. Forman, vol. 7, pp. 97–144.

—— 'Essay on Christianity', in *The Works of Percy Bysshe Shelley*, ed. Forman, vol. 6, pp. 338–74.

—— *Essays, Letters from Abroad, Translations and Fragments*, ed. by Mary Shelley, 2 vols (London: Edward Moxon, 1840).

—— 'Hymn to Intellectual Beauty', in *The Works of Percy Bysshe Shelley*, ed. Forman, vol. 1, pp. 371–75.

—— 'Mont Blanc', in *History of a Six Weeks' Tour*, pp. 175–83.

—— *The Necessity of Atheism*, in *The Works of Percy Bysshe Shelley*, ed. Forman, vol. 5, pp. 305–09.

—— 'Ode to Heaven', in *The Poetical Works of Percy Bysshe Shelley*, ed. Mary Shelley, vol. 2, pp. 415–17.

—— 'On a Future State', in *The Works of Percy Bysshe Shelley*, ed. Forman, vol. 6, pp. 271–80.

—— 'On the Devil, and Devils', in *The Works of Percy Bysshe Shelley*, ed. Forman, vol. 6, pp. 381–406.

—— 'On Life', in *The Works of Percy Bysshe Shelley*, ed. Forman, vol. 6, pp. 255–63.

—— *Poems and Prose*, ed. by Timothy Webb and George E. Donaldson (London: J. M. Dent, 1995).

—— *The Poetical Works of Percy Bysshe Shelley*, ed. by Mary Shelley, 4 vols (London: Edward Moxon, 1839).

—— *The Poetical Works of Percy Bysshe Shelley*, ed. by William Michael Rossetti, 3 vols (London: John Stark, 1885).

—— 'Prometheus Unbound', in *Shelley's Poetry and Prose*, ed. Reiman and Fraistat, pp. 202–86.

—— *Queen Mab*, in *The Works of Percy Bysshe Shelley*, ed. Forman, vol. 4, pp. 379–536.

—— *A Refutation of Deism: In a Dialogue*, in *The Works of Percy Bysshe Shelley*, ed. Forman, vol. 6, pp. 29–80.

—— *Shelley's Poetry and Prose*, ed. by Donald H. Reiman and Neil Fraistat (New York and London: W. W. Norton, 2002).

—— *The Works of Percy Bysshe Shelley in Verse and Prose*, ed. Harry Buxton Forman, 8 vols (London: Reeves and Turner, 1880).

——, with Mary Shelley, *History of a Six Weeks' Tour Through a Part of France, Switzerland, Germany, and Holland, with Letters* (London: T. Hookham, jun., and C. and J. Ollier, 1817).

SHINER, LARRY, 'The Meanings of Secularization', in *International Yearbook for the Sociology of Religion*, 3 (1967), 51–62.

SHUCK, GLENN, *Marks of the Beast. The Left Behind Novels and the Struggle for Evangelical Identity* (New York: New York University Press, 2004).

SHUTE, NEVIL, *On the Beach* (Toronto: Random House, 1974).

SMITH, JANE I., 'Afterlife: An Overview', in *Encyclopedia of Religion*, editor in chief Lindsay Jones, 2nd edn, vol. 1 (Detroit: New York, Thomson Gale, 2005), pp. 128–35.

SMITH, QUENTIN, 'Atheism, Theism and Big Bang Cosmology', *Australasian Journal of Philosophy*, 69 (1991), 48–66.

SNYDER, ROBERT LANCE, 'Apocalypse and Indeterminacy in Mary Shelley's *The Last Man*', in *Studies in Romanticism*, 17 (Fall 1978), 435–52.

SÖLLE, DOROTHEE, 'Atheistisch an Gott glauben', in *Gesammelte Werke*, ed. by Ursula Baltz-Otto and Fulbert Steffensky, vol. 3: *Stellvertretung* (Stuttgart: Krenz, 2006), pp. 217–33.

—— 'Theologie nach dem Tod Gottes' (first published in 1964), in *Gesammelte Werke*, ed. by Ursula Baltz-Otto and Fulbert Steffensky, vol. 3: *Stellvertretung* (Stuttgart: Krenz, 2006), pp. 195–217.

—— *Untersuchungen zur Struktur der 'Nachtwachen von Bonaventura'* (Göttingen: Vandenhoeck & Ruprecht, 1959).

SONNENBERG, FRANZ VON, *Donatoa*, 2 vols (Halle: Neue Societätsbuch- und Kunsthandlung, vol. 1 1806, vol. 2 1807).

—— *Franz von Sonnenbergs Gedichte*, ed. by J. G. Gruber (Rudolstadt: Hof-Buch- und Kunsthandlung, 1808).

—— *Das Welt-Ende*, Part I (no further parts published) (Vienna: [n.pub.], 1801).

SONTAG, SUSAN, *As Consciousness is Harnessed to Flesh. Diaries 1964–1980*, ed. by David Rieff (London: Penguin, 2013).

—— 'The Imagination of Disaster', *Commentary* (October 1965), pp. 42–48.

—— *Reborn. Early Diaries 1947–1963*, ed. by David Rieff (London: Penguin, 2009).

SPARK, MURIEL, *Child of Light. A Reassessment of Mary Wollstonecraft Shelley* (Hadleigh: Tower Bridge Publications, 1951).

SPINOZA, BENEDICT DE, *Ethics* (London: Penguin, 1996).

—— *Tractatus Theologico-Politicus, Tractatus Politicus*, trans. by R. H. M. Elwes (London and New York: George Routledge and Sons, [n.d.]).

STABLEFORD, BRIAN, 'Man-Made Catastrophes', in *The End of the World*, ed. by Eric Rabkin, Martin Greenberg et al. (Carbondale: Southern Illinois Press, 1983), pp. 97–138.

—— 'Science fiction before the genre', in *The Cambridge Companion to Science Fiction*, ed. by Edward James and Farah Mendlesohn (Cambridge: Cambridge University Press, 2003), pp. 15–31.

STAFFORD, FIONA, *The Last of the Race. The Growth of a Myth from Milton to Darwin* (Oxford: Oxford University Press, 1997, first published 1994).
STEFFEN, WILL, PAUL J. CRUTZEN and JOHN R. MCNEILL, 'The Anthropocene: Are Humans Now Overwhelming the Great Forces of Nature?', *Ambio*, 36 (December 2007), 614–21.
STEIN, GERTRUDE, 'Reflection on the atomic bomb', in *Les Cahiers du GRIF*, 41–42 (1989), p. 149.
STEMPEL, DANIEL, 'Revelation on Mount Snowdon: Wordsworth, Coleridge, and the Fichtean Imagination', *The Journal of Aesthetics and Art Criticism*, 29 (1971), 371–84.
STERN, J. P., 'Marxism on Stilts', *The New Republic*, 9 March 1987, 38–42.
STEWART, GEORGE R., *Earth Abides* (New York: Ballantine Books, 1983, first published 1949).
STOSCH, KLAUS VON, *Theodizee* (Paderborn: Schöningh, 2013).
SUNSTEIN, EMILY, 'Shelley's Answer to Leslie's *Short and Easy Method with the Deists* and Mary Shelley's Answer, "The Necessity of a Belief in the Heathen Mythology to a Christian"', in *Keats-Shelley Memorial Bulletin*, 32 (1981), 49–54.
SUVIN, DARKO, *Metamorphoses of Science Fiction: On the Poetics and History of a Literary Genre* (New Haven and London: Yale University Press, 1979).
SWINBURNE, RICHARD, 'For the Possibility of Miracles', retrieved at <http://www.orthodoxytoday.org/articles2/SwinburneMiracles.php>, accessed 3 April 2013.
—— 'A simple theism for a mixed world: response to Bradley', *Religious Studies*, 43 (2007), 271–77.
T., D., review of *Le dernier Homme, ouvrage posthume*, in *Esprit des Journaux, français et étrangers*, vol. 5 (May 1811), pp. 84–102.
TACKETT, TIMOTHY, 'The French Revolution and Religion to 1794', in *The Cambridge History of Christianity*, vol. 7: *Enlightenment, Reawakening, and Revolution*, ed. by Stewart J. Brown and Timothy Tackett (Cambridge: Cambridge University Press, 2008 (*Cambridge Histories Online*)), pp. 536–55.
TAYLOR, CHARLES, *A Secular Age* (Cambridge, MA: Harvard University Press, 2007).
THOMAS, SOPHIE, 'The Ends of the Fragment, the Problem of the Preface: Proliferation and Finality in *The Last Man*', in *Mary Shelley's Fictions. From 'Frankenstein' to 'Falkner'*, ed. by Michael Eberle-Sinatra (Basingstoke: MacMillan, 2000), pp. 22–38.
THORNE, CHRISTIAN, 'The Revolutionary Energy of the Outmoded', *October*, 104 (2003), 97–114.
THROWER, JAMES, *Western Atheism. A Short History* (Amherst: Prometheus Books, 2000).
TITTMANN, JOHANN AUGUST, *Über Supranaturalismus, Rationalismus und Atheismus* (Leipzig: Fleischer, 1816).
TOULMIN, STEPHEN, and JUNE GOODFIELD, *The Discovery of Time* (London: Hutchinson, 1965).
TOUROUDE, ALFRED, *Les Écrivains havrais* (Le Havre: Librairie de E. Touroude, 1865).
TOWNSEND, GEORGE, *Armageddon. A Poem in Twelve Books. The First Eight Books* (London: J. Hatchard, 1815).
TURNER, SHARON, *The Sacred History of the World, as displayed in the Creation and subsequent events to the Deluge, attempted to be philosophically considered in a series of letters to a son* (London: Longman, et al., 1834).
VAIL, JEFFREY, '"the Bright Sun was Extinguish'd": The Bologna Prophecy and Byron's "Darkness"', *Wordsworth Circle*, 28 (Summer 1997), 183–92.
VAN PROOYEN, KRISTINA, 'The Realm of the Spirit: Caspar David Friedrich's Artwork in the Context of Romantic Theology, with special reference to Friedrich Schleiermacher', *Journal of the Oxford University History Society* (Winter 2004), 1–16.
VERSINS, PIERRE, *Encyclopédie de l'Utopie des Voyages Extraordinaires et de la Science Fiction* (Lausanne: L'Age d'Homme, 1972).
VIJN, J. P., *Carlyle and Jean Paul. Their Spiritual Optics* (Amsterdam: John Benjamins, 1982 (Utrecht Publications in General and Comparative Literature, vol. 18)).

VOLNEY, CONSTANTIN FRANÇOIS CHASSEBŒUF, COMTE DE, *Les Ruines, ou Méditation sur les révolutions des empires* (Paris: Desenne, Vollard and Plassan, 1791).
—— *The Ruins: Or A Survey of the Revolutions of Empires*, 2nd edn (London: J. Johnson, 1795).
VOLTAIRE, 'Poem on the Lisbon Disaster', trans. by Joseph McCabe, retrieved at <https://en.wikisource.org/wiki/Toleration_and_other_essays/Poem_on_the_Lisbon_Disaster> on 16 April 2016.
—— 'Poème sur le désastre de Lisbonne', critical edition by David Adams and Haydn T. Mason, in *Les Œuvres Completes de Voltaire*, vol. 45A (Oxford: Voltaire Foundation, 2009), pp. 269–358.
—— *The Works of Voltaire. A Contemporary Version* (Akron: The Werner Company, 1906).
VONDUNG, KLAUS, *Die Apokalypse in Deutschland* (Munich: DTV, 1988).
WAGAR, W. WARREN, 'The Rebellion of Nature', in *The End of the World*, ed. by Eric Rabkin, Martin Greenberg et al. (Carbondale: Southern Illinois Press, 1983), pp. 139–72.
—— 'Round Trips to Doomsday', in *The End of the World*, ed. by Eric Rabkin, Martin Greenberg et al. (Carbondale: Southern Illinois Press, 1983), pp. 73–96.
—— *Terminal Visions. The Literature of Last Things* (Bloomington: Indiana University Press, 1982).
WASSERMAN, EARL S., *Shelley. A Critical Reading* (Baltimore and London: Johns Hopkins University Press, 1971).
—— *The Subtler Language. Critical Readings of Neoclassic and Romantic Poems* (Baltimore: Johns Hopkins University Press, 1950).
WATT, IAN, *The Rise of the Novel. Studies in Defoe, Richardson and Fielding* (Harmondsworth: Penguin, 1974, first published 1957).
WEBB, TIMOTHY, *Shelley. A Voice not Understood* (Manchester: Manchester University Press, 1977).
WEBER, JOHANNES, *Goethe und die Jungen: Über die Grenzen der Poesie und vom Vorrang des wirklichen Lebens* (Tübingen: Niemeyer, 1989).
WEINBERG, STEVEN, 'A Designer Universe?', *New York Review of Books*, 21 October 1999; cited from Lawrence M. Krauss, 'Religion vs. Science?', in *The Religion and Science Debate. Why Does It Continue?*, ed. by Harold W. Attridge (New Haven and London: Yale University Press, 2009), pp. 125–53 (p. 125).
WEINRICH, HARALD, 'Literaturgeschichte eines Weltereignisses: Das Erdbeben von Lissabon', in *Literatur für Leser. Essays und Aufsätze zur Literaturwissenschaft* (Stuttgart: Kohlhammer, 1971), pp. 64–76.
WELLS, H. G., 'The Star', in *The Short Stories of H. G. Wells* (London: Ernest Benn, 1957), pp. 644–55.
—— *The World Set Free. A Story of Mankind* (New York: E. P. Dutton, 1914).
WENINGER, ROBERT, 'Letzte Menschen und der Tod Gottes. Eine philosophische und literarische Genealogie', in *Abendländische Apokalyptik. Kompendium zur Genealogie des Untergangs in der europäischen Kultur*, ed. by Veronika Wieser, Christian Zolles, Catherine Feik, Martin Zolles and Leopold Schlöndorff (Berlin: Akademie Verlag, 2013), pp. 75–100 [= expanded reprint with a new introduction of 'Letzte Menschen und der Tod Gottes. Eine philosophische und literarische Genealogie', *Arcadia*, 35 (2000), 2–24].
WESLEY, CHARLES, *The Cause and Cure of Earthquakes. A Sermon preach'd from Psalm xlvi.8* (London: n. pub.], 1750).
—— [?], *Hymns occasioned by the Earthquake, March 8, 1750. To which are added an Hymn upon the pouring out of the Seventh Vial, Rev. xvi, xvii, etc. Occasioned by the Destruction of Lisbon* (Bristol: E. Farley, 1756).

WESLEY, JOHN, *Serious Thoughts Occasioned by the Earthquake at Lisbon, to which is subjoin'd An Account of all the late Earthquakes there, and in other Places*, 6th edn (London: [n. publ.], 1756).

WILLIAMS, HELEN MARIA, *A Tour in Switzerland; or, A View of the Government and Manners of those Cantons with Comparative Sketches of the Present State of Paris*, 2 vols (London: G. G. and J. Robinson, 1798).

WOLF, NORBERT, *Caspar David Friedrich 1774–1840. Der Maler der Stille* (Cologne: Taschen, 2007).

WORDSWORTH, WILLIAM, *The Prelude. A Parallel Text*, ed. by J. C. Maxwell (London: Penguin, 1986 (Penguin Classics)).

WUKADINOVIĆ, SPIRIDION, *Franz von Sonnenberg* (Halle: Niemeyer, 1927).

YOUNG, EDWARD, *Le Jugement dernier, poëme en trois chants, imité d'Young*, trans. by J. L. Boucharlat (Paris: Le Normant, 1806).

—— *Le jugement dernier. Poème en trois chants, traduit d'anglais, en vers français*, trans. by M. Jolin (Orléans: Guyot, 1804).

—— *A Poem on the Last Day* (Oxford: Edward Whistler, 1713).

ZINS, DANIEL L., 'Exploding the Canon: Nuclear Criticism in the English Department', in *Papers on Language and Literature*, 26 (1990), 13–40.

INDEX

12 Monkeys, film directed by Terry Gilliam 511
1984, novel by George Orwell 413, 425–26, 436
2012, film directed by Roland Emmerich 352–53, 490–91

Abe, Kobo xi
Abrams, M. H. 79–80, 82–83, 85, 131, 184–85, 262
Achituv, Yosef 369
Adam (biblical character) 33, 36, 71, 87, 108–10, 114, 147, 158–59, 166, 169–72, 240, 315–17, 320, 326, 336, 403, 463–64, 506, 508, 522
Adams, Douglas 466
Adelung, Johann Christoph 153–54, 255
Adenauer, Konrad 414
Adler, H. G. 368
Adorno, Theodor W. 361–64, 367–69, 382, 384, 395–96, 398–401, 421, 445, 519
Aeschylus 322
After London or Wild England, novel by Richard Jefferies 436, 485, 519
Alas, Babylon, novel by Pat Frank 422–25, 427, 439–42, 444, 452, 513, 519, 535
Aldiss, Brian 319, 328, 356
Alkon, Paul K. 37, 43, 111–13, 118–19, 136, 144, 158–60, 169–70, 328, 344, 350, 354
Allen, Graham 342, 351
Altizer, Thomas J. J. 372–76, 442
Amery, Carl 514
Anders, Günther 2, 367, 369, 381–88, 390–99, 408, 419, 421–22, 424–26, 431, 434–35, 439, 444–45, 459, 470–71, 502, 504
Angelus Silesius, *see* 'Silesius, Angelus'
Ape and Essence, novel by Aldous Huxley 5, 350, 411, 446–53, 459, 462, 467, 519, 535
Apocalypse xi–xii, xiv, 3, 30, 37, 41–42, 44, 48, 50, 54, 56, 64–65, 81–83, 88–91, 101, 104, 108, 112, 117, 120, 144–45, 149–50, 158–60, 162, 165, 170–72, 188, 191–92, 198, 231, 280–82, 311, 328–29, 351–53, 356, 359, 365, 387–88, 391, 393–95, 401, 403–04, 423–25, 434–37, 445–46, 450–52, 459, 467–77, 493, 518–19, 531
see also 'Armageddon, Nuclear'
Apocalypse-Blindness 390–98
Arendt, Dieter 204
Arendt, Hannah 369, 382, 392
Aristotle 62, 77
Armageddon 36, 144, 280–82, 351, 398, 413, 468, 477–78, 482
see also 'Armageddon, Nuclear', 'Last Judgment'

Armageddon, Nuclear xi, 365, 380–81, 390, 397–98, 403, 409, 422–23, 435, 438, 440, 446, 452, 455, 459, 463–64, 467, 524
Armageddon, film directed by Michael Bay 353, 490
Armageddon, verse epic by George Townsend 36, 280–83, 471, 478, 481
Armageddonists 380–81
Aronofsky, Darren 491
Aronson, Ronald 369
Asimov, Isaac 466
Assante, Armand 413
Astaire, Fred 413
Atheism xii, xv, 17, 32, 35–36, 38–41, 53–54, 57 n. 37, 59, 72, 84–85, 90, 93–94, 98, 101, 105, 117, 130, 133, 140, 150–52, 155–56, 163, 166, 171, 175–80, 183–89, 194, 204–20, 224, 231, 233–37, 242–43, 251, 255–66, 272–77, 283–85, 294, 296, 318–20, 322–24, 327–28, 334, 337, 342, 345, 348, 350, 353–54, 359–60, 371–77, 381, 387, 396, 439, 456, 465, 479, 481, 495–501, 507, 515–17, 520, 535–36
Atom(ic) bomb, *see* 'Nuclear bomb'
Atwood, Margaret 486–88, 519, 535
see also 'Oryx and Crake'
Aubuisson de Voisins, Jean François de 271
Auerbach, Erich 445
Augustine 370 n. 23
Auschwitz (includes 'Holocaust' and 'Shoah') 359, 368–71, 377–78, 380–82, 385, 391–92, 398–400, 428, 460, 462, 517 n. 84
Austen, Jane 75

Bachmann, Ingeborg 415
Bacon, Francis 259, 269–70, 272
Baker, Carlos 262
Ballard, J. G. 490
Balmer, Edwin 490
Balzac, Honoré de 75, 125, 219
Banks-Smith, Nancy 429
Barbauld, Anna Laetitia 299 n. 123
Barber, Lynn 340
Bay, Michael 353
see also '*Armageddon*'
Baudelaire, Charles 219
Becker, Claudia 214 n. 53, 219
Beckett, Samuel xi, 379–80, 420, 468, 512
Benedict XVI (Cardinal Joseph Ratzinger) 516 n. 83
Benson, Robert Hugh 478 n. 16
Bentley, Richard 179 n. 157

Bergerac, Cyrano de 353
Berkovits, Eliezer 378
Berman, David 206 n. 33, 261–62, 265–66
Bichsel, Peter 399
Birnbacher, Dieter 522–23
Birus, Hendrik 222 n. 69
Blake, William 51, 68–74, 199, 375
Bloch, Ernst 514–20, 522
Bloom, Harold 299, 312
Blount, Charles 151
Blumberg, Jane 329 n. 192, 333–34, 348
Blumenberg, Hans 254, 268, 286, 370, 388, 496
Böhme, Hartmut 518–19
Böhme, Jakob 280
Boileau-Despréaux, Nicolas 160
Böll, Heinrich 399
Bollnow, Otto Friedrich 189, 498, 510
Bonaventura, see 'Klingemann, August'
Bonneville, C. M. Le Roy 149, 158
Born, Max 414
Boubée, Nérée 290
Boucharlat, Jean-Louis 46, 122 n. 42
Bourguet, Louis 10
Bowie, Andrew 189 n. 6
Box, Jason E. 503
Boyd-Bowman, Susan 429
Braiterman, Zachary 377–78
Brentano, Clemens 60, 194–98, 228
Brew, Claude 324
Brewer, William D. 271 n. 54, 338
Brians, Paul 416, 438
Brinken, Friedrich Ernst von 202
Brinkmann, Richard 224, 227
Brocchi, Giovanni Battista 338–39
Brongniart, Alexandre 56 n. 32, 290
Broocks, Rice 207
Brothers, Richard 51
Brown, Stewart J. 57–58
Brun, Friederike 310, 313
Buber, Martin 369
Büchner, Georg 5, 204, 211–14, 224, 234–35, 257 n. 12, 308
Buckland, William 56 n. 32, 284–88, 340
Buckley, William F. 428
Buffon, Georges-Louis Leclerc Comte de 100, 162–64, 166, 170, 240, 242, 248, 274, 289–90, 337–38
Bugg, George 294
Bulkeley, John 43 n. 4
Bülow, Vicco von (aka Loriot) 415
Bultmann, Rudolf 371
Bunyan, John 180
Burke, Edmund 199–200, 202–04, 527
Burnet, Thomas xv, 54–56, 89, 169, 188, 248, 255, 289, 308–10, 512
Burton, Robert 151
Butler, Samuel 355

Byrne, Peter 154
Byron, George Gordon Lord 5, 36, 78–79, 164–66, 175, 242–43, 248, 250, 280, 299–300, 312, 314, 321–25, 329, 335–36, 338–39, 342–43, 354, 512, 534
see also 'Darkness'

Cabanis, Jean-Pierre 270
Cage, Nicolas 473
Cambacérès, Étienne Hubert de 143
Camerarius, Rudolph Jacob 288
Cameron, Kenneth Neill 177, 258, 261–62, 264, 297–99, 304 n. 136, 307 n. 141, 313, 339
Cameron, Lauren 349 n. 246
Campbell, Archibald 337
Campbell, Thomas 248, 250, 335–36
Camping, Harold 54
Camus, Albert 350, 359, 368, 373, 471, 497–500, 502, 510, 519
Cannon, George 258, 328
Čapek, Karel 403–04
Carlson, Carol C. 477
Carlson, David 476
Carlyle, Thomas 215, 248, 290
Carus, Carl Gustav 202
Carus, Paul 507
Casey, Timothy J. 219 n. 63
Celan, Paul 368
Cervantes Saavreda, Miguel de 322
Chadwick, Owen 285, 288, 295
Chambers, Ephraim 151, 179
Chateaubriand, François-René de 58, 74, 146, 292
Cherbury, Herbert of 151
Chernobyl 369, 503
Children of Men, film directed by Alfonso Cuarón 353, 455
The Children of Saturn, novel by Jens Rehn, see '[Die] Kinder des Saturn'
Cicero 322
Clairmont, Claire (Jane) 322–24, 342
Clark, David Lee 262
Clark, William 258, 260, 263
Clarke, Arthur C. 466, 482
Clarke, I. F. 43, 112, 118–20, 145, 449
Coast with Fisherman, painting by Caspar David Friedrich, see 'Meeresstrand mit Fischer'
Cohen, Arthur Allen 369, 377
Coleridge, Samuel Taylor 51, 59, 77, 79, 84–85, 121, 210, 217, 249, 264, 298, 310–14, 322
Collins, Anthony 151
Collins, (William) Wilkie 75
Collum, John 427
Colman, Samuel 199
Comte, Auguste 162
Condorcet, Nicolas Marquis de 112, 161–62, 170, 208
Contagion, film directed by Steven Soderbergh 353

Conybeare, William 284–85, 287–88, 340
Cooper, James Fenimore 75, 242, 455–56, 512
Cornils, Ingo 5 n. 7, 200 n. 24, 514 n. 73
Cowper, William 480, 512
Craig, William Lane 272–75, 277, 471–72
Creuzé de Lesser, Augustin-François 113–14, 117, 351, 471
Croce, Benedetto 445
Cromie, Robert 404
Crowe, Russell 491
Cuarón, Alfonso 353, 455
    see also 'Children of Men'
Curie, Marie 404
Cuvier, Georges 56 n. 32, 270–71, 284, 290–96, 337–40, 491, 494

Dahl, Johan Christian 194
Dalton, John 56 n. 32
Danby, Francis 199
Danton, Georges 50
Darby, John Nelson 477
Dark Mirrors, short novel by Arno Schmidt, see 'Schwarze Spiegel'
'Darkness', poem by Gordon Lord Byron 5, 36, 164–66, 175, 242, 248, 250, 335, 513
Darwin, Charles 33–34, 56 n. 32, 57, 115, 162, 255, 274–75, 287–88, 296, 441–42, 461, 512
Darwin, Erasmus 274–76, 321
Dath, Dietmar 445 n. 175
Däubler, Theodor 76
David, Jacques-Louis 140
Davy, Humphry 304 n. 136, 321–22, 337
The Day After, film directed by Nicholas Meyer 360, 427–34, 469, 511, 513
Death of God xi–xii, 5, 7–8, 37–40, 186, 188, 190, 219, 222, 224, 227, 238, 255, 347–48, 371–79, 438, 442, 465–66, 494, 499, 520, 535–36
Death of God Theology 371–80, 499
de Beer, Gavin 322–23
Deep Impact, film directed by Mimi Leder 353, 490, 511
Defoe, Daniel 180, 344, 354–55, 483 n. 25, 512
    see also 'Robinson Crusoe'
Deism xii, 8, 17–18, 20, 23–25, 28, 32, 35–36, 58, 89–90, 94, 97, 106–07, 130–34, 140, 149–58, 163, 166–80, 186, 188, 194, 234, 242–43, 254–56, 261–66, 272–74, 277, 283, 293, 302, 317, 324–28, 331, 336–37, 340, 348, 353–54, 371–72, 439, 535
de Luc, Jean-André 292
Deluge, see 'Flood, Biblical'
Demachy, Pierre-Antoine 140–41
Le Dernier Homme, epic by Jean-Baptiste Cousin de Grainville xv, 8, 36–37, 43, 46, 49, 73, 77, 102, 105, 107–25, 129–30, 134–36, 143–50, 158–60, 164, 166, 168–74, 180, 186, 210–11, 219, 224, 231, 247, 280, 318, 347, 353, 423, 455, 463, 478–81, 490, 512

Derrida, Jacques 351 n. 252, 374, 394–98, 400–01, 408, 416, 424
Descartes, René 189, 238 n. 99, 269, 319, 527
Desmarest, Nicolas 294
Desmoulins, Camille 50
de Vries, David 504
Dick, Philip K. 445 n. 175
Dickens, Charles 75
Diderot, Denis 17, 35–36, 40, 152, 164, 265, 297
Didier, Béatrice 117 n. 30, 137 n. 69
Dissipatio H.G., novel by Guido Morselli 355, 505, 523–24
Dolomieu, Déodat de 292
Domian, Jürgen 505
Donatoa, 1805–06 verse epic by Franz von Sonnenberg xv, 3, 36, 42, 46, 49, 60–62, 64–79, 83, 85–90, 95, 98–102, 104–05, 108, 120–21, 125, 129, 144–48, 162, 180, 186, 224, 231, 280, 347, 358, 365, 423, 455, 471, 478, 480–81, 516 n. 83
Doré, Gustave 245, 247
Dostoevsky, Fyodor Mikhailovich 125, 373, 377, 499, 515 n. 74
Dowling, David 360–61, 368, 398, 400, 413, 421, 423–24, 435, 438, 468–69, 508
Doyle, William 139, 141–42
Dr. Strangelove or: How I learned to Stop Worrying and Love the Bomb, film by Stanley Kubrick 6, 381, 502, 512–13, 519, 530
Draper, John William 272
Drummond, William 337
Dryden, John 43 n. 4
Dubois, Louis 158–59
Dumont, André 139
Dyer, John 242

Eagleton, Terry 38, 255, 347
Earth Abides, novel by George R. Stewart xi, 5, 350, 355, 437, 483–88, 513–14, 519, 522, 535
Eatherly, Claude 383
Eckardt, A. Roy 369, 517 n. 84
Eckermann, Johann Peter 103
Eich, Günther 415
Einstein, Albert 367, 409, 414
Eliade, Mircea 131–32, 134–35, 214, 495–96, 498, 500
Eliot, George 44, 75, 156, 345 n. 234, 501
Eliot, T. S. 132, 187, 358, 411, 413, 445
Emmerich, Roland 352–53, 490
Encyclopedie ou Dictionnaire Raisonné des Sciences, des Arts et des Métiers 30–31
The End of the World, 1801 verse epic fragment by Franz von Sonnenberg, see '[Das] Welt-Ende'
Enlightenment xii, 2 n. 4, 7–8, 15–18, 28, 35, 42, 47, 49–51, 54, 57–63, 86, 89, 97, 100–01, 104, 112, 134, 161, 171, 178, 184, 217, 238 n. 99, 243, 267, 274, 293, 296, 322, 347, 350–51, 356, 361–64, 367–69, 385, 395, 421, 496

Evans, Arthur B. 117–18
Evans, Ifor 74, 79–80
Evans, Mary Ann, *see* 'Eliot, George'
Eve (biblical character) 4, 71, 158–59, 240, 297, 316–17, 330, 403, 454, 463–64, 508, 513, 522

Fackenheim, Emil 369
Feldman, Stanley 431
Ferguson, Frances 436
Feuerbach, Ludwig 156, 175, 235, 345, 358, 501, 536
Fichte, Johann Gottlieb 60, 62–63, 84, 91 n. 107, 101, 180, 184, 189, 220, 224, 228–29, 234–38, 244–45, 255, 269, 307, 465
Fiedler, Leslie 1, 444–45
Films, *see* '*12 Monkeys*', '*2012*', '*Armageddon*', '*Children of Men*', '*Contagion*', '*The Day After*', '*Deep Impact*', '*Dr. Strangelove*', '*I am Legend*', '*Noah*', '*La Jetée*', '*Outbreak*', '*The Omega Man*', '*The Road*', '*Threads*'
Flammarion, Nicolas Camille 5, 20 n. 27, 36, 114–18, 134, 240–42, 248, 347, 490
Flaubert, Gustave 75, 219
Fleig, Horst 229
Fleming, William F. 14 n. 14
Flood, Biblical xiv, 24–25, 33, 199, 227, 238, 245, 287, 290–92, 339–41, 343, 353–54, 491, 493
Fontenelle, Bernard le Bovier de 20, 266–69, 281, 297, 322, 337, 353
Forster, E. M. 403
Forster, Harold 45
Fossils 221, 284, 287–88, 290–96, 337–41, 347, 354
  see also 'Geology'
Foucault, Michel xii, 40–41, 252–55, 293, 337, 347, 354
France, Anatole 115 n. 25
Frank, Manfred 254–55
Frank, Pat 422–27, 439–42, 444, 452, 468, 513, 519, 535
  see also '*Alas, Babylon*'
Frankenstein, novel by Mary Shelley xii, 3, 7, 41, 165, 274, 314–23, 326–28, 337, 346, 349–50, 356–57, 359–63, 382, 384, 396, 403, 468, 491
Franklin, H. Bruce 360–61
Franzen, Jonathan 1
Frederick the Great 96–97, 196
Frederick William II 96–97
French Revolution 46, 50–51, 54, 57–59, 81, 83, 112 n. 18, 137–43, 145–46, 161, 168, 184, 243, 246, 296
Freud, Sigmund 366–67, 377, 384, 524, 527–33
Friedländer, Saul 475–76
Friedrich, Caspar David 73, 190–204, 211, 214, 245, 308, 351–52, 493
  see also '[*Der*] *Mönch am Meer*', '*Meeresstrand mit Fischer*', '*Wanderer über dem Nebelmeer*'
Frisch, Max 366
Fulford, Tim 51

Füssli, Johann Heinrich (John Henry Fuseli) 199, 222

Gadamer, Hans-Georg 143, 145
Gagne, Élise 113, 117, 149, 171, 353, 471
Gagne, Paulin 113–14, 117, 149, 351, 471
Galbreath, Robert 117, 134, 185
Galilei, Galileo 270 n. 51
Galvani, Luigi 321, 337
Gardner, Ava 412–13
Gauchet, Marcel 59, 134
Gautier, Théophile 219
Geology xii, 33, 57 n. 34, 162–64, 271, 284–96, 304, 334, 337–42, 346, 359, 448, 491, 494
  see also 'Fossils'
Gibbon, Edward 177, 242, 322, 337
Giesy, John Ulrich 409
Gilbert, Sandra M. 315–17, 320, 322
Gillespie, Gerald 225 n. 79, 226, 229 n. 87
Gillespie, Michael Allan 236, 238 n. 99
Gillispie, Charles Coulson 286–88, 296
Gisborne, John 261
Glavinic, Thomas 240, 505
Gleim, Wilhelm Ludwig 50
Glorious Appearing. The End of Days, novel by Tim LaHaye and Jerry B. Jenkins 57, 99–100, 473–79, 481
Godfrey, Hollis 404, 409
Godwin, William 177, 208, 256–57, 260, 265, 270, 308, 320, 322, 327–28, 331–35, 348–49, 384, 500–01
Goethe, Johann Wolfgang 8–10, 43, 50, 61–62, 66 n. 58, 73–76, 84–85, 103, 125, 127–30, 157, 178, 180–85, 187, 202, 214, 217–18, 224, 229, 237, 245, 255, 322, 331, 354, 388–89, 461, 468, 535
  see also '*Wilhelm Meisters Lehrjahre*'
Goldsmith, Steven 355–56
Goodfield, June 150, 268
Goya, Francisco 222
Grainville, Guillaume-Balthazar Cousin de 143
Grainville, Jean-Baptiste François Xavier Cousin de 5, 8, 36, 43, 46–47, 54, 102, 105–24, 129–30, 134–50, 158–71, 174, 180–82, 186, 188, 210–11, 214, 222 n. 69, 240, 242, 245, 249–51, 255, 282, 336 n. 209, 347, 478–81, 500
  see also '[*Le*] *Dernier Homme*'
Grant, Matthew 383, 433–35
Grass, Günter 5, 350, 416, 445–46, 455, 464–67, 535
Green, A. Lincoln 240, 403
Gregory, Brad S. 272–75, 277
Gribbin, John 490
Grippen, Ross P. 136, 138, 143, 158
Gruber, Johann Gottfried 48–49, 62–66, 69, 84, 91–92, 94, 99–100, 136
Gubar, Susan 315–17, 320, 322
Guha, Anton Andreas 398–99, 416, 535
Gumbrecht, Hans-Ulrich 254 n. 8
Gutzkow, Karl 212

H (Hydrogen) bomb, *see* 'Nuclear bomb'
Haag, Ruth 229
Hackett, Timothy 137–38, 141
Hagel, Chuck 468
Hahn, Otto 414
Hall, Spencer 264 n. 34
Haller, Albrecht von 202
Hamacher, Bernd 10 n. 11
Hamilton, William 372–76, 379, 442
Hamlet (figure) 1, 224, 232–33
Hammon, William 265
Hare, Peter H. 369
Harrasser, Karin 530 n. 111
Harrison, Ted 54
Hartman, Geoffrey 85–86
Harvey, Warren Zev 369
Hastie, W. 24 n. 34
Haushofer, Marlen xi, 5, 355, 506
  see also '[Die] Wand'
Hébert, Jacques 140
Hegel, Georg Wilhelm Friedrich 76–77, 81, 83–84, 125–27, 157, 162, 236, 269, 286, 349, 363–64, 375–77, 502, 520
Heidegger, Martin 188–89, 371, 382, 499, 520, 523
Heine, Heinrich 60, 76, 156–58, 178, 234, 236
Heinlein, Robert A. 445 n. 175
Heise, Ursula K. 520–21
Heisenberg, Werner 367, 414
Helvétius, Claude Adrien 265
Hennell, Charles 501
Herder, Johann Gottfried 50, 66, 157–58, 354
Herder, Luise 66, 69
Herschel, William 56 n. 32, 270–71, 297, 303
Heydenreich, Karl Heinrich xv, 204–08, 210–11, 214, 228, 235, 255, 265, 279, 347, 500–01
Hildesheimer, Wolfgang 399, 526–27
Hillcoat, John 353, 506
Hiroshima 2, 360, 366–69, 379–80, 382–83, 385–86, 392, 409, 411, 415, 424, 437, 449, 452, 464, 477, 502
Hitchener, Elizabeth 264, 278 n. 68, 339
Hobbes, Thomas 522
Hoffmann, E. T. A. 228
Hofmann, Werner 191–92, 198, 202, 214
Hogg, Thomas Jefferson 271, 337
Holbach, Paul-Henri Thiry 17, 32, 40, 72, 101, 156–57, 177, 207–08, 217, 255, 259–60, 264–65, 270, 272, 274, 285, 297–98, 308, 322, 331, 337, 535
Holder, Rodney 272–75, 277, 471–72
Hölderlin, Friedrich 75, 85, 207, 209, 211, 214, 349
Holmes, Richard 257–58, 322–23
Holocaust, *see* 'Auschwitz'
Holocaust, U.S. television miniseries 395
Hölscher, Lucian 334–35
Homer 63, 115 n. 25, 123–25
Hood, Thomas 250, 335

Hopkins, Anthony 491
Horkheimer, Max 361–64, 367–69, 382, 384, 395–96, 421, 445
Horn, Eva 120 n. 39, 170–71, 185, 355, 400–02, 508–13, 518, 530
Hugo, Victor 219
Hume, David 24, 32, 151, 154–56, 169, 177, 272, 277 n. 64, 337, 522
Hume, Fergus 355
Hutton, James 163–64, 173, 205, 287, 289, 291, 296–97, 302–03, 334, 339–40, 500
Humboldt, Wilhelm von 56 n. 32
Huxley, Aldous 5, 350, 360, 368, 409–11, 446–53, 459, 462, 467, 481, 502, 519–20, 535
  see also '*Ape and Essence*'

I am Legend, film directed by Francis Lawrence 353
Ionesco, Eugène 359
Ireton, Sean 308
Israel, Jonathan 63, 150 n. 99, 154, 178

Jackson, Mick 429
  see also '*Threads*'
Jacobi, Friedrich Heinrich 235–38, 255, 269, 465
James, Clair 402
James, P. D. 353, 455, 490
Jameson, Fredric 469
Jameson, Robert 291–92
Jaspers, Karl 382, 498, 510
Jauß, Hans Robert 254
Jean Paul (Johann Paul Friedrich Richter) 75, 192, 214–22, 224–25, 229, 231–32, 234, 237–38, 240, 244, 248, 250, 255, 301, 307–08, 465–66, 471, 535–36
  see also 'Rede des todten Christus vom Weltgebäude herab, daß kein Gott sei'
Jefferies, Richard 436–37, 485, 519
  see also '*After London or Wild England*'
Jenkins, Jerry B. 36, 57, 99–100, 188, 280, 353, 413, 472–78, 480–82
  see also '*Glorious Appearing. The End of Days*' and '*Left Behind*'
Jenner, Edward 119, 170
Jesus (including 'Christ') 3, 29, 53, 57, 63–64, 68–72, 87–89, 100, 111, 131, 135, 148–49, 154, 156–58, 169, 172, 180, 186, 216–20, 224, 234, 258, 261, 287, 297–99, 308, 319, 346, 372, 374–76, 439, 464–67, 472–76, 482, 501, 507, 516–17
Johnson, Barbara 351
Johnson, Lyndon B. 418
Johnson, Samuel 45
Joliot-Curie, Frédéric 404, 414
Jonas, Hans 369, 371, 378–79
Jones, Frederick L. 271
Joyce, James xi, 89, 130–33, 148
  see also '*A Portrait of the Artist as a Young Man*'

Jungk, Robert 382
Jürgens, Kai U. 445 n. 175

Kahn, Herman 402
Kant, Immanuel 15–28, 30–32, 35–36, 62–64, 84, 91–92, 94–101, 104, 106–08, 135, 150, 152–53, 157, 172–74, 204–05, 221, 224, 235–36, 238, 244, 255, 268–69, 274, 281–82, 289–90, 297, 354, 392, 395, 461, 463, 514, 522
Kardec, Allan (Hippolyte Rivail) 117
Kästner, Erich 415
Keats, John 51
Keller, Gottfried 75
Kendrick, T. D. 29 n. 42
Kennedy, John F. 415, 418
Khrushchev, Nikita 415
Kincheloe, Joe L. 472
Die Kinder des Saturn, novel by Jens Rehn 355, 416, 452–54
King-Hele, Desmond 277
Kissinger, Henry 428
Klein, Richard 401
Kleist, Heinrich von 194 n. 17, 195, 197–98, 200
Kleßmann, Eckart 59
Klingemann, August 5, 224–35, 237–38, 244–45, 250, 255–56, 275, 335, 351, 353, 374 n. 34, 443
 see also '[Die] Nachtwachen des Bonaventura'
Klopstock, Friedrich Gottlieb 43, 46, 61, 63–64, 72, 75, 77, 84–85, 121, 123–25, 149, 158–59
Knight, Mark 285, 471
Koeppen, Wolfgang 415
Kohlschmidt, Werner 224
Koppel, Ted 428
Koppenfels, Werner von 351 n. 253, 356
Kosegarten, Gotthard 192, 196
Koselleck, Reinhart 254–55, 295
Koyré, Alexandre 189 n. 4
Kramer, Stanley 426
Kren, George M. 377
Kubrick, Stanley 6, 381, 502–03, 512, 519, 530
 see also 'Dr. Strangelove'
Kuhn, Thomas S. 33, 254
Küng, Hans 376 n. 38, 495
Kupiec, Anne 108, 112–13, 118, 120, 137 n. 69

LaHaye, Tim 36, 57, 99–100, 188, 280, 353, 413, 472–78, 480–82
 see also 'Glorious Appearing. The End of Days' and 'Left Behind'
La Jetée, film directed by Chris Marker 511
Lamarck, Jean-Baptiste 34, 284, 292–94, 296, 339–40
Lambe, William 270
La Mettrie, Julien Offray de 32, 72, 101
Laplace, Pierre-Simon 56 n. 32, 259, 270–71, 297, 303
Larsen, Svend Erik 15–16, 25
Last Judgment (including Day of Judgment and Second Coming) xiv, 3, 5, 28–29, 33, 36–37, 43–57, 67–71, 88–89, 94–100, 102, 104–08, 110–12, 118, 121–22, 124, 130, 134, 140, 148–49, 158–60, 162, 168–74, 186, 188, 192, 216, 222, 227, 229–30, 232, 242, 280–82, 287, 295, 302, 330, 335, 346–47, 351, 353, 380, 454, 465–66, 470–82, 491, 516–18, 520, 535
 see also 'Armageddon', 'Armageddon, Nuclear'
The Last Man, 1805 prose epic by Jean-Baptiste François Xavier Cousin de Grainville, see '[Le] Dernier Homme'
The Last Man, 1826 novel by Mary Shelley xi–xii, xv, 3–5, 8, 17, 34–37, 39–41, 118, 144, 188, 240, 250–51, 255, 317, 320, 328–60, 365, 384, 411, 436, 454, 457, 482–84, 488, 490–91, 512, 514, 519, 522, 529, 531, 534–35
 see also 'Verney, Lionel'
The Last Man, early 1830s watercolour painting by John Martin 202, 493–94, 512
The Last Man, 1849/1850 oil painting by John Martin 493–94, 512
'The Last Man', 1823 poem by Thomas Campbell 248, 250, 335–36
'The Last Man', anonymous 1826 short story in *Blackwoods Edinburgh Magazine* 248–50, 335
'The Last Man', 1826 satirical ballad by Thomas Hood 250, 335
Lauer, Gerhard 16–17
Lawrence, Francis 353
 see also 'I am Legend'
Leask, Nigel 296 n. 110, 302, 304, 309, 312–13
Leavis, F. R. 445
Left Behind, novel series by Tim LaHaye and Jerry B. Jenkins 36, 57, 188, 280, 413, 472–82
Leibniz, Gottfried Wilhelm 10–14, 16, 21, 23, 91–92, 370, 443–44
Lem, Stanislaw 466
Lenz, Jakob Michael Reinhold 204, 211–14, 234
Lenz, novella by Georg Büchner 204, 211–14, 224, 234, 257
Lepenies, Wolf 162, 255, 288
Leslie, Charles 324–26
Lessing, Gotthold Ephraim 74 n. 68, 237, 273 n. 56
Level 7, novel by Mordecai Roshwald 6, 355, 411, 416–22, 433, 442–44, 452, 454, 467, 513, 519, 525, 529, 531, 535
Leviathan, short novel by Arno Schmidt 459–63
Levinas, Emmanuel 369
Lewis, C. S. 78
Libhart, Byron R. 219
Lichtenberg, Georg Christoph 42, 229 n. 87
Lifton, Robert Jay xiii–xiv, 358, 368, 380–82, 385, 393–94, 467, 471, 482, 502–03, 524–27
Lindsey, Harold Lee 477–78
Linné, Carl 255
Lionel Verney, see 'Verney, Lionel'

Lisbon Earthquake xv, 8–17, 23–31, 36, 47, 369, 371, 378–79, 444
Littell, Franklin 369
Locke, John 151, 322
Lokke, Kari E. 359
Lomax, William 345, 349
London, Jack 5, 355, 483–88, 513, 519, 535
  see also 'The Scarlet Plague'
Louis XVI 50, 138
Loutherberg, P. J. de 199–200
Löwith, Karl 15, 223, 286
Löwy, Michael 515 n. 74
Luc, Jean-André de, see 'de Luc, Jean-André'
Lucanus, Ocellus 302 n. 132
Lucifer's Hammer, novel by Larry Niven and Jerry Pournelle 489–90, 519, 522
Lucretius 177, 207, 211
Lukács, Georg 125–34, 180–83, 185, 189, 214, 354, 514–15
Lund, Roger D. 151
Luther, Martin 59
Lyell, Charles 56 n. 32, 252, 287, 293, 338

Macpherson, James, see 'Ossian'
Majewski, Henry 119
Major, Thomas 242
Malraux, André 219
Malthus, Thomas 170, 348–49
Mandel, Emily St. John 5, 437, 482, 486–88, 513, 519, 535
  see also 'Station Eleven'
Mann, Thomas 75, 308, 386 n. 59
Marat, Jean-Paul (Mara) 50, 140
Marcus, Paul 381
Marie Antoinette 50
Marker, Chris 511
  see also 'La Jetée'
Markson, David xi, 355, 446, 505
  see also 'Wittgenstein's Mistress'
Marovitz, Sanford E. 449
Marquard, Odo 15, 101, 243–44, 286, 499
Martin, John 32–33, 44 n. 7, 199–200, 202, 353, 492–94, 512
Marx, Karl 156, 162, 175, 235, 265, 286, 514
Mason, Emma 285, 471
Matheson, Robert 353
Mauthner, Fritz 92 n. 111, 140 n. 80, 207
Mayr, Ernst 254–55, 293
McCabe, Joseph 14 n. 14
McCarthy, Cormac 2, 5, 240, 353, 355, 506–08, 512, 525, 535
McFarland, Thomas 91 n. 107
McGrath, Alister 262, 500–01
McMahon, Darrin 50
McManners, John 137 n. 70, 139, 141
McNamara, Robert 417, 428

Medwin, Thomas 257, 324
Meeresstrand mit Fischer (*Coast with Fisherman*), painting by Caspar David Friedrich 190–91
Mellor, Anne K. 321, 332–34, 342, 345, 350–51, 360
Melville, Herman 75, 377
Mercier, Louis Sébastian 242, 247–48
Merle, Robert 446
Metz, Johann Baptist 369
Meyer, Nicholas 427, 429, 431
  see also 'The Day After'
Michelet, Jules 219
Miller, J. Hillis 214
Miller, Walter M. 437, 519
Milton, John 43, 46, 63, 68, 72–73, 75, 77, 79–80, 83, 118, 121, 123–25, 149, 280, 315–17, 320, 322, 362, 479–81
Mitscherlich, Alexander 369
Moltmann, Jürgen 369, 517–19
Momoro, Antoine-François 140
Der Mönch am Meer (*The Monk by the Sea*), painting by Caspar David Friedrich 74, 190–94, 198, 200, 202–03, 214, 493
The Monk by the Sea, painting by Caspar David Friedrich, see '[Der] Mönch am Meer'
'Mont Blanc', poem by Percy Bysshe Shelley 204, 256, 264, 284, 296, 299–314, 332, 334, 357, 479, 494
Montaigne, Michel de 321
Montesquieu, Charles-Louis de Secondat 322
Morell, André 11
Moritz, Karl Philipp 75, 85, 322
Morselli, Guido 355, 505, 523–24
  see also 'Dissipatio H.G.'
Moses (biblical character) 202, 223, 290, 308, 319, 326, 346
Murray, John 324
Musset, Alfred de 219
Myers, David B. 273 n. 57

Die Nachtwachen des Bonaventura (*The Night Watches of Bonaventura*), Romantic satire by August Klingemann 5, 224–34, 237–38, 244–45, 250, 256, 275–76, 335, 351, 353, 374 n. 34, 443
Napoleon Bonaparte 42, 48, 57, 109–10, 142–43, 246, 259, 292
Nash, Edward 323
The Necessity of Atheism, religious treatise by Percy Bysshe Shelley xv, 177, 256–57, 259, 261–62, 264–65, 302, 308, 467 n. 200, 497
Negative Theology 374
  see also 'Death of God Theology'
Nerval, Gérard de (Gérard Labrunie) 219
Newton, Isaac 19, 21, 56 n. 32, 98, 160, 185, 208, 269, 272, 274, 304, 492, 494
Newton, John Frank 270
Nicholson, William 270
Nicolson, Harold 404, 409

Nietzsche, Friedrich 38–40, 175, 215–16, 219, 222–25, 235–36, 238–40, 244, 308, 347, 372–73, 377, 443, 462, 494, 513, 519–20, 522, 526
The Night Watches of Bonaventura, Romantic satire by August Klingemann, *see* '[Die] Nachtwachen des Bonaventura'
Niven, Larry 489–90, 519
  see also 'Lucifer's Hammer'
Noah (biblical character) 33, 284, 308, 339, 341, 343, 346, 352, 452–55, 464–65, 491
  see also 'Flood, Biblical'
Nodier, Charles 49, 113, 118, 120–21, 123, 136, 219
Norton, Roy 404
Nothingness 5, 204, 208, 210, 217, 226–27, 231, 234, 236, 241, 279, 495 n. 41, 535
  see also 'Atheism'
Novalis (Friedrich von Hardenberg) 58–60, 74–75, 85, 125, 183, 224, 234
Noyes, Pierrepont 404
Nuclear bomb 1, 2, 41, 132, 358–60, 366–69, 380, 382–87, 391–93, 400, 404, 406–09, 414–19, 425–27, 429–37, 443, 446–47, 450, 455–57, 462, 467–69, 477, 502, 530

Oberlin, Johann Friedrich 211, 213
The Omega Man, film directed by Boris Segal 353
O'Neill, Michael 305
Onfray, Michel 507
On the Beach, novel by Nevil Shute xi, 350, 355, 411–16, 422, 424, 426, 433, 438–39, 441–42, 444, 467, 511–13, 519, 529, 531, 535
Orgill, Douglas 490
Orwell, George 359, 413, 425–26, 436
  see also '1984'
Oryx and Crake, novel by Margaret Atwood 486–88, 519, 522, 535
Ossian 196, 198, 242, 246, 512
Outbreak, film directed by Wolfgang Peterson 353
Overpeck, Deron 432
Ovid 354

Pace, Joel 81
Paine, Thomas 153–54, 177, 255, 274, 337
Paley, Morton D. 51 n. 22, 82–83, 112, 124, 158, 165, 168 n. 138, 199, 250 n. 114, 332–33, 336 n. 209, 346, 493
Paley, William 130, 154, 274–77, 279–80, 284–85, 287–89, 467
Pantheism 8, 96, 115 n. 25, 154, 156, 178–80, 184, 186, 194, 204–05, 237, 255, 258, 262–64, 314, 496, 535
Park, Mungo 337
Parkinson, James 339–41, 491
Pauling, Linus 414–15
Peacock, Thomas Love 300–01
Peck, Gregory 412–13
Penn, Granville 294, 340

Perrault, Charles 160
Petrarch 63
Philipse, Herman 156 n. 116, 210–11
Pichois, Claude 219
Piercy, Marge 360
Plantinga, Alvin 272, 308, 471–72
Playfair, John 163, 287, 296, 302
Plutarch 317, 322
Poe, Edgar Allan 77–78, 490
A Poem on the Last Day, poem by Edward Young xv, 36, 43–46, 71, 88–90, 121–22, 160, 188, 232, 280, 471
Pollok, Robert 209–10, 351, 471, 478–80
Pomfret, John 43 n. 4, 160
Pope, Alexander 10–14, 16, 20–23, 43, 460
Popper, Karl 270 n. 51,
Porter, Jeffrey L. 424–25
A Portrait of the Artist as a Young Man, novel by James Joyce 89, 130–33, 148
Pournelle, Jerry 489–90, 519
  see also 'Lucifer's Hammer'
Praz, Mario 215 n. 53
The Prelude, poem by William Wordsworth 79–86, 183–85, 199, 203, 224, 243, 300 n. 123, 313–14, 343, 494
Priestley, Joseph xv, 51, 207–08, 265, 287
Priestman, Martin 184, 257 n. 13, 314, 318
Pullman, Philip 466

Queen Mab, poem by Percy Bysshe Shelley xv, 177, 256–66, 269–70, 297–98, 308, 320, 322, 324 n. 178, 333–34, 337

Raffles, Thomas 323
Ramdohr, Freiherr Friedrich Wilhelm Basilius von 194
Ramsay, William 405
Ransmayr, Christoph 308
Ratzinger, Cardinal Joseph, *see* 'Benedict XVI'
Ray, John 90, 274
Reagan, Ronald 427–29, 432–33
'Rede des todten Christus vom Weltgebäude herab, daß kein Gott sei', text by Jean Paul 192, 214–20, 224, 234, 248, 301, 471
Reed, Terence James 496–97
Rees, Abraham 270
Rees, Martin 503
A Refutation of Deism, religious treatise by Percy Bysshe Shelley 177, 256, 261, 264–65, 277, 328, 334
Rehn, Jens 355, 416, 446, 452–54, 513, 519, 535
  see also '[Die] Kinder des Saturn'
Reid, William Hamilton 151
Renan, Ernest 219
Richardson, Samuel 322
Richter, Hans Werner 415
Rink, Friedrich Theodor 25 n. 37

The Road, novel by Cormac McCarthy 2, 5, 240, 353, 355, 506–08, 512, 525, 535
Robards, Jason 427
Robespierre, Maximilien 50, 140, 142
Robinson Crusoe, protagonist of Daniel Defoe's novel *Robinson Crusoe* 4, 78, 344, 455, 483 n. 25, 512
Rogers, Neville 262
Ronsin, Charles Philippe 140
Roosevelt, Franklin Delano 409
Rosenberg, Alan 381
Rosendorfer, Herbert 505
Roshwald, Mordecai 5–6, 355, 411, 416–26, 433–34, 442–44, 452, 454, 467–68, 513, 519, 525, 529, 535
 see also 'Level 7'
Rotblat, Joseph 414
Rotermundt, Rainer 37
Rothko, Mark 200 n. 24
Rousseau, Jean-Jacques 140, 262 n. 31, 313, 322
Rowling, J. K. 78
Rubenstein, Richard L. 376–77
Rudwick, Martin J. S. 57 n. 34, 163, 283, 291–96, 302, 334, 339–40
Runge, Philipp Otto 73–74, 192
Russell, Bertrand 382–83, 410–11, 414, 416, 434, 436, 441, 450
Russell, Colin 163–64
Rutherford, Ernest 404–05

Sacks, Jonathan 369
Sagan, Carl 428
Saint John the Divine (author of the 'Book of Revelation') 434
Saint John the Evangelist 241
Saint-Pierre, Bernard de 136
Sambrook, A. J. 208
Sansal, Boualem 496 n. 44
Sartre, Jean-Paul 71–72, 372–73, 377, 383, 499, 502, 510
Saumier, Octave 245
Saussure, Horace-Bénédict de 56 n. 32
The Scarlet Plague, novel by Jack London 5, 355, 483–88, 513, 519, 522, 535
Schaumann, Caroline 202, 308
Scheff, Werner 490
Schell, Jonathan 360, 382, 387, 417, 455
Schelling, Friedrich 59–60, 63, 84, 91 n. 107, 94, 101, 180, 225, 229
Schillemeit, Jost 229
Schiller, Friedrich 60–61, 66 n. 58, 68 n. 61, 77, 83–84, 98, 101, 126–29, 215, 322
Schipper, Bernd U. 517–18
Schlegel, August Wilhelm 60, 193, 229
Schlegel, Friedrich 59–60, 75, 85, 127, 131, 184, 193, 224, 229, 349
Schlegel-Schelling, Caroline 229
Schleiermacher, Friedrich 60, 193

Schmerl, Rudolf B. 449
Schmid, Susanne 261, 346 n. 241
Schmidt, Arno xi, 5, 350, 355, 445–46, 455–64, 467, 524
 see also '*Leviathan*' and '*Schwarze Spiegel*'
Schopenhauer, Arthur 207, 211, 265, 461, 463, 497
Schücking, Lida 66, 69
Schwarze Spiegel (*Dark Mirrors*), short novel by Arno Schmidt xi, 5, 350, 355, 446, 455–64, 467
Schweitzer, Albert 382, 414–17, 422, 424
Schwenger, Peter 402, 409, 438, 459, 469
Scofield, Cyrus I. 477
Scott, Walter 78, 181, 183, 242, 246–48, 322, 328, 512
Scowcroft, Brent 428
Scrivener, Michael Henry 256 n. 11, 262
Sebald, W. G. 308
Sedgwick, Adam 340
Segal, Boris 353
 see also '*The Omega Man*'
Senhouse, Humphrey 323–24
Shaffer, Elinor 50, 82, 470
Shaftesbury, Anthony Ashley Cooper, third Earl of 151
Shakespeare, William 61, 224, 226, 488
 see also 'Hamlet'
Shelley, Mary xi–xii, xv, 3–5, 8, 17, 34–37, 39–41, 118, 144, 165, 188, 222 n. 69, 240, 249–51, 255, 257, 279, 300–01, 314–38, 340, 342–51, 353–63, 365–66, 384, 403, 411, 436–37, 454, 457, 468, 482–83, 488, 490–91, 500, 512, 514, 519, 521–22, 529, 534–35
 see also '*Frankenstein*' and '*The Last Man*'
Shelley, Percy Bysshe xv, 5, 41, 51, 83, 156, 163 n. 127, 165, 175, 177–78, 204, 245–46, 251, 255–66, 269–72, 274–75, 277–84, 288, 296–314, 320–26, 328, 330, 332–34, 337–40, 342, 346, 348–49, 351, 357, 384, 467 n. 200, 479, 494, 497, 500–01, 534–35
 see also 'Mont Blanc', 'The Necessity of Atheism', 'Queen Mab', 'A Refutation of Deism'
Shiel, Matthew Phipps 240, 355
Shiner, Larry 286 n. 85
Shoah, *see* 'Auschwitz'
Shute, Nevil xi, 5, 350, 355, 411–16, 422–26, 433–34, 438–39, 441–42, 444, 467–68, 512, 519, 529, 535
 see also 'On the Beach'
Sigelman, Lee 431
Silesius, Angelus 507
Smith, David Nichol 79
Smith, Jane I. 519 n. 90
Smith, Quentin 273
Snyder, Robert Lance 335 n. 206, 355
Soddy, Frederick 405
Soderbergh, Steven 353
 see also 'Contagion'
Sölle, Dorothee (also Dorothee Sölle-Nipperdey) 234, 369, 374–75
Soloveitchik, Joseph B. 369
Sonnenberg, Franz von xv, 3, 5, 36, 42–43, 46–50, 54, 60–81, 83–94, 97–102, 104–05, 108, 121, 125, 129–

30, 135–36, 144–49, 162, 169, 172, 175, 180–82, 186, 188, 224, 231, 243, 255, 280, 347, 358, 365, 423, 455, 471, 478–81, 516 n. 83
 see also '*Donatoa*' and '[*Das*] *Welt-Ende*'
Sontag, Susan 4 n. 6, 6, 364–65, 389, 397–98, 401, 409, 480–81
Southey, Robert 177, 242, 246, 260, 264, 298, 323, 327, 512
Spark, Muriel 342 n. 225, 355
'Speech of the dead Christ from atop the World's Edifice', text by Jean Paul, *see* 'Rede des todten Christus vom Weltgebäude herab, daß kein Gott sei'
Spengler, Oswald 520
Spinoza, Benedict de 154–56, 177–80, 189, 205, 237, 255, 257 n. 12, 259, 270, 501, 522
Stableford, Brian 248 n. 111, 328, 356, 404
Staël, Anne-Louise-Germaine Necker, Madame de 60, 113, 157, 215, 219, 322
Stafford, Fiona 89, 118–19, 243, 246, 512
Stapledon, Olaf 36, 466, 482
Station Eleven, novel by Emily St. John Mandel 437, 482, 486–88, 513, 519, 522, 535
Stein, Charlotte von 61
Stein, Gertrude 435
Steinberg, Shirley R. 472
Stendhal (Henri Beyle) 75
Stern, J. P. 514–15
Stewart, George R. xi, 5, 350, 355, 437, 483–88, 513, 519, 535
 see also '*Earth Abides*'
Stirner, Max 207
Stoddard, Brandon 429
Strauß, David Friedrich 156, 180, 376, 501
Stroberle, João Glama 8
Sublime, the (including: nuclear sublime) 92, 110–11, 121, 135, 163 n. 127, 186, 194, 196, 198–205, 211, 221, 243, 268, 280, 299–309, 313–15, 323, 343, 346, 354, 357, 436, 459, 479–80, 493–94, 500, 527, 530–31, 536
Sunstein, Emily 324–25
Suvin, Darko 479
Swift, Jonathan 322
Swinburne, Richard 272, 471–72
Szczesny, Gerhard 415
Szilard, Leo 409

Tacitus 322
Tackett, Timothy 50 n. 18
Tasso 63
Taylor, Charles 57, 59, 133–35, 150–51, 174, 178, 184–85, 205, 208–09, 214, 255, 271–72, 373, 471–72, 495–500, 520, 536
Tell, Wilhelm 68
Theism xii, 8, 17, 20, 23 n. 31, 25, 28–33, 36, 57 n. 34, 89, 94, 97–98, 101, 130, 150–56, 166, 168–72, 175, 177–81, 186, 188, 194, 205–08, 242, 255, 259–60, 263–64, 272–74, 279–80, 283–84, 289, 292–93, 369–72, 376 n. 38, 448, 497, 515, 535
 see also 'Atheism', 'Deism', '*Left Behind*', 'Pantheism', 'Theodicy'
Thelwall, John 210
Theodicy 10–12, 15, 21, 23, 91–92, 95, 99, 101, 158, 184, 369–71, 373, 377–78, 440, 444, 450, 462
Thomson, James 43 n. 4
Thorne, Christian 475–76
Threads, film directed by Mick Jackson 360, 429, 432, 434, 513
Thrower, James 179
Tieck, Ludwig 60, 74–75, 85, 215, 229
Tindall, Matthew 151
Tittmann, Johann August 175–78
Toland, John 151
Tolkien, J. R. R. 78
Tolstoy, Count Lev Nikolayevich 125, 515 n. 74
Toulmin, Stephen 150, 268
Touroude, Alfred 123–24
Townsend, George 36, 280–83, 471, 478–79
Train, Arthur 409
Troeltsch, Ernst 286
Trotter, Thomas 270
Trump, Donald 503
Turner, Sharon 56, 288–92, 491
Turner, J. M. William 199, 493

Unger, Thorsten 16–17
Ure, Andrew 294
Ussher, James, Archbishop 19, 51–52, 248

van Prooyen, Kristina 192–93, 202
Verne, Jules 1 n. 1, 118, 466
Verney, Lionel, protagonist of Mary Shelley's novel *The Last Man* 3–4, 39, 41, 316, 329–34, 337, 340, 342–45, 347, 353–57, 359, 421, 454–55, 457, 483–84, 521, 534
Versins, Pierre 119–20, 144–45, 350
Vico, Giambattista 520
Vigny, Alfred de 219
Vijn, J. P. 219
Villers, Charles de 219
Villiers de l'Isle-Adam, Auguste comte de 219
Vincent, François-Nicolas 140
Viret, Pierre 151
Virgil 63
Volney, Constantin François Chassebœuf, Comte de xv, 166–68, 242, 245–46, 318–19
Voltaire 10–17, 23–24, 26, 28, 30, 35, 58, 77, 96, 136, 150, 161, 228, 322, 330 n. 195, 337, 369–71
Vondung, Klaus 398, 434
Vonnegut, Kurt 445 n. 175
Voß, Johann Heinrich 61

Wagar, W. Warren 2 n. 4, 7, 104, 112, 115, 119, 328, 344, 346, 404, 409, 436–38, 490–91, 494–95, 502, 527
Wakefield, Gilbert 51
The Wall, novel by Marlen Haushofer, see '[*Die*] *Wand*'
Wallis, George C. 240, 490
Die Wand, novel by Marlen Haushofer xi, 5, 355, 506
Wanderer above the Sea of Fog, painting by Caspar David Friedrich, see '*Wanderer über dem Nebelmeer*'
Wanderer über dem Nebelmeer, painting by Caspar David Friedrich 201–02, 211, 245, 352
Ward, Rachel 413
Wasserman, Earl S. 177, 262, 264 n. 34, 279 n. 69, 306 n. 140
Watson, Emma 491
Watt, Ian 75, 180–81
Webb, Timothy 298 n. 118
Weber, Johannes 73–74
Weber, Max 59, 134, 214
Weinberg, Steven 252
Weinrich, Harald 15 n. 15
Weisman, Alan 504
Weizsäcker, Carl Friedrich von 367, 382, 414
Wells, H. G. 1, 5, 36, 240–42, 248, 355, 405–11, 426, 466, 490, 492–93, 512, 535
   see also '*The World Set Free. A Story of Mankind*'
Das Welt-Ende, 1801 verse epic fragment by Franz von Sonnenberg 49, 64–65, 75, 86, 95, 100
Werner, Abraham Gottlieb 56 n. 32, 271, 288, 296
Wesley, Charles 28–29, 36
Wesley, John xv, 28–31, 33, 36
West, Benjamin 199
Whewell, William 340
White, Andrew Dickson 272
Wieland, Christoph Martin 61, 66 n. 58, 322, 461
Wiesel, Elie 428
Wilhelm Meister's Years of Apprenticeship, novel by Johann Wolfgang Goethe, see '*Wilhelm Meisters Lehrjahre*'

Wilhelm Meisters Lehrjahre, novel by Johann Wolfgang Goethe 75, 85, 180–84, 215
William, Edward 342
Williams, Helen Maria 309–10, 313
Wilson, John 354
Wittgenstein's Mistress, novel by David Markson xi, 355, 446, 505
Wolf, Norbert 192–94
Wolfe, Gary K. 145
Wolfram von Eschenbach 125
Wollaston, William 56 n. 32
Wood, Allen W. 97
Wood, Robert 242
Wood, Robert Williams 409
Woods, John E. 460
Wordsworth, William 5, 51, 59, 79–86, 100, 183–85, 199, 203, 224, 243, 255, 262 n. 31, 300 n. 123, 306–07, 310–14, 322, 343, 494
   see also '*The Prelude*'
The World Set Free. A Story of Mankind, novel by H. G. Wells 405–09, 411, 426, 535
Wright, Charles 58
Wukadinović, Spiridion 60 n. 41, 66 n. 58, 73, 91 n. 100, 99, 149
Wylie, Philip 490
Wyschogrod, Edith 369
Wyschogrod, Michael 369

Yeltsin, Boris 417
Young, Edward xv, 5, 36, 43–48, 54, 71, 88–90, 121–22, 160, 172, 188, 198, 232, 242, 255, 280, 471, 480
   see also '*A Poem on the Last Day*'
Yukawa, Hideki 414

Zins, Daniel L. 393
Zola, Émile 75

www.ingramcontent.com/pod-product-compliance
Lightning Source LLC
Chambersburg PA
CBHW080436170426
43195CB00017B/2797